OXFORD PAPERBACK REFERENCE

The Oxford Companion to
Twentieth-Century Poetry in English

The author of two books of verse, Ian Hamilton has written
biographies (of Robert Lowell and J. D. Salinger) and literary
criticism: his *Keepers of the Flame* appeared in 1992 and *Walking
Possession*, a collection of essays and reviews, was published in
1994. From 1962 to 1979 he edited *The Review* and *The New
Review* and for three years, from 1984, he presented BBC TV's
Bookmark series.

Oxford
Paperback
Reference

The most authoritative and up-to-date reference books for both students and the general reader.

The Oxford Companion to
Twentieth-Century Poetry in English

IAN HAMILTON

Oxford   New York

OXFORD UNIVERSITY PRESS

1996

Oxford University Press, Walton Street, Oxford ox2 6dp

Oxford New York
Athens Auckland Bangkok Bombay
Calcutta Cape Town Dar es Salaam Delhi
Florence Hong Kong Istanbul Karachi
Kuala Lumpur Madras Madrid Melbourne
Mexico City Nairobi Paris Singapore
Taipei Tokyo Toronto

and associated companies in
Berlin Ibadan

Oxford is a trade mark of Oxford University Press

First published 1994 by Oxford University Press
First issued as an Oxford University Press paperback 1996

British Library Cataloguing in Publication Data
Data available

Library of Congress Cataloging in Publication Data
Data available
ISBN 0-19-866147-9 (hbk.)
ISBN 0-19-280042-6 (pbk.)

10 9 8 7 6 5 4 3 2 1

Printed in Great Britain by
Mackays Ltd
Chatham, Kent

Introduction

This *Companion* is offered both as a reference work and as a history, a map of modern poetry in English. It may be thought that the territory has already been well mapped, in anthologies and textbooks, but I can think of no other single-volume publication that runs from 1900 to the present day and covers topics, movements, magazines, and genres as well as individual poets, dead and alive.

Over the five years that I have worked on the *Companion* I have more than once paused to remind myself how speedily such maps can change, how fashions rise and dive. Imagine a similar compilation put together in, say, 1950. Dylan Thomas would have had more space than he gets here, and so too would Nicholas Moore, Karl Shapiro, Sidney Keyes, and other big-name figures of that time. Surrealism would have bulked larger, and there would have been a more tender deference to periodicals like *Poetry Quarterly* and *Poetry London*. The precise contours would of course have depended on who had done the mapping, but the general shape would surely have reflected the epoch's taste for the florid and religiose, its lack of any real interest in technique, its suspicion that the political poets of the 1930s had somewhat let the side down, and so on.

Ten years later, the map would have changed again, with Auden and Empson restored to favour. We would note a new respect for the output of the American academies and for those writers of the 1940s who had kept their wits about them and not turned to God, or Jung. Overall, there would have been more braininess than ecstasy, more common sense than communal subconscious. In covering these bygone decades, I have tried to keep in mind some notion of how things must have seemed *then*, and to balance this against what I take to be history's subsequent or current valuation. At the same time, I have been wary of the passage-of-time school of literary judgement. It isn't true that 'if it's good, it will survive'; someone, somewhere has to keep saying that it's good—or if not good, exactly, then at least worthy of a small piece of the historical jigsaw, the map. There are poets discussed in this *Companion* who would probably not get into any 'up-to-date' anthology of modern verse. Their inclusion, though, should not be viewed as merely archivistic. Who knows how things will look in ten years' time?

Perhaps the first thing to be confessed of this 1994 *Companion* is that it comes from England (or Britain: 'England', in this introduction, should be taken to mean the United Kingdom as a whole). Forty years ago this would not have seemed like much of a confession; after all, the book is meant to be about poetry in *English*, is it not? Indeed, when I imagined a pre-1960 version of it, I automatically did the imagining in terms of poetry in England, with only parenthetical

Introduction

reference to the United States. In spite of all the movable road signs, London was still the metropolis that mattered. Take it on to the mid-Sixties, though, and there is a serious effrontery in this assumption. A *Companion* done in 1965 would have needed to acknowledge Boston or New York or San Francisco—or even Liverpool, alas. Nowadays, London is but one of several capitals, and most people are agreed that 'poetry in English' can no longer be thought of in the singular.

If the *Companion* has a plot, then, it is to do with this shift from 'poetry' to 'poetries'. And in order to make sense of this shift, the plot inevitably centres on the relationship between the poetries of England and America. It tells of a courtship, a marriage, a divorce. In the first third of the century we have a lively interplay between the English and American traditions, each seeming to vitalize the other; in the middle third there is a struggle for control; the final third shows a gradual decline of interest, so that in the end even the rivalry seems to have died.

And if we look beyond England and America to the poetries of Australia, Canada, and the several other English-speaking territories covered in this book, we can see that they too have an involvement in the central romance: they have invariably felt the need to take one side or the other, however determined they have been to establish identities which they can call their own. These identities are already distinctive and describable, as I hope the *Companion*'s coverage makes clear, and can only become more so as the poets of these territories continue to explore the ways in which *their* English differs from the English of England and America. And this is to talk only of language-differences—differences of sensibility we take to be already well-declared. At the moment, it is hard to imagine the poetries of Australia, Canada, and so on, making a complete break with their Anglo-American parentage. There is a wish to make that break, and a wish not to. It is perhaps from this conflict that distinctiveness currently ensues. To which someone will no doubt retort: try telling that one to the Aborigines.

People talk about modern poetry being different from other, earlier poetry. When asked what they mean, they usually reply that it is less accessible, less disciplined in its technique: modern poets, they say, care little for their audience and are contemptuous of tradition. None of these definitions can be made to stick. 'Difficulty' is not a twentieth-century invention, nor is the wish to make innovations in technique. And as for questions of 'audience' and 'tradition', it could be argued that these are topics on which modern poets have worried themselves almost to excess.

It could further be contended that the insistency of such worries was what first marked off modern poetry from the poetry we had before. At no earlier period, it could be said, were the makers of poems required so nakedly to ask themselves: why poems? At no earlier period was the potential audience so thrillingly immense and yet (or therefore) so depressingly neglectful. At no period were the tribal bard's tribe-altering pretensions so cheerfully disdained. For a poet in, say, 1920, there was real, sometimes exquisite anguish in perceiving what the new 'mass literacy' was likely to amount to, in terms of the survival of his art. Edmund Wilson's essay 'Is Verse a Dying Technique?' appeared in 1928. It was all very well for Eliot to extol poetry as civilization's 'highest point of consciousness, its greatest power and its most delicate sensibility', but which 'civilization', exactly, did he have in mind? In his own poems, the consciousness, both powerful and delicate, is one of exclusion and defeat, as if a doctor were prohibited from tending his sick patient—with the prohibition coming from the patient.

But Eliot's cultural idealism (and Pound's too) was American in origin, and when we try to define the differentness of modern poetry this is perhaps where the investigation should begin: at the point when English poetry became Anglo-American. No earlier English poetry took much cognizance of outsiders, unless those outsiders were long dead and came from Greece or Rome. By the 1920s, though, the two most impressive and influential poet-critics in London were writing with at least one eye on their own, far-away backyards—in Massachusetts or Idaho. And from those backyards there was an answering alertness. When William Carlos Williams read *The Waste Land*, he said: 'I had to watch him carry my world with him, the fool, to the enemy.' The enemy was Europe, and 'my world' was 'the local conditions in America'—what Williams called 'the American grain'.

As Ezra Pound saw it, Williams's sense of betrayal sprang from a kind of fake primitivism, from envy and ignorance, the sort of backwardness, or backyardness, that had driven Pound to Europe in the first place. To him, Williams—or 'little Bill', as he liked to call him—was no more than a 'village cutup', the 'most bloody inarticulate animal that ever gargled'. And yet, from their opposing standpoints, both Pound and Williams dreamed of an American Renaissance. For Pound this could only be achieved by treating the United States as medieval, lagging 500 years behind the Europeans. For Williams, America was more than just a cultural condition, it was an actual place, 'a world of great beauty and ripest blossom'. It was also a 'hard, truculent, turbulent mass' that had yet to be properly, open-mindedly explored. Europe and its art had 'painted over, smeared' the mysteries of the New World. The newness of America had never been grasped or understood on its own terms by native artists because the cultural assumptions and ambitions of those artists had not actually been native. The ethnic-American poetries that are so trumpeted today have their roots in Williams's start-afresh polemic. After all, did not Pound also mock Williams as a 'dago immigrant'? Williams's mother, he seemed to recall, came from Santo Domingo.

The quarrel between Williams's nativism and Pound's cosmopolitanism was an American quarrel, and it is chiefly in the history of American poetry that we can see its consequences acted out: in the proudly reactionary attitudinizing of Ransom, Tate, and the Southern Agrarians; in the New Criticism on the one hand and Black Mountain on the other; in the split between a poetry of the academy and a poetry of the soil—the Paleface versus Redskin, cooked versus raw face-offs identified by Robert Lowell—and in the continuing argument between readers and performers, page and stage. The Lowell generation was probably the last on either side of the Atlantic to believe in the continuity of the Anglo-American collaboration, and in *Life Studies* Lowell nobly tried to get the best of 'his' two worlds: to write a European poetry under the influence of William Carlos Williams. When Lowell moved from strict metres to *vers libre* he was deferring not to Pound's Europe but to Williams's America. We can, if we wish, now view *Life Studies* as even more comprehensively elegiac than it seemed in 1959.

There have of course been post-Lowell Americans who looked to England for their models, but they have been marginalized in their own culture or, as with the current New Formalists, they have been obliged to make a stately song-and-dance about their reverence for Tradition or Antiquity. And there are today British poets who cut a dash by imitating Ashbery or Merrill. But English poetry since Auden has, on the whole, tried to make Englishness a virtue. The Amis–Larkin generation chucklingly made a point of declaring its contempt for all things transatlantic—or, come to that, cross-channel. Would they have been more stylistically adventurous, more feelingful and eloquent, if the American irritant had not been there? Has 'being English' in this sense actually been shaped by the wish not to be American? The English native tradition has been kept intact and is seemingly vigorous, but is it not too arrogantly static?

Every so often the English have gone in for a bout of transatlantic yearning—A. Alvarez's 1963 anthology *The New Poetry* more or less told English poets to learn from America or die—in Pound's words—'piecemeal of a sort of emotional anaemia'—and these bouts will now and then recur. There is a solemnly programmatic strain in American letters which will always attract the undriven, the good learners. But the Americans are less impressed than they used to be by English imitations, and their critical rhetoric these days tends to be aggressively home-spun. Helen Vendler introduces her Faber (or Harvard, depending where you are) anthology of *Contemporary American Poetry* with the warning that her book 'will be able to extend its charm only to those who genuinely know the American language—by now a language separate in accent, intonation, discourse and lexicon, from English'. This is not so very different from what Auden said in 1956 when he introduced *his* Faber book of *Modern American Verse*. Speaking of the difference between American and English, Auden called it 'the most subtle difference of all and the hardest to define . . . what the secret of the difference is I cannot put my finger on', but he could tell it when he heard it, in Robinson or Frost, and did not in the least feel that it debarred him from responding to those poets' charms.

It is Vendler's tone of 'Keep off, this is now *ours*' that makes one hesitate to suggest a speedy reconciliation. Maybe American poets *need* fifty years of freedom from English constraints. And maybe the English need a break from having to reaffirm their Englishness. We'll see. But the two languages still have much in common, much that the one can borrow from the other; so that I do now and then find myself entertaining the pious hope that this *Companion* might help to rekindle an old spark. It seems to me that each side should at least know what the other side is up to, and have some sense of the ins and outs of the historical relationship.

It will perhaps be thought that I am straining for a narrative that isn't/wasn't there. If I am, then you can blame it on *my* taste—a taste shaped in the early to mid-1960s, when the examples of Europeanized Americans like Lowell, Snodgrass, Berryman, Roethke, and Plath really did seem to be urging a renegotiated treaty. The 'enemies' in those days were twofold: in America, the academic-experimental, with its theories about breath, pulse, the open field of the white page, and sundry other elaborations or distortions of the Williams line; in England, the Beatlish ingratiators, with their student-union poetry readings, their 'disaffiliate' life-styles, and their wide-eyed insistence that 'most people ignore most poetry because most poetry ignores most people'—a cry both electrifying and anaesthetizing, as it proved. These enemies are still abroad, in various new guises, and several of them will be found to feature in this book. They have to; they are on the map.

In other words, this is not a critical anthology; nor is it a textbook. I want it to be seen as serious and useful, but I will not at all mind if it is read for fun, as a kind of documentary-entertainment. For those who like making lists, as I do, I here offer a few leads (all figures are approximate, and susceptible to computerized riposte). The *Companion* covers about 1,500 poets, 100 subjects. Of the poets, 550 are British, 550 American. Other territories break down as follows: Australia (120), Canada (110), Africa (60), Asia (40), New Zealand (35), Caribbean (30). There are about 200 women and 100 black writers. Twenty-seven poets had nervous breakdowns, fifteen committed suicide, and fifteen were/are diagnosed as alcoholic. Nineteen served time in jail, fourteen died in battle, three were murdered, one executed. Zany professions include lumberjack, tax inspector, furniture remover, carpet salesman, and policeman, but of course the vast majority of poets earn their living in universities. The most popular off-campus day-job is that of doctor or psychiatrist. Only one poet has played hockey for his country.

Ezra Pound is most often mentioned as an influence on other poets, with Auden, Yeats and Williams runners-up. Eliot is named less often than Lowell and Stevens. Rilke is the most influential foreign poet. More poets died in their seventies than at any other time of life. More lived past the age of 80 than died young (that is, before the age of 40). The most popular year to be born in was 1947, with 1934 not far behind. The dominant poetic star-sign is . . .

Enough, though. To qualify for inclusion in this *Companion*, a poet needs to have lived in the twentieth century, if only for a month or so. Thus, Stephen

Introduction

Crane sneaks in but Hopkins is omitted. A poet also has to be over 30, if still living; the youngest in the book was born in 1963. He or she must have published at least one substantial collection of poetry. There may well be poets who have been unjustly overlooked, and reviewers will no doubt tell me who they are. In some instances, the poets themselves will bear the news. The choice of subjects and contributors, the allocation of space, and the general orientation of the book have been my responsibility. The opinions expressed by individual contributors are not always opinions that I share.

Attempting to cover such a vast field has of course meant soliciting lots of advice, and I am grateful to many of my contributors for their informal guidance. In particular, I would like to acknowledge the help of Douglas Dunn (on Scotland), Peter Porter (Australia), and Mario Relich (Caribbean). For the American coverage I have sought assistance from numerous quarters, and most of my US contributors have at one time or another been conscripted as editorial consultants (unofficial and unpaid): I have appreciated their forbearance even though I have not always followed their advice. On US matters I have also had useful comment from Donald Hall, Richard Howard, Mary Gray Hughes, Stanley Plumly, Mark Strand, and David Wojahn. On Commonwealth poets, Alistair Niven of the Arts Council of Great Britain gave me many useful leads, and I should also mention with gratitude Guy Butler, J. M. Coetzee, Patrick Cullinan, James Curry, C. J. Driver, Lloyd Fernando, Andrew Gurr, Dennis Lee, Alan Lawson, Leslie Monkman, John Robinson, Elizabeth Richie, and Kelwyn Sole.

The original idea for the *Companion* came from Kim Scott Walwyn of the Oxford University Press, and I am grateful to her for helping to set out the guidelines, so to speak, and for generally getting the thing moving. In the later stages, Frances Whistler and Andrew Lockett have kept it on the rails and Jeff New has made numerous mechanical—and some not-so-mechanical—adjustments; in their different ways each has saved me a few blushes, for which I am most thankful. My chief debt, though, has been to my day-to-day assistant Charis Ryder. She has managed the administration with her customary thoroughness, but her vigilance has extended to all aspects of the undertaking so that she has been, in effect, co-editor.

Ian Hamilton

Selection of Anthologies

American Poetry since 1945, ed. S. Stepanchev (New York, 1965).

And Now the Poets Speak: Poems Inspired by the Struggle for Zimbabwe, ed. N. Zimunya and M. Kadhani (Harare, 1981).

An Anthology of Twentieth-Century New Zealand Poetry, ed. Vincent O'Sullivan (Oxford, 1987).

Australian Poetry 1957, ed. Hal Porter (Sydney, 1957).

Australian Poetry Now, ed. T. Shapcott (Melbourne, 1970).

Birthright: A Selection of Poems from Southern Africa, ed. M. Zimunya (London, 1989).

Black Poets in South Africa, ed. Robert Royston (London, 1973).

The Blue Wind: Poems in English from Pakistan, Introduced by Peter Dent (Budleigh Salterton, 1984).

Canadian Poetry Now: Twenty Poets of the 80s, ed. Ken Norris (Toronto, 1984).

Contemporary American Poetry, ed. Donald Hall (Harmondsworth, 1962, 1971).

Contemporary Australian and American Poetry, ed. T. Shapcott (St Lucia, Qld., 1976).

Contemporary Australian Poetry, ed. John Leonard (Boston, 1990).

Contemporary Indian Poetry in English, ed. Kaiser Haq (Columbus, Ohio, 1990).

Contemporary [Indian] Poetry in English: An Assessment and Selection, ed. S. Peeradina (*Quest* 74, 1972; repr. as a book, Bombay, 1977).

A Controversy of Poets, ed. Paris Leary and Robert Kelly (New York, 1965).

The Direction of Poetry, ed. R. Rickman (Boston, 1988).

Ecstatic Occasions, Expedient Forms, ed. David Lehman (New York, 1987).

The Faber Book of Contemporary Scottish Poetry, ed. Douglas Dunn (London, 1992).

The Faber Book of Irish Verse, ed. John Montague (London, 1974).

The Faber Book of Modern American Verse, ed. W. H. Auden (London, 1956).

The Faber Book of Modern Australian Verse, ed. Vincent Buckley (London, 1991).

The Faber Book of Twentieth-Century Women's Poetry, ed. Fleur Adcock (London, 1987).

The Fate of Vultures: New Poetry of Africa, ed. M. Zimunya, P. Porter, and K. Anyidoho (Oxford, 1989).

From Our Yard: Jamaican Poetry since Independence, ed. Pamela Mordecai (Kingston, 1987).

The Fugitive Poets: Modern Southern Poetry in Perspective, ed. W. C. Pratt (New York, 1965).

The Generation of 2000, ed. William Heyen (Princeton, NJ, 1984).

Georgian Poetry, ed. James Reeves (Harmondsworth, 1962).

The Golden Apples of the Sun, ed. C. Wallace-Crabbe (Melbourne, 1980).

A Group Anthology, ed. E. Lucie-Smith and P. Hobsbaum (London, 1963).

Harper's Anthology of Twentieth-Century Native American Poetry, ed. Duane Niatum (San Francisco, 1987).

The Heinemann Book of African Poetry in English, ed. Adewale Maja-Pearce (Oxford, 1990).

Hinterland: Caribbean Poets from the West Indies and Britain, ed. E. A. Markham (Newcastle upon Tyne, 1989).

The Home Book of Modern Verse, ed. B. E. Stevenson (New York, 1963).

Selection of Anthologies

The Imagist Poem: Modern Poetry in Miniature, ed. W. C. Pratt (New York, 1963).

Indian Poetry in English since 1950, ed. Vilas Sarang (Bombay, 1989).

A Land Apart [South Africa], ed. André Brink and J. M. Coetzee (London, 1986).

Landfall Country: Work from 'Landfall', 1947–1961, ed. Charles Brasch (Christchurch, NZ, 1962).

London Magazine Poems, 1961–1966, ed. Hugo Williams (London, 1966).

The Longman Anthology of Contemporary American Poetry, ed. S. Friebert and D. Young (New York, 1989).

The Liverpool Scene, ed. Edward Lucie-Smith (London, 1967).

Mamba Book of Zimbabwean Verse in English, ed. C. and O. Style-Gwern (Harare, 1986).

The Mid-Century: English Poetry 1940–1960, ed. David Wright (Harmondsworth, 1965).

Modern American Poetry, ed. Louis Untermeyer (New York, 1962, 1969).

Modern Poetry from Africa, ed. Ulli Beier and Gerald Moore (Harmondsworth, 1963; rev. as *The Penguin Book of Modern African Poetry*, 1984).

The Morrow Anthology of American Poetry, ed. David Smith (New York, 1985).

Naked Poetry: Recent American Poetry in Open Forms, and *Naked Poetry 2*, ed. Stephen Berg and Robert Mezey (Indianapolis, Ind., 1969, 1974).

The New American Poetry, 1945–1960, ed. Donald M. Allen (New York, 1960).

The New Australian Poetry, ed. J. Tranter (St Lucia, Qld., 1979).

A New Book of South African Verse in English, ed. Guy Butler and Chris Mann (Cape Town, 1979).

The New Canadian Poets 1970–1985, ed. D. Lee (Toronto, 1985).

New Impulses in Australian Poetry, ed. T. Shapcott and R. Hall (St Lucia, Qld., 1968).

The New Oxford Book of Australian Verse, ed. Les Murray (Melbourne, 1986).

The New Oxford Book of Canadian Verse in English, ed. Margaret Atwood (Toronto, 1982).

The New Oxford Book of Irish Verse, ed. T. Kinsella (Oxford, 1986).

The New Poetry, ed. A. Alvarez (Harmondsworth, 1962, 1966).

The New Poetry, ed. Michael Hulse, David Kennedy, and David Morley (Newcastle upon Tyne, 1993).

New Poets of England and America, ed. Donald Hall, Robert Pack, and Louis Simpson (Cleveland, Ohio, 1957).

New Signatures, ed. Michael Roberts (London, 1932).

New Zealand Writing since 1945, ed. M. P. Jackson and V. O'Sullivan (Auckland, 1983).

The Norton Anthology of Modern Poetry, ed. Richard Ellmann and Robert O'Clair (New York, 1973).

Oral Poetry from Africa, ed. J. Mapanje and L. White (London, 1983).

The Oxford Book of American Verse, ed. F. O. Matthiessen (Oxford, 1950).

The Oxford Book of Canadian Verse: In English and French, ed. A. J. M. Smith (Toronto, 1960, 1965).

The Oxford Book of Contemporary New Zealand Poetry, ed. Fleur Adcock (Auckland, 1982).

The Oxford Book of Scottish Verse, ed. John MacQueen and Tom Scott (Oxford, 1966).

The Oxford Book of Twentieth-Century English Verse, ed. Philip Larkin (Oxford, 1973).

The Oxford India Anthology of Twelve Modern Indian Poets, ed. A. K. Mehrotra (New Delhi, 1992).

The Penguin Book of Canadian Verse, ed. Ralph Gustafson (Harmondsworth, 1958, 1967, 1975).

The Penguin Book of Caribbean Verse in English, ed. Paula Burnett (Harmondsworth and New York, 1986).

The Penguin Book of Contemporary British Poetry, ed. Blake Morrison and Andrew Motion (Harmondsworth, 1982).

The Penguin Book of Contemporary New Zealand Verse, ed. I. Wedde and H. McQueen (Harmondsworth, 1985).

The Penguin Book of Contemporary Verse, 1918–1960, ed. Kenneth Allott (Harmondsworth, 1962).

The Penguin Book of Modern Australian Poetry, ed. J. Tranter and P. Mead (Harmondsworth, 1991).

The Penguin Book of New Zealand Verse, ed. Allen Curnow (Harmondsworth, 1966; revd. edn., ed. Douglas Stewart, 1966).

The Penguin Book of Southern African Verse, ed. Stephen Gray (Harmondsworth, 1989).

Pergamon Poets 2: Poetry from Africa, ed. Howard Sergeant (Oxford, 1968).

Poems from East Africa, ed. D. Cook and D. Rubadiri (London, 1971).

Poems from India, Sri Lanka, Malaysia and Singapore, ed. Y. Gooneratne (Hong Kong, 1979).

Poems of Black Africa, ed. Wole Soyinka (London, 1975).

Poems of the Second World War, ed. V. Selwyn (London, 1985).

Poems since 1900, ed. Colin Falck and Ian Hamilton (London, 1975).

The Poetry Anthology: 1912–1977, ed. Daryl Hine and Joseph Parisi (Boston, 1978).

Poetry by Canadian Women, ed. Rosemary Sullivan (Toronto, 1982).

Poetry from Oxford in Wartime, ed. William Bell (London, 1945).

Poetry of the Thirties and *Poetry of the Forties*, ed. Robin Skelton (Harmondsworth, 1964, 1965).

The Poetry of War, ed. Ian Hamilton (London, 1965).

Puerto Rican Writers at Home in the USA, ed. Faythe Turner (Seattle, 1991).

The Rattle Bag, ed. Seamus Heaney and Ted Hughes (London, 1985).

Samora, ed. M. Zimunya and C. Hove (Harare, 1987).

Strong Measures, ed. P. Dacey and D. Jauss (New York, 1986).

Ten Twentieth-Century Indian Poets, ed. R. Parthasarathy (New Delhi, 1976).

The Terrible Rain: The War Poets, 1939–1945, ed. Brian Gardner (London, 1966).

A Treasury of Asian Literature, ed. J. D. Yohannan (New York, 1956).

Twelve Poets of the Pacific, ed. Yvor Winters (Norfolk, Conn., 1937).

Two Centuries of Australian Poetry, ed. M. O'Connor (Melbourne, 1988).

Two Decades of Indian Poetry: 1960–1980, ed. K. N. Daruwalla (New Delhi, 1989).

Under 35: The New Generation of American Poets, ed. Nicholas Christopher (New York, 1989).

The Vintage Book of Contemporary American Poetry, ed. J. D. McClatchy (New York, 1990).

The Voice That is Great Within Us, ed. Hayden Carruth (New York, 1970).

Key to Contributors

AB	Alan Brownjohn	CWo	Catherine Woeber
AC	Amit Chaudhuri	DBa	Douglas Barbour
AF	Anne French	DBr	David Brooks
AG	Arthur Gregor	DD	Douglas Daymond
AH	Andrew Hudgins	DED	Douglas Dunn
AHa	Alamgir Hashmi	DES	Donald E. Stanford
AJ	Alan Jenkins	DeVS	De Villo Sloan
AKM	Arvind Krishna Mehrotra	DG	Dana Gioia
ALRC	Angus Calder	DH	Daniel Hoffman
AM	Andrew Motion	DHa	Dennis Haskell
AM-P	Adewale Maja-Pearce	DHe	David Headon
ARL	A. Robert Lee	DJ	Dan Jacobson
AS	Anne Stevenson	DK	David Kennedy
AST	Anthony Thwaite	DL	David Lehman
AT	Ann Thwaite	DM	David Mason
ATT	A. T. Tolley	DR	David Rampton
AU	Alan Urquhart	DRB	Donald R. Bartlett
AW	Andrew Wallace	DS	David Staines
BB	Bruce Bennett	DStJ	David StJohn
BK	Bruce King	DWF	D. W. Fenza
BM	Bill Manhire	EB	Edward Butscher
BMe	Bruce Meyer	EC	Eleanor Cook
BO'D	Bernard O'Donoghue	EDF	Elaine D. Foster
CAR	Carol Rumens	EG	Emily Grosholz
CB	Christopher Benfey	EH	Eamonn Hughes
CF	Colin Falck	EHF	Edward Foster
CH	Christopher Hope	EJ	Evan Jones
CHa	Cliff Hanna	EMcM	Elizabeth McMahon
CJR	Christopher Reid	ETL	Edward T. Larrissy
CKS	C. K. Stead	FA	Fadzilah Amin
CLB	Charles Bainbridge	FKA	Fleur Adcock
CM	Clive Meachen	FMcK	Frank McKay
CMW	Charlotte M. Wright	FO	Femi Oyebode
CP	Christopher Pollnitz	GB	Gillian Boddy
CPH	Claire Harman	GC	Graham Clarke
CR	Clay Reynolds	GE	Gavin Ewart
CS	Colin Smythe	GF	Giles Foden
CW	Clive Wilmer	GG	Gary Geddes
CW-C	Chris Wallace-Crabbe	GHB	George Bowering

GM	Glyn Maxwell	LD	Laurence Donovan
GMacB	George MacBeth	LdeS	Lakshmi de Silva
GS	Grace Schulman	LM	Les Murray
HC	Henri Cole	LMacK	Lachlan MacKinnon
HH	Hugh Haughton	LMcM	Lynne McMahon
HL	Herbert Lomas	LR	Liam Rector
HMcQ	Harvey McQueen	LRi	Lynn Risser
HV	Helen Vendler	LS	Leon Stokesbury
HW	Hugo Williams	LT	Lewis Turco
IES	Ian Sansom	MacDJ	MacDonald Jackson
IMcM	Ian McMillan	MB	Marianne Boruch
IS	Iain Sharp	MCB	Matthew C. Brennan
IW	Ian Wedde	MF	Mark Ford
JB	James Booth	MG	Michael Gnarowski
JC	James Campbell	MH	Michael Heller
JCr	Julian Croft	M-HM	Mpalive-Hangson Msiska
JD	Jeff Doyle	MHu	Michael Hulse
JDB	Jonathan Barker	MI	Mick Imlah
JG	Jamie Grant	MJ	Mark Jarman
JGS	Julian Symons	ML	Michele Leggott
JH	John Haffenden	MLe	Marcia Leveson
JHS	Jon Stallworthy	MLo	Mary Lord
JKK	Janice Kulyk Keefer	MLR	M. L. Rosenthal
JL	John Lucas	MO'N	Michael O'Neill
JLa	John Lang	MP	Michael Palmer
JM	John Mole	MQA	Michael Q. Abraham
JP	Jay Parini	MR	Mario Relich
JPr	John Press	MRu	Mark Rudman
JR	Jonathan Raban	MRW	Mark Wormald
JRa	Jarold Ramsey	MS	Meic Stephens
JRo	Judith Rodriguez	MS-S	Martin Seymour-Smith
JS	Jennifer Strauss	MW	Mark Williams
JSt	James Steele	NB	Neil Besner
JT	Jeff Titon	NC	Neil Corcoran
JTC	Jane Todd Cooper	NE	Nicholas Everett
JTFT	James T. F. Tanner	NG	Noreen Golfman
KBS	Koh Buck Song	NJ	Nicholas Jenkins
KG	Kevin Goddard	NP	Neil Powell
KGo	Ken Goodwin	NW	Nigel Wheale
KH	Kevin Hart	PB	Peter Bland
KI	Kevin Ireland	PBM	Blake Morrison
KJ	Kai Jensen	PD	Peter Dale
KO	Kole Omotoso	PDH	Philip Hobsbaum
KS	Kirpal Singh	PF	Peter Forbes
LA	Lionel Abrahams	PK	Paul Kavanagh
LCS	Lim Chee Seng	PL	Paddy Lyons

Key to Contributors

PM	Philip Mead	SG	Stephen Gray
PMcC	Patricia McCarthy	SH	Seamus Heaney
PMcD	Peter McDonald	SK	Sandra Kemp
PMS	Peter Sanger	SMcK	Susan McKernan
PMStP	Paul Matthew St Pierre	SMI	S. Manzoorul Islam
PNFP	Peter Porter	SO'B	Sean O'Brien
POM	Pierre Maldive	SPB	Sven Birkerts
PP	Peter Pierce	SPG	Sharmani Patricia Gabriel
PS	Peter Stitt	SS	Shaista Sonnu
RA	Ranjana Ash	SW	Stephen Watson
RB	Reg Berry	TC	Tom Clark
RBH	Ronald B. Hatch	TDeP	Thomas DePietro
RF	Robert Fraser	TJGH	T. J. G. Harris
RG	Roger Gilbert	TP	Tom Paulin
RGa	Roger Garfitt	TS	Timothy Steele
RGr	Robert Gray	TSw	Thomas Swiss
RH	Ron Horning	TW	Ted Weiss
RHa	Rachel Hadas	TWi	Terence Winch
RJG	Richard Gray	TWS	Tom Shapcott
RL	Richard Lansdown	VS	Vivian Smith
RMcD	Robert McDowell	WC	William Corbett
RMcP	Robert McPhillips	WG	William Gillies
RP	Robert Polito	WGS	W. G. Shepherd
RPa	Rajeev Patke	WHN	W. H. New
RR	Roger Robinson	WHP	William Pritchard
RS	Richard Stull	WM	Wes Magee
RSG	R. S. Gwynn	WMcK	Wayne McKenna
RSP	Robert S. Phillips	WMY	Wong Ming Yook
RW	Ronald Warwick	WP	Wyatt Prunty
RWB	R. W. Butterfield	WS	William Scammell
RZ	Robert Zaller	WSB	W. S. Broughton
SB	Stewart Brown	WT	William Toye
SbinH	Shuaib bin Hasan	YG	Yasmine Gooneratne
SEG	Sherrill E. Grace		

Alphabetical List of Contributors

Michael Q. Abraham (MQA), Lionel Abrahams (LA), Fleur Adcock (FKA), Fadzilah Amin (FA), Ranjana Ash (RA), Charles Bainbridge (CLB), Douglas Barbour (DBa), Jonathan Barker (JDB), Donald R. Bartlett (DRB), Christopher Benfey (CB), Bruce Bennett (BB), Reg Berry (RB), Neil Besner (NB), Sven Birkerts (SPB), Peter Bland (PB), Gillian Boddy (GB), James Booth (JB), Marianne Boruch (MB), George Bowering (GHB), Matthew C. Brennan (MCB), David Brooks (DBr), W. S. Broughton (WSB), Stewart Brown (SB), Alan Brownjohn (AB), Edward Butscher (EB), R. W. Butterfield (RWB), Angus Calder (ALRC), James Campbell (JC), Amit Chaudhuri (AC), Tom Clark (TC), Graham Clarke (GC), Henri Cole (HC), Eleanor Cook (EC), Jane Todd Cooper (JTC), William Corbett (WC), Neil Corcoran (NC), Julian Croft (JCr), Peter Dale (PD), Douglas Daymond (DD), Thomas DePietro (TDeP), Lakshmi de Silva (LdeS), Laurence Donovan (LD), Jeff Doyle (JD), Douglas Dunn (DED), Nicholas Everett (NE), Gavin Ewart (GE), Colin Falck (CF), D. W. Fenza (DWF), Giles Foden (GF), Peter Forbes (PF), Mark Ford (MF), Edward Foster (EHF), Elaine D. Foster (EDF), Robert Fraser (RF), Anne French (AF), Sharmani Patricia Gabriel (SPG), Roger Garfitt (RGa), Gary Geddes (GG), Roger Gilbert (RG), William Gillies (WG), Dana Gioia (DG), Michael Gnarowski (MG), Kevin Goddard (KG), Noreen Golfman (NG), Ken Goodwin (KGo), Yasmine Gooneratne (YG), Sherrill E. Grace (SEG), Jamie Grant (JG), Richard Gray (RJG), Robert Gray (RGr), Stephen Gray (SG), Arthur Gregor (AG), Emily Grosholz (EG), R. S. Gwynn (RSG), Rachel Hadas (RHa), John Haffenden (JH), Cliff Hanna (CHa), Claire Harman (CPH), T. J. G. Harris (TJGH), Kevin Hart (KH), Shuaib bin Hasan (SbinH), Alamgir Hashmi (AHa), Dennis Haskell (DHa), Ronald B. Hatch (RBH), Hugh Haughton (HH), David Headon (DHe), Seamus Heaney (SH), Michael Heller (MH), Philip Hobsbaum (PDH), Daniel Hoffman (DH), Christopher Hope (CH), Ron Horning (RH), Andrew Hudgins (AH), Eamonn Hughes (EH), Michael Hulse (MHu), Mick Imlah (MI), Kevin Ireland (KI), S. Manzoorul Islam (SMI), MacDonald Jackson (MacDJ), Dan Jacobson (DJ), Mark Jarman (MJ), Alan Jenkins (AJ), Nicholas Jenkins (NJ), Kai Jensen (KJ), Evan Jones (EJ), Paul Kavanagh (PK), Janice Kulyk Keefer (JKK), Sandra Kemp (SK), David Kennedy (DK), Bruce King (BK), Koh Buck Song (KBS), John Lang (JLa), Richard Lansdown (RL), Edward T. Larrissy (ETL), A. Robert Lee (ARL), Michele Leggott (ML), David Lehman (DL), Marcia Leveson (MLe), Herbert Lomas (HL), Mary Lord (MLo), John Lucas (JL), Paddy Lyons (PL), George MacBeth (GMacB), Patricia McCarthy (PMcC), Peter McDonald (PMcD), Robert McDowell (RMcD), Frank McKay (FMcK), Wayne McKenna (WMcK), Susan McKernan (SMcK), Lachlan MacKinnon (LMacK), Elizabeth McMahon (EMcM), Lynne McMahon (LMcM), Ian McMillan (IMcM), Robert McPhillips (RMcP), Harvey McQueen (HMcQ), Wes Magee (WM), Adewale Maja-Pearce (AM-P), Pierre Maldive (POM), Bill Manhire (BM), David Mason (DM), Glyn Maxwell (GM), Clive Meachen (CM), Philip Mead (PM), Arvind Krishna Mehrotra (AKM), Bruce Meyer (BMe), John Mole (JM), Blake Morrison (PBM), Andrew Motion (AM), Mpalive-Hangson Msiska (M-HM), Les Murray (LM), W. H. New (WHN), Sean O'Brien (SO'B), Bernard O'Donoghue (BO'D), Kole Omotoso (KO), Michael

Alphabetical List of Contributors

O'Neill (MO'N), Femi Oyebode (FO), Michael Palma (MP), Jay Parini (JP), Rajeev Patke (RPa), Tom Paulin (TP), Robert S. Phillips (RSP), Peter Pierce (PP), Robert Polito (RP), Christopher Pollnitz (CP), Peter Porter (PNFP), Neil Powell (NP), John Press (JPr), William Pritchard (WHP), Wyatt Prunty (WP), Jonathan Raban (JR), David Rampton (DR), Jarold Ramsey (JRa), Liam Rector (LR), Christopher Reid (CJR), Mario Relich (MR), Clay Reynolds (CR), Lynn Risser (LRi), Roger Robinson (RR), Judith Rodriguez (JRo), M. L. Rosenthal (MLR), Mark Rudman (MRu), Carol Rumens (CAR), David St John (DStJ), Paul Matthew St Pierre (PMStP), Peter Sanger (PMS), Ian Sansom (IES), William Scammell (WS), Grace Schulman (GS), Lim Chee Seng (LCS), Martin Seymour-Smith (MS-S), Tom Shapcott (TWS), Iain Sharp (IS), W. G. Shepherd (WGS), Kirpal Singh (KS), De Villo Sloan (DeVS), Vivian Smith (VS), Colin Smythe (CS), Shaista Sonnu (SS), David Staines (DS), Jon Stallworthy (JHS), Donald E. Stanford (DES), C. K. Stead (CKS), James Steele (JSt), Timothy Steele (TS), Meic Stephens (MS), Anne Stevenson (AS), Peter Stitt (PS), Leon Stokesbury (LS), Jennifer Strauss (JS), Richard Stull (RS), Thomas Swiss (TSw), Julian Symons (JGS), James T. F. Tanner (JTFT), Ann Thwaite (AT), Anthony Thwaite (AST), Jeff Titon (JT), A. T. Tolley (ATT), William Toye (WT), Lewis Turco (LT), Alan Urquhart (AU), Helen Vendler (HV), Andrew Wallace (AW), Chris Wallace-Crabbe (CW-C), Ronald Warwick (RW), Stephen Watson (SW), Ian Wedde (IW), Ted Weiss (TW), Nigel Wheale (NW), Hugo Williams (HW), Mark Williams (MW), Clive Wilmer (CW), Terence Winch (TWi), Catherine Woeber (CWo), Mark Wormald (MRW), Wong Ming Yook (WMY), Charlotte M. Wright (CMW), Robert Zaller (RZ).

A

ABERCROMBIE, Lascelles (1881–1938), was born just outside Manchester, at Ashton upon Mersey; he was educated at Malvern College and at Victoria (later Manchester) University. He worked as a journalist for several years but at the age of 38 became a lecturer at the University of Liverpool; subsequently, he was professor of English at Leeds (from 1922) and Goldsmith's Reader in English at Oxford (from 1935).

In an essay entitled 'The Function of Poetry in the Drama' (1912), Abercrombie sought to redefine the possibilities of verse drama, but his own attempts at the genre are unhappily innocent of stagecraft. A clue to his more fruitful development as a poet is provided by the publication, also in 1912, of his study of Thomas *Hardy: at his best, he is less a stereotypical *Georgian than a second-class Hardy, fond of combining muscular rural imagery with lyric or ballad forms. This mixture, in poems such as 'The Fear' and 'The Stream's Song', evidently appealed to *Yeats, who included eight pages of Abercrombie's work in the *Oxford Book of Modern Verse* (1936).

Though his poetry lacks the distinction of a major talent, it is enjoyable, capably written, and now unjustly neglected. It was collected as *The Poems of Lascelles Abercrombie* (London, 1930), and a supplementary volume, *Lyrics and Unfinished Poems*, appeared in 1940, two years after the author's death. [NP

ABSE, Dannie (Daniel) (1923–) has a Jewish background, is Welsh, and a doctor: biographical facts which feature in his poems. Abse has an immediately likeable poetic voice, compassionate, humorous, observant. But the poems are not content with likeableness, nor are they satisfied with the merely personal. 'Return to Cardiff', one of his better-known pieces, describes Abse's feelings on revisiting his native city: loss, brief retrievals of the past, a sense of identity's oddness. The writing is conversational; it is also sharp and intelligent. Its rhythms win an unpredictable music from the musing hesitations of Abse's speaking voice.

'Return to Cardiff' was included in his 1962 book, *Poems, Golders Green*. Abse had by then sloughed off an initial weakness for rhetoric. Subsequent volumes blend a keen appetite for the everyday with an appalled, unmelodramatic awareness of suffering. 'A Night Out' revolves round watching a film about Auschwitz. Troubled, resilient, and anchored in the particular, the poem shows Abse's honesty to advantage. 'Hunt the Thimble' illustrates his interest in the riddle or parable; the repeated questions and answers mimic a child's game but generate a potently obscure menace. These two poems were included in *A Small Desperation* (London, 1968); as the self-deprecating title suggests, Abse's imagination finds suburbia frustrating yet stimulating territory.

Some of Abse's tonally surest work occurs in his most recent volumes, *Way Out in the Centre* (London, 1981; in the US as *One-Legged on Ice*, Athens, Ga., 1983) and *Ask the Bloody Horse* (London, 1986; in the US, as *Sky in Narrow Streets*, Princeton, NJ, 1987). Both his alertness to the strangeness at the heart of familiarity and his wry grappling with the numinous (especially evident in *Ask the Bloody Horse*) find supple expression here. The most convenient single volume of Abse's poetry is *White Coat, Purple*

1

Coat: Collected Poems 1948–1988 (London, 1989; New York, 1990). *A Strong Dose of Myself* (London, 1983) contains essays about poets and poetry. Critical studies of his work include Joseph Cohen (ed.), *The Poetry of Dannie Abse: Critical Essays and Reminiscences* (London, 1983) and Tony Curtis, *Dannie Abse* (Cardiff, 1985).

[MO'N

ACHEBE, Chinua (1930–), is one of the foremost literary figures in Africa. He was born in Ogidi, in rural Eastern Nigeria, where, alongside his family's Christianity, he absorbed the still-vigorous traditions of his Igbo people. He was educated at Government College, Umuahia, and University College, Ibadan, and after working for a time as a teacher, joined the Nigerian Broadcasting Company in Lagos. *Things Fall Apart* was the first of four major novels published between 1958 and 1966. In 1969, during the Civil War, Achebe toured the United States with fellow writers to promote the Biafran cause. He turned to different forms of writing: essays, short stories, and poems. After the war he became professor of literature at Nsukka and editor of the journal *Okike*. A long-awaited fifth novel, *Anthills of the Savannah*, appeared in 1987. In 1990 he was severely paralysed in a road accident.

Lucidity and self-possession characterize Achebe's poems as they do his prose. His Igbo conviction that 'nothing is absolute' imparts a wry detachment to his philosophizing. While 'Beware Soul Brother' blends Christian spirituality and Igbo communalism, other poems satirize both religions. 'Lament of the Sacred Python' shows 'cannibal' Christians blasphemously dining on the divine snake, while 'Those Gods are Children' exposes Igbo prudence in sacrificing only the smallest yams to the ancestors. His most moving poems focus on wry or poignant real-life incidents: the struggle of a mango seedling to root itself on a concrete roof, the deadpan stare of a starving child confronted by a rose-cheeked baby in a Christmas crib-scene.

Achebe's poems are collected in *Beware Soul Brother* (Enugu and London, 1972; in the US,

Christmas in Biafra and Other Poems, New York, 1973). See also *Chinua Achebe: Novelist, Poet, Critic*, by David Carroll (2nd edn., London, 1990). [JB

ACKERMAN, Diane (1948–), was born in Illinois, and received her doctorate from Cornell University; she writes regularly for *The New Yorker*. Eclectic, witty, and impetuous, her poetry collects its vocabulary from Hollywood and Donne, NASA and Einstein's letters, and Egyptian hieroglyphs. *Reverse Thunder* (New Brunswick, NJ, 1988) continues to celebrate the visionary appetites expressed in *Wife of Light* (New York, 1978) and the visceral imaginings of *The Planets* (New York, 1976).

Ackerman cultivates the combination of opposites. In her poems, the most abstract concepts are hitched to the plumpest, most redolent images: 'An event is such a little piece of time-and-space | you can mail it through the slotted eye of a cat.' God hidden in his universe becomes a soft-shelled crab, and Venus in her atmosphere 'a buxom floozy with a pink boa; | mummy, whose black | sediment dessicates within'. Conversely, her poems of love securely lodged in the body tend to ally themselves with moon and ghost, things bloodless, luminous, atmospheric: 'the popsongs, | the gone-sours, | the setbacks, the blights, | the cartwheel heart | where love careens, | all the little dismals | and the giant dreams.'

The Planets in particular shows Ackerman grafting dry scientific vocabulary on to sensuous images. She makes us see how close the modern exploration of space has brought us to the heart and visage of each planet. See also: *Jaguar of Sweet Laughter* (New York and London, 1992) [EG

ACORN, Milton (1923–86), was born in Charlottetown, Prince Edward Island. Seriously wounded in the Second World War, he returned home and worked as a carpenter until *In Love and Anger*, his first volume of poems, was published privately in 1956. He then quit carpentry and devoted himself to writing. In 1962 he married poet Gwendolyn *MacEwen; the marriage failed the following year. After living in Toronto, Vancouver, and Toronto again, Acorn returned to Charlottetown and spent the remainder of his life there. *The Island Means Minago* (1975) won the Governor-General's Award for poetry.

Idealistic and at times angry, this Marxist-Leninist poet occasionally falls into political rhetoric. In his best political poems, however, he is a sincere and passionate denouncer of social injustice. 'I've Tasted My Blood' and 'Knowing I Live in a Dark Age' are masterful poems of this kind. But Acorn is not a poet of a single theme. 'Charlottetown Harbour' and 'November' are superb descriptive lyrics in which the language is evocative and the images precise.

Acorn's many volumes of poetry include *In Love and Anger*, *I've Tasted My Blood* (1969), *More Poems for People* (1972), *The Island Means Minago* (1975), *Jackpine Sonnets* (1977—all Toronto); *Captain Neal MacDougal and the Naked Goddess* (Charlottetown, 1982), *Dig Up My Heart: Selected Poems of Milton Acorn 1952–83* (Toronto, 1983), and *Whiskey Jack* (Toronto, 1986) with and edited by James Deahl. Deahl has also edited and published three other volumes of Acorn's poems: *I Shout Love and Other Poems* (1987), *The Uncollected Acorn* (1987), and *Hundred Proof Earth* (1988—all Toronto). [DRB

ADAMS, Arthur H(enry) (1872–1936), was born in Lawrence in the Otago province of New Zealand's South Island, the son of a Tasmanian-born surveyor and astronomer. After graduating BA from Otago University in 1894, he lived by his pen as journalist, novelist, playwright, librettist, and poet. He travelled to China as war correspondent for the Christchurch *Press* during the Boxer Rising, spent the years 1902–5 in England, and settled in Australia, editing the Red Pages (the literary section) of the Sydney *Bulletin* and becoming editor of the Sydney *Sun*.

As a poet Adams is best known for 'The Dwellings of our Dead', by which he is represented in the Oxford *Anthology of Twentieth Century New Zealand Poetry*, ed. Vincent O'Sullivan (Auckland, 1970; 3rd edn., 1987). Despite some florid Romantic diction, this poem carries, by

way of its mournful music, a strong emotional charge. Adams's other verse has not been reprinted since *The Collected Verses of Arthur H. Adams* (Melbourne, 1913), which includes nothing from either *The Nazarene: A Study of a Man* (London, 1902) or *London Streets* (London, 1906). But Adams is significant in the history of New Zealand poetry for having brought deep personal involvement to a poetic tradition that had been dominated by earnest dilettantes. His verse, which may recall work by Rupert *Brooke or by such British *fin de siècle* poets as Arthur *Symons and John *Davidson, engages with disturbing and ugly areas of experience ignored by his more complacent predecessors, offers a heterodox view of Christ, shows compassion for the downtrodden, and can exhibit a sensuality that seemed bold in the early twentieth century. [MacDJ

ADAMS, Léonie (1899–), was born in New York City and educated at Barnard College. Her second book, *High Falcon*, was published in 1929 to critical acclaim, but her *Poems: A Selection* (New York) did not appear until 1954, with twenty-four new poems. It won the Bollingen Prize in Poetry. Like her friend Louise *Bogan, Adams is a painstaking, severe, and not prolific poet.

Adams's work might well be called Platonic, for it is a poetry of forms, schematic and elegant, from which the messy details of private life or historical accident have been abstracted. The most successful poems embed their metaphysical reflection in natural forms. Although Adams disdains the particulars of history, she gives her poetry a welcome concreteness in terms of tree, flower, and evening star. 'The moon above the milky field | Gleaning moves her one slant light; | Wind weeps from out its cloud. | Then, weeping wind, unshroud | Pale Cassiopeia.'

This obsessive use of natural emblems creates an odd tension, however, since ultimately Adams's poetry is about the weather in her own rather isolated and changeable soul. Agnostic, uncertain of the claims of art, having no reason to suppose a correspondence between nature and self, Adams uses the pathetic fallacy not to expand into the world but to contract into self-reflection. 'The will shall learn itself alone, | For walking by the waters' side.' The only comfort offered by nature is cold, since its recurrences are blind to the human face, deaf to its voice; the most one can ask for is forgetfulness.   [EG

ADAMSON, Robert (1943–), grew up in Sydney but while a young teenager ran away to live as a fisherman on the Hawkesbury River. This is how he lives today, after periods spent in remand homes and prison.

Adamson first made his mark, in *Canticles on the Skin* (1970), with poems that reflected these experiences but played with the roles that the experiences offered. Adamson's poetry has had three strands: imagistic celebrations of nature, particularly of the Hawkesbury River, its birds and fish; extravagant celebrations of existence as mythological quest; and a modern scepticism which directs irony at this penchant for romantic celebration.

All these elements have been apparent in his work from the beginning. His poems in *The Clean Dark* (1989) are perhaps his most serene. Gone are the jumpy rhythms and sardonic rhymes frequent in his poems about drugs and prison. Yet even here a degree of restlessness and self-consciousness is frequent. Adamson's poems are sometimes allusive, and his books provide many epigraphs drawn from major writers, but this is not the most convincing aspect of his work.

For a decade Adamson was influential in contemporary Australian poetry through his editorship of the magazine *New Poetry*. He is a brilliant book designer and has published one novella, *Zimmer's Essay* (1974). His poems are most readily accessible in *Selected Poems* (Sydney, 1977) and *The Clean Dark* (Sydney, 1989).   [DHa

ADCOCK, Fleur (1934–), was born in Auckland, spent the war years as a child in various parts of England, and in 1947 returned to live in Wellington, where she was educated at Victoria University. For a brief period she taught in the classics departments at Victoria and Otago universities. She then became a librarian. In 1963

she settled in London, working in the library of the Foreign and Commonwealth Office. Since 1979 she has been a free-lance writer, with London as her base.

It was in Dunedin and Wellington in the late 1950s and early 1960s that Adcock began publishing poetry. In fact, as she writes in 'In Memoriam: James K. Baxter', she 'married . . . into the art', marrying part-Polynesian poet Alistair *Campbell at the age of 18. She has two sons. Her first collection, *The Eye of the Hurricane*, was published in Wellington in 1964. She is now widely regarded as one of the two or three best women poets writing in Britain. New Zealand anthologists also continue to claim her. In several of her poems questions of identity are touched on in terms of allegiance to one or the other hemisphere.

Adcock's poems range from tightly controlled rhymed structures to relaxed conversational pieces in looser forms. Her characteristic manner is decorous, urbane, and poised, but may also be astringent, and many of her strongest poems are tense with intuited menace, their composure holding nightmare at bay: it is as though the writing of poems were a strategy for maintaining the cool persona who delivers them. She is a shrewd observer of personal, especially sexual, relations.

Adcock's *Selected Poems* (Oxford, 1983, 1991) draws on six volumes. Her main subsequent collections have been *The Incident Book* (Oxford, 1986) and *Time-Zones* (Oxford, 1991). She also edited *The Faber Book of Twentieth Century Women's Poetry* (London, 1987) and has done translations from Romanian and from medieval Latin. She was interviewed for *Landfall*, 143 (1982), and for *Talking about Ourselves*, ed. Harry Ricketts (Wellington, 1986); an autobiographical essay appeared in *Beyond Expectations*, ed. Margaret Clark (Wellington, 1986).   [MacDJ

AE (1867–1935), pseudonym of George William Russell, poet, painter, mystic, agronomist, and editor, born in Lurgan, Co. Armagh. Moved to Dublin in 1878. At the Dublin Art School he met W. B. *Yeats, and they were close friends for many years, united by interests in the Irish literary revival and in magical-theosophical matters, though they later became partially estranged.

Russell's pseudonym was adopted from a compositor's query 'AE–?', failing to read his original mystical nom-de-plume 'Aeon'. His first poems, *Homeward. Songs by the Way* (1894) resembled Yeats's early 'Celtic Twilight' poetry. But his work did not develop much; Frank *O'Connor noted AE's career-long 'habit-forming' tendency to produce the same misty, Donegal poems and paintings. Though AE's second *Collected Poems* (1919) does display some advance, what is frustrating is how rarely he exercised his more concrete poetic vernacular, reminiscent of the developed Yeats, displayed in poems such as the longer narrative 'Michael' or 'On Behalf of Some Irishmen not Followers of Tradition', which ends with the adjuration to young writers: 'Against the sceptred myth to hold | The golden heresy of truth.' But mostly he did hold to the sceptred myth.

AE was irreproachable in several capacities: as an encourager of young writers; as a socially responsible opponent of the repressive magnates of Dublin in the 1912–13 strikes; as Horace Plunkett's manager of the successful development of the co-operative agricultural movement; above all, as an excellent editor (helped by Susan Mitchell) of two of Plunkett's enlightened cultural journals, *The Irish Homestead* (1905–23) and *The Irish Statesman* (1923–30).

A collected edition of AE's writings, which will include a volume of poems, is to be published by Colin Smythe in England and the Humanities Press in the USA. See H. Summerfield, *That Myriad-Minded Man: A Biography of G. W. Russell—A.E.* (Gerrard's Cross, 1975) and John Eglinton's 1937 *Memoir*.   [BO'D

AGARD, John (1949–), was born in British Guiana (now Guyana). Together with Linton Kwesi *Johnson and Benjamin *Zephaniah, he can be considered a 'dub' poet, for many of his poems use vernacular and dialect modes and are written to be performed, though they display a hard-edged wit which loses nothing in print. The link with performance and musical accompaniment is emphasized by his own description of himself as a 'poetsonian', and is strongest in *Man to Pan* (Havana, 1982), which won the Casa de las Américas prize. It contains poems which continually allude to the music of steel bands in an often delightful, occasionally disturbing, but always unpredictable manner. In 1977 he came to England, where he has been working as a Touring Lecturer with the Commonwealth Institute in London.

Mangoes & Bullets: Selected and New Poems 1972–84 (London and Sydney, 1985) is his best, and most representative, collection. The poems in which a limbo dancer functions as an elusive persona through which Agard probes the pain and alienation bequeathed by history in the Caribbean are among his most effective, and were first published in *Limbo Dancer in Dark Glasses* (London, 1983). Recent books include *Life Doesn't Frighten Me at All* (1989) and *Laughter is an Egg* (1990—both London).   [MR

Agenda. Founded in 1959, William Cookson's refreshingly plain, purposeful-looking magazine has pursued its clearly defined poetic programme in an admirably resilient manner. Its presiding genius—some would unfairly say its editorial obsession—is Ezra *Pound, but a glance through back issues quickly shows that the magazine's pages have been open to a surprisingly wide variety of styles and views. There have been plenty of solid special numbers, on poets ranging from Thomas *Hardy to David *Jones, and on thematic subjects such as criticism, myth, and rhythm. Reviews are often stronger on passion than on professionalism, but that is part of the magazine's characteristic, excitable flavour. A series of Agenda Editions has collected work by poets closely associated with the magazine, including Peter *Dale and Michael *Hamburger. *Agenda*, published in London, is now co-edited by William Cookson and Peter Dale.   [NP

Agrarianism, a movement among men of letters in the American South of the late 1920s and 1930s to defend its traditional agricultural way of life against the industrialization and urbanization that were fast overwhelming it. The 'Twelve Southerners' who contributed essays to the most substantial Agrarian publication, *I'll Take My Stand: The South and the Agrarian Tradition* (1930), were Donald *Davidson, John Gould *Fletcher, Henry Blue Kline, Lyle Lanier, Andrew Lytle, H. C. Nixon, Frank Lawrence Owsley, John Crowe *Ransom, Allen *Tate, John Donald Wade, Robert Penn *Warren, and Stark Young. As Agrarians they had no formal affiliation with Vanderbilt University, although ten of them had either taught or studied there. The book urged southerners not to adopt the industrial ideal, its essays variously pointing out the adverse effects of industrialism (on attitudes to labour, religion, and the fine arts) and the exemplary and civilized qualities of a society, like that of the Old South, which refuses to deify technological improvement and material prosperity. As its critics quickly realized, the volume failed to show how Agrarianism could be properly implemented, let alone compete with industrialism. So, in the following decade, in several public debates and many articles, the Agrarians attempted to justify its practicability. In *Who Owns America? A New Declaration of Independence* (edited by Tate and Herbert Agar, 1936) they united with economists from elsewhere to question the value of large corporations and centralized power.

Contemporary attacks on Agrarian writing accused it of being a romantic apology for slavery and a nostalgic dream of restoring plantation life. More recent attacks see it as a Utopian exercise which ignored the more vexing realities of southern history and experience. Certainly it did not succeed in its explicit objectives: after the Depression the South was rapidly urbanized and industrialized. Tate, however, later thought the movement had been successful, if only in convincingly demonstrating that the dehumanizing results of modern industrialism could—and should—be tempered by religious humanism.

Like Tate, the other Agrarian poets, Ransom, Davidson, and Warren, had all originally become interested in defending the South in 1925 in response to the northern ridicule poured on the Tennessee Anti-Evolution Bill (which had prohibited the teaching of Darwin's evolu-

tionary theory in all public schools and universities). But ultimately only Davidson was committed to the South above all else. For the others, as Louis D. Rubin shows in *The Wary Fugitives: Four Poets and the South* (Baton Rouge, La., 1978), Agrarianism had actually been an expression of other—religious, social, and aesthetic—imperatives. See also, for a mixture of group biography and intellectual history, *The Southern Agrarians*, by Paul K. Conkin (Knoxville, Tenn., 1988).   [NE

AHMED-UD-DIN, Feroz (1950–), was born in Dhaka and attended schools throughout Bangladesh (where his police-officer father happened to have been posted). He graduated from Dhaka University in 1975 with an MA in English.

Ahmed-ud-Din writes tellingly about the loss of vision in contemporary life, and in his work he attempts to revitalize the self through a series of epiphanic resolutions. His poems are mostly short and intense; they address the common problems of humanity but are rich in local reference. His only collection, *This Handful of Dust*, was published in Calcutta in 1975 by Writers Workshop.   [SMI

AI (1947–), was born in Tucson, Arizona, of mixed Native American, African American, and Japanese heritage; she studied writing with Galway *Kinnell at the University of California at Irvine. The author of four books of poems—*Cruelty* (Boston, 1973), *Killing Floor* (Boston, 1978), *Sin* (Boston, 1986), and *Fate* (Boston, 1991), Ai lives in Cambridge, Massachusetts.

All Ai's work is stark, harsh, and dramatic in style. But as her preoccupations move from personal violence to historic atrocity, her imagination opens out into the public arena; the domestic turns political. Throughout her poetry, a stripped-down diction conveys an underlying, almost biblical indignation—not, at times, without compassion—at human misuses of power and the corrupting energies of various human appetites.

Although virtually all the poems present themselves as spoken by a particular character, Ai makes little attempt to capture individual styles of diction, personal vocabularies; the result, if monotonous, is also striking. A Mexican revolutionary, an old woman with a young lover, the dead Robert Kennedy, a Vietnam veteran—all speak with a sullen, deadpan passion that galvanizes our attention through the voice's intensity rather than by the accumulation of realistic detail. The foreshortened, nearly parodic vividness of Ai's characters makes them closer to types than to historical portraits.

[RHa

AIDOO, Ama Ata (1942–), Ghanaian playwright, short-story writer, and poet, was christened Christina Ama Aidoo, but now uses her African name. She read English at the University of Ghana, Legon, and made an early reputation with her plays, *The Dilemma of a Ghost* (1965) and *Anowa* (1969), which placed her among the most original of modern African dramatists. Her poems and short stories appeared first in the journals *Okyeame*, *Black Orpheus*, and *Presence africaine*. She has pursued a career as writer and university teacher in Ghana, Kenya, and the United States. Recently she has been living in Zimbabwe.

Aidoo's work is strongly influenced by oral tradition, and her writing is intended primarily to be heard. Sometimes, like the traditional *griot*, she makes no clear distinction between prose and verse, and her novel *Our Sister Killjoy: or Reflections from a Black-Eyed Squint* (1977) moves constantly between prose and loose free verse. The work takes the form of the indignant tirade of a Ghanaian student on an officially sponsored cultural visit to Germany. She attacks the polite racism of Europe, the corrupt leaders of neo-colonial Africa, educated Africans who waste their skills in First World countries, and the sexism of both western and African societies. As 'our sister' she demands the licence accorded to one of the family to speak her mind frankly, even bad-temperedly, to her fellow Africans.

Aidoo's verse is most accessible in *Our Sister Killjoy* (London, 1977). A volume of poems, *Someone Talking to Sometime*, was published in Harare in 1985. See also Lloyd W. Brown, *Women Writers in Black Africa* (Westport, Conn. and London, 1981).

[JB

AIKEN, Conrad (Potter) (1889–1973), was deeply affected throughout his life by the tragedy in his childhood. He was 11 years old when he heard, from the next room, the sound of the shots with which his father had killed both the boy's mother and himself. The early years in Savannah (to which he returned in old age) were changed to life with an ancient aunt in Massachusetts. He was educated at Concord and Harvard, where he became friendly with T. S. *Eliot. Aiken's finest novel, *Great Circle*, deals directly with his parents' violent deaths, and his interest in psychoanalysis sprang from the need to explain or exorcise the most crucial event of his life.

Aiken's output began with *Earth Triumphant* (1914) and in the next decade he produced almost a book of verse a year. The *Selected Poems*, which excluded almost all of his first, second, and fourth books, appeared in 1933, and was followed by another *Selected* (New York, 1961) and a *Collected* (New York, 1953; 2nd edn., 1970). Aiken was married three times, and had three children by the first marriage. His autobiographical excursion *Ushant* appeared in 1952. Books about him include Houston Peterson's largely psychoanalytical *The Melody of Chaos* (1931) and *Conrad Aiken: A Life of his Art*, by Jay Martin (Princeton, NJ, 1962).

Writing to Malcolm *Cowley in 1941, Aiken called himself 'an almost unique phenomenon, a poet who has acquired a Reputation, or a Position, or what have you, without ever having been caught in the act': that is, the act of writing anything considered by critics as poetry. It is true that although Aiken was loaded with prizes and awards (the Pulitzer Prize, National Book Award, Gold Medal for Poetry, etc.), much critical writing about him has been dismissive or slighting. This is in part because of a deadly facility, combined with a liking for conventionally musical rhythms, in part because of his tendency to treat historical themes or myths as subjects for dramatic rhetoric. The result was long poems like *Punch: The Immortal Liar* (1921) and *The Kid* (1947), which contain fine passages yet are unmistakably failures taken as a whole. There is some truth in Randall *Jarrell's comment that Aiken was 'a kind of Midas: everything he touches turns to verse', with the corollary that 'everything *blurs* into everything else'.

At least that is true of Aiken's easiest and most nostalgic writing. His finest poetry, however, achieves in places the grandeur he was always looking for, and in others gets beyond the fluent expression of nostalgia to what comes through as genuine anguish. *Preludes for Memnon* (1931), his finest volume, was apparently intended, along with its lesser successor *Time in the Rock* (1936), as a single work attempting to fix many 'fragments of consciousness . . . so that the life which the consciousness reflects may be known and judged'. The idea has a typically Aikenian vagueness, but these preludes are best seen as individual poems, most of them using the forms of Elizabethan and Jacobean dramatic verse as a springboard for wholly original work. Many of the poems deal at one or two removes with aspects of the poet's life and loves, others play with a constant concern for 'the ding-an-sich, | The feeling itself, the round bright dark emotion'. The idea of poetry as a 'thing in itself', outside feeling but still part of it, along with the belief that *words* can never express *things*, never ceased to fascinate Aiken. In *Preludes for Memnon* the expression of these preoccupations is all the more convincing because it is joined to jokes and outrageous puns. The prelude that begins 'Two coffees in the Español, the last | Bright drops of golden Barsac in a goblet, | Fig paste and candied nuts', and goes on to reflections about age, love, and death, is one of the grandest, most successful examples of his rhetoric.

Some of the other late poetry is accomplished and personal without being totally original, but a sizeable selection could still be made of poems that could have been written by nobody else, in particular those where his characteristic nostalgia is laced with irony. 'King Borborigmi' (who is 'King of infinite space in a walnut shell— | But has bad dreams; I fear he has bad dreams'), 'The Wedding', and 'Psychomachia' are three examples of the variety of manners Aiken could command. His talent lost something by being diffused instead of concentrated, but was still remarkable.   [JGS

ALDINGTON, Richard (christened Edward Godfree) (1892–1962), was born in Portsmouth (a town of suffocating dullness, according to his self-pitying poem 'Childhood'), the son of a solicitor, and was educated at Dover College and (for one year) London University. In 1911 he met the American poet H.D. (Hilda *Doolittle), six years his senior, and the pair were taken up by Ezra *Pound, who coined the term *Imagistes* (see IMAGISM) for them, sent their work to Harriet Monroe for *Poetry* magazine in Chicago, and published them in his own anthology *Des Imagistes* (1914).

Aldington married H.D. in 1913, but they were soon estranged (though the marriage was not annulled until 1938, to enable him to remarry). He stayed a proclaimed Imagist when the group was appropriated by Amy *Lowell (his second and third volumes were *Images of War* and *Images of Desire*), and from 1914 to 1917 he edited the literary pages of the *Egoist*, which became the movement's main organ; T. S. *Eliot replaced him as literary editor when Aldington went to the Western Front. After his experiences in the trenches he was diagnosed neurasthenic, and through the Twenties, feeling broken and embittered, he scraped a living as a free-lance writer and translator (see *Fifty Romance Lyric Poems*, 1931). Publication in 1929 of his angry war novel, *Death of a Hero*, made him famous. Quitting England, he spent the Second World War in America, but eventually settled in Montpelier, where in his last years he wrote controversial biographies of D. H. *Lawrence (whose poems he had edited), Norman Douglas, and T. E. Lawrence.

Only Aldington's very earliest poems, collected in the volume *Images* (1915), are now much regarded. The book is Hellenistic in spirit, and in its yearning vocatives (four consecutive poems begin 'Potnia, Potnia . . .', 'O you, O you most fair . . .', 'O Artemis . . .', 'Pan O Pan . . .') and the preponderance of colour effects there are unexpected echoes of the Tennyson of 'Oenone'. These lean pieces of imitation marble are offset by a group of contemporary urban poems, 'Cinema Exit', 'In the Tube', 'Hampstead Heath', and others.

Of subsequent volumes, *Images of War* is an unrewarding clash between theory and terror (though 'Blood of the Young Men' is still often anthologized). The poems of *Exile* show a developing interest in the verse paragraph, and *Words for Music* even includes some 'Metrical Exercises'. His most characterful extended work, ridiculed on publication, is the phantasmagoric *Fool i' the Forest* (1925), which owes much to *The Waste Land*. The poem, which presents three figures ('I', the Conjuror, and the fool Mezzetin) as aspects of a single person, is an unstable amalgam of dream, allusion, and Poundian satirical rant at the capitalist system: 'And Helen's married to a Guggenheim. | (Sweet Helen, make me immortal with a kiss).'

See the autobiography, *Life for Life's Sake* (London, 1941) and the introduction to *The Complete Poems* (London, 1948). H.D.'s *Bid Me to Live* (London and New York, 1960) contains a vivid portrait of Aldington as 'Rafe Ashton'.

[MI

ALI, Agha Shahid (1949–), was born in Delhi. His father is a professor of education and Ali was educated in American, Indian, and Kashmiri schools and universities. After teaching at Delhi University and in Kashmir, Ali settled in the United States as a professor of English and creative writing. One of the few Indians from an Islamic family to write poetry in English, Ali blends the traditions of the Urdu *ghazal* with contemporary American verse. His themes are the unrootedness, fears, joys, incongruities, and surprises of exile alongside memories and imagining of a past which has increasingly become distanced and which continues to evolve without his presence. There is also amusement with his life in America and an existential insecurity resulting from having left the protecting comfort of his family.

Ali's first two volumes were heavily drenched with the sadness of Urdu poetry and T. S. *Eliot's sense of loss. *The Half-Inch Himalayas* (1987) is carefully composed of linked images, allusions, and recurring situations. It expresses the anxieties, fantasies, and discoveries of the continual traveller who imagines lives

he and others might have had. *A Walk Through the Yellow Pages* (1987) uses a highly American idiom, advertising slogans, and parodies of folktales to reveal nightmarish fears hidden by the commonplace. Ali has also translated Faiz Ahmed Faiz from Urdu.

His poetry is available in *Bone-Sculpture* (Calcutta, 1972), *In Memory of Begum Akhtar* (Calcutta, 1979), *A Walk Through the Yellow Pages* (Tucson, Ariz., 1987), *The Half-Inch Himalayas* (Middletown, Conn., 1987), and *A Nostalgist's Map of America* (New York, 1992). He has written *T. S. Eliot as Editor* (Ann Arbor, Mich., 1986).

[BK

ALLEN, Dick (1939–), was born in Troy, New York, and grew up in Round Lake Village, a rural community north of Albany. At Syracuse University he became editor-in-chief of the college newspaper, before graduating in 1961. He was a graduate student in writing at Brown University in the early Sixties, studying there with *Berryman, and in 1964 went on to teach at Wright State University in Dayton, Ohio, where he co-founded *Mad River Review*. In 1968 he joined the faculty at the University of Bridgeport in Connecticut, where he currently holds the Charles A. Dana Endowed Chair of English.

The influence of science fiction on his poetry has been apparent from his first volume, *Anon and Various Time Machine Poems* (New York, 1971), highlighted by the long 'pop epic' of Anon, an American Everyman of the Sixties making a surreal journey through the contemporary American landscape and, via time travel, backwards and forwards through American culture and history. The shorter 'Time Travel Poems' established the type of lyric that characterizes his subsequent volumes, *Regions with No Proper Names* (New York, 1975), *Overnight in the Guest House of the Mystic* (Baton Rouge, La., 1984), and *Flight and Pursuit* (Baton Rouge, 1987). They are by turns erotic and mystical, rooted in the matrix of his life in New York State, Ohio, Rhode Island, and Connecticut, as in 'The Poet at Eighteen', 'Visit', and 'Janes Avenue', even as they explore other lives in narratives like 'Cliff Painting', and veer from the quotidian in 'Crossing the Stars on New Year's Eve' and 'Barge Lights on the Hudson'.

Since 1981 Allen has become increasingly associated with the revival of narrative and metre in American poetry, and in 1988 he edited a special issue of *Crosscurrents* containing poems and essays pertaining to the *New Formalism and the *New Narrative. This involvement has given his recent poetry a technical polish that tempers the frenetic wildness of his inventive but uneven earlier work.   [RMcP

ALLISON, Drummond (1921–43), was born at Caterham in Surrey, and educated at Bishop's Stortford College and Queen's College, Oxford, where he took a wartime shortened degree in history before joining the army. He served as an Intelligence Officer with the West Surrey Regiment, and was killed in action between Naples and Rome in December 1943.

At Oxford, Allison became a close friend of John *Heath-Stubbs and Sidney *Keyes, both of whom were at Queen's College. The only poems by Allison to appear in his lifetime were those included in *Eight Oxford Poets* (1941), edited by Michael Meyer and Keyes. After his death a collection of his poems, *The Yellow Night*, was published (London, 1944), and several appeared in the anthology *Poetry from Oxford in Wartime* (London, 1945), ed. William Bell. *The Poems of Drummond Allison* (Reading, 1978), ed. Michael Sharp, added to these twelve further poems from manuscript.

Unlike Heath-Stubbs, Keyes, and the rest of that circle in early wartime Oxford, Allison was an admirer of W. H. *Auden, whose work he had first read at school. This is clear from such poems of 1940/1 as 'Come let us pity Death', 'The Seaside Hotel', 'One finds in leaves his solace', 'The gardener rises restive', and 'For Karl Marx'. But Allison's poems are certainly not just Audenesque pastiche. His work has a tough and yet supple intellectual sinew, and enjoys a vocabulary both wide and apt.

Chaucer, Malory, and Arthurian myth supplied him with some material, but there is also plenty of the ordinary world he knew: the suburbs, Oxford, the army, all treated wittily,

wryly, and sometimes with elegiac power of a surprising and authoritative kind, as in 'Dedication', 'My Sister Helen (1917)', and 'The Brass Horse'.   [AST

ALLOTT, Kenneth (1912–73), spent his childhood and youth in Cumberland, took First Class Honours in English at Durham University, and emerged as a poet at Oxford, where he was co-editor of the little magazine *Programme*. He made a poetic reputation in the Thirties as one of the principal contributors to *New Verse, published in collaboration with Stephen Tait a comic novel, *The Rhubarb Tree* (1937), in which the heroine is no more than a voice on the telephone, and then *Poems* (1938), followed by another collection, *The Ventriloquist's Doll* (1943). He later became a professor at Liverpool University, where he edited the standard edition of Matthew Arnold's poems, and also *The Penguin Book of Contemporary Verse* (1950, revised and enlarged 1962). He was twice married.

Allott was the most deliberately stylish poet of the Thirties, always verbally witty, at times almost too careful and thoughtful. He used surrealistic effects brilliantly, as in one of his best-known poems, 'Lament for a Cricket Eleven', but with a deliberation alien to a true surrealist. His skilful rhetoric was always under control, so that the indignation expressed in such a poem as 'Exodus' ('From this wet island of birds and chimneys | Who can watch suffering Europe and not be angry?') was genuine but seemed calculated. The general tone of his first collection is elegiac, regretting the past, seeing little hope in the future, and taking conscious refuge in personal happiness. 'The Professor' blends a controlled surrealism in the image of a wild professor meditating on death, with an arbitrary but wonderfully effective final couplet: 'Heaven is full of clocks which strike all day. | It is to music we are put away.' *The Ventriloquist's Doll* does not fail in wit or stylishness, but adds little of importance to *Poems*.

Like almost all other English poets of his generation Allott was influenced by *Auden, but he was one of the few who absorbed the influence and produced, not imitation Auden, but poems individual to himself and unique in the decade during which he was a poet. His *Collected Poems* appeared in 1975 (London).   [JGS

ALURISTA (1947–), by birth Alberto Baltazar Urista Heredia, moved with his family from Cuernavaca and Acapulco, Mexico, to San Diego in 1960. Much influenced by the example of César Chávez and his United Farm Workers, in 1967 he helped to found MECHA (Movimiento Estudiantil Chicano de Aztlán), the Chicano Student Movement of Aztlán. If he is indeed the poet laureate of Chicano culture, as he has been dubbed, it rests upon several counts: his celebration of 'Aztlán' as the mythic, south-western homeland of the Chicano people; his creation of an 'interlingual' verse which switches between Spanish (whether Mexican or the *caló* of the barrio), English (mainstream or black), and Amerindian (Náhuatl or Mayan); and his adeptness in the use of pre-Columbian folklore and imagery.

Floricanto en Aztlán (1971), with its amalgams of English and Spanish, set the note in which a poem like 'when raza' typically calls for an end to alienation ('mañana doesn't come|for he who waits'). But Alurista's versatility also extends to the Maya-influenced incantatory verse of *Nationchild Plumaroja, 1969–1972* (1972), the language experiments and puns of *Spik in Glyph* (1980), and the European poems of *Dawn's Eye* (1982). Principal collections include *Floricanto en Aztlán* (Los Angeles, 1971), *Nationchild Plumaroja* (San Diego, Calif., 1972), *Timespace Huracán* (Albuquerque, New Mexico, 1976), *A'nque* (San Diego, 1979) and *Return: Poems Collected and New* (Ypsilanti, Mich., 1982). See also *Understanding Chicano Literature*, by Carl R. Shirley and Paula W. Shirley (Columbia, South Carol., 1988).   [ARL

ALVAREZ, A(lfred) (1929–), was born in London and educated at Oundle School and Corpus Christi College, Oxford. After a brief academic career, which produced *The Shaping Spirit* (London, 1958), a study of modern poetry, and *The School of Donne* (London, 1961), he became a free-lance writer and Poetry Editor of The

Observer. In his influential Penguin anthology *The *New Poetry* (Harmondsworth, 1962) he urged the superiority of such American moderns as *Lowell, *Berryman, and *Plath to *Larkin and British 'gentility'. *Under Pressure: The Writer in Society* (London, 1965) is a useful set of interviews with East European and American writers, originally broadcast on the BBC. *Beyond All this Fiddle* (London, 1968; New York, 1969) is a collection of essays written 1955–67.

As a critic Alvarez identified himself closely with *Confessional Poetry, coming to regard emotional breakdown or extremism as a virtual criterion of seriousness, and arguing that poetry itself was a 'murderous art'. This line of thought culminated in *The Savage God* (London, 1971; New York, 1972), a study of suicide among writers and artists, remembered now chiefly for its memoir of the last months of Sylvia Plath. A mixture of perspicacity and dubious special pleading, his criticism is perhaps better at locating intensity than at explaining its workings, or distinguishing between suffering and self-pity. What is lasting in the poetry he endorsed, though, is not its sickness but its health. His critique of British poetry's tendency to slip back into neo-Georgian cosiness and inhibition was timely and acute, as was his insistence that honesty should take precedence over received good taste.

His own poetry is collected in *Lost* (London, 1968) and *Autumn to Autumn* (London, 1978). Blood and death figure largely. 'God is a cannibal' ('The Killing'); 'The skull in my hands is my life's. It stares at me' ('The Survivor'); 'Death| like homesickness|like homecoming after captivity' ('Dying').

Outside literature, he is known for his interest in rock-climbing and poker. Other books include the novels *Hers* (1974) and *Hunt* (1978), and *Offshore: A North Sea Journey* (1986), *Feeding the Rat: Profile of a Climber* (1988), and *Rainforest* (with Charles Blackman, 1988).   [WS

American Poetry Review or *APR* (Philadelphia) is the most widely circulated poetry journal currently published in the United States. Established in 1971, it immediately distinguished itself from other journals like *Poetry* (Chicago) by means of its tabloid format, which was doubtless intended to counter the image of literary magazines as stodgy and academic. It is perhaps most notorious for publishing large photographs of the poets it prints, a practice that for some epitomizes the aspect of contemporary American poetry known as 'Po Biz'. The practice may also reflect the bias of its editors, Stephen *Berg, Arthur Vogelsang, and David Bonnano, towards more personal poetic modes, chiefly those that centre on the poet's own reported experience; Berg co-edited the influential anthology *Naked Poetry*, which helped to codify and canonize those modes in the Sixties. While *APR* prints much mediocre poetry of the 'workshop' variety, it has also published virtually all of the best contemporary American poets at one time or another, and it regularly includes valuable portfolios of translations from major poets working in other languages.   [RG

AMIS, Kingsley (1922–), was born in South London and educated at the City of London School and St John's College, Oxford, where Philip *Larkin was a fellow undergraduate and close friend. He served in the army during the Second World War, and was a university teacher at Swansea, Princeton, and Cambridge, becoming a full-time writer in 1963. Publication of two early volumes of poems, *Bright November* (1947) and *A Frame of Mind* (1953), preceded *Lucky Jim* (1954), the first of the many entertaining novels for which he is better known. There followed *A Case of Samples* (1956), a pamphlet, *The Evans Country* (1962), and *A Look Round the Estate* (1967). The *Collected Poems 1944–1979* (London, 1979) contains six poems from *Bright November*, almost everything from the later books, and some previously uncollected poems. As editor, Amis has compiled the *New Oxford Book of Light Verse* (1978) and the *Faber Popular Reciter* (1978).

Amis's early verse did more than the work of any of the contemporaries with whom his name was linked (Larkin, John *Wain, D. J. *Enright, Elizabeth *Jennings, and others in Robert *Conquest's *New Lines* anthology of 1956) to set the tone for the 1950s *Movement in poetry. Clear, and assiduously crafted, it upheld traditional forms and devices, debunked intellectual or emotional pretentiousness, and sought to demonstrate that common experience invariably undermines romantic (including erotic) aspiration. At the same time, to write about love and personal disillusionment at all (sometimes movingly, and with unexpected vulnerability in poems like 'Masters' and 'Sources of the Past') is to acknowledge that poetry is still a suitable repository for feeling; and a persisting sub-romantic note can still be detected in Movement verse. This remains in Amis's poetry even when, from the mid-1950s onwards, he brought his comic talents into play, hinting ruefully at an inability to produce love poems ('A Bookshop Idyll') and envying the sexual conquests of a commercial traveller ('A Song of Experience'). But he was steadily developing his distinctive identity as a poet: that of the no-nonsense, more than averagely sensual man who can curb undue romantic tendencies but will still poignantly register regret and nostalgia ('A Chromatic Passing-Note', 'In Memoriam W.R.A.'), and deplore the disappointments of love ('Sight Unseen', 'A Point of Logic'). By the time he reached *The Evans Country*, a group of bawdy cameos set in a philistine, lower-middle-class South Wales (anticipating his much-later novel, *The Old Devils*), this identity was firmly established. The sexual adventures of the ordinary, unintellectual Evans may be fast and furtive, but (by implication the question challenges great lovers, poets, and his own readers): 'Who's doing better, then?' The last twenty poems in *Collected Poems* are the work of twenty years; their mood is by turns nostalgic ('A Reunion'), acerbic ("Their Oxford'), and fearful ('Drinking Song'). But the bluff, abrasive humour, and technical adroitness leave his admirers regretting that Amis has not produced more verse in this period.   [AB

AMMONS, A(rchie) R(andolph) (1926–), was born and raised in rural North Carolina, the youngest of a tobacco farmer's three surviving children. Ammons started writing poetry on board a United States destroyer escort in the South Pacific during the Second World War. Upon his return to civilian life he majored in science at Wake Forest University and later did graduate work in English at the University of California, Berkeley. For a year he was principal of the tiny elementary school in the island village of Cape Hatteras. For the better part of a decade he worked as a sales executive in his father-in-law's biological glass company on the southern New Jersey shore.

Ammons published *Ommateum*, his first book, at his own expense in 1955; sixteen copies were sold in the next five years. In 1964, the year he joined the English faculty at Cornell University in Ithaca, NY, he published his second collection and rather rapidly went from total obscurity to wide acclaim. *Collected Poems 1951–1971* (New York, 1972), which won the National Book Award in 1973, capped an astonishingly productive period. Other high honours attended the publication of *Sphere* (New York, 1974) and *A Coast of Trees* (New York, 1981). Despite a variety of physical maladies, Ammons remains a genial presence on the Cornell campus, where he continues as poet-in-residence.

Ammons is a maverick talent, utterly distinctive in voice, marked by high poetic ambition yet capable of whimsy. A nature poet, with a highly developed scientific acumen that sets him off from his contemporaries, Ammons often seems intent on making the consciousness of the poet the secret or real subject of the poem. In many cases, meticulous observation of the natural world is put at the service of abstract investigations and themes, such as the question of the one and the many; Ammons is constantly on the search for a unifying principle among minute and divergent particulars. The much-anthologized 'Corsons Inlet' is characteristically peripatetic, chronicling the poet's thoughts as he walks along the shore, where he celebrates fluid forms and disdains artificial enclosures. The critic Harold Bloom has championed Ammons as a transcendentalist, 'the most direct Emersonian in American poetry since Frost'. Like *Frost, Ammons loves nature too deeply to sentimentalize it or flinch in the face of its cruel-

ties. But he is warmer; where Frost is a poet of terror, Ammons would convert fear into praise. He aspires, as he writes in 'The City Limits', to a transcendent 'radiance' that illuminates equally a sublime landscape or the scene of a natural slaughter.

Among his long poems, *Tape for the Turn of the Year* (Ithaca, NY, 1965; New York, 1972) is a notable experiment in form. The poem's skinny lines are the result of Ammons's decision to type out the poem, without revision, on a long roll of adding-machine paper. The buoyant and discursive *Sphere* (1974), Ammons's masterpiece, displays his formal and prosodic originality. Consisting of 155 sections, each containing four three-line stanzas, *Sphere* enacts 'the form of a motion' (the book's subtitle). The colon is used as an all-purpose punctuation mark, with the effect that closure is continually postponed. The three-line stanzas resemble a species of *terza libre*—a rhymeless version of the stanza unit of Shelley's 'Ode to the West Wind'. Ammons writes in the American idiom, has a 'democratic' bias in favour of lower-case letters, switches rapidly from high to low diction, and in one mood may remind his readers that 'magnificent' in North Carolina comes out 'maggie-went-a-fishing'. But his sly wit doesn't obscure the visionary nature of his poetry, the aim to affirm the magnificence of creation, however lowly in appearance, however dark in design.

Ammons's *Selected Poems* (1987) and *Selected Longer Poems* (1980—both New York) offer an excellent introduction to his work. See also *The Really Short Poems of A. R. Ammons* (New York, 1991), 'A. R. Ammons: The Breaking of the Vessels' in *Figures of Capable Imagination*, by Harold Bloom (New York, 1976) and 'A. R. Ammons' in *Alone With America*, by Richard Howard (New York, 1980).   [DL

ANDERSON, Ethel (1883–1958), born in England but educated in Sydney, was married to an officer in the Indian Army and hence lived for some time in India, a fact which is reflected in *Indian Tales* (1948), as in some of her poetry. She returned to Australia in 1926, her husband serving on the staff of several governors and with the governor-general at Yarralumla. Her other collections of short stories are *The Little Ghosts* (1959) and the brilliantly idiosyncratic *At Parramatta* (1956); there are two volumes of essays.

Her collections of poetry are *Squatter's Luck* (1942) and *Sunday at Yarralumla* (1947). In the former she develops a distinctively Australian version of pastoral on a loose Virgilian model. Her style is mannered, sometimes a little archaic, and decidedly witty. Although seldom noticed by the literary mainstream, she had an effect on the more substantial work of David *Campbell.

Except for a new edition of *At Parramatta* (Melbourne, 1985; with an afterword by Paul Salzman), Anderson's work is out of print. Chris *Wallace-Crabbe discusses her pastoral poetry in *Falling into Language* (Melbourne, 1990).

[CW-C

ANDERSON, Jon (Victor) (1940–), born in Somerville, Massachusetts, is currently associate professor of English at the University of Arizona. Married three times, he has written, with frequent elegiac turns, about the impermanent boundaries of selfhood, desire, and personal relationships.

Although his badly titled first book *Looking for Jonathan* (Pittsburgh, 1968) misled some reviewers to pigeonhole Anderson as a merely confessional poet, the collection included a number of cunning, allegorical inventions; it also established the terse lyricism he was to refine in his later works, *Death & Friends* (Pittsburgh, 1970) and *In Sepia* (Pittsburgh, 1974). *The Milky Way: Poems 1967–1982* (New York, 1983) demonstrated that, overall, he is a resourceful, meditative poet. While Rilke is, perhaps, the strongest influence evident in his poems, Anderson's humanism is lonelier and more secular, and less consoled by any literary aestheticism. Obsessed with defining the mutable limits of the self, Anderson is also, necessarily, obsessed with death. He provides the sting and satisfaction of a life undergoing keen examination and smart prescriptions, as in the poem 'In Autumn': 'We who have changed, & have | No hope of

change, must now love | the passage of time.'

Discussions of *The Milky Way* appeared in the *Times Literary Supplement* (10 June 1983; a review by William Logan) and the *Nation* (7 Apr. 1984; a review by Elizabeth Frank). [DWF

ANDERSON, Patrick (John McAlister) (1915–79), was born in Ashtead, Surrey and educated at Sherborne School, Dorset, as well as Oxford and Columbia. He spent ten fruitful and influential years (1940–50) in Canada as a schoolmaster and member of the avant-garde poetry circles of Montreal. After leaving Canada, Anderson travelled widely in Egypt, Malaya, and Greece. He took a position in 1957 with the English Department at Trent Park College of Education, Barnet, Hertfordshire, where he remained until his retirement.

Anderson's Canadian stay is noteworthy for his strong involvement in the little magazine culture of Montreal, his Marxist politics, and his emergence as a poet. His poems appeared in the key anthologies of the period and he published two accomplished collections of verse, *A Tent for April* (Montreal, 1945), and *The White Circle* (Toronto, 1946), while *The Colour as Naked* (Toronto, 1953) appeared after he had left Canada. A skilful if, on occasion, derivative poet with a clear debt to *Auden and *Spender, Anderson made a genuine contribution to Canadian poetry with his energy and creative verve.

In the middle 1950s he turned to prose, and published several works of autobiography and travel. In the 1970s he made a number of return visits to Canada; these rekindled his interest in poetry and resulted in *A Visiting Distance. Poems: New, Revised and Selected* (Ottawa, 1976), and *Return to Canada: Selected Poems* (Toronto, 1977).

[MG

ANDREWS, Bruce. See Language Poetry.

ANGELOU, Maya (1928–), was born in St Louis, Missouri, and grew up in Arkansas and California. She toured Europe in *Porgy and Bess* before moving to New York where she worked as a night-club singer and performed in Genet's

The Blacks. After becoming involved in Black struggles in the Sixties she was editor of the *African Review* in Ghana. She has written six books of autobiography and now holds a lifetime appointment as Reynolds Professor of American Studies at Wake University, North Carolina.

Her first collection of poetry, *Just Give Me a Cool Drink of Water 'Fore I Diiie* (New York, 1971), was combined with her second, *Oh Pray My Wings Are Gonna Fit Me Well* (New York, 1975), under the former title for publication in London in 1988. In the same way *And Still I Rise* (New York, 1978) was published with *Shaker, Why Don't You Sing?* (New York, 1983) under the title of the former collection (London, 1986). Her most recent collections are *Now Sheba Sings the Song* (New York and London, 1987) and *I Shall Not Be Moved* (New York and London, 1990). The strength of her lyrics, with their unashamed and passionate use of iambic rhythm and full rhyme, lies in the combination of blues and gospel traditions with strong emotional and political insight.

She was chosen to read her lengthy poem starting 'A Rock, A River, A Tree' and ending 'Very simply, | With hope | Good morning', at President Clinton's inauguration ceremony.

[CB

ANGIRA, Jared (1947–), was born in Kenya. He took a degree in commerce at the University of Nairobi and represented Africa on the executive committee of the World University Service. He now works at the Harbours Corporation. Angira has published five volumes of poetry, including *Silent Voices* (London, 1972), *Cascades* (London, 1979), and *The Years Go By* (Nairobi, 1980). He writes wittily, sometimes cynically, about life in the slums of Nairobi. Several of his poems are included in Wole *Soyinka's definitive *Poems of Black Africa* (London, 1975).

[KO

Angry Penguins, a journal of art and culture edited by Max *Harris and John Reed (1943–6), who encouraged a radical modernist movement in art and literature. The 'Ern Malley' hoax (1944) brought it notoriety and was to rein-force literary caution and conservatism in Australian poetry for over two decades. 'Ern Malley' was a fictitious experimental poet concocted by James *McAuley and Harold *Stewart, young poets who parodied concepts of free association in a set of 'posthumous' works which were submitted to *Angry Penguins*. Ern Malley was acclaimed in a special issue (Autumn 1944), featuring the poems, major articles, and a cover painting by Sidney Nolan. The hoax was leaked to the press and received great attention. 'Intellectuals' were pilloried as pretentious dupes. A court case followed in which Max Harris was fined £5 for publishing obscene material. *Angry Penguins*, despite overseas admirers (e.g., Sir Herbert *Read), never really recovered. It was succeeded by *Ern Malley's Journal* (1952–5) edited by Max Harris, John Reed, and Barrie Reid (former editor of *Barjai* (1943–7) a similarly innovative Brisbane journal).

The Penguin Book of Modern Australian Poetry ed. J. Tranter and P. Mead (1991) has reproduced all the Ern Malley poems, and Angus and Robertson have published *Collected Poems of Ern Malley*, introduced by Albert Tucker and Max Harris (Sydney, 1993). See also Michael Heyward's *The Ern Malley Affair* (London, 1993) [TWS

ANSEN, Alan (1922–), was born in Brooklyn, grew up on Long Island, and took both his BA and MA at Harvard in 1944. Back in New York, Ansen, asked by W. H. *Auden to go over the drafts of *Age of Anxiety*, developed enduring friendships with Auden and Chester *Kallman, as well as with William Burroughs, Allen *Ginsberg, Gregory *Corso, and other figures in the *Beat movement. Ansen moved to Europe in 1954 and has lived there—first in Venice, then in Athens—ever since.

The double dedication of Ansen's first book of poems, *Disorderly Houses* (Middletown, Conn., 1959), shows his twofold heritage from Auden and Burroughs. Pattern and chaos; fervent homage to tradition and a truculent stance towards society—Ansen's idiosyncratic, learned, and gloomily exuberant poetry embraces such oppositions with gusto. Scholarly and critical tones, and an encyclopedic knowledge of Western culture, blend surprisingly with confessional and experimental modes, as in the poem entitled 'Imperfect Tributes: A Shriek, a Song and a Discourse'. A notable influence on such writers as Kerouac and Corso, Ansen appears in various guises in their work.

Several volumes of Ansen's poetry were privately printed in Athens, but an excellent selection of his work is now available in *Contact Highs: Selected Poems* (Elmwood Park, Ill., 1989), which includes a biographical introduction and a bibliography. Ansen has collected his memories of conversations with Auden in *Auden's Table Talk* (New York, 1989; London, 1991).

[RHa

ANTONINUS, Brother. See EVERSON, WILLIAM.

ANYIDOHO, Kofi (1947–), was born in Ghana. He attended teacher-training college before taking a degree in English at the University of Ghana, and then pursued postgraduate studies in America. In spite of this educational background, Anyidoho's development as a poet is almost totally home-grown, drawing on his Ewe background and his reading in Ewe poetry, both modern and traditional. He is at present teaching at the University of Ghana in Accra. His first volume, *Elegy for the Revolution* (New York, 1978) is a lament for Ghana's failed military revolution. His next collection, *A Harvest of Our Dreams* (London, 1984), is more personal, although it includes poems from the first book and shares its communal concerns. In 1985 Anyidoho published *Earthchild, with Brain Surgery* (Accra). [KO

ARASANAYAGAM, Jean Solomons (1934–), daughter of a Dutch burgher family with roots in colonial Sri Lanka, married to a Tamil Hindu, she combines her European and Asian heritages in her poetry. A university-educated teacher, Arasanayagam is also a painter, batik artist, linoprint maker, fiction writer, and poet, whose early verse recorded painterly impressions of Sri Lankan life and landscape (especially of the mountain country of Kandy, her birthplace).

The tranquil surface of Arasanayagam's poetry changed dramatically following Sri Lanka's ethnic disturbances in 1983. Much of her recent work expresses the fear and despair experienced by prisoners, exiles, and refugees from ethnic violence. Honoured by two Sri Lanka Arts Council awards for poetry and nonfiction, she received in 1990 an international award in the Ninth 'Salute To The Arts' poetry contest sponsored by Triton College, Illinois.

Published in magazines in Sri Lanka and abroad, Arasanayagam's work is included in Y. Gooneratne (ed.) *Poems from India, Sri Lanka, Malaysia and Singapore* (Hong Kong, 1979) and the 1990 *Triton Anthology*. Her own publications include *Kindura* (1973), *Poems of a Season Beginning and a Season Over* (1977), *Apocalypse 83* (1984), *A Colonial Inheritance* (1985), all printed privately in Sri Lanka; and *Trial by Terror* (Hamilton, NZ, 1987). [YG

ARMITAGE, Simon (1963–), was born in Huddersfield, West Yorkshire. He studied geography at Portsmouth Polytechnic and social work at Manchester University. He is a probation officer and lives in Marsden near Huddersfield. He received an Eric Gregory Award in 1988.

Armitage is one of the most talented of those northern English poets of the 1980s who are associated with Huddersfield, Britain's 'alternative poetic capital'. His full-length debut, *Zoom* (Newcastle upon Tyne, 1989) employs a distinctively northern and youthful demotic alongside 'official' literary language, often to deadpan effect. It is notable that while he has obvious social and political concerns, the problems of linguistic status and deracination which vex the older northern-born poet Tony *Harrison do not figure largely in his work.

Armitage's poems are both firmly grounded in place and wide in their imaginative, emotional, and technical range, moving easily between anecdote, larger narrative, art, and politics. The influence of Paul *Muldoon is sometimes apparent, but the strongest impression is of a considerable talent going confidently about its business.

In 1992 Armitage published *Xanadu* (Newcastle upon Tyne), the text of a BBC poem-film set in a Rochdale housing estate, and *Kid* (London), his second full collection. The latter sustains the narrative and comic elements of *Zoom*, while attending more closely to matters of identity (in a series of poems employing the character of Robinson, originally created by Weldon *Kees, and showing a deepening historical and political interest ('Lines Thought to have been Written on the Eve of the Execution of a Warrant for his Arrest').

Armitage has published a number of pamphlets, *Human Geography* (Huddersfield, 1986), *The Distance Between Stars* (Sheffield, 1987), *The Walking Horses* (Nottingham, 1989), and *Around Robinson* (Nottingham, 1991). His work is represented in *Poetry With an Edge*, ed. Neil Astley (Newcastle upon Tyne, 1988).   [SO'B

ARROWSMITH, William (1924–92), was born in New Jersey and spent his boyhood in Massachusetts and Florida. He graduated from Princeton University, attended Oxford University on a Rhodes Scholarship, and embarked on a career as professor of classics, essayist, translator, editor, and film critic. A teacher of legendary force and the author of widely hailed articles on educational reform, he held many teaching appointments, including at the University of Texas at Austin (1958–70), Yale University, Johns Hopkins University, New York University, Emory University, and Boston University (1986–92).

His learned and racy translations from the classics gained a wide audience. In particular, his version of Petronius's *Satyricon* (Ann Arbor, Mich., 1959; repr. 1961), his many plays of Euripides, and his translations of *The Birds* (New York, 1961; repr. 1962) and *The Clouds* (New York, 1962) of Aristophanes brought classical literature to life for several generations of readers and theatre-goers. In later years Arrowsmith turned to modern Italian literature. His *Hard Labor*, poems by Cesare Pavese (New York, 1976; repr. 1985) influenced the development of the hard-bitten, anti-lyrical poetics in the United States in the late Seventies, and by the time of his death he had translated all the books of poems

which Eugenio Montale published in his own lifetime.

Arrowsmith was equally influential as an editor and essayist, founding some of the liveliest journals in the United States (*The Chimera*, *The* *Hudson Review*, *Arion*). In his editing, as in his scholarship and translation, he wedded imaginative vigour to erudition. His edition and translations of Nietzsche (*Unmodern Observations*, 1990) and his essays on T. S. *Eliot and Antonioni show his consistent devotion to the dynamism within the European tradition.

Arrowsmith's many honours include the Landon Translation Prize from the Academy of American Poets for Montale's *The Storm and Other Things* (1986), and the International Montale Prize. His later volumes are Montale's *The Occasions* (1987) and the posthumous *Cuttlefish Bones* (1993).   [RW

Art and Letters. This quarterly magazine first appeared in July 1917 but had been planned much earlier, in the spring of 1914. The editors of the first two issues were the art critic Frank Rutter and the artists Charles Ginner and Harold Gilman; thereafter, Rutter alone. It concentrated, naturally enough, on the visual arts, and in the first four issues poetry was confined to short poems by Herbert *Read, Laurence *Binyon, H. Austin Petch, and M. de Holewinski. Read, who was closely connected with the magazine, contributed to No. 3 an article offering 'definitions towards a modern theory of poetry' that made cautious moves in the direction of free verse, suggesting that 'rhyme, metre, cadence, alliteration, are various decorative devices to be used as the vision demands'. Vision was defined as 'the recognition of emotions possessing an aesthetic value'. Aesthetic value remained undefined, but Read's conclusion was that the poet's 'duty and joy' was to 'express the exquisite among his perceptions'.

The 'new series' which began in 1919 shortly after the war ended, was different, and poetically more interesting. Osbert *Sitwell put some money into the magazine and became poetry editor, publishing poems by himself and his sister, as well as work by *Huxley, *Hueffer,

Richard *Aldington, and Siegfried *Sassoon. Other contributions showed a marked shift in the direction of modernism. Osbert Sitwell's work was in his early pacifist or socialist vein: 'We will not buy Art and Letters, | It is affected! | Our sons | And brothers | Went forth to fight, | To kill | Certain things— | 'All this poetry and rubbish'— | We said | We will not buy Art and Letters.'

And not enough people did buy the maga- zine, in spite of interesting prose pieces by *Eliot, Firbank, and Wyndham *Lewis, and poems by Eliot, Isaac *Rosenberg, Wilfred *Owen, Read, and of course the Sitwells. With the appearance of *Coterie, which had several of the same contributors, it was no doubt felt that there was danger of duplication, and the Spring 1920 issue was the last. The contents of the two magazines give a good idea of the most lively art and writing produced at the end of the war, and for a year or two after it.   [JGS

ASH, John (1948–), was born in Manchester, and studied at the University of Birmingham then worked as an elementary-school teacher and research assistant before moving to New York in 1985. He co-wrote a book on the effects of the tourist trade in underdeveloped nations, and has published six volumes of poetry, the most recent of them Disbelief (1987) and The Burnt Pages (1992—both New York and Man- chester). In addition to his poetry, Ash has writ- ten numerous articles and reviews for literary journals.

Ash's chief source of inspiration has come not from his native tradition but from the more experimental strains of French and American poetry. In his earlier work Ash openly evokes the decadent phase of French symbolism; his more recent writing derives heavily from the *New York School, especially the poetry of his friend and homonymous mentor John *Ash- bery. Despite the unmistakeable debts that Ash owes to Ashbery, his poetry has a visual clarity and phonic lushness that distinguish it from that of other New York School disciples. Ash's imag- ination is drawn to culture rather than nature; his poems evoke both the beauty and the

fragility of human constructs. This is most clearly evident in his frequent recourse to an imagery of crumbling architecture. Ash is an urban elegist, at once romantic in his sense of the city's pathos and nobility, and postmodern in his concern with surface, ambiguity, and dis- solution.   [RG

ASHBERY, John (1927–), was born in Rochester, New York, and brought up on a farm in Sodus nearby. He attended Harvard College, graduating in 1949, and afterwards enrolled in graduate school at Columbia University, New York, receiving his MA in 1951. His first book, Some Trees, was published in 1956 in the Yale Younger Poets series with an introduction by W. H. *Auden. He spent 1955/6 studying in Paris on a Fulbright Scholarship, and returned to Paris in 1958 where he was employed as art critic for the Paris Herald Tribune. He returned to New York in 1966, working until 1972 as Execu- tive Editor of Art News. In 1974 he was appointed to a teaching post at Brooklyn College.

Ashbery's first volume, Some Trees, is in- fluenced by the work of Wallace *Stevens and W. H. Auden, and reflects also Ashbery's read- ing of avant-garde French poets such as Ray- mond Roussel, Pierre Reverdy, and Max Jacob. In its most famous poem, 'The Instruction Manual', the poet is supposed to be writing an instruction manual 'on the uses of a new metal', but instead he drifts into a pastel travelogue- style reverie about the Mexican city of Guadala- jara. After his move to Paris Ashbery began experimenting with more radical styles of poetic disjunction. His second volume, The Tennis Court Oath (Middletown, Conn., 1962), contains a number of cut-up poems composed out of seemingly arbitrary fragments of lan- guage. The long poem 'Europe' is the most extreme of these. Even some of Ashbery's most fervent admirers have been puzzled by this book, and Harold Bloom, one of his earliest champions, has called it 'a fearful disaster'. Ash- bery himself has said that in these poems he was 'taking poetry apart to try to understand how it works', while in his next volume, Rivers and Mountains (New York, 1966), he set out 'to fit it back together'. Over half of *Rivers and Mountains* is taken up by the long poem 'The Skaters', in which Ashbery expansively develops a beguiling series of possible fictions for the poetic self, though without ever identifying a supreme one. Its long lines and extreme openness have provoked various critics to see this poem as Ashbery's 'Song of Myself'.

In his next collection, *The Double Dream of Spring* (New York, 1970)—the title is borrowed from a painting by Giorgio de Chirico, whose work Ashbery greatly admires—he explores more obviously lyrical modes of poetry. In the poem 'Soonest Mended' he characterizes his poetic stance as 'a kind of fence-sitting | Raised to the level of an esthetic ideal'. In this poem in particular, which he has called his 'one-size-fits-all Confessional poem', Ashbery is able to transform his sense of life's ability to escape all imposed formulations into a resonant and fertile uncertainty: 'For this is action, this not being sure, this careless | Preparing, sowing the seeds crooked in the furrow, | Making ready to forget, and always coming back | To the mooring of starting out, that day so long ago.'

Ashbery's willingness to experiment is well illustrated by his following volume, *Three Poems* (New York, 1972), which is in fact three long prose pieces, with occasional interspersed lyrics. *Self-Portrait in a Convex Mirror* (New York and London, 1976), undoubtedly Ashbery's most popular and successful volume, was awarded three of America's most prestigious literary prizes, including a Pulitzer. Its long title poem is a meditation based on the Mannerist painter Parmigianino's famous self-portrait. Although the poem is not Ashbery's own favourite, most critics see it as his seminal work, and this is probably because it eschews many of the surrealist and disjunctive effects with which so much of his work is inflected. In the poem Ashbery broods on his familiar themes—the relationship between art and life, the instability of any sense of self, the impossibility of a single coherent narrative, the passing of time—with a clarity and directness unusual for him.

Later Ashbery volumes have found new ways of approaching such dilemmas. The enormous, seventy-page poem 'Litany' from *As We Know* (New York and London, 1978) is in double columns, 'meant to be read as simultaneous but independent monologues' (Author's Note). *Shadow Train* (New York and Manchester, 1981) consists of fifty sixteen-line poems. Recent collections, *A Wave* (1984), *April Galleons* (1987), and *Hotel Lautréamont* (1992—all New York and Manchester), are a less deliberately formatted mixture of the lyrical and meditative.

Ashbery has also written three plays, and co-written a novel with James *Schuyler called *A Nest of Ninnies* (New York, 1969; Manchester, 1987). [MF

Asian-American Poetry. 'Asian-American', as much as 'Indian' or 'Hispanic', if an improvement on the racially loaded 'oriental', has never been a less-than-vexatious designation. Americans of Chinese, Japanese, Korean, Filipino, Indo-Pakistani, and recently of Vietnamese and other Asian origins, poets or not, have found themselves aggregated into the one term, a single, encompassing marker. For they all can look back not only to their own respective Asian culture and language but to their own hard-won 'American' histories. The inscription of each of these histories, especially in poetry, has been voluminous, and at no time more so than in the liberating cultural aftermath of the 1960s.

'Today in hazy San Francisco, I face seaward | Towards China . . .' begins Marilyn Chin in 'We Are Americans Now, We Live in The Tundra', a moving invocation of her double heritage in her best-known collection, *Dwarf Bamboo* (1987). Other Chinese-American poetry which equally explores this hyphenation of East and West, of pictograph and word, would include: Alex Kuo, *The Willow Tree* (1971) and *Changing The River* (1986); George Leong, *A Lone Bamboo Doesn't Come From Jackson Street* (1977); Fay Chiang, *In The City of Contradictions* (1979); Stephen Liu, *Dream Journeys to China* (1982); Amy Ling, *Chinamerican Reflections* (1984); Mei-Mei *Berssenbrugge, *The Heat Bird* (1983) and *Packrat Sieve* (1983); Cathy Song, *Picture Bride* (1983); Nelly Wong, *The Death of Long Steam Lady* (1986); Diana Chang, *What Matisse Is After*

(1984); Wing Tek Lum, *Expounding The Doubtful Points* (1987); Shirley Geok-Lin *Lim, Modern Secrets* (1988); John Yau, *Corpse and Mirror* (1983) and *Radiant Silhouette: New and Selected Work 1974–1988* (1988); and David Mura, *After We Lost Our Way* (1989).

Whether written by second-generation *nisei* or third-generation *sansei*, Japanese-American poetry has also increasingly won prominence—rarely, however, without reference to the legacy of Pearl Harbor and the camps. For as Richard Oyama writes in 'Untitled', in the anthology *Transfer 38* (1979): 'When we were children, | you spoke Japanese | in lowered voices . . . .It is the language| of silence within myself.' 'Unsilencing' Japanese-America can be met with in verse-collections like: Lawson Fusao *Inada, Before The War* (1971) and 'Four Songs for Asian America' (1973); *Ai, Cruelty* (1973), *Killing Floor* (1979), and *Sin* (1986); Mitsue Yamada, *Camp Notes* (1976) and *Desert Run* (1988); James Mitsui, *Crossing Phantom River* (1978); Geraldine Kudaka, *Numerous Avalanches at the Point of Intersection* (1978); Janice Mirikitani, *Awake in the River* (1978) and *Shedding Silence* (1987); and Ronald Tanaka, *Shino Suite* (1981). Likewise a Korean-American gallery emerges with a daring, inward prose-poem like Theresa Hak Kyung Cha's *Dictée* (1982), and Chungmi Kim, *Selected Poems* (1982) and Alison Kim, *Mirror Mirror (Woman Woman)* (1986). Filipino-American poetry finds its own virtuosity of voice in Jessica Hagedorn, *Dangerous Music* (1975) and *Petfood and Tropical Apparitions* (1981); Myrna Peña-Reyes, *The River Singing Stone* (1983); and Virginia Cerenio, *Without Names: A Collection of Poems* (1985). The poetry of a Sri Lankan-American/Canadian like Michael *Ondaatje, or a Vietnamese-American like Thich Nhat-Hanh, suggests Asian-American dispensations still to come.

Anthologies include: Jeffery Paul Chan, Frank Chin, Lawson Fusao Inada, and Shawn Wong (eds.), *Aiiieeeee! An Anthology of Asian-American Writers* (Washington DC, 1974) and *The Big Aiiieeeee!: An Anthology of Chinese American and Japanese American Literature* (New York,

1991); Janice Mirikitani *et al.* (eds.), *Ayumi: A Japanese American Anthology* (San Francisco, Calif., 1980); Joseph Bruchac (ed.), *Breaking Silence: An Anthology of Contemporary Asian American Poets* (Greenfield Center, NY, 1983); Shirley Geok-lin Lim, Mayumi Tsutakawa, and Margarita Donnelly (eds.), *The Forbidden Stitch: An Asian American Women's Anthology* (Corvallis, Oreg., 1989); L. Ling-chi Wang and Henry Yiheng Zhao (eds.), *Chinese-American Poetry: An Anthology* (Seattle, Wash., 1991). Critical scholarship includes: Elaine H. Kim, *Asian American Literature: An Introduction to the Writings and their Social Context* (Philadelphia, Pa., 1982); King-Kok Cheung and Stan Yogi (eds.), *Asian American Literature: An Annotated Bibliography* (New York, 1988); and Shirley Geok-lin Lim and Amy Ling (eds.), *Reading the Literatures of Asian America* (Philadelphia, 1992).   [ARL

ATWOOD, Margaret (Eleanor) (1939–), was born in Ottawa, Canada. She grew up in Ottawa and Toronto, but as a child spent the summers with her family in northern Quebec. She received her BA from the University of Toronto in 1961 and her MA from Radcliffe College, Harvard, in 1962. She won a Governor-General's Award for her first book of poetry, *The Circle Game* (1966), and went on to become one of the finest and most prolific of contemporary writers. To date she has published twelve volumes of poetry, seven novels, three collections of short stories, one critical study of Canadian literature, one volume of collected essays, and has edited other works, including *The New Oxford Book of Canadian Verse in English* (1982). Two of her novels, *Surfacing* (1972) and *The Handmaid's Tale* (1985), have been made into films. She has been active in such organizations as the Writers' Union of Canada, Amnesty International, and PEN, and has lectured widely around the world. Atwood has won many prizes, including a Guggenheim Fellowship and the Molson Prize (both in 1981), and has received several honorary degrees.

Atwood's poetry is characterized by the vivid precision of her language and the power of her imagery. In her short, laconic lyrics she provides sharp insights into the consciousness of the speaker, while in her series of connected poems she develops symbolic and visionary explorations of the ironic dualities of existence. Her interest in the politics of human relationships has led her to explore a wide range of subjects, from the conflicting attitudes towards Canada of the pioneer, Susanna Moodie, in *The Journals of Susanna Moodie* (Toronto, 1970) to the myths and deceptions of romantic love in *Power Politics* (Toronto, 1973); to the ambiguities of myth in *You Are Happy* (Toronto, 1974) and the horrors of torture and repression in *True Stories* (Toronto, 1981). Her fiction is equally varied. *Surfacing* (1972) is a moving narrative of a woman's rediscovery of herself in the wilderness, while *Lady Oracle* (1976) is a comic satire on the trials of growing up in the 1950s and a parody of romance fiction. *Bodily Harm* (1981), in which the Canadian protagonist experiences the terror of a Third World country revolution, is her most explicit treatment of the issues of personal and national responsibility and culpability. In her feminist dystopia, *The Handmaid's Tale*, Atwood portrays present social and political trends in a convincing story of future disaster; while her most recent novel, *Cat's Eye* (1988) is a complex exploration of the life of the artist.

Collections of her poetry are available in *Selected Poems* (Toronto, 1976; New York, 1978) *Selected Poems II* (Toronto, 1986; Boston, 1987); and *Selected Poems: 1966–1984* (Toronto, 1990). See also *Violent Duality* (Montreal, 1980), by Sherrill Grace; *Margaret Atwood* (Boston, 1984), by Jerome Rosenberg; and *Margaret Atwood: Vision and Forms* (Carbondale, Ill., 1988), ed. Kathryn Van Spanckeren and Jan Garden Castro. [SEG

AUDEN, W(ystan) H(ugh) (1907–73), was born on 21 February 1907 into a provincial English world still Tennysonian in outlook. He was the third son of a gentle, cultivated family doctor and a domineering former nurse who had once wanted to go to Africa as a missionary. Auden was by nature a versatile, polymorphous writer, one who felt that, amongst other things, poetry

was 'a game of knowledge'. The odd geometry of his parents' marriage seems to have added an intellectual openness and restlessness, even as it left him personally extremely anxious. He boarded at Gresham's School in Norfolk, then in 1925 went up to Christ Church, Oxford, where he soon switched from reading biology to English.

For a collected edition made late in his career, Auden divided his poetry into broad phases; each constituted, he felt, a 'chapter'. The first stretches from 1927 until the end of 1932, and in it Auden emerges from the sacred ground of English Romanticism, the Lake District. The landscape of these guarded, archaic-sounding poems is the same as Wordsworth's, though in Auden the area is desolate and the solitary is numbed by feelings of intense isolation and disappointment. Even the shared resources of English are denied: conjunctions and pronouns have flaked away, leaving a language of glittering, compacted hardness.

A pamphlet, *Poems*, was cranked out on a hand-press by his friend Stephen *Spender in 1928. The same year Auden left Oxford and spent the next nine months in Germany (mainly Berlin), writing, reading widely in psychology, and brothel-crawling. At a moment when Europe's foundations were starting to shudder, he also became concerned about political issues. In September 1930, a few months after Auden had returned to England, T. S. *Eliot at Faber and Faber published Auden's first full-length book, again austerely called *Poems* (London, 1930). Meanwhile, Auden had gone off to teach at a seedy Scottish prep-school.

In *Poems* (1930) there is a dark, autistic vein of love poetry; there is also a kind of admonitory satire, castigating Britain's spiritual torpor. His next book, *The Orators* (London, 1932), is the culmination of both these tendencies and it reads like a surrealist explosion of language. There are hints of a narrative involving a failed insurrection against the governing class, but the real subject of *The Orators* is its own bristling verbal energy.

Despite the obscurity of his early work, Auden was hailed by critics as the leader of a group of young, left-wing, writers that included Louis *MacNeice, Spender, and C. *Day Lewis. Backed by Eliot, and fuelled by a growing literary confidence, Auden seems to have felt for a while that he could have a role to play in the country's renewal. This belief soon evaporated, and by the end of the decade he was to feel trapped by his sense of responsibility. None the less, the revolutionary 'movement' was an important means of self-definition for these poets as they were crawling out of the shadow of *Yeats and Eliot. It also gave Auden a clearly defined audience to write for and a reason to try and forge an accessible public style.

He soon came to see *The Orators* as a botched effort, and his work, which shows a strong evolutionary urge, began to move forward. In the autumn of 1932 he started teaching at the Downs School in Herefordshire. In that mellow world his poetry opened like a bud, becoming more expansive and much richer in surface detail. This is the start of the second 'chapter', the phase when Auden, drawing on Marx and Freud, was able to make a brilliant stream of connections between individual guilts and pleasures and the crisis that seemed to be eating away at European civilization. Simultaneously, his interest in the possibilities of verse-forms burst out in a profusion of beautifully adroit sonnets, sestinas, and ballads.

Auden was a homosexual, but in 1935 he married Thomas Mann's daughter, Erika, a fugitive from Nazi persecution, in order to get her an English passport. The same year he left the Downs. In search of a wider field of vision he joined a documentary film company, where he worked briefly and unhappily. For six years after that he was a free-lance writer. A second collection of lyrics, *Look, Stranger!* (London, 1936)—the American edition is *On This Island* (New York, 1937)—extended his reputation.

So did his plays. Auden had composed a long charade, 'Paid On Both Sides' (1928), and a polemical 'masque', *The Dance of Death* (London, 1933). In the later Thirties he and Christopher Isherwood turned out a string of dramas: *The Dog Beneath the Skin* (London and New York, 1935), *The Ascent of F6* (London, 1936;

New York, 1937), and *On the Frontier* (London, 1938; New York, 1939). Although none of the plays is a fully integrated work, they contain flashes of great poetry. The choruses in *The Dog Beneath the Skin* offer huge panoramas of English life, and *F6* contains an allegory of Auden's early fantasy of himself as a healer and redeemer of society. He later said it was while working on the play that he realized that, for the sake of his artistic growth, he would have to leave England.

Auden's pre-war years were a period of fertility in many media and of almost continuous wandering. In 1936 he went with MacNeice to Iceland (where he liked to believe his ancestors had come from), a trip that resulted in their *Letters from Iceland* (London and New York, 1937). The volume contains Auden's masterpiece of autobiographical light verse, 'Letter to Lord Byron'. Then, in January 1937, he went to observe the Spanish Civil War. Auden was never a member of the Communist Party, and he seems to have been shunted aside by the party bosses in Spain. Immediately after he returned, though, he wrote his most famous call to action, 'Spain', a poem full of local brilliance but one that cannot now be separated from knowledge of the Civil War's tragically convoluted history. Auden hardly ever spoke about his experiences in Barcelona, but in the wake of the visit his poems darkened; many from the later Thirties are bleakly pessimistic, shielding themselves from the historical turmoil behind layers of stylization and irony. In early 1938, after he had hurriedly assembled his *Oxford Book of Light Verse* (London, 1938), Auden went abroad again, this time with Isherwood. They travelled to China to write about the Sino-Japanese War. Their book, *Journey to a War* (London and New York, 1939) became a parable about the difficulty of politically engaged writing: as Isherwood recounts it, they could never find any clearly drawn lines of battle in China. The problem is developed in the volume's sonnet sequence 'In Time of War', which finds the war going on everywhere, all the time. The sonnets show an important broadening of Auden's moral imagination, and throughout, Christian symbolism begins to bubble to the surface. On their voyage to England in mid-1938 Auden and Isherwood stopped off in New York. In January 1939 they went back there.

Going to America was another turning-point, and Auden began purging himself of a rhetoric that he felt had now been exhausted. The next phase of his career, initiated by a series of elegies and psychological portraits, is a period of much more intimate writing, concerned above all with subjectivity and loneliness. He had fallen in love with a younger American writer, Chester *Kallman, and his happiness seems to have released a flood of other feelings, including what were only half-suppressed religious impulses. *Another Time* (New York and London, 1940) contains some of his best work, though, as the title indicates, the poems already seemed to him to belong in a vanished era. The book includes 'September 1, 1939', a lyric written the weekend war was declared, which tries to come to terms with the failure of the 'clever hopes' of a 'low dishonest decade' for social and personal renewal, and attempts a new, modestly heroic, role for the writer. Auden later came to dislike the sanctimoniousness of the piece.

The suggestions of religious and poetic conversion were strengthened in *The Double Man* (New York, 1941; published in London the same year under the title *New Year Letter*). Again admitting the failure of the utopian hopes of the Thirties, the volume's main element, a long neo-Augustan verse epistle, is a dissection of man's spiritual predicament and of the dualism in European secular thought which Auden believed had ultimately led to the catastrophe of war. It ends with a petition for aid from a mysterious—though still unnamed—power. Around October 1940, just after he finished the book, Auden began going to church.

Although he remained a Christian for the rest of his life, Auden never became pious or dogmatic, at least in his poems. In fact his faith seems to have increased his intellectual appetite. By inclination his mind was speculative, synthesizing, and eclectic—he was probably the only poet from the earlier half of the century well acquainted with the most advanced thought of

the day—and Christianity allowed him to order this vast store of knowledge from philosophy, history, and theology into a harmonious and poetic world-view.

In the next few years he produced three more long poems. Each addresses the situation created by the 'crisis' of the war and of his conversion to Christianity, and each deals with its implications for his art. It is a retrenchment in the form of an enormous, almost forbidding, flowering: Auden's developing artistry feeds off his complex feelings about literature, and particularly about his own early writing. Two of these poems, 'For the Time Being', a Christmas Oratorio dedicated to his mother who had died in 1941, and 'The Sea and the Mirror', a verse 'commentary' on *The Tempest* that Auden described as his 'Ars Poetica', were published together in *For the Time Being* (New York, 1944; London, 1945). His final long poem is *The Age of Anxiety* (New York, 1947; London, 1948). This ornate, rather Joycean work, which won the 1948 Pulitzer Prize, is an interior portrait of the average twentieth-century city-dweller, cast in the form of a meeting between four New Yorkers in a bar on All Souls' Night, 1944.

Between 1939 and early 1947 much of his time was taken up with work on these long poems and earning a living as a university lecturer. In 1945, though, he spent a few months in Germany as an observer with the US Air Force's 'Strategic Bombing Survey', studying the effects of aerial bombardment. Amongst the ruins of Darmstadt and Munich his interest in rebuilding cities took on renewed urgency, and some of his most ambitious works of the post-war years open out into an investigation of how to unify the contemporary world. The most important in this respect are the poem 'Memorial for the City' (1949), and a series of anti-Romantic lectures, *The Enchafèd Flood* (New York, 1950; London, 1951).

In 1946 Auden became a US citizen. The following year was one of artistic uncertainty, a time when he was again casting around for a new literary direction. Once more a fresh 'chapter' began with a change of air. From 1948 until 1957 Auden summered—and wrote most of his poetry—on Ischia, an island in the Bay of Naples. This period, during which Auden became the first truly rootless, international poet since Byron, was inaugurated by the elegiac syllabics of 'In Praise of Limestone'. The poem appeared in the transitional *Nones* (New York, 1951; London, 1952). The Mediterranean breathed a restrained, 'classical' feeling into Auden's work, and renewed his interest in the natural world and in the great movements of human history. The poems are more relaxed, but there is no slackening of artistic authority: his writing is both colloquial and gracefully elevated.

Auden believed that every poem should pose a new technical challenge for the poet. Thus, formal precision is balanced in the Fifties by a great deal of formal experimentation. The main thematic preoccupation is with the humanist task of defining Man through his relations with the world around him, and this culminates in a pair of major sequences from mid-decade: 'Bucolics' and 'Horae Canonicae'. Both were published in *The Shield of Achilles* (New York and London, 1955), along with that book's title poem, a meditation on the West's culture of violence. The final pieces from the period were gathered into *Homage to Clio* (New York and London, 1960).

As his verse became more conversational, Auden found an outlet for his love of the grand style by writing opera libretti. (He had already worked on an operetta, *Paul Bunyan*, with Benjamin Britten in 1939–1941.) He and Kallman now produced the words for Stravinsky's *The Rake's Progress* (1951). Later they collaborated on *Elegy for Young Lovers* (1961) and *The Bassarids* (1966), both by Hans Werner Henze, and *Love's Labour's Lost* (1973) by Nicolas Nabokov.

Auden's activities were not confined to poetry and opera, though. He also produced a torrent of critical prose and, with Norman Holmes Pearson, edited a five-volume anthology of verse, *Poets of the English Language* (New York, 1950; London, 1952). From 1956 to 1961 he was Professor of Poetry at Oxford, countering the authority of his lectures in the Sheldonian with a stream of baroque occasional verses and academic clerihews.

In 1958 he and Kallman moved again, this time to a summer cottage outside Vienna. Increasingly Auden's poetry came under the influence of Herbert and Dryden, becoming dryer and more sober, though he set even the most apparently parochial of his poems in the sweep of long historical vistas. In fact, Auden was now beginning to produce a subtle, highly crafted poetry of old age, crankier, but also much more topical and political than it had been for several decades. He continued to seek out new formal challenges as well, and his long, chatty meditations are interspersed by showers of brilliantly sharp haiku diary-jottings. Both sides of this Goethean persona are represented in *About the House* (New York, 1965; London, 1966), which contains another major sequence, a poem for every room in his home, except—their relations continued to be complicated—Kallman's bedroom.

Auden's final books, *City Without Walls* (London, 1969; New York, 1970), *Epistle to a Godson* (New York and London, 1972), and the posthumous *Thank You, Fog* (London and New York, 1974) are the completion of the curve. Each of these books contains important poems: wry, ego-less musings in which extinction—feared, witnessed, and, occasionally, inflicted—is a frequent subject. Auden maintained that poets died once they had finished their historically appointed task. He spent the summer of 1973 in Austria and had planned to fly back to Oxford, where he now spent his winters. However, on 28 September 1973, in the middle of his last night in Vienna, he suffered a fatal heart-attack.

Since his death Auden's polemical aura, whether in its early political or in its later High-Churchy form, has faded. He now seems an extraordinarily comprehensive and various writer; not one voice, but many. He was a master of the sparkling detail who also loved the vast, inhuman overviews of geography and history, a poet of great technical finesse who was ambivalent about the worth of literature, the century's wittiest public versifier who could also sound the note of someone speaking out into an unpeopled silence. Only a major poet could have mingled and brought to perfection so many different styles, and only a great one could have been so ready to throw away his successes and move on.

The bulk of his work is part of its meaning, too. In historical terms, his importance lies in his reaction against Modernism's tortured sense of stasis and restriction. Auden is a self-effacing poet: the nearest he got to an autobiography was *A Certain World* (New York and London, 1970), a vast collection of his favourite texts from other writers. Looked at from one point of view, this distaste for personal revelations and visionary extremity can be traced to the accidents of his psychological make-up. Looked at from another, though, his encyclopedic intellectual scope, his polyglot linguistic inclusiveness, and his insistence that all forms and subjects are still available to the contemporary poet, look like the dynamic of poetry working itself out through him. Auden is a powerful precursor-figure for later poets, and his voice reverberates in writing as different as *Lowell's churning sonnets and *Ashbery's cool, loose webs.

The bibliographical situation is tangled, and no one book can represent all the important facets of Auden's career. The bedrock is the *Collected Poems* (2nd edn., New York and London, 1991). However, when Auden was trying to discover what sort of poems he wanted to write next, he often looked back sourly on earlier work and even cut out several key poems, notably 'Spain' and 'September 1, 1939'. This means that the *Collected Poems* must be supplemented by two anthologies. *The English Auden: Poems, Essays and Dramatic Writings 1927–1939* (London, 1977; New York, 1978) provides a much broader picture of the first decade or so, and includes *The Orators*. For the original version of 'Spain', the reader needs the *Selected Poems* (New York and London, 1979). All three are edited by Auden's literary executor, Edward Mendelson. A multi-volume, historically oriented edition, *The Complete Works of W. H. Auden*, also under Mendelson's editorship, is under way. To date, a volume of the dramas written with Isherwood, *Plays and Other Dramatic Writings 1929–1938* (Princeton, NJ, 1988; London, 1989), and a volume of the libretti

composed with Kallman, *Libretti* (Princeton, NJ, and London, 1993) have appeared. In addition to *The Enchafèd Flood* (see above), there are three collections of fairly late prose: *The Dyer's Hand* (New York, 1962; London, 1963), based on Auden's lectures as Professor of Poetry at Oxford; *Secondary Worlds* (London, 1968; New York, 1969), the 1967 T. S. Eliot Memorial Lectures; and *Forewords and Afterwords* (New York and London, 1973). However, a huge quantity of valuable material is still buried in the back-numbers of little magazines. For guidance, consult *W. H. Auden: A Bibliography 1924–1969*, by B. C. Bloomfield and Edward Mendelson (2nd edn., Charlottesville, Va., 1972). Information on work from the final few years of Auden's life and on discoveries made since his death can be found in Mendelson's 'W. H. Auden: A Bibliographical Supplement', in Katherine Bucknell and Nicholas Jenkins (eds.), *W. H. Auden: 'The Map of All My Youth'* (Oxford, 1990). The best account of Auden's life is Humphrey Carpenter's *W. H. Auden: A Biography* (London and Boston, 1981); Alan Ansen's *The Table Talk of W. H. Auden* (New York, 1990; London, 1991) gives a good impression of his witty, playful intelligence. Critical works include *A Reader's Guide to W. H. Auden*, by John Fuller (London, 1970), *The Auden Generation*, by Samuel Hynes (London, 1976; New York, 1977), *Early Auden*, by Edward Mendelson (New York and London, 1981), and *W. H. Auden*, by Stan Smith (Oxford, 1985). Auden left instructions that after his death his friends should burn all letters from him. In fact not much seems to have been destroyed, but until publication of the *Complete Works* is finished no edition of his correspondence will appear. [NJ

AUSTIN, Alfred (1835–1913), was born in Leeds, son of a wool stapler. He was called to the bar (1857), but gave up the law for political journalism. He stood twice for Parliament. He co-founded and edited the Tory *National Review*. Only one of his works, *The Garden That I Love*, (London, 1894), enjoyed anything like popularity. Remarkably, Austin has the reputation of having been the worst, most unread English poet; more remarkably, examination of his works bears out this verdict. He became Poet Laureate in 1896 because Lord Salisbury, the Prime Minister, was careless and ignorant of poetry ('no one else asked for it'), and he was a figure of fun amongst his contemporaries, including *Hardy, who once sent him an ironic letter of congratulations on a collection. Lines from one or two of his official poems—for example, on the Prince of Wales's illness: 'He is no better, he is much the same'—have entered the language by virtue of their ludicrousness. He firmly believed in his genius: *Autobiography* (London, 1911) is an astonishing record of unaware mediocrity. See *Songs of England* (London, 1898) and *Alfred Austin, Victorian* (London, 1953), by N. B. Crowell. [MS-S

AVISON, Margaret (1918–), was born in Galt, Ontario, brought up on the Canadian prairie, and educated at the University of Toronto. She worked as a librarian and teacher, but after a profound Christian vision she took up her vocation as a social worker at a church mission in downtown Toronto. As a poet she has written steadily but has not rushed into print, producing only four books in forty years since her first poems were published.

Often characterized as 'metaphysical', sometimes 'difficult', Avison's poetry is intensely modern. It is improvised according to the play of sound, and nearly always concerned with the act of seeing. The poems are Christian but not doctrinaire. Avison looks for images among poor people, strangers, and the lonely wanderers of the city. She looks at them carefully, and humanizes them in their singularity. Her sympathy and her skill have won over writers and readers who will never share her faith.

Avison has always discouraged the makers of reputation, especially the literary press and the academics. Thus she has a greater following among poets than among critics. Her first two books were published outside Canada, and her last two by a nearly unknown press in Nova Scotia. Yet there is a tacit agreement across the country that she is one of Canada's most accomplished poets.

Avison's first two volumes were gathered as *Winter Sun / The Dumbfounding: poems 1940–1966* (Toronto, 1982). This was followed by *No Time* (Hantsport, NS, 1989) and *Selected Poems* (Toronto, 1991). A collection of essays about her work, and a bibliography, can be found in '*Lighting up the Terrain*': *The Poetry of Margaret Avison*, ed. David Kent (Toronto, 1987).

[GHB

AWOONOR, Kofi (1935–) (formerly George Awoonor-Williams), was born in Wheta, Ghana, and educated at the famous Achimota School and the University of Ghana at Legon, from which he graduated in 1960. He lectured in English at the School of Administration until 1963, and at the Institute of African Studies until 1967, when he left to take an MA at the University of London. He travelled to the United States the following year on a scholarship from the University of California at Los Angeles and Columbia, and was subsequently appointed chairman of the department of comparative literature at the State University of New York at Stony Brook, where he taught until his return to Ghana in 1975 to take up a post at the University of Cape Coast. In January 1976 he was imprisoned without charge for almost a year for harbouring a fugitive at a time of political uncertainty in the country, an experience which he later recorded in *The Ghana Revolution* (New York, 1984). After his release he resumed teaching at the University until 1984, when he was appointed Ghanaian ambassador to Cuba.

An intensely lyrical poet, Awoonor has spoken of the necessity for the writer in contemporary Africa 'to provide . . . a certain articulate vision, which must order his society because otherwise social life would be a very sterile and a very futile exercise'. Although very much a modern poet who has drawn heavily from the poetry of other societies and cultures, he has attempted to incorporate elements from the Ewe oral tradition to give his poetry a more African feel.

In 1971 Awoonor published an influential novel (or 'prose-poem', as he terms it), *This Earth, My Brother* (New York, 1971; London,

1972), and he has also written on African culture in *The Breast of the Earth* (New York, 1972), and on Ewe traditional poetry in *Guardians of the Sacred Word* (New York, 1974). There are five collections of his verse: *Rediscovery* (Ibadan, 1964); *Night of My Blood* (New York, 1971); *Ride Me, Memory* (New York, 1973); *The House by the* *Sea* (New York, 1978); and *Until the Morning After: Collected Poems, 1963–1985* (New York, 1986). His poetry has appeared in the major anthologies of African poetry. A critical appreciation of his work can be found in Robert Fraser, *West African Poetry: A Critical History* (Cambridge, 1986).

[AM-P

B

BACA, Jimmy Santiago (1952–), of mixed Chicano and Apache origins, had a disastrous childhood—his mother murdered by her second husband, his father dead of alcoholism. He then absconded from a New Mexico orphanage, drifted unto a violent 'street' and drug-affected adolescence, and found himself early in penitentiaries from San Quentin to Arizona. The inmate writing which he turned to in default of any better path he has said 'bridged my divided life of prisoner and free man'. It also found a supporter in Denise *Levertov, then poetry editor for the radical periodical *Mother Jones*. That led on to *Martín & Meditations on the South Valley* (New York, 1987), a richly localized journey-poem centred on the south-west. For its 'de-tribalized Apache' narrator, the new-found encounter with land and heritage becomes restorative. A similar sense of self-discovery runs through his *Black Mesa Poems* (New York, 1989), whether remembered poverty and drift, the different landscapes of Mexico and Texas, the life of the *pueblo* with its *ristras* and *curanderas*, or even, as in a poem like 'I Am Here', the fevers of prison life. Baca's verse reads much in the tradition of the chronicle, a poetry of witness made the more affecting by his clarity of image. His essential collections remain *Martín & Meditations on the South Valley* and *Black Mesa Poems*, but see also the essays in *Working in the Dark: Reflections of a Poet of the Barrio* (Santa Fe, New Mexico, 1992).   [ARL

BAIN, Donald (1922–), was born in Liverpool and educated at King's College, Cambridge, where he was a contemporary of Nicholas *Moore, Hamish *Henderson, and Alex *Com-fort. While at Cambridge he edited *Oxford and Cambridge Writing* (1942) and had his first poems published in *Folios of New Writing*. During the war he served in the Royal Artillery and the Gordon Highlanders until he was invalided out. His few published poems come from those years. After the war he took up a career as an actor.

His poems were stylish but neither compelling nor memorable, with the exception of the brief but frequently anthologized 'War Poet'. Its unheroic tone of puzzled and ironic acceptance reflects the feeling about the Second World War of so many who were caught up in it. The poem's last line is one that stays in the mind as a telling epitome of contemporary attitudes: 'We do not wish to moralize, only to ease our dusty throats.' There is no book of poems by Bain. His few anthologized poems can be found in *Poetry from Cambridge in Wartime*, ed. G. Moore (London, 1946), *The Poetry of War: 1939–1945*, ed. I. Hamilton (London, 1965), and *Poems of the Second World War*, ed. V. Selwyn (London, 1985).   [ATT

BAKER, Howard (1905–90), was born in Philadelphia, but was educated in the west, receiving his BA in 1927 from Whittier College, California; his MA in 1929 from Stanford; and his Ph.D in 1937 from the University of California at Berkeley. He studied at the Sorbonne, 1929–31.

At Stanford he became acquainted with Yvor *Winters, and was one of the first members of the *Stanford School, editing, with Winters and Janet *Lewis, *The Gyroscope* (1929–30). He published eight poems in Winters's anthology *Twelve Poets of the Pacific* (1937). In the early

Thirties he was an editor of *The Magazine*. He had planned to be a teacher but, discontented with academic life, he settled at Terra Bella, California, and established a successful orange-growing and packing business.

His poems are highly crafted, perceptive, intellectual, and witty. There are frequent references to Greek myths and literature, with which he became increasingly absorbed in his later years. Among his most memorable poems are 'Pont Neuf', 'Ode to the Sea', 'Psyche' (inspired by Robert *Bridges's 'Eros and Psyche'), and 'Letter from the Country', written as 'advice to a young editor', warning him to avoid popular fads in contemporary poetry and to set his standards by the models of Greek literature.

His prose works include the novel *Orange Valley* (New York, 1931), his scholarly *Introduction to Tragedy: A Study in the Development of Dramatic Form* (Baton Rouge, La., 1939), and *Persephone's Cave: Cultural Accumulations of the Early Greeks* (Athens, Ga., 1979). Most of his best poetry is in his *Ode to the Sea and Other Poems* (Denver, Col., 1966). [DS

BALDWIN, James Arthur (1924–67), was born in Harlem, New York City, the son of poor immigrants from the American South. Baldwin attended De Witt Clinton High School, where he edited the school magazine, *The Magpie*, and was taught by the *Harlem Renaissance poet Countee *Cullen. Baldwin is known for his prose, but his first literary efforts were in verse, and in a few poems written in the 1940s he exhibited a facility no less remarkable for having been influenced by black literary forebears such as Langston *Hughes. Baldwin continued to write poems occasionally, sometimes reading them in public to jazz accompaniment, and in 1983 he published *Jimmy's Blues* (London and New York, 1986), a collection of mostly free-form, epigrammatic verses, many of them dedicated to family and friends.

For a discussion of Baldwin's juvenilia, see *Talking at the Gates: A Life of James Baldwin*, by James Campbell (London and New York, 1991). [JC

BANNING, Lex (Arthur Alexander) (1921–65), was born in Sydney. Although more than one of Lex Banning's teachers recognized the boy's intelligence, his formal education was hampered by the cerebral palsy over which he would eventually triumph. Unable to master handwriting, he learned to type and persuaded Sydney University to let him enrol in an arts course, where he won distinction in English and philosophy. An interest in philosophical questions and language is one constant of his poetry, and perhaps reflects the influence of Professor John Anderson, whose libertarian thinking and logical rigour shaped at least two generations of Sydney intellectuals.

From the mid-1940s to the early 1960s Banning was a leading and seminal figure around the Push, as Sydney's Bohemia was then called. His verse is typically formal and succinct, though also strongly experimental within those limits. Fond of learned allusion, archaizing language, and the very simplest stanza forms, he abhorred the merely personal, though it is possible to discern a moving trace of self-portraiture in his poem 'Nursery Rhyme,' which begins 'There was a crooked man | who walked a crooked mile'.

Poetry had a talismanic quality for Banning. When a fellow poet in a public lecture called it 'the wine of literature', he gulped a characteristic throatful of air and interjected 'no! the cognac!' Publishing only two pamphlets and one slim volume in his lifetime, Banning has not been lucky in his immortality. As a nearly apolitical exponent of the Forties *poème bien fait*, and lacking a secure measure of fame when he died, he was quickly eclipsed by the politicizing shift in literary sensibility which occurred soon afterwards. A retrospective collection of all his work, plus a short biography, was brought out by Angus and Robertson in 1987: *There Was a Crooked Man*, by Richard Appleton. [LM

BARAKA, Amiri Imamu (1934–), was born Everett LeRoi Jones in Newark, New Jersey, where he attended school and began college at the Newark branch of Rutgers University. He transferred to Howard University subsequently and took his BA there in 1954. He was a member of the US Air Force from 1954 to 1956. He married a white Jewish woman in 1958, a union which was discussed in his first wife's book, *How I Became Hettie Jones* (New York, 1990). He was divorced in 1965 and married again the following year. His teaching career included academic positions at the New School for Social Research in New York City from 1961 to 1964 and shorter appointments at Columbia and San Francisco State universities.

Preface to a Twenty Volume Suicide Note (New York, 1961) was LeRoi Jones's first collection of poems; subsequent volumes were *The Dead Lecturer* (New York, 1964); *Black Art* (Newark, NJ, 1966), *Black Magic: Poetry 1961–1967* (Indianapolis and London, 1969), and *It's Nation Time* (Chicago, 1970). By the publication of *Spirit Reach* (Newark, NJ, 1972) Jones had changed his name and his religion to Black Muslimism and was well established as the premier black militant of the world of poetry. He had also become a playwright, written a novel, a collection of short stories, and edited or written many other titles, most of them on social issues. His *Selected Poetry* (New York) was published in 1979.

Although Baraka's is a militant black poetry, his primary influences were the modernist poets *Pound and *Williams, via Charles *Olson and his quondam *Black Mountain school of poetry. Baraka's earliest work was lineated prose, and it remained so, though as his work matured he sometimes used the longer lines of Whitman and *Ginsberg. Jones's sojourn for a summer in the 'Little Black Mountain' of the State University of New York at Buffalo in 1964, where Olson was teaching, enabled him to absorb directly from their source theories of *Projective Verse, Vorticism (see BLAST), the 'open form', and 'breath-pause' lineation. If Baraka had little in common with the formalism of such Afro-American poets as Robert *Hayden, Gwendolyn *Brooks, or even Langston *Hughes, his practice approached those of his older black contemporaries when it came to the influence of jazz forms, for his poems are often a sort of 'scat' which renders the poem more suitable to public performance than to reading on the printed page.

Baraka has inspired more scholarship since 1973 than any other black poet in America. William J. Harris's *The Poetry and Poetics of Amiri Baraka: The Jazz Aesthetic* (Columbia, Mo., 1985) examines the poet's ethnic literary-musical roots, as does Baraka's own *The Music: Reflections on Blues & Jazz* (New York, 1987). Theodore Hudson in *From LeRoi Jones to Amiri Baraka* (Durham, NC, 1973) wrote that young blacks look to him as a culture hero. He is seen as a revolutionary both in literature and in politics, and he draws large audiences wherever he speaks. He is arguably the most widely read contemporary Afro-American poet. His *Autobiography of Le Roi Jones—Amiri Baraka* (New York) was published in 1984. [LT

BARBOUR, Douglas (1940–), born in Winnipeg, has spent all but a decade of his life on the prairies. Resident in Edmonton from 1969, he has become, with Robert *Kroetsch, one of the leading prairie poets, and a distinguished critic of Canadian poetry. He began initially to work in a Poundian open-field poetics expanded by reading *Creeley, *Duncan, and *Levertov. His earlier poems—collected in *Land Fall* (1971) and *White* (1972)—announce his investigation of the prairie landscape within this tradition. His long poem, *Visions of My Grandfather* (1977), showed the influence of bp *Nichol and Phyllis *Webb.

Collaboration with Stephen Scobie in the sound/performance poetry duo Re:Sounding resulted in *The Pirates of Pen's Chance* (Toronto, 1981), a collection of 'homolinguistic' (English to English) translations produced associatively from source texts. Subsequent works, particularly *Story for a Saskatchewan Night* (Edmonton, 1990), uncover the open field of both prairie and page, displaying a generative tension between lyric and anti-lyric elements.

Visible Visions (Edmonton, 1984) selects from his first eight volumes and adds twenty new poems with a useful introduction by Kroetsch; *Story for a Saskatchewan Night* selects from the later explorations. [RB

BARKER, George (1913–91), was born in Loughton, Essex, educated at Marlborough Road, Chelsea, and Regent Street Polytechnic, London. For a period in his early life (1939–41) he held an academic post in Japan; but, with a few exceptions (appointments briefly attached to universities in Britain and the United States), he worked as a free-lance writer. He has sometimes been seen as 'the last Romantic'—or at any rate the last of the Bohemians.

Barker emerged almost as a boy prodigy, and at about the same moment as two other prodigies, Dylan *Thomas and David *Gascoyne, in the early 1930s. With no advantages except his own talent and wayward charm, he published his first book at the age of 20 (*Thirty Preliminary Poems*, 1933), a novel that same year, and in 1935 both a book of poems and a work of prose fiction with T. S. *Eliot at Faber. In 1936, when W. B. *Yeats published his *Oxford Book of Modern Verse*, Barker was the youngest poet whom Yeats included: 'a lovely subtle mind', wrote Yeats, 'and a rhythmical invention comparable to Gerard Hopkins.'

His career through the 1930s was indeed charmed, and for several years Barker was seen as one of the most important poets of the generation that immediately succeeded *Auden and *MacNeice. *Poems* (1935) was followed by the long poem *Calamiterror* (1937), *Lament and Triumph* (1940), and, after his return to Britain during the war, *Eros in Dogma* (1944). What characterized all these poems was a fluent, heady, occasionally absurd rhetoric, often imitated and as often parodied: when the reactionary drama critic, James Agate, wanted to make mockery of 'modern poetry', all he needed to do was to quote a few lines of George Barker.

Barker's reputation became most controversial at the moment when part of his *True Confession of George Barker* (1950) was broadcast on the BBC Third Programme: this long, Villonesque work had originally been rejected by Barker's usual publisher, Faber, on grounds of obscenity, and then was the subject of shocked questions in Parliament after some of it had been broadcast. After Dylan Thomas's death in 1953 Barker's

standing seemed somehow to diminish, as if the literary public could not cope with two doomed romantics at the same time. Though Barker went on publishing (another ten volumes for adults between 1950 and 1978), he was in eclipse.

The publication, first, of his long poem *Anno Domini* (London and Pittsburgh, Pa.) in 1983, and then of his *Collected Poems*, ed. Robert Fraser (London), in 1987, has helped to build and consolidate his later reputation. He can no longer be conventionally seen as a standard New Romantic, or member of the *'New Apocalypse': his range, from elegiac rhetoric to proverbial plainness, is impressively wide, and his many masks and poses over many years need to be carefully and sympathetically examined. See also *Street Ballads* (London, 1992). [AST

BAUGHAN, Blanche (Edith) (1870–1958), was born in Putney and graduated from the University of London in 1892 with a BA in Classics, the top first-class student of her year. She migrated to New Zealand in 1900, taking a job as housekeeper on a farm on Banks Peninsula in Canterbury, and spent most of her remaining life in that area. There is no collected edition of her poems, but she has been represented in major New Zealand anthologies.

'A Bush Section', over 250 lines of verse influenced by Whitman, is the most impressive poem written in New Zealand before the 1920s, capturing a colonial sense of being spiritually marooned but also offering hope for the future. Although 'A Bush Section' was first published in Baughan's 'volume of New Zealand verse', *Shingle-Short and Other Verses* (Christchurch, n.d. [1908]), its distinctive exclamatory and interrogative rhetoric is foreshadowed in her *Verses* (London, 1898) and *Reuben and Other Poems* (London, 1903). In most of her best poems Baughan draws on a lively Victorian tradition of verse narrative and dramatic monologue.

After an illness (1909–10) Baughan found that 'the poetic impulse . . . vanished'. Influenced by Hindu philosophy, she turned to voluntary welfare work and founded the New Zealand Howard League for Penal Reform. Her *Poems from the Port Hills* (Auckland, n.d. [1923]) shows the decline in her powers as poet. There is an article on her verse and prose sketches by Peter Alcock in *Landfall*, 102 (1972). [MacD]

BAXTER, James K. (1926–72), was born at Dunedin, New Zealand. His father was a pacifist farmer of Scottish descent and his mother took degrees in languages at Sydney and Cambridge. Baxter began to write verse at 7 and his elegy-dominated first volume, *Beyond the Palisade*, was published in 1944 when he was 18, manifesting the influence of *Yeats and Dylan *Thomas; the following year Allen *Curnow singled him out for praise in the introduction to his *A Book of New Zealand Verse 1923–45*. He entered the University of Otago in 1944 but soon gave up, largely (by his own admission) because of excessive drinking. From an early age he claimed various mystical experiences which turned Christian in his late teens. He became a fervent Roman Catholic at the age of 32, but this did not lessen the pace of his hard-lived life; his major conflict was with the Calvinism in which he said he had been brought up, claiming that 'New Zealand society (and, indeed, modern Western society in general) carries like strychnine in its bones a strong unconscious residue of the doctrines and ethics of Calvinism'. He remained a self-styled figure of the 'wilderness' who always saw the artist as a tribesman cut off from his tribe, even when he returned to Otago University as Burns Fellow. Latterly he lived in the small Maori settlement of Jerusalem; he died at the age of 46 while on a visit to Auckland.

Despite his breaches of taste, his repetitiveness, and his excessive output, Baxter is a major figure in twentieth-century English poetry: in New Zealand only Allen Curnow can rival his achievement. Curnow's urbanity and self-consciousness contrast markedly with the more inspirational wildness of Baxter; Baxter attacked Curnow fiercely for being stuck in the politically anxious Thirties, when writers agonized over the imperialist ill-treatment of the Maoris, ignoring the new poets who 'in the late Forties and Fifties . . . seceded from the self-conscious New-Zealandism . . . and began to write simply

as people who happened to live in a given time and place'. It is an ironic charge for Baxter to level, since his poetry, though founded in personal observation and experience of nature, is always socially aware (he was lastingly affected by the poverty of Japan and India, which he visited on a UNESCO grant in 1958), and his later poetry is suffused with Maori words and themes. Paradoxically, too, his attacks on Calvinism cover a Calvinist contempt for modern culture's shoddy acquisitiveness. His poetry is hectoring, vatic, and often sexist; but it is never dull, because nearly every line has urgency and verbal life. He was a fine critic, and he wrote good pieces on 'Tam O' Shanter' and on Wilde.

Baxter's *Collected Poems* have been excellently edited by J. E. Weir (Oxford, 1980). A useful bibliography is J. E. Weir and B. A. Lyon, *A Preliminary Bibliography of Works By and Works About James K. Baxter* (Christchurch, 1979) and there are two good introductory studies: V. G. O'Sullivan, *James K. Baxter* (Wellington, 1976), and J. E. Weir, *The Poetry of James K. Baxter* (Wellington, 1970); as well as a biography, *The Life of James K. Baxter*, by Frank McKay (Auckland, 1990). [BO'D

Beat Generation, a group of poets and writers who rose to prominence during the 1950s and exerted considerable influence on literary fashions over the subsequent ten or fifteen years. The key members of this group were Allen *Ginsberg, Jack Kerouac, William Burroughs, and Gregory *Corso; other poets more loosely associated with the Beats, particularly during their sojourn on the West Coast, were Gary *Snyder, Michael *McClure, Lawrence *Ferlinghetti, Diane *di Prima, and others involved in the *San Francisco poetry renaissance (though the latter is usually considered a distinct movement extending well beyond the Beats).

In its purest form Beat writing is characterized by a distinctive blending of comic exuberance and prophetic aspirations. Neither as wholly playful as the work of New York poets like Frank *O'Hara nor as earnestly visionary as the poetry of San Franciscans like Robert *Duncan, Beat poetry tries, and at its best is able, to walk a narrow line between camp and mysticism, comedy and apocalypse. The very term 'Beat', a rare instance of a self-bestowed label, captures some of this precarious doubleness, combining as it does a colloquial sense (as in 'beat up', 'beaten down', raffish and socially outcast) with an almost religious sense ('beatific', angelic)—perhaps with overtones also of jazz rhythm, a significant influence on Beat poetics. The key event in the emergence of the Beats (as poets rather than fiction writers) was probably the famous group reading at the Six Gallery in San Francisco, at which Ginsberg gave the first public performance of *Howl*. Thanks to the rather bemused attention of magazines like *Time* and *Life*, and the publicity generated by the obscenity trial over the publication of *Howl*, the Beats quickly became notorious figures, literary versions of James Dean, Marlon Brando, and other popular embodiments of rebellious youth. With their disdain for bourgeois values and their readiness to shock middle-class sensibilities, the Beat writers opened the way for the much broader counter-culture of the 1960s, within which Ginsberg served as a kind of fatherly icon. For collections of Beat writings and comments, see Park Honan, *The Beats* (London, 1987) and the series of anthologies edited by Arthur and Kit Knight from California.

[RG

BEAVER, (Victor) Bruce (1928–), was born in Manly, New South Wales, Australia. With its arcades, malls and beaches, Manly has become the setting for much of his later poetry, which consists largely of meditations and personal explorations of both social and metaphysical concerns.

Like Patrick White, Beaver has a well-developed intuition for the outcasts of society, as well as for the humanizing features of life, even the life of those kicked and trampled by city living. A contemporary of Peter *Porter and Vincent *Buckley, he first came to literary prominence with his fourth collection of poems *Letters to Live Poets* (Sydney, 1969), awarded three major prizes. This book-length sequence was the first landmark in the 'new' Australian poetry that found expression in the Vietnam War years, and the volume remains crucial to an understanding of later Australian poetic developments.

His novel, *You Can't Come Back* (Adelaide, 1966, repr., 1984), was based on Beaver's early experience as a surveyor's linesman. Its tough depiction of working-class life and its laconic recognition of a brutalizing environment implicitly established the context from which the author's own later search for values and spiritual meanings was to strike out. Most important of his later books are *Lauds and Plaints: Poems 1968–1972* (Sydney, 1974), *As It Was* (St Lucia, Qld., 1979), and *Charmed Lives* (St Lucia, 1988). In these works Beaver's essentially pluralist concept of spiritual striving is most ardently articulated. *As It Was*, which won for him the Patrick White Prize, is in many ways his most accessible book. In two sections, it explores with grace and often playful detail the many-layered levels of childhood and adolescence in the depression years of Manly.

Charmed Lives contains some of the author's most rich and expressive writing and concludes with a major sequence, 'Tiresias Sees', which surveys with raunchy wit the cavalcade of living from the point of view of age and the close-felt presence of death.

Although a *Selected Poems* was published by Angus & Robertson (Sydney) in 1979, the later and more definitive edition from the University of Queensland Press in 1991 illustrates clearly the significance of his work in the 1980s. See also 'Bruce Beaver: A Survey', in *Biting The Bullet: A Literary Memoir*, by Thomas Shapcott (Sydney, 1990). [TWS

BECKETT, Samuel (Barclay) (1906–89), was born in Dublin to a prosperous, Protestant, Anglo-Irish (originally French Huguenot) upper-middle-class family, and was educated at Portora Royal School, Enniskillen, and Trinity College, Dublin. During two years (1928–30) he spent as *lecteur d'anglais* at the École Normale Supérieure in Paris he formed close attachments to James *Joyce, Thomas McGreevy, Nancy

Cunard, and the circle of writers who contributed to the avant-garde magazine *transition*. Returning to Dublin he was made an MA and resigned a Trinity lectureship in French after teaching for four terms. This abandonment of a promising academic career began a period of great uncertainty, dominated by Beckett's difficult relationship with his mother, his struggle to establish himself as a writer against her determination that he should enter the family business (quantity surveying), bouts of heavy drinking, various ailments and illnesses, probably psychosomatic in origin, solitary travels between Germany, France, and Ireland, and 'two bad years' (1933–5) in London, during which Beckett made several abortive ventures into literary journalism and underwent psychoanalysis. In 1938, the year in which his first novel, *Murphy*, was published (after rejection by forty-two publishers), Beckett settled in Paris where, with Suzanne Deschevaux-Dumesnil, he remained for the rest of his life (apart from an interruption in the Second World War when Beckett, a member of the Resistance, narrowly escaped capture by the Gestapo and went into hiding in unoccupied France); there he wrote, for the most part in French and translating himself, the novels and plays that brought him international renown and (in 1969) the Nobel Prize for Literature.

Like his earliest stories, the free-verse poems Beckett wrote in English before he was 30—with titles like 'Whoroscope' (on the life of René Descartes), 'Echo's Bones', and 'Sanies'—brandish their learned author's admiration for Dante and the extravagantly punning Joyce of *Finnegans Wake*; nevertheless, they anticipate in a harsher manner some of his much more disciplined later prose works. There are echoes of Rimbaud (whom Beckett translated, along with Apollinaire and Eluard), but the phrasing and the frame of reference are Irish (with touches of London and Paris), the idiom strenuously modernist in its disruptions of continuity, and full of a violence not yet subordinated to syntax, veering wildly between throw-away exactness and arch punctilio. In all this there are glimpses of raw—all too raw—material that fuels the

novels' and plays' ferocious comedy of 'ignorance and impotence'. Poems in French of the late 1930s and 1940s, some of them translated by the author, achieve a bleaker, barer statement of recognizably Beckettian despairs (but with scarcely Beckettian solemnity), and move inexorably towards the brevity of 'Mirlitonnades' and the translations from the maxims of Sébastien de Chamfort ('how hollow heart and full | of filth thou art'). *Collected Poems in English and French* (London and New York, 1982) contains all the original poems and translations that Beckett wished to preserve.   [AJ]

BEER, Patricia (1924–   ), was born in Exmouth, Devon, of a Plymouth Brethren family. Educated at Exmouth Grammar School, Exeter University, and Oxford, she lived in Italy, lecturing in English, from 1946 to 1953; from 1962 to 1968 she taught at Goldsmith's College, London. In 1964 she married Damien Parsons, an architect, and has now settled once more in Devon.

Beer's poems bring a wary, observant, wry, and well-read intelligence to bear on a relatively narrow range of themes and subjects: mortality, the workings of good and evil, the mysterious ways of God, and religious belief; love, nature, the passing of time and of generations, small but exalted moments of illumination. Her verse may have grown more casual and comprehensible with each volume, but her approach has remained tenaciously modest and domestic. In the introduction to her *Collected Poems* she comments on her first encounter, at university in the 1940s, with modern poetry, and her own early attempts, on her return from Italy in 1953, to write it. 'The poetic scene I stepped into was inevitably a death-trap. It was really the scene of the Forties still . . . The myth-kitty had not been sneered out of existence; to many it was still Aladdin's cave.' She is harsh towards her early poems; but in fact those that survive into the first part of her *Collected* seem less like the 'verbal debauchery' she accuses herself of than a fairly disciplined adumbration of later work. In first-person lyrics and brief historical monologues, Beer has written about Devon, Italy, literature, landscape, the lives of ancestors, and the death of parents—above all, about death, the insecurity and fearfulness that surround an apparently comfortable existence, and the various ways in which the dead haunt the living.

Her verse often sounds more instinctive than regular (though this conceals considerable artfulness—an enduring attachment to unostentatious syllabics, an equally firm preference for neat stanzaic forms with loose or irregular rhyme), and her tone is resolutely colloquial and informal. She herself remarks that she has 'never been accused of imitating any other poet', and though 'imitation' is certainly not in question, it is possible to detect echoes in Beer of a long tradition of English verse, from medieval charms to nineteenth-century hymns; of *Hardy; and perhaps of Stevie *Smith, with whom 'There had been friendship, not close, coming late in the day', and with whom Beer shares an element of whimsical, *faux-naïf* surprise and sly, dark humour.

Beer's *Collected Poems* (Manchester, 1988 and 1990) assembles, in chronological order, the pared-down contents of her seven collections (including the *Selected Poems*, London, 1979), and adds fourteen previously uncollected pieces. She has also published an autobiography, *Mrs Beer's House* (London, 1968); a volume of literary criticism, *Reader: I Married Him* (London and New York, 1974); and *Moon's Ottery*, a novel (London, 1978). [AJ]

BELITT, Ben (1911–), was born in New York City, where he spent several years in an orphanage before rejoining his mother, an orthodox Jew. He attended the University of Virginia, and since 1938 has been a professor of English at Bennington College. During his long career he has received relatively little critical attention, in part, no doubt, because of his scanty output, but more centrally because his poetry's mixture of high Romanticism and extreme, uncompromising difficulty has placed it outside the various fashions of the past five decades. By the same token, however, he has attracted a small group of dedicated admirers, among them the poet Howard *Nemerov and the critic Harold Bloom.

Belitt's poetry combines an austere, abstract vision of human alienation with a loving and sensuous attention to scene and locality—an unlikely conjunction, and one that may account for the poet's ongoing obsession with duality and doubleness, as evinced in the title of his book *The Double Witness* (Princeton, NJ., 1976). Upon his essentially Jewish resignation to a tragic universe he grafts a romantic celebration of nature's beauty and abundance, and the result, while at times elusive in tone and affect, is a rich, densely worked, and strikingly intelligent body of poetry that deserves more praise than it has had. Belitt has also been a prolific translator of Spanish, Italian, and French poetry, particularly of Pablo Neruda. His oeuvre can be surveyed in *Possessions: New and Selected Poems* (Boston, 1986). [RG]

Bell, The, an Irish literary and cultural periodical, founded by Sean O'Faolain in October 1940 and edited by him until 1946 when the novelist Peadar O'Donnell succeeded him until its demise in 1954. Its principal self-definition was as a liberal opponent of censorship in Ireland. As a counter to what it saw as the chimerical Gaelic ideals of the new state, it dealt with the actualities of political life (economics and industry), as well as with literature. O'Faolain's editorship made most impact in promoting short-story writers such as Frank *O'Connor and Bryan MacMahon. Among its poetry editors were Frank O'Connor and Louis *MacNeice, who published established writers (*Kavanagh, *Rodgers, *Hewitt, *Gogarty, as well as O'Connor and MacNeice themselves) and helped establish a few new writers (*Iremonger, Roy *McFadden). For contents, see R. Holzapfel, *The Bell: An Index of Contributors* (Dublin, 1970). [BO'D

BELL, Julian (Heward) (1908–37), was born in London, the son of Clive and Vanessa Bell and the nephew of Virginia Woolf. He was educated at Leighton Park School, a Quaker institution, and at King's College, Cambridge, where he was a contemporary of John *Lehmann and William *Empson. While at Cambridge, he contributed to *The Venture*, and was elected to the élite Apostles society. His *Winter Movement* (1930) was greeted as one of the most promising first books of its day, comparable with W. H. *Auden's *Poems* (1930).

Winter Movement was dedicated to Richard Jefferies and consists largely of poems about the English countryside. They are finished and controlled performances, though their inspiration was *Georgian rather than modernist. The book ends with a set of 'Characters in the manner of Pope'; and a modernized version of Pope's style was Bell's aim for the next two years.

Poems by Bell appeared alongside those of Empson, Auden, and Stephen *Spender in *New Signatures* in 1932; but Bell did not belong with Auden and Spender, either artistically or politically. In 'A Brief View of Poetic Obscurity' he had set out in 1930 his unsympathetic view of modernism; and, as a Socialist, Bell felt that Auden and Spender were romantic in seeing the salvation of society in Communism. His own contribution to *New Signatures*, 'Arms and the Man', was a satire on disarmament written in couplets.

In 1933 Bell experienced another spurt of creativity, which led to the poems collected in *Works for Winter* (1936). This book had none of the vividness of *Winter Movement*, though there are some touching personal poems. Everything in it was written before he departed for China in 1935 to be professor of English at Wuhan University, a position he accepted after his thesis was rejected at Cambridge. When he returned from China he went to Spain as an ambulance driver in the Civil War. He was killed in 1937. In his last two years he wrote no poetry.

His life is told in *Journey to the Frontier*, by P. Stansky and W. Abrahams (London, 1966). *Essays, Poems and Letters*, ed. Q. Bell (London, 1938) is a selection of his work.   [ATT

BELL, Martin (1918–78), was born in Southampton and educated at Taunton's School and University College, Southampton. He was an exemplar of Thirties poetic enthusiasm, a follower of *Auden, and a member of the Communist Party. But he was also (much more unusually) an intellectual of the working class, an enthusiast for French poetry, especially the Surrealists, and a lover of Italian opera. Later Bell was to write of a Southampton friend killed in the war, that he was 'a pattern of accomplishments,|And joined the Party first, and left it first' ('Letter to a Friend'). He could have been describing himself. Bell's poetry was both late-arrived, as one of Auden's epigoni coming into flower in the age of the *Movement, and prescient of what was to come, in its defence of Leftish humanism against the dismantling of the Welfare State. Bell died in poverty in Leeds in 1978.

Bell's first successful poem was a translation of Gérard de Nerval's celebrated sonnet 'El Desdichado', written while he was serving in the Royal Engineers in Italy. He wrote slowly and rarely on his return to civilian life and work as a schoolteacher in London. His creative time began when he joined The *Group, and encouraged by his reception there, especially the advocacy of Philip *Hobsbaum and Peter *Redgrove, he produced a string of powerful poems in the decade 1955 to 1965. This included 'Headmaster: Modern Style', 'Reasons for Refusal', 'Winter Coming On' (after Laforgue), 'Ode to Himself', 'High Street, Southampton', and 'Ode to Groucho'. In the last decade of his life he produced a substantial number of stylish translations of the French Surrealist poets Reverdy, Desnos, Peret, and Max Jacob.

Bell's poetic legacy is contained in the one book he produced during his lifetime, his *Collected Poems* (London and New York, 1967). Although a selection of his work appeared in *Penguin Modern Poets, 3* (1962), and his posthumously published *Complete Poems* (Newcastle upon Tyne, 1988) gathered together fragments from his later life, all his finest poetry fits into that span of one hundred pages which was both his debut and his apotheosis.   [PNFP

BELL, Marvin (Hartley) (1937–), born in New York City, is both poet and academic; he is Flannery O'Connor Professor of Letters at the University of Iowa and has been associated since his debut (*Two Poems*, Iowa City, 1965) with the *Iowa Writers' Workshop. He is an autobiographical, not to say *confessional, poet, writing in the tradition of *Snodgrass and *Lowell, but with a deliberate emphasis on the comic and the trivial in the manner of *Rothenberg, Jonathan *Williams, and other allied poets. *Seques* (Boston, 1983) consists of a correspondence in verse with the poet William *Stafford, and contains his most interesting and concentrated work, in which he can be seen reacting to the often amusing 'probes' of the older poet. His verse is conversational, diffuse, often jokey, much concerned with the intimate details of his family and domestic life, and with many echoes of *Roethke's manner, but without Roethke's regard for traditional form. *New and Selected Poems* appeared in New York in 1987.   [MS-S

BELL, William (1924–48), grew up in Derbyshire and was educated at Epsom College and at Merton College, Oxford, where he at first read physics. After a period in the Fleet Air Arm he returned in 1946 to read English. While at Oxford, Bell edited *Poetry from Oxford in Wartime* (1945) and *More Poetry from Oxford* (1946), the first of which contained poems by John *Heath-Stubbs, Philip *Larkin, Christopher *Middleton, and David *Wright. In 1946 he published his first book, *Elegies*. He was killed climbing the Matterhorn in August 1948 at the age of 24 and his second book, *Mountains Beneath the Horizon*, appeared posthumously in 1950.

Bell was an admirer of W. B. *Yeats and Ezra *Pound, and this may account for his penchant for mythological imagery and for complex and traditional forms. The virtues of his work are a firmness and naturalness of diction and a controlled amplitude of movement. While his poetry evinces a considerable potentiality, it is often marred by a mannered avoidance of direct reference to experience. *Mountains Beneath the Horizon* (London, 1950) contains a brief memoir.   [ATT

BELLERBY, Frances (1899–1977), née Parker, was born and brought up in Bristol. Reticent about personal details, she knew much hardship and illness and published her first book of verse, *Plash Mill* (London, 1946), when in her forties. Her work was never widely read or anthologized, but had many devotees, such as Charles *Causley, who edited her *Selected Poems* (London, 1970). She wrote a novel, *Hath the Rain a Father?* (London, 1946), and three books of stories. The most potent influences on her work are the counties of Cornwall and Devon, in which she lived for much of her life. She was a religious and contemplative nature poet much akin to Ruth *Pitter, but quieter and without the oddities, quirks, and prolificity. At the age of 30 poetry (she wrote) 'seeped away, unregretted'; then, some fifteen years later, it returned 'for no known or surmised reason'. Her taut and disciplined poems almost always depict landscapes—usually with a quiet sense of menace and mystery. See *The Sheltering Water and Other Poems* (Gillingham, Kent, 1970) and *The First-Known and Other Poems* (London, 1974).   [MS-S

BELLOC, Hilaire (Pierre René) (1870–1953), was born in Paris, the son of a French lawyer and his English wife. He was educated at Oxford. In the Edwardian era—during which he was a Liberal MP—he, Wells, Shaw, and *Chesterton were known as the 'big four'; but his reputation gradually faded, owing in part to the extreme truculence of his Roman Catholic polemic, and to diminishing powers. He wrote two kinds of poetry, serious and light. The serious, included in *Collected Verse* (London, 1958), is melodious and skilfully crafted: 'Tarantella' remains the best-known example. As an author of light verse Belloc is outstanding. He exploited this vein from *The Children's Bad Book of Beasts* (1896) until 1930; all is collected in *Cautionary Verses* (London, 1939) and in *Hilaire Belloc's Cautionary Verses* (New York, 1959). Here he displayed the more relaxed, 'English' side of himself. The mock-solemn, deliberately bathetic manner arose from Belloc's affectionate parodying of the often-moralizing nursery rhymes of Jane and Ann Taylor (*Original Poems for Infant Minds*, London, 1804). The tone of his tales (do not, for example, play with matches or you will be burned to death) is always light and charmingly inconsequential, rather than satirical of over-strict Victorian morality; they act as a counterpart to Belloc's unbridled ferocity in polemic. See *The Life of Belloc* (London, 1957), by R. W. Speaight, and *Hilaire Belloc* (London, 1984), by A. N. Wilson. [MS-S

BENEDIKT, Michael (1935–), was born in New York. He served as poetry editor of the *Paris Review* (1974–8), and has made his living as editor, co-editor, or correspondent of various magazines, such as *Art International* and *Art News*, and as a visiting professor or poet-in-residence. An eclectic writer, he is interested in prose-poetry and in contemporary film and theatre, which he says have influenced him as much as any movements in poetry. His poetry is conversational and casual, and many of his poems have struck critics as loose to the point of carelessness; but his rejection of 'seriousness' as a desirable quality is well in keeping with the early European surrealist methods he espouses. Benedikt has translated surrealist poets such as Jean L'Anselme and Desnos, and his own manner reflects theirs. He is a successful performer of his own works, some of which resemble libretti for stand-up comic turns. When he is not writing in a markedly surrealist style, Benedikt can seem trite and banal: 'O come to me, true | beloved, so that you can go away in a hurry again!' The Grilled Flowers Press of Tucson has published a study of his work, *Benedikt: A Profile* (Tucson, Ariz., 1978). Other collections are *Night Cries* (Middletown, Conn., 1976) and *The Badminton of Great Barrington; or Gustav Mahler and the Chattanooga-Choo-Choo* (Pittsburgh, Pa., and London, 1980). [MS-S

BENÉT, Stephen Vincent (1898–1943), younger brother of the poet and critic William Rose *Benét, was born in Bethlehem, Pennsylvania, and (his father being a colonel in the army) raised in New York, California, and Georgia. He published his first two books of poems, *Five Men and Pompey* (1915) and *Young Adventure* (1918), while still an undergraduate at Yale. In 1920 he went to Paris to write his first novel, *The*

Beginning of Wisdom (1921), and on his return the following year married Rosemary Carr. Thereafter he made a living writing stories, novels, and, for two years, film scripts, but always considered himself chiefly a poet.

John Brown's Body (which won the Pulitzer Prize in 1928), an epic poem of the Civil War, displays Benét's full thematic and formal range, using loose five- and six-foot lines for the main narrative, blank verse for Lincoln's soliloquies, and rippling heroic couplets to suggest the gallantry of the antebellum South. His most ambitious shorter poems are the 'Nightmare' poems in *Burning City* (1936), which imagine various forms of urban catastrophe; the ballads in *Tiger Joy* (1925), however—such as 'The Mountain Whippoorwill: A Georgia Romance', strongly influenced by William Morris—have been much more popular. Benét's prolixity and his lack of wit, irony, or symbolic intensity place him in the 'genteel' tradition of American poetry stemming from Longfellow and Bryant. He has received little critical attention, and is now remembered mainly for his patriotism: he wrote *A Book of Americans* (1933), verse biographies, with his wife; and propaganda for the Writer's War Board during the Second World War. *Western Star* (winner of the Pulitzer Prize in 1943), an epic poem describing the colonization of America, was left unfinished at his death.

See *John Brown's Body* (New York, 1928; repr. 1982) and *Selected Poetry and Prose*, ed. Basil Davenport (New York, 1964); and for a thorough critical biography, *Stephen Vincent Benét: The Life and Times of an American Man of Letters, 1898–1943*, by Charles A. Fenton (New Haven, Conn., 1958). [NE

BENÉT, William Rose (1886–1950), the older brother of Stephen Vincent Benét, was born at Fort Hamilton, New York, educated at Albany Academy, and graduated from Yale in 1907. After various editorial jobs and a stint in the US Air Service, he became an associate editor at the New York *Post*'s Literary Review in 1920. Four years later he was one of the founders of the *Saturday Review of Literature*, writing 'The Phoenix

Nest' column. His early poetry, always facile, exuberant, and highly romantic, included ballads, historical pageantry, and quasi-mystical fantasies of various kinds, as evidenced in *Merchants from Cathay* (1913), *The Falconer of God* (1914), *The Great White Wall* (1916), and the more solemn *Perpetual Light* (1919), a memorial to his first wife. His second wife, the poet and novelist Elinor *Wylie, together with the influence of Robert *Frost, encouraged a needed paring of his verse, as seen in *Man Possessed* (1927), although the ballad 'Jesse James: American Myth' remains his most popular poem.

Benét co-edited *The Oxford Anthology of American Literature* (1938) with N. H. Pearson, and his *The Dust Which Is God* (1941), a thinly disguised verse autobiography, won the 1942 Pulitzer Prize. A representative sampling of Benét's stronger work can be found in *Modern American Poetry*, ed. Louis Untermeyer (New York, 1969).

[EB

BENNET, Louise (1919–), Jamaican poet and folklorist, was born in Kingston. In 1945 she won a British Council Scholarship to study at the Royal Academy of Dramatic Arts in London, and subsequently worked as a comedienne for repertory companies in England, and also for the BBC. She returned to Jamaica in 1955, and from 1959 to 1961 lectured in drama and Jamaican folklore at the University of the West Indies. Among the many honours she has received is an MBE.

Bennet was famous in the Caribbean for her performances as 'Miss Lou', and her poems, written in dialect employ various comic personae. They are informed by the oral tradition, making use of such devices as the 'Anancy' tales of the cunning spider, familiar proverbs, and cautionary tales. As a consequence, they have tended to be underrated as the work of an amusing, but not quite 'respectable' entertainer. In fact, Bennet's poems at their best display great mastery of characterization and complex irony, as well as serious social comment. The closest English equivalent might well be *Kipling, also a master of common speech, though perhaps he would not have appreciated 'Colonisation in Reverse'.

This poem is a witty, mocking, and buoyantly good-humoured tilt at the irrational fears of many in the 'mother country'.

Some of Bennet's poetry is available on records, and much of her best in *Selected Poems*, ed. Mervyn Morris (Kingston, Jam. 1982).

[MR

BENTLEY, E(dward) C(lerihew) (1875–1956), English novelist and humourist, was born in London, son of an official in the Lord Chancellor's Department. He went to school with G. K. *Chesterton, a lifelong friend. After a distinguished career at Oxford he was called to the bar (1902), but soon afterwards devoted himself to journalism, working for the *Daily Telegraph* from 1912. Most famous for the superior detective novel, *Trent's Last Case* (London, 1913), Bentley also invented a new (light) verse form, the clerihew (so called from his second name). A collection of these, *Biography for Beginners* (London, 1905), illustrated by Chesterton, was published as by Edward Clerihew. The clerihew, still a frequently attempted form, was defined by Bentley as a 'sort of formless four-line verse'. It consists of two rhyming couplets. The most quoted is: 'The art of Biography | Is different from Geography. | Geography is about maps, | But Biography is about chaps.' See *Clerihews Complete* (London, 1951).

[MS-S

BERG, Stephen (1934–) was born in Philadelphia and educated at the University of Pennsylvania, Boston University (where he was taught by Robert *Lowell), and the University of Iowa (where he attended the *Iowa Writers' Workshop). Between 1959 and 1961 he lived in Mexico. Since 1972 he has, as co-founder, been co-editor of *American Poetry Review. He has taught at Princeton and Haverford College, and is currently professor of the humanities at the University of the Arts, Philadelphia. He married Mildred Rutherford Lane in 1975 and has two daughters.

Berg's early poems deal with personal experience without insisting on the biographical facts of the poet's identity. A long immersion in the work of Anna Akhmatova reflected a poetic uncertainty about the self he wanted to present, but led to more than one volume. Subsequently, the prose poems of 'Shaving' and the extended 'Homage to the Afterlife' show, respectively, debts to Lowell and *Ginsberg which are repaid with a more naked and specific examination of personal disquiet.

Berg's poems are generously represented in *New and Selected Poems* (London and Washington, DC, 1992). His individual collections are *The Daughters* (Indianapolis, Ind., 1971), *Grief* (New York, 1972), *Akhmatova at the Black Gates* (Chicago, 1981), and *In It* (Chicago, 1986). He has also published, often in collaboration, translations from the Japanese, Aztec, Eskimo, Greek, and Hungarian.   [LMacK

BERNSTEIN, Charles. See LANGUAGE POETRY.

BERRIGAN, Daniel (J.) (1921–), was born in Minnesota. He was jailed, along with his brother Philip, for anti-war activities in 1968, and became for a short while an international *cause célèbre* as one of the Catonsville Nine. His play *The Trial of the Catonsville Nine* was produced in Los Angeles in 1970. His early devotional verse, although unconventional in Catholic terms, showed the influence of George Herbert, but dispensed with the English poet's formalism; clearly Berrigan had been affected by the radical American Catholic Dorothy Day, and by Caroline Gordon's sympathetic portrait of her in her novel *The Malefactors*. The poetry written after he had founded Clergy and Laymen Concerned about Vietnam is more direct and programmatic, in keeping with the man who poured blood on, and burned, draft papers; there were later similar poems arising from his imprisonment: *Trial Poems* (Boston, 1970), *Prison Poems* (Greensboro, NC, 1973). This is the poetry of an activist rather than that of a poet contemplating activism, but it is eloquent none the less. He has now largely abandoned poetry, he says, in favour of creating a society in which it may properly be written. See also *False Gods, Real Man* (New York, 1966); *Daniel Berrigan: Poetry, Drama, Prose*, ed. M. True (New York,

1988); *The Writings of Daniel Berrigan*, ed. R. Labrie (Lanham, Md., 1989).   [MS-S

BERRIGAN, Ted (Edmund Joseph Michael) (1934–83), was born in Providence, Rhode Island. He served in the army from 1954 to 1957, then attended the University of Tulsa before moving to New York City in the early 1960s. In New York he met poets and painters, published art criticism and book reviews, and wrote, during a three-month period in 1963, a series of short poems, most of them fourteen lines long, which he brought out the following year as *The Sonnets* (New York, 1964). Their themes are the conventional ones of love, friendship, art, and how they play and prey upon each other, but Berrigan explodes the sonnet form's conventions—literally, by repeating, varying, and scrambling lines, many lifted from other poets; and figuratively, by taking perceptions and insights as he finds them rather than where sonnets of the past might have led him to place them.

Although none of Berrigan's later books can touch the luxurious brilliance of *The Sonnets*, all are characterized by an engaging emotional directness and a bracing command of everyday speech. Twice married and the father of four children, he taught at universities across the United States and in England, and died unexpectedly of blood poisoning caused by a perforated ulcer. The most comprehensive collection of his work is *So Going Around Cities: New and Selected Poems 1958–1979* (Berkeley, Calif., 1980).   [RH

BERRY, Francis (1915–), born in Malaya, held chairs in English at the University of Sheffield, 1947–70, and at Royal Holloway College, University of London, 1970–80. Since retiring he has had visiting appointments in the United States, the West Indies, India, Australia, Malawi, and Japan. In addition to criticism, radio plays, and a novel, he has published some nine volumes of verse: *Galloping Centaur: Poems 1933–1951* (London, 1950), selected from four earlier volumes, was followed by *Morant Bay and Other Poems* (London, 1961), *Ghosts of Greenland* (London, 1966), and *From the Red Fort* (Bristol, 1984). He writes mainly long narrative poems, usually with a historical setting: for example, 'Murdock' is the story of a feud between two brothers, 'Morant Bay' describes a negro uprising in Jamaica in 1865, 'Illnesses and Ghosts at the West Settlement' is set in Greenland in the time of Erik the Red, and 'The Singing Dome' is about Shah Jehan, builder of the Taj Mahal.

[POM

BERRY, James (1924–), was born in Boston, a coastal village in Jamaica. He spent his late teens working in America, but moved to 'dislocated' London, as he put it, in 1948, and has been in Britain ever since, now living in Brighton. After having worked for Post Office International Telegraphs from 1951 to 1977, he went on to become a full-time writer, an opportunity which began with his C. Day Lewis fellowship (1977–8). His poem, 'Fantasy of an African Boy', won first prize in the National Poetry Competition for 1981. He is an accomplished reader of his own work.

Berry's poetry not only reflects both Jamaican and British culture, but also merges them 'to make it new'. He owes something to Louise *Bennet in his use of Jamaican dialect, proverbs, and folk-tales but he also excels in poetry about the experience of being black in Britain, particularly in *Lucy's Letters and Loving* (London, 1982), in which 'Lucy' is an unlettered immigrant woman. In *Chain of Days* (London, 1985), he occasionally echoes the younger generation of 'dub' poets like Linton Kwesi *Johnson and Benjamin *Zephaniah. Poems like 'My Father' and 'Faces Around My Father' are clear-eyed in their self-analysis.

Other collections include *Fractured Circles* (1979) and *When I Dance* (1988—both London). His books of short stories include *A Thief in the Village* (1987) and *Anancy-Spiderman* (1989—both London).

[MR

BERRY, Wendell (1934–), was born and raised on a farm in Kentucky. Having taught for several years in California and New York, Berry returned to the Kentucky River region where he has lived for two decades, writing and farming

on seventy-five acres in Henry County with his wife and children. His poems, which often have a quietly meditative aura, are characterized by simplicity of line and a straightforward narrative structure. The poet returns frequently to themes that have interested him from the beginning, such as the power of natural cycles, family responsibility, and the importance of community. His language is always unaffected, finely tuned to the cadences and rhythms of common speech, though he avoids the use of local dialects. A fair number of his poems, such as 'At a Country Funeral', are written in traditional (almost Wordsworthian) blank verse, but he is a versatile poet who has worked in any number of forms, including free verse. A strong conservationist and defender of small-scale farming, he often infuses his poems with political passion, as in 'Dark with Power'. Throughout the years he has written a number of poems that protest against war, industrialism, and the interruption of traditional agriculture in America.

Each of these themes has been taken up separately in books of essays too, such as *The Unsettling of America* (1977) and *Standing by Words* (1983). In his essays, as in the poetry, he is by turns social critic, naturalist, and prophet. A strong religious bent underlies everything Berry has written; as he says in *Standing by Words*: 'The imagination is our way to the Divine imagination, permitting us to see wholly—as whole and holy—what we perceive as scattered, as order what we perceive as random.' In addition to the poems and essays, Berry has also written several novels and one volume of connected short stories.

Berry has published his work in numerous collections, including *Openings* (1968), *The Country of Marriage* (1973), and *Clearing* (1977—all New York), and *Sabbaths* (San Francisco, 1987). His *Collected Poems: 1957–1982* (San Francisco, 1985) remains the most comprehensive collection of his verse.

[JP

BERRYMAN, John (1914–72) was born John Smith Jr. in rural Oklahoma, the result of a miserable marriage between a feckless, small-town banker and a schoolteacher who thought she

Berryman

deserved better. His father, John Allyn Smith Sr., drifted toward the Florida land boom when his banking career foundered. The Smiths opened a restaurant in Tampa in 1925, and closed it the following year when the boom collapsed. John Smith Sr. died of a gunshot wound that, despite questionable details, was ruled a suicide. His father's death haunts all of Berryman's books, and biographers have taken it to be a key to his life and work (as, indeed, did the psychoanalytically inclined poet himself). Smith's widow remarried, this time to a dapper Georgian called John Berryman. The couple moved to New York, and John Smith Jr. became John Berryman Jr.

Berryman attended the South Kent School and Columbia, where he came under the courtly influence of the poet and critic Mark *Van Doren. Berryman dressed like a dandy, attended strip shows and speakeasies, and memorized the lyrics of 150 popular songs—a plausible source, so far unexamined, for the forms and diction of his later lyrics. Upon graduation, he won a Columbia fellowship to spend two years at Cambridge University. He spent an hour with *Yeats, got drunk with Dylan *Thomas, and returned to New York, in 1938, with a beard, fine tweeds, and a clipped British accent.

After false starts in journalism and high-school teaching, Berryman became what he despised, a college professor, with stints through the Fifties and Sixties at Princeton, Harvard, Iowa, and, tenured at last, at Minnesota. He was notorious for his sweating, spitting lecture style and for his capacity for drink, which played havoc with his professional and marital life—he was married three times. Not until 1969, however, did Berryman admit to himself or his friends that he was an alcoholic; his unfinished novel *Recovery*, published posthumously in 1973, records his struggles with alcoholism.

While his famous contemporaries—Robert *Lowell, Elizabeth *Bishop, Delmore *Schwartz —have begun to settle in the imagination, Berryman has remained, since he leaped to his death from a bridge above the Mississippi River in 1972, elusive, changing shape in the mind

as he constantly changed shape during his life. His imaginative life seems, in retrospect, a ventriloquist's search for an appropriate dummy. He was drawn to the great impersonators in literature: Shakespeare (whose biography he tried for twenty years to write), Yeats, and Stephen *Crane (whose biography he did write). His interest in the extra-marital affair commemorated in *Sonnets to Chris* (1947, published as *Berryman's Sonnets* in 1966) cooled early, but to give the sonnet sequence the requisite twists he purposefully, like an improvising (and rather heartless) actor, prolonged and complicated the relationship. In his first major poem, *Homage to Mistress Bradstreet* (1953, 1956), Berryman impersonated a seventeenth-century woman poet. Although he despised Ann Bradstreet's poetry ('all this bald | abstract didactic rime I read appalled'), it was her body, not her words, that he appropriated for his seduction fantasy. The centre-piece of the poem is a childbirth scene written with Joycean gusto and lack of punctuation.

What redeemed the disintegration of his own life, Berryman always assured himself, was the poetry. But by the time he began writing his loosely autobiographical *Dream Songs* (1969), the book he is famous for, redemption by art no longer seemed so certain to him. He announced that he was 'down on Rilke and the hieratic boys just now'—especially Yeats—for not mixing with real men and women. Whitman became his model, and, in his last poems, a woman poet whose words he did not despise: Emily Dickinson. But he was coming to seem increasingly unreal to himself—such were the effects of prolonged alcohol abuse—finding himself 'less impressed than I used to be by the universal notion of a continuity of individual personality'. The *Dream Songs* are conceived as a sort of running minstrel show, with its hero sometimes in black face. The book has moments of jaunty brilliance and piercing clarity, especially in the many elegies for Berryman's contemporaries. 'I'm cross with god who has wrecked this generation', he wrote in one song. But occasionally the songs sound like a drunk who stayed too long at the party.

Berryman wrote some of his best poetry during the last years of his life, when he seemed willing, finally, to drop his disguises, letting the circus animals go home. Some of these poems seem almost posthumous in their disillusioned gravity, like the Yeatsian 'He Resigns' of summer 1970. The undertow of his father's death tugs at many of these late poems, as though some reconciliation were at hand.

Berryman's poetry, except for *The Dream Songs* (New York, 1969; London, 1990), is collected in Charles Thornbury (ed.), *John Berryman: Collected Poems, 1937–1971* (New York, 1989; London, 1990). There are two full-length biographies of Berryman: John Haffenden's *The Life of John Berryman* (London, 1982) and Paul Mariani's *Dream Song: The Life of John Berryman* (New York, 1990). Notable critical studies include Haffenden's *John Berryman: A Critical Commentary* (London and New York, 1980) and Joel Conarroe's *John Berryman: An Introduction to the Poetry* (New York, 1977). There is a fascinating memoir by Berryman's first wife, Eileen Simpson, *Poets in Their Youth* (New York, 1982). Berryman's own best critical work is collected in *The Freedom of the Poet* (New York, 1976). [CB

BERSSENBRUGGE, Mei-Mei (1947–), was born in Beijing to a Chinese mother and a Dutch-American father. She grew up in Massachusetts and then attended Reed College and the School of the Arts at Columbia University. Since then she has lived in New Mexico and in New York.

Berssenbrugge's early poems were imagistic, almost classically Chinese in their bias towards objects and description, but with her second book, *Random Possession*, she began to let her images fan out, expand, and in the process became a philosophical poet, questioning being and language simultaneously. By the time of her most recent book, *Empathy* (Barrytown, NY, 1989), she had developed a long line that breaks the 'normal' horizontal border of the page. Her work is rescued from preciousness by precision, and by a vision which goes beyond the iteration of particulars. She is an experimental writer in the sense that the poems do not have different

'subjects' as such. She is experimenting with getting the language of philosophy into her work, making poems that ask questions about representation, what it means to engage the world with language.

Her other books include: *Summits Move with the Tide* (New York, 1974), *The Heat Bird* (Providence, Rhode Island, 1984), and *Hiddenness* (New York, 1987). [MRu

BETHELL, (Mary) Ursula (1874–1945), was born in England to wealthy parents who had already made their home in New Zealand and soon returned there. She grew up in the South Island, was educated there and in Europe, and devoted herself to social work in, alternately, Christchurch and London. After the First World War she went back to New Zealand, built a house in the Cashmere Hills overlooking Christchurch, where she lived with her friend Effie Pollen from 1924 to 1934, and began writing poetry. Her first collection, *From a Garden in the Antipodes* (published under the pseudonym Evelyn Hayes in 1929), is literally about her garden, with detailed descriptions of plants, weather, and seasonal events. The poems are mostly in free verse (Arthur *Waley was an influence) and have a lively freshness of style, not without irony, humour, and occasional whimsy. Although Bethell felt drawn to England (planting primroses to remind her of the English spring), her poetry is physically rooted in the New Zealand landscape, which she presents as it is and not, like her predecessors, with the eyes of an outsider. The poet D'Arcy Cresswell wrote: 'New Zealand wasn't truly discovered . . . until Ursula Bethell, "very earnestly digging", raised her head to look at the mountains.' Bethell's work stands at the beginning of modern poetry in New Zealand.

Her later books (*Time and Place*, 1936; *Day and Night, Poems 1924–34*, 1939) show an alteration of style which could be viewed as a regression to more stilted *Georgian and Victorian models; the verse is formal, the diction more artificial, the impulse less spontaneous. Bethell was a devout Anglican much exercised by her spiritual struggles and anxious to direct her poetry towards devotional aims. This, and her increasing technical ambition, had the effect of subduing much of what was instinctive in her writing. Nevertheless, there are attractive and successful poems among her uneven later output. After Effie Pollen's death in 1934 Bethell wrote little poetry, apart from the agonized 'Six Memorials' to her friend. *Collected Poems*, ed. Vincent O'Sullivan, is published by Oxford University Press (Auckland, 1985). [FKA

BETJEMAN, Sir John (1906–84), was born in Highgate, the son of a manufacturer of Dutch descent who made luxurious household articles. His childhood was marred by school bullies, a sense of social inferiority, and a sadistic Calvinist nurserymaid who appalled him with tales of eternity and hell: 'I caught her terror then. I have it still.' He was happy at the Dragon School, Oxford, but fear of bullying made his life wretched at Marlborough, although he loved the countryside and numbered among his friends Louis *MacNeice, Bernard *Spencer, Ellis Waterhouse, and Anthony Blunt. At Magdalen College, Oxford he plunged into the pleasures of sex, drink, party-going, and the purchase of books beyond his means, while his study of architecture was facilitated by rich and aristocratic friends through whom he gained entry into English and Irish country houses. Failure in Divinity Moderations entailed his being sent down: he nurtured a lifelong hatred for his tutor, C. S. *Lewis, who at this crisis displayed a total lack of sympathy. After Betjeman had caused his father acute distress by refusing to enter the family firm, Oxford connections secured him a post in 1931 on the *Architectural Review*, which he left in 1933 to become a freelance journalist. During the war he worked for various government departments, and after 1945 lived by journalism and by engagements on radio and television.

His first book of poems, *Mount Zion* (1931), was published by his rich friend Edward James, a patron of surrealism and husband of Tilly Losch, a beautiful, rapacious Viennese dancer. *Ghastly Good Taste*, a study in architectural fashion, appeared in 1933, the year of Betjeman's mar-

riage to Penelope, the daughter of Field-Marshal Sir Philip (later Lord) Chetwode. Three volumes of verse, *Continual Dew* (1937), *Old Lights for New Chancels* (1940), and *New Bats in Old Belfries* (1945), increased Betjeman's reputation in the small, sophisticated coteries of his admirers, and W. H. *Auden's introduction to his choice of Betjeman's verse and prose, *Slick but not Streamlined* (1947), advanced Betjeman's claims to be regarded as a serious poet, a judgement echoed by John Sparrow in his preface to Betjeman's *Selected Poems* (1948). *A Few Late Chrysanthemums* (1954), his finest collection, foreshadowed the enormous success of *Collected Poems* (1958). His verse-autobiography, *Summoned by Bells* (1960), was more interesting for its revelations about the poet than for the quality of its poetry, nor did *High and Low* (1966) and *A Nip in the Air* (1974) compare with his earlier work.

In his Preface to *Old Lights for New Chancels* Betjeman spoke of his 'topographical predilection': throughout his career he was a masterly painter of landscapes and townscapes with figures, whom he portrayed with love, affection, or satire, or with a mixture of all three. Some of his best-known characters, such as Pam, that 'great big mountainous sports girl', Miss J. Hunter Dunn, silken Myfanwy, and the girl in the liquorice fields at Pontefract, are young and amorous. But his sympathies encompass older women who are not particularly likeable: the elderly nun in 'Felixstowe, *or* The Last of her Order', the dying nightclub hostess in 'Sun and Fun'. For Betjeman the topographical and the emotional are inextricably conjoined. In 'Middlesex' the sight of 'Fair Elaine the bobby-soxer' evokes the countryside of his childhood and the more distant vision of Victorian England, as enshrined in *The Diary of a Nobody*, and of those who lie 'Long in Kensal Green and Highgate silent under soot and stone'. That note of mortality sounds more often and more deeply in Betjeman's later verse.

His mastery of metre, rhyming, and stanzaic patterns offers continual delight, and he showed considerable skill in the handling of blank verse. He was often content to employ traditional forms or to compose variations on other men's themes; but his original tunes are among the most dazzling examples of his metrical resourcefulness and delicacy. 'Wantage Bells', 'Ireland with Emily', 'A Shropshire Lad', and the intricate 'I. M. Walter Ramsden' display his art at its most assured.

His poetry enjoyed immense popularity; his knighthood in 1969 and his appointment as Poet Laureate in 1972 were almost universally welcomed; he accumulated honours and public appointments; he achieved fame as an eccentric, and as a virtuoso performer on television. Some of his poetry, including what he came to regard as 'merely comic verse', is forced and feeble, but his lyrical cunning, his gusto, the originality of his topographical and amatory verse, his resonant melancholy, and his power to evoke an idiosyncratic world have secured him a place among the most gifted poets of his generation.

See *Collected Poems* (London and Boston, 4th edn., 1979) and Bevis Hillier's *Young Betjeman* (London, 1988), the first volume of the authorized biography.   [JPr

BHATT, Sujata (1956–), was born in Ahmedabad, but grew up in America where her scientist father had settled. Part of her university education was at Iowa University's creative writing department. She lives in Germany, is married to a German, and is a free-lance writer.

Bhatt employs her native Gujarati for onomatopoeic effect, and because for her certain subjects cannot be described in English. In 'Search for my Tongue' she writes of the anguish of immigrants when they start to lose their first language and interweaves Gujarati and English into a successful bilingual poem. Bhatt travels through many cultures, using myth and symbol from Greek mythology, Hinduism, Buddhist history, Nordic lore, and science. She connects across the cultures—the Kama Sutra connects with Leda and the swan in an erotic love poem; Parvati, the goddess, connects with Twinings, the tea merchants, in a sardonic commentary on colonialism.

Her two collections are *Brunizem* (1988) and *Monkey Shadows* (1991—both Manchester).
                                                   [RA

BIDART, Frank (1939–), grew up in Bakersfield, California, and was, he claims, infected from earliest youth onward with the dream of making great movies. While the choice of expressive medium has changed over the years, the impulse toward a dramatic staging of material has not. Bidart's work to date, now gathered in *In the Western Night: Poems 1965–90* (New York, 1990), shows the poet moving the locus of dramatic tension steadily inward.

After a childhood riven by family conflicts, Bidart moved east to attend Harvard. As he wrote in the early poem, 'California Plush', 'I made myself an Easterner'. At Harvard, Bidart formed important friendships with Elizabeth *Bishop and Robert *Lowell. *Golden State* (New York, 1973), Bidart's first collection, reflects the Lowell influence—the terse lines recount the particulars of family history and have a harsh, fluorescent glare: 'You punished Ruth | when she went to Los Angeles for a weekend, by | beginning to drink.'

The fascination with exacerbated states grew stronger, but by *The Book of the Body* (New York, 1977), Bidart had freed himself from any traces of the Lowell stance. In his well-known poem 'Ellen West', the poet uses the mask of an anorexic woman to explore the soul's conflicting impulses towards salvation (bodilessness) and the necessary penance of physicality. Bidart appears drawn to existential and religious themes, even as he refuses the consolation of any doctrine.

In his third book, *The Sacrifice* (New York, 1983), Bidart continued to utilize the dramatic confrontations made possible by the adoption of a persona. 'The War of Vaslav Nijinsky', the *tour-de-force* of the book, projects the torments of madness and spiritual obsession upon a larger screen—that of a world on the verge of war. The lines effectively transmit the deranged fury of an innocent-become-martyr flaying himself: 'I said to myself: | I must join MY GUILT | to the WORLD'S GUILT.' The poem makes full use of Bidart's staggered lineation and emphatic capitalizations.

Bidart lives in Cambridge, Massachusetts, and teaches at Wellesley College and Brandeis University.   [SPB

Big Table. In 1958 *The Chicago Review*, a literary quarterly subsidized by the university, published a selection of writing by the *Beats and the *San Francisco Group poets in its spring issue; in its fall issue of the same year, it extended this allegiance by publishing a nine-page section of William Burroughs's *Naked Lunch*, complete with swear-words and its assertive homosexuality. This was duly attacked by Jack Mabley of the *Chicago Daily News*, with the result that the university asked for the contents of the third issue and then suppressed it. The editor, Irving Rosenthal, and the poetry editor, Paul Carroll then resigned and started their own magazine. Using a suggestion of Jack Kerouac's, they named it *Big Table*, and in March 1959 they published the first issue, subtitling it: 'The Complete Contents of the Suppressed Winter 1959 Chicago Review'. The Chicago Post Office impounded the magazine, thereby creating sufficient publicity to ensure that *Big Table* sold all the issues left available to it. The American Civil Liberties Union took the Post Office to court. It was ruled that the magazine was not obscene, a decision which helped to pave the way for the eventual publication of *Naked Lunch*, though it still had to suffer a further obscenity trial in order to free itself entirely from suppression. *Big Table* ran for five issues, gracefully retiring once its initial aims had been achieved. Contributors included Robert *Creeley, Robert *Duncan, Kenneth *Koch, and Allen *Ginsberg, whose *Kaddish* appeared in *Big Table*'s second issue. See Paul Carroll's *The Poem In Its Skin* (1968), which was referred to on its cover as a 'Big Table Book'.   [CM

BINYON, (Robert) Laurence (1869–1943), was born in Lancaster, the son of a clergyman, and educated at St Paul's and Trinity College, Oxford. He worked in the British Museum in the Department of Prints and Drawings, where he became an authority on Oriental Art; his *Painting in the Far East* (1908) was the first book on the subject in any European language.

His first volume of verse, *Lyric Poems*, was published in 1894; early poems show him experimenting (after *Bridges and Hopkins) with the natural stress-accent of English (see, for example, the anthologized lyric 'The Little Dancers'). During the First World War he wrote a number of poems collected as *The Four Years*, one of which, 'For the Fallen', is among the best-known of all war poems; the fourth stanza provided the inscription for thousands of memorials. Other poems from that collection have been undeservedly neglected: 'The Zeppelin', 'The Witnesses', and 'The Bereaved' are good examples of a discredited genre, the war poem from the Home Front; 'Guns at the Front', 'Dark Wind', and 'The Arras Road', while still celebrating 'the beauty of the dead', are physically closer to the reality of battle. After these, two long traditional odes written in the 1920s, 'The Sirens' (1924) and 'The Idols' (1928), read somewhat remotely. Aside from his lyric poetry, Binyon wrote nine verse plays, including *Arthur* (1923)—one of several treatments of Arthurian legends—which was staged at the Old Vic with music by Elgar.

After the publication of the *Collected Poems* in two volumes in 1931 (London), Binyon embarked on a fine translation of the whole of Dante's *Divine Comedy* in terza rima—completed in 1943 (London), and rougher in texture than most of his original verse—in which some commentators have found the best use of his craft. Elsewhere his grave, academic style has been judged too monotonously refined. Poems in the posthumous *The Burning of the Leaves* (London, 1944) show that half-a-century made little impact on his stubbornly pure technique; on the other hand, the timely title sequence (formerly published as 'The Ruins') and the beautiful fragment 'Winter Sunrise' are some of the best (if also the last) of all 'Edwardian' poetry.

[MI

BIRNEY, (Alfred) Earle (1904–), was born in Calgary, Alberta. Birney grew up in Calgary and on a farm in Erickson, British Columbia. His 1981 memoir, 'Child Addict in Alberta', tells of the influence of Calvinism and of his early infatuation with words. An honours student at the University of British Columbia, he went on to doctoral study in Old and Middle English at the

University of Toronto, after which he taught at the University of Utah. His involvement in Trotskyite causes during the 1930s, however, led to his leaving the USA. After severing his left-wing political connections, he served actively with the Canadian Army to 1945. From 1946 to 1965 he taught at the University of British Columbia, in later years setting up Canada's first creative writing programme. In 1965 he moved east, took up various writer-in-residence positions, and performed with the sound poetry and jazz group Nexus. Until disabled by a severe heart attack in the mid-1980s, he published regularly. He currently lives in Toronto with his companion Wai-lan Low.

David and Other Poems (Toronto, 1942) exemplifies Birney's early verse, though many lyrics from these years were substantially rephrased when gathered in the two-volume *Collected Poems* (Toronto, 1975). 'David', Birney's most popular narrative poem, recounts a mountain-climbing accident which leads the young narrator to an acute ethical choice. 'Anglosaxon Street', combining Old English metrics with modern political slogans, exposes the wartime attitudes of urban Toronto. *The Strait of Anian* (Toronto, 1948), the first of several volumes of selected verse, illustrates the poet's continuing fascination with the fact of war and the idea of wilderness.

With *Ice Cod Bell or Stone* (Toronto, 1962) and *Near False Creek Mouth* (Toronto, 1964), Birney turned in different formal directions, using non-linear meditation and colloquial idiom to confront the disparity between his community's post-war values and the continuing value of community. His travels abroad led to some of his most evocative lyrics, including 'The Bear on the Delhi Road', and some of his most barbed social critiques, including 'Billboards Build Freedom of Choice'. Satirist as well as metaphysical lyricist, Birney twice updated his mordant national analysis, 'Canada: Case History', and he experimented increasingly with visual design and verbal play. Along with other late volumes, *Rag & Bone Shop* (Toronto, 1971) wittily condemns inequities but equally muses on the passing of time.

Altogether, Birney has published thirty-six books of poetry, fiction, radio plays, and commentary. Several literary essays appear in *Spreading Time* (1980). *The Creative Writer* (1966) and *The Cow Jumped Over the Moon* (1972) comment on the reading and writing of poetry. Two novels—the picaresque *Turvey* (1949; unexpurgated edn., 1976) and the realist *Down the Long Table* (1955)—respectively satirize military bureaucracy and condemn McCarthyism.

[WHN

BISHOP, Elizabeth (1911–79), was born in Worcester, Massachusetts, the only child of an American father with Canadian antecedents, and a Canadian mother. Her father died when she was 8 months old; her mother then suffered a series of mental breakdowns which led to her being permanently confined. From the age of 5 Bishop was looked after by relatives, first her maternal grandparents in Nova Scotia, then members of her father's family in Worcester and South Boston, and she never saw her mother again. After boarding at Walnut Hill School near Boston, she entered Vassar, intending to study music (composition and piano), but she soon switched to English and graduated in 1934. The rest of her life was characterized largely by a sense of uprootedness and—in spite of a number of close friendships with other writers, a poetry consultantship at the Library of Congress in Washington in 1949/50, and a post at Harvard in her last years—detachment from literary and academic centres of power. She travelled widely and had homes, successively, in New York, Florida, Brazil, and Boston.

The loss of Bishop's parents and abrupt changes of home in childhood seem to have been decisive in the formation of her later habits of mind and poetic practice. As a young girl she made her own discovery of the poems of George Herbert, and his influence may be traced through both her juvenilia and her mature work. It is most clearly evident in her first published collection, *North & South* (Boston, 1946), whether in her witty transplanting of Herbert's own words ('Wading at Wellfleet'), or in a more thorough adaptation of

47

his poetic procedures to her special require-
ments ('The Weed'); and this lends the book
some of its distinctiveness. North & South
already shows a voice unlike that of any other
American poet, and it lays claim to themes that
its author was to explore more fully in subse-
quent volumes.

Much has been made of Bishop's indebted-
ness to Marianne *Moore, and the value of the
older poet's friendship and encouragement is
fondly acknowledged by Bishop herself in a
prose piece, 'Efforts of Affection: A Memoir of
Marianne Moore'. But apart from a shared
enthusiasm for accurate observation, the two
poets have little in common, either formally or
materially, beyond what might have been
expected from the accidental overlapping of
their lives. Moreover, it appears that it was
Bishop's need to find in poetry a means of
addressing her unique experience of alienation
that drove her to Herbert and other English
writers of the seventeenth century, rather than
to any closer example, specifically because they
stood at such a fixed distance from the culture of
her own time. Another identifiable strain in
North & South, also markedly un-American, but
serving to counterbalance any tendency to
mere antiquatedness, was that of surrealism—
used, too, for the purpose of distancing.

Visual representations and artefacts, whether
real or imaginary, play a significant part in many
of these early poems. In 'The Map' and 'Large
Bad Picture', the inadequacy or misleading sug-
gestiveness of certain images stands figuratively
for the broader perils of intercourse with the
perceived world. The 'Monument' supplies
scrupulously detailed information about a
strange wooden structure of unyielding incom-
prehensibility. The toy horse and its acrobat
rider, which are described in 'Cirque d'Hiver',
allow, surprisingly, for a meditation on the soul,
while elsewhere ('The Weed', 'Sleeping Stand-
ing Up') the attempt to objectify inner states has
inevitably bizarre or disconcerting results. Even
those poems in North & South which purport to
deal directly with the real world are prone to
hints of bafflement and futility, as expressed by
the oddly assorted inventory of domestic trap-

pings in 'Jerónimo's House', or the unedifying
riot of nature in 'Florida'.

In exploring and signposting her poetic
domain, Bishop's first book is like that of many
another writer. What distinguishes it is the
assurance with which she sets about the task—
an assurance sometimes ironically at odds with
a quiet and professedly tentative manner—and
the richness of the material she finds there.
Significantly, the book won her the admiration
of, among others, two fellow poets: Randall
*Jarrell, who discussed it perceptively in *Parti-
san Review, and Robert *Lowell, who became a
lifelong friend and literary confidant. Lowell's
later debt to Bishop's example is a matter of
record; whether she learned as much from him
is more doubtful.

North & South was followed by three further
collections of new work within Bishop's life-
time: an incorporation of North & South with A
Cold Spring under the title Poems (Boston, 1955;
London, 1956), Questions of Travel (New York,
1965), and Geography III (New York and Lon-
don, 1976). As at least three of the titles indicate,
the problem of establishing one's place in the
world continued to be of central interest to her.
The practice of taking extraneously given
images and artefacts as pretexts for meditations
on the subject was gradually dropped, although
it still supplies the focus of the argument in an
important poem, 'Over 2,000 Illustrations and a
Complete Concordance'. Bishop came to
depend less, too, on overtly surrealistic devices.
Instead, her travels and foreign domicile
afforded her the opportunity to look at land-
scapes whose strangeness was simply a fact, and
to use her powers of vivid description and ani-
mistic metaphor as a means of co-ordinating
and fixing the abundance of sensations to which
she was exposed.

The tension generated by the clash between
extravagantly proliferating imagery and the
modesty of the mind set on putting it in order is
what lends point to the most successful of the
poems in this category—'The Bight', 'At the
Fishhouses', and 'Questions of Travel' among
them. Traditional metres, which Bishop han-
dled skilfully elsewhere, would have been inap-

propriate here. So she evolved her own, idiosyncratic system of lines governed less by considerations of prosody than by an ear finely attuned to the music of assonance, colloquial pacing, and aptly judged pauses and breaks. The mimetic purpose is to show the poet's mind as it improvises its way towards a resolution, in so far as that may be said to occur. The method is one of unflappable diffidence. It appears that Hopkins's metrical experiments gave Bishop the incentive to pursue her own, but she took a far different course from his in her cultivation of looseness and avoidance of insistent stress. Only occasionally does her voice modulate to something like declamation, as in the visionary last lines of 'At the Fishhouses'.

A notable feature of Bishop's later poems is their more frequent use of biographical material. In the section of *Questions of Travel* headed 'Elsewhere', she includes a number of poems about childhood experiences that seem taken from life. 'Sestina' and 'First Death in Nova Scotia' relate troubling incidents in the lives of children, while 'In the Waiting Room', from *Geography III*, offers a startling account of a moment of traumatic self-awareness in Bishop's own seventh year. But while such poems are a long way in spirit from the studied obliqueness of *North & South*, it would be a mistake to think of Bishop's development as a straightforward homing-in on early experiences. Besides the autobiographical poem cited here, *Geography III* contains exercises in dramatic monologue ('Crusoe in England'), rueful comment, and metaphorical fantasy, as well as her characteristic anecdotal and descriptive modes ('The Moose', 'Poem'). The scope is as wide as ever; nuance and intimation are still the preferred means. When Bishop wished to reflect on her misfortunes as a child she was more likely—whatever the reasons may have been—to choose prose, whether in the form of a short story (e.g. 'In the Village'), or of a memoir ('The Country Mouse').

Bishop's output of poems was a small one, by the standards of her time. Apart from her translations (from the Portuguese, Spanish, and French), *The Complete Poems 1927–1979* contains just over one hundred titles, and this is counting juvenilia and occasional light verse. The quality, however, is formidably high. It is perhaps for this reason that Bishop was so admired by her peers and came to have the reputation of being something of a 'poet's poet'. The impression is of a creative intelligence bent solely on satisfying the strictest inner demands, writing only what was necessary, and undeflected by fashion. The assiduously cultivated uniqueness of Bishop's style set her apart from her contemporaries and has made her a dangerous poet to imitate, but her example will no doubt continue to be an inspiration, and her poems read. Although she was recognized in her own day and her books won her such signs of esteem as the Pulitzer Prize and the National Book Award, her standing has, if anything, risen since her death, and it is not uncommon to hear her placed among the greatest of American poets.

A *Complete Poems* was published in 1969, but *The Complete Poems 1927–1979* (New York and London, 1983) now gives the standard text of Bishop's poetical works. *The Collected Prose* (New York, 1984) contains short stories and writings under the heading, 'Memory: Persons & Places'. *The Diary of 'Helena Morley'* (1957) was translated from the Portuguese by Bishop, and has an introduction by her. She also collaborated with Emanuel Brasil in editing *An Anthology of Twentieth-Century Brazilian Poetry* in her own translations. A biography, *Elizabeth Bishop: Life and the Memory of It* (Berkeley, Calif. and London) by Brett Miller, appeared in 1993.

[CJR

BISHOP, John Peale (1892–1944), was born in Virginia, the son of a physician. He was set to become a painter, but during his years at Princeton (1913–18), where he was a close friend of Edmund *Wilson, he distinguished himself as a writer and, in particular, as a poet of great promise. His first collection was *Green Fruit* (New York, 1917). Wilson described him at that time as one 'who lived for poetry', and his reputation was then legendary. After active service with the American army in France—an experience which left an indelible mark—he returned to New York and became managing editor of *Vanity Fair*, then a literary periodical. He subsequently spent much time in France, but finally returned to America—Cape Cod—in 1933; he died of heart disease. He was the original of the 'genius' Thomas Parke D'Invilliers in Scott Fitzgerald's novel *This Side of Paradise*.

Bishop's finely wrought, fastidious, formally strict poetry has been somewhat neglected, although two or three critics have thought him 'essentially second-rate'; this opinion seems to have been accepted by anthologists, and he is now scarcely read. Associated, if only vaguely, with *Ransom and the *Agrarians, his poems often demonstrate the decorum and sophistication achieved by those poets. Allen *Tate in particular valued him for his expression of the tension between the South and the rest of the modern world. He was a neurotic, perfectionist, and excessively literary poet, who sometimes wrote in the style of others—in particular the English metaphysical poets of the seventeenth century—because (he claimed) he did not want to be himself. He found it hard to finish poems. He influenced British poetry of the 1940s for a very brief period, through his admirer Nicholas *Moore. See *Collected Poems* (New York and London, 1948).   [MS-S

bissett, bill (William Frederick) (1939–), was born in Halifax, Nova Scotia, but since the late Fifties has lived in Vancouver, British Columbia, where in the Sixties he became a leader among counter-culture writers, founding the radical magazine *Blew Ointment* (1963) and beginning his prolific career as a poet. His work has been attacked by politicians as pornographic and sensational. By 1990 he had published over fifty volumes of poetry, much of it in small presses like his own Blew Ointment Press, which he founded in 1967.

bissett's refusal to capitalize his name is consistent with his attacks on conventional spelling, punctuation, and typography. His radical poetics celebrate the shamanic potential of language, always emphasizing the visual, oral, and aural elements of words so that their significance does not emerge univocally from

their conventional meanings, but strikes the senses more immediately through their sight and sound. bissett is one of Canada's best-known *sound poets, frequently performing and chanting his verse, which often depends on repetition and incantation for its power.

On the page, bissett's language forces readers to look at familiar words with new eyes: 'the' becomes 'th', 'and' becomes 'nd', 'some' becomes 'sum', 'station' becomes 'stashun'. Often words are run together and lines repeated until a visual pattern is established, only to be disrupted by a deft typographical variation. bissett often illustrates his poems with his own drawings.

A latter-day romantic visionary, bissett wishes to recover essential ecstasy and purity through rapt invocations of the body and spirit. His poems deplore the mundane, attack sophistry, and exalt revolutionary simplicity.

Beyond Even Faithful Legends: Selected Poems 1962–1976 (Vancouver and Los Angeles, 1980) offers a generous collection of bissett's work.
                    [NB

BLACKBURN, Paul (1926–71), son of the poet Frances Frost, was born and raised in St Albans, Vermont. He remained there until he was 14, when his mother brought him to New York. Though he spent some years at the University of Wisconsin (where he began corresponding with Ezra *Pound), and travelled extensively in Europe, Blackburn remains largely associated with New York City and the alternative poetry scene that flourished there throughout the 1960s.

The publication of *The Collected Poems of Paul Blackburn* (New York, 1985) did much to bring this poet into larger public awareness. For Blackburn had been, hitherto, a poet of fugitive small-press appearances, largely neglected by the critical establishment. But he is increasingly seen, along with his friend Robert *Creeley, as an important link between the modernist innovations of Pound, the experimentalism of the *Black Mountain poets, and the peculiarly American celebrations of the *Beats.

Blackburn's oeuvre can be seen to fall into at least three distinct phases. The earliest work, much of it written while he travelled in Europe in the early 1950s, reflects the influence of Creeley (with whom he had an extensive correspondence) and of Pound's troubadour renderings. The poems from this period are lyrical and subdued, extremely effective in playing off sound patterns and pauses—already Blackburn is using white space to maximal expressive advantage.

The 1960s find the poet living in New York, working to open his prosody to the energies and collisions of an urban subject-matter. The early calm has yielded to the clamour of streets, voices; the surface is increasingly making room for diary-like notations. The poet himself, however, elects to remain largely absent—certainly we hear next to nothing from the inner man. Blackburn has become an extraordinarily effective medium for the transmission of daily moments excerpted from time: 'The loudest sound in this public room | is the exhaust fan in the east window | or the cat at my back | asleep there in the sun | bleached tabletop, golden | shimmer of ale' (from 'The Island'). Blackburn's collection *The Cities* (New York, 1967) is the apotheosis of this phase of his development.

In early 1970 Blackburn was diagnosed as having cancer of the throat. In the time before his death the following year his poetry becomes more and more like an extended personal journal. The poems—entries—are likely to baffle the first-time reader, but those familiar with the earlier work will find the ease and immediacy thrilling.

Some of Blackburn's small-press publications are: *Early Selected Y Mas* (Los Angeles, 1972); *In . On . Or About the Premises* (London and New York, 1968); *The Journals* (Santa Barbara, Calif., 1975). [SPB

BLACKBURN, Thomas (Eliel Fenwick) (1916–79), son of an Anglican clergyman (see his autobiography *A Clip of Steel*, London, 1969, his best book), was born in Cumbria. After leaving Cambridge as a result of alcoholism, and a spell of psychotherapy, Blackburn took a degree in English from Durham University. He became a schoolmaster and, eventually, lecturer at a teacher-training college. Poems in early collec-

tions are eloquent and carefully crafted, but the influences of *Yeats and Jung, on style and content respectively, are over-obtrusive. *Selected Poems* (London, 1975) demonstrates that he eventually achieved an occasionally impressive bareness of utterance. But as he cast off the habit of pastiche his technical powers diminished, and the content of his poetry tended more towards the commonplace. However, his posthumous volume, *Bread for the Winter Birds* (London, 1980) is moving and memorable as a candid, painful sequence recording his final mental and physical disintegration under the effects of alcohol and unsuitable medication. As fully self-critical and *confessional as the poems of *Lowell, and perhaps influenced by him, these are less lyrical and more strictly personal. Blackburn is seen at his most individual in such balefully meditative poems as 'Teaching Wordsworth' and 'En Route' (both in *Selected Poems*).

[MS-S

Black Mountain Poets, the poets associated with Black Mountain College, a small, experimental, democratically run college in North Carolina, in the late 1940s and early 1950s. Charles *Olson was its rector, Robert *Creeley and Robert *Duncan were members of staff, and Edward *Dorn, Joel *Oppenheimer, John *Wieners, and Jonathan *Williams studied there. Paul *Blackburn, Paul Carroll, Larry *Eigner, and Denise *Levertov never attended the college but their work was also given its first significant American publication in *Origin (1951–7) and *The Black Mountain Review* (edited by Creeley, 1954–7), and later included in Donald Allen's influential anthology, *The New American Poetry* (1960), which first recognized the poets as a group.

Like many other American poets who emerged in the 1950s, the Black Mountain poets reacted against the poetic 'closure' and compression advocated by the *New Criticism. Their models were not the seventeenth-century 'metaphysical' poets and *Eliot, but Blake, Whitman, *Lawrence and, above all, *Pound and William Carlos *Williams whose work they found exemplary of what they called 'open' or 'organic' form. In fact the word 'open' described their ideal not only for a poem's form but also for its substance and even for the process of its composition. The speaker of an open poem, according to Olson, is neither a fictional persona nor the poet's autobiographical personality but the part of the poet's self, beyond his ego, that provides an open channel through which impersonal nature can speak. It followed that grammatical and poetic conventions (including ordinary lineation, straight left-hand margins, and regular metres) should be discarded so that a poem's form could spontaneously adapt to its substance as it progressed. The resulting poems are open because provisional and because they show little evidence of rational selection: art, said Duncan, is not an 'achievement' but an 'adventure'.

The Black Mountain poets were much more united in theory, however, than in practice. Each responded to different qualities in Pound and Williams. Olson wanted to revise Pound's historiography, Duncan to emulate his 'sublime and ecstatic' poetry. Creeley turned to the more 'sincere' style of Williams, and Levertov also wrote variations on the Williams lyric. None of the others, except perhaps Dorn, has been as widely read, though Blackburn, Jonathan Williams, and Oppenheimer deserve mention as the most engaging, accessible, and humorous of the group.

All seven issues of *The Black Mountain Review* have been collected in three volumes (New York, 1969), but *The New American Poetry: 1945–1960*, ed. Donald Allen (New York, 1960) is still the best short selection of the group's early work. *Black Mountain: An Exploration in Community*, by Martin Duberman (New York, 1972) is a comprehensive history of the college.   [NE

BLACKMUR, R(ichard) P(almer) (1904–65), was born in Springfield, Massachusetts. After high school, instead of going to university he worked in the Dunster House bookshop in Boston and, in 1929, edited *Hound & Horn* with Lincoln Kirstein before the magazine moved from Harvard to New York. In 1930 he married Helen Dickson, an artist from Harrington, Maine, where they lived on and off until 1951

when they divorced. From 1928 to 1940 Blackmur was a free-lance critic and poet; then Allen *Tate, who liked his 'vigorous, tough-minded' criticism, appointed him to assist in the newly established course in creative English at Princeton. He remained at Princeton—first as resident fellow (1940–8), then as professor (1948–65)— for the rest of his life.

Two Guggenheim Foundation grants, in 1936 and 1937, had enabled Blackmur to research a large-scale work on the historian Henry Adams, but the book was never completed (although various studies have been gathered posthumously in *Henry Adams*, 1980); the medium best suited to his deliberately provisional insights was always the essay, not the monograph, and modern poetry and criticism the subjects on which he wrote most persuasively. In his first two books of essays, *The Double Agent: Essays in Craft and Elucidation* (1935) and *The Expense of Greatness* (1940), he advocates the 'technical approach' to poetry, which is 'concerned, first and last—whatever comes between—with the poem as it is read and as what it represents is felt'. Typically, his own readings (of *Stevens, *Moore, and *Yeats, among others) are brilliant analyses of the techniques good poems use to exceed discursive statement and create, rather than merely reflect, sensibility. Later books of criticism include *Language as Gesture* (1952), which prints both new and previously published essays, *The Lion and the Honeycomb* (1955), and *Form and Value in Modern Poetry* (1957). Blackmur's prose is fluent and entertaining, and it is generally agreed that of all the *New Criticism his essays will have the most lasting influence.

His poetry, first published in *From Jordan's Delight* (1937), *The Second World* (1942), and *The Good European and Other Poems* (1947), consists mainly of lyric sequences on personal and intellectual themes. 'Dedications' is about the end of a relationship and 'A Labyrinth of Being' about marriage and fatherhood, while 'Judas Priest', a sequence of four sonnets, celebrates 'all those who shun the dogma's dreadful weight', and 'The Cough' considers the respective claims of non-verbal and verbal expression, the cough and the word. Blackmur's poetry, unlike his prose, has never been widely enjoyed, a fact which he attributed to his 'own defects—of style and sensibility and scope'. His sequences weave subtle and paradoxical arguments; but their considerable moral intelligence is often obscured by archaic syntactical inversions, formal diction, and wooden obedience to traditional (usually iambic) metres.

Blackmur's poetry has been collected in *Poems of R. P. Blackmur* (Princeton, NJ, 1977); the best selections of his prose are *Language as Gesture* (New York, 1952; repr., 1981) and *Selected Essays of R. P. Blackmur* (New York, 1986).

[NE

Black Orpheus, the pioneering African arts and literature journal, was published in Nigeria. It was founded in 1957 by Ulli Beier, and under the expatriate European regime of Beier, Jahnheinz Jahn, and Gerald Moore its editorial stance was 'inspirational' rather than critical. Early issues introduced francophone writers, and published work by *Soyinka, J. P. *Clark, La Guma, Mphahlele, and *Aidoo. Beier affected the 'primitive' (Onitsha Market literature, sign-painting), but also promoted modernist complexity. He has been criticized for publishing his own work under the Nigerian pseudonym Sangodare Akanji. Nevertheless, his editorship was very successful. By 1963 circulation had reached 3,500 and Longmans of Nigeria took over publication.

After Beier left for Papua New Guinea in 1966, the editorship fell to the Nigerians, Abiola Irele and J. P. *Clark, who adopted a new approach: 'there was no point any more in presenting African literature as new literature that had to be defended and all that' (Irele). In 'The Legacy of Caliban' (Issue 2 : 1), Clark attacked European distortion of Africa. Issues 2: 2 and 2: 3 focused on traditional African literature and on politics. But Longmans had withdrawn, and it emerged that the Fairfield Foundation, one of the journal's backers, was funded by the CIA. Amid multiplying organizational problems, Irele left in 1974 (to found the *Benin Review,*

which died after one issue), Clark left in 1975, and publication was transferred to the University of Lagos Press. The new editor, Theo Vincent, produced two issues, dated 1978 and 1980, but not published until 1981. Since then *Black Orpheus* has been dormant. [JB

BLAND, Peter (1934–), was born in Scarborough, Yorkshire, and went to school in the Midlands; he emigrated to New Zealand in 1954 after the deaths of his parents and lived in Wellington, where he worked as a clerk, social worker, journalist, and broadcaster, and read English at Victoria University. He became friendly with the poets James K. *Baxter and Louis *Johnson, and with them edited the literary journal *Numbers* in the early 1960s. Johnson was a particularly significant influence; Bland shared his views on the importance of social realism in poetry, using imagery from suburban life and popular culture. With these *Wellington poets he argued against the loftier, chthonic vision of New Zealand poetry advocated in anthologies and periodicals by the Auckland group.

In 1964 Bland became one of the co-founders of the Downstage Theatre Company and worked as a writer, director, and actor; in 1968 he returned to England with his wife and three children, and has since earned his living as an actor, mostly in Britain but with another interlude in New Zealand from 1985 to 1989.

His poems feed on exile and displacement. The eponymous persona of *Mr Maui* (London, 1976) is described in a prefatory note as 'a young tribal outcast' who later returns to the country of his birth as head of his own tribe; cultural dislocation and the struggle for survival are recurring themes. In *The Crusoe Factor* (London, 1985) a different returned wanderer is used as a mouthpiece for commentary on social conditions in Britain. A later poem, in memory of Louis Johnson, discusses the question of place and the importance of travelling and not 'digging in'.

One of Bland's strategies is humour; he has remarked on the fact that he does not write about acting and the theatre, but the techniques of comedy and timing learnt from his stage and film work find a place in his poetry, together with a relaxed colloquial tone which does not preclude literary and historical allusions. His most recent collections are *Selected Poems* (Dunedin, 1987) and *Paper Boats* (Dunedin, 1990). [FKA

Blast. There were only two issues of this magazine, edited by Wyndham *Lewis. The first, a 'great puce monster' as he later called it in reference to its bright pink cover, measured twelve inches by nine, and had the title printed at an angle across the cover in block capitals more than three inches high. The second, the 'War Number', had Lewis's painting 'Before Antwerp' on the cover. The page-size was the same, but the number of pages and of reproductions of paintings and drawings was considerably reduced. It is said that 1,700 copies of the first number were printed, although probably less than half that number were sold. The number printed of *Blast 2* is not known. The first issue appeared in June 1914, the second in July 1915.

Although *Blast* was called a 'Review of the Great English Vortex', it was almost entirely a display case for Lewis's art and ideas. That is true, even though Ezra *Pound invented the name 'Vorticism' and C. R. W. Nevinson claimed to have suggested the magazine's title. The outsize sans-serif typography, and the lists of 'Blasts' and 'Blesses' captured, as was intended, a lot of attention, and if the typography astonished, the harshly vigorous reproductions, with their insistence on the mechanical nature of human beings, sometimes repelled. 'A vast folio in pink paper covers, full of irrepressible imbecility' said the *Morning Post*, although there were others who found the reproductions of drawings and sculptures remarkable. The wartime issue was less flamboyant, with only a few Blasts and Blesses, but it contained a page of gnomic injunctions by Lewis about the importance of duality: 'You must talk with two tongues if you do not wish to cause confusion' is one among a series of commendations of the double personality.

Among the other contributors were Rebecca West with a short story, and the beginning of Ford Madox *Hueffer's *The Good Soldier*, along with reproductions of work by Vorticists and their allies. T. S. *Eliot made his first public appearance as a poet with 'Preludes' and 'Rhapsody on a Windy Night', and there were several poetic hiccoughs by Pound, some witty, one anti-Jewish. Near the end of his life Lewis said that in 1914 he would have insisted on the creation of an artistic language 'absolutely distinct from what was handed us by nature—such as stones and trees or men and women . . . What I should have put in place of trees and stones, and men and women, would have been invented shapes, with no direct connection with nature'. In old age he rejected most of these views, but along with the social ideas about the machine-like nature of most human beings, they were the springs of the Vorticist movement and the reason for *Blast*. [JGS

BLESSING, Richard (1939–83), was born in Bradford, Pennsylvania. His first two books were studies of Wallace *Stevens and Theodore *Roethke. He also published a novel, *The Passing Season* (Boston, 1982). At the time of his death, from a brain tumour, he was chairman of the graduate programme in English at the University of Washington.

There are fine poems in his first two collections—some of them tart ('Teaching You to Think'), some lyrical ('The Eagle'), and some ('Elegy for Elvis') both at once. And there are effective touches in the numerous poems about his father. Frequently, however, the poems seem willed rather than achieved, marked by easy surrealism, evasive use of the second person, and piled details that do not always cohere. But the fifteen poems in his last book, *Poems and Stories*, published almost simultaneously with his death, are easily his best. In 'State of Women', 'Late News' (about a mass murderer), and especially the ten-poem sequence on his illness and attempts at recovery, he writes with a sureness and power not previously seen in his work. The poems of this sequence are reflective, resonant, and rich with word-play and allusions that reinforce, rather than disrupt, the seriousness of theme. Stoic in the assimilation of the worst that life can offer, and cheerful in the resolve to go on as best one can, they are a well-wrought and moving testament to the human spirit.

Blessing's three collections are *Winter Constellations* (Boise, Idaho, 1977), *A Closed Book* (Seattle and London, 1981), and *Poems and Stories* (Port Townsend, Wash., 1983).   [MP

BLIGHT, John (1913–95), was born in South Australia but lived most of his life in Southern Queensland, whose coast of sunken river valleys, mangrove swamps, coral reefs, and sand dunes provided him with much of his poetic inspiration. For many years he ran a sawmill near Maryborough. He lived in Brisbane.

Blight was a sort of mystic biologist of poetry. He recorded the natural world with materialist concentration which amounts to ecstasy. His 'Sea Sonnets' in *A Beachcomber's Diary* (Sydney, 1964) and *My Beachcombing Days* (Sydney, 1968) re-create the ever-changing turbulence of the Queensland coast just before the beginnings of the Great Barrier Reef. He was entirely at home with such subjects as a beached whale, a bee's sting, or the shadowy world of mangroves.

Blight's early books, *The Old Pianist* (Sydney, 1945) and *The Two Suns Met* (Sydney, 1954), his two *Beachcombing* volumes, and *Hart* (Melbourne, 1975) make up the bulk of his poetry, which was brought together in *Selected Poems 1939–1975* (Melbourne, 1976).   [PNFP

BLOOM, Valerie. See PERFORMANCE POETRY.

BLUMENTHAL, Michael (1949–), grew up in a German-speaking household in Washington Heights, New York City. After graduating with a degree in economics from the State University of New York in Binghamton (1969), he took a law degree at Cornell (1974) and practised for a year as an attorney for the Federal Trade Commission. His interest in writing led him successively to an arts administration position with the National Endowment for the Arts, writing positions at Time-Life Books and the National Endowment for the Humanities, and a television production post with West German Televi-

sion, before he went to Harvard as a teacher of creative writing (1983–92). He has had Fulbright Fellowships to Israel (1987) and Hungary (1992), and a Guggenheim Fellowship (1988).

Blumenthal has written five books of poetry: *Sympathetic Magic* (New York, 1980); *Days We Would Rather Know* (New York and London, 1984); *Laps* (Boston, 1984); *Against Romance* (New York and London, 1987); and *The Wages of Goodness* (St Louis, 1992); he has also edited an anthology of marriage poems, *To Wed and to Woo* (New York, 1992). Though Blumenthal is a poet of deft social commentary (see 'Jungians and Freudians at the Joseph Campbell Lecture') and of social protest ('The Heart of Quang Duc'), he writes most often of the conflict between idealization ('romance') and disillusion. A marriage followed by a divorce, and a subsequent marriage followed by the birth of a son, have given Blumenthal material for a series of poems for and against romance, while his own uncertain status as a bilingual child in a family of German-Jewish refugees has given him an abiding interest in foreignness, family dynamics, marginalization, and solitude.

His poems often display a poignant mixture of melancholy and comedy, bewilderment and resolve. He casts himself frequently as a *naif* enduring painful enlightenment; or an erring 'Puer Aeternus' (as one poem has it) resolving to do better; or an analysand coming, perhaps too late, to a revealing truth. Blumenthal's affinities for the moralist literature of aphorisms and *pensées* can sometimes tinge his poems with the homiletic or the sentimental. In *Laps*, he writes a prologue putting himself under the patronage of Aristippus of Cyrene, who believed in 'the primacy of pleasure as a source of moral good'. The conflict between law and pleasure is one of Blumenthal's chief themes, down to his most recent meditations on 'the wages of goodness'.

[HV

BLUNDEN, Edmund (Charles) (1896–1974), was educated at Christ's Hospital and Queen's College, Oxford, served in the First World War from 1916 to 1918, and was awarded the Military Cross. *The Waggoner* (1920) and *The*

Shepherd (1922), for which he won the Hawthornden Prize, included poems from five slender volumes published in 1914 and 1916. *Undertones of War* (1928), a chronicle of the war in verse and prose, gained him a wider reputation that was enhanced by *The Poems of Edmund Blunden 1914–1930* (1930).

Blunden is underestimated today as a war poet, largely because the work of *Owen, *Rosenberg, and *Sassoon has overshadowed his achievement. Ironically enough, it was Blunden's edition of Owen's poems in 1931 that inaugurated the revival of interest in his work. Blunden's war poems are more restrained than those of the other three men, but his hatred of the war and his grief for the dead, whom he commemorated in an elegy of passionate lyricism, 'Their Very Memory', were as intense as theirs. Moreover, he expressed a horror at the devastation of the French countryside that is almost absent from their poetry: 'I have seen a green country, useful to the race, | Knocked silly with guns and mines, its villages vanished.' He was unique also among his fellow poets in acknowledging that there were moments of happiness amid the insensate slaughter. 'In Senlis Once' celebrates a brief interval of rest and refreshment, just as 'Concert Party: Busseboom' recalls an hour of innocent entertainment 'While men in the trenches below Larch Wood | Were kicking men to death'.

Blunden's poems about the English countryside are among his finest. They combine a formal, at times almost archaic, utterance with an exact portrayal of the scene, a delicacy of perception, and an air of unease and foreboding. His sympathies embrace alms-women, lovers young and old, village forefathers, midnight skaters, even the cornered weasel in 'Winter: East Anglia' that 'stands his ground | And hard as winter dies'.

Between the wars Blunden lived by literary journalism, as professor of English literature at Tokyo University from 1924 to 1927, and as a fellow and tutor in English at Merton College, Oxford, from 1931 to 1943.

During the ten years after the outbreak of war in 1939 Blunden published three volumes.

Poems 1930–1940 (1940) bore traces of his preoccupation with the earlier conflict. In the Preface he denied 'morbidly wishing to go back that road', yet 'that tremendous time does not easily give up its hold'. *Shells by a Stream* (1944) and *After the Bombing* (1949) reflected his sombre meditation on the darkness of the times, lightened by his belief in traditional values and the hope of renewal.

After leaving Merton, Blunden worked for the *Times Literary Supplement* until he joined the UK Liaison Mission in Tokyo in 1948. In 1950 he began a second spell with the *TLS*; and was appointed emeritus professor of English literature at Hong Kong University in 1953, returning to England in the early 1960s. When living in Hong Kong he was permitted by the Chinese authorities to visit the Great Wall of China. His terse, poignant sonnet about the Wall describes how it stretches for thousands of miles, defending the frontier with 'stairway, sally-port, loop, parapet'. The parallels between the Wall and the trenches of the 1914–18 war, though never spelled out, pervade the sonnet. And 'This new-set sentry of a long dead year', whom the poet half-knows, is the brother of the sentries on the Western Front.

A Hong Kong House: Poems 1951–1962 (1962) and *Eleven Poems* (1965) were Blunden's last two volumes. He was elected Professor of Poetry at Oxford in 1966, but ill health forced him to resign in 1968. He spent his final years with his third wife, Claire, and their four daughters in the Suffolk village of Long Melford, writing a guide in 1966 to its magnificent parish church.

Blunden devoted much time to editing, biography, and criticism. His editions of John Clare in 1920 (with Alan Porter) and of Ivor *Gurney in 1954 performed for them the service he had rendered Owen in 1931. His most important studies were of writers major and minor who flourished between the later seventeenth and mid-nineteenth centuries. He had a particular affection for Shelley, Keats, Lamb, Leigh Hunt, their friends and, among later authors, Thomas *Hardy.

Yet it is by his poetry that he will be longest remembered. In his preface to his 1930 collection he spoke of the Great War as an experience so early 'as to mould and colour the poetry throughout this book'. It continued to do so throughout all his poetry. His other major theme was the English countryside in which he was born and to which he returned after his wanderings.

See *Poems of Many Years*, ed. Rupert Hart-Davis (London, 1957); *The Poetry of Edmund Blunden*, by Michael Thorpe (Wateringbury, Kent, 1971); *Selected Poems*, ed. Robyn Marsack (Manchester, 1982). [JPr

BLUNT, W(ilfred) S(cawen) (1840–1922), was born in Petworth, Sussex. As a young man he worked in the diplomatic service. In 1869 he married Byron's granddaughter, and three years later began the travels in North Africa, the Middle East, and India which confirmed a strong antipathy to colonialism. In 1875 he published his first volume of poems, *Sonnets and Songs by Proteus*; *The Love Sonnets of Proteus* followed in 1880. He argued successively for Egyptian, Indian, and Irish independence; his stance on Ireland earned him the approval of Shaw and two months in Irish gaols, an experience treated in the sonnet sequence *In Vinculis* (1889).

A selection of Blunt's poems made in 1898 by W. S. Henley (whose introduction sets Blunt's 'natural elegance' and 'careless, high-bred swing' over his 'little faults of time and tune') suppressed political poems, like 'The Wind and the Whirlwind' (1883) about the crushing of the revolt in Egypt; such items were restored in the two-volume *Poetical Works* of 1914 (London; New York, 1923), whose publication Blunt supervised himself and which included the controversial verse play *Satan Absolved* (1899)— 'Absolved' because the sins of the British Empire are judged to exceed Satan's.

Philip *Larkin printed a sonnet of Blunt's as the first item in his *Oxford Book of Twentieth-Century English Verse*; but though he was obviously a political and moral progressive, Blunt dated himself rather (in 1914) as a 'mid-Victorian poet a little ahead of his epoch'. His most characteristic works are his sonnet sequences, those in the guise of the philanderer 'Proteus', and *Esther*,

which forms a narrative about a young Englishman's sexual initiation at the hands of a French actress. The licence assumed by privilege in the Proteus poems ('The day of love is short, and every bliss | Not tasted now is a bliss thrown away') is worth contrasting with the more familiar *mores* of (say) Patmore's *The Angel in the House*. Blunt's pioneering translations from classical Arabic were also admired in their time.

See *My Diaries* (two vols., London, 1919–20) and a biography, *A Pilgrimage of Passion* by Elizabeth Longford (London, 1979). [MI

BLY, Robert (1926–), is an important figure in contemporary American poetry—because of his own writings, because of his influence on such poets as James *Wright, and because of his prominence as a public figure. Bly was born on a farm in western Minnesota and, though he graduated from Harvard University and has given poetry readings and attended conferences all over the United States and in Scandinavia, has lived all his life in Minnesota. He is the author of nine volumes of poetry—ranging from *Silence in the Snowy Fields* (Middletown, Conn., 1962; London, 1967) to *Selected Poems* (New York, 1986)— and is the founding editor of a magazine called, depending upon the decade, *The Fifties, The *Sixties, The Seventies*, and *The Eighties*. At times the figure of Bly as teacher, preacher, and reformer has seemed to dominate that of Bly the poet. The public donation of his National Book Award money (received in honour of *The Light Around the Body* (New York and London) in 1968) to the anti-war group Resistance was an entirely typical gesture for Bly; much of his poetry is outwardly political, a result largely of his concern over the war in Vietnam.

Bly has always tended to view the world in terms of dualities, polarities. Throughout his career he has argued, with an almost Messianic fervour, that there exists an opposition between the poetry of the Cartesian mind—logical, empirical, straightforward, businesslike—and the poetry of the subconscious mind. He strongly feels that the former type is characteristic of the American literary tradition, just as Cartesian thought is typical of the American mind; thus his programme of searching out and translating the work of exemplars of the latter type—Neruda, Tranströmer, Jiménez, Vallejo, Trakl, and others.

It is largely because of Bly's efforts in this direction that America has recently had a poetry of the *'deep image'—an image that comes from the unconscious mind and that communicates a meaning that is not logical. Such images create bridges between the two layers of the mind, making them one: 'We are approaching sleep: . . . | . . . a tunnel softly hurtling into darkness.' In the outer world, too, Bly sees dualities; just as man's mind has both its conscious and unconscious aspects, so the natural world has both its physical and its spiritual aspects: in the poem 'Driving Toward the Lac Qui Parle River' are soybeans 'breathing on all sides', water 'kneeling in the moonlight', and lamplight falling 'on all fours on the grass'. The desire to unite all these elements is the major impetus behind both Bly's poetry and his public career. Though predominantly good-natured, even humorous, in his writings, Bly has his more sombre side, as can be seen in his volume *The Man in the Black Coat Turns* (New York, 1981; London, 1983).

Bly's *Selected Poems* (1986) contains a relatively small number of poems presented to illustrate ideas developed in several short essays. The serious reader needs to consult the individual volumes mentioned above. See also Howard Nelson, *Robert Bly: An Introduction to the Poetry* (New York, 1984), Richard Jones and Kate Daniels (eds.), *Of Solitude and Silence: Writings on Robert Bly* (Boston, 1981), and Joyce Peseroff (ed.), *Robert Bly: When Sleepers Awake* (1984).

[PS

BODENHEIM, Maxwell (1892–1954), was born in Mississippi, the only child of Carrie and Solomon Bodenheimer, but the family moved to Chicago by 1900. Expelled from high school, he joined the army in 1908, where he altered his name and served a term at Leavenworth for going AWOL. After his release he became part of Chicago's 'renaissance' until his cynical paranoia alienated even close

friends, causing him to flee to New York in 1915. He married Minna Schein three years later and published his first book of poems, *Minna and Myself* (1918), followed by seven others over the next twelve years, ending with *Bringing Jazz!* (1930), although he also wrote twelve sensationalist novels between 1923 and 1934.

Despite *Imagist roots, Bodenheim's early poetry was an impressionistic *vers libre* obsessed by oxymorons, essentially sentimental, often romanticizing urban scenes. His later work is much more conventional, including a number of technically competent but uninspired sonnets. He and his third wife were murdered in their Greenwich Village flat by a deranged guest.

Selected Poems (New York, 1946) has Bodenheim's major verses. See also *Maxwell Bodenheim* (New York, 1970), by Jack B. Moore.   [EB

BOGAN, Louise (1897–1970), one of three children, was born in Maine to parents of Irish descent and spent her early life in a series of New England mill towns, victimized by parental battles. She would lose one brother to the First World War, and the other to alcoholism at the age of 33. She began writing poetry as a 'life-saving process' at the Girls' Latin School in Boston, and went on to Boston University. She won a scholarship to Radcliffe but married Curt Alexander instead, accompanying him as an army wife to Panama in 1917, where her daughter Mathilde was born. In 1919 she left Alexander, who died a year later, and moved to Manhattan to pursue a literary career. She married Raymond Holden, an affluent poet and novelist, in 1925, but they were separated by 1934 and divorced in 1937.

Bogan's first three collections of verse, *Body of This Death* (1923), *Dark Summer* (1929), and *The Sleeping Fury* (1937), presented the melancholy insights of a strict formalist much influenced by W. B. *Yeats but lacking his genius. Even her most successful lyrics, such as 'Medusa', 'Knowledge', and 'Women', suffer from a remote fastidiousness and relentless intellectuality, though these same qualities helped make her an acute and important poetry critic. Starting in the 1930s and continuing until her death, she wrote most of *The New Yorker*'s poetry reviews. A number of these appeared in *Selected Criticism: Poetry and Prose* (1955) and doubtless underlay *Achievement in American Poetry, 1900–1950* (1951), her incisive critique of modernism's variegated impact on the poets of her era.

Bogan's *Poems and New Poems* (1941) and *Collected Poems 1923–1953* (1954) failed to generate the sort of broad acclaim she thought they deserved, although she did share the 1954 Bollingen Prize with Léonie *Adams. Her last years were harrowed by several bouts of clinical depression, and she died alone in her apartment from a coronary occlusion early in the morning of 4 February 1970.

Her poetry is available in *The Blue Estuaries: Poems, 1923–1968* (New York, 1968; repr. 1977), and much of her criticism in *A Poet's Alphabet: Reflections on the Literary Art and Vocation*, ed. Robert Phelps and Ruth Limmer (New York, 1970). See also *What the Woman Lived: Selected Letters of Louise Bogan 1920–1970*, ed. Ruth Limmer (New York, 1973) and *Louise Bogan: A Portrait* (New York, 1985), by Elizabeth Frank.

[EB

BOLAND, Eavan (Aisling) (1944–), is the youngest daughter of the painter Frances Kelly and the Irish diplomat F. H. Boland. Though born in Dublin, her school-days were in the main passed outside Ireland—in London, where her father was Irish Ambassador, and in New York, where he was Representative at the United Nations. In 1966 she graduated in English from Trinity College Dublin, and lectured there until 1968. She has taught creative writing in Ireland and in America, and collaborated with the actor Micheál MacLiammóir on a study of W. B. *Yeats. A noted reviewer and award-winning broadcaster, she is a member of the Irish Academy of Letters, and lives in Dublin with her husband and two daughters.

New Territory (1967) dealt largely with what it might mean to be a poet, and was remarkable for suppleness and ingenuity of rhythm. It included translations from the Irish; she has since made distinguished verse translations after Horace, Mayakovsky, and Nelly Sachs. During the 1970s she took on themes of Irish identity, engaging with history and with the marginalization of women, enlarging and complicating lyric forms to accommodate voices of oppression and insult alongside protest against indignity. In the 1980s her poetry began a disengagement from these wider social concerns, focusing instead on details of home-making and domesticity, politics giving way to issues of aesthetics and philosophy.

Selected Poems (Manchester, 1989) provides an overview of her work, but is meagre in its representation of the translations which appeared in *The War Horse* (London, 1975; Dublin, 1980).

[PL

BOLD, Alan (1943–), born and brought up in Edinburgh, has been a tireless all-round man-of-letters since his graduation from his home town's university in 1965, the year of his first collection, *Society Inebrious*. By 1971 he had published four more collections, with Chatto & Windus, appeared in *Penguin Modern Poets 15*, and edited *The Penguin Book of Socialist Verse* (1970). Encouraged from the beginning by C. M. Grieve ('Hugh *MacDiarmid'), that rush of books looked like a rate of productivity worthy of Bold's mentor.

Although Bold has continued to write and publish—*In This Corner: Selected Poems 1963–1983* (Edinburgh, 1983), for example, contained new work as well as old—his initial energy seems to have subsided. Earlier poems, while often clumsy, displayed a confident directness when facing large themes, as in 'June 1967 at Buchenwald'. Later work, although still too direct to be lyrical in the ways in which it might be aiming for, is almost meditative by comparison (e.g. 'Markinch Hill' and 'Grass').

As critic, literary commentator, editor, and biographer, Bold has been astoundingly productive. Among his books are studies of George Mackay *Brown (1978), the ballad (1979), Muriel Spark (1986), and *A Burns Companion* (1990). His *MacDiarmid: A Critical Biography*

(London, 1989; new edn. 1990) is outstanding, and supported by a critical study, *MacDiarmid: The Terrible Crystal* (London, 1983), a general survey, *Modern Scottish Literature* (London, 1983), as well as *The Letters of Hugh MacDiarmid* (London, 1984) and *The Thistle Rises: A Mac-Diarmid Miscellany* (London, 1984). He has edited many anthologies, as well as collections of critical essays on, among others, Smollett, Scott, Byron, *Spark, *Pinter, and *Auden. He is a frequent reviewer.   [DED

Bollingen Prize in Poetry, established in 1948 by the Bollingen Foundation, financed by Paul Mellon, was initially given annually but became biennial after 1963. For the first award, in 1949, the Fellows in American Letters of the Library of Congress recommended *Pound's *Pisan Cantos*, but the ensuing controversy caused the Library to discontinue its patronage; the prize has since been administered by Yale University Library. Prizewinners include most of the major American poets of the period. Between 1961 and 1968 the Foundation also awarded a Bollingen Poetry Translation Prize.   [POM

BOOTH, Philip (1925–), was born in Hanover, New Hampshire. His father was a professor at Dartmouth College, and Booth grew up in an environment both bookish and athletic. He was a varsity skier at Dartmouth until the Second World War interrupted his undergraduate education. He served in the US Army Air Force, 1944–5, then returned to Dartmouth and took his AB in 1948. The following year he received his Master's degree from Columbia University. He has taught at Bowdoin, Dartmouth, Wellesley, and finally Syracuse University, where he remained from 1961 until his retirement twenty-five years later as senior poet in the creative writing programme. He now lives in Castine, Maine, in the house that has belonged to his family for five generations.

Booth's first collection, *Letter from a Distant Land*, appeared in 1957, when the poet was 32. It won the Lamont Poetry Prize. It was characteristic of the seven collections which were to follow. Written in a spare and colloquial style, the poems fell into short lines as laconic as New England conversation. The Maine Coast was a metaphor for man living on the edge. In Booth's later books the ebb and flow of tides become associated with the give and take of time.

The fullest edition is *Relations: Selected Poems, 1950–1985* (New York, 1986). It contains selections from six previous collections, plus thirty-one new poems. To date there is no biography or autobiography.   [RSP

Botteghe Oscure was an international literary magazine devoted to the publication of work in the native language of the writers it included; it published roughly 650 writers drawn from thirty different nationalities, supplementing its basic issues with a number of books and pamphlets of translation. It was founded in Rome in 1949 by Princess Marguerite Caetani (1880–1963), who had previously edited *Commerce* in Paris (1924–32), a magazine which focused on some of the central writers of the day, such as *Joyce, Woolf, and Rilke. *Botteghe Oscure* was more catholic in its approach, publishing work by Alexander Trocchi and Carson McCullers as well as writers like *Auden, Bataille, Hölderlin, *Muir, E. E. *Cummings, Italo Calvino, and Gunter Grass. Its twenty-five issues were all substantial, possessing a distinctive design and evincing a fresh approach to the problems of internationalism in literature. It was alert to changes in the literary landscape and managed to include the early writings of many figures who went on to build significant reputations. It ceased publication in 1960.

[CM

BOTTOMLEY, Gordon (1874–1948), was born in Keighley, Yorkshire. His health was wretched from the age of 19 and, as he once said, he 'had no biography'. He made his life's work the revival of the English *verse drama, but only the amateur stage was influenced by his example, although his plays were well crafted. It has often been asserted that they are superior to those of Christopher Fry; but, whether this is true or not, they lacked commercial appeal. In essence Bottomley remained quintessentially *Georgian, but he manifested the best aspects of this movement, and was a skilled metrist. There is little unusual in the content of his poems, except for a rather solemn note. His best work is to be found in the plays, which by a few (notably Lascelles *Abercrombie) were taken up as pioneering. *King Lear's Wife* (London, 1915) and *Gruach* (London, 1921) both treat Shakespearian themes; these and others were designed for performance in small rooms, or halls, without scenery. He anticipated *Yeats in drawing on Japanese Noh plays to reinforce his technique. He is well represented in Edward Marsh's series of anthologies *Georgian Poetry. Poems and Plays* (London, 1953) is a good retrospective selection. See also *Letters to Gordon Bottomley* by Edward Thomas (London, 1968), ed. George R. Thomas.   [MS-S

BOTTOMS, David (1949–), was born in Canton, Georgia, the only child of a funeral director and a registered nurse. Educated at Mercer University, West Georgia College, and Florida State University, Bottoms became an associate professor of English in 1987 at Georgia State University, where he teaches creative writing.

Bottoms gained critical recognition with his first book of poetry, *Shooting Rats at the Bibb County Dump* (New York, 1980), which was chosen by Robert Penn *Warren as winner of the 1979 Walt Whitman Award of the Academy of American Poets. In this work Bottoms draws from his strong Southern background—his childhood in a small town, his life on the road as a bluegrass and country-and-western musician, and his knowledge of the outdoors—to create characters and situations which capture the eccentricity and isolation of many contemporary Southern lives. The voices in his poems are those of the people of his region; images of Southern swamps, creatures, and cultural oddities predominate. His other collections are *In a U-Haul North of Damascus* (New York, 1983) and *Under the Vulture-Tree* (New York, 1987). He is also the author of two well-received novels, *Any Cold Jordan* (New York, 1988) and *Easter Weekend* (Boston, 1990).   [LRi

BOTTRALL, Ronald (Francis James) (1906–89), was born in Cornwall. He won a scholarship to Cambridge, and spent his working life abroad. His few successful poems occur amongst a mass of intelligent work which seldom comes into focus. He wrote too rapidly and too much under the influence of *Pound. He was insecure, and tended to rely on the goodwill of other poets to advertise his talents. But these (e.g. *Eliot and *Graves) were only ever half convinced, although there was justice in G. S. *Fraser's remark that they could not all be 'entirely wrong'. He was not 'rediscovered', along with Graves, *Empson, and *Cameron, in the post-war period. *Collected Poems* (London, 1961) made little impact. His best work is to be found in later volumes, in particular *Poems 1955–1973* (London, 1974), which contains a vivid narrative, 'Talking to the Ceiling', and a number of almost surrealistic short poems. See also *Against a Setting Sun* (London, 1984).

[MS-S

BOWERING, George (Henry) (1935–), was born in Penticton, British Columbia, and educated in schools in the Okanagan Valley. After high school he served in the RCAF as an aerial photographer (1954–7), then enrolled in the University of British Columbia, where he received a BA in history in 1960 and an MA in English in 1963. While at university Bowering discovered the work of William Carlos *Williams, and readily fell under the influence of the creative theories and compositional practices of the American poets Charles *Olson, Robert *Creeley, and Robert *Duncan. The latter two were visitors to his university in the early 1960s, and Creeley was an adviser on Bowering's creative writing thesis, *Points on the Grid*, which was published in 1964.

Bowering was a founding co-editor of an important avant-garde magazine of poetry *Tish* (1961–3), and from 1964 to 1974 published his own occasional journal, *Imago*. He has also published widely in little magazines and has since 1965 been a contributor to the postmodernist journal, *Open Letter*.

Bowering's creativity has been closely associated with the little-press movement in Canada, while his career as a writer has been nurtured by academic life, with teaching appointments at several universities. He is now a professor of English at Simon Fraser University in Burnaby, British Columbia.

Since the appearance of his first book of poems, *Sticks and Stones* (Vancouver, 1963), with a preface by Creeley, Bowering has produced a prolific stream of poetry, prose fiction, and criticism. He won the Governor-General's Award for poetry in 1969 for two collections, *Rocky Mountain Foot* (1968) and *The Gangs of Kosmos* (1969—both Toronto). *Touch: Selected Poems 1960-1970* (Toronto) appeared in 1971, and an ampler *Selected Poems: Particular Accidents* (Vancouver) in 1980. His long poems are collected in *West Window* (Toronto, 1982), with later work in *Kerrisdale Elegies* (Toronto, 1984).

An opinionated yet skilful critic, Bowering has published a small book on the Canadian poet Al *Purdy (1970), and several collections of essays, including *A Way with Words* (1982), *The Mask in Place: Essays on Fiction in North America* (1983), and *Imaginary Hand: Essays* (1988). He has also published six volumes of prose fiction.

[MG

BOWERING, Marilyn (1949–), was born in Winnipeg, and raised in Victoria, British Columbia. She took her BA and MA degrees at the University of Victoria, where she now teaches in the creative writing department.

Bowering's first collection, *The Liberation of Newfoundland* (1973), employs graphic images of whaling to depict the violence implicit in male–female relations. Her next several books continue to break down the boundaries of form through a surreal use of imagery. *The Sunday Before Winter* (Toronto, 1984) offers a good selection from this first phase of her development. After the mid-1980s she turned to poetry of a quasi-historical bent. *Grandfather was a Soldier* (Victoria, BC, 1987) tells of her own journey to the battlefields of the First World War where her grandfather fought. *Calling All the World* (Victoria, BC, 1989) recounts the story of the dog Laika sent into space by the Soviets in 1957. *Anyone Can See I Love You* (Erin, Ont., 1987) offers a first-person portrait of Marilyn Monroe.

In 1977 Bowering co-edited with David Day the collection *Many Voices: An Anthology of Contemporary Canadian Indian Poetry* (Vancouver). She has also published two books of fiction, *The Visitors Have All Returned* (1979) and *To All Appearances a Lady* (1989).

[RH

BOWERS, Edgar (1924–), born in Georgia, served with the US Army in Europe during the Second World War. He took his BA in 1947 from the University of North Carolina and his Ph.D in 1953 from Stanford University, where he studied with Yvor *Winters. Since 1958 he has been a professor of English at the University of California, Santa Barbara. His main collections are *The Form of Loss* (Denver, Col., 1956), *The Astronomers* (Denver, 1965), *Living Together* (Boston, 1973; Manchester, 1977), and *For Louis Pasteur* (Princeton, NJ, 1989). In 1989 Bowers was awarded the Bollingen Prize.

A poet of great intellectual sophistication and historical awareness, Bowers is perhaps chiefly concerned with the human spirit as it relates to nature and as it expresses itself in different times, places, and cultures. Such earlier poems as 'Aix-la-Chappelle' and 'The Stoic' deal with the Second World War and with the vulnerability of culture in the face of ignorance and violence; such later poems as 'Thirteen Views of Santa Barbara' evoke the beauties of the natural world and speak of the threats posed to them by human indifference and greed. Other poems examine interconnections between durable forms of existence and their transient manifestations in individual lives and events. Certain of these poems (e.g. the 'Autumn Shade' sequence) explore the relationship between the real self, which is necessarily involved in the corruptions and disappointments of life, and an ideal self, which serves as an exemplar to which the real aspires but which it can never fully attain.

Bowers writes in traditional forms, which he employs with unmannered dexterity. The earlier work generally features rhymed stanzas, whereas the later work is principally in blank verse. If the earlier poems, such as the eerily beautiful 'Astronomers of Mont Blanc', are striking in their concentration, the later work shows a greater range of circumstantial detail.

Anthologies featuring Bowers's poems include *New Poets of England and America* (New York, 1957) and *Five American Poets* (London, 1963). Among critical studies are those in Yvor Winters's *Forms of Discovery* (Denver, Col., 1967) and Richard Howard's *Alone with America* (New York, 1969). [TS

BOWES LYON, Lilian (1895–1949), first cousin to Queen Elizabeth, the Queen Mother, was brought up at Ridley Hall, Bardon Mill, Northumberland, and that terrain characterizes her poems.

With good judgement, Philip *Larkin put what is probably her best poem, 'The White Hare', into *The Oxford Book of Twentieth-Century English Verse*: 'At the field's edge, | In the snow-furred sedge, | Couches the white hare'. Attractive also are 'Duchess', about a trace-horse in a blizzard; 'Snow Bees' about the first flakes of winter; and 'Death and Snow'—'when no foot, when no breath even, had smudged | the big white field'. Lilian Bowes Lyon may seem limited in diction and too much attached to literary decorum, but her authentic vision of snow, winter, and the Northumbrian landscape deserves to endure.

Her first book was *The White Hare* (London, 1934). Her *Collected Poems* appeared in London in 1948. [PDH

BOYLE, Charles (1951–), was born in Leeds and educated at Loretto School and St John's College, Cambridge, where he graduated in English in 1972. He taught English first in a Sheffield comprehensive school and then in North Africa, in Cairo and Rabat (1976–9). North African subjects appeared in his first collection, *Affinities* (Manchester, 1977), and Boyle returned to them in *House of Cards* (Manchester, 1982) and in *Sleeping Rough* (Manchester, 1987). Previously he had appeared in the anthology *Ten English Poets*, edited in 1976 by Michael Schmidt; although his empiricism is characteris-

tically English, Boyle's ironic, urbane poetry of instability and alienation has more in common with the work of Michael *Hofmann and Stephen *Romer than with that of the writers he originally appeared with. He also has affinities with the American poet Louis *Simpson and the short-story writer Frederick Barthelme. His most recent collection is *The Very Man* (Manchester, 1993). In 1981 Boyle won a Cholmondeley Award. Since 1980 he has been married to the painter Madeleine Strindberg and living in London, where he has worked as an editor with Time-Life Books and Faber and Faber. [MHu

BOYLE, Kay (1903–), was born in St Paul, Minnesota, lived in Europe for thirty years, and then took up academic appointments in America. She married three times, was twice divorced, and widowed in 1963. Although she is far better known as a novelist and story-writer, Kay Boyle has always insisted that she is primarily a poet. This is true in the sense that the fervent but humorous spirit of her verse has always informed her fiction, from the novel *Plagued by the Nightingale* (New York, 1931) onwards. As a poet, she acknowledged the influences of William Carlos *Williams, James *Joyce, D. H. *Lawrence and Padraic *Colum. These influences are perhaps too evident. Hers is an intelligent and readable body of work, but the ability to condense thought is largely absent. She is seen at her most rewarding in 'A Complaint for Mary and Marcel', in which the narrative parts are in prose, and in which her humour is to the fore. See *Collected Poems* (New York, 1962), and *This is Not a Letter* (Los Angeles, 1985). [MS-S

BRACKENBURY, Alison (1953–), was born in Lincolnshire and educated at Brigg High School and St Hugh's College, Oxford, where she read English. Since 1976 she has lived on the outskirts of Cheltenham, with her husband and daughter, and now works in the family electroplating business.

Alison Brackenbury won a Gregory Award in 1981. She is a prolific poet whose three Carcanet

(Manchester) collections, *Dreams of Power* (1981), *Breaking Ground* (1984), and *Christmas Roses* (1988), are all twice as long as the average collection. This is the key to her relative neglect, because the volumes have a diffuse feel; they are under-edited, but she has written a clutch of poems which place her firmly in the tradition of Edward *Thomas, Ivor *Gurney, and more recently P. J. *Kavanagh and E. J. *Scovell. Unfashionably for a poet who emerged in the urban Eighties, she is a countrywoman, apparently uninterested in the urban *Zeitgeist*. Like *Larkin, she writes of provincial lives—people who work in shops, watch a once-desired house grow derelict, drive home on wet Friday nights and find a frog in the road, balance the books at home—and these neglected byways become luminous in her poetry.

Stylistically, Brackenbury's poems have a strong rhythmic momentum, and a reek of the pathos of things: the hot dust of electric fires, forlorn assemblages of junk, an industrial piggery, are as familiar presences in her work as fields and horses.

See *Selected Poems* (Manchester, 1991). She is also represented in *Some Contemporary Poets of Britain and Ireland*, ed. Michael Schmidt (Manchester, 1984) and *Making for the Open*, ed. Carol Rumens (London, 1985).   [PF

BRASCH, Charles (1909–73), was born into an established mercantile family in Dunedin, and educated at Waitaki Boys' High School and St John's College, Oxford. He lived and worked overseas from 1931 to 1946, when he returned to permanent residence in New Zealand.

His first three books of poetry—*The Land and the People* (1939), *Disputed Ground, Poems, 1939–45* (1948), and *The Estate and other poems* (1957) associate him with that group of poets who were exploring issues of national identity and treating the concerns of the settler-migrant establishing a European society in New Zealand. Brasch's own verse style had a conservative reticence that distinguished it from some of the more exuberant and experimental work of his contemporaries. His last three books spanning the 1960s—*Ambulando* (1964), *Not Far*

Off (1969), and the posthumously published *Home Ground* (1974)—show an innovative change of poetic style and direction, and a new voice, less discursive, speaking of personal themes with a distinctly modernist tone.

As important as his verse was Brasch's editorship of the quarterly *Landfall*, which he established in 1947 and edited for its first eighty issues. A man of wide cultural interests, he was a generous benefactor of the arts, particularly in his home city Dunedin. See *Collected Poems*, edited by Alan Roddick, (Auckland, 1984), and Brasch's autobiography to 1947, *Indirections* (Auckland, 1980). See also James Bertram, *Charles Brasch* (Wellington, 1976).   [WSB

BRATHWAITE, E(dward) K(amau) (1930–), was born in Bridgetown, Barbados. He was educated at Harrison College, and at Pembroke College, Cambridge (on an island scholarship) where he read history. His doctoral dissertation at Sussex University was on *The Development of Creole Society in Jamaica, 1770–1820* (Oxford, 1971). From 1955 to 1962 he taught in Ghana, which was a great formative experience for a poet who identifies so strongly with his African roots. He was subsequently professor of Social and Cultural History at the University of the West Indies and is at present teaching in New York.

His poetic techniques include allusiveness, loosely linked imagery, and multiple voices. In this, he resembles early modernists like *Eliot and *Pound, but where they detected disintegration and decay in Western civilization, Brathwaite seeks to revive, and synthesize with other strands, African traditions and culture. Sections in dialect and rhythms derived from jazz further enrich his poetry. *The Arrivants* (Oxford, 1973) is generally considered to be his finest work. Subtitled 'A New World Trilogy', it combines three earlier volumes, *Rights of Passage* (1967), *Masks* (1968), and *Islands* (1969). Expansive in its range, both historical and stylistic, the trilogy can be described as an open-ended epic of the black diaspora; hence, of the African contribution to the varied cultures and societies of the Americas.

Other volumes include *Other Exiles* (Oxford, 1975). *Mother Poem* (1977), and *Sun Poem* (1982) and *X-Self* (1987—all Oxford and New York) comprise a second trilogy. *Third World Poems* (London, 1983) is mainly a selection from previous volumes. His most recent book is *Middle Passages* (Newcastle upon Tyne, 1991). Brathwaite's views on dialect are expounded in *History of the Voice: The Development of Nation Language in Anglophone Caribbean Poetry* (London and Port of Spain, 1984). [MR

BRAUN, Richard Emil (1934–), a native of Detroit, took a master's degree in Latin from the University of Michigan and a doctorate from the University of Texas. He taught classics for many years at the University of Alberta in Canada, and is thus neither fish nor fowl in either country. He is, in addition, a difficult poet in offbeat, even macabre ways.

Braun is often a narrative poet, but the stories he tells are enigmatic. The interests of his lyrics are similarly unconventional. Things on their surfaces appear to be normal; details are crystalline, hard-edged—yet at the peripheries of vision existential terrors loom.

These are features of Braun's first three collections, *Companions to Your Doom* (n.p. 1961), *Children Passing* (Austin, Tex., 1962) and *Badland* (Penland, NC, 1971). In his fourth volume, *The Foreclosure* (Urbana, Ill., and London, 1972), he began to modify the nightmare, modulating to a point where it was not so overtly surreal, and the effects became more subtle. He has also published translations of Euripides, Persius, and Sophocles. [LT

BRAUTIGAN, Richard (1933–84), was born in Tacoma, Washington. He was best known for his strange and original fiction; poetry, although he wrote a good deal of it, was little more to him than an agreeable recreation. A large number of his brief poems are simply jokes. Some hypothesize crazy or fanciful situations, which are amusing, but few possess, or pretend to possess, substance. They do, however, help to illuminate his achievement as a literary personality, a kind of modern Thoreau, who struggled,

through his happiness-seeking prose, against the constitutional depression which eventually led to his suicide. His main collections are *The Pill Versus the Springhill Mining Disaster: Poems 1957–1968* (San Francisco and London, 1970), and *Loading Mercury with a Pitchfork* (New York, 1976). [MS-S

BRENNAN, Christopher (1870–1932), born in Sydney, the son of an Irish brewery worker, was educated by Jesuits as a scholarship boy and at the University of Sydney. He won a fellowship to the University of Berlin, became engaged to his landlady's daughter while there, and discovered the poetry of Mallarmé, which was the most important influence on his work. Returning to Sydney, he worked for a decade in the public library, passed over for appointment to the university even though his scholarship was such that he could have 'graced', a colleague later said, the chairs of philosophy, classics, modern languages, or literature in any institution. His drunkenness, 'immoral' poems, and unconventional behaviour were already held against him. When he was eventually appointed professor of German and comparative literature, Brennan's lectures were hugely popular, but before long had to be scheduled for early in the day, because of his drinking.

Three years after his return, Brennan's fiancée came to Australia. They were married and had four children, but eventually Brennan left home to live in sailors' hotels. With his family he was something of a tyrant, but in Sydney's bohemia he was sought after for his wit, erudition, and ebullience. A massive figure, with a great hooked nose and vast meerschaum pipe, he became the legend of a thousand brilliant and drunken nights; conversing in, quoting from, construing six languages. When the university heard that he had deserted his family and was living with a much younger woman he was dismissed, but the blow came some months after his companion had been killed, run down by a tram, and when Brennan was still in the depths of grief. From then on he degenerated rapidly, becoming filthy and gross, and living without any support except charitable contributions. Certain Catholic clergy helped, giving him occasional teaching work, and old friends bought him drinks and food so as to hear his often still-marvellous talk. He lived amongst the *demi-monde* of Kings Cross, moving between the prostitutes and the nuns, and finally returned to the Church, which he had dismissed since schooldays, as he was dying.

The main body of Brennan's work is in *Poems 1913* (Sydney and London), a sometimes contrived *livre composé*, which records his Symbolist quest for an absolute reality, an intimation of which will transform this world for the initiate. Such an experience is called, after Mallarmé, 'Eden'. Mallarmé wrote admiringly to him ('Poet, wonderful Poet') in response to the gift of Brennan's first book, and chose to defend him against a hostile Parisian reviewer. Brennan's poems often have fresh, Whitmanesque flourishes as their opening lines—'Once, when the sunburst flew'; 'My heart was wandering in the sands'; 'The banners of the king unfold'; 'I saw my life as whitest flame'; 'O life, O radiance'; 'Fire in the heavens, and fire along the hills'— but the promise, again and again, fails, lost in tangled syntax, portentousness, archaism, generalizations, and ponderous, sub-Miltonic rhetoric.

His best poem, by far, is 'The Wanderer', in which the quest for an Absolute is abandoned, and the material world and its sufferings accepted with a calm resignation. The language in the sequence is generally less pretentious and the rhythm more supple than in anything else that Brennan wrote. There are perhaps four or five other poems, lyrics, in which something of his potential was realized.

Frank Kermode has written appreciatively of 'The Wanderer'; Clive James, in his book of essays, *Snakecharmers in Texas* (1989) is interested by Brennan but disappointed by the poetry; Axel Clark's *Christopher Brennan* (1980) is the definitive biography; and G. A. Wilkes's *New Perspectives on Brennan's Poetry* (1953) is an outstanding study. *Selected Poems* (Sydney, 1992) includes *Poems 1913* together with letters between Brennan and Mallarmé. The anthology *Christopher Brennan* (St Lucia, Qld, 1984), edited by Terry Sturm, contains, as well as the poetry, selections of Brennan's still-excellent literary criticism on the Symbolist movement.

[RGr

BREW, (O. H.) Kwesi (1928–), was born in Cape Coast, of an old Gold Coast family whose connections with the Fante-speaking area of what is now central Ghana go back as far as 1745. Educated locally, he embarked on a career as diplomat, serving in his country's foreign service in Britain, France, India, and Germany. The title of his volume of 1968, *Shadows of Laughter* (London), suggests the ambience of his verse, which is of a pictorialism etched by menace. The poetry is multivalent, subtly ambiguous. In 'The Executions Dream' he employs the almost Daliesque image of a disembodied eye sticky in the palm of a hand, 'Glittering, wet and sickening| Like a dull onyx of thorns'. The poem is a supplication, but whether from the victim to his executioner or the executioner to his victim we are not sure. In 'Plea for Mercy' a group of wanderers return to an ancestral shrine, but their faith is unrewarded, their requests unheard. In 'Locusts' the brilliant pink of an approaching swarm presages ruin, while in 'Questions of Our Time' the inquiries of the title are addressed, not as custom would demand to an elder, but to a child playing in the dust, who answers gnomically 'perhaps'. Most famously, in 'The Sea Eats our Lands', Brew evokes the continual erosion of the sea coast around Keta in Eweland in the country's eastern region. A frequent theme is that of return, but it is to a domain blasted by poverty and decimated by ruin. A reductionist account of his verse would interpret it as an expression of the destruction of Ghana's national aspirations at the hands of her immediately post-colonial governments, but the delicacy and remoteness with which these anxieties are expressed carry his work well beyond the preoccupations of any one period or stage of political growth. Brew is a traveller who writes about home, a pessimist whose sadness is redeemed by beauty, and a religious poet whose appeals are addressed to shrines which lie empty. [RF

BREWSTER, Elizabeth (1922–), was born in the small lumber town of Chimpman, New Brunswick. She received her first degree at the University of New Brunswick and her Ph.D at the University of Indiana in 1962. For many years she worked as a librarian. In 1972 she joined the English department at the University of Saskatchewan, where she taught until 1990.

From the time she began publishing in the 1940s, Brewster has taken for her subject-matter the small events of everyday life. In her first poems she employed rhymed quatrains, but soon forsook rhyme for free verse and the verse tale. Frequently her short stories in verse portray people isolated within their communities by their inability to express themselves. Her earlier poetry resembles that of the eighteenth-century English poet George Crabbe, on whom she wrote her doctoral dissertation. During the 1960s she increasingly turned to events in her own life as her main subject. Her usual procedure is to voice a personal anxiety and then undermine its importance by placing it in the wider human context.

A good selection of her work can be found in the two-volume *Selected Poems* (1944–1977 and 1977–1984: Ottawa, 1985). Brewster has also written two novels, *The Sisters* (1974) and *Junction* (1983), as well as three short-story collections, *It's Easy to Fall on the Ice* (1977), *A House Full of Women* (1983), and *Visitations* (1987). Paul Denham's 'Speeding Towards Strange Destinations: A Conversation with Elizabeth Brewster', in *Essays on Canadian Writing*, 18/19 (Summer/Fall 1980) offers a good introduction to Brewster's poetry.   [RBH

BRIDGES, Robert (1844–1930), son of a landowner, was born in Walmer, Kent, and educated at Eton and Corpus Christi College, Oxford, where he first met Gerard Manley Hopkins. Bridges trained to be a medical doctor at St Bartholomew's Hospital, London, and after working as a physician at other London hospitals he retired to Yattenden, Berkshire, in 1881. From 1907 until his death he lived at Boar's Hill, Oxfordshire. In 1913 he succeeded Alfred *Austin as Poet Laureate.

Though at Yattenden he wrote long poems (*Prometheus the Firegiver*, 1883, and *Eros and Psyche*, 1885) and eight plays (1885–94), his early reputation was built on his short poems. These, almost devoid of memorable meaning or strong feeling, are beautifully crafted and display a rare gift for verbal melody; as *Yeats wrote of one of them: 'Every metaphor, every thought a commonplace, emptiness everywhere, the whole magnificent.' Determinedly un-Victorian, Bridges harks back instead to the chaste lyrics of Campion and the young Milton. (He had a life-long interest in words for music, and provided lyrics for four works by Parry.) The second book of short poems was dedicated to Hopkins, whose influence can occasionally be felt in much-anthologized pieces like 'London Snow' and 'On a Dead Child'; and Bridges was himself an innovator of an academic sort, ambitious to loosen the traditional metres of English verse and write 'by the rules of a new prosody'.

In the late part of his career he wrote largely in a flexible twelve-syllable line with variation in the placing of the accents, what he called a 'loose alexandrine' (see SYLLABICS). *The Testament of Beauty*, his last work, is a long philosophical poem in four books ('Introduction', 'Selfhood', 'Breed', and 'Ethick'); but the central myth of 'the Chariot of the Soul' is not interesting, and the frigidity of thought and style obscures the work's technical virtues. The twentieth century has expressed more gratitude for his edition of Hopkins's poems (1918) than for his own writings.

The Testament of Beauty was added to the *Poetical Works* (London) in 1953. See also *A Choice of Bridges' Verse* (London, 1987). Bridges did not want a biography, and destroyed his documents; Catherine Phillips's scholarly life (Oxford, 1992) defies him respectfully. (See also DARYUSH, ELIZABETH.)   [MI

BRINGHURST, Robert (1946–), was born in Los Angeles of Canadian parents and has lived variously in Alberta, Beirut, London, Montana, Utah, and (since 1973) on the British Columbia coast. Two suites of multiple lyric meditations on thinking, one about the Pre-Socratics ('The

Old in Their Knowing', 1973–82), and the other using ancient Taoist and Buddhist writers ('The Book of Silences', 1986), are among his finest representative poems. He has also worked with the elders of native North American thought in poems ('Tzuhalem's Mountain', 1982) and in his prose versions of Haida mythology, *The Raven Steals the Light* (with Bill Reid, 1984). Poetry with complex musical and prosodic structures which attends centrally to the human intelligence is his particular contribution to Canadian poetry.

Bringhurst's selected poems, *The Beauty of the Weapons* (Toronto, 1982; Port Townsend, Wash., 1985), has the major poems to 1982; *Pieces of Map, Pieces of Music* (Toronto, 1986; Port Townsend, 1987) has the subsequent poems with two important autobiographical essays.

[RB

BRISSENDEN, R(obert) F(rancis) (1928–91), was born in Wentworthville, Sydney, the son of a schoolteacher. Educated at the universities of Sydney and Leeds, he taught principally in Canberra from 1953 until his retirement, in 1984, as reader in English at the Australian National University. As a writer, editor, critic, teacher, and arts administrator he played a significant role in the development of contemporary Australian literature.

A lyric poet, he had a gift also for comic and satiric verse. Although his subjects range from major issues of the 1970s and 1980s (the Vietnam War, the conservation movement) to the classical world and more personal preoccupations (literature, jazz), he returns most repeatedly and effectively to the shorescapes and fauna of the south coast of New South Wales.

His principal collections are *Winter Matins* (Sydney, 1971), *Building a Terrace* (Canberra, 1975), *The Whale in Darkness* (Canberra, 1980), *Sacred Sites* (Canberra, 1990), and a posthumous selected poems, *Suddenly Evening* (Melbourne, 1993). Other significant publications are *Virtue in Distress* (on Samuel Richardson; Melbourne, 1974), and two thrillers, *Poor Boy* (Sydney, 1987; New York, 1988) and *Wild Cat* (Sydney, 1991). He co-edited *The Oxford Book of Australian Light Verse* (1991).   [DBB

BROCK, Edwin (1927–   ), was born in London and is one of the few poets to have served as a policeman (1951–9). He has also worked in advertising, and has been poetry editor of *Ambit* magazine since 1960. His poetry, mainly autobiographical (or, as he has put it, 'self-defining') offers an interesting and revealing British contrast to the American *confessional genre; it has more affinities with prose than has most of the latter. Where many poets omit what they feel to be the too-mundane, Brock supplies it in detail. Rough-hewn, dogged, deliberately unsubtle, and full of incongruous echoes from other poets, his work is also disarmingly genuine. See *Penguin Modern Poets* 8 (with Geoffrey Hill and Stevie Smith, Harmondsworth, 1966), *Invisibility is the Heart of Survival: Selected Poems* (New York, 1972)—with its introduction by Alan Pryce-Jones—and *Five Ways to Kill a Man: New and Selected Poems* (Petersfield, Sussex, 1990); also his autobiography *Here, Now. Always.* (London and New York, 1977).

[MS-S

BROCK-BROIDO, Lucie (1956–), grew up in Pittsburgh; her hyphenated name combines her mother's maiden name and her father's name. She received her BA and MA from the writing seminars at Johns Hopkins, and took an MFA in writing at the School of the Arts of Columbia University. She has subsequently taught writing at Wheaton College, Tufts, and Harvard. Knopf published her first volume of poetry, *A Hunger*, in 1988 (2nd edn. 1992).

Brock-Broido's poems often show a ventriloquist's talent exerted through arresting personae (a survivor of the police bombing of the MOVE group—a black clan—in Philadelphia; two mad female twins, 'elective mutes', who share a private language and commit murder; a child who has fallen down a well). Brock-Broido's 'domestic mysticism' declares that her work is 'peopled by Wizards, the Forlorn, | The Awkward, the Blinkers, the Spoon-Fingered Agnostic Lispers . . . | The Charlatans. I am one of those.' The stagey and the coy are weapons in her arsenal, which also uses irony and the theatrical to stage dramas of a life where 'a hunger' is obsessive but strange rewards attend its vigils. Recently, Brock-Broido has written a series of poems inspired by Emily Dickinson's letters to an unknown man whom she addressed only as 'Master'. In Brock-Broido's hands the Master can be God, a lover, or an interior exaction; and the language of the letter-writer can range from Amherst archaic to postmodern eclectic.

[HV

BRODSKY, Joseph (1940–), was born in Leningrad to Russian-Jewish parents. The family shared a communal apartment while Brodsky attended public schools, which he quit at 15. In the decade that followed he changed jobs many times, along the way working as a milling-machine operator at a factory which produced cannons and at a hospital morgue where he cut and sewed up bodies. For a time, like his mother, he was able to support himself as a translator. This hand-to-mouth existence was not satisfactory in the view of Soviet authorities, who arrested him in 1964 on the charge of social parasitism. In 1960 he met Anna Akhmatova (1889–1966), who, when Brodsky was sentenced to five years' forced labour on a state farm in Siberia, championed his cause. This, along with transcripts of his trial smuggled to the west, helped to make Brodsky's plight internationally known. He was released in 1965 after serving eighteen months of his sentence. In 1972 he was expelled from the Soviet Union. That same year he was hired as poet-in-residence at the University of Michigan. In 1980 he moved to New York City's Greenwich Village. In 1987 he received the Nobel Prize for literature.

In his introduction to Brodsky's *Selected Poems* (New York and Harmondsworth, 1973), translated by George L. Kline, W. H. *Auden identified Brodsky as 'a tradionalist . . . interested in what lyric poets of all ages have been interested in . . . encounters with nature . . . reflections upon the human condition, death, and the meaning of existence'. Certainly Brodsky has benefited from his gifted poet-translators, most conspicuously in *A Part of Speech* (New York and Oxford, 1980), his second major collection in English, which includes transla-

tions by Anthony *Hecht, Howard *Moss, and Richard *Wilbur. His own translations have been criticized for turgidness, lacking a native sense of musicality. Brodsky's third collection in English is *To Urania* (New York and London, 1988). He has also published *Less than One: Selected Essays* (New York and London, 1986).

[HC

BRONK, William (1918–), was born in the small upstate town of Hudson Falls, New York, into an old Dutch patrician family whose name goes back to the early Dutch settlement that later became the borough of New York City called the Bronx. Except for occasional travel, in particular his important visits to the pre-Columbian ruins of Tikal and Machu Picchu, he has lived in Hudson Falls, running a family-owned lumber business.

Bronk's poetry, austere and consummately metaphysical in tone, is a sustained, brooding body of work which seeks to articulate the most fundamental questions, the nature of human consciousness, of desire, time, and location. Though often linked by critics to the work of *Stevens, Bronk's poems proceed by more naked, stripped-down means: a preference for direct statement over metaphor, and a fierce, almost syllogistic logic. Bronk's remarkable imagery, subdued and bleak, often drawing on the winter-struck landscapes of the American north-east, is suggestive of the fragile nature of perception and thought. As in his essays, collected in *The New World* (New Rochelle, NY, 1974), where he ponders the meaning of archaic culture and our encounters with its otherness, Bronk's aim in his poems is to investigate the paradoxical nature of existence, our need to construct mental or physical worlds by which we confirm who we are and that we do exist. Ambitious in theme, Bronk's poetry is simultaneously a contemplation of, and eloquent quarrel with, the human condition.

The most complete collection of Bronk's poetry is *Life Supports: New and Collected Poems* (Berkeley, Calif., 1981). The recent volume, *Manifest: and Furthermore* (Berkeley, 1987) is an important addition to his work. See also

Parnassus: Poetry in Review (Spring–Summer 1977), and the William Bronk issue of *Sagetrieb* (1989). [MH

BROOKE, Rupert (Chawner) (1887–1915), was born in Rugby, where his father was a house-master at Rugby School, and grew up in the comfortable security of a home dedicated to ideals of 'godliness and good learning'. Having discovered the power of poetry—from a chance reading of Browning—at the age of 9, Brooke entered his father's school in 1901. From the start, he did well both in the class-room and on the playing-field; for although early on he adopted the pose of the decadent aesthete, win-ning the school poetry prize in 1905, he found time to play in the cricket XI and the rugger XV. He was strikingly handsome, and his physical presence was matched by a sharpness of intel-lect, a charm and vitality of manner that affected everyone with whom he came into contact. Popular and successful at Rugby, he was even more so at King's College, Cambridge, where he went as a scholar in 1906. He read vora-ciously, and threw himself into acting and the activities of the University Fabian Society, of which he became president.

Having gained a second class in the Cam-bridge Classical Tripos, Brooke established him-self in the house afterwards made famous by his poem 'The Old Vicarage, Grantchester', and began to work at a dissertation on Webster and the Elizabethan dramatists. His pastoral exist-ence, however, was interrupted by an unhappy love affair, and in 1912 he travelled through France and Germany in search of peace of mind. Partially recovered, he returned to England and was elected to a Fellowship at King's. He divided his time between Cambridge and Lon-don literary and political circles.

Falling in love again, Brooke decided that he needed a change of scene while considering what to do with his life, and in May 1913 he sailed for America. He had been commissioned by the *Westminster Gazette* to write a series of articles on his impressions of the United States and Canada, and over the coming months sent back a dozen vivid dispatches. After an idyllic

interlude in the South Seas (that resulted in some of his best poems), he returned to England and enlisted within weeks of the outbreak of the First World War. He served with the Royal Naval Division in the retreat from Antwerp, and was on his way to Gallipoli when he contracted blood-poisoning, from which he died on 23 April 1915.

England at this time needed a focal point for its griefs, ideals, and aspirations, and Brooke was promptly iconized by Church and State: his son-net 'The Soldier' read aloud in St Paul's Cathed-ral, his *Times* obituary appearing over the initials of Winston Churchill. His *1914 and Other Poems* and subsequent *Collected Poems* sold 300,000 copies over the next decade. This elevation into a tragic figure of almost mythical stature is highly ironic, since his friends—who included Violet Asquith, Frances *Cornford, Henry James, Geoffrey and Maynard Keynes, and Vir-ginia Woolf—would remember him above all for his laughter and the laughter he induced in them. Brooke once quoted the remark of Hugo to Baudelaire, 'You have created a new shud-der', and went on to suggest that one might say of Ernest Dowson: 'He has created a new sigh.' Similarly, we might say of Brooke that he cre-ated a new laugh. Laughter is audible in no less than a third of the poems and fragments in Keynes's edition of the *Poetical Works*, a statistic doubly surprising given the nature of his central subject: the place of love and life and laughter after death. This is the theme of the best of his early poems, such as 'Oh! Death will find me' and 'The Hill', and the elegant satires 'The Fish' and 'Tiare Tahiti', in which he engages Chris-tianity and Platonism with 'the sword of laugh-ter'.

Brooke's 1914 sonnets celebrate the discov-ery of a cause, a vision—found also in the con-temporary poems of *Owen, *Rosenberg, and others—of an exhausted civilization rejuven-ated by conflict. The start of the war prompted what he had earlier, ironically, described as 'Nineteenth Century grandiose thoughts, about the Destiny of Man, the Irresistibility of Fate, the Doom of Nations, the fact that Death awaits us All'. Forsaking Marvellian tetrameters for Tennysonian pentameters, he yielded to the temptations of a high style that in his better poems he had resisted. He should not, however, be seen as a 'war poet'. He is a poet of peace, a celebrant of friendship, love, and laughter.

The standard edition of the poems is *Rupert Brooke: The Poetical Works*, ed. Geoffrey Keynes (London, 2nd edn., 1970). Keynes also edited *The Letters of Rupert Brooke* (London, 1968). The standard biography is *Rupert Brooke*, by Christopher Hassall (London, 1964). See, too, *Rupert Brooke: A Reappraisal and Selection from his Writings, Some Hitherto Unpublished*, ed. Timothy Rogers (London, 1971) and *The Neo-Pagans: Friendship and Love in the Rupert Brooke Circle*, by Paul Delany (London, 1987).   [JHS

BROOKS, Gwendolyn (1917–   ), was born in Topeka, Kansas, and graduated from Chicago's Wilson Junior College in 1936. She married Henry Blakely in 1939, and they have two children. In 1971 she was made Distinguished Professor of the Arts at New York's City College. Her first three books of poetry, *A Street in Bronzeville* (New York, 1945), *Annie Allen* (New York, 1949), winner of a Pulitzer Prize, and *Bronzeville Boys and Girls* (New York, 1956), treated urban black life with satiric rage and erudite objectivity, utilizing ballads, dramatic monologues, and lyric forms to simulate novelistic sweep.

Her basic approach, except perhaps for a sharper protest note, changed little in later volumes such as *In the Mecca: Poems* (New York, 1968) and *Aloneness* (Detroit, 1971). Although 'The Womanhood' and similar poems are usually praised for their ambitious reach, Brooks does best in terser, simpler efforts—in 'The Empty Woman', for instance, a few Bronzeville portraits, and salutes to *Frost and Langston *Hughes. Her *Selected Poems* (New York, 1963) contains important early work. See also *Gwendolyn Brooks: Poetry and the Heroic Voice* (Lexington, Ky., 1989), by D. H. Melhem, and *A Life Distilled: Gwendolyn Brooks, Her Poetry and Fiction*, ed. Maria K. Mootry and Gary Smith (Champaign, Ill., 1989).   [EB

Broom (November 1921–January 1924), one of the group of little magazines edited or part-edited by American expatriates, or published from European cities. *Broom* was founded and first edited by the bookseller Harold Loeb and the poet and critic Alfred *Kreymborg, once described as the 'patron saint of the modern "little magazine" movement'. It appeared from Rome, Berlin, and finally New York. Kreymborg had previously published other little magazines such as *Glebe* (1913) and *Others* (1914). *Broom*, essentially a continuation of these ventures, although more elaborate and sumptuous in appearance, was well known and, for a little magazine, successful, but at first fairly conservative in its context. It gave equal space to European and to American writers such as *Pound and British ones such as *Aldington. When it fell into new hands it became more erratic, and soon ceased to appear. See *The Little Magazine* (New York, 1947), by F. Hoffman, C. Allen, and C. Ulrich.   [MS-S

BROWN, George Mackay (1921–   ), is a native of the Orkney Islands, from which he has been absent only to attend Newbattle Abbey College (where Edwin *Muir was Warden) and the University of Edinburgh (1956–60; 1962–4) as a mature student. His subjects almost invariably pertain to his remote northern homeland. Not only in his prose account *An Orkney Tapestry* (London, 1969) is he a scholar and historian of his place, but also in his poetry (and novels, short stories, and plays). Norse sagas, the Catholic liturgy, Hopkins, Dylan *Thomas, and the ballads are among the sources of a poetry which at its best assumes pellucid imagery and narrative as its ideals.

Real and imagined histories overlap in Brown's lyrical evocation of his islands and the traditions from which their sense of community stems. A narrowness of range might seem to follow from a position so firmly located to the point of a determined rootedness. However, the time-scale of Brown's poetry stretches from prehistory to the present day. There is a good deal in his work about the Vikings and the pre-Reformation past of the Orkneys, of voyages and the

71

sea. As a historical vision, Brown's is omnibus and kaleidoscopic, as well as densely populated with characters and incidents. It might only be by sleight-of-hand that Brown can be claimed as a Scottish poet: like Edwin Muir, he has admitted to feeling more Norse than Scottish, and, therefore, untroubled by the usual questions of nationality which tend to beset many Scottish writers.

Loaves and Fishes (London, 1959) introduced the town of Hamnavoe (his name for Stromness, where he lives), and it has reappeared consistently ever since. *The Year of the Whale* (London, 1965) saw him perfect the kind of poem with which he has come to be associated—a narrative lyric, often focusing on one or more characters, as in 'The Funeral of Ally Flett', 'Farm Labourer', 'Old Fisherman with Guitar', 'Trout Fisher', and 'Hamnavoe Market'. The first and last of these risk an obvious listing of events, or, in the case of 'Hamnavoe Market', seven kinds of consequence of heavy drinking. Runes, bestiaries, calendars, seasonal lists, and so on occur frequently enough to become repetitive. Taken in quantity, Brown's poems can at times feel as if they depend on too much of the same thing. Duplicated sensations, however, are by and large redeemed by scrupulous writing, clarity, certainty of diction, and an engaging honesty.

Fishermen with Ploughs (London, 1971) is an ambitious cycle, convincing in its individual parts, but doctrinally insecure. By the end of the book a 'Black Pentecost', or apocalypse, is imagined as having obliterated most of the world. An Orcadian rescue of humanity is witnessed through the agency of women and a return to the old ways of farming and fishing.

Poems New and Selected (London and New York, 1973) was followed by *Winterfold* (London, 1976), *Selected Poems* (London, 1977), *Voyages* (London, 1983), *The Wreck of the Archangel* (London, 1989), and a new *Selected Poems* (London, 1991). Brown has also written lyrics and opera libretti for the composer Sir Peter Maxwell Davies, and edited *Selected Prose of Edwin Muir* (1987). His novels include *Greenvoe* (1972), *Magnus* (1973), and *Time in a Red Coat*

(1984). There is a study by Alan Bold (Edinburgh, 1978).   [DED

BROWN, Pete. See PERFORMANCE POETRY.

BROWN, Sterling A. (1901–89), was born in Washington DC, the son of a professor of religion. He was educated at Harvard and in 1926 began a lifelong career in teaching, most of it spent at Howard University. Brown began publishing during the 1920s, the era of the *Harlem Renaissance, but he always resisted being labelled a Renaissance poet. In his first volume, *Southern Road* (New York, 1932), he exhibited the range of his poetic voice. The book includes some pastoral lyrics written in a plain English with archaic echoes ('Grief has been hers, before this wintry time. | Death has paid calls, unmannered, uninvited'), but has many more of the dialect poems for which Brown is better known. These draw on mainly musical sources, the ballad, the work-song, and the blues. Certain stanzas from poems such as 'Odyssey of Big Boy', 'Long Gone', and 'Southern Road' could fit easily into the blues lyrics sung by Brown's contemporaries, such as Blind Lemon Jefferson. In a cycle of poems chronicling the adventures of a character called Slim Greer, Brown incorporates elements of fable as he sets his ironic hero loose among the black world, the white world, and the after world.

After *Southern Road* Brown published only sporadically, though he continued to write verse. His *Collected Poems*, ed. Michael S. Harper, was published in 1980 (reissued Chicago, 1989). See also the 1941 anthology, *The Negro Caravan*, ed. by Brown, Arthur P. Davis, and Ulysses Lee (reissued New York, 1969).   [JC

BROWN, Wayne (Vincent) (1944–), was born in Trinidad. He was educated at St Mary's College, Port of Spain, the University of the West Indies, and the University of Toronto. His father was a distinguished judge but, as his mother died giving birth, he was brought up mainly by relatives. As an only child he spent many holidays alone exploring shorelines, and indeed seascapes are prominent in his poems. He held the Gregory Fellowship in Poetry (1975–6) at the University of Leeds. At present he writes a column for the *Trinidad Guardian* and teaches part-time at the University of the West Indies, St Augustine Campus.

Derek *Walcott was one of his mentors when he first started writing poetry, and a poem like 'Ballad of the Electric Eel', though distinctively elegant and supple, could not have been written without the example of Ted *Hughes. One of his best poems, 'Noah', wears its archetypal symbolism lightly, and reveals the poetic imagination in blinding flashes of imagery. *On the Coast* (London, 1972) won the Commonwealth Prize for Poetry. Brown has also written a biography of *Edna Manley* (London, 1975), a prominent Jamaican literary figure. [MR

BROWNE, Michael Dennis (1940–), a native of Walton-on-Thames, England, became a naturalized American in 1978, more than a decade after enrolling at the University of Iowa. Before taking an MA there in 1967 he was educated at Hull University and Oxford. Since 1971 he has taught at the University of Minnesota.

Browne's first volumes contain poems of spare narrative context, fractured syntax, and startlingly juxtaposed metaphors. 'The King in May', for instance, creates a surrealistic effect by combining a mythic, unnamed speaker and setting with a series of vivid, unpredictable figures of speech, while 'The Delta' (set in Vietnam) conveys the nightmarish unreality of war by means of archetypal imagery and unpunctuated syntactic repetitions. Browne's newer work also reveals his interest in dreams, but his style has become more direct, more personal, and more accessible, without sacrificing psychological depth, as a poem like 'Her Garden' demonstrates.

Browne's publications include *The Wife of Winter* (London, 1970; revised edn., New York, 1970), *The Sun Fetcher* (Pittsburgh, 1978), and *Smoke From the Fires* (Pittsburgh, 1984). [MCB

BROWNJOHN, Alan (1931–), was born in London, which has been his home for most of his life. He was educated there and at Oxford; he has been a lecturer in English at colleges of further education, poetry critic on the *New Statesman*, a member of the Arts Council Literature Panel, a Labour borough councillor and parliamentary candidate, chairman of the Greater London Arts Association Literature Panel, and chairman of the Poetry Society. He is now a free-lance writer and broadcaster. He has a son by his first wife, Shirley Toulson, whom he married in 1960 (the marriage ended in divorce in 1969); in 1972 he was married again, to Sandra Willingham.

Brownjohn's political sympathies and domestic concerns inform a poetry that aims for, and achieves, stylistic correctness, emotional reticence, modest understatement: qualities frequently associated with English poetry of the 1950s and (though Brownjohn was a member of the *Group) particularly with the *Movement. Brownjohn's early work did not appear in either of Robert *Conquest's *New Lines* anthologies, though it would have looked, with its touches of *Auden, *Graves, and *Empson, perfectly at home there. His *Collected Poems* is arranged chronologically by decades, beginning with the 1950s, and there are no radical departures in the 1960s, 1970s, or 1980s. There is, though, a steady deepening and darkening of the poems' 'virulent proprieties', 'moments of disquiet', and 'meticulous disenchantment' (all phrases from the poems themselves); and a growing confidence and conviction in the approach to social, personal, and philosophical themes—the failures and follies of 'progress' in post-war England, the pressures on love and marriage, and an acutely self-questioning sense of moral and epistemological doubt. Trim and orderly stanzas, a facility with moralized anecdote and metaphorical exempla, have never been abandoned; nor, more damagingly, has the tendency to a baldly abstract diction and a philosophizing-in-verse.

The most rewarding developments have been in Brownjohn's gift for elliptical narrative (as in his longer sequences) and in his mastery of tonal nuance, his trust in the ability of a deliberate plainness to suggest much that the poem leaves unsaid. An ear for the accents of social tact and the discreetly avoided 'painful subject' is pertinent here, as is his own comment on his 'styles of reticence': 'I don't feel like making apology for this because I greatly admire certain English puritan values and feel that English rationalism, democracy and humanity would be our best post-imperial contribution to the world at large.' The 'puritan values' have always been evident in the ordinariness of Brownjohn's subjects, his acknowledgement of unexceptional happiness, his sober facing-down of futility and fear. More recently, 'post-imperial' overtones have entered his work, along with a plangent insistence on the inexpressible (often associated with the sea or seaside settings), and a muted, stoical compassion that does not exclude irony.

Collected Poems 1952–1983 (London, 1983) was reissued in 1988, to include most of the poems published in a subsequent volume, *The Old Flea-Pit* (London, 1987); the most recent collection is *The Observation Car* (London, 1990). Brownjohn has also published a novel, *The Way You Tell Them* (London, 1990); a novel for children (as John Berrington), *To Clear the River* (London, 1964); a critical study, *Philip Larkin* (London, 1975); and a translation (with Sandy Brownjohn) of Goethe's *Torquato Tasso* (London, 1985). [AJ]

BRUCE, George (1909–), a native of north-east Scotland, was educated at the University of Aberdeen. He taught for some years before joining the BBC. Since his retirement he has held a number of visiting posts in American and Australian universities. *Sea Talk* (Glasgow, 1944), was followed by *Selected Poems* (Edinburgh, 1947). *Perspectives: Poems 1970–1986* (Aberdeen, 1987) continues from *Collected Poems* (Edinburgh, 1971).

Bruce's work is spare, distrustful of sensuous phrase-making, perhaps even of lyricism itself, and succeeds in the avoidance of interesting rhythm. 'No grace here, nor riches, but authority', he writes in 'Landscapes and Figures'. Statements like these have been claimed as a truthful imitation of human values found in the region

around Fraserburgh. They could also be excuses for a poetic interpretation of place and character in which the usual demands of artistry have been subordinated to a local ethos, impressive and understandable in itself, but too stern, perhaps even perversely presbyterian in its approval of 'authority', to permit 'grace', plenitude of feeling, or secular harmonies.

In his role as a Scottish cultural middleman, Bruce has written much criticism. He is the author of *Festival in the North: the Story of the Edinburgh Festival* (London, 1975) and *'To Foster and Enrich': The First Fifty Years of the Saltire Society* (Edinburgh, 1986). He edited *The Scottish Literary Revival: An Anthology of Twentieth Century Poetry* (London and New York, 1968). He is co-editor of an excellent anthology about rural Scotland, *The Land Out There* (Aberdeen, 1991). [DED

BRUTUS, Dennis (1924–), was born in Salisbury (Harare), Zimbabwe, of South African parents, and in early life moved with them back to South Africa. He studied at Fort Hare and the University of Witwatersrand, and taught for fourteen years in South African high schools. Classified as Coloured, he campaigned and protested against the Apartheid regime, and this led to his arrest in 1963. He escaped whilst on bail but was re-arrested and shot in the back during a further escape attempt. He was sentenced to eighteen months hard labour and served his sentence at the penal colony of Robben Island. He emigrated to England in 1966 and then to the USA, where he is now professor of literature at Northwestern University. He has been president of SANROC (South African Non-Racial Olympic Committee), acting chairman of the International Campaign Against Racism in Sport, and United Nations Representative for International Defence and Aid.

Brutus's volumes of poetry, *Sirens Knuckles Boots* (Ibadan, 1963, Evanston, Ill., 1964), *Letters to Martha* (London, 1968), *Poems from Algiers* (Austin, Tex., 1970), and *Thoughts Abroad* by John Bruin (Del Valle, Tex., 1970) were republished with additional poems in *A Simple Lust* (London and New York, 1973). His other published works are *Stubborn Hope* (London and Washington, DC, 1978) and *Airs and Tributes* (Camden, NJ, 1989). In *Letters to Martha* Brutus excelled: gracefully poised lines, unextravagant emotions, perceptive observations of prison life. See *Understanding African Poetry* (London, 1982), by Ken Goodwin. [FO

BUCKLEY, Vincent (1925–88), was born at Romsey, Victoria (Australia), and educated at the universities of Melbourne and Cambridge. The first of his eight volumes of verse, *The World's Flesh*, appeared in Melbourne in 1954, while *Last Poems* was published posthumously in 1991, also in Melbourne. In this long career Buckley maintained grave central concerns: with provenance—his roots in rural Victoria and in Ireland—asking: 'How can I find my fathers in this darkness?'; with the Roman Catholic faith; with wives and families; with politics, especially its formal hypocrisies and the tactics of totalitarian regimes. In *Masters in Israel* (Sydney, 1961), Buckley described his father and himself as: 'Two small, self-wounding, fearful men.' Their relationship is treated at more length in the sequence 'Stroke', influenced by Robert *Lowell, in *Arcady & Other Places* (Melbourne and London, 1966). In that volume a group of political poems anticipated his autobiographical work *Cutting Green Hay* (1983), which dealt with sectarian and party politics in the 1950s, and *Memory, Ireland* (1985), an account of time spent in that country.

Buckley held a personal chair in English at Melbourne University for more than two decades and was an influential teacher. His literary criticism, including *Essays in Poetry, Mainly Australian* (Melbourne, 1957), *Poetry and Morality* (London, 1959), *Poetry and the Sacred* (London and New York, 1968), belongs to his younger days. From 1958 to 1964 he edited the pluralistic Catholic quarterly *Prospect*, and was also poetry editor of the *Bulletin* in this period. His volume of verse, *Golden Builders* (Sydney, 1976) showed Buckley in experimental vein, echoing Blake's prophetic poetry in his exploration of urban fragmentation. Later books dealt with Ireland—*The Pattern* (Dublin, 1979)—

and with the birth of a daughter—*Late-Winter Child* (Dublin, 1979). [PP

BUCKMASTER, Charles (1950–72), was born in the country town of Gruyere, Victoria (Australia), and left school shortly before matriculating. He worked briefly at various manual jobs and at the Source Bookshop in Melbourne. He became one of the leaders of the youthful poetry 'explosion' in the Vietnam War years, and edited the short-lived mini-mag *The Great Auk*. Although he travelled widely through Australia he is associated with the Melbourne avant-garde of the late 1960s. He committed suicide in 1972.

Because of his early death Buckmaster was seen as a tragic and representative figure of the confrontationalist period when a whole generation of Australian 19-year-olds were conscripted for active service in a war to which they had no commitment. Established values were challenged and alternatives explored. Buckmaster's life and his literary activities illustrate both romantic defiance and tragic self-doubt.

It was not until the publication of his *Collected Poems* (St Lucia, Qld., 1989), edited by Simon MacDonald, that a proper survey of Buckmaster's poetic output became possible. Not surprisingly for someone who died at 22, there is much ephemera, but his poems about his home area (most notably the long poem 'A history of the father') have gained a secure place in the poetry of his epoch. For further reference, see *Parnassus Mad Ward: Michael Dransfield and the New Australian Poetry*, by Livio Dobrez (St Lucia, Qld., 1990). [TWS

BUKOWSKI, Charles (1920–94), was born in Germany, and moved to America at the age of 2. For most of his life he has lived in and around Los Angeles, where he worked at a variety of menial jobs before gaining recognition as a writer in the Sixties. He stands at the centre of a group of Los Angeles-based writers who glorify a gritty street life that encompasses bars, race-tracks, and other seedy urban haunts. Bukowski thus represents the antithesis of the academic poet. Instead he hints at the possibility of a genuinely popular poetry; in the US he has a wide following among readers who do not generally keep up with contemporary poetry, and he is also much admired in Europe. This is undoubtedly to do with the candour and ease of his style, coupled with the raunchiness of his subject-matter; in many ways his work has more in common with rock music than with literature.

Yet Bukowski cannot be dismissed as a poet simply because he is popular, or because his poems are easy to read and full of racy or seamy items from his private life. In a sense his work is a natural culmination of the ongoing revolt against formalism, the academic, and the intellectual that has periodically energized American poetry since its inception. For Bukowski the poem is manifestly not sacred; its purpose is simply to record events and emotions with a compression and directness not available in prose (though he also writes novels and stories). While it is possible to detect in his work vestiges of modernist poetics, these elements are integrated within a seemingly artless, improvised utterance that exhibits no discernible formal structure. Bukowski makes fairly obvious use of free-verse devices like enjambment and indentation, but for the most part he shows little interest in technique. His effects are primarily narrative, and involve the collision of his own gruff, funny, idiomatic voice with the random incidents of his daily life.

His many books of poems have been published by small presses like Black Sparrow in Santa Barbara; his work is also included in *Penguin Modern Poets* 13 (1969).   [RG

BUNTING, Basil (1900–85), was born into a Quaker family in Northumberland, where he grew up and spent the latter part of his life. In between, however, he lived an adventurous, cosmopolitan existence. Educated at a Quaker boarding school in Yorkshire, he served six months in prison as a conscientious objector in 1918. The following year he went to London, where he did odd jobs and spent a year at the London School of Economics. In 1923 he went to Paris, met Ezra *Pound and worked for Ford

Madox *Ford on the *Transatlantic Review*, and then followed Pound to Rapallo in 1924. He worked for a time as a sailor, and subsequently spent a nomadic life in London, Germany, Italy, the United States, and the Canary Islands. During this period, with Pound's encouragement, he began publishing poetry and brought out his first book, *Redimiculum Matellarum*, in Milan in 1930. Pound's Faber *Activist Anthology* (1933) contained fifty pages of Bunting, and he became closely acquainted with another Poundian protégé, Louis *Zukofsky.

Bunting joined the RAF on the outbreak of war and was posted to Persia, partly on the strength of his having taught himself classical Persian in Rapallo. He fell deeply in love with the country and became Vice-Consul in Isfahan in 1945, marrying a Persian woman in 1948. His *Poems 1950* was published in Texas in 1950. After another stint in Italy, this time as a journalist, he returned to Persia as a correspondent for *The Times*, but was eventually expelled by Mosaddeq. He spent the rest of his life in Northumberland, doing odd jobs and working as a journalist on the local paper. With the encouragement of Tom *Pickard in 1963 he began to write again after a period of dryness, publishing in England for the first time in the 1960s: his name was made with the long poem *Briggflatts* in 1966. His *Collected Poems* was published in 1968. In the latter part of his life he was much in demand as a visiting poet at various American universities, and also had close ties with the University of Newcastle upon Tyne, which awarded him a D. Litt in 1971. There is a Bunting archive at the University of Durham.

Bunting's many short 'odes' make frequent reference to the scenes and episodes of his nomadic and bohemian life in France, Italy, and Persia, one of the finest (no. 36) being a meditation on the forms of Persian poetry compared to mosque architecture; and his many translations and versions, which he calls 'Overdrafts', testify to an exceptional inwardness with a number of different languages and cultures. His long poem *The Spoils* (1951) is a vivid evocation of historic and contemporary Persia, containing a powerful critique of the results of British imperialism in that country. The longer poem held a continual fascination for Bunting, from *Villon* (1925) to *Briggflatts* (1966), presumably partly as homage to Pound, whose *Cantos* he celebrated in 'On the Fly-Leaf of Pound's Cantos', referring to them as 'the Alps'. In the *Collected Poems* all his long poems are grouped under the general title 'Sonatas'; and, although he talks rather speciously in interviews about musical form in relation to poetic composition, the analogy does have force. Repeated images, reiterated motifs, the sense of variations being performed on central themes, all help to give his work an integrity of organization rare in the modernist long poem, and certainly not apparent in Pound's *Cantos*.

One of Basil Bunting's major themes is the necessity for leaving home and the constant desire to return there. *Briggflatts* employs a number of Northumbrian dialect words; in several sections it takes elements of the Dark Age history of the north of England as its theme; it uses, in places, a heavy alliteration and abrupt syntax which strongly recall Anglo-Saxon poetic forms. These obeisances to Bunting's origins are combined, however, with elaborate notations of his travels and reading: the poem's imagery of voyaging takes in references to his life in London, Italy, and Persia which justify its subtitle, 'An Autobiography'. If there is an element of Poundian inclusiveness in this, the poem is also indebted to one of Bunting's other poetic heroes, Wordsworth, for its return, across the years, to a 'spot of time' from Bunting's childhood. Having lived most of his life well outside the usual framework of literary production and reception, Bunting had to wait until late in life for any acclaim in his own country; but his has since come to seem a significant modern reputation. A revised edition of the *Collected Poems* was published in London and New York in 1978, and a volume of *Uncollected Poems*, ed. Richard Caddel, appeared in 1991 (Oxford). See also Carroll F. Terrell (ed.), *Basil Bunting: Man and Poet* (1981), and Peter Makin, *Bunting: The Shaping of his Verse* (Oxford, 1992). *The Complete Poems* (combining *Collected and Uncollected Poems*) is due to appear in 1994 (Oxford and New York).

[NC

BURKE, Kenneth (1897–1986), was born in Pittsburgh, Pennsylvania, and educated at Ohio State and Columbia universities. His wide intellectual interests and talents were evident from the start: he studied Marx and Freud; did research for the Laura Spellman Rockefeller Foundation (1926–7) and editorial work for the Bureau of Social Hygiene (1928); was music critic for the **Dial* (1927–9) and the *Nation* (1934–6); and translated several German books (including Mann's *Death in Venice*, 1925; revised edn., 1970). His first book of critical essays, *Counter-Statement* (1931), was shortly followed by his only novel, *Towards a Better Life* (1932). Since 1938 he taught and lectured at several universities and published many critical books. *Permanence and Change: An Anatomy of Purpose* (1935) was an attempt to reconcile his growing Marxist sympathies with his earlier aestheticism. His search for an all-inclusive intellectual framework, however, culminated in 'dramatism', the purposive theory of language described in *A Grammar of Motives* (1945) and *A Rhetoric of Motives* (1950), which sees—and analyses—all forms of language as revelations of motive.

Burke began writing as a poet but has been much more prolific, and widely read, as a literary and philosophical critic. His poems are all lyrics, as he defines the term: terse summaries of momentary moods and motives. They are accessible, light, playful, and witty, despite their frequently abstract and metaphysical themes; 'ideally', he says, 'the complete lyrist would love ideas at least as strongly as sensations, and preferably more'. His criticism has often been attacked for its proliferation of abstract terms, abstruse arguments, and frivolous associative leaps; but his analysis of rhetoric is now seen to have anticipated the cross-disciplinary and highly theoretical work of Michel Foucault and other post-structuralists.

See *Collected Poems, 1915–67* (Berkeley, Calif., and London, 1968); *The Complete White Oxen: Collected Shorter Fiction* (Berkeley, 1968); *The Philosophy of Literary Form: Studies in Symbolic Action* (Berkeley, 1941; revised edn., New York, 1957; London, 1959); and for assessments of all his writing, *Critical Responses to Kenneth Burke, 1924–1966*, ed. William Rueckert (Minneapolis, 1969).

[NE

BURNSHAW, Stanley (1906–) was born in New York City. He attended Columbia University, the University of Poitiers, and the University of Paris, and received a BA from the University of Pittsburgh in 1925 and an MA from Cornell in 1933. From 1933 to 1936 he was an editor of *New Masses*; from 1939 to 1958 founder, president, and editor-in-chief of the Dryden Press; and from 1958 to 1967 vice-president at the publisher Holt, Rinehart, and Winston. He received the National Institute of Arts and Letters award for literature in 1971.

Burnshaw's varied literary output includes verse (*In the Terrified Radiance*, New York, 1972), criticism (*The Seamless Web*, New York and London, 1970, 1991), fiction (*The Refusers*, New York, 1981), translation (*The Poem Itself*, New York, 1960, 1989; London, 1964; *The Modern Hebrew Poem Itself*, New York, 1965; Cambridge, Mass., 1989), and biography (*Robert Frost Himself*, New York, 1986). Central to his work is an insistence on the indissoluble unity of mind and body in all human experience, including the production of art; this forms the theme of *The Seamless Web* and, together with the evocation and acceptance of mortality, the preoccupation of much of his poetry. *A Stanley Burnshaw Reader* (Athens, Ga., 1990) conveniently samples his work. [RZ

BURNSIDE, John (1955–), was born in Dunfermline, Fife, and read English and European studies at Cambridge College of Arts and Technology. He works as a risk analyst in computers and lives in Bramley, Surrey. He received a Scottish Arts Council Literary Award for his first collection *The hoop* in 1988.

The hoop (Manchester, 1989) combines autobiographical elements with history and natural observation. These staple ingredients are refreshed by quiet intensity and meticulous detail. Burnside offers a highly personal account of parts of England and Scotland, rarely touching on public themes. He dramatizes the pleasures and anxieties of ordinariness and privacy: a lamplit study and its hoarded objects ('The hoop') are in one way a defence against the terrors of the past and the uncertainties of identity;

in another they are the imagined threshold of a quite different place: 'everybody, knows | magic is somewhere else, where no one goes' ('Inside'). His romanticism is intensified in *Common Knowledge* (London, 1991), where a religious dimension clearly emerges (for example, in the prose poems 'Annunciations'). Burnside's most recent collection, *Feast Days* (London, 1992) continues this development, negotiating between the loss of religious assurance ('a life recalled, that could not happen now') and the persistence of the uncanny. Stylistically, Burnside is walking the line between scruple and hyperaesthetic affectation. [SO'B

BUTLER, Guy (1918–), was born at Cradock, Cape Province, and educated at Rhodes University, Grahamstown. During the war he served with the South African forces in the Middle East and Italy, after which he took up a scholarship at Oxford. From 1948 to 1950 he lectured at the University of Witwatersrand, and from 1952 until 1983 he was professor of English at Rhodes University. He served as English editor of the Afrikaans journal *Standpunte*, and helped found the poetry journal *New Coin*. Several of his plays have been performed by the South African National Theatre.

Butler's poems reflect the tension between his two 'homes': the civilized Europe of art and literature; the artless Africa of savage, history-less landscapes and barbarous native peoples. He considers 'old-fashioned techniques' most suitable for Africa's shallow cultural soil; and his forms are regular, his imagery often literary in origin. In 'Myths' the alien veld is suddenly familiarized by the pastoral vision of a guitar-strumming black Orpheus with his Eurydice. In 'Cape Coloured Batman' Butler evokes the exotic romance of his servant's mixed ancestry, and the pathos of one whom a 'touch of the tarbrush' has cast into history's shade. In 'Home Thoughts', failing to find himself on Europe's maps, he resumes the dubious task of imposing Apollonian order on the Dionysiac barbarity of his African home.

A *Selected Poems* was published in Johannesburg in 1975, and a number of Butler's poems are included in *A New Book of South African Verse in English*, ed. Guy Butler and Chris Mann (Cape Town, 1979). See also *African English Poetry: A Modern Perspective*, by Michael Chapman (Johannesburg, 1984). [JB

BUTLIN, Ron (1949–), lives in Edinburgh where he was born. Brought up in Hightae, a small village near Dumfries, he was educated at Edinburgh University and has held a number of writer-in-residence posts in Scotland.

Butlin's poems often view things from unusual angles, and have accordingly been variously tagged surrealist, imagist, and erotic, but he is essentially a lyric poet. Music is a recurrent theme, as in the longish title-poem of *Ragtime in Unfamiliar Bars* (London, 1985), and Butlin employs a range of subtle free-verse rhythms. The bleak side to his work is evident in the stories in *The Tilting Room* (Edinburgh, 1983) and his first novel, *The Sound of My Voice* (Edinburgh, 1987), the latter on the nervous breakdown of an alcoholic businessman 'thirty-four years old and already two-thirds destroyed'.

Butlin's first two booklets, *Stretto* (Edinburgh, 1976) and *Creatures Tamed by Cruelty* (Edinburgh, 1979), contained some poems in Scots, but he now writes exclusively in English. He has translated poems from a number of other languages, including Chinese in *The Exquisite Instrument: Imitations from the Chinese* (Edinburgh, 1982). [JDB

BYNNER, Witter (1881–1968), is most commonly remembered as one of the perpetrators of 'Spectrism', perhaps the century's major literary hoax. Writing as Emanuel Morgan, Bynner published with Arthur Davison *Ficke (as Anne Knish) the poems collected in *Spectra: A Book of Poetic Experiments* (New York, 1916), which found enthusiastic support among poets as radically different as Edgar Lee *Masters, John Gould *Fletcher, and William Carlos *Williams. William Jay *Smith's *The Spectra Hoax* (Middletown, Conn., 1961) contains the complete text of *Spectra* as well as other 'Spectric' poems by Bynner, Ficke, and their subsequent collaborator 'Elijah Hay' (Marjorie Allen Seiffert).

Although Spectrism was initially intended as a spoof of literary movements like *Imagism, Bynner found that writing under the mask of Emanuel Morgan freed him from the restraints he had felt in his early poems and so continued using it in such works as those collected in *Pins for Wings* (New York, 1920).

Shortly after the Spectra episode, Bynner, in collaboration with the Chinese scholar Kiang Kang-hu, began translating poems from the Chinese anthology *Three Hundred Pearls of the T'ang Dynasty*. These translations, collected in *The Jade Mountain* (New York, 1929), may be Bynner's major achievement. Few have translated Chinese poetry as well. One who did was Kenneth *Rexroth, whose translations of Tu Fu were undertaken largely at Bynner's instigation.

Bynner was capable of a great range of poetry, from witty social verse to deeply expressive lyrical works dealing with his homosexuality and, as he said in 'No Anodyne', 'perfect loneliness'.

The Works of Witter Bynner (New York, 1978–9) include *Selected Poems, Light Verse and Satires, Prose Pieces*, and *The Chinese Translations*. The first of these volumes offers an extensive biographical introduction by James Craft and a judicious critical introduction by Richard *Wilbur. [EHF

C

Calendar of Modern Letters, The. In 1933 F. R. Leavis, introducing a selection from the critical work in the *Calendar of Modern Letters*, said the approach could 'fairly be held up as a model for a critical journal'. Frank Kermode, reviewing a reissue of the journal many years later, called it a paradigm. Their praise does not seem exaggerated.

The *Calendar* lasted for no more than two-and-a-half years. It first appeared in March 1925 as a monthly, became a quarterly in April 1926, and closed its doors in July of the following year with 'A Valediction Forbidding Mourning', asserting the validity, not necessarily of all the work printed, but of the attitude behind the editorial choice: 'The value of a review must be judged by its attitude to the living literature of the time (which includes such works of the past as can be absorbed by the contemporary sensibility) and there should naturally be some homogeneity of view among the more regular contributors.'

Such homogeneity, more easily recognized than described, certainly marked the approach of the editors Edgell *Rickword and Douglas Garman, and their chief coadjutor Bertram *Higgins. It showed in an approach to imaginative writing that adopted no particular social or political stance, yet was aware that to consider any literary work outside the context of its time must leave a yawning gap of interpretation and some inadequacies of understanding. Both in their sympathies and their sharpness, the editors and their principal reviewers produced critical views of the best writing in the period that remain interesting and valid. What was something like corporate criticism can be seen at its finest in the 'Scrutinies' of established reputations that began to appear from the first number with Rickword on Barrie, and were later embodied in the two volumes of *Scrutinies* that gave Leavis a title for his periodical, *Scrutiny*.

The Scrutinies are not, however, the prime beauty of the *Calendar*, although it was an almost unerring critical sense that chose the fiction and poetry. The list of contributors reads like a roll-call of the best writers in that brief period, writing usually at the top of their form. *Lawrence's 'The Princess', boldly run over three issues, stories by William Gerhardi, Mary Butts, Stephen Hudson, Liam O'Flaherty, and translations from Babel, Leonov, Pirandello, and Chekhov; Aldous *Huxley on Breughel and long extracts from Wyndham *Lewis's *The Lion and the Fox* and *The Dithyrambic Spectator*; that long, curious comic poem 'The Marmosite's Miscellany' by Robert *Graves masquerading as John Doyle, and poems by Laura Gottschalk (later *Riding) and Hart *Crane, *Ransom, and *Tate, Americans then almost unknown in Britain.

Was it true, as Leavis suggested, that since the *Calendar* could not find support, 'what hope can there be for any serious critical journal?' The 'Valediction' does not say that the financial position enforces the periodical's closure, but that an unspecified 'different organization' is needed, which will avert the problem of having 'the leaks periodically stopped by a generous patron'. It says also that a '"political" attitude' might be economically helpful, although it would be 'an abuse of function'. It must surely be relevant that within a few years Garman had become a Communist Party functionary, and Rickword a very active sympathizer. A magazine like the *Calendar* could not have been edited by those who no longer thought of an emphatically 'political' attitude as an abuse of function.

[JGS

Cambridge School, The. Individual poets and informal movements of writers emerge continuously from Oxford and Cambridge, but the term 'Cambridge School' refers to a particular grouping who began writing in the later 1960s, some of whom studied or worked in the city. J. H. *Prynne is a central figure, together with Andrew Crozier, John James, Wendy Mulford, Douglas Oliver, and Peter Riley, all of whom continue to write. These poets initially used self-publication as a means of encouraging an active interchange of poetry and ideas within a diffuse network of writers and readers. *The English Intelligencer* (1967–8) was the circulating worksheet which provided the forum for this exchange. The term 'school', applied to this loose association of individuals, is only a retrospective category, as is so often the case.

Self-publication was partly dictated by the singularity of their aims and of the poems which they wrote. The group drew on a wide range of American and European influences, reacting against the state of poetry then prevailing in Britain. Their poetry at its best articulates a new sense of subjectivity in relation to the world as if freshly received, and combines lyric intensities with ethical concerns. The Ferry Press, edited by Andrew Crozier, published collections of poems in striking format and to a very high standard. Tim Longville and John *Riley edited the *Grosseteste Review* and Press (1966–75) with similar energy. *A Various Art* (Manchester, 1987), edited by Crozier and Longville, offers a representative selection of the poetry. *Poets on Writing. Britain, 1970–1991* (London, 1992), edited by Denise Riley, collects statements from writers involved in the initial activity, and also from poets subsequently influenced by their work.

[NW

CAMERON, (John) Norman (1905–53), the son of a Scottish cleric who was senior presidency chaplain in Bombay, went to school at Fettes, and then to Oriel College, Oxford. He published poems in *The Fettesian* and *Oxford Poetry*, and later became one of the most frequent contributors to *New Verse*. In person he was tall, thin, and fair, a bohemian but slightly intimidating character, contemptuous (Geoffrey *Grigson said in a brief memoir) of most kinds of literary ambition, 'a literate original, not a literary man'. He spent the years from 1930 to 1932 as an education officer in Southern Nigeria, and later became an advertising copy-writer, work which he enjoyed. He is said to have been the inventor of the expression 'Night Starvation', a condition curable by taking Horlicks, and he wrote for the *Graves-*Riding magazine *Epilogue* an article on 'The Fairy-Tale Element in Advertising'.

In the Second World War he worked with a small group that included the film director Alexander Mackendrick and the literary editor T. R. Fyvel, producing political propaganda. He married three times, was a hard drinker, and became a Roman Catholic convert two years before his death. *The Winter House* (1935) was the only original collection published during his lifetime. *Collected Poems*, with an introduction by his close friend Robert Graves, appeared in 1957, and the *Complete Poems*, which contains a dozen more poems, in 1985 (both London). He was also a notable translator, of Rimbaud and Villon and much French prose, including *Candide, Cousin Pons*, and Stendhal's letters.

Cameron's total poetic output, including his juvenilia, amounted to no more than seventy-odd short pieces, several ironic or deliberately comic, yet the slightest of them makes an impact, and the earliest are marked by the Manichaean struggle between puritanism and paganism that ordered his life. An early poem, 'Nunc Scio Quid Sit Amor' expresses his longing for and terror of the 'fierce outlander' who visits him from the land 'where the wild rainbow like a great giraffe | Curves down its neck to drink upon the sea . . . I fear you and I fear you, barbarous Love. | You are no citizen of my country.'

But Cameron's poetic country was just this divided land. The outrageous images, like that of the 'wild rainbow', are always under the strict control of what Graves called the Presbyterian moralist; the metres are definite, the rhymes exact, the insoluble problem stated over and over in various forms but always sharply and with a sense of style. 'The Dirty Little Accuser' is condemnatory about an unnamed Dylan *Thomas, but the poet reflects that when the 'crapulous lout' has been ejected his accusation can never be answered. 'The Invader' contemptuously dismisses Nazism in terms of its greed, not for conquest but for love. In technical terms Cameron owed a debt to Graves, perhaps something to Laura Riding, yet he hardly wrote a derivative or conventional phrase. There is something merciless about the way in which he turned his deepest feelings into demeaning comedy: 'When you confess your sins before a parson, | You find it no great effort to disclose | Your crimes of murder, bigamy and arson, | But can you tell him that you pick your nose?' Below the surface this is no more lighthearted than *Larkin, and behind the metronomic exactness, the contempt for casualness and concern for style, was a passionate seriousness that gives his few poems their strange authority.

Collected Poems and Selected Translations, ed. Warren Hope and Jonathan Barker, came out in 1990 (London).   [JGS

CAMPBELL, Alistair (Te Ariki) (1925–), was born at Penrhyn, Cook Islands, of a Rarotongan mother and a New Zealand father. At the age of 8 he emigrated to Dunedin where he lived for eleven years. The landscape of Central Otago furnished images for his first book, *Mine Eyes Dazzle* (Christchurch, 1950). After moving to Wellington in 1944 he joined the school publications branch of the Department of Education, where he remained until his retirement in 1972. He married the poet Fleur *Adcock, with whom he had two sons, and after their divorce married Meg Andersen. They have three children.

Following a period in a psychiatric hospital he moved to Pukerua Bay overlooking the island of Kapiti, former stronghold of the famous Maori fighting chief Te Rauparaha who became a powerful presence in his poetry. Other Polynesian themes followed. Campbell is a lyric poet in the tradition of *Yeats, but for him feelings matter more than ideas. His *Collected Poems* (Martinborough) appeared in 1981.   [FMcK

CAMPBELL, David (1915–79), was born near Adelong in the Monaro district of New South Wales, and educated in Australia and at Cambridge. He served with distinction in the Second World War in the RAAF, and after the war lived on various properties in the Canberra area, dividing his life between farming and writing. In 1964 he became poetry editor of the *Australian*, and edited *Australian Poetry 1966* and *Modern Australian Poetry* (1970).

Like other emerging poets of the 1940s, Campbell used traditional forms in his attempt to link popular Australian subject-matter to the European tradition of pastoral and the metaphysical lyric. He focused on characteristic Australian subjects ('Harry Pearce', 'The Stockman') in an attempt to capture a vanishing world. He also experimented with the ballad, the tall story, and the pastoral sequence in 'Cocky's Calendar' and 'Works and Days'. The lyricism of early poems like 'Night Sowing' and 'Who Points the Swallow' gives way in his post-1970 volumes to restless experiment. *The Branch of Dodona* (1970) reinterprets classical myth to comment on the modern world; sequences like 'Starting from Central Station' and 'Deaths and Pretty Cousins' are autobiographical variations on life-studies themes, influenced by *Roethke and *Lowell, while series like 'Ku-Ring-Gai Rock Carvings' and 'Letters to a Friend' experiment with haiku-like arrangements. Campbell's later volumes free themselves from the formal polish of his early work and have the qualities of notebook entries and sketches. Part of his work consisted of translations and imitations from the Russian (published in collaboration with Rosemary *Dobson). He also wrote two volumes of short stories, *Evening Under Lamplight* (1959) and *Flame and Shadow* (1976). *Collected Poems*, (Sydney, 1989.)   [VS

CAMPBELL, George (1916–), was born in Panama of Jamaican parents, and educated in Kingston and New York. In the 1940s he was one of the poets associated with Edna Manley's *Focus* group.

Often biblically allusive, his poems tend to have a liturgical flavour, but at the service of a secular, and politically radical outlook. 'Holy', which opens with the lines, 'Holy be the white head of a Negro | Sacred be the black flax of a black child', was quoted by Derek *Walcott in *Another Life*, very much as a tribute. 'In the Slums', on the other hand, ends with great simplicity of imagery: 'Here | Here is | The world we accept | From our glass houses.' Another poem, 'History Makers', graphically describes women stone-breakers, and focuses on them as symbolic of women's endurance in general.

Collections include *First Poems* (Kingston, Jam., 1945), which was reprinted in vol. 10 of the Yale series, *Critical Studies on Black Life and Culture* (1981), and *Earth Testament* (Kingston, 1983). See also *From Our Yard: Jamaican Poetry Since Independence*, ed. Pamela Mordecai (Kingston, 1987). [MR

CAMPBELL, (Ignatius) Roy(ston) (Dunnachie) (1902–57), was born in Natal, came to England in 1918 and published in 1924 *The Flaming Terrapin*, an allegory in which the terrapin stands for the renewal of life. After returning to South Africa he joined forces in 1926 with William *Plomer and, later, Laurens van der Post to produce *Voorslag* (Whiplash), a literary magazine that satirized everything held sacred by the Afrikaners. He compounded the offence with *The Wayzgoose* (1928), a satirical poem about South African life.

Adamastor (1930) a volume of exuberant lyrical power, written after his move to Provence, was followed by *The Georgiad* (1931), a long, virulent attack on the Bloomsbury Group in which his contempt for their work was sharpened by his fury at his wife's involvement with Vita *Sackville-West and her associates. *Flowering Reeds* (1933) marked a return to a gentler lyricism, and a further collection of poems, *Mithraic Emblems*, was published in 1936.

In *Broken Record* (1934), a prose autobiography, Campbell paraded his sympathies with Fascism and in 1935 he became a Roman Catholic.

Flowering Rifle (1939), a strident eulogy of Franco as the upholder of Christian values, is one of the nastiest and worst poems ever written by a man of Campbell's gifts. His claim, made in this mixture of rodomontade and religiosity, to have fought for General Franco is false; but, greatly to his credit, he volunteered in 1942 for the British army in the Second World War and spent most of his military service in East Africa as a coast-watcher, after training briefly with Wingate's commando force.

Sons of the Mistral (1941) is a selection of his poems. *Talking Bronco* (1946), a disappointing volume, contains a number of accomplished but lightweight poems about East Africa, of which the liveliest are 'Heartbreak Camp' and 'Dreaming Spires', Campbell's playful name for giraffes.

There are, however, two poems in the collection that rank among the finest verse he ever wrote. One is the sonnet, 'Luis de Camões', in which he claims an affinity with the sixteenth-century Portuguese poet, the author of *The Lusiads*, who had, like himself, been a Catholic and a servant of Spain, and had sailed past Fort Jesus to endure the life of a common soldier in Mombasa: 'He shouldered high his voluntary Cross, | Wrestled his hardship into forms of beauty, | And taught his gorgon destinies to sing.'

The second poem of outstanding merit in *Talking Bronco*, a version of *En Una Noche Oscura* by St John of the Cross, foreshadows Campbell's major post-war undertakings. He translated a dozen Spanish and Portuguese works of fiction, among them *Cousin Basilio*, the nineteenth-century masterpiece of Eca de Quieroz. Campbell's verse translations are the crown of his poetic achievement. *The Poems of St John of the Cross* (1951) and his version of Baudelaire's *Les Fleurs du Mal* (1952) are worthy of the originals. His translations and appraisal of Lorca in 1952 may seem an unlikely tribute from an aggressively heterosexual Roman Catholic apologist for General Franco to a Communist homosexual murdered by the General's supporters. But apart from the aberrations of *Flowering Rifle* and of the autobiographies—the second, *Light on a*

Dark Horse (1951), reiterated the old beliefs—all Campbell's work was inspired by a generous love of poetry and a pursuit of imaginative truth.

Some readers find certain of Campbell's most celebrated poems, such as 'Tristan da Cunha' and 'Choosing a Mast', too self-consciously heroic and elaborately rhetorical. Yet their exuberance and élan carry them irresistibly to their triumphant conclusions, and his shorter lyrics, such as 'The Serf', 'The Zulu Girl', and 'The Sisters', burn with a controlled sensuousness.

Campbell was a quarrelsome and, at times, a truculent figure. He fell out with his co-editors of *Voorslag*; he pursued a variety of literary vendettas; and his married life was stormy. Although some of his accusations against Bloomsbury may have been justified, his diatribes against Communists, homosexuals, and wowsers (a favourite term of abuse) were often ludicrous and wearisome. Yet all these flaws were powerless to spoil the vein of pure lyricism and the nobility of mind that inform the finest of his poems.

Campbell died in a car crash in Portugal. His *Collected Poems* were published in three volumes in 1949, 1957, and 1960 (London), the third volume being devoted to his translations. See also *Selected Poems* (Oxford, 1982), ed. Peter F. Alexander, author of *Roy Campbell* (Oxford, 1982).   [JPr

CAREW, Jan (Rynveld) (1925–), was born in Agricola, British Guiana (now Guyana), and educated at Berbice High School and at several universities in the United States and Europe. Professor of African and American studies at Northwestern University, he has travelled widely and now lives in Chicago.

Though best known as a prolific novelist, he has been writing poetry throughout his career. His poems, in fact, tend to explore in purer form than the novels the historical layers which make up the West Indian identity. 'The Cliffs at Manzanilla', for instance, is a sombre meditation on the Carib Indians, whose prayers to their gods 'were lost like echoes of the thrashing surf | in a green indifferent hinterland of silence'. Elegiac

in tone, the poem's intensity would have been difficult to sustain in terms of prose fiction. Aphoristic conciseness characterizes other poems; for instance, 'The memory of home is like the bread of life | to those who roam' ('Requiem for My Sister').

His poems have been published in *Streets of Eternity* (Georgetown, Guyana, 1952) and *Sea Drums in My Blood* (Port of Spain, Trinidad, 1980). Among his most notable novels are *Black Midas* (London, 1958), *The Last Barbarian* (London, 1961), and *Moscow is Not My Mecca* (London, 1964).   [MR

CARROLL, Paul. See *Big Table*.

CARRUTH, Hayden (1921–), born in Connecticut and educated at the universities of North Carolina and Chicago, has spent most of his life in New England and upper New York state; he began publishing collections of his work in 1959. Several well-regarded books followed, particularly *The Bloomingdale Papers* (Athens, Ga.), published in 1975 but written twenty-two years earlier when he was a patient in an asylum.

With the publication of *Brothers, I Have Loved You All* (Riverdale, NY, 1978), Carruth found his own voice. Utilizing New England character and diction with a facility equal to Robert *Frost's, many of his strongest poems in this and subsequent volumes involve stoic resolve in the face of hardship and defeat.

In his introduction to *Effluences from the Sacred Caves* (Ann Arbor, Mich., 1983), a collection of essays and reviews, he said that he defined himself 'only *against* the Platonic and Romantic aspirations', which, none the less, held for him 'a powerful, though I think false, allure'. In this he turned against the transcendental ambitions characteristic of many of his New England predecessors. Carruth's New England is a land of pragmatists and sceptics. Given his very hardedged sensibility, it is not surprising that he also includes William Carlos *Williams and Ezra *Pound among his masters.

See his *Selected Poetry* (New York and London, 1985) and *Collected Shorter Poems: 1946–1991*

(Port Townsend, Wash., 1992). See also his long meditative poem, *The Sleeping Beauty* (New York, 1982).   [EHF

CARSON, Ciaran (1948–), was born in Belfast into an Irish-speaking family, and educated at Queen's University Belfast. He worked in the Civil Service, as a teacher, and as a musician, before becoming Traditional Arts Officer for the Northern Ireland Arts Council.

The New Estate (1976), his first collection, though promising, consisted largely of a poetry of domesticity. His distinctive voice appeared in his second collection, *The Irish for No* (1987). There he began to use with assurance the long line which is a hallmark of his writing and which allows him the room to develop his free-wheeling narratives. This trend was continued in his third volume, *Belfast Confetti* (1989), in which his concern with Belfast was also intensified. Through an attentiveness to representation Carson avoids sensationalism and sentimentality. He considers that maps and language can never capture the shifting urban landscape: language is always turned aside into digression; maps show roads which no longer exist. The only mode of narrative is digressive, the only map of the city is the city itself. The metaphor 'Belfast confetti'—the name given to the bricolage of nuts, bolts, and half-bricks used by rioters—balances the elements of danger and celebration which Carson successfully combines in poetry which is exhilarating, funny, and exact.

The New Estate and Other Poems (Oldcastle, Co. Meath, 1988) reprints his first collection with additional poems; his other collections are still in print: *The Irish for No* (Newcastle upon Tyne, 1987); *Belfast Confetti* (Oldcastle, Co. Meath, 1989).   [EH

CARTER, Martin (Wylde) (1927–), was born in Georgetown, British Guiana (now Guyana), and educated there, at Queen's College. He was actively involved in the nationalist movement, and a spell of three months in detention for his political activities led to *Poems of Resistance* (London, 1954), the collection which established his reputation. This volume reflects Carter's commitment to the People's Progressive Party of Dr Cheddi Jagan, and its Marxist orientation. The stark, militant rhetoric of a poem like 'I Clench My Fist', however, is counterbalanced by the compassion and startling imagery of one like 'Cartman of Dayclean'. Carter at his best also fuses the confessional and the political, as in 'I Come from the Nigger Yard'.

After independence, Carter joined the cabinet of Prime Minister Forbes Burnham as Minister of Public Information and Broadcasting, and represented Guyana at the United Nations. His later poetry loses some of its political urgency, but it gains in sibylline irony.

Poems of Succession (London and Port of Spain, 1977) also contains poetry from his earlier books. His last collection to date is *Poems of Affinity: 1978–1980* (Georgetown, 1980). *Hinterland: Caribbean Poetry from the West Indies and Britain*, ed. E. A. Markham (Newcastle upon Tyne, 1989), contains a substantial selection of his poems, and also a probing interview with Peter Trevis.   [MR

CARVER, Raymond (1939–88), is best known as a short-story writer, but his interest as a poet is oddly independent of his prose, though perhaps a growth from it, at least in terms of a certain spare and tight-lipped style. The stories of Carver operate often in a low-keyed, blue-collar world, where a stark ashcan brilliance illuminates a sort of bleak heroism. These stories take place in the darkness at the edge of town.

The best of Carver's stories are likely to last, but his poems remain more controversial. Most of them strike the ear with a deliberate flatness of diction, an absence of metaphor, and an air of being arranged in roughly chopped lengths, as if a backwoodsman has been at a copse of prose with an axe. But his plain look is part of a sound American tradition, rooted in *Frost and *Jeffers, flowering in Robert Penn *Warren. Indeed, the very extremity of Carver's drive towards casualness—his conscious willingness to leave his finished text with the freshness of a first draft or note for a poem—is what gives his work its genuine originality and importance.

We are being invited to accept in verse what was once very difficult to accept even in prose when we had it offered first by Hemingway: the gas turned down towards its lowest level without the flame going out.

The justification for this bare style can perhaps be found most easily in the poignant and bitter experiences from which Carver has taken his material. We form a relationship with a persona—close to Carver but not quite him—who has endured alcoholism, loves hunting and the American wilderness, and is dying of cancer. This last element dangerously qualifies our responses, but inevitably so. We watch a brave man counting out his time, seeing this happen through a verse medium as clear as glass, the perfect, neutral focus for our emotions.

Carver's collections include: *Near Klamath* (Sacramento, Calif. 1968), *Winter Insomnia* (Santa Cruz, Calif. 1970), *At Night the Salmon Move* (Santa Barbara, Calif. 1976), *In a Marine Light: Selected Poems* (London, 1987), and *A New Path to the Waterfall* (New York and London, 1989); see also *Fires: Essays, Poems, Stories* (London, 1985).   [GMacB

CASSITY, Turner (1929–), was born in Jackson, Mississippi, where he grew up, and was educated at Millsaps College, BA 1951; Stanford University, MA, 1952; and—after two years in the US Army—at Columbia University, MS, 1955. At Stanford University he became associated with Yvor *Winters's *Stanford School.

Cassity's extensive travels include South and Central America, Russia, Hong Kong, Europe, the West Indies, Australia, and West Africa. He lived for three years in Johannesburg and Pretoria. In 1991 he retired as catalogue librarian in the library of Emory University after twenty-nine years of service.

The locales of his poems are as geographically far-flung and exotic as his travels, but the extreme variety of place and subject is given unity by several dominant themes—social injustice, greed, vanity, hypocrisy, lust, and vulgarity of taste. He is primarily a satirist. In his poetic procedure he employs logical structure and conventional prosody, but in the confines of his strict forms there is a variety of rhythm and an impressive display of exotic and unconventional imagery and diction. Occasionally there are poems of serious metaphysical substance, such as his meditations on chance and determinism in 'Calvin at the Casino'; on time versus beauty, in the ingenious 'A Clock with a Mirror Face, Presented to a Lady'; and on death in 'Allerseen', all from his first book, *Watchboy, What of the Night?* (Middletown, Conn., 1966). Caustic comment on contemporary culture continues in *Steeplejacks in Babel* (Boston, 1973), notably in 'Off the Freeway', and 'The Shropshire Lad in Limehouse'. There is a heartless dissection of the heritage of imperialism in the South African poems and in the play on Cecil Rhodes in *Yellow for Peril, Black for Beauty* (New York, 1975). *The Defense of the Sugar Islands* (Los Angeles, 1975) is a psychological study of an American soldier who, during the Korean War, is stationed in Puerto Rico, far from the military action. *Hurricane Lamp* (Chicago, 1986) and *Between the Chains* (Chicago, 1991) are Cassity's most recent books.   [DS

CATALANO, Gary (1947–), was born in Brisbane but soon moved to Kellyville, on the outskirts of Sydney, where his Italian father was a market gardener. He attended Trinity Grammar School in Sydney, but left at the age of 16 to begin an intensive course of self-education. Without any formal training he managed to become one of Australia's leading art critics, an achievement recognized in 1986 when he was appointed by the Melbourne *Age* as its art correspondent. He has published three volumes of art criticism and a collection of short stories, in addition to his poetry.

Catalano's early poems, in *Remembering the Rural Life* (St Lucia, Qld., 1978), are touchingly detailed childhood recollections, but this first book already bore indications of the minimalist direction his poetry was later to take, concluding with a group of tersely introspective meditations. In *Heaven of Rags* (Sydney, 1982) and *Slow Tennis* (St Lucia, 1986) his verse became increasingly abstract, cryptic, and refined, its form attenuated in ultra-short lines and repetitive two- or three-line stanzas, until, in *Fresh Linen* (St Lucia, 1989), he produced a volume of prose poems from which even content had been omitted.   [JG

CAUDWELL, Christopher (Sprigg, Christopher St John) (1907–37), was born in London and educated at Ealing Priory School, which he left in 1922 to work as a journalist. Between then and his death he wrote eight thrillers and five books on aviation under his own name. At the end of 1935 he joined the Communist Party; and in December 1936 drove an ambulance to Spain. There he joined the International Brigade. He was killed on 12 February 1937, his first day in action.

At his death, Caudwell left studies of science, literature, and society written under the influence of Marxism: *Illusion and Reality* (1937); *Studies in a Dying Culture* (1938); *The Crisis in Physics* (1939); and *Further Studies in a Dying Culture* (1949). Of these, *Illusion and Reality*—'A Study of the Sources of Poetry'—is his outstanding and lasting work.

From an early age Caudwell wrote poetry, and a selection appeared as *Collected Poems* in 1939. Because of his death in Spain, Caudwell became a figure of legend; and the legend is supported by *Illusion and Reality*, but not by the poems. His poetry is bright and energetic; but its intellectual radicalism is not assimilated to an individual use of imagery, diction, or form. *Collected Poems* (Manchester, 1986) has an informative introduction.   [ATT

CAUSLEY, Charles (1917–), was born in Launceston, Cornwall, and has lived there ever since. He attended the local grammar school, and later worked in an office before serving in the Royal Navy, 1940–6. On demobilization Causley trained as a teacher and subsequently worked in schools ('thirty years in chalk Siberias') before resigning in his fifties to become a full-time author. He remains based in Cornwall but has increasingly ventured across the world to take up literary appointments in Australia, Canada, and the USA.

Causley published plays in the Thirties—*Runaway* (1936), *The Conquering Hero* (1937)—but had to wait until 1951 before his first collection of poems was printed—*Farewell, Aggie Weston*. Since then he has produced an abundance of verse for adults and for children; his principal publisher (Macmillan, London) brought out a *Collected Poems* in 1975 and another in 1992.

Experiences gained in the navy offered Causley a meaty subject-matter, as did the Cornish landscape and its people. He stands quietly apart from the machinations and in-fighting of the poetry world, and has consistently eschewed trends and fashions, preferring instead to use traditional forms to create a readable poetry which appeals to a wide audience. Causley's strengths are his clarity, sensitive use of rhyme, freshness of language and imagery, and an ability to combine recognizable poetic forms with contemporary reference-points. The collections of poems for children include a generous slice of humour.

Recent work, such as the collection *A Field of Vision* (London, 1988), offers great diversity of material as Causley records his childhood, and includes observational poems gathered from his literary travels around the globe. *Causley at 70* (Calstock, Cornwall, 1987) is a compilation of appreciative poems and prose contributed by leading literary figures, while *The Young Man of Cury* (London, 1991) is a rich and rewarding collection for young people.   [WM

CERAVOLO, Joseph. See NEW YORK SCHOOL.

CERVANTES, Lorna Dee (1954–), has been called by *Alurista 'probably the best Chicana poet active today'. Both *Emplumada* (Pittsburgh, Pa., 1981) and *From the Cables of Genocide: Poems on Love and Hunger* (Houston, Tex., 1992), and the work published in magazines like *Mango*, the *Revista Chicano-Riqueña*, and *Red Dirt*, exhibit considerable skill and variety. She can be toughly unsentimental yet lyric, as in 'Beneath the Shadow of the Freeway', a recollection of her cross-blood Chicano and Native American welfare-family upbringing in California. She can speak forcefully, as in 'Barco de Refugios/

Refugee Ship', about America's non-recognition of her *mestiza* heritage, causing her to feel 'orphaned from my Spanish name'. She can assume an intimate, teasing tone as in her love poem 'The Body As Braille'. In 'Cannery Town in August' she invokes nameless women 'who smell of whiskey and tomatoes, | peach fuzz reddening their lips and eyes', working through the night to can California fruit and vegetables. And though 'political' only in the most oblique fashion, she can write with well-placed irony of cultural outsiderness, as in 'Poem for the Young White Man Who Asked Me How I, an Intelligent, Well-Read Person Could Believe in the War between Races'. Few contemporaries, chicano/a or otherwise, match her powers of articulating *barrio* and blue-collar family life and labour—or the intimacies of a hard-won, anti-patriarchal femininity. See also *Chicana Poetry: A Critical Approach to an Emerging Literature*, by Marta Ester Sánchez (Berkeley and Los Angeles, 1985). [ARL

CHALLIS, Gordon (1932–), was born in Wales and emigrated to New Zealand in 1953. He studied at Victoria University College in Wellington in the later 1950s, completing a degree in psychology in 1960. He published extensively in the small periodicals associated with Wellington's literary activities in those years, and was recognized as one of the emerging poets of his generation.

His poetry was often metaphysical, developing conceits that explore the metaphorical attributes of a persona created out of what Kendrick *Smithman called 'nominal unreality'. The figures of his poems are often grotesque and allegorical, but they always suggest insightful awareness of human behaviour and temperament.

The editor of *Landfall* presented him as one of four new 'poets of the sixties' in the first issue of the decade (issue 53, Mar. 1960), and Challis's first book, *Building* (Christchurch, 1962), was well-reviewed. Smithyman wrote on him in his study of New Zealand poetry, *A Way of Saying* (Auckland, 1965), but Challis himself did not publish for many years after 1964. [WSB

CHAPPELL, Fred (1936–), was born in Canton, a mill town in the mountains of western North Carolina, and raised on the family's farm. Educated at Duke University, he has taught creative writing at the University of North Carolina at Greensboro for over twenty-five years.

Chappell's early reputation was based on the four novels he published between 1963 and 1973, one of which, *Dagon* (New York, 1968), received France's Prix de Meilleur des Livres Étrangers. His first volume of poems, *The World Between the Eyes* (Baton Rouge, La., 1971), earned little recognition. Not until the publication of the tetralogy *Midquest* (Baton Rouge, 1981), which reprinted four previously published books (*River*, *Bloodfire*, *Wind Mountain*, and *Earthsleep*), did Chappell's poetry attract significant critical attention. In 1985, largely on the strength of *Midquest's* achievement, Chappell was named, along with John *Ashbery, co-recipient of the Bollingen Prize. His other publications in the 1980s included a collection of short stories, two novels, and three additional books of poems.

Chappell's art derives from two major sources: his childhood and youth in the Appalachian mountains and his wide reading in the books, philosophical as well as literary, that have shaped Western culture. Among the most notable qualities of his poetry are its carefully crafted variety of forms, its fine story-telling and creation of character, its humour, and its serious moral intent. Chappell's poems reveal both enormous erudition and a profound commitment to what he has called 'folk art'. In addition to the mountain community whose life *Midquest* records, the book also creates a striking sense of literary community and of a vital literary tradition through its varied poetic forms, its verse epistles to contemporary author-friends, and its countless references to other writers, especially Dante, whose spiritual quest Chappell's persona emulates. *Castle Tzingal* (Baton Rouge, La., 1984), a moral allegory presented through a series of voices, *Source* (Baton Rouge, 1985), and *First and Last Words* (Baton Rouge, 1989), a volume largely composed of prefaces and afterwords to Chappell's reading, confirm his poetic range and power.

The Fred Chappell Reader (New York, 1987) reprints thirty-four of the author's poems, including over a third of *Midquest*, together with a generous selection from his fiction. [JLa]

CHARLES, Faustin (1944–), was born in Trinidad, and educated at the universities of Kent and London. He has lived in England since 1962, has been a visiting lecturer for the Commonwealth Institute, and works as a part-time teacher in London. Richly imagistic, his poems tend to be lush and fertile with implication, but also elegant in execution. He excels in phantasmagoric effects, most strikingly in 'Nude Black Nymph Riding a Black Stallion at Midnight'. His aims as a poet are strongly suggested in 'Calypso Cricketer' and 'Cricket's in my Blood'.

His collections include *The Expatriate* (London, 1969), *Crab Track* (London, 1973), and *Days and Nights in the Magic Forest* (London, 1986). He has also written two novels, *Signposts of the Jumbie* (London, 1981) and *The Black Magic Man of Brixton* (London, 1985). *Tales from the West Indies* (London, 1985) is a collection of short stories. [MR]

CHENEY-COKER, Syl (1945–), was born in Freetown, Sierra Leone. He studied at the universities of Oregon and Wisconsin before returning to Africa, where, after working as a journalist in Sierra Leone, he taught for many years at the University of Maiduguri in Nigeria. He also taught for two years at the University of the Philippines, but eventually returned to live in Freetown, where he edits and publishes the radical newspaper *The Vanguard*. He has published one novel, *The Last Harmattan of Alusine Dunbar* (Oxford, 1990) and three collections of poetry: *Concerto for an Exile* (London, 1973) which was reissued as a part of his second collection, *The Graveyard Also Has Teeth* (London, 1980), and *The Blood in the Desert's Eyes* (Oxford, 1990).

Syl Cheney-Coker's poetry has always seemed an adjunct to his calling as a radical, campaigning journalist. His are poems of causes, essentially intended as interventions into the various debates that his life's wanderings and his intellectual enquiries have touched

on—so he has written about South Africa, black America, the Arab–Israeli conflict, the duties and fates of poets everywhere, as well as the struggles in Sierra Leone, about which he has always been outspoken. Cheney-Coker is unashamedly opinionated, rhetorical, and verbose. His work is characterized by a surging, discursive, long-lined verse that at times teeters on the verge of the prosaic. His best poems, however, assume the force of poetic manifestos on behalf of the world's 'sufferers'. [SB]

CHESTERTON, G(ilbert) K(eith) (1874–1936), was born in London. He made his first reputation with his comic drawings, but had become a well-established journalist by the turn of the century. He was associated in the public mind with his Roman Catholic friend Hilaire *Belloc ('The Chesterbelloc'); but he was not actually received into the Roman Catholic Church until 1922. Chesterton is most famous as the creator of the priest-detective Father Brown, and as a capable, witty, paradoxical essayist. His profundity has been questioned, but never in regard to his poetry, which is unashamedly lightweight. He wrote in the tradition of Browning, and never made the slightest effort to accommodate himself to modernism, which he regularly mocked (his last radio broadcast, 'We Will End With a Bang', pokes fun at *Eliot). The chief influences upon him were Walt Whitman and Belloc, the nonchalance of whose light verse he at first tried to emulate. At its worst Chesterton's poetry declines into trite doggerel. At its best ('The Donkey' has been much anthologized, but 'The Rolling English Road' is more characteristic) it has a pleasant charm and sincerity, although—perhaps surprisingly—Chesterton could never express paradox in poetry as successfully as he could in prose. *Collected Poems* (London, 1933) is the most complete edition. [MS-S]

CHIMOMBO, Steve (1945–), was born at Zomba, Malawi, and studied at the universities of Malawi, Wales, Leeds, and Columbia. He joined the staff of Chancellor College, University of Malawi, in 1972, where he is currently professor of English. He has published a play, *The Rainmaker* (1978), a novel, *The Basket Girl* (1990), and a critical study of Malawian oral literature. He also edits a literary journal, *Wasi Writer*. *Napolo Poems* (Zomba, 1987), his only collection to date, received honourable mention in the prestigious 1988 Noma Award for publishing in Africa. A selection of the poems from this volume, as well as a previously unpublished poem, 'A Death Song', appeared in the *Heinemann Book of African Poetry in English* (1990).

According to the poet himself, the Napolo of the title is 'the mythical subterranean serpent residing under mountains and associated with landslides, earthquakes and floods in Malawi'. The last serious manifestation of this mythical serpent was in 1946, when Zomba mountain erupted and thousands of people were killed. The local population thought it was a sign of the end of the world, and still talk of it to this day. At an immediate level, the poems in the collection draw on the newspaper reports, folk-songs, and stories associated with the event; at a deeper level, however, they form an oblique commentary on one of the most ruthless dictatorships anywhere in the world. [AM-P

CHIPASULA, Frank (1949–), was born in Malawi and studied at Chancellor College, University of Malawi, until he was forced into exile in 1973. He lived for one year in Tanzania, then moved to Zambia. He obtained a BA from the University of Zambia in 1976, and for the next two years worked as an English editor for NECZAM, the national publishing house. He moved to the United States in 1978. He studied first at Yale University, where he obtained an MA in 1982, and then at Brown University, where he obtained a Ph.D in 1987. He is currently an associate professor in the Black Studies Department at the University of Nebraska at Omaha. He has edited an anthology of poetry from Central and Southern Africa, *When My Brothers Come Home* (Middletown, Conn., 1985), and published four volumes of poetry: *Visions and Reflections* (Lusaka, 1972); *O Earth, Wait for Me* (Johannesburg, 1984); *NIGHTWATCHER,*

Nightsong (Peterborough, 1986); and *Whispers in the Wings* (Oxford, 1991). His prize-winning poem, 'Manifesto on *Ars Poetica*', was published in *The Fate of Vultures* (Oxford, 1989), an anthology of new African poetry from the 1988 BBC Arts and Africa Poetry Award. Chipasula's work is banned in his own country.

Living in exile has enabled Chipasula to write openly against the dictatorship of Life-President Dr H. Kamuzu Banda, who has ruled Malawi since independence in 1964. In the 'First Word' to his three-part poem, *NIGHTWATCHER*, *Nightsong*, he speaks of the need to 'break out of [the] vicious shell of silence' that is 'familiar to our people'. In 'Manifesto on *Ars Poetica*', he promises to 'undress our raped land and expose her wounds'. [AM-P

CHITRE, Dilip Purushottam (1938–), was born in Baroda, where he had his early education. His family moved to Bombay when he was 13. After taking a degree in English from Bombay University in 1959, he went to Ethiopia for three years to teach in schools, and in the late Sixties and Seventies he was associated with the magazine *Quest* (now *New Quest*), for which he wrote essays, reviews, and a regular column of comment. He has edited *An Anthology of Marathi Poetry: 1945–65* (Bombay, 1967), doing most of the translations himself, and his translations of Tukaram (seventeenth century) are collected in *Says Tuka* (New Delhi, 1991). He has also directed a film and held exhibitions of his paintings.

A prolific writer in two languages, Marathi and English, Chitre has created a large body of work, much of it uncollected. *Travelling in a Cage* (Bombay, 1980), his only book in English so far, contains merely a fraction of his English poems. The title poem was written between 1975 and 1977, when he lived in the United States. Its epigraph, 'The heart is placed obliquely in the chest' is from Gray's *Anatomy*, and a sexual encounter, not always obliquely dealt with, appears to be at the heart of the sequence. Chitre sees language, sex, even death, as a prison or cage, with self-murder, 'the greatest of all forms', holding the key to freedom. The book's shorter poems play down his *De Profundis* side, and employ a plainer, less inward-turning voice and a raconteur's tone.

Travelling in a Cage might be difficult to find, but poems from it are available in two recent anthologies, *Indian English Poetry since 1950*, ed. Vilas Sarang (Bombay, 1989), and *The Oxford India Anthology of Twelve Modern Indian Poets*, ed. Arvind Krishna Mehrotra (Delhi, 1992). For a discussion of his work, see *Modern Indian Poetry in English*, by Bruce King (Delhi, 1987).

[AKM

CHRISTOPHER, Nicholas (1951–), was born in New York; his life and work have centred on that city. He attended the Horace Mann School and Harvard, where he studied with Robert *Lowell and Anthony *Hecht. Two strains are discernible in his work: a tough, urban temperament, alert to the bizarre juxtapositions and speed of modern life; and a lyrical, sensuous strain, traceable perhaps to Christopher's Greek ancestry. His first book of poems, *On Tour with Rita* (New York, 1982), was remarkable for its striking imagery and cosmopolitan geography; Christopher is fascinated by the romantic figure of the wanderer, the traveller, the artist perpetually 'on tour'.

The related theme of the essential solitude of the artist is at the core of his vision; two sections of *On Tour with Rita* are titled 'Solos', and the book opens with a poem called 'Double Solitaire' and has, as its penultimate poem, 'The Soloist'—the title, as well, of Christopher's novel (1986) about a concert pianist. A second book, *A Short History of the Island of Butterflies* (New York, 1986), develops further the twin themes of wandering and solitude. A more unusual work, his most original and challenging to date, is the long poem, *Desperate Characters*, subtitled 'A Novella in Verse' (New York, 1988). Christopher has always had a rich sense of popular culture—comic strips, films, rock music. His long poem, set mainly in Hollywood, is nourished by his interest in film culture, especially *film noir*. Written in a taut free verse, it is a vivid, fast-moving narrative of shady characters living on the edge.

[CB

CHUILLEANÁIN, Eiléan Ní (1942–), was born in Cork, the daughter of the writer Eilis Dillon and Cormac Ó Chuilleanáin, professor of Irish at University College, Cork. She was educated at UCC, and lectures in Medieval and Renaissance English at Trinity College Dublin. Her first volume of poems was *Acts and Monuments*, published by Gallery Press (Dublin, 1973), and she has published three further volumes with Gallery, the most recent being *The Magdalene Sermon* (1989). *The Second Voyage: Selected Poems* (Manchester and Winston-Salem, NC) came out in 1986. She has also written *Irish Women: Image and Achievement—Women in Irish Culture from Earliest Times* (Dublin, 1985) which is regarded as the authoritative overview of its subject.

Ní Chuilleanáin's early poems were written in a free form, and their virtues (which made her a prize-winner from the first) were evocativeness and imaginative imagery. These gifts were well exemplified, for example, in her volume *Cork* (1977), which was accompanied by Fintan Lalor's drawings. Her later poetry is more ambitious and has more direction to it. Like other Irish women poets of her era, such as Eavan *Boland, this more recent work is an absorbing mix of mythology, mostly Irish and centring on female archetypes, and contemporary domestic experience. As the objective has become more focused, the style has become more precise. Edna Longley in *The Irish Review*, 8 (Cork, Spring 1990) characterized Ní Chuilleanáin's poetry as 'even-paced and temperate . . . inclined to repeat structural patterns', but saw it moving beyond her usual concerns (national identity and femininity) in a metaphysical direction in the strange, imaginative 'Observations from Galileo'.

[BO'D

CIARDI, John (1916–86), was born in Boston and graduated from that city's Tufts College in 1938, followed by a year at the University of Michigan. He was in the Air Force from 1942 to 1945 and married in 1946. Although he taught at college level, his most important posts were as director of the Bread Loaf Writers' Conference and *Saturday Review*'s poetry editor.

Homeward to America (1940) and *Other Skies* (1947), his first two collections, as well as *As If: New and Selected* (1955), are deftly traditional in lyric formulas but modern in their conversational ease, excessive at times in lexical acrobatics. He exerted greater impact on the literary scene with his poetic rendition of Dante's *The Divine Comedy* (1979), begun in 1954, and editorship of *Mid-Century American Poets* (1950) and *How Does a Poem Mean?* (1960), still a standard college text.

The most substantial edition of his work remains *The Achievement of John Ciardi: A Comprehensive Selection of His Poems with a Critical Introduction*, ed. Miller Williams (Chicago, 1969). [EB

CLAMPITT, Amy (1920–94), was born in New Providence, Iowa, and pursued a career in publishing and librarianship, mainly in New York, before her richly intelligent poems began to attract attention in the 1970s. Her debut with *The Kingfisher* (New York) came as late as 1983, when she was 63. This long incubation period suggests two things: an intelligence that has ripened into a learned and mature sensibility, and a stubbornly maintained fastidiousness during the 'confessionalist' 1960s.

Amy Clampitt's elegantly crafted meditations, more cultured and less eccentric than Marianne *Moore's, manifest a profound feeling for nature. A biographer's gift for re-creating character and situation informs long poems on Keats, George Eliot, and other writers with whom she identifies. Chiefly, however, Clampitt is a moralist. Her openly baroque, complex stanzas are usually sustained by the working out of a gradually revealed idea. In more personal poems, like 'The Cove' in *The Kingfisher*, the fine stitching of the verse creates distinctive, womanly interiors: 'cross-stitch | domesticates the guest room', while outside, warblers 'flirt' through foliage which is 'all ombre | and fine stitchery'. In 'Gradual Clearing' the sea, which had been a 'wavering | fishnet plisse', takes on the 'smoothness | of peau-de-soie or just-ironed | percale, with a tatting | of foam out where the rocks are'. In the

best of her long poems, such as her meditation on life and death in 'A Procession at Candlemas', the accumulated effect of forty-eight three-line stanzas is grand and unfussy.

Clampitt's second major collection, *What the Light Was Like* (New York, 1985; London, 1987) consists chiefly of elegies dedicated to the memory of her brother. A subsequent collection, *Archaic Figure* (New York, 1987; London, 1989) dwells on European travel, with the usual accompaniment of sympathetic reflection on art, artists, migraine, and time. See also, *Westward* (New York and London, 1992) [AS

CLARK, Tom (Thomas Willard) (1941–), served as poetry editor for the *Paris Review* from 1963 until 1973. Much of his verse (he had published thirty-six collections by 1990) has been issued by small presses in small editions. His main inspiration comes from European surrealism; presentation is based on various models, ranging from the comedian Lenny Bruce to the laid-back, conversational procedures of Ted *Berrigan, with whom Clark, together with Ron *Padgett, shared an early collection, *Back in Boston Again* (Philadelphia, 1972). Most of Clark's poems are anti-literary in all senses, and they are often throw-away, without regard for or interest in conventional technique. Many deal with baseball, as in *Baseball* (Berkeley, Calif., 1976). See also: *Paradise Revisited: Selected Poems 1978–1984* (Santa Barbara, Calif., 1984); *Fractured Karma* (Santa Rosa, Calif., 1990). [MS-S

CLARK BEKEDEREMO, J(ohn) P(epper) (1935–), was born of Ijo and Urhobo parents in Kiagbodo, mid-western Nigeria. He studied at Government College, Ughelli, and later obtained a BA in English at University College, Ibadan. He has held fellowships at Princeton University and at the University of Ibadan. Formerly professor of English at the University of Lagos, he is now artistic director of PEC repertory theatre in Lagos.

A selection of his earlier works, *Poems* (Ibadan, 1962), *A Reed in the Tide* (London, 1965), and *Casualties* (London, 1970), have been collected together in *A Decade of Tongues* (London,

1981). His latest volume of poetry is *State of the Union* (London, 1985). He has also written four plays, two critical works, and a travelogue. His translation of an Ijo oral epic poem, *The Ozidi Saga*, is highly regarded, and two of his poems, 'Ibadan' and 'Abiku', have already become classics of modern African poetry and are widely known by schoolchildren in Nigeria. He is at his best when capturing the essence of a place or phenomenon in a few descriptive lines. For critical reviews, see *Understanding African Poetry* (London, 1982), by Ken Goodwin and 'J. P. Clark's Poetry', in *Perspectives on Nigerian Literature* (Lagos, 1988), ed. Yemi Ogunbiyi. See also entry on *Black Orpheus*.   [FO

CLARKE, Austin (1896–1974), was born in Dublin and lived there throughout his life, except for a period in London from 1921 to 1937. Although he wrote nearly twenty verse plays, three novels, two literary autobiographies, and a substantial body of criticism and journalism, his principal significance is as a poet. He disputes with *MacNeice and *Kavanagh the title of the leading Irish poet in the generation after *Yeats. He was born to a relatively well-off family in Dublin, although six of his nine siblings died in infancy. He was given a first in his English MA at University College, Dublin, in 1917, and succeeded to the lectureship made vacant there by the execution of Thomas *MacDonagh for his part in the 1916 Easter Rising. In 1919 he had a mental breakdown (on which he drew for what is perhaps his greatest poem, 'Mnemosyne lay in dust' in 1966). After a brief first marriage in 1920, he lost his UCD lectureship in 1921 and subsequently lived mostly by his writing.

In 1917 his first collection of poems, *The Vengeance of Fionn*, was warmly received. It is an eloquent, epic-styled evocation of Irish legend in the manner of early Yeats, whom Clarke then revered. His fifth volume of poems, *Pilgrimage* (1929), mixes with this earlier legendary style a new spare realism and eroticism, representing a departure from the prevailing modes in Irish poetry of the time. Its principal stylistic innovation is to attempt (with varying success) to incorporate into poetry in English the asson-

antal patterns of Gaelic poetry, as prescribed by Larminie and MacDonagh. After his first *Collected Poems* in 1936, the short confessional volume *Night and Morning* (1938) introduced what were later to be his principal themes: sexual freedom and conscience, and the constricting effects of the Church, which he saw in operation in his medieval 'Celto-Romanesque' world as well as in contemporary Ireland. But *Night and Morning* was followed by a seventeen-year poetic silence, which is not fully explained by Clarke's statement that he was working on plays in that period. He returned to poetry with the angrily topical and public *Ancient Lights*, published in 1955 when he was nearly 60. The best of these forceful pieces are much admired as a flourish of 'lust and rage' in old age, as prescribed by Yeats, though they often seem too willed.

Clearly an important figure, with gifts of style and imagination that few can match, Clarke remains often uncompelling. It has been suggested that politically inclined Irish writers were disablingly marginalized by Irish neutrality in the Second World War. In any case, Clarke's unvaryingly Irish perspective, combined with his anticlericalism and distaste for the politics of the new state (which Clarke saw as a disastrous failure of republican idealism), meant that he had no obviously sympathetic catchment area. But, pending a full-scale biography and a detailed critical account that is more than introductory, his reputation remains to be established conclusively.

See: *Collected Poems* (Dublin, and London and New York, 1974); *Selected Poems*, ed. Hugh Maxton (Dublin, 1991); and *Twice Round the Black Church: Early Memories of Ireland and England* (London, 1962); also Susan Halpern, *Austin Clarke: His Life and Works* (Dublin, 1974); G. Craig Topping, *Austin Clarke: A Study of His Writings* (Dublin, 1981—this has a useful appendix listing Clarke's journalism); M. Harmon, (ed.), *Irish University Review: Austin Clarke Special Issue*, 4: 1 (Spring 1974).   [BO'D

CLARKE, Gillian (1937–   ), was born and educated in Cardiff, where she took a degree in

English. After two years in London as a news researcher for the BBC, she returned to Wales in 1960. She has since lectured in art history, and from 1976 to 1984 edited the *Anglo-Welsh Review*.

The Sundial, Clarke's first collection, was published by a small Welsh press in 1978, and immediately established the territory of her work as both isolated and luminous. Bleak meditations on the passing of time, of journeys made by car through a landscape of slate and coal-mines, modulated into a lyricism associated with the experience of giving birth, and the 'tugging pleasure' of its 'bruised reordering'. In the long title-poem of *Letter From a Far Country* (1982) there was still a promise of lyricism, yet the bruises suffered in comparative silence by generations of Welsh women proved the more emphatic preoccupation. Writing home in English from her ancestors' future, she commemorated but also identified herself with their confinement: her letter of release remained 'unfinished, unposted'. *Letting in the Rumour* (1989) struck a more positive note. Still, 'At One Thousand Feet' on her hillside, Clarke now mined her family's history to celebrate its affinity with a contemporary world of 'glasnost, | golau glas, | a first break of blue'.

For a representative sample of her work, see *Selected Poems* (Manchester, 1985).   [MRW

CLARKE, John Cooper. See PERFORMANCE POETRY.

CLEMO, Jack (Reginald John) (1916–94), was born the son of a Cornish clay-worker in a granite cottage near St Austell which, in the first of two autobiographies (*Confessions of a Rebel*, 1949), he describes as 'a fitting birthplace for me, being dwarfed under Bloomdale clay-dump, solitary, grim-looking, with no drainage, no water or electricity supply, and no back door'. With little formal education, and for most of his writing career, both deaf and blind, Clemo lived there all his life, though the conditions improved.

Clemo first came to attention with his novel *Wilding Graft* (1948) which was admired by T. F.

Powys, and writing of Powys in his second volume of autobiography (*Marriage of a Rebel*, 1980) Clemo stressed an affinity in that both men had 'chosen the unworldly borderline, the terrible wrestle with God'. Like Powys, too, Clemo had become preoccupied by 'the struggle between the ascetic and the sensualist'.

Dominated by the stark landscape of the clay-pits, Clemo's best-known poems explore the forces of nature and the workings of a hard-won grace. His earliest work, of which the characteristically titled 'Christ in the Clay-Pit' is a good example, is marked by the self-wounding, exclusively tortured spirit of Calvinism, and his development as a poet has been informed by a search for reconciliation which he describes as 'mystical-erotic' in poems full of a charged, evangelical language. Powerful, intense, and often chillingly austere, his poetry nevertheless became mellower in later years and more reconciled to the human condition.

In a telling portrait by Charles *Causley which introduces Clemo's 1961 collection *The Map of Clay*, the poet's cottage is seen to contain a portrait of Billy Graham on the mantelpiece and volumes of D. H. *Lawrence and Karl Barth in the bookcase, suggesting vividly the components of his vision. Clemo's *Selected Poems* was published by Bloodaxe Books (Newcastle upon Tyne, 1988), as was his latest collection, *Approach to Murano* (1992).   [JM

CLIFTON, Lucille (1936–), was born in Depew, New York, to a working-class family. Educated at the State University of New York at Fredonia and Howard University, she married Fred James Clifton, an educator, in 1958, and raised six children. She is distinguished professor of humanities at St Mary's College, Maryland.

Clifton gained national attention in 1969 with her first volume, praised for its craft and its evocation of urban black life. Thus her early work is significant to the Black Arts Movement; however, four subsequent volumes demonstrate that hers is a poetry not of race but of revelation, in the manner of Denise *Levertov. Characterized by brevity, simplicity of language, and polyrhythmical phrasing, her work celebrates the spiritual revealed in the ordinary. Many poems (e.g. the 'two-headed woman' and 'Lucifer' sequences) depend on voice for their dramatic situation, yet they are not dramatic monologues, like those of Gwendolyn *Brooks, but rather voiced meditations. Clifton writes that she hears characters speak, including family members and mythic figures.

Good Woman (Brockport, NY, 1987) collects the memoir and poems from 1969–80, followed by *Next* (1987) and *Quilting* (1991). [JTC

CLOUTS, Sydney David (1926–82), was born in Cape Town, and educated there at the South African College School and the University of Cape Town, where he studied law and philosophy. He married Marjorie Leftwich in 1952. His poetry first appeared in South African magazines during the 1950s, and in 1961 he departed for the UK to become a literary agent. Some poems were broadcast by the BBC in 1965, and in 1966 his volume *One Life* was published in South Africa. On completion of an MA at Rhodes University in Grahamstown in 1969, he returned to the UK, where he worked as a librarian until his death in 1982.

Clouts's prominence in South African poetry is assured but controversial. Criticism has ranged from descriptions of him as South Africa's 'purest poetic talent', to readings of the poetry as 'blinkered' because it tends to ignore social issues or deals with them from a position of naïve romanticism. These ideological difficulties are compounded by what for many is an unnecessary impenetrability, often the result of the poet's attempt to reduce language to the barest minimum. See his *Collected Poems* (Cape Town, 1984), ed. Marjorie and Cyril Clouts, and *English in Africa*, 11: 2 (1984), dedicated to him. [KG

COBBING, Bob. See SOUND POETRY.

COLEBATCH, Hal (1945–   ) is the son of a former premier of Western Australia. After completing a degree in politics at the University of

Western Australia he enrolled in a law course, graduating to become a solicitor. In his student days, he worked as a journalist and radio script-writer, and even offered himself as a political candidate for a state election in the 1970s: at his electoral rallies he read his poetry to captive audiences. He is also the Australian manager for Debrett's Peerage.

Two early books, *Spectators on the Shore* (Melbourne, 1975) and *In Breaking Waves* (Melbourne, 1979), are incorporated in Colebatch's third published book *Outer Charting* (Sydney, 1985). It is not to Colebatch's discredit that there is no sign of development from his first book to his fourth and latest, *The Earthquake Lands* (Sydney, 1990): he established a distinctive and successful style from the outset and has persisted with it ever since. His poems are all in rhyming forms, most commonly quatrains and sonnets, though the rhythm is that of the plainest discursive prose. A number of his poems are dispassionate descriptions of seascapes, but more deal with political matters as Colebatch rails against the left-wing orthodoxies of present-day Australia. [JG

COLERIDGE, Mary (Elizabeth) (1861–1907), was the great granddaughter of Samuel Taylor Coleridge's elder brother. She was born in London, educated at home, and lived throughout her life with her family, helping her sister to care for their father after their mother's death in 1898. She published five novels and a volume of essays, as well as four small pseudonymous books of poems in her lifetime. Her *Collected Poems*, with a preface by Henry Newbolt, went through five editions in less than two years shortly after her death.

In one of her essays Mary Coleridge wrote that infants are happy because they do not think, adding 'it is because in sleep we cannot think, or only think distortedly, that in sleep we are happy'. The dubiously accurate statement reflects the melancholy of her short poems, none longer than forty lines. At its best her work has just a little of Emily Dickinson's wit and edge, but lacks altogether the American poet's intensity, substituting for it too often a lack-lustre or genteel sentimentality. Her most successful poems are those of a dozen lines or less on subjects to do with lost or illicit love.

See *Collected Poems*, ed. Theresa Whistler (London, 1954). [JGS

COLES, Don (1928–), was born in Woodstock, Ontario and educated at the University of Toronto and at Cambridge, from which he received an MA in 1954. He spent the next ten years in various European centres before returning to Canada. He now teaches creative writing at York University, Toronto. Coles is also poetry editor at the Banff Centre for the Fine Arts.

Coles's poetry is notable for its elegance, sophistication, and urbane intelligence. These qualities are as evident in his first book, *Sometimes All Over* (Toronto, 1975) as in his last, *K. in Love* (Montreal, 1987), a series of concentrated 'notes' inspired by a reading of Kafka's letters and journals. Coles is equally at home in the Europe of Munch and Mann and in the Canada of his Bergmanesque childhood; combining lofty eloquence with wry off-handedness, he can produce a *tour de force* on subjects as disparate as Pushkin's fiancée and Major Hoople. *Landslides: Selected Poems 1975–1985* (Toronto, 1986) shows an impressive range of subject-matter and technique.

Coles's other books of poetry include. *Anniversaries* (Toronto, 1979), *The Prinzhorn Collection* (Toronto, 1982), and *Little Bird* (Montreal, 1991). [JKK

COLUM, Padraic (1881–1972), was born at Longford in Ireland, the son of the master of the workhouse there. As a young man he associated with *Yeats, *Joyce, James *Stephens, Lady Gregory, and a host of others. Later he worked for the state of Hawaii on a folklore programme for schoolchildren, and he and his wife, the writer Mary Colum (née Maguire), whom he had married in 1912, became American citizens. But he journeyed regularly to Ireland for the remainder of his life.

Colum's poetry is almost all in traditional forms, and based in Irish lore; but it was never in the artificial, later Celtic Twilight style of the minor poets of the first decades of the twentieth century who were content to imitate the early Yeats. Colum achieved such genuine simplicity that he was universally respected; but his work seldom drew the attention it deserved. On the other hand, such poems as 'She Moved Through the Fair' became so well known that they went back into the tradition. Others, such as 'Ploughing', are starkly contemplative. *Carricknabauna,* a musical based on his poems, was produced in New York in 1967. See his *Collected Poems* (New York, 1953) and *Life and the Dream* (New York, 1947), by Mary Colum. Also *The Dublin Magazine,* 6 (Spring, 1967). [MS-S

COMFORT, Alex(ander) (1920–), was born in London and educated at Highgate School and Trinity College, Cambridge, where he was a contemporary of Nicholas *Moore and Hamish *Henderson. He was a conscientious objector in the Second World War, and his pacifist views are evident in his early work, particularly in his third volume of poetry, *The Signal to Engage* (London, 1947).

Comfort spoke of the awareness of death as differentiating his generation from the left-wing poets of the Thirties. His third volume of poetry, *Elegies* (London, 1944), taking its example from Rilke, seeks to move towards an acceptance of death. Yet, while Comfort's poetry of the period seems impressive, it diffuses rather than resolves the pressures it attempts to contain.

By 1951 Comfort had published six volumes of poetry, seven of fiction, two of literary criticism, and two plays, and had edited several anthologies. However, his career was in medicine, and his literary output became sparser. He returned to poetry with *Haste to the Wedding* (London, 1962; Chester Springs, Pa., 1964)— poems that celebrated sexuality—and in 1972 gained fame for his best-selling prose book *The Joy of Sex. Poems for Jane* (London, 1978: New York, 1979), consisting of poems of personal experience, is in many ways his most interesting collection.

Alex Comfort (Boston, 1978) by A. Saloman is a

study of his work. He is represented in the *Oxford Book of Twentieth-Century English Verse* (1973) and the Penguin *Poetry of the Forties*, ed. R. Skelton (1968).   [ATT

Concrete Poetry is an umbrella term for a multilingual body of verbal explorations written, drawn, and otherwise recorded since the middle of the century by poets and artists around the world. The international character of the movement is perhaps best indicated by the fact that the expression 'concrete poetry' itself was coined independently and more or less simultaneously, in 1952, by a group of Brazilian poets and theorists that included Augusto de Campos, Haroldo de Campos, and Décio Pignatari, and by the Swedish poet, playwright, and artist Oyvind Fahlström. By converting words, type, and white space into drawing tools, sculptural vocabularies, and sonic environments, they hoped to strip away the formal conventions and historical associations which, they believed, threatened to overwhelm, disfigure, or simply trivialize the phenomenon of poetic immediacy.

Among the influences discernible in their works and those of other early concrete poets, such as Carlo Belloli, Eugen Gomringer, Diter Rot, Carlfriedrich Claus, Daniel Spoerri, Kitasano Katue, and Ernst Jandl, are the typographical experiments of the Italian futurists and Russian constructivists; the ideogrammatic methods of *Pound's later Chinese cantos; the word-play of *Joyce's *Finnegans Wake*; the rhythms of Gertrude *Stein's poems, plays, and novels; the soundscapes of Dadaists Hugo Ball and Kurt Schwitters; the *musique concrète* of Varèse, Cage, Stockhausen, and Boulez; the concepts of permutational game theory and their early applications to cybernetics; the anti-grammar of advertisements and newspaper headlines; and the linguistic philosophy of Ludwig Wittgenstein. In Great Britain and in the United States, where the first influential concrete poets (Ian Hamilton Finlay, John Furnival, Aram Saroyan) did not appear until the early 1960s, the movement was for the most part either ignored or dismissed by reviewers and literary critics. See *An Anthology of Concrete Poetry*, ed. Emmett Williams (New York, Villefranche, and Frankfurt, 1967); *Concrete Poetry: An International Anthology*, ed. Stephen Bann (London, 1967); and *Concrete Poetry: A World View*, ed. Mary Ellen Solt (Bloomington, Ind., 1968).

[RH

Confessional Poetry is verse in which the author describes parts of his life which would not ordinarily be in the public domain. The prime characteristic is the reduction of the distance between the persona and the author.

Confessional poetry derives from the Romantics, from such poems as Wordsworth's 'Nutting' and Coleridge's 'Dejection: An Ode'. More immediately, it relates to Ezra *Pound's 'Hugh Selwyn Mauberley' and 'Pisan Cantos', where intimate references to friends are worked into the verse.

The term 'confessional verse' was first made current in a review of Robert *Lowell's *Life Studies* by M. L. *Rosenthal (*The Nation*, 19 Sept. 1959, revised version repr. in M. L. Rosenthal, *The New Poetry*, New York, 1967). Rosenthal points out that Lowell's speaker in his poems is unequivocally himself. When that speaker attacks his father for lack of manhood, or refers to his breaking marriage, we are in no doubt that it is Lowell's own father who is under attack and Lowell's own marriage that is in reference. Other poets of the Confessional school are John *Berryman, Anne *Sexton, W. D. *Snodgrass, and Sylvia *Plath.

At its worst, Confessional poetry is a kind of therapy that thrusts private experience upon an unwilling reader. At its best, as in Lowell's *Life Studies*, it is a way of creating character so as to inform the trauma of the past with understanding and, sometimes, compassion.   [PDH

CONN, Stewart (1936–), was born in Glasgow, and his first book, *Stoats in the Sunlight* (London, 1968), identified him as a fastidious recorder of the landmarks, relatives, and farms of his boyhood. His reunions with the past elicited measurements of personal and agricultural change. What emerged was the image of a dwindling rural Lowland Scotland worked out in crafted lines and stanzas.

An Ear to the Ground (London, 1972) and *Under the Ice* (London, 1978) saw him extend his range, but with a similar appreciation of form applied to different subjects. 'Family Visit' and 'To My Father' drew from the family concerns of some of the earlier work. Much in these two volumes was domestic and marital, with an unnerving sense of the fragility of life as well as an unmodish awareness of its decencies and delights. By and large, these have been Conn's chief poetic interests since; see, for example, the third part of *In the Kibble Palace: New and Selected Poems* (Newcastle upon Tyne, 1987). Subdued rhythms, half-rhymes, and a plain vocabulary are characteristic of his unassertive but attractively honest voice.

Conn is also the author of many plays for stage and television. He worked as a drama producer for BBC Radio from 1962 to 1992 and was head of BBC Radio Scotland's drama department. In that capacity, his contribution to Scottish poetry, and Scottish writing in general, has been significant. His most recent book is *The Luncheon of the Boating Party* (Newcastle upon Tyne, 1992). [DED

CONNOR, Tony (John Anthony Augustus) (1930–), was born in Manchester and left school at the age of 14. He worked as a textile designer until 1960, and the following year joined Bolton Technical College as a liberal studies assistant. His first collection of poems, *With Love Somehow*, appeared in 1962 (London). He spent the academic year 1967/8 as visiting poet at Amherst College, Massachusetts, and subsequently became visiting poet, lecturer, and (from 1971) professor of English at Wesleyan University, Middletown, Connecticut.

Connor's early books established him as an acute and wide-ranging social poet, with an engagingly bluff sense of wit. A change of tone was signalled by his *Twelve Secret Poems* (published as a pamphlet, 1965, and incorporated in *Kon in Springtime*, London, 1968) with their journeys into the 'suburbs of Hell', which preceded his permanent move to the USA. *In the Happy*

Valley (London, 1971) presents his adopted country with sometimes baffled admiration as a brilliantly fragmented, almost surreal mosaic. His *New and Selected Poems* (London and Athens, Ga.) were published in 1982. [NP

CONQUEST, (George) Robert (Ackworth) (1917–), was educated at Winchester and Magdalen College, Oxford, served in the army from 1939 to 1946, and then spent ten years in the foreign service. Subsequently he has been a free-lance writer and reviewer, literary editor of the *Spectator*, and more recently has become famous as an expert on Russian affairs. He has held various posts at American universities, and since 1981 has been based at the Hoover Institution, Stanford University. *The Great Terror* (1968) and *The Harvest of Sorrow* (1986), the first dealing with Stalin's organized terror and persecution in the late Thirties, the second with the death by starvation of millions in the Ukraine, have made him internationally known.

Conquest's poetry has been little touched by his other interests. Indeed, the work of his that is most nearly political comes in his first collection and, as in poems like 'A Minor Front' and 'On The Danube', is perhaps implicitly left-wing, and so at odds with his later prose writings. In general, he is a personal rather than a social poet, his characteristic tone lyrically enthusiastic, the verse vigorous and varied, the appreciation of the visible world powerful. A lesser strain in his poetry is ironic or satiric, and he is capable also of fanciful, near-metaphysical speculation, as in 'On an X-Ray Photograph of the Poet's Skull' or 'The Phases of Venus'. His early master was *Auden, and there are residual traces in his later work of *Graves's offhand and quirky humour. At times his rhetoric is too high-flown for his subject, occasionally he ties himself up in verbal or metaphysical knots, but his best work celebrates the acts and emotions of love in a manner clear, elegant, and easy.

Poems (London and New York, 1955) was succeeded by *Between Mars and Venus* (London and New York, 1962), *Arias from a Love Opera* (London and New York, 1968), and *Forays* (London, 1979). *New and Collected Poems* appeared in London in 1988. Conquest also championed the *Movement poets in the Fifties, when he edited the anthology *New Lines, and he has produced a vigorous translation of Solzhenitsyn's *Prussian Nights* (London, 1977; New York, 1978).

[JGS

CONSTANTINE, David (1944–), was born in Salford; he lectured in German at the University of Durham from 1969 to 1981, and is now a fellow in German at the Queen's College, Oxford. He has translated Hölderlin and written a book about him, and the German poet's 'Half of Life', with its balance between celebration and anxiety, classical restraint and romantic longing, might be a manifesto for Constantine's own work. *A Brightness to Cast Shadows* (Newcastle upon Tyne, 1980) uses an impassioned, skilful lyricism to clarify a vision of experience that is both light and dark: love is affirmed, yet social wretchedness—the subject of a novel by Constantine, *Davies* (1985)—is treated with straightforward tenderness and Brechtian irony. *Watching for Dolphins* (Newcastle upon Tyne, 1983) demonstrates a poignant obsession with loss and longing, often revivifying traditional myth. *Madder* (Newcastle upon Tyne, 1987)—Constantine's best collection—is written in a leaner, seriously playful style that is responsive both to the sombre 'noise | And shadow' of history and to the 'manifest beauty of breathing'.

[MO'N

Contemporary Poetry and Prose, a magazine inspired by the 1936 Surrealist Exhibition in London. The second issue included nine poems and an enigmatic 'statement' by Paul Eluard, plus work by André Breton, Dali, René Char, and other well-known figures in the *Surrealist movement, together with very short stories by a boy of 5 and a girl of 7. Britain was represented by contributions from Kenneth *Allott and the youthful David *Gascoyne, as well as the editor Roger Roughton. This second number, together with a Picasso issue (4/5), represented the magazine's most typical productions, although other young British poets, including Gavin *Ewart and Dylan *Thomas (with a

poem and near-surrealist story), appeared in its pages. The magazine lasted for ten issues and a little more than twelve months. 'This is the last Number as the Editor is going abroad for some time', said a note in number 10. Roughton, who financed the magazine, gassed himself in Ireland in 1941.

[JGS

COOLIDGE, Clark. See NEW YORK SCHOOL.

COOPER, Jane (1924–), was born in Atlantic City, New Jersey, and educated at Vassar College, the University of Wisconsin, and the University of Iowa. From 1950 to 1987 she taught at Sarah Lawrence College. She lives in New York City.

The relative sparseness of Cooper's poetic oeuvre is matched by the economy of individual poems: her work has a sinewy, thought-through quality. In cool language, careful syntax, and controlled structures, she looks steadily at family, love, work, cities and loneliness.

A journal passage from the early 1950s which Cooper retrieved for her 1974 essay, 'Nothing Has Been Used in the Manufacture of This Poetry That Could Have Been Used in the Manufacture of Bread', captures the integrity with which she has approached her art: 'I have a very old-fashioned idea of what poetry should do. It is the soul's history and whatever troubles the soul is fit material for poetry.'

Like her friends and contemporaries, Adrienne *Rich, Jean *Valentine, Grace Paley, and other New York women writers, Cooper has been intensely concerned since the late 1960s with the problems, themes, and achievements of women's writing, which is the subject of her 'Poetry . . . Bread' essay. Cooper's books of poetry are *The Weather of Six Mornings* (New York, 1968), *Maps and Windows* (New York, 1974), and *Scaffolding: New and Selected Poems* (London, 1984).

[RHa

COPE, Wendy (1945–), was born in Kent, took a history degree at St Hilda's College, Oxford, and was a primary-school teacher for some years, specializing in music. Her two collections of poetry, *Making Cocoa for Kingsley Amis*

(London, 1986) and *Serious Concerns* (London, 1991), quickly reached the best-seller lists, and established her as the most popular English poet of the Eighties.

Cope writes skilfully in such traditional verse-forms as the ballade, rondeau redouble, villanelle, and triolet, and, in *The River Girl* (London, 1988), a children's poem which originated as a puppet-play, demonstrates an ease with the longer narrative. She is a gifted parodist, and has invented a memorable comic character in the shape of the pretentious suburban poet, Jason Strugnell, author of numerous sonnets and, more recently, a sequence of song lyrics, 'Strugnell Lunaire'. Though conservative in form, Cope has an attractively subversive vision, particularly of male sexual behaviour, and enjoys debunking the fashionable forms of worthiness, such as the Green movement. While she excels at the self-mocking tone, her more personally charged poetry seems less sure of its voice. [CAR

CORMAN, Cid (Sidney) (1924–), was at first associated with Charles *Olson, Robert *Creeley, and Louis *Zukovsky, whose poetry he published in his magazine, *Origin, or at the Origin Press. In 1958 he went to Japan and set up his publishing activities there, returning to America in the early 1980s. By 1987 he had published over seventy volumes of verse, most of them being short collections from small or private presses. He is still better known for his early and influential advocacy of William Carlos *Williams, Creeley, and other poets who were not accepted in America in the 1950s and 1960s than for his own poetry, for which he makes few claims, asking only that it 'sing into you a little moment'. It resembles the work of the *Black Mountain school, being in very short lines, and consisting mainly of momentary impressions, most of these personal and frequently verbless. The latter feature became increasingly pronounced, doubtless owing to his long residence in Japan and the effect of its poetry on him. He has translated much French and Japanese poetry. See *Aegis: Selected Poems 1970–1980* (Barrytown, NY, 1980). [MS-S

CORN, Alfred (1943–), was born in Georgia, where he graduated from Emory University. Following doctoral studies in French literature at Columbia, Corn began writing poetry and literary criticism for numerous magazines and quarterlies. He has since taught at Yale, Columbia, and UCLA (among others), and has edited a book of essays by contemporary writers on The New Testament, *Incarnation* (New York, 1990). A collection of critical essays on fiction and poetry, *The Metamorphoses of Metaphor* (New York, 1987), includes pieces on many of the poets who influence his work most consistently: *Stevens, *Ashbery, Robert *Lowell, *Bishop, and Hart *Crane.

Corn's first book, *All Roads at Once* (New York, 1976), ranges formally from imagistic short lyrics to an ambitious narrative poem ('Pages from a Voyage'), and reflects his interest in the relation of art to experience. His subsequent four volumes similarly balance autobiographical episode and anecdote with his wide knowledge of art and literature. If his first book emphasizes natural observation, his second, *A Call in the Midst of the Crowd* (New York, 1978), celebrates the urban landscape of New York City in its long title sequence. With *The Various Light* (New York, 1980), Corn achieves a smoother syntax and greater clarity in lyric poems about loss and impermanence. His fourth book, *Notes from a Child of Paradise* (New York, 1984), is a full-length narrative poem, partly written in *terza rima*, which chronicles Corn's courtship, marriage, and divorce, and, less successfully, aspires to a grand vision of America in the Sixties. A prolific poet, Corn departs somewhat from his previous mandarin work in the long poem 'An Xmas Murder' (in *The West Door*, New York, 1988), a chilling and plain-spoken tale diminished only by its weak narrative frame. [TDeP

CORNFORD, Frances (née Darwin) (1886–1960), was born in Cambridge, and privately educated. She was a granddaughter of Charles Darwin, the wife of the classical scholar, F. M. Cornford, and the mother of the poet, John

*Cornford, who was killed in the Spanish Civil War.

She was comparable at her best with Walter *de la Mare and W. H. *Davies. But neither the advocacy of Rupert *Brooke nor that of J. C. *Squire could persuade Edward Marsh to put her work into his *Georgian anthologies.

Her poems rejoice at the tranquillity of life in Cambridge where she lived almost all her life. But, at the same time, she shows a quirky apprehension of decay and death. Best of all, perhaps, is 'Childhood', with its perception of the mutual incompetence of a small child and a senile great-aunt. Her poignant epitaph for Charlotte Brontë sits alongside her mock-epitaph for a reviewer, the latter chirping 'I hope to meet my Maker brow to brow | And find my brow the higher'.

Frances Cornford's first book was *Poems* (London, 1910), and this was followed by five others, consolidated into a *Collected Poems* (London, 1954). She also published a morality play, *Death and the Princess* (Cambridge, 1912).

[PDH

CORNFORD, (Rupert) John (1915–36), was born in Cambridge, the son of the classicist Francis Cornford and the poet Frances *Cornford, and studied at the London School of Economics and Trinity College, Cambridge. He joined the Young Communist League in 1933, and the Communist Party in 1935. He graduated in June 1936, a month before the Spanish Civil War began, and in August left for Spain, where he was one of the first Englishmen to join the Anarchist POUM. He was in the battles for Madrid and Boadilla, and was killed in December on the Cordoba front on his twenty-first birthday or the day after.

Cornford's precocious achievements and his early death in Spain have made him a literary legend, though he in fact left about two-dozen poems, only half of which were written after he was 18. His writings, which consisted largely of political essays and letters, were brought together as *John Cornford: A Memoir* (London, 1938: enlarged as *Understand the Weapon, Understand the Wound*, Manchester, 1976) and *Collected Writings*, ed. J. Galassi (Manchester, 1988).

Cornford saw his poems as instrumental to his political views; yet 'Full Moon at Tierz' remains a work of remarkable power, largely because of its directness and the intensity of its conviction. The firmness and simplicity of its diction is also a feature of 'To Margot Heinemann', one of the most touching personal poems of the period. See also, *Journey to the Frontier* (London, 1966), by P. Stansky and W. Abrahams, an authoritative study. [ATT

CORSO, (Nunzio) Gregory (1930–), was born in New York City to a poor family. He was one of the original *Beats, along with *Ginsberg and Kerouac. It has been said that 'if Kerouac was the father-figure and Ginsberg the rabbi-figure, Corso was the child-figure and the clown'. Corso, less noticed in recent years, still writes, and has managed to hang on to his hard-won immaturity (or, in original Beat terms, innocence). As a young man he got into trouble with the police and served three years in prison for an attempted robbery. He read much there, and on his release was supported by a number of Harvard students, who helped him to publish his first book, *The Vestal Lady on Brattle and Other Poems* (Cambridge, Mass., 1955). Then Ginsberg discovered him. His earliest verse was outrageous, often funny, very much that of an autodidact (full of 'hard' words), and sometimes touching. Later, under the influence of Kerouac, with his philosophy of spontaneity and do-it-yourself-satori, his poems became more grandiose; it also became clear that he had been reading Hart *Crane, and wished to emulate his singing line. One of his most prominent personae began to resemble that of Charles *Bukowski, but was more self-consciously literary. But he remains, as he has said, 'un-Faustian . . . naive . . . strange—sweet—smart—why not'. Unlike his old associates, he has refused to succumb to the White House or literary agents and, for many, his is the only surviving authentic Beat voice—beat up, certainly, and now faded, but still full of good-hearted hatred for the establishment. See *Selected Poems* (London, 1962); *Penguin Modern Poets 5* (1963)—with *Ferlinghetti and Ginsberg; *Mindfield: New* *and Selected Poems* (New York, 1989). Also G. Stephenson, *Exiled Angel: A Study of the Work of Gregory Corso* (London, 1989).   [MS-S

Coterie. The first issue of this quarterly appeared on May Day 1919, the double (and last) number 6/7 in the winter of the following year. It was both a companion and a rival to *Art and Letters*, distinguished from it by a greater emphasis on poetry. The principal contributors, some of whom wrote in almost every number, were Aldous *Huxley, A. E. Coppard, T. W. Earp, H. J. Massingham, L. A. G. Strong, F. S. *Flint, Herbert *Read, Russell Green, Edith *Sitwell, and Conrad *Aiken, who acted as American editor, although almost the only other American contributor was Aiken's friend John Gould *Fletcher. T. S. *Eliot's 'A Cooking Egg' appeared in the first number, and Richard *Aldington, Edmund *Blunden, Wilfred *Owen, Royston Dunnachie (later Roy) *Campbell, and the other *Sitwells also had poems printed. The editor for all except the last issue was Chaman Lall, with an editorial committee including Aldington, Huxley, Eliot (for two issues), and Wyndham *Lewis (for one). There were reproductions of work by artists as varied as William Rothenstein and Zadkine.

Most of the *Coterie* poets are now forgotten, or became celebrated as fiction writers. It seems surprising now that the *Daily Herald* should have deplored their work as part of 'the plague of verse-publication which continues like an everlasting Spanish influenza epidemic'. Nowadays there seems little to stir enthusiasm or indignation. But much of the poetry printed ran counter to what was still the prevailing *Georgian mode: some of it was wayward or flippant, and a little was gently or savagely ironical. The magazine was succeeded by the less interesting *New Coterie*, which appeared quarterly from 1925 to 1927, concentrating much more on prose fiction than on verse.   [JGS

COULETTE, Henri (Anthony) (1927–88), was born in Los Angeles, where he lived almost all of his life, except for a short stint in the army (1945–6) and the time he spent in graduate school at the University of Iowa. On his graduation from Iowa he returned to his alma mater, California State University, Los Angeles, and taught there until his death from an apparent heart attack at his home in South Pasadena.

Coulette's best-known book, *The War of the Secret Agents and Other Poems* (1965), received the Lamont Poetry Award of the Academy of American Poets. The book's title poem is about a ring of spies operating in occupied France during the Second World War. The poem depicts the sadly comic delusions of the spies and reveals the larger web of interlocking duplicities that destroys them. At the end of the poem the author addresses the reader, saying 'there is no meaning|or purpose; only the codes'. Coulette's second book, *The Family Goldschmidt* (1971), was accidentally shredded by the publisher before it was widely distributed.

Usually written in traditional verse forms but sometimes in carefully wrought free verse, Coulette's poetry often looks to popular culture for its subject-matter—spy novels, Hollywood movies, computer poets, life in the 1960s—but considers it with classical wit and contemporary ambivalence. His tone might best be characterized as serio-comic.

Posthumously published by the University of Arkansas Press, *The Collected Poems of Henri Coulette* (Fayetteville and London, 1990) contains the two published books, along with a new book that Coulette had readied for publication and a small selection of uncollected poems.

[AH

COWLEY, Malcolm (1898–1989), was born in western Pennsylvania and raised in Pittsburgh, where he became a lifelong friend of Kenneth *Burke. At Harvard, Cowley met Conrad *Aiken and E. E. *Cummings, and attended the literary salons of Amy *Lowell, who gave him much practical advice on his early poetry. Although he is best known as an editor, a literary critic, and a cultural historian, Cowley began his illustrious career in letters as a poet, and was influenced early on by the French Dadaist and *Surrealist poets, many of whom he met in Paris, where he translated their poetry into English. *Blue Juniata: A Life* (New York, 1985) incorporates his three earlier volumes of poetry (*Blue Juniata*, 1929; *The Dry Season*, 1941; and *Blue Juniata: Collected Poems*, 1968) into an autobiographical sequence modelled on Whitman's *Leaves of Grass*, which Cowley celebrated as a critic.

Following the 'shapes of his childhood, patterns of his growth', Cowley recalls, in many poems, his idyllic boyhoood, a simpler time marred only by the death of his adoptive sister ('The Pyre' and 'The Red Wagon'). 'Tomorrow Morning' captures the revolutionary fervour of literary radicalism in the Thirties, when Cowley uncritically supported the Soviet Union. His best poems, like his best prose writings, are generational portraits. 'The Flower and the Leaf' and 'Ezra Pound at the Hôtel Jacob' profile his renowned friends with the same verve as his unforgettable prose memoir of Hart *Crane in *Exile's Return* (1951), his definitive chronicle of the so-called lost generation of expatriate American writers.

A selection of Cowley's poems and his prose about poets can be found in *The Portable Malcolm Cowley*, ed. Donald Faulkner (New York, 1990).

[TDeP

CRANE, (Harold) Hart (1899–1932), was born in Garrettsville, Ohio, of continually quarrelling parents and committed himself to a poetic career after having had one of his poems accepted by a New York magazine when he was 16. He was encouraged in his ambition by the widow of William Vaughn *Moody, and when his parents separated in 1916 he moved to New York, abandoned his intentions of preparing for college, and plunged into the Greenwich Village world of poetry, painting, avant-gardisme, and moral and ideological unorthodoxy.

After making many literary contacts, Crane returned to Ohio in late 1919 to try to support himself by menial work in his father's chocolate business while reading and writing in the little spare time that was left to him. During this time he acquainted himself with a wide range of writers who had come to his notice through the criticism of T. S. *Eliot and Ezra *Pound. In 1922 he

obtained work as an advertising copy-writer, which he believed would free him from his enslavement to the business world and be congenial to his poetic abilities. He was drawn back to New York in 1923, and from this time onwards made a precarious living, mostly from copy-writing, and came to feel increasingly isolated from the values of 1920s America, both because of his homosexual life-style and deepening alcoholism, and also because of his unproductive and socially non-respectable vocation as a poet.

Crane's reaction against the poetic pessimism of Eliot's *The Waste Land* was partly responsible for his determination to 'launch into praise' in an affirmative and visionary poem about America which eventually became *The Bridge*. A personal grant from the banker Otto Kahn allowed him time to work on this project; meanwhile his first collection of lyrics, *White Buildings*, was published in 1926. The disorder of his personal life continued to intensify, while his private faith in the meaning and value of his optimistic poem steadily declined. On a short trip to Europe in 1928 he spent most of his time in Paris among American expatriate writers and artists. Awarded a Guggenheim Fellowship after the publication of *The Bridge* in 1930, he embarked for Mexico in 1931 with the intention of writing an epic poem about the Spanish conquest of that country. This last phase of his career included an attempt to establish a heterosexual identity for himself in an affair with the estranged wife of Malcolm *Cowley, Peggy Baird. On a return trip to the United States in April 1932 he committed suicide by leaping overboard from the stern of his ship.

Like much of the poetry of the period, Crane's very earliest lyrics exhibit many 1890s-ish qualities, and they have usually been dismissed rather patronizingly by critics. These poems nevertheless possess a lyrical delicacy and fragility which may define the true nature of Crane's talent better than most of his later, more willed and declamatory work. Poems like 'My Grandmother's Love Letters', 'Pastorale', or 'Voyages I'; the more obviously derivative and literary 'Legende' or 'Forgetfulness'; or the piece of seasonal imagery 'October–November', written when he was 17, show a sensitivity in the handling of free verse which is unsurpassed by any other English-language poet. If he had been more sure of the real nature of his poetic powers, and if he had been able to assimilate more of his twentieth-century subject-matter within his lyric capacities (as he occasionally did in *The Bridge*) without doing violence to them, it seems possible that Hart Crane might have marked out a more Romantic and intuitive path for American poetry than the one which it in fact took.

Crane's sensitivity to the connotative or associational dimension of words is a noticeable characteristic of his earlier poems, but it also helped to open the way to his later poetic undoing. Partly under the influence of the Elizabethan poets and dramatists, but also that of the French Symbolists, and particularly of Rimbaud, he gave himself over in many poems to the creation of complex knots of meaning which were not easily intelligible without some kind of accompanying interpretation from the poet himself. Some of the later lyrics of *White Buildings* such as 'Possessions', 'Lachrymae Christi', or 'Recitative', embody a great sense of visionary aspiration and occasional lines of intense beauty, but without yielding any clearly graspable overall significance. Crane also abandoned his earlier delicate free verse for blank verse, and thereby laid the basis for the rather oratorical idiom which became the anchoring mode of his major poem, *The Bridge*. This 'turn' in Crane's work took place around 1922, principally in his three-part poem 'For the Marriage of Faustus and Helen', which was an attempt to relate these archetypal or mythic figures to the actual circumstances of modern city life.

Crane's ambition in *The Bridge* was to write a visionary poem about America in which America's past history since the Spanish conquest and its present-day realities of business, engineering, and democratic optimism would be held together by one over-arching and exaltational symbol—the Brooklyn Bridge—in an almost Dantesque manner. Other emblems which serve to integrate the poem on a symbolic level include Columbus, Pocahontas, Rip Van Winkle, Walt Whitman, the clipper ship *Cutty Sark*, the Mississippi river, and the New York subway. From the start, the success of such an enterprise seemed doubtful, even to Crane himself, but the large-scale and loose framework of the long poem nevertheless allowed him room to explore many different poetic styles and materials, and between its opening 'Proem' and its closing 'Atlantis'—both of them written in high-toned and annunciatory blank verse—*The Bridge* contains extended passages and many individual lyrics which are both easily readable and poetically successful. 'The Harbor Dawn' is one of Crane's most subtle and authentically modern lyrics. 'The Rivers', set firmly in the twentieth-century world of railroads and railroad hobos, perhaps comes closest to Crane's aim of tracing living links between America's past and its present, and does so by making historical and psychological, rather than merely symbolic connections. 'Cutty Sark' contains some interesting formal experiment, 'National Winter Garden' has some sharp contemporary observation, 'Virginia' is a playful and innocent love lyric. 'The Tunnel', set in the New York subway—cast in the role of a Dantean hell or purgatory—is persuasively infernal, but at the same time reveals the main flaws of Crane's method in so far as this subterranean symbol of desolation is of course realistically a product of the very same forces which produced its would-be uplifting counterpart, the Brooklyn Bridge. Crane's last collection, assembled shortly before his death, shows a successful return to simplicity in such lyrics as 'Island Quarry', or even the Hopkinsesque 'The Hurricane', but by this time his life was in chaos and his talent largely destroyed.

The key to Crane's 'failure' to do all that he might have done is almost certainly to be found in his continuing, if largely unconscious, acceptance of the American bourgeois values which surrounded and beset him. By these criteria he could only see himself as a non-achiever, and his attempts by way of compensation to achieve a public affirmation in his poetry (rather than authentically and more personally to register despair or defeat, as he had done in a poem like his homage to Chaplin, 'Chaplinesque') led to a distortion of his talent and a loss of poetic direction; meanwhile his life, and his talent, were being undermined by real-life forces which he tried to ignore as he toiled away at his mystical bridge-building. The many mid-century poets (for example, Robert *Lowell) who have been fascinated by Crane have perhaps seen him as anticipating some of their own conflicts with twentieth-century American society.

The most recent edition of Crane's poetry is *The Poems of Hart Crane*, ed. Marc Simon (New York, 1986). Crane's letters and few critical writings are well represented in the *Complete Poems and Selected Letters and Prose*, ed. Brom Weber (New York and London, 1966); a revised paperback edition of the *Complete Poems*, without the letters and prose, was published from Newcastle upon Tyne in 1984. The biographies by Philip Horton (*Hart Crane*, New York, 1937) and Brom Weber (*Hart Crane*, New York, 1948) are still of interest, while that of John Unterecker (*Voyager*, New York, 1969) is as thorough and definitive as any biography is now likely to be. There is little good criticism of Crane's work, and the most penetrating comments are perhaps still to be found in the essays of such poet-critics of his own generation as Allen *Tate, Yvor *Winters, and R. P. *Blackmur.   [CF

CRANE, Stephen (1871–1900) was descended from Methodist clergymen and a hero of the Revolutionary War; these martial and evangelical strains helped to shape his sensibility. In his teens already a journalist, he attended Lafayette College in Pennsylvania and Syracuse University for only one year; in a fraternity house he drafted *Maggie: A Girl of the Streets* (1893), the first American naturalistic novel of slum life. Crane sought and gained the endorsement of William Dean Howells, influential novelist and editor of *Harper's Monthly*. But Crane was unacquainted with writers or poets, consorting with art students in New York City, writing freelance feature articles for newspapers. In 1895 *The Red Badge of Courage* appeared; it made him instantly famous. This is still perhaps the best

war novel and study of fear in American literature. Crane was sent as a war correspondent to cover the Cuban insurrection of 1897. Before boarding the gun-running tugboat whose sinking led to his story, 'The Open Boat', Crane met the undivorced wife of a son of the governor-general of India, who had abandoned her on the Florida coast where she set herself up as a madam. From then on Crane, the preacher's boy, led a life of scandal, passing Cora Taylor off as his wife when they moved to England. Living beyond their means in a country house in Surrey, they entertained Henry James, H. G. Wells, Conrad, and other notables. By then suffering from tuberculosis and ever deeper in debt, Crane desperately wrote hack work until his death in 1900. He was 28.

Among his voluminous writings Crane published only two slim books of verse: *The Black Riders* (1895) and *War is Kind* (1899). He called his work 'lines', to distinguish it from the vapid poems then in fashion. Despite the appearance in the 1890s of the last edition of Whitman's *Leaves of Grass* and the first publication of Emily Dickinson's poems, the period valued Richard Watson Gilder and other versifiers later described by T. S. *Eliot as 'nimbly dull'. *Santayana has written of the promising young poets of the 1890s—William Vaughn *Moody, Trumbull *Stickney, George Cabot Lodge, all students at Harvard—that they were undone by gentility and submission to conventional taste. By contrast, the relatively untutored Crane's lines were unmetered, unrhymed, abjured poeticisms, and used a much plainer language than did his own colourful, imagistic prose. 'There was a man with tongue of wood | Who essayed to sing' he wrote. His principal themes in verse are rebellion against a vengeful God; the insignificance and isolation of man in a universe of force; and the irony of courage. His poems are brief, epigrammatic, allegories or parables; their structures are borrowed from the prose fables of Olive Schreiner and the parables of the Bible.

In his vision of man's aloneness in a faithless, mechanical, and uncaring universe, as in his abjuring poetic diction and verse conventions,

Crane anticipated the repudiations to be made two decades later by *Pound, *Eliot, William Carlos *Williams, the *Imagists and the *vers libristes. Amy *Lowell introduced his poetry in the first collected edition, *Work*, vol. 6 (New York, 1926). A selection appears in *The Portable Stephen Crane* (Harmondsworth and New York, 1977), ed. Joseph Katz. The definitive edition, including uncollected poems, is *Works of Stephen Crane*, vol. 10, *Poems and Literary Remains* (Charlottesville, Va., 1975); this text is reprinted in *Stephen Crane: Prose and Poetry*, ed. J. C. Levenson (New York and Cambridge, 1984). See also *Stephen Crane*, by John Berryman (New York, 1950); *The Poetry of Stephen Crane*, by Daniel Hoffman (New York, 1957); *Stephen Crane: A Biography*, by R. W. Stallman (New York, 1968); and *A Reading of Stephen Crane*, by Marston LaFrance (Oxford, 1971).   [DH

CRAPSEY, Adelaide (1878–1914), born in Brooklyn Heights and named for her mother, was the third child of the Revd Algernon Crapsey, a free-thinking Episcopal minister, who moved his family to Rochester, New York, soon after her birth. Crapsey grew up in a hectic but intellectual household as her father's favourite. She graduated in 1901 from Vassar College and taught prep school for two years before attending Rome's School of Archaeology, returning in 1905 for her father's widely reported heresy trial. She also accompanied him to the 1907 Hague Peace Conference, but bouts of fatigue forced her to resign another teaching post. She spent two more years abroad, researching a study of English metrics.

Her own poetry was conventionally Romantic, often Keatsian, but exposure to recently translated Japanese *tanka* and haiku, as well as to Emily Dickinson and Landor, encouraged a new tautness. Early in 1911, while teaching at Smith College, she invented the cinquain: an unrhymed, five-line poem with a 1,2,3,4,1 accentual scheme. She also learned that tuberculin meningitis was ravaging her brain, and passed her last year in a sanatorium.

Though a minor poet, anticipating the *Imagists, Crapsey was a pioneer in the shift away from Victorian rhetoric and sentimentality, as the sardonic 'To the Dead in the Grave-Yard under my Window' confirms. Pressured by death, her modest gift forged a group of cinquains—'November Night', 'Trapped', 'The Guarded Wound', 'Amaze', 'The Warning', 'Night Winds', 'Triad'—that have entered the canon. Her unfinished thesis was published as *A Study in English Metrics* (New York, 1918), and Susan Sutton Smith has edited *The Complete Poems and Collected Letters of Adelaide Crapsey* (Albany, NY, 1976). See also *Adelaide Crapsey* (Boston, 1979), by Edward Butscher and *Alone in the Dawn* (Athens, Ga., 1989) by Karen Alkalay-Gut.   [EB

CRASE, Douglas (1944–   ), was born in Battle Creek, Michigan, and received a BA from Princeton University. He dropped out of law school at the University of Michigan in order to write campaign speeches for the Democratic candidate for governor of the state. He then moved to Rochester, New York, where he spent three years working as a speech-writer for Eastman Kodak. He now lives and works in New York City as a free-lance writer.

To date Crase has published only one volume, *The Revisionist* (Boston, 1981), yet that has been enough to establish him as one of the most important poets of his generation, displaying a rare ambition and an explicitly Whitmanian concern with American landscape and history. As Crase himself acknowledges, his major influence among living poets has been *Ashbery; unlike other second-generation *New York School poets, however, Crase picks up not Ashbery's playfully surrealist mannerisms but the deeply American strain in his work that reaches back through Hart *Crane, *Stevens, and Whitman to its ultimate origins in Emerson (whose essays Crase has recently edited). Where older poets like *Ginsberg, *Simpson, and James *Wright have bemoaned what they regard as modern America's betrayal of Whitman's vision, Crase steadfastly continues to affirm the sense of infinite possibility, in however attenuated a form, that has been at the centre of American mythology since Emerson. As the title of his book suggests, the renewal of American possibility depends for Crase on revision in all its senses, political as well as literary; in his poems he explores these modes of revision as they connect with specific landscapes. Crase is a topographical poet in an almost eighteenth-century sense; he writes lovingly and meticulously about places as such, rather than incidents or epiphanies for which they provide convenient backdrops. His style is discursive, argumentative, at times verging on the prosaic in its abstract diction and pursuit of intricate logical structures; but these qualities (which may reflect and to some extent parody his work as a corporate speech-writer) are balanced by an intense lyricism that breaks out unexpectedly in the midst of dry patches, much like the beauty Crase continues to find cropping up in the barren landscapes of *fin-de-siècle* America. [RG

CRAWFORD, Robert (1959–), was educated at the universities of Glasgow and Oxford, and is now lecturer in Scottish literature at St Andrews. This academic background sets up expectations which are agreeably confounded by Crawford's poetry. His work is lively, sentient, and eclectic—Scottish qualities, perhaps, but rarely found controlled by such a wide-ranging and astute critical intelligence. *A Scottish Assembly* (London, 1990) was followed by *Talkies* (London, 1992), which shows a similar scope as well as a Scottish particularity but with an enhanced confidence. His growth as a poet can be sensed in the bravura inventiveness of two longer poems, 'Z' and 'Customs'. His work is also topical within the context of the recent regeneration of the Scottish cultural and political scene, especially in his critical but positive engagement with Scottish subjects and personalities.

Crawford also writes in a densely textured Scots, as in *Sharawaggi* (Edinburgh, 1990) which he shared with W. N. Herbert.

Crawford has published *The Savage and the City in the Work of T. S. Eliot* (Oxford, 1987) and *Devolving English Literature* (Oxford, 1992), and has co-edited collections of essays, *About Edwin Morgan* (Edinburgh, 1990) and *The Arts of Alas-*

dair Gray (Edinburgh, 1991). Crawford is also a founder and co-editor of the poetry magazine *Verse*. [DED

CREELEY, Robert (White) (1926–), was born in Arlington, Massachusetts. He lost his father, and the use of his left eye, before he was 5, and was subsequently brought up on a farm in West Acton. A year with the American Field Service in India and Burma (1944/5) interrupted his time at Harvard; on his return he married, left Harvard without graduating, and, in 1948, went to New Hampshire to try subsistence farming. His attempt two years later to launch his own magazine failed, but prompted a long correspondence with Charles *Olson and provided material for Cid *Corman's journal, *Origin. In search of a cheaper way of life, the Creeleys moved in 1951 to France and the following year to Mallorca (the setting for Creeley's only novel, *The Island*, 1963), where they stayed until their divorce in 1955. There they set up the Divers Press and printed books by Creeley himself (including *The Gold Diggers*, 1954; eleven stories), Robert *Duncan, Olson, and others. At Olson's invitation Creeley taught at Black Mountain College (spring 1954 and autumn 1955) and founded and edited the *Black Mountain Review* (1954–7: see BLACK MOUNTAIN POETS).

His first three books of poetry, *Le Fou* (1952), *The Kind of Act of* (1953), and *The Immoral Proposition* (1953), appeared in quick succession while he was in Europe, and his next two, *All That is Lovely in Men* (1955) and *If You* (1956), shortly after his return to America. In 1956 Creeley settled in Albuquerque, New Mexico, where he remarried, taught at a boy's school until 1959, and took an MA from the University of New Mexico in 1960. Having worked as a tutor on a Guatemalan plantation, in the early 1960s he began a new academic career—which led him in later years to the State University of New York, Buffalo—and became nationally known with *For Love: Poems 1950–1960* (1962). He divorced again, and married for the third time in 1977.

Creeley's poetry is predominantly concerned with love and the emotions attending intimate relationships. Among his strongest influences he lists not only poets, like Olson, William Carlos, *Williams, and *Ginsberg, who reassured him that 'you can write directly from that which you feel', but also jazz musicians, who demonstrated that feelings could be expressed no less powerfully for eschewing prescribed forms. Creeley's early poems, collected in *Poems 1950–1965* (1966), are minutely detailed—often obscure—analyses of feelings, their verse invariably free, their lines and stanzas short, and their sentences terse. A new disillusionment with analytical thinking is evident in *Words* (1967), *Pieces* (1969), and *A Day Book* (1972), and a less exalted view of love in *Later* (1978) and *Echoes* (1982). More notable for its continuities than for its changes, however, his poetry has sustained its unique brand of vigilant minimalism for the last four decades. Most of it is gathered in *The Collected Poems 1945–1975* (Berkeley, Calif., 1982; London, 1983), most of his criticism in *Was That a Real Poem and Other Essays*, ed. Donald Allen (Bolinas, Calif., 1979), and all of his fiction in *The Collected Prose* (New York and London, 1984). See also *Charles Olson and Robert Creeley: The Complete Correspondence*, ed. George F. Butterick and Richard Blevins, 9 vols. (Santa Barbara, Calif., 1980–90), and *Robert Creeley's Poetry: A Critical Introduction*, by Cynthia Dubin Edelberg (Albuquerque, N. M., 1978). See also *Selected Poems 1945–90* (London and New York, 1991). [NE

CRONIN, Jeremy (1949–), grew up in Simonstown, South Africa, where his father was a naval officer. He became a Marxist during his student years at the University of Cape Town and the Sorbonne, where he gained his MA in philosophy. In 1976 he was arrested for distributing pamphlets for the banned African National Congress. His seven years in gaol as a political prisoner gave rise to the poems of his only volume, *Inside* (Johannesburg, 1983), which won the Ingrid Jonker Prize in 1984. He spent three years in exile in London and Lusaka before returning home in 1990, and is on the executive of the South African Communist Party.

Prison freed Cronin from the fear that lyricism is self-indulgent in a context of oppression:

his personal suffering became part of the collective suffering and resistance of his comrades. This African humanism is enhanced in many of his poems by indigenous diction and oral repetition, and his work is perhaps best encountered in performance.

In 1987 *Inside* was published in London, and eight poems from *Inside* appeared in *TriQuarterly*, 69 (Evanston, Ill.). See Keith Gottschalk's review in *Critical Arts*, 3: 2 (1984).

[CWo

CROZIER, Lorna (1948–), was born and raised in Swift Current, Saskatchewan, where she worked as a teacher (1972–7) after graduating from the University of Saskatchewan, Saskatoon. Crozier has taught creative writing, held a number of writer-in-residence positions, worked as a radio correspondent with the Canadian Broadcasting Corporation, and in 1986 was appointed a Special Lecturer at the University of Saskatchewan.

Crozier's early verse, *Inside Is the Sky* (Saskatoon, 1976), *Crow's Black Joy* (Edmonton, 1978), and *Humans and Other Beasts* (Winnipeg, 1980), explores the landscape of poetry and celebrates the simple virtues and vices of prairie people. Her recent poetry, in *The Weather* (Moose Jaw, Sask., 1983), *The Garden Going on Without Us* (Toronto, 1987), *Angels of Flesh, Angels of Silence* (Toronto, 1988), and *Inventing the Hawk* (1992) analyses gender and sexual politics, anatomizes the lifeline from foetus to angel to death, and questions the seeming invulnerability of nature.

[PMStP

CRUZ, Victor Hernandez (1949–), born in Aguas Buenas, Puerto Rico (where he now lives), grew up in Spanish Harlem. Early *Beat- and black-influenced collections like *Papo Got His Gun* (New York, 1966) and *Snaps* (New York, 1969) established him as a leading *nuyoriqueño* (or New York-Puerto Rican) poet. His adeptness in Spanish and English, and in using a blend of both, has served a now considerable body of poetry whose key theme has been the contrasting worlds of Manhattan and Puerto Rico, an American metropolis of the *barrio* and the tenement as against a Caribbean homeland as luxuriant in its people as its topography. Thus an early poem like 'urban dream', in *Snaps*, can speak of New York apocalypse ('things blowing up. | times square | electrified'), while a later poem, like 'Areyto', in *Red Beans* (1991), can invoke a Puerto Rico at once Arawak-Indian, Afro-Caribbean, and eclectically 'Spanish'. A similar multi-cultural vibrancy and reference marks out all his stronger poetry, as, for instance, in his New York-inspired 'Mountain Building', or his lyric, Puerto Rico-inspired 'Geography of the Trinity Corona', both in *By Lingual Wholes* (San Francisco, 1982). From the 1960s on, Cruz has been a major energy in America's Latino renaissance, able to shift from an oral street voice to an almost Wallace *Stevensish versatility. The principal collections include *Mainland* (New York, 1973), *Tropicalization* (New York, 1976), *Rhythm, Content & Flavor* (Houston, Tex., 1989), and *Red Beans* (Minneapolis, 1991). [ARL

CULLEN, Countee (1903–46), was probably born in Louisville, Kentucky. He was adopted by a Harlem preacher and his wife at the age of 15, and later attended both New York University and Harvard. With the publication of his first volume of poems in 1925, *Color*, Cullen assumed the place of a central figure in the *Harlem Renaissance. The book stated the themes—the injustice of colour-prejudice, the black man's African legacy, religious doubt and belief—that were to dominate his work over the twenty years until his death. A frequently anthologized poem is 'Incident', in which an 8-year-old boy has his visit to a strange city spoiled when he is called 'nigger'.

Cullen had other interests besides race, however, and a wider formal range than most of his Renaissance contemporaries. His verse is often crisp, subtle, and intelligent at once, taking special pleasure in manipulating the paradoxes thrown up by the modern treatment of the black man brought forcibly to the Land of the Free.

A selected poems was published as *On These I Stand* (New York, 1947); a group of eight of

Cullen's poems is included in the anthology *Black Voices*, ed. Abraham Chapman (New York, 1968); see also *A Many-Colored Coat of Dreams: The Poetry of Countee Cullen* (Detroit, 1974), by Houston A. Baker, Jr., and *Harlem Renaissance*, by Nathan Irvin Huggins (New York, 1971).

[JC

CULLINAN, Patrick (1932–), was born in Pretoria and educated at Charterhouse and Oxford. He has worked as a saw-miller in the Eastern Transvaal and, latterly, as a lecturer in English at the University of the Western Cape.

First coming to prominence in the 1960s, Cullinan rapidly established himself as one of South Africa's leading poets. Since then he has also distinguished himself as an editor of the influential journal, *The Bloody Horse*, as a translator of Montale, and an historian of early European explorers in South Africa.

In his first collection, *The Horizon Forty Miles Away* (1973), many of the distinctive concerns of the white South African poet find expression. But Cullinan gives new resonance to these through a verse that is so unadorned as to be almost a form of anti-poetry. He also reveals a gift, rare in South Africa, for the use of myth and parable.

Throughout this first volume there is a note of controlled anguish which is all the more powerful in his second collection, *Today Is Not Different* (1978). Although Cullinan has never been a 'protest' poet, here he uses past South African history to reflect, albeit indirectly, upon present troubles. Moreover, in such poems as 'The Billiard Room', he shows himself also to be a striking historian of family relations.

As a poet, Cullinan early showed the type of concern with language which marked him as something other than a realist. This is all the more conspicuous in *The White Hail in the Orchard* (1984). In this volume his themes become ever more metaphysical. At the same time, his skilful focusing on questions of language and reality, particularly in a poem like 'Mimesis', has served to underline his position as one of the few genuine modernists in English South African poetry.

Selected Poems (Cape Town, 1992) contains the best of his work.   [SW

CUMMINGS, E(dward) E(stlin) (1894–1962), was born in Cambridge, Massachusetts, to liberal, indulgent parents who from early on encouraged him to develop his creative gifts. While at Harvard, where his father had taught before becoming a Unitarian minister, he delivered a daring commencement address on modernist artistic innovations, thus announcing the direction his own work would take. In 1917, after working briefly for a mail-order publishing company, the only regular employment in his career, Cummings volunteered to serve in the Norton-Harjes Ambulance group in France. Here he and a friend were imprisoned (on false grounds) for three months in a French detention camp. *The Enormous Room* (1922), his witty and absorbing account of the experience, was also the first of his literary attacks on authoritarianism. *Eimi* (1933), a later travel journal, focused with much less successful results on the collectivized Soviet Union.

At the end of the First World War Cummings went to Paris to study art. On his return to New York in 1924 he found himself a celebrity, both for *The Enormous Room* and for *Tulips and Chimneys* (1923), his first collection of poetry (for which his old classmate John Dos Passos had finally found a publisher). Clearly influenced by Gertrude *Stein's syntactical and Amy *Lowell's imagistic experiments, Cummings's early poems had nevertheless discovered an original way of describing the chaotic immediacy of sensuous experience. The games they play with language (adverbs functioning as nouns, for instance) and lyric form combine with their deliberately simplistic view of the world (the individual and spontaneity versus collectivism and rational thought) to give them the gleeful and precocious tone which became a hallmark of his work. Love poems, satirical squibs, and descriptive nature poems would always be his favoured forms.

A roving assignment from *Vanity Fair* in 1926 allowed Cummings to travel again and to establish his lifelong routine: painting in the after-

noons and writing at night. In 1931 he published a collection of drawings and paintings, *CIOPW* (its title an acronym for the materials used: charcoal, ink, oil, pencil, watercolour), and over the next three decades had many individual shows in New York. He enjoyed a long and happy third marriage to the photographer Marion Morehouse, with whom he collaborated on *Adventures in Value* (1962), and in later life divided his time between their apartment in New York and his family's farm in New Hampshire. His many later books of poetry, from *VV* (1931) and *No Thanks* (1935) to *Xaipe* (1950) and *95 Poems* (1958), took his formal experiments and his war on the scientific attitude to new extremes, but showed little substantial development.

Cummings's critical reputation has never matched his popularity. The left-wing critics of the 1930s were only the first to dismiss his work as sentimental and politically naïve. His supporters, however, find value not only in its verbal and visual inventiveness but also in its mystical and anarchistic beliefs. The two-volume *Complete Poems*, ed. George James Firmage (New York and London, 1981) is the standard edition of his poetry, and *Dreams in the Mirror*, by Richard S. Kennedy (New York, 1980) the standard biography. *e. e. cummings: The Art of His Poetry*, by Norman Friedman (Baltimore and London, 1960) is still among the best critical studies of his poetic techniques.   [NE

CUNNINGHAM, J(ames) V(incent) (1911–85), was born in Cumberland, Maryland, to Irish Catholic parents. The family moved to Montana, then to Colorado, where at 16 Cunningham graduated from a Jesuit high school. His father having died the year before in an industrial accident, Cunningham drifted from job to job, making several abortive attempts at college. He settled at Stanford University, studying with Yvor *Winters and W. D. Briggs, and publishing poems as an undergraduate in prominent magazines. Cunningham received an AB in classics in 1934, a Ph.D in English eleven years later. *The Helmsman*, his first of six poetry collections, appeared in 1942. In a long career Cunningham taught at numerous universities, including Harvard and Brandeis, where he remained from 1953 until retirement in 1980. He was married three times and had one child, a daughter.

Perhaps because his work is severe and his oeuvre small, Cunningham has not been as widely read as he deserves to be. When he is praised it is usually as a great epigrammatist, but Cunningham was a poet (he preferred to be called a verse-maker) of complex vision, confronting the incongruities of modern life with directness and purifying anger. His quest for virtue in 'sinuous exacting speech' suggests that he found little virtue elsewhere. If his poems display the plain style associated with Winters and the *Stanford School, they are also the best and most searching poems that school has produced. Cunningham was unafraid of the pithy abstraction, yet his sequences, 'Doctor Drink' and 'To What Strangers, What Welcome', as well as short poems like 'Montana Pastoral', are full of incisive images.

Cunningham's critical and scholarly essays discuss Shakespearean tragedy, Dickinson, *Stevens, and poetic form. In 'The Quest of the Opal' and 'The Journal of John Cardan' he poses questions of technique in relation to the uncertainty and dividedness of human nature.

The Collected Poems and Epigrams (Chicago and London, 1971) lacks several good poems found in *The Exclusions of a Rhyme* (Denver, Col., 1964). *The Collected Essays* (Chicago, 1976) includes both scholarly and critical work. See also *The Poetry of J. V. Cunningham*, by Yvor Winters (Denver, 1961), and 'An Interview with J. V. Cunningham' by Timothy Steele, in *The Iowa Review* (Fall 1985). [DM

CURNOW, Allen (1911–), was born in Timaru, New Zealand, of Scottish and English stock. He did not move directly to a university education but first became a journalist and then studied for the Anglican ministry, returning before ordination to newspaper work. More significant than his early career moves were the friendships he made with New Zealand writers, including Denis *Glover, R. A. K. *Mason and A. R. D. *Fairburn. From the outset Curnow

was perceived to be a key figure in the emergence of an authentic New Zealand literature. Later involvements with James K. *Baxter and C. K. *Stead helped confirm Curnow's importance as a catalyst to newer generations of poets, until now, entering his eighties, he is the unquestioned doyen of his country's writing. He has edited two of the landmark anthologies of New Zealand poetry, *A Book of New Zealand Verse* (1945 and 1951) and the *Penguin Book of New Zealand Verse* (1960). Soon after the Second World War he came to England and worked on Fleet Street, after which he was invited to join the English department of Auckland University. Curnow's life since the Fifties has been devoted to university teaching, with extended periods travelling in the United States and Europe. He has also worked on compiling a definitive canon of his poetry.

Curnow's first book, *Not in Narrow Seas* (1939), with its determination to add to 'the anti-myth about New Zealand', is, significantly, reprinted entire in his Penguin *Selected Poems* of 1982. Poets' first published collections often distil an essence they later deplore but recognize as important. This Penguin culls Curnow's prodigious forty-year output severely and may be seen to mark the two-thirds point of his career. The later volumes drawn upon by the selection show the remarkable development of Curnow as a quirky, experimental, perhaps even 'post-modernist' poet. This phase is summed-up in his second collection, *Continuum* (Auckland, 1988), sub-titled 'New and Later Poems, 1972–1988', to which must also be added a further book of *Selected Poems, 1940–1988* (London, 1990), containing his most recent work. The title of one of his late poems serves as a clue to those qualities in his poetry which tend to elude criticism—'An Incorrigible Music'. In his hands, the English language makes music continually, and yet he is faithful to that journalistic particularity which resists any too-ready recourse to the sublime.

In all his verse Curnow reveals herself as a quiet virtuoso with a complete command of poetic resource. He combines a vernacular diction with a high baroque tone, and never wrenches the tessitura of his language even over an extended range. His collected work has a consistent feeling of maturity, a philosophical calm which also manages to include the scabrous, the vulgar, and the sheerly ordinary. His poetry has got more, not less, audacious with age, so that *Continuum* and its successors constantly surprise the reader, being skittish and profound by turns. [PNFP

CURTIS, Tony (1946–), was born in Carmarthen and educated at University College, Swansea, and Goddard College, Vermont. He is now Senior Lecturer in English at the Polytechnic of Wales. His four collections of verse are *Album* (1974), *Preparations* (1980), *Letting Go* (1983), and *The Last Candles* (1989). Many of his poems are concerned with his family (especially his dead father) and friends, but they are more celebratory than elegiac, and tender-hearted rather than sentimental. A wide range of historical and contemporary perspectives is brought to play in some of his longer narrative poems, such as 'The Death of Richard Beattie—Seaman' and 'Soup'.

Tony Curtis's *Selected Poems 1970–85* (Bridgend), together with an American edition, *Poems: Selected and New* (Santa Cruz, Calif.) appeared in 1986; see also the interview the poet gave to Robert Minhinnick in *The New Welsh Review*, 2: 4 (Spring 1990), and the article by Tony Brown on the poetry of Tony Curtis in the same number of that magazine. [MS

D

DABYDEEN, Cyril (1945–), was born in British Guiana (now Guyana), and educated at Queen's College in Georgetown, and the University of the West Indies. He moved to Canada in 1970, eventually becoming a Canadian citizen. In keeping with the Canadian cultural ethos, his poetry has gradually mellowed and become more relaxed in tone, the concluding couplet of 'As An Immigrant' being characteristic: 'And let the beaver draw me closer | As I quarry silence and talk | In riddles so that the maple leaf | Itself will understand.' He could not have chosen two more familiar symbols of Canada than the beaver and the maple leaf, but by doing so he paradoxically secures his own distinctive vision as a Guyanese who grew up on the periphery of a wilderness. Dabydeen's poetry in general explores borderlines of all kinds, keeping at bay inscrutable tropical and arctic landscapes. His latest collection is titled *Coastland: New and Selected Poems 1937–1987* (New York and London, 1989), and his collection of short stories, *Still Close to the Island* (Ottawa, 1980). [MR

DABYDEEN, David (1955–), was born in British Guiana (now Guyana), and educated at the universities of Cambridge and London, completing his doctorate in 1982. Academic appointments have included a research fellowship at Wolfson College, Oxford, and a lectureship at the Centre for Caribbean Studies, University of Warwick.

The poems in *Slave Song* (Mundelsrup, Denmark, 1984), are distinguished by innovative use of Guyanese Creole dialect. Primarily dramatic monologues, the poems deal with the harsh lives and frustrated sexual fantasies of sugarcane cutters. The cumulative effect is that of an anti-pastoral inferno, the protagonists trapped in physical and spiritual pain, though still capable of being gripped by tender emotion. More wide-ranging and autobiographical, the poems in *Coolie Odyssey* (London, 1988) explore the experience of East Indians, both in Britain and in the Caribbean. Dabydeen's views on forms of English, and their often hidden political and cultural implications, are expounded in 'On Not Being Milton: Nigger Talk in England Today', his contribution to *The State of the Language,* ed. Christopher Ricks and Leonard Michaels (London and Berkeley, Calif., 1990).

Other books include the studies *Hogarth's Blacks* (Manchester, 1987) and *Hogarth, Walpole and Commercial Britain* (London, 1987), and *The Intended* (London, 1991), his first novel. [MR

D'AGUIAR, Fred(erick) (1960–), was born in London of Guyanese parents. He grew up in Guyana, and returned to London in 1972. He later trained and worked as a psychiatric nurse before reading English and Caribbean studies at the University of Kent.

D'Aguiar's poems are deeply rooted in Caribbean folk-wisdom, reinterpreting its homilies in terms of the contemporary world. They are also informed by a humane humour quite different from any kind of steely wit, but not at all sentimental. In his first collection, *Mama Dot* (London, 1985), the title refers—as E. A. *Markham put it—to the archetypal grandmother, an elemental force'. The ostensibly anecdotal poems about her, some in the vernacular, are in fact subtly rhetorical in structure.

The poems in *Airy Hall* (London, 1989) survey his early years in Guyana, often capturing the vivid sensuousness of childhood vision.

The 'Black British Poetry' section of *The New British Poetry* (London and Sydney, 1988) was edited by him. A selection of his poems, and a short essay on his childhood, 'Zigzag Paths', are available in *Hinterland: Caribbean Poetry from the West Indies and Britain*, ed. E. A. Markham (Newcastle upon Tyne, 1989).   [MR

DALE, Peter (John) (1938–), is co-editor of the magazine *Agenda. His main achievement has undoubtedly been as translator of François Villon (*The Legacy, The Testament and Other Poems*, London, 1973), in which he attempts to reproduce the metres of the originals. He has also written imitations of Tamil poetry in *The Seasons of Cankam* (London, 1975), in the tradition of *Pound's adaptations from the Chinese, and versions of Laforgue. Forthcoming is his verse translation of Dante's *Divine Comedy*. As an original poet Dale is quiet and, essentially, neo-*Georgian. His lack of energy is in part offset by his evident sincerity. He writes, usually, in a controlled free verse. His most interesting work is to be found in *Mortal Fire* (London, 1970; rev., London, 1976), and in the sonnet-sequence *One Another* (London, 1978). Later poems, which show little development in method, are collected in *Too Much of Water: Poems 1976–1982* (London, 1983). See also *Earth Light* (Frome, Somerset, 1991).   [MS-S

DALLAS, Ruth (1919–), born in New Zealand's southernmost city, Invercargill, has lived most of her life in Dunedin. She began publishing in local papers as a child, and was the most frequent woman contributor to the literary quarterly *Landfall during the period of Charles *Brasch's editorship (1947–67). Six volumes of her verse were published by the Caxton Press, Christchurch, between 1953 and 1979, and *Song for a Guitar and Other Songs* by Otago University Press, Dunedin, in 1976. She has also written stories and several children's books. In 1968 she held the Robert Burns Fellowship at the University of Otago, which in 1978 awarded

her an honorary D.Litt. *Walking on the Snow* (1976) won the 1977 New Zealand Book Award for Poetry.

Dallas's poems characteristically focus on natural phenomena—whether within the Southland countryside or Dunedin's gardens and parks—to meditate on the cycle of the seasons and on human transience. She peoples her landscapes with figures who are apt to be representative rather than individual. Receptive to oriental influences, she will address a Chinese poet, emulate a Japanese potter or printmaker, or respond to the spirit of Buddhist sculpture. In some of her later volumes she cultivates a vein of dream imagery.

Her development may be traced in *Collected Poems* (Dunedin, 1987). An autobiographical account of her 'Beginnings' as a writer was published in *Landfall*, 76 (1965), and reprinted in *Beginnings*, ed. Robin Dudding (Wellington, 1980).   [McDJ

DANGOR, Achmat (1948–), was born and educated in Johannesburg. In 1973, following years of anti-apartheid campaigning, Dangor was declared a banned person by the South African Government. After the ban was rescinded in 1978, he worked as a manager for a multinational company in Johannesburg. More recently he has been director of the Kagiso Trust, an agency providing humanitarian and educational aid to the victims of apartheid.

Dangor has so far published one volume of verse, *Bulldozer* (Johannesburg, 1983), and it bears the stamp of his political commitment. The poetry moves from the lyricism of 'The Colour of Love' and 'My Africa' to the more explicitly political 'Die Patriot' and 'Leila', where the voice is thunderously public, merging Afrikaans street-talk with standard English. Dangor has published a short-story collection, *Waiting for Leila* (Johannesburg, 1981), and a novella, *The Z Town Trilogy* (Johannesburg, 1990). He has also written for the stage, and his play *Majiet* has won him critical acclaim.   [M-HM

DARUWALLA, Keki Nasserwanji (1937–), was born in Lahore into a Parsee family, completed his

Masters degree in English literature at Punjab University, and has since worked as assistant to the inspector-general of police in Uttar Pradesh and, latterly, as a career diplomat. His most recent posting was to the Indian High Commission in London.

Since his first collection of poems, *Under Orion* (Calcutta, 1970), he has published six volumes. He won the prestigious Sahitya Akademi Award for *Keeper of the Dead* (Delhi, 1982) and the Commonwealth Poetry Prize (Asia Region) for *Landscapes* (Delhi, 1987). He is a discriminating anthologist himself, and the introduction to his selection *Two Decades of Indian Poetry* (New Delhi, 1980) provides a concise and stimulating overview of recent developments.

Daruwalla's poetry evinces an intensity of vision, an ability to evoke landscape and environment that won the praise of Robert *Graves. *Crossing of Rivers* (Delhi, 1976) is a sequence of linked poems recording a personal pilgrimage along the River Ganges. Written in a taut style, it weaves a web of allusion, drawing upon Hindu, Zoroastrian, and personal myth, but there is also a satirical edge.

Unlike many of his contemporaries who write in English, Daruwalla is untroubled by notions of 'Indian authenticity', perhaps because of his own minority status as a Parsee and his peripatetic life-style. His attitude towards the language he writes in is summarized in a witty and elliptical poem, 'My Mistress'. [RW

DARYUSH, Elizabeth (1887–1977), was born in London, the daughter of Robert *Bridges, the future Poet Laureate, and Monica Waterhouse, whose father Alfred was the famous architect. She was brought up in the family manor house, Yattendon, and at Boar's Hill, Oxford, where under the guidance of her father she developed an early interest in the flowers of rural England. She refers to her father's teaching in her moving memorial verses 'Bye Flowers'. In 1923 she married Ali Akbar Daryush whom she met while he was engaged in Persian studies at Oxford. They lived in Persia until 1926, when they moved to their permanent home, Stockwell, on Boar's Hill, close to the home of her parents.

In her first book, *Charitesse 1911* (Cambridge, 1912) and throughout the many volumes published by the Oxford University Press and later by the Carcanet Press, she established herself as a traditionalist poet writing in conventional prosody but (like her father) willing to experiment in non-traditional forms. One of her best-known poems, 'Still-Life', an ironic critique of the false security of the idle rich, is written in *syllabic verse. The subject-matter of her best poems is moral without being didactic—a stoic acceptance of impermanence, the need for discipline, self restraint, and dignity in the face of tragic loss. Among her finest poems are 'Autumn, dark wanderer' (on the feeling of loss brought about by seasonal change), 'Faithless familiars', 'Fresh spring', and 'Eyes that queenly sit'.

Perceptive critical and technical comments on her poetry are to be found in Yvor Winters, 'Robert Bridges and Elizabeth Daryush', *American Review*, 8 (1936–7); in Winters's foreword to her *Selected Poems* (New York, 1948); and in Donald Davie's introduction to her *Collected Poems* (Manchester, 1976). [DS

DAS, Kamala (1934–), was born in Punnayurkulum, Kerala, into an aristocratic Nair family. Married off while still an undergraduate, she did not publish any poetry until the Sixties. She received the PEN Asia prize in 1963. She has three collections: *Summer in Calcutta* (Delhi, 1965), *The Descendants* (Calcutta, 1967), and *The Old Playhouse* (Bombay, 1973). Hers is a personalized poetry of marital unhappiness, the quest for love outside of marriage, the terrors of mental illness, and the joys of childhood memories. Much of her verse is written with a sense of urgency in a language she describes as half-English, half-Indian, its distortions and queernesses hers alone. Some of her strongest poems, like 'The Old Playhouse' and 'Sunshine Cat', describe the husband persona as a jailer. In others, like 'The Freaks', she discovers love to be 'grand, flamboyant lust'. When she turns despairingly to her matriarchal roots—as in her most anthologized work, 'My Grandmother's House'—she finds it lying in silence with snakes moving about the books.

Das's poetry is available in her *Collected Poems*, vol. 1 (Trivandrum, 1984). Her autobiography, *My Story* (Bombay, 1976), translated by her from the Malayalam, provides the context for her verse. [RA

DATTA, Sanjib (1919–), alias Sanjib Datza, was born in Comilla, Bangladesh, the son of a lawyer and freedom fighter in the undivided India. He took an MA in English at Calcutta University. His only book of verse, *Eyeless in the Urn* (Dhaka, 1975), takes its title from the murder of his father, Dhirendranath Datta, in 1971 by the Pakistani Army, after prolonged torture and blinding. The army camp in which these horrors took place was ringed by low hills, suggesting an urn. The book is an attempt on Datta's part to come to terms with his personal loss, but it also succeeds in subsuming the loss under a larger philosophical understanding of death itself.

Datta has worked as a journalist in Bangladesh and Calcutta, and in the mid-1960s he edited *Levant*, a literary quarterly. For some years he retreated into the hills of tribal Nagaland, editing an English newsweekly, but is now settled in Calcutta, where his novel, *Judas Tree*, appeared in 1984. [SMI

DAVENPORT, Guy (1927–), was born in Anderson, South Carolina, and educated at Duke, Oxford, and Harvard universities. Apart from two years in the United States Army Airborne, he has spent all his adult life in academic surroundings, since 1963 as professor of English at the University of Kentucky at Lexington. He has published, all from Berkeley, California, numerous volumes of criticism, short stories, translations (especially from ancient Greek), and poetry, including *Eclogues: Eight Stories* (1981); *The Geography of the Imagination* (1981), which collects many of his literary and artistic salutations and homages; and *Thasos and Ohio: Poems and Translations, 1950–1980* (1986).

Davenport is a man of multifarious learning, who preserves the aesthetic spirit of those high modernists he celebrates, such as *Joyce, *Pound, *Eliot, Marianne *Moore, David *Jones, *Zukofsky, and *Olson, but his independent-minded eclecticism is demonstrated by the high opinion he also holds of quite other kinds of writer such as Eudora Welty and the formalist poet, J. V. *Cunningham. His own poetry, which employs a variety of modes, including rhyming couplets and iambic metre, is witty, packed with historical and cultural reference, and possessed of the 'passion for objectivity' that in the work of the modernist masters he so cherishes. [RWB

DAVEY, Frank(land Wilmot) (1940–), was born in Vancouver and brought up in the nearby Fraser Valley. He was educated at the University of British Columbia and University of Southern California, where he wrote a dissertation on Charles *Olson's poetics. For two decades he taught English and writing at Toronto's York University, before going to University of Western Ontario (London) in 1990.

Like his modernist predecessor, Louis *Dudek, Davey favours the long poem or sequence, is wary of metaphor and lyric, and has always published his books with selected literary presses. But Davey sees himself as a postmodernist. He has said that the serious poem cannot be finished but must be abandoned.

His subject in books such as *Popular Narratives* (Vancouver, 1991) is often childhood, adolescence, and young manhood, but his re-creating of those personal years is always related ironically to issues in history, politics, industry, and education. He fashions links between individual pathology and public crises.

Davey has devoted a large part of his time to criticism and editing. He was the central force in the successful 1980s attack on the thematic criticism of Northrop Frye, whose influence dominated the Canadian critical and academic worlds in the 1970s. His several critical books and collections consider literature as ideological and discursive. Recent texts, such as *Reading Canadian Reading* (Winnipeg, 1988), expound on the relationships between writing and the economics of publishing.

Davey was managing editor of the poetry-poetics newsletter *Tish* (1961–3), and since 1965 has been editor of *Open Letter*, a journal of postmodern theory and criticism. A key guide to his ideas at mid-career can be found in a long interview, 'Starting at Our Skins', in a 1979 issue of *Open Letter*.   [GHB

DAVIDSON, Donald (Grady) (1893–1968), was born in Tennessee and taught at Vanderbilt University from 1920. He was one of the founders and editors of the *Fugitive* magazine, and one of the foremost Southern *Agrarians, contributing to the manifesto *I'll Take My Stand*. He was also the close friend and confidant of such poets as Allen *Tate and John Crowe *Ransom. He wrote the libretto to the opera *Singin' Billy* (produced 1952), to music by Charles Faulkner Bryan. As a poet in his own right, Davidson has not been reckoned one of the outstanding Fugitives. He was more important to the movement as an austere influence and setter of guide-lines, especially in the early and more conservative years.

His poetry, like his prose, is noted for its lucidity and its chiselled correctness. After a collection of shorter poems, *An Outland Piper* (New York, 1924), he published *The Tall Men* (New York, 1927), a blank-verse narrative. *Lee in the Mountains* (New York, 1938) contained short poems about Southern figures. Of all his group Davidson remained the most steadfastly committed to Agrarian principles (*Still Rebels, Still Yankees* (1957) consists of essays which some thought were reactionary). Some of the poems in *The Long Street* (New York, 1961), however, intelligently view the conflict in Davidson between nostalgia for an old order and awareness of the contemporary situation, and this is his best collection. See *Poems 1922–1961* (New York, 1966).   [MS-S

DAVIDSON, John (1857–1909), was born in Barrhead, Renfrewshire, the son of a minister. At thirteen, he entered a Greenock chemical works; his later works give evidence of a lasting scientific curiosity. He resumed his education in 1872 as a pupil-teacher at the Highlanders' Academy, and held various teaching posts from 1877 to 1889. His first notable publication was *Bruce*, an Elizabethan-style chronicle play (Glasgow, 1886). Other plays followed, the best of

them the pantomimic *Scaramouch in Naxos* (1890), as well as novels and stories; but by the time he moved to London in 1890, seeking literary fame, his preferred forms were the ballad and dramatic monologue, which he applied to contemporary urban subjects. *Yeats praised *In a Music Hall and Other Poems* (1891) as an example of a new writer seeking out 'new subject matter, new emotions'; Yeats's temperamental dispute with Davidson is recounted in his *Autobiographies*. *Fleet Street Eclogues* (1893) was a critical and (modest) popular success; but sales of *Ballads and Songs* (1894), *Fleet Street Eclogues* (second series, 1896), *New Ballads* (1897), and *The Last Ballad* (1899) were insufficient to support him as he believed they should. The last ten years of his life, soured by poverty and 'a strain of angry pride' (Ernest Rhys) were largely devoted to two blank-verse projects: his anti-Christian philosophical poems called *Testaments*, and the huge, unfinished dramatic trilogy *God and Mammon*. He was awarded a civil-list pension in 1906, but want, illness, and the decline of his powers continued to oppress him. The onset of cancer and the strain of financial indebtedness to G. B. Shaw drove him to suicide by drowning off Penzance.

Davidson wrote too much too quickly, and his reputation now rests largely on a single successful poem, the satiric Cockney monologue 'Thirty Bob a Week'. T. S. *Eliot described this in the foreword to Maurice Lindsay's *John Davidson: A Selection of his Poems* (London, 1961) as 'a great poem for ever', and acknowledges a personal debt to it and to other of Davidson's poems which treat the world of 'dull tasks in uncongenial spheres' (e.g. 'In the Isle of Dogs', 'A Northern Suburb'). Hugh *MacDiarmid has praised him more broadly and objectively. In Lindsay's *Selection* the remarkable science-poem 'Snow' is a further proof of Davidson's originality; but much of the book is made up of extracts from longer poems whose uneven wholes are judged unreadable.

Davidson's essay 'On Poetry' was included in the volume *Holiday* (1906). There is a bio-critical study by Mary O'Connor (Edinburgh, 1987).

[MI

DAVIE, Donald (1922–95), was born in Barnsley, Yorkshire, spent his childhood in the industrialized West Riding, and received his earliest education at Barnsley Holgate Grammar School. In 1941 his studies at St Catharine's College, Cambridge (which he had entered in 1940), were interrupted by service in the Royal Navy, which posted him to Murmansk and Archangel until 1943. He married Doreen John in 1945, returned to Cambridge University to receive his BA in 1947, his MA in 1949, and his Ph.D in 1951. His career as a university teacher began in Trinity College, Dublin, in 1950, and he became a fellow in 1954. He resigned his fellowship in 1957, and subsequently taught as a visiting professor at the University of California, Santa Barbara, and at Gonville and Caius College, Cambridge. In 1964 he was a co-founder of the University of Essex and a professor of English there. In 1968 he accepted a professorship at Stanford University, where he remained until 1978 when he removed to Nashville, Tennessee, as Andrew W. Mellon Professor in Humanities at Vanderbilt University. He retired from Vanderbilt in 1987 and lived in Devonshire.

Davie was born of Baptist parentage and for a number of years considered himself to be a conservative member of the English dissenting tradition, with an admiration for the hymns of Isaac Watts and Charles Wesley and a dislike for bohemianism, Bloomsbury, and 'sentimental leftists'. There is, therefore, a strong ethical element in much of his verse, expressed in its plain style. At Cambridge he considered himself to be a disciple of F. R. Leavis, and his native tendencies towards moralism and plain writing and speaking were reinforced by contacts with Yvor *Winters's* Stanford School—he read Winters very early in his career, and established personal contacts with the Winters group when teaching in the States. In England Davie was a leading member of the *Movement, of which he considered his critical book, *Purity of Diction in English Verse* (London, 1952; New York, 1953), to be a manifesto. Of his numerous volumes of verse, perhaps the best-known are *Essex Poems* (1969) and *The Shires* (1974), where as a traditionalist he develops one of his most cherished themes—

the importance of a sense of place in life and in poetry. Among his best-known poems are 'Woodpigeons at Raheny', 'The Fountain', 'Remembering the Thirties', 'A Winter Landscape near Ely', 'Iona', 'Lowlands', and 'In the Stopping Train'.

Davie held several lectureships in Europe which enabled him to pursue his interest in Polish, Hungarian, and Russian literature, and which resulted in his verse translations and adaptations. *The Forests of Lithuania* (Hessle, Yorks., 1959) is an adaptation of the Polish poet Adam Mickiewicz's romantic epic *Pan Tadeusz*. *The Poems of Dr Zhivago* (Manchester and New York, 1985) and *Pasternak: Modern Judgements* (London, 1969; Nashville, 1970), edited by Davie and Angela Livingstone, contain his verse translations of poems by Boris Pasternak, whom Davie considered to be among the greatest poets of our time. Among Davie's most important books of criticism are *Articulate Energy: An Inquiry into the Syntax of English Poetry* (London, 1955; New York, 1958); *Ezra Pound: Poet as Sculptor* (New York, 1964; London, 1965); *Thomas Hardy and British Poetry* (New York, 1972; London, 1973); and *Under Briggflatts: A History of Poetry in Great Britain, 1960–1988* (Manchester, 1989). Among his critical books on European literatures are *Czeslaw Milosz and the Insufficiency of the Lyric* (Knoxville, Tenn., 1986) and *Slavic Excursions: Essays on Russian and Polish Literature* (Manchester, 1990). Among volumes he has edited are Elizabeth Daryush's *Collected Poems* (Manchester, 1976); *Collected Poems of Yvor Winters* (Manchester, 1978; Athens, Ohio, 1980); and the *New Oxford Book of Christian Verse* (Oxford and New York, 1981). The bulk of his shorter poems are in *Collected Poems 1950–1970* (London and New York, 1972) and *Collected Poems 1970–1983* (Manchester and Notre Dame, Ind., 1983). Biographical information is in Davie's *These the Companions: Recollections* (Cambridge, 1982). [DS

DAVIES, Idris (1905–53), was born at Rhymney, in Monmouthshire. He left school at the age of 14 to work in a coal-mine, but after the General Strike of 1926 he studied at the University of Nottingham and became a teacher in London and Wales.

His first volume of verse, Gwalia Deserta (1938), is concerned with the dereliction of industrial south Wales during the years of the Depression. All the poems in it are either short lyrics in the style of A. E. *Housman or in the accumulative, long-line form which was to become characteristic of his later work. They include the poem which, set to music by Pete Seeger, became famous as the song 'The Bells of Rhymney'.

The long poem entitled 'The Angry Summer' (1943) consists of fifty short, untitled sections, and is a loosely chronological record of the General Strike, from the high spirits of its beginning to the miners' ignominious return to work. A further volume appeared during the poet's lifetime under the title Tonypandy and Other Poems (1945).

Early judgements of Idris Davies tended to emphasize his integrity as man and poet while criticizing the somewhat narrow range of his work, but the wry humour and passionate indignation which inform the best of his poems are now recognized as self-imposed limitations which help to throw his main themes into relief.

The fullest edition of Idris Davies's poems is to be found in the volume of his Collected Poems compiled by Islwyn Jenkins (Llandysul, 1972). Islwyn Jenkins has also written a monograph on the poet in the Writers of Wales series (Cardiff, 1972) and a book-length study, Idris Davies of Rhymney (Llandysul, 1986). See also Glyn Jones, The Dragon has Two Tongues (London, 1968); Anthony Conran, The Cost of Strangeness (Llandysul, 1982); and the special number of Poetry Wales, 16: 4 (Spring 1981), which is devoted to his work.   [MS

DAVIES, W(illiam) H(enry) (1871–1940), was born in Newport, Monmouthshire, and brought up by his grandparents in the Church House Inn there. He left school at 14, was apprenticed to a picture-framer, read avidly, and attended classes in the evening. At the age of 22 he received a small weekly legacy from the estate of his grandmother, and sailed for Amer-

ica, where he spent six years tramping back and forth. In 1899, he injured his right foot when jumping a moving train in Canada and had to have his leg amputated above the knee. From then on he wore an artificial limb. These years are re-created in Davies's The Autobiography of a Super-Tramp (London, 1908), a modern classic of autobiography. Davies returned to Newport, then settled in London where he lived in cheap lodging-houses and concentrated on writing full time. In 1905 he published The Soul's Destroyer and Other Poems at his own expense under the imprint: 'Of the Author, Farmhouse, Marshalsea Road, S.E.' The book was favourably reviewed by Edward *Thomas, who encouraged Davies to write Super-Tramp. In 1923 Davies married Helen Matilda Payne, a young countrywoman in her early twenties whom he had picked up in a London street. The story is vividly told in Young Emma (London, 1980), a book written in 1924 but impossible to publish at the time due to its candour. The couple settled in the Cotswold town of Nailsworth where they lived until Davies's death in 1940.

In his lifetime Davies wrote just under 800 poems published in twenty individual volumes, which generally sold well. He was quick to find his own style: his first book, The Soul's Destroyer, contained 'The Lodging House Fire', a portrait of a poor lodging-house. Other realist urban poems include the violent picture of urban degradation in 'Saturday Night in the Slums', the down-and-out of 'The Heap of Rags', and 'The Bird of Paradise', on the delusions of a dying prostitute. These poems can be set against work such as his best-known poem 'Leisure' ('What is this life if, full of care, | We have no time to stand and stare'), or 'In the Country', which counterbalances urban squalor with an idealized rural world of lost innocence: 'This life is sweetest; in this wood | I hear no children cry for food.'

See: Richard J. Stonesifer, W. H. Davies: A Critical Biography (London, 1963); Complete Poems, intro. Osbert Sitwell, foreword Daniel George (London, 1963); Selected Poems, ed. Jonathan Barker (London, 1985); The Autobiography of a Super-Tramp, preface George Bernard Shaw

(London, 1908; repr. Oxford, 1980); *Later Days* (London, 1925; repr. Oxford, 1985; *The Essential W. H. Davies*, ed. Brian Waters (London, 1951); *Young Emma*, foreword by C. V. Wedgwood (London, 1980). [JDB

DAVIS, Dick (1945–), was born in Portsmouth. After graduating from King's College, Cambridge, he worked as a teacher in, among other places, Iran, and gained a doctorate in Persian from Manchester University in 1989. He teaches Persian at Ohio State University, Columbus.

An early passion—and one that has not been lost—was for Edward Fitzgerald's *Rubáiyát of Omar Khayyám*, a new edition of which Davis edited in 1989; this passion may explain the most obvious characteristic of his own poetry: its dependence on traditional metrical skills. But it was evident from his first collection, *In the Distance* (1975), that Davis uses metre and rhyme in no outdated manner. He creates with them intricately wrought poems that move in a quiet and measured way. There is a notable exactness of thought and perception.

Davis has translated works by Natalia Ginzburg, Attar's *The Conference of the Birds* (with Afkham Darbandi), and *The Legend of Seyavash* (a translation of part of Ferdowsi's *Shahnamah*). His second collection of poems was *Seeing the World* (1980). There are both British and American selections: *Devices and Desires: New and Selected Poems 1967–1987* (London, 1989) and *Selected and New Poems* (Fayetteville, Ark., 1991). [TJGH

DAVIS, Jack (1917–), was born in Perth, Western Australia and spent his early childhood in the small country town of Yarloop, one of a family of eleven Aboriginal children in a white community. Neither of his grandfathers was Aboriginal—one was a Sikh, the other a Scotsman. His parents were taken from their Aboriginal mothers as children. Davis himself was sent to the Moore River Nature Settlement for education and training. His experience there is recalled in his poems and plays, and in Keith Chesson's *Jack Davis: A Life-Story* (Melbourne,

1988).

Davis's three books of poems are *The First-Born and Other Poems* (Sydney, 1970); *Jagardoo: Poems from Aboriginal Australia* (Sydney, 1978); and *John Pat and Other Poems* (Melbourne, 1988). In each of these books an Aboriginal persona speaks for his people, lamenting their tragic defeat by the white invaders, reflecting on a loss of identity and purpose among contemporary Aborigines, especially in the cities. [BB

DAVISON, Peter (1928–), was born in New York, grew up in Colorado, and was educated at Harvard College and Cambridge University. From 1956 until 1985 he was a book editor at the Atlantic Monthly Press; since then he has been a senior editor at Houghton Mifflin; he has also been poetry editor of *The Atlantic* for many years. His first wife, writer Jane Davison, died in 1981; he married Joan Edelman Goody, an architect, in 1984. His first book of poems was *The Breaking of the Day*, which won the Yale Series of Younger Poets Award in 1963. It was characterized by a sharp wit and strongly physical sense of language. Then, as now, Davison has been drawn to traditional forms.

Much influenced by Robert *Frost, Davison has been increasingly attracted to rural images and has relied heavily on iambic patterns broken up by the patterns of ordinary speech. His quietly sophisticated, contemplative voice recalls the English *Georgians, a school of poets with whom his father, Edward Davison, was often associated. Though essentially a nature poet, Davison has in recent years written poems about his family and personal life; this *'confessional' vein has been mined most fully in his autobiography, *Half Remembered: A Personal History* (New York, 1973; London, 1974). Since then, he has published another eight volumes, including *Dark Houses* (New York, 1971), a volume dedicated to his father; *Walking the Boundaries: Poems 1957–1974* (New York and London, 1974); *Praying Wrong: New and Selected Poems, 1957–1984* (New York, 1985); and *The Great Ledge* (New York and London, 1989). For criticism, see Guy Rotella, *Three Contemporary Poets of New England* (Boston, 1983). [JP

DAWE, (Donald) Bruce (1930–), was born in Geelong, Victoria, Australia, to working-class parents. He left school at 16 to begin a series of short-lived, mostly unskilled jobs. After a year at Melbourne University, Dawe returned to unskilled jobs until 1959, when he began a nine-year period of service with the Royal Australian Air Force, working in the education section in Australia and Malaysia, and rising to the rank of sergeant. In 1964 he married Gloria Blain; their four children are the subject of poems. After his Air Force service, Dawe worked as a teacher. He completed his Arts degree, and subsequently, through part-time study, gained other degrees, including a Ph.D.

From his very first volume, *No Fixed Address* (Melbourne, 1962), Dawe's work has been popular with critics and the public. He is probably Australia's best-selling poet and has won many awards. His collected poems, *Sometimes Gladness*, was the only volume of poetry included in a list of the ten best Australian books of the decade in 1984.

Dawe has always acknowledged his indebtedness to the small-town ordinariness of Edgar Lee *Masters and Edwin Arlington *Robinson, an influence evident not only in his poems but also in his stories. His sympathies are with the 'bottom-dog', the 'battler', the person puzzled and overwhelmed by life. He writes about cities, suburbs, and—perhaps most tellingly—about the places on the outskirts where city and country meet.

World events, especially those involving war or injustice, figure in some poems, notably the Vietnam War poem, 'Homecoming'. Over the past twenty years he has written many satirical poems about Australian politics, especially concerning Queensland's long-serving populist premier, Sir Joh Bjelke-Petersen. Other poems have concerned the ill-treatment of Australian Aborigines. His commonest form is the dramatic monologue, of which 'A Victorian Hangman Tells His Love' (a black-humour protest against capital punishment spoken by the hangman) is typical.

No edition of Dawe's poetry has been published outside Australia, though he is substantially represented in the *Norton Anthology of Modern Poetry*, ed. Richard Ellmann and Robert O'Clair (New York, 2nd edn., 1988). His current collected volume is *Sometimes Gladness: Collected Poems, 1954–1987* (Melbourne, 1988). *Bruce Dawe: Essays and Opinions*, ed. Ken Goodwin (Melbourne, 1990), contains a set of prose statements and a bibliography. *Over Here, Harv! and Other Stories* (Melbourne, 1983) contains short stories. The main critical work is Ken Goodwin, *Adjacent Worlds: A Literary Life of Bruce Dawe* (Melbourne, 1988). [KGo

DAY LEWIS, C(ecil) (1904–72), was born in Ireland. Proud of his Anglo-Irish connections, he moved with his family to England in 1905. He was educated at Sherborne and at Wadham College, Oxford, where he read classics. His first two volumes of verse, *Beechen Vigil* (1925) and *Country Comets* (1928), were slight. *Transitional Poem* (1929), *From Feathers to Iron* (1931), *A Time to Dance* (1935), and *Noah and the Waters* (1936) deployed images of comrades, frontiers, blood, red dawns, and saviours. Day Lewis excluded a number of these poems from his *Collected Poems* (1954).

He turned to prose in *A Hope for Poetry* (1934) and edited a left-wing symposium, *The Mind in Chains*, in 1937, the year in which he joined the Communist Party. Although the imminence of war did not alter Day Lewis's beliefs, it awakened certain ideas and emotions not hitherto expressed in his poems. The title of his volume *Overtures to Death* (1938) indicates his prevailing mood. In 1940 he joined the Home Guard, and from 1941 to 1946 worked for the Ministry of Information. Many of the poems in *Word Over All* (1943) and *Poems 1943–47* (1948) concerned his childhood and the turbulence of his emotional life; they show also the influence of *Hardy and, to a lesser extent, of Edward *Thomas that marked his later verse.

After the war Day Lewis became influential in academic and orthodox literary circles. His 1946 Clark Lectures at Cambridge were published as *The Poetic Image* (1947); he was the elected Professor of Poetry at Oxford from 1951 to 1956; and *The Poetic Impulse* (1965) was based on his 1964 Charles Eliot Norton Lectures at Harvard. After the ending of his first marriage and of his long association with Rosamond Lehmann, he married the actress Jill Balcon in 1951. They gave many readings together, often under the auspices of the Apollo Society.

Collections of verse appeared regularly. *An Italian Visit*, a lyrical narrative poem (1953), was succeeded by *Pegasus* (1957), *The Gate* (1962), *The Room* (1965), and *The Whispering Roots* (1970). The craftsmanship of these poems was not disputed, but some critics believed that he had ensconced himself in a bland conservatism, sadly at variance with his youthful ardour.

He lavished skill and metrical ingenuity on his translations of Virgil's *Georgics* (1940), *Aeneid* (1952), and *Eclogues* (1963), and published in 1946 a version of Valéry's *Le Cimetière Marin*. He wrote three mainly autobiographical novels and, from 1935 onwards, a score of detective tales under the pseudonym of Nicholas Blake.

Appointed Poet Laureate in 1968, he brought to his office a fine presence, courtesy, eloquence and administrative ability. Like most of his predecessors though, he was unfitted to write poems on major public themes.

See *Poems of C. Day Lewis 1925–1972*, ed. Ian Parsons (London, 1977) and *Collected Poems of C. Day Lewis*, ed. Jill Balcon (London, 1982); his autobiography, *The Buried Day* (London and New York, 1960); and *C. Day-Lewis* (London, 1980), by Sean Day-Lewis, the elder son of his first marriage. [JPr

DEANE, Seamus (1940–   ), was born in Derry, Northern Ireland, and educated at Queen's University, Belfast, and Cambridge University. He is currently professor of English and American Literature at University College, Dublin. Deane is a director, along with fellow poets Seamus *Heaney and Tom *Paulin, of the Field Day Theatre Company.

Deane's earliest poetry—in, for example, *Gradual Wars* (Shannon, 1972)—was serious, intelligent, and overwrought. In *Rumours* (1977) and *History Lessons* (1983—both Dublin) his work has matured and sweetened, and he has begun to explore political and social themes

through humour, narrative, and indirection, as in the much-praised poems 'Guerillas' and 'Christmas at Beaconsfield'.

His works of criticism include *Celtic Revivals: Essays in Modern Irish Literature 1880–1980* (London, 1985) and *A Short History of Irish Literature* (London, 1986). An analytic study of Deane's work, usefully comparing it with the work of Paulin and Heaney, can be found in C. C. Barfoot and Theo D'haen (eds.), *The Clash of Ireland: Literary Contrasts and Connections* (Amsterdam, 1989). [IES

Deep Image is a term that has come to be associated with certain American poets, above all Robert *Bly and James *Wright, who practise a variety of image-based verse that emphasizes not the empirical and the concrete, as in Objectivism, but the connections between images and the unconscious. Strongly influenced by Carl Jung's thought on archetypes, Bly has been the most polemical spokesman for such poetry, in various essays published in his journal *The Fifties*, *The *Sixties*, and *The Seventies*. Bly calls for American poets to abandon rational, discursive thinking and to cultivate the associational modes of imagery found in poets like Lorca, Trakl, Neruda, and Transtomer. Other poets loosely associated with this mode include Galway *Kinnell, Louis *Simpson, Donald *Hall, Jerome *Rothenberg, and Robert *Kelly, who coined the term 'deep image'; its influence among younger American poets has been widespread, particularly during the 1970s. [RG

DEHN, Paul (Edward) (1912–76), was born in Manchester and educated at Shrewsbury School (for whose 400th anniversary he wrote a masque) and at Brasenose College, Oxford. From 1936 to 1963 he wrote film criticism for the London newspapers, except during the war years, when he was with the Special Operations Executive. He later wrote scripts for films, among them *The Spy Who Came in from the Cold*.

The poems in his first collection, *The Day's Alarm* (London 1949), were urbane and accomplished and had a well-sustained style somewhat reminiscent of that of C. *Day Lewis, to whom the title-poem of Dehn's second volume, *Romantic Landscape* (1952), is dedicated. He shared with Day Lewis a gift for the nostalgic evocation of the past; and there is much that is attractive in his best poems, though little that is disturbing.

The Fern on the Rock: Collected Poems appeared in 1965 (London), and Dehn published no further book of poetry. The majority of the non-dramatic poems of any consequence in his *Collected Poems* in fact come from his first volume, *The Day's Alarm*, which must sustain whatever reputation he has.   [ATT

DE HOYOS, Angela (1940–), Mexican-born but raised in San Antonio, Texas, announced her poetic debut with *Arise, Chicano: and Other Poems* (Bloomington, Ind., 1975), strong Chicano-nationalist 'protest' verse written from the late 1960s onwards. Its title-poem speaks from the vantage-point of the migrant worker trapped doubly by 'the shrewd heel of exploit' and by an English language in which 'not even your burning words are yours'. That compares with 'The Final Laugh', a bold, keenly satirical and anti-racist soliloquy, in which she treats the key Chicano issues of assimilation and loss of cultural pride. With *Chicano Poems for the Barrio* (Bloomington, 1975) her range increases—especially in bilingual poems like 'Hermano', an extolling of Chicano heritage which takes the Alamo and the white American triumphalism which surrounds it as its presiding metaphor, and in 'Small Comfort', which treats the issue of language and custom, the 'burial', as she says, of *chicanismo* beneath an overlay of 'Anglo' Americanism. De Hoyos, too, has shown considerable skill in developing the use of personae, not least in 'One Ordinary Morning' from *Selecciones* (Veracruz, Mex., 1976), metaphysical verse both in form and theme, or 'Ex Marks The Spot' from *Woman, Woman* (Houston, Tex., 1985), a careful (and bilingual) lament at the loss of a close feminine friendship. Promised volumes include *Dedicatorias* and *Gata Poems*.

Criticism includes *The Multi-faced Poetic World of Angela de Hoyos*, by Marcela Aguilar-Henson (Austin, Tex., 1985) and *Angela de*

Hoyos, A Critical Look, by Luis Arturo Ramos (Albuquerque, New Mexico, 1979).   [ARL

DE LA MARE, Walter (1873–1956), was born at Charlton, Kent, and educated at St Paul's Cathedral Choir School in London. In 1890, aged 16, he began work in the statistics department of the London office of Anglo-American Oil. He married Constance Elfrida Ingpen in 1899; they had four children. His first book of poems, *Songs of Childhood* (London, 1902), was published under the pseudonym Walter Ramal. He was author of nineteen books of poems published between 1902 and 1953, two of the best-known of which are *The Listeners* (London, 1912) and *Peacock Pie* (London, 1913), the latter for children. De la Mare's poems were included in each of Edward Marsh's *Georgian Poetry* anthologies between 1912 and 1922. He was made Companion of Honour in 1948 and awarded the Order of Merit in 1953.

De la Mare is essentially an inward-looking poet of escape, skilled at depicting atmosphere and mood as in his elliptical narratives such as 'The Railway Junction', 'The Listeners', or the remarkable 'The Feckless Dinner Party', a poem written almost entirely in dramatic voices. The best poems are shot through with a disturbing sense of mystery and unease in which dream can shift into nightmare. He writes chillingly on supernatural and unearthly themes.

De la Mare's writing is technically assured. It is conservative in form yet capable of a wide range of subtle and virtuoso effects. His variations on established verse forms helped direct modern British poetry away from the experiments of early modernism, and back to the traditional methods into which W. H. *Auden was to breathe new life in the 1930s.

De la Mare's poems for children are models of their kind and include numerous small masterpieces, such as 'The Song of the Mad Prince', 'Old Shellover', 'Hi!', and 'Tit For Tat', collected in *Collected Rhymes and Verses* (London, 1944). What starts out as a children's poem can, in a few lines, turn unexpectedly into an exercise in controlled terror, as in 'John Mouldy', 'smiling there alone' in his rat-infested cellar.

Graham Greene praised the best of de la Mare's short stories for 'a prose unequalled in its richness since the death of James, or dare one, at this date, say Robert Louis Stevenson', and it may indeed be argued that de la Mare is overall even more interesting as a prose writer than a poet. The language of the stories is generally sharper and avoids the archaic diction of the poems, and his novels are overdue for rediscovery—in particular *Henry Brocken* (1904) and *The Return* (1910). *Memoirs of a Midget* (1921) was reprinted in 1982, with a preface by Angela Carter.

De la Mare was also a compendious, original, and influential poetry anthologist, keen to include the out-of-the-way along with the well known. *Come Hither; A Collection of Rhymes and Poems for the Young of All Ages* (London, 1923) contains everything from mainstream poems to anonymous border ballads, folk songs, children's chants, and nursery rhymes. In 1939, Auden commented that it, 'more than any book I have read before or since, taught me what poetry is'. Other brilliant, labyrinthine anthologies are *Desert Islands* (London, 1930), *Behold This Dreamer* (London, 1939), and *Love* (London, 1943). De la Mare's two books of literary criticism, *Pleasures and Speculations* (London, 1940) and *Private View* (London, 1953), are full of unexpected insights, as in the lecture 'Rupert Brooke and the Intellectual Imagination'.

See also: Forrest Reid, *Walter de la Mare: A Critical Study* (London, 1929); *Tribute to Walter de la Mare on his Seventy-Fifth Birthday* (London, 1948); Walter de la Mare, *Collected Poems* (New York, 1941; London, 1942); *Collected Rhymes and Verses* (London, 1944, 1989); *Walter de la Mare: A Selection from his Writings*, ed. Kenneth Hopkins (London, 1956); *The Complete Poems of Walter de la Mare* (London, 1969); *Selected Poems*, ed. R. N. Green-Armytage (1st edn. London, 1954; repr. London, 1973); *A Choice of de la Mare's Verse*, ed. W. H. Auden (London, 1963); Theresa Whistler, *Imagination of the Heart: The Life of Walter de la Mare* (London, 1993). [JDB

DENBY, Edwin (1903–83), was born in Tientsin, China, where his father was the American Consul. After attending the Hotchkiss School in Connecticut he entered Harvard, but although he appears to have been academically brilliant he dropped out of college and travelled to Europe with a friend. He spent the Twenties and early Thirties as a dancer, choreographer, and librettist in Austria, Germany, and France. After returning to New York in 1935, he concentrated on writing poems, opera and ballet libretti, and dance criticism. He is now known as one of the most influential dance critics of this century. Denby's literary significance lies chiefly in his having provided a link between Hart *Crane and Frank *O'Hara, the two major twentieth-century poets of Manhattan. While Denby's own poetic output was sporadic and uneven, it displays striking originality and inventiveness. In it we can see him gradually pushing Crane's high rhetoric, clotted diction, and pseudo-rational syntax toward the looser, more vernacular idiom of O'Hara's 'lunch poems'. The result is a poetry that retains traditional formal values (most of Denby's poems are sonnets or rhymed stanzas) while opening itself to the contingencies and dislocations of city life. At its best his work offers an effortless blending of intelligence and immersion; at its weakest these two elements fail to cohere, and the poems become knotted and opaque.

His first book of poems, *In Public, In Private*, appeared in 1948, and was followed by only two more small-press collections. Horrified at the prospect of senility, Denby committed suicide on 12 July 1983. His poetry is available in *The Complete Poems*, ed. Ron Padgett (New York, 1986). [RG

DENNIS, C(larence) J(ames) (1876–1936), was born in South Australia. After a varied career as clerk, barman, and journalist, he moved to Toolangi near Melbourne in 1908, where he remained to the end of his life. He is especially popular for his dramatic monologues in verse: *The Songs of the Sentimental Bloke* (1915; new edn. Sydney, 1992), *The Moods of Ginger Mick* (1916), and *Digger Smith* (1918). He married Olive Herron in 1917.

Dennis is most noted for his mastery of the larrikin slang that defines the voices of his main characters. Sentimental and nationalistic, his vernacular captures the aspirations of a mythical Australian lower class, contemptuous of the 'self-made slaves' of the middle and ruling classes, while aspiring to their values.

The best available collection of Dennis's verse is *The Sentimental Bloke and Other Selected Verse* (Sydney, 1973). A. H. Chisholm's *The Making of the Sentimental Bloke* (Melbourne, 1946) is a helpful biography, while G. W. Hutton's *C. J. Dennis, The Sentimental Bloke* (Melbourne, 1976) provides a useful modern appraisal. [AU

Desert Poets and *Personal Landscape*. During the Second World War a surprisingly large and heterodox number of British writers found themselves, for a variety of reasons, in the Middle East. Not all were combatants, and these included R. D. Smith, Olivia Manning, Robert Liddell, Bernard *Spencer, and Lawrence *Durrell. Together with Robin Fedden, the latter two founded the Cairo-based poetry magazine *Personal Landscape*, whose first number appeared in January, 1942. Among the magazine's regular contributors were most of the writers already mentioned, together with George Seferis, Terence *Tiller, and Keith *Douglas.

Personal Landscape was the best-known of the literary magazines to come out of the Middle East, but it was by no means the only one. *Salamander*, for example, had been started by Keith Bullen from his flat in Cairo as an offshoot of his 'Salamander Society', a Sunday-morning literary gathering, and its contributors included the poets John Waller and G. S. *Fraser. Fraser, indeed, tried to run his own monthly magazine for soldier writers, called *Orientations*.

See *Return to Oasis: War Poems and Recollections from the Middle East, 1940–1946* ed. Victor Selwyn, Erik de Mauny, Ian Fletcher, G. S. Fraser, and John Waller, with an introduction by Lawrence Durrell (London, 1980). Other army-based periodicals of the Middle East included *Citadel* (edited by David Hicks from

the Anglo-Egyptian Institute) and *Parade*, to both of which Douglas contributed. [JL

DE SILVA, Alfreda (1920–), was born in Sri Lanka, and has worked as a free-lance journalist, broadcaster, and television script-writer. Her poems are published in *Out of the Dark the Sun* (Moratuwa, 1977) and *The Unpredictable Blood* (Colombo, 1988). She has also written books of verse for children. Her most notable pieces are 'Collages', a frightening sketch of personal relationships; 'First-Born', which involves the reader in the violence of birth; and 'Crows and Children', in which the creatures of the title compete for food at a garbage can: 'Someone has willed them the dark | The Sun goes on without them.' [LdeS

DE SOUZA, Eunice (1940–), was born into a Goan Catholic family in Bombay and is a graduate of both the University of Bombay and Marquette University, Wisconsin. She currently lectures in English literature at St Xavier's College, Bombay. Her journalism is widely appreciated in India for its impatient and acerbic tone, and her poetry criticism is seen as a healthy reaction against a tradition of derivative, lifeless, 'Indo-Anglian' verse.

Although she is not a prolific poet, de Souza's voice is individual and challenging. The poems in her first collection, *Fix* (Bombay, 1976), are firmly located in the Goan Catholic community of her childhood. They are direct, often witty, always iconoclastic. Her targets, as identified by a range of contrasting personae, are the casual tolerance of social injustice, the sexual mores inculcated by Jansenism, and the omnipresent oppression of women. Many of her funniest pieces reproduce the dated argot of the period and ambience in which they are set.

De Souza's second collection, *Women in Dutch Painting* (Bombay, 1988), is more personal, betraying a wider range of sympathies and interests. Both collections have recently been published in a new volume, *Ways of Belonging* (Edinburgh, 1990), together with some new material. [RW

DEUTSCH, Babette (1895–1982), was born in New York City and studied at Barnard College where she started to publish her writing in literary magazines. For a time she was a secretary to the economist and social commentator Thorstein Veblen, and was also on the Committee for Cultural Freedom with the American philosopher John Dewey. She taught at college in New York City and translated German and Russian poetry, in collaboration with her husband, Avrahm Yarmolinsky. Her poetry is socially alert, relating the terms of individual existence to larger political and philosophical questions. Her *Collected Poems: 1919–1962* (Bloomington, Ind., 1963) brought together *Banners* (1919), *Epistle to Prometheus* (1931), and *Animal, Vegetable, Mineral* (1954). She also wrote novels (*In Such a Night*, 1927 and *Rogue's Legacy*, 1942, for example), as well as some significant literary criticism. The most notable examples are her study of Walt Whitman (1941) and *Poetry in Our Time* (1952), a general view of the modern poem. Her major critical text is perhaps the *Poetry Handbook: Dictionary of Terms* (New York, 1957; London, 1958). [GC

DEVLIN, Denis (1908–59), was born in Greenock, Scotland, to an Irish family which returned to Ireland in 1918. He was educated at Belvedere College, University College, Dublin, Munich University, and the Sorbonne. Between Belvedere and UCD he spent a year at All Hallows College, a seminary, but decided against the priesthood. As a student, he was one of an academically brilliant and artistically outward-looking generation of the Thirties in Ireland, which also included Brian O'Nolan (Flann O'Brien), Mervyn Wall, Brian Coffey (with whom Devlin published *Poems*, Dublin, 1930), and somewhat more marginally, Samuel *Beckett, who considered Devlin one of the most interesting poets of his generation. He took a degree in languages, but despite a period of research and a spell as an assistant lecturer in English at UCD, he joined the Irish Foreign Service in 1935. Thereafter his life was that of a successful career diplomat. He became Irish ambassador to Italy in 1958.

Devlin's early work was highly cerebral—not to say precious and obscure. Later on his poems, although still densely packed, became more accessible and better controlled, and they adopted a distinct but surprisingly rare Irish Catholic perspective. His central themes are exile and love. In each case Devlin identifies both a secular and a divine aspect without merely reiterating that time-worn opposition. Thus, exile is both the life of the diplomat and the condition of humanity, expelled to the vale of tears that is the fallen world. Human and divine love, similarly, have secular and divine aspects: the love of God, given and received by humanity, is subject to secular transformations, while mortal love can achieve timelessness, as in 'The Colours of Love'. In Devlin's thought, metaphysical and physical passion are not just reflections of each other—they are mutually dependent components, brought together only rarely, as in the figure of Christ in the sequence 'The Passion of Christ'. Throughout his life Devlin translated widely from the French, notably from St John Perse (also a diplomat). His translations are not a separate part of his work but an extension of it, for they deepen his concern with language as negotiation: between cultures, between lovers, between consciousness and silence, and between God and humanity.

Because of Devlin's erratic publication history and constant revisions, both of his own poetry and of his translations, Brian Coffey's editions of the *Collected Poems* (Dublin, 1964) and *The Heavenly Foreigner* (Dublin, 1967) need to be supplemented by the *Selected Poems*, ed. Robert Penn Warren and Allen Tate (New York, 1963). This situation will be rectified if J. C. C. Mays's edition of the *Collected Poems of Denis Devlin* (Dublin, 1989) is, as promised, supplemented by a further volume of posthumous work (some of which is already available in the other editions cited here). [EH

Dial, The. F. F. Browne founded this literary periodical in Chicago in 1880, choosing a title in deliberate recall of a journal run by the American Transcendentalists from 1880 to 1884.

Despite this, the journal remained an essentially safe, conservative product until 1919, when it was taken over by Scofield Thayer and J. S. Watson. By this time, the periodical's base had switched to New York and the new editors opened up the contents in order to include the more progressive thinkers and writers of the post-war era. With associates like Thomas Mann, T. S. *Eliot and James *Stephens, it became the finest American periodical of its era; *Yeats, William Carlos *Williams, H. D. (Hilda *Doolittle), D. H. *Lawrence, E. E. *Cummings, and many others appeared in its pages. It also reproduced the work of important European sculptors and painters, a legacy suggested by Thayer's collection of 450 works of art, including work by Munch, Picasso, and Matisse, which came to be known as 'The Dial Collection'. Due to Thayer's ill health, Marianne *Moore became editor in 1926, retaining her role until its demise in 1929. Despite its success, the periodical did not preclude controversy; Williams, although he was given the Dial Award in 1926, kept a critical distance and Moore managed to arouse the wrath of some by completely revising a poem of Hart *Crane's before letting it be published. With essays and reviews by Ezra *Pound, T. S. Eliot and Yvor *Winters, the periodical was of crucial importance in sharpening the advance of critical procedures, advocating the kind of close attention to text which later became the realm of the *New Criticism. Eliot's *The Waste Land* was first published in its pages, a fitting testimony to its centrality and importance. [CM

DICKEY, James (1923–), was born in Atlanta, Georgia. After serving as a pilot in the Second World War, he attended Vanderbilt University. Having earned an MA in 1950, Dickey returned to military duty in the Korean War, serving with the US Air Force. Upon return to civilian life Dickey taught at Rice University in Texas and then at the University of Florida. From 1955 to 1961, he worked for advertising agencies in New York and Atlanta. After the publication of his first book, *Into the Stone* (Middletown, Conn., 1962), he left advertising and began teaching at various colleges and universities. He is currently poet-in-residence and Carolina Professor of English at the University of South Carolina.

Dickey's third volume, *Buckdancer's Choice* (Middletown, 1965), won the prestigious National Book Award in Poetry. From 1966 to 1968 he served as poetry consultant to the Library of Congress. In 1977 Dickey read his poem 'The Strength of Fields' at President Carter's inauguration. The Hollywood film of his novel *Deliverance* (Boston, 1970) brought Dickey fame not normally enjoyed by poets.

Dickey's poems are a mixture of lyricism and narrative. In some volumes the lyricism dominates, while in others the narrative is the focus. The early books, influenced obviously though not slavishly by Theodore *Roethke and perhaps Hopkins, are infused with a sense of private anxiety and guilt. Both emotions are called forth most deeply by the memories of a brother who died before Dickey was born ('In the Tree House at Night') and his war experiences ('Drinking From a Helmet'). These early poems generally employ rhyme and metre.

With *Buckdancer's Choice*, Dickey left traditional formalism behind, developing what he called a 'split-line' technique to vary the rhythm and look of the poem. Some critics argue that by doing so Dickey freed his true poetic voice. Others lament that the lack of formal device led to rhetorical, emotional, and intellectual excess. The truth probably lies somewhere between these two assessments, and it will be left to the reader to decide which phase of Dickey's career is most attractive.

Dickey's most comprehensive volume is *The Whole Motion* (Hanover, NH, and London, 1992). His early poems are collected in *The Early Motion* (Middletown, 1981). Recent individual volumes include *The Eagle's Mile* (Hanover and London, 1990) and *Falling, May Day Sermon, and Other Poems* (Hanover and London, 1982). Dickey has also published collections of autobiographical essays, *Self Interviews* (Garden City, NY, 1970; repr. New York, 1984) and *Sorties* (Garden City, 1971; repr. New York, 1984).

[RS

DICKEY, William (Hobart) (1928–), was born in Bellingham, Washington state, and attended Harvard, the University of Iowa, and Oxford. He has taught at Cornell and Denison University in Ohio, and since 1962 at San Francisco State University. From formal beginnings, markedly influenced by *Auden—who chose his first book, *Of the Festivity* (New Haven, Conn., 1959), for the Yale Series of Younger Poets—and Richard *Wilbur, Dickey has moved to an 'open' style, including 'multimedia poems combining text, graphics, sound recordings and animation on computers', and has taught a course on this subject. The transition was not abrupt: poems of the late 1960s and early 1970s, such as those collected in *More under Saturn* (Middletown, Conn., 1971), owe an obvious debt—perhaps too obvious—to *Imagism and to *Pound. But in *Rainbow Grocery* (Amherst, Mass., 1978), Dickey's most widely read collection, he leaves tradition behind altogether, and displays a shift towards 'local' (San Francisco) poetry and the subject of homosexuality. See also *The King of the Golden River* (Cumberland, Iowa, 1986). [MS-S

DICKINSON, Patric Thomas (1913–94), was born at Nasirabad in India. His father was killed early in the First World War, and he was educated at St Catherine's College, Cambridge, where he won a blue for golf. After teaching at a preparatory school he served in the Artists' Rifles from 1939 to 1940, but was invalided out. He joined the BBC in 1942, working in the Feature and Drama Department until he resigned in 1948 to become a free-lance writer.

He has published more than twenty volumes of poems and verse translations since 1946. All his poetry is lyrical but the early romanticism and *Yeatsian symbolism have given way to a tauter, darker, more concentrated utterance. *This Cold Universe* (London, 1964) presents, as the title suggests, a characteristically sombre view of lonely man in an impersonal world, lost and despairing unless redeemed by love.

Dickinson published translations of Aristophanes in 1959 and 1970, and of *The Aeneid of Vergil* (London and New York, 1960). He has written and produced many radio poetry programmes, including the series 'Time for Verse', and a number of feature programmes, of which those on Keats and on Wilfred *Owen were particularly memorable. [JPr

DIDSBURY, Peter (1946–), was born in Fleetwood, Lancashire, but moved to Hull at the age of 6 and has been closely associated with that city ever since. He read English and Hebrew at Oxford, taught English for eight years, and worked at Hull museums for two. In 1987 he became a research assistant with Humberside County Council's Archaeological Unit, writing reports on Roman and medieval pottery. The 'historical imagination', historical erudition, a thorough immersion in the urban-domestic life of Hull and in its estuarial hinterland of rain-drenched farms, drains, ditches, and dykes: all these are powerfully present in Didsbury's poems. But his most characteristic genre is playful invention, and his fictions often depend on little more than a 'necessary premiss' (though this may be arbitrary or fanciful) and authorial whim to sustain them. Intimations of dread or compassion, wonder and disenchantment; nods to *Surrealism and Sterne, John *Ashbery and John Keats; visionary disjunctions and flurries of archaic or pedantically formal diction; inconclusive revelations or portentously offhand gestures: these have secured Didsbury an academic following which has made much of his 'postmodernism' and 'subversiveness' (though in fact the poems are traditionally 'poetic' in their reliance on metaphor and a lyricism of the surprising statement or image).

Didsbury's collections are *The Butchers of Hull* (Newcastle upon Tyne, 1982) and *The Classical Farm* (Newcastle upon Tyne, 1987). [AJ

DI MICHELE, Mary (1949–), was born in Lanciano, Italy, and has lived in Canada since 1955. Educated at the universities of Toronto and Windsor, Ontario, she teaches creative writing at Concordia University in Montreal. A strong feminist, she edited an anthology of Canadian women poets, *Anything is Possible* (Oakville, Ont. 1984); a visit to Pinochet's Chile inspired a strong group of poems examining the interconnections between sexual and power politics. They have been published in her latest collection, *Luminous Emergencies* (Toronto, 1990).

Lyrical, metaphorical, yet also interrogative and unsettling, Di Michele's poetry explores the transformative powers of language, memory, and love. Influenced by artists as diverse as Rilke, Frieda Kahlo, and Leonard Cohen, her writing also acknowledges the work of other women poets, notably Bronwen *Wallace, with whom she co-published *Bread and Chocolate/Marrying into the Family* (Ottawa, 1980).

Di Michele's publications include *Mimosa and Other Poems* (Oakville, 1981); *Necessary Sugar* (Ottawa, 1983); and *Immune to Gravity* (Toronto, 1986). [JKK]

DIPOKO, Mbella Sonne (1936–), was born in Douala, Cameroon and grew up in Western Cameroon and Nigeria. He joined the Nigerian Broadcasting Corporation in 1958 as a news reporter but has lived in France since 1960. He studied law for a time at Paris University. He now devotes himself to poetry and painting.

Dipoko's articles, short stories, and poems have been published widely; his first poems were broadcast by the BBC African Service. His only volume of poetry, *Black and White in Love* (London, 1972), was published following his trip from England through France and Spain to Morocco. He has also published two novels and a play. His most accomplished work is the title-poem, 'Black and White in Love'. The structure is free verse; the language is evocative and accessible; the concerns are urbane and liberal. There is tenderness and sensitivity in his poetry, but his political ideas are unrefined and fragmentary. [FO

DI PRIMA, Diane (1934–), was born in New York City and educated at Swarthmore College, Pennsylvania. Married with three children, she has acted as contributing editor to *Kulchur* magazine, editor of *Signal* magazine, and editor, with LeRoi Jones (Amiri *Baraka), of *Floating Bear* magazine. With her husband, Alan Marlowe, she has also been editor and publisher of

Poets Press, based in New York. Her first collection of poetry, *This Kind of Bird Flies Backward*, was published in 1958 (New York); and since then she has produced many volumes, the more significant or representative of which include *The New Handbook of Heaven* (San Francisco, 1963), *Revolutionary Letters* (New York, 1969), and *Kerhonkson Journal, 1966* (Berkeley, Calif., 1971). Her prolific output also includes several novels and plays.

Sometimes described as one of America's 'street poets', di Prima was prominent as a counter-cultural voice in the 1960s. Her work has been particularly concerned with American life outside the middle-class mainstream: with the culture of travellers and hobos, ethnic minorities, outsiders. However, even the political polemics of *Revolutionary Letters* are punctuated by more intimate moments concerned with friends and family, while *New Handbook of Heaven* is full of magic and incantation, and the poems in *Kerhonkson Journal* are notable for their tenderness and lyricism. See, in particular, *Selected Poetry: Nineteen Fifty-Six to Nineteen Seventy-Six* (New York, 1977). [RJG

DISCH, Tom (Thomas Michael) (1940–), was born in Iowa, grew up in Minnesota, moved to New York City after graduating from high school in 1958, and became a full-time writer after dropping out of New York University four years later. Versatile and prolific, Disch has long enjoyed a commanding international reputation for his science-fiction novels, such as *Camp Concentration* (1968), *334* (1972), and *On Wings of Song* (1979). Recognition for his poetry came first in England: three of his collections, including *Burn This* (1982), were published in London. *Yes, Let's*, a volume of new and selected poems (Baltimore, 1989), confirmed his growing stature in America.

The virtues of Disch's prose—wit, invention, boyish wonder, and intellectual sophistication—are to be found in his verse too. He writes in a wide range of forms: sestinas and villanelles, songs and sonnets, the abecedarius and its opposite, the zewhyexary (a Disch coinage). His approach to form is jubilant in the *New York

School manner; he has a flair for clever internal rhymes and an ability to stretch out a conceit to the furthest limit of ingenuity. Disch has written inspired parodies as well as chatty and urbane verse essays (such as 'On the Use of the Masculine-Preferred') that recall *Auden's efforts in this vein. The novels and poems he has written jointly with other writers may help persuade sceptics of the value of literary collaboration.

Disch is the author of *Amnesia*, an 'interactive' computer fiction, in addition to children's books, collections of short stories, historical fiction, and verse plays. He has served as fiction critic for *Playboy*, and is at present the theatre critic for *The Nation*. In September 1990 Disch found himself at the centre of a controversy when a New York City production of his short play, *The Cardinal Detoxes*, caused the Roman Catholic Archdiocese of New York to lodge strong protests.   [DL

DOBSON, Rosemary (de Brissac) (1920–), was born in Sydney. Her paternal grandfather was the English poet Austin Dobson (1840–1921). After studying design, which she regarded as a valuable discipline, and attending university, she became a publisher's editor in Sydney. Later she lived abroad with her husband before settling in Canberra. Douglas *Stewart encouraged publication of *In a Convex Mirror* (Sydney, 1944).

Dobson shares the classicist and formalist orientation of such contemporaries as James *McAuley and A. D. *Hope. Its simplicity, clarity, detachment, and precision give her work a contemplative stillness—what Hope calls 'passionate serenity'—which reflects her love of early Renaissance painting. Her effects derive from quiet irony, wit, and formal finesse rather than visual imagery; her sensibility is spare and austere.

Although her career spans five decades, Dobson is neither prolific nor broad in scope. Her chief preoccupation has always been time and its implications for individual experience (notably parenthood) or, more often, art. *Child With a Cockatoo* (Sydney, 1955) contains her best-known poems, mostly dramatic mono-

logues pertaining to Renaissance paintings. Some poems are informed by a sense of loss ('Cock Crow', 'Jack'), or by a sense of the mystery beyond that which can be apprehended and expressed. But Dobson is resolutely anti-transcendental, as 'Over the Frontier' demonstrates.

With her friend David *Campbell she has translated Mandelstam and other Russian poets. *Selected Poems* (Sydney, revd. edn., 1980) reprints much of five earlier volumes. *The Three Fates* (Sydney, 1984), influenced by Chinese poetry, contains impressive work in the free verse she now favours. *Collected Poems* appeared (Sydney) in 1991.   [AW

DOBYNS, Stephen (1941–), was born in Orange, New Jersey, and teaches at Warren Wilson College. Though primarily a poet, he is also the author of ten novels, including five chronicling the adventures of Saratoga detective Charlie Bradshaw. Whatever medium he happens to write in, Dobyns is always a story-teller, for all his work is based upon narrative. Even in the volume that ought to be his most static, *The Balthus Poems* (New York, 1982), where each poem is based upon a single one of the French artist's paintings, Dobyns brings the characters to life by creating dynamic stories for them.

Perhaps because he was a newspaper reporter early in his life, Dobyns does not look inside his own psyche for the subject-matter of his poems; he writes primarily in the third person. Many of his poems contain traditional stories that bite their own tails, resolving at the end conflicts established at the beginning. Others —for example, 'The Invitation', from his most recent book, *Cemetery Nights* (New York, 1986; Newcastle upon Tyne, 1992)—move in a linear fashion, leaving behind the characters and situations with which they begin. Still others are created like spider-webs; their stories are sticky, confusing, in danger of being broken and flung, at any moment, 'into heaven's blue and innocent immensity'.

Dobyns's first volume, *Concurring Beasts* (New York), was the Lamont Poetry Selection for 1971; his fifth, *Black Dog, Red Dog* (New

York), was chosen for the National Poetry Series in 1984. His other volumes are *Griffon* (1976) and *Heat Death* (1980—both New York).   [PS

DONAGHY, Michael (1954–), was born in New York, and educated at Fordham University and the University of Chicago. He was poetry editor for the *Chicago Review* before moving to London, where he now lives. His first collection, *Shibboleth* (Oxford, 1988), earned him the year's Whitbread Poetry Prize, and also the Geoffrey Faber Memorial Award of 1989. *Errata* (also Oxford) followed in 1993.

Shibboleth records an intelligent literary apprenticeship: Donaghy recalls his precocious childhood with affectionate irony, parades a wide range of learning lightly, and views the oddities of real life—a man carrying a man-length mirror along a girder, or an especially fruitful *Guardian* misprint—with wry amusement. He is fond of unsettling juxtapositions (*Yeats and an angel, Purcell and a twelve-speed bike), and perhaps over-fond of poetic riddles which implicate the reader without troubling to teach him the rules of the game. His allusiveness, too, can become overburdened, as when his precise reference to a cadenza in Mozart (K.285a) is called upon to support an entire poem. In love poems, such as 'The Present', there is a more subtly rewarding blend of intimacy and intellect.

A poet who tries on so many suits of clothes is always in danger of looking like a coat-hanger: the poems in his second collection, *Errata*, find Donaghy beginning to settle for longer, more fluent-looking forms (as in the substantial narrative spoken by Benvenuto Cellini), although his imagination remains dartingly anecdotal and often bewilderingly frenetic.   [NP

DOOLITTLE, Hilda (H.D.) (1886–1961), was born in Bethlehem, Pennsylvania. Her mother was a Moravian artist, her father a professor of astronomy. The posthumous memoir, *End to Torment*, describes how, as a student at Bryn Mawr College, she fell in love with Ezra *Pound, who was then a postgraduate student at the University of Pennsylvania, and who gave

her a hand-bound sheaf of poems entitled *Hilda's Book*. She left college in her sophomore year with poor grades. In 1911 she travelled to London, where Pound was established, intending to stay for the summer; but she never returned, and lived in England and Switzerland for the rest of her life. Instead of Pound she married her fellow-Imagist Richard *Aldington in 1913; they separated in 1919, though they were not divorced until 1938. After Aldington left her she lived with Bryher (Winifred Ellerman) from 1919 to 1946.

It was Pound who labelled her 'H.D. Imagiste' when, in 1912, he sent her poems (and Aldington's) to Harriet Monroe for publication in *Poetry*. She continued to subscribe to *Imagism when the movement was taken over by Amy *Lowell; and her spare, clear, sculptural early poems, like 'Pear Tree' and the famous 'Oread' ('Whirl up, sea— | Whirl your pointed pines . . .'), are among the most successful embodiments of Imagist principles.

After the breakdown of her marriage her poetry began to serve a more complex personal purpose, and the purely Imagist phase of her career can be considered closed by the publication in 1925 of the (first) *Collected Poems*. *Red Roses for Bronze* (1931) shows her moving towards a more discursive treatment of psychic and religious archetypes, a tendency accelerated by her visits to Vienna, in 1933 and 1934, to be analysed by Freud—(see the memoir, *Tribute to Freud*, (1956), and the poem 'The Master', which transplants their relationship typically to ancient Greece and describes how the Freud-figure sets her free to 'prophesy', to voice her proto-feminist repudiation of 'man-strength'. Subsequent volumes of note include the wartime *Trilogy* (composed 1942–4 and published 1944–6) and the 300-page poem *Helen in Egypt* (1961), her re-creation, composed in the guise of the ancient Sicilian poet Stesichorus, of the Helen–Achilles myth.

H.D. has been variously dismissed as a poet of minor gifts, narrow range, and esoteric concerns, and promoted (especially in America) as the great female modernist in verse. Though the cult of H.D. may be more political than literary, several poets have expressed a debt: see Robert *Duncan's unfinished *H.D. Book*, and Denise *Levertov's elegy in her volume *O Taste and See*.

A *Collected Poems* was published in New York in 1983 (Manchester, 1984), and *Selected Poems*, ed. Louis L. Martz, in 1989 (Manchester). *Bid Me to Live* (London and New York, 1960) is an auto-biographical novel with lively portraits of Aldington and D. H. *Lawrence.   [MI

DORN, Ed(ward) (1929–), was born and grew up in eastern Illinois, on the banks of the River Embarrass (a tributary of the Wabash). He never knew his father. His mother was of French ancestry, his grandfather a railroad man. He attended a one-room school, while in high school played billiards with the local undertaker for a dime a point, and after two years at the University of Illinois and two stops at *Black Mountain College, travelled through the trans-mountain West following the winds of writing and employment. From 1965 to 1970 he lived in England, where he lectured at the University of Essex. He has since taught in Kansas, Chicago, and San Francisco; throughout the 1980s he taught in the Creative Writing Program of the University of Colorado, Boulder, and with his wife Jennifer edited the newspaper *Rolling Stock*.

Dorn's early work is notable for lyrical, gestural style, his later for a humorous and increasingly abrasive moral satire. The American West has been his special subject; the various phases of his writing have in common a strict and angular attention to the particularities of its landscapes and culture. The anti-post-industrial-capitalist mock-epic *Gunslinger* (Durham, NC, and London, 1989) is for Dorn a sort of transitional marker, demonstrating the best qualities of both his early and late modes. Eight years in the making (1967–75), this ambitious, inventive, multi-voiced allegorical narrative plays off pop song and cowboy ballad in assembling an outrageous outlaw metaphysics, extravagantly updating pre-Socratic philosophies and the myths of comic-book gunman and Hollywood/TV frontier hero to fit the subjectivist ethics of the Vietnam War-era drug culture.

Among Dorn's works are *The Collected Poems, 1956–1974* (San Francisco, 1975; enlarged edn. 1983); *Hello, La Jolla* (Berkeley, Calif., 1978); *Yellow Lola* (Santa Barbara, Calif., 1980); and *Abhorrences* (Santa Rosa, Calif., 1990). His prose writings include *The Rites of Passage* (Buffalo, Col., 1965; rev. edn. issued as *By the Sound*, Mt. Vernon, Wash., 1971); *The Shoshoneans* (New York, 1966); and *Views* (San Francisco, 1980).
                                    [TC

DOUGLAS, Lord Alfred (Bruce) (1870–1945), is mostly remembered now for his association with Oscar Wilde from 1891 until Wilde's death in 1900. Douglas, the third son of the Marquess of Queensberry, either was or became soon after meeting Wilde an enthusiastic homo-sexual, and after Wilde's trial and imprisonment shocked many liberal-minded figures (and angered Wilde) by an article attacking the British Government, and expressing pride that Wilde had recognized his 'beautiful body' and 'beautiful soul'. In 1900 Douglas married, gave up homosexual practices, and in 1911 became a Roman Catholic. A year later he learned that *De Profundis*, published in 1905, was in fact an edited version of a letter written him by Wilde in prison, full of bitter reproaches for Douglas's behaviour. His anger at what he regarded as Wilde's betrayal was expressed in the partly ghost-written *Oscar Wilde and Myself* (1914). His *Autobiography* (1929) and *Oscar Wilde: A Summing Up* (1940) show how much the affair continued to obsess him. There are biographies by Rupert Croft-Cooke (1963) and Montgomery Hyde (1984).

Douglas's *Poems* appeared in France in 1896. Two poems favouring homosexuality were omitted when the collection was anonymously published in England as *The City of the Soul* (1899). *In Excelsis*, a sonnet sequence written while Douglas was in prison for libelling Winston Churchill, appeared in 1923, the *Complete Poems* (London) in 1928. Douglas has had a very bad press as a poet, his serious work excluded from almost all anthologies, his nonsense poems ignored in collections of light verse. He is remembered, ironically enough, by a single line he came to regret: 'I am the Love that dare not speak its name'.   [JGS

DOUGLAS, Keith (1920–44), was born in Kent, and brought up near Cranleigh, where his father drifted in and out of work (settling for a while as a chicken-farmer) and his mother succumbed to *encephalitus lethargia*, or 'sleepy sickness'. As soon as he was eligible, Douglas was bundled off to boarding school—in Guildford, first, then in 1931 to Christ's Hospital.

By the time he went up to Merton College, Oxford, in 1938—where his tutor was Edmund *Blunden—the disruptions of home had forced him to evolve a style of living which would remain constant for the rest of his life: rational and pragmatic in thought, hard-hitting and hard riding in deed, brisk and vigorous in his pursuit of affection. The stories and poems he wrote as an undergraduate (for a while he edited *The Cherwell*) show similar qualities: taking their lead from *Auden, they relate private feelings to public issues in a way which allows the poet's sensitivity to be mined but at the same time defended and deflected.

When war broke out Douglas relished the chance it gave him to dramatize these tensions. After training at Sandhurst and Wickwar (the time was heavily punctuated by games-playing and girl-chasing) he was posted in 1941 to Palestine with the Nottinghamshire (Sherwood) Rangers. The history of his time in North Africa is dashingly told in his memoir *Alamein to Zem Zem* (1946), where he is at pains to appear casual and raffish—deserting in order to see action, living it up in Alexandria and Cairo, chasing the enemy across the desert as though they were competitors in a gymkhana. When he returned to England in late 1943 his brave face was still intact. In June the following year he was sent to France, and four days after landing he was killed. He was 24.

As a soldier, Douglas managed to conceal his finer feelings until the very end of his life. His poems—to their credit—are not so sanguine. In an early letter he anticipated that 'one day cynic and lyric will meet and make a balanced style', and from 'Simplify me when I'm dead' (1941) to

his last poem, 'On a return from Egypt' (1944), he gives many examples of their conjunction. 'These grasses, ancient enemies' is characteristic: 'devil and angel do not fight,|they are the classic Gemini|for whom it's vital to agree| whose interdependent state|this two-faced country reflects.' Douglas knew that it was his own mind which contained the 'arguments of hell with heaven', but realized that their terms and resolution were reflected in the actual circumstances of battle. 'Cairo Jag' is typical of several poems in juxtaposing the seedy world of the base town with the battlefields a mere 'day's travelling' away, and explores the truce they are forced to make between their apparent similarities. 'The streets dedicated to sleep|stenches and sour smells' are parodied by the 'new world', where 'the vegetation is of iron|dead tanks, gun barrels split like celery'.

This animation of war by its opposite (the same process occurs in 'Dead Men', 'Landscape with Figures', and 'Vergissmeinicht') produces another of Douglas's major themes. As an undergraduate he wrote that poetry 'is like a man, whom thinking you know all his movements and appearance you will presently come upon in such a posture that for a moment you can hardly believe it is a position of the limbs you know', and as a soldier he regularly finds himself testing the unreality of his impressions. In *Alamein to Zem Zem* he draws images from the 'normal', civilian world to perform this function, admitting that he went to fight 'a little like a visitor from the country going to a great show'. The explosions of gunfire which give the impression of 'watching a magician's trick'; the wounded men 'in an attitude like the humble and resigned attitude of people in long queues'; and the dead Italian soldiers who look 'like trippers taken ill' all bear the same sinister resemblance to scenes of peace as the corpse in 'Vergissmeinicht', who is 'sprawling in the sun' like a sunbather.

In their oblique way these comparisons provide the 'pity' which admirers of First World War poetry find lacking in Douglas. His repeated transformation of people into things (a casualty into a 'cleverly posed waxwork') testifies to war's dehumanizing effect, and redirects the compassion of his predecessors rather than merely re-creating it—which he realized 'a modern poet on active service' would be tempted to do. His heroes are not tortured, sensitive souls, advertising their distress, but the 'obsolescent breed' of his poem 'Sportsmen', who 'under these stones and earth lounge still | in famous attitudes of unconcern'. At the same time that Douglas realizes their stupidity, he admires their nonchalance—the very quality on which so many of his own best poetic strategies depend. The more marked his detachment, the more it suggests his involvement. It is a tone of considerable subtlety, a fine balance of disinterest and commitment, which ably carries out his own commands: 'To be sentimental or emotional now', he stated in a letter, 'is dangerous to oneself and to others. To trust anyone or admit to any hope of a better world is criminally foolish, as foolish as it is to stop working for it.'

See, *Complete Poems*, ed. Desmond Graham (Oxford, 1987); *Keith Douglas: A Prose Miscellany*, ed. Desmond Graham (Manchester, 1985); and *Keith Douglas 1920–1944*, by Desmond Graham (Oxford, 1974). [AM

DOVE, Rita (1952–), was born in Akron, Ohio, and educated in Ohio and at the universities of Tübingen and Iowa. She ends her first book, *The Yellow House on the Corner* (Pittsburgh, 1980), by pointing out, in the poem 'Ö', how the finding of a perfect word can allow a writer to 'start out with one thing, end | up with another, and nothing's | like it used to be, not even the future'. The poems in that book begin in the author's childhood neighbourhood in the industrial city of Akron, but reach to worlds as far away as Sweden, Germany, Tunisia, literature, music, geometry, and the American South where Dove encounters her enslaved ancestors—a meeting that helps to shape her identity but does not limit the vision of her work. Her second book, *Museum* (Pittsburgh and London, 1983), is her most cosmopolitan, containing poems that range in reference from 'Shakespeare Say', which tells the story of a black American blues-singer in Paris, to 'The Copper Beech', which describes the significance of the most rococo tree 'in the park of the castle | at Erpenberg'.

Dove's third collection, *Thomas and Beulah* (Pittsburgh), for which she was awarded the Pulitzer Prize in Poetry in 1986, uses the lives of the poet's maternal grandparents in order to explore the experiences of those mid-twentieth-century American blacks who journeyed from the South to search for jobs in the industrial North. In addition to containing the most personal poems Dove has yet published, *Grace Notes* (New York, 1988; London, 1992) also deals with the black experience in America and includes a remarkable section on words ('grace notes') and the possibilities of language.

In addition to her books of poems, Dove is also the author of one collection of short stories *Fifth Sunday* (1985), and is working on a novel.

[PS

DOWNIE, Freda (1929–93), was born in London and educated in Northampton, Australia, and Kent. Her first pamphlet collection, *Night Music*, appeared in 1974, and she subsequently published several small-scale editions of her poetry—most recently *Even the Flowers* (1989) —as well as two full collections: *A Stranger Here* (London, 1977) and *Plainsong* (London, 1981).

Freda Downie's poems—elegant, full of gently spiked irony, and oblique, wistful glances at everyday events and familiar landscapes—relish oddity, sometimes skirmishing with the whimsical, but their hallmark is a sharp, controlling intelligence which seldom permits mere eccentricity. Her poem 'Pastime' carries an epigraph from Montaigne—'When I play with my cat, who knows if I am not a pastime to her more than she is to me?'—and this kind of unsettling, contemplative wisdom gives her writing its distinctive edge. As she observes in the title-poem of *A Stranger Here*: 'I wait, every detail waits | For something—for someone recognizable | Approaching with special lotions and explanations.' In her best poems the lotions and explanations she provides herself are refreshingly unexpected. [JM

DRANSFIELD, Michael (1948–73), divided his life between 'bohemian' areas of his native Sydney and restless motor-bike wanderings round rural east-coast Australia. His poetry reflects the division. Hailed as a harbinger of a Sixties poetic—urban-based; aesthetically, socially, and politically radical—he became a major figure in the 'new' poetry promoted by the *University of Queensland Press Paperback Poets and the anthologies of Thomas *Shapcott, *Australian Poetry Now* (Melbourne, 1969) and John *Tranter, *The New Australian Poetry* (Brisbane, 1979). However, his city poems speak tellingly of personal and social anomy, of angry despair at environmental degradation and the Vietnam War, and of the ecstasies and desolations of drug-taking. From the beginning he turned to the city's antonym for contrast; not, however, to the bush of social realism, but to idealized lost worlds, those of the cultured graziers of 'Courland Penders' and the spiritually rich aboriginal inhabitants ('On the Land').

In 1973 Dransfield died of a drug-related tetanus infection, leaving the largely prepared *Memoirs of a Velvet Urinal* and some 600 poems. Rodney *Hall's literary executorship culminated in *Collected Poems of Michael Dransfield* (St Lucia, Qld., 1990). For a retrospective view of this 'Rimbaud of the suburbs', see 'Remembering Michael Dransfield', in *Literary Memoirs: Biting the Bullet*, by Thomas Shapcott (Brookvale, 1990). [JS

DRINKWATER, John (1882–1937), was born in Leytonstone, London. He was one of those poets who may safely be described as quintessentially *Georgian, and he is well represented in all five volumes of *Georgian Poetry*. But his work, unlike that of *Graves, *de la Mare, and even (very occasionally) J. C. *Squire, has failed to last. He had a more distinguished theatrical career. At 25 he met Barry Jackson, and with him formed the Pilgrim Players, which led to the founding of the Birmingham Repertory Theatre, of which Drinkwater became manager in 1913. The Pilgrims gave his first verse-play, *Cophetua* (1913); and this was followed in 1918 by the highly successful *Abraham Lincoln*, given

by the Repertory. Although the verse of this, and others resembling it, was flat and undistinguished, it had competence, and played well enough in its time. Drinkwater produced a stream of popular biographies and autobiographies. His greatest interest in later life was philately, and he owned a notable collection. *Collected Poems* (London, 1923); *Collected Plays* (London, 1925). [MS-S

DRIVER, C(harles) J(onathan) (1939–), was born in Cape Town, the son of a clergyman-schoolmaster. He was educated at St Andrews College, Grahamstown, the University of Cape Town, and Trinity College, Oxford.

As an active participant in student politics, and president of the National Union of South African Students, Driver was detained in 1964 under a ninety-day detention law. While at Oxford (1965–7) his South African passport was withdrawn, effectively forcing him into exile. He has been a teacher in Kent and Humberside, a headmaster in Hong Kong and at Berkhamstead School, Hertfordshire, and is at present headmaster of Wellington College, Berkshire.

Driver's poems are characterized by a search for a home, both actual and artistic, as a way of finding meaning, defeating time, and overcoming a lurking sense of absurdity in ordinary life. They sometimes seem occasional, and at times self-conscious, but this is offset by a rigorous honesty and a careful craftsmanship that is nevertheless always aware of aspects of human experience the craft cannot fully tap.

He is better-known as a novelist than a poet, having published four novels, the best-known of which are *Elegy for a Revolutionary* (1969) and *Send War in Our Time, O Lord* (1971), both of which were banned by the South African authorities. His volumes of poetry include *Occasional Light*, published in a Mantis edition with Jack Cope (Cape Town, 1979), *I Live Here Now* (Lincoln, 1979), and *Hong Kong Portraits* (1986). [KG

DUBIE, Norman (1945–), was raised in isolated communities in New England with books for entertainment. A graduate of Goddard

College and the University of Iowa, he has come to write some of the most learned and allusive poetry of his generation. His poems are most often based on stories and characters drawn from history, literature, and art. In technique he is a postmodernist and feels free to alter and combine his materials according to the demands of the imagination; at the beginning of his *Selected and New Poems* (New York, 1983) he quotes Randall *Jarrell approvingly: 'What the wish wants to see, it sees.' In choosing his materials, Dubie favours the nineteenth century and often turns to Russia. His first book, *Alehouse Sonnets* (Pittsburgh, 1971), which he has mistakenly repudiated, engages the poet in a dense, amusing, and learned dialogue with William Hazlitt; characters from twentieth-century Vermont intermingle with others from nineteenth-century England.

A listing of subjects from another of Dubie's books, *The City of the Olesha Fruit* (New York, 1979), indicates the range of his interests: in 'The Infant', the dead Kafka is berated by his father; in 'The Seagull', Chekhov meditates in his garden at Yalta; in 'The Old Asylum of the Narragansetts' we see the everyday life of an early American Puritan settlement; 'The Ambassador Diaries of Jean de Bosschere and Edgar Poe' is addressed to Conrad *Aiken and draws parallels between his life and theirs.

Dubie's selected poems is parsimonious; in addition to the volumes listed above, the reader is encouraged to consult *In the Dead of the Night* (Pittsburgh, 1975); and *The Illustrations* (1977), *The Everlastings* (1980), *The Springhouse* (1986), and *Groom Falconer* (1989—all New York).

[PS

DUDEK, Louis, (1918–), was born and educated in Montreal, receiving his BA from McGill University in 1939. Upon graduating, Dudek looked for work as a journalist and tried his hand at free-lance writing before settling into a job in advertising. His early poems began to appear in 1941–2 in the *McGill Daily* and at about the same time he became involved with the group editing the avant-garde magazine *First Statement*, which marked the beginning of a long history of active participation in the little-press and little-magazine movement in Montreal. In 1944 he married Stephanie Zuperko and moved to New York City, where he studied history and comparative literature at Columbia University. In 1951 Dudek returned to Montreal and took up an appointment in the English department at McGill University where he spent the rest of his academic career. In the following year, Dudek, together with Raymond *Souster and Irving *Layton, launched Contact Press—destined to become one of the most important little presses in Canada—with the publication of a joint collection of their poetry, *Cerberus* (Toronto). At the same time, Dudek became involved with a series of avant-garde literary magazines: *Contact* in 1952; *CIV/n* in 1954; and finally his own poetry magazine, *Delta* (1957–66). He was also a co-founder of the little press, Delta Canada (1963–1971).

Dudek's own poetry, which was characterized initially by colloquial lyricism and strong social concerns, as evidenced in *East of the City* (Toronto, 1946), has developed into the long, meditative statement which began with *Europe* (Toronto, 1954), and went on to *The Transparent Sea* (Toronto, 1956) and *En Mexico* (Toronto, 1958). He had become (much like his friend and correspondent, Ezra *Pound) a writer concerned with preserving civilization and the values of serious art. Repelled by the literary histrionics and cultural excesses of the 1960s, Dudek retreated into his own work, publishing a long and ruminative poem, *Atlantis* (Montreal), in 1967 and a *Collected Poetry* (Montreal) in 1971. Between 1965 and 1969 he wrote reviews and a column on the arts for the two English-language dailies in Montreal. In 1967 he co-edited (with Michael Gnarowski) *The Making of Modern Poetry in Canada*. This was followed by several volumes of essays and criticism.

The later Dudek, as exemplified in *Continuation I* (1981) and *Continuation II* (1990–both Montreal), is someone engaged in writing 'the poem without end', which takes the form of recording the fragmentary, poetic instant, and suggests a natural creative process rather than the willed structures of conventional poetics. *Infinite*

Worlds (Montreal, 1988), the definitive selected poetry, was edited by Robin Blaser, while his cultural journalism has been collected as *In Defence of Art* (Kingston, Ont., 1988).   [MG

DUFFY, Carol Ann (1955–), was born in Glasgow, and spent her childhood in Staffordshire. She graduated in philosophy at the University of Liverpool in 1977. Though reluctant to style herself a playwright, Duffy has had two plays performed at the Liverpool Playhouse, and her well-crafted monologues suggest a strong dramatic talent. The social criticism of her poetry is never mere polemic, but is channelled through the sensibilities—and the rich fantasy-lives—of various characters: the artist's model of 'Standing Female Nude', frazzled housewives, lager-sodden husbands, nervy young delinquents, and the shabby-genteel stewing in their repressions. Sometimes, perhaps, Duffy aims her poetic fire at obvious victims, easy targets; but her best work combines lyric intensity with plain-speaking.

She has published several booklets and three full-length collections, *Standing Female Nude* (1985), *Selling Manhattan* (1987), and *The Other Country* (1992—all London).   [CAR

DUGAN, Alan (1923–), was born in New York and works as a staff member at the Fine Arts Work Centre at Provincetown, Massachusetts. His first book, *General Prothalamion in Populous Times* (1961), was privately printed, but his second, *Poems* (New Haven, Conn., 1961) won both the Yale Younger Poets Award and the Pulitzer Prize, and was greeted with unusually wide praise. The stark, usually unrhymed poems in this and succeeding volumes have been aptly described as 'directly stated, dry, bleak'. They were fluent, but the gloomy poet distrusted his own fluency, and questioned himself in every way: 'I guess there is a garden named | "Garden of Love". If so, I'm in it | I am the guesser in the garden.'

Apart from faintly echoing (or resembling) Robert *Creeley's laconic manner, Dugan's work offered a sharp contrast to contemporary American poetry at the time, being on the one hand formal and over-academic, and on the other loose to the point of spilling into undisciplined, impressionistic prose. Dugan was disciplined, but eschewed both extremes, and tended only to write when he was moved to do so. Greatly respected for his honesty and restraint, he has disappointed only inasmuch as he has not developed (or tried to develop)—almost as if he regarded the notion of development as a kind of artificiality. What has been called the 'stinging note of self-contempt' is still apparent, and so is an extreme pessimism: we are offered the conscientious and intelligent reportage of a spirit which sees itself as dead, or about to die: 'Oh it is here | that I propose to build | it, the Cathedral "Abattoir" . . .'

Dugan's work lacks variety and he is sometimes too fearful to explore his lyrical potential; but his austerity and plainness continue to impress. See *Collected Poems* (New Haven, 1969; London, 1970); *Poems 6* (New York, 1989).

[MS-S

DUGGAN, Eileen (1894–1972), the fourth daughter of Irish immigrant parents from County Kerry, was born in the small settlement of Tua Marina in the South Island province of Marlborough, New Zealand. She attended Wellington Teachers' College and Victoria University College in Wellington, and taught for a brief period before becoming a free-lance journalist. For forty-five years she edited 'Pippa's Page' for women in the *New Zealand Tablet*.

Duggan's first two small volumes of poetry, *Poems* (1922) and *New Zealand Bird Songs* (1929), were published in New Zealand, while the subsequent three, *Poems* (1937), *New Zealand Poems* (1940), and *More Poems* (1951), were published in England and America. For some time she was New Zealand's best-known poet, and certainly the first to be internationally recognized. Yet there has never been a collected edition of her poetry. Complicated circumstances also resulted in her omission from the two important New Zealand anthologies edited by Allen *Curnow.

Duggan's profound religious faith is central

to her poetry. Many of her early poems were concerned with Ireland and its dispossessed people. There is, however, no sense of exile from 'Home'. She was firmly committed to New Zealand; many of her poems focus on her feelings for its people, both Maori and Pakeha, its emerging nationalism, and the landscape which provided her with appropriate symbols and imagery. A number of her ballads celebrate the strength and courage of pioneer women, while she was also one of the first New Zealand writers to incorporate Maori myth and language into her poetry. Her work is uneven, at times marred by an old-fashioned literariness and an excessive romanticism. At its best, for example in her best-known lyric, 'The tides run up the Wairau', it achieves an impressive economy of thought and image.   [GB

DUGGAN, Laurie (1949–), was born in Melbourne and studied at Monash University (with a brief sojourn at the University of Sydney). He has had various occupations: lecturing in media studies at Swinburne College (1976) and the Canberra College of Advanced Education (1983), free-lancing as a script-writer (1977–82), and writing art criticism for *The Times on Sunday* (1986). He is currently working as a research assistant and living in Melbourne.

Like many Australian poets of his generation, Duggan was drawn to modernism in its American embodiment: *Pound is an obvious forebear, but Duggan's commitment to open forms, his play with fragmentation, and his fascination with popular culture show an affinity with William Carlos *Williams. Lyricism and satire have been Duggan's touchstones from his first collections, *East* (Melbourne, 1976) and *Under the Weather* (Sydney, 1978). *Adventures in Paradise* (Adelaide, 1982) shows him trying a relaxed, amusing autobiographical poem; it marks the culmination of *The Great Divide* (Sydney, 1985).

With *The Ash Range* (Melbourne, 1987), Duggan ventured into a longer, more complex work, what he calls an epic in Pound's sense, a 'poem including history'. The work is a collage in verse and prose of journal entries, newspaper

clippings, local histories, and other documents relating to Gippsland culture and history: while its content is solidly Australian, its technique has been learned from the *Black Mountain school.

In *The Epigrams of Martial* (Melbourne, 1989), Duggan proved himself to be an incisive translator; many of the poems allude to contemporary writers and literary politics, and are wickedly funny. *Blue Notes* (Melbourne, 1990) also contains translations from the Italian, chiefly of Ardengo Soffici, and revisits the epigram and the lyric. Several lyrics from this collection have also appeared in a pamphlet, *All Blues* (London, 1989).   [KH

DUNCAN, Robert (1919–88), was born in Oakland, California. After his mother died he was adopted by a couple who practised orthodox theosophy. He attended the University of California at Berkeley, then spent several years in New York City as part of Anais Nin's circle. After a brief marriage, he returned to Berkeley for graduate work. In 1951 he met the artist Jess Collins, with whom he lived until his death. During the Sixties Duncan was among the most vocal of the poets writing against the Vietnam War.

Duncan's oeuvre constitutes a sustained and powerful exploration of visionary possibilities. Resolutely clinging to a high, at times archaic style, tempered only by the quirks of spelling associated with the *Beats, he produced a large body of poetry charged with mystical energies, celebrating modes of transcendence ranging from the erotic and the aesthetic to the religious. His inspiration derives from poets like Pindar, Dante, and Blake, and from more recent experimental writers like *Stein, *Pound, and especially H. D. (Hilda *Doolittle), about whom he wrote a critical book. But he is most immediately associated with the group of poets gathered under Charles *Olson's tutelage at *Black Mountain College in North Carolina, where Duncan briefly taught. Through Olson's theories of *projective verse Duncan came to his own understanding of poetic form as process rather than shape or structure; this, together with his Neo-Platonic concern with higher vision, accounts for the general murkiness of his work, its way of moving from topic to topic without providing clear narrative or logical links. At times this penchant for flowing leads to long, amorphous dithyrambs that offer no clear subject beyond a vague mysticism.

His books include *The Opening of the Field* (New York, 1960; London, 1969), and most recently *Ground Work II: In the Dark* (New York, 1987). The fullest study of his work is Mark Andrew Johnson, *Robert Duncan* (Boston, 1988).

[RG

DUNMORE, Helen (1952–), was born in Yorkshire. After graduating from the University of York in 1973, she spent some time teaching in Finland, and now lives in Bristol.

Dunmore has a good ear for phrasing and cadence, even in her most irregularly structured work, and a strong visual, even cinematic, sense. Her poems often give the effect of a panning movement between distance and close detail. Although at times a sharp miniaturist, she is usually at her best in more expansive, medium-length forms. Despite her preoccupation with the organic and domestic worlds and with maternity, she has a range of political and philosophical concerns.

She has published four volumes of verse (all from Newcastle upon Tyne): *The Apple Fall* (1983); *The Sea Skater* (1986); *The Raw Garden* (1988); and *Short Days, Long Nights* (1991). [CAR

DUNN, Douglas (Eaglesham) (1942–), born and brought up in Renfrewshire and educated at the Scottish School of Librarianship and the University of Hull, for long worked as a librarian at the University of Hull. His widely noticed first book, *Terry Street* (London, 1969), was regarded as coming from 'Larkin territory'—fresh and original for all that. Many lines, quoted and praised by critics for their graphic qualities, dourly described such things as 'Old men's long underwear | (Dripping)' and (most notably) frozen dogshit, as well as other appurtenances of working-class Hull.

The bright, sour early poems were indignant, deeply felt, and full of effective description; but *Terry Street* was both poster-colour-promising

and immature. Dunn's next two collections, *The Happier Life* (London, 1972) and *Love or Nothing* (London, 1974), disappointed most critics: it was felt that he had failed to develop his own voice, had included too much frivolous light verse, and was too often wilfully obscure. *Barbarians* (London, 1979), however, confirmed his reputation: he developed his technique and powers of concentration, and was more self-critical. The descriptions of physical and mental squalor had become more sharply focused and suggestive, although the intellectual dimension of the poetry as a whole remained, as it does now, faintly suspect, and is hardly accounted for by an alleged 'Marxist presence'.

St Kilda's Parliament (London, 1981) marked a further advance, despite the inclusion in it of a number of patently weak or insufficiently realized poems. *Elegies* (London, 1985), a series of poems in memory of his wife, perhaps overinfluenced by *Hardy, was undoubtedly moving, but praised in perhaps too superlative terms: time has served to deepen some critics' doubts about Dunn's lack of subtlety and depth. But the poetry of later collections (including *Northlight*, London, 1988) is valued for its honesty, eschewal of rhetorical embellishment, and humanity. His latest volume is *Dante's Drum-Kit* (London, 1993).

Dunn has edited a selection from the American poet Delmore *Schwartz, and translated Racine's *Andromache* (London, 1990). See *Selected Poems 1964–1983* (London, 1986); *New and Selected Poems 1966–1988* (New York, 1989).

[MS-S

DUNN, Stephen (1939–), was born in New York City and educated at Hofstra University, the New School for Social Research, and Syracuse University. He served in the army, played professional basketball for a year, and worked as an advertising copy-writer before starting a teaching career. He is a professor at Stockton State College in New Jersey.

Dunn is one of America's foremost poets of middleness, in all its aspects: social, cultural, psychological, stylistic. His poetry is consistently intelligent and even-tempered, rejecting equally the blandishments of illusion and disillusionment. He does not write with the descriptive or sensual fullness common to his generation, instead choosing to pursue a discursive style in which metaphor functions as a kind of logic. Dunn is primarily concerned with the ways we find to live in a world of other people, and hence his imagination is more moral than aesthetic, though he would no doubt find the distinction a false one. He features in his own poems as an almost comic protagonist, stumbling towards a self-conscious wisdom through a series of parabolic encounters with strangeness. Dunn's choice of reason, responsiveness, and responsibility over extravagance makes him one of the less conspicuous but more appealing poets of his generation. His most recent book is *Between Angels* (New York and London, 1989).

[RG

DURCAN, Paul (1944–), was born in Dublin and studied archaeology and medieval history at University College, Cork. In his first book, *O Westport in the Light of Asia Minor*, published in 1975, he already displayed in his zany verse-narratives the dislocated, conversational vernacular which is his hallmark. Everyday language is made disconcerting by defeating idiomatic expectation, and by whimsical titles such as 'Archbishop of Kerry to have Abortion'. Beginning with the Patrick Kavanagh Award in 1974, Durcan has enjoyed considerable and increasing recognition, culminating in the prestigious Whitbread Poetry Prize for *Daddy, Daddy*, (1990). His work has been variously characterized as mystical, surrealist, or facetious. Despite his violent yoking together of heterogeneous ideas and registers (biblical repetition in colloquial contexts, for example), his vivid narratives are more atmospheric than metaphysical. The principal difficulty is deciding how seriously to take the poetry's politics, and how far the narrator of these extravagant stories is to be identified with the poet. There is no doubting Durcan's genuine compassion, for example in the impressive poems about his broken marriage in *The Berlin Wall Café* (1985). He has plausibly been called feminist, and his opposition to the violence of contemporary Northern Ireland is unwavering. Despite the success of some earlier volumes, including two selections—*The Selected Paul Durcan* (1982) and *Jesus and Angela* (1988)—*Daddy, Daddy* has been greeted as a major advance in range and seriousness, suggesting that his work is still developing. It was followed in 1991 by *Crazy About Women* (Dublin). Since 1982 his primary publisher has been The Blackstaff Press, Belfast.

[BO'D

DURRELL, Lawrence (1912–90), was born in India to an English-Irish family. Although sent back to England for a conventional education, Durrell turned naturally to bohemianism. The eccentric life he lived in childhood and manhood is best known through his zoologist brother Gerald's autobiographical books, and via his own celebrations of places and people, including travel books on Corfu and Rhodes, letters and memoirs of Henry Miller, and that *tour-de-force* of diablerie, *The Black Book* (1938). In many ways, Durrell resembles the British poets of the last century who lived expatriate lives but directed their works back to their homeland—Browning, Landor, Eugene Lee-Hamilton—with the necessary rider that Durrell has always seen Americans and English-speaking Continentals as part of his audience. His tangential relationship with England (he never lived there for any length of time) did not prevent his being employed in various official British capacities, both in wartime and after, chiefly in the Eastern Mediterranean. Durrell's novels, travel books, and comic forays into diplomatic life are better known than his verse. Indeed, the author of *The Alexandria Quartet* is probably not known to many of his readers as a poet.

And yet few poets of any generation have started as brilliantly as Lawrence Durrell. His precocious early verse culminated in his first book from a major publisher, *A Private Country*, in 1943. This may claim to share with Wallace *Stevens's *Harmonium* and W. H. *Auden's *Poems* (1930) the title of most accomplished debut of the century. But Durrell was to prove more a Mendelssohn than a Mozart: his poetry did not mature and produce the masterpieces his readers had every reason to expect from such youthful achievement. Even so, his next two books, *Cities, Plains and Peoples* (1946) and *On Seeming to Presume* (1948), make the decade of the Forties a time of rich harvest for Durrell. This was the period when his celebration of Mediterranean life was coupled with a fine satirical vision of his English inheritance, and before the sway of the exotic overwhelmed his lyrical impulse.

The beauty of his early poetry, written in and about Greece and Egypt, has not staled. 'Nemea', 'At Epidaurus', and 'On Ithaca Standing' breathe the sharp-edged reality of timeless Greece, its lives and options as hard as the light of the country. The exotic had not turned into the picturesque at this juncture. Early Durrell celebrates more than the genius of place. His sequence 'The Death of General Uncebunke' is the most (perhaps the only) successful example of surrealism in British poetry, David *Gascoyne notwithstanding. His scabrous and satirical poems are brilliant, as 'The Ballad of the Good Lord Nelson' and 'Pressmarked Urgent' show. Perhaps Durrell's greatest gift is his celebration of the antinomy of past and present, of classical persistence and contemporary emotion. For this reason, 'On First Looking into Loeb's Horace' may be considered his most characteristic poem. He finds a copy of the Loeb crib of Horace's poetry annotated by a former lover's hand, and the poem is both a sympathetic analysis of the Roman poet's life, and a lament for vanished love and the Mediterranean civilization that nurtured it.

A revised edition of the *Collected Poems* was published in London in 1980.   [PNFP

DUTTON, Geoffrey (Piers Henry) (1922–), was raised on a South Australian sheep station founded by pioneer ancestors. He was a wartime pilot and English lecturer before becoming a publisher. While his social privilege, education (Magdalen College, Oxford), and extensive travels oriented him towards the culture of England and Europe, he came to realize the depth of his attachment to Australia, a subject addressed in such poems as 'A Finished Gentleman' and 'An Australian Childhood'. Retaining an antipathy for Australia's philistine timidity, he became a republican and campaigner against censorship. Only the first of seven volumes reflects his association with the self-consciously modernist *Angry Penguins movement. Thereafter his poetry is not only accessible but unashamedly conventional. He handles rhyme with facility; the verse is assured, fluent, and usually good-humoured. His many love poems often show a metaphysical or cavalier influence. In some respects the poetry is that of a patrician gentleman, a view belied by his other writings and literary activities. His settings range from Russia to the South Pacific; a talent for description of nature is particularly evident in *Selective Affinities* (1985). *Findings and Keepings: Selected Poems 1939–1969* (Adelaide, 1970) collects the best of the earlier work.

[AW

DYLAN, Bob (1941–), was born Robert Allen Zimmerman in Duluth, Minnesota. When he was 6 his family moved even further north to Hibbing, near the Canadian border. Although in his early years in New York Dylan invented a host of improbable stories about his upbringing—that he was part of a travelling circus, a New Mexico orphan, that he had Indian blood—he in fact grew up in a reasonably prosperous middle-class Jewish family. He entered the arts college of the University of Minnesota on a state scholarship in 1959, but dropped out after six months. He travelled east to New York in 1961 where he made friends with his earliest hero, folk-singer Woody Guthrie, to whom he dedicated his first original composition, 'A Song to Woody'. Dylan played small folk-clubs and quickly built up a reputation. The first of his thirty-one albums, simply called *Bob Dylan*, was released the following year. Major events in his life and career include his move into electric rock in 1965, his marriage to Sara Lowndes the same year, his motor-cycle accident in 1967, his country-music period of 1970–2, his divorce from Sara—with whom he had five children—in 1977, and his conversion to Christianity in 1978.

Dylan brought to both the folk-song and the rock lyric an intelligence, verbal complexity, and self-consciousness that were wholly new and distinctive. Throughout the multiple shifts of direction that characterize Dylan's career, his powers as a song-writer have never been in doubt. Critics such as Christopher Ricks and Michael Gray have shown how Dylan's use of language is more subtle and expressive than perhaps even his most ardent fans have realized. The highest points in his achievement are probably the 1965/6 albums *Highway 61 Revisited* and *Blonde on Blonde*, full of surreal wit and extraordinary manipulations of language, and the more directly emotional *Blood on the Tracks* (1975).

The Songs of Bob Dylan 1966–1975 were published in New York in 1976. He has also written a novel, *Tarantula* (1971).   [MF

DYMENT, Clifford (1914–71), was born of Welsh parents in Alfreton, Derbyshire. His home town was Carleon upon Usk until, on the death of his conscripted father in 1918, his mother moved to West Bridgford, near Nottingham. Educated at Loughborough Grammar School, he then ran a cycle-shop, tried commercial travelling, and ended writing film-scripts. During the Second World War he wrote and directed military-training films; afterwards, films on civics and agriculture for the Ministry of Information. Later he worked in BBC radio and television.

Dyment's topics are nature, childhood, personal experience. Religion is also a preoccupation—mostly in the sense of questioning man's role and purpose on earth, though many samples seem purely doctrinal and devotional. His theme is the loneliness of the individual in society and in nature. He writes free and formal verse, uses traditional and modern rhyming, claiming an organic rightness of rhythm where metre deviates from expected norms. The two extremes of Dyment's work are best shown in 'The Axe in the Wood', an unrhymed sonnet, not harmfully reminiscent of Edward *Thomas, and 'The Hedgehog', in free verse. His more direct religious verse is well represented by 'Pietà'. In his last phase, he ventured into poems derived from dream experience: these were appended to his *Collected Poems* (London, 1970). An autobiography, *The Railway Game*, appeared in 1971.   [PD

E

EBERHART, Richard (1904–), was born in Austin, Minnesota, the son of a well-off midwestern businessman who worked for a meatpacking company. Eberhart graduated from high school in 1921 and briefly attended the University of Minnesota, before making his way east to Dartmouth College, where he graduated with a BA in 1926. After graduation, Eberhart had a succession of temporary jobs until he signed on to a tramp steamer to sail around the world. He eventually jumped ship and made his way to England, where he enrolled in St John's College, Cambridge, taking another BA in 1929. At Cambridge, he studied with I. A. *Richards and befriended William *Empson. Returning to the States, Eberhart studied in the graduate school at Harvard (1932–3), then took a position as an English instructor at St Mark's School, near Boston, where he taught for seven years; during this time, one of his pupils was Robert *Lowell. During the war, Eberhart served as an aerial-gunnery instructor for the US Navy. This experience led to the writing of his most famous poem, 'The Fury of Aerial Bombardment'. Eberhart married Elizabeth Butcher, the daughter of a wealthy manufacturer, just before the war; after the war he served for several years as an executive of his father-in-law's floor-wax company. Leaving the business world for academe in the early 1950s, Eberhart taught English literature at Princeton, then at Dartmouth, where he remains poet-in-residence. Recognition came slowly to Eberhart, though he had an early champion in F. R. Leavis, who was reminded of Blake when he read Eberhart's compact early lyrics, such as 'For a Lamb' and 'The Groundhog'. Leavis also noted a mystical strain in Eberhart which has continued throughout the years.

Eberhart's collections of poetry have usually been greeted with mixed reviews; critics have most often complained of unevenness in the volumes, which contain too many ill-formed, awkward poems. But he has been widely praised for his best work, which is marked by a peculiar fierceness, a willingness to grapple with issues of human mortality and sin. Eberhart's poems are often set in highly symbolic, northern landscapes. In recent years the coast of Maine has often been the setting for his work, as in *The Long Reach* (New York, 1984). In all, Eberhart has published nearly thirty books since *A Bravery of Earth*, his first volume, appeared in 1930. His *Collected Poems, 1930–1986* (New York, 1986), remains the most comprehensive collection of his work. Among his numerous awards and prizes are the Bollingen Award (1962), the Pulitzer Prize for Poetry (1966), and the National Book Award (1977). In addition to the poetry, Eberhart has also written verse dramas and criticism. For criticism of his work, see Joel Roache, *Richard Eberhart* (New York, 1971) and Bernard F. Engel, *Richard Eberhart* (Boston, 1971). [JP

ECHERUO, Michael (1937–), was born in Okigwi in the Owerri Province of the former East Central State of Nigeria. After studying at Stella Maris College, Port Harcourt, and at the newly established University College of Ibadan, he embarked on a career as a university teacher, firstly at the University of Nigeria at Nsukka, then back at Ibadan, where he holds the chair of English. He took further degrees at Cornell

University, and has some distinction as a critic, especially of English fiction in its relation to Africa, his 1973 study *Joyce Cary and the Novel of Africa* being probably his *chef-d'oeuvre*. But in the early Sixties he slowly established a reputation as a poet in a quiet, if erudite, mould, contributing to one of the early issues of the journal **Black Orpheus*, and publishing the collection *Mortality* with Longman in 1968. He has been compared to his fellow countryman Christopher **Okigbo, but where Okigbo is a poet of cycles, Echeruo is a poet of moods: declining seasons, the crisis and promise of death. Throughout *Mortality* the controlling images are of autumn and harvest, the melancholy and fruitfulness of which are explored in their private, mythic, and political dimensions.   [RF

EDGAR, Stephen (1951–), was born in Sydney. From 1971 to 1974 he lived in London, working as a library assistant. After returning to Australia, he worked in libraries in Sydney and Hobart. He read classics at the University of Tasmania, graduating BA in 1978 and Dip. Lib. in 1985.

To date, Edgar has published two collections of poetry, *Queuing for the Mudd Club* (Hobart, 1985) and *Ancient Music* (Sydney, 1988). A third collection, *Corrupted Treasures*, has recently been completed. Amongst the younger Australian poets, he is distinctive for a firm commitment to closed forms and for showing considerable panache in handling them. Although he draws strength, in this regard, from writers as various as **Frost, Gwen **Harwood, A. D. **Hope, and **Stevens, his voice is in no way muted by theirs. His writing is by turns lyrical and meditative, guided by music as an exemplary discipline, yet drawn towards exuberance and phantasmagoria. Three main themes recur in his work: rereadings of folk-tales (Sleeping Beauty, the Pied Piper, and Bluebeard); the dislocations and fitful illuminations offered by travel; and the pathos arising from family relations. Throughout his work mordant (and sometimes hilarious) observations of contemporary culture cut figures against a background of classical myth.

[KH

EDMOND, Lauris (1924–), was born in Hawkes Bay, New Zealand, and educated at Victoria University. She says she always wrote poems and kept them in the cupboard, but her first published book came out only in 1975. Since then she has been very prolific, and *Summer Near the Arctic Circle* (1988) was her ninth collection.

Edmond is a personal poet; her most memorable successes—such as 'Epitaph' from *Salt from the North* (1980) and 'Hymns Ancient and Modern' from *Seasons and Creatures* (1986)—are about family tragedy or happiness. The poetry's prevailing tone is one of humane observation, expressed in quiet, direct language. Her later volumes are divided into three sections, dealing with travel, ageing, and family. But her best poems (such as 'The Outward and Visible Signs' from *Summer Near the Arctic Circle*) cross over all such categoric boundaries as they become a remarkable kind of wisdom poetry.

All Edmond's volumes have been published in New Zealand by Oxford University Press, and all except *Seasons and Creatures* (Newcastle upon Tyne, 1986) by Oxford in England. *Selected Poems* was published by Oxford in 1984, to be followed by *New and Selected Poems* (Auckland, 1991; Newcastle upon Tyne, 1992).   [BO'D

EDMOND, Murray (1949–), was born in Hamilton, New Zealand. He took a degree at Auckland University in 1971, and since then has worked in theatre, publishing poetry at regular intervals. In the late Sixties and early Seventies he published in, and edited, two issues of the short-lived magazine *The Word is Freed*, whose title displays its generation's messianic hopes. In 1974–6 Edmond lived in England and toured Europe, then returned to New Zealand, where he continued to work in experimental and educational theatre. He was writer-in-residence at Canterbury University, Christchurch, in 1983. Since 1985 he has taught at Auckland University, where he is at present working on a thesis on experimental theatre in New Zealand. Edmond has written several plays and a full-length musical, *A New South Pacific*.

Edmond's own writing is rhapsodic and linguistically dense, with dramatic and narrative qualities which owe much to his life in the theatre. His books of poetry include *Entering the Eye* (Dunedin, 1973); *Patchwork* (Christchurch, 1978); *End Wall* (Auckland, 1981); and *Letters and Paragraphs* (Christchurch, 1987). With his wife, Mary Paul, he edited *The New Poets: An Anthology of Initiatives in Recent New Zealand Poetry* (Auckland, 1987). [IW

EDSON, Russell (1935–), was born in New York City, son of Gus Edson, a cartoonist who drew Andy Gump. An accomplished printmaker himself, Edson showed his talent early, winning at 16 the Kimon Nicolaides Scholarship at the Art Students League in New York, an event which triggered his leaving school in the tenth grade. He studied writing briefly at *Black Mountain College before settling in Connecticut with his wife Frances. His eleven books include a collection of plays and two novels, though he is most celebrated for his prose poems for which he has received several awards.

Edson's poems are brief, strange narratives of an inverse world. Although deeply surreal and never confessional, they have a life-like, offhand clarity, even as they record the odd and the monstrous—a man grown so fat he spills completely out of his shoes; another who tells his father he's about to marry his car. Edson writes fables, some grim, some hopelessly funny, rich with non-sequiturs and transforming, mysterious connections. The work is original, a lyric mix of Dante and Warner Brothers. *The Intuitive Journey and Other Works* (New York, 1976) is representative, including new and earlier work. *The Wounded Breakfast* (Middletown, Conn., 1985) is the most recent collection. [MB

EE, Tiang Hong (1933–90), was born in Malacca, the ancestral home-state of the Babas, or Straits-born Chinese. His birthplace figures prominently in his verse, serving as a metaphor for the early splendour and eventual decline of the Baba epoch. Ee received his education at the Universities of Malaya and Reading. He was a lifelong educationist.

Ee's early poetry was written during his undergraduate days in the 1950s. His first small collection of verse, *I of the Many Faces* (Malacca, 1960), pays heed to the individual's place in Malaya's plural society. In his second volume, *Lines Written in Hawaii* (Honolulu, 1973), Ee's 'Malaysianness' gives way to his musings on life in general and the nature of human relationships.

Ee's Baba ancestry shaped his view of himself as a poet. The Babas, although they had assimilated the Malay tongue and culture over generations, were still identified with the more-recent immigrant Chinese. This lack of acceptance gave rise to the note of protest and the theme of dislocation which characterized Ee's best poetry, found in his third publication, *Myths for a Wilderness* (Singapore, 1976). His disenchantment and growing feelings of helplessness at the gradual erosion of his community's roots finally caused Ee to emigrate to Perth, Australia, with his wife and four children in late 1975.

In *Tranquerah* (Singapore, 1985), Ee's last book of verse, the poet, still speaking in strong Malaysian accents, re-examines his past in order to come to terms with his present status as an 'exile'. *The Second Tongue: An Anthology of Poetry from Malaysia and Singapore* (Singapore, 1976) contains poems from Ee's third volume.

[SPG

Egoist, The. See ALDINGTON, RICHARD, and IMAGISM.

EIGNER, Larry (1927–), critically palsied as a result of forceps delivery at birth, has spent most of his life in bed or in a wheelchair. Until 1978 he lived with his family in Massachusetts, but then moved to Berkeley, California, where he was cared for by the poet Robert Grenier. The example of William Carlos *Williams can be felt in Eigner's attention to detail and precision of observation. His work characteristically derives from sights and sounds in the vicinity of his home—clouds, birds, crickets, cars, rain—but words in the poems are arranged in visual patterns of great elegance and complexity, much as in the work of one of his principal masters, Charles *Olson. Eigner does not merely duplicate Olson's *projectivist manner, however. In Ron Silliman's introduction to his anthology of *Language Poetry, *In the American Tree* (Orono, Me., 1986)—dedicated to Eigner—he identifies this poet as one who has 'transcended the problematic constraints' of Olson's speech-based projectivist poetics. Eigner has himself pointed out that his poetry originates in 'thinking' rather than speech.

Eigner's *Selected Poems* (Berkeley, Calif.) was published in 1972. Among many subsequent collections are *Things Stirring Together or Far Away* (Los Angeles, 1974) and *Waters, Places, a Time* (Santa Barbara, Calif, 1983). His critical writings were edited by Benjamin Friedlander in *Areas Lights Heights* (New York, 1989). An earlier selection is *Quiet Harbor Quiet Act Around* (Kensington, Calif., 1978). Some of his letters were gathered by Robert Kocik and Joseph Simas in *Larry Eigner Letters* (Paris, 1987). See Irving P. Leif, *Larry Eigner: A Bibliography of His Work* (Metuchen, NJ, 1989). [EHF

ELDER, Anne (1918–76), was born at Auckland and moved to Australia at the age of 3. In 1938 she joined the Borovansky Ballet, eventually becoming a soloist. After her marriage in 1945 she settled at Eaglemont, Melbourne. Her first poems were published in newspapers and periodicals from 1956, but near the end of the decade diffidence led her to stop writing, and she did not resume until the late 1960s. Of her three volumes of verse—*For the Record* (Melbourne, 1972), *Crazy Woman* (Sydney, 1976; London, 1978), and *Small Clay Birds* (Melbourne, 1988)—two were published posthumously. The last drew on the first two and on unpublished poems. Its title comes from the poem 'Apologia', where Elder spoke of the pains of translating into words 'my hard brown-shrouded seed of thoughts'. With a whimsy that she usually kept at bay, Elder called those words 'small clay birds'. More often her verse was elliptical, its tone detached but grieving as she addressed an extensive range of subjects—the death of her father and her own illness, small creatures, the ambience of Spain. The dichotomy between the 'pitiful' and the 'terri-

ble' exercised her, as did obscure menaces to the self and unrealizable desires. Elder's small corpus is technically skilled and temperamentally melancholy; no myth has yet been made of her. [PP

ELIOT, T(homas) S(tearns) (1888–1965), was born in St Louis, Missouri, the youngest child of Charlotte Champe Stearns Eliot and Henry Ware Eliot, a southern businessman from a distinguished Bostonian family, then president of the Hydraulic Brick Company. Eliot's grandfather, Walter Greenleaf Eliot, was a prominent Unitarian minister who had moved from Boston to St Louis with a strong sense of educational mission, and his example cast a long shadow over Eliot's childhood and career. Eliot's schooldays were largely spent in and around St Louis, punctuated by long annual holidays on the Massachusetts coast. In 1906 he entered Harvard University and completed his BA in 1909 and MA in 1911, beginning work on a doctoral thesis on the philosophy of F. H. Bradley in 1912 (eventually published as *Knowledge and Experience in the Philosophy of F. H. Bradley,* 1964). Seemingly set on an academic career, in 1912 he was appointed an assistant in philosophy at Harvard. While a student, however, he encountered Symons's *The Symbolist Movement in Literature,* which he later described as a 'revelation', and during these years he began writing his own ironic and Bostonian versions of symbolist poems, such as 'Spleen' and 'Humoresque' after the manner of Jules Laforgue, and then his Jamesian 'Portrait of a Lady', a super-subtle adaptation of the Browning poetic monologue to the climate of the new century.

Eliot's Harvard career was interrupted by a 'romantic year' in Paris (1910–11), in which he attended Bergson's lectures on personality at the Sorbonne, took part in the demonstrations of the *camelots du roi,* a right-wing, anti-Dreyfusard organization, and became friends with Jean Verdenal, to whom he later dedicated his first book of poems. He returned to Europe again in 1914, as a travelling fellow in philosophy at Merton College, Oxford, and though neither Oxford nor academic philosophy was to prove satisfactory, England was henceforward to become Eliot's permanent home. Though he returned to the United States for brief visits in later life, this Bostonian Southerner was to spend the rest of his career in England, and it was with what he called 'the mind of Europe' rather than the literature of his native land that he chose to align himself.

It was in London in 1914 that Eliot met another émigré American poet, Ezra *Pound, the most conspicuous and successful entrepreneur of the literary and artistic experimentalism which flourished in the British capital during the period of the aggressively avant-gardiste journal *Blast (1914) and the poetic anthology Des *Imagistes (1914), and associated with such figures as the writer and painter Wyndham *Lewis, the brilliant reactionary critic T. E. *Hulme, and the iconoclastic sculptor Henri Gaudier-Brzeska. Pound, on reading Eliot's 'The Love-Song of J. Alfred Prufrock', the culminatory poem of his discreet American poetic apprenticeship, proclaimed that Eliot had 'modernized himself on his own' and promoted him to a starring role in the modern movement in literature. He arranged for the publication of 'Prufrock' in *Poetry (1915), and acted as agent and editor for Eliot's work, a role that culminated in his decisive editorial contribution to The Waste Land (1922). Despite subsequent periods of estrangement and disagreement, Eliot was later to act as an advocate and publisher of Pound's work too, publishing his Selected Poems and Cantos with Faber, and lobbying for his release from St Elizabeth's in the late 1950s. The literary careers of the two expatriate Americans came to be profoundly intertwined.

In 1915, after a two-month courtship, Eliot married Vivien Haigh-Wood, an English girl from a conventional upper-middle-class family. The marriage, though it was to prove extremely unhappy, contributed to Eliot's commitment to living in England as well as to his unnerving vision of marital unhappiness in poems and plays. During this difficult time Eliot earned a living, first as a schoolteacher in High Wycombe and Highgate, then, after 1917, in the colonial and foreign department of Lloyd's Bank in London. In his spare time he continued to oscillate between literature and philosophy. Through his friendship with Bertrand Russell he did some reviewing for philosophical journals, while in the evenings he gave lectures on literature, including a course on modern French literature in 1916. After several unsuccessful attempts to be inducted into the US Navy in 1918, Eliot found himself representing Lloyd's Bank in the complex financial negotiations involved in the Treaty of Versailles at the close of the war. At the same time, with the publication by The Egoist of Prufrock and Other Observations (1917), the harvest of his first and primarily American poetic phase, Eliot's literary career finally began to take shape. It was followed by the publication of Poems (1919) and Ara Vos Prec (1920), which included 'Sweeney among the Nightingales' and 'Burbank with a Baedeker: Bleistein with a Cigar', as well as the cunningly contrived historical allegory of 'Gerontion'. They mark a new stage of Eliot's poetic development, predominantly in the form of suavely grotesque exercises in lyric satire of English and European post-war culture, in the severely regular rhymed stanzas prescribed by Pound as a 'remedy' for the 'dilutation of vers libre'. As assistant editor of The Egoist (1917–19), Eliot was beginning to play an increasingly influential role as critic as well as poet. He published his first book of criticism, The Sacred Wood (1920), which through such important early essays as 'Tradition and the Individual Talent', with its notorious claim that poetry is not 'the expression of personality, but an escape from personality', and 'Hamlet', with its idea of an 'objective correlative', proved to be not only a touchstone for Eliot's poetic thinking but a milestone in the establishing of a peculiarly twentieth-century 'historical sense' of literature.

The strains of professional, literary, and personal responsibilities took a severe toll on Eliot and in 1921 he applied for leave from the bank, then suffered a physical and mental breakdown, going first to Margate and then to Lausanne to recuperate. It was in these months that he wrote the bulk of what was to become The Waste Land

(1922). A vocal collage of 'fragments shored' against his and his culture's 'ruin', written in a musically unerring and psychologically unnerving idiom, the poem is the culmination of his early work, and its publication, in the year of the appearance of *Joyce's Ulysses, marks the key moment in the cultural legitimation of Eliot and 'modernism'. With its hallucinatory iconography of post-war London and stammering vision of psychic disintegration, it is one of the inescapable landmarks of twentieth-century poetry. Much of Eliot's later career can be understood as an attempt to escape its consequences.

The Waste Land was published in the first issue of *The Criterion*, a cultural quarterly sponsored by Lady Rothermere, which Eliot founded and edited until 1939. Through his commentaries in *The Criterion*, his decisive editorial role in the publishing firm of Faber and Faber, which he joined in 1925, and his contributions to other literary periodicals, Eliot soon became an established spokesman for the avant-garde, and probably the most influential literary critic of the twentieth century. In 1924 he published *Homage to John Dryden*, studies of Dryden and the metaphysical poets, which outlined the myth of a 'dissociation of sensibility' occurring in the late seventeenth century, and declared that 'poets in our civilization . . . must be *difficult*'—views which shed as much light on Eliot's need to justify his own poetry as on earlier literary history. This was followed by *For Lancelot Andrewes: Essays on Style and Order* (1928), in which he announced himself to be 'classical in literature, royalist in politics, and Anglo-Catholic in religion'. Thereafter Eliot's criticism and poetry sought to establish an authoritative alignment with 'tradition' and 'orthodoxy of sensibility'. His *Selected Essays* (1932) confirmed his status as conservative controversialist and arbiter of his generation's taste, while with *The Use of Poetry and the Use of Criticism* (1933), a survey of poetry criticism from the Renaissance to the modern period, and the subsequently unreprinted *After Strange Gods: A Primer of Modern Heresy* (1934), a diagnosis of what he found disturbing in contemporary cul-

ture, Eliot mapped out his fatefully persuasive sense of the use of poetry and criticism in and for his time.

For Lancelot Andrewes proclaimed Eliot's unrepentantly traditionalist solutions to his problems of cultural identity. He had in fact become a member of the Anglican Church and a British citizen in 1927. In 1932/3 he partially resolved the difficulties of his troubled marriage when he formally separated from his wife Vivien, who later died in a private mental hospital in 1947. In the years following his 'conversion' he published a series of lyrical meditations on religious themes ('Journey of the Magi', 'A Song for Simeon', and 'Marina'), and with his essay on Dante (1929) and *Ash Wednesday* (1930)—a purgatorial Dantesque sequence which impersonally dramatized, in almost liturgical form, the poet's conversion crisis—Eliot's poetry entered a new phase. *The Idea of a Christian Society* (1939) articulated its theology, and 'The Music of Poetry' (1942) its poetics. During the early years of the war Eliot wrote a series of quasi-musical and Christian meditations built around and named after places of symbolic importance to the poet, *East Coker* (1940), *Burnt Norton* and *Dry Salvages* (1941), and *Little Gidding* (1942). They were published together as *Four Quartets* (1943), the culminating work of Eliot's later career, constructed within a rhetoric of traditional mystical paradox and permeated by a profoundly nostalgic and Anglican vision of history, culminating in a vision of seventeenth-century Little Gidding framed by the broken London of the Blitz. For some readers this represents the climax of Eliot's poetic oeuvre; for others, its anti-climactic betrayal.

Eliot's early poetry, as evinced in poems such as 'The Love-Song of J. Alfred Prufrock' and *The Waste Land*, was dramatic, lyrical, ironic, and brilliantly discontinuous. His later poetry is marked by a dissociation of that precariously unified sensibility: the 'metaphysical' intelligence issued in the solemn discursiveness of *Four Quartets*, while the poetic playfulness was siphoned off into the virtuoso light verse of *Old Possum's Book of Practical Cats* (1939), and the dramatic imagination into a series of experiments in verse drama. Much of

Eliot's criticism was devoted to verse theatre, and his later career was largely taken up by attempts to resurrect poetic drama in the wake of *Yeats. These began with the satirical and jazzily demotic fragment *Sweeney Agonistes* (1932), and two church plays—a laboured ecclesiastical pageant, *The Rock* (1934), and *Murder in the Cathedral* (1935), a ritual drama based on the murder of Thomas à Becket which was to prove Eliot's most theatrically effective work. There followed a set of cleverly contrived but rarely convincing attempts to reconcile Christianity and classical drama, modern poetry, and the well-made play—*The Family Reunion* (1939), *The Cocktail Party* (1950), *The Confidential Clerk* (1954), and *The Elder Statesman* (1959). Though these plays earn Eliot a place in the problematic history of modern *verse drama, relatively few readers have found them to succeed either as verse or drama. After *Four Quartets*, Eliot published little of poetic significance. Despite the award of the Nobel Prize for Literature and the Order of Merit in 1948, and his belated personal happiness after his marriage to Valerie Fletcher in 1957, Eliot's postwar role was very much that of an elder statesman and successful man of letters. His later prose, from 'What is a Classic' (1945) and *Notes towards the Definition of Culture* (1948) to *On Poetry and Poets* (1957), a collection of later lectures and essays, reflects his own status as a 'modern classic' and confident definer of 'culture', but has little of the polemical energy or provocative clarity of the pre-war criticism. He died on 4 January 1965, and his remains were buried at East Coker. A finally Europeanized American—and Eliot was nowhere more American than in his Europeanism—he was buried in the English village from where his family had emigrated to America in the seventeenth century.

At the end of his life Eliot noted, with characteristically sly modesty, that he would 'perhaps have a certain historical place in the literary history of our period'. It would be more truthful to say that, for better and worse, the canonical literary history of the first half of the twentieth century has been largely shaped by and around T. S. Eliot—with his contemporaries, Pound and Joyce. As poet first and foremost, but also as

literary and cultural critic, playwright, and publisher, Eliot's influence on modern literature has been profound, controversial, and irreparable. Eliot's poetic output, including the belatedly published *Poems Written in Early Youth* (1950, 1967), remains relatively meagre, but his *Collected Poems 1909–62* embodies one of the most complete and cunningly contrived oeuvres in twentieth-century literature. John *Berryman named 'Prufrock' the first 'modern' poem, and *The Waste Land* quickly became established as the archetypal monument of poetic modernity in English. During his later career Eliot became a thoroughly establishment figure, an embodiment of cultural conservatism and the doyen of academic criticism. Perhaps as a result, much of the most interesting subsequent poetry and criticism in the USA and Britain appeals to other values and directions than those he came to represent, especially in these later years. Eliot's reactionary politics, religious orthodoxy, cultural élitism, and mandarin temperament have done much to render his work suspect to later readers on both sides of the Atlantic. Eliot, the Wordsworth or Tennyson of our era, has become a modern 'classic' and must suffer the fate of the classic—to be demolished and avoided for a while, in order to be resurrected in another guise.

The standard edition of Eliot's poetry comprises *Collected Poems, 1909–1962* (London and New York, 1963) and *Collected Plays* (London, 1962). For his correspondence, see *The Letters of T. S. Eliot*, vol. 1, *1898–1922*, ed. Valerie Eliot (London, 1988). See also *The Waste Land*, with biographical introduction by Valerie Eliot (London, 1971) and Helen Gardner, *The Composition of 'Four Quartets'* (London, 1978). There is still no satisfactory biography, but the most useful biographical introduction is *T. S. Eliot* (London, 1984), by Peter Ackroyd. See also Lyndall Gordon's two volumes, *Eliot's Early Years* (1978) and *Eliot's New Life* (1988—both Oxford).

[HH

ELLIOT, Alistair (1932–), was born in Liverpool. Between the ages of 8 and 13 he lived, with his two sisters, in America. Subsequently he was educated at Edinburgh and Oxford, where he studied classics. From 1965 to 1967 he lived in Iran. He retired from his position at the Newcastle University Library in 1982, and immediately afterwards went back to America for a visit, writing a number of poems about the experience.

Elliot's forms are traditional, his subjects various, though travel and meditations in connection with writers of the past are favourite themes. These themes are brought together in the entertaining long poem *On the Appian Way* (1984), an account of a journey from Rome to Brindisi in the footsteps of Horace, who made the same journey in 37 BC and wrote about it in his Fifth Satire. Elliot's writing is consistently lively and unlaboured, and rhythmically subtle; the perceptions are quick, sociable, and exact. There is throughout his work a strong feeling for the continuities of European culture.

Elliot's most celebrated book is his translation of Verlaine's two clandestine volumes of erotic poetry, *Femmes/Hombres, Women/Men* (London, 1979). Other translations are *The Lazarus Poems*, by Heinrich Heine (Ashington, Northumberland, and Manchester, 1979) and *French Love Poems* (Newcastle upon Tyne, 1991). *My Country: Collected Poems* (Manchester, 1989) includes work from Elliot's first five collections and a number of previously uncollected poems.

[TJGH

ELMSLIE, Kenwood. See NEW YORK SCHOOL.

EMPSON, William (1906–84), was born at Yokefleet Hall near Howden in Yorkshire. In 1920 he won a scholarship to Winchester College, and five years later a Milner Scholarship to Magdalene College, Cambridge, where he took mathematics. He gained a first in Part 1, but his enthusiasm had waned by the time he took Part II, when he was placed only Senior Optime. But he was unusually allowed a fourth year to read English, under the direction of I. A. *Richards; and in 1929 he gained a 'starred' first in Part I of the English Tripos.

His prospects changed forever in 1929, however, when the Master of Magdalene chose to make a scandal out of an inadvertence: contraceptives were discovered in Empson's possession, and he was debarred from taking up a Bye-Fellowship. But he promptly won himself world-wide fame by publishing his first book at the age of 24. *Seven Types of Ambiguity* (1930), 'a grammatico-critical essay' which grew out of a paper written for Richards, changed the course of literary criticism by elucidating in creative detail the effects, the meanings, and implications, achieved in English poetry. From 1931 to 1934 he taught English literature at Tokyo University of Literature and Science, in an ethos of perniciously developing nationalism. Then in July 1937 he went off to teach at the National University in Peking, where the Japanese invasion obliged him to spend two years as a refugee with the Southwest Associated Universities, ending up in the province of Yunnan. From 1940 he was with the BBC, first in the Monitoring Department and then as Chinese Editor in London (where he befriended Orwell and *MacNeice), organizing short-wave broadcasts to China and writing features for the Home Service; the effectiveness of his work stung the Nazi propagandist Hans Fritzsche into dubbing him a 'curly-headed Jew'. In 1941 he married Hetta Crouse, who bore him two sons. From 1947 to 1952 he taught at Peking University, where he was caught up in the civil war; he was trapped during the siege of Peking, and witnessed the Liberation of 1949 and the advent of Communist China. From 1953 until his retirement in 1971 he held the Chair of English Literature at Sheffield University. He was knighted in 1979.

It was the success of *Seven Types of Ambiguity* that prompted Chatto & Windus to issue *Poems* (1935), though Empson had already gained a high reputation with a selection in *Cambridge Poetry 1929* which was singled out for praise by Leavis. Other critics were impressed by the poet's intellectual precision and the dense wit of his work. The early poetry is difficult because Empson's apprehension of the place of science in the modern world charged his work (according to his contemporary Kathleen *Raine) with radical questions about the way in which man tries 'to impose order on fields of knowledge and experience so contradictory as to threaten the mind that contains them with disintegration—the compulsion, as Empson writes, to "learn a style from a despair" ' ('And learn a Style from a Despair', *New Statesman & Nation*, 5 Nov. 1955). So far from being the product of sterile over-intellectualization, the poems strive painfully to cope with the contradictions that arise from what Empson called 'the strangeness of the world, in which we are often tripped up and made helpless'. This poetry tended to be undervalued in the 1930s because it seemed not to be engaged with the political divisions embodied in the work of *Auden and others, but later critics came to see that Empson's small body of verses concerned a subject perhaps less topical but no less profound and urgent, the need for a new imaginative synthesis in a non-traditional society. Certainly the poems of his second volume, *The Gathering Storm* (1940), are infused with a baleful sense of cultural crisis and a mood of courageous renunciation.

'I imitated Donne only, which made me appear pointlessly gawky or half undressed', he declared; arguments were what his poetry was made out of. Indeed, so many of his early poems deal with what he called the 'neurotic (uncaused) fear' of individual isolation, the wish to escape that fear through love, and the wish also to transcend the oppressive facts of the known physical world, that the challenge of new knowledge about the universe puts him in a position of remarkable affinity with Donne. He is a 'metaphysical in the root sense', as Richards insisted; not just in the sense of being witty and erudite but also in the sense of passionately enquiring into and arguing about the nature of existence and experience. Adverse critics stress his putatively impersonal concern with ideas; favourable critics, by contrast, have shown that he commands a large, humane, and stoical view of life.

Eliot, Allen *Tate, *Betjeman, and *Larkin enormously admired his poetry; and several poets of the 1950s, notably those associated with the *Movement, took his work as a model. Robert *Lowell called him the most intelligent poet writing in the English language. But

Empson ended his career as a poet when he brought out *Collected Poems* (New York, 1948; London, 1955).

A posthumous collection of poems is included in *The Royal Beasts and other works* (London, 1986; Iowa City, 1987). Empson's critical works include *Some Versions of Pastoral* (London, 1935—published as *English Pastoral Poetry* in the USA), *The Structure of Complex Words* (London, 1951), *Milton's God* (London, 1961), *Using Biography* (London, 1984), and *Argufying* (London and Iowa City, 1987). See also *William Empson: The Man and His Work*, ed. Roma Gill (London, 1974) and *The God Approached: A Commentary on the Poems of William Empson*, by Philip and Averil Gardner (London, 1978). [JH

ENGLE, Paul (1908–91), was born in Cedar Rapids, Iowa. He attended Coe College there, graduating in 1931. He had studied for the Methodist ministry and preached at Stumptown church at the edge of town, but he heard no call and took an MA from the University of Iowa in 1932 instead. In the same year he published what may have been the first creative thesis ever submitted anywhere for a graduate degree, *Worn Earth* (New Haven, Conn., 1932), in the Yale Series of Contemporary Poets. Subsequently he studied at Columbia and then travelled to Oxford on a Rhodes Scholarship, taking another set of degrees there.

In 1937 he returned to the University of Iowa as a faculty member and eventually became director of the *Iowa Writers' Workshop, the oldest programme of its kind in the world. Under his aegis the Workshop became world-famous as a training ground for young writers. Towards the end of his career Engle founded Iowa's Translation Workshop which draws young poets and novelists from around the globe.

Always a traditionally formal poet, Engle's books include: *American Song* (New York, 1934; London, 1935); *Break the Heart's Anger* (Garden City, NY, and London, 1936); *New Englanders* (Muscatine, 1940); *West of Midnight* (New York, 1941); *American Child* (New York, 1945); *The World of Love* (New York, 1951); *Book and Child*

(Iowa City, 1956); *Poems in Praise* (New York, 1959); *Christmas Poems* (n.p., 1962); *A Woman Unashamed and Other Poems* (New York, 1965); and *Embrace: Selected Love Poems* (New York, 1969). Notwithstanding these and many other publications including plays and two novels, Engle has never been a celebrated poet, perhaps because he has attempted generally to be popular rather than literary, as many of his titles attest. Nevertheless, he has played a major role in post-Modernist poetry, for it was his workshop that provided the model for nearly every creative-writing programme in the United States, and the people who have passed through his hands academically include nearly everyone of consequence in American literature for the past half-century.   [LT

English Review, The. See FORD, FORD MADOX.

ENRIGHT, D(ennis) J(oseph) (1920–), was born in Leamington, Warwickshire, and educated at Leamington College and Downing College, Cambridge, where he studied English under F. R. Leavis. After taking his doctorate at the University of Alexandria (1949), Enright spent many years teaching abroad in Egypt, Japan, West Berlin, Bangkok and Singapore, experiences recorded in his *Memoirs of a Mendicant Professor* (London, 1969). From 1975 to 1980 he was honorary professor of English at the University of Warwick. He was co-editor of *Encounter* from 1970 to 1972, and editorial adviser and director of Chatto & Windus from 1971 to 1982; he won the Queen's Gold Medal for Poetry in 1981.

Enrights's early poems bring a cool, undeceived voice to bear on exotic locations and subject-matter. *The Laughing Hyena and Other Poems* (London, 1953), *Bread Rather Than Blossoms* (London, 1956), and *Some Men Are Brothers* (London, 1960) contain quizzical explorations of oddity yet are warmly humanist in tone, satirizing human pretension, endorsing the unsung kindness of those 'Rooted in precious little, without benefit of philosophy, | Who grew the rice, who deliver the goods, who | Sometimes bear the unbearable' ('Tea Ceremony'). Prolific

but uneven, he published five more books in the next thirteen years, including *Unlawful Assembly* (London and Middletown, Conn., 1968) and *The Terrible Shears* (London, 1973; Middletown, 1974), about his working-class childhood in the Twenties, which is so prosaic as almost to constitute a kind of anti-poetry. Increasingly throwaway and ironic in manner, *Paradise Illustrated* (London, 1978) and *A Faust Book* (Oxford, 1979) are dry, postmodernist annotations of two cultural monuments. Enright's determination to avoid rhetoric and position-taking means that the poetry tends to court bathos and the exact opposite of the singing line. *Collected Poems* (Oxford and New York, 1987) exhibits his variousness, from early achievements like 'How right they were, the Chinese poets' ('Suffering exists, and most of it is not yours') to the gentle humour of 'Agape', which ruminates slyly on the lightning that struck York Minster in 1985. See also *Under the Circumstances* (1991) and *Old Men and Comets* (1993—both Oxford).

He has published four novels, three children's books, and many volumes of criticism and reviews, including *The Apothecary's Shop* (London, 1957), *Conspirators and Poets* (London, 1966), and *A Mania for Sentences* (London, 1983; Boston, 1985). He has also edited *the Oxford Book of Contemporary Verse* (1980) and *the Oxford Book of Death* (1983).   [WS

ENSLIN, Theodore (1925–), may be Thoreau's truest descendant among contemporary American poets. A resident of New England since the 1940s and a resident of Maine since 1960, Enslin writes a poetry attentive to setting and the seasons and the ways in which they transform and define the self. Enslin studied musical composition with Nadia Boulanger when she was living in the United States during the Second World War, and his work is profoundly musical, one of the finest instances in American poetry of what *Pound called *melopoeia*.

In 1975, Enslin characterized the poem as 'a life process'. Thoreau would have understood that definition, but whereas Thoreau wrote chiefly as an observer, Enslin has found ways to transform observation, or the experience of observation, into the experience of poems.

Enslin has been one of the more prolific poets of his generation. For the early work, see *The Median Flow: Poems 1943–1973* (Los Angeles, 1975). Among other works, the five volumes of *Forms* (New Rochelle, NY, 1970–3) and two volumes of *Ranger* (Richmond, Calif. 1978, 1980) deserve particular notice. A collection of essays on Enslin was edited by John Taggart and published in *Truck*, 20 (1978).   [EHF

ESHLEMAN, Clayton (1935–), was born in Indianapolis and educated at Indiana University. He writes an intensely autobiographical poetry shaped in large part by Reichian theory and attention to myth. He was influenced at the outset of his career by Rilke's assertion in *Letters to a Young Poet* that poetry arises from the self. Eshleman's midwestern values and background were stripped away as he went deeper into a poetic exploration of the fundamental self, which he understood as specifically sexual—a view intensified through his encounter with Reichian therapy in the 1960s. He read James Hillman's *The Dream and the Underworld* in the late 1970s, and this, combined with his investigations of Palaeolithic art, led to an increased understanding of archetypes and to the poems collected in *Hades in Manganese* (Santa Barbara, Calif., 1981), *Fracture* (Santa Barbara, 1983), and *Hotel Cro-Magnon* (Santa Rosa, Calif., 1989).

Eshleman's principal achievements are as a poet, but he has also edited two of the most respected journals of postmodern poetry, *Caterpillar* (1967–73) and *Sulfur* (1981–). He is an admired translator of, among others, Pablo Neruda, Aime Cesaire, Antonin Artaud, and César Vallejo. Eshleman has been an enormously productive poet, but *The Name Encanyoned River: Selected Poems, 1960–1985* (Santa Barbara, 1986) provides a good introduction. His selected prose is available in *Antiphonal Swing: Selected Prose, 1962–1987* (Kingston, NY, 1989). For a study of his work and its place in the development of postmodern American poetry, see Paul Christenson's *Minding the Underworld*

(Santa Rosa, 1991). See also Martha J. Sattler, *Clayton Eshleman: A Descriptive Bibliography* (Jefferson, NC, 1988).   [EHF

ESPADA, Martín (1957–), born in Brooklyn of Puerto Rican parents and currently a tenant lawyer in Boston, writes a socially aware poetry which from the outset has marked his identification with the Spanish-speaking migrant in America. Pablo Neruda has been a key influence. *The Immigrant Iceboy's Bolero* (Maplewood, NJ 1982) set the note—typically, 'Mrs. Baez Serves Coffee on The Third Floor', about a deranged arsonist setting fire to a Latino tenement building; 'Waiting For the Cops', a portrait of drugs and street violence which 'waits' for its larger solution; or 'Red Buzzard of Light Circling in the 25th Precinct', an East Harlem story of false arrest and Puerto Rican victimization. In *Trumpets from the Islands of their Eviction* (Tempe, Ariz., 1987), a more personal note enters, as in 'We live by what we see by night' or 'From An Island You Cannot Name', tributes to his father's life as an early immigrant *puertorriqueño*. Even so, he remains essentially a city poet, not least in his wry, vivid account of everyday Puerto Rican life in 'Tony Went to the Bodega but He Didn't Buy Anything'. Espada's third collection, *Rebellion is the Circle of a Lover's Hands* (Willimantic, Conn., 1990) favours an increasing economy of form, notably in 'Clemente's Bullets', his memoir of the struggle for Puerto Rican independence, and, 'Latin Night at the Pawnshop', a terse comment on Puerto Rican poverty amid the affluence of Boston.   [ARL

EVERSON, R(onald) G(ilmour) (1903–92), was born in Oshawa, Ontario, of United Empire Loyalist stock, and educated at the University of Toronto and Osgoode Hall Law School. He chose not to practise law at the beginning of his career, preferring instead to try his hand at professional writing. This led him into thrillers and western fiction, a good deal of which he published pseudonymously in the pulp market. Everson then moved into public relations, becoming a partner in a prominent Montreal firm which specialized in advertising and business communications; he worked there until his retirement.

Everson began to write verse seriously in the 1920s, and in spite of their occasional nature, his poems continued to appear steadily in American and Canadian magazines, eventually leading to the appearance of his first, privately published collection, *Three Dozen Poems* (Montreal, 1957) which was closely followed by *A Lattice for Momos* (Toronto, 1958). These were poems of a mature sensibility reflecting Everson's thoughtful but cryptically matter-of-fact manner, a quality which became the hallmark of his writing. Variously described as possessing an 'innocent vision' and being 'almost greatly gifted', Everson has shown adroitness in reconciling his innate philosophic conservatism with an entirely modern spirit. In 1963 he published *Blind Man's Holiday* (Toronto), and later that year, he helped found in Montreal, with Louis *Dudek, Glen Siebrasse, and Michael Gnarowski, a small literary press called Delta Canada (1963–71), the first publication of which was his collection of poems, *Wrestle with an Angel* (1965). His *Selected Poems 1920/1970* appeared in 1970 (Montreal) and was followed by *Indian Summer* (Ottawa, 1976), *Carnival* (Ottawa, 1978) and *Everson at Eighty* (Ottawa, 1983). The later collections, heavily dependent upon reminiscence, a strong sense of history, and the impressions garnered during extensive travel, became more elaborate in their delivery and more sombre in their mood. Everson's last collection, *Poems About Me*, came out in 1990 (Ottawa). [MG

EVERSON, William (1912–), was born in Sacramento, California, to Francelia and Louis Everson, a Norwegian composer. He dropped out of Fresno State College, where he had ingested Robinson *Jeffers's 'mystical pantheism', to marry a high-school sweetheart. Drafted as a conscientious objector, he spent the war years in Oregon work camps, then gravitated to the San Francisco *Beat circle orbiting Kenneth *Rexroth. A Catholic convert in 1949, he became

a Dominican monk two years later, teaching and writing under the name Brother Antoninus.

His first volume, *The Residual Years: Poems 1934–1948* (1948, revd. edn. 1968), established his bold poetic signature: Jeffers's muscular metaphysical quest entwined with the Beats' hatred of both formalism and American materialism. A potent sensuality also marked that signature, as evident, for instance, in *The Hazards of Holiness: Poems 1957–1960* (1962) and *The Rose of Solitude* (1967). He left the Dominicans late in 1969, an event treated in *Man-Fate: The Swan Song of Brother Antoninus* (1974). Everson has since published two critical texts and several poetry collections, including *The Veritable Years: 1946–1966* (1978) and *The Masks of Drought* (1980—both Santa Barbara, Calif.). [EB

EWART, Gavin (Buchanan) (1916–), had poems published in *New Verse* while still a schoolboy at Wellington and was later an exhibitioner at Christ's College, Cambridge. He served in the Royal Artillery from 1940 to 1946, and later worked for the British Council and in advertising. After the publication of *Poems and Songs* in 1938 his next volume did not appear until the Sixties, when *Pleasures of the Flesh* (1966) disgusted or angered some readers by its explicit and sly sexual references. Among the 'Eight Awful Animals' described in this collection were the Dildo, the Masturbon, and the Panteebra ('The Panteebra rhymes with zebra and is a very slinky cockteaser'). A joke about Virginia Woolf's last period (the name changed later to Emily Brontë) gave much offence.

'Its bad taste jokes are myriad', Ewart said of 'The Dildo', and a deliberate outrageousness has remained a conspicuous element in the several collections he has published since breaking public silence. *The Collected Ewart 1933–1980* appeared in 1980, a completely new collection called *The New Ewart* only two years later, a volume of clerihews, another of very short poems, and *Penultimate Poems* more recently (all published in London). Two selections have appeared in the USA: *The Gavin Ewart Show* (Cleveland, Ohio, 1986), and *Selected Poems 1933–1988* (New York, 1988).

Ewart's fecundity is extraordinary, and so is his technical skill. He is ready, and indeed eager, to experiment with any verse-form, rhyme-scheme, or metre. When a reviewer suggested that he wrote two or three poems a week, Ewart responded that he produced far more than that. He refuses to be selective about his work, believing that time will do the necessary editorial weeding. He has expressed a preference for light over heavy poetry, saying that 'Good light verse is better than bad heavy verse | any day of the week', but his refusal to contemplate any grandeur of style or manner has inevitably limited his achievement. Many of the comic poems are delightful, the high spirits with which they are written persuasive, and it is easy to accept that 'by writing the one-line sagas | and fooling about with the norm | the Poet Ewart may have answered | the vexing Question of Form'.

But there remains the question of content, and here Ewart's self-imposed restrictions are regrettable. His best poems are those in which the tone remains light but the material is seriously treated, like the sonnets about his parents and his children, or 'Lovers in Pairs', which tells of old lovers keeping each other warm in 'the penultimate bed | before the one with the gravestone'. But it would be wrong to be stuffy about a poet who on his chosen level offers such a varied and emotionally generous comic view of twentieth-century English manners, beliefs, and behaviour.   [JGS

EZEKIEL, Nissim (1924–), was born into a Jewish (Bene-Israel) family in Bombay. He studied philosophy at Birkbeck College, London and has had a distinguished academic career teaching English literature at Bombay University. As an undergraduate he was a member of the Radical Democratic Party and an intense concern for social justice is seldom far from the surface of his writing. He has also worked as an advertising copy-writer and was the first editor of the celebrated intellectual bi-monthly, *Quest* (now *New Quest*). He has served as a member of the council of Indian PEN and of the Lalit Kala Akademi and the Sahitya Akademi, India's national academies of art and literature. He was for a time the editor of *Poetry India*, which was generally regarded as the most important Indian poetry journal. He has published widely on Indian art and literature. In 1983 he was presented with the much-coveted Sahitya Akademi Award and in 1988 with the Padma Shri for his contribution to Indian literature in English.

Despite his achievements in so many different fields, it is almost certainly for his poetry that Ezekiel will be remembered. Many critics regard him as the first major Indian poet to write in English. Since the publication of his first collection, *A Time to Change* (London, 1952) there have been seven further volumes. These have now been gathered into one volume, *Collected Poems* (Delhi, 1989), which includes a preface by the poet Gieve *Patel, who provides a perceptive introduction to Ezekiel's work.

Ezekiel's poems exhibit a varied range of tone and concerns. His personal use of religious metaphor in *Hymns in Darkness* (Delhi, 1976) and *Latter-day Psalms* (Delhi, 1982) suggests a return to earlier questionings of the problematics of identity, but now being reworked within the imagery of a distinct Indo-Judaic tradition. Other motifs are supplied by the teeming cosmopolitan life of Bombay and the ambiguities of personal and sexual relationships. The fastidious craftsmanship, urbanity of tone, and habitual understatement make many of the poems appear simple, but often the full implications of the myth and metaphor woven into the narration are reserved for the final verse or line.

Another aspect of Ezekiel is revealed in the broad humour of his 'Very Indian Poems in Indian English' and 'Goodby Party for Miss Pushpa T.S.'. In these he exploits the comic incongruities that arise from an imperfectly acquired veneer of western culture at work upon a type of Indian sensibility.

The most extended studies of Ezekiel as a poet are Chetan Karnani, *Nissim Ezekiel* (New Delhi, 1974), and a special issue of *Journal of South Asian Literature*, 11: 3–4, guest-edited by Inder Nath Kher.   [RW

F

Faber Book of Modern Verse, The (London, 1936), edited by Michael *Roberts, is a guide to the poetry enjoyed by intellectuals at the time of publication. The editor's introduction proved to be a piece of criticism as prescriptive as the *Poetics* of Aristotle. Henceforward, poetry would use intricate ideas, condense and compress metaphors, and deploy words in modes which were deliberately fantastic. Exemplars that were put forward included T. S. *Eliot, W. H. *Auden, William *Empson, Edith *Sitwell, and Laura *Riding. All were strongly represented in the first edition of the anthology.

As important as what Michael Roberts put in was what he left out. He said in the introduction that he recognized the merit of Walter *de la Mare, Edmund *Blunden, and Edwin *Muir. But he had decided to exclude these poets because they made no notable development in poetic technique. He did not even mention *Hardy, Edward *Thomas, and Robert *Frost, substantial figures conspicuous by their absence.

Roberts had a wonderful confidence in his judgement. But the *Faber Book* is not an exemplification of absolute excellence, whatever that may be. Rather, it represents the taste of one man in his own era. It is to be hoped that the first edition, untrammelled by the revisions of later editors, will continue to be reprinted in its pristine state. The *Faber Book* mirrors the indifference of its period to much that helped in shaping the poetry of a later age. But it also encapsulates, as no other literary document quite does, the innovative quality of the 1930s.   [PDH

FAHEY, Diane (1945–), was born in Melbourne, where she was educated. After spending some years abroad she has returned to live in South Australia. Her first collection, *Voices from the Honeycomb* (Brisbane, 1986), established her as a new poet of considerable strength and flexibility, writing through a range of subjects drawn from art, cinema, personal observation, and with an eye for the quirky newspaper report. Her second collection, *Metamorphoses* (Sydney, 1988) draws on Greek myths to 'tell the story of contemporary woman journeying from patriarchy to reclaim her own space and authenticity'. The book includes an extended section of 'Notes and Illustrations'. Diane Fahey expanded on her preoccupations as developed in this book in a prose essay published in *Poetry and Gender: Statements and Essays in Australian Women's Poetry and Poetics*, ed. Brooks and Walker (1989). Her latest collection is *Mayflies in Amber* (Sydney, 1993).

Although the reinterpretation of classical myths has been at the heart of much twentieth-century invention and pastiche, Fahey's work in Australia has gained from recent feminist theory and from the poet's own belief in poetry as 'an integrating process'.   [TWS

FAINLIGHT, Harry (1935–82), was born in New York of Jewish parents, his father being English and his mother American. He grew up in England but was evacuated to the United States during the Second World War. After reading English at Cambridge, he moved to New York to join the *Beat poets.

He returned with a celebrated long poem, 'The Spider', an account of an LSD trip. He performed it at the Albert Hall reading in London in 1965 which was filmed as *Wholly Communion*. In a state of drug-induced paranoia, he later suppressed the poem.

The one pamphlet he allowed to be published in his lifetime, *Sussicran* (London, 1965), reflects another suppression that must also have left its mark: the English law's suppression of male homosexuality. Poems like 'Meeting', a bleak variation on *Owen's 'Strange Meeting', evoke the homosexual underworld as it was before the law changed in 1963.

His reworking of Owen, as of Shelley, shows the poetic ambition that underlay his suppressions and his recurrent breakdowns. He ended in a remote cottage in Wales where he was found dead of pneumonia. He had lived out the role of the poet as Saul Bellow imagines it in *Humboldt's Gift*: incompetent in the world's terms, but keeping imagination's gate.

His *Selected Poems* (London, 1986) were edited by his sister, Ruth *Fainlight.   [RGa

FAINLIGHT, Ruth (1931–), was born in New York, educated at schools in the USA and England, and at art colleges in Birmingham and Brighton; in 1985 she was poet-in-residence at Vanderbilt University, Tennessee. She married the novelist Alan Sillitoe in 1959.

Ruth Fainlight's poetry combines fidelity to the complicated realities of life with an intense, almost mystical apprehension of the woman poet's role as seer: 'Sibyls' is an extended sequence about just such women. Yet, perhaps because she has also published short stories, her most assured pieces seem often to be vignettes of people observed, with thoughtful candour, in their characteristic contexts. Undeterred by apparently intractable subject-matter, she has even recycled a poem from 'The New Science of Strong Materials'.

Her first full-length collection, *Cages* (London and Chester Springs, Pa.), appeared in 1967. Since then she has published six further books of poetry—the most recent is *The Knot* (London, 1990)—several pamphlets, and a *Selected Poems* (London, 1987); *Daylife and Nightlife* (London, 1971) is a volume of her short stories, and she has edited the *Selected Poems* of her brother, Harry *Fainlight (London, 1986).   [NP

FAIRBURN, Arthur Rex Dugard (A.R.D. or Rex) (1904–57), was among the most vigorous and forceful personalities to emerge in New Zealand poetry in the years between 1930 and 1950. He was always associated with Auckland, where he lived all his life except for two years in England, and where he worked at a variety of jobs from journalism to university tutoring. An essayist and polemicist as well as a poet, he contributed prolifically to local journals on matters relating to art, politics, and society.

The youthful effusion of his first volume, *He Shall Not Rise* (London, 1930), gave way to a more mature poetry in the years of the Depression. Those years produced the long poem 'Dominion', published first in 1938, and many of his best shorter poems. Though much of his satire and comic work retains its force, his most enduring verse is lyrical, expressing a Romantic belief in human experience being at its most vital when it is in harmony with nature. Fairburn's concerns seem to owe much to Blake and *Lawrence, but also much to his eclectic enthusiasm for the art, literature, and popular philosophical writings of his own time.

His best poems are found in *Poems 1929–1941* (1943) and *Strange Rendezvous* (1952—both Christchurch). *Three Poems* (Wellington, 1983) contains his longer works, 'Dominion' and the post-war poems 'The Voyage' and 'To a Friend in the Wilderness'. See also *Collected Poems* (Christchurch, 1966); *The Woman Problem and other prose*, selected essays, (Auckland, 1967); *The Letters of A. R. D. Fairburn*, ed. Lauris Edmond (Auckland, 1981); and Denys Trussell, *Fairburn* (Auckland, 1984).   [WSB

FALCK, Colin (1934–), was born in London. He was educated at Magdalen College, Oxford, where he took degrees in philosophy, psychology, and economics. He has made his living as a lecturer in sociology and humanities. He was one of the group associated with *The *Review* and *The New Review*. The unusually coherent poetics he worked out is reminiscent of *Graves as well as of the approach of *The Review*, but it is independent and lacks Graves's mythographical paraphernalia: it appeals to 'genuineness' and to *frisson* in *Housman's sense, but carefully refines this to avoid mystical elaborations. His honesty has demanded that his output be restricted to a relatively few brief poems, since he refuses to 'versify attitudes'. His adaptations from Antonio Machado, in *The Garden in the Evening* (Oxford, 1964), remain the best of the many that have been attempted; they well reflect the Spanish poet's exquisiteness of phrase and mood, the changes of which are discriminatingly recorded in *Backwards into the Smoke* (Manchester, 1973) and *In This Dark Light* (London, 1978). There are fastidious poems and, latterly, cautious excursions into more sociological areas of concern. He has been called 'minimalist', but such poems as 'Lyme Regis Station' are admired for their emotional resonance, perfection of phrase, and technique, and for the fruitful manner in which they extend the original precepts of the *Imagism to which he was initially indebted. His latest publication is *Memorabilia* (London, 1992). [MS-S

FALLON, Padraic (1905–74), was born in Athenry, Co. Galway, Eire. He was educated at St Joseph's School, Roscrea. At 18 he moved to Dublin and became a customs official, working until 1939 in Dublin and subsequently in Wexford. In Dublin, *AE encouraged him and helped him get his first poems published. His work appeared regularly in the *Dublin Magazine* until it folded in 1958. He died during a visit to England at Aylesford, Kent. His body was taken back for burial in Kinsale, Co. Cork, where he had settled after retirement. In the same year the first extensive collection of his work, *Poems*, was published.

With Austin *Clarke's and *Kavanagh's, Fallon's work marks the emergence of a specifically Irish, as opposed to Anglo-Irish, sensibility in poetry written in English, an emergence that involved standing against the tremendous example of *Yeats, though Fallon was in some ways less successful in this than the former two poets. He was helped in his struggle to achieve stylistic independence by the example of *Pound, though he never became a modernist

in the Poundian mould. There is often a stylistic faltering even in Fallon's best work, but throughout his oeuvre can be found fine, coherent poems that display a subtle ear for cadences and a freshness of thought and perception.

The fullest edition of the poems, including a number of poems from the plays he wrote for Radio Eireann as well as translations, is *Collected Poems* (Manchester and Oldcastle, Co. Meath, 1990), which has an introduction by Seamus *Heaney and an afterword by the poet's son, Brian Fallon. [TJGH

FANTHORPE, U(rsula) A(skham) (1929–), was born in London and studied at St Anne's College, Oxford (1949–53) and the University of London Institute of Education (1953–4). She became an assistant English teacher, and later head of English, at Cheltenham Ladies' College, Gloucestershire, and from 1972 to 1983 did hospital clerical work in Bristol. In 1983–5 she was Arts Council Writing Fellow at St Martin's College, Lancaster, and in 1987–8 she was Northern Arts Literary Fellow at the universities of Newcastle and Durham.

U. A. Fanthorpe is a notable exponent of a tendency in English poetry which Harry Chambers's Peterloo Press has done much to encourage—wry, observant, humane, inclined to the proverbial, faithful to place and experience, sharing some of *Larkin's attitudes, if not his habitual formality. Fanthorpe's poems often begin in the everyday, working to disclose the common experience—frequently the expectation of death. Her hospital work has enabled her to observe the stripping of identity and the importance of ritual in the face of mortality ('Lament for the Patients').

Attachment to 'ordinary' people is matched by love of 'this narrow island charged with echoes | and whispers' ('Earthed'), her account of which is anecdotal rather than political. Place also provides access to myth: her account of London's lost rivers, 'Rising Damp', ends by naming the rivers of Hell. The more directly mythological poems seem less successful, working towards a point rather than a discovery, but her best work (for example, 'Seminar: Felicity and Mr Frost') succeeds by noticing, overhearing, and divining.

Fanthorpe's collections (all published from Liskeard, Cornwall) are: *Side Effects* (1978); *Standing To* (1982); *Voices Off* (1984); *A Watching Brief* (1987); and *Neck-Verse* (1992). *Selected Poems* (Harmondsworth) appeared in 1986.   [SO'B

FAULKNER, William (1897–1962), was born and raised in Oxford, Mississippi, attending local schools. Although he joined the British Royal Air Force in Canada, the war ended before he saw action. He married Estelle Oldham in 1929, and they had one surviving daughter. His first love was poetry, and he completed *Vision of Spring* in 1921 but could not find a publisher. *The Marble Faun* (pastoral lyrics) appeared in 1924, two years before his first novel, *Soldiers' Pay*.

Both *Vision of Spring* and *The Marble Faun* are clearly derivative of Keats, Verlaine, and other Romantic and Symbolist figures, the strongest American influences being Conrad *Aiken and T. S. *Eliot. But Faulkner's poetic gift was limited, and in *Sartoris* (1929) and *The Sound and the Fury* (1929), he began translating modern techniques learned from poets (and James *Joyce) into his brilliant cycle of Yoknapatawpha novels. *Salmagundi* (1932), *This Earth* (1932), and *A Green Bough* (1933) represent his last attempts at poetry.

Faulkner's verse can be found in *Early Prose and Poetry*, ed. Carvel Collins (Boston, 1962; London, 1963) and the reissue of *The Marble Faun* and the 1933 volume *A Green Bough* (New York, 1965). Judith Sensibar's *The Origins of Faulkner's Art* (Austin, Tex., 1984) traces the poetic roots of his fiction. See also *Selected Letters of William Faulkner*, ed. Joseph Blotner (New York and London, 1977) and *William Faulkner: American Writer* (New York and London, 1989), by Frederick R. Karl.   [EB

FEARING, Kenneth (Flexner) (1902–61), was born in Oak Park, Illinois, the son of a Chicago attorney. After leaving the University of Wisconsin he did a variety of jobs, including millhand, salesman, and sports reporter, and later worked as a journalist on *Time*, the magazine

serving as background for his crime story *The Big Clock*, the best of his several novels. His first collection of poems *Angel Arms* (1929) was followed by four others, and *New and Selected Poems* (Bloomington, Ind.) appeared in 1956. He was twice married, and had one son.

'For practical purposes I should say I was in the Whitman tradition', Fearing said, but this obvious derivation took a personal colouring from a simplistic but strongly held radicalism, and use of current slang, advertising slogans and copy, phrases on posters, and neon signs. There are a few poems justifying the comment that Fearing converted the bromides of tabloid journalism into art, but sentimentality is never far away. Radical Fearing can sometimes carry a reader along on his Whitmanesque wave, lyrical Fearing is to be avoided. Yet although the form of the verse was derivative, from Carl *Sandburg as well as Whitman, the result was sometimes original. Nobody else wrote like Fearing in the Thirties and Forties. In manner he was a forerunner of the *Beats, although he would have found their nihilism deeply uncongenial.   [JGS

FEINSTEIN, Elaine (1930–), was born in Bootle, Lancashire. She took her degree at Newnham College, Cambridge, and began to read for the bar. She began writing under the influence of various American poets, notably William Carlos *Williams, Wallace *Stevens, and Emily Dickinson. But it was through translating the poems of Marina Tsvetaeva (*Selected Poems*, London, 1971, 4th edn. Oxford and New York, 1993) that she discovered the way to a more open, fluid syntax, immediately responsive to shifts of narrative and mood. Tsvetaeva's influence is visible in her first novel, *The Circle* (1970), and throughout her subsequent fiction. The directness and freshness of tone in her poems link them to the same source. She can create strong emotional atmosphere, though sometimes her bold strokes lead to a rather generalized approach to form and content.

Feinstein has written nine novels to date, and five verse collections, all published in London: *In a Green Eye* (1966); *The Magic Apple Tree* (1971);

The Celebrants, and Other Poems (1973); *Some Unease and Angels* (1977); and *Badlands* (1987). She has also written plays, screenplays, and biographies, including *A Captive Lion: The Life of Marina Tsvetayeva* (London and New York, 1987). [CAR

FEINSTEIN, Frederick. See NEW NARRATIVE, THE.

FELDMAN, Irving (1928–), was born in Coney Island, New York, and educated at City College and Columbia University. He has lived in Puerto Rico, France, and Spain, and the echo of European literary styles, especially *Surrealism, is evident in his work. Yet the profoundest influence on his poetry is not a fashion but an event, the Jewish Holocaust. A teenager in New York during the early 1940s, Feldman suffered the destruction of European Jewry at a distance that was none the less close to home, as the title-poem of his book *The Pripet Marshes* (New York, 1964) makes clear. And in the middle of the poem which follows it, 'To the Six Million', he writes: 'There is someone missing. | Is it I who am missing?'

His *New and Selected Poems* (New York, 1979) shows a mastery of tone and style and a broadening circle of concerns, always, however, fretted by a pessimistic wisdom. Lyrics, aphorisms, tales, psalms, prose poems, jokes, and disquisitions range over the whole sad, funny backlot of modern life, from 'The Handball Players at Brighton Beach', to poetry readings in the Hamptons, to Bette Davis, 'fantastic and compelled', slamming the door behind her. Feldman never ceases to wonder over the way we freely invent our lives and yet are driven by powers looming behind or within us. [EG

Feminist Criticism. It is a curious historical fact that it has been harder for female poets to write and to get published than for their more 'substantial sister novelists' (Jan Montefiore, *Feminism and Poetry*, London, 1988). Jeni Couzyn's introduction to the *Bloodaxe Book of Contemporary Women Poets* (Newcastle upon Tyne, 1985)

describes how tradition has relegated female poets to three securely marginalized sterotypes: Miss Dedication (Elizabeth Barrett Browning), Miss Eccentric Spinster (Emily Dickinson, Stevie *Smith), and the Mad Woman (Sylvia *Plath). All brands of female poet are apparently busy running between bedrooms and prayer-meetings, and—as Theodore *Roethke has it—spend a great deal of time 'caterwauling'. Twentieth-century anthologies of poetry are punctuated by male regrets. Thus Geoffrey Summerfield in his anthology *Worlds* (Harmondsworth, 1974): 'I regret the omission of women poets from this book . . . Britain in the last fifteen years has not produced a woman poet of real stature.' Recent anthology statistics (eleven pages of poems by women out of a total of 462 pages in John Hayward's 1960 *Faber Book of English Verse*; twenty-nine poems by women out of a total of 884 in Helen Gardner's 1972 *New Oxford Book of English Verse*; and, perhaps worse, three female poets out of a total of forty poets in D. J. Enright's 1980 *Oxford Book of Contemporary Verse, 1945–1980*) tell their own story.

The poets' sister novelists have encouraged polemical readings of their work. There is no equivalent approach to women's poetry. What criticism there is is divided between the academic, which is concerned with a feminist aesthetics of poetry—for example, *Shakespeare's Sisters: Feminist Essays on Women Poets*, ed. Sandra Gilbert and Susan Gubar (New Haven, Conn., 1979); *Feminism and Poetry*, by Jan Montefiore (London, 1987); and the non-institutional, which attempts to promote radical political uses for women's poetry—for example, journals like *Conditions, Sinister Wisdom*. Both camps, however, share certain key concerns. First, accessibility: a vexed issue, for availability to a wide audience militates against the cultivation of prestigious experimental modes, rejected as élitist or difficult, or as undesirable and 'male'. Secondly, value: again, a vexed issue, for political and aesthetic values may be at odds. Jan Clausen believes that her poetry should be underpinned and justified by her lesbianism. Anthologists offer collections which feminist critics may regard as inferior poetry, but as valuable social documentary—see, for example, Montefiore's analysis of *Scars Upon My Heart*, a collection of women's poetry of the First World War (London, 1981). Clausen herself acknowledges that this kind of poetry may be limited to 'a knee-jerk anti-patriarchal stance' which itself simply imposes new taboos. Finally, the development of a specifically female language. This new language is normally defined in relation to notions of subjectivity, as worked out by the French feminist theorists Helène Cixous, Luce Irigaray, and Monique Wittig. But many poets and critics, such as Anne *Stevenson, have argued in favour of a tradition which transcends gender. Research into *écriture féminine* is haunted by the spectre of essentialism: the notion that there is a unique and unified female experience.

For all that, female poets are now waving from the sea in which many of their earlier and less fortunate sisters drowned. They are buoyed up by ideological diversity, and by the sense of different audiences (women of colour, lesbians, working-class women, the old, the young . . .). Yet, as Elizabeth *Jennings points out, there is still a long way to go: 'My mind is raided by a dazzling light, | Sun is where I belong | But I'm an expert on night.' [SK

FENTON, James (1949–), was born in Lincoln and educated at Repton and Magdalen College, Oxford, where he followed a degree course in psychology and philosophy and won the Newdigate Prize with 'Our Western Furniture', a sonnet-sequence about European influences on Japan. *Terminal Moraine* (London, 1972), a first volume of high promise, displayed a variety of forms and unconventional subject-matter, ranging from topical satire (his 'Open Letter to Richard Crossman') to startling assemblages of recondite and alarming detail from anthropology ('The Pitt-Rivers Museum, Oxford'), biology ('A Frog'), or horticulture ('The Fruit-Grower in Wartime').

The title-poem of this first book touches on an important element in Fenton's writing: a restless yearning for changing scenes and experiences. This is treated entertainingly in 'The Skip', in his second volume, *The Memory of War*

(Edinburgh, 1982; reprinting several poems from *Terminal Moraine* and including everything in his 1978 pamphlet, *A Vacant Possession*). Here, as before, he can be abundantly mysterious and sinister, with the same strong hint of intellectual games-playing (in 'Nest of Vampires' or 'A Staffordshire Murderer'). But between books he had worked in Germany and south-east Asia, and he now writes from personal experience with a new authority and emotional strength. 'A German Requiem' is a laconic and formal exploration of collective memory and collective forgetfulness in post-1945 Germany. 'In a Notebook', like the later 'Children in Exile', draws movingly on his Cambodian journeys and their aftermath.

Manila Envelope (1989), published from the Philippines where he was a correspondent, comprised a book of thirteen substantial poems, a poster of one of them, and a broadsheet poetic manifesto, advocating different, even reckless directions in poetry and attacking prescriptive critics. His abandoned, surreal word-play threw off constraints of prosody and even meaning (in 'Here Come the Drum Majorettes' and 'The Ballad of the Shrieking Man'), though both the topical, and the personal and reflective poet are still present, in 'Jerusalem' and 'The Mistake'.

Fenton has also published collections of his theatre criticism and reportage, travel writing (with Redmond O'Hanlon), and a collaboration with John *Fuller in a collection of satirical poems, *Partingtime Hall* (London, 1987). [AB

FERLINGHETTI, Lawrence (Mendes-Monstanto) (1919–), was born in Yonkers, New York. The publisher of Allen *Ginsberg's *Howl* (City Lights Books), Ferlinghetti is indelibly identified with the San Francisco *Beat movement. He was a co-founder of the movement, and remains its chief apostle. Like Ginsberg, he has a shrewd business sense, and his poetry has immense popular appeal: *A Coney Island of the Mind* (New York, 1958) was one of the big poetry best-sellers of the century. The poems in *A Coney Island of the Mind* owe considerable debts to Carl *Sandburg and Vachel *Lindsay, as well as the less likely E. E. *Cummings, but were original in their time for use of explicit language and direct, no-holds-barred attacks on the 'Terrible People' (i.e. politicians and bankers). Ferlinghetti does write with the 'immediacy, power and passion' that have been claimed for him; but as society has changed so his message has come to look less startling. Abrasiveness and bad language have begun to look ordinary, too. Thus, *To Fuck is to Love Again*, published by Fuck You Press in New York (1985), has quite lost its revolutionary impact. But Ferlinghetti's persistence impresses, and his earlier poems were often, above all, funny. Such a volume as *Endless Life: Selected Poems* (New York, 1981) still has appeal when it is taken as a whole, for its freshness. But Ferlinghetti aims for mass appeal and thus loses the psychological and rhythmical subtleties of his best models. Collections include *An Eye on the Birds: Selected Poems* (London, 1967), and *Wild Dreams of a New Beginning* (New York, 1988). See also B. Sileski, *Ferlinghetti: The Artist in his Time* (New York, 1990).   [MS-S

FERNANDO, Patrick (1931–83), combined a career in Sri Lanka's Department of Inland Revenue with the writing of a meticulous, mannered poetry shaped by his classical education and Roman Catholic upbringing. Often ironic in its perceptions, as in 'The Late Sir Henry' and 'Obsequies of the Late Antonio Pompirelli, Bishop', it evinces a concern for discipline and precision in matters of technique.

Although his inspiration was rooted in Western classical literature, Fernando strove during the 1950s to find common ground with Sri Lanka's Sinhala-speaking majority culture. He worked on doggedly during a period of chauvinistic cultural resurgence that was openly hostile to Western arts and letters, describing his situation in those years as one of 'unhelpful isolation'.

During his lifetime Fernando published one collection, *The Return of Ulysses: Poems* (London, 1955). *Selected Poems* was published posthumously by OUP (India) in 1984. See also: Y. Gooneratne (ed.), *Poems From India, Sri Lanka, Malaysia and Singapore* (Hong Kong, 1979); Y. Gooneratne (ed.), 'The Poetry of Sri Lanka', *Journal of South Asian Literature* special

issue, 12:1/2 (Fall–Winter 1976), Asian Studies Center, Michigan State University.   [YG

FERRY, David (1924–), was born in Orange, New Jersey. He is professor emeritus of English at Wellesley College in Massachusetts, where he began teaching in 1952. His wife Anne, whom he married in 1958, is a well-known critic of English poetry of the sixteenth and seventeenth centuries.

Ferry's two collections are brief (together they comprise only seventy-three pages), and unified in tone, style, and theme. *On the Way to the Island* (Middletown, Conn., 1960) employs a style of conscious artifice, with occasional echoes of *Yeats, *Stevens, and *Ransom. In *Strangers* (Chicago and London, 1983), the writing is quieter and the imagery more wide-ranging. The best poems—'out at Lanesville', 'After Spotsylvania Court House', and others— impress with the richness of their human concerns, but impress also, as the title suggests, with the knowledge that our deepest longings for connection and fulfilment cannot, in the nature of things, be satisfied. He has also published a verse translation of *Gilgamesh* (New York and Newcastle upon Tyne, 1992). In addition to his poetry, he is the author of *The Limits of Mortality: An Essay on Wordsworth's Major Poems* (Middletown, 1959).   [MP

FICKE, Arthur Davison (1883–1945), was born in Iowa, his father an eminent lawyer with whom he travelled around the world. He attended Harvard where he was a classmate of Wallace *Stevens and Witter *Bynner, and after graduation worked for eight years in his father's office, turning out eight volumes of verse and two treatises on Japanese art. In 1907 he married Evelyn Blunt, and they had one son, but he divorced her to marry the painter Gladys Brown in 1923. Ficke was a lyric traditionalist and had collaborated with Bynner on the *Spectra* hoax in 1914, producing a volume of supposed 'poetic experiments' (much praised by several eminent poets), to vent his anti-modernist disdain, though guilty himself of writing free verse on occasion. His most ambitious work was *Sonnets* *of a Portrait Painter* (1914, revd. edn., 1922), and *Selected Poems* appeared in 1926, but none of his poetry is particularly memorable or easy to find. *The Home Book of Modern Verse*, ed. Burton Egbert Stevenson (New York, 1963), offers five examples. [EB

FIELD, Edward (1924–), was born in Brooklyn, New York. He attended New York University and served in the US Army Air Force during the Second World War. He won the Lamont Poetry Award for his first book, *Stand Up Friend, With Me* (New York, 1963).

Writing a conversational, unadorned poetry, Field takes on a variety of unlikely subjects, including aliens from outer space, faith-healers, spiritual gurus, and televised football games, creating entertaining exposés of contemporary life in America. He also explores more traditional subjects, such as his own Jewish heritage and troubled love affairs. His sensitive examination of his family and their effects on one another and him is given its fullest treatment in 'Visiting Home', a long poem in his volume *A Full Heart* (New York, 1977).

Field combines a self-deprecating, painful, even at times maudlin voice with the keen ability to look at extremely personal material with an objective eye. He is, furthermore, a poet unbound by intellectual systems, either philosophical or psychological, and in fact examines such thought patterns with a deft scepticism in a number of poems.

The best source of his poems is the recent *New and Selected Poems* (New York, 1987). Other volumes include *Stars In My Eyes* (New York, 1978) and *Variety Photoplays* (New York, 1967; 2nd edn., 1979). [RS

FIGUEROA, John Joseph Maria (1920–), was born in Kingston, Jamaica. He was educated at St George's College, Jamaica, a Jesuit institution. He went on to study at Holy Cross College, Worcester, Massachussets, and do postgraduate work at the University of London. He has had many academic appointments, the last one at the Open University (UK). He has also contributed to the BBC's 'Caribbean

Voices' programme, and to early recordings of 'West Indian Poets Reading Their Own Work' (Caedmon TC 1379).

At their best, Figueroa's poems tend to be sensuous, yet formally stringent, and expansive in their breadth of reference. He can be precise about 'Chartres Window', for instance, or subtly ironic in 'Christmas Breeze', which counterpoints religious observances in England and Jamaica. As Spanish is his second language he has also written adaptations of Lorca and St John of the Cross. Sensitivity to cultural crosscurrents leavens his most effective imagery. In this respect, Derek *Walcott's poems may owe something to Figueroa's practice.

His last collection, which also includes poems from earlier ones, was *Ignoring Hurts* (Washington DC, 1976). Some of his work is also available in *News for Babylon*, ed. James Berry (London, 1984). [MR

FINCH, Peter. See SOUND POETRY.

FINKEL, Donald (1929–), husband of the poet and novelist Constance *Urdang, is a native of New York City. He left New York early in his career, however, and accepted a series of university teaching positions, culminating with his appointment to the faculty of Washington University in 1960, where he has been the poet in residence since 1965. He has also recently taught at Bennington College and Princeton University.

In spite of his Eastern background, Finkel seems pre-eminently a Midwestern poet, and it is in this landscape and diction that much of his work occurs. His poems may borrow from classical myth or a very extensive and profound knowledge of Western culture, but they repeatedly return to the concerns of the emotionally parched world associated with the Midwest. His stronger poems include 'The Detachable Man', a sequence collected in a volume of that name (New York, 1984), in which the title figure identifies himself as one who does *'without'*. Richard *Howard, in an essay on Finkel in *Alone with America* (New York, 1969, 1980), argues that the poetry's 'prime compulsion' is 'the escape from myth into individuality, history and death'.

See Finkel's *Selected Shorter Poems* (New York, 1987). Among well-regarded works not included there is *Adequate Earth* (New York, 1972), a long poem which draws on a visit which Finkel made to Antarctica in 1969. He returned to Antarctica for subject-matter in another long poem, *Endurance: An Arctic Idyll* (New York, 1978). [EHF

FINLAY, Ian Hamilton. See CONCRETE POETRY.

FISHER, Roy (1930–), was born at Handsworth, Birmingham, and educated at Handsworth Grammar School and Birmingham University. He taught at Midlands schools and colleges from 1953 to 1971, and as senior lecturer in American Studies at the University of Keele, 1972–82. Since then he has worked as a freelance writer and musician.

Fisher is an elusive, skilful poet who has absorbed an unusual number of influences. 'I get used as a between-worlds counter in reviewers' debates', he has said, the worlds in question being those of the 'underground' and the 'establishment'. This is borne out by his publishing history: his early *Collected Poems: The Ghost of a Paper Bag* (London, 1969) was published by Fulcrum Press, noted for its championship of neglected figures; his later *Poems 1955–1980* (London, 1980) and *Poems 1955–1987* (London, 1988) by Oxford University Press.

The Fulcrum *Collected* demonstrates his variousness. Fisher can write traditional, well-made poems such as 'The Hospital in Winter', wittily metaphysical poems such as 'The Billiard Table' and 'Starting to Make a Tree', and ambitious modernist poems like 'City', an extended meditation in prose and verse on his native Birmingham. This has been likened to William Carlos *Williams's Paterson. It began as a series of discrete short poems and prose observations, and was only later fused or agglomerated into one. 'The openness of my preferred forms', he has remarked, 'is . . . imaginative self-preservation as well as . . . a political attitude'—i.e. a rejection

of metrical closure and consensus politics. One of his constant themes is the nature of perception itself, and the role of an imperious imagination. 'The human mind makes the world. The examination of this organism that makes the world is of paramount interest.' In lesser poems, for example in much of *The Thing About Joe Sullivan* (Manchester, 1978), this reflexivity seems rather cloudy and whimsical, a means of evading the emotions that lie beneath the quiet surface of his best work.

Jazz, 'violent and ordinary', is clearly one influence on his method of composition, West Coast and *Black Mountain poetry another. Fisher himself insists that he is a 'realist'; the element of surreal caprice in his poems simply mirrors that of our perceptual apparatus and the world at large. 'On the Neglect of Figure Composition', a recent, witty poem containing proposals for 'a fresh Matter of Britain', is both playful and serious, and far from indifferent to conceptual thought. [WS

FITTS, Dudley (1903–68), was born in Boston. He was early associated with John *Wheelwright and Richard *Blackmur, and with the magazine *Hound & Horn*. He was instructor in English at Phillips Academy, Andover, Massachusetts, from 1941 until his death. Best known for his translation, with Robert *Fitzgerald, of Sophocles's *Oedipus Rex*, and of other Greek plays, and for his useful *An Anthology of Contemporary Latin American Poetry* (New York, 1942), with its skilful translations and parallel texts, Fitts also wrote original verse. His main (and considerable) solo achievement was his colloquial translation of Aristophanes's *Lysistrata* (New York, 1953; London, 1955), but his own poetry, while it attracted little attention, and was hardly anthologized, was sensitive, graceful, and carefully made. It was less influenced by classical models than by modern Spanish poetry. It struck many critics as wilfully obscure, perhaps on account of its elliptical style; but others praised it for its style and integrity. See *Poems (1926–1936)* (New York, 1937). [MS-S

FITZGERALD, R(obert) D(avid) (1902–86), was born in Sydney into two distinguished families. His father's family were colonial civil servants, and his mother's, the le Gay Breretons, included his uncle John, professor of English at Sydney University and a poet himself. FitzGerald qualified as a land surveyor in 1925 and followed that profession in Fiji and Australia for the rest of his life.

He published poetry consistently from the early 1920s to the 1980s, acquiring a reputation by the time he was in his late twenties. His standing was at its highest in the 1950s, but his classical forms and uncompromising metrics were not popular in the last few decades of his life.

FitzGerald attempted most of the traditional forms of poetry—the lyric, the long narrative, the meditation, and the ballad. He was least successful with the lyric, but his long meditative poems were some of the finest written in Australia. His subjects were often domestic and personal, but his major contribution was in uniting speculation in aesthetics with the new theories of physics. FitzGerald's ideas grew out of late nineteenth-century vitalism and twentieth-century notions of time. In combining them, he added to what has been called the 'metaphysical' tradition in Australian poetry. These ideas are best seen in such poems as 'The Hidden Bole' (1938), 'Essay on Memory' (1938), and 'The Face of the Waters' (1944). He was also one of the initiators of what became known as 'Voyager Poems'—poems about Australia's history which stress heroism and national creative energy—for example, 'Heemskerk Shoals' (1944) and his most anthologized poem, the convict portrait, 'The Wind at Your Door' (1958). His views on politics and history were illustrated in 'Between Two Tides' (1952), an epic-length poem about Tonga in the early nineteenth century. His spare, elliptical style and jagged rhythms have alienated some readers, but they have the attraction of individuality and the immediacy of the struggle to articulate complex thought.

The most recent edition of FitzGerald's poetry, together with a selection of his prose, may be found in *Portable Australian Authors: Robert D. FitzGerald*, ed. Julian Croft (St Lucia, Qld., 1987). [JCr

FITZGERALD, Robert (Stuart) (1910–85), was born in Geneva, New York, but grew up in Springfield, Illinois. His Irish-American parents were actors who had met in a road company. Fitzgerald's early life was marked by tragedy. His mother died when he was 3; his only sibling five years later. When he was 17 his long-invalided father also died. Despite these losses, Fitzgerald became a model scholar-athlete whose literary ambitions received early encouragement from his fellow townsman Vachel *Lindsay. Before attending college, Fitzgerald spent an extra year of preparation at The Choate School where he met the Latin master, Dudley *Fitts, with whom he would eventually collaborate on their widely performed translations of Euripides's *Alcestis* (1935) and Sophocles's *Antigone* (1938) and *Oedipus Rex* (1948). At Harvard Fitzgerald took honours in English and Greek. Graduating in 1933, he worked first as a reporter for the *New York Herald Tribune*. In 1936 he joined the staff of *Time*. In the Second World War he served in the US Navy at Guam and Pearl Harbor. In 1945 he returned to the Catholic Church, an experience which suffuses his subsequent poetry. Quitting *Time* in 1949, Fitzgerald divided his time between teaching in the USA and writing in Italy, where he eventually settled his large family. In 1965 he was appointed the Boylston Professor of Rhetoric and Oratory at Harvard, where his charismatic teaching proved influential to the younger poets who would later become known as the *New Formalists. He won many honours, including the first Bollingen Prize in translation. He died in Hamden, Connecticut.

Fitzgerald is generally acknowledged as his generation's pre-eminent translator of classical poetry. His reputation rests primarily on his celebrated versions of Homer's and Virgil's epic poems, *The Odyssey* (1961), *The Iliad* (1974), and *The Aeneid* (1983), but is equally supported by his commanding translations of Sophocles and Euripides. Fitzgerald's *Odyssey* demonstrates the combination of virtues which made his translations invaluable: he created a compelling narrative line, which makes every character and incident memorable, without ever sacrificing the poetry. Cast in flexible but resonant blank verse, Fitzgerald's language mixes archaic and contemporary diction to achieve a lucid but dignified tone capable of both narrative speed and lyric expansion. Showing how the classical epic could be re-created as living contemporary poems, Fitzgerald's translations have not only become the standard against which later versions have been measured; in their form, tone, and texture they have also provided an influential example of how contemporary narrative poems might be written.

Fitzgerald's achievements as a translator have tended to overshadow his genuine talent as a lyric poet. His most powerful early poems are elegiac meditations on particular landscapes. In 'Midsummer' he considers the small-town neighbourhoods of his lost youth. In 'Souls Lake' and 'Colorado' the natural scene becomes a mirror for philosophical speculation. If Fitzgerald's early work reflects spiritual longing, his deeply Catholic later poetry—like 'Solstitium Saeculare'—displays a radiant religious peace.

Spring Shade: Poems 1931–1970 (New York, 1971) remains the definitive collection of Fitzgerald's verse. His translations of *The Odyssey* (New York, 1961; London 1962), *The Iliad* (New York and London, 1974), and *The Aeneid* (New York and London 1983) have stayed continuously in print since publication. Fitzgerald's interview in *The Paris Review* (Winter, 1984) is a rich source of biographical and critical information.   [DG

Fitzrovia is the name (arrived at by ironic parallel with Belgravia, and only recently made official by the local borough) given to the district just north of London's Oxford Street and west of Tottenham Court Road, centred on the pubs, cafés, and restaurants in and around Charlotte Street. The name derives, not from Fitzroy Square a few blocks to the north, but from the Fitzroy Tavern, whose proprietors between

1919 and 1956, first Judah Kleinfeld and then his daughter and son-in-law Annie and Charlie Allchild, made it a celebrated meeting place for writers, painters, and leftist politicians. Hugh Gaitskell (who met his future wife there, and borrowed a pound from the publican to celebrate his engagement), Dylan *Thomas, Augustus John, Nye Bevan, and Tom Driberg were among its famous, or soon-to-be famous habitués; and it was Driberg, writing as William Hickey in his *Daily Express* column in 1946, who used the name 'Fitzrovia' and thus gave it wide circulation.

Though the Fitzroy continued popular, it was the Wheatsheaf the younger writers of the 1940s most favoured. Tambimuttu, editor of *Poetry London*, told one of them, Julian Maclaren-Ross, that Fitzrovia was 'dangerous': 'You will stay there . . . day and night and get no work done'—a warning Maclaren-Ross recorded but did not heed.

Alan *Ross (*London Magazine*, Dec. 1961) and Julian Maclaren-Ross (*Memoirs of the Forties*, London, 1965) have recorded impressions of Fitzrovia in its literary heyday during the 1940s, a time when those meeting-places seemed to Ross 'enormously exciting and savagely happy'.
                                                        [CKS

FLECKER, James (originally Herman) Elroy (1884–1915), was born at Lewisham, South London. He went up to Trinity College, Oxford, in 1902, on a classical scholarship. While there he became well known for his agnosticism, his *fin de siècle* style, and for the promising precociousness of his poetry. He later studied modern languages, became friendly with Rupert *Brooke, and worked in the consular service (Constantinople, Beirut). Flecker was one of the more gifted poets of the Edwardian era; there is reason to suppose that he might have developed had he not fallen victim to tuberculosis. He had fruitfully studied French poets, Heredia in particular, and the colourful style he evolved, while over-lush and devoted to verbal effect at the expense of content, was more than competent. He had a reliable ear, and certain phrases in his work (there are twenty in the *Oxford Dictionary* *of Quotations*) are memorable and shot through with genuinely fervent, if diffused and sometimes commonplace, feeling. 'The Dying Patriot' offers a good example of his strengths and weaknesses. Flecker was best known for his play *Hassan* (London, 1922), which had a vogue some years after his death; but, although agreeably luxuriant in its faintly decadent manner, it has dated and is now read less than individual poems such as 'The Old Ships' and 'To a Poet a Thousand Years Hence'. He served as a role-model for the *Georgians. See *Collected Poems* (London, 1946), and *James Elroy Flecker: From School to Samarkand* (Thames Ditton, Surrey, 1952), by T. S. Mercer. [MS-S

FLETCHER, Ian (1920–88), was born in London and educated at Dulwich College. Soon after the outbreak of the Second World War he joined the British Army and was posted to the Middle East. Here he met a number of poets who were to become lifelong friends, among them Bernard *Spencer and G. S. *Fraser. Fraser provides a memorable account of the young Fletcher in his autobiography, *A Stranger and Afraid* (Manchester, 1983). After the war he became first a children's librarian and then lecturer in English at Reading University, rising eventually to the position of professor. At the time of his death Fletcher, who had taken early retirement from Reading, was professor at the State University of Arizona.

Fletcher's first volume of poems *Orisons* (London, 1947) was followed by the editorship of the literary magazine *Colonnade*, whose first number proved also to be its last. This was perhaps appropriate for a man who had begun to establish himself as a leading authority on the 1890s. His next volume of poems, *Motets* (Reading, 1962) showed something of his abiding concerns with the music and architecture of the Baroque period. He published no further full volume, although there were to be several pamphlet collections, including *The Milesian Intrusion: A Restoration Comedy Version of Iliad XIV* (Nottingham, 1968), a typically witty and *recherché* performance. Many of his major literary-

historical essays were gathered together in *W. B. Yeats and His Contemporaries* (1987). There is a brief memoir by Derek Stanford in *London Magazine*, 29: 11/12 (1990). [JL

FLETCHER, John Gould (1886–1950), was born in Little Rock, Arkansas, the son of a banker and Confederate Civil War veteran, and educated at Harvard. Like several contemporaries, he abandoned America for the richer culture of Europe, living in London, 1909–14 and 1918–33. Finding no takers for his copious early poems, he published five volumes simultaneously at his own expense in 1913 (he later pulped all the unsold copies). In the same year he met *Pound in Paris, but found him too stern a critic, and it was not until Amy *Lowell took over the *Imagist movement that he was ushered into that fold, appearing in each of her three anthologies (1915–17). His five-movement 'Blue Symphony' in the first of these is typical of his early work, whose formal innovations have artistic or musical models (or both). In fact Fletcher was too individual a spirit to embrace the Imagist programme: in 1916 he wrote to Lowell: 'I do not believe that a poem should present an "image". I do not believe in cadence but in rhythm.' In America during the war years, he wrote a series of pieces on American subjects in what he called 'Polyphonic Prose' (see, for example, 'Clipper Ships'), as well as a number of poems influenced by Oriental art, later collected in *Japanese Prints* (1918). He was still incorrigibly over-productive, and his fortunes took a down-turn when three separate volumes were rejected by publishers in 1917. The next distinct phase of his career, beginning in the mid-Twenties, was religious, its most significant product the Blakean long poem *Branches of Adam* (1926). After a nervous breakdown in 1932 he returned for good to Arkansas, where he followed the *Fugitives in affirming a Southern agrarian culture against Yankee materialism; his last books, *South Star* (1941) and *The Burning Mountain* (1946) have strong regional associations. In 1950 a recurrence of mental illness caused him to drown himself.

Fletcher's *Selected Poems* (New York, 1938) won him the Pulitzer Prize; but even within this volume, as a contemporary reviewer remarked, '[his] best and most concentrated work is often lost in the wide reaches of a diffuse whole'. Prose works include *Paul Gauguin* (1921), the first biography of the painter in English, and the autobiography *Life is My Song* (1937). [MI

FLINT, F(rank) S(tuart) (1885–1960), was born in Islington, north London, the son of a commercial traveller, and was brought up in what he later described as 'fleabitten' poverty. He left school at 13 and, after a succession of odd jobs, joined the civil service as a typist at 19; he studied French and Latin at night school, and eventually became proficient in ten languages. At 24 he married, and, already a contributor—chiefly of articles on contemporary French literature—to journals such as the *New Age* and the *English Review*—published his first book of poems, *In the Net of the Stars*. This records, for the most part in conventional late-Romantic terms, with occasional flashes of French Symbolism and *Georgian rural nostalgia, the yearnings and disenchantments of a sensitive soul dismayed by urban squalor and redeemed by passionate love; the rhyming stanzas may be unadventurous, the inversions and poeticisms those of an exhausted idiom, but the poems have an affecting awkwardness and sincerity.

It was in this year too—1909—that Flint first came into contact with T. E. *Hulme; out of their close friendship and shared stylistic preoccupations grew an informal group of poets whose attachment to *vers libre* and 'the Image' made them precursors of the movement that Ezra *Pound (who was introduced to Hulme and Flint at about the same time) later christened *Imagisme. Flint, in fact, collaborated in the first printed statement of Imagist precepts, in *Poetry* for March 1913 ('Pound's direct treatment of the "Thing", whether subjective or objective', and so on); his poems appeared in the Imagist anthologies and he remained—despite a bitter falling-out with Pound—a loyal supporter of the movement's aims and principles.

Many of the poems in his collection *Cadences* (London, 1915) seem merely pared-down versions of the themes—and sometimes even the subject-matter, as in 'The Swan'—of *In the Net of the Stars*: clearer, plainer, and undoubtedly more 'modern', but thinner in texture and less spontaneous in feeling. When he came to publish *Otherworld: Cadences* (London, 1920), Flint was as stalwart as ever in his defence of the free verse he now called 'unrimed cadence', and just as dismissive of rhyme and metre, which he called 'dead or dying devices' that 'strangle and stifle the natural cadence of our emotion'. Almost all trace of the other Imagist virtues has, however, disappeared from the prolix, ruminative title-poem of this book, which provides Flint's fullest exploration of his distinctive theme—defeated aspiration, the contrast between drab reality and a lushly idealized 'otherworld' based on domestic affections; though some of the shorter pieces find more concrete correlatives for Flint's characteristic mood of wistful (self-) disappointment. He published no more collections, and seems to have stopped writing poetry, after *Otherworld* (though his miniature verse-drama, 'The Making of Lilith', was included in *Imagist Anthology*, London, 1930); instead, he rose to a senior position in the statistics division of the Ministry of Labour and steadily contributed articles and reviews to periodicals such as the *Chapbook*, *Poetry Review*, and the *Times Literary Supplement*. He also published two volumes of translations from the French of Jean de Bosschère (London, 1917) and Émile Verhaeren (London, 1916).

[AJ

FORBES, John (1950–), was born in Melbourne but endured a peripatetic childhood in New Guinea and Malaya before undergoing a Catholic education at De La Salle College in Sydney. He was briefly at Monash University in Melbourne, where he associated with Alan *Wearne, Laurie *Duggan, and John A. *Scott, before graduating from Sydney University with a degree in fine arts.

A long poem by Forbes, 'Four Heads & How To Do Them', was the most frequently anthologized piece in Australia for the 1970s, but his first full-length book, *Stalin's Holidays* (Sydney, 1980), did not appear until the end of that decade, and eight more years elapsed before his second collection, *The Stunned Mullet* (Sydney, 1988). A *New and Selected Poems*, which in fact includes nearly all the poetry he has written, was published (Sydney) in 1991.

Despite his small output, Forbes has been an influential and imposing figure since the Monash Readings of 1968, his *annus mirabilis*. His achievement consists of the introduction of a style, since widely imitated by lesser writers, to Australian poetry. It is a style which invites postmodernist exegesis, a hectic mixture of deliberate non-sequiturs, mixed metaphors, meaningless similes, and private jokes. It moves with a dream-like inevitability, combining sophistication and boyishness, all in a depersonalized tone. The effect can be amusing, exhilarating, and involving. The style is remarkably similar to that of the New York poet Frank *O'Hara, whose work was the subject of a thesis Forbes wrote as a student; but its content is Australian. [JG]

FORCHÉ, Carolyn (1950–), was born Carolyn Sidlosky in Detroit, Michigan, and grew up in its suburbs. She attended Michigan State University and Bowling Green University. Forché's first book of poems, *Gathering the Tribes* (New Haven, Conn., and London, 1976), was chosen for the Yale Series of Younger Poets by Stanley *Kunitz, who admired the unabashed eroticism in poems such as 'Taking Off My Clothes' and the Sapphic narrative, 'Kalaloch'. In many of these free-verse poems she meditates on the kinship bonds of Native Americans, and links their tribal rites and rituals to her own ethnic roots in Eastern Europe.

A few weeks spent in civil-war-torn El Salvador inspired a group of sombre poems in Forché's second book, *The Country Between Us* (New York and London, 1981), which includes the often-reprinted prose piece, 'The Colonel', a journalistic account of a dinner with a Salvadoran military man who collects the ears of his victims. Poems about oppression in Czechoslovakia ('Letter From Prague, 1968–78'), a

scarred Vietnam veteran ('Joseph'), and an American expatriate in Paris ('Expatriate') all blend the personal and the political. Without irony or humour, many poems in the volume emphasize the naïvety of the poet in the face of world events she cannot fully understand. Forché has also published translations of Claribel Alegria and Robert Desnos. [TDeP]

FORD, Ford Madox (1873–1939), was born Ford Madox Hueffer (all his books are thus signed until 1923) in Merton, Surrey, the son of a German music-critic and his English wife. His poetry has not been widely read or noticed, although it was often published in his lifetime. Ford put much less effort into it than into his prose; but it is not negligible, either as an indispensable guide to a complex man or for its intrinsic qualities. It is free and flowing, usually careless, almost wilful in its lack of concentration; he showed little grasp of the technical side of verse-making; but it is also genuinely modest, charming, and (like most things he did) unusual. He had a good enough natural ear to preserve him from rhythmical barbarities. He wrote poetry throughout his life, from *Poems for Pictures and for Notes of Music* (London, 1900) to *Collected Poems* (New York, 1936), which is incomplete. His best work is in *Antwerp* (London, 1914), which *Hardy found 'delightful in its spontaneity', and in the sequence of nine poems called 'Buckshee', occasioned by his pleasure and gratitude at being loved by a young woman when he was a sick old man. See *Selected Poems* (Cambridge, Mass., 1971), ed. Basil Bunting (an excellent selection), and *English Poetry 1900–1950* (Manchester, 1981) by C. H. Sisson. [MS-S

FORD, Mark (1962–) was born in Nairobi, Kenya. He was educated at St Paul's School, Lincoln College, Oxford, and Harvard. He has taught at University College, London, and is currently visiting lecturer at Kyoto University (Japan).

Ford's vivacious poems range between the oblique social commentary of 'Passion Play', in which football provides a morose refrain, and the surrealistic exuberance of 'A Swimming-pool Full of Peanuts'. The highly intelligent evasiveness of the verse is influenced by *Ashbery. Metaphors which seem entirely private, as in 'Winter Underwear', use objects of public discourse as hollow symbols, ones beyond decoding, in a way which insists on the primacy of the poet's imagination. Ford brings to British poetry a *New York School style of take-it-or-leave-it breeziness which reflects his academic experience yet shows a sharp ear for contemporary idiom. It was this ear in particular which brought Ford early acclaim.

Ford's first collection is *Landlocked* (London, 1992); a selection appears in *New Chatto Poets: Number Two* (London, 1989).   [LMacK

FORD, R(obert) A(rthur) D(ouglass) (1915–), was born in Ottawa, and educated at the University of Western Ontario and Cornell. Determined to live a normal life despite a debilitating muscular disease, he joined the Department of External Affairs in 1940. In 1946 he married Maria Thereza Gomez, a Brazilian delegate to the United Nations, and was appointed Secretary to the Canadian Embassy in Moscow. He eventually became Canada's Ambassador to the USSR, a post he occupied from 1964 to 1980. A lifelong interest in Russian history and culture have made him one of his country's most thoughtful commentators on East–West affairs.

His first book of poems, *A Window on the North* (1956), won the Governor-General's Award for poetry. Critics noted the influence of Bliss Carman and D. C. Scott, particularly in the lovingly described emptiness of the northern landscapes and the fascination with the consolations of bleakness. Translations and adaptations of Russian and Portuguese poetry helped Ford extend the somewhat limited range of this early volume. He has published six books of poetry since, in which he has essentially explored the same territory: the dark and silent spaces whose oppressiveness can be held at bay by signs of human order—love, memory, cultural artefacts, patterns of meticulously noted details. Ford's laconic suggestiveness often creates a kind of lyric minimalism, a quiet self-assertion in the presence of the century's large and poten-

tially soul-destroying movements and concerns. The vision in the later volumes has become, if anything, darker and more personal. Ford's technical and political conservatism makes him something of an anomaly in Canadian poetry of this period, and helps explain the relative neglect in which his verse has languished. He has added Serbo-Croatian, Spanish, French, and German poems to his published work as a translator. Now retired, he lives in a chateau near Vichy, France.

The most recent, and fullest, edition of Ford's poetry is *Coming From Afar: Selected Poems 1940–1989* (Toronto, 1990). See also *Our Man in Moscow: A Diplomat's Reflections on the Soviet Union* (Toronto, 1990), an autobiographical account of Ford's years as Canadian Ambassador in Moscow.   [DR

FORREST-THOMSON, Veronica (1947–75), grew up in Glasgow and was educated at the universities of Liverpool and Glasgow. Her poetry has particularly attracted interest since the posthumous publication of her critical work, *Poetic Artifice* (1978), which is influenced by formalism, structuralism, the criticism of William *Empson, and the philosophy of Wittgenstein, but which is always trenchant and original. Her earlier poems in *twelve academic questions* (1970) and *Language-Games* (1971) were concerned to explore the conventions which decree that a poem is a poem. But under the influence of Empson her work reverted to more traditional models, and the poems became dense with ambiguity, irony, and allusion: so dense with allusion in fact, that some read like a self-conscious inventory of quotations. They are sometimes flippant in tone, and maladroit in their handling of form, especially when emotional suffering is the source of inspiration. Nevertheless, there are some poems where all these factors work successfully together: 'Pastoral' is one such. Her collected poems are in *On the Periphery* (Cambridge, 1976).   [ETL

FOULCHER, John (1952–), was born in Sydney and educated at Macquarie University.

He has worked mainly as a schoolteacher, latterly in Canberra, and since 1990 has been poetry editor of the *Canberra Times*.

The first of his three volumes of verse, *Light Pressure*, appeared in 1983 (Sydney). The poetry was technically skilled and careful, in the service of precise notations of scenes from the poet's emotional life. The range of Foulcher's work widened in *Pictures from the War* (Sydney, 1987), winner of the National Library Poetry Award, in which human conflict, 'cruelty, and poverty, and war', was the broad ground of his concern. The death of his father, marriage, and the advent of his own children are conventional subjects that Foulcher treats detachedly. Passive, acted upon, 'kidnapped from school | in the alien craft of university', he writes at length of the self observed, though this egoistic concentration features more strongly in *Paperweight* (Sydney, 1991). Perceived from outside ('I sit', 'I lean', 'I recall'), as an actor in his difficult marriage, Foulcher parries the impulse to *confessional poetry by restricting himself to description of the incidentals and externals of his life. All that he presently needs for a supple and intelligent, not quite self-indulgent poetry, is there, and larger gestures—for instance towards his religious beliefs—are not so successfully handled. See also *New and Selected Poems* (Sydney, 1993).

[PP

FRAME, Janet (1924–), was born in Oamaru, New Zealand, the daughter of a railway worker. Frame's childhood was marked by tragedy: her two sisters were drowned and her younger brother was epileptic. As a young woman Frame suffered a breakdown and was admitted to Seacliff Hospital outside Christchurch. She spent eight years in psychiatric hospitals and narrowly escaped a leucotomy.

Frame's writing carries the marks of this background, but we should be wary of projecting on to the poetry the images of distress and loneliness associated with her life. In the poems light and dark are always in balance, shifting continually from comic to tragic modes and from the sublime to the ridiculous, often within a single sentence. Popular speech-forms, the language of advertising, and suburban clichés are set alongside echoes of Shakespeare or *Masefield's 'Sea-Fever'. Pastiche abounds, along with a Joycean predilection for puns and *double entendre*. Above all, there are continual deflations of the 'poetic' by the mundane. There are also images of death, loss, and terror, but these are controlled by a richly comic delight in language-play.

Frame has published only one book of poems, *The Pocket Mirror* (New York and London, 1967). But to focus on the work published under the category 'poetry' while ignoring the wealth of poetry worked into her novels is to misrepresent her. She will surely be remembered as a novelist rather than as a poet; nevertheless, she is not one of those novelists who happen to have written poems which are mere footnotes to the major work. All her writing challenges the distinction between poetry and prose. Her novels include *The Lagoon* (1951), *Owls Do Cry* (1961), and *The Carpathians* (1988); her three volumes of autobiography were made into a film by Jane Campion under the title of the second volume, *An Angel at my Table*.

[MW

FRANCIS, Robert (Churchill) (1901–87), was born in Upland, Pennsylvania, and attended Harvard. From 1926 until his death he lived in Amherst, Massachusetts. His home since 1940, a small, tree-shaded house he called 'Fort Juniper', inspired the name of the Juniper Prize for Poetry, which the University of Massachusetts Press established in his honour.

Although he enjoyed his seclusion in Amherst, he often travelled to Europe and taught variously at home and abroad. He served as Phi Beta Kappa poet at Tufts and at Harvard, and he taught at the American University in Beirut, Lebanon. He spent a year in Rome, having won the Rome Prize of the American Academy of Arts and Letters, 1957–8.

From his first collection, *Stand with Me Here* (New York, 1936), the poems of Robert Francis are marked by an excited curiosity about ordinary things. In them, passion is restrained by a clipped, conversational tone and an original use of form. 'Altitude', in *The Face Against the Glass* (published by the author, 1950), begins with a startled perception of a hawk circling around shrieking crows, and gains momentum as the birds rise and disappear. Much of his later work deals with the drama of human perception as related to art: remarkable poems in this genre are 'Part for the Whole' (1950), 'Exclusive Blue' and 'Three Darks Come Down Together' (1960).

His ten volumes of poetry are represented in *Collected Poems, 1936–1976* (Amherst, Mass., 1976). Among his seven prose works are a novel, *We Fly Away* (New York, 1948), a book of essays, *The Satirical Rogue on Poetry* (Amherst, 1968), and an autobiography, *The Trouble with Francis* (Amherst, 1971). [GS

FRASER, G(eorge) S(utherland) (1915–80), was born in Glasgow. After graduating from St Andrews in 1937 Fraser worked as a journalist in Aberdeen. He spent most of the Second World War in Egypt, where he was associated with Lawrence *Durrell (about whom he wrote a study, 1968), Terence *Tiller, and Bernard *Spencer. His posthumously published autobiography, *A Stranger and Afraid* (1983), takes his story up to the 1940s. A frequent reviewer in the post-war years, Fraser was a figure of considerable influence on the literary scene before taking up a university appointment at Leicester in 1958, where he continued to work until the year before his death. His literary 'evenings' in his London period have been referred to frequently by memoirists of his generation.

Experience as a free-lance found its critical expression in *The Modern Writer and His World* (London, 1953; revd. edn. 1964; New York, 1955) which is still interesting as an early book in the field. Much of *Vision and Rhetoric* (1959) reappears in *Essays on Twentieth-Century Poets* (1978). University teaching led to *Alexander Pope* (1978), and to *A Short History of English Poetry*, which is readable, but largely routine except for the attention paid to Scottish poetry.

His first collection was *The Fatal Landscape* (1943). It was followed by *Home Town Elegy* (1944) where the title-poem shows more conviction than most of his work, with the possible

exception of 'Lean Street' in the same volume. *The Traveller Has Regrets* (1948) and *Conditions* (1969), while fluent, did little to assert the presence of an important talent. *Poems of G. S. Fraser*, ed. I. Fletcher and J. Lucas, and with an appreciative introduction (Leicester, 1981), represents the full range of his work. By the 1950s and later the impression is not exactly of a gift worn out by literary journalism and teaching, but of one unable to rise above its initial forms and concerns. 'A Napkin with Veronica's Face, Not Christ's', six sonnets in memory of Veronica *Forrest-Thomson, is a moving exception. He is likely to be remembered as an understander and encourager of poetry who was unable to live up to the promise of the best of his earlier work.

[DED

FRENCH, Anne (1956–), was born in Wellington. She graduated from Victoria University of Wellington in 1980 and moved to Auckland as managing editor of Oxford University Press in New Zealand. In 1993 she became Massey University's inaugural Writer's Fellow. Her first collection of poems, *All Cretans are Liars* (Auckland, 1987), won the 1988 New Zealand Book Award for Poetry. Its title, which alludes to the famous paradox of Epimenides, acknowledges the tricksiness of language and the tendency of truth to recede even as one attempts to formulate it. And it points to the poet's concern with the evasions and subterfuges of verbal communication, and to the witty, paradoxical, game-playing qualities of her poems. French is candid, sophisticated, literate, and sharp. She is an effective commentator on sexual politics. Her second book, *The Male as Evader* (Auckland, 1988), recognizes that women collude in the drama of deception. Her third collection, *Cabin Fever* (Auckland, 1990), while still concerned with 'knowledge and belief', ventures into the outdoors, to range widely around northern New Zealand and its coastal waters.

French is well represented in the Oxford anthology, *Yellow Pencils: Contemporary Poetry by New Zealand Women*, ed. Lydia Wevers (Auckland, 1988). There is a long interview with her in *Landfall*, 171 (1989). [MacDJ

FRIED, Michael (1939–), was born in New York City and educated at Princeton (BA) and Harvard (Ph. D). In between Princeton and Harvard, he served time as a Rhodes Scholar at Merton College, Oxford and was a major influence on the poets who later came to be associated with *The *Review*. Fried's brief, intense and sharply visual lyrics have been collected in two pamphlets—*Other Hands* (Oxford, 1962); *Appetites* (Oxford, 1964)—and one full-length collection, *Powers* (Oxford, 1973). Since the mid-Seventies, he has become better known for his art criticism than for his poetry, although his *Absorption and Theatricality: Painting and Beholder in the Age of Diderot* (Berkeley, Calif., 1980) has plenty to reveal about his practice as a poet. A second volume of verse, *To the Center of the Earth*, is expected in 1994.   [POM

FROST, Robert (1874–1963), was born in San Francisco, where he spent his first eleven years. After the death of his father, a journalist, he moved with his mother and sister to eastern Massachusetts near his paternal grandparents. He wrote his first poems while a student at Lawrence High School, from which he graduated as co-valedictorian with the woman he was to marry, Elinor Miriam White. He entered Dartmouth College in the fall of 1892 but stayed for less than a term, returning home to teach school and to work at various jobs, including factory-hand and newspaperman. In 1894 he sold his first poem, 'My Butterfly: An Elegy', to a New York magazine, *The Independent*. That same year, unable to persuade Elinor to marry him (she wanted to finish college first), he headed south on a reckless journey into Virginia's Dismal Swamp. After emerging unscathed he came home to Lawrence where he and Elinor were married in December 1895.

Both husband and wife taught school for a time, then in 1897 Frost entered Harvard College as a special student, remaining there just short of two years. He performed well at Harvard, but his health was uncertain and he rejoined his wife in Lawrence, where she was about to bear a second child. In October of 1900

he settled with his family on a farm just over the Massachusetts line in New Hampshire, purchased for him by his grandfather. There, over the next nine years, he wrote many of the poems that would make up his first published volumes. But his attempt at poultry farming was none too successful, and by 1906 he had begun teaching English at Pinkerton Academy, a secondary school in New Hampshire. That same year two of his most accomplished early poems, 'The Tuft of Flowers' and 'The Trial by Existence', were published. Meanwhile he and Elinor produced six children, two of whom died in infancy. After a year spent teaching at the State Normal School in Plymouth, New Hampshire, he sold the Derry farm and in the fall of 1912 sailed with his family from Boston to Glasgow, then settled outside London in Beaconsfield.

Within two months of his arrival in England, Frost placed his first book of poems, *A Boy's Will* (1913) with a small London publisher, David Nutt. He also made acquaintances in the literary world, such as the poet F. S. *Flint, who introduced him to Ezra *Pound, who in turn reviewed both *A Boy's Will* and *North of Boston*, which followed it the next year. He became friends with members of the *Georgian school of poets—particularly with Wilfred *Gibson and Lascelles *Abercrombie—and in 1914, on their urgings, he moved to Gloucestershire to be nearer them and to experience English country living. The most important friend he made in England was Edward *Thomas, whom Frost encouraged to write poetry and who wrote sharply intelligent reviews of Frost's first two books. While many reviewers were content to speak of the American poet's 'simplicity' and artlessness, Thomas recognized the originality and success of Frost's experiments with the cadences of vernacular speech—with what Frost called 'the sound of sense'. His best early poems, such as 'Mowing', 'Mending Wall,' and 'Home Burial,' were composed under the assumption that, in Frost's formulation from one of his letters, '*the ear does it*. The ear is the only true writer and the only true reader.' The best part of a poet's work, he insisted, was to be found in the sentence-sounds poems made, as of people talking. Like Wordsworth (as Edward Thomas pointed out in one of his reviews of *North of Boston*), Frost boldly employed 'ordinary' words and cadences ('I have sunk to a diction even Wordsworth kept above', he said in another letter) yet contrived to throw over them—in Wordsworth's formulation from his preface to the *Lyrical Ballads*—'a certain colouring of imagination'.

England's entry into the First World War hastened Frost's return to America early in 1915. By the time he landed in New York City, his American publisher, Henry Holt, had brought out *North of Boston* (Holt would continue to publish Frost throughout his life). He was fêted by editors and critics in the literary worlds of both New York and Boston, and he continued shrewdly to publicize himself, providing anthologists and interviewers with a vocabulary to describe his poetic aims. A third volume of verse, *Mountain Interval*, published in 1916 but still drawing on poems he had written in England and before, showed no falling off from his previous standard. In fact such poems as 'The Road Not Taken,' 'An Old Man's Winter Night,' 'The Oven Bird,' 'Birches,' 'Putting in the Seed,' and 'Out, Out —' were among the best he had written or was to write. Like the somewhat late-coming and even drab oven bird of his poem, Frost knew in 'singing not to sing', and a century after the ecstatic flights of romantic poets like Keats and Shelley, Frost's bird remained earthbound (the oven bird, in fact, builds its nests on the ground) and, like the poet who created him, sang about the things of this world.

Soon after he re-established himself in America, Frost purchased a farm in Franconia, New Hampshire (he would purchase a number of farms over the course of his life) and then, at the behest of President Alexander Meiklejohn, joined the faculty of Amherst College in Massachusetts. Frost was later to teach at the University of Michigan and at Dartmouth College, but his relationship to Amherst (sometimes a troubled one) was the most significant educational alliance he formed. Meanwhile he had begun the practice of reading his poems aloud—or

rather, 'saying' them, as he liked to put it—at public gatherings. These occasions, which continued throughout his life, were often intensive ones in which he would read, comment on, and reflect largely about his poems and about the world in general. Particularly at colleges and universities he commanded the ears and often hearts of generations of students, and he received so many honorary degrees from the academy that he eventually had the hoods made into a quilt.

Frost won the first of four Pulitzer Prizes in 1924 for his fourth book, *New Hampshire*, and followed it with *West-Running Brook* (1928) and *A Further Range* (1936), which also won a Pulitzer. Yet the latter volume occasioned, from critics on the left, the first really harsh criticism Frost's poetry had received. One of those critics, Rolfe *Humphries, complained in *New Masses* (his review was titled 'A Further Shrinking') that Frost no longer showed either a dramatic or a sympathetic attitude toward his New England characters; that in setting himself against systematic political and social reforms (especially Franklin Roosevelt's New Deal), he had become querulous and sarcastic, all too personally present in his quarrel with the way things were going. It is true that, for one reason or another, Frost no longer wrote poems like the dramatic monologues and dialogues in *North of Boston*, and that poems from *A Further Range*, such as 'Two Tramps in Mud Time' or 'Provide, Provide', were argumentative and at times didactic in their thrust. But he had become expert at composing poems that had affinities with light verse and that consisted of a pointed, witty treatment of issues and ideas. Such a treatment purchased its surface brilliance at the cost of deeper sympathies and explorations.

Those deeper concerns were to make themselves felt once again, however, in what was to be Frost's last truly significant book of verse, *A Witness Tree* (1942). During the 1930s, as he became ever more honoured and revered, Frost endured a terrible series of family disasters. In 1934 his youngest and best-loved child, Marjorie, died a slow death from the puerperal fever contracted after giving birth to her first child; in

1938 his wife Elinor died suddenly of a heart attack; then, when he seemed to be pulling things together once more, his son Carol committed suicide in 1940. Another daughter, Irma, suffered—as did Frost's sister Jeannie—from mental disorders and was finally institutionalized. A number of poems in *A Witness Tree* undoubtedly derived their dark tone from the family tragedies suffered over the decade; but at any rate lyrics such as 'The Silken Tent', 'I Could Give All to Time', 'Never Again Would Birds' Song Be the Same', and 'The Most of It' stand in the top rank of Frost's work (he himself thought that some of his best poetry was contained in this book). In words from his prose essay 'The Figure a Poem Makes', they exhibit both 'how a poem can have wildness and at the same time a subject that shall be fulfilled'.

Except for the publishing of a major poem, 'Directive', in his 1947 volume, *Steeple Bush*, Frost's poetry after the Second World War was mainly occasional, a relaxation from earlier intensities. He made a triumphant return to England in 1957 to receive honorary degrees from Oxford and Cambridge; he expended his efforts to have Pound released from St Elizabeth's Hospital; and under the Kennedy administration he made a somewhat less-than-satisfactory visit to Russia, in which he attempted, in conversation with Premier Khrushchev, to mediate between the superpowers. His last reading was given to a large audience in Boston in December 1962; the following day he went into hospital for a prostate operation and suffered a severe heart attack while convalescing, then a series of embolisms, one of which killed him in January of 1963.

Frost once wrote about Edwin Arlington *Robinson that 'his life was a revel in the felicities of language', and surely the claim could be made, even more appropriately, of Frost himself. While standing apart from the modernist work of his famous contemporaries—*Eliot, Pound, *Stevens—his own poetry, in its complication of tone and its delicate balancing of gravity and wit ('I am never more serious than when joking', he said more than once), asks for constant vigilance on the reader's part: a listening ear for the special postures of speech and the dramatic effects of silences. Like the works of his great predecessor, Emerson, Frost's poetry has never been sufficiently appreciated in England, the country which gave him his start. This neglect may be in part a reaction to the rather promiscuous admiration he inspired from so many different sorts of American readers (and non-readers), many of whom would have no time for Eliot or Stevens. But if, for some Americans, the homely nature of Frost's materials—cows, apples, and snow-covered woods—predisposes them to like his poetry, such readers are no more narrow than the 'cosmopolitan' ones who accept mythical allusions in Eliot or Pound but disdain stone walls as a fit vehicle for serious poetry. Frost's own formulation to an American friend in 1914 is helpful in thinking about his achievement: he told the friend, Sidney Cox, that the true poet's pleasure lay in making 'his own words as he goes' rather than depending upon words whose meanings were fixed: 'We write of things we see and we write in accents we hear. Thus we gather both our material and our technique with the imagination from life; and our technique becomes as much material as material itself.' It was this principle that Pound saluted in Frost when, in his review of *North of Boston*, he remarked conclusively: 'I know more of farm life than I did before I had read his poems. That means I know more of "Life".'

The Poetry of Robert Frost, ed. Edward Connery Latham (New York and London, 1969) collects Frost's poems but is marred by questionable editorial tampering with punctuation and orthography. *Robert Frost: A Biography*, by Lawrence Thompson and R. H. Winnick (New York, 1981), is a one-volume edition of Thompson's three-volume biography. A selection of Frost's letters is *Selected Letters of Robert Frost*, ed. Lawrence Thompson (New York, 1965). See also *Robert Frost: The Work of Knowing*, by Richard Poirier (New York, 1977) and *Frost: A Literary Life Reconsidered*, by William H. Pritchard (New York, 1984; London, 1985).

[WHP

FRY, Christopher. See VERSE DRAMA.

Fugitive

Fugitive, The, a poetry magazine, nineteen issues of which were published in Nashville, Tennessee, from April 1922 to December 1925, was edited jointly by the self-designated Fugitives who had been meeting weekly for several years to read and discuss each other's poems. The original Fugitives were Walter Clyde Curry, Donald *Davidson, William Yandell Elliott, James Frank, William Frierson, Sidney Hirsch, Stanley Johnson, John Crowe *Ransom, Alec B. Stevenson, and Allen *Tate. They were later joined by Merrill *Moore, Laura *Riding (Gottschalk), Alfred Starr, Robert Penn *Warren, and Jesse and Ridley Wills. All but Hirsch, Frank, Riding, and Stevenson were either students or teachers at Vanderbilt University, which would not, however, support the magazine. Not until the fourth issue were its pages opened to outside contributors. Thereafter the most notable of these were Hart *Crane, John Gould *Fletcher, and Robert *Graves.

The Fugitives were committed to no particular programme but did agree on some basic points: that poetry should avoid the sentimentality and 'local colour' of the standard Southern literature of the time, and be intellectual and demanding as well as emotional: 'not the act of a child', as Ransom later said, 'but the act of an adult mind.' The magazine's poetry received much enthusiastic, and some adverse, criticism both for its dense and intricate verse and for its gloomy vision of modernity. Ransom, Davidson, and Tate always stood out from the rest of the group as ambitious, professional literary men. They conducted critical debates about modernism (to which most of the others were not sympathetic) in the magazine, developing what would later become the tenets of the *New Criticism; they went on to enjoy successful literary careers; and for them, as well as for Warren (the youngest Fugitive), *Fugitives: An Anthology* (edited by Davidson, 1928) marked the watershed between their involvement as Fugitive poets and as *Agrarian Southerners. Every issue of the magazine is reprinted in *The Fugitive: A Journal of Poetry* (New York, 1966). *The Fugitive Group: A Literary History*, by Louise Cowan (Baton Rouge, La., 1959) is still the best

account of its history, while *The Wary Fugitives: Four Poets and the South*, by Louis D. Rubin (Baton Rouge, 1978) is a more detailed study of Ransom, Davidson, Tate, and Warren.   [NE

FULLER, John (1937–), was born in Ashford, Kent, the son of the poet Roy *Fuller and Kathleen Fuller (née Smith). He was educated at St Paul's School and New College, Oxford and in 1966 became a fellow of Magdalen College, Oxford.

In his first book, *Fairground Music* (London, 1961), he showed a remarkable facility for composing poetry in a variety of conventional verseforms, a talent for vivid descriptive writing, and a sophisticated wit and verbal virtuosity, as in the outlandish rhymes of 'Snapshot'. Of the expertly written sonnets, 'A Kiss in Galloway' is the most moving. Wit and verbal pyrotechnics are prevalent in Fuller's next volume, *The Tree that Walked* (London, 1967), as in 'De Sade', a sequence of eight limericks. *Epistles to Several Persons* (London, 1973), written in Burns stanzas, are random satirical comments on the fads and pretensions of contemporary culture. They were published simultaneously with annotation in *Poems and Epistles* (Boston, 1973), together with a group of poems including 'The Two Sisters', a sombre character-portrayal reminiscent of *Masefield, and 'The Art of Love', a devastating comment on a world dominated by feminism and sexual permissiveness. *Lies and Secrets* (London, 1979) is notable for 'The Most Difficult Position', a study of the complex psychological rivalry between two nineteenth-century chess masters—Howard Staunton, British chess expert for the *Illustrated London News*, and the American master from New Orleans, Paul Morphy. The quarrel is famous in chess history. Staunton's part is spoken in blank verse, first in a monologue to his wife, later in soliloquy as epilogue. The style is Browning pastiche, but it is first-rate pastiche. Morphy's part is in hexameters, an epistle written in the summer and fall of 1858, to his mother. 'The Most Difficult Position' is perhaps Fuller's best poem.

The best introduction to Fuller's poetry is

Selected Poems 1954 to 1982 (London, 1985) which reveals a modern sensibility expressing extremely eclectic subject-matter in a variety of traditional verse-forms. More recent collections are *Partingtime Hall* (with James *Fenton) (1987), *The Grey among the Green* (1988), and *The Mechanical Body* (1991—all London)   [DS

FULLER, Roy (Broadbent) (1912–91), was born in Failsworth, Lancashire, and grew up in Blackpool, where he attended Blackpool High School and later qualified as a solicitor. After a spell in private practice he joined the Woolwich Equitable Building Society in 1938, becoming a director in 1969. He was legal adviser to the Building Societies Association, of which he was a vice-president, and at one time a governor of the BBC. His lectures as Oxford Professor of Poetry (1968–73) are published under the titles *Owls and Artificers* (London, 1971) and *Professors and Gods* (London, 1974). He received many prizes and awards, including a CBE and the Queen's Gold Medal for Poetry, both in 1970; he was also chairman of the Literature Panel of the Arts Council and of the *Poetry Book Society.

During the war Fuller served as a radar mechanic in East Africa and then as a radio and radar officer at the Admiralty in London, experiences commemorated in his first books: *Poems* (London, 1939), *The Middle of a War* (London, 1942), and *A Lost Season* (London, 1944). *Auden's powerful influence is visible throughout, but is gradually subsumed into Fuller's own flexible voice. 'The Middle of a War' and 'During a Bombardment by V-Weapons' are minor classics, expertly condensing all the mixed, unheroic emotions induced by war, and distinguishing between 'ridiculous detonations' and 'the permanent and real | Furies . . . settling in upstairs'. Less death-haunted and less lyrical than his fellow war poets Alun *Lewis and Keith *Douglas, his poetry coolly but honestly records the boredoms and deprivations suffered by most civilians during the aftermath of the Blitz, anticipating *Larkin sometimes in its wry colloquialism ('The 'Nineties would have seen me thrive, | Dyspep-

tic, bookish, half-alive') and refusal to make large gestures. With *Epitaphs and Occasions* (London, 1949), *Counterparts* (London, 1954), and *Brutus's Orchard* (London, 1957), he settled into the middle style that continued to serve him throughout a prolific and distinguished career.

Politically, he moved from Thirties neo-Marxism to an undogmatic, left-of-centre Welfare Statism. His poetry characteristically pits reason and a well-stocked mind against lust and terror, a wry stoicism against 'amatory botherations', concluding that 'the world belongs to the obtuse and passionate, and that the bosom's small | But noticeable curve subtends its tall | Explosions and orations of mad abuse' ('The Perturbations of Uranus'). Linguistically too the dialectic is always between the decorous and the rude, 'ruminant . . . art' attempting to digest a world 'weltering in blood'.

'Poetry is something between the dream | And its interpretation', he has said. Fuller cherished art for its coherence and lucidity, but persistently worried about its ability to deal with the quotidian: 'Girl with fat legs, reading Georgette Heyer, | Shall I arrange you in my pantheon?' ('Romance'). Another girl spotted at the baker's eyeing 'a bogus | Farm-house cob' has 'gathered herself together from | The chaos of parturition and | Appears now with a lacquered bouffant | Top-knot and her old wiles unimpaired' ('Metamorphosis'). Fuller rejoiced in the mixture of savagery and civilization that characterizes urban life. He also seized on the posthumous tense, as it were, with Hardyesque relish: 'My photograph already looks historic'; 'Already one's actions smack of the legendary, | If only to oneself'. Like Auden and *Hardy too he was a dedicated experimenter, using a wide variety of poetic forms, including syllabics, though the pentameter remained his norm.

There are perhaps rather too many quirky meditations and journeyman pieces on favourite topics—gardening, music, poetry, birds, cooking, dreams, insomnia, bits and pieces of science—in the 550 pages of *New and Collected Poems 1934–84* (London, 1985), but this is merely to say that Fuller benefits from selection. His last substantial collection, *Available for Dreams* (London, 1989), recording the 'unegotistical sublime' of illness and old age and the pleasures of the daily round, showed little diminution of his remarkable powers. See also *Last Poems*, ed. John Fuller (London, 1993).

Fuller also published eight novels, eight children's books, and three volumes of memoirs, *Souvenirs* (London, 1980), *Vamp Till Ready: Further Memoirs* (London, 1982), and *Home and Dry: Memoirs 3* (London, 1984). [WS

FULTON, Alice (1952–), was born and raised in Troy, New York, where she lived until the age of 25; the industrial, northern city of Troy and its mythic homonym loom large in her second book of poems, *Palladium* (Urbana, Ill., 1986). Here she transforms her Catholic, working-class background into the stuff of myth through her inventive and evocative language. Fulton loves words—the sections in this book are prefaced by six distinct sets of meanings for the word 'palladium'—and her poems are full of triple-*entendre* and coinages. She re-creates speech at all levels of diction: the scientist, nun, pimp, and child sing equally in her poems. Her most recent book, *Powers of Congress* (Boston, 1990), is even more ambitious in its inventiveness. She makes the least aspect of modern life seem poetic: computers, hotel decor, junk bonds. And she reveals the cruelty of everyday life, of childbirth and war, with an uncommon fierceness. [EG

FULTON, Robin (1937–), was born on the Isle of Arran and educated at Edinburgh University. Although he has published steadily over the past thirty years, Fulton's reputation as a translator, especially of modern Swedish poetry, may have overshadowed his own work.

Many of his poems attempt to elicit states of mind, thoughts and perceptions, which are only just on the edge of consciousness. 'Each has stepped into | the outer darkness of his own company', he writes of fellow train passengers in 'Travelling Alone' (*Selected Poems 1963–1978*, Edinburgh, 1980). 'Reality, so plain and inescapable. | I leave it again without noticing I'm going', he says in 'Waking in the Small Hours'. 'Something I can't see is being interrogated'—'Home Thoughts' (*Fields of Focus*, London, 1982). Understated but discreetly affecting personal dilemmas seep from his poems. At its best, his work succeeds through the simple statement of the unexpected. He is a poet of lying awake, listening to 'sounds behind sounds', of 'the pause | clock-hands make at midnight', almost, it could be said, a poet predisposed or addicted to the feelings of exile—'Home Thoughts' and 'Listening to Rachmaninov in a New House' are two examples. His most recent collection is *Coming Down to Earth and Spring is Soon* (London, 1990). He has lived in Norway since the mid-1970s.

Besides his original poetry and translations (especially of Tranströmer, Lagerkvist, Aspenström, Harding), Fulton has published a critical study, *Contemporary Scottish Poetry* (Edinburgh, 1974) and a collection of essays and reviews, *The Way the Words are Taken* (Edinburgh, 1989). He edited *Lines Review* from 1967 to 1976. [DED

Furioso, was a magazine devoted to the expression and cultivation of the urban, modern, secular temperament. Edited by Reed *Whittemore, it was published in Northfield, Minnesota, and lasted for some fourteen years (1939–53), adding Howard *Nemerov as co-editor for its last issues. The paper shortage kept its wartime issues relatively brief, but it flourished in the post-war context, its delightful and irreverent tone constituting an effective tonic in a difficult age. Whittemore was interested in the 'intelligent private individual at work on the world of his immediate environment', and this stance proved to be a flexible one, as can be gauged from the fact that its contributors included not only William *Faulkner but also Wayne C. Booth, whose contributions were in a satirical mode which pre-dated his later concentration on literary theory. It is remembered with great affection by those who read it, the quality and consistency of its humour being perhaps its most prized asset. [CM

FURNIVALL, John. See CONCRETE POETRY.

G

GALLAGHER, Tess (1932–), was born in Port Angeles, Washington. she was taught creative writing by Theodore *Roethke at the University of Washington, and the poems of *Stepping Outside* (Lisbon, Iowa, 1974) and *Instructions to the Double* (Port Townsend, Wash., 1976) combine Roethke's verbal exuberance with his metaphysical inclinations, but without at all trying to imitate his style or manner. The poems about 'doubles', which may mean, for the author, either 'reflections' or 'things with which I identify', are often interesting but, with a few exceptions, confused. Her third husband, Raymond *Carver, died in 1988. *Willingly* (Port Townsend, 1984) consists of poems about and to Carver, and lovingly mirror his style and approach to life, although they lack his subtle touch. Gallagher's avowed methods, to write poems resembling the little prayers she sent out as a child, for fish to bite, may irritate some as too fey; but of those practising such methods she is perhaps paramount. See *Amplitude: New and Selected Poems* (St Paul, 1987).   [MS-S]

GARDNER, Isabella (Stewart) (1915–81), was born in Newton, Massachusetts, daughter of an investment banker. After attending private schools, she studied drama, first in East Hampton, New York, and then in London. She was a professional actress from 1939 to 1942. Her first poetry collection did not appear until 1955, when she was 40.

From 1950 to 1956 she was associate editor of *Poetry* magazine in Chicago. The last of four marriages was to poet-critic Allen *Tate, who was in residence at the University of Minnesota. After divorcing Tate, Gardner made her home in Ojai, California, and later in New York City, where she died. A slow, often blocked writer, Gardner produced four collections in her lifetime. Her lyrics are admired for their spontaneity of voice, playfulness and economy of language, and formal accomplishment. Her best poems, like 'The Widow's Yard', deal with personal relationships and the failure of love.

The fullest edition of Gardner's poetry is *Isabella Gardner: The Collected Poems* (Brockport, NY, 1990). It includes all previously collected poems as well as thirty unpublished or uncollected.   [RSP]

GARFITT, Roger (1944–), was born in Melksham, Wiltshire, and educated at Merton College, Oxford. He edited *Poetry Review*, 1978–81 and was poetry reviewer for the *London Magazine*, 1973–6.

Landscape is the centre of Garfitt's work. He is both a meticulous re-creator of, for example, the effects of light, and a sociable poet who sees place as expressive of its inhabitants. His most recent collection, *Given Ground* (Manchester, 1989), concentrates on the unsung lives of the many whom official history excludes ('Hares Boxing', 'Lover Lumb Mill') and extends into the mythological ('The Hooded Gods' are three unnamed household deities). The minuteness of his attention is often rewarding. Clearly socialist in outlook, and combining formality with freer verse, Garfitt is an intriguing counterpart to the more public work of Douglas *Dunn and Tony *Harrison.

His collections are: *Caught on Blue* (Oxford, 1970); *West of Elm* (Cheadle, Cheshire, 1974); *The Broken Road* (Newcastle upon Tyne, 1982);

and *Given Ground* (Manchester, 1989). He has collaborated on *Rowlstone Haiku*, with Frances *Horovitz and Alan Halsey (Madley, Herefordshire, 1982) and *Walt*, edited by Noel Connor (Brampton, Cumbria, 1983), and has edited the *Collected Poems* of Frances Horovitz (Newcastle upon Tyne, 1985). [SO'B

GARIOCH, Robert (Sutherland) (1909–87), was born in Edinburgh and educated at that city's Royal High School and University. He began publishing in newspapers in the 1930s. *Seventeen Poems for Sixpence* (1940) was a slender collection shared with Sorley *MacLean. Conscripted in 1941, Garioch spent the rest of the war as a POW. The experience is recorded in 'The Wire', a harrowing poem virtually medieval in atmosphere and amounting to a chilling vision of captivity. *Two Men and a Blanket* (written 1946, published 1975)—he referred to it as 'that *Kriegsgefangenschaft* book'—is a prose evocation of his years as a prisoner.

Writing of Garioch's 1940 pamphlet in 1955, George Kitchin referred to Garioch's 'rough-tongued satire, and his language reeking of the closes of Edinburgh'. He went on to state that they 'should not blind us to his real talent'. Kitchin meant the poems in English in *Chuckies on the Cairn* (1949). Garioch's English poems are far from negligible ('Chalk Farm 1945', 'Property', 'Now I Remember You, McAlister') but his 'real talent' turned out to be for poetry in Scots. His literary affections owed much to Robert Fergusson (1750–74), the precursor of Burns; he is addressed in 'To Robert Fergusson' and commemorated in the sonnet 'At Robert Fergusson's Grave'. The first of these poems employs the 'Standard Habbie' or Burns Stanza, first used by Robert Sempill of Beltrees in the seventeenth century (see LALLANS). Hugh *MacDiarmid's revival of poetry in Scots in the 1920s deliberately avoided Burnsian and other older verse-forms as part of his strategy of dissociating new Scottish poetry from the taint of Burns's trivializing imitators and the thoughtless populism which had grown around Scotland's national poet. Reintroducing these

stanzas with contemporary verve rather than archeological piety constitutes a large part of Garioch's achievement. 'Embro to the Ploy', for example, a high-spirited dig at the pretensions of the Edinburgh Festival, makes use of the bob-and-wheel stanza of the fifteenth-century poems 'Peblis to the Play' and 'Christis Kirk on the Grene'. Stanzas like these support the classically indigenous force of Garioch's work; they are perfect foils for a craftsmanship that is at times stunning in its vernacular confidence, and rarely if ever inadequate. They also assisted him to tap the directness and fast tempos of Scottish verse, in keeping with his persona as Edinburgh's Everyman, a wry, observant, satirical, witty, and elusive figure, whose puzzled smile disguised a wealth of erudition.

Much of Garioch's poetry is humorous; he had a sharp eye for modernist affectation, fakery, hypocrisy, and unearned magnitude of self. Poems like 'The Wire' and 'The Muir', however, could have been undervalued as a consequence. The outcome of his attempt to understand the 1953 Reith Lectures by J. Robert Oppenheimer, 'The Muir' is especially interesting as a meditation on science written in Scots.

Garioch taught in England from 1946 to 1959, which might help to explain the relative slowness with which he came to an established reputation, although he was well known in Scottish literary circles since the newspaper publication of *The Masque of Edinburgh* as early as 1933. A new and expanded version of that work appeared in 1954. Subsequent volumes, as well as cherished public readings, extended his work to a wider readership and considerable popularity. *Collected Poems* (Manchester, 1977) is replaced by *Complete Poetical Works*, ed. R. Fulton, (Edinburgh, 1983). *A Garioch Miscellany* contains brief memoirs, letters, reviews, and the text of *The Masque of Edinburgh*. His translations, of which there are many, especially his versions of Belli's sonnets, are included in *Complete Poetical Works*. [DED

GARLICK, Raymond (1926–), was born in London and educated at the University College of North Wales, Bangor. He later taught English at Pembroke Dock and at Blaenau Ffestiniog. He was the founder of *Dock Leaves* and edited the magazine (later *The Anglo-Welsh Review*) from 1949 to 1961, when he left Wales to teach at an international school in the Netherlands. Six years later he returned to Wales to take up a post as senior lecturer in the English department at Trinity College, Carmarthen, and he remained there until his retirement.

As editor and critic he made a significant contribution to the study of Anglo-Welsh literature, arguing in numerous essays, and in his *An Introduction to Anglo-Welsh Literature* (Cardiff, 1970), that from the late fifteenth century there has been a tradition of writing by Welshmen in the English language which deserves wider recognition, particularly in the schools of Wales. He has also edited, with Roland Mathias, an influential anthology, *Anglo-Welsh Poetry 1480–1980* (1984).

Before his departure for the Netherlands, Garlick published two volumes of his verse, *Poems from the Mountain-House* (1950) and *The Welsh-speaking Sea* (1954), as well as a long poem for radio, *Blaenau Observed* (1957). Since his return he has published a trilogy of verse collections: *A Sense of Europe* (1968), *A Sense of Time* (1972), and *Incense* (1976). The unity of these three volumes is in their verse-forms, often intricately structured, and in their common themes, which include a nationalist view of Wales, the poet's adopted country, as an integral part of European civilization, a passionate concern for justice and an admiration for the non-violent campaigns of *Cymdeithas yr Iaith Gymraeg* (The Welsh Language Society), and a preoccupation with language, especially English as one of the languages of a fully bilingual Wales.

A number of new poems, written since he left the Roman Catholic Church, appeared in Raymond Garlick's *Collected Poems 1946–86* (Llandysul, 1987). There is an autobiographical essay by the poet in *Artists in Wales*, ed. Meic Stephens (Llandysul, 1973). [MS

GARRETT, George (1929–), was born in Orlando, Florida, and educated at Columbia and Princeton. Since the mid-1950s he has held a number of academic appointments, most prominently at Hollins College, the University of South Carolina, and the University of Virginia, where he was appointed Henry Hoyns Professor of Creative Writing in 1984. Garrett is a complete man of letters who has published in all genres, including short stories, screenplays, and literary criticism, and who has edited anthologies and literary reviews. His first collection of poems, *The Reverend Ghost*, appeared in 1957 in Scribner's Poets of Today series. Since then he has published six collections, including *For a Bitter Season: New and Selected Poems* (Columbia, Mo., 1967) and *The Collected Poems of George Garrett* (Fayetteville, Ark., 1984), as well as numerous chapbooks and broadsides.

Garrett's wit, literary sophistication, and deft handling of traditional forms link him to the academic poets of the 1950s, like *Nemerov and *Wilbur, but he has also written a substantial number of free-verse lyrics. He is at his best as a writer of intelligent light verse, satirical epigrams and invectives, and topical poems, all genres that have become rare in contemporary American poetry. A lifelong Episcopalian, Garrett draws on religious subjects for poems like 'Revival', which describes ironically the fervour of Southern fundamentalists. 'Buzzard', a frequently anthologized poem, depicts a predatory bird as the appropriate emblem of both religious and poetic inspiration. He is also the author of a number of sensitive love poems. In recent years Garrett has concentrated on writing fiction, which includes *An Evening Performance: New and Selected Short Stories* (1985); *Poison Pen* (1986), an entertaining work of social and literary satire; and a trilogy of novels about Elizabethan England. [RSG

GARRIGUE, Jean (1912–72), was born in Evansville, Indiana. Her pre-Revolution ancestry was of mixed French, English, and Scottish origin. She received her BA degree at the University of Chicago, and in 1943 an MFA at the University of Iowa. She settled in New York's Greenwich Village and taught occasionally at various colleges, and from 1968 to 1970 she was appointed scholar, Radcliffe Institute for Independent Study. She died of Hodgkins disease in December 1972.

The individuality evident from her first publication in the Fall 1941 issue of the *Kenyon Review* accounted for her swift emergence as one of her generation's leading poets. In addition to the seven volumes of poems that followed, she also published a novella, *The Animal Hotel* (New York, 1966), and the collection *Chartres and Prose Poems* (New York, 1971). Among American poets her strongest affinities were with Hart *Crane, and among English poets with Keats. She also admired greatly *Stevens and Marianne *Moore on whose poetry she published a highly regarded monograph *Marianne Moore* (Minneapolis, 1965; London, 1966).

In her poetry Garrigue relates to all things ephemeral with an intensity so charged that only language which aims to exceed itself is adequate. That she managed to combine excess with the strictness of art remains her triumph. She detects the unseen not as absence but as felt reality. This vision, running through much of her work, is suggested by the title of what was perhaps her best book, *Country Without Maps* (New York, 1964). By the time of her death, attention to her work had somewhat declined—she had little appeal for a criticism concerned solely with feminist causes—but a revival of interest is under way. Her papers have been acquired by the prestigious Berg Collection (New York) and articles on her have appeared in recent scholarly journals, including a symposium in *Twentieth Century Literature* (Hempstead, NY, 1983).

Her most representative collection remains *New and Selected Poems* (New York, 1967). For critical studies see the chapter on Garrigue in *Unassigned Frequencies*, by Laurence Lieberman (Urbana, Ill., 1977), and *Jean Garrigue, A Poetics of Plentitude*, by Lee Upton (Madison, NJ, 1991).

[AG

GASCOYNE, David (Emery) (1916–), was born at Harrow and educated at Salisbury Cathedral Choir School and Regent Street Polytechnic in London. In 1932, while still at school, he published his first book of poems, *Roman Balcony*. In 1933 his poems appeared in *New Verse*, and his semi-autobiographical novel, *Opening Day*, was published. On the advance of royalties he visited Paris, home of the *Surrealist movement that he already admired. In *A Short Survey of Surrealism* (1935) he gave one of the first accounts of the movement published in England. He was then 19. He was one of the few British poets to be strongly influenced by the movement, as is evident from his second book of poems, *Man's Life Is This Meat*, published in 1936, the year of the Surrealist Exhibition in London. In September he joined the Communist Party, and the following month went briefly to Spain.

In the autumn of 1937 he came upon Pierre Jean Jouve's *Poèmes de la Folie de Hölderlin* (1930), which had a profound effect on him, as described in *Paris Journal* (1978); and in 1937 he published a volume of original poems and translations, *Hölderlin's Madness*. The influence of Jouve was an abiding one and is felt in Gascoyne's most important book, *Poems 1937–42*, where there is a new, religious quality.

During the latter years of the Second World War Gascoyne worked as an actor and wrote little poetry. In 1947 he returned to Paris, out of which came the title-poem of his next book, *A Vagrant* (1950). It contained some powerful poems, but was marred by what the author called 'make-weight verse'. By this time he was much engaged by Existentialism, particularly the work of the Russian philosopher Leon Chestov.

In the early Fifties he was commissioned to write a long poem for radio, which was finally broadcast in 1955 and published the following year as *Night Thoughts*. During the Fifties he lived in France and suffered medical and psychological problems due to the use of amphetamines, to which he alludes in *The Sun at Midnight* (1970). He has written hardly any poetry since *Night Thoughts*.

Gascoyne is an uneven writer, but his work includes visionary poems of an often harrowing religious and philosophical intensity, unusual in poets of his generation. His work is marked by a depth of response, seldom encountered in British writing, to modern European poetry, his translations from which appeared as *Collected Verse Translations* (Oxford, 1970). His *Collected Poems 1988* (Oxford, 1988) contains a valuable memoir that serves as an introduction to the poems. [ATT

GEDDES, Gary (1940–), was born in Vancouver and grew up in British Columbia and Saskatchewan. Educated at the University of British Columbia and the University of Toronto, he was once writer-in-residence at the University of Alberta. He now lives in Dunvegan, Ontario, and commutes to Montreal where he teaches at Concordia University. The settings of his poems reflect his wide travel—notably in the Far East.

Political, but not in any partisan way, Geddes is deeply concerned with 'what we can't afford to forget about our private and collective pasts'. Like Al *Purdy, he often finds himself among graves, archaeological relics, and 'lost manuscripts | charting connections'. There is a strong narrative element in his poetry: see, in particular, 'Sandra Lee Scheuer' and longer, fragmented poems such as *War & other measures* (Toronto, 1976) and *The Terracotta Army* (Ottawa, 1984). 'Sandra Lee Scheuer' is about a student killed at Kent State University on 4 May 1970 by the Ohio National Guard. *War & other measures* is a collection of related lyrics and narrative fragments imaginatively reconstructing the life of Paul Joseph Chartier, who died in the men's washroom of the Canadian House of Commons on 18 May 1966, when the bomb he was carrying accidentally exploded. *The Terracotta Army* is a series of dramatic monologues in which the imagined speakers are clay soldiers from China of the third century BC.

Geddes's other volumes are: *The Acid Test* (Winnipeg, 1981) which includes 'Letter of the Master of Horse', published as a separate volume in 1973; *Changes of State* (Moose Jaw, Sask., 1986); *Hong Kong Poems* (Ottawa, 1987); *No Easy Exit* (Lantzville, BC, 1989); and *Light of Burning Towers: Poems New and Selected* (Montreal, 1990). [DRB

Generation of '68, a term now largely accepted as applying to a radical shift of poetic perspectives in Australia, stimulated by official government commitment to the Vietnam War. This released strong protest movements among young Australians (and many of their elders), and coincided with the beginnings of the 'drug culture'. The emerging poets bypassed normal channels to produce their own publications, inspired by American models. They were first given prominence in the anthology *Australian Poetry Now*, edited by Thomas *Shapcott in 1970. As a poetic movement, the 'Generation of '68' served to challenge existing conventions of poetic style and form and had a profound influence on major older poets, such as John *Blight and David *Campbell, as well as creating a wide audience for the young poets involved. Although John *Tranter in his 1979 anthology *The New Australian Poetry* assumed the role of spokesman (male poets predominated), two talented poets who died young—Michael *Dransfield and Charles *Buckmaster—perhaps best exemplify the freshness and vulnerability of the period. What is of particular importance, however, is that many poets whose writing first found its focus in the specific politics of the time were to continue to develop as writers (e.g. Robert *Adamson, Alan *Wearne, John Tranter) and now occupy a central position in Australian poetry. [TWS

Georgian Poetry, was a term coined by Edward Marsh in 1911 to signal a reaction against the expansive sententiousness of the Victorians and to proclaim his belief that 'English poetry is now once again putting on new strength and beauty', as he said in his preface to *Georgian Poetry 1911–1912*. This anthology, published by Harold *Monro in 1912, was followed by four further volumes, the last of which appeared shortly before *The Waste Land* in 1922, a chronological misfortune which partly explains the common perception of 'Georgian Poetry' as a species of lightweight, sentimental lyricism catapulted into deserved oblivion by modernism; furthermore, attention lavished on the 'war poets' in general, and on Wilfred *Owen in particular, has prevented many readers from noticing the other poets who were writing in the second decade of the century. Yet the Georgians were considered daring and indeed revolutionary in the literary context of their time: the anthologies included poets as controversial as D. H. *Lawrence and as considerable as Robert *Graves, who later vigorously denounced the movement; other contributors included Edmund *Blunden, Rupert *Brooke, W. H. *Davies, Walter *de la Mare, John *Masefield, and Siegfried *Sassoon. In his Penguin anthology Georgian Poetry (Harmondsworth, 1960), James *Reeves argued plausibly for the exclusion of Lawrence and for the inclusion of Owen and Edward *Thomas, thus defining Georgianism in terms of style rather than as a label for anyone who appeared in the anthologies: this strategy, by extending the range of subject-matter and by emphasizing the poets' formal qualities, presented the movement in its most coherent and persuasive light.   [NP

GHISELIN, Brewster (1903–), was born in Webster Groves, Missouri, and for most of his life worked as a teacher of English at the University of Utah, Salt Lake City, where from 1971 he was emeritus professor. Although admired during the 1950s by such poets as W. S. *Merwin and, later, James *Dickey and Kathleen *Raine, his poetry, the bulk of which may be read in Windrose: Poems 1929–1979 (Salt Lake City, 1980), has not reached an international audience. He has written that his 'central subject' is 'man's struggle for breath, for being and light', and his poetry is concomitantly fervid—although always in a disciplined manner—owing much to *Eliot, Hopkins, and, perhaps above all, to St-John Perse. It is never less than carefully and conscientiously written. Ghiselin's earlier verse, as in his first collection, Against the Circle (New York, 1946), was polished and elegant, reflecting the then prevailing *New Criticism; this later gave way to a broader and more (as it has been described) 'tidal' style. Ghiselin was editor of the Rocky Mountain Review, which later became the Western Review, and he was a member of the editorial advisory board of

Concerning Poetry from 1968. See also The Dreamers (Winston-Salem, NC, 1981), and Brewster Ghiselin Issue, Blue Hotel, 1 (Lincoln, Nebr., 1980).   [MS-S

GHOSE, Zulfikar (1935–), was born in Sialkot, Pakistan. He took a degree in English and philosophy at Keele University, and, before becoming a teacher in London, was cricket correspondent of the Observer. He is now professor of English at the University of Austin, Texas. He has written some dozen novels—including one, The Texas Inheritance (London, 1980), under the name of William Strang—and two books of criticism as well as five collections of poetry. At first associated with B. S. *Johnson, with whom he co-authored a book of stories (Statement Against Corpses, London, 1964), and with Johnson's somewhat misconceived poetic experimentation, he has recently—especially in his fiction—gravitated to more sophisticated genres, demonstrating the influence of his philosophical studies. Philip *Hobsbaum has said that Ghose's 'precision of detail is a pattern about a void'. But students of 1960s so-called *'syllabics' and of predominantly intellectual poetry, such as was most notably and polemically practised by the Romanian mathematician Ion Barbu (called by him 'passion on ice'), would find his work rewarding. See his autobiography, Confessions of a Native Alien (London, 1965), Penguin Modern Poets 25 (with Gavin Ewart and B. S. Johnson, Harmondsworth, 1974), and A Memory of Asia (Austin, Tex., 1984).   [MS-S

GIBBON, (William) Monk (1896–1987), was born in Dublin. He fought in the First World War and went on to Keble College, Oxford. He was an associate of *AE, and edited his The Living Torch (London, 1937). Gibbon is less well known for his poetry than for his revealing memoirs of his friend *Yeats, The Masterpiece and the Man: Yeats as I Knew Him (London, 1959), which was taken, at the time of its appearance, as 'refractory'—the great poet had found Gibbon 'argumentative'. His own poetry, not much noticed, but respected, was little influenced by Irish models, but rather, in the manner of its presentation, by late Victorians and Edwardians such as Robert *Bridges. It is unashamedly replete with poeticisms, inversions, archaisms, and commonplace emotions—which he has defended as proper to poetry—but is nevertheless graceful and well made. At his occasional best he has achieved, in poetry, a terse epigrammatic quality, rather at odds with his less-inspired although technically deft conventional manner. See *The Branch of Hawthorn Tree* (Dublin, 1927) and *The Velvet Bow and Other Poems* (London, 1972).   [MS-S

GIBSON, Wilfred Wilson (1872–1962), was born in Hexham. He was four times rejected for service in the First World War on account of his poor sight, but eventually he did serve as a private (1917–19). He founded, with Rupert *Brooke and Lascelles *Abercrombie, *New Numbers*, a short-lived magazine of *Georgian poetry. With Abercrombie and *de la Mare he benefited from Brooke's will. Gibson, a too-prolific and typical Georgian if ever there was one, specialized in dour dramatic poems, often with artificial surprise endings modelled (it has been suggested) on the American short-story writer O. Henry. Although he was briefly well known as a 'realist', and for his active participation in the Georgian movement, it must be recorded that Gibson's work was consistently uninspired and rhythmically flat. It reads, at best, like a prose blend of Edward *Thomas, *Frost, and de la Mare. Claims that a few war poems, such as 'Long Tom', are exceptional, do not stand up to investigation. But he was conscientious, honest, and dogged. Many volumes succeeded the large *Collected Poems 1905–1925* (London, 1926).   [MS-S

GILBERT, Jack (1925–), was born in Pittsburgh, Pennsylvania, and educated at the University of Pittsburgh and at San Francisco State College. Recipient of the Yale Younger Poets Award for *Views of Jeopardy* (New Haven, Conn., 1962), he served as chief lecturer on American Literature for the US State Department in the 1970s. His second collection, *Monolithos: Poems, 1962–1982* (New York, 1982),

chronicles his later migratory and reclusive life in Italy, Japan, and Greece, where he lived with the poet Linda *Gregg.

His preference for writing brief, elliptical, understated poems is best understood as a corrective to the discursive excesses of *Beat and conversational poetry. Despite his distrust of artfulness, many of his most memorable poems, like 'The Abnormal Is Not Courage', 'Don Giovanni on His Way to Hell', and 'In Dispraise of Poetry', focus on literary and historical subjects. Narrating the frustrations of a self seeking to build a redeeming spirituality through Eros, asceticism, and travel, his best poems gain depth and resonance from their allusive Aegean settings. His work is unified in theme and tone; but with two sparing collections published over thirty years, it is also fragmentary, mysteriously incomplete, like the statuary of the Mediterranean vistas he often describes.

Discussions of *Monolithos* appeared in *The New York Review of Books* (23 Sept, 1982; a review by Helen Vendler) and *The New York Times Book Review* (12 Sept. 1982; a review by Richard Tillinghast).   [DWF

GILBERT, Kevin J. (1933–), was born in Condobolin, New South Wales, the son of an English-Irish father and Aboriginal-Irish mother. His mother's Wiradjuri people fiercely resisted the white invasion. Orphaned at 7, Gilbert remembers seven Wiradjuri elders 'who knew of the old things'—namely the language, customs, sacred spots, and massacre sites. In 1957 he was charged with the murder of his white wife; no defence witnesses were called, he was given life, and spent the next fourteen-and-a-half years in some of the state's worst gaols. His first play (and the first by an Aboriginal), *The Cherry Pickers* (written 1970; pub. 1988) and many poems were written while he was incarcerated.

His release, after a public campaign, coincided with the publication of his first volume of poems, *End of Dream-Time* (1971), and a new wave of Aboriginal militancy. Gilbert played a pivotal role: in 1972 he helped organize the Black Moratorium and the famous Aboriginal

Embassy on the lawns of Parliament House; he was charged (and exonerated) with threatening to kill the queen; and he published *Because a White Man 'Il Never Do It* (1973), his first attempt to contribute to 'the regeneration of the Aborigine'. In the last twenty years, through his passionate espousal of Aboriginal rights and the publication of *Living Black—Blacks Talk To Kevin Gilbert* (1977; repr. Ringwood, Victoria, 1978), *Inside Black Australia—an Anthology of Aboriginal Poetry* (1988), and *Aboriginal Sovereignty Justice the Law and Land* (1988), Gilbert has emerged as the most political and iconoclastic of all Aboriginal writers. He ran the Treaty '88 Campaign, and in 1990 began Australian Aboriginal Community Aid Incorporated.

Like virtually all Aboriginal creative writers in Australia today, Gilbert is an activist first and a writer second. His poetry in the 1970s falls broadly into four categories—Aboriginal character studies, strident social protests, indictments of 'Jackies' (career Aboriginals, 'lickin' smilin' lyin''), and calls to action, such as 'Mister Man', 'The Flowering . . .', 'Look Koori', and 'Me and Jackamari Talkin' About Land Rights'. His more recent poems maintain the rage but he is now more positive, at times even cautiously optimistic.

The Blackside—People Are Legends and other poems (St Lucia, Qld., 1990) is the most substantial collection in print. It is complemented by Gilbert's essays (and new poems) in *Imagining the Real: Australian Writing in the Nuclear Age* (1987) and *Looking Beyond Yesterday: The Australian Artist and New Paths to Our Future* (1990).

[DH

GILLIES, Valerie (1948–), was born in Canada, but was brought up and educated in Edinburgh, where she attended the University. A year at the University of Mysore in southern India provided the subjects of the best poems in her first collection *Each Bright Eye* (Edinburgh, 1977).

Whether about people, places, children, animals, or objects, Gillies's poetry hinges on uncluttered observations and insights, often delivered in moods of puzzled affection. Disclosures of a more unnerving kind run through her work too; however, its general effect is gentle, settled and benign, although without an excess of understatement or soft-hearted benevolence. The unshowy lyricism of her first two collections stems from a technique that is essentially one of free verse leaving room for the possibilities of a near-musical tonality. Some poems in *Bed of Stone* (Edinburgh, 1984) attempt more organized rhythm and rhyme ('The Pause', 'Eagle', 'The Drill'). Her relaxed, scrupulous formality is extended in *The Chanter's Tune* (Edinburgh, 1990). [DED

GILMORE, Mary (Mary Jean Cameron) (1865–1962). Born into a family of pioneer settlers in southern New South Wales, Mary Gilmore was the first woman member of the Australian Workers Union and the first woman on its executive. In 1893 she helped to found the socialist New Australia settlement in Paraguay; marrying there, she returned to Australia with her husband and son in 1902. Editor for many years of the women's page of the *Worker* newspaper, she became famous for her essays and articles, which often rise to the quality of prose poetry, especially in the reminiscences she collected in the volume *Old Days: Old Ways* in 1933. Through her own and other newspapers Mary Gilmore championed many causes over the years, from invalid pensions to a proper status for illegitimates.

Her reputation as a poet began to grow with the publication of her first collection, *Marri'd*, in 1910, and was consummated by the rapturous reception of her second volume, *The Passionate Heart*, in 1918. Of a reformist rather than a revolutionary temper, fiercely patriotic, with a real love for the downtrodden of all periods of Australian history, she could extol the convicts and pioneers and yet write with clearer eyes than any of her contemporaries about the great glossed-over crime of settlement days, the wholesale slaughter of the Aborigines. In the latter half of her long life she became the legendary elder and remembrancer of the Labor movement, then of the nation, and even thirty years after her death her legend continues, to a degree, to inhibit a clear assessment of her published work. The beloved figure of Dame Mary may be hiding a better poet than recent criticism has allowed. Since the 1960s, she has tended to be represented fairly sparsely in anthologies, and very often by the same few short, concentrated lyrics: 'Nationality', 'Old Botany Bay', sometimes 'Never Admit the Pain'. All of these do represent one side of her verse, a side equally well illustrated by the less familiar but deeply moving elegy 'The Little Shoes That Died'.

Perhaps surprisingly for a cradle Presbyterian and lifelong socialist, Mary Gilmore at times evinced a mystical and rather Catholic spirituality, which not only allowed her to contribute simultaneously, in the 1950s, to the Communist paper *Tribune* and the *Catholic Weekly*, but evoked several fine religious poems, notably the title-poem of her 1931 collection *The Rue Tree*. Living across a great span of literary epochs, and tugged this way and that by the impulses of Victorian romanticism, bush balladry, and the pre-modernist modernity of contemporary newspaper verse, she seems at times uncertain in her diction, veering between the colloquial, the poeticizing, and many usually unfortunate strains of dialect. On the other hand, there is a lesser-known side of her verse which connects with the manner and sensuous particularity of her best essays, and achieves the supple density of poems such as 'The Harvesters'.

A *Collected Poems of Mary Gilmore* is still reprinted fairly regularly by Collins/Angus and Robertson, and her *Old Days: Old Ways* has gone through many editions, but truly comprehensive editions of her prose and verse are still awaited. [LM

GINSBERG, Allen (1926–), was born in New Jersey to Naomi and Louis Ginsberg, high-school teacher and poet. He attended Columbia University, which he used as a base for forays into Greenwich Village, befriending William Burroughs, Jack Kerouac, and other members of the *Beat generation. After graduation he moved to San Francisco, where poet Lawrence *Ferlinghetti published his extraordinarily popular *Howl and Other Poems* (1956), its outrageous, Whitmanesque title poem a *vers-libre* anthem for the entire Beatnik revolt against middle-class mores and the political establishment's 'death culture', quite explicit anent Ginsberg's promiscuous homosexuality. Ginsberg himself emerged as the youth movement's most visible guru, and his frequent public performances were more 'happenings' than poetry readings, as he chanted, made music, smoked pot, and did not hesitate to strip naked.

His earliest poetry, later gathered in *Empty Mirror* (1960), had been influenced by William Blake and the seventeenth-century Metaphysicals, but Western mysticisim and elaborate design gave way to Zen Buddhism and a devotion to the 'thing itself' poetics of William Carlos *Williams, which Ginsberg translated into a kind of spontaneous composition. *Kaddish and Other Poems* (1961), especially the powerful title poem, reflected the impact of Robert *Lowell's *Life Studies* (1959) in its headlight-harsh approach to intimate family matters, in this case his mother's insanity. The books published over the next decade or so, including *Reality Sandwiches* (1963), *Planet News: 1961–1967* (1968), and *T.V. Baby Poems* (1968), as he roamed the globe as unofficial youth ambassador and anti-war spokesman (being elected 'King of the May' by a vast gathering of Czechoslovakian students in 1965), offer little more than mildly clever observations from a raw travel diary, with the exception of 'At Apollinaire's Grave' and 'To Aunt Rose' in *Reality Sandwiches*.

As the latter poem suggests and *Kaddish* had proven, Ginsberg's self-indulgent aesthetic requires the harness of profound grief and fear to ride it into memorable verse. It is not surprising, then, that transcending familiar tourist litanies, *The Fall of America: Poems of These States* (1973) represents something of an artistic recovery, its elegiac bass chord resonant with mid-life nostalgia and an intensifying existential anxiety, best realized by 'Consulting I Ching Smoking Pot Listening to the Fugs Sing Blake', and continued into *Plutonian Ode* (1981), National Book Award winner.

Ginsberg's influence has declined, generally restricted to ageing members of the *New York School and San Francisco's college radicals. The recent surge of interest in formal verse has not aided his cause, though his fame as historic rebel and star performer has actually grown. Poetically, however, despite a refreshing refusal to mature, he has lapsed into comic self-parody, incanting against the evils of tobacco, for example, or provoking his large bourgeois audiences with a hymn to his love-torn anus.

Harper and Row (New York) published his *Collected Poems 1947–1980* in 1984. See also *On the Poetry of Allen Ginsberg*, ed. Lewis Hyde (Ann Arbor, Mich., 1984) and *Allen Ginsberg* (New York, 1989), by Barry Miles.   [EB

GIOIA, Dana (1950–), was born in Los Angeles of Italian and Mexican descent and raised in the blue-collar suburb of Hawthorne. He attended Catholic schools before moving on to Stanford University, where he edited its literary magazine *Sequoia*. He spent two years doing graduate work in comparative literature at Harvard where he studied with Robert *Fitzgerald and Elizabeth *Bishop and received his MA in 1975, before returning to Stanford for his MBA. Since 1977 he has worked as a business executive in New York while contributing poetry and critical essays to such journals as *The New Yorker* and *The Hudson Review*. In addition, he has edited the stories of Weldon *Kees, co-edited two anthologies of Italian poetry, and translated Montale's *Mottetti: Poems of Love* (St Paul, Minn., 1990).

Gioia's poems range in subject-matter from meditations on the landscape of California ('California Hills in August') and his youth spent there ('Cruising with the Beach Boys') to ones on his life as a business man in suburban Westchester County ('Eastern Standard Time' and 'In Cheever Country'); from poems that examine the 'Lives of the Great Composers' to such brief lyrics on the evanescence of love and the nature of mortality as 'Parts of Summer Weather' and 'The Gods of Winter'. 'The Room Upstairs' and 'Counting the Children' are psychologically astute dramatic monologues whose isolated speakers contemplate the com-

plexities and varieties of love. His sequence, 'Daily Horoscope', is a philosophical musing on how to accept the limitations of everyday existence in the context of brief epiphanic glimpses into a world of ideal beauty. A man adeptly juggling, like *Stevens, business and poetic careers, Gioia makes this his animating theme. His poetry is grounded in traditional metrics and characterized by distinct musical cadences and technical virtuosity, gifts which, in conjunction with his essays, especially the much-reprinted 'Notes on the *New Formalism', place him at the front of that movement.

His collections are *Daily Horoscope* (St Paul, 1986), and *The Gods of Winter* (St Paul and Calstock, Cornwall, 1991). See also: *Can Poetry Matter? Essays on Poetry and American Culture* (St Paul, 1992).   [RMcP

GIOVANNI, Nikki (1943–), was born Yolande Cornelia Giovanni, Jr., in Knoxville, Tennessee. Entering Fisk University in 1960, she edited the university literary magazine and founded a chapter of SNCC (Student Non-Violent Coordinating Committee) on campus. Previously a right-wing Republican, she became involved in radical and black-power movements and, after studying further at the universities of Pennsylvania and Columbia, she immersed herself in black community and cultural projects. Her first two books, *Black Feeling, Black Talk* (New York, 1967) and *Black Judgement* (Detroit, 1969) grew out of this activity and reflect her commitment at the time to the development of a separate African-American identity.

Her third collection *Re: Creation* (Detroit, 1970) was not notably different from her first two. In 1969, however, Giovanni gave birth to a son to whom she dedicated her first book of poems for children, *Spin a Soft Black Song* (New York, 1970); and in 1971, after travelling to the Caribbean, she published *Gemini: An Extended Autobiographical Statement on my First Twenty-Five Years of Being a Black Poet* (Indianapolis and London, 1976). These two books reveal a more introspective style and approach. 'I'm into a very personal thing now . . . and I'm more settled', she said at the time of the publication of her next collection *My House* (New York, 1972). She was also achieving wider fame thanks to the popularity of her album, *Truth Is On Its Way* (1971), on which she reads some of her poetry against the background of gospel music. Work published since has continued to tap a more personal vein while also promoting ideals of universal human relatedness. Notable recent collections include *Cotton Candy on a Rainy Day* (New York, 1978) and *Those Who Read the Night Winds* (New York, 1983). Useful biographical and critical material is to be found in *African-American Poets since 1955*, ed. Trudier Harris and Thadious M. Davis (Detroit, 1985).   [RJG

GLASSCO, John (Stinson) (1909–81), was born in Montreal of a prominent family, was educated in private schools and briefly attended McGill University before going to Paris in 1928, an experience fictively retold in his *Memoirs of Montparnasse* (1970).

He published his first collection of verse, *The Deficit Made Flesh*, in 1958 (Toronto), and this was followed by *A Point of Sky* (Toronto, 1964), *Selected Poems* (Toronto, 1971), and *Montreal* (Montreal, 1973), a long satire/parody. As a writer of prose, Glassco, who had a highly adaptable style, tried his hand at completing Aubrey Beardsley's (1872–98) *Under the Hill* (1959), and went on to more titillating work in *The English Governess* (1960), *The Temple of Pederasty* (1970), *Fetish Girl* (1972), and *The Fatal Woman* (1974). In addition, Glassco had a distinguished career as a sensitive and skilful translator of French-Canadian writing, beginning with an early interest in Saint-Denys Garneau (1912–43), whose *Journal* he translated in 1962 and *Complete Poems* in 1975. He also edited (translating many of the selections himself) a landmark anthology, *The Poetry of French Canada* (Toronto, 1970).

In his poetry Glassco has shown himself to be a traditional stylist concerned with the decaying landscape of a particularly stony but picturesque part of rural south-eastern Quebec. Widely read, occasionally decadent in spirit and given to the fine phrasings of a genuinely elegant sensibility, Glassco has fashioned a strong if elegiac statement out of the tension between a

remembered, relic-strewn past and the acquisitive stresses of contemporary life.   [MG

GLOVER, Denis (1912–80), born in Dunedin, New Zealand, was both poet and printer, and he began both careers at Canterbury University College. The Caxton Press, which he established first as a university club press in 1933 and then as a commercial venture in Christchurch, gave to a generation of New Zealand writers the chance of publication with a quality of typography that commanded international respect. In the Second World War he served with the Royal Navy, and helped interest John *Lehmann, the editor of *Penguin New Writing*, in New Zealand authors of the time.

Glover's poetry celebrates the vitality of individual toil and delights in the sea and his country's landscape. It also reflects his pleasure in sport and his wide knowledge of classical and renaissance literature. But, like many of his generation, Glover reveals a melancholy in his treatment of mortality and human insignificance in the presence of the landscape. Though parts of his prolific output are ephemeral, the best of his work—the 'Sings Harry' cycle and the 'Arawata Bill' poems—remain valued, while his ironic ballad 'The Magpies' may now be the single most-recognized poem in his own country.

Selections of Glover's poems were published in his lifetime in *Enter Without Knocking* (Christchurch, 1964 and 1971) and posthumously in *Selected Poems*, introduced by Allen Curnow (Auckland, 1981). See also his autobiography *Hot Water Sailor* (Wellington, 1962), and J. E. P. Thomson, *Denis Glover* (Wellington, 1977).   [WSB

GLÜCK, Louise (1943–), was born in New York and raised on Long Island. Glück, who is married to John Dranow, a writer, has made her home in Plainfield, Vermont, for many years. From this base she has taught at various American colleges and universities, including Columbia, the University of Iowa, and Williams College. Her first book of poems, *Firstborn*, appeared in 1968. That volume, deeply influenced by the poetry of Sylvia *Plath, dealt in images of contemporary wastelands and focused on lost lives, figures moving through a postmodern suburban landscape with severe physical or emotional damage. 'The poison| that replaces air took over', she writes in 'The Chicago Train', which opens this collection of harsh, elliptical poems. Though many of the poems centre on domestic scenes, they consistently reach for a larger, symbolic meaning, as in the title-poem, 'Firstborn', where even a 'lone onion' in a bowl of soup is seen to be 'floating like Ophelia, caked with grease'.

Glück's breakthrough came with *The House on Marshland* (New York, 1975), which began the work of turning the family circle into a kind of symbolic galaxy, with biblical and other mythical allusions underpinning the literal level of the poems. Glück's characteristic style: terse, hard, deeply imagistic and lyrical, emerges here in full force. One of the best poems of this volume, 'The Pond', opens with a haunting image typical of Glück: 'Night covers the pond with its wing.' The pond becomes emblematic—of memory, the reservoir of all myths, hopes, and dreams. Having by now moved to Vermont, Glück begins to rely heavily on natural imagery, as in 'Flowering Plum', where she says in a typical line: 'In spring from the black branches of the flowering plum tree | the woodthrush issues its routine | message of survival.'

This 'message of survival' is consistently mixed with a harsher message of despair in Glück's work. *Descending Figure* appeared in 1980, taking up again the themes of family life and human loss, and featuring a memorable sequence, 'The Garden', a subtle meditation on the theme of human solitude and death in the context of the poet's origins and love relations. Glück's fourth collection was *The Triumph of Achilles* (New York, 1985), a volume dedicated to issues of 'knowing' and 'clarifying' the poet's sense of the world, whose title-poem ends with Achilles grieving for Patroclus in his tent, 'a victim of the part that loved, | the part that was mortal'. It was followed by *Ararat* (New York, 1990), and *The Wild Iris* (New York, 1992), which won the Pulitzer Prize. For criticism, see

Helen Vendler, *Part of Nature, Part of Us* (Cambridge, Mass., 1980). [JP

GOGARTY, Oliver St John (1878–1957), was born in Dublin. After a leisurely education, which included a term at Oxford as well as medical school in Dublin, he qualified as an ear-and-throat surgeon. For a time, owing to the demands of medical etiquette, he was obliged to keep his literary persona, such as that of playwright for the Abbey, under wraps. He was most famous for his bawdiness and wit, and for being the model for Buck Mulligan in *Joyce's Ulysses*. In verse he was a gifted epigrammatist, but *Yeats was scarcely justified in describing him as 'one of the great lyric poets of our age'. Now his graceful, if old-fashioned verse is a little neglected. His much-anthologized 'Leda and the Swan' is often quoted as evidence of his mastery of form, as are 'Ringsend' and 'The Crab Tree'. Insistently anti-modernist, he could be ponderous and, for an esteemed wit, portentous and 'poetical'; but at his best he is sonorous, if never wholly original. He lived in America from 1939 till his death. See *Collected Poems* (London, 1951) and *Unselected Poems* (Baltimore, 1954). See also, J. B. Lyons, *Oliver St John Gogarty* (Lewisburg, 1976) and U. O'Connor, *Oliver St John Gogarty: A Poet and his Times* (London, 1964). [MS-S

GOLDBARTH, Albert (1948–), was raised in Chicago and studied at the universities of Illinois, Iowa, and Utah. He has taught at Cornell and the University of Texas: he is currently Distinguished Professor of Humanities at Wichita State University.

Albert Goldbarth is one of the most prolific poets of his generation, having published numerous volumes and chapbooks since 1973, sometimes as many as two a year. This fact is not merely incidental to his poetry, but has everything to do with its identifying traits, above all its almost manic prolixity. Goldbarth was one of the first poets to revolt against the minimalist poetics established in the 1960s by poets like James *Wright, *Bly, *Merwin, and *Strand. Rather than offering quiet, bare epiphanies insulated from the chaos and vulgarity of contemporary America, Goldbarth wades into his cultural surroundings with equal measures of glee and disgust. In his poetry the 'discursive' style called for by the slightly older poet Robert *Pinsky takes on a nearly pathological quality; Goldbarth's many essay-poems seem less interested in their ostensible subjects (the history of glass, novelty stores, etc.) than in their own compulsion to generate language as profusely as possible. In a wry self-critique appended to his long poem *Opticks* (New York, 1974), Goldbarth writes that his 'radical style consists of never using one word where three can be substituted', a principle that seems expressly designed to flout writing-workshop conventions. What makes Goldbarth's poetry engaging is its dense and intricate texture, which is achieved in part through his ear for bizarre words from diverse vocabularies, some technical ('syzygial', 'defalcation'), and some colloquial ('rinkydink'), and in part through his eye for eccentric particulars of all kinds: kitsch objects, outlandish news items, odd scientific or historical facts. These strands are skilfully woven together, always with some central thread of earnest meditation serving to unify, however tenuously, the motley fabric. Reading Goldbarth can be both exhilarating and fatiguing; few poets offer a greater sense of profusion, yet ultimately his poems are more concerned with the enervating effects of culture than with its capacity to nourish. Among his more recent books are *Popular Culture* (Columbus, Ohio, 1990) and *Heaven and Earth: A Cosmology* (Athens, Ga., 1991). [RG

GOLDSWORTHY, Peter (1951–) was born in Winlaton, South Australia, and educated in medicine at the University of Adelaide. He has sought since then to combine medical practice with writing, in more or less equal measures. In 1982 he published both his first book of verse, *Readings from Ecclesiastes*, and his first collection of short stories, *Archipelagoes*. His novel *Maestro* (1989) approaches the racing wit of his best poetry.

The small, skinny poems in Goldsworthy's earlier volume give little hint of the intellectual sharpness which distinguishes the prize-winning *This Goes with That* (Sydney, 1989). These stylishly chiselled poems offer rueful ironies at the expense of the universe. Reaching into parody, domestic lyricism and an inventive use of kennings, they spell out an acute, if modest, epistemology. In every line the poet strives to make language elegant enough to do justice to the world as comedy. In the process he is frequently self-dismantling. [CW-C

GONZALES, Rodolfo 'Corky' (1928–), literally fought his way out of the *barrio* in Denver, Colorado, by becoming a one-time Golden Gloves boxing champion and national prizefighter. In the early 1950s, however, he turned to politics, founding, in 1966, the influential Denver Crusade for Justice. In 1967 he published *I Am Joaquín/Yo Soy Joaquín*, a bilingual, free-verse history-in-small of *chicanismo* in which 'Joaquín' serves as the everyman voice of *la raza*, the people. Beginning from the defeat and Hispanicization of the Mayan and Aztec civilizations, Joaquín delineates each stage in the Amerindian-Spanish history of *los chicanos*—through, in turn, Mexican Independence (1821), the ceding of much of northern Mexico to the United States (1848), the Mexican revolution (1910–20), and, finally, the modern 'border' Mexico-America of the American south-west. As the persona for his community, Joaquín ends with a near Whitmanesque flourish against poverty and exploitation: 'La Raza! | Mejicano! | Español! | Latino! | Hispano! | Chicano! | or whatever I call myself, | I look the same | I cry | and | sing the same.'

The complete text is to be found in *I am Joaquín/Yo Soy Joaquín* (New York, 1967).

[ARL

GOODISON, Lorna (1947–), was born in Kingston, Jamaica. She studied at the Jamaica School of Art and at the School of the Art Students' League in New York. Now a free-lance writer living in Kingston, she has previously worked as an artist, designer, painter, and illustrator. Many of her poems allude to modern art and mythological subjects. 'The Mulatta and the Minotaur', for instance, is an exploration of the nature of poetry, in which feminine and masculine principles interlock. It ends by mocking Picasso's patriarchal pretensions. Her elegy, 'For Don Drummond', a musician who committed suicide after killing his girl-friend, confronts Jamaican social tensions. Her poems have become increasingly more mystical and religious, but she is a seeker rather than a dogmatist.

Goodison's books are all graced by covers illustrating her paintings; they include *Tamarind Season* (Kingston, 1980), *I Am Becoming My Mother* (London, 1986), and *Heartease* (London, 1989). [MR

GOODMAN, Paul (1911–72), was born in New York City. He was at first a teacher in a progressive school, later a lay psychologist. Acknowledged even by his admirers as an often poor and 'intellectually fractured' writer, Goodman was, as a literary-radical bohemian, none the less provocative. In the 1960s he was a notorious dissident figure, and an influential guru for the student young. He published, beginning with *Ten Lyric Poems* (New York, 1934), eighteen collections of poetry. This poetry consists of what are essentially jottings, in segments of prose, written in an awkward slang or imitation antiquated style. Much of its appeal had to do with its obsessive attention to various homo-erotic dilemmas, stated with extreme directness. Goodman, twice married and with children, was much influenced by Wilhelm Reich (despite Reich's dislike of homosexuality or ambisexuality), and the ideas of Reich dominate his poetry. See *Collected Poems* (New York, 1974), ed. Taylor Stoehr. [MS-S

GOONERATNE, Yasmine (1935–), was educated at the universities of Ceylon and Cambridge and is the foundation director of the Post-Colonial Literatures and Language Research Centre of Macquarie University, Sydney. She has published critical books on Jane Austen, Pope, and on the novelist Ruth Prawer Jhabvala. In her first book of verse, *Word, Bird, Motif* (Kandy, 1971), she captures tones varying

from the trenchant to the tender, the poignant, or the suavely savage. *The Lizard's Cry* (Kandy, 1972) employs the Sanskrit and Sinhala message-poem convention and reveals a keen, if anguished, perception of the socio-economic factors behind the 1971 insurgency. *6000 ft Death Dive* (Colombo, 1981), published after nine years' domicile in Australia, exploits a lucent sensuousness without sacrificing wit or pith. [LdeS

GOULD, Alan (1949–), was born of British-Icelandic parents; he graduated from the Australian National University in 1971. He has travelled widely and worked as a teacher, a nuclear-physics technician, and an agricultural labourer.

Gould's poetry revolves around themes of necessity and will; memory and observation; space, time, and the sea; myth-making and history. His accounts of journeys by sea and air stress a sense of continuity between the individual self and other life-forms, and the universe.

Icelandic Solitaries (1978) and *Astral Sea* (1981) both contain poetic sequences featuring Icelandic myth. Further volumes of poetry (all from Sydney) include *The Pausing of the Hours* (1984), *The Twofold Place* (1986), *Years Found in Likeness* (1988)—part of which is a libretto, 'The Great Circle', written for a choral symphony by Graham Hair—and *Formerlight* (1992). He has also published three books of fiction. [PK

GRAHAM, Jorie (1951–), daughter of sculptress Beverly Pepper, grew up in Italy and was educated at the Sorbonne, Columbia University, and the University of Iowa, where she currently teaches.

Graham's first collection, *Hybrids of Plants and of Ghosts* (Princeton, NJ, 1980) suffered from intellectual vagueness. But *Erosion* (Princeton, 1983) conveyed a sense of liberated coherence. The poems chronicled a longing for spiritual attainment in the clamorous here and now, often making use of an ingenious inventory of Donne-like conceits: 'we | stitch the earth, | it seems to me, each time | we die, going | back under, coming back up . . .' (from 'I Watched a Snake').

The End of Beauty (New York, 1987) departs radically from her previous volumes. The poems reflect the influence of Michael *Palmer and certain of the *Language poets. Connections are attenuated, leaps between fragmented sections often require reserves of faith in the leaper.

[SPB

GRAHAM, W(illiam) S(ydney) (1918–86), was born in Greenock, on the Clyde. He worked for a while as a structural engineer. His first book of verse, *Cage Without Grievance*, came out in 1942. This was followed by *The Seven Journeys* (1944) and *2nd Poems* (1945). But it was *The White Threshold* (London, 1949) and *The Nightfishing* (London, 1955) that secured his reputation, and these were followed by *Malcolm Mooney's Land* (London, 1970) and *Implements in their Places* (London, 1977). His *Collected Poems 1942–1975* came out in 1979, and, posthumously in 1993, *Aimed at Nobody*, forty-four poems in notebook and worksheet form, ed. Margaret Blackwood and Robin Skelton (both London).

Graham is often described, aptly enough, as a Romantic, for his celebration of moments of intense significance, especially those of love, in a lyrical, and sometimes bardic manner. The manner is especially at issue. For since the Forties, when Graham's work first appeared, the term 'Romantic' in discussion of contemporary poetry has come to encompass a technique associated particularly with the work of Dylan *Thomas: a high density of metaphor, especially metaphor created through the surprising use of misapplied parts of speech. Graham's early verse is very much of its time in this respect, as in 'Explanation of a Map': 'Near farms and property of bright night-time | By mileaway dogbark how there is means to say | What unseen bargain makes heavier where I walk | The meanwhile word . . .'.

The purified style of *The Nightfishing* dramatizes the uncertainty of individual identity in the context of a night fishing for herring. 'To work at waking. Yet who wakes?' The sea becomes a metaphor for the protean nature of the 'I', a flux against which credible identity can occasionally be defined in successful action. This concern becomes linked to an anxiety about the difficulties of communicating from such uncertainty. In 'Malcolm Mooney's Land' the difficulty is symbolized by the narrator's isolation in an arctic landscape where the snow and ice are 'the obstacle | Of language'. In true Romantic fashion, Graham sees the self as subject to unconscious drives. This belief, together with his interest in words, produces the memorable poem, 'What is the Language Using Us For?' The answer, it seems, is hard to find. As for the question, it only matters when we want to tell 'Each other alive about each other | Alive', as we want to do in love. Love is one of Graham's chief subjects, and he conveys a considerate tenderness in his elusive rhythms.

[ETL

GRANT, Jamie (1949–), was born in Melbourne, Australia, and has worked in publishing and bookselling. He has done occasional editing and book reviews and has toured England with a national cricket team (and has written on that subject).

Grant has become associated with a small group of poets who have claimed allegiance to Les *Murray, whose concept of a 'vernacular republic' has stressed the endurance of rural and family values as against the eclecticism of city modishness. Grant's own verse is wry, sharply observed, and with a quasi-ruminative discursiveness that is perhaps closer in spirit to the work of Geoffrey *Lehmann, a friend and contemporary of Murray. In the feuds and factions of contemporary Australian poetry, Grant's work represents an essentially conservative urban vision—nervous about expressing emotional commitment, taut, habitually ironic, but its strengths are in its uncluttered imagist decorum and selection of detail, and in a sometimes rueful self-recognition in poems that are ostensibly maps of social behaviour.

Grant's two major verse collections, both published by Angus & Robertson (Sydney), are *The Refinery* (1985) and *Skywriting* (1989).

[TWS

GRAVES, Robert (von Ranke) (1895–1985), was born in Wimbledon, the son of the Irish poet and folklorist Alfred Perceval Graves and his second wife. He began to write poetry while still at Charterhouse School, being encouraged by one of his schoolmasters there, the mountaineer George Mallory, as well as by Edward Marsh. When war broke out, he joined the Royal Welch Fusiliers. He came to know Siegfried *Sassoon while serving in France, where he was wounded and supposed dead. He became known as one of the war poets with his first collection, *Over the Brazier* (1916). His war poetry was not, however, of the calibre of Sassoon's or *Owen's, and later he suppressed it. During the war Graves married Nancy Nicolson, daughter of William Nicolson and sister of the painter Ben Nicolson. He went up to St John's College, Oxford, where one of his tutors was Percy Simpson, whose *Shakespearean Punctuation* influenced his and Laura *Riding's analysis of Shakespeare's Sonnet 129 in their *A Survey of Modernist Poetry* (1927), which in turn influenced the critical methods of the young William *Empson, and thus the course of English criticism.

Graves's poetry appeared regularly in Marsh's *Georgian Poetry* anthologies, but by 1922 it had become apparent, in volumes such as *The Pier Glass* (1921), that, although traditional in form—as it always remained—it was by no means typically Georgian. The early Graves wrote in complex experimental schemes often derived from Welsh prosody, depended heavily on nursery rhyme and ballad, and explored his feelings of guilt on lines (as his critical study *Poetic Unreason* (1925) made clear) heavily influenced by Freud. In 1925 he met the American poet Laura Riding, and from that time his attitude and style changed. He was affected not by her poetic procedures, which he never sought to imitate, but by her unique and antinomian personality, by the fact that he was in love with her, and by her major role in relieving him from the post-war trauma, or 'neurasthenia' as it was then called, from which he suffered. He began to distrust everything that had been imposed upon him by convention, and to defend some aspects of modernism (for example, the poetry of E. E. *Cummings and

Gerard Manley Hopkins, then regarded as modernistic). His poetry became a means of self-critical exploration of his own psyche. Riding became the muse to whom he submitted all his work for judgement, and his belief in her powers was, for many years, absolute. After a scandal involving her attempted suicide, Graves and Riding went to the island of Majorca (1929–36), where they carried on with publishing activities on their Seizin Press (mostly their own work, but also that of Gertrude *Stein, James *Reeves, and one or two others), and issued three volumes of the miscellany *Epilogue*. They returned to England at the outset of the Spanish Civil War, and then went to America (1939), where they parted company.

The experience of Riding soon became the basis for Graves's 'historical grammar of poetic myth', *The White Goddess* (London and New York, 1948; revd. and enlarged, 1952, 1961), a highly individualistic and influential variation on themes explored in Mario Praz's *The Romantic Agony*, and for his theory—to which he more or less adhered throughout his life—that every poet must have a muse actively destructive of all but his capacity to love. The rationale behind this is not masochistic, but rather an almost mystical desire to be purified of the kind of 'grossness' described in such poems as 'The Succubus': a reappearance, albeit in a more sophisticated form, of Graves's pre-Riding dedication, first to the Christian faith he lost in the war, and then to conventional morality. No poet, he had solemnly told Peter *Quennell at Oxford, could possibly be successful if he did not observe strict conventional morality. Many of the poems of his first phase, together with a few of his second, are collected in *Poems 1914–27* (1927). In *Poems* (1929) the new, harder manner, purged of whimsicality and sentimentality, is fully in evidence. From this time onwards Graves subjected his poems to continual revision in a series of *Collected Poems* published some in London, some in New York, some in both (1938, 1948, 1955, 1959, 1961, 1965, 1966, 1975). They first appeared in separate small collections. There is as yet no variorum edition tracing these revisions, and little detailed account of them. The poems' uniquely pungent quality comes less, perhaps, from their preoccupation with romantic love than from the poet's resistance, often ironically, sceptically, or even cynically expressed, to its demands and existential inconveniences. Thus, in Graves's best poetry, mostly written between 1930 and 1950, a naturally lyrical voice is undercut and challenged by a down-to-earth, gritty, paradoxical enlightenment on the subject of the poet's own motives and desires. Graves's more obvious exemplars include Skelton, the Metaphysicals, and, in particular, Rochester. *Hardy was the chief contemporary influence. But the flavour is Graves's own. In the last twenty-five years of his poetic activity his work became more lapidary, a textbook demonstration of poetic devotion to the muse. But it retained its epigrammatic force and its technical mastery.

Graves was a gifted translator from the classics (Apuleius's *The Golden Ass* (1950), and others), a powerful historical novelist (*I, Claudius* (1934), and many others), and a stimulating but unreliable critic. Much of the best of his criticism was done in collaboration with Riding; the rest is collected in *The Common Asphodel* (1949). His Clark Lectures, *The Crowning Privilege* (1959), and his lectures as Oxford Professor of Poetry, *Oxford Addresses on Poetry* (1962), are best approached as guides to his own idiosyncratic approach, although they contain indispensable insights. He himself privately acknowledged that the stresses of the muse, in her various appearances to him, had taken their toll of his later criticism so far as thoroughness and accuracy were concerned. His *Greek Myths* (1955) has delighted general readers and enraged scholars. The anthropological assumptions of the unscholarly *The White Goddess* are dubious, but the book remains a classic statement of an unusual and drastic romantic thesis. *Goodbye To All That* (1929, revd. edn. 1957), the least self-consciously literary of all the British First World War memoirs, also has classic status. Martin Seymour-Smith's full biography, *Robert Graves: His Life and Work* (London and New York, 1982) is based on extensive personal knowledge; Richard Perceval Graves's *The*

Assault Heroic and *The Years with Laura* (London, 1986–90), which cover the years 1895–1939 add family lore and some other detail.   [MS-S

GRAY, Sir Alexander. See LALLANS.

GRAY, John (1866–1934), was born in London. Taken out of school in 1879, he was successively a metal-turner, civil servant, aesthete, Catholic convert, and, from 1901, priest. His *Silverpoints* (subsidized by Oscar Wilde, designed by Charles Ricketts, published by the Bodley Head, 1893) contained sixteen poems and thirteen translations from the French Symbolists; as both text and object, it was the quintessential Nineties volume. After two decades of silence following his ordination, he resumed writing and publishing in his last years. His novella *Park: A Fantastic Story* (1932) was reissued in 1966 and again in 1984. Gray died four months after the death of his lifelong friend and benefactor André Raffalovich.

'The Barber' and 'Mishka' stand out from the merely decorative effects of his earliest verse, as does 'The Tree of Knowledge' from the mass of devotional poetry written between his conversion and ordination; 'The Flying Fish' (1896) is also notable. His late work is compressed, precise, and individual (at times eccentric); 'Quatrains' and 'Ode' show to especially good effect his reading of modernist poetry.

Gray's *Collected Poems* have been edited by Ian Fletcher (London, 1974; Greensville, NC, 1988). Fr. Brocard Sewell has compiled *Two Friends* (1963; essays on Gray and Raffalovich) and written *Footnote to the Nineties* (1968) and *In the Dorian Mode: A Life of John Gray* (1983). Jerusha Hull McCormack's *John Gray: Poet, Dandy, and Priest* (1991) is a critical biography.   [MP

GRAY, Robert (1945–), grew up in a rural environment on the north coast of New South Wales, which provides most of his settings, and left school without matriculating. Gray's poetry is notable for its clarity and objectivity; it evokes mood (often melancholy) through carefully selected sensory details and often manifests the static, epiphanic quality of *haiku*. Indeed this is a favourite form, though Gray is also given to leisurely, loosely structured meditations or narratives in free verse. While drawn to nature, he also addresses the morose patterns of lower-class life (urban and rural), family relationships, and the corruptions of civilization.

For Gray the world apprehended by the senses is real, sufficient, and autonomous. He is attracted to those principles of Buddhism consistent with materialism and positivism; these are adduced in several poems which extol non-attachment, the mind 'light-footed upon all things'. Contemplation of the world involves both escape from self and a salutary empathy, hence Gray's ideal of 'disinterested care', which has social and aesthetic dimensions, justifying both his socialism and his meticulous craftsmanship.

Selected Poems (Sydney, 1985) represents four earlier volumes. See also *Piano* (Sydney, 1988). Gray's chapter in *The American Model* (Sydney, 1982) outlines his aesthetic position.   [AW

GRAY, Stephen (1941–), was born in Cape Town. After studying at the University of Cape Town, he proceeded to Queens' College, Cambridge, where he edited *Granta* and produced Shakespeare. He took an MA at the *Iowa Writers' Workshop, then travelled briefly in Chile before settling back in South Africa where he teaches at the Rand Afrikaans University in Johannesburg.

Gray is highly conscious of belonging to the South African tradition of Roy *Campbell and William *Plomer; indeed his verse, which is always versatile and idiomatic, can be seen as an attempt to extend that tradition by applying it to the developing South African scene and thus to produce 'a history of local endeavour'. His first collection, *It's about time* (Claremont, Cape Province, 1974), inclined towards the derivative, but in *The Hottentot Venus* (London, 1979), and above all in *Love Poems, Hate Poems* (London, 1982), he evolved a style which is fluent, racy, aurally astute but innocent of commas. He is at his best when wedded to tighter forms, as in *Love Poems, Hate Poems*, where a protracted variety of sonnet allows him just the right vehicle

for meditations on love, violence, and betrayal. He is above all a poet of process, of becoming, an interpreter of *actualités*. While others fled the country, or indulged in furious sniping from within, Gray preferred to stay and observe. His latest collection, *Apollo Café* (Claremont, 1989), confirms him as a bitter eulogist of his own torn land, 'my nourishment and obsession'.
                                                                    [RHF

GREACEN, Robert (1920–), was born in Derry, Northern Ireland, and educated at the Methodist College, Belfast, and Trinity College, Dublin. Having once worked for the UN, Greacen went on to teach and work as a free-lance writer. His early work was overwhelmed by the influence of *Auden, *Thomas, and *Yeats, and he did not discover his own voice until quite late, in the sequence of poems that make up *A Garland for Captain Fox* (Dublin, 1975). In the inscrutable figure of the fictional Captain Fox, Greacen finds a focus for his energies and attentions, and he produces a mischievous and captivating portrait. Significantly, Greacen's work as an anthologist of Northern Irish poetry and prose helped to establish the distinctive voice of the province.

Greacen's collections of verse include *The Bird* (Dublin, 1941), *One Recent Evening* (London, 1944), *The Undying Day* (London, 1948), *A Garland for Captain Fox, Young Mr. Gibbon* (Mornington, 1979), and *A Bright Mask* (Dublin, 1985). He has also published an autobiography, *Even Without Irene* (Dublin, 1969), and has edited a number of anthologies of work from Northern Ireland, including *Northern Harvest* (Dublin, 1944) and, with Valentin *Iremonger, the Faber *Contemporary Irish Poetry* (London, 1949).   [IES

GREENBERG, Samuel (1893–1917), was born in Vienna. His father, a Jewish worker of gold and silver brocade, emigrated to America with his wife and children when the poet was 7, and the family settled in New York City's lower East Side, where Greenberg attended public schools until his parents' distressed circumstances made it necessary for him to begin working in a sweatshop at the age of 12. Poverty and long hours of tedious labour notwithstanding, he read vora-ciously, graduating from dime novels to Keats, Shelley, and Emerson, and on weekends he went to concerts, took sketching lessons, and studied paintings in museums. As his intellectual world expanded, the landscape of his life contracted: his mother died in 1908 and his father in 1913, a year after Greenberg himself was diagnosed tubercular. His last four years were spent largely in charity hospitals, and in these bleak surroundings he wrote most of his exuberantly mystical poetry. After his death, his brothers and a friend, the art critic William Murrell Fisher, managed to preserve several hundred poems and prose fragments, and in 1923 Fisher showed some of the manuscripts to Hart *Crane, who recognized the originality underlying the awkwardness and incoherences that were the result of poor schooling and worse health. Especially impressed by the dead poet's highly charged vocabulary, replete with curious archaisms and idiosyncratic coinages, and by his densely impacted musical sentence structure, Crane composed and published a collage of lines taken almost verbatim from several of Greenberg's 'Sonnets of Apology', and it was the story of this appropriation that led to the publication of *Poems from the Greenberg Manuscripts*, ed. James Laughlin (Norfolk, Conn., 1939), which led in turn to a much larger collection, *Poems by Samuel Greenberg*, ed. Harold Holden and Jack McManis (New York, 1947). See also Marc Simon, *Samuel Greenberg, Hart Crane and the Lost Manuscripts* (Atlantic Highlands, NJ, 1978).

[RH

GREGER, Debora (1949–), was born in Walsenburg, Colorado, and raised in Richland, Washington, the eldest of seven children. Since 1974 she has lived with William *Logan, the poet and critic. She attended the University of Washington and the University of Iowa, and has taught at the University of Florida, where she is an associate professor of English, since 1985. With the assistance of the Amy Lowell Poetry Travelling Scholarship and awards from the National Endowment for the Arts and the Ingram Merrill Foundation, she has travelled and lived in England.

Greger's poems are reticent autobiographically, employing a fanciful, cerebral mode, while making use of fairy-tale, description, and both memory and myth, but not in any traditional narrative sense. Rather, the poems seem cleverly conjured, and are sometimes as hermetic as symbols on a cave wall.

Greger has published three collections of poetry: *Movable Islands* (Princeton, NJ, 1980), *And* (Princeton, 1986), and *The 1002nd Night* (Princeton, 1990).
[HC

GREGG, Linda (1942–), was born in Suffern, New York, and soon moved in 1943 to Marin County in California. Her parents were both active educators, and her father was also an architect and an author.

Gregg has travelled widely, living for times in Greece, Sweden, Nicaragua, and elsewhere, and has kept up an intermittent life as a teacher, taking up residencies at the universities of Syracuse, Iowa, and Houston, and other literary centres throughout America. Even more than most of her peripatetic generation, Gregg has been one to 'burn with the speed | of endless departures', as the poet W. S. *Merwin, an aesthetic compatriot of Gregg's, has put it. She received a BA (1967) and MA (1972) from San Francisco State University, where she studied with the poet Jack *Gilbert, an important influence on her life and work. But her poetry also has about it a pared-down and elliptical motion reminiscent of George *Oppen.

She has published three books to date: *Too Bright to See* (Port Townsend, Wash., 1981); *Alma* (New York, 1985); and *The Sacraments of Desire* (St Paul, Minn., 1991).
[LR

GREGOR, Arthur (1923–), emigrated to the United States from Vienna in September 1939, two weeks after the Second World War had broken out in Europe, a refugee from Nazism. His first book of poems, *Octavian Shooting Targets*, appeared in New York in 1954. After a trip to India he discovered the theme of self-realization that was to unfold in his eight subsequent volumes, from *Declensions of a Refrain* (New York, 1957) to *Secret Citizen* (1989).

From 1974 to 1988 Gregor directed the creative writing programme at Hofstra University; since 1989 he has been poet-in-residence there for one semester each year, while spending the remaining months in France. There is a selected edition of his work, *Embodiment and Other Poems* (New York, 1982). Gregor's own description of his life and work, 'Basic Motivations', appears in *Contemporary Authors Autobiography Series*, 10.

[GS

GREGORY, Horace (Victor) (1898–1982), was born in Milwaukee and studied Lucretius and Catullus at the University of Wisconsin. From the first his work seemed modern—spare in form, urbane in tone, urban in imagery—yet deeply rooted in classical influences. As Winfield Townley *Scott wrote, Gregory 'employed his spirit not to avoid the confusing modern world but to clarify and enrich it'. Gregory was a true man of letters: he published ten collections of poetry, three books of translations (Catullus and Ovid), eight books of literary criticism, an autobiography, edited or co-edited ten anthologies, and co-wrote with his wife, the poet Marya *Zaturenska, the controversial *History of American Poetry, 1900–40*. His *Collected Poems* received the Bollingen Award. Gregory was also a distinguished teacher. From 1934 to 1960 he lectured on classical literature in translation and modern poetry at Sarah Lawrence College.

All this he accomplished while in frail or precarious health. He was born with tuberculosis of the bone that left him partially paralysed, as well as causing a tremor in the right hand. When he walked he was unstable, and later in life he was confined to a wheelchair. Due to illness, he was first educated at home by a tutor. Later he went to a private school, the German-English Academy. For three summers he attended the Milwaukee School of Fine Arts, and thought he would become a painter. ('I decided to switch when I found myself writing poems on canvas', he said. Later he wrote a book-length study of James McNeill Whistler.) When he attended the University of Wisconsin (1919–23), he met his future wife.

After graduation, in what was to be the most important influence on his work, Gregory turned his back on Milwaukee and his affluent family. He moved to New York City, where he lived in the Chelsea district among the artistic and the poor. What he saw there motivated him to destroy the manuscript of his first book of poems, composed of highly conventional lyrics. In its place he wrote *Chelsea Rooming House* (New York, 1930; published in London in 1932 as *Rooming House*), one of the strongest and most individual first books by a modern poet. Its free-verse dramatic monologues of the underdog set the tone for the entire body of his poetry.

The most complete edition is *Collected Poems* (New York, 1964), though it omits certain admired early works and all of *Another Look* (New York 1976). See also *The House on Jefferson Street, A Cycle of Memories* (New York, 1967) and *Spirit of Time and Place: Collected Essays* (New York, 1972). [RSP

GREIG, Andrew (1951–), was born in Bannockburn, raised in Fife, and attended the University of Edinburgh.

Self-preening is not entirely absent from Greig's earlier work, and crops up too in his second collection, *Surviving Passages* (Edinburgh, 1982) in a poem like 'Last Night's Poems'. Predecessors to that collection were *White Boats* (1972) and *Men on Ice* (1977). *Surviving Passages*, however, demonstrates an essential liveliness, at its best in a firm free verse (see 'In the Tool-Shed') which allows his imagination to work.

A Flame in Your Heart (Newcastle upon Tyne, 1986), written with Kathleen Jamie, is an interesting poetic fiction about the love affair between a Second World War fighter pilot and his girl-friend. Greig's work, however, begins to find its achievement in *The Order of the Day* (Newcastle upon Tyne, 1990). American (such as John *Berryman) and other influences on his work have become truly digested and fructifying. They help to provide Greig with a poetic manner which diverges from Scottish averages without ignoring the insistent priorities of recent Scottish culture. What has now begun to make his work distinctive is a hard and vivid contemporary diction.

An experienced mountaineer and inveterate traveller, Greig has also published two prose works which reflect his love of the high places, *Summit Fever* (London, 1985) and *Kingdoms of Experience* (London, 1986), and a novel, *Electric Brae* (Edinburgh, 1992).   [DED

GRENFELL, Julian (1888–1915), heir of Lord Desborough, was educated at Eton and Balliol College, Oxford. He joined the regular army in 1910, was sent to France in 1914, and was killed at Ypres. 'Into Battle', published in *The Times* on 28 May 1915, and much anthologized since, exemplifies the kind of poetry written by the now vanished aristocratic British officer-and-gentleman type, so many of whom fell in the First World War. Grenfell wrote only a few more poems, none of them comparable to 'Into Battle'. He was an amateur poet, with few literary connections and no literary aspirations. Many have found shallow elements in the patriotic verse of Rupert *Brooke and in similar, less-skilfully made effusions; but most responsible anthologists of the war period have felt compelled to consider 'Into Battle': it cannot be labelled specious and it almost perfectly expresses the warrior spirit which has persisted in poetry from Homer onwards. See *Julian Grenfell* (London, 1976), by Nicholas Mosley. See also *Some Soldier Poets* (London, 1919), by T. Sturge Moore, which reprints Grenfell's other poems.   [MS-S

GRIFFITHS, Bill. See PERFORMANCE POETRY.

GRIGSON, Geoffrey (1905–85), was born the seventh son of a Cornish vicar in the parish of Pelynt and educated in Devon, Surrey, and at St Edmund Hall, Oxford. In his autobiography *The Crest on the Silver* (1950), with a characteristic blend of acerbity and affection, he describes his elderly father as 'a sample of the negative, passive culture which passed for scholarship', and from an early age Grigson took up the contrary position, regarding himself as 'a childish and

hungry sensualist, finding and finding and, as I still am, unsatisfied'. His passion for discovering, for noticing the overlooked, and—as an anthologist—rescuing the single good poem by an otherwise indifferent author is matched by a savagely critical desire to scorn the mediocre and pillory the inadequate.

Between 1933 and 1939, while literary editor of the *Morning Post*, he held to the view expressed by Coleridge—that praise of the unworthy is robbery of the deserving, and during the same period, as editor of the magazine *New Verse*, he put this maxim ever more forcefully into practice. Although he claimed to have come to recognize that 'the tactic was too uncharitable, and dust lies down sooner or later of its own accord', age can hardly be said to have mellowed Grigson the journalist and critic. There was something increasingly predictable about his cantankerous spleen and paying-off of old scores, and his last collection of essays, *Blessings, Kicks and Curses* (1982), though thoroughly readable, relishes the benediction rather less than putting the boot in.

It is, however, in his poetry—the first volume of which appeared in 1939—that Grigson's keen-eyed, unsentimental appreciation of nature, his eclectic curiosity, his reverence for hallowed objects, and what he describes in the autobiography as 'a localized sense of life and a sense of history' come to the fore. Many of the poems are occasional, quirkily conversational jottings, their syntax strained by inversion and multiple parentheses, but they sound the authentic note of instant speech—vivid, declaratory, much more carefully shaped than might at first appear. Their visual accuracy has much in common with the poems and notebooks of Clare and Hopkins, about both of whom Grigson wrote with insight, and it should be remembered that as well as championing *Auden and *MacNeice, Grigson did much to draw attention to the work of Ben Nicholson and Henry Moore, and to the paintings of Samuel Palmer.

Grigson's poems, too, are of a piece with his own notebooks. Although he maintained that *Notes from an Odd Country* (1970) should be seen as the best gloss on his poems, *A Private Art* (1982) is equally illuminating. Both books are full, like the poems, of precise observation, idiosyncratic opinion, high relish, and quick temper. His *Collected Poems 1963–1980* (London, 1982) was followed by several individual volumes, the last of which—*Persephone's Flowers* (London, 1986)—contains five poems written during the last few weeks of his life and found among his papers. One of these poems recalls his awkward relationship with his father. Grigson was prolific and argumentative to the very end.   [JM

GROSHOLZ, Emily (1950–), was born in Bryn Mawr, Pennsylvania. She was educated at the universities of Chicago and Yale. She is a member of the philosophy department at Pennsylvania State University and serves as an advisory editor for the *Hudson Review.

Grosholz's poetry ranges from relatively short meditative pieces to narrative (see her 'Cypress and Bitter Laurel'). Much of her work is about absence of one kind or another, and a significant number of her poems deal with paintings. Another preoccupation is travel. Travel is a figure for process, and pausing to visit a place often means taking stock of the self. Often this process is broadened as the speaker addresses someone not present. Many of Grosholz's poems are epistolary and are the occasions for meditations about the way relationships evolve, especially within the changing circumstances of travel. Recently she has moved from the singular meditative stance of her earlier poems to a perspective that entails the presence of others, and this increased objectivity has produced some deft love poems.

Grosholz's collections of poetry to date are *Sailboat, Flower, Child* (Baltimore, Md., 1992); *Shores and Headlands* (Princeton, NJ, 1988); *The River Painter* (Champaign, Ill., 1984); and a pamphlet, 'Cypress and Bitter Laurel' (*The Reaper*, 17). Her *Cartesian Method and the Problem of Reduction* was published by Oxford University Press in 1991.   [WP

GROSS, Philip (1952–), was born at Delabole, Devon, 'beside the slate mine'. His father was an Estonian refugee and Gross has written memorably of the Holocaust and the world of the wartime refugees. His mother was the village schoolmaster's daughter. He read English at the University of Sussex and worked as a librarian before moving to Bristol in 1984.

There is a touch of the chameleon about Philip Gross, which is not to say that he is derivative; rather, that he has an extraordinarily plastic imagination, and his technique is tuned to the occasion of each poem. He is an animist, apparently able to get under the skin of any being or phenomenon. In this he resembles Ted *Hughes, but Gross's muse is less musclebound. If influences are sought, Craig *Raine was a presence in his first full collection, *The Ice Factory* (London, 1984). (There was an earlier short volume from Peterloo, *Familiars* (1983), which contains a few poems not in *The Ice Factory*.) This *Martian influence is largely absent, though, from his second book, *Cat's Whisker* (London, 1987), which the publisher advertised as a miscellany, there being no recurrent themes. Further evidence of his versatility can be found in *The Air Mines of Mistila* (Newcastle upon Tyne, 1988), written in collaboration with Sylvia *Kantaris.   [PF

GROSSMAN, Allen (1932–), was born in Minneapolis and studied at Harvard and Brandeis universities. He was until recently the Paul E. Prosswimmer Professor of Poetry and Education at Brandeis; he now teaches at Johns Hopkins University.

Though he has never received the kind of attention given to many other poets of his generation, Grossman has over the years become something of a legend in certain circles, particularly in the Boston area. This cult status doubtless reflects his power and eloquence as a teacher passionately committed to the redemptive functions of poetry; his recent book *The Sighted Singer* (Baltimore, Md., 1992) comprises a series of fascinating conversations with the poet Mark Halliday and a remarkable work of 'speculative poetics', 'Summa Lyrica', which outlines a conception of poetry at once fiercely Romantic and profoundly humane. His own poetry is uncompromising in its engagement of the high style, as derived chiefly from such modernist giants as *Yeats, *Stevens, and Hart *Crane. His insistence on the visionary, prophetic dimension of poetic speech, and the intense rhetoric that accompanies it, may have led some readers and critics to dismiss him as an anachronism. But Grossman does not simply repeat Romantic modernism; he also corrects it, particularly in the sphere of morality. Rejecting the notion that vision and prophecy entail a solipsistic withdrawal from other selves, Grossman has evolved a subtle and moving ethic based on the idea of care—an ethic that may owe something to his Judaism, which he frequently invokes. Poetry, in his view, is one of the primary ways in which human beings 'affirm one another', preserving their voices and images 'against our vanishing'. Thus Grossman's most striking departure from his high modern forebears lies in his frequent reference to other people, who are always granted full humanity—his childhood nurse; a woman seen on the street; most especially his parents, Louis and Beatrice, who figure in many of his poems. Stylistically Grossman's poetry has moved from an austere, stark mode to a more baroque and playful manner that verges on pastiche yet never relinquishes its fundamental seriousness. His poetry may be read in *The Ether Dome and Other Poems: New and Selected 1979–1991* (New York, 1992). [RG

Group, The, was a deliberately antithetical response to the supposedly tame, formalist poetics of the *Movement, which were exemplified in the anthology *New Lines. However, unlike the Movement, whose members never assembled in any organized way, the Group was from the start a tightly knit, even a local affair, originating in Cambridge in 1952 when a number of poets connected with the magazine *Delta* began holding regular meetings to read and critically analyse each other's recent work. Subsequently the focus moved to London, where poets met at the homes of Philip *Hobsbaum and, later, Edward *Lucie-Smith. After the Group disintegrated as a formal entity during

the 1960s, it was resurrected as Poets' Workshop, and its members remained influential in organizations such as the Poetry Society.

The Group may have been socially more coherent but it was poetically more diverse than the Movement: perhaps its most widely shared characteristics were an interest in natural and violent imagery, and a corresponding suspicion of gentle irony and closed forms. Among the poets who have been associated with it at different times are Alan *Brownjohn, Philip Hobsbaum, Ted *Hughes, Edward Lucie-Smith, George *MacBeth, Peter *Porter, and Peter *Redgrove, most of whom would have broadly supported the 'anti-gentility' stance of A. *Alvarez in his Introduction to *The New Poetry* (1962). *A Group Anthology*, edited by Hobsbaum and Lucie-Smith, appeared in 1963 (London).

[NP

GUEST, Barbara (1923–), was born in Wilmington, North Carolina, and attended the University of North Carolina as well as the University of California at Los Angeles and Berkeley.

The only female member of the so-called *New York School, she has affinities with Frank *O'Hara. Like much of O'Hara's poetry, Guest's is alive to the possibilities of the moment and yet insists on the domestic continuities, the fascinations of the everyday. Her publications include *Poems: The Location of Things* (New York, 1962), *The Blue Stairs* (New York, 1968), *I'Ching: Poems and Lithographs* (Paris, 1969), *Moscow Mansions* (New York, 1973), and *Quilts* (New York, 1981). In addition to her verse she has written plays, fiction, and a biography of H.D.: *Herself Defined: The Poet H.D. and her World* (New York, 1984; London, 1985).

[GC

GUNN, Thom(son William) (1929–), was born in Gravesend and raised principally in Hampstead. His father was a journalist, as his mother had been before her marriage. In 'My Life Up to Now', an autobiographical essay written in 1977, Gunn warmly recalls growing up in a household full of books and playing with friends on the Heath. However, his parents divorced, and his mother, with whom he lived after the divorce and who encouraged his interest in reading and writing, took her life when he was 15. It is possible that the emphasis, in certain of his poems, on self-definition and self-reliance reflects not only such literary influences as the French existentialists, but also personal circumstances that required independence and resilience of him while he was still relatively young.

After two years of national service in the army, Gunn went in 1950 to Cambridge. Here he attended lectures by F. R. Leavis, who impressed him with his passion for literature, his belief in the value of realized imagery, and his insistence on the expressive significance of verse rhythm. Gunn also discovered Donne and read all of Shakespeare, both authors contributing to the formation of his early style, which is exemplified in 'Tamer and Hawk' and 'The Beach Head', and which is characterized by a masterful control of the metaphysical conceit, the extended metaphor or analogy. In 1954 he travelled to California, where he held a fellowship at Stanford University and studied for a year with Yvor *Winters, about whom he has written a fine reminiscence, 'On a Drying Hill'. After living and teaching briefly in Texas, Gunn returned to the San Francisco Bay area, settling in San Francisco itself in 1961. From 1958 to 1966 he taught at the University of California at Berkeley, but resigned his professorship to devote more time to writing. He subsequently held occasional visiting appointments at different schools; since the late 1970s, he has taught at Berkeley for one term a year.

While at Cambridge, Gunn wrote most of the poems that appeared in his first collection, *Fighting Terms* (1954; revd. edns. 1958, 1962). Impressive for their concentration, their vigour, and their effective fusion of traditional metre with contemporary idiom, these poems established him as one of the most arresting voices of his generation. Though critics associated him with the *Movement, his predilections were never as sharply anti-modernist as those of such Movement poets as *Larkin and *Amis. Indeed, Gunn

soon began to investigate different tonalities, a development encouraged by his move to the United States and by his reading of Williams Carlos *Williams, *Stevens, and other American experimentalists. Gunn's second book, *The Sense of Movement* (1957), and more especially his third, *My Sad Captains* (1961), feature poems in *syllabic measures, poems which, like 'Vox Humana' and 'Considering the Snail', show the poet speaking in a quieter, more tentative manner. Gunn has remarked that syllabics provided him with a transitional form to work his way into free verse, and *Touch* (1967) contains his earliest free-verse poems.

Unlike many of his contemporaries, however, who began with conventional forms and switched exclusively to free verse, Gunn continued to work in metre too; and *Moly* (1971), with such memorable poems as 'At the Centre' and 'Sunlight', employs strict forms to render illuminations related to experiences with hallucinogenic drugs. *Jack Straw's Castle* (1976) in part explores darker aspects of these experiences. The title piece, a sequence of poems examining consciousness nightmarishly isolated from its customary contexts, recalls Gunn's earlier 'Misanthropos' sequence, which appears in *Touch* and which has as its protagonist a man who has survived a terrible world war and who believes himself to be the only survivor, 'the last man' on earth. *The Passages of Joy* (1982) shows a growing concern with friendship and its social virtues. Gunn is a homosexual and in the mid- and late 1980s he wrote a number of powerful poems about the AIDS epidemic, collected in *The Man with Night Sweats* (London, 1992).

Overall, Gunn's poetry has evolved towards a more directly humane treatment of its subjects. This evolution may be seen in the changing aspects of two abiding qualities in his work: his sympathy with the outsider-rebel and his interest in the nature of courage. Whereas the outsider-rebels of earlier poems tend to exhibit, as do the motorcyclists in 'On the Move', romantic self-sufficiency, those in later work are more likely to be injured or lost, as with 'Sparrow' or 'Slow Walker'. And if the characteristic gesture of courage in early poems like 'Lerici' and 'In Santa Maria del Popolo' is that of opening the arms wide to the existential void, in the later work courage is perhaps best expressed by the comforting embrace that the man dying of AIDS in 'Memory Unsettled' confers on a friend more sick than he.

Gunn has also collaborated with his brother, the photographer Ander Gunn, on *Positives* (1966), supplying verse to accompany his brother's photographs. *The Occasions of Poetry, Essays in Criticism and Autobiography*, (ed. Clive Wilmer (1982; enlarged edn., 1985) displays the wide range of Gunn's reading and literary sympathies.

Key writings on Gunn include the autobiographical essays in *The Occasions of Poetry*. Jack W. C. Hagstrom and George Bixby's *Thom Gunn, A Bibliography 1940–1978* (London, 1979) offers, as well as data on the poems, a list of interviews with Gunn and entries for his uncollected book-reviews. *Three Contemporary Poets: Thom Gunn, Ted Hughes and R. S. Thomas*, ed. A. E. Dyson (London, 1990) reprints George Fraser's fine 1961 essay, 'The Poetry of Thom Gunn', and Wilmer's illuminating 'Definition and Flow: Thom Gunn in the 1970s'. Gregory Woods's *Articulate Flesh* (New Haven, Conn., 1987) has a chapter on Gunn as a gay poet. In addition, an issue of *PN Review* (No. 70, 1989) devoted chiefly to Gunn contains useful discussions of his work. His poems are widely anthologized; the most comprehensive selection of them is his *Selected Poems 1950–1975* (London, 1979), winner of the W. H. Smith Award in 1980.   [TS

GURNEY, Ivor (1890–1937), was born in Gloucester, the son of a tailor. His musical abilities were recognized early and in 1906 he enrolled as an articled pupil to the cathedral organist. Even at this early age the stabilizing influence of musical colleagues (one of them was Herbert Howells), his intoxication with what his friend Will Harvey called 'the very fact of being Gloucester bred', and his deep love of the local countryside were disturbed by poor health, reckless solitariness, and a confused egoism which made him passionately independent in his impulses but vulnerably derivative in his utterance.

In 1911 he won a scholarship to the Royal College of Music in London to study composition under Stanford, and here he achieved his first real success: a setting of five Elizabethan lyrics. Here too his sense of Englishness was sharpened—in music by his increased exposure to the work of Elgar and Vaughan Williams, and in poetry by the opportunity to meet and hear the *Georgian poets whom Edward Marsh was promoting. 'Our young men must write on a diet largely composed of Folk Song and Shakespeare', he told his friend Marion Scott.

When war broke out his career as a composer was stunted. After he had reached France (in 1916, as a private in the 2nd/5th Gloucesters) he found time to compose no more than five songs. Instead, he intensified his interest in writing poems, and his two collections (*Severn and Somme*, 1917, and *War's Embers*, 1919), contain several of the lyrics on which his reputation still rests—notably 'To His Love' and 'Song' ('Only the wanderer . . .'). In 1917 he was gassed at Ypres and posted back to England, where he suffered a breakdown in the late spring of the following year. In 1922 he was incarcerated in the City of London Mental Hospital at Dartford, suffering from schizophrenia. He died fifteen years later.

Gurney wrote a great deal of poetry during his asylum years, and it was only when the poems were collected and edited by P. J. *Kavanagh (Oxford, 1982), and later, the best selected (Oxford, 1990) that Gurney's status as a major war poet became apparent. His preoccupations were those of the Georgians—the sanctity of place, the threat of change, the delights of seclusion, the barbarism of conflict—but his treatment is recognizably modern: broken rhythms, buckled diction (he had read Hopkins in Robert *Bridges's anthology *The Spirit of Man*), idiosyncratic syntax, breathless celebration (in 'Cotswold Ways', for instance), undermined by despairing regret. Like Edward *Thomas, whom he greatly admired, his work forms a link between Victorian and contemporary sensibilities, and the pressures and problems of occupying such a position give his work its power as well as being the means by which it was overwhelmed. See Michael Hurd, *The Ordeal of Ivor Gurney* (Oxford, 1978).   [AM

GUSTAFSON, Ralph (1909–), was born of Anglo-Swedish stock in Lime Ridge, Quebec. He studied at Bishop's University, then at Oxford. After a brief stint at teaching in Canada he returned to England, where he published his first two collections of poetry and remained from 1933 to 1939. During the war he worked for the British Information Services in New York, summarizing attitudes to Britain in the American press. Since 1963 he has lived in North Hatley, Quebec, where he has worked as writer-in-residence at Bishop's, as a music critic for radio, and as a free-lance writer and anthologist, editing various editions of the *Penguin Book of Canadian Verse*.

Gustafson's critical writings in *Plummets and Other Partialities* (1987) provide clues to some of his poetic concerns. His early work is notable for its craftiness, particularly its compression, verbal wit, and musicality, although feeling and idea are at times overwhelmed by form in these somewhat overwrought poems. In mid-career Gustafson explored longer forms, experimenting with sequences, or what he called 'the poem by sections'. His later work has been characterized by a mix of what he calls witness poems, on significant public events, and quiet, meditative pieces about the life and landscape of the Eastern Townships of Quebec where he lives.

Gustafson has also written two books of stories, *The Brazen Tower* (1974) and *The Vivid Air* (1980). The best selection of his poetry is to be found in *The Moment Is All: Selected Poems* (Toronto, 1983) and *The Collected Poems of Ralph Gustafson* (Victoria, BC, 1987).   [GG

GUTHRIE, Ramon (1896–1973), was born in New York City and served in the American Field Service and US Army Air Corps from 1916 to 1919. He married Margarite Maurey in 1922 and pursued an expatriate life in Paris through most of the 1920s. Beginning in 1930, he taught French and comparative literature at Dartmouth College. He also wrote two novels and, with George E. Diller, edited *French Literary Thought since the Revolution* (1941) and *Prose and Poetry of Modern France* (1964).

Guthrie's first books of verse, *Graffiti* (1959) and *Asbestos Phoenix* (1968), seem to have been preparations for his minor masterpiece in satiric melancholia, *Maximum Security Ward: 1964–1970* (New York, 1970). Influenced by Laforgue, *Pound, and young *Eliot—the main voice in the 'poem' echoes Prufrock's self-conscious estrangement—this work builds a dramatic collage of affects, tropes, and literary references around the interior monologue of a doomed but erudite member of Gertrude *Stein's 'lost generation', which helps explain its archaic aura of Baudelairean posturing.

For a sympathetic explication of Guthrie's poetic sequence, see *Ramon Guthrie's Maximum Security Ward: An American Classic* (Columbia, Mo., 1984), by Sally M. Gall.   [EB

GUTTERIDGE, Bernard (1916–85), was educated at Cranleigh School. During the war he served with Combined Operations, a fellow officer being Alun *Lewis, whose death he recorded in his poem 'Burma Diary'.

All but half-a-dozen of the poems in *Traveller's Eye* (1947) were written between 1939 and 1945, the great majority being descriptions of the places Gutteridge had known during his military service in Madagascar, India, and Burma. They are vivid evocations of landscapes, towns, and people, the reports of a traveller who perceives the squalor beneath the picturesqueness. 'Patrol Buonamary' is an amusing sketch, written on the spot, of an almost comic engagement in Madagascar. 'The Enemy Dead' is a much grimmer poem: 'It's not a man, the blood-soaked | Mess of rice and flesh and bones . . .'.

The Angry Game (1954), a novel about advertising, his own profession, was followed by *Old Damson-Face* (London, 1975), which contained two-dozen new poems and a selection from *Traveller's Eye*. These final poems command a bare, hard directness. The mood is sardonic, the glance in the mirror is unsmiling and unflinching. Drink, sex, death are faced without comforting illusions.   [JPr

GWALA, Mafika Pascal (1946–), was born in Verulam, near Durban, in South Africa's Natal province and educated at Vryheid where he matriculated. He has worked as a legal clerk, secondary-school teacher, factory worker, and publications researcher, notably as the editor of *Black Review* in 1973, in which he appeared as a leading exponent of the Black Consciousness philosophy in South Africa. In the black township of Hammarsdale in 1982 he was a founder member of the Mpumalanga Arts Ensemble which has contributed substantially to the ensuing working-class poetry and arts movement. In the early 1990s he was a student at the University of Manchester. He is married and has several children.

He is often grouped by critics with the Johannesburg-based poets, Oswald *Mtshali, Mongane *Serote, and Sipho *Sepamla, as a leader of the 'Soweto poets' group which came to prominence after the Soweto uprising of 16 June 1976, but, although his work deals in protest terms with the Soweto condition, it is not literally Soweto-based. His poems began to appear in journals like *Ophir* (Pretoria) from 1970 and his first collection was published in 1977— *Jol'iinkomo* (Johannesburg). This was followed by his only other collection to date, the substantial *No More Lullabies* (Johannesburg, 1982), No. 15 in the Staffrider series. His work is characterized by a bluesy-jive idiom that stresses black African creative usages of English, and is often strongly satirical of the pretensions of bourgeois urbanites.

His later work is well represented in *Exiles Within*, an anthology produced in 1986 by the Writers Forum in Johannesburg. A fair summary of his career is John Povey, 'The Poetry of Mafika Gwala', *Commonwealth*, 8: 2 (Dijon, Spring 1986).   [SG

GWYNN, R(obert) S(amuel) (1948–), was born in Eden, North Carolina, of a middle-class family which had been in the South for generations. A high-school athlete, Gwynn attended Davidson College on a partial football scholarship until a sports injury forced him to abandon the game. He completed his education at the University of Arkansas. Since 1976 he has taught at Lamar University in Beaumont, Texas.

Gwynn's early collections, *Bearing and Distance* (1977) and *The Narcissiad* (1981), revealed a poet almost entirely at odds with the literary temper of his times. Formal and satiric, his poems pilloried the excesses of contemporary American culture. *The Narcissiad*, a mock epic, recounts the adventures and apotheosis of Narcissus, an ambitious but talentless poet. In *The Narcissiad* American poets simultaneously realize that to achieve artistic pre-eminence in the overcrowded field of verse they must kill all competitors. After a series of outrageous battles, fought by caricatures of fashionable American poets, Narcissus ineptly triumphs.

The Drive-In (Columbia, Mo., 1986) stands as one of the representative volumes of the *New Formalist movement. Gwynn's metres are traditional but his language is aggressively contemporary and colloquial. The volume is a small encyclopedia of historical genres—elegy, satire, anacreontic, epistle, dialogue, ode, sonnet-sequence—but Gwynn usually employs the forms in deliberately irreverent, even obscene ways. The early cynicism remains but now is balanced by a lyrical impulse. *The Drive-In*'s signature piece, 'Among Philistines', retells Samson's downfall in a lurid American setting of shopping malls and tabloid journalism. This dark, comic poem unexpectedly rises to a lyric epiphany as the captive hero finds redemption in his mutilation. *Body Bags* (1990) further explores the lyric potential of the ludicrously doomed, especially in the title sequence of three vernacular sonnets about the pointless deaths of high-school acquaintances.

Gwynn has also been an active critic. His monograph-length summaries of 'The Year in Poetry', which have appeared in the *Dictionary of Literary Biography Yearbook* since 1987, have made him perhaps the only critic in America who reviews every significant new collection of verse. He has also edited *American Poets Since World War II: Dictionary of Literary Biography*, vol. 105 (Columbia, 1992).   [DG

HACKER, Marilyn (1942–), was born in New York City and educated at the Bronx High School of Science, Washington Square College of New York University, and the Art Students League. The author of five books of poems and winner of the National Book Award (1974), Hacker has taught at several universities, including the State University of New York at Binghamton. She divides her time between New York City and Paris.

Hacker's fluent command of technique, fully evident in her first book, *Presentation Piece* (New York, 1974), has been maintained in subsequent collections. Her sonnet-sequences, villanelles, and various stanzaic poems share a restless, dynamic quality and a conversational tone: this is a poetry largely addressed to friends and lovers which usually transcends the merely intimate exchange. Meditations on love and grief arise from sketched city-scapes, notes on meals, weather, travels, furnished interiors.

Hacker's lesbianism is increasingly explicit in her recent *Love, Death, and the Changing of the Season* (New York, 1986) and *Going Back to the River* (New York, 1989). These alert and sensuous accounts of urban love affairs have an urgent yet casual rapidity and wit. Yet the later books are perhaps less ambitious than Hacker's earlier work, notably *Separations* (New York, 1976) and *Taking Notice* (New York, 1980). Technical expertise was there from the first, but the subject-matter now seems somewhat more limited to rapid, detailed notations of a busy life.

[RHa

HADAS, Rachel (1948–), spent her childhood in New York City. She was educated at Radcliffe College, Johns Hopkins University, and Princeton, and is now associate professor of English at Rutgers University. She has published two books of literary essays. During the early Seventies she spent four years in Greece, and was trained as a classicist, so the real and imagined landscape of Greece looms large in her poetry, especially in the book *Slow Transparency* (1983). These earlier poems bear traces of Seferis's metaphysical re-imagining of sea and island, the accidents of history, and the essence of time; and James *Merrill's word-play, textual abridgements, borrowings, and bridgings.

Her later poetry, however, has become all her own. Playful diction is controlled by a sober consciousness of limits, the scope of the Aegean spiralled back into glints on a Manhattan window-pane. In *Pass It On* (Princeton, NJ, 1989), her themes are friendship, marriage, and (most centrally) the connections that persist between parent and child. Her poems on bearing and nursing a child, reading to him, and watching him begin to speak, are touching but unsentimental, inventive and yet steeped in literary and family tradition. To pass on what we know and love, she says, we have 'no way but words'.

[EG

HAINES, John (Meade) (1924–), was born in Norfolk, Virginia. He served in the US Navy, 1943–6, and homesteaded in Alaska, supporting himself by hunting and trapping, 1946–69. Since 1972, he has held positions as poet-in-residence at several universities.

Well known for his deft renderings of Alaskan frontier life, his range of subjects has broadened steadily since the publication of his first book, *Winter News* (Middletown, Conn, 1966). His poetry indicts post-industrial culture for making the non-essential seem essential, for its despoiling of nature, and for its wilful delusions and selfish offices. Despite the heftiness of such themes, Haines's poems seldom lose their winsome lyricism, wit, or concision. His poetry is celebratory as well. In each of his books Haines evokes the Alaskan wilderness—beautiful, generous, and unspoiled—and can thus afford understatement; post-industrial life appears, in comparison, hideous and aberrant. Where other American poets adopt an elemental vocabulary and archetypal imagery merely as components of a fashionable style, Haines speaks of wind, stone, ice, leaf, and branch as a true initiate. His is the hard-earned language of an original and self-reliant naturalist.

His other books of poetry include *The Stone Harp* (Middletown, 1971; repr. London, 1971); *Cicada* (Middletown, 1977); *News from the Glacier: Selected Poems 1980* (Middletown, 1980); and *New Poems 1980–88* (Brownsville, Oreg., 1990). See also his own essays and autobiographical stories, *Living off the Country: Essays on Poetry and Place* (Ann Arbor, Mich., 1981), and *The Stars, the Snow, the Fire* (St Paul, Minn., 1989).   [DWF

HALL, Donald (1928–), was born in New Haven, Connecticut, and educated at Phillips Exeter Academy, New Hampshire, Harvard, and Oxford, where his poem 'Exiles' won the Newdigate Prize (1952). In 1952 he married Kirby Thompson, by whom he has two children, and was made creative-writing fellow at Stanford University the following year. He spent another three years at Harvard, this time as a junior fellow, and from 1957 was a professor of English at the University of Michigan.

Hall's first two books of poetry—*Exiles and Marriages* (New York, 1955) and *The Dark Houses* (New York, 1958)—harness moral arguments and social observations to traditional forms. Ideas, ironies, and metres give way to images, emotions, and free rhythms in *A Roof of Tiger Lilies* (New York and London, 1964) and *The Alligator Bride* (New York, 1969); the latter's fragmented syntax and surrealist juxtapositions

make it Hall's most experimental work. *The Yellow Room: Love Poems* (New York, 1971) and *Kicking the Leaves* (New York, 1978; London, 1979), elegies and memories, reflect Hall's growing conviction that 'the poem is a vehicle for self-discovery'. Later collections include *The Twelve Seasons* (Deerfield, Mass., and Dublin, 1983), *Great Days in the Cow's House* (Mt. Carmel, Conn., 1984), and *The One Day and Poems 1947–1990* (Manchester, 1991).

In 1975 Hall retired from Michigan and, with his second wife, the poet Jane *Kenyon, returned to his ancestral farmhouse in Danbury, New Hampshire, to live by his writing alone. He was made Poet Laureate of New Hampshire in 1984. He has published books on baseball, a critical biography of the sculptor Henry Moore (1966), a critical study of Marianne *Moore (1970), personal and literary reminiscences, and books for children. His strongest influence, however, has been as an editor: of poetry for the *Paris Review* (1953–62); and of numerous widely read selections and anthologies, most notably *Contemporary American Poetry* (Harmondsworth, 1962; rev. edn., 1971), the *Oxford Book of American Literary Anecdotes* (1981), and the *Oxford Book of Children's Verse in America* (1985). See also *A Blue Wing Tilts at the Edge of the Sea: Selected Poems 1964–74* (London, 1975) and *The Weather for Poetry: Essays, Reviews and Notes on Poetry, 1977–81* (Ann Arbor, Mich., 1982).

[NE

HALL, J(ohn) C(live) (1920–), was born in London and educated at Leighton Park School, Reading, and Oxford. While at Oxford, Hall was an editor of *Fords and Bridges* and contributed to its successor, *Kingdom Come*. He was a friend of Keith *Douglas; and, while Douglas was in Egypt, arranged the publication of *Selected Poems* (London, 1943) by K. C. Douglas, J. C. Hall, and Norman *Nicholson. Of strong Quaker sympathies, Hall was exempted from military duties and did farm-work during the Second World War. After the war he made his career in publishing and was for some years on the staff of *Encounter*.

From 1943 to 1947 he seems to have written

little or no poetry; and he has been a very sparse poet throughout his career. In 1952 he edited Edwin *Muir's *Collected Poems*; and Muir's influence is particularly felt in his third book, *The Burning Hare* (London, 1966). Keith Douglas said that Hall's early poetry could do with a little more cynicism; and thirty years later, in *A House of Voices* (London, 1973), Hall seemed to find himself in a style more direct and less involved with conventional rhetoric than was his earlier poetry. He can be sampled in *Selected and New Poems* (London, 1985). [ATT

HALL, Rodney (1935–), was born in Solihull in England of Australian parents. His father died when he was six months old, and the family returned to Australia after the Second World War. Hall went to Queensland, where he left school at 16, later taking a degree from the University of Queensland in 1971. He has worked as a script-writer, actor, film critic, youth officer for the Australian Council for the Arts, and as teacher of music and creative writing. From 1967 to 1978 he was poetry editor of the *Australian*, and from 1972 to 1975 adviser to Angus and Robertson, both influential positions. Since 1981 he has concentrated on prose: among his six novels, *Just Relations* (1982) won the Miles Franklin Award; he has also written studies of artist Andrew Sibley (1968), writer John *Manifold (1978), a number of accounts of Australia, libretti, and has edited numerous anthologies, most notably, with Tom *Shapcott, *New Impulses in Australian Poetry* (1968), as well as three volumes of Michael *Dransfield's poetry.

His poetry is witty, detached, and wears considerable learning with an easeful grace. Often ironic, it is technically flexible and well crafted. His first publication was *Penniless till Doomsday* (London, 1961), followed in Australia with a small selection in *Four Poets* (Melbourne, 1962). Eight volumes followed in the next thirteen years. His *Selected Poems* (St Lucia, Qld., 1975), extracts the best of his first eight books, excepting *The Law of Karma* (Canberra, 1968). See also: *Black Bagatelles* (St Lucia, 1978), and *The Most Beautiful World* (St Lucia, 1981). [JD

HALPERN, Daniel (1945–), was born in Syracuse, New York, and grew up in Los Angeles and Seattle, the eldest of four children. His father was a scrap-metal dealer. He was educated at California State University at Northridge and Columbia University. For two years, from 1969 to 1970, he lived in Tangier, where he met the composer and writer Paul Bowles. With financing from Bowles, together they founded the international literary magazine *Antaeus*, which Halpern continues to edit. He is also editor-in-chief of the Ecco Press in New York City. As Halpern's artistic mentor and friend in those early years, Bowles introduced him to the avant-garde in contemporary literature and music. Since 1976 he has taught at Columbia University.

Like the work of his teachers Stanley *Kunitz and Mark *Strand, Halpern's poetry is spare in its diction. Often his poems are studies in *film noir* surfaces. But there are also poems of Maine light and New York urbanity, where the senses are continually stimulated by landscape, mood, and gastronomic delights.

Halpern has published seven volumes of poetry, of which the most recent are *Foreign Neon* (New York, 1991), *Tango* (New York, 1987), and *Seasonal Rights* (New York, 1982). Also *Songs of Mririda*, by Mririda n'Ait Attik, from a French translation of the original Berber and (co-translated) *Orchard Lamps*, by Ivan Drach, from the Ukrainian. He has edited *The American Poetry Anthology* (New York, 1975), *The Antaeus Anthology* (New York, 1986), and *The Art of the Tale: An International Anthology of Short Stories* (New York, 1986). [HC

HAMBURGER, Michael (1924–), was born in Berlin and emigrated to England in 1933. He was educated at schools in Edinburgh and London, and studied modern languages at Christ Church, Oxford. During the war he served as an infantryman, non-commissioned officer, and lieutenant in the Royal Army Educational Corps, 1943–7. After the war he held posts at University College, London and the University of Reading. Since 1964 he has been a guest lecturer and visiting professor at various American universities, but has mostly devoted himself to free-lance writing and translation. His translations have won many distinguished prizes and awards.

Hamburger's memoirs, *A Mug's Game* (Manchester, 1973 and—retitled *Spring of Beginnings*—1991) tell his life story up to the early 1950s. His contemporaries at Oxford included *Larkin and the wartime generation of Sidney *Keyes, Drummond *Allison, David *Wright, and John *Heath-Stubbs. Later he became an admirer of Herbert *Read. Much of his poetry shows the pervasive influence of T. S. *Eliot. He has explored social dilemmas, personal loneliness, and the impersonal sanities of nature: 'Come late into the freedom his from birth, | To breathe the air, and walk the ownerless earth' ('Confirmist'). *Collected Poems 1941–1983* (Manchester, 1984) offers a large conspectus of his best work. His most recent volume is *Roots in the Air* (Manchester, 1991). His critical books include *The Truth of Poetry* (London, 1969; New York, 1970), *A Proliferation of Prophets: German Literature from Nietzsche to the Second World War* (Manchester, 1983), and *Testimonies* (Manchester, 1989).

As a translator of classic and modern German poetry Hamburger has made a significant contribution to Anglo-American understanding of the German poetic canon. Some of his better-known works include *Hölderlin: Poems and Fragments* (various editions: currently London, 1994); *Decline: 12 Poems by George Trakl* (London, 1952); *Selected Poems* of Hans Magnus Enzensberger (London, 1968); *Selected Poems* of Paul Celan (with Christopher Middleton, London, 1972); *German Poetry 1910–1975* (New York, 1976; Manchester, 1977); *Poems* by Paul Celan (Manchester, 1980); *An Unofficial Rilke: Poems 1912–1926* (London, 1981); *Poems and Epigrams* of Goethe (London, 1983). [WS

HAMILTON, George Rostrevor (1888–1967), the only son of a clergyman, was born in London and educated at Exeter College, Oxford. In 1912 he joined the Inland Revenue and there pursued a distinguished career, for which he was knighted in 1951. He settled in London, living first by the Thames at Chiswick then moving to Blackheath, where he was a friend of Roy *Fuller, another poet and man of letters committed to the professional world.

The first of eighteen volumes of verse, *Escape and Fantasy*, appeared in 1918, the year of Hamilton's marriage to Marion Hermine; *The Making*, a selection of his poetry to 1925, was significantly dedicated to Henri Bergson, a study of whose philosophy Hamilton published in 1921. He claimed that Bergson taught him 'immediacy of sight', and to 'immerse [his] life's movement . . . in a living, streaming universe'; but Hamilton's verse rarely repaid the debt. In later life Plato replaced Bergson as a presiding influence in his somewhat mannered meditations on nature, in which the Thames continued to figure, uneasily, as a unifying presence. His taste for formality was perhaps best suited to the polished epigrams he produced in great numbers. His study of *The English Verse Epigram* appeared in 1965; but his most impressive criticism is in *The Tell-Tale Article* (1949), an acute, admirably focused discussion of language in T. S. *Eliot and W. H. *Auden.

Selected Poems and Epigrams (London, 1945) represents Hamilton's poetic career. For a brief memoir, see Roy Fuller, *Spanner and Pen* (London, 1991). [MRW

HAMILTON, Ian (1938–), editor of this *Companion*, was born in King's Lynn, Norfolk, and educated at Darlington Grammar School and Keble College, Oxford. He edited *The *Review*, 1962–72 and *The New Review*, 1974–9. Publications include (verse) *The Visit* (1970) and *Fifty Poems* (1988–both London); (prose) *A Poetry Chronicle* (London and New York, 1973); *The Little Magazines: A Study of Six Editors* (London, 1976), *Robert Lowell: A Biography* (New York, 1982; London, 1983); and *Keepers of the Flame* (London, 1992; New York, 1993). [POM

HAMPTON, Susan, (1949–) was born in Inverell, New South Wales. Her published poetry includes *Costumes* (1981) and *White Dog Sonnets: a novel* (1987), and her most recent work is a collection of monologues, prose poems, stories, and performance pieces, *Surly Girls* (1989). With Kate *Llewellyn, she edited the *Penguin Book of Australian Women Poets* (1986) and worked with the Aboriginal writer, Ruby Langford, on Langford's autobiography *Don't Take Your Love to Town* (1989). Hampton has also written, with Sue Woolfe, a teaching textbook *About Literature* (1984). In 1979 her poem 'Stockton' won the Mary Gilmore Poetry Competition.

Hampton's poems 'The Crafty Butcher' and 'Yugoslav Story' are most often anthologized, possibly because they do not call attention to her commitment to a lesbian feminist aesthetic. Hampton has assembled an eloquent statement of her feminism in David Brooks and Brenda Walker's *Poetry and Gender* (1990). Though she is committed to challenging representations of women, and to creating a poetry which breaks down genre barriers, Hampton consistently writes about relationships and examines the failure of romantic, monogamous love. At the same time, she attends to the social and political implications of personal life, and her writing about lesbian women, particularly in *Surly Girls*, has a polemical intent.   [SMcK

HAQ, Kaiser (1950–), was born in Dhaka and educated at St Gregory's School, Dhaka College, and Dhaka University. In 1971 he joined the Bangladesh Liberation Army when the war of liberation broke out. After liberation he resigned his commission to resume his studies at Dhaka University, and in 1975 joined the English department as a lecturer.

Haq writes about the contemporary Bangladeshi scene, exposing life's little incongruities and ironies, exploiting a form of colonial English which, even so many years after the departure of the British, still seems to dominate academic and media discourse. His poetry relies heavily on irony and understatement. It combines flashes of insight with a journalistic detailing of objects; it is moving and insightful but smart and refreshingly witty at the same time. Haq likes to see himself as belonging to an Indo-Anglian tradition which has attained a distinct

identity and idiom of its own, and one of his favourite themes is the alienation and rootlessness of the educated middle class.

Haq has appeared widely in poetry reviews and journals at home and abroad, including *London Magazine* and *Cambridge Review*, and has published two volumes of poems, *A Little Ado* and *Starting Lines* (both Dhaka, 1978). He has also edited an anthology, *Contemporary Indian Poetry in English* (Columbus, Ohio, 1990), and translated many Bengali poems into English.

[SMI

HARDY, Thomas (1840–1928), was born in Higher Bockhampton, Dorset, a hamlet three miles from the county town of Dorchester. His father, also named Thomas, was an independent builder; his mother, Jemima, was in domestic service at the time of her marriage. Both were members of families with extensive connections throughout southern and western Dorset. Thomas Hardy senior was a gifted amateur musician; Jemima, who was far more energetic and ambitious than her husband, encouraged all her children—her bookish and delicate older son in particular—to seek the best education available to them, within the family's limited means.

Hardy left school at 16 and was apprenticed to a local architect. In 1861 he moved to London, where he was to live for the next five years, and took a job as an architect's assistant. A notebook he kept shows that it was during this period that he began to write verse. His first novel, *Desperate Remedies*, was published in 1871. By then he was once again in Dorset (he made his home there for the rest of his life), and was engaged to be married to Emma Gifford, whom he had met during a visit to Cornwall. Over the next twenty-six years he published a large number of novels, of which the most famous are probably *Far From the Madding Crowd*, *Tess of the D'Urbervilles*, and *Jude the Obscure*.

Throughout these years he continued to write poems, or to jot down lines and ideas for poems. However, he published nothing of what he had written in this form until the last of his novels, *The Well-Beloved*, had appeared in 1897. *Wessex Poems and Other Verses* came out the year after; it was followed by a further eight volumes of verse, the last of which, *Winter Words*, was published posthumously. He also wrote a verse drama on the Napoleonic Wars, *The Dynasts*, which appeared in three parts between 1904 and 1908. Hardy's decision to give up fiction and confine himself to verse owed something to the hostile reception given to *Jude the Obscure*, on the grounds of the novel's supposed obscenity; but the biographical and literary evidence shows that poetry was anything but a *pis aller* for him. Rather, it could be called his earliest as well as his last calling.

Anyone looking into the *Complete Poems* for the first time might well be struck by two apparently contradictory features of the massive volume in his hands. The first is of the uniformity of Hardy's poetry; the second is of its variety. What is meant by 'uniformity' here is that it is impossible to trace any kind of development, any growth or decline in power, any change in subject-matter, technique, or even emotional tone, from the beginning to the end of Hardy's poetic career. No doubt this is in part due to the fact that he had been accumulating poems or drafts of poems for so long before appearing in public as a poet; these were then drawn in irregular fashion into his successive collections. The felicities of his verse are manifest as frequently in the first volume as in the last; so are the lapses into awkwardness and bathos to which he was always prone; so are those turns of phrase and rhyme which somehow combine the felicitous and the awkward in a manner which is quite unlike anything to be found elsewhere in English poetry.

There are, of course, sequences of poems which plainly belong to one or another specific period of Hardy's life—those he wrote during the Anglo-Boer War, for example; or even more notably, those written after Emma Hardy's death, which celebrate and mourn the brief period of happiness he and she had known together, as well as the decades of conjugal misery that had followed. However, groups of poems like these do not differ in style or vocab-

ulary from the rest of his output; even the themes, moods, and preoccupations which they explore with their own special intensity are familiar from other contexts and in other guises.

As for the 'variety' of his verse: he wrote hundreds of lyrics and love-songs, ballads, sonnets, dramatic, descriptive, and meditative poems of all kinds, drinking songs, character sketches, poems on public issues and events (the sinking of the *Titanic*, the outbreak or the ending of wars, an eclipse of the moon), tributes to other poets (Shakespeare, Shelley, Keats, Swinburne) —as well as poems which combine these genres, or elements of them, in often unexpected ways. In addition, the verse-forms, rhythms, and rhyme-schemes used by the poet vary from poem to poem in what seems to be a positively compulsive manner. No particular form is matched consistently to any particular genre or type of subject-matter. (Blank verse, however, is found only in *The Dynasts*; all Hardy's other poetry is rhymed.) To complicate matters yet further, he will frequently begin a poem in one elaborate stanzaic form, very possibly a form newly invented for the occasion, only to switch to another half-way through; sometimes he will then return to the original form before the end of the poem, sometimes not.

The effect of all this on the reader is bound to be, intermittently at least, one of bewilderment. The formal restlessness of the poet, and the strained ingenuities and improbabilities of rhyme and vocabulary into which it occasionally drives him, can make an almost childlike impression at times. Nor does it seem unfair to call childlike some of the delight which Hardy takes, in his dramatic and narrative verse especially, in malign, melodramatic coincidences, or in a generalized, sepulchral spookiness, or in moments of heavily contrived self-disclosure on the part of his protagonists. These faults will, of course, be familiar to readers of his novels and short stories too. When Hardy gives the name *Satires of Circumstance* (1914) to one collection, the reader is entitled to fear that all too many of its poems will mechanically fulfil the ominous promise of the title; and this indeed turns out to be the case. Yet that particular volume also contains the sequence of poems about the death of Emma Hardy, which (under the sub-heading 'Poems of 1912–13') includes many examples of his finest and most heartfelt work. One cannot help feeling that there is something typically perverse and Hardyesque in his choosing to link together in so uncritical a manner some of the best and the worst of which he was capable.

However, all criticisms made, Hardy remains for his admirers an indispensable poet: one of that smallish group of whom one might say that his absence would be felt not just as a depletion of the canon of English poetry but as a personal loss. That his work was to affect so deeply successors as different as W. H. *Auden and Philip *Larkin is perhaps just one illustration of this point. The sources of his appeal may be identified, crudely enough, in threefold fashion: first, in the delicacy of his observations of the natural world; secondly, in his capacity to stare straight into the duplicities of human passion; and thirdly, in the philosophical scope of his mind. But one must at once add that his greatest strength as a poet ultimately shows itself not by way of a movement in his verse from one to another of these elements, but in the unique and indissoluble fusion of them which it again and again offers.

For Hardy, nature is never inert—neither in itself as a theatre of continual change; nor as the terrain, begrudging and generous in turn, from which we and all other animals have to glean a living; nor in the ever-renewed power it has to evoke a response in those who regard it. In fact, a paradox that the verse presses upon us—and here we come on one of its philosophic dimensions—is that even when it is at its harshest, bleakest, its apparently most remote and indifferent, nature is to be understood as having these aspects only because we ourselves are compelled to see it as such. Thus, almost in spite of ourselves, we remain a part of it, and it remains a part of us. ('We' in this context refers not only to the human race, incidentally: Hardy is always sensitive to the possibility that the humblest animals are conscious of more than we dare to credit them with. See, for instance, the little poem 'An August Midnight'.)

If Hardy looks on both nature and our relations to it as continually undergoing a process of change, he is positively obsessed with the instability and transience of all human emotions—and hence of all human life. Here again, however, the essentially philosophic nature of his verse makes itself apparent. To say that he is preoccupied with transience is also to say that he is constantly engaged in a search for permanence; or for such permanence as we are capable of experiencing. Recurrence across the generations is one form of it; memory is another; both are at once beyond all value and yet inherently and ironically subversive of value. We possess our memories only at the cost of knowing that we can never recover or go back to that which we are remembering; the individuality we treasure, and all the passions which sustain it, turn out to be nothing but an ineluctable miming of the lives of the dead and the yet-to-be born.

In the light of all this, and given also Hardy's unflinching (if often aggrieved) refusal of the comforts offered by religious belief, it is hardly surprising that the emotions and states of mind most eloquently expressed in his verse are those of bewilderment, dismay, regret, remorse, loss, failure, and misunderstanding; a longing for times past together with an exacerbated sense of opportunities not taken or simply not noticed when that same past was actually present, available, malleable; a consciousness of motives wholly or partly hidden at times of action, and revealed or understood too late to be of any use; above all, a never-to-be-evaded awareness of mortality. Feelings like these are inevitably taken both to reflect and to account for Hardy's famous 'pessimism'; and that pessimism is in turn commonly identified with his 'philosophy' (Hardy himself does it from time to time). Enough has been said here, however, to suggest that the latter word should be used both more widely and more carefully in thinking about his work.

In the end, what makes Hardy a philosophic poet is something more than his bleak view of human possibilities, however deeply he held that view and however central it was to his overall achievement. He is a philosophic poet because he struggles so hard to extend the range of the sayable, and hence of the thinkable, whether it be by the poet himself or by anyone who reads his work. What is the true nature of the relation between animate creatures and an apparently inanimate world, and in what terms can it best be described? Is it possible for conscious beings to imagine an absence of consciousness—and if so, how? What is it of the dead that lives in us and in what forms does it manifest itself? How are we able to apprehend the limits of our own knowledge and experience; and what kind of knowledge, what kind of experience, is it to feel that very apprehension within us? These are the questions which his verse asks of itself and of its readers, even as it talks (or sings) of hedgehogs and thrushes, raindrops, birch trees, fresh love, embittered love, and a long-dead sister 'laughing, her young brown hand awave'.

See the *Complete Poetical Works*, ed. Samuel Hynes, in three volumes (Oxford and New York, 1982–5), and *Thomas Hardy: A Selection*, also ed. Samuel Hynes, (Oxford, 1984). See also Robert Gittings's *The Young Thomas Hardy* (1975) and *The Older Hardy* (1978—both London); and Michael Millgate's *Thomas Hardy: A Biography* (Oxford, 1982). Hardy's novels are readily available in various editions; his deeply uninteresting *Collected Letters*, ed. R. L. Purdy and Michael Millgate, were published in seven volumes between 1978 and 1988.   [DJ

HARFORD, Lesbia (1891–1927), was born Lesbia Keogh in Melbourne, where she studied philosophy and law, being one of the first women graduates in law at Melbourne University. Both her life and her art were shaped to conform to her commitment to the socialism of the radical labour movement. Despite congenital heart disease, she spent years in manual work in clothing factories; despite seriousness about writing, she published few of her often untitled poems, and remained remote from Sydney's literary world, although maintaining Melbourne contacts with Frank *Wilmot and Nettie Palmer; aware of contemporary movements in poetry, she chose

to write 'little fresh songs', accessible to the fellow-workers she frequently made her subject-matter.

Palmer edited a selection in 1941, and national anthologies like Serle's *An Australasian Anthology* (London, 1927) kept some poems in circulation, but major attention came with feminist criticism, attracted by her expression of the tensions and contradictions experienced by women seeking independence in work, politics, and love. *The Invaluable Mystery*, her novel on these themes, was finally published (Ringwood, 1987), following *The Poems of Lesbia Harford* (Sydney, 1985), a complete edition with a comprehensive introduction by Drusilla Modjeska.
[JS

Harlem Renaissance, The, occurred during the 1920s, a result of the confluence of black American writers and artists in a district which was already fashionable among the white smart set as the music-and-entertainment capital of New York. The early years of the century had seen the publication of works such as W. E. B. DuBois's *The Souls of Black Folk* and Booker T. Washington's *Up From Slavery*, indicating the future role of black people in America. In 1925, Alain Locke, a professor at Howard University, brought together a collection of short stories, poems, and prose by divers hands, under the title *The New Negro*. As the abstraction was held to characterize the 'spiritual Coming of Age' of the black race, so the volume itself could be seen as a mark of its cultural maturity.

Major figures in the Harlem Renaissance were Langston *Hughes, Arna Bontemps, James Weldon *Johnson, Nella Larsen, Countee *Cullen, Claude *McKay, Jean *Toomer, and Zora Neale Hurston, many of whom treated the themes of black life in a way that felt modern, while borrowing elements from the folk literature of black tradition. Visual artists of the Renaissance, including Aaron Douglas and William H. Johnson, incorporated African and primitive motifs into their work. Among the magazines founded at the time which devoted themselves to 'Negro studies' were *Crisis* (edited by DuBois), *Opportunity*, and the *Messenger*.

These magazines were not exclusively literary, but the significance of the Harlem Renaissance did not lie solely in its literary impact. Although much that was produced from Harlem in the 1920s is of greater historical than artistic importance, the Renaissance made white America aware for the first time of the modern art of a people it had not long before kept in slavery.

For an account of this development see *Harlem Renaissance*, by Nathan Irvin Huggins (New York, 1971). *When Harlem Was in Vogue*, by David Levering Lewis (New York, 1981) is a study of broader scope, with less emphasis on the literary life of the 1920s.   [JC

HARPER, Michael S(teven) (1938–), was born in Brooklyn, but received his high-school education in Los Angeles. He took degrees from the City College and California State College there, and from the *Iowa Writers' Workshop. He taught in several colleges and universities on the West Coast, but since 1973 has taught at Brown University in Providence, Rhode Island, with honorary stints at many schools.

His first book of poems was *Dear John, Dear Coltrane* (Pittsburgh, 1970), and he has published several collections since, including *Song: I want a Witness* (Pittsburgh, 1972), *Nightmare Begins Responsibility* (Urbana, Ill., 1974), and *Images of Kin: New and Selected Poems* (Urbana, 1977). Harper writes out of his black heritage, using the referents and rhythms of jazz and blues, but his language does not seek to exclude; rather, he writes to include, to initiate and welcome. His most recent book is *Healing Songs for the Inner Earl* (Urbana, Ill., 1985).

[LT

HARRIS, Max (1921–95), was born in Adelaide but grew up in Mount Gambier, a large country-town near the border between South Australia and Victoria. A nearby town appears in the name of perhaps his best-known poem, 'The Tantanoola Tiger'. Harris worked briefly as a journalist, then completed a degree in economics at Adelaide University.

In 1944, when still a student, he gained inadvertent celebrity as the victim of Australia's most spectacular literary hoax. *Angry Penguins*, the literary magazine he had founded two years earlier, invited some such treatment: its content, much of it written by Harris himself, consisted mainly of clumsy imitations of Dylan *Thomas and T. S. *Eliot, while its editorial stance was precociously pompous. James *McAuley and Harold *Stewart, young poets only a few years older than Harris, resolved to deflate his pomposity by inventing a non-existent poet whose verse was even worse than Harris's own; they named their creation 'Ern Malley' and submitted his work to *Angry Penguins*, where Harris swallowed the bait. In the subsequent fracas Harris was prosecuted for publishing 'indecent advertisements', and his career as an avant-gardist ended in humiliation. It was not, however, the end of his literary career. Ten years later he completed *The Coorong and Other Poems* (Adelaide, 1955) in which he revealed himself as an impressively mature and accomplished, if somewhat conservative, poet. *A Window at Night* (Kensington Park, NSW, 1967) overlaps the previous book but adds new poems as well. The quality of Harris's best poetry tends to be overlooked in the face of his other pursuits, from his youthful misadventures, through his appearances as a television personality in the 1960s, to his latter-day manifestation as a crusty newspaper columnist.

[JG

HARRIS, Wilson (1921–), was born in New Amsterdam, and educated in British Guiana (now Guyana). Until he moved to Britain in 1958 he was a government surveyor, exploring the wild hinterland of Guyana which features so prominently in his work. His writing career began as a poet, under the pseudonym 'Kona Waruk', in Guyana. *Fetish* (Georgetown, 1951), his first volume of verse, was published in A. J. *Seymour's Miniature Poets Series.

The 'cross-cultural imagination', as Harris himself called it, so evident in his poems, foreshadowed the many novels he wrote in Britain, all dense with archetypal imagery, allegory, and mythic overtones. The poems often revitalize ancient Greek myths, and graft them on to a tropical setting, and modern conditions. 'Laocoön', for instance, converts the destructive snakes of the myth from Virgil's *Aeneid* into the horrors revealed by newspaper headlines.

Eternity to Season (Georgetown, 1954, revd. edn., London, 1978) is his most accomplished volume, and was preceded by *The Well and the Land* (Georgetown, 1952). His best novels include *Palace of the Peacock* (1960), *The Secret Ladder* (1963), and *Carnival* (1985—all London).

[MR

HARRISON, Jim (James Thomas) (1937–), was born in Grayling, a small county seat in northern Michigan, the state in which he has spent most of his life. After attending Michigan State University, where he studied comparative literature, he taught for two years at the State University of New York, Stony Brook, before returning to live on a farm in the region of his birthplace. He has been poetry editor of the *Nation* and co-editor of *Sumac*. His local rootedness and rural loyalties are disclosed in several titles of his eight volumes of poetry, which, in addition to *Selected and New Poems, 1961–1981* (New York, 1982), include *Locations* (New York, 1968), *Returning to Earth* (Ithaca, NY, 1977), and *The Theory and Practice of Rivers* (Seattle, 1986). He is also the widely acclaimed author of nine volumes of prose fiction, from which may be singled out *Legends of the Fall* (New York, 1979; London, 1980), three novellas exploring the ways of violent revenge.

Characteristically a free verse of short, imagistic lines, Harrison's is a poetry both of natural particulars and the universals of human experience. Though most happily grounded close to home, he is a poet of large sympathy and concern, who names amongst the primary influences upon him Whitman, *Yeats, Rilke, Lorca, Neruda, and *Pound, and whose *Letters to Yesenin* (Fremont, Mich., 1973) enact a passionate correspondence between the contrasting kinds of Russian and American anguish.

[RWB

HARRISON, Tony (1937–), was born in Leeds and educated at Leeds Grammar School (1948–55) and Leeds University (1955–60), where he read classics and took a diploma in linguistics. He lectured in English at Ahmadu Bello University, Nigeria, 1962–6 and at Charles University, Prague, 1966–7. In 1968–9 he co-edited *Stand*. In 1977/8 he was resident dramatist at the National Theatre.

Tony Harrison's achievement springs from apparent contradiction: he is a classicist from the working class; a writer of considerable scholarship seeking a mass audience in the theatre and on television; a poet of great technical accomplishment whose work insists that it is speech rather than page-bound silence; a pessimist with a relish for life; above all, perhaps, a poet repeatedly troubled by the knowledge that the very gift which enables him to speak for his class is what separates him from it. These shaping tensions have bred Harrison's conviction that poetry 'is not something I can take for granted': hence, perhaps, the scale and ambition of his work.

Harrison's first full collection, *The Loiners* (London, 1970) showed a ready transition between the personal and the larger stage of power in history—from sex on a Leeds tombstone to the burning victims at Philip of Spain's wedding in 'The Nuptial Torches'. It is in the ongoing series *The School of Eloquence* (London) that he begins to make a history for himself, turning to address language as a form of power and exclusion (for example, 'Them & [uz]'). To 'occupy' the 'lousy leasehold poetry' involves not only the inclusion of supposedly unpoetic materials, but also mastery of the forms tradition has proposed as the possession of the élite—notably the sonnet. A struggle is waged both by and in the poems, and Harrison's emotional frankness, while sometimes risking sentimentality, has an undeniable force. At the same time, his travels, notably to the USA, have provided him with a less class-burdened context from which a more ample and sensual poetry has emerged (for example, 'A Kumquat for John Keats').

Harry

The 1987 television broadcast of the controversial V (new edn., Newcastle upon Tyne, 1989) a meditation on death and division in a vandalized Leeds graveyard, written during the 1984–5 miners' strike, brought Harrison wide attention. He has continued to use television as a medium for poetry in *Loving Memory* (1987) and *The Blasphemers' Banquet* (1989). His conviction that poetry is a public art is further demonstrated by the publication of his Gulf War poems, 'Initial Illumination' and 'A Cold Coming' in the *Guardian* on 5 and 18 March 1991, during the conflict.

Harrison has also worked extensively as a theatre poet and as a librettist, writing acclaimed versions of Racine, Molière, and Aeschylus, as well as *The Mysteries* (London, 1985) and *The Trackers of Oxyrhynchus* (London, 1990). A new original play, *Square Rounds*, was published in 1992 (London).

A revised edition of the *Selected Poems* (Harmondsworth, 1984 and New York, 1987) appeared in 1987 (Harmondsworth). *V and Other Poems* (New York, 1990) contains some previously uncollected work. *A Cold Coming: Gulf War Poems*, and *The Gaze of the Gorgon*, which won the Whitbread Award, both came from Newcastle upon Tyne in 1992.

Dramatic Verse 1973–1985 (Newcastle upon Tyne, 1985) appears in paperback as *Theatre Works 1973–1985* (Harmondsworth, 1986). *Tony Harrison: Bloodaxe Critical Anthologies 1* (Newcastle upon Tyne, 1991), ed. Neil Astley, is a comprehensive critical introduction to his work.[SO'B

HARRY, J(an) S. (1939–), was born in Adelaide, South Australia. A reclusive and unpredictable poet, J. S. Harry has been praised for her 'wit and lyrical argumentation', and for her stylistic versatility. Each new volume has seemed like a leap into the dark, or a demonstration of her ability to range from experimental modishness to formal tautness, from scintillation to savagery. There is sometimes an unevenness of pace, but Harry is perhaps best read in volume form, rather than for individual poems. Because of this, perhaps, her work has been difficult to anthologize adequately.

Her collections to date are *The Deer under the Skin* (St Lucia, Qld., 1971); *Hold for a Little While*, *and Turn Gently* (Sydney, 1979); and *A Dandelion for Van Gogh* (Sydney, 1985). Her Selected Poems is due from Penguin.   [TWS

HARSENT, David (1942–), was born in Devonshire. From his first collection, *A Violent Country* (London, 1969), his central subject has been the relationship, or non-relationship, between men and women. This he treats with a deftly tuned bleakness; his lines are often short, his words and syllables always weighed. Typically, 'Home Movies' sketches an emotional drama by focusing on the act of seeing, yet leaves its implications suggestively unstated; less typically, observation points the way towards release from unhappiness for both watcher and watched at the end of the poem. An intent record of moods close to desperation, 'The Woman's Soliloquies' moves skilfully between speech and silence, 'she' and 'I'. Here as elsewhere in Harsent's work, the human and the natural interact, sharing a need for endurance.

After Dark (London, 1973) includes more ventilated lines and poems about parents and childhood, of which 'Two Postscripts to my Father' and 'Encounter' are impressive examples, the first unsentimentally direct, the second haunting. The slow-motion, cinematic clarity of Harsent's images marks his third collection, *Dreams of the Dead* (London, 1977). By now he had mastered the art of making larger wholes out of short pieces. Two sequences of brief poems, 'Dreams of the Dead' and 'Moments in the Lifetime of Milady', reach inner states by way of an inventive documentation of externals: weather, a Berlin bar, spiders, deathbed silks. Narcissism is a risk the volume faces and surmounts.

Harsent's next volume, *Mister Punch* (Oxford, 1984), extends the poet's fascination with dream, nightmare, lust, and loss in a sequence of grimly humorous poems featuring Punch, a trickster-like persona who challenges comparison with *Berryman's 'abominable' Henry. But Harsent's dream songs eschew the fractured idiom patented by Berryman in favour of a polished, bitter control (evident in the virtuoso rhyming of 'Rouault: A Portrait'). David Harsent's *Selected Poems* (Oxford, 1989) was compiled by the author and draws on the four collections mentioned above. Since then he has published *News from the Front* (Oxford, 1993).

[MO'N

HART, Kevin (1954–), was born in London, grew up in Brisbane, and was educated in Canberra. He has taught both philosophy and English at universities in Victoria. Apart from his distinction as a poet, he is the foremost literary theorist of his generation in Australia. At present he is Associate Professor of Comparative Literature and Theory at Monash University. He has examined the relations between deconstruction and mysticism in his challenging book, *The Trespass of the Sign: Deconstruction, Theology and Philosophy* (Cambridge, 1989).

Hart's own poetry started out quietly enough among the Canberra formalists. However, in *The Lines of the Hand* (1981) and *Your Shadow*, three years later (both Sydney), his mature characteristics emerged: passionate declaration, purity of diction, and a hunger for ontology. Hart's fondness for tercets can suggest a Wallace *Stevens turned Christian, but he is more physical than Stevens. Often he bypasses modernist irony altogether at the behest of Eros or Agape.

The best essay on Hart's work is Peter Steele's 'Kevin Hart', *Overland*, 122 (1991), which links the poetry with the criticism and with the translations from Ungaretti. The poems can be found in *Peniel* (Melbourne, 1990) and in most anthologies of Australian poetry.

[CW-C

HARTIGAN, P. J. ('John O'Brien') (1878–1952), was born in Yass, a New South Wales country town, of Irish immigrants. He was ordained a Roman Catholic priest in 1903 and worked as a pastor in rural areas of New South Wales until retirement in 1944. Hartigan's verse provides a humorous yet sympathetic record of the lives of his congregations, mainly Irish settlers, and their responses to Australian outback life. His collection *Around the Boree Log* (1921), published under the pseudonym 'John O'Brien', was immensely popular and reprinted five times in as many years, most recently in *Around the Boree Log and Other Verses* (Sydney, 1988). Hartigan's unpublished verse appeared posthumously in *The Parish of St Mels* (1954).

The subjects and form of Hartigan's verse locate it in the popular tradition of the Australian rural ballad, epitomized by A. B. (Banjo) *Patterson. His most enduring piece, 'Says Hanrahan', satirizes the pessimism of the farmer whose refrain: 'We'll all be rooned', echoes throughout the poem, regardless of dramatic, positive changes in fortune.

For a detailed discussion of Hartigan's life and work see *'John O'Brien' and the Boree Log*, by James Mecham (Sydney, 1981). A brief assessment is given in *The Oxford Companion to Australian Literature*, ed. William Wilde, Joy Hooton, and Barry Andrews (Melbourne, 1985). 'Says Hanrahan' is printed in the *Penguin Book of Australian Ballads*, ed. Russel Ward (Melbourne, 1964).

[EMcM

HARTNETT, David (1952–), read English at Oxford and went on to write a D Phil on James *Merrill. He shares with Merrill a formal resourcefulness exemplified by 'Prehistories', four villanelles included in his second collection, *House of Moon* (London, 1988). Their skills communicate an emotional depth typical of this poet; exact and daring metaphors explore rather than decorate. Hartnett's work combines delicacy and force, figurative brilliance and trust in feeling, acute self-consciousness and openness to experience. His first collection, *A Signalled Love* (London, 1985), unsentimentally affirms, even as it investigates, the significance of the personal. Especially affecting is the title-poem, a sequence concerned with the birth of the poet's son. *House of Moon* builds on and extends the thematic and stylistic range of *A Signalled Love*. Rooted in the actual yet suffused with symbolic nuance, 'The Other Side of the Mountain', the second collection's final poem, moves hauntingly between a childhood self and 'Europe—

|Her wars, this last exhausted peace'. His latest collection is *Dark Ages* (London, 1992).

[MO'N]

HARTNETT, Michael (1941–), was born on a farm in Newcastle West, County Limerick. He is recognized as one of the principal Irish poets of his era, but he has suffered critical neglect. The reasons for this are evident: Hartnett does not fit very neatly into the various schools of Irish-English poetry—post-Yeatsian or Ulster—and his principal influences are not from English or Anglo-Irish literature at all but from classical Irish-language poets, like Daibhi Ó Bruadair (from Hartnett's locality and translated by him in 1985), and from Lorca (also translated by Hartnett, who lived for a time in Spain). In addition, his work badly needs authoritative editing: initially, perhaps, in a corrected selected poems, because his poetry varies greatly, from the loose, adolescent extravagance of his first volume, *Anatomy of a Cliché* (1968), to the exact spareness of the translations from his own Irish lyrics in *A Necklace of Wrens*.

In 1975 Hartnett declared his intention to write only in Irish in the title-poem of what remains his most substantial volume, *A Farewell to English*, and he has kept primarily true to that principle. His powerful manifesto-poem, 'A Small Farm' (1970), takes an un-nostalgic, anti-pastoral view of rural life. Again, both of these features have led to his neglect; it remains ironic that his reputation was highest when his writing was least impressive.

See: *Collected Poems*, vol. 1 (1984/5), and vol. 2 (1986/7—both Dublin and Manchester), and *A Necklace of Wrens. Selected Poems in Irish with English Translations by the Author* (Dublin, 1987).

[BO'D]

HART-SMITH, William (1911–90), was born in Tunbridge Wells, England, emigrated to New Zealand in 1924, and moved to Australia in 1936. He earned his living as a radio mechanic in Sydney before enlisting in the Australian army in 1940. After the war he went back to New Zealand as an adult-education tutor and returned to Australia again in the early 1960s as a radio technician.

Hart-Smith was associated with the *Jindyworobak movement in the 1940s which aimed at linking white and aboriginal Australia. He was drawn to its use of anthropology and myth in the depiction and interpretation of landscape and the spirit of place, but his abiding affinities were with the *Imagists and the early poetry of Ezra *Pound, D. H. *Lawrence, William Carlos *Williams, and Marianne *Moore. Immensely productive, Hart-Smith was one of the most experimental, eclectic, and individual poets in the Australia of his time. He wanted his poems to be 'poems of discovery, recording brief moments of insight and understanding' in language spare and unadorned. His best lyrics, like 'Boomerang', 'Kangaroos', 'Gulls at Pareora', 'Native Violets', and 'Bathymeter' are usually short, astringent, and imagistic. A verse-sequence *Christopher Columbus* (1943) was an important contribution to the historical narrative (the voyager poem) in Australia and New Zealand. He is the author of ten collections, and three selections have appeared: *Poems of Discovery* (1959) and *Selected Poems* (1985), and *Hand to Hand: Selected Poems 1935–90* (1991—all Sydney).

[VS

HARWOOD, Gwen (1920–), was born in Brisbane but since 1945 has lived in Tasmania. Her education prepared her for a career in music, and she has subsequently combined the careers of music teacher and poet. The sequence of poems about the drunken, disreputable, self-pitying but ultimately sympathetic musician, Professor Krote, gives a painfully comic insight into the predicaments of all those forced to earn a living from receiving 'an earful|of Gounod' with their pupils' scales.

Throughout a long writing life Harwood has repeatedly turned to music as the subject-matter for her elegant, invariably closely rhymed, lyrical poems, but she is by no means confined to the one subject. Apart from a number of fine occasional poems, of which the one to A. D. *Hope is outstanding, she is capable of lively social satire, as in 'Cocktails at Seven'; of acute and almost *Larkin-like observation and commentary, as in 'Home of Mercy', and 'In the Park', and—perhaps most remarkably—of deeply felt and powerfully executed love poetry. This ranges from the teasing out of dark ambiguities in 'Triste, Triste', to the unabashed eroticism of 'Carnal Knowledge I and II' and the second 'Meditation on Wyatt'. Harwood's most recent collection is *Bone Scan* (Sydney), which won the 1989 Victorian Premier's Literary Award. Her *Selected Poems* (Sydney) was published as *Collected Poems* (Oxford and New York) in 1992. She has composed several libretti, working with contemporary composers. [JL

HARWOOD, Lee (1939–), was born in Leicester and attended London University. He has published fifteen books of poetry, given readings and lectures in Europe and North America, and edited various little magazines. His name is sometimes coupled with that of Tom *Raworth, with whom he shares an accessible, un-literary manner, and a concern with the present moment. More than Raworth, however, and like his friend the American poet John *Ashbery, he cultivates a loose, flowing, sometimes flippant, and often lyrical style in which to depict the movement of the mind on the spot. There are surprises and surreal moments, but these tend to be folded into the smooth flow of the poem. Much of his work seems 'painterly' in the sense that it displays a keen sensitivity to colour and a careful attention to landscape—his work has a pastoral bias—enacted through a broad and detailed survey of a scene. These qualities are well displayed in *Landscapes* (London, 1969). But in the end Harwood's concern is to let his consciousness take him where it will. His selected poems, *Crossing the Frozen River* (London), were published in 1988. [ETL

HASHMI, Alamgir (1951–), was born in Lahore, educated in Pakistan and the United States, and has worked as a professor of English, editor, and broadcaster. His early work, which includes a collection of love poems, *Oath and Amen* (Philadelphia, Pa., 1976), and a long poem recording his travels across America, *America is a Punjabi Word* (Zurich, 1979), is characterized by a terse, witty, imagistic style, and reveals a recurring preoccupation with language, time, and place. The poet's peripatetic career in America, Europe, and Pakistan is reflected in the concerns of his subsequent collections, *My Second in Kentucky* (1981), *This Time in Lahore* (1983), and *Neither This Time/Nor That Place* (1984—all Lahore). As Hashmi has developed, there has been a broadening of human sympathies and an emerging political awareness which have modified the virtuosity and self-absorption of some of his earliest writing. His most recent publications are *Inland and Other Poems* (1988), *The Poems of Alamgir Hashmi* (collected poems) (1992), and *Sun and Moon and Other Poems* (1992—all Islamabad). [SS

HASKELL, Dennis (1948–), was born and raised in the working-class western suburbs of Sydney. After completing a commerce degree in 1968, he worked as an accountant over the next few years in Sydney and London, travelled in America and Europe, married, and developed an interest in philosophy and literature. He completed an arts degree in 1976, received his doctorate in 1982, and presently lectures in English at the University of Western Australia.

His first book of poems, *Listening at Night* (Sydney, 1984), exhibits a religious sensibility in an essentially godless world, celebrated as the search for the extraordinary in a mundane urban environment. While many of Haskell's earlier poems are imagist in technique, he also writes more abstract pieces that explore his philosophic concerns, especially in his second book, *Abracadabra* (Fremantle, 1993). His academic writing includes many articles on modern poetry, and a study, *John Keats* (1991). He has edited (with Hilary Fraser) an anthology of contemporary Western Australian verse, *Wordhord* (1989) and an edition of *The Poems of Kenneth Slessor* (1991). Haskell also co-edits the magazine *Westerly*. [AU

HASLUCK, Nicholas (1942–), was born in Canberra, Australia, son of Dame Alexandra and the late Sir Paul Hasluck, both of them authors. He graduated from the University of Western Australia in 1963 and Oxford in 1966, and currently practises law in Perth. Hasluck has become recognized as one of the notable fiction stylists in Australia, but his poetry, too, is important, particularly in its relation to an energetic regional 'explosion' of creativity in Western Australia from the end of the 1970s and into the 1980s.

Anchor and Other Poems (Fremantle, 1976) initiated the West Coast Writing series from Fremantle Arts Centre Press and was to establish that press as one of Australia's leaders in small-press activity, an exemplar of its kind. Hasluck's poetry set a standard of urbanity and specific vividness of observation. The title-poem, 'Anchor' is a sequence in thirteen sections exploring an essential Australian theme of shoreline and littoral; in this it presages the two major sequences in his second book of poems, *On The Edge* (Claremont, 1980; poems by William Grono and Nicholas Hasluck). The most substantial of these, 'Rottnest Island', balances precision of image with an edgy, open-ended reflectiveness.   [TWS

HASS, Robert (1941–), was born in San Francisco and studied under Yvor *Winters at Stanford University in the 1960s. The recipient of the Yale Series of Younger Poets Award in 1972, Hass has taught at various American universities, including the State University of New York at Buffalo and the University of Virginia. His first book, *Field Guide*, was published in 1973 (New Haven, Conn.) and was followed by *Praise* (New York and Manchester, 1981). In addition to his volumes of original poetry, he is also well-known as a critic and essayist (his collection *Twentieth Century Pleasures* (New York) won the National Book Critics Circle award in 1984) and, especially in England, as co-translator of the work of the Nobel Prize-winning Polish poet Czeslaw Milosz, whose monumental *Collected Poems 1931–1987* was published in 1988.

It is easy to see why Hass would respond to the intense lyrical fantasia of Milosz, in which a history of suffering and oppression is carried with great tact and grace along the fine lines of a sensibility which, for all its privacy, stays engaged, alert, and lucid. Hass's own best poems strive for a comparable lucidity. Their evocations of place, particularly California, are always suffused with a vividly responsive human consciousness, making it apparent why one of his favourite forms is the haiku. Yet his intensely rendered states of nature and consciousness are rarely entirely innocent of history: the fate of the American Indian, the lot of working-class Polish-Americans, the Vietnam war, and the squalor of contemporary urbanization all provide a context of anxiety and unease; it is unsurprising to find Hass writing passionately about Robert *Lowell. His tone, however, is usually meditative, ruminative, occasionally almost entranced, one of its major signatures being a bitter-sweet, Chekhovian sadness (Chekhov is himself the hero of more than one of the poems). It is hard to manage this at length without affectation or complacency, and Hass is certainly a poet of variable quality; but the distilled eroticism, all yearning and nostalgia, of a poem such as 'Meditation at Lagunitas', goes well beyond any mere absorption of earlier Romantic models.   [NC

HAY, George Campbell (1915–84), was brought up in Tarbert Loch Fyne by his mother and her aunts. Here he learned Gaelic and developed a lifelong love of the landscape and seascapes of Kintyre, admiration for the Tarbert fishermen, and a fascination for their boats. Hay's linguistic talents were nurtured through a classical education at Fettes and Oxford. By then, however, his interests embraced many other languages and literatures, including Irish Gaelic and Welsh. He translated poetry into and out of all of these, and composed in many. War service widened the scope of his linguistic explorations, and he became especially interested in Arabic language and culture. Surviving the war, he was seriously injured by a bomb-blast in Greece in 1946. His health never really recovered, and he was hospitalized several times during his later years, which were spent in Edinburgh.

Hay's most productive period began when he joined the circle of Oxford Scots led by Douglas

*Young, and continued until his injury. His poetry shows both an ardent nationalism and a wider concern for the common man. He is a connoisseur of languages, enthralled by the challenge of creating and of translating the creations of others. His Gaelic and Scots poems are distinguished by a consistent and occasionally overwhelming musicality.

Hay's poetry is best-known through the collections *Fuaran Sléibh* ('Upland spring': Glasgow, 1947), *Wind on Loch Fyne* (Edinburgh, 1948), and *O na Ceithir Airdean* ('From the Four Airts': Edinburgh, 1951). A selection with introduction appears in the bilingual anthology *Nuabhàrdachd Ghàidhlig/Modern Scottish Gaelic Poems*, ed. D. MacAulay (Edinburgh, 1976). Hay's collected works are being edited by M. Byrne (Edinburgh, forthcoming). [WG]

HAYDEN, Robert (1913–80), was born in Detroit and educated at Wayne State University and at the University of Michigan, where he took his MA in 1944. He began teaching at Fisk University, a predominantly black college, in 1946, and he ended his career back at Michigan.

Hayden was always a formal poet, but his formalism was not—except in his earliest work—of a traditional nature, for he experimented with language approaches; however, unlike some of his ethnic contemporaries, he was not radically politicized by the Civil Rights Movement of the 1960s. Hayden did not want to be judged by specialized, 'Negro-only' criteria. On the other hand, he did not shrink from utilizing his heritage and his family background.

Heart-Shape in the Dust (Detroit, 1940) was his first book, and *The Lion and the Archer*, with Myron O'Higgins (n.p., 1948), his second. Only one collection appeared during the next decade, however: *Figures of Time* (Nashville, Tenn., 1955). Two collections were issued during the 1960s—*A Ballad of Remembrance* (London, 1962) and *Selected Poems* (New York, 1966). In the next decade there were *Words in the Mourning Time: Poems* (New York, 1970) and *The Night-Blooming Cereus*, (London, 1972). *American Journal: Poems* (New York, 1982) appeared posthumously. There is a study by Robert Feltrow, *Robert*

Hayden (Boston, 1984). [LT

H.D. See DOOLITTLE, HILDA.

HEANEY, Seamus (1939–), was born in Mossbawn, Co. Derry, Northern Ireland, the eldest of nine children and the son of a Catholic farmer and cattle-dealer. In 1951 he won a scholarship to St Columb's College, where he was a boarder, and then in 1957 to Queen's University, Belfast, where he returned as a lecturer, after some years schoolteaching, in 1965. That same year he married Marie Devlin, and in 1966 published his first book of poems, *Death of a Naturalist* (London and New York). After two more collections, and a year in California, he became a full-time writer and moved to Co. Wicklow in 1972, returning from the countryside to live in Dublin in 1976. In 1984 he was appointed Boylston Professor of Rhetoric and Oratory at Harvard, and in 1989 he became Professor of Poetry at Oxford, two prestigious lecturing posts that have taken him away from Dublin for extensive periods but have also allowed him time to pursue his own work. He was winner of the Nobel Prize for Literature in 1995.

Richly physical in its descriptions of rural life (digging, blackberry-picking, churning, thatching, etc.), Heaney's early work in *Death of a Naturalist* and *Door into the Dark* (London and New York, 1969) shows the influence of both Ted *Hughes and Patrick *Kavanagh. At its freshest, it conveys a country-boy's first troubled encounters with sexuality, responsibility, and death; at its most pious, a merely sentimental affection for a disappearing, peasant-simple world. Beyond the rustic homage can be glimpsed Heaney's anxiety about how he can best keep faith with the values of his tribe and ancestors while not lapsing into their grunting curtness and silence.

Similar concerns were brought to a head by political events in Northern Ireland in the early 1970s, as Heaney, in solidarity with his fellow Catholics during the civil-rights marches, bombings, and terrorism of the Troubles, found himself searching 'for images and symbols adequate to our predicament' while not wishing to become a mere propagandist. *Wintering Out* (London, 1972; New York, 1973) lovingly rolling its tongue round childhood words and place-names, finds a deeper structure for the present hostilities by uncovering a history of linguistic and territorial dispossession. The verse-form—narrow, two-stress, unrhymed quatrains which owe something to William Carlos *Williams and which run like mine-shafts down the page—becomes a means of drilling into the past. A recurrent image is that of the peat-bog which, with its unique preserva-tive properties, Heaney sees as a kind of 'mem-ory bank', spectacularly so in the case of the 'bog people' of northern Europe, about whose remarkably intact Iron Age corpses Heaney composes a number of his finest poems both in this collection and its successor, *North* (London, 1975; New York, 1976).

Divided into two parts, the first (historical and highly wrought) tracing the invasions of Ire-land from the Vikings to the Elizabethans, the second (contemporary and journalistic) attempting a colloquial, head-on reportage of the Troubles, *North* is Heaney's most politically overt book, a myth by which to understand the history of Ireland. It is hardly surprising that his next, *Field Work* (London and New York, 1979), should have been a self-conscious retreat or 'escape from the massacre', its core a group of sonnets about living in the Wicklow country-side, the 'hedge-school' of Glanmore, though in fact his finest political poem, 'Casualty', is to be found here, and it is—despite the quieter, more celebratory domestic note sounded in the two fine love poems, 'The Skunk' and 'The Otter'—his most troubled, elegiac, questioning book.

Heaney's more recent work moves into a more allegorical and spirit-haunted terrain, with the influence of Homer and Dante, and Milosz and *Brodsky, more telling than that of Hughes and Kavanagh. But even his most grandiose or elliptical work none the less retains its roots in his childhood. The central sequence of *Station Island* (London, 1984; New York, 1985) is about Lough Derg, an ancient place of pilgrimage, and includes a series of ghostly encounters, one of them with *Joyce, who urges

Heaney to strike out on his own. *Sweeney Astray* (London and New York, 1984) is his version of the medieval Irish *Buile Suibhne*. *The Haw Lantern* (London and New York, 1987) contains a moving sonnet-sequence about his mother's death, and *Seeing Things* (London and New York, 1991) a number of poems about his dead father. This last collection is Heaney at his most buoyant to date, discovering miracles at 50 and regaining some of the palpability and physicality of his first book—another twist in the develop-ment of a poet whose constant struggle is to honour his origins without surrendering to the restraints he fears they place on him.

Heaney's two books of essays, *Preoccupations: Selected Prose 1968–1978* (London and New York, 1980) and *The Government of the Tongue* (London and New York, 1988), are useful companions to the work and fascinating in their own right. Critical studies include Blake Morrison's *Seamus Heaney* (London, 1982), Robert Buttel's *Seamus Heaney* (London, 1985) and *The Art of Seamus Heaney*, ed. Tony Curtis (Bridgend, 1982).   [PBM

HEATH-STUBBS, John (1918–), was born in London and educated at Worcester College for the Blind and Queen's College, Oxford. He has often been described as a Romantic, perhaps because any serious interest in Romanticism seemed highly unusual in the early 1940s, when he began to be published (*Eight Oxford Poets*, 1941, *Wounded Thammuz*, 1942). In fact, he might just as well be called a Classicist if one were to be guided by his call in 1941 for 'the return to the classical tra-dition of English poetry'. During this period, when he was an undergraduate, he published an article on the poetry of John Gay. His early work is indebted to the Augustans, to the minor Roman-tics, and to Milton's shorter poems. His originality was to weave a distinctive modern, pastoral style out of these unexpected strands. His admiration for Leopardi (a selection of translations from whom he published in 1946) is in part owing to the fact that the Italian poet is 'at once a Romantic and a Classicist', but also to his sense that Leopardi was one who had to construct a system of his own from past mythologies, from 'erotic passion', and from 'natural beauty'. For the same reason he admired the French Symbolists and Hart *Crane. This view of poetry might seem to align him with *Yeats more than with any other modern poet, and he can strike a note redolent of Yeats's power, and of his confidence with symbolism, as in 'Titus and Berenice'. But the characteristic tone of Heath-Stubbs, from the mid-Fifties, has been dry and ironic, as in the 'Epitaph' in *A Charm Against the Toothache* (London, 1954). Increasingly he comes to seem like a neoclassicist, albeit one who often chooses to write in free verse. He is sometimes reminiscent of Cavafy, whose work he admires. But he remains a master of traditional forms: 'Sestina', from *The Watchman's Flute* (Manchester, 1978) offers only one among many examples of his versatility. A more ambitious and less ironic side of his work is displayed in the long Arthurian poem *Artorius* (Providence, RI, 1970; London, 1972). See *Collected Poems 1943–1987* (1988) and *Selected Poems* (1990—both Manchester). His criticism includes *The Darkling Plain* (London, 1950), a study of Victorian Romantic poetry. [ETL]

HECHT, Anthony (1923–), was born in New York City. He graduated from Bard College in 1944 and served in the army in Europe and Japan. After the war he studied at Kenyon College, where he began a long and distinguished career as a professor, most recently at Georgetown University, Washington. His second collection, *The Hard Hours*, won the Pulitzer Prize for poetry in 1968; his many other awards include the Bollingen Prize and the Librex-Guggenheim Eugenio Montale Award. Apart from five poetry collections, he has published critical essays (*Obbligati*, 1986), light verse (*Jiggery-Pokery*, 1967, with John *Hollander), and translation, most notably of Aeschylus (*Seven Against Thebes*, 1973, with Helen Bacon) and Joseph *Brodsky.

Some recent editions of his work (*Collected Earlier Poems* and *The Transparent Man*, both New York and Oxford, 1990) employ on their covers a photograph of the poet's face reflected in a mirror—on the latter book a photographic negative—most appropriate images for his substantial and remarkable oeuvre, which holds the glass up to this worst of centuries and looks it squarely in the eye, neither glossing its beauty nor flinching from its horror. The work of Anthony Hecht shatters the cosy notion that a fragmented, fractured age should be reflected in the forms of its art, that ugliness and shapelessness demand payment in kind. Like *Auden, he has absorbed the evils and grotesqueries of his unhappy century into a verse both highly formal and all-encompassing, stitching wounds with iambs, sculpting pentameters of sustained, Latinate beauty, sounding a healing music.

Thirteen years after his first book (*A Summoning of Stones*, 1954) in which, as he rightly admits, 'advanced apprenticework', craft, and polish have priority, Hecht published *The Hard Hours*, where pity and terror rise to the placid surface of his tones, sometimes an even simplicity (as in the famous ' "It Out-Herods Herod. Pray you, avoid it" ', where he counterpoints the innocence of his children in front of the television with the observation that he 'could not, at one time, | Have saved them from the gas'); sometimes a numbed lyricism: 'Father, among these many souls | Is there not one | Whom thou shalt pluck for love out of the coals? | Look, look, they have begun | To douse the rags' ('Rites and Ceremonies'). In the latter poem Hecht goes further towards confronting the Holocaust than perhaps any other English-language poet. Elsewhere, he weaves together biblical and classical history, modern America, myth, and fine art with a painter's detailed observation and transformation of the physical.

Millions of Strange Shadows (1977) continues and expands the work, notably into love poems which are all the more intense and conquering for being part of the same dread world as the cruelty, tyranny, and spiritual inertia by which such love is encircled and threatened. The Horatian range and dexterity of Hecht's lines also allow some happy ventures into comedy ('The Ghost in the Martini') and current affairs ('Black Boy in the Dark'), always anchored on the twin foundations of the poet's historical awareness and his generous, embracing intelligence.

These strands continue through *The Venetian Vespers* (1980) and *The Transparent Man* (1990). See in particular 'The Short End' and the title-poem in the former, one a tragicomedy of an American woman, the other an exile's monologue of childhood memory, aspiration, and decay; and in *The Transparent Man*, the enchanting 'Love for Four Voices', a masque of the lovers from *A Midsummer Night's Dream*. In 1993 he published a long study of Auden, *The Hidden Law* (Cambridge, Mass. and London). [GM

HEGLEY, John. See PERFORMANCE POETRY.

HEJINIAN, Lyn. See LANGUAGE POETRY.

HENDERSON, Hamish (1919–), was born in Blairgowrie, Scotland, and educated at Blairgowrie High School, Dulwich College, and Downing College, Cambridge, where he was a contemporary of Nicholas *Moore and Alex *Comfort. He saw his generation as growing up for war: he was 22 at the time of the Battle of El Alamein, which he viewed as one of the major formative events of his life. From his experiences of the desert war came his only volume of poetry, *Elegies for the Dead in Cyrenaica* (London, 1947; new edn. 1978), one of the few impressive attempts to write a long poem about the Second World War.

For Henderson the conflict seemed to be between the dead, who were innocent, and the living who must seek to expiate their survival. The elegies suggest the unity of all those dead in war by juxtaposing memories of the desert campaign with echoes of real and legendary wars, especially those of the Scottish Highlands. The poems are more impressive individually than as a whole, and are most telling in their evocation of the desert war and the desert scene.

Since 1948 Henderson has largely devoted himself to the study of Scottish literature and folklore. See *The Chapman*, 42 (1985) for recent (and earlier) poems and for an essay in the same issue which confirms his authorship of such war-time songs as 'The D-Day Dodgers' and 'The Highland Division's Farewell to Sicily'. [ATT

HENDRIKS, (Michael) A(rthur) L(emière) (1922–), was born in Kingston Jamaica, of West Indian and French parentage, and educated at Jamaica College, Jamaica, and Ottershaw College, England. Now dividing his time mainly between Britain and America, he has travelled widely in Europe and the Americas. Executive posts have included: general manager of the Jamaican Broadcasting Corporation; international director of Thomson Television International; chairman of the Arts Council of Jamaica; and president of the Jamaican Centre of International PEN.

His poetry has much in common with that of John *Figueroa in its cosmopolitan outlook, sensuousness, and sacramental imagery. He is particularly effective when he writes about the sea, even finding epic similes for it, like 'pathways of the fish' and 'Sandless highways'. His attachment to the ocean, and fascination with how it has shaped the lives of West Indian islanders, he shares with Derek *Walcott.

Two long sequences, 'The Islanders' and 'D'où Venons Nous? Que Sommes Nous? Où Allons Nous?' (after the Gauguin painting) are particularly distinctive. The former quietly imposes its dream-like logic on the reader, as the poet carves out a landscape of meditation on Caribbean realities; the latter achieves a prophetic intensity of vision. His later poems are more spare, almost bitter in tone, but also lucidly detached. 'Ennui' and 'Where It's At' are especially powerful in this bleak vein.

Collections include *On This Mountain* (London, 1965); *These Green Islands* (Jamaica, 1971); *Muet* (Walton on Thames, 1971); *Madonna of the Unknown Nation* (London, 1974); and *To Speak Simply: Selected Poems 1961–1986* (Sutton, Surrey, 1988). [MR

HENDRY, J(ames) F(indlay) (1912–86), was born in Balgrayhill near Glasgow and educated at Whitehill School, Dennistoun, and Glasgow University, which he left without taking a degree. During the Second World War he was with Army Intelligence. After the war he was a translator and founded the School of Translating and Interpreting at Laurentian University in Canada. He died in Toronto in 1986.

Hendry is best known as the principal founder of the *New Apocalypse movement, and his essays 'Myth and Social Integration' and 'The Art of History' remain insightful and stimulating. Herbert *Read thought well of him and published his first two books of poems *The Bombed Happiness* (1942) and *The Orchestral Mountain* (1943).

Hendry's first two volumes of poetry did not measure up to the ambitions for literature expressed in his essays. Many of the poems are clumsily pretentious. *Marimarusa* (Caithness, 1979) and *World Alien* (Dunfermline, 1980) are linguistically plainer, but seldom show a sustained verbal felicity. *Aquarius*, 17/18 contains 'An Interview with J. F. Hendry'.   [ATT

HENRI, Adrian (1932–), was born in Cheshire. He has made his living as a member of the Liverpool scene and as a lecturer. Henri, one of the *Liverpool Poets, has designed his verse for public performance to the accompaniment of musical instruments; it has attracted little attention from critics, unless as a sociological phenomenon (e.g. John Willett's *Art in a City*, London, 1967). He claims to have been influenced by *Eliot, Mallarmé, and Tennyson, but a more evident debt is to the *Beat poets. He values spontaneity above concentration. Recently he has published verse for children, but still with the live audience in mind. *Collected Poems 1967–1985* (London, 1986).   [MS-S

HERBERT, W. N. See LALLANS.

HEWETT, Dorothy (1923–), born in Perth, Western Australia, was brought up on a wheat and sheep farm at Malyalling via Wickepin in the Great Southern Region of Western Australia. Hewett discovered in these childhood years a basis for her pastoral vision of 'the Garden', a place of dangerous innocence against which she counterpoints, in her poetry and plays, 'the City' of Sydney, where she lived for a time in the late 1940s, and returned to live in 1974.

Hewett's poetry of the 1960s was strongly influenced by the ideology of the Communist Party, which she joined at 19 and left in 1968. Theatrical and romantic by temperament, she has written poetry and plays which incline towards the personal and *confessional, though the early populist ballads and socially critical verse also reflect a desire to upset conservative social attitudes and practices. Poems such as 'Legend of the Green Country' and 'The Puritans' in *Windmill Country* (1968) recall Robert *Lowell's *Life Studies*, but dramatize an undeniably Australian ruralism. Hewett's poetry of the 1970s is more urban, influenced by Sydney 'new romantics' Robert *Adamson, John *Tranter, and others and the American *Black Mountain poets Charles *Olson, *Creeley, and *Duncan. A third phase, in the 1980s, is notable for this poet's experiments with myth and legend.

Hewett has published five volumes of verse (all Sydney): *What About the People!* (with Merv Lilley, 1963); *Windmill Country* (1968); *Rapunzel in Suburbia* (1975); *Greenhouse* (1979); and *Alice in Wormland* (1987; Newcastle upon Tyne, 1990). A recent selection of her poetry is *A Tremendous World in her Head* (Sydney, 1990).

Hewett's mythologizing of personal experience reaches its apogee in her *Wild Card: An Autobiography, 1923–1958* (Melbourne, 1990).

[BB

HEWITT, John (1907–87), was born and grew up in Belfast where his parents were teachers of nonconformist Protestant background. From 1930 to 1957 he worked in the Belfast Museum and Art Gallery, and from 1957 to 1972 he was director of the Herbert Museum, Coventry. His last fifteen years were spent back in Belfast. Hewitt always avowed socialist principles and a lack of religious affiliation, although his sense of community identification was unwavering ('my own' is a recurrent construction in his writing). In the *Irish Times* in 1974, he declared himself to be 'an Ulsterman of planter stock . . . born in the island of Ireland, so secondarily . . . an Irishman. I was born in the British archipelago and English is my native tongue, so I am British . . . I'm European. This is my hierarchy of values.'

This hierarchical order of identifications explains much about Hewitt's poetry and its reception. Though of *Auden's era, his poetry was largely ignored for most of his career. (Geoffrey *Grigson included him in his 1949 anthology, *Poetry of the Present*.) But the Ulster poets since the 1960s have all claimed Hewitt as a standard-bearer of non-sectarian, northern regionalism, with the result that in the last decade of his life he was regarded as a major figure, recognized by the founding of a summer school in his name in 1988.

The adjective used by Hewitt of himself, picked up by most commentators, is 'mannerly', which suggests well the low-key Augustanism of his poetry, in form and tone. His poetry also manifests a marked sense of place, as physical location and native region; the place is always Ulster, and the identity always the Protestant settler. This is first strikingly stated in one of Hewitt's best-known poems 'The Colony' (1950), in which the Ulster planters are represented as Roman legionaries, garrisoned on the native 'barbarians', 'squatting at our gates'. As well as political allegories, Hewitt wrote fine personal and nature lyrics like 'The swathe uncut' and 'The little lough'. His edition of the Rhyming Weavers, *The Rhyming Weavers, and Other Country Poets of Antrim and Down* (Belfast, 1974), has been an important influence in current Ulster writing, broadening the literary community.

Hewitt's *Collected Poems* (Belfast) appeared in 1992, ed. Frank Ormsby. A good introductory essay is '"The Dissidence of Dissent": John Hewitt and W. R. Rodgers', by John Wilson Foster, in *Across a Roaring Hill: The Protestant Imagination in Modern Ireland: Essays in Honour of John Hewitt*, ed. Gerald Dawe and Edna Longley (Belfast, 1985). See too T. Clyde (ed.), *Ancestral Voices: The Selected Prose of John Hewitt* (Belfast, 1987).   [BO'D

HIGGINS, Bertram (1901–74), was born in Melbourne, son of a hotelier. After a year at Newman College, Melbourne, in 1918, he read languages at Oxford. From 1922 to 1930 he worked in London as a book reviewer and was closely associated with the *Calendar of Modern Letters*, which published a number of his poems

and articles. From 1930 to 1933 he lived in Australia, publishing there his most important poem 'Mordecaius' Overture' (1933). He then returned to Europe and served in the RAF during the Second World War. After the war he and his family settled permanently in Australia. Higgins was greatly influenced by the French Symbolists and the literary milieu of London in the 1920s. It has been claimed that he wrote the first and finest modernist poem in Australia—'Mordecaius'. His style was richly allusive in the manner of *Pound and *Eliot, but utilized a late-nineteenth-century diction. He had little influence in Australia and his poetry was generally ignored until 1981, when the first collection of his poems, *The Haunted Rendezvous* (Geelong, Vic.) appeared.   [JCr

HIGGINS, Brian (1930–65), was born in Batley, Yorkshire. He was a gifted mathematician and, briefly, a professional Rugby footballer. He then became a schoolteacher; but soon abandoned this for a literary career, at which he was also unsuccessful. After living from hand to mouth for some years, he died of a rare heart disease. His poetry, to be found in *The Only Need* (London, 1962), *Notes While Travelling* (London, 1964), and the posthumous *The Northern Fiddler* (London, 1966), mainly satirical, is frequently inchoate and over-influenced by Patrick *Kavanagh, George *Barker, and David *Wright—all of whom encouraged him. But in some twenty poems, including 'Snow and Poetry' and 'A Slight Unease', he achieved a surprisingly precise, elegant and metaphysical voice that might well have been developed had he lived.   [MS-S

HIGGINS, F(rederick) R(obert) (1896–1941), was born in Foxford, County Mayo, son of a Protestant engineer. He founded the Irish Clerical Workers' Union, and was the editor of trade-union journals, and of Ireland's first magazine for women. His first significant collection was *The Dark Breed* (London, 1927); this was followed by *Arable Holdings* (Dublin, 1933) and *The Gap of Brightness* (London, 1940). Higgins believed that poetry should resemble music, and so, although never incoherent or even very mannered, he tended to allow the sense of his poems to look after itself. His verse achieved a considerable degree of musicality. His poems are usually wistfully erotic or celebratory of the Irish folk. After 1933 Higgins tried to abandon lyricism, and, under the influence of his by-then close friend *Yeats, attempted a more symbolic style (e.g. 'Auction!' from the final volume), but this won him little subsequent admiration. His best poems, such as 'The Grief' (from *The Dark Breed*) and 'The Wife of the Red-Haired Man' (from *Arable Holdings*), with their evocative, song-like diction, are now neglected.   [MS-S

HILL, Geoffrey (1932–), was born in Broms-grove, Worcestershire. Educated at Oxford, he subsequently taught in the University of Leeds, where he was elected to a professorship in English literature in 1976. He has since been a fellow of Emmanuel College, Cambridge, and in 1988 moved to the United States. He currently holds a post at Boston University. His critical essays appeared in *The Lords of Limit* (London and New York, 1984).

Hill won an Eric Gregory Award for his poetry, the first of many plaudits, in 1961; in the glare of the esteem now surrounding him, it is worth recalling that his early work, *For the Unfallen: Poems 1952–1958* (1959), defeated as many readers as it fascinated. Hill began his book with a sternly formal treatment of the Genesis creation myth; neither the subjects of his poems nor the voices he chose to approach them had much in common with the work of his contemporaries. While other university poets of the 1950s reacted against modernist difficulty by standing under the banner of accessibility, Hill had other, older objects in mind. 'Against the burly air I strode, | Crying the miracles of God': the combination this work presented of a personal investment in explicitly religious struggle, a daunting breadth of scholarly allusion, and the clear suggestion that such expression cost him genuine pain, seemed to forbid its assimilation by a reading public. Even his 'Two Formal Elegies', the first of many poems on Nazi atrocities and the persecution of the Jews in Europe,

deterred the easy response. They contained instead dark ironies directed, by a motivation that was as yet obscure, at 'the pushing midlanders' who survive in wilful, complicit ignorance of the horrors Hill memorialized.

Not until the publication of *King Log* (1968) did Hill's reputation begin to spread. He continued to address the tensions between history, myth, legend, and the more personal imperatives of memory, giving agonized voice—in sequences such as 'Funeral Music'—to victims of a violence that the compelling density of his work refused to consign to its ostensibly remote historical context, and developing a cold, impassioned, Yeatsian rhetoric to address the horrors which Hill believes, after *Pound, it is the poet's duty to address. He continued to insist that contemporary Europe is irredeemably burdened with its past, and that lyric poetry must confront the uncomfortable fact of such territory's status as both 'nest and holocaust'. But his insistence carries another weight, that of personal conviction. Hill's disgusted fascination for the inevitable horrors of the individual human body, alive as well as dead, makes an enemy of himself, and, indeed, of his own corpus. His celebration, in *The Mystery of the Charity of Charles Péguy* (1983), of the French Catholic intellectual who intervened disastrously in the Dreyfus affair before dying heroically in the first days of the First World War, makes Hill's distrust of poetry's commemorative and potentially political rhetoric more explicit, as it does his own attitude to the relationship of poetry to action.

Neither that poem, nor the collection *Tenebrae* (1978), constitutes his masterpiece. *Mercian Hymns* (1971), a series of thirty formally innovative prose poems reanimating and reinhabiting the life of the eighth-century King Offa, comes closer than any of Hill's other work to achieving the atonement he has continually sought of the currency of historical chronicle, devotional religious lyric, and twentieth-century poetic idiom. Allusive, inventive, but also surprisingly exuberant, the collection represents a remarkable late addition to the two traditions—of doubting Romanticism and of modernism—to which Hill has such close affinities.

Hill's poetry is gathered in *Collected Poems* (London, 1985; New York, 1986). For critical studies, see Christopher Ricks, *The Force of Poetry* (Oxford, 1984); Peter Robinson (ed.), *Geoffrey Hill: Essays on His Work* (Milton Keynes, Bucks., 1985); and Vincent Sherry, *The Uncommon Tongue: The Poetry and Criticism of Geoffrey Hill* (Ann Arbor, Mich.,1987). [MRW

HILL, Selima (1945–), was educated at the University of Cambridge. She lived in London for some years before settling on the Dorset coast. She has received several awards for her work, and won first prize in the 1988 Arvon International Poetry Competition for a poem-journal charting the life of a schizophrenic, *The Accumulation of Small Acts of Kindness* (London, 1989). Her two previous volumes are *Saying Hello at the Station* (London, 1984) and *My Darling Camel* (London, 1988).

Selima Hill creates a poetic world that is hermetic but inviting. Her knack is to concentrate imagery and narrative into a teasing, attractive microcosm, often suggestive of an extremely compressed short story. A fascination with remote geographical and archeological space (Ancient Egypt, for example) adds colour and exoticism to much of her work, but her relaxed homeliness of tone guards against guide-bookishness, and her subtle, oblique views are never touristic. While, like Medbh *McGuckian, she aims to subvert the rational, and raise eccentricity to art, her mood is usually less dream-like, her imagery less fluidly suggestive. Small, wry forays against sexual kitsch and a light touch of ecological conscience give social resonance to her later work. [CAR

HILLYER, Robert (1895–1961), was born in New Jersey but belonged to an old Connecticut family. He graduated from Harvard in 1917, the same year his first volume appeared, *Sonnets and Other Lyrics*. After serving as an ambulance driver in the First World War, he returned to teach at Harvard. In 1926 he married Dorothy Hancock Tilton, and they had one son. Though friends with John Dos Passos and Conrad *Aiken, Hillyer was an adamant foe of mod-

ernism in any form, describing himself as 'a conservative and religious poet in a radical and blasphemous age.' He did attempt to inject some measure of the harsher realism gleaned from E. A. *Robinson and *Frost into his technically deft traditional verses. Satire was more suitable to his minor talent and aristocratic temperament, however, as in the mildly witty use of Pope's heroic couplets in a series of poetic 'letters'. His *Collected Verse* (1933) won a Pulitzer Prize. Divorced in 1943, he resigned from Harvard the next year and served as president of the conservative Poetry Society of America, leading the fight against the 'new estheticism' represented by *Pound, *Eliot, and other 'expatriate' intellectuals—he protested against awarding the first *Bollingen Prize to Pound in two vituperative articles for the *Saturday Review of Literature*.

Hillyer's *Collected Poems* (New York, 1961) contains the bulk of his verses. [EB

HINE, Daryl (1936–), was born in Burnaby, British Columbia. He was educated at McGill University in Montreal and, after several years in France on a fellowship, at the University of Chicago where he taught until 1968, when he assumed the editorship of *Poetry* magazine. Since leaving that post in 1978 he has continued to teach in the Chicago area.

Hine is one of those North American poets who, along with others like Anthony *Hecht and John *Hollander, is sometimes classed as a 'university wit'. While the label accurately suggests the enormous erudition his work displays, it fails to do justice to both its formal brilliance and its emotional and meditative depth. Hine's poetry can be forbidding in its technical polish, its allusiveness, and frequent lack of clear narrative occasion; above all in its abstract diction and difficult syntax. He has quite consciously refused the various counter-traditional modes and idioms of modernism in favour of a verse modelled in form on the seventeenth century, and in elegance and urbanity on the Alexandrian school of Theocritus (whom Hine has translated). Yet for all his emphasis on craft and finish, Hine's poetry often has a muted but eloquent pathos, particularly when it takes up erotic themes, that keeps it from becoming too dry or brittle. Though he has never abandoned his devotion to strict verse-forms, his poetry has gradually moved closer to his own experience, culminating in his long autobiographical poem *Academic Festival Overtures* (New York, 1985), which centres on the poet's adolescent confrontation with his own homosexuality. Hine's earlier work can be surveyed in *Selected Poems* (New York, 1981). [RG

HIRSCH, Edward (1950–), was educated at Grinnell College in Iowa and at the University of Pennsylvania, where he studied with the poet Daniel *Hoffman. He has won a number of awards, including the Delmore Schwartz Award for his first book, *For the Sleepwalkers* (1981), and the National Book Critics Circle Award in Poetry for his second collection, *Wild Gratitude* (New York, 1986). In Hirsch's first volume the world is seen through the eyes of a magic realist and rendered by a skilful rhetorician. The book has a playful beginning, dominated by verbal experimentation and insincerity ('The guardian | Angel of poetry sits in a wicker chair . . . | Ceaselessly trying to astonish us: | To astonish, yes, and to offend'), and progresses to an elegiac ending. The two impulses are intimately related through Hirsch's view of poetry, as expressed in one of his elegies: 'These imaginings make it possible | To survive, to endure the hard light, | Though darkness is floating in.' Feeling seems mostly to replace playfulness in Hirsch's second and third books (*The Night Parade* (New York) was published in 1989), even—in the eyes of some critics—to the point of sentimentality. *Wild Gratitude* in particular was criticized for its reliance on modifiers to convey nuance. In addition, each volume shows an increasingly autobiographical subject-matter; Hirsch seems to be leaving behind his early regard for pure imagination. [PS

HOBSBAUM, Philip (1932–), was born in London and educated at Bellevue Grammar School, Bradford. He read English at Downing College, Cambridge, under F. R. Leavis, and took his doctorate at the University of Sheffield, under William *Empson. Since then he has taught at Queen's University, Belfast and at the University of Glasgow, where he is reader in English.

Hobsbaum founded the *Group (with Edward *Lucie-Smith, George *MacBeth, Martin *Bell, Peter *Porter, and others) in London in 1955, and took its principles with him to form other groups in Belfast and Glasgow. In Belfast Hobsbaum's arrival coincided with, and may have helped the emergence of, young Northern Irish poets such as Seamus *Heaney, Michael *Longley, and Derek *Mahon.

Hobsbaum's first book of poems, *The Place's Fault* (London, 1964), takes its title from a *Larkin poem, and that indicates its general tenor and indebtedness. *In Retreat* (London, 1966) varies the ordinary-life poems with a number of dramatic monologues. *Coming Out Fighting* (London, 1969) tells the story of a failed love affair with a younger woman. Despite the *confessional subject-matter, it lacks drama and real verbal energy. *Women and Animals* (London, 1972) is about the poet's subsequent divorce.

Hobsbaum has also published critical works on Dickens, *Lawrence, *Lowell and *Essentials of Literary Criticism* (London, 1983). [WS

HODGINS, Philip (1959–95), was born in Shepparton, a country town in Victoria, and grew up on a dairy farm at Katandra West, a place-name which figures in several of his poems. He was educated at Geelong College, and then worked in publishing for seven years. At the age of 24 he was diagnosed as having leukemia, and was told that he could expect to live for as few as three more years. He survived for twelve.

Though he had already begun to publish poetry of promise, Hodgins was galvanized as a writer by this news. He rapidly completed his first book, *Blood and Bone* (Sydney, 1986), in which many of the poems deal with the prospect of an early death; the calm, reasoned tone of these poems, and the impressive command of technique in them, makes them all the more wrenching to read. Hodgins's second book has a humorous title, *Down the Lake With*

Half a Chook (Sydney, 1988), and expands his range from the hospital ward to memories of his country childhood and boarding-school life. Hodgins's third book, *Animal Warmth* appeared in 1990 (Sydney). Three further books were published: *Up on All Fours* (1993), *Dispossessed* (1994) and a posthumous work, *Things Happen* (1995). [JG

HODGSON, Ralph Edwin (1871–1962), born in Darlington, Co. Durham, the son of a coal merchant. He was a recluse with a strong sense of privacy, and little is known about his early life: adept at boxing and billiards, he worked in the theatre in New York and as a draughtsman on a London evening paper. In 1913 he founded (with Lovat Fraser) the publishing house The Sign of the Flying Fame; his own *Eve and Other Poems,* with coloured cuts, was one of its first productions. His appearance in the second volume of *Georgian Poetry* won him admirers, and he enjoyed the friendship of *de la Mare, *Sassoon, and *Eliot, whose affectionate 'Lines to R. H. Esqre.' refers to his love of dogs (he bred bull-terriers, and judged them at Cruft's).

Hodgson was editor of *Fry's Magazine* for a while, but he mistrusted literary cliques and left England in 1924 to take up the post of lecturer in English Studies at Tohoku University at Sendai in Japan. Edmund *Blunden records an eccentric, inveterate talker, quick to take offence, who referred to himself as 'The Last of the Fancy'. From his retirement in 1938 he lived in Minerva, Ohio.

Hodgson's reputation, once considerable, was based on a relatively small body of work: *The Last Blackbird* (1907) and *Poems* (1917). The latter furnished the anthologists of two decades with standards like 'Time, you old Gipsy Man', 'Stupidity Street', and 'The Bells of Heaven', with their simple rhythms and clear sentiments, though 'The Bull' (especially), 'The Moor', and others are subtler and more substantial. After the First World War, however, Hodgson stopped writing poetry until he was in his seventies, when he began to send out broadsheets or 'Flying Scrolls' to his friends. Colin Fenton collected these in *The Skylark and Other Poems* (London, 1958).

Hodgson's main inspiration was always the enchantment of nature, and man's idiotic abuse of it. His most-praised poem, 'The Song of Honour' (modelled on Smart's 'Song to David') is a rapturous recital of the world's harmonious hymn of being; his longest finished poem, 'To Deck a Woman', is an angry attack on trade in furs and feathers, originally published (in 1910) as propaganda in favour of prohibitive legislation. In style, however, his late poems differ markedly from those of his *'Georgian' period; they are humorous and cryptic, and make much use of direct speech (see 'Tobit', 'Hever Picnic', and all the miniatures collected in *The Skylark*). His last long poem, 'The Muse and the Mastiff', is a curiosity. Ten years in the writing and not finished, it takes off from a single line of Coleridge's 'Christabel' and is as vigorous and strangely charming as it is cranky and incoherent.

Hodgson's *Collected Poems* was published in London in 1961. There is no biography. [MI

HOFFMAN, Daniel (1923–), was born and grew up in Larchmont, New York. He attended Columbia University, with three years (1943–6) out for active service in the US Army Air Force. After receiving his doctorate he taught at Columbia and at Swarthmore and is now poet-in-residence at the University of Pennsylvania.

In his eight books of poems Hoffman has explored the fragile bond between man and nature in language which veers sharply from the vernacular to the heroic. He writes of the contemporary scene with a spiritual integrity that is akin to that of the Transcendentalists. Hope, for Hoffman, is a live issue: he 'defies desolation'. These concerns are mirrored in the title of his *New and Selected Poems: Hang-Gliding from Helicon* (Baton Rouge, La., 1988). Equally at home in formal and free verse, Hoffman is never afraid to go to an extreme, to risk the outrageous. He knows how to spin believable tales. He is an expert mimic and a parodist of the obvious. Nowhere is history or nature taken straight: it is always sifted through myth and folklore. Hoffman is responsive to 'things | whose archetypes | have not yet been dreamed' ('On the Industrial Highway').

In *Brotherly Love* (New York, 1980), he gives his interest in folklore and myth an historical setting. The poem's hero is William Penn, founder of the city of 'brotherly love', and Hoffman's task is to construct a poem in the same spirit as Penn. 'Penn, in the Quaker tradition, was trying to found a commonwealth in which everyone could live by the light of Divine grace. That's why his treaty with the Indians, whom he approached as his spiritual equals, became the governing image of my whole shebang' (from 'Daniel Hoffman: Education of the Poet', in *Envoy*, 53). In an age of deconstruction Hoffman is reconstructing, like Penn, what the 'age' has torn apart. He sees his task as picking up the pieces in search of a new country.

Hoffman's other collections include *An Armada of Thirty Whales* (New Haven, Conn., 1954); *The City of Satisfactions* (New York and London, 1963); and *The Center of Attention* (New York, 1974). [MRu

HOFMANN, Michael (1957–), was born in Freiburg, Germany. He is the son of the novelist Gert Hofmann, some of whose works he has translated. He came to Britain at the age of 7 and was educated at schools in Edinburgh and Bristol, and then at Winchester College. He took an English degree at Magdalene College, Cambridge, and pursued graduate studies at the University of Regensburg and Trinity College, Cambridge. Since 1983 he has worked as a freelance writer.

Hofmann's first book, *Nights in the Iron Hotel* (London, 1983), announced an unusual talent, one given to wringing poetry out of flat, prosaic rhythms and containing many elisions and ironies, somewhat in the manner of Robert *Lowell's later poems. The title-poem is a sad and witty reflection on a stalled love affair in which sex is characterized as 'a luxury, | an export of healthy physical economies'. His second book, *Acrimony* (London, 1986), confirmed the promise of the first, and largely avoided its occasional thinness. The first half is devoted to modern urban life. Even the titles of poems— 'Between Bed and Wastepaper Basket', 'From Kensal Rise to Heaven'—suggest a slightly off-

beat, surreal approach to experience. It is in the second half of the book, however, entitled 'My Father's House', that Hofmann shows a real deepening of his art. This explores the uneasy son-father relationship—complicated in Hofmann's case by literal divisions of language and culture, and by the fact that both are writers— with memorable honesty and precision.

K. S. in Lakeland: New and Selected Poems was published in New York in 1990. Hofmann's translations include *The Legend of the Holy Drinker* by Joseph Roth (London, 1989) and *Castle Gripsholm*, by Kurt Tucholsky (London, 1985). [WS

HOLBROOK, David (Kenneth) (1923–), was born in Norwich, and has worked in education all his life. He is now an emeritus fellow of Downing College, Cambridge. His reputation as a poet has inevitably, if a trifle unfairly, been compromised by his often denunciatory reactions to pornography and pop-culture. The quietness and exactness of much of his poetry, mostly dealing with 'ordinary, everyday' existence—his explicitly chosen subject-matter—has therefore come as a surprise to many readers who had avoided it, being under the impression that it would reflect his position as cudgel to philistine culture. He is an avowed atheist, but an understanding of Catholic existentialist psychiatry (e.g. of Victor Frankl), as well as the writings of the anti-Freudian psychoanalyst Ian Suttie, is essential to his poetry, as is his debt to his teacher F. R. Leavis. His point of view as a poet is best stated in *The Quest for Love* (London, 1964) and *The Masks of Hate* (Oxford, 1971). See also *Chance of a Lifetime* (London, 1978) and *Selected Poems 1961–1978* (London, 1980).

[MS-S

HOLDEN, Molly (1927–81), was born in Peckham, South London, the granddaughter of Henry Gilbert, a novelist and children's author. When she was 13 her family moved to Swindon, and the broad spaces and historical resonance of the Wiltshire landscape proved to have a lasting influence on her work. She was educated at King's College, London, taking her MA in 1951.

In the 1960s, when her two children were still young, she was stricken by the multiple sclerosis which led to her paralysis and death. She had always written poetry, but it was during the years of illness that she became most consistently productive. Her pamphlets *A Hill Like a Horse* (1961) and *Bright Cloud* (1964) were followed by *To Make Me Grieve* (1968), *Air and Chill Earth* (1971), and *The Country Over* (1975), as well as four novels for children.

Primarily a nature poet, she was first influenced by Thomas *Hardy. Her work has the same painstaking quality of vision, though *Housman seems an obvious presence behind the bitter-sweet simplicity of the shorter lyrics. Some of her unrhymed work shows an abrupt or casual method of enjambement, as if she deliberately wished the impulse to describe to overrule niceties of cadence. Some of her most moving poems are those in which she confronts with candour the sadness and frustration her disablement caused her. (She acknowledges too, though, the value of the watchful stillness it encouraged.)

Selected Poems (Manchester, 1987) contains a variety of work from the earlier volumes and the uncollected MSS, together with a memoir by her husband, Alan Holden. [CAR

HOLLANDER, John (1929–), was born in New York, and took two degrees at Columbia before moving on to further graduate study at the University of Indiana. He was elected a junior fellow of the Society of Fellows at Harvard University and later taught at Hunter College of the City University of New York, before taking up his current position as A. Bartlett Giamatti Professor of English at Yale University.

Hollander's career as a poet began when W. H. *Auden chose his first volume, *A Crackling of Thorns*, for the Yale Series of Younger Poets Award in 1958. Auden's poetic kinship is evident throughout Hollander's poems; one finds in them a deep commitment to traditional forms joining an effort to bring contemporary issues, private and public, to bear in original ways. Since publishing that first volume Hollan-

der has written more than fourteen collections. In some of these, Hollander—like the seventeenth-century poets he admires—writes poems in concrete figures, using, for instance, the shapes of a key, a crescent moon, an umbrella, or a swan while writing poems focused on those images. He often begins a poem with an ordinary image and proceeds, through a sequence of elaborate metaphysical turns, to widen the scope of the poem. His best-known early poem, for instance, is 'the Great Bear', in which the poet contemplates the sky at night, searching for patterns in a patternless splay of light.

The best of Hollander's early work is collected in *Spectral Emanations: New and Selected Poems* (New York, 1978). More recent volumes include *Powers of Thirteen* (New York, 1983), *In Time and Place* (Baltimore, Md., 1986), and *Harp Lake* (New York, 1988). The final poem in this highly accomplished volume is 'The Mad Potter', a Yeatsian meditation that becomes, in the end, an elegy for the poet himself and an exploration of the relation of art and language to human mutability. Hollander's books of criticism include *The Untuning of the Sky* (1961), *Vision and Resonance* (1975), *The Figure of Echo* (1981), and *Melodious Guile* (1988). He has also written two books for children. [JP

HOLLO, Anselm (1934–), was born in Helsinki, Finland, and attended the universities of Helsinki and Tübingen, Germany, before moving first to England, where he worked for the BBC, and then to the United States, where he has been visiting professor at numerous universities and latterly, since 1989, lecturer at the Naropa Institute, Boulder, Colorado. He has published more than forty volumes of poetry, including *Sojourner Microcosms: Poems New and Selected, 1959–1977* (Berkeley, Calif., 1977) and most recently *Outlying Districts* (Minneapolis, 1990). He has also published many volumes of translated poetry, from Finnish, Russian, Swedish, German, and French.

Energy, versatility, and continuous movement are the hallmarks of Hollo's poetry and character of mind. Expatriated, he has made his home in 'the new American poetry . . . a very real place to be . . . It moved me here, & it's still moving, faster and more variously than ever.' Light-hearted, agile-witted, open-spirited, essentially joyful and benign, Hollo is tolerant of and receptive to all kinds of experience. 'Phew! wow! pow! zat voss somsink', exclaims his 'professor albert hofman', as he 'inadvertently inhaled' and thus discovered LSD. Yet he is also a poet who can convey poignantly the haphazard forlornness of transient American lives, where 'in the neverness motels of the bitter country | lovers lie sleeping & loving in fits & starts'. [RWB

HOLLOWAY, (Christopher) John (1920–), was born in London. He is a life fellow of Queens' College, Cambridge. He published his first book collection, *The Minute and Other Poems* (Hessle, 1956) in the year of Robert *Conquest's *Movement anthology *New Lines*, to which he contributed, and he was at first (vaguely) regarded as a 'Movement poet', if only on account of his attachment to traditional forms. *The Victorian Sage* (London, 1953) is his major critical work. The writing of poems has increasingly been seen as a sideline, in the sense that, although he is a careful and conscientious craftsman, idea rather than language is primary in his verse, which lacks urgency. The chief influences on the early, mythopoeic poems were *Graves and, in particular, Edwin *Muir. In *The Landfallers: A Poem in Twelve Parts* (London, 1962), written in *terza rima*, he used poetry, not unskilfully, as a means to a philosophical end (he had read philosophy at Oxford), whose nature most readers found obscure. The poems in *Wood and Windfall* (London, 1965) have been praised for their evocation of Greek landscape. See also *New Poems* (New York, 1970) and *Planet of Winds* (London, 1977). [MS-S

HONGO, Garrett (Kaoru) (1951–), was born in Volcano, Hawaii, grew up there and in Southern California, and spent one year studying in Japan. He attended Pomona College, studying with the late Bert Meyers, and the University of Michigan, and received an MFA in writing from the University of California at Irvine. Since graduating, he has taught poetry at UC Irvine, the University of Southern California, the University of Missouri at Columbia (where he also served as a poetry editor for *The Missouri Review*), and the University of Oregon, where he currently directs the creative-writing programme.

His first book of poetry, *Yellow Light* (Middletown, Conn., 1982), presents ruminative lyric portraits of family and childhood set against the suburban Los Angeles of the Fifties and early Sixties. Often nostalgic and melancholy, the poems strive both to celebrate and preserve a coherent record of the poet's own bi-cultural history and the older Japanese heritage preceding it. The poems of his second book, *The River of Heaven* (New York, 1988), focus this dual effort on the Hawaiian branch of the poet's family and display a greater willingness to call on narrative techniques to tell their stories.

[RMcD

HOOKER, (Peter) Jeremy (1941–), was born in Warsash near Southampton. A career lecturing in English and creative writing has taken him to Wales, the Netherlands, and Somerset, as well as his native Hampshire. *A View from the Source* (Manchester, 1982) selects poems from four previous collections; he has since published *Master of the Leaping Figures* (Petersfield, 1987). His extensive criticism includes essays on David *Jones and John Cowper *Powys, both writers central to his outlook.

Though Hooker's poetry touches on his travels, it is dominated by his feeling for his home territory: the chalk downs, forest paths, and muddy estuaries of the region he celebrates in *Solent Shore* (Manchester, 1978), which is, like nearly all his poetry, an integrated sequence of short lyrics. He has called his work a 'poetry of place', which partly means a poetry of fact, shaped from and by the substance of the world. But his facts grow from invisible roots—in a shared human history and the mysterious otherness of non-human creation. Much of Hooker's originality as a poet derives from his very English use of historically resonant language in the spacious forms of American modernism. [CW

HOPE, A(lec) D(erwent) (1907–), was born in Cooma, New South Wales, the son of a Presbyterian minister. He spent most of his childhood in rural Tasmania, where his parents fostered his interest in the classics and in English poetry. Despite an early interest in science, he graduated in 1928 from Sydney University with an arts degree and took up a scholarship at Oxford, returning to Australia in 1931. He has followed an academic career, eventually holding the chair of English at the Australian National University, Canberra, from which he retired in 1968. As emeritus professor he remained closely associated with the university.

Hope wrote his first poem at the age of 8, and continued to write thereafter, though almost all his early work was lost in a fire a few years before his first collection of verse, The Wandering Islands, appeared in 1955. This collection, however, made a great impact in a country to some extent still parochial in outlook. Though Hope's poetry is largely traditional in form, and reminiscent in this respect of *Yeats, *Frost, and *Graves, his voice is more powerfully satiric than any of these poets, and his sexual explicitness, combined with his erudition, has often been analysed unsympathetically when it has been analysed at all. His poetry is much concerned with man's ambiguous and often adversarial relationship with nature, which is seen either to succumb to, or to ignore, his urge to master her through ingenuity, blind destructiveness, or both. This opposition is frequently translated into terms of sexual struggle and conflict, themselves illustrated by mythological and biblical material. Similarly, the seriousness with which Hope regards the role of poetry in the world manifests itself in a reverence for, and a familiarity with, poets of the past which some readers will not share. This seriousness is by no means incompatible with an unforgiving, sardonic brand of humour, quite un-Australian in nature. A combination of these factors has led to Hope's having a slightly uneasy relationship with his native literary culture. In a country with its own particular idea of the democratic vistas writers should address, he has been accused, wrongly, of being élitist, misogynist,

and anti-Australian in attitude. This last accusation is particularly unjust: as an academic Hope has consistently supported the teaching of Australian literature at Australian universities.

Hope's love for traditional verse-forms can occasionally seem self-indulgent; his vision of man's struggle with nature portentous, and his view of sex both old-fashioned and wilfully 'poetic'. His scepticism and the ferocity of his wit, however, are provocative in the fullest sense. They transcend the purely satirical, and betray a compassionate impatience with human folly which is both traditional and timely.

Hope's Collected Poems (Sydney, 1972) was followed by A Late Picking (Sydney, 1975), A Book of Answers (Sydney, 1978), The Age of Reason (Carlton, Victoria, 1985), and Orpheus (Sydney, 1991). See also Selected Poems, ed. Ruth Morse (Manchester, 1986), and a new Selected Poems to mark his eighty-fifth birthday (Sydney, 1992). His essays have been collected in The Cave and the Spring (Adelaide, 1965); Native Companions (Sydney, 1974); and The Pack of Autolycus (Canberra, 1979). The New Cratylus (Melbourne, 1979) is a study of the craft of poetry. See also A. D. Hope, by Leonie Kramer (Melbourne, 1979).
[RL

HOPE, Christopher (1944–), was born in Johannesburg and studied at the universities of the Witwatersrand and Natal. Before leaving South Africa in 1975 he worked as a journalist in Durban and also played an important part in Bolt, the liveliest little magazine of the period. Since then he has lived in London, establishing himself as one of the most distinguished of South Africa's expatriate writers.

Many of Hope's preoccupations as a novelist find an earlier expression in his poetry. Particularly in his first collection, Cape Drives (London, 1974), he explores the historical dilemmas of his own kind, the white, English-speaking minority in South Africa. In a verse that is tightly controlled, tough-minded, and astringent, he dissects the compromised lives and troubled identities of people who no longer feel they have a place in Africa. This culminates in 'The Flight of the White South Africans', a poem in which Hope would seem to be saying a personal goodbye to his native land even as he prophesies the collective demise of his own people.

Hope's poetry has retained its obsession with the complex fate of being a South African. However, in his next collection, *In the Country of the Black Pig* (London, 1981), his concerns are distanced, as well as controlled, through the use of a less realistic, more allegorical mode. At the same time, Hope has continued to elaborate his distinctive vision of South Africa. It is one in which all conventional distinctions between the comic and tragic are repeatedly blurred. The complex humour generated by this is evident once again in the long poem *Englishmen* (London, 1985). Here, through skilful use of narrative, South African history is seen as a nightmare in which the farcical and brutal are indissolubly linked.

Hope is included in all the representative South African anthologies, including André Brink and J. M. Coetzee's *A Land Apart* (London, 1986). The most useful background to the poetry is to be found in the discussion of his South African youth in his travelogue, *White Boy Running* (1988). His novel *Serenity House* was on the Booker Prize short list in 1992.   [SW

HOPKINS, Kenneth (1914–88), was born in Bournemouth, England, the son of a greengrocer and shoe-repairer. At 14 he was apprenticed to an ironmonger, but at 21 he decided to devote himself to literature after receiving encouragement from John Cowper *Powys. In 1938, with a knapsack full of his poems, he made his way to London, peddling his work from door to door. In 1939 he married Elizabeth Coward and during the next half a century addressed over two hundred poems to her. During the Second World War he created the Grasshopper Press, which published poems by contemporary poets, including R. C. *Trevelyan who, in correspondence with Hopkins, criticized his work and also published him in the *Abinger Chronicle*. During the period after the war his energetic literary life included publication (sometimes under pseudonyms) of eight crime novels, eight volumes of the Books of the

Film series, parodies, an autobiography, and numerous volumes of verse. He was a visiting professor at the University of Texas and elsewhere, and a proprietor of the Warren House Press. He died in Norwich.

Hopkins is noted for his poems of love and passion, as in *Love and Elizabeth* (London, 1944). His favourite verse-form was the sonnet.

His *Collected Poems: 1935–1966* and *Collected Poems 1966–1977* have recently been reprinted by the Warren House Press, Cheshire. His autobiography, *The Corruption of a Poet* (London, 1954) and Paul Roberts's 'Love, Death, and Wit: An Introduction to the Life and Work of Kenneth Hopkins', *Papers on Language and Literature* (University of Southern Illinois, Summer 1990) are sources for his biography.   [DS

HORAN, Robert (1922–) is known for a single book, *A Beginning* (New Haven, Conn., 1948), selected by W. H. *Auden for the Yale Series of Younger Poets. Horan was among the poets who gathered in the 1940s around Lawrence Hart, a teacher at the University of California at Berkeley, who argued for a derivative poetry indebted largely to English and American modernism. One favoured model was Hart *Crane, whose work is strongly echoed in Horan's. Auden called Hart's group the Activists because of their proclivity for intense, driven styles— which is very much what one finds in Horan's work. In the Foreword to *A Beginning*, Auden singled out Horan's dexterity as a versifier, and it is, in fact, his technical virtuosity which places his densely textured poems among the more interesting from the immediate postwar era.

In the late 1940s Horan was a member of the circle around Gian Carlo Menotti, to whom, with Samuel Barber, *A Beginning* was dedicated, but he soon withdrew from that group as well as from the Activists. Although his work was often anthologized and a few scattered poems were subsequently published, there was no second book; yet *A Beginning* remains, beside the work of Rosalie Moore and Jeanne McGahey, one of the principal accomplishments of the Activists.   [EHF

HOROVITZ, Frances (1938–83), was born in London in 1938 and educated at Bristol University and the Royal Academy of Dramatic Art. Her career as a poet was paralleled by that as a distinguished reader and presenter of poetry, and she made a number of recordings for BBC Radio 3 and the Open University. She published the first of several pamphlets, *Poems*, in 1967. Her first full-length collection, *Water Over Stone* (London, 1980) was followed by *Rowlstone Haiku* (Hereford, 1982) and *Snow Light, Water Light* (Newcastle upon Tyne, 1983). In 1982 she moved to Herefordshire where she died, after a long illness from cancer, in 1983. *Collected Poems*, ed. Roger Garfitt, came from Newcastle upon Tyne in 1985.

Perhaps not surprising in the work of a poet drawn to the haiku form, there is a Japanese quality in her tough delicacy of outline and sparingness of detail. Usually happiest working on a miniature scale, she shapes her poems with an instinctive rather than formal sense of prosody. Her best work conveys a feeling of organic wholeness, reminiscent of the landscapes and natural objects that are often its subject-matter.

[CAR

HOROVITZ, Michael. See PERFORMANCE POETRY.

HOUEDARD, Dom Sylvester. See SOUND POETRY.

Hound & Horn (1927–34), a quarterly magazine of literature and the arts, was edited by Lincoln Kirstein with the help at different times of Varian Fry, R. P. *Blackmur, Bernard Bandler, A. Hyatt Mayor, Allen *Tate, and Yvor *Winters. It was founded by Kirstein and Fry when they were students at Harvard, as its final editorial recalled, 'as a college paper based on the London *Criterion*', which aimed to make Americans more aware and appreciative of the latest experimental developments in the arts. Having severed its ties with Harvard in 1929 (dropping its subtitle, 'A Harvard Miscellany') and moved to New York City in 1930, it became one of the most highly regarded—and elegantly pre-

sented—periodicals of its kind, attracting contributions from almost every prominent American Modernist, including T. S. *Eliot, Ezra *Pound (whose poem 'The White Stag' provided its name), William Carlos *Williams, Marianne *Moore, E. E. *Cummings, Wallace *Stevens, and Gertrude *Stein.

Committed to no consistent ideological stance, the magazine addressed a series of topical issues. Humanism received particularly extensive discussion for two years (1928–30), communism for two more (1931–3) and Southern *Agrarianism and Pacific neoclassicism featured strongly from 1932 when Tate and Winters became regional editors. Most enduring and influential, however, were the critical essays and reviews, by Blackmur and others, which advocated and practised a purely aesthetic approach, thus helping to develop the *New Criticism. *The Hound & Horn* by Leonard Greenbaum (The Hague, 1966) is a thorough account of the magazine's history, and *The Hound and Horn Letters*, ed. Mitzi Berger Hamovitch (Athens, Ga., 1982), a selection of correspondence by its editors and contributors.

[NE

HOUSMAN, A(lfred) E(dward) (1859–1936), was born in Fockbury, Worcestershire, and educated at Bromsgrove School and St John's College, Oxford. After taking first-class honours in classical moderations, he disastrously failed his final examinations and took a clerical job in the Patent Office, London, for the next ten years. However, he kept up his own rigorous classical studies, was awarded his MA, published in specialist journals, and took up the chair of Latin at University College, London, in 1892. In 1911 he was elected a fellow of Trinity College, Cambridge, and Kennedy Professor of Latin in the university, posts he held until his death.

Housman's gifts as a poet have sometimes been seen as being much like his gifts as a classical scholar: narrow, profound, isolated, brooding, and on occasion ferocious. He brought his highly trained and subtle powers as a textual critic to bear on one of the least-considered (some would say least-rewarding) Roman writers, Manilius, and guarded him as a dragon would its cave. In the same way, he guarded his poems and the emotional wounds from which they welled: wounds he suffered in his youth, and which he could hardly bring himself to mention except through the obliquities of his apparently stark and simple verse.

His first book, A Shropshire Lad (1896), was originally published at his own expense, before being taken up by Grant Richards, who continued to be his publisher. Its poems soon began to become popular, the South African war helping to draw attention to Housman's memorable mixture of patriotic pride and stoical gloom, pessimism, and nostalgia. The 'Shropshire' of the book's title and its poems, though often apparently reinforced with place-names (Clun, Ludlow, Wenlock Edge), is a region of evocative emotions rather than an actual locality. This is a 'land of lost content'. Housman was not a rural writer; instead, he based a personal mythology (of country lads betrayed in love, drinking themselves into oblivion, committing suicide, being hanged for nameless crimes) on a pastoral tradition which he helped to rediscover.

In his lifetime, Housman published only one other book of poems, the decisively titled Last Poems (1922). This is a gathering of pieces from the 1890s until the end of the First World War. It shows no real development from A Shropshire Lad: its strengths, and its few weaknesses (an occasional mawkishness, and what might be called a hopeless emotional vulgarity—'Little is the luck I've had | And oh, 'tis comfort small | To think that many another lad | Has had no luck at all'), are the same, virtually interchangeable. The almost marmoreal words are matched with an extraordinarily seductive, though simple, rhythmical inspiration: 'In gross marl, in blowing dust, | In the drowned ooze of the sea, | Where you would not, lie you must, | Lie you must, and not with me.'

After Housman's death, his brother Laurence, as his literary executor, gathered together More Poems (London, 1936). There then appeared a Collected Poems (London, 1939, paperback, 1967), edited by John Carter, which included a few 'Additional Poems'. In 1988 Christopher Ricks edited a Collected Poems and Selected Prose (London). A new collected poems, which will attempt a chronological ordering, is in preparation. Another important text is Housman's Leslie Stephen Lecture at Cambridge, The Name and Nature of Poetry (1933), in which he spoke about his basic attitude to poetry—chiefly, that it strikes to the pit of the emotions and bypasses 'thought'. This simple intuitiveness is not as simple as it looks. Nor, indeed, is Housman's poetry, which has been sporadically carped at by critics who find it 'adolescent'; but the popularity of the poetry cuts across many boundaries and barriers, of age and taste. See also John Bayley, Housman's Poems (Oxford, 1992); Norman Page, A. E. Housman: A Critical Biography (London, 1983); and Richard Perceval Graves, A. E. Housman: The Scholar Poet (London, 1979). [AST

HOUSTON, Douglas (1947–), was born in Cardiff and read English at Hull University. He now lives near Aberystwyth.

Houston's work is striking in its combination of large and local themes in language both literary and vernacular, and for a vein of fantasy by turns amusing and disquieting. Apocalyptic pieces like 'Sic Transit' are juxtaposed with comic monologue ('To the Management'), bizarre ritual ('Devotions') with imaginative additions to history ('Horst Wessel on Alcatraz'). An atmosphere of nightmare pervades a number of poems dramatizing dreams or madness ('From the Corner', 'After the Anaesthetic').

An admirer of both W. H. *Auden and Derek *Mahon, Houston also looks back to Baudelaire and Keats: an aspiration to Romantic grandeur is habitually checked by irony and humour. At his best, when philosophical leanings are bedded in the particular, Houston is a poet of strangeness and charm.

Houston's first collection of poems is With the Offal Eaters (Newcastle upon Tyne, 1986). Selections of his work are contained in A Rumoured City: New Poets from Hull, ed. Douglas Dunn (Newcastle upon Tyne, 1982) and Poetry with an

Edge, ed. Neil Astley (Newcastle upon Tyne, 1988). [SO'B

HOUSTON, Libby (1941–) was born in London, brought up in the West Country, and educated at Lady Margaret Hall, Oxford. In 1966 she married the artist Malcolm Dean, who illustrated her early books. She was widowed in 1974 and returned to Bristol, where she works in local research and is a regular contributor to BBC Radio schools programmes.

Especially in her first two books, *A Stained Glass Raree Show* (London, 1967) and *Plain Clothes* (London, 1971), her poetry typifies in many ways the spirit of the 1960s, and shows the influence of the American *Beat poets. At the same time her use of traditional vernacular forms such as the ballad and limerick, the debunking humour, flights of pastiche, and the comic-sympathetic approach to the animal world, all help to create a feeling of Englishness. In her more recent volumes, *At the Mercy* (London, 1981) and *Necessity* (Nottingham, 1988), her mood is darker and more meditative, and she is drawn to the longer, mythological narrative poem. Though she can be an obscure and uneven writer, her refusal to find the easy answer or the pleasant cadence can be rewarding: an unusual metaphysical intelligence is at work and continuing to develop. [CAR

HOVE, Chenjerai (1956–), was born in Mazvihwa, Zimbabwe (then Rhodesia), and educated at the University of Rhodesia. A former teacher, he worked as a cultural journalist in Harare until his two-year appointment as writer-in-residence at the University of Zimbabwe in 1990. His novel, *Bones* (Harare, 1988), won the 1988 Zimbabwean Publishers/Writers Literary Award, as well as the 1989 Noma Award for publishing in Africa. He has published two volumes of poetry: *Up In Arms* (Harare, 1982) and *Red Hills of Home* (Gweru, 1985).

Much of Hove's poetry is informed by the natural world to an extent that is unusual in modern African poetry. Only the Nigerian, Niyi *Osundare, communicates the same depth of feeling for the landscape of his birth, as is evi-

dent in the opening stanza of the title-poem from his second collection: 'Father grew up here | tuning his heart | to the sound of the owl from the moist green hills, | beyond, the eagle swam in the air | while mother-ant dragged | an unknown victim to a known hole | printed on the familiar unreceding earth . . .'

Hove also contributed to *And Now the Poets Speak: Poems Inspired by the Struggle for Zimbabwe* (1981). Some of his poems can be found in the *Mambo Book of Zimbabwean Verse in English*, ed. Colin and O-lan Style (Gweru, 1986) and in the principal anthologies of African poetry. [AM-P

HOWARD, Richard (1929–), was born in Cleveland, Ohio, and educated at Columbia University and the Sorbonne. A prolific translator from French, Howard was made a Chevalier de l'Ordre National du Gouvernement Français (1980) for his many translations from authors including Gide, Barthes, Baudelaire, and (in progress) Proust. Honoured by the Pulitzer Prize in poetry (1970), Howard has taught at many universities, including Johns Hopkins and the universities of Houston and Cincinnati. He lives in New York City.

The formal versatility and fluent ease with abstractions of Howard's early poetry recall *Auden, but as early as *The Damages* (Middletown, Conn., 1967) many poems begin to locate either historical or imagined characters in vividly evoked settings. Howard's voice has moved steadily away from the directly personal; rather, a poem may feature Goliath addressing Donatello's David, or the aged Browning holding forth in Florence, or a figure in a Caspar David Friedrich canvas musing, or a pair of fictional Americans in Paris describing the (apocryphal) visit to that city of the old Wallace *Stevens.

In such dramatic guises, and in suave, sinuous, and often witty language, Howard offers meditations on art and society, mortality and love. The poems are rich in aphorisms and cultural history alike, but transcend such ingredients; most tend toward a melancholic abstractness very different from the verve and bustle of a dramatic monologue by Browning. The urbane voice is recognizably Howard's.

Howard's translations from French are too numerous to list. Notable volumes of poetry are *Two-Part Inventions* (New York, 1974) and *Misgivings* (New York, 1979). Howard is also the author of a capacious study of America poetry in the mid-twentieth century, *Alone with America* (New York, 1969, expanded edn. 1980).   [RHa

HOWE, Susan. See LANGUAGE POETRY.

HOWES, Barbara (1914–) was born and raised in Boston, and attended Bennington College. In the mid-Forties she edited the literary journal *Chimera* in New York, but for many years she has lived in North Pownal, Vermont. Her book *The Blue Garden* (1972) reveals in smaller compass what *A Private Signal: New and Selected Poems* (1977) shows in full, a poetic world located between the geographical poles of New England and the island of Tobago in the Caribbean. That world is rich in the lore of nature, and of neighbours described with a naturalist's precision and sympathy.

Howes is a formalist of sorts, though inventive and self-determined. Her formalism is not so much a refusal of free verse as the expression of a taste for symmetry and complication; she usually chooses forms that work against the grain of any easy, unimpeded flow of thought or speech. The more she hems and dams her poems, the more interesting they become, and the more insistent their music.

Her Vermont poems are naturally more inward and personal, reflecting the farmers and animals she lives among, her children and memories. Her pastoral poems are not sentimental, but candidly reveal the violence and physical hardship of winter and mud-season in the green mountains: the dog shot by hunters, the old cow and her untimely calf dead together in the field, the 'windmares' brought on by blizzard, the abused child who shot his father four times. All these sombre themes, together with life's ordinary celebrations, she finds worthy of poetry.   [EG

HUDGINS, Andrew (1951–), was born in Kileen, Texas, and holds degrees from Huntington College and the University of Alabama. Since 1985 he has been on the faculty at the University of Cincinnati.

Hudgins's first volume, *Saints and Strangers* (New York, 1985), is divided into four unequal parts containing a total of thirty-three poems. Characters of familiar name appear throughout, including St Francis, Audubon, Zelda Fitzgerald, as well as biblical figures. The fourth section comprises an eight-part poem from which the volume takes its title. The poems deal with death and images of horror, and most of his narrators are ironic angels at best: the best tend to be pathetically mad or significantly depressed. His collection of personae—drunk drivers, female convicts, murdered girls—suggest a sense of the grotesque that is in good company with the Southern Gothic poets he says he admires.

In his second book, *After the Lost War: A Narrative* (New York, 1988), Hudgins focuses on a single figure, a poet, Sidney Lanier, and follows Lanier's sensibility through the American Civil War and the knowledge of his own, impending death.   [CR

Hudson Review, The (1948–), was founded by three young graduates of Princeton University, Frederick *Morgan, Joseph Bennett, and William *Arrowsmith. Over the years, Morgan (who is now co-editor with his wife, Paula Deitz) has had the central role in running the magazine and has published both established and emerging writers of substance. Himself a poet of some distinction, Morgan has been especially attentive and receptive to serious poetry: early issues of *Hudson Review* featured Ezra *Pound and Wallace *Stevens; later on, poets such as A. R. *Ammons, W. S. *Merwin, Louis *Simpson, Anne *Sexton, and William *Stafford appeared first—or early in their careers—in the magazine. Nor is the emphasis exclusively American; Charles *Tomlinson has been a regular contributor of poems and translations, while Continental theorists such as Jean Starobinski and E. M. Cioran have frequently shown up in

Hudson's pages. The magazine has successfully avoided both the strongly political atmosphere of *Partisan Review* and the at times provincial, regional quality of university-based periodicals like the *Sewanee* or the *Southern Review*. *Hudson Review* has always existed apart from any university subsidy, has a very small staff, and has never exceeded a circulation of four or five thousand.

In addition to poetry, it has regularly published fiction and has shown a discriminating eye for such original prose writers as James McConkey, Wendell *Berry, Guy *Davenport, and Susan Kenney. But perhaps even more impressive are the magazine's so-called 'back pages'; since from its inception *Hudson Review* has provided quarterly 'omnibus' accounts of recent fiction and poetry, along with reviews of current performances on the stage, on film, and in dance. The list of distinguished critics who have reviewed regularly for the magazine is a long one and includes Hugh Kenner, Marvin Mudrick, Robert M. Adams, and Marius Bewley. For many years B. H. Haggin provided regular reports of concerts and ballets, as did John Simon of film. These reports, and those of their successors, have been notable for an often polemical edge, which reflects an editorial willingness to let contributors speak their minds about what they see and hear. In one of his infrequent editorials, Frederick Morgan once alluded to forces in society 'that would pervert art and stifle responsible criticism'. Thus it was all the more necessary 'for an independent literary review to exercise its lonely prerogatives: of remaining accessible to the new and unexpected, of joining no coterie . . . and of maintaining the cleansing function of criticism as the revealer and scourge of fraud'. In the continuing liveliness of its critical tone, *Hudson Review* has lived up to such ideals.   [WHP

HUEFFER, Ford Madox. See FORD, FORD MADOX.

HUGHES, Glyn (1935–), was born in Middlewich, Cheshire, and educated at Altrincham Grammar School and the Regional College of Art, Manchester. He taught art and liberal studies at schools and colleges in Lancashire and Yorkshire until 1972, since when he has been a free-lance writer.

His poems are largely set in 'that block of the Pennines made of millstone grit, and ringed with the Yorkshire wool towns to the east and the Lancashire cotton towns to the west' vividly described in his prose book *Millstone Grit* (London, 1975). In his first collection, *Neighbours* (London, 1970), he explores both the landscape and its people, dour, uningratiating, taciturn, more concerned with survival than with the niceties of friendship or love. Occasionally northern stereotypes intrude, and the tone of voice probably owes something to his namesake Ted *Hughes, but the chaos and poetry of the high moors is subtly realized, mirroring personal and national (post-industrial) hardship.

Rest the Poor Struggler (London, 1972) circles round similar places and themes, showing some American influence in its free-verse rhythms, and a greater interest in narrative. *Best of Neighbours: New and Selected Poems* (Sunderland, 1979) reprints the best of the earlier work and begins to explore the Nonconformist, evangelical world—'mills for souls called "chapels"'—he has gone on to write about at greater length in his novels and plays.

His prize-winning novels include *Where I Used To Play On The Green* (London, 1982), *The Hawthorn Goddess* (London, 1984), and *The Rape of the Rose* (London, 1987). He has also written stage plays and verse plays for radio.   [WS

HUGHES, Langston (1902–67), was a native of Joplin, Missouri, but he grew up in various places in the American Midwest and in Mexico, where he taught and was a ranch-hand for his father. He moved on to manual labour in New York City, France, and Washington, DC; however, Hughes was also the first American black to make a living as a writer. Although he began as a poet, his literary output was enormous, covering drama, fiction, autobiography, libretti for musicals, opera, and a cantata. Furthermore, Hughes wrote in a variety of styles and techniques: he was as capable of penning a traditionally formal poem as a prose poem in the style of Whitman.

Although Hughes is associated with the *'Harlem Renaissance' of the 1920s and 1930s, he lived into the Decade of Protest and served as a model for postmodernist blacks such as Robert *Hayden, Gwendolyn *Brooks, Amiri *Baraka, and Don L. *Lee. Hughes was accused by some critics, both black and white, of not writing enough consciousness-raising material, but he was in fact the first black American to write civil-rights protest poetry that was identifiable as such, and he did it when it was quite dangerous to do so.

Hughes tried hard to bring into American literature not only the black experience, but Afro-American musical traditions as well, for many of the poems he wrote were conceived of as 'jazz' poems, as Steven C. Tracy discussed in *Langston Hughes and the Blues* (Urbana, Ill., 1988). Hughes is given credit for making the 'blues' as much a part of American literature as it had become of American music. Blues first appeared as a consciously literary form in Hughes's poem, 'The Weary Blues', which won *Opportunity* magazine's poetry prize in 1925 and, in the following year, was the title-poem of his first book (New York, 1926). The synthesis of these efforts was *Montage of a Dream Deferred* (New York, 1951) which is a 'street epic' full of all sorts of jazz effects, as is *Ask Your Mama: 12 Moods for Jazz* (New York, 1961). His autobiographies are *The Big Sea* (New York, 1940) and *I Wonder As I Wander* (New York, 1956). His most comprehensive collection is *Selected Poems* (New York, 1959); the most recent is the posthumous *The Panther and the Lash* (New York, 1969). Jemie Onwuchekwa's book *Langston Hughes: An Introduction to the Poetry* (New York, 1976) provides a good overall view of the poet's work, as does Arnold Rampersad's *The Life of Langston Hughes* (New York and London, 1986–8) of his career.

[LT

HUGHES, Ted (Edward James) (1930–), was born in Mytholmroyd in Yorkshire. His father, William Hughes, was a carpenter who fought in the First World War (he was one of only seven-

teen survivors of an entire regiment which perished at Gallipoli). The family moved to Mexborough, a coal-mining town in South Yorkshire, when Hughes was 7, and his parents took a newsagent's and tobacconist's shop. In 1948 he won an Open Exhibition to Pembroke College, Cambridge. Before attending university he did two years' National Service in the RAF. After leaving Cambridge, he worked as a rose-gardener, night-watchman, and a script-reader for Rank at Pinewood, before becoming a teacher.

He married the American poet Sylvia *Plath in 1956 and the couple went to the USA in the following year. Hughes taught English and creative writing at Amherst College, and Plath taught literature at Smith College. After spending several months in the writers' colony of Yaddo in Saratoga Springs, the couple returned to England in December 1959.

Hughes's first collection of poems, *The Hawk in the Rain*, was published in 1957, and its vigorous vernacular won immediate acclaim. Its terse celebration of raw natural energies contrasted with the rational ironies of *Movement verse and since the late 1950s Hughes has been viewed as a nature poet. His appointment as Poet Laureate in 1984 sealed his essentially shaman-like conception of his poetic mission and enabled him to speak out on environmental issues while celebrating royal weddings and babies.

During a prolific writing career, Hughes has been regarded as a poet who writes about the natural world rather than society, but the feral forces he celebrates are disguised metaphors for a series of historical struggles—Reformation, Industrial Revolution, First World War—which echo and combine in his radically unsettled imagination. Rooted like D. H. *Lawrence in dissenting culture, Hughes follows Lawrence both as a literary model and as a writer who attempts to abolish society by locating the self-justifying act of individual witness in a primordial wilderness. Hughes's primitivism embodies this wounded search for an original wholeness and forms the basis of his writing for children (a gifted children's writer, his story, *The Iron Man*, is widely popular).

In his early poems, Hughes sometimes uses rhyme, but he does so uneasily. Drawing on Walt Whitman and Robinson *Jeffers, his verse-line is most confident when unconstrained by the demands of formal rhyme or metre. His imagination is drawn to horizons, open space, the impacted bunching of strong monosyllables ('short fierce fuse' in 'The Jaguar', 'sudden sharp hot stink of fox' in 'The Thought-Fox'). Locating North American wilderness poetry in England, he expresses a type of puritan, entrepreneurial striving, a visceral populism which scorns what Hughes has termed the 'crippled court-artifice' of polite speech. His second volume, *Lupercal* (1960), aims to challenge the cultural dominance of southern English culture by designing heroically English figures on recognizably Yeatsian principles. Like *Yeats, Hughes likes to set up imaginative polarities—salt-bleached Viking warriors against the 'elaborate, patient gold of the Gaels'.

In his verse, Hughes has constructed a myth in which the Germanic/puritan/masculine is eternally at war with the Celtic/catholic/feminine. The driven, gruelling texture of his poems is intensely puritan—they are written to the moment in a type of absolute present tense. Hughes's poems do not develop; instead, he appears to have been endlessly re-drafting the same poem. His visionary spontaneity is a form of born-again evangelical earnestness which is integral to Yorkshire dissent. In their fascination with an elemental energy, his poems may also be read as protests against the post-war consensus which was challenged by the election of a radical conservative government in 1979. By coincidence, Hughes's most assured volume, *Moortown*, was published that year. The poems in the opening sequence are elegies for an island economy which is self-reliant and not 'at the mercy of foreign politicians' (this remark is taken from Hughes's introduction to *Moortown Diary*, the reprint of the volume's opening sequence which was published in 1989). Insistently, these poems enact the means by which individual enterprise reclaims a natural wilderness. Paradoxically, they also express the desire to occupy a primal natural world before 'indus-trial servitude'. Such a wish is an expression of Hughes's primitivist imagination, his celebration of what Nietzsche terms 'the free powers without ethics'. The volume is dedicated to the memory of Jack Orchard, whose daughter, Carol, Hughes married in 1970 (Sylvia Plath committed suicide in 1963).

Hughes has won many literary awards and in 1968 he set up the Arvon Foundation to encourage new writing. His most important volumes are *The Hawk in the Rain* (London and New York, 1957); *Lupercal* (London and New York, 1960); *Wodwo* (London and New York, 1967); *Crow* (London, 1970, revd. edn. 1972; New York, 1971); *Gaudete* (London and New York, 1977); *Remains of Elmet* (London and New York, 1979); *Moortown* (London, 1979, New York, 1980; title-sequence reprinted separately as *Moortown Diary*, 1989); *Wolfwatching* (London, 1989). In 1992 he published *Rain-Charm for the Duchy and Other Laureate Poems* and a prose work, *Shakespeare and the Goddess of Being* (both London). See also, Ekbert Faas, *Ted Hughes: The Unaccommodated Universe* (Santa Barbara, Calif, 1980), Terry Gifford and Neil Roberts, *Ted Hughes: A Critical Study* (London, 1981), and Thomas West, *Ted Hughes* (London, 1985).

[TP

HUGO, Richard (1923–82), was born in Seattle and educated at the University of Washington. He is sometimes said to have taken a radical turn in his poetry with the volume *31 Letters and 13 Poems* (1977), from a distanced formality to something like*confessionalism. The change is more apparent than real, however; Hugo is both more personal in his early work and more formal in his later work than is generally perceived. What he did in 1977 was not so much change his style as expand the range of his subject-matter, making it franker and more inclusive. He was always an unusually self-analytical poet; but before *31 Letters and 13 Dreams* he presented his feelings largely through persons and objects separate from himself. With that volume he began to speak much more directly of his own life. The story that gives psychological energy to Hugo's poems is by turns painful, tragic, and triumphant. His father, a man named Hogan, abandoned Hugo's mother shortly after the poet was born. She then married a man named Hugo and left the baby with her parents, who raised him within a strict and emotionally impoverished environment. Out of this childhood, not surprisingly, came feelings of worthlessness, guilt, and shame, all of which were, for years, projected outward on to the surrounding landscape. This is why Richard Hugo is so famous for the many early poems—like 'Degrees of Gray in Philipsburg'—that he wrote on the abandoned, failed small towns of the Pacific Northwest; they are a mirror to his soul. And yet Hugo is no literalist; as explained in his collection of essays, The Triggering Town (New York, 1979), he followed a principle of composition that resembles the process of psychoanalysis: 'when you are writing you must assume that the next thing you put down belongs not for reasons of logic, good sense, or narrative development, but because you put it there. You, the same person who said that, also said this.' In 31 Letters and 13 Poems Hugo relaxed his forms in order to say things he could not say otherwise. A kind of balance is achieved in White Center (1980), which revisits territory covered earlier but from a happier perspective.

All of Hugo's individual books are republished in Making Certain It Goes On: The Collected Poems (New York and London, 1984). See also Michael S. Allen, We Are Called Human: The Poetry of Richard Hugo (1982), Jack Myers (ed.), A Trout in the Milk: A Composite Portrait of Richard Hugo (1982), and Donna Gerstenberger, Richard Hugo (1983).   [PS

HULME, T(homas) E(rnest) (1883–1917), was born in Endon, Staffordshire, and educated at the High School, Newcastle under Lyme, and St John's College, Cambridge. He was sent down in his second year, for—in one account—'indulging in a brawl'. Pugnacity in one form or another seems to have characterized many of Hulme's public dealings—he is said to have carried a brass knuckleduster made for him, at his request, by Gaudier-Brzeska. Hulme was killed in action with the Royal Marine Artillery;

though fascinated by military strategy, he appears not to have approached warfare with the same truculent relish he showed for argument. Before this he worked in Canada and Brussels; while living in London he joined the 'experimental' Poets' Club (in 1908) and published (in the New Age for January 1912) 'The Complete Poetical Works of T. E. Hulme', five poems, the longest of which is nine lines. He published only six poems during his lifetime. Some two dozen other poems and fragments survive, but like his prose writings these remain uncollected, and Hulme might seem a very marginal figure were it not for the considerable impact he had made on twentieth-century taste. In his own words a 'philosophic amateur', influenced both by Bergson and L'Action française, Hulme developed the 'classical, reactionary and revolutionary' outlook later embraced by T. S. *Eliot; he championed the semi-abstract, geometrical art of Wyndham *Lewis, Henri Gaudier-Brzeska, and Jacob Epstein; and his propaganda on behalf of *vers libre and the primacy of the image in poetry was effectively taken up (along with Hulme's combative stance) by Ezra *Pound. Hulme was not among the contributors to Pound's or Amy *Lowell's 'official' *Imagist anthologies, but Pound signalled an affinity (or acknowledged a debt) by reprinting the 'Complete Poetical Works' as an addendum to his own 1912 volume, Ripostes.

In his attack on Romanticism, on conventionally poetical subject-matter, and outworn expression, in his repeated demands for a 'visual, concrete language' to convey 'vividly felt actual sensation', Hulme provided polemical buttressing for the kind of poetry that he and others such as F. S. *Flint and Pound had begun to write. His own poems, which predate his most 'classical' phase, are graceful mood pieces, focusing a 'state of soul' through striking but homely images, reaching towards the rhythms of conversational speech while retaining the inversions of a more antiquated style. Yet their very modesty and charm could now be seen—along with his insistence on freshness, novelty, 'an accidentally seen analogy or unlooked-for resemblance', and on keeping to 'the exact curve of the thing' or feeling—to anticipate the tendencies of much British post-war poetry.

Speculations: Essays on Humanism, and the Philosophy of Art, ed. Herbert Read (London, 1924; last repr. 1987) contains a selection from Hulme's prose and the five poems that comprise 'The Complete Poetical Works'; more poems and fragments, with textual details, are published in *The Life and Opinions of T. E. Hulme*, by Alun R. Jones (London, 1960); see also *T. E. Hulme*, by Michael Roberts (London, 1938 and Manchester, 1982). [AJ]

HULSE, Michael (1955–), is by profession a university lecturer. His background is Anglo-German. He first came to attention when his poem 'Dole Queue', a dramatic monologue, won the Poetry Society Prize in 1978. The collection of the same title (London, 1981) disappointed many critics, after the promise shown by the lively, if brash, title-poem, by much that was, in the words of one of them, 'flat and wilfully inane'. Later volumes attempt to articulate what Hulse calls 'my atheism, my liberal humanism, my Anglo-German background'. His juxtaposition of the erotic and the comic has its admirers, as has the honesty of his relaxed uncertainty, implied in such lines as 'I really ought to do more of this narrative stuff'. His collection *Eating Strawberries in the Necropolis* (London, 1991) is more assured, especially in technique, but its rather cerebral effort to be 'European' is made at the expense of verbal energy. See also *Propaganda* (London, 1985). In 1993 Hulse co-edited an anthology of *The New Poetry* (Newcastle upon Tyne).

[MS-S]

HUMMER, T. R. (1950–), was born and raised in Macon, Mississippi. He received a BA and MA in English literature from the University of Southern Mississippi in Hattiesburg, and later a PhD in English and creative writing from the University of Utah. He has served as editor of several literary periodicals, including *Quarterly West*, the *Cimmarron Review*, the *Kenyon Review, and the *New England Review*. He is currently a professor of creative writing and literature at Middlebury College in Vermont.

From the publication of his first book, *The Angelic Orders* (1982), to the present, T. R. Hummer's poetry has been characterized by moral seriousness. He has written personal narratives and dramatic monologues exploring the complexities of politics, labour, racism, and other themes. But he has proved most successful in the substantial number of poems in each of his four full collections that deal with the meaning and mystery that love and sexuality have for human beings at the end of the twentieth century. In these, Hummer has sought to combine both passion and philosophy. His books include *The Passion of the Right-Angled Man* (Urbana, Ill., 1984), *Lower-Class Heresy* (Urbana, 1987), and *The 18,000-Ton Olympic Dream* (New York, 1990). [LS

HUMPHREYS, Emyr (1919–), is best-known for his television plays and for the score of novels he has written since the 1950s, when he won the Somerset Maugham Award for *Hear and Forgive* (1952) and the Hawthornden Prize for *A Toy Epic* (1958). His prose-works are his major achievement, but he also has a reputation as a poet, having published four volumes of verse: *Ancestor Worship* (Denbigh, 1970); *Landscapes* (Beckingham, Kent, 1979); *The Kingdom of Brân* (1979); and *Pwyll a Riannon* (1980—both London). His verse is more direct than his prose (which is subtle and finely wrought) and more personal. It nevertheless shares with the novels a concern with 'the Welsh condition', often from a nationalist and Protestant point of view, and it makes little concession to readers who are not familiar with the history, literature, and legends of Wales.

A selection of Emyr Humphreys's verse (with that of John *Ormond and John *Tripp) appeared in *Penguin Modern Poets* (1978). A study of his work has been contributed to the Writers of Wales series (1980) by Ioan Williams; see also the article by Roland Mathias in The *Anglo-Welsh Review*, 70 (1982). [MS

HUMPHRIES, Rolfe (1894–1969), was born in Pennysylvania; the family moved to California in 1912, but he graduated from Amherst in 1915. Influenced by his schoolteacher mother, he was attracted to strong women, and both Genevieve *Taggard and Louise *Bogan became close friends after he moved to New York City in 1923. He began teaching Latin at the Woodmere Academy on Long Island in 1925, the same year he married Dr Helen Spencer. Over his career he produced six volumes of poetry—controlled, well-executed lyrics more intelligent than intense—but he is better known for his vigorous translations, especially Lorca's *The Poet in New York* (1940), Virgil's *The Aeneid* (1951), and Ovid's *Metamorphoses* (1955).

A liberal, concerned with the dangerous world situation in the 1930s, and not above writing political verses, Humphries joined the Communist Party but left in 1940. His reputation for integrity was confirmed in 1948 when he refused to remove a reference to *Pound's anti-Semitism from his introduction to that poet's *Selected Poems* (1949), which was then published without the introduction. He returned to Amherst as a lecturer in English in 1957, though he also gave a seminar in translation at Yale.

All of Humphries's poetry is in his *Collected Poems* (New York, 1965) and *Coat on a Stick* (New York, 1969). See also *Poets, Poetics, and Politics: America's Literary Community Viewed From the Letters of Rolfe Humphries, 1910–1969*, ed. Richard Gillman and Michael Paul Novak (Lawrence, Kan., 1992). [EB

HUNT, Sam (1946–), was born in Auckland, New Zealand. After being expelled from school he worked at various jobs around the country, mainly truck-driving and labouring, before settling at Bottle Creek, an estuary north of Wellington. He has lived in this area ever since, making his living almost entirely from writing, publishing, and performing. A troubadour poet with a gravelly voice, Hunt travels New Zealand reading his poems and singing his songs in schools, theatres, and taverns, where he reaches a wide popular audience. With his sheepdog Minstrel (d. 1988) he rapidly became a national figure. He has also toured Australia and the United States.

His poetry is simple, personal, and strongly autobiographical. It is performance material, Romantic in nature, with a strong sense of place. His first small handbound collection of poems, *Between Islands* (1964) was followed in quick succession by thirteen further volumes which sold very well. *Collected Poems* (1980) and *Selected Poems* (1987—both Auckland) contain his major work. See also *Introducing Sam Hunt*, by Peter Smart (Auckland, 1981) and *Angel Clear: On the Road with Sam Hunt*, by Colin Hogg (Auckland, 1989). [HMcQ

HUXLEY, Aldous (Leonard) (1894–1963), is remembered as a novelist and essayist, but he began as a poet and published four volumes, *The Burning Wheel* (1916), *The Defeat of Youth* (1918), *Leda* (1920), and *The Cicadas* (1931). His *Collected Poems*, with an introduction by Richard Church, appeared in 1971 (London). His early poems were published in the intellectually fashionable magazines of the Twenties, like *Art and Letters* and *Coterie*, but T. S. *Eliot's remark that he had been 'unable to show any enthusiasm for Huxley as poet' came to be generally shared, perhaps even by the poet himself.

It is easy to agree with Eliot. Huxley's most ambitious poems, like the lengthy 'Leda', are choked with knowledge, limply classical in diction, and verbose rather than energetic, while shorter pieces like 'A Sunset' or 'A Melody by Scarlatti' strain effortfully to be sensitive. Yet there are memorable pieces, the savagely or biliously ironic poems Huxley himself perhaps valued least. Among them are the various Philosopher's Songs ('Unchecked the cancer gnaws our tissues, | Stops to lick chops and then again devours'), the wholly successful 'Complaint of a Poet Manqué' ('We judge by appearance merely: | If I can't think strangely I can at least look queerly'), and something like a dozen other poems, including one or two of the poetic fragments embedded in the novels. Several of them are worth a place in any modern collection of satiric verse. [JGS

HYDE, Robin (1906–39), pseudonym of Iris Guiver Wilkinson, was born in South Africa of an English father and Australian mother who shortly took her to Wellington, New Zealand, where she grew up and began work as a journalist. She suffered from recurrent ill health, including mental breakdowns, depression, and a painful physical illness which left her permanently lame and caused her to become intermittently addicted to morphine. She had two children, one of whom died in infancy. Until her health made it impossible she worked for newspapers in several parts of the country; she then struggled to earn her living by writing (five novels, two other prose books, and much journalism). All the time she was writing poetry, which she regarded as her true work. In 1938 she set out for England but stopped on the way to visit China and report on the Sino-Japanese war; after gruelling experiences there she travelled to London, where some months later, suffering from depression, poverty, and a tropical disease caught in China, she committed suicide.

The collections of poems published in her lifetime—*The Desolate Star* (1929), *The Conquerors* (1935), and *Persephone in Winter* (1937)— tended to be over-pretty and marred by 'poetic' language; they were based on faded literary models and contained little reference to her New Zealand surroundings. Often they resorted to historical, biblical, or literary subject-matter. However, she left a great deal of unpublished work, much of which showed more vigour and flexibility; in this she brought her novelist's skills to bear on subject-matter which was familiar to her or genuinely experienced; her verse-forms became less rigid and her language more straightforward. A substantial selection from this later work was published as *Houses by the Sea & The Later Poems* (Wellington, 1953), ed. Gloria Rawlinson. It includes the title sequence, a vivid evocation of her childhood, and poems written in New Zealand, China, and England. Her *Selected Poems*, ed. Lydia Wevers, is published by Oxford University Press (Auckland, 1984).   [FKA

I

IGNATOW, David (1914–), was born in Brooklyn, the only son of Jewish-Russian immigrants. The onset of the Depression forced him to leave college in his freshman year and take a series of low-paying jobs. He married artist Rose Graubart in 1938, and they have two children. Showing the clear influence of William Carlos *Williams, his first book, *Poems* (1948), was as simple and direct as its title, mostly urban, spare free verse in service of a 'hard core realism literally presented'.

The main literary current, still under the spell of *Eliot and *Pound's neoclassic modernism, ran against him, but a second volume, *The Gentle Weight Lifter* (1955) had the help of a positive review by Williams himself. The next few decades, which included publication of his strongest work, *Figures of the Human: Poems* (1964) and *Rescue the Dead* (1968), involved editing and teaching, while recognition grew as Ignatow deepened his naturalistic mode with surreal invention, narrative functioning as metaphor to limn an unjust world. His verse became a species of social protest but also explored domestic, even *confessional themes, particularly fierce father-son conflicts.

Ignatow won the Bollingen Prize in 1977. Robert Bly edited his *Selected Poems* (Chicago, 1975), and parts of his candid journals have been published as *The Notebooks of David Ignatow*, ed. Ralph J. Mills, Jr. (Chicago, 1973). The fullest collections of his work are *Poems 1934–69* (1970) and *New and Collected Poems, 1970–1985* (1986 — both Middletown, Conn).　　　　　　[EB

Imagism, a poetical movement instigated by American poets in London, roughly coterminous with the First World War. There were four numbers of an annual anthology, 1914–17. Its main associates were the Americans Ezra *Pound, H. D. (Hilda *Doolittle), John Gould *Fletcher, and Amy *Lowell, and the Britons Richard *Aldington (who for a time edited the movement's chief organ, the *Egoist*) and F. S. *Flint.

T. E. *Hulme was a seminal figure. Flint describes meetings in 1909 where Hulme, he, and some others discussed how contemporary poetry might be revivified by *vers libre*, by the influence of the *Symbolistes*, and by forms derived from the Japanese tanka and haiku. Among Hulme's circle was Pound, newly arrived from America. Two years later Pound's former fiancée, H.D., also came to London, and with her future husband Richard Aldington began to sculpt poems whose severity Pound admired ('Straight talk, straight as the Greek!'). In 1912 Pound told these two that they were '*Imagistes*', and sent their work to Harriet Monroe's *Poetry*. The word *Imagiste* first occurred in print in Pound's prefatory note to the poems of Hulme; and the first statements of an evolving programme appeared in *Poetry* for March 1913: 'Imagisme', printed over Flint's signature and purporting to be an interview with an Imagiste (in fact all contrived by Pound); and 'A Few Don'ts by an Imagiste' signed by Pound himself. The first enumerated the cardinal rules of the movement as '1. Direct treatment of the "thing" . . . 2. To use absolutely no word that did not contribute to the presentation. 3. . . . to compose in sequence of the musical phrase, not in sequence of the metronome'; 'A Few Don'ts', meanwhile, proscribed superfluous words, abstractions, and iambs.

Pound edited the first anthology, *Des Imagistes*, published in March 1914 with poems by himself, Aldington, H.D., and Flint, and one each from Skipwith Cannell, John Cournos, Ford Madox Hueffer (see Ford), James *Joyce, Amy Lowell, Allen Upward, and William Carlos *Williams, not all of whom would have subscribed in full to Pound's principles. These received a further exposition (by now using the English form 'Imagist') in his essay on 'Vorticism' in the *Fortnightly Review*, September 1914, with its useful distinction between image and symbol: 'The symbolist's *symbols* have a fixed value, like numbers in arithmetic, like 1, 2 and 7. The imagist's images have a variable significance like the signs a, b and x in algebra . . . the author must use his *image* because he sees it or feels it, *not* because he thinks he can use it to back up some creed or some system of ethics or economics.'

But Pound was already chafing at his partners. He and Flint had fallen out when Amy Lowell arrived from America to put her promotional energy and financial backing at the group's disposal. Pound refused to contribute to the anthologies on her democratic terms, so it was she who oversaw the volumes *Some Imagist Poets* for 1915–17. Her first volume's 'Preface' contains a six-point credo derived from Pound and Hulme, but Pound thought what he called 'Amy-gism' a debasement of his own ideas, and it is true that she had a broader policy of promoting *vers libre* of all sorts. (Fletcher credited her with pioneering one variety—'Polyphonic Prose'—in which he himself experimented.) She was able, for instance, to convince D. H. *Lawrence that he was an Imagist.

By 1917 the movement was felt to have served its purpose. (A nostalgic fifth 'Imagist Anthology', with new work by most of the original contributors, was edited by Aldington on a whim in 1930.) Its limitations are perhaps suggested by the fact that the same pair of miniatures—H. D.'s 'Oread' and Pound's 'In a Station of the Métro'—are invariably cited to represent its achievement; and even of these Harold *Monro's contemporary objection is arguable: 'It is petty poetry . . . such images should appear by the dozen in poetry.' Equally valid, however, is a *Times Literary Supplement* review of 1917 which suggests that 'even when it is not very good in itself, it seems to promise a form in which very good poetry could be written'; and the fulfilment of the Imagist promise may best be located in Pound's *Cantos*, Eliot's *The Waste Land*, and H.D.'s *War Trilogy*, works which absorb certain elements of Imagist practice into effective larger structures. At the very least, Imagism introduced several of the prominent features of modernist poetics—organic form, elimination of personality, rejection of public themes—to the élite audience it sought for itself. *Imagist Poetry*, ed. Peter Jones (Harmondsworth, 1972), has an authoritative introduction and useful appendices.   [MI

IMLAH, Mick (1956–), was brought up in Milngavie and London. He read English at Magdalen College, Oxford, where he did research on Victorian poetry and was junior lecturer in English. He was founding editor of *Oxford Poetry* (1983) and editor of *Poetry Review* 1983–6. From 1989 to 1993 he was poetry editor for Chatto & Windus.

Imlah's first full collection, *Birthmarks* (London, 1988), is the work of an accomplished technician with an appetite for eccentric and at times baroque narrative ('Goldilocks', 'The Zoologist's Bath'), blackly and at times cruelly humorous. An overt literariness and pleasure in the play element of poetry, along with his formal skill, suggest the influence of his former college tutor, John *Fuller. He shares the current widespread interest in monologue while making his interest in Browning more apparent than most of his contemporaries. The subjects of his work to date might seem academic but the effect is quite otherwise: at once fastidious and extravagant.

A pamphlet collection, *The Zoologist's Bath and Other Adventures*, was published by the Sycamore Press (Oxford) in 1982.   [SO'B

INADA, Lawson (Fusao) (1938–), was born in Fresno, California; he attended the University of California at Berkeley and Fresno State College, where he took his BA in 1959. Subsequently he attended the *Iowa Writers' Workshop and the University of Oregon, where he received an MFA in 1966. He began his teaching career at the University of New Hampshire, and went to Southern Oregon State College in 1966.

His first substantial publication was a group of poems in *Three Northwest Poets*, with Albert Drake and Doug Lawder (Madison, Wis., 1970). His first, and so far his only solo book is *Before the War* (New York, 1971). Inada edited *Aiiieeeee!: An Anthology of Asian-American Writers* (Washington, DC, 1974) and *The Big Aiiieeeee!* (New York, 1990). He shared another book, *The Buddha Bandits Down Highway 99* (San Francisco, 1977) with Garrett *Hongo and Alan Lau. Despite Inada's intense involvement with Asian-American poetry, his own work owes more to American sources than to Asian; the five-poem sequence 'Since When As Ever More', for instance, is an even stricter catalogue of parallel structures than most Walt Whitman pieces—as strict, in fact, as Allen *Ginsberg's *Howl* or Christopher Smart's *Jubilate Agno*, but the catalogues are fragmentary in nature and they rely heavily on repetitions.   [LT

INGAMELLS, Rex (1913–55), was born in Orraroo, South Australia, and read history at the University of Adelaide. He worked in turn as an adult-education tutor, a high-school teacher, and a publisher's agent. Ingamells was the driving spirit of the Jindyworobak Club which he founded in 1938 and which developed into the influential and controversial *Jindyworobak movement. *Jindyworobak*, an Aboriginal word which Ingamells paraphrased as 'to annex, to join', encapsulated for him the means of developing a uniquely Australian poetry: he advocated rejecting the forms and directions of other world literature, focusing on the Australian environment and distinctively Australian experience which he divided into three eras: 'primaeval, colonial and modern'.

Ingamells's poetry, conventionally lyric in form and tone, attempts to apprehend the Aboriginal experience, but he was also inspired by records of the early European explorers and

their quest for the mythical *terra australis*, which he describes in poems such as 'Luis De Torres' and 'The Great South Land'.

Ingamells published eight collections of poetry, one novel, and critical works. *The Jindyworobaks*, ed. Brian Elliott (St Lucia, Qld., 1979) gives a selection of Jindyworobak poetry, including that of Ingamells, and discusses its impact on later poets   [EMcM

Iowa Writers' Workshop, the oldest and best-known creative writing programme in the United States, was founded in 1937 at the University of Iowa by the poet Paul *Engle. Many prominent American poets have been associated with the programme, either as faculty (Donald *Justice, Marvin *Bell, Gerald *Stern, Jorie *Graham) or as graduates (Rita *Dove, James *Tate, Michael *Harper, Philip *Levine, W. D. *Snodgrass, William *Stafford). Some critics accuse large programmes like Iowa's of producing homogenized poems that conform to stultifying 'workshop' conventions; Donald *Hall derisively calls these 'McPoems'. Certainly the Iowa Workshop has encouraged certain strains of poetry—the autobiographical, the *'Deep Image'—at the expense of others, but the diversity and accomplishment of its alumni suggest that it is more than a literary assembly-line. At their best the workshops help to create a community of writers and readers engaged in a common enterprise; at their worst they foster competitiveness and careerism.

[RG

IRELAND, Kevin (1933–) was born in Auckland, New Zealand, of pioneer Irish and English stock. He was educated at Auckland University College, leaving in 1952 in protest at the position the Students' Association took during the Waterfront Strike. In 1959 he travelled to Australia and on to England and Eastern Europe. In London he took a job at *The Times*, where he found a literary bolthole as a printer's reviser for almost twenty years. During that time he published eight books of poetry, all with New Zealand publishers, although he rarely visited

New Zealand during his self-imposed 'exile'. His sixth book, *Literary Cartoons*, won the New Zealand Book Award for Poetry in 1978. Ireland returned to New Zealand in 1985, and has held several writing fellowships and published three more books.

The strongest influence on Ireland's early poetry was the New Zealand poet, R. A. K. *Mason, whose short, spare, unpunctuated lines and gruff unsentimentality he admired. By his second book Ireland had found his subject and his own distinctive voice: this book and the next half-dozen conduct a wry, urbane, self-deprecating examination of love and lovers' folly. The elegant wit of *Literary Cartoons* (1977) was repeated in *Tiberius at the Beehive* (1990), where the satirist's attention turned from literature to politics. Ireland's earlier poetry was largely unpunctuated, and was just as often in regular stanzas, using varieties of half-rhyme, as it was *vers libre*. More recently he has attempted longer poems, much longer punctuated lines, and he now writes with greater detachment, often on historic subjects.

See *Selected Poems* (Auckland and Oxford, 1987).   [AF

IREMONGER, Valentin (1918–), was born in Dublin and made his career in the Irish diplomatic service. From 1949 to 1951 Iremonger was poetry editor of the magazine *Envoy*, which published his first solo collection, *Reservations*, in 1950. Later he became ambassador to various countries, including India. *Reservations*, direct and confident, made an impact; the poem 'Icarus' in particular was widely anthologized. Since then he has written little. *Horan's Field and Other Reservations* (Dublin, 1972) consists for the most part of poems from the earlier volume. The 'reservation' of his title meant a jealously guarded imaginative area away from, perhaps, just the kind of matters he confronted in his working life. There was a bitter note but this early sharpness gave way, in *Horan's Field*, to a fashionable pessimism. See also *On the Barricades* (Dublin, 1944), his earliest collection, shared with Robert *Greacen and Bruce Williamson.   [MS-S

JACKSON, Alan (1948–), born in Liverpool, was educated in Edinburgh and has lived there all his life, working mostly as a free-lance writer. There is a strong sense of personality in his poems, but few of them make sense as individual works of art. Words such as 'heart', 'fire', 'light', 'death', and 'pain' are reiterated with an insistence that can become tiresome. Jackson is best as a poet of short spurts: either in two- or three-lines *pensées*, or striking moments in longer poems.

A retrospective assemblage, *Salutations: Collected Poems 1960–1989* (Edinburgh, 1990), has been published, but poems have been left out which are more articulated than some of those that got in. The book should be read alongside the selection of Jackson's work in *Penguin Modern Poets 12* (1968), and with his best collection, *The Grim Wayfarer* (London, 1969).　　[PDH

JACKSON, Michael (1940–), is by education and experience a social anthropologist. Born in New Zealand at Inglewood, Taranaki, and educated at Auckland and Cambridge universities, he taught anthropology at Massey University before moving to Australia in 1982 to teach and write. Since 1989 he has held an endowed research professorship at Indiana University, where he is able to combine scholarly research with his creative work.

His first collection, *Latitudes of Exile*, won the 1976 Commonwealth Poetry prize. While conservatively following in the tradition of *Yeats and *Eliot, and unaffected by the debate about form in New Zealand poetry, the poems typically show the intersection of an educated Western mind with the facts of strange cultures, or

with remembrances of family things past. In *Wall* (1980), the poems open up more, are less constricted by tradition. *Going On* (1985) is a logbook of the illness and death of his wife; the poems are hard-edged, yet do not always escape sentimentality or preciousness. Of related interest is Jackson's recent fiction, *Barawa, and the Way Birds Fly in the Sky* (1986), an 'ethnographic novel', and *Rainshadow* (1988), in which the forgotten past of a Taranaki childhood is reconstructed.

Duty Free: Selected Poems 1965–88 (Dunedin, 1989) covers the three volumes, adding a dozen new poems.　　[RB

JACOB, Violet. See LALLANS.

JAMES, Clive (1939–), was born in Sydney and educated at Sydney and Cambridge universities. He has achieved fame as a television personality, but it was as a writer of verse that he first attracted literary attention: his four mock-epics *Peregrine Prykke's Pilgrimage* (1976), *The Fate of Felicity Fark* (1975), *Britannia Bright's Bewilderment* (1976), and *Charles Charming's Challenges* (1981—all London), appeared before his fictionalized autobiography began to be published in best-selling instalments. While extravagant claims cannot be made for these epics—their author, with his habitual self-deprecation, says of the last of them that 'the West End critics demanded that its perpetrator be transported to Botany Bay, and were not to be mollified by the information that he was born there' —they established James as the most adept practitioner of light verse in his generation of Australians.

Had he not left Australia for England as soon as he graduated from Sydney University his epics might not have been published, even if they had been written. In the years of James's absence from Australia, light verse has fallen there into intellectual disrepute. Few of his other accomplishments would have been possible, either, if he had stayed at home. Liberated by success, he published *Other Passports* (London, 1986), an interim 'collected poems'. To those readers who did not feel obliged to sneer at his public persona, a customary treatment for Australia's successful expatriates, it was apparent that his poetic skill extended beyond light verse. He is a considerable poet with a voice all his own, versatile, witty, and technically rigorous.   [JG

JARMAN, Mark. See NEW NARRATIVE, THE.

JARRELL, Randall (1914–65), was born in Nashville, Tennessee, moved with his parents to Los Angeles soon after, then returned to Nashville with his mother after his parents divorced. In 1926–7 a visit to his paternal grandparents in Los Angeles would provide him, decades later, with the remembered sensations and experiences that inform 'The Lost World' the three-part title-poem of his last and best book of verse. Jarrell graduated from Vanderbilt University in Nashville, where he studied with Robert Penn *Warren and John Crowe *Ransom. (Later his mentor would be, for a short time, another Vanderbilt graduate, Allen *Tate.) These poet-critics were associated with the *Fugitive group of writers that had come together in Nashville in the 1920s; but Jarrell showed little interest in Fugitive or 'Southern' political and cultural ideas. His early poetry, some of it published while he was still an undergraduate, is apocalyptic, surreal, and humourless—much indebted to *Auden's example, though lacking Auden's wit and formal brilliance.

When Ransom accepted a job at Kenyon College in Ohio, Jarrell followed him as an assistant, taught courses in the English department, and wrote his Master's thesis on A. E. *Housman's poetry. At Kenyon he roomed first with Robert *Lowell, then with a group of talented literary people which included Lowell and the fiction writer Peter Taylor, who later became Jarrell's closest friend. After two years at Kenyon he took a job at the University of Texas, married Mackie Langham in 1940, and brought out his first book of poems *Blood for a Stranger*, in 1942. Meanwhile, encouraged by Edmund *Wilson, who published him in *The New Republic*, he made a reputation for himself as a fierce and fiercely humorous critic of other poets. His penchant for the devasting one-line dismissal (e.g. Oscar Williams's poems give the impression of 'having been written on a typewriter by a typewriter') caused recipients acute pain, but established Jarrell, in his twenties, as a highly readable force to be reckoned with.

In 1942 he entered the Army Air Force, but failed to qualify as a flyer and became a celestial training navigator in Tucson, Arizona. During his nearly four years of service he wrote many poems about the army and the war, accumulating the bulk of his next two books, *Little Friend, Little Friend* (1945) and *Losses* (1948). In these poems his earlier, Audenesque style modulated into a flatter, greyer, more homely idiom, appropriate for re-creating the dailyness of barracks life as well as the disasters of combat. During the latter part of his service, in 1945, he wrote a number of letters to Lowell about the manuscript of Lowell's soon-to-be-published book of poems, *Lord Weary's Castle*—letters filled with valuable suggestions for improving what Jarrell thought would be the most important poetry collection since Auden's *Poems* (1930). After the war Jarrell spent a year as literary editor of the *Nation*, whose back pages he filled with poems and reviews from many of the best writers in America and England. He also taught at Sarah Lawrence College, which he would later make use of as a model for the mythical Benton College in his satiric novel, *Pictures from an Institution* (1954).

Jarrell's post-war appreciations of Lowell, Elizabeth *Bishop, and William Carlos *Williams helped to establish their reputations as significant American poets; they also marked a change of emphasis in his criticism, in that he now mainly celebrated poets rather than awarded them demerits. His essays on *Frost (whose influence on his own poems was significant), Whitman, Marianne *Moore, *Stevens, Williams, Ransom, and others (mainly collected in *Poetry and the Age*, 1953) remain classics of clear-eyed, informed, and loving description, written in a wholly accessible and always humorous prose. His poetic reputation however did not keep pace with his critical one, and it was not until *The Woman at the Washington Zoo* (1960), which won the National Book Award, and *The Lost World* (1965) that he showed how original and attractive a poet he could be. The best of his later poems—like 'The Woman at the Washington Zoo', 'Next Day', 'The Lost Children', 'The Lost World', and 'Thinking of the Lost World', are narratives, frequently spoken by women, which have some of the strength and human compassion of Frost's dramatic monologues (much admired by Jarrell). They also express, in a distinctive way, what Karl *Shapiro called 'the common dialogue of Americans'.

Jarrell married his second wife, Mary von Schrader, in 1952, and for most of his remaining years taught, with notable success and pleasure, at the University of North Carolina at Greensboro. He was an active poetry consultant at the Library of Congress in Washington for two years, and—during periods in the late 1950s and early 1960s when his rate of poetry production was low—he translated *Faust*, Part I, a Chekhov play, and several of Grimm's tales. Near the end of his life he wrote some remarkable children's stories, of which *The Bat Poet* (1964) and *The Animal Family* (1965) are pre-eminent. Soon after completing *The Lost World* he became mentally ill, first elated and later depressed, and eventually attempted suicide by slashing his wrist. Recovering, he went back to teaching in the fall of 1965, then entered a hospital in Chapel Hill for therapy on his wrist. While there, and while walking at dusk on a nearby highway, he was struck by a car and killed immediately. The coroner's verdict was accidental death, although the circumstances will never be entirely clear.

Jarrell will be remembered for his poems which, as Lowell claimed, rank with 'the best lyric poets of the past'; for his brilliantly engaging and dazzling criticism; and for his passionate defence, in what he termed 'the age of criticism', of writing and reading poems and fiction. *The Complete Poems* (New York, 1969) includes hitherto uncollected and unpublished work; while *Selected Poems*, ed. William H. Pritchard (New York, 1990) contains fifty of his best. *Poetry and the Age* (New York, 1953) and *Kipling, Auden & Co.* (New York, 1980) are collections of essays and reviews. *Randall Jarrell's Letters*, ed. Mary Jarrell (Boston, 1985; London 1986), has much valuable commentary. See also *Randall Jarrell: A Literary Life*, by William H. Pritchard (New York, 1990). [WHP

JEFFERS, Robinson (1887–1962), is one of the few American poets of the twentieth century who can be approached in terms of ideas rather than technique. As a classical scholar, Jeffers was able to absorb the principles of repetition and antithesis without feeling a need to retain the division into feet of the traditional British metric line. The result is a long-winded, clamorous free verse which manages a rare dignity and ease in the handling of large themes. For Jeffers, these large themes were summed up in his philosophy of Inhumanism, with its symbols of the falcon and the rock: violent energy and stoic endurance, 'bright power, dark peace'. In the course of the 1920s, while other American writers were travelling to Paris and London, or seeking a home base in the great cities of the east, Jeffers retired into the wild ocean landscape of north California, where he built himself a stone tower with his own hands. There, living in comparative isolation with his wife Una, Jeffers began work on a dual series of poems: long verse narratives basing their emotions—and occasionally their plots—on the dramas of the Greek tragedians, and short meditative poems arising out of personal experience in the wilderness.

These two extremes might be illustrated by the book-length poem *The Women At Point Sur*, and the brief lyric 'Hurt Hawks', with its liberal-challenging line: 'I'd sooner, except the penalties, kill a man than a hawk'. Inevitably, this kind of statement made Jeffers enemies. His best book, *The Double Axe*, appearing in 1948 just after the Second World War (revd. edn., New York, 1977), carried a disclaimer from the publishers, who wanted to disassociate themselves from the views expressed in some of the (apparently) pro-Nazi poems. In fact, Jeffers was years ahead of his time in noting the bitter ferocity of the Allied Powers in victory. Poems like 'The Bloody Sire' were perhaps provoking, and remain so, but there is an almost sublime detachment from worldly affairs in a lyric like 'The Eye', about the Pacific Ocean: 'what it watches is not our wars.' What can surprise and may survive best of Jeffers's copious output are the moments where satire and tenderness meet, as in poems like 'Original Sin', where early men are seen slaughtering a mammoth.

See *Selected Poetry of Robinson Jeffers* (New York, 1931; paperback, 1965) and *Selected Poems*, ed. Colin Falck (Manchester, 1987).

[GMacB]

JENKINS, Alan (1955–), was born in London and read English and French at Sussex University. Since 1981 he has worked for the *Times Literary Supplement* and is presently deputy editor.

Love, sex, violence, and relations between the personal and political are central themes in Jenkins's poetry. His first collection, *In The Hothouse* (London, 1988) ranges from oblique erotic reminiscence to the ambitious narrative centrepiece, 'Or Would You Rather Not Be Saved'. The latter's elliptical structure and multiple allusiveness show the influence of Paul *Muldoon, as do Jenkins's rhythmic flexibility and ingenuity of rhyme.

Unabashed by the uncertainties of tone allegedly discovered by some reviewers of his debut, in the title poem of *Greenheart* (London, 1990) Jenkins produced a *tour de force* of exotic horror in which elements of postmodernist play coexist with an attempt to uncover the roots of violence by recasting *Heart of Darkness* in the drug economy of South America. Alongside this, a series of poems about the author's father

indicate growing confidence in the more direct expression of feeling. A stylish, inventive, highly literary poet with an appetite for risk, Jenkins is in the process of discovering his potential.

Jenkins's work is anthologized in *New Chatto Poets* (London, 1986). He has edited *Essential Reading* (London, 1986), the selected poems of Peter *Reading. [SO'B]

JENNINGS, Elizabeth (1926–), was born in Boston, Lincolnshire, and educated at St Anne's College, Oxford. She worked first in advertising, then in Oxford City Library, and briefly in publishing before becoming a full-time writer. Her early work in volumes like *Poems* (1953), *A Way of Looking* (1955), and *Song for a Birth or a Death* (1961) won praise for its clarity and orderliness. It avoided the incoherence and formlessness of much contemporary neo-Romantic poetry, and revealed (in poems like 'The Climbers', 'Kings', and 'The Storm') a preference for regular verse-forms and an allegorical approach deriving from *Muir, *Graves, and occasionally *Auden. But although she was included in Robert *Conquest's *Movement anthology, *New Lines* (1956), her verse did not share the academic wit of some poets in that book, or the ironic, down-to-earth tone of others. Jennings's individual, highly sensitive treatment of love, childhood, or religious experience (as in her sequence 'Notes for a Book of Hours') does, however, show the quality of mature restraint often advocated by Movement poets and critics. The address of this quietly rhymed, finely crafted work is intimate, but real persons are not named and actual situations not developed. Jennings's poems about illness and hospital scenes, in *Recoveries* (1964) or *The Mind Has Mountains* (1966), sometimes register acute personal suffering but never go beyond a proper reticence. Conscious, perhaps, that her technical skill and imaginative resource might be further stretched, she has made some successful attempts in later books, like *Growing Points* (1975) and *Extending the Territory* (1985), to vary the shape and diversify the subject-matter of her poems (examples are 'Thunder and a Boy' and 'A Time Ago'). The *Collected Poems* (London, 1967) was revised and extended for its reissue (Manchester, 1987); some of the preceding individual volumes are only lightly represented, others more substantially. *Selected Poems* (Manchester, 1979) is a narrower personal choice of her work up to that stage. Her latest collection is *Times and Seasons* (Manchester, 1992). *Every Changing Shape* (London, 1961) contains critical essays, she has translated *The Sonnets of Michelangelo* (London, 1961), and there are two books of poems for children. [AB

JENSEN, Laura (1948–), was born in Tacoma, Washington. Her grandparents emigrated from Scandinavia in the 1880s. The first literary influence on Jensen was Laura Ingalls Wilder's *Little House* series read aloud to her in childhood, stark accounts of American frontier life. Other influences were David *Wagoner and Mark *Strand at the University of Washington (BA 1972), before she entered the *Iowa Writers' Workshop (MFA, 1974). Jensen has published three poetry collections and many chapbooks, and has taught for extended periods at Tacoma Community College and in residencies at the University of Minnesota and elsewhere. A 1989 Guggenheim Fellowship enabled her to travel to Scandinavia and work on her fourth collection.

Although drawing from the *imagist and *surrealist traditions of the last half-century, Jensen remains a poet of high originality, from her first book *Bad Boats* (New York, 1977) through to her third, *Shelter* (Townsend, Wash., 1985). Her work is characterized by an intensely private yet impersonal vision. Never sensational in her subject-matter, Jensen none the less transforms the most ordinary situation into mystery, finding occasion there for wonder. Her dramatic design is elliptic rather than rational, austere rather than wily or lush. Gradually her work has opened toward more public concerns, such as war and poverty. [MB

JILES, Paulette (1943–), was born in Salem, Missouri. She grew up in Blackwater and other towns, and received a BA in Spanish Literature from the University of Missouri (1968). Emigrating to Canada in 1969, Jiles worked briefly

as a free-lance journalist with the Canadian Broadcasting Corporation. Her first poems appeared in the anthology *Mindscapes* (1971), edited by Ann Wall. After travelling in Europe and Africa (1970–2), and publishing *Waterloo Express* (Toronto, 1973), she spent the years 1973–83 in the Canadian Arctic, working in aboriginal communications. Here she explored the themes of silence–utterance, wilderness–community, and dream–nature that distinguish her verse, notably *Celestial Navigation* (Toronto, 1984), which won a Governor-General's Award (1985). *Blackwater* (New York, 1988), *The Jesse James Poems* (Winlaw, BC, 1988), and *Song to the Rising Sun* (Winlaw, BC, 1989) followed. Jiles is the author of a novel, *The Late Great Human Road Show* (1986), and a prose sequence, *Sitting in the Club Car Drinking Rum and Karma-Kola* (1986). She has been a lecturer at David Thompson University Centre in British Columbia, and writer-in-residence at Phillips Academy in Massachusetts. [PMStP

Jindyworobak Movement. An Australian poetic development named after the Jindyworobak Club, founded by Rex *Ingamells in Adelaide (1938) with his prose statement *Conditional Culture*. The movement sought to incorporate an Aboriginal sense of 'place' within the developing English-language culture of the time. Its preoccupations ran counter to currents of international modernism, and the last vestiges of the Bush Ballad tradition still evident in the national weekly the *Bulletin*. The Jindyworobaks sometimes incorporated Aboriginal words into their poems, and this led to charges of primitivism. The wealth and spiritual wholeness of Aboriginal culture was not to be widely appreciated for another forty years. If, in retrospect, only a few of the poets involved produced outstanding work (e.g. Roland *Robinson), they were prescient in seeking intellectual and cultural nourishment from within rather than from without. Later movements of the 1950s (A. D. *Hope and the academic claimants of poetry) and the late 1960s (post-Vietnam internationalism) continued to sneer at the Jindyworobaks, who produced annual anthologies from 1938 to

1953. The 1980s, more environmentally self-conscious and responsive to Aboriginal heritage, began to recognize in the Jindyworobak movement important precedecessors, not only in these areas but in the movement's more general identification with a laconic 'Australian' speech cadence (e.g. in poems by Ian *Mudie) that anticipated the acknowledged breakthrough of later poems by Bruce *Dawe and Les *Murray.   [TWS

JOHNSON, Amryl (*c*.1960–), was born in Tunapuna, Trinidad. She came to England when she was 11, and now lives in Oxford. Her degree from the University of Kent is in African and Caribbean studies, and she has given many poetry readings and writing workshops in schools. What she said in *Sequins for a Ragged Hem* (London, 1988), her memoir of a return visit to Trinidad, is applicable to her poetry: 'My emotions would knot and turn, twist and fragment in the whirlpool of existence. At times, I felt like a ghost who was haunting herself.' Many of her poems endow the Trinidad Carnival with archetypal significance, and one of her finest, 'The Wheel', displays Yeatsian authority in its sense of history as recurring agony: 'It stood silhouetted against the sky | drawing in the pain and suffering.' A note explains: 'In Tobago a gigantic iron wheel, now reclaimed by nature, is almost all that remains of what was once a sugar mill.' Amryl Johnson's first book of poems was *Long Road to Nowhere* (Oxford, 1982), but a second volume of the same title, published in London in 1985, contains work that is entirely new.   [MR

JOHNSON, B(ryan) S(tanley William) (1933–73), was born in London, and worked as a bank clerk before reading English at King's College, London University; he was subsequently a teacher, and was made poetry editor of the *Transatlantic Review* when it moved to London in 1964. In 1970/1 he was arts fellow at the University of Wales at Aberystwyth. He committed suicide at his home in Islington at the age of 40.

Johnson's verse, a slim output of sixty-three pieces in all, is collected in two volumes, *Poems*

(1964) and *Poems Two* (1972—both London), and is considerably outweighed by his prose fiction. (He wrote seven novels, in a reflexive, Shandean spirit; *The Unfortunates*, 1969, came in a box.) Both books give an impression of a mind expressing itself more ambitiously elsewhere. The movement between them is from the shapely, literary address of the first (which features a group of sonnets and poems in *syllabic stanzas) towards a pinched, hurt, colloquial utterance ('Yes, I shall write it down, you old cow'); the written and the spoken voice contend and briefly agree in the stoical 'Distance Piece'. The most distinctive poems make up the final section, called 'Rotting', of *Poems Two*: cheerless conceits around his mother's cancer and his own mortality.

Johnson's film in verse, *You're Human Like the Rest of Them*, was produced by the British Film Institute in 1967, and the text published in *New English Dramatists* 14 (Harmondsworth, 1970).
                                                          [MI

JOHNSON, Colin (Mudrooroo Narogin) (1938–), was born in East Cuballing near Narrogin, in the south-west of Western Australia. He is a member of the Nyoongah people and is one of the leading figures in the second generation of Australian Aboriginal writers in English.

Johnson is the author of three novels, *Wild Cat Falling* (1975), *Long Live Sandawara* (1979), and *Doctor Wooreddy's Prescription for Enduring the Ending of the World* (1983). His two volumes of poetry to date are *The Song Circle of Jacky and Selected Poems* (Melbourne, 1986) and *Dalwurra, the Black Bittern* (Nedlands, WA, 1988). Both volumes adapt aspects of traditional Aboriginal song-cycles to the author's understanding of contemporary realities. One of these realities is that the fourteen tribes of south-west Australia have now gone and only one tongue remains: that of the Nyoongah or Bibbulman people, a distinctive version of Australian English, on which Johnson draws.

Like Jack *Davis, Johnson recognizes the facts of change but introduces a more defiant voice. His poems in *The Song Circle of Jacky* recall traditional tribal perceptions and customs from the perspective of a fringe-dweller of both Aboriginal and European Australia. *Dalwurra, the Black Bittern* uses the symbolic figure of this now-displaced bird to trace the author's travels through Asia, Europe, and back to Australia. Significant in these travels is India, where the author himself lived for some years as a Buddhist monk.   [BB

JOHNSON, Denis (1949–), was born in Munich, and works as a free-lance writer. His first two collections, *The Man Among the Seals* (New York, 1969) and *Inner Weather* (Port Townsend, Wash., 1976), demonstrated that he was an obliquely satirical poet with a preference for odd subjects seen from weird perspectives.

Where *Ginsberg's *Howl* speaks for a generation invigorated by rebellion and self-expression, Johnson's *Incognito Lounge* (New York, 1982) speaks for a generation dissipated by its own self-gratification; it is a raw and original examination of contemporary suburban and urban life, of secular humanism becoming mere consumerism. Intimate and surreal, the poems are confessions of an Everyman turned Any-customer, who tries to dissipate his failures through cinematic fantasies, shopping, drinking, and changing sexual accomplices. Johnson's subsequent book of poetry, *The Veil* (New York, 1987), is neither as concentrated nor as unified a book, although it contains a few splendid dramatic monologues, such as 'The Monk's Insomnia' and 'Talking Richard Wilson Blues'.

Narrating similar themes of the alienated and self-destructive, his novels include *Angels* (New York, 1983), *Fiskadoro* (New York, 1985), and *The Stars at Noon* (New York, 1986).   [DWF

JOHNSON, James Weldon (1871–1938), was born in Jacksonville, Florida, studied law, and became the principal of the grammar school he had attended. He moved to New York City and in 1900 collaborated with his brother, J. Rosamond Johnson, on 'Lift Every Voice and Sing', extremely popular among black Americans, as well as on a number of other songs and musicals.

The multi-talented Johnson served the US consular service in Venezuala and Nicaragua between 1906 and 1913, and his novel about 'passing', *The Autobiography of an Ex-Colored Man* (1912), published anonymously, caused a stir, although *God's Trombones* (1927), sermons by a black preacher in free-verse paragraphs that simulated impelling oratory rhythms, had a greater critical impact. He rejected the minstrel dialect employed in early poems, and among his later successes are 'O Black and Unknown Bards', a tribute to the creation of the spiritual, and 'Brothers', a graphic account of a black man burned to death by a white mob that echoes Edwin Markham and foreshadows *Faulkner.

Ever conscious of his historic racial mission, Johnson compiled *The Book of American Negro Poetry* (1922), a pioneering anthology, and with his brother edited *The Book of American Negro Spirituals* (1925). He also served as field secretary for the NAACP (National Association for the Advancement of Colored People) then became its general secretary. In 1930, however, he resigned to assume the post of professor of creative literature at Fisk University. He was killed in a car accident.

Johnson's verses can be found in *The Poetry of the Negro 1746–1970*, ed. Langston Hughes and Arna Bontemps (New York, 1970) and *The Black Poets*, ed. Dudley Randall (New York, 1971).

[EB

JOHNSON, Linton Kwesi (1952–), was born in Chapleton, Jamaica, and educated at Tulse Hill Comprehensive School (Brixton) and Goldsmiths' College of the University of London, where he took a BA in sociology. As a political activist with the Black Panther Movement, he organized a poetry workshop which was expanded to include musicians, the group calling itself Rasta Love. The poetry he performed with this band was influenced by reggae rhythms, but the poems stand on their own, though performed with musical accompaniment. These poems of articulate, if highly demotic, protest came to be called 'dub poetry' by Johnson. They display the authentic voice of young urban blacks in Britain today, and the style of 'dub poetry' has been described by James *Berry as 'over-compensation for deprivation'. Rage and belligerent overstatement are its keynotes, but also optimistic vitality, energy, and exuberance. Other prominent practitioners include John *Agard and Benjamin *Zephaniah.

Johnson's work includes *Voices of the Living and the Dead* (London, 1974), *Dread Beat An' Blood* (London, 1975), *Inglan is a Bitch* (London, 1980), and *Tings an Times: Selected Poems* (Newcastle upon Tyne, 1991). His recordings include, on the Virgin label, *Dread Beat An' Blood* (1978) and, on the Island label, *Forces of Victory* (1979), *Bass Culture* (1980), and *Making History* (1984).

[MR

JOHNSON, Louis (1924–88), was born in Feilding, New Zealand, son of a policeman. In the late 1940s he entered Wellington Teachers' College and quickly became the angry young man of the capital's literary life during a drab period of post-war austerity and repression. He was a leading member of the socially conscious *Wellington Group of poets, and in 1951 he published a collection of poems, *Roughshod Among the Lilies*, with the Pegasus Press (Christchurch). He was editor of two important literary magazines of the period, *Arachne* and *Numbers*, established the *New Zealand Poetry Yearbook* (1951–64), and founded the Capricorn Press.

In 1968, feeling that New Zealand had become 'an unacceptably suppressive society', Johnson moved to Papua New Guinea. This was followed by a long period as a lecturer in creative writing at the Mitchell College of Advanced Education in New South Wales. He published two collections in Australia, the second of which, *Fires and Patterns* (Brisbane), was awarded the New Zealand Book Award in 1975. He returned to Wellington in 1980 to take up the annual literary fellowship at Victoria University, serving on the New Zealand Literary Fund Advisory Committee from 1982 until his death in England in November 1988. He was awarded the OBE in 1987.

As a poet Louis Johnson looked beyond the historical and landscape-painting poetry of the Thirties and Forties and opened up a new urban subject-matter. Probably his best collection is *Bread and a Pension* (Christchurch, 1964) in which the influence of *Auden is augmented by a growing feeling for the vernacular. He was a passionate, sometimes clumsy, and often witty poet, dedicated to his own creative sources, with a recognizable voice and 'a concern with the *what* of a poem rather than the How'.

[PB

JOHNSTON, George (Benson) (1913–), was born in Hamilton, Ontario, and educated at the University of Toronto. From 1950 to 1979 he taught English at Carleton University in Ottawa, specializing in Old English and Old Norse. In 1971 he was awarded an honorary degree by Queen's University, and in 1979 by Carleton University.

Johnston started as a writer of fiction, and began to write poetry regularly only after the Second World War, publishing in journals. By the time he was almost 60 he had published only two small volumes of original poetry. *The Cruising Auk* (Toronto, 1959) revealed his talent for serious light verse as it wittily, and with a kind of melancholy comedy, depicted an almost surreal landscape, a small city and its characters through childhood, innocence, domesticity, happiness, adult disappointments, and doom. The same qualities are displayed in *Home Free* (Toronto, 1966), which includes two long poems, 'Under the Tree', about capital punishment, and a narrative poem, 'Love in High Places'. These two collections, along with new poems—lyrics and brief narratives—made up *Happy Enough: Poems 1935–1972* (Toronto, 1972), in which Johnston's true nature as a serious poet of personal and domestic themes became clear. Since then he has published *Taking a Grip* (Ottawa, 1978), perhaps his best book; *Ask Again* (Moonbeam, Ont., 1984); and his collected poems, *Endeared by Dark* (Erin, Ont., 1990).

In Johnston's later volumes many poems are of a valedictory nature, and in their lack of formal ostentation and their relaxed, unpretentious diction, they seem to come as close to the commonplace and the prosaic as they can. In the introduction to *Endeared by Dark* he emphasizes the importance of knowing the medium intimately in terms of its history, diction, syntax, and rhythms. The naturalness of his art hides such a sophisticated awareness, and a density of suggestion is attained in his seemingly uncontrived presentation of experience.

Johnston has translated from the Old Norse *The Saga of Gisli* (1963), *The Faroe Islanders' Saga* (1974), and *The Greenlanders' Saga* (1976). He has also translated works by modern Norwegian, Icelandic, and Faroese writers, including an anthology of Faroese poetry, *Rocky Shores* (1981). He emphasizes the importance of translation, both as a cultural act and as a creative discipline. [ATT

JOHNSTON, Martin (Clift) (1947–90), was the son of the writers George Johnston and Charmian Clift. He was born in Sydney but grew up and went to schools on the Greek islands of Kalymnos and Hydra where the Johnston family lived and worked between 1954 and 1964. Johnston's adult life was divided between Sydney and Greece, before his untimely death in Sydney in 1990, and his writing often reflects these cross-cultural experiences. While a student at Sydney University in the late 1960s Johnston was heavily involved in anti-Vietnam protests; he became an important figure in the young generation of Australian intellectuals and writers who began to publish in the early 1970s.

Johnston's earliest poetry is surreal in its imagery and dazzlingly erudite, qualities which his writing displays throughout. The elegance of his lyricism is never compromised by his eye for exotic detail or the swiftness and complexities of his thought. (The analogy between Johnston's poetry and his expert interest in chess is one that reviewers have noticed.) As well as intellectuality and allusiveness, there is an underlying elegiac mood, present from early poems such as the one in memory of his father, 'The Sea-Cucumber', which breaks through at moments with great power, as in these lines from the posthumously published 'Grief': 'Love is the subject and love's loss the text. | Grief

breaks the heart and yet the grief comes next.'

Johnston's poems are represented in most anthologies of contemporary Australian poetry. He published three collections during his lifetime, *Shadowmass* (Sydney, 1971), *The Sea-Cucumber* (Brisbane, 1978), and *The Typewriter Considered as a Bee-Trap* (Sydney, 1984), and a series of translations *Ithaka: Modern Greek Poetry in Translation* (Sydney, 1973). He also published an experimental novel *Cicada Gambit* (Sydney, 1983). *Selected Poems and Prose*, ed. John Tranter, came out in 1993 (St Lucia, Qld.). See also *George Johnston: A Biography*, by Garry Kinnane (Melbourne, 1989). [PM

JONES, Brian (1938–), was born in London, and is a schoolmaster by profession. His first two collections, *Poems* (London, 1966) and *A Family Album* (London, 1968), attracted a good deal of attention and had unusually high sales for poetry. Here, it seemed to many readers and reviewers, was an energetic, blunt poet using conventional procedures without recourse to clichés, archaisms, or poeticisms. Critics discerned the intelligently exploited influence of Edward *Thomas, as well as potentialities for narrative. The contents of *A Family Album*, especially the 'Aunt Emily' poems, demonstrated an ability for lucid characterization not often seen in English poets at the time. Expectations were maintained with *Interior* (London, 1969), which contained similar work, and with *For Mad Mary* (London, 1974), whose title-poem evoked wide praise. But Jones did not develop his narrative powers, or deepen his approach, and his two succeeding collections, *The Island Normal* (Manchester, 1980) and *The Children of Separation* (Manchester, 1985) contained, for the most part, either repetitious lyrics in the old manner, or more experimental narratives. The satirical view taken by Jones of the acquisitive society and of art threatened by commercialism, while moderately effective and deeply felt, seemed predictable and less original than the personal note sounded in the first poems. His most recent book of verse is *Freeborn John* (Manchester, 1990). *The Spitfire on the Northern Line* (London, 1965) is a collection for children. [MS-S

JONES, David (Michael) (1895–1974), was born in Brockley, Kent, to an English mother and Welsh father. He attended Camberwell School of Art and joined the Royal Welch Fusiliers as a private in 1914, serving until 1918. His experiences in the earlier phase of the war became the basis for his long poem, *In Parenthesis*, eventually published in 1937 (London; New York, 1961). In 1921, he became a Roman Catholic, and the following year joined Eric Gill's community of artists and craftsmen at Ditchling, Sussex, remaining there, at Capel-y-ffin in Wales, and at Pigotts in Buckinghamshire for a number of years, and being briefly engaged to Gill's daughter, Petra. In 1928 he visited Lourdes and Salies-de-Bearn, country which figures prominently in his paintings, and in 1934 he went to Cairo and Jerusalem with Gill, a trip influential on both the conception and imagery of his later writings, *The Anathemata* (London, 1952; New York, 1963) and *The Sleeping Lord and Other Fragments* (London, 1974). He subsequently lived a fairly solitary life in Sidmouth, Devon, and, after 1939, in London, occasionally suffering depression and breakdown and becoming increasingly withdrawn, but maintaining his output as poet, painter, engraver, and calligrapher; he was supported partly by various kinds of patronage. From 1940 he also wrote an increasing number of reviews, radio talks, and essays, primarily on the arts, mythology, and aesthetic theory: they are collected in *Epoch and Artist* (London and New York, 1959) and *The Dying Gaul* (London, 1978). Praised by T. S. *Eliot (who wrote an introduction for the paperback edition of *In Parenthesis* in 1963, calling it 'a work of genius') and W. H. *Auden, he was awarded the CH in 1974.

All of Jones's work is essentially interdependent, drawing on a central fund of preoccupations and motifs, deriving partly from heterogeneous and arcane sources: Welsh mythology, particularly *The Mabinogion*; Malory; the liturgy and forms of his heterodox Catholicism; certain key texts of archaeology and anthropology. Motifs from sources such as these are woven into *In Parenthesis*, where they create a rich verbal texture and place the First World War in a large historical and mythological perspective. *In Parenthesis* is his only narrative poem: both *The Anathemata* and *The Sleeping Lord* are more fragmentary and episodic. *The Anathemata* comes with a lengthy introduction, dense annotation, and Jones's own illustrations. It is an attempt to define his own complex cultural identity as an Anglo-Welshman; to articulate a view of the history of Britain and a Christian understanding of the relationship between history and the Incarnation; and to celebrate various manifestations of man as artist. The individual poems of the *Sleeping Lord* sequence are more straightforwardly approachable, being dramatizations of historical moments, particularly that of the Cruxifixion, and monologues spoken in the characters of, for instance, Roman centurions. Both these works, however, depend on an even larger conception which Jones never brought to realization: its remaining fragments were edited by Harman Grisewood and René Hague and published in 1981 as *The Roman Quarry and Other Sequences*. A late British modernist, indebted to Eliot and *Joyce (though not to *Pound, with whom he has more frequently been compared), Jones has never been fully assimilated by English literary criticism, though his strength and significance have been attested by such later poets as Seamus *Heaney, Geoffrey *Hill, and John *Montague. His letters are available in *Dai Greatcoat: A Self-Portrait of David Jones in His Letters* (London 1980). See also John Matthias (ed.), *David Jones: Man and Poet* (Orono, Maine, 1989).   [NC

JONES, D(ouglas) G(ordon) (1929–), was born in Bancroft, Ontario, and educated at McGill University and Queens University, Kingston, bastions of Anglo-Canadian tradition. He teaches English in Quebec, at Sherbrooke, a French-language university. He was one of the founding editors of *Ellipse*, a magazine in which Canada's English and French poetries are translated.

Jones has published six books of poetry since the mid-Fifties. He also translated a volume of selected poems by the Quebec poet Paul-Marie Lapointe, for publication in the United States.

Recently the Quebec journal *Urgences* published a Jones poem, 'Rock Garden: October', along with forty translations of it by Quebec's prominent poets.

Jones's poetry is lyrical and imagist, marked by economy and precision. Typically he attends to the details of seasonal change, especially around his home in Quebec's Eastern Townships. But as did one of his literary sources, William Carlos *Williams, he has also found fellowship and energy in the works of painters, such as the Canadian painter David Milne in *Under the Thunder the Flowers Light Up the Earth* (Toronto, 1977), and most recently Balthus, in *Balthazar and Other Poems* (Toronto, 1988). Jones might best be described as a meditative poet, but one who resembles a painter or a composer more than a philosopher. His longer poems are suites rather than excursions.

In 1970 Jones published *Butterfly on Rock* (Toronto), a thematic study of Canadian literature which has become a standard work of criticism. It explores biblical echoes in Canadian writing, especially images of the expulsion of Adam and Eve. Jones honours Northrop Frye and prizes human courage that will face down the human fear of the other: 'The only effective defence for a garrison culture is to abandon defence, to let down the walls and let the wilderness in, even to the wolves.' [GHB

JONES, Evan (1931–), born and brought up in Melbourne, is a product of Melbourne University and taught there, in the English department, for many years. His first book, *Inside the Whale* (Melbourne, 1960) and its successor *Understandings* (Melbourne, 1967) are filled with skilfully wrought lyrics, songs, extended odes, and a variety of forms such as villanelles and nursery rhymes. In these poems Jones moulds the vernacular with great verve and displays an eye for exact observation, together with a wide knowledge of western European myth. His early 'Address to the Pure Scholars' and his late 'Insomnia' are those rare things, sestinas which are not otiose.

Jones held a Stanford Writing Fellowship in the period 1958 to 1960 and the influence of Yvor *Winters, succeeding that of *Auden, confirmed him in his didactic and heuristic approach to poetry. Thus his work was at variance with the tone which prevailed in Australian poetry during the Sixties and Seventies, a time when his technical skill and pre-eminenace as a formal master should have afforded him wide recognition and influence. There is an irony inherent in Evan Jones's position as a formalist among a people which distrusts tradition and virtuosity. He, more than any of his colleagues, celebrates ordinary human emotions in the vernacular mode.

See also: *Recognitions* (Canberra, 1978) and *Left at the Post* (St Lucia, Qld., 1984). [PNFP

JONES, Glyn (1905–95), was born in Merthyr Tydfil, Glamorgan, and worked for most of his life as a teacher at schools in Cardiff.

His early work, published as *Poems* (1939), shows in its alliteration the author's lifelong fascination with poetic disciplines in Welsh and attempts to reproduce in English the effects of Welsh prosody and the Welsh praise-tradition. The long poem *The Dream of Jake Hopkins* (1944), originally written for broadcasting, deals with his often unhappy experience as a teacher, while 'Merthyr' takes as its subject (as does the work of Leslie *Norris) the town in which he grew up. The short stories and novels of Glyn Jones reveal the same qualities as his poetry: full of pathos and humour, they are essential for an understanding of the themes and special effects of his verse. Among his other works are the translations *The Saga of Llywarch the Old* (1955) and two collections of Welsh harp-stanzas.

Although his output as a poet was comparatively small, Glyn Jones continued to write well into old age. His *Selected Poems* (Llandysul, 1975) reprints his early work; a second edition, subtitled *Fragments and Fictions* (Bridgend, 1988), presents a further eighteen poems.

There is an essay on Glyn Jones in the Writers of Wales series (Cardiff, 1973); see also the author's memoir of literary life in Wales, *Setting Out* (Cardiff, 1982). Most important of all is his autobiography, *The Dragon has Two Tongues* (London, 1968). [MS

JONES, LeRoi. See BARAKA, AMIRI.

JONES, Rae Desmond (1941–), was born in the mining town of Broken Hill in western New South Wales, a city memorably depicted in his first novel, *The Lemon Tree* (1990). He graduated at 35 from the University of Sydney, by which time he was well established as one of a new, urban generation of Australian writers loosely centred on himself and John *Tranter, and now generally tagged as the *Generation of '68.

Jones helped project the image of the 'new poetry' through personal performances of his work in a wide range of settings, especially in venues not normally associated with literature. In his private life he took a number of casual jobs before joining the Commonwealth Employment Service and, later, becoming an English and history teacher at Granville Boys' High School in Sydney's western suburbs. He has released an LP, *Two Voluminous Gentlemen* (1977) with Norman Talbot, and a video, *Rae Jones: Poet With A Tuba* (1985). He was founding editor of the journal *Your Friendly Fascist*, which appeared for several years.

In his early poetry Jones projected a violent and anarchic persona with strong self-destructive attitudes but also an underlying sensitivity of response, echoing a background later developed with clarity in his first novel. *The Mad Vibe* (Sydney, 1975), his second collection, tellingly enunciates this stage of his creative development. It was succeeded by *Shakti* (Brisbane, 1977), which retains the tone of personal assertiveness but focuses more on the external world. *Walking the Line* (1979), a collection of short stories, may be seen as an exploration of more extended forms and of prose as a device for 'poetic' expression.

Jones's work is discussed in two books that explore the poetry of this period: *A Possible Contemporary Poetry: Interviews with Thirteen Poets from The New Australian Poetry*, ed. M. Duwell (1982), and *Parnassus Mad Ward: Michael Dransfield and the New Australian Poetry*, ed. L. Dobrez (1990).   [TWS

JONES, Rodney (1950–), was born in Falkville, Alabama, and reared in rural northern Alabama.

He attended the University of Alabama where he met the poet Everette *Maddox, an early formative influence on his poetry. Jones graduated from the University of Alabama in 1971 with a degree in English literature. He then attended the University of North Carolina at Greensboro, receiving an MFA in creative writing in 1973. Since that time he has taught English and creative writing in public schools and universities. He has been on the faculty of the department of English at Southern Illinois University since 1984.

Like many poets of the southern United States, Jones writes often about the power of the past. A theme that runs through his work is the ability of the imagination to give meaning to personal memory and thus define the present in terms of the past. This theme is central to his first book, *The Story They Told Us of Light* (1980), although most poems in the book seem to be well-made apprentice works. It was not until the publication of *The Unborn* (1985), that Jones found his own voice, using a longer line combined with devices of conversational poetry as diverse as those employed by Robert *Frost and C. K. *Williams. Since the publication of his second book he has received a number of grants and awards. Most significant of these is the 1990 National Book Critics Circle Award given to his third book, *Transparent Gestures* (Boston, 1989).
                                                        [LS

JONES, Sally Roberts (1935–), was born in London but brought up in north Wales and educated at the University College of North Wales, Bangor. Formerly a reference librarian, she lives in Port Talbot, West Glamorgan, where she and her husband own the Barn Owl Press, a children's books imprint. Many of her precise, ironical poems deal with the darker side of everyday life, often in an urban setting, but she is also concerned with aspects of local history and with her family over several generations. Her four volumes of verse are *Turning Away* (1969), *Strangers and Brothers* (Port Talbot, 1977), *The Forgotten Country* (Llandysul, 1977), and *Relative Values* (Bridgend, 1985). She has also published a monograph on the novelist Allen Raine in the Writers of Wales series (1979).   [MS

JONES, T. Harri (Thomas Henry) (1921–65), was born on a hill-farm near Llanafan Fawr, Builth, Breconshire. He was educated at the University College of Wales, Aberystwyth, where he read English, and his first teaching post was at the Naval Dockyard Apprentices' School in Portsmouth. In 1959 he emigrated to Australia where he became a lecturer at the University of New South Wales in Newcastle.

His first volume, *The Enemy in the Heart* (1957), showed promise in its exploration of the tension between a young man's sexual passion and the curbing influence of a narrowly religious upbringing. In Australia he was active in literary and academic circles but suffered from depression and the problems associated with heavy drinking. He nevertheless began to free himself in his next volume, *Songs of a Mad Prince* (1960), from the influence of Dylan *Thomas and R. S. *Thomas and from the metaphysical conceits on which he had relied too much in his early work. In *The Beast at the Door* (1963) there are a number of memorable love-portraits and some moving evocations of the Wales from which he had escaped but which he could not put out of mind. In the complexity of its emotions and its mastery of colloquial language this volume was his best achievement. Among his other themes were the sea, war, and the loss of religious belief. The *confessional mode of his later writing, collected in the posthumous volume, *The Colour of Cockcrowing* (1966), pointed towards the possibility of further development which was not to be. The poet was found drowned in a disused bathing-pool near his home on 29 January 1965.

The *Collected Poems* of T. Harri Jones was edited by Don Dale-Jones and Julian Croft (Llandysul, 1977); the latter also contributed an essay on the poet in the Writers of Wales series (Cardiff, 1976). [MS

JOSEPH, Jenny (1932–), was born in Birmingham. She was educated at St. Hilda's College, Oxford. She has worked as a newspaper reporter, an adult-education lecturer, and a pub landlady, and has lived in South Africa. Her first collection of poems, *The Unlooked-for Season* (Northwood, Middx., 1960) won an Eric Gregory award. Since then, in addition to a number of books for children, she has published *Rose in the Afternoon and other poems* (1974), *The Thinking Heart* (1978) and *Beyond Descartes* (1983—all London,), and an experimental poem-novel, *Persephone* (Newcastle upon Tyne, 1985). A *Selected Poems* came from Newcastle upon Tyne in 1992.

Intellectually astringent, intense, occasionally prolix, Jenny Joseph's work sometimes evokes the bluestocking's earnest, questioning energies and artlessness. She has always been drawn to the longer poem, an interest that culminates in the diffuse but often engrossing counterpoint of *Persephone*. Though perhaps temperamentally drawn to philosophical generalization, she rarely forgets her reporter's skill of homing in on the human detail. [CAR

JOSEPH, M(ichael) K(ennedy) (1914–81), was born in Chingford, Essex, but spent much of his post-war childhood in Belgium and France, gaining the international range of sympathy and polyglot cultivation which enrich his work. His parents settled in 1924 in New Zealand, where he became a professor of English at Auckland University. He died there shortly after retirement.

The only interruption was artillery service in the Second World War, an experience which dominated his literary and moral thought. Usually regarded as a poet of scholarly elegance, and indeed skilled in word-play, satire, and learned meditation, Joseph also brought an intense visual memory to his treatment of war and other contemporary subjects. He borrowed forms from film and a sense of cosmic scale from science-fiction (in which he was a superior novelist), notably the awesome Wellsian montage of past and future in 'Epilogue to a Poetry Reading'. In novels like *A Soldier's Tale* (1976) and in varied poems, including the Owen-like 'Elegy on the Unburied Dead', Joseph is a truthful and powerful writer on war.

Eschewing *confessional intimacies, his work more obliquely frames personal feeling, as in pastiches such as 'Meditation on a Time-Piece'. Most distinctive, however, is his habitual confrontation of the moral complexities of cruelty and mercy, apocalypse and hope, based in, but not constrained by, his Catholic faith.

Inscription on a Paper Dart (Auckland and Oxford, 1974) is his selected poems.   [RR

JOYCE, James (Augustine Aloysius) (1882–1941), was born in Dublin and educated in Jesuit schools there. He studied English, French, and Italian at University College, and took Gaelic League Irish classes under Padraig Pearse. In 1904 he and Nora Barnacle (they married in 1930) left Ireland for Trieste, where he wrote *Dubliners* (1914) and *A Portrait of the Artist as a Young Man* (1916). He lived in Zurich from 1915 to 1919, and in 1920 moved to Paris where he spent most of the rest of his life. At the outbreak of the Second World War he left Paris for Zurich, where he died. His major works are the novels *Ulysses* (1922) and *Finnegans Wake* (1939); he published a play, *Exiles*, in 1918.

Joyce's first literary ambitions were in poetry but his gift for detailed circumstantiality was more suited to the extensive novel form. Attempts have been made to describe *Finnegans Wake* as poetry because of its highlighting of language rather than narrative (and *Giacomo Joyce* can be seen as a linked series of elegant prose poems, describing a love-affair). Joyce published two slight volumes of lyric poems: *Chamber Music* (1907: his first published work), and *Pomes Penyeach* (1927). These are formally tight and conventional in diction, remote from the experimental language of *Finnegans Wake*. The persona in the thirty-six poems of *Chamber Music* (single-voiced like a Schubert song-cycle: Joyce called the collection 'a suite of songs' and set one of the poems to music himself) is the young lover, alternately lovelorn and sensual, as he serenades his beloved. The cycle has been variously interpreted as codedly suggestive (chamber-pots) or symbolic (the chamber-size constrictions of the lover's mind).

Apart from several Swiftean broadsides on the Irish literary revivalists, most notably 'The Holy Office' (1904) and 'Gas from a Burner'

(1912), and the exquisite '*Ecce puer*' marking the birth of his grandson (1932), *Pomes Penyeach* (1927) collects the rest of Joyce's poetic output. These thirteen poems illustrate Joyce's enduring taste for the nostalgic (*Pound told him they were not worth publishing), and 'Tilly' is the only one which is much anthologized.

The best guide to Joyce's poems is Richard Ellmann, *James Joyce* (revd. edn., New York and Oxford, 1982). They are included in R. Ellmann, A. Walton Litz, and John Whittier-Ferguson (eds.), *James Joyce: Poems and Shorter Writings* (New York and London, 1991).   [BO'D

JUSSAWALLA, Adil Jehangir (1940–) was born in Bombay and educated at the Cathedral School there. He read English at University College, Oxford, and returned to India in 1970. Between 1972 and 1975 he was lecturer in English at St Xavier's College, Bombay. He has edited *New Writing in India* (Harmondsworth, 1974), still the best introduction to the country's post-independence literature. During the past fifteen years he has worked for various Bombay newspapers and magazines, and has also been associated with two small presses, Clearing House and Praxis.

Though he tends to be dismissive about his first book, *Land's End* (Calcutta, 1962) is a remarkably confident volume. Its anxieties and attitudes may belong to a young man, but a much older person seems to have handled the verse. Jussawalla wrote these poems in England or some part of Europe, and has said they are 'about a resentment' at being abroad. This is not entirely true, for many of them are strongly affected by the sense of place. His longest and most ambitious work so far, however, is the title sequence of *Missing Person* (Bombay, 1976). 'Missing Person' is a metaphor for the Indian bourgeois intellectual, 'our two-bit hero', for whom English, the language learnt in school, becomes, for the rest of his life, 'a piece of tin' aimed at his throat. The sequence maps an area of historical rifts few Indian poets have looked at.

Jussawalla's collections are now out of print, but poems from them are included in two recent anthologies, *Indian English Poetry since*

1950, ed. Vilas Sarang (Bombay, 1989), and *The Oxford India Anthology of Twelve Modern Indian Poets*, ed. Arvind Krishna Mehrotra (Delhi, 1992). For a discussion of his work, see *Modern Indian Poetry in English*, by Bruce King (Delhi, 1987).   [AKM

JUSTICE, Donald (1925–), was born and raised in Miami where he attended the public schools and studied piano, eventually with the composer Carl Ruggles at the University of Miami from which he graduated in 1945. After receiving his MA from North Carolina, he studied for a year at Stanford with *Winters, from whom he learned much about poetic metre, before going on to receive his Ph.D from Iowa in 1954. He taught at the *Iowa Writers' Workshop from 1957 to 1982, remaining firmly committed, as the interviews and essays in *Platonic Scripts* (Ann Arbor, Mich., 1984) attest, to the idea of the poem as a crafted work of art. In 1982 he returned to Florida, and since then has taught at the University of Florida in Gainesville.

Having spent many of his childhood summers on his grandparents' farm in Georgia during the Depression, his view of the South differed from that of the *Fugitives and *Agrarians, despite early admiration for the work of *Ransom. He does not share their idealization of the area as a lost paradise, knowing primarily its poverty, and eventually ceased to consider himself a Southern writer. Nevertheless, it is to the Florida and Georgia of his childhood that he returns again and again with a Wordsworthian ambition to poetically memorialize this landscape. If his first book, *The Summer Anniversaries* (Middletown, Conn., 1960) is notable for its mastery of such forms as the sonnet and the sestina, it also begins to sketch in the Southern

landscape from which he emerged in such poems as 'Landscape with Little Figures', 'Sonnet: The Poet at Seven', and 'Tales from a Family Album'. The volume's strongest poems are 'Sestina: Here in Katmandu', an experimental piece contrasting the poet's successful quest for sublime transcendence with the subsequent necessity of living in the flat, real world, and the brief, resonant elegy, 'On the Death of Friends in Childhood'. His next two books, *Night Light* (Middletown, 1967) and *Departures* (New York, 1973), extend his vision to encompass his adult experiences in places as various as Kansas, Syracuse, San Fransisco, and Iowa City in such poems as 'American Sketches', 'Bus Stop', and 'Men at Forty'. *Departures* is his most experimental book, though his forays into free verse are always kept in check by his formal decorum. Here he also began to imitate musical forms in poetry, as in 'Sonatina in Green' and 'Sonatina in Yellow'.

The publication of his *Selected Poems* (New York, 1979; London, 1980), which won the Pulitzer Prize, and *The Sunset Maker* (New York and London, 1987) confirmed his reputation as one of the pre-eminent American lyric poets of his generation. The previously uncollected poems in the former book return to traditional form while extending his evocation of his childhood in such poems as 'First Death', 'Memories of the Depression Years', and his most luminous evocation of Miami in the Thirties, the prose-annotated 'Childhood'. The new poems in the latter collection combine with two stories and an essay to give a portrait of the artist as both a young and an older man, highlighted by elegies to old music teachers and fellow poets, the most moving being his villanelle, 'In Memory of the Unknown Poet, Robert Boardman Vaughn'.

[RMcP

K

KALLMAN, Chester (1921–75), was born in Brooklyn and educated at Brooklyn College and the University of Michigan. Kallman met W. H. *Auden in 1939 and became the elder poet's life-long companion, although the two men spent much time apart and the relationship was sometimes stormy. After Auden's death in 1973, Kallman's life, already dissolute and disorganized, went even more out of control; he died in his sleep in his Athens apartment.

Kallman's three volumes of poetry—*Storm at Castelfranco* (New York, 1956), *Absence and Presence* (New York, 1963), and *The Sense of Occasion* (New York, 1971)—show a gift for terse, often astringently witty lyrics whose prevailing tone is one of disenchantment. Kallman's twofold histrionic gift for aria-like effects and for impersonation appears in such poems as 'The Solitudes: A Little Cantata' and 'The African Ambassador: A Suite', the latter a series of monologues about experience and estrangement. Kallman is probably best known for the opera libretti on which he collaborated with Auden, notably those for Stravinsky's *The Rake's Progress* (1951) and Hans Werner Henze's *Elegy for Young Lovers* (1961) and *The Bassarids* (1966). With Auden, Kallman also translated opera libretti, including those of Mozart's *Don Giovanni* and *The Magic Flute* and Brecht and Weill's *The Rise and Fall of the City of Mahagonny* and *The Seven Deadly Sins*. On his own, Kallman translated the libretti of Monteverdi's *The Coronation of Poppea*, Donizetti's *Anna Bolena*, and Bartok's *Duke Bluebeard's Castle*. An interesting account of Auden and Kallman's years together is Dorothy J. Farnan's *Auden in Love* (New York, 1984),

written by Kallman's long-time friend and step-mother. [RHa

KAMAL, Daud (1935–87), was born in Abbottabad, Pakistan, received his early education at a public school, and later attended the universities of Peshawar and Cambridge. He was professor of English in the University of Peshawar. During an academic tour in December 1987 he died of heart failure in New York.

Kamal published two volumes of translations of Urdu poetry before his own first collection, *Recognitions*, appeared in England (Budleigh Salterton, 1979) with an introduction by Anthony *Thwaite, who wrote of Kamal's unsentimental wistfulness and of his concern for 'the fragments of the past, summoned up in brilliant but reticent images'. In his second book, *A Remote Beginning* (Budleigh Salterton, 1985), Kamal continued to join imagist practice to the poetics of the Urdu *ghazal* and the haiku. Sadness alternates with outrage, and two styles are discernible throughout: lyric-narrative, as in 'The Street of Nightingales' and 'Water Carrier', and the staccato-telegraphese of 'River Mist'. [AHa

KANTARIS, Sylvia (1936–), was born in the Derbyshire Peak District, and now lives in Cornwall. She studied at Bristol University and at Queensland, Australia, where she was influenced by the French Surrealists, on whom she wrote her MA and Ph.D theses. She has been a tutor for the Open University, and was Cornwall's first Writer in the Community. Her collections are *Time and Motion* (Sydney, 1975; Helston, Cornwall, 1986); *The Tenth Muse*

(Liskeard, Cornwall, 1983, 1986); *The Sea at the Door* (London, 1985); *Dirty Washing: New and Selected Poems* (Newcastle upon Tyne, 1989; Chester Springs, Pa., 1990), and *Lad's Love* (Newcastle upon Tyne, 1992). A narrative fantasy, *The Air Mines of Mistila* (Newcastle upon Tyne, 1988), co-written with Philip *Gross, reveals the playful aspects of her imagination.

Generally, Kantaris deals with unpretentious, everyday subjects in fluent, loosely structured verse. Her strengths are her emotional directness and ready humour, but she is sometimes in danger of relaxing into prosiness. Often at her best when she risks seriousness, she can be a moving love poet and yet often shows a lively streak of feminist rebellion (see *News from the Front*, 1983, written in collaboration with D. M. *Thomas, and her two autobiographical essays in *Delighting the Heart*, 1989).　　　　[CAR

KAVANAGH, P(atrick) J(oseph Gregory) (1931–), was born in Sussex; his father was Ted Kavanagh, noted for his ITMA sketches on radio. Kavanagh read English at Merton College, Oxford, after National Service in Korea. He has worked as an actor, in publishing, and in television. He now works as a free-lance writer and has a column in the *Spectator*, for which he is also the poetry editor.

Although Kavanagh's influences (Edward *Thomas, *Auden, *MacNeice) place him squarely in the English mainstream, he is a maverick poet, an outsider, affiliated to no group. He has spoken admiringly of MacNeice's 'wristy manner' and this is present in the best of his own poetry and prose. He has written pastoral, eclogues, and satires, but the shorter lyrics are his finest achievement. See, in particular: 'Perfection Isn't Like a Perfect Story', 'The Temperance Billiards' Room', and 'On the Way to the Depot'.

Kavanagh's crucial subject was his first wife Sally (daughter of Rosamond Lehmann), who died two and a half years after their marriage. Kavanagh's prose account of his life up to her death, *The Perfect Stranger* (London, 1972), is a classic. It is the story of an insouciant misfit (in Korea he had deliberately courted death), redeemed by a rare woman.

At the time of writing, Kavanagh's latest book is *Finding Connections*, an enquiry into his Irish background. Kavanagh's five collections of poetry, from *One and One* (London, 1959) to *Life Before Death* (London, 1979) are out of print; *Presences: New and Selected Poems* (London, 1987) has poems from each volume and his *Collected Poems* was published in Manchester in 1992. He has also edited the *Collected Poems* of Ivor *Gurney (Oxford, 1982).　　　　[PF

KAVANAGH, Patrick (1904–67), was born in the parish of Inniskeen, Co. Monaghan, and succeeded his father as a cobbler and small farmer. He is the most popular and influential Irish poet of the generation after *Yeats, but the controversy that he fomented and suffered throughout his life survived him. He is the century's most prominent representative of the 'rural' as against the 'urban' side of an established Irish literary dichotomy—at least before Seamus *Heaney, whose consistent championing of Kavanagh has helped to stabilize his high standing.

Kavanagh finished his Irish national primary schooling at the age of 12, coming from an entirely unbookish background, but he says he was already writing verses at that stage. His first book, *Ploughman and other Poems* (1936), was uneven, not surprisingly, but it contained some of his now most admired lyrics, especially 'Inniskeen Road: July Evening', which has his hallmark: a rough immediacy combined with a feeling for the transcendent power of the imagination. In 1938 he published *The Green Fool*, a loosely autobiographical novel which he later deplored as 'stage-Irish', but which some readers still regard as the most successful of his three versions of that material—the other two being *Tarry Flynn* (1948), which Kavanagh called 'the only authentic account of life as it is lived in Ireland this century', and *By Night Unstarred* (published by his brother Peter in 1978).

In 1939 he moved to Dublin, a step he later called 'the worst mistake of my life'. There he published his most famous poem, *The Great Hunger* (1942), a powerful, if over-long, account of the spiritual and social privation of the Irish

kayak

small farmer. Kavanagh later criticized it for its too-explicit concern 'with the woes of the poor'.

The poems of Kavanagh's middle period often lack objectivity, being too concerned with the role and reception of the poet. In 1952 he and Peter used the latter's American savings to launch *Kavanagh's Weekly*, which ran for thirteen issues between April and July, extending into polemic Kavanagh's resentments at the Dublin literary establishment and the pettinesses of Irish politics. There followed a disastrous period in his life: he sued the insignificant weekly the *Leader* for libel and was treated with contemptuous hostility in the courts, and in 1953 he developed lung cancer. But then, miraculously, followed his happiest years, referred to as his 'Canal Bank' period from a 'rebirth' he says he underwent one summer's day in 1955 on the banks of the Grand Canal in Dublin, when he learnt the virtues of 'simplicity' and 'not to care'. The poems of his last decade were again uneven, often prosodically unconvincing or tending towards reductiveness after the magnificent sonnets of the 'Canal Bank'. In April 1967 he married Katharine Moloney.

Paradoxically, Kavanagh has been underrated because of the immediate appeal of his most popular poems ('Kerr's Ass', 'On Raglan Road', 'Shancoduff'), which has tended to establish them as the measure of his achievement. Recently the corpus has been read as a whole, balancing sentimentality, touchiness, and pomposity about 'art', against philosophical insight and social generosity. He gave Irish poetry a salutary shift towards reality, away from its Celtic high ground.

See: *Collected Poems* (London, 1972); *Collected Pruse* (London, 1973); *The Green Fool* (London, 1938; Harmondsworth, 1975); *Tarry Flynn* (London, 1948; Harmondsworth, 1978); *By Night Unstarred*, ed. Peter Kavanagh (The Curragh, 1978); *Kavanagh's Weekly* (complete in one volume, Newbridge, 1981). Also, Antoinette Quinn's Life, *Patrick Kavanagh* (Dublin, 1991), and, for background, Anthony Cronin, *Dead as Doornails: A Chronicle of Life* (Dublin, 1976).

[BO'D

kayak. From 1964 to 1984, arguably the preeminent little poetry magazine in the United States. Founded by George Hitchcock and edited and produced by him, though sometimes with assistance, *kayak* began in San Francisco where Hitchcock taught himself to print on a multilith-addressograph offset press bought from the Pacific Steamship Line, where it had been used to print shipboard menus. This surreal touch extended to other aspects of *kayak's* production—one issue was printed on US Army target paper—and to the editorial policy as well. Usually printed somewhere in each issue, this policy read: 'A kayak is not a galleon, ark, coracle, or speedboat. It is a small watertight vessel operated by a single oarsman. It is submersible, has sharply pointed ends, and is constructed from light poles and the skins of furry animals. It has never yet been employed as a means of mass transport.'

During the Vietnam War, *kayak* published some of the strongest anti-war poetry, much of it exhibiting the American brand of surrealism called *deep imagism. Poets who published some of their finest work in *kayak* included Margaret *Atwood, Robert *Bly, Philip *Levine, W. S. *Merwin, and Anne *Sexton. The magazine also featured surrealist collages by Nanos Valaoritas, John Digby, and Hitchcock himself. Also famous were *kayak's* graphics, many taken from nineteenth-century wood engravings, and Hitchcock's rejection slips.

In its twenty years *kayak* published sixty-four issues. After Issue 22 Hitchcock moved to Santa Cruz, California. There he expanded production to include a book series and published first volumes of poetry by such notable writers as Charles *Simic and Raymond *Carver. [MJ

KEENE, Dennis (1934–), was born in London and educated at Sheen Grammar School and St John's College, Oxford. He has spent most of his adult life abroad, teaching in Malaysia, Ethiopia, and Japan, and is now professor of English literature at Japan Women's University, Tokyo.

Keene first made a name as a poet while an undergraduate at Oxford. In his mid-twenties he stopped writing poetry, beginning again in his fortieth year. His first book, *Surviving*, appeared in 1980. His poetic practice is linked intimately with his apprehension of temporal experience, which accounts for the circling, repetitive mode he often employs. There is also, throughout his work, an argument with Romantic and symbolist modes of comprehending and representing experience. Keene's major achievement is the long poem 'Universe', which combines deliberately prosaic blank verse, prose passages, and traditional verse-forms, and deals with astronomy, atomic physics, history, and personal experience, not drawing them into any factitious and comforting relationship, but holding them in their incomprehensibility and irreducibility.

See *Universe and Other Poems* (Manchester, 1984). Keene's many translations of twentieth-century Japanese work include *The Modern Japanese Prose Poem* (Princeton, NJ, 1980) and the novel *Singular Rebellion*, by Saiichi Maruya (Tokyo, 1986; London, 1988).

[TJGH

KEES, Weldon (1914–55), was born in Nebraska and, growing up in the Depression, his obsessions were the Communist Party (he was a Trotskyite) and the stupidities of middle-class America.

Kees published his first story when he was 16. A novel, *Slow Parade*, went the rounds in 1937 and another, *Fall Quarter*, met a similar fate (since rectified by Story Line Press). His first poem, 'Subtitle', was published in the same year. His first book of poems, *The Last Man*, was published in San Francisco in 1943, though the poems have less to do with the horrors of war than those of a man 'alone in a worn out town in wartime'. Less obviously indebted to *Auden, his second book, *The Fall of the Magicians*, was published in New York in 1947. By this time he had quit his job as a librarian and taken up painting. Kees was also a competent jazz pianist and composer, and in later years made films and put on revues. He earned his living writing for *Time*, *The New Yorker*, and the *Nation*.

Kees's last book, *Poems 1947–1954*, was published just before his death and contains an epi-graph from Hawthorne: 'those dark caverns into which all men must descend, if they would know anything beneath the surface and illusive pleasures of existence.' On 18 July 1955 his car was found near the entrance to the Golden Gate Bridge. The body was never found.

Today Kees is known for a smaller body of work, about 150 poems, than any other poet of comparable standing in America. Indeed, he is best known for just four poems, the strange 'Robinson' poems, which pre-date and prefigure John *Berryman's 'Henry' dream songs. Where Berryman's poems are perversely modernistic, Kees's are urbane and accessible: 'Through sounds of ice cubes dropped in a glass, an osteopath, | Dressed for the links, describes an old Intourist tour | —Here's where old Gibbons jumped from, Robinson.'

This is the period of *ciné noir*: betrayal, corruption, and murder in the public sector, the lone gumshoe, possibly called Robinson, going about his hopeless but poetic calling, alone, terminally depressed, and inevitably drunk.

Weldon Kees was largely ignored by anthologists during his life and even now is usually represented by one or two poems. A notable exception was Conrad *Aiken's *Twentieth Century American Poetry*, which printed nine poems, more than by any other poet after *Eliot and *Pound. Kees's *Collected Poems*, ed. Donald Justice, were published by the University of Nebraska Press (revd. edn. 1975, London, 1993).

[HW

KEESING, Nancy (Hertzberg) (1923–93) was born in Sydney, Australia, and graduated from the university there. She was most widely known as a free-lance writer and active executive member of numerous literary organizations. She was a founding member of the Literature Board and chairman from 1944 to 1947. She was made a Member of the Order of Australia in 1979.

Keesing's poetry remains the key to her literary activity. She was one of a generation of poets who emerged in the 1940s under the shadow of the Second World War and who revitalized the craft, combining lyrical exactitude with a quality of wit and playfulness notably absent in the work of many writers in that period. Her later poetry is suffused by her warm concern for people and by the telling, idiosyncratic detail.

As a poet, she published *Imminent Summer* (Sydney, 1951), *Three Men and Sydney* (Sydney, 1955), *Showgrounds Sketchbook* (Sydney, 1968) and *Hails and Farewells* (Sydney, 1977). She edited, with Douglas Stewart, the important anthologies *Australian Bush Ballads* (Sydney, 1955) and *Old Bush Songs* (Sydney, 1957). There are also books of criticism and social commentary, historical monographs, and children's fiction. Her book of memoirs, *Riding the Elephant* (Sydney, 1988) is a colourful personal document.   [TWS

KEFALA, Antigone (1935–) was born in Romania of Greek parents and has lived in Romania, Greece, New Zealand, and Australia. She graduated from Victoria University in 1960 and has worked as a librarian, English teacher, and arts administrator.

Although she has published several works of fiction, it is as a poet that Kefala has established a reputation. She is one of the increasingly influential writers in Australia who uses the English language to reveal a poetic sensibility profoundly influenced by non-English origins. Her subject-matter is often the characteristic theme of displacement, alienation, and rootlessness found in much writing of the diaspora, but Kefala refines this with a lyrical delicacy and she has a subtle understanding of antipodean nuances.

Her three verse collections are *The Alien* (Sydney, 1973), *Thirsty Weather* (Sydney, 1978) and *European Notebook* (Sydney, 1988).   [TWS

KELL, Richard (Alexander) (1927–), was born in Youghal, Co. Cork, and educated at Trinity College, Dublin. He lectured in English at Isleworth Polytechnic 1960–70, and was senior lecturer at Newcastle Polytechnic 1970–83. From 1960 to 1973 he reviewed poetry for the *Guardian*.

Linked at times both with the *Movement and the *Group, Richard Kell shares a background in the Irish Protestant clergy with Louis*MacNeice and is similarly drawn to dualisms. A strong sensuous appetite ('River') is matched by a sense of order enlivened by paradox and wit, as in the sequence *Humours* (Sunderland, 1978). *Heartwood* (Newcastle upon Tyne, 1981) is an extended examination of bereavement following the death of the poet's wife by drowning. Kell's humanistic attempt to reconcile reason and emotion is nowadays unusual, and is matched by his formal accomplishment and the elegance of his improvisations.

Kell's other main collections are *Control Tower* (London, 1962); *Differences* (London, 1969); *The Broken Circle* (Sunderland, 1981); and *In Praise of Warmth: New and Selected Poems* (Dublin, 1987). Pamphlets include *Poems: Fantasy Poets 35* (Oxford, 1957).   [SO'B

KELLY, Robert (1935–), was born in Brooklyn, New York, and educated at the City College of New York and Columbia University. After a brief career as a translator he took a series of posts as lecturer or writer-in-residence at various institutions, including Tufts University, the California Institute of Technology, and Bard College. The editor of *Chelsea Review* from 1958 to 1960, he also helped to launch *Trobar*, an influential poetry magazine, and Trobar books; and with seven other poets he formed The Blue Yak, a poet's co-operative, in New York. He has also been editor of *Matter* magazine and Matter publishing company.

The first of his many collections, *Armed Descent*, appeared in 1961. During the 1960s he published no fewer than twenty-five volumes, with some of his best work to be found in *Finding the Measure* (Los Angeles, 1968) and *A California Journal* (London, 1969). Kelly has described his poetry as 'news from nowhere', adding 'my work is not *my* work . . . my personality is its enemy'. Experimenting with a variety of forms, and using language that always pivots on an image, he tries to dramatize life as process, impersonal energy. Deploying a technique that offers a haunting mixture of dream, chant, and ritual, he attempts to translate the interpenetra-

tion of things into intelligible, although not nec-
essarily paraphraseable, sounds. He has contin-
ued to be a prolific writer of plays, novels, and
essays as well as poems. His many volumes of
poetry since the 1960s include *Flesh: Dream: Book*
(Los Angeles, 1971); *The Convections* (Santa Bar-
bara, Calif., 1978); *Spiritual Exercises* (Santa Bar-
bara, 1981); and *Not This Island Music*
(Santa Rosa, Calif., 1987).   [RJG]

KENNEDY, X. J. (1929–), the pseudonym of
Joseph Charles Kennedy, was born in Dover,
New Jersey. Raised as a Roman Catholic, he
attended Seton Hall, Columbia, and the Univer-
sity of Michigan, where he completed all work
for a doctorate except the dissertation. In 1977
he gave up his tenured professorship at Tufts in
order to devote himself full time to writing and
editing. His college textbooks, a few of which
are co-written with his wife, Dorothy, are best-
selling introductions to literature and composi-
tion, and include *Literature* (5th edn., New York,
1990) and *An Introduction to Poetry* (7th edn.,
Boston, 1990).

Kennedy likes to refer to himself as 'one of an
endangered species: people who still write in
meter and rime'. Though formal verse was
unpopular in the early Seventies, he and his wife
published the little magazine, *Counter/
Measures*, a short-lived but influential refuge for
traditional poets. Kennedy's first volume, *Nude
Descending a Staircase* (Garden City, NY, 1961),
which won that year's Lamont Award, estab-
lished him as a technical virtuoso who combines
metaphysical wit with idiomatic diction. *Cross
Ties* (Athens, Ga., 1985) selects the best from this
and subsequent volumes, and includes every-
thing from limericks to sonnets, as well as epi-
grams, elegies, heroic couplets, and villanelles.
Many of his finest poems express an irreverent,
sometimes profane, view of religion ('First Con-
fession', 'Nothing in Heaven Functions As It
Ought', 'The Aetheist's Stigmata', and 'Hang-
over Mass'). His frank sexual humour surfaces
in poems about flagellation, masturbation, and
his own buttocks.

An expert at parody and satire ('Among Stool
Pigeons' and 'Emily Dickinson in Southern Cal-

ifornia'), Kennedy excels at verse set to popular
music, such as his often-anthologized lamenta-
tion on fading beauty, 'In a Prominent Bar in
Secaucus One Day'. Mocking much about the
poetry trade, Kennedy bemoans the bleak state
of American culture. Not strictly a nay-sayer, he
also celebrates the richness of everyday life with
its simple epiphanies. He elevates the vulgar
with his effortless technique and deflates pre-
tence with his sardonic wit. Since the mid-Sev-
enties Kennedy has written mostly children's
verse, work full of sophisticated nonsense and
much inspired silliness, including *Brats* (New
York, 1986) and *Ghastlies, Goops, and Pincushions*
(New York, 1989).

Breaking and Entering (London, 1971) is
Kennedy's only volume to appear in England,
and is a selection from all his work at the time.
                                          [TDeP

KENNELLY, Brendan (1936–), was born in
Ballylongford, Co. Kerry, and educated at Trin-
ity College, Dublin, where he became professor
of modern English literature, and at Leeds Uni-
versity. His first four books of poetry were pub-
lished jointly with Rudi Holzapfel; his
reputation was established by his impressive
second solo volume, *My Dark Fathers* (1964).
After four further volumes in fairly rapid succes-
sion and the AE Memorial Prize for Poetry
(1967), his *Selected Poems* were published in 1969.
He published two early novels and edited his
acclaimed *Penguin Book of Irish Verse* in 1970. The
volumes of the next twelve years demonstrate
the same characteristics as this earlier poetry: a
free-form, individualistic, romantic expression-
ism which is forceful but can seem flat and unre-
lieved. *Cromwell* (1983) changed Kennelly's
status dramatically: this series of 160 poems on
the themes and obsessions of Irish history con-
fronts that history's bogeyman, Cromwell, with
Buffán, its hapless consumer. Kennelly's graphic
force was ideally suited to this clamorous
sequence, of which there is a stage version, and
which is now regarded as one of the principal
poetic commentaries on the recent vestigial
turbulence of the Irish past. A new selected, *A
Time For Voices* was published by Bloodaxe

(Newcastle upon Tyne) in 1990, as was *Cromwell* in 1987, and a 400-page epic poem *The Book of Judas* (1991). A good short introduction is Gerard Quinn's 'Brendan Kennelly: Victors and Victims', *The Irish Review*, 9 (Autumn 1990).

[BO'D

KENNEY, Richard (1948–), was born in Glen Falls, New York and graduated from Dartmouth College in 1970. After graduation Kenney studied Celtic lore in Ireland and Scotland, then worked for several years as a school-bus driver and house painter in Winooski, Vermont. Married to botanist Mary Hedberg, he is currently teaching at the University of Washington, in Seattle.

Kenney's first book of poems was *The Evolution of the Flightless Bird* (1984), selected by James *Merrill for the Yale Series of Younger Poets; Merrill writes in his introduction to that volume that Kenney 'is not out to disguise the liveliness of his mind or the breadth of his learning. He has read science and history and philosophy as well as Hopkins and Browning, Crane and Frost.' Kenney's deeply allusive, elliptical but firmly drawn work is marked by a recondite, often inward, diction and an interest in myth and language. 'The Hours of the Day', a sonnet-sequence that opened his first volume, is a meditation on the echoes between self and world that haunt the poet's 'hero' through twenty-four hours and sonnets in a complex, interrupted narrative of loss and recovery. Kenney's preference for the long poem is seen in 'Notes from Greece', the elaborate final poem of that first volume centred on a visit to the Byzantine monastic communities at Mount Athos. *Orrery* (New York, 1985) is Kenney's second collection, which opens with a narrative 'crown' of sonnets; 'Apples' is an extended sequence of lyrics that moves through a single year on a cider-milling farm in Vermont.

[JP

KENYON, Jane (1947–), was born in Ann Arbor, Michigan, and educated at the university there. In 1972 she married the poet Donald *Hall, and by 1975 they had left Ann Arbor to take up residence in Hall's ancestral farmhouse in Danbury, New Hampshire. Kenyon's first book of poems, *From Room to Room* (Cambridge, Mass., 1978), was marked by meditations on the subject of *residing*—both in terms of locale and of character—in the life of the country. Her translation of *Twenty Poems*, by Anna Akhmatova (St Paul, Minn., 1985) further framed the progress of her work, which then went on to find a more solid voice in *The Book of Quiet Hours* (St Paul, 1986).

Kenyon has made something of an aesthetic of quiet, and her poems have a brooding introversion. Rare among American poets, she is also able to infuse her poetry with a lightly worn sense of Christian humility, and an active—if worried—sense of mercy. These are among the qualities which give her verse both the tones and the turns of serious prayer. Within the subtle, yet dramatic, use of rhyme and sound in *Let Evening Come* (St Paul, 1990), she evokes not only the drama of her need to speak, but also the deep communion and solace within any reader's need to listen.

[LR

Kenyon Review, The, an influential journal of poetry, fiction, and criticism established at Kenyon College in Gambier, Ohio, in 1939. Although its founding editor was John Crowe *Ransom, who came to Kenyon from Vanderbilt University in 1937, Ransom himself credited Roberta Teale Swartz, a poet who was married to Kenyon president Gordon K. Chalmers, as the driving force behind its inception. The first issue featured two of Robert *Lowell's earliest poems, Randall *Jarrell's 'A Winter's Tale', John Peale *Bishop's 'The Sorrows of Thomas Wolfe', and reviews by R. P. *Blackmur and Yvor *Winters. Subsequent issues in the first volume included poetry by John *Berryman, Dylan *Thomas, Muriel *Rukeyser, and Allen *Tate. During the *Kenyon Review*'s first twenty-five years, poets as diverse as John *Ashbery, James *Dickey, Anthony *Hecht, James *Merrill, Theodore *Roethke, Wallace *Stevens, and William Carlos *Williams appeared there.

Under Ransom's editorship, the *Kenyon*

Review became the leading organ of the *New Criticism, publishing important articles on poetry by Tate, Cleanth Brooks, Robert Penn *Warren, William *Empson, and Ransom himself, who contributed to virtually every issue during the magazine's first decade. Of this great period Lowell once remarked that, 'when a good critical essay came out it had the excitement of a new imaginative work'. With Ransom's retirement in 1958 the editorship was offered to Jarrell, who declined. It was edited until 1967 by Robie Macauley, who was succeeded by George Lanning and Ellington White. The magazine ceased publication in November 1969, at the end of its thirty-first year; Kenyon's refusal to subsidize further deficits was cited as the ostensible reason, but the sense that the magazine had lost its unique identity during the turbulent 1960s may have also played a part. With considerable backing from private sources a new series was begun in 1979, with Frederick Turner and Ronald Sharp as co-editors. Since then the magazine has been edited variously by Philip D. Church and Galbraith M. Crump, T. R. *Hummer, and Marilyn *Hacker, who took control in 1990. One of Hacker's first acts as editor was to refuse a grant from the National Endowment for the Arts on the grounds that the magazine could not subscribe to vague governmental guide-lines on obscenity.

The Kenyon Critics, edited by Ransom in 1951, collected important essays and book reviews. *Gallery of Modern Fiction: Stories from the* Kenyon Review (1966) was edited by Macauley. An anthology of poems from the magazine, *The Kenyon Poets*, edited by Crump, appeared in 1989 as part of the magazine's fiftieth anniversary. An index to the magazine's first twenty-five years was published in 1964.   [RSG

KEYES, Sidney (Arthur Kilworth) (1922–43), was educated at Tonbridge School and Queen's College, Oxford. An elegy on his grandfather, written when Keyes was 16, is an example of his precocious talent, which he extended and deepened at Oxford, where he became the centre of a group of poets and edited with Michael Meyer

Eight Oxford Poets (1941). He wrote with astonishing fluency: for example, he composed the first of his Oxford poems, 'Remember Your Lovers', in an examination room, having finished his papers early. He came to dislike the poem for its 'lush sensuality'.

Keyes, an omnivorous reader and lover of paintings, found inspiration in such visionaries as El Greco, Blake, Hölderlin, and Schiller and in masters of the macabre, notably Webster, Goya, Beddoes, Picasso, and Rouault. He loved also Wordsworth, Clare, *Hardy, *Housman, and Edward *Thomas, regretting that he had not been born in nineteenth-century Oxfordshire or Wiltshire, 'because then I might have been a good pastoral poet, instead of an uncomfortable metaphysical poet without roots'. His early poems were influenced by *Yeats (overwhelmingly) and Rilke, especially an ambitious poem of over 400 lines, 'The Foreign Gate', written in February and March 1942.

Even more potent than his intellectual allegiances was his intense but unreciprocated passion for Milein Cosman, a refugee from Düsseldorf who had come to Oxford when the Slade School had moved there from London. The epitaph on his love for Milein is 'North Sea', written in October 1942.

In April 1942 Keyes joined the army and one month later was posted to the Officer Cadet Training Unit at Dunbar. Between then and the end of the year he wrote some of his finest verse, including two linked poems, 'Dido's lament for Aeneas' and 'Rome Remember', which celebrates 'the singers | That cry with dead voices along the African shore'. He wrote a long poem in December 1942 and January 1943, 'The Wilderness' which, like 'The Foreign Gate' is immensely ambitious but a partial failure. He thought both his 'nearest misses'.

Keyes was killed in action in Tunisia towards the end of April, fighting with great gallantry. A posthumous collection of poems, *The Cruel Solstice*, was published in 1943.

See *Collected Poems*, ed. Michael Meyer (London, 1945, paperback, 1988). J. Guenther's *Sidney Keyes* (London, 1965) is a biographical study.   [JPr

KEYT, George (1901–93), son of a Sri Lankan Indo-European family, was educated at Trinity College, Kandy. Far better known as a painter than as a poet, he is regarded as one of the most brilliant figures in contemporary Asian art. He lived for long periods in India and Nepal, and his painting and poetry were influenced by his deep interest in Indian music and philosophy, and Indian and Kandyan dancing.

Keyt's poetic oeuvre consists of three volumes of original verse, *Poems* (1936), *Image in Absence* (1937), and *The Darkness Disrobed* (1937), all published privately in Kandy and long out of print; a volume of translations, *Poetry from the Sinhalese* (1939); and a frequently reprinted rendering into English verse of Sri Jayadeva's Sanskrit pastoral poem *Gita Govinda* (1940), the amorous and spiritual themes of which inspired a large number of his paintings. Though he published no poetry after 1940, the cultural influence he exerted through his painting has been considerable. Keyt also published an illustrated volume of Sinhalese folk-tales, retold in English (Colombo, 1974).

See Y. Gooneratne (ed.), *Poems From India, Sri Lanka, Malaysia and Singapore* (Hong Kong, 1979); A. Halpe (ed.), *George Keyt: A Felicitation Volume* (Colombo, 1977); and J. D. Yohannan (ed.), *A Treasury of Asian Literature* (New York, 1956), which reprint selections from Keyt's poems; also H. A. I. Goonetileke, *George Keyt: A Life in Art* (Colombo, 1989), which includes a bio-bibliography of the artist-poet, 1923–88.

[YG

KILMER, Joyce (1886–1918), son of a chemist, was born in New Brunswick, New Jersey, and attended Rutgers between 1901 and 1906, but earned his AB from Columbia in 1908, the same year he married Alice Murray. After teaching Latin for a year, Kilmer worked on the *Standard Dictionary* and served as literary editor with the *Churchman*, an Episcopal outlet, before joining the staff on the Sunday Magazine and Book Review sections of the *New York Times*. His first book of poems, *Summer of Love* (1911), showed the strong influence of early *Yeats and the Celtic poets. He converted to Roman Catholi-

cism after his daughter contracted infantile paralysis, which in turn inspired 'Trees', the only poem of his still remembered. *Trees and Other Poems* appeared in 1914 (it was reissued in London in 1941), followed by a book of prose, *The Circus and Other Essays* (1916), *Main Street and Other Poems* (1917), and, posthumously, *Joyce Kilmer: Poems, Essays and Letters* (New York, 1918). Kilmer enlisted as a private when the United States entered the First World War and was killed at the second Battle of the Marne.

[EB

KINNELL, Galway (1927–), was born in Providence, Rhode Island, and studied at Princeton and the University of Rochester. He served in the United States Navy and then visited Paris on a Fulbright Fellowship. Returning to the United States, he worked for the Congress on Racial Equality and then travelled widely in the Middle East and Europe. He has taught at several colleges and universities, including California, Pittsburgh, and New York. The poems of his first volume, *What a Kingdom It Was* (1960), were informed by a traditional Christian sensibility. However, while retaining a sacramental dimension, his later work burrows fiercely into the self away from traditional sources of religious authority or even conventional notions of personality. 'If you could keep going deeper and deeper', he has said, 'you'd finally not be a person . . . you'd be a blade of grass or ultimately perhaps a stone. And if a stone could read poetry would speak for it.'

The poems issuing from this conviction may be found in such collections as *Flower Herding on Mount Monadnock* (1964), *Body Rags* (1968), *The Book of Nightmares* (1971), and *Mortal Acts, Mortal Words* (1980). Short, chanting lines, a simple, declarative syntax, emphatic rhythms, bleak imagery, and insistent repetition: all are used here to generate the sense of the poet as shaman who throws off the 'sticky infusions' of speech and becomes one with the natural world, sharing in the primal experiences of birth and death. *Walking Down the Stairs* (1978) is a useful selection of interviews with Kinnell; he has also published a number of translations. His *Selected*

Poems (Boston, 1982; London, 1984) won a Pulitizer Prize and is the best introduction to his work. [RJG

KINSELLA, Thomas (1928–), was born in Dublin and abandoned a science degree at University College, Dublin, to work in the Irish Civil Service until 1965 when he retired from the Department of Finance. Since then he has taught at various universities in the United States. He has been a director of the Dolmen and Cuala presses in Dublin; in 1972 he started his own Peppercanister Press which has published most of his work before publication in larger volumes by Dolmen and by Oxford University Press in Oxford and New York. His first volume *The Starlit Eye* (Dublin, 1952) is lyrical but already somewhat cryptic because of its breadth of mythological and literary allusion, from *Eliot to medieval Irish legend. *Another September* (1958) was enthusiastically received in Ireland, England, and America (his poetry has always shown American influence), and his standing as a principal figure in contemporary poetry was confirmed by the reception of *Nightwalker and other poems* in all three centres in 1968. The tendency towards greater crypticism and more subdued imagery of that intellectual volume has continued, through *Notes from the Land of the Dead and other poems* (1972) to the various numbered brief Peppercanister volumes up to *Open Court* (17) in 1991.

The lack of an extensive collection since *Poems 1956–1973* has obscured Kinsella's drift. Moreover, his writing is increasingly allusive and the symbolic coding has become even more internalized, with his eye on Jung, Irish myths, and his own Joycean Dublin topography. The principal interest lies in watching Kinsella building towards a definitive structure as he attempts (like *Yeats) to make of his work a myth of modern Irish life. This is not a self-indulgence but a painstaking record of the accumulation of experience and sensation from an internal vantage-point.

Kinsella's second major significance in Irish literary history is his translating of earlier Irish poetry, both of the medieval period (*The Táin*) and the classical period (*An Duanaire*), in a campaigning attempt to give a clear vernacular hearing to poets who have lacked it. He has famously (and controversially) defined the Irish tradition as 'gapped': that is, as a single national culture which is fragmented by a change of vernacular—an idea that nowadays seems recognizably modernist, in Eliot's tradition. He has also occasionally turned aside from his psychic odyssey towards public events, most famously in *Butcher's Dozen* (1972: Peppercanister only), an impassioned broadside against the Widgery Tribunal's anodyne judgement on the events of 'Bloody Sunday' in Derry. Less sensationally, he has sustained Austin *Clarke's hostilities against Dublin's architectural planners.

Kinsella's crypticism means that he benefits from being read with an informed guide, such as Maurice Harmon's *The Poetry of Thomas Kinsella* (Dublin, 1974), or the chapter 'Clarke and Kinsella' in Dillon Johnston's *Irish Poetry after Joyce* (South Bend, Ind., and Dublin, 1985). Since *Poems 1956–1973* (Dublin; Oxford; and Winston-Salem, NC, 1980), he has published *Blood and Family* (Oxford, 1988); *From Centre City*, which includes the Peppercanister pamphlets to date, is forthcoming. He edited The *New Oxford Book of Irish Verse* (Oxford, 1986), and his principal translations are *The Táin*, with illustrations by Louis le Brocquy (Dublin, 1969; Oxford, 1970) and, with Seán Ó Tuama, *An Duanaire, 1600–1900: Poems of the Dispossessed* (Dublin and Oxford, 1981). [BO'D

KINZIE, Mary (1944–), was born in Montgomery, Alabama, and raised in the South. She was divorced in 1992 and has one child, Phoebe, born in 1985. Kinzie attended Northwestern University and Johns Hopkins University, and is a professor of English at Northwestern.

Kinzie's poems surprise the reader as much with verbal complexity as with the human story they disclose. They are often lyrics in the truest sense, for their revelation of a tragic element; and can seem 'masculine' and 'feminine' at once in their thematic domains: war, passion, history, and motherhood.

Kinzie has published four volumes of poetry: *The Threshold of the Year* (Columbia, Mo., 1982), which won the 1982 Devins Award; *Masked Women* (New York, 1990); *Summers of Vietnam* (New York, 1990); and *Autumn Eros* (New York, 1991). For many years she was a staff reviewer for the *American Poetry Review*, and she has published a book of critical prose entitled *The Cure of Poetry in an Age of Prose* (Chicago, 1993).   [HC

KIPLING, Rudyard (1865–1936), was born in Bombay, sent (at the age of 6) with his sister to horrible foster-parents in Southsea, and then to an equally horrible public school. He returned to India to work as a journalist, and, by way of short prose pieces and poems, embarked on a literary career.

Somebody once said of Kipling: 'Even if he's not a great poet, he's certainly a great *something*!' His best novel, *Kim*, could be called great, and the same contentious epithet could be applied to the best short stories. The poetry is a different matter. *Eliot regarded it as 'verse', though he did admit that Kipling could write 'poetry' accidentally. Kipling, from the first, wrote in strict forms, the forms of ballads and music-hall songs: light verse at first, then with moral and political purpose—like Brecht. However, by these simple means, he could achieve remarkable effects. Eliot has shown how the variations of pace in 'Danny Deever' (probably his best poem) enhance the total effect. Orwell contended that Kipling's Cockney verse would have sounded better in standard English, more dignified and more stately. Lines like 'When 'Omer smote 'is bloomin' lyre' don't inspire confidence, because they suggest that Kipling's soldiers are only puppets expressing Kipling's opinions.

Kipling's poetry was always overwhelmingly popular with the English middle classes. 'If' has been elevated almost to the height and dignity of an alternative Creed. But most of his poems—including 'If'—are 'political' in some sense, and unless you agree with Kipling's line, you may not like the poem. He once gave a talk on literature to senior boys at Wellington College, in which he recommended them, when

they met people who advocated the reading of *lurid* literature, to think to themselves whether 'they strike you as the kind of men you'd like to be with in a tight place'. In other words (this was in 1912) the virtues of junior officers are the key virtues: courage, awareness of danger, improvisation.

Kipling's Indian knowledge and experience was not beneficial only for the writing of *Kim* and the Indian stories. 'Arithmetic on the Frontier', an early poem, compares the Afghan tribesman with his inaccurate rifle ('a ten-rupee *jezail*') to the Sandhurst-trained infantry subaltern, trained for seven years ('Two thousand pounds of education'), and concludes: 'The odds are on the cheaper man.' Nor does the soldier-talk always seem theatrical. See 'Mandalay'. Kipling also wrote overt political satires. 'Gehazi' (on the Marconi scandals) now depends too much on knowledge of the case, and of the Old Testament. He also wrote one fine 'prophetic' poem, warning of the troubles to come—'The Storm Cone', written in 1932, four years before his death.

The best introduction to the poems, with a long essay, is T. S. Eliot's *A Choice of Kipling's Verse* (London, 1941; many later impressions).
[GE

KIRKUP, James (Falconer) (1923–), was born in South Shields, Co. Durham. Since 1977 he has lived mostly in Japan and Andorra. Kirkup began as a much-heeded young English poet until, not long after the publication of *The Prodigal Son: Poems 1956–1959* (London, 1959), and true to the spirit of the comic and casual which always flourished in him, he began to divert his energies into minority causes (e.g. *The Bad Boy's Bedside Book of Do-It-Yourself Sex*, Tokyo, 1978). The reliable translator of many notable authors, Kirkup had technical ability, and his earlier poetry abounded in difficult verse-forms. His first collection was *The Drowned Sailor* (London, 1947), and his reputation was at its apogee when he published the less rhetorical *A Correct Compassion* (London, 1952), the long, documentary title-poem of which describes a heart-operation. Those who waited to see how this efficient poet was going to develop were disappointed. Later work, published in small editions, has concentrated on oriental or homo-erotic themes; one poem about Christ achieved a brief notoriety when it was prosecuted for alleged blasphemy. Further collections are *The Refusal to Conform* (London, 1963) and *The Body Servant: Poems of Exile* (London, 1971). [MS-S]

KIZER, Carolyn (1925–), was born in Spokane, Washington, and educated at Sarah Lawrence College. She has held a number of positions both in and out of the academy, including teaching appointments in the *Iowa Writers' Workshop.

Her first book was *The Ungrateful Garden* (Bloomington, Ind., 1961). The long poem, 'Pro Femina', from *Knock Upon Silence* (Garden City, NY, 1965), was an early feminist work which, in the opinion of some critics, has not been excelled by any poem on the same subject since.

Kizer's poems are formal and lyrical, but a particular element of her success is her sense of narrative, as in *Yin: New Poems* (Brockport, NY, 1984). She gets and keeps the reader's attention without resorting to the sensational or the hortatory. In 'Semele Recycled', for instance, the poet tells a tale out of Greek myth, but makes it familiar and compelling: a narrative embodiment of the war between the sexes and the truce that is eternally struck.

Although she published a book entitled *Mermaids in the Basement: Poems for Women* (Port Townsend, Wash., 1984), Kizer's work is not aimed at a 'special interest' audience. *The Nearness of You* (Port Townsend, 1986) is her most recent volume, but the largest collection is her third, *Midnight Was My Cry: New and Selected Poems* (Garden City, NY, 1971). [LT

KLAPPERT, Peter (1942–), was born in Rockville Center, New York, and grew up in Connecticut. He was educated at Cornell University and the University of Iowa and is an associate professor at George Mason University. His first collection, *Lugging Vegetables to Nantucket* (New Haven, Conn., 1971), won the Yale Series of Younger Poets competition. 'The Babysit-

ters', the book's central poem, displays his characteristic qualities and concerns: satire, wordplay, structural experimentation, and a sense of alienation. In *Circular Stairs, Distress in the Mirrors* (Marlboro, Vt., 1975), a shorter collection, he explored the theme of the double.

With *The Idiot Princess of the Last Dynasty* (New York, 1984), Klappert produced a work of epic proportions. The book is a long series of poems in the form of monologues by 'Doc' Dan Mahoney, a character based on Dr Matthew O'Connor from Djuna Barnes's 1936 novel *Nightwood*. In its setting (1939–40), structure, allusiveness, and metaphysical perspectives, *Idiot Princess* is a product of late modernism, recalling *Eliot, *Pound and other influences. Mahoney is the archetypal outsider—abortionist, homosexual, alcoholic—whose complex, multi-valenced voice allows Klappert to make full use of his own heterogeneous talents. The large ambition, moral intensity, omnivorous learning, and technical accomplishment that mark *Idiot Princess* have attracted widespread praise. [TWi

KLEIN, A(braham) M(oses) (1909–72), was born in Ratno, Ukraine, to Jewish parents who moved to Montreal in 1910. While studying at McGill (1926–30), he published poems and essays in Canadian and American periodicals. He graduated from the Université de Montréal law-school in 1933, and practised law until his retirement in 1956. During the 1920s and 1930s he was actively involved in the Zionist youth group Young Judaea. From 1938 to 1955 he edited the *Canadian Jewish Chronicle*. During this time he was also employed by the Jewish philanthropist, Samuel Bronfman, as a speech-writer and public-relations consultant. Teaching as a visiting lecturer in poetry at McGill (1945–8) and running unsuccessfully for the Federal Socialist Party (1949) added pressures to a busy life. In 1955 Klein suffered a mental breakdown from which he never fully recovered.

As a Jew living in a French-Canadian province, which in turn was surrounded by an English-speaking majority, Klein was acutely conscious of his vulnerable minority status. His first verse collection, *Hath Not a Jew . . .* (1940), gathered over a decade of poems on Jewish themes. Enthusiastic reception led to a second collection, *Poems* (1944) and *The Hitleriad* (1944), a mock-epic indictment of Nazi Germany. *The Rocking Chair and Other Poems* (1948) conveyed the tensions of life in Quebec with characteristic wit and affection. The highly wrought novella, *The Second Scroll* (1951), an expression of his Zionism, reflected his deep knowledge of *Joyce's *Ulysses*. There were also numerous essays, reviews, editorials, stories, and translations from Hebrew and Yiddish.

The most recent and authoritative edition of Klein's poetry is *A. M. Klein: The Complete Poems*, ed. Zailig Pollock (Toronto, 1990). See also: *A. M. Klein: Literary Essays and Reviews*, ed. Usher Caplan and M. W. Steinberg (Toronto, 1987); *A. M. Klein: Short Stories*, ed. M. W. Steinberg (Toronto, 1983); *A. M. Klein, Beyond Sambation: Selected Essays and Editorials 1928–1955*, ed. M. W. Steinberg and Usher Caplan (Toronto, 1982); *Like One That Dreamed: A Portrait of A. M. Klein*, by Usher Caplan (Toronto, 1982); and *A. M. Klein and His Works*, by Noreen Golfman (Toronto, 1990).   [NG

KNIGHT, Etheridge (1931–), was born in Corinth, Mississippi. Self-educated, he served in the US Army (1947–51), and while recuperating from shrapnel wounds, he began a life-long cycle of drug-addiction and recovery. Three marriages (to poet Sonia *Sanchez, Mary Ann McAnally, and Charlene Blackburn) ended in divorce. During Knight's incarceration for robbery at Indiana State Prison (1960–8), Dudley Randall, founder of Broadside Press in Detroit became his mentor.

Knight's aesthetic emphasizes the relationship between the poet, the poem, and the people: the poet witnesses through his own experience the truth of the collective vision of the people and returns it to them as the poem. Like Whitman, as well as many poets of the African-American oral tradition, he views the poet as one with the people, rather than a 'poet-preacher', such as *Baraka. Knight's commitment to the spoken poem is notable, although

he has published widely. Technically, he combines traditional metrical devices with accentual rhythms of black street-talk, blues, and toasts (rhyming, humorous, often vulgar narratives extolling the subculture's power).

A dominant motif in Knight's poems is the tension between love, freedom, and various forms of imprisonment, especially in the earlier collections *Poems from Prison* (Detroit, 1968) and *Belly Song and Other Poems* (Detroit, 1973). In later collections an expanded thematic and technical range does not diminish his life-affirming tone. *Born of a Woman: New and Selected Poems* (Detroit, 1980) received a Pulitzer Prize nomination and won the National Book Award; the most comprehensive collection, *The Essential Etheridge Knight* (Pittsburgh, Pa., and London, 1986), won the American Book Award.   [JTC

KNISTER, (John) Raymond (1899–1932), was born in the village of Ruscomb, Ontario. He attended, briefly, the University of Toronto and Iowa State University. His peripatetic life took him to Iowa City where he became involved as associate editor with the Midwestern avant-garde literary magazine, *The Midland*. Knister's stories, sketches, and poems appeared in the popular press as well as in avant-garde publications such as *This Quarter* in Paris. A rural background which included work on the family farm was balanced by the experience of big-city life in Chicago, Toronto, and Montreal. Knister's tragically shortened life as a professional writer was one of struggle burdened by the responsibilities of a young family.

Knister was not only a practitioner of new literary modes in the modified imagism of his poetry and the psycho-realism of his fiction, but he was also actively engaged in furthering modernism in Canada. He edited a landmark anthology, *Canadian Short Stories* (1928), and engaged in thoughtful critical journalism. He died in a tragic drowning accident while vacationing with his family. In 1949 the Canadian poet Dorothy *Livesay published his *Collected Poems* (Toronto). Six of his best stories were collected by Michael Gnarowski and published as *Selected Stories of Raymond Knister* (1972), and

David Arnason edited *Raymond Knister: Poems, Stories, and Essays* (1975). Anne Burke assembled *Raymond Knister: An Annotated Bibliography* (1981).

[MG

KNOTT, Bill (William Kilborn) (1940–), was born in Michigan, and spent some of his childhood on a Michigan farm. His mother died when he was 6, his father when he was 11, and he spent the years between 8 and 16 in an orphanage. After serving in the US Army as a medic, he made his way to Chicago where he studied with poets Gwendolyn *Brooks and John *Logan. Knott has since gone on to take an MFA from Vermont College, and has held appointments at a number of colleges, including Emerson College in Boston, where he now teaches.

Knott published his first book of poems, *The Naomi Poems: Book One: Corpse and Beans* (Chicago, 1968) under the pseudonym of St Geraud (who, according to Knott, was the hero of a French pornographic novel, the head of an orphanage who debauched his charges). After this auspicious beginning Knott went on to publish *Aurealism: A Study; Autonecrophilia; The Poems: Book 2; Love Poems to Myself;* and, with the poet James *Tate, a collaborative prose-work titled *Lucky Darryl*.

Much is written about *'language poetry' in America, and if by that we mean an essentially language-based, self-referential world of words in the tradition of the Surrealists, *Stein, *Joyce, and others, then Knott's work partakes of that lineage. His influences are decidedly European: Desnos, Eluard, and Michaux. But as Knott published *Becos* (New York, 1983), *Outremer* (Iowa City, 1989), and *Poems 1963–1988* (Pittsburgh, Pa., 1989), it became apparent that he had long ago outlived any 'surrealist' or 'language' label that might have been conferred upon him. His work is individual, not to say eccentric, and has about it an inner logic which is now self-generative. In the recent volume of selected poems he pared down some poems to as little as one line or one phrase from their former, published incarnations, and this kind of ongoing revision and reassemblage—

reinvention, as from his beginning—remains a signature of Knott's aesthetic. [LR

KOCAN, Peter (1947–) was born in Newcastle, New South Wales, and in 1966 was sentenced to life-imprisonment for the attempted assassination of Arthur Calwell, leader of the Australian Labour Party. *The Other Side of the Fence* (1975) was completed before his release, after nearly ten years in Morisset Mental Hospital. He now lives on the Central Coast, north of Sydney.

The core of Kocan's first volume is a gallery of institutional portraits. *Armistice* (1980) handles this material more steadily, while tracing an affinity with poets of the First World War. Only in the prose vignettes of two novels, *The Treatment* (1980) and *The Cure* (1983), is Kocan fully in command of his Morisset experience, which he bids farewell to in *Freedom to Breathe* (1985), poems displaying a firm if pessimistic historical sense. *Flies of a Summer* (1988), a somewhat Wellsian dystopia, allows its characters to forge viable group loyalties and identities. Despite his acquaintance with the pathological personality, Kocan displays a pre-modernist sense of character, in verse hallmarked by a technical and political conservatism.

The Other Side of the Fence (St Lucia, Qld., 1975) and *Freedom to Breathe* (Sydney, 1985) are his two main collections. A prize-winning sequence, 'The Private Poems of Governor Caulfield', appeared in *Lines from the Horizon*, ed. Christopher Pollnitz (Newcastle, NSW, 1982). [CP

KOCH, Kenneth (1925–), was born in Cincinnati, Ohio, and served as a rifleman in the Pacific theatre during the Second World War. After graduating from Harvard in 1948 he moved to New York City, where his close circle of friends included the poets John *Ashbery and Frank *O'Hara and the painters Jane Freilicher and Larry Rivers. In France and Italy, where Koch spent three fellowship years, he found inspiration in the ambience of foreign languages imperfectly understood, and he set out to communicate the same 'incomprehensible excitement' in his poetry.

Thank You (New York, 1962) remains Koch's most influential collection. Radiating comic energy, the book illustrates *par excellence* certain seminal strategies associated with the *New York School, such as the 'list' poem, where the inventory as a structural device serves an ideal of inclusiveness and a delight in humorous incongruity. Koch's tone, often imitated, is one of exclamatory exuberance and hyperbolic wit, as in his invention of a conceptual artist who plans to paint the Pacific Ocean and has, to this end, ordered 16 million tons of blue paint.

If the spirit of pastiche is definitive of postmodernism, Koch must be considered one of that movement's pioneers. A gifted and versatile parodist, he built his comic epic *Ko, or a Season on Earth* (New York, 1959) on *ottava rima*, the stanza of Byron's *Don Juan*. *The Art of Love* (New York, 1975), a spoof on pedagogy, offers unconventional instruction on matters of aesthetics and love. *One Thousand Avant-Garde Plays* (New York, 1988)—actually consisting of 112 miniature verse plays—takes on the concept of avant-garde art, mindful that it may be beautiful and ridiculous at once.

At Columbia University, where he has taught for thirty years, Koch developed innovative techniques for teaching the writing of poetry. He attained a degree of celebrity when he applied these methods to schoolchildren and elderly nursing-home residents. The best-known of his books on education are *Wishes, Lies, and Dreams* (1970) and *Rose, Where Did You Get That Red?* (1973—both New York). Koch's *Selected Poems* appeared in New York in 1985 and in Manchester in 1991. [DL

KOETHE, John (1945–), was born in San Diego, California. He attended Princeton University as an undergraduate, and took a Ph.D in philosophy at Harvard. He is a member of the philosophy department at the University of Wisconsin in Milwaukee, where he lives with his wife.

In his recent poetry Koethe has perfected and purified the autobiographical lyric mode developed by John *Ashbery. The subtle relations between time and desire form Koethe's primary

theme; for this reason his poetry offers few tangible objects or landscapes, instead evoking the abstract yet intimate space of life itself, as experienced by an intensely introspective mind. Yet in Koethe's hands the medium of language itself takes on a silken sensuality. The influence of his work as a professional philosopher is clear in his poetry, but it does not lead to sterility; for Koethe, ideas themselves are infused with pathos. If his work thus far has a major flaw it is a lack of variety, of tone as well as subject. Like other disciples, Koethe has successfully siphoned off and distilled one current in Ashbery, but at the cost of his master's range and abundance. His most recent book is *The Late Wisconsin Spring* (Princeton, NJ, 1984). [RG

KOLATKAR, Arun Balkrishna (1932–), was born in Kolhapur and works as a graphic artist in a Bombay advertising agency. He is one of the few genuinely bilingual poets of contemporary India, writing in both English and Marathi. Although his poems have appeared in a number of anthologies and journals in India, Britain, and the United States, his only two published collections to date are *Arun Kolatkarchya Kavita* (a selection of his Marathi verse) and a collection of thirty-one linked poems in English, *Jejuri* (Bombay, 1976). For this volume, he was awarded the Commonwealth Poetry Prize. Notable among his uncollected verse is the long poem, 'The Boatride' which was originally published in Arvind *Mehrotra's short-lived little magazine, *Damn You*. It has subsequently been published in R. *Parthasarathy's *Ten Twentieth Century Indian Poets* (Delhi, 1976).

Kolatkar's most sustained achievement, *Jejuri*, ostensibly records a pilgrimage to the temple of Khandobi at Jejuri, a small town in Western Maharashtra. The poet views Hindu tradition sceptically. His laconic verse borrows something from the medieval *bhakti* poets of Maharashtra, especially Tukaram (who Kolatkar has translated into English), and juxtaposes this with the relaxed diction of the American *Beat poets. An idiosyncratic humour pervades much of Kolatkar's writing; it derives some of its force from viewing commonplace detail at an unaccustomed angle. In the short poems this can produce original, surreal effects. Longer poems, notably 'Ajamil and the Tigers', display a skilfully sustained handling of narrative and irony.   [RW

KOMUNYAKAA, Yusef (1947–), was born in Bogalusa, Louisiana, served in Vietnam as correspondent and editor of the *Southern Cross*, and received the Bronze Star. He is now associate professor of English at Indiana University.

Highly compressed, Komunyakaa's poetry has the virtues of both lyrical and narrative poetries: lush cadences, dense imagery, and dramatic conflicts. Discordant then melodic, riffing across a range of dialects, gritty then opulent in its imagery, his work is inspired by blues, jazz, and the historic suffering of black Americans. In his first major collection, *Copacetic* (Middletown, Conn., 1984), the conflicts are usually those of racism, but despair and rage are abated by a will to persevere and to sing. Where *Copacetic* often deals with the rural South during the first half of this century, *I Apologize for the Eyes in My Head* (Middletown, 1986) relates episodes of class-strife in present day urban America, dramatizing the enduring aftermath of slavery: poverty and the psychic violence of more repressed—but still insidious—forms of racism. Some of Komunyakaa's most memorable poems appear in *Dien Cai Dau* (Middletown, 1988): 'Re-Creating the Scene', 'To Do Street', and 'Facing It' are among the most moving poems written about the Vietnam war.
                                                       [DWF

KREYMBORG, Alfred (1883–1966), was a native of New York City who, during the earliest period of modernism, became an editor and literary entrepreneur on a par with Ezra *Pound, whom he met in Paris in 1921 after a correspondence of eight years. Originally an experimental poet and the editor of *Broom*, which was published in Rome beginning in 1921, and other pioneering modernist magazines including *The Glebe* (New York, 1913) and the *Others* anthologies (New York, 1916–19), Kreymborg wrote the first comprehensive history of American poetry, *Our Singing Strength* (New York, 1929). Those sections concerning the modernist poets were full of insights into the work of his contemporaries; they often read like insiders' gossip which, indeed, they were. In his later life he suffered from Parkinson's disease and wrote little.

Kreymborg is neglected, perhaps because, though he began as an offbeat writer of *imagist and impressionist poems, he turned away from avant-garde work quite early and became a strict formalist. His *Love and Life* (New York, 1908) and *Apostrophes* (New York, 1910), which he straightforwardly called 'prose poems', were among the century's earliest examples of *vers libre. Mushrooms* (New York, 1916) and *Blood of Things* (New York, 1920) were typified by aphoristic, often imagistic work, such as 'Vista' or 'Theology'. 'Overheard in an Asylum' is a remarkable anti-war poem; other work was epigrammatic and whimsical, as for instance 'Race Prejudice'.

Traditionally formal work began to make inroads into *Less Lonely* (New York, 1923), and by the time of *Scarlet and Mellow* (New York, 1926) Kreymborg's transformation was virtually complete. Other books of his poetry were *The Lost Sail* (1928); *Manhattan Men* (1929); *The Little World* (1932); *Two New Yorkers*, with Alexander Kruze (1938); *Ten American Ballads* (1942); and *The Selected Poems 1912–1944* (1945— all New York). *Man and Shadow, an Allegory* (New York) appeared in 1946. A lifelong pacifist, Kreymborg's last book was, appropriately, *No More War and Other Poems* (New York, 1950). Kreymborg also scripted and produced many plays and puppet plays, from *Lima Beans* in 1918 through *The Four Apes* of 1939. He wrote a novel, two novelettes, and an autobiography, *Troubadour* (New York, 1925).   [LT

KROETSCH, Robert (1927–), was born in Heisler, Alberta. After graduation, he worked for the US Army as a civilian education and information specialist in Labrador. He holds graduate degrees from Middlebury College and the University of Iowa. After teaching for several years at the State University of New York at

Binghampton and editing *Boundary 2*, a journal of postmodern literature, he returned to Canada, where he has taught mainly at the University of Manitoba. Kroetsch's critical writings are to be found in *The Lovely Treachery of Words: Essays Selected and New* (1989).

In his poetry, Kroetsch moves from fairly traditional beginnings in *The Stone Hammer Poems* (Lantzville, BC, 1975) to vigorous experimentation in *Seed Catalogue* (Winnipeg, 1977) and the remaining texts collected in *Field Notes* (Don Mills, Ont., 1981). His best-known and most interesting long poem is *Seed Catalogue*, which explores history and place in comic-opera or mock-epic fashion. Using the flat and, at times, commercial diction of seed catalogues and their testimonials as a counterpoint to his lyrical and anecdotal meditations on place, growing up, family, and the advent of sexual awareness, Kroetsch is able to construct a touching, evocative, and at times hilarious patchwork quilt of life in the vanished prairie that is at once both a portrait of the artist as farm-boy and a testament to the perennially transforming power of art.

Kroetsch has published seven novels. Other collections of poetry are *The Ledger* (London, Ont., 1975) and *The Sad Phoenician* (Toronto, 1979). [GG

KUMIN, Maxine (1925–), was born and raised in Philadelphia, the daughter of prosperous Jewish parents, and educated at Radcliffe College. Kumin's friends in Boston included Sylvia *Plath and Anne *Sexton. The versatile author of novels, short stories, essays, and children's books as well as poetry, Kumin won the Pulitzer Prize in 1973. She has taught at Columbia, Brandeis, and Princeton, has served as poetry consultant to the Library of Congress, and now lives in New Hampshire, where she is currently state poet laureate.

Increasingly since her move to the country, Kumin's poetry has concerned itself with the natural world. In matter-of-fact tones sometimes darkened by elegy, her work chronicles the lives and deaths of animals and the cycle of the seasons. The fragile state of the environ-ment is another compelling theme. Except as an occasion for mourning illnesses and deaths (the later poems abound in dark dreams), the human world seems marginal in Kumin's imagination, in contrast to the rural poems' rootedness in daily experience.

Kumin's work is less daring and stylistically distinctive than that of such contemporaries as Plath and Sexton (Kumin has a poem about surviving her friend Sexton). The tone is steady, grounded, almost stoical in comparison; the language less likely to transcend its occasion and engage in lyric flights. Kumin's early work is more concerned with formal structures than her later work, but always her language is subordinated to observation and thought.

Notable collections are *Up Country: Poems of New England* (New York, 1973) and *The Retrieval System* (New York, 1978). Kumin's thoughts on poetry are collected in *To Make a Prairie* (Ann Arbor, Mich., 1979). [RHa

KUNENE, Mazisi (*c.*1930–), was born in Durban, South Africa, and took his MA at the University of Natal. In 1956 he won the Bantu Literary Competition and in 1959 went to the School of Oriental and African Studies, University of London, where he wrote a dissertation on Zulu Poetry. While there, he helped found the Anti-Apartheid Movement in Britain. Upon his return to Southern Africa he became the head of the Department of African Studies at the University of Lesotho. He later taught African studies at the University of California. He has represented the African National Congress both in Europe and the United States.

More than any other African writer, Kunene is clearly an indigenous poet who sees himself as part of a specific African tradition of written and oral culture. Most of his poetry in English was in fact first written in Zulu. Kunene employs such traditional genres as the funeral dirge, the war song, the praise-song, and the elegy. He also includes elements of traditional religion and cosmology, such as ancestor-worship.

Above all, Kunene's poetry is political; it describes the inhumanity of the Apartheid regime in South Africa and looks back to the values of pre-colonial Africa. He has published the following anthologies: *Zulu Poems* (London, 1970); *Emperor Shaka the Great* (London, 1979); *Anthem of the Decades* (London, 1981); and *Ancestors and the Sacred Mountain* (London, 1982).

[M-HM

KUNITZ, Stanley (1905–), was born in Worcester, Massachusetts, where he grew up; he studied at Harvard College, receiving a BA in 1926 and an MA in 1927. He then moved to New York, taking a job with the H. W. Wilson company as an editor of the *Wilson Library Bulletin*; he also began at this time the work of collaboration with Howard Haycraft on four important biographical dictionaries of English and American authors. His first book of poems, *Intellectual Things* (1930) was barely recognized, and Kunitz did not publish his second book, *Passport to War*, for another fourteen years. The Second World War interrupted his career as editor, and when he was released from the army he joined the faculty of Bennington College, the first of several academic jobs. Real recognition came slowly to Kunitz, culminating in his receiving the Pulitzer Prize for Poetry in 1958 for his first *Selected Poems*.

The witty, even defiantly intellectual first poems of Kunitz gave way, gradually, to a more autobiographical verse (as in *The Testing Tree*, 1971), which reminded some critics of Randall *Jarrell and Robert *Lowell in their *confessional phases. The poems of recent years have been restrained but quietly passionate, as in 'The Layers', where Kunitz writes: 'I have walked through many lives, | some of them my own, | and I am not who I was, | though some principle of being | abides, from which I struggle | not to stray.' Always, Kunitz writes with an almost passionate clarity and with attention to formal details.

Kunitz has also worked as a translator, creating deft English versions of Russian poems by Mandelstam, Yevtushenko, Stolzenberg, Akhmatova, and Akhmadulina. His critical essays are collected in *A Kind of Order, A Kind of Folly* (Boston, 1975). Collections of verse include *The Poems of Stanley Kunitz* (Boston, 1979) and *Next-to-Last Things* (Boston, 1985). For criticism, see Marie Henault, *Stanley Kunitz* (Boston, 1980) and Gregory Orr, *Stanley Kunitz* (New York, 1985).

[JP

KUPPNER, Frank (1951–), was born in Glasgow and educated at the university there. A set of 501 unrhymed quatrains, prefaced by ten more in a 'Technical Note' on the unrhymed quatrain, seems a less-than-ideal approach to a first book, especially when it's called *A Bad Day for the Sung Dynasty* (Manchester, 1984). Kuppner's first collection has an off-beat, subdued, and often tedious humour. *The Intelligent Observation of Naked Women* (Manchester, 1987) is— yet again—composed entirely in unrhymed free-verse quatrains. The title-poem, however, exerts a considerable, if slow-working charm, and Kuppner's first-person singular feels like a voice to be trusted. 'Passing Through Doorways' is a leisurely evocation of where Kuppner lived in Glasgow, and again, the voice feels honest. At times, though, Kuppner appears to confuse poetry or mystery with vagueness. While his work relies on 'a speaking voice', it is one liable to give in to a defensive prosiness. Rhythm, figuration, and other sonorous and visual effects have yet to earn a place in his work. Languor, perhaps even a dandified or willed fatigue, predominate.

Ridiculous! Absurd! Disgusting! (Manchester, 1989) includes prose, as well as yet more quatrains. Kuppner has also published a novel 'of sorts' (as he says), *A Very Quiet Street* (1989).

[DED

L

LAING, Kojo (1946–) was born in Kumasi, Ghana. After taking an MA at Glasgow University in 1968 he spent nine years in administrative positions in provincial Ghana, followed by a year in Accra. From 1980 to 1985 he was secretary to the Institute of African Studies at the University of Ghana, and at present he is chief executive of a private school in Accra founded by his mother.

Laing describes his poetic medium as 'verbal fireworks'. One poem has a different poem inserted into it in single capitalized words every other line; another places the same five lines in a different order in each of its first three stanzas. His themes are unusually varied. 'The same corpse' is a robust satire on the corruption of Ghanaian society. 'Africa sky' is a lyrical mood piece. 'I am the freshly dead husband' is the quirky monologue of a dead man in his coffin, observing the false grief of his fashionable widow. In 'Funeral in Accra' clocks become 'anachronistic' and the deceased is sung 'slowly to death'. The relentless flow of witticism may irritate, but it can also seem imaginatively liberating.

Laing's poetry is collected in *Godhorse* (Oxford, 1989). [JB

Lallans. Other names for the language of Lowland Scotland have included Scots, Braid Scots, the Scots Vernacular, Aggrandized Scots, Synthetic Scots, and Plastic Scots. Doric, now seldom used, properly applies to the dialect of north-east Scotland, especially Aberdeenshire.

After the revival of poetry in Scots in the eighteenth-century, by Allan Ramsay, Robert Fergusson, Alexander Ross, and Robert Burns, poetry continued to be written in Lallans, or Lallan as it was called by R. L. Stevenson, who can be credited with lending the term a new currency. Much of this subsequent verse rarely aspired to a level above that of dialect and the districts associated with it. Supernatural themes were especially common, in, for example, the poetry of Violet Jacob (1863–1946). Lewis *Spence (1874–1955) introduced a diction with more historical resonance, harking back to the Scotland of the sixteenth century. More successful, however, were Sir Alexander Gray's (1882–1967) translations into Scots from Heine (*Songs and Ballads, Chiefly from Heine*, 1920).

Christopher Murray Grieve, better known as Hugh *MacDiarmid, published his first Scots lyrics in his collection *Sangschaw* in 1925. In such poems as 'The Bonnie Broukit Bairn', 'The Watergaw', and 'The Eemis Stane,' he produced a startling modernity in terms of imagery and psychology together with a strongly ancestral note conveyed by Scots diction. In editorials in his magazine *The Scottish Chapbook* (15 issues, 1922–3), MacDiarmid justified Scots in terms of modernity, psychology, and indigenousness. Equally important to him was the extent to which its 'speculative and imaginative tendencies' were superior to those of English, especially as used by 'Anglicized Scots'.

MacDiarmid's Scots, or Lallans, and that of writers after him, has been called Synthetic Scots. To some extent the phrase is an attempt to escape the belittling associations of dialect, but what it describes is the practice of using in the same poem words which originate from two or more districts. In recovering a language in which, MacDiarmid noted, there was embedded 'a vast unutilized mass of lapsed observation', dictionaries were, and continue to be, indispensable. Philological acumen is peculiarly important to any poet attempting to write Scots verse. Indeed, it should be apparent that Lallans is by now a literary or poetic language. Its relationship to contemporary Scottish speech is ideal, tangential, and retrospective, rather than a reflection of how Scottish people actually speak.

Poetry in Lallans can be seen as an attempt to preserve a linguistic and poetic tradition of very considerable antiquity. Political as well as literary factors enter the picture. The Scots language is associated by many with political independence, as well as with perhaps the greatest period of Scots poetry, that of the 'Makars', Henryson, Dunbar, Douglas, and Lindsay. However, there are specific qualities to Scots which underline its distinctiveness. Especially in native stanzas, such as Standard Habbie (or the Burns stanza), or that of the old poem 'Christis Kirk on the Grene', or the elaborate stanza of Montgomerie's 'The Cherry and the Slae' (c.1597), it lends itself to a remarkable directness, precision, and fast tempo. Qualities such as these can be seen in the plainer measures of MacDiarmid's long poem *A Drunk Man Looks at the Thistle* (1926). They come through strongly in Robert *Garioch's artfully stanzaic verse, as well as his sonnets, especially those translated from Belli. Satirical and comic effects suit Lallans well, too, as does tenderness, which can hardly be surprising in a tradition which includes the song-maker Robert Burns. Good examples are William *Soutar's 'The Tryst' and Sydney Goodsir *Smith's 'Aa My Life'.

Others who have used Scots include Douglas *Young, Maurice *Lindsay, George *Bruce, Alasdair Mackie, and Alexander *Scott. Edwin *Morgan has used Scots in his translations (see, especially, his versions of Mayakovsky). It is used by William Neill (b. 1922), Raymond Vettese (b. 1950), Robert *Crawford (b. 1959), and by W. N. Herbert (b. 1961), whose tonal base is Dundonian speech, to which he adds an extraordinary diction gleaned from lexicons. While the literary perpetuation of Scots (or Lal-

lans) seems more or less secure, a language's detachment from the actual speech of a country remains a problem with potentially serious consequences. Lallans has no standardized orthography.   [DED

LAMANTIA, Philip (1927–), was born in San Francisco and educated at public schools there. At the age of 15 he saw his work published by Henri Ford and Parker Tyler in their magazine *View*. André Breton described him at the time as 'a voice that rises once in a hundred years'. His first collection was published in 1946. Lamantia then travelled extensively and, of the younger *San Francisco group poets, became one of the first to experiment with altered states of consciousness. He was initiated into the Washo Indian peyote rites in Nevada in 1953 and afterwards spent three years in Mexico, living for a while with the Cora Indians of Nayarit. At the end of his wanderings he tried to destroy all his earlier work: this was, however, eventually published in 1962. Beginning to write again in the late 1950s, Lamantia claimed that 'he broke with surrealism in 1946'. Nevertheless, the volumes that followed, among them *Ekstasis* (1959), *Destroyed Works: Hypodermic Light, Manic Notebook, Still Poems, Spansule* (1962), and *Touch of the Marvelous* (1966), all have the essential surrealistic quality of revealing the inner life via explosive patterns of imagery. A useful selection of the work from these years is to be found in *Selected Poems 1943–1966* (San Francisco, 1967). In the 1960s Lamantia travelled in Europe and continued to publish: the work sustaining a development noticeable in his 1966 collection away from an almost obsessive consciousness of cruelty and towards a poetry of affirmation. Notable recent volumes include *The Blood of Air* (1970), *Becoming Visible* (1981), and *Meadowlark West* (1986—all San Francisco).   [RJG

Landfall, a New Zealand quarterly, was started by Charles *Brasch in 1947. Scion of a wealthy Dunedin family, Brasch had gone to Oxford in the 1930s and stayed on in Britain during the war. He returned to put his time and money into a periodical which would be 'distinctly of

New Zealand without being parochial', and literary, but not solely literary. It would be like *Horizon*, which Brasch read and admired, but guided, as the *Criterion* was and, Brasch felt, *Horizon* was not, by 'general ideas' about 'imaginative truth . . . truth in history, philosophy, religion'.

The seriousness, and at the same time an element of the grandiose and the vague in Brasch's commitment, help to explain both *Landfall's* importance and its limits under his guidance. It became without a doubt the best literary periodical New Zealand has ever had. It was the focus for literary performance and debate, a platform and a means by which writers scattered down the length of the two islands could get to know one another's work. The standard was always high, without ever being adventurous. Anything of importance published in or by New Zealand writers was at least intelligently reviewed, and sometimes discussed at length. Almost every New Zealand writer of consequence during the Fifties and Sixties appeared there. But many young writers chafed against the authority of *Landfall*, resenting what they saw as Brasch's prissiness, his solemnity, his inflexibility.

After twenty years and eighty issues, Brasch handed over to Robin Dudding, a talented but saurian editor whose ability was not in meeting deadlines or keeping to schedules, and who in 1972 fell out with the Caxton Press, *Landfall's* publishers. Dudding then started up his own periodical, *Islands*, taking, at least for a time, virtually the complete *Landfall* stable of writers with him. For the next decade *Landfall* limped along, edited first by Leo Bensemann, an employee of the Caxton Press, then by Peter Smart, a schoolmaster and writer of school textbooks, always in the shadow of *Islands* where all the exciting work was appearing.

Islands has now faded, and once again *Landfall* is New Zealand's principal literary magazine. Respectable and often interesting, it has a slightly academic flavour, and lacks the centrality and authority it had under its founder. The magazine was to have ceased publication late in 1992, but has been given a new lease of life under the aegis of the Oxford University Press.

[CKS

LANE, Patrick (1939–), was born in Nelson, British Columbia, into a working-class family and educated at the University of British Columbia. After working at a variety of jobs, including carpet-salesman and medic in a lumber camp, Lane took up poetry as a serious vocation following the death in 1964 of his elder brother, Richard Stanley 'Red' Lane, a pop poet of the early Sixties who has assumed a slightly mythic standing in Canadian poetry, and who Patrick Lane memorialized in an early chapbook, *Carnival Man* (1966).

From his early collections—*The Sun Has Begun to Eat the Mountains* (Montreal, 1972), *Passing into Stone* (Vernon, BC, 1973), and *Beware the Months of Fire* (Toronto, 1973)—to his most recent works—*The Measure* (Windsor, Ont., 1980), *Old Mother* (Toronto, 1982), *A Linen Crow, A Caftan Magpie* (Saskatoon, 1984), *Selected Poems* (Toronto, 1987; Oxford, 1988—an update of his *Selected Poems*, 1978), and the sequence *Winter* (Regina, Sask., 1990)—Lane has stressed that, although he is not a political writer in the overt sense, he is a writer of the working class, a witness and chronicler, not only of the political world, but of the private domestic tensions shared by two people.

Throughout his poetry Lane has professed a voice in search of a home, whether that home is found in the remains of his parents' house in the interior of British Columbia, or in the prairie, or in distant lands and times. His travels to South America in the early 1970s led to *Unborn Things: Poems of South America* (Madeira Park, BC, 1975), which chronicles the blurred distinction between barbarity and culture. Anarchy and violence are at the heart of Lane's early poetry. For him, history is something which dies in the vastness, the obliqueness of working-class Canada; the memory of the poet is its only, somewhat ambivalent, repository. In an early essay, 'To the Outlaw', Lane writes that the poet is both trapped and defined by history, and the voices which survive it are essentially pathetic.

In *No Longer Two People* (Winnipeg, 1981), which Lane co-wrote with the poet Lorna *Crozier, what begins as a male-female argument is synthesized, humanized, and ultimately unified, and in his more recent works, such as the poems at the conclusion of *Selected Poems* and those in *Winter*, a more pensive, less vernacular voice has emerged. [BM

Language Poetry is not so much a movement as a theory-generated method of poetic composition that has emerged from the postmodernist tendency in contemporary North American poetry. First formulated and practised in New York City and San Francisco in the early 1970s, Language poetry has risen from a highly intellectual but renegade brand of urban verse to a recognized practice that stands in direct opposition to the *New Formalism. Inherent in the practice of Language poetry is the desire to move beyond and resolve the poetic contradictions of the preceding generation, specifically the work of Frank *O'Hara and the *New York School and, to a lesser extent, Allen *Ginsberg and the *Beat poets. Writers who established and are currently identified with language poetry include Bruce Andrews, Charles Bernstein, Lyn Hejinian, Susan Howe, Bob Perelman, Stephen Rodefer, and Ron Silliman.

Language poets are known for their prolific output of poetic theory as well as poetry. Scanning this immense body of work in prose and verse, a number of defining characteristics can be isolated: (1) the use of open forms (free verse) as formulated and practised in the lineage of Whitman, *Pound, and *Olson; (2) a devaluation of the spoken (oral) and an emphasis on the written (visual) dimensions of poetry; (3) the employment of various techniques practised by the twentieth-century avant-garde, such as William Burroughs's 'cut-up' method, to disrupt conventional narrative and syntax; (4) a removal of the self—a deconstruction of what language poets uniformly believe to be the false consciousness of individualism that has evolved in the Euro-American poetic tradition; (5) an insistence on the indeterminacy of meaning; and (6) a preoccupation with the medium of language as an end in itself, so that representations of the self in poetry are replaced by chains of self-referential language, this practice showing the influence of Gertrude *Stein.

Language poetry has a strong connection with the North American poetic tradition, despite its seeming rejection of the past. An important and acknowledged influence comes from the *Objectivist movement of the 1930s. *Zukofsky's modernist epic poem *A*, with its fractured language and theory-in-verse, is an acknowledged cornerstone in the language canon. The work of the *Black Mountain poets, specifically Robert *Creeley's poetry, fiction, and essays, are cited by members as the first clear indications of language poetry and theory.

Early essays and poetry by the language poets appeared in the journals *This*, *Roof*, and *L=A=N=G=U=A=G=E* and have been collected in the anthologies *The L=A=N=G=U=A=G=E Book* (Carbondale and Edwardsville, Ill., 1984) and *In the American Tree* (Orono, Me., 1986).

[DeVS

LANSDOWN, Andrew (1954–), was born in Pingelly, a small town south-east of Perth in Western Australia. He gained arts degrees from both the Western Australian Institute of Technology and the Murdoch University before becoming for a time a tutor in creative writing at the former institution, which later was renamed the Curtin University. Since then he has worked as an education officer in various prisons in Western Australia, a grim occupation which has done surprisingly little to affect his work.

Few Australian poets have been so prolific and consistent. At 37 he has already published six collections of verse, with a seventh ready for publication. From his first book *Homecoming* (Fremantle, 1979) he has adopted a Christian stance and, perhaps as a result, his work has been neglected and undervalued. A collection of poems for children, *A Ball of Gold*, was followed by *Counterpoise* (Sydney, 1982), *Windfalls* (Fremantle, 1984), *Waking and Always* (1987), *The Grasshopper Heart* (1991), and *Horse with Lipstick* (1992—all Sydney). Lansdown is a miniaturist, a poet attentive to the smallest details of nature, and to subtle domestic emotions. The effect of his work is cumulative, so that his poems can seem slight when considered separately; their style is precise and direct, and never ostentatious. Unusually for a poet of the late twentieth century, the mood in his poems is generally one of contentment or joy, causing fashion-conscious readers to overlook his consistent technical excellence.   [JG

LARKIN, Philip (1922–85), grew up in Coventry (where his father served as City Treasurer), attended King Henry VIII School, and went up to read English at St John's College, Oxford, in 1940—the austere, war-disrupted atmosphere of his undergraduate years in Oxford, during which he formed a lasting friendship with Kingsley *Amis, is evoked in his novel *Jill* (1946). After graduating, Larkin went to the small town of Wellington, where he ran the local library, 'single-handed and untrained', and still found time to write both *Jill* and his second novel, set in a small-town library, *A Girl in Winter* (1947); a third novel was begun and worked at for five years, but never completed. Temperamentally, Larkin seems to have needed a full-time job, and without realizing it he had already embarked on the career which was to last to the end of his life, and which took him subsequently to the university libraries of Leicester (1946–50), Belfast (1950–5), and Hull (1955–85). Hull was where he spent the second half of his life, and he wrote vividly about the place in his poem 'Here', but even after thirty years would have hesitated to call it home. He never married, and liked to portray himself as a hermit-like bachelor, despite several important relationships with women. As a reviewer he wrote perceptively about both poetry and jazz, often taking the side of the 'pleasure-seeking audience' against the drabness and difficulty of modernism, though his own work's relationship with modernism was a good deal more complex than he liked to pretend. In the autumn of 1984, a year before his death, he was offered the Poet Laureateship but turned it down.

Regarded for much of his career as a minor poet with a narrow range of subject-matter, Larkin now seems to dominate the history of English poetry in the second half of the century much as *Eliot dominated it in the first. Though detractors continue to speak of his gloom, philistinism, insularity, and anti-modernism, the authority and grandiloquence of his long poems, and the grace, sharpness, or humour of his shorter ones now seem indisputable, as does his clear-eyed engagement with love, marriage, freedom, destiny, ageing, death, and other far from marginal subjects. The appearance of his *Collected Poems* in 1988, while turning up no new masterpieces, added over eighty poems to the Larkin canon, considerably enlarging our sense of a poet who had published only four slim volumes in his lifetime.

For all the seriousness of his early ambitions as a novelist, Larkin's achievement and reputation were made as a poet: he liked to say, not that he chose poetry, but that it chose him. Yet there was little maturity in his first volume, *The North Ship* (1945), which if anything seems to go backwards from the tough, witty Audenesque verse he wrote as a schoolboy. Its frail, inward, Yeatsian rhetoric of hearts and silences and stony places has a consistency of tone he might have been pleased with for a time, but which he soon tried to toughen and correct, in part through the flatter, less deceived manner of Thomas *Hardy. He was blocked and seemingly depressed through the late 1940s (when his father died), but in 1950, in the autumn of which he moved to Belfast, he wrote 'At Grass', 'Deceptions', 'Spring', 'Wants', 'No Road', and a number of other poems that were to appear in *The Less Deceived* (1955).

It was in this collection that Larkin constructed the poetic persona—plain-speaking, sceptical, modest, unshowy, awkward, commonsensical, even rather dry and dull—that was to be associated not only with him but with the *Movement, the post-war generation of poets anthologized in Robert *Conquest's *New Lines* (1956). It is a persona that owes something to modernist forebears like Laforgue and Eliot, but also to the Englishness of *Betjeman and

Orwell. There can be something faintly comic in the Larkin narrator's miserable exclusion from the joys of sex, or the consolations of religion, or the excitements of social rebellion, his life compromised or squatted on by 'the toad work'. But at best Larkin makes matters of obsessive concern to him—whether to marry, how to face the idea of death, what we owe to others (especially our parents) and ourselves, to what extent we control our lives—into rich dramatic monologues, inviting the reader to listen in as he thinks aloud, venturing one tentative explanation then overturning it with another, filling his speech with the hesitations and self-corrections ('Yes, true; but . . .', 'No, that's not the difference: rather, how . . .') that seem to guarantee the speaker's honesty. The Larkin persona is a subtle and elaborate construct, even a mask, though he was perhaps right to feel that his work was far more direct, emotional, and even naïve than critics acknowledged.

The effect of a man speaking to other men (rather less, perhaps, to women) is even more pronounced in Larkin's two other mature collections, *The Whitsun Weddings* (1965) and *High Windows* (1974), which in nearly all respects are a refinement of the manner and enlargement of the scope of *The Less Deceived*, not a departure (Larkin remained as contemptuous of the idea of 'development' as he did of free verse or poetry in translation). In these volumes, the close pact with the reader is enhanced by Larkin's use of the vernacular, the slangy familiarities and obscenities not only counterpointing and holding down more elevated diction but also delivering some of his most famous lines ('Books are a load of crap', 'They fuck you up, your mum and dad'). The epigrammatic quality of Larkin's verse would be hard to overemphasize: many of his best lines seem to float magnificently free of their immediate context— 'Life is first boredom, then fear', from 'Dockery and Son', for example; or 'Nothing, like something, happens anywhere', from 'I Remember, I Remember'; or 'What will survive of us is love', from 'An Arundel Tomb'—but he would rarely allow himself to fire his big guns without first patiently winning the reader's trust: the verse-

form which dominates the poems on which his reputation seems likely to rest—'Church Going', 'The Whitsun Weddings', 'Dockery and Son', 'The Old Fools', 'Aubade'—is spacious (eight-to-twelve lines), complex-rhyming, and can run to as many as eight stanzas. The pattern is nearly always the same: the siting of the speaker in a particular place, then the slow opening out of one man's tentative musings into a large, confident, universal statement.

The mood of Larkin's poems is often sombre, glimpsing the loneliness, emptiness, and mortality that lie underneath social rituals. The ideas in his poems, baldly stated, can sound chilling and depressing, nearer to *Beckett than Betjeman: that we always make the wrong choice, supposing we have any choice at all; that the sense we have of a 'life lived according to love' makes the compromised, loveless reality almost unendurable; that human existence is only bearable because the prospect of death is worse. But his gloom is often overstated by critics. He rather relished the role of misanthrope, and there is something energetic and life-enhancing about his determination to find phrase-making, disabused summations of everything from childhood ('A forgotten boredom') to marriage ('two can live as stupidly as one'). Even his darkest poems have their element of black comedy, and there are, besides, a number of exercises in light verse, whether satirical about social mores ('Sexual intercourse began | In nineteen sixty-three'), sardonic about human relationships ('He married a woman to stop her getting away | now she's there all day'), or gently mocking of academic life ('Jake Balokowsky, my biographer | Has this page microfilmed'). The tone here is affectionate rather than scabrous, and though Larkin has been accused of loftiness and condescension—as in his image of the 'cut-price crowd, urban yet simple'—this is to ignore his imaginative engagement with ordinary lives: the empathy he shows towards the young mothers in 'Afternoons', pushed to the side of their own lives, or towards the patients and stretcher-cases in 'Ambulances' and 'The Building'. Larkinesque affirmation of another kind comes from the metaphors of air and light, the transcendent Utopian gleams which appear throughout his work, highlighting the limitations of the real world, yet offering a vision of hope and integrity which is more than merely cruel.

Never a prolific writer, Larkin published little after 1974, feeling that poetry had given him up, turning increasingly to drink, becoming partially deaf (and so losing the consolations of jazz), and deriving professional comfort only from the acclaim for his collected prose, *Required Writing*. Apart from 'Aubade' (the definitive statement of his fear of death) and 'Love Again' (a haunting poem of sexual jealousy), he wrote almost nothing worth preserving in his last ten years. Though his work repeatedly denies the possibility of life after death, Larkin survives through his art as an original, obsessive, deep-feeling poet who courageously refused the consolations of conventional belief.

Larkin's *Collected Poems*, ed. Anthony Thwaite (London, 1988; New York, 1989), contains most of his published and unpublished poetry. *Required Writing* (London, 1983; New York, 1984) is a collection of miscellaneous prose and critical pieces, 1955–82, and *All What Jazz* (1970) a collection of his jazz reviews. *Selected Letters of Philip Larkin*, ed. Anthony Thwaite, came out in London in 1992 (New York, 1993), and Andrew Motion's biography, *Philip Larkin: A Writer's Life* in London in 1993. Useful biographical information is contained in *Larkin at Sixty*, ed. Anthony Thwaite (London, 1982) and *Philip Larkin, 1922–1985: A Tribute*, ed. George Hartley (London, 1988). Andrew Motion's short study, *Philip Larkin* (London, 1983) and Janice Rossen's *Philip Larkin: His Life's Work* (London, 1989) provide useful introductions.   [PBM

LASDUN, James (1958–), was born in London and read English at Bristol University. He now lives in New York and teaches at New York University. He has won an Eric Gregory Award for his poetry and the Dylan Thomas Award (in 1986) for the stories in *The Silver Age* (London, 1985).

Lasdun combines brilliant, dense-packed imagery reminiscent of Anthony *Hecht with deft rhythmic control. In style and mood he is a poet of the Eighties: not the Eighties of urban dereliction, graffiti, and cardboard cities, but its brittle antipode of decadent wealth.

Lasdun's reputation rests on two books so far: *The Silver Age* and the collection of poems, *A Jump Start* (London, 1987). Both display his neo-Jacobean sensibility, *The Silver Age* in rather cruel stories of spoilt people, told in a conventional style but with considerable panache. In his poems, similar people and places are rendered in a style that is particularly good at fleshing out indeterminate states: the feathery evocation of 'On the Road to Chenonceaux', the bravura metaphysics of 'Vanishing Points'.

A Jump Start is very much a young man's book—Lasdun is brilliant on the way women's bodies pack the clothes they wear. Like the youths in his poem 'Vindice at the Oyster Bar' he is 'tuned to the brine of sex'. How he will develop is uncertain, but it is rare for a writer to make more or less simultaneous debuts in fiction and poetry to equal acclaim, as he has done.   [PF

LATTIMORE, Richmond (Alexander) (1906–84), was born in Paotingfu, China. A Rhodes Scholar, he was a distinguished classicist whose sensitive English interpretations of Pindar, Homer, Hesiod, and other Greek poets helped to educate more than one generation. For much of his life he taught classics at Bryn Mawr College, Pennsylvania. His own poetry, although often graceful and well made, is much less important.

Lattimore was not only a meticulous scholar but also remarkably well educated in modern poetry and criticism. His *Iliad* (Chicago, 1951) and *Odyssey* (New York, 1962) have been the preferred versions of the majority of readers, critics, and classicists. The choice lies between the short and more colloquial lines of Robert *Fitzgerald's versions, and Lattimore's six-stress, slower-paced ones. Lattimore was responsible, with David Grene, for the best collection of the plays of the three Greek tragedians, *Complete Greek Tragedies* (Chicago, 1959); he contributed to this versions of the *Oresteia* and four plays by Euripides. His own poems, collected in *Poems from Three Decades* (New York, 1972), draw mainly on classical themes, and are a little awkward when they determinedly introduce newer ones: Lattimore was a scholar disenchanted by modern life, but without much compulsion to express his feelings about it. His grasp of the habits of modern speech was sound, but his excursions into free verse are unconvincing. He was better when, a self-consciously modern Theocritus, he employed forms such as the sestina and the sonnet. On these occasions he described landscapes, many of them with classical associations. He was more successful, though, in finding unusual descriptive adjectives in his translations than in his original poetry, which is cliché-prone.   [MS-S

LAUGHLIN, James (1914–), was born in Pittsburgh and attended Harvard University, at the end of his freshman year there visiting Ezra *Pound in Rapallo. Pound advised the wealthy young Laughlin that he could make his best contribution to literature as a publisher of new writing, rather than as a poet. Subsequently in 1936 Laughlin established New Directions, publishing first Pound and William Carlos *Williams and thereafter a wide range of American and international work, until New Directions became, as it has remained, the foremost disseminator of modernist and related writing in the English-speaking world.

However, he has also continued throughout his life to write and publish his own poetry, some twenty volumes in all, including *Selected Poems, 1935–1985* (San Francisco, 1986). His poems, sometimes in what he himself calls 'long and languid' lines, but more usually in shorter, regularly defined, but freely measured couplets or triplets, employ a language that is cool, clear, unstrained, and unaffected. They call to mind most often, amongst his immediate seniors, Williams and *Cummings. Laughlin is modest about his own poetic achievement. Yet he is a poet capable of considerable beauty of image

and movement, of good-humoured irony and bitter-sweet reminiscence, of compassion for 'the succession of the generations'.   [RWB

LAWRENCE, D(avid) H(erbert) (1885–1930), was born in Eastwood, Nottinghamshire, the fourth son of a coal-miner. His mother, whose influence dominated the first half of his life, belonged to the middle class and had been a teacher. In 1898 he won a scholarship to Nottingham High School, and in 1906 went to University College, Nottingham.

Lawrence, according to his own note in the *Collected Poems* (1928), wrote his first two poems, 'if poems they were, when I was nineteen'; he identifies them as 'To Guelder-Roses' and 'To Campions'. Though these pieces suffer from *Georgian and Romantic diction, and a rather clumsy handling of traditional form (a limitation we find in much of Lawrence's poetry), they nevertheless have certain unmistakable features—for instance, a choice of adjectives and nouns evoking colours, textures, and sensations—which foreshadow the later verse; here we find Lawrence on his way to creating his personal poetic language without yet having anything to say in it. An account of his reading in his youth can be found in *A Personal Record* (1935), by Jessie Chambers (whom he portrayed as Miriam in *Sons and Lovers*). He apparently knew most of the poems in Palgrave's *Golden Treasury of Songs and Lyrics*, but what she remembers most vividly are his recitations of Shelley, Wordsworth, and Keats. A crucially important influence on his poetry was that of Walt Whitman. According to Chambers, 'Whitman's *Leaves of Grass* was one of his great books. He would sometimes write, "I'm sending you a Whitmanesque poem," when he was enclosing one of his own.' Lawrence later used Whitman's free, brimming long line and his extrovert poetic voice for his own purposes in his verse; his vision—mythopoeic and sceptical at once— was, however, very different from the American poet's. An acute and characteristically idiosyncratic essay by him on Whitman can be found in *Studies In Classic American Literature* (1923).

Lawrence

In 1909 Lawrence's poetry was published in the *English Review*, after Jessie Chambers sent three poems—'Discipline', 'Dreams Old and Nascent', and 'Baby Movements'—to the journal's editor, Ford Madox Hueffer (later *Ford). Hueffer was deeply impressed, and wished to meet Lawrence personally; thus was formed the latter's first literary friendship, and through Hueffer came his initial contact with London's literary world. *The White Peacock*, his first novel, was published in 1911, and a book of verse, *Love Poems and Others*, in 1913. Among the succesful pieces here are the ones based on his experiences as a schoolteacher at Croydon, and poems that explore themes of love and sexuality while subtly attending to the details of the Midlands landscape. Also in this volume is 'End of Another Home-Holiday', in which a smoky, understated mood of parting (in this case, from his mother) lies beneath the scrupulously observed and casually animated particulars of a small town; moreover, that important Lawrentian symbol the moon is suggestively present. All this is developed through finely judged rhythmic and prosodic variations which both preserve and liberate the ambiguity of the moment; there is a balance of subject-matter and a form not quite traditional and not quite *vers libre* which Lawrence seldom achieves again until the poems in *Birds, Beasts and Flowers* and his last poems about death. For an interesting reading of this poem, see A. *Alvarez's essay on Lawrence in *The Shaping Spirit* (1958). We also find in *Love Poems and Others* the dialect poems, which reveal insights into the small-scale tragedies and the unexpected humorousness of working-class life reminiscent of *Hardy's novels; these poems were much admired by Ezra *Pound. The book was critically well-received, Pound calling it 'the most important book of poems of the season', and Edward *Thomas welcoming it as 'the book of the moment in verse'.

Amores (1916), his next collection of poetry, once more has some powerful pieces about family life ('Discord In Childhood'; 'Sorrow', a slight and touching elegy on his mother); some of the events recorded here are to be found in a more realized form in the novel *Sons and Lovers* (1913). In 1912 Lawrence eloped with Frieda Weekley (the aristocratic German wife of his former modern-languages tutor) to Germany; they were married after returning to England, in July 1914. *Look! We Have Come Through* (1917) is a sequence of poems mostly about married love and happiness: two themes relatively rare in modern poetry. 'Gloire De Dijon', 'Song Of A Man Who Is Loved', and 'Song Of A Man Who Has Come Through' represent, after his mother's death, a phase of renewal and creativity, and suggest a profound, albeit slightly threatened, conjugal calm; what is most wonderfully expressed, perhaps, is the sense of *gratitude* to the woman in the poems. By now Lawrence had also discovered his aims and desires as a poet. In his nervously sensitive but forcefully conversational manner, he articulates his ideas (which owe something to his reading of F. T. Marinetti and the Italian Futurists) in his remarkable essay, 'Poetry of the Present', in *New Poems* (1918). His intention, he says, is to write a 'poetry of that which is at hand: the immediate present', of the 'moment' in which there is nothing 'fixed, set, static', and to employ a Whitmanesque free verse that would do away with 'clichés of rhythm as well as phrase'.

Meanwhile, Lawrence's novel *The Rainbow* was completed in 1915; it was banned on publication. After the war he travelled extensively with Frieda in search of societies that could offer him an alternative to the modern Western civilization he had come to hate. Most of the poems in *Birds, Beasts and Flowers* (1923), which he (and many others) considered his 'best book of poems', are set in places as diverse as Italy, Sicily, Australia, New Mexico, and Ceylon. Some of his most impressive poetry—'Almond Trees', 'Bat', the tortoise-sequence, and the much-anthologized 'Snake', among others—is to be found here, written in an unprecedented, flickering free verse, in a style at once celebratory and wittily hectoring. They convey, through their peculiar language, an almost occult empathy with the landscape; 'empathy', however, is an inadequate word for the complex Lawrentian relationship with natural phenomena. The energy of many of these poems also derives from a concealed misanthropy, an intense and irrational longing for a 'world empty of people', converted here, through the healing power of the imagination, into a positive feeling of reverence for non-human life.

In 1925, the Lawrences returned to Europe, and in 1928 *Lady Chatterley's Lover* was banned. *Pansies* (1929)—from the French *pensées*, thoughts—contains poems that show a deepening disgust with English society; in some, however, the disgust provides the impulse for genuinely funny satire. After Lawrence's death of tuberculosis in Vence, Richard *Aldington published *More Pansies* and *Last Poems* in 1932 from manuscripts found among his last writings. Besides some memorable pieces about the sea, God (a distinctively Lawrentian, excitable, and amoral God), and the Etruscans, are, in *Last Poems*, the great sonorous poems on death, including 'The Ship of Death' and 'Bavarian Gentians'. These poems, which divulge his personal myth of death and the afterlife, interweaving images from Etruscan culture and the Etruscan tombs, are perhaps the most serene and affirmative he ever wrote, and are full of a haunting and even tragic optimism about a 'new life'—an idea always precious to Lawrence. They remind us that his poetry (even on the eve of death) is essentially a poetry of wonder, of possibilities, and of departures. See *Complete Poems*, ed. V. de S. Pinto and W. Roberts (London and New York, 1964; paperback, 1967), and also two full-length studies of Lawrence's verse: *Acts Of Attention* (Ithaca, NY, and London, 1972), by Sandra M. Gilbert, and *Thinking In Poetry* (London, 1987), by M. J. Lockwood. [AC

LAWSON, Henry (1867–1922), was born on the Grenfell (New South Wales) gold-fields. Educated in country schools, he worked as a coach- and house-painter. By 1883 he had joined his mother Louisa (later editor of the feminist journal *Dawn*) in Sydney. His first published poem, 'A Song of the Republic', appeared in the *Bulletin* in 1887. The early bent of his verse was radical (as spokesman for 'the Army of the Rear') and

nationalist (warning against the danger of 'old-world errors and wrongs and lies | Making a hell in a Paradise'). Lawson's poems of outback life mingled celebration of bush characters with a realistic appraisal of hardship. In his 1892 verse debate with A. B. 'Banjo' *Paterson in the *Bulletin* he took the pessimistic side. A note of threnody informs Lawson's outback poems, for instance in the lament of how 'The mighty Bush with iron rails | Is tethered to the world'.

Lawson published many, sometimes best-selling, volumes of verse. These have been valued less highly than his short fiction. A. A. Phillips referred to the 'ventriloquial folk-voice' that spoke through Lawson's poetry. Like his contemporary Rudyard *Kipling, Lawson's ballads were a rich fount of aphorism, apparent crystallizations of popular feeling, even if a racist and militarist strain was pronounced in his later years. See *Poetical Works of Henry Lawson* (Sydney and London, 1918, new edn. 1979). Phillips's *The Australian Tradition* (1958) and Brian Matthews's *The Receding Wave* (1972) contain important criticism. George Mackaness's *An Annotated Bibliography of Henry Lawson* (1951) and Colin Roderick's *Henry Lawson Criticism 1874–1971* (1972) are significant, if not recent, reference works. Lawson survives through his writing and in legend, but not yet in a considerable biography. [PP

LAYTON, Irving (Peter) (1912–), was born Israel Pincas Lazarovitch in Romania, and was brought to Montreal by his immigrating parents who settled in the working-class ghetto of that city. Educated at local schools, Layton received a B.Sc. from Macdonald College and an MA in political science from McGill University. He taught school at various levels, and evening classes at Sir George Williams College. His success as a poet led to a professorship of English at York University, Toronto, from which he retired in 1978. He now lives in Montreal.

Layton harboured strong left-wing ideals from his college days which found an outlet in the 1940s in his association with a modernist little magazine called *First Statement*. This was the beginning of a series of involvements with the little-press movement, most important of which was Layton's connection with Contact Press in the early 1950s which, in turn, led to a friendship with the Americans Robert *Creeley and Jonathan *Williams, the latter publishing Layton's breakthrough collection, *The Improved Binoculars* (1956) with an enthusiastic foreword by William Carlos *Williams. In 1959 Layton won the Governor-General's Award for *A Red Carpet for the Sun*, a collection which established his reputation and standing in the literary community. The frank and passionate rhetoric of his poems disturbed the critics of the day, and led Layton into a war of words with reviewers and anthologists, whom he accused of smothering the creative process. His poetry shows great swings between a Dionysian celebration of life on the one hand and much tenderness and sorrowing about the dark side of existence. Given to the self-conscious verbal strut, the occasional vulgarism, the declamatory posture of poet and prophet, Layton won a large audience both for himself and for contemporary poetry in Canada. Well read in Marx, D. H. *Lawrence, and Nietzsche, Layton took upon himself the various roles of social rebel, raunchy poet, and poetic will personified. A slow publishing start in the Forties with two slim collections led to a productive decade in the Fifties, and ultimately would see Layton as the author of some fifty volumes of verse and a memoir, *Waiting for the Messiah* (Toronto, 1985). His first *Collected Poems* came out in 1965 (Toronto). With the advent of the Seventies, Layton began to exhibit a growing social conservatism coupled with a self-conscious Jewishness, tendencies characterized by support for American politics and anti-Christian rhetoric. A major volume, *The Collected Poems of Irving Layton* (Toronto) appeared in 1971, while his *Uncollected Poems 1935–1959* (Oakville, Ont.) was published in 1976. *Engagements: The Prose of Irving Layton* (Toronto, 1972) was followed by *Taking Sides: The Collected Social and Political Writings* (Oakville) in 1977. There are three collections of letters: *An Unlikely Affair* (Oakville, 1980), *Wild Gooseberries: The Selected Letters of Irving Layton* (Toronto, 1989), and *Irving Layton and Robert Creeley, The Complete Correspondence*

1953–1978 (Kingston, Ont., 1990). Layton was inducted into the Order of Canada in 1976.

[MG

LEA, Sydney (1942–), grew up in the affluent suburbs of Philadelphia, and graduated from Yale University with a BA and Ph.D before taking up teaching positions at Dartmouth College, Yale, and Middlebury College. In 1976, Lea co-founded, with Jay Parini, *New England Review*, a literary journal, which he edited until 1989.

Lea's poetry is densely concrete, often formal in structure and style. His affection for the woodland areas of New England, especially New Hampshire and Maine, and his interest in hunting and fishing, provide a regional aspect to his poems, which frequently move in autobiographical directions, as in 'The Tracks on Kenyon Hill' or 'For My Son Creston at the Solstice', both of which affect an outdoor, woodsy setting that becomes increasingly symbolic. In Lea's best work outer landscape merges with inner to create a sense of the physical presence of the spiritual world—much in the American tradition of Emerson and Thoreau.

Lea's second book, *The Floating Candles* (Urbana, Ill., 1982) contains a memorable long narrative, 'The Feud', which depends on a strongly colloquial voice and finely tuned dramatic sense for its effects. The narrative impulse continues through Lea's more recent volumes, including *No Sign* (Athens, Ga., 1987) and *Prayer for the Little City* (New York, 1989), which take his poetry in an explicitly Christian direction. Lea's first novel was *A Place in Mind* (New York, 1988). He has also edited a volume of essays on Anthony *Hecht's poetry. [JP

LEDWIDGE, Francis (1887–1917) was born in Slane, Co. Meath, where for a time he worked as a labourer and clerk. From boyhood Ledwidge wrote poetical, untutored verses. Lord Dunsany, local landlord and an aspiring writer of the Celtic revival, introduced him to *Yeats's poetry and to Katherine Tynan with whom he corresponded. Ledwidge was an organizer of the Irish Volunteers; like many of the Volunteers, he enlisted in the British Army in 1914, in Dunsany's regiment. His years in the war were marked by homesickness, highlighted by news of the 1916 Rising (his best-known poems are 'Thomas McDonagh' and 'The Blackbirds', elegies for the executed poet-leaders of the Rising, *MacDonagh and Plunkett). He was killed near Ypres in 1917.

Ledwidge is like a lesser Keats: his stylized diction and syntax are vivified by colloquial idiom ('The Singer's Muse' 'made a poet of her servant boy'), in a mixture that anticipates Patrick *Kavanagh or early *Heaney. The poeticisms too are often vivid: the 'spider-peopled wells'; 'this poor bird-hearted singer of a day'. His mixed language is perhaps learned from Yeats; its archaizing recalls Mangan. Neither his poeticality nor his national sentiments have current appeal; but it is sad that his nature poetry has not been discovered by Clare's readership. Ledwidge's *Complete Poems* were edited by Alice Curtayne (London, 1974); she also wrote *Francis Ledwidge: A Life of the Poet* (London, 1972).

[BO'D

LEE, Don L. See MADHUBUTI, HAKI R.

LEE, Laurie (1914–), was born, the eleventh of twelve children, in Stroud in Gloucestershire, where he went to school. He described those among whom he grew up as the country's first literate peasantry, the inheritors of an oral tradition of language. He left home at 19 and walked to London, where he worked as a labourer. In 1935 he went to Spain, supporting himself by playing his violin in the streets or cafés. In the Second World War he worked as a script-writer and in the Ministry of Information. His first volume of autobiography, *Cider With Rosie* (1959) brought him fame and independence.

Although a number of his poems were written in the 1930s, he had almost no contact with the literary world during those years. His poems were included in the third volume of John *Lehmann's *Poets of Tomorrow* in 1944; and his first book, *The Sun My Monument*, appeared that year (London; New York, 1947). Lee's second book, *A Bloom of Candles*, twelve 'verses from a

poet's year' (London), came out in 1947. His last book of new poems, *My Many-Coated Man* appeared in 1955 (London; New York, 1957). He has written two verse dramas, *Peasants' Priest* (1947) and *The Voyage of Magellan* (1948).

Although Lee had little education and wrote about the life from which he came, the imagery of his early poems shows the influence of the sophisticated poetry of *Auden and *Spender and possibly of the Spanish poet, Federico Garcia Lorca. His best work has a sharpness and brightness of imagery and a lightness of movement that are unmistakable; but these effects are also a measure of his limited range. He is none the less a poet of enduring charm. His work can be explored in *Selected Poems* (London, 1983).   [ATT

LEE, Li-Young (1957–), was born in Jakarta, Indonesia, of Chinese parents. In 1959 his father, who was personal physician to Mao Tse-tung, fled Indonesia with his family after spending a year as a political prisoner in President Sukarno's jails. They travelled throughout Hong Kong, Macau, and Japan, before arriving in America in 1964. Lee studied at the University of Pittsburgh, the University of Arizona, and the State University of New York, Brockport.

Lee has written, 'I think immigrants have beautiful stories to tell. But the problem is to make art out of it.' His critics fault the work for its slackness, both emotionally and linguistically; his admirers speak of his modesty and of the unsentimental intimacy with which he handles his often sensational subject-matter.

Li-Young Lee is the author of two collections of poetry, *Rose* (Brockport, NY, 1986), which received the Delmore Schwartz Memorial Poetry Award, and *The City in Which I Love You* (Brockport, 1990), which was the Lamont Poetry Selection of the Academy of American Poets. Lee lives in Chicago with his wife Donna and their two children.   [HC

LEE, Tzu Pheng (1946–), began writing poetry while still at school. During her undergraduate years at the University of Singapore her poems came to the attention of Edwin *Thumboo, among others, and she was encouraged to publish. Essentially a private poet, she made a public impact with the appearance in 1966 of her 'My Country and My People'. Many Singaporean readers saw this piece as encapsulating the peculiar history of the nation in its convoluted progress from British colony to independent republic. Lee's later work is more personal. Both *Against the Next Wave* (Singapore, 1988) and *The Brink of an Amen* (Singapore, 1991) register emotional anguish, but they also celebrate the embracing of a religious faith which has intensified over the years, and now provides the secure emotional basis of her work. See also *Prospect of a Drowning* (Singapore, 1976). [KS

LEHMAN, David (1948–), was born in New York City and educated at Columbia University and Cambridge, writing a dissertation at Columbia on the prose poem. He has taught at Brooklyn College and Hamilton College. He currently lives with his wife and son in Ithaca, New York, where he works as a free-lance writer, editor, and book-reviewer. Recently Lehman has instigated an annual series of anthologies titled *Best American Poetry*.

Lehman's own poetry began in the mode of the *New York School, with obvious debts to Frank *O'Hara, Kenneth *Koch, and John *Ashbery. But in his most recent book, *Operation Memory* (Princeton, NJ, 1990), his imagination is drawn to the nightmares of twentieth-century history. Lehman eschews a literal accounting of horrors, opting instead for a mythopoeic mode that converts the traumas of war and genocide into slippery dream narratives. His poems draw freely on popular culture, especially movies, and the result is an uneasy mixture of the conventional and the unspeakable, as though the truth of history could only be glimpsed through the protective gauze of cliché. His first book was *An Alternative to Speech* (Princeton, 1986).

[RG

LEHMANN, Geoffrey (1940–), grew up at McMahon's Point on Sydney Harbour, his father the owner and pilot of a small ferry. He attended Shore (Sydney Church of England

Boys' School) and graduated in arts-law from the University of Sydney. At university he met Les *Murray and co-edited a literary magazine with him. They published a joint first volume of their own poetry, *The Ilex Tree* (1965). Lehmann practised as a solicitor until 1976, then taught law in the faculty of commerce at the University of New South Wales. He is now a partner in an international accounting firm, working in Sydney. He has published six volumes of poetry, a *Selected Poems* (Sydney, 1976), a novel, a book on Australian naïve painters, has edited or co-edited four anthologies of poetry, and is co-author of the major treatise on Australian tax law. Married twice, he has five children.

Lehmann has a predilection for exploring a subject in a series of poems, and has written in this way on his family background, Roman history (including a book in the persona of the Emperor Nero, who is depicted sympathetically), and the daily life of his then father-in-law, Ross McInerny, a farmer in inland New South Wales, whose anecdotes become a vehicle for the author's own liberal-humanist attitudes (*Ross's Poems*, Sydney, 1978). The earlier poetry is mostly in a supple, plain-spoken blank verse, with a somewhat formal tone; the later eases its limbs in *vers libre* and relaxes its diction. Lehmann can be seen as continuing the ethos of the Sydney 'vitalist' school, of which the artist Norman Lindsay was the theorist and Kenneth *Slessor the leading exponent: his work, like theirs, celebrates 'pagan' values—sensuousness, aestheticism sexuality, vitality, and considerations of quality above those of equality. He combines successfully the influence of Slessor and of C. P. Cavafy. His most recent book, *Children's Games* (Sydney, 1990), appearing after a ten-year silence, contains some of his best work, particularly the title-poem. [RGr

LEHMANN, John (Frederick) (1907–87), was born in Buckinghamshire and educated at Eton and Trinity College, Cambridge, where he was a contemporary of William *Empson, Kathleen *Raine, and Julian *Bell. His early admirations were the *Georgian poets and T. S. *Eliot; and the economy of style of the best Georgian poetry was reflected in his first book, *A Garden Revisited*, in 1931. Left-wing political leanings emerge in *The Noise of History* (1934), whose Rilkean prose poems communicate the feeling of menace underlying middle-European life in the 1930s. In 1936 Lehmann started the periodical *New Writing*, and during the late Thirties wrote little poetry. He began writing again during the Second World War, producing *Forty Poems* (1942) and *The Sphere of Glass* (1944), his best single volume.

During the rest of his career, he ran his own publishing house, founded the *London Magazine*, wrote his autobiography and many works of criticism, biography, and history, but produced little poetry. However, his last book of new poetry, *The Reader at Night* (1974), contains one or two of his best poems.

Despite a certain conventionality of diction, his poems have an unostentatious directness and economy. He was one of the few British poets to attempt the prose poem—at length in *Christ the Hunter* (1965), but most successfully in *The Noise of History*.

He may be sampled in *New and Selected Poems* (London, 1985). See also *John Lehmann: A Tribute*, ed. A. T. Tolley (Ottawa, 1987).   [ATT

LEITHAUSER, Brad (1953–), was born in Michigan where he also grew up. After graduating from Harvard College and Harvard Law School, he married the poet Mary Jo *Salter and spent several years in Japan as a research fellow at the Kyoto Comparative Law Centre. Since then Leithauser has travelled widely in Europe and has lived for short periods in Rome, London, Reykjavik, and Paris.

Leithauser is a formalist. He specializes in urbane, detailed descriptions of the minutiae and exotica of life. His poems frequently record strange incidents or artefacts he comes across on his travels. Like Marianne *Moore, whom he deeply admires, Leithauser delights in the oddness of unfamiliar things; a stuffed tortoise, a Japanese moss garden, a Bonsai nursery. He excels also in capturing the peculiarities of animals, reptiles, and fish. One of his best poems is a fanatically precise evocation of sea-horses,

while others describe rabbits, snakes, an ostrich, fireflies, and a toad and a damselfly who momentarily confront one another on an empty road.

Leithauser has also applied his deft poetic craftsmanship to longer narrative poems. 'A Ghost of a Ghost' is a dramatic monologue delivered by a ghost condemned to haunt the house of his bereaved family. In 'Two Incidents On and Off Guam' the protagonist watches with a crowd on the beach the rescue by helicopter of two drowning swimmers. Later in the poem he goes snorkelling, and the bubbles emitted by some scuba divers below suddenly overwhelm him with a sense of the miraculousness of everything: 'a breath- | taking incandescence so intense the | body is as nothing in the path | of its streaming . . .'.

Leithauser's collections are *Hundreds of Fireflies* (New York, 1982) and *Cats of the Temple* (New York, 1986). A selection from both books, *Between Leaps*, was published in Oxford in 1987; and see *The Mail from Anywhere* (Oxford and New York, 1990). He has also written three novels, the most recent of which is *Seaward* (New York, 1993).   [MF

LEONARD, Tom (1944–), was born and educated in Glasgow and took an MA at Glasgow University. *Six Glasgow Poems* and *A Priest Came on at Merkland Street* (both Glasgow, 1970) established Tom Leonard as an uninhibited and original writer whose innovation was the serious use of working-class Glasgow speech. It was apparent from the beginning that the language he used amounted to more than a comically notated dialect based on near-phonetic misspelling. Glasgow's unique accent, its phrasings and cadences, were accurately reproduced, but an early poem like 'The Good Thief' was seen as poetic rather than a sub-biblical jest located in the environs of a football stadium.

Leonard uses humour to serve his critical indignation. 'The Voyeur', 'Pffff', 'No Light', 'Unrelated Incidents', and parts of 'Ghostie Men', for example, seem calculated to leave the reader (or listener) in a state where amusement rubs against worried shock. Leonard's work in this vein has a linguistic unexpectedness from start to finish.

Intimate Voices: Selected Work 1965–1983 (Newcastle upon Tyne, 1984) is Leonard's essential book to date. His approach to language is illuminated there by an essay on William Carlos *Williams—'What I like about Williams is his presentation of voice as a fact, as a fact in itself and as a factor in his relationship with the world as he heard it, listened to it, spoke it . . .'. Leonard seems to have found much of his own release in that recognition. In its turn, his urban Scots has helped to instill confidence in younger writers as far as 'voice' is concerned, and its helpful, and unhelpful, links with English-English.

Situations Theoretical and Contemporary (1986) and *Nora's Place* (1990) are in 'ordinary' English. His anthology *Radical Renfrew* (Edinburgh, 1989) unearths a neglected, virtually suppressed tradition of working-class poetry in the west of Scotland from around 1790 to the early twentieth century. [DED

LEPAN, Douglas (1914–), was born in Toronto and educated at the universities of Toronto and Oxford. After serving with the Canadian Army during the Second World War he joined the Canadian Department of External Affairs, and later he served as principal of University College at the University of Toronto. In addition to his poetry he has written one book of fiction, *The Deserter* (1964), and a collection of memoirs, *Bright Glass of Memory* (1979).

Characterized by elaborate language and a highly figurative style, LePan's poetry meditates on the longing of the human spirit for freedom and dignity in a hostile world. Essentially traditional in form and formal in diction, several poems in his first book, *The Wounded Prince and Other Poems* (1948), examine a quest through the Canadian landscape for both a personal and a national identity. In contrast, the poems of *The Net and the Sword* (1953) are set in wartime Italy where LePan's heroes struggle to maintain their ideals in a bleak world of entrapment, violence, and death. Although the self-conscious ornateness of these earlier volumes is less apparent in

two more-recent collections, *Something Still to Find* (1982) and *Far Voyages* (1990), these later poems reveal a similar search for love, peace, and justice amidst moral confusion and brutality.

LePan's achievement is well represented in *Weathering It: Complete Poems* (Toronto, 1987). See also 'The Wounded Eye: The Poetry of Douglas LePan' by J. M. Kertzer, *Studies in Canadian Literature*, 6 (1981), and S. C. Hamilton, 'European Emblem and Canadian Image: A Study of Douglas LePan's Poetry', *Mosaic* (Winter, 1970). [DD

LERNER, Laurence (David) (1925–), was born in Cape Town. After more than twenty years at the University of Sussex, he now teaches at Vanderbilt University. Lerner is a valued critic and instructor, but his conscientious and intelligent, if pallid poetry—of which there exists a considerable quantity—provides an interesting guide to his methods and preferences. Much of his work has the air of having been 'done' rather than sweated out of the poet, yet in certain respects it is admirable: well-argued, and 'complex' in the sense demanded by the old *New Criticism. 'When humans talk they split their say in bits | And bit by bit they step on what they feel. | They talk in bits, they never talk in all' ('The Merman') is an acceptable way of echoing *Empson, but lacks feeling and urgency. See: *A.R.T.H.U.R. & M.A.R.T.H.A: or, The Loves of the Computers* (London, 1980); *Selected Poems* (London, 1984); and *Rembrandt's Mirror* (London and Nashville, 1987). [MS-S

LEVERTOV, Denise (1923–), was born in Ilford, Essex, her mother being 'descended from the Welsh tailor and mystic Angel Jones of Mold' and her father 'from the noted Hasid, Schneour Zaiman, "the Rav of Northern White Russia"', although he himself had converted to Christianity and become an Anglican priest. Levertov's own heterogeneous spirituality is, therefore, in the first instance very much an ancestral inheritance. She was educated privately in a bookish home enlivened by many and diverse visitors. A nurse in wartime London, in 1946 she published her first volume of poems in thoroughly English, neo-romantic vein. In 1948 she emigrated to the United States, where by her husband, Mitchell Goodman, she was introduced to Robert *Creeley, Cid *Corman, who published her poems in *Origin, the organicist and objectivist poetics of William Carlos *Williams and Charles *Olson, and to Robert *Duncan, to whom, because of his mystical and mythic way of perceiving, she felt an especial affinity. By 1955, when she became an American citizen, she was already a distinctly American poet, on her way to becoming one of the significant voices of the age. Levertov has published some fifteen volumes of poetry, including the broadly representative *Selected Poems* (Newcastle upon Tyne, 1986) and *Breathing the Water* (New York, 1987; Newcastle upon Tyne, 1988). Her prose is gathered in *The Poet in the World* (New York 1973) and *Light Up the Cave* (New York, 1981). She has taught at numerous universities and since 1982 has been professor of English at Stanford University.

Levertov writes as both a maker and a seer, as a proponent of both scrupulous craftsmanship and organic form, whereby 'the poet can discover and reveal' the form that is in all things. Her poem 'September 1961' celebrates 'the old great ones', specifically *Pound, Williams, and H.D. (Hilda *Doolittle), whilst elsewhere she names Duncan and Creeley 'as the chief poets among my contemporaries'; and, very roughly to locate her, it might be said that, just as she is more etherially inclined than Williams or Creeley, so she is more materially grounded than H.D. or Duncan. 'The world is | not with us enough. | *O taste and see'*, she writes in the title-poem of one of her volumes: 'bite, | savor, chew, swallow, transform . . .'. But though a poet possessed continually of spiritual curiosity, she is also a poet of personal experience and relationships, who has strenuously explored the conflicting claims of the domestic and the artistic; a poet of memory and commemoration, who, expatriated in the United States, recalls her Essex childhood in radiant detail, and who, many years later, celebrates her mother enduring, then dying, at great old age in Mexico; and a

poet of public statement and witness, who is outraged by all forms of destruction but who came less precociously and self-tormentingly to political consciousness than her elder sister, Olga, whose premature death is hauntingly mourned in the 'Olga Poems' of 1967. However, Levertov's radical politics are always to be seen within the larger context of her fundamentally religious, sacramental sense of the holiness of all things: 'Blessed | be the dust. From dust the world | utters itself. We have no other | hope, no knowledge.'

Levertov's most industrious critical reader has been Linda Wagner, who published her study, *Denise Levertov* (New York), in 1967, edited *Denise Levertov: In Her Own Province* (New York, 1979), and, as Linda Wagner-Martin, edited *Critical Essays on Denise Levertov* (Boston, 1990). Bibliographies include Robert A. Wilson, *A Bibliography of Denise Levertov* (New York, 1972) and Liana Sakelliou-Schulz, *Denise Levertov: An Annotated Primary and Secondary Bibliography* (New York, 1989).   [RWB

LEVI, Peter (Chad Tigar) (1931–), born in Middlesex, was a Jesuit priest until he resigned orders in 1977. He was elected Professor of Poetry at Oxford (1984–9). His abundant verse, now presented as consecutively numbered (from the beginning) instead of titled, has not yet been widely studied. Most attention was paid to his early poems, particularly those in *The Gravel Ponds* (London, 1960) and *Water, Rock and Sand* (London, 1962). These, although they displayed the debt to Wallace *Stevens apparent throughout his work, were more conventional in form than those written later, and sounded a more personal note, sometimes reminiscent of *Graves, at others of *Auden. Succeeding collections see the growing influence of Greek surrealism (Levi has translated modern Greeks such as Elytis), and of a multitude of European poets. Levi's later verse is open to the strictures that have been levelled at his prose: over-enthusiastic and hasty. That he has much of interest to say is undoubted; the general effect is blurred. *The Noise Made by Poems* (London, 1977) is a critical commentary. See: *Collected Poems 1955–1975*

(London, 1976); *Goodbye to the Art of Poetry* (London, 1989). [MS-S]

LEVINE, Philip (1928–), was born in Detroit, Michigan, and educated in local schools and at Wayne State University. He is now Professor of English at California State University in Fresno. Levine has periodically lived in Spain, a country whose people, landscape, and history remain a strong presence in his poems.

A prolific poet, Levine has published collections at regular intervals since *On the Edge* appeared in 1963. His earliest poems were relatively formal in character, but *Not This Pig* (1968), his second book, marks the emergence of Levine's mature style, characterized by a haunting lyricism, an inward sense of the natural world (frequently invoked for symbolic purposes), and a strong identification with ethnic and working-class issues. There is an undertone of rage and defiance throughout this, and other, volumes. (In 'Animals Are Passing from Our Lives', for instance, a pig refuses to be butchered, crying in the last line: 'No. Not this pig.')

Levine is particularly well known for his poems set in Detroit, a blighted urban landscape about which he has written with visionary intensity. *1933* (1974) was his most explicitly autobiographical work, in which family members and the physical geography of Detroit were uniquely invoked. 'Letters for the Dead', 'Uncle', and '1933' are among the finest poems of his maturity, followed in *The Names of the Lost* (1976) by more poems set in Detroit, such as 'Belle Isle, 1949', which describes a young couple who 'baptize' themselves in the polluted Detroit River with its 'brine | of cars parts, dead fish, stolen bicycles, | melted snow'.

Levine's strong identification with the antifascist side of the Spanish Civil War has given his poetry a decidedly left-populist political slant, as in his elegy for a Republican soldier, 'To P.L., 1916–1937', which appeared in *They Feed They Lion* (1972), one of Levine's strongest collections. Another strong poem focused on this period is 'On the Murder of Lieutenant Jose Del Castillo by the Falangist Bravo Martinez, July 12, 1936'—a vivid historical piece, published in *The Names of the Lost*. Here, as in Levine's best work generally, he re-creates a particular milieu with freshness and originality.

Though he has written well about Spain and Detroit, Levine has lived much of his adult life in northern California, and a number of his poems reflect the dry dust and hot climate of the Fresno Valley, as in 'A Sleepless Night', which begins: 'April, and the last of the plum blossoms | scatters on the black grass | before dawn'. Levine is, ultimately, a religious poet, and he invests whatever landscape he chooses to write about—geographical or mental—with a fervent spirituality. A volume called *Ashes* (1979) contains many of his most explicitly religious poems, many of which explore his Jewish roots, as in 'On a Drawing by Flavio', which summons the image of the Rabbi of Auschwitz, who 'bows his head and prays | for us all'.

Levine's *Selected Poems* (New York, 1984) is a major collection of the poet's work. Recent books include *Sweet Will* (1985) and *A Walk with Tom Jefferson* (1988—both New York). For criticism, see *Cry of the Human*, by Ralph J. Mills, Jr. (Urbana, Ill., 1975). [JP

LEVIS, Larry (Patrick) (1946–), was born, raised, and educated in Fresno, California. He received an MA from Syracuse University and a Ph.D from the University of Iowa. After many years at the University of Missouri, he currently teaches at the University of Utah.

Levis may fairly be described as a typical exponent of the mainstream *Iowa Writers' Workshop/*American Poetry Review* style that has dominated American poetry for the past twenty years. In so far as that style has changed, Levis's poetry has changed with it, though not in far-reaching ways: his lines have grown longer and correspondingly more discursive, his rhetoric is a touch more flamboyant, his subjects are more narrative, but essentially he continues to write a hybrid of *confessional and *deep image poetry—labels one might ordinarily prefer to avoid, but which seem quite appropriate for a poet as generic as Levis. Bits of anecdotal reminiscence centred on family or lovers, an indiscriminately reverent tone, a programmatic emphasis on loss and equally programmatic turns toward reconciliation, gratuitous phrases that create little dramatic frames ('I think', 'You can almost believe', 'Look'): these are the ingredients of the period style as Levis and many other workshop-based poets practise it. Levis's success, measured in the many prizes and fellowships he has received, reflects the skill with which he deploys this shared style. His books include *The Afterlife* (Iowa City, 1977), *Winter Stars* (Pittsburgh, 1985), and *The Widening Spell of the Leaves* (Pittsburgh, 1991).   [RG

LEWIS, Alun (1915–44), was born and grew up in Cwmaman, a small mining village near Aberdare in Mid-Glamorgan, the eldest son of two Welsh schoolteachers. He was educated at Cowbridge Grammar School as a boarder, and Aberystwyth College, where he took a first in history and contributed poems and stories to the college magazine. This was followed by a miserable period in Manchester, where he lived in a slum and did postgraduate research on thirteenth-century religious and economic history.

From an early age he was torn by conflicting private and public impulses, which occasionally led to severe depression. Social injustice was all around him, exacerbated by the Depression. Lewis's strong sense of duty, socialist and nonconformist, urged him to put his talents to public use as a journalist, teacher, or academic. His private emotional life, however, rich and confused, pulled him in the opposite direction, towards literature and the contemplative life, 'alone in a People's Age'. The declaration of war solved, or rather postponed, his dilemma, and in 1940 he enlisted in the Royal Engineers. But 'the perversions of Hitler . . .', he wrote, 'affected me less profoundly than my own destructive impulses'.

He married Gweno Ellis in July, 1941 and transferred to the 6th Battalion, South Wales Borderers, eventually rising (after a characteristic struggle as to whether he should become an officer or stay in the ranks) to the rank of captain. The army kept training and retraining him in various skills, and he spent most of his time moving around England, far from action, writing stories and poems, which began to attract the attention of Robert *Graves and other writers. Eventually the battalion was sent to India, on a long sea voyage via South Africa, and finally on to Burma to engage with the Japanese. While in India he fell in love with a married woman, Freda Akroyd, and also came increasingly under the spell of eastern religious attitudes, especially Buddhist renunciation of material reality. 'Acceptance seems so spiritless, protest so vain. In between the two I live', he wrote to Gweno. And, in a late poem, 'I am seeking less and less of world'. He died in mysterious circumstances, possibly by his own hand, in March 1944, near Goppe Bazar, Burma.

Two of the strongest influences on his poetry are Keats and Edward *Thomas, to the latter of whom he addressed such fine early poems as 'All Day It has Rained . . .' and 'To Edward Thomas'. Both mentors were death-haunted, in their different ways, and both clearly spoke to Lewis's own troubled nature. His early work is marred by over-reliance on capitalized abstractions such as Death, Love, Time, Beauty, and by sub-Yeatsian plangency, but shows also a remarkable lyric strain which deepened throughout his short life. *Raiders' Dawn* (London, 1942), his first book of poems, captured many of the experiences of enlisted men and went through several editions, as did his collection of stories *The Last Inspection* (London, 1943). *Ha! Ha! Among the Trumpets* (London, 1945), published posthumously, shows him absorbing India, turning inwards more and more, working towards a sort of testament in his late poem 'The Jungle', whose 'green indifference' and 'jungle pool | That drowns its image in a mort of leaves' mirror his own predicament as soldier-predator and dreamer-prey: 'The killing arm uncurls, strokes the soft moss'. It ends in large rhetorical questions about death, which recall both Rilke and the *Yeats of 'Among School Children'. Together with the very different Keith *Douglas—Douglas asserts, Lewis questions—he is probably the finest of the poets who fought in the Second World War.

Lewis's publishing history has been unfortunately scrappy. *Letters from India*, ed. Gweno Lewis and Gwyn Jones (Cardiff, 1946), and *Letters to Gweno*, ed. Gweno Lewis (Bridgend, 1989) contain much of his voluminous correspondence. *In the Green Tree* (London, 1948) contains poems and extracts from Lewis's excellent journals. The best critical introduction to his work is *Alun Lewis: Selected Poetry and Prose*, ed. Ian Hamilton (London, 1966). *Selected Poems of Alun Lewis*, ed. Jeremy Hooker and Gweno Lewis (London, 1981) is a useful sampler, and much interesting uncollected work is available in *Alun Lewis: A Miscellany of his Writings*, ed. John Pikoulis (Bridgend, 1982). *Alun Lewis: A Life*, by John Pikoulis (Bridgend, 1984) is the first full biography to date. Collected editions of the poems and short stories have been announced for publication in the early 1990s by the University of Wales Press. [WS

LEWIS, C. Day. See DAY LEWIS, C.

LEWIS, C(live) S(taples) (1898–1963), was born in Belfast and served for twenty years as a fellow of Magdalen College, Oxford. From the mid-1950s he was professor of medieval and Renaissance English at Cambridge. He published his poetry under the pseudonym of Clive Hamilton. In the biography *C. S. Lewis* (London, 1990), A. N. Wilson writes that, although Lewis long harboured the ambition to be a major poet, it 'is extraordinary that someone . . . with such an unfailing eye for the excellent in other poets could have gone on writing poetry of such appalling quality'. This is in essence a correct judgement, although a little overstated: Lewis was metrically competent in his shorter poems, although deficient at length. His major effort, alas, was a long narrative poem, *Dymer* (London, 1926), which he reprinted in 1950 when he hoped (but failed) to win the 1951 election for the Oxford Chair of Poetry. See *Poems* (London, 1964), ed. Walter Hooper, and *The Inklings*, by Humphrey Carpenter (London, 1978). [MS-S

LEWIS, Janet (1899–), was born near Chicago. Her father, Edwin Herbert Lewis, professor of English at the Lewis Institute, Chicago, encouraged her early interest in writing. Growing up in the Chicago suburb of Oak Park, she spent her summers with her family in northern Michigan and Canada where, from childhood on, she became well acquainted with the Indians and their culture, drawing on these experiences for her first book of poems *The Indians in the Woods* (Bonn, Germany 1922; repr. Palo Alto, Calif., 1980) and her first novel, *The Invasion* (New York, 1932). She married the poet and critic Yvor *Winters in Santa Fe in 1926 and settled in semi-rural surroundings in Los Altos, California, near Stanford University where her husband taught until his death in 1968.

Although she experimented with free verse early and late in her career, most of her luminous and resonant lyrics are written in conventional prosody. Her subjects are love, protracted illness (she was at a Santa Fe sanatorium for tuberculosis for several years), death of friends, friendship, domestic duties, and other themes of universal scope. Among her best-known poems are 'Earth-Bound', 'During Illness', 'In an Egyptian Museum', 'Love Poem', and 'To Helen'. She began a series of librettos in verse with *The Wife of Martin Guerre: An Opera* (Denver, Col., 1958), drawn from her second novel published in 1941. Her volume of poems *The Ancient Ones* (Portola Valley, Calif., 1979) reflects a lifelong interest in the native cultures of New Mexico.

Her poems have been collected in *Poems Old and New, 1918–1978* (Athens, Ohio, 1981). See also Mitzi Berger Hamovitch, 'My Life I Will Not Let Thee Go Except Thou Bless Me: an Interview with Janet Lewis', *Southern Review*, 18 (Apr. 1982). [DS

LEWIS, (Percy) Wyndham (1882–1957), made many enemies during a career as visual artist, social philosopher, polemical critic (see BLAST), and novelist. He is little regarded as a poet, but the 2,000-line *One-Way Song* (1933) is an accomplished and wholly individual work. As a statement of Lewis's socio-political stance and an argument about the reactionary nature of those who clung to what Lewis regarded as the mock-revolutionary idea of 'Progress', the poem is often unclear, but the parts are much more eloquent and effective than the whole.

The opening section, 'Engine Fight-Talk', is genially critical of the Audenic poetic concern with machinery; 'Song of the Militant Romance' looks at the extravagant verbalism of Joyceans; 'If So The Man You Are' is a statement of Lewis's own position. The verse-forms used are the old-fashioned fourteener and the heroic couplet, both handled with freshness, humour, and an at times overwhelming vigour.

See *Collected Poems and Plays* ed. Alan Munton (Manchester, 1979). Jeffrey Meyers's *The Enemy* (London, 1980) is a comprehensive biography, and *The Essential Wyndham Lewis* (London, 1989) a useful introduction to the various aspects of the work.   [JGS

LIEBERMAN, Laurence (1935–), was born in Detroit, Michigan, and educated at the University of Michigan, Ann Arbor, and the University of California, Berkeley. His teaching career has included a post at the College of the Virgin Islands, St Thomas (1964–8), where he developed the interest in life in the Caribbean and the underwater world of the coral reefs which has remained a persistent theme in his poetry. Since 1970 he has been a professor of English at the University of Illinois, Urbana, and poetry editor for its press.

Drawing on Whitman, Lieberman has developed a long cadenced verse line and an emphasis on narrative uncommon in twentieth-century poetry. An inveterate traveller, he views the customs and scenery of the Caribbean—and, in *God's Measurements*, Japan —with the eye of a tourist / poet.

His collections include *The Osprey Suicides* (New York and London, 1973); *God's Measurements* (New York, 1980); *Eros at the World Kite Pageant: Poems 1979–1982* (New York, 1983); and *The Mural of Wakeful Sleep* (New York, 1985). His criticism can be found in *Unassigned Frequences: American Poetry in Review 1964–77* (Urbana, Ill., and London, 1977).   [LD

LIM, Shirley Geok-lin (1944–), was born and raised in Malacca, Malaysia, the only daughter

in a family of five sons. She was educated in the University of Malaya, and remained in Malaysia until the late 1960s, when she left to study in America. Although she has since settled there, her poetry has maintained strong links with her Malaysian past. Lim's first and best-known collection of poems, *Crossing the Peninsula and Other Poems* (Kuala Lumpur), won the 1980 Commonwealth Poetry Prize. This was the first time the prize had been won by an Asian and a woman. Her subsequent publications include *Another Country and Other Stories* (Singapore, 1982), *No Man's Grove and Other Poems* (Singapore, 1985), and *Modern Secrets: New and Selected Poems* (Aarhus, 1989).

Of Chinese origins in a non-Chinese cultural landscape, Lim writes best about the culturally colonized and marginalized individual. Her poetry is dominated by sharp delineations of fragmented identities, and sustained by a strong, penetrating style and an ironic, unsentimental delivery. She has furthered this theme significantly by addressing the question of her female identity within the context of her received patriarchal culture.

Lim's work has appeared in various anthologies, including *A Private Landscape*, ed. David Ormerod (Kuala Lumpur, 1967); *The Second Tongue*, ed. Edwin Thumboo (Kuala Lumpur, 1976); and *Under Another Sky*, ed. Alistair Niven (London, 1987). See also *The Writer's Sense of the Contemporary*, ed. Bruce Bennet *et al.* (Perth, 1982), for Anne Brewster's essay on Lim.

[WMY

LIMA, Frank. See NEW YORK SCHOOL.

LINDOP, Grevel (1948–), was born in Liverpool, studied English at Oxford, and teaches at Manchester University. After a romantic and bookish pamphlet, *Against the Sea* (1969), he published his first full-size volume, *Fools' Paradise*, in 1977, demonstrating a harder and more achieved technique, especially in two poems about manual work, 'The Spot-Welder's Song' and 'The Barrel-Dance'. His second full volume, *Tourists* (1987), was more wide-ranging and ambitious. This has more public concern than its predecessors, but its principal merit is its power of precise observation and description, as in the long title-poem, set on a South-East Asian island, and in a series of poems illustrating twenty-one wood engravings by Bewick. Lindop's easy and exact vernacular is the vehicle for a perceptiveness and intelligence which, perhaps because of his slow rate of production, have still to be accorded proper recognition.

Lindop's collections have all been published by Carcanet Press (Manchester); he is also the author of *The Opium-Eater; a life of Thomas de Quincey* (Oxford, 1981). [BO'D

LINDSAY, (John) Maurice (1918–), was born in Glasgow and educated at Glasgow Academy and the Scottish National Academy of Music. *Collected Poems: 1940–1990* (Aberdeen) selects from some twenty volumes, some of them 'collected' or 'selected' editions. Much of the work is occasional. Latterly it has been celebratory (marriage, domestic life, comforts, complacencies) or satirical (feckless Glaswegians, Scottish excesses, etc.) and managed with light-hearted crustiness. 'A Net to Catch the Winds', an autobiography in 127 *ottava rima* stanzas, complete with Byronic rhymes, some of them snappy, is his most sustained as well as his most achieved performance. Much of his poetry is, however, marred rather than enlivened by his generational displeasures.

Lindsay's contribution to Scottish poetry lies chiefly in his work as an editor, critic, and historian, in which fields he has been prolific as well as substantial. For example, he edited *Modern Scottish Poetry: An Anthology of the Scottish Renaissance 1920–1945* (London, 1946), revised in 1966, 1976 (with Carcanet Press), and 1986 (with Hale). Another notable book is *History of Scottish Literature* (London, 1977). [DED

LINDSAY, Vachel (1879–1931), was born in Springfield, Illinois, to religious-fundamentalist parents. He entered Hiram College in 1897 but left after three years to study art in Chicago and New York until 1905. Fired by a desire both to preach temperance and bring verse to the masses, he tramped around the country beg-

ging, and bartering broadsides of his poems. He was part of the literary revival hailed as America's 'poetry renaissance' and anchored in the Midwest by Harriet Monroe's 1912 founding of *Poetry magazine.

Lindsay's first book, *General Booth Enters Heaven and Other Poems* (1913) was a popular success, aided by its author's dramatic readings of the title-poem and of the naïvely racist title-poem of his second collection, *The Congo and Other Poems* (1914). Like his lectures on 'The Gospel of Beauty', the public readings were sincere, evangelical attempts to elevate national taste. If his jingle-rhymed and syncopated poems were not profound, they were genuinely modern in their reformist (populist) stance, conversational ease, and readiness to experiment, scoring the Booth poem, for instance, with a revival hymn, or apeing popular music in *The Daniel Jazz* (1920).

Lindsay, however, was victimized by success, forced to perform the same poems repeatedly even as he lost faith in their worth. Always prey to self-doubts, he was hurt by criticisms of his third volume, *The Chinese Nightingale and Other Poems* (1917), and the flop of *The Golden Book of Springfield* (1920), prose revelations. The 1922 death of his mother led to a total, if temporary, collapse, and in 1924 he learned he was epileptic. Marriage a year later only deepened his depression. He swallowed a bottle of Lysol in a hotel room during yet another reluctant reading tour.

Lindsay's *Collected Poems* (New York, 1923, revd. edn. 1925) remains available, as is his *Johnny Appleseed and Other Poems* (New York, 1981). See also *Letters of Vachel Lindsay*, ed. Marc Chenetier (New York, 1979) and *City of Discontent: An Interpretive Biography of Vachel Lindsay* (New York, 1975), by Mark Harris. [EB

Little Review, The, first appeared in March 1914 with an introductory piece by the editor Margaret Anderson saying that 'Life is a glorious performance' and that 'this eager, panting Art shows us the wonder of the way as we rush along'. Anderson, a girl from Indiana, had no literary or social ideas at this time beyond a vague feeling for anarchism, but her enthusiasm kept the magazine going during a period when Sherwood Anderson, Vachel *Lindsay and Eunice *Tietjens were the best-known contributors.

The transformation of the periodical from one of purely parochial interest into a paper printing the finest contemporary work then being written in English came with the appointment of Ezra *Pound as foreign editor. In her autobiography *My Thirty Years' War* (1930) Anderson told the story, and included several of Pound's exclamatory and extraordinary letters. Poems by *Eliot and *Yeats, stories and articles by Wyndham *Lewis, contributions from Richard *Aldington, Hart *Crane, Djuna Barnes—every monthly issue had material in it justifying the boast on the masthead: 'Making No Compromise With The Public Taste.' The ultimate refusal to compromise, and the magazine's greatest glory, was the printing of extracts from *Joyce's *Ulysses*.

The prosecution of *Ulysses* made the *Little Review* famous, or notorious, in the United States. One issue had been confiscated because of a story by Lewis, but the prosecution of *Ulysses* put Anderson and her fellow editor jane heap (who did not acknowledge capital letters for names) under the spotlight in a way that delighted them, although they were disappointed to be fined rather than imprisoned, and dismayed by the legal order that no more of Joyce's book should appear in the magazine. By 1921 Pound's interest was fading, and when in the following year Anderson and Heap moved the magazine to Paris he became no more than an occasional contributor.

The *Little Review* continued to exist until 1929, but without the animating passion and individual taste of Pound became just another high-brow magazine. Between 1924 and 1927 Heap carried on the paper alone from New York, and fluttered from interest in Expressionism and Surrealism to Russian Constructivism. The editorial in the final number said space had been given to '23 new systems of art (all now dead), representing 19 countries'. The intention had been to provide 'a trial-track for racers . . . But you can't get race horses from mules.' Anderson complemented Heap's disillusion by saying that

in 1929 'even the artist doesn't know what he's talking about'. Perhaps an equal bafflement was shown by editors who believed there were twenty-three new systems of art. In this final editorial Heap announced that she was saying goodbye to art in favour of 'pursuits more becoming to human beings'. As for Anderson, at the end of her autobiography she was still making 'vows to achieve an increasingly beautiful life'. See Ian Hamilton, *The Little Magazines: A Study of Six Editors* (London, 1976). [JGS]

Liverpool Poets, The, the name given to a group of three poets, Brian *Patten, Adrian *Henri, and Roger McGough (1937), who performed their verses in the aftermath of the success of the Beatles. They form a part of sociological rather than literary history, and, while *The Mersey Sound* (London, 1967) and *The Liverpool Scene* (London, 1967) were widely bought anthologies, *New Volume* (London, 1983) went by without much comment. Their work was always designed for a public audience, usually for musical accompaniment, and was characterized by a vaguely aggressive but cheerful attitude towards the establishment and official education. It sounded, as was intended, more effective in performance than when it was read, and none of the poets concerned developed a literary technique—nor did they supplant, as might have been a part of their intention, literary poets who write primarily for the reader. [MS-S

LIVESAY, Dorothy (1909–), was born in Winnipeg, Manitoba, of a family with strong interests in writing and journalism. She was educated at Glen Mawr private school for girls and, with interruptions, at the University of Toronto and the Sorbonne. Strongly influenced by a free-thinking father and left-wing ideas and personalities—Engels, Marx, Emma Goldman, and Shaw—Livesay embarked on a career in social work and joined the Communist Party. Her first book of poems, *Green Pitcher* (1928) was a precocious effort showing considerable craft and a developing social conscience. In 1932 she published *Signpost*, in which a demonstrated technical skill is matched by a growing sense of her own persona. The 1930s saw Livesay working actively for leftist causes as a social worker, organizer, and contributor to left-wing periodicals. Committed to the ideal of the working class and its contribution to the war effort, Livesay published *Day and Night* (1944) and the appropriately named, *Poems for People* (1947). Much of her literary effort of the Thirties and Forties is marred by the stereotypical language of leftist rhetoric.

After the death of Livesay's husband in 1959 she went to teach in Zambia, and returned in the early 1960s to enter her most impressive phase as poet, teacher, and pioneer feminist. Two collections, *The Unquiet Bed* (1967) and *Plainsongs* (1969) reveal a mature, sensual, and outspoken writer. There is also the beginning of an unabashed self-awareness which, appropriately enough, serves as a rehearsal for the strong autobiographical elements that colour her later work. In 1968 she published *The Documentaries*, which stands as an important contribution to the long poem in Canada. Her major collection, *Collected Poems: The Two Seasons* (Toronto) appeared in 1972. Intense and confessional in her old age, Livesay's output and energy are truly remarkable. She has remembered herself and her times in a series of reminiscences: *Beginnings: A Winnipeg Childhood* (1973); *The Raw Edges: Voices from our Time* (1983); and, latterly, *Journey with my Selves* (1991). Livesay has edited the anthology, *Forty Women Poets of Canada* (Montreal, 1972), and helped to found *CV/II*, a magazine of poetry and criticism. She is an Officer of the Order of Canada.   [MG

LIVINGSTONE, Douglas (1932–), was born in Kuala Lumpur, and went to Africa at the age of 10. He lived for a time in the old Federation of Rhodesia and his poems reflect something of the energy, if not the optimism, of that short-lived experiment. Marine biologist, diver, sometime pugilist, jazz *aficionado*, Livingstone in his verse is a scrupulous craftsman. There is broad humanity, though his interest in microscopic organisms suggests that he might see them as more successful than anything to be found in the human species.

His early poems, which appeared in the pamphlet *The Skull in the Mud* (London, 1960), set out what were to become continuing themes of blood and bone, the destructive energies of African wildlife, human and animal, set against the indifference of the continent and the violent shifts in its history. This last is evident in his verse play *The Sea My Winding Sheet* (Johannesburg, 1978), which looks at the myth of Adamastor.

Livingstone is the only contemporary South African English poet who can stand comparison with Roy *Campbell, a position he has held since the appearance of *Sjambok, and Other Poems from Africa* (London and New York, 1964), which established his reputation. The curious, distinctive combination of large, sometimes violent, themes with a meticulous eye for the telling detail is evident in his *Poems* (London and New York, 1968) and dramatically reinforced in *Eyes Closed Against the Sun* (London and New York, 1970), the best collection published in South Africa since the war.

Menacing gallantry and steely lyricism are Livingstone's trade-marks. The poems in *A Rosary of Bone* (Cape Town, 1975; rev. edn., 1983) seem pallid after the intensity of his earlier work, and Livingstone omits many of them from his *Selected Poems* (Johannesburg, 1984). *The Anvil's Undertone* (Johannesburg, 1978) was a welcome return to form. His strengths as a satirist are to be seen in the Giovanni Jacopo meditations, a series of mordant reflections on his life and times which have appeared over the past twenty years. His scientific interests are summarized in his *Microbial Studies in the Sea off Durban, 1964–88* (Natal, 1988).

For a critical study of Livingstone's work, see: 'Douglas Livingstone', in *South African English Poetry: A Modern Perspective*, by Michael Chapman (Johannesburg, 1981).   [CH

LLEWELLYN, Kate (1940–), was born in Tumby Bay, South Australia. She gained early qualifications as a registered nurse and later a BA in history and classics from the University of Adelaide (1978). From 1965 to 1972 she was an owner/director of various Adelaide art galleries. She began writing poetry in the mid-1970s. Her *Trader Kate and the Elephants* (Adelaide, 1979) won the Anne Elder Award for a first book of poetry. She has published three subsequent collections (*Luxury*, Sydney, 1985; *Honey*, 1988; and *Figs*, 1990), as well as a *Selected Poems* (1992—all Hawthorn, Victoria). She is the author of a prose trilogy (*The Waterlily*, 1986; *Dear You*, 1988; and *The Mountain*, 1989) based on diaries of her life in the Blue Mountains of New South Wales, where she now lives, and in 1991 published *Angels and Dark Madonnas*, an account of travels in India and Italy. With Susan *Hampton, she edited the influential *Penguin Book of Australian Women Poets* (1985). Her poetry, 'with all its precise moments of bitterness and ecstasy, lust and folly, irony and grief' (Marie Tulip), reflects the *Confessional and *Deep Image poetries of North America, and is known for its candour, sensuality, and what some construe as a stubborn disregard for the prevailing, predominantly patriarchal, Australian poetic.   [DBr

LOCHHEAD, Douglas Grant (1922–), was born in Guelph, Ontario, and educated at the universities of McGill and Toronto. His father was a distinguished bacteriologist. Through his mother's family, the VanWarts, Lochhead experienced life in rural New Brunswick. Childhood summers were spent in Fredericton and on the shore of the Bay of Fundy. Since academic retirement in 1987 Lochhead has continued to live in Sackville, New Brunswick, a small university town surrounded by the Tantramar Marshes which have provided one of the landscapes in much of his later work.

Lochhead's early poetry was influenced by Dylan *Thomas, *Auden, *Yeats, and *Roethke. His mature work starts with *Millwood Road Poems* (1970). This collection's seemingly improvisational airs about domestic, small city, and small wildlife matters are partly indebted to *Souster and W. C. *Williams, but Lochhead's free verse here, as elsewhere, is distinguished not only by convincing line-breaks, accurate stresses, and cogent forms but also by an unpre-

tentious yet insistent attempt to balance nature and humanity, love and the poetic imagination. Lochhead's work is often spry, elegant, and comic. At other times, and increasingly so in later collections such as the prose-poem sequences of *High Marsh Road* (1980) and *The Panic Field* (1984), his work is abrupt and sardonic. It deals with personal loss, guilt, blocked metaphysical ambition, self-betrayal, and with the survival of a beleaguered poetics still based upon generosity and trust.

Tiger in the Skull: New and Selected Poems, 1959–1985 (Fredericton, NB, 1986) remains the single most wide-ranging collection. But later volumes, including *Upper Cape Poems* (Fredericton, 1989) and *Dykelands* (Montreal, 1989), more than double its contents. See also *The Red Jeep and Other Landscapes: A Collection in Honour of Douglas Lochhead* (Fredericton, 1987), ed. Peter Thomas, and *As the Eyes of Lyncaeus: A Celebration for Douglas Lochhead* (Sackville, NB, 1990), by Peter Sanger.   [PMS

LOCHHEAD, Liz (1947–), was born and brought up in industrial Lanarkshire. She attended the Glasgow School of Art and taught for several years. *Memo for Spring* (Edinburgh, 1972) introduced her up-tempo, bitter-sweet, feminine self-awareness to the male-centred Scottish poetry world.

Dreaming Frankenstein and Collected Poems (Edinburgh, 1984) draws from *Memo for Spring*, with more recent work added. 'What the Pool Said, On Midsummer's Day', 'The Grim Sisters', 'My Mother's Suitors', and a number of other poems demonstrate that the range of Lochhead's talent can work at levels deeper than those of audience-nudging entertainment. Couplets in 'Fourth of July Fireworks', for example, have a Lowellian hardness. At times, too, she writes a singing line which seems as much haunted by the lyrics of popular songs as by more formal poetry. Expert timing and a natural narrative-dramatic gift have contributed to her success as a public performer of her work.

True Confessions and New Clichés (Edinburgh, 1985) is a selection of monologues, songs, and other pieces for revue performance. It is poetry in cabaret mood and often extremely funny. *Bagpipe Muzak* (London, 1991) contains a section of similar 'recitations' (as she calls them), which, if anything, are satirically sharper and more achieved. The theatre seems a natural home for such work and Lochhead, unsurprisingly, is the author of several plays, notably *Mary Queen of Scots Got Her Head Chopped Off* (1989). However, *Bagpipe Muzak* also contains a section of poems. Here too there is an increased assurance, a seriousness which can handle the paraphernalia of contemporary life with jaunty affection as well as a critical, measuring eye for its darker side. [DED

LOEWINSOHN, Ron(ald William) (1937–), was born in the Philippines. He first went to the United States in 1945, living in Los Angeles and the Bronx before settling with his parents in San Francisco. After graduating from high school in 1955 he spent two years travelling around America. Returning to San Francisco, he then married in 1957. Work as a lithographer was followed by undergraduate and graduate study at San Francisco State College, the University of California, Berkeley, and Harvard. Having taught writing in California and at Harvard, he became a member of the Department of English at Berkeley in 1970. He has also edited a number of little magazines, including *Change*, *Sum*, and *R.C. Lion*.

His first volume of poetry, *Watermelons*, was published in 1959, with a prefatory commendation from William Carlos *Williams and an introduction by Allen *Ginsberg that described Loewinsohn as part of the 'great wave of Poetry . . . breaking over America now'. Deeply indebted to Williams, Loewinsohn dwells on the local, the minute particulars of the ordinary world, meditating on the beauty, violence, and the surprises of everyday life in poems that are notable for their tender feelings and colloquial vigour. Some of his work is particularly memorable for its sexual frankness (one of his poems bears the title, 'The Romaunt of the Rose Fuck'); but a more frequent mode is a pellucid, unforced lyricism, the desire, as Loewinsohn has put it, 'to fill our days with beauty | from

whatever faucet's available'. Other volumes include *The World of the Lie* (1963); *The Sea, Around Us* (1968); *The Step* (1968); and *The Leaves* (1973). A useful selection is to be found in *Meat Air: Poems 1957–1969* (New York, 1970). [RJG

LOGAN, John (1923–87), was born in Red Oak, Iowa. He earned a BS in zoology at Coe College in Cedar Rapids and an MA in English at the University of Iowa. The father of nine children, he taught at St John's College in Maryland and the University of Notre Dame (Indiana) before becoming a professor of English at the State University of New York in Buffalo. His first book, *Cycle for Mother Cabrini* (1955), was metrically and religiously conventional, influenced as much by Rilke as by the Old Testament. His second and third collections, *Ghosts of the Heart: New Poems* (1960) and *Spring of the Thief: Poems 1960–1962* (1963), evinced a technical loosening into syllabics and slant rhymes, though still concentrated on a metaphysical vision. The latter collection also introduced a bolder note of sensuality as it explored the lives of poets and religious figures.

This sexual motif intensified in both *The Zig-Zag Walk: Poems 1963–1968* and *The Anonymous Lover: New Poems* (1973), often amplified or mocked by witty rhymes and absurd puns, as Logan's orthodox Catholicism acquired a Zen openness. His prose has been collected in *A Bullet for the Ear: Interviews, Essays, and Reviews*, ed. A. Poulin, Jr. (Ann Arbor, Mich., 1983) and his verse in *The Collected Poems* (Brockport, NY, 1989). See also *Dissolve to Island: On the Poetry of John Logan*, ed. Michael Walters (Houston, 1984). [EB

LOGAN, William (1950–), was born in Boston, and grew up in the north-eastern United States. He attended Yale and the University of Iowa, where he studied with Donald *Justice, later a colleague at the University of Florida. Logan divides his time between his academic job in Gainesville and a home in Cambridge, England.

Logan distinguishes himself from his American contemporaries by his unfailing commitment to a poetry of impersonality and statement. In vigorous, simple diction, his first book, *Sad-Faced Men* (Boston, 1982) reflects a classical sensibility in poems about fate, abandoned gods, and the dullness of the material world. Nature, as manifest in imagery of water throughout the volume, is a source of awe, discomfort, and cruelty ('Ice' and 'Maelstrom'). *Difficulty* (Edinburgh, 1984; Boston, 1985) declares its denser textures in its title, and supports Logan's complex philosophical intentions with its linguistically demanding verse. As sombre as his previous volume, Logan's more mature work displays a hard-earned wit in cynical poems about loneliness, betrayal, and decay ('Hard Waters', 'Cartography', and 'Dream Contract'). Many of these poems resume the poet's ongoing struggle against his true 'enemy', silence. In Logan's strongest volume yet, *Sullen Weedy Lakes* (Boston, 1988), he turns to politics, but only in the abstract. His poems on affairs of state explore corruption, conspiracy, and tyranny, and he peoples these narratives with unnamed mercenaries, generals, emperors, assassins, and exiles ('The Ancient Economy', 'Methods of Empire', 'Banana Republics'). [TDeP

LOGUE, Christopher (1926–), was born and educated in Portsmouth, and served in the British Army 1944–8. In 1951 he moved to France, where his first book of poems, *Wand and Quadrant*, was published in 1953; since 1956 he has lived in London, where until recently he edited the 'True Stories' column for the satirical magazine *Private Eye*. He has also worked as a playwright, screen-writer, anthologist, and actor.

Logue's interest in verse had cosmopolitan beginnings; he was among the first English writers to appreciate Pablo Neruda, whom he translated and adapted in the late Fifties. He was equally responsive to world events and to trends in youth culture, so that his poems, both in their straightforwardly political content and in their slangy, jazzy address, are strongly affixed to their particular time. Typical of his career in the Sixties were a series of poster poems, distributed by Turret Books, London, including *I Shall Vote*

Labour (1966), and the readings he gave, with Adrian *Mitchell and others, in protest against the Vietnam War. He has more than thirty verse publications, in various forms, to his credit; the more durable of these are preserved in *Ode to the Dodo: Poems from 1953 to 1978* (London, 1981). He is nowadays best known, however, not for his 'popular' contemporary work but for his racy, clangorous adaptations (including extraneous elements from later history) of some books of the *Iliad*: these are collected in two volumes, *War Music* (London, 1981; New York, 1987) and *Kings* (London, 1991). [MI

LO LIYONG, Taban (1938–), was born of Southern Sudanese and Ugandan parents and grew up in Uganda. He studied at Howard University and at Iowa, where he was the first African to receive an MFA from the *Iowa Writers' Workshop. He has taught at the universities of Nairobi, Kenya, and Papua New Guinea, and now works as a director of cultural affairs in Juba, Southern Sudan.

Lo Liyong has published three volumes of poetry: *Frantz Fanon's Uneven Ribs: Poems, More and More* (London, 1971), *Another Nigger Dead* (London, 1972), and *Ballads of Underdevelopment* (Kampala, 1978). He is an authority on the oral literature of the Lwo and Masai and has published his own transmutation of Lwo oral poetry, *Eating Chiefs* (London, 1970), and a collection of short stories from the oral tradition.

Lo Liyong's approach to poetry is highly individualistic. The poems take the form of unedited stream-of-consciousness material. The literary allusions are endless and the content often clever and infuriating. However, it is arguable whether his ideas work as poetry. Lo Liyong is aware of this, and in response to the charge that 'all this is prose' he argues that 'prose is poetry now'. See *Understanding African Poetry* (London, 1982), by Ken Goodwin, for a sympathetic critical review of Lo Liyong's work. [FO

LOMAS, Herbert (1924–), grew up in Southport, Lancashire. He served in the army in India

(1943–6) and read English at Liverpool University (MA, 1952), before lecturing at the University of Helsinki (1952–65) and Borough Road College, London (1966–82). Married with two children, he lives in Aldeburgh, Suffolk.

Lomas is an idiosyncratic poet. His language is both meticulous and conversational, blending sometimes surreal imagery with anecdote and meditation. He is an adept improviser in received forms. His interests extend beyond poetry—*Who Needs Money?* (London, 1972), is a work on economic reform—and his attitude is characteristically enquiring, as he ranges over love, sex ('The Groves of Academe'), music, family history (the sequence 'Todmorden'), and religious belief—the subject of *Letters in the Dark* (London, 1986)—via vampires, photography, and translations from Valéry, Horace, and Finnish poets. At once urbane and astonished, lyrical and down-to-earth, Lomas's is an attractive voice.

Lomas's other collections are *Chimpanzees are Blameless Creatures* (London, 1969); *Private and Confidential* (London, 1974); *Public Footpath* (London, 1981); *Fire in the Garden* (Oxford, 1984), and *Trouble* (London, 1992). A prolific translator of Finnish, he edited *Contemporary Finnish Poetry* (Newcastle upon Tyne, 1991).

[SO'B

London Magazine, The, a monthly literary journal, was established by John *Lehmann in 1954, three years after the collapse of Lehmann's famous Penguin *New Writing*. It was intended to fill the gap left by that and the demise of Cyril Connolly's *Horizon*. It took its name from the periodical which, between 1820 and 1829, published some of the most celebrated work of Hazlitt, Keats, De Quincey and Leigh Hunt, and was backed by the newspaper magnate Cecil King of the *Daily Mirror*. The intention was that it should discover and encourage new writers as well as publishing established names, and that it should carry the work of American and Commonwealth along with English writers, and also Europeans in translation. Its editorial board included John Hayward, Elizabeth Bowen, William *Plomer, Rex *Warner, C. V. Wedgwood, and Thom *Gunn. New stories and poems were to be the principal offerings each month, together with reminiscences and confessions by contemporary authors. There would be a substantial reviews section, where 'lucidity, seriousness and freshness of approach' were required of the contributors. Lehmann was determined not to let his magazine become a vehicle either for academic theory or for political ideology. 'There are no Keep Out notices', he wrote in his first issue, 'except for those who *in their writing* put political propaganda—or any kind of propaganda—before art, and those who should never have strayed into the field of literature at all.'

Lehmann edited the magazine for seven years, after which it was taken over by Alan *Ross. Under Ross the magazine was to change from being 'a review of literature' to 'a review of the arts'. Painting, sculpture, music, film, photography, and theatre would all be considered; and it would be designed to have a more noticeable visual effect. 'Gravity . . . but never solemnity. Astringency but not malice. And at all costs experiment, the hopefulness that the best, even most melancholy art, always must generate, even in despite of itself'—these were what Ross aimed for.

Since the magazine began, an impressively large list of the most notable of modern writers have published work in its pages. In recent years it has appeared bi-monthly. 'Experiment' is less in evidence than it once was; the same old hands appear and reappear; there is inevitably a sameness about a magazine which keeps one editor over many decades. But in a time when academic journals nominally devoted to literature publish mostly what must seem to outsiders private conversations, the *London Magazine* continues to be readable and interesting.

Apart from the files of the magazine itself, information about it can be found in John Lehmann's *The Ample Proposition* (London, 1966), and in Alan Ross's *Coastwise Lights* (London, 1988).

[CKS

LONGLEY, Michael (1939–), was born in Belfast and educated at Trinity College, Dublin, where he read Classics. He worked as a schoolteacher in Dublin, London, and Belfast until, in 1970, he joined the Arts Council of Northern Ireland, eventually becoming director of literature and the traditional arts. He published his first volume, *No Continuing City* (London and Chester Springs, Pa.), in 1969. He is married to the critic Edna Longley, who has written widely on the contemporary poetry of Northern Ireland. He shares with her a devotion to the work of Louis *MacNeice, and his advocacy resulted in his revisionist edition of MacNeice's *Selected Poems* in 1988.

Michael Longley is a poet of the personal life, a quiet, punctilious observer of love and landscape (particularly that of Co. Mayo). His exact and elegant notations, often minimalist in their brevity, are nevertheless enlivened by a certain disconcerting strangeness in which realism may bewilderingly swerve into fantasy or even the surreal, natural description into emblem, the quotidian into parable, topographical into imaginary location. In *An Exploded View* (London, 1973), his verse letters to Seamus *Heaney, Derek *Mahon, and James *Simmons (with whom he was associated in the Belfast 'Group') suggest that the discursive is not his most successful mode. Reticent, tentative, and unpresuming, he is more memorable as an elegist, where his capacity to disconcert produces a number of exceptional poems. In 'Wounds', from *An Exploded View*, he links his father's experience in the Ulster Division at the Somme with contemporary terrorist atrocities to produce a deeply poignant sense of hapless involvement in political process; and in probably the best known of his poems, 'The Linen Workers', from *The Echo Gate* (London, 1979), he complicates a relationship between his father, the eponymous victims of sectarian assassination, and a chillingly surreal Christ, 'fastened for ever | By his exposed canines to a wintry sky'. Refusing to settle for any appropriate *gravitas*, the poem achieves a far more appropriate terror, disgust, and helplessness. A *Selected Poems 1963–1980* was published in Winston-Salem,

NC, in 1980. See also *Poems 1963–1983* (Edinburgh, 1985). His latest collection is *Gorse Fires* (London, 1991). [NC

LORDE, Audre Geraldin (1934–92), was born in New York City and educated there at Hunter College and Columbia University, where she took a master's degree in library science which she practised until 1968 when she began a career as an academic at Tougaloo College. She later held various academic posts, including that of Thomas Hunter Professor at Hunter College. She was a member of the editorial staffs of various periodicals and received sundry awards.

Audre Lorde's first book was *The First Cities* (New York, 1968); this was followed by eight others including *Coal* (New York, 1976), *The Black Unicorn* (New York, 1978), and *Chosen Poems—Old and New* (New York, 1982). It is hard to fault Lorde's range of personal experience, for the jacket copy of her latest book reads: 'As Marilyn *Hacker has written, "Black, lesbian, mother, cancer survivor, urban woman: none of Lorde's selves has ever silenced the others."' But her rendition of these states is too often flat and prosy. Lorde died of cancer in 1992; her last volume was *Our Dead Behind Us* (New York, 1986; London, 1987). [LT

LOW, Jackson. See SOUND POETRY.

LOWBURY, Edward (Joseph) (1913–), son of a Hampstead doctor, was educated at St Paul's School and University College, Oxford, where he won the Newdigate Prize and the Matthew Arnold Memorial Prize. He did his clinical studies at the London Hospital and took a medical degree at Oxford before specializing in pathology. After spending three years of the Second World War in the RAMC in East Africa, Lowbury began his long career in Birmingham working under the auspices of the Medical Research Council. For his distinction as a pathologist he was awarded the OBE and received honorary doctorates from the universities of Aston and of Birmingham.

Edward Lowbury's poetry reflects his scientific knowledge, his love of music, and his wide reading in literature and philosophy. His shorter poems combine lyrical purity, meditative subtlety, and technical assurance; while the epistolary poems exhibit narrative strength, the power to portray complex characters, and a sense of history.

His first book, *Port Meadow* (London, 1936), was followed in 1947 by *Crossing the Line* (London), which had won a competition organized by Hutchinson and judged by Edmund *Blunden and Louis *MacNeice. *Time for Sale* (London, 1961) assembled his best work of the previous decade and a half. His *Selected and New Poems 1935–89* (Frome, Somerset, 1990) superseded an earlier selection published in 1978.

[JPr

LOWELL, Amy (Lawrence) (1874–1925), poet and foster-parent of the *Imagist movement. Born in Brookline, Massachusetts, of an aristocratic family and educated privately, she came late to poetry after years of travel, voluntary work, and society life. Her first volume, *A Dome of Many-Coloured Glass* (1912), is derivative late Romanticism, thought 'fluid, fruity, facile stuff' by Richard *Aldington. In January 1913, however, she took as a 'revelation' the signature 'H.D. Imagiste' which she came upon in *Poetry* magazine; and in the following year she arrived in England to link up with Aldington, H.D. (Hilda *Doolittle), and *Pound (who published one of her poems in his 1914 anthology *Des Imagistes*) in promoting and directing the new movement. As Pound grew fed up with her headstrong 'democratizing' methods, she assumed leadership and edited three volumes of the anthology *Some Imagist Poets* (1915–17).

Pound derided what he called 'Amy-gism', and the movement certainly changed under her influence. In the first place, her own verse, while it has its (somewhat long-winded) versions of Imagist formulae ('Do you think you see a young man in a swallow-tailed coat leading an orchestra? | I tell you it is a white, pointed flame in a silver dish'), is better described as a mystical sort of impressionism. Secondly, though her

1915 'Preface' restates Pound's principles of exactness, clarity, and concentration, she was principally concerned, as he foresaw, to promote *vers libre* of all sorts. The Preface to her own *Sword Blades and Poppy Seeds* (1914) expresses a debt to the French Parnassians for their example (borrowing F. S. *Flint's phrase) of 'unrhymed cadence'; in 1915, J. Gould *Fletcher credited her with the innovation of 'Polyphonic Prose', restoring to the Imagist 'skeleton' the panoply of 'assonance, alliteration, rhyme and return'. Lowell herself ascribed this form to Paul Fort; in her own work, it has been applied both to her lush prose poems and to the method of alternating prose and verse used in 'Guns as Keys: and the Great Gate Swings' in *Can Grande's Castle* (1920).

Lowell's flamboyant wealth, large figure, and eccentric behaviour (she smoked cigars and slept on sixteen pillows) set her up for ridicule. D. H. *Lawrence's estimate of her as 'a good amateur' embodies a general suspicion of one who seemed to play at poetry. Yet she maintained a prolific output after the dispersal of Imagism, producing twelve volumes (three published posthumously) in her thirteen active years; one of these, *Men, Women and Ghosts*, runs to 360 pages, even while excluding the 'purely lyrical' part of her recent writing. *The Complete Poetical Works* was published in 1955 in Boston, and while it confirms the durability (for example) of her oriental fixation, it also records aspirations to a broader formal and thematic range—see the colloquial dramatic poems of *East Wind* (1926)—than she is normally allowed. The major task of her later years was her two-volume Life of Keats (1925), largely based on MS materials. Lives of Lowell include those by S. Foster Damon (1935), Horace Gregory (1958), and Jean Gould (1975). [MI

LOWELL, Robert (Traill Spence) (1917–77), was born in Boston, descended on his mother's side from the Winslows who arrived on the *Mayflower*, and related through his father to the poets James Russell Lowell (his great-great-uncle) and Amy *Lowell (his cousin). Educated first at St Mark's School, where his English teacher was the poet Richard *Eberhart (Eberhart would recall being shown a manuscript of some sixty poems, full of 'raw power'), he entered Harvard College in 1935. This Lowell, however, was not set to follow the family tradition of smooth academic passage and comfortable installation within the cultural and civic life of Boston. After an unsatisfactory freshman year, he got himself engaged to a woman five years his senior, and at Christmas 1936 found himself in a quarrel with his father, during which he famously knocked the parent to the floor. The episode was probably brought on by one of those bouts of mania which would recur with cruel regularity until his death, so Lowell was lucky to have been attended at the time by his mother's psychiatrist, the poet Merrill *Moore. Moore directed his patient away from Harvard towards a more intensely literary milieu, one which included the distinguished poet-professors Allen *Tate and John Crowe *Ransom. Under Ransom's supervision, Lowell studied classics at Kenyon College in Ohio, and there met two of his lifelong friends and mentors, the short-story writer Peter Taylor and the poet-critic Randall *Jarrell. During this time he also met and married the novelist Jean Stafford, who remained a vital energy in his writing life until the couple separated in 1946.

After graduating in 1940, Lowell went south to Louisiana State University, worked with the famous *New Critics, Cleanth Brooks and Robert Penn *Warren, developed a Southern accent, and, more drastically, converted to Catholicism. Further deliberate swerves from the paths of convention ensued: in 1943 he declared himself a conscientious objector to the United States' participation in the Second World War, and was duly incarcerated. The overall result was that when *The Land of Unlikeness* appeared in 1944, its tone of rancorous disaffection and its symbolist habits of baroque Catholic allusion and elaboration had been thoroughly underwritten by this rite of passage from blue-eyed boy to blue-blooded *enfant terrible*. Already Lowell was marked by his aura of great distinction, and from then until his death his name would remain synonymous with the

effort by a contemporary poet to attain classic status, to pitch the force of his pugnacious intellect and his traditional 'European' sensibility against the grain of media-dominated, consumerist–oriented, imperially inclined late-twentieth-century America. (*Imitations*, his book of translations from great poets in different European languages, appeared in 1961, and constituted an oblique assertion that he placed his own career under the aegis of such masters.)

Lowell's second volume, *Lord Weary's Castle* (1946), won great critical esteem and many literary honours: its author seemed to have secured a history for American poetry after the achievements of the modernists. Poems like 'The Quaker Graveyard in Nantucket' served notice that this voice was equal to the burden of the past. Along with Elizabeth *Bishop, John *Berryman, Sylvia *Plath, and, to a lesser extent, Theodore *Roethke, Lowell would create the fashion and generate the force of American poetry for the next three decades. Only Allen *Ginsberg and the *Beats would possess anything like the same impact and glamour, and it was partly in response to the head-on simplicity of the Beats that Lowell's style changed in the 1950s, and he produced his greatest single volume, the epoch-making *Life Studies*, in 1959. This collection initiated an autobiographical project which would henceforth dominate his oeuvre, and resembled both a cubist self-portrait and a gallery of ancestral busts. It is the book of 'a man who has come through', a firmly braced utterance combining the strict feel of traditional form with the free-hanging voice of *vers libre*, and its subjects include the whole private matter of mental collapse and recovery. It felt intimate, new and powerful, and it created the need for a new critical term, *'confessional poetry', which nominated the genre *Life Studies* had established.

With poems like 'Man and Wife', 'Skunk Hour', 'Waking in the Blue', and 'Memories of West Street and Lepke', Lowell had invented a way of getting at life, of making poetry kick and freak at the edge of contemporary reality, and his next two books of original poems, *For the*

Union Dead (1964) and Near the Ocean (1967), extended the effort to arrive at an inclusive, rhetorically heightened contemporary art, one that pushed beyond the domestic and the psychic into the realm of the political. The crises of the Civil Rights movement and the Vietnam War, arising to trouble the aftermath of the Kennedy years, provide the background for poems like 'Fall 1961' and 'Waking Early Sunday Morning', but they also provide a kind of enhanced acoustic which sustains the poetry's aspiration towards a nobler, unconstrained state of being.

During these years Lowell was very much a public figure. His Catholicism behind him, remarried since 1949 to the writer Elizabeth Hardwick, he now lived in New York and enjoyed the status of unofficial poet laureate. He spent his summers writing in Maine and, in the early Sixties, began to teach poetry courses at Harvard every spring; yet he also continued to undergo regular periods of hospitalization, to the great distress of his friends and his deeply afflicted self.

It has been suggested that the drug prescribed for his illness contributed to the change of style which became evident in Lowell's 1969 volume, the aptly entitled Notebook 1967–68. This is a massive accumulation of unrhymed sonnets, poems of immediate, unprepossessing, blunt-edged force, which record not so much the public events of those days as the reactions which the events provoked in Lowell's consciousness. Certainly, the writing is different from the more pointed articulation of the earlier books; his poetic intelligence is on the rampage, swooping into all kinds of biblical, classical, and historical sources for analogies and omens, and deliberately shunning the old, orchestral melodiousness.

Notebook 1967–68 was subsequently revised, reorganized, and vastly extended into three more thematically coherent volumes, History, For Lizzie and Harriet, and The Dolphin, all published in 1973. The content and focus of the second and third of these books reflect yet another upheaval in Lowell's affairs. This occurred when he left New York and Elizabeth Hardwick to become resident in England with the novelist and essayist Lady Caroline Blackwood, whom he married in 1972. These books represent the extreme of Lowell's push to get at life and 'say what happened', making use of letters from Elizabeth ('Lizzie') Hardwick, and generally opening to the scrutiny of readers an intimate world of pain which he had both endured and inflicted. 'Is art worth this?' Elizabeth Bishop asked, and many others contended that it was not. For Lizzie and Harriet and The Dolphin showed Lowell at the height of his wilfulness and daring. Secular, knowing, incriminatory, unconcerned to cajole the ear or to win sympathy, the best poems in them, such as 'Fishnet' and 'Dolphin', manage to acknowledge all the self-awareness and belatedness of the postmodern consciousness, yet they reconfirm poetry as a value-challenging and value-producing activity.

Even so, his next book made it look as if he had been preparing for diminuendo. The mood of Day by Day (1977) is autumnal, ruminant, uninsistent, indulgent. 'We are poor passing facts', he says in 'Epilogue', one of the several self-epitaphs which this last collection contains. There is a mood of general absolution, of simultaneous comprehension and renewal. From the opulent, resurgent poème-à-clef which opens the collection ('Ulysses and Circe', a mythological treatment of the Lowell/Blackwood/Hardwick triangle), to the elegiac valediction of 'Marriage', the poetry is steadily a-tremble between stylistic self-denial and debilitated impulse—a poetry which only Robert Lowell could write, and only at this stage of his life, a life with which (as he acknowledged in 'Dolphin') he 'plotted perhaps too freely'.

Lowell's oeuvre also contains critical essays, tough-minded, knottily composed autobiographical prose, and brilliant memoirs of his personal friends and literary mentors. He also made adaptations for the stage of a trilogy of stories by Melville and Hawthorne, published as The Old Glory in 1964. He did a translation of Racine (Phaedra, 1961) and versions of Aeschylus (Prometheus Bound, 1969, and The Oresteia, 1978). Even so, it is as a poet that he has established his sure place in literary history: his achievement is major, original and undislodgeable. Beginning with aspirations that were Marlovian and impatient of limit, he ended by coming to accommodations that were virtually Chekhovian. All through his career he believed in the mystery of the resonant line, and achieved many that had the formal conclusiveness and proverbial density of major poetry from the past. The strain of the ambition often shows, however, and the price he paid for such magnificence appears in a certain rhetorical assertiveness, an overweening triumphalism of tone which can provoke resistance by its very assuredness. Towards the end of his life and after his death his reputation suffered because of a reaction in critical and academic circles against those New Critical qualities which had originally made him pre-eminent. In a period when the poetics of indeterminacy were in the ascendant, and critics were intent upon exposing the discriminations entailed by a writer's gender or minority status, Lowell's 'canonical' steadfastness and cultural certitudes did not win many advocates. Indeed, the new climate favoured the more tentative art of his great friend and influence Elizabeth Bishop, a poet whom he unfailingly honoured and inevitably overshadowed when he was alive. But there is a linguistic foundedness and perfected form about Lowell's always-intelligent art which secures its inherent poetic value and guarantees its survival.

So far, there has been no collected edition of Robert Lowell's poems. *Selected Poems* (New York, rev. edn., 1977) may be supplemented by the individual volumes noted above and by *Poems 1938–49* (London, 1950); and by *Collected Prose*, ed. Robert Giroux (London, 1987). See also *Robert Lowell: A Biography*, by Ian Hamilton (New York, 1982; London, 1983) and *Robert Lowell, Interviews and Memoirs*, ed. Jeffrey Meyers (Ann Arbor, Mich., 1988).   [SH

LOWRY, Malcolm (1909–57), was born in New Brighton and went to school and university in Cambridge. He is most famous for the novel *Under the Volcano* (London, 1947), but he left many poems, which are now at the University of British Columbia. He planned a collection, to be called *The Lighthouse Invites the Storm*, and in *Selected Poems of Malcolm Lowry* (San Francisco, 1962) Earle Birney observes Lowry's own arrangement. The poems are more choate and formally exact than might be expected. There is even a near-successful villanelle ('Death of a Oaxaquenian'). Many are eloquently descriptive of the agonies of alcoholism, and the fear which prompts it. There is also an interesting comment on the success he achieved with *Under the Volcano* (he wishes he 'had been left in darkness forever to founder and fail'), and a brilliant poem about printing errors ('Strange Type'). Lowry did not take his verse seriously enough fully to locate his own voice, and the redemptive qualities hidden in his major fiction are absent from it. But a gaily ironized note of pain is not, and Birney's capable selection is at least worthy of wider circulation. *The Collected Poetry of Malcolm Lowry*, ed. Kathleen Scherf appeared in Vancouver in 1992. See 'The Unknown Poetry of Malcolm Lowry', by Earle Birney, *British Columbia Literary Quarterly*, 24 (1961).

[MS-S

LOWTHER, Pat(ricia Louise) (1935–75), was born in Vancouver and raised there in a working-class suburb. After leaving school at 16, she worked in the office of a shipbuilding company for two years, then married and had two children. In 1968, having divorced the husband of her first marriage, she married Roy Lowther, an elementary-school teacher and poet with strongly left-wing political views. Deeply committed to socialism herself, Pat Lowther actively supported the New Democratic Party. She also taught creative writing at the University of British Columbia and, just before her death, was elected co-chair of the League of Canadian Poets. Lowther was murdered by her second husband in 1975.

Most of Lowther's verse is written from a feminist perspective. Its expressive power is partly a product of strong contrasts (as in 'Remembering How'), suggestive metaphors (as in 'Seven Purgative Poems'), delicate analogies (as in 'Amphibia'), and variety of descriptive detail (as in 'Two Babies in Two Years'). Several of her poems are concerned with the politics of exploitation from an historically materialist perspective (e.g. 'Regard to Neruda', 'The Dig', 'Chacabuco, The Pit'); one of them ('Coast Range') suggests that simple natural things are the basis of all truth about life.

Lowther's best work may be found in *This Difficult Flowering* (Vancouver, 1968) and in the posthumously published volume, *A Stone Diary* (Toronto, 1977). Her other publications include *Milk Stone* (Ottawa, 1974) and a short—and rather cryptic—broadside, *The Age of the Bird* (Burnaby, 1972). Her juvenilia was published in *Final Instructions: Early and Uncollected Poems*, ed. Dona Sturmanis and Fred Candelaria (Vancouver, 1980). [JSt

LOY, Mina (1882–1966), was born in London into a well-to-do middle-class English family descended from Hungarian Jews and English Protestants. She studied art in Europe and England and developed a style of painting resembling that of the Decadents.

She lived in Florence with her husband Stephen Haweis from 1907 to 1916, divorced him, and married in 1918 Arthur Craven, a heavyweight boxer who survived three rounds with Jack Johnson. Within a year of the marriage Craven was murdered in Mexico. Loy lived in New York for a few years and then settled in Paris. She numbered among her friends avant-garde painters and writers including Carl Van Vechten, Guillaume Apollinaire, Mabel Dodge, Djuna Barnes, and William Carlos *Williams.

Her highly experimental free-verse poems began appearing from 1914 on in *Others*, the *Dial*, and *The *Little Review*. Her most important book of poems, *Lunar Baedeker*, was first published in 1923. Biting satire and caustic cynicism expressed in savage, violent imagery are characteristic of her verse, as in 'Apology for Genius' and 'Der Blinde Junge'.

In 1936 she moved to New York City, which is the scene of much of her later poetry, and in 1954 to Aspen, Colorado, to be with her daughters. She died in Aspen.

The definitive edition of her work is *The Last*

Lunar Baedeker, ed. and intro. Roger L. Conover, and published by the Jargon Society (Highlands, NC, 1982). Virginia M. Kouidis, *Mina Loy: American Modernist Poet* (Baton Rouge, La., 1980) is a critical biography. [DS

LUCIE-SMITH, (John) Edward (McKenzie) (1933–), was born in Kingston, Jamaica. His earliest verse, as exemplified in *A Tropical Childhood* (London, 1961), was largely *Georgian in inspiration. Later he was a leading figure in the *Group, experimenting with dramatic monologues in the manner of Browning; some of these appeared in *Confessions and Histories* (London, 1964). In the early 1970s, after the appearance of his collection *Towards Silence* (London, 1968), he announced that he was tired of 'conventional verse forms' and 'their lack of real flexibility', and that he 'hated the term "poet"'; he began to experiment with poster and *concrete verse, and poems written to be recited, by his friends, to the accompaniment of musical instruments. His themes, he has said, are 'erotic . . . historical and aesthetic . . . and occasionally religious'. Most of his recent collections, with the exception of *The Well Wishers* (London, 1974), have been limited editions containing only a few poems, and he has lately been active in the field of art criticism. [MS-S

LUDVIGSON, Susan (1942–), was born in Rice Lake, Wisconsin. In her twenties she moved to North Carolina and has lived in either North or South Carolina since that time. She is currently professor of English at Winthrop College in South Carolina, and spends half of each year in southern France.

Ludvigson's early poetry, collected in her first two full collections, *Northern Lights* (1981) and *The Swimmer* (1984), was written in short, carefully crafted lines. The subjects were various, ranging from the concerns of women in both the modern world and throughout history to comic views of life and love in the late twentieth century. Occasionally the poems would take on a satirical or even grotesque quality, as in the often-anthologized 'Man Arrested in Hacking Death Tells Police He Mistook Mother-in-Law for Raccoon'. In her later work Ludvigson abandons the devices of satire and comedy in an attempt to come to serious conclusions about the meanings of life and death in what she perceives to be a faithless world. In her most recent poems she focuses on both art and love as the sources from which the meaning that she seeks can be discovered.

Ludvigson's most recent volumes of poetry are *The Beautiful Noon of No Shadow* (Baton Rouge, La., 1986) and *To Find the Gold* (Baton Rouge, 1990). [LS

LUX, Thomas (1946–), was born in Massachusetts and educated at Emerson College. He presently teaches creative writing at Sarah Lawrence College in New York.

Lux casts a scathing eye on the human experience, especially the chaotic version manifest in the United States during the decades following the Second World War. Cruelties inflicted, both consciously and unconsciously, degradations and sorrows borne, misguided aspirations, and above all confusion about how to live—these are the subjects of his poems, but Lux neither judges nor condemns.

His books include *The Drowned River* (1990), *Half Promised Land* (1986), *Sunday* (1979), *The Glassblower's Breath* (1976), and *Memory's Handgrenade* (1972—all Boston). [RS

M

McAULEY, James (1917–76) was born at Lakemba, New South Wales. He wrote his first poems as a teenager at Fort Street High School and his first journalism for student publications while at the University of Sydney (1935–40). In 'Self-Portrait, Newcastle 1942' he described himself at a frustrated time in his life, teaching dull classes in his first job, talking anarchism with friends, and reading Rilke. That year he married.

In 1943 McAuley was transferred to the Directorate of Research and Civil Affairs, and a first visit to New Guinea the following year began a long-standing concern with the affairs of that country. The next year saw his first fame, or notoriety, when (with Harold *Stewart) he perpetrated the Ern Malley hoax, in the magazine *Angry Penguins*, publishing the quasi-apocalyptic poems (titled *The Darkening Ecliptic*) of an imaginary Australian modern bearing a resemblance to George *Barker and Henry *Treece.

McAuley's traditionalist antipathy to modernism was to be thoroughly documented in subsequent critical writing, particularly *The End of Modernity* (1959). A Roman Catholic convert (in 1952), McAuley held many hieratic, antiegalitarian views; but his more personal writings also revealed a man of considerable compassion and affection. These qualities mark the best of his poetry in *Under Aldebaran* (1946), *A Vision of Ceremony* (1956), *Captain Quiros* (1964), *Surprises of the Sun* (1969), and *Time Given* (1976). The widely anthologized 'Because' (remembering his parents), 'Pietà' (remembering the death of a day-old son), and 'Terra Australis' are written in the rhyme and iambic metre McAuley preferred. His symbolism is most effective when at its lightest.

A prolific critic (*The Grammar of the Real*, 1975) and editor (*A Map of Australian Verse*, 1975), James McAuley founded the Sydney magazine *Quadrant* in 1956 (remaining its sole editor till 1963) and from 1961 was Reader in Poetry at the University of Tasmania. *Collected Poems* (Sydney, 1993) is introduced by Leonie Kramer, who edited *James McAuley: Poetry, Essays and Personal Commentary* (St Lucia, Qld., 1988); this has a valuable introduction and notes. There are useful books on McAuley by Vivian Smith (Melbourne, 2nd edn., 1970) and Peter Coleman (Sydney, 1980), and helpful essays by David Bradley in Geoffrey Dutton (ed.), *The Literature of Australia* (Melbourne, 2nd edn., 1976), and by Judith Wright in *Preoccupations in Australian Poetry* (Melbourne, 1965).   [MHu

MacBETH, George (Mann) (1932–92), was born in Shotts, Lanarkshire, the son of a miner and an antique-dealer's daughter. When MacBeth was 3 the family moved to Sheffield, where he was educated at the King Edward VII School, later going to New College, Oxford. From 1957 he lived in London as a producer of talks and poetry programmes for BBC radio, and was an influential member of the *Group; from 1976 he earned his living as a free-lance writer. MacBeth's first two marriages, to Elizabeth Robson and Lisa St Aubin de Téran were both dissolved; in 1989 he married Penelope Ronchetti-Church and settled in Ireland, where he died of motorneurone disease three years later.

MacBeth's admirers have seen a boldly experimental and playful poetic intelligence behind his copious output in a wide variety of styles and forms, while others have found in it a succession of self-dramatizing poses and evidence of 'extra-ordinary gifts extravagantly wasted'. Some of the lighter 'performance' pieces are ingenious, accurate and amusing, but the relish for pain and violence, the addiction to sick jokes and unconvincing slang, the modish properties and themes, all of which marked much of MacBeth's work in the Sixties and Seventies, have worn less well. MacBeth's most interesting writing is obsessively autobiographical. The early experiences that shaped his adult life and work (the death of his father in an air-raid in 1941, and of his mother ten years later; his own bout of rheumatic fever at the age of 12, which left him an invalid for much of his adolescence) are described in a memoir, *A Child of the War* (London, 1987). His long poem, *A War Quartet* (London, 1969), evokes the experience of combatants in the Second World War. Again and again, in shorter poems, MacBeth returns to the war, his parents' deaths, or the pre-war years of their prime in the attempt to untangle the 'war-tied knot' of 'illness or guilt' that presses through his marital crises or sexual unhappiness. Despite the lugubrious tone and *confessional charge of such poems, MacBeth's language is apt to remain stubbornly external, padded or contorted to fit unyielding rhyme- and stanza-schemes or syllabic patterns; the stiffness of this stylized self-revelation not lessened by over-reliance on portentous symbolic diction. Later poems attempt—and sometimes achieve—a spacious pastoral elegance (though often seeming tricked out in traditional dress) and a more scrupulous, tentative approach, celebrating 'the luck of settlement, of finding a piece of land to feel secure on' and 'someone to live there with'; later still, MacBeth evoked the bitter break-up of this idyll (always troubled by undercurrents of sado-masochistic fantasy), resettlement in Ireland, and a new relationship.

Collected Poems 1958–1982 (London, 1989) supersedes *Collected Poems 1958–1970*, and is a fairly rigorous selection from fourteen books of verse, four others—*A War Quartet*; *Lusus: A Verse Lecture* (London 1972); *The Cleaver Gardens* (London, 1986); and *Anatomy of a Divorce* (London, 1988)—being unrepresented. *Trespassing:*

Poems from Ireland (London, 1991) and *The Patient* (London, 1992) appeared subsequently. MacBeth also published *My Scotland: Fragments of a State of Mind* (London, 1973), several novels, and books for children; and edited a number of anthologies, notably the *Penguin Book of Sick Verse* (London, 1963), the *Penguin Book of Animal Verse* (London, 1965), and the *Penguin Book of Victorian Verse* (London, 1969).   [AJ]

McCAFFREY, Steve. See Sound Poetry.

MacCAIG, Norman (1910–) (orig. McCaig), was born in Edinburgh. After graduating in classics from the University of Edinburgh in 1932, MacCaig entered on a career as a primary-school teacher. It was interrupted by the Second World War, during which he was a conscientious objector and suffered the usual penalties. He continued to teach until 1970 when he became Lecturer, and then Reader in Poetry, at the University of Stirling.

MacCaig's first collections were *Far Cry* (1943) and *The Inward Eye* (1946). Both were heavily influenced by the *New Apocalypse school. MacCaig has described his disenchantment with encrusted obscurity in an anecdote. A friend, having read both books, asked: 'When are you publishing the answers?' There then followed what MacCaig has called 'the long haul back to lucidity'. Nothing from his first two books has survived in selected and collected editions published since.

Riding Lights (1956) established the mature style which he has developed and modified in subsequent phases of his work. His poems are usually short, and, in the four books preceding *Surroundings* (1966) neat metricality, rhyme, and stanza were matched with habits of mind and figuration which soon attracted the label 'metaphysical'. As well as Elizabethan and Jacobean conceited poetry, Wallace *Stevens has been cited as an influence. More enabling affections could be poetry by Andrew *Young, John Crowe *Ransom, W. H. *Auden, and Louis *MacNeice.

MacCaig's poems are informed by agnostic common sense, sensuous wonder, and a generous, welcoming sanity. His freer style, its looseness markedly different from that of earlier poems like 'Byre', 'Summer Farm', or 'Fetching Cows', has not prevented his ingenious similes. Free verse, though, from *Surroundings* on, has been accompanied by a tendency to question the metaphor-making once typical of his work. But it is the instinctive if also reasonable free play of the 'five senses' (see 'Centre of Centres') which is close to the animating force of his poetry, and to its figurative techniques. For example, a trout jumping is seen as having 'hung high its drizzling bow | For a count of three— | Heraldic figure on a shield of spray.' A scene is observed, then transformed; an accurate perception is noted and then ornamented. Examples of his ingenious precision are plentiful. Unusually for a Scottish poet, he is a disinterested pictorializer as well as a writer whose imagination is profoundly ethical. Many of his poems celebrate Assynt in north-west Scotland—to some extent his background is that of a Gael disinherited of the Gaelic language. However, many poems also describe Edinburgh; his imagery is more than adaptable to the urban scene.

MacCaig has called history 'filthy', and a strong anti-political thread runs through his work from the mid-1960s ('Old Edinburgh' and 'No Interims in History' are two examples). Along with a number of satirical pieces (chastising pedants, dullards, the sanctimonious, etc.), these bring about a complicating contrast with his many poems about creatures, places, lochs, rivers, mountains, weather, country people, love, and friendships. Intellectually nimble lyricism is, however, the strongest feature of his poetry. Over the range of his work his dextrous imagery, intelligence, compassion, unpredictable similes, metrical skill, and unflagging lyrical energy cumulate into a substantial body of work which has yet to receive the critical attention it deserves.

In the Scottish, and every other, context MacCaig has maintained a characterful, garrulous independence. 'Patriot', for example, declares: 'My only country | is six feet high | and whether I love it or not | I'll die | for its independence.'

Although little more than a squib, 'Patriot' suggests that personal autonomy is not always an easy stance for a Scottish poet to take. It could be the more remarkable in MacCaig's case when it is kept in mind that he was a close friend of Hugh *MacDiarmid, whose poetry MacCaig admires without sharing its underlying beliefs and designs. His work has been influential on younger Scottish writers.

Collected Poems (London, 1990) replaces the 1985 edition. Criticism of MacCaig's poetry includes: Erik Frykman, *Unemphatic Marvels* (Gothenburg, Sweden, 1977), and J. Hendry and R. Ross (eds.), *Norman MacCaig: Critical Essays* (1990). [DED

McCLATCHY, J(oseph) D(onald) (1945–), was born in Bryn Mawr, Pennsylvania and educated at Georgetown University and Yale. He has written three collections of poetry, *Scenes from Another Life* (1983), *Stars Principal* (1986), whose title derives from Gerard Manley Hopkins's 'Spelt from Sybil's Leaves', and *The Rest of the Way* (1990—all New York). McClatchy's verse is intricately wrought in a variety of complex rhyme-schemes. His best poems combine a rich bravura surface with a sophisticated dialectic or narrative. In the ambitious 'Ovid's Farewell', for instance, he develops a complex parable about the poet's ambivalent relations with art and life in flowing verse. In the poem Ovid relates how, knowing his younger brother was about to be bitten by a poisonous snake, he spell-bound the boy with verse, allowing the snake to strike. Occasionally McClatchy's poems can seem too fastidious in their perceptions, and rather complacent about their own powers of formal ingenuity, but often he is a delicate and intriguing poet. He edited *The Vintage Book of Contemporary American Poetry* (New York, 1990); he is also an influential poetry critic, and has written interestingly on Robert *Lowell, Elizabeth *Bishop, and James *Merrill. A collection of his essays, *White Paper*, was published in 1989. He has taught creative writing at a number of American universities, including Princeton and Yale. [MF

McCLURE, Michael (Thomas) (1932–), was born in Kansas, and is now professor at the California College of Arts and Crafts, Oakland. A prolific poet and playwright, and one who is highly thought of among those who attend poetry readings, McClure believes that poetry 'is a muscular principle—an athletic song or whisper of fleshly thought'. He has been an associate of *Ferlinghetti's, and writes in a style sometimes reminiscent of *Creeley and Charles *Olson, but he never gives an impression of being quite as serious or earnest as these two exemplars. Kenneth *Rexroth in his political mood is another influence. There are scores of broadsides, posters, and graphic poems. See *Selected Poems* (New York, 1986).   [MS-S

McCRAE, Hugh (1876–1958), was born in Melbourne into a literary family. He left school early to become a free-lance writer and illustrator, but married the daughter of a pastoralist when barely in his twenties. He could then spend his life cultivating his 'gift for idleness', waiting for the rare bursts of inspiration in which his poems were written. He was in the United States for a few years as an actor, and was for a while a magazine editor in Australia, but seems mainly to have been occupied with his correspondence, which he illustrated, and which gives accounts of his many practical jokes. (A selection of his letters appeared in 1970.) McCrae's last years were spent by the river at Camden, south of Sydney, surrounded by his family of daughters. His wife is said to have developed a 'worn and worried look' from the days of his womanizing. To his friends in Sydney he was 'the gayest of companions'; 'tall and handsome as the sunlight', in Douglas *Stewart's words.

McCrae's poetry was influenced by *fin de siècle* paganism, but with the strange addition of an Australian healthiness. Kenneth *Slessor called it the first real poetry written in Australia, because of its uncompromised aestheticism. McCrae's earliest volume, *Satyrs and Sunlight* (1909), contains almost all of his significant work. It is filled with whimsical caricatures of Greek mythology, with satyrs, fauns, nymphs,

and centaurs, or with historical pantomime figures—cavaliers, wenches, vagabonds—all given a jaunty, larrikin quality, as if they inhabit the Australian sunlight. There are no more than five or six charming pieces of décor which survive out of McCrae's work (anachronistic though these always were); most of his poetry is only successful in fragments, or was left by him fragmentary and without direction.

McCrae's importance for Australian poetry lay in his insistence on sensuousness, physicality, the image, and on musical delicacy as the whole nature of poetry; on pleasure as its entire *raison*. This he held to within an overwhelmingly philistine, mercantile society, where almost all of the rest of literature was sermonizing or of a naturalistic grimness.

A new selection of his verse and prose, projected by Angus & Robertson (Sydney), has been postponed.   [RGr

McCUAIG, Ronald (1908–). Born in Newcastle, New South Wales, Ronald McCuaig resembles his friend and admired contemporary Kenneth *Slessor in two respects: he spent his working life in journalism, and he ceased writing poetry in middle life. His conceits and madrigals in the manner of the seventeenth century have not worn well; where he shines is in colloquial realistic monologues and satires, usually of urban life and clearly influenced by the strongly proletarian tradition of his native city. A fear of censorship on the part of publishers caused him to publish his first collection, *Vaudeville*, privately in 1938, though its sexually explicit passages, as usual in his work, were fairly mild and the attitude to sex hardly joyous.

In all, McCuaig published four collections of verse and one of essays and short stories (*Tales out of Bed*, 1944). All are long out of print. They relate strongly to the half-innocent, half-deeply sophisticated world of urban low-life in Australia before the present era of multiculturalism, and are thus out of fashion now, but a *Selected Poems* was published in Sydney in 1992.   [LM

MacDIARMID, Hugh, pseudonym of Christopher Murray Grieve (1892–1978), was born, a postman's son, in Langholm, Dumfriesshire. MacDiarmid's formal education ended with his father's death in 1911 when the poet was training to be a schoolteacher in Edinburgh. Between 1912 and enlistment in the Royal Army Medical Corps in 1915 he worked on local newspapers in Scotland and South Wales. War service followed, including periods in the Balkans and France where he seems to have enjoyed sufficient leisure to form energetic literary and cultural plans. *Northern Numbers* (1920–2) was followed by his periodical *Scottish Chapbook*. Editorials under the name C. M. Grieve promulgated justifications for writing in the Scots language (see especially, 'A Theory of Scots Letters', repr. in A. Bold (ed.), *The Thistle Rises*, 1984 and A. Riach (ed.), *Hugh MacDiarmid: Selected Prose*, 1992), while he published lyrics in Scots under his pseudonym. In Grieve's case a pseudonym was a liberating device more than a sly disguise. Self-publication indicates something of the provincial climate which the dichotomous poet-critic was determined to sweep away. The Scots language was expounded for its modernist opportunities. He described it as 'an inchoate Marcel Proust—a Dostoevskian debris of ideas—an inexhaustible quarry of subtle and significant sound'.

Annals of the Five Senses, six prose pieces and six poems in English, appeared in 1923 but was written earlier; 1925 saw the publication of his Scots lyrics, *Sangschaw*, followed in 1926 by *Penny Wheep* and his long, audacious, and compelling masterpiece *A Drunk Man Looks at the Thistle*. Using J. Jamieson's *Etymological Dictionary of the Scottish Language* (1808; new edn. in four vols., 1879–82) and Warrack's *Chambers' Scottish Dictionary* (1911) as well as memory, MacDiarmid 'synthesized' his diction by taking words and expressions from the dialects of different districts of Lowland Scotland. The practice has now become established, but MacDiarmid's poetry of the 1920s has not been surpassed (see LALLANS).

Outspoken fervour and incautious ambition typified MacDiarmid's career from beginning to end, and was matched by prodigious productivity. Norman *MacCaig has suggested that Mac-

Diarmid's motto might have been 'excess is not enough'. Inconsistency, recklessness, and passionate intellectualism were among the risks MacDiarmid took. 'I'll hae nae hauf-way hoose, but aye be whaur | Extremes meet' expresses perfectly his aesthetic, and perhaps also his temperamental delight in turbulence. In politics, a thoroughly foregrounded concern, his extremism is more controversial. His use of Scots was perhaps inseparable from nationalist passion, although not its primary motive. In the early 1920s he advocated Italian fascism; he was a founder member of the National Party of Scotland (1928), from which he was expelled in 1933 on grounds of communism. He joined the Communist Party soon after and was expelled in 1938 on grounds of nationalism. He rejoined in 1956 as a gesture of support for the Soviet invasion of Hungary.

His personal circumstances in the 1930s reflected the poetic, philosophical, and political turmoil into which his work led him and to which his mind always seemed predisposed. The ruthless 'First Hymn to Lenin' and adamant but sweeping 'On a Raised Beach' express his political and private determination. He was divorced in 1931, married Valda Trevlyn soon after, and in 1933 moved to the remote Shetland island of Whalsay. He suffered a nervous breakdown in 1935. Not far off 50, in 1942, he was conscripted for war work in Clydeside industry.

MacDiarmid ceased writing in Scots around 1934 and the collection of that year, *Stony Limits*, marks the extent to which he chose to engage with philosophy, science, linguistics, communism, and facts as poetic material. 'A poetry full of erudition, expertise, and ecstasy', was how he stated his ambition for an intellectual epic in which Mind would be the hero and which was to be called *Mature Art*. Parts of this largely unrealized *magnum opus*—the work of a poet who believed in 'giganticism'—came out separately as *In Memoriam James Joyce* (1955), 'The Kind of Poetry I Want', 'Cornish Heroic Song for Valda Trevlyn', and others.

Although acknowledged in Scotland as crucial to Scottish poetry, culture, and politics (see

SCOTTISH RENAISSANCE), MacDiarmid's signifi-
cance as a major figure of modernism has been
harder to establish. In England particularly he is
little more than a reputation assembled from
misleading reports and unsympathetic assess-
ments.

The Complete Poems, 2 vols. (London, 1978) was
reissued in 1985 with an appendix of ten addi-
tional poems. Carcanet (Manchester) published
a Selected Poems in 1992, and also a Selected Prose.
There is an annotated edition of A Drunk Man
Looks at the Thistle, ed. K. Buthlay (1987). Alan
Bold edited The Letters (London, 1984; see also
C. Kerrigan (ed.), The Hugh MacDiarmid—
George Ogilvie Letters, 1988). There is a biography
by Alan Bold (London, 1988). Selections of Mac-
Diarmid's essays and fiction will be found in The
Uncanny Scot, ed. K. Buthlay (1968); Selected
Essays, ed. D. Glen (1969); and The Thistle Rises,
ed. A. Bold (1984). [DED

MacDONAGH, Thomas (1878–1916), was
born in Cloughjordan, Co. Tipperary. After var-
ious periods of teaching, he took his BA (1910)
and wrote an MA on Thomas Campion for Uni-
versity College, Dublin, where he was a lecturer
from 1912. He joined the Gaelic League in 1901
and in 1908 began teaching with Pádraig Pearse
at St Enda's School. A leader of the Easter Rising
and one of the seven signatories of the procla-
mation of a provisional Irish Republic, he was
executed in May 1916.

MacDonagh had plays performed at the
Abbey and in Edward Martyn's Irish Theatre.
He published several volumes of poems from
1903 onwards—collected by James *Stephens
as The Poetical Works of Thomas MacDonagh
(Dublin and London, 1916). His earlier poetry is
slight and conventional, but from Songs of Myself
(1910) onwards his manner becomes less
artificial. His best collection was Lyrical Poems
(1913), and the best of those are translations
from the Irish where (most famously in 'The
Yellow Bittern') he reproduces Irish metrical
forms in English. Of related importance are the
chapters in Literature in Ireland: Studies Irish and
Anglo-Irish (Dublin, 1916) where he acutely
identifies 'the Irish mode'—the prosody of Irish

English induced by the Irish language. His the-
ory and practice here influenced later writers
such as Austin *Clarke (who succeeded to his
lectureship at UCD). [BO'D

MacDONALD, Cynthia (1928–), was born in
New York City. After graduating from Benning-
ton College, she pursued a career as an opera
and concert singer. In 1970 she earned an MA
from Sarah Lawrence College and began a new
career as poet and teacher. She taught at Johns
Hopkins University before settling at the Uni-
versity of Houston, Texas, where she is now a
professor; she has also been a research fellow
at the Houston/Galveston Psychoanalytic
Institute.

Macdonald's extra-literary vocations as opera
singer and psychoanalyst together hint at the
distinctive flavour of her poetry, which features
a gaudy theatricality placed in the service of a
thorough anatomy of human compulsions. She
writes with great wit and a refreshing freedom
of invention; for Macdonald poetry is not con-
fession or documentary but a peculiarly fabu-
lous species of fiction. Her poems are populated
by a variety of grotesque and comic types, from
circus freaks to cheerleaders, each one becom-
ing an allegorical caricature of some essential
human trait. In form her poetry is generous,
making full and expressive use of the page-as-
stage; and while precision is not one of her most
notable qualities, the energy of her imagination,
by turns boisterous and ominous, gives her lan-
guage its own baroque contours. Macdonald's
most recent books are (W)holes (New York,
1980) and Alternate Means of Transport (New
York, 1985). [RG

McDONALD, Nan (1921–74), was born at East-
wood in Sydney, graduated from the University
of Sydney in arts, and worked for the publishers
Angus and Robertson as an editor. McDonald
published three volumes of poetry and a Selected
Poems (Sydney, 1969). She was unmarried, lived
always with members of her family, and died of
cancer when she was 52.

McDonald's poetry is mostly sombre and
deathward-drawn. Its style is muted and aus-

tere, refined and unpretentious, and it exults in cold, inhuman places (like the smoky blue vistas of the coast south from Sydney, the alpine country of New South Wales, and the steep Hawkesbury River area). Her relatively early death was evidently long anticipated and accepted. A stoic, Protestant religion underlies much of her work.   [RGr

McDONALD, Roger (1941–), was born at Young, New South Wales, and educated at Scots College, Sydney. He worked as a teacher, then as a producer with ABC radio and television in Hobart, 1967–9, before becoming an editor with the *University of Queensland Press in Brisbane. During his years there (1969–76) he supervised the Paperback Poets series, which was an important place of publication for the self-styled poetic *'Generation of '68'. McDonald's two volumes of verse—*Citizens of the Mist* (1968) and *Airship* (1975)—were published by the press (St Lucia, Qld.). The latter includes prose poems, notably the sequence 'Night, day, metal, water' on themes of war, which anticipate both his abandonment of verse and the subject of his first novel, *1915* (1979). Set principally at the Gallipoli landings, the book was turned into a television series. McDonald's subsequent novels are *Slipstream* (1982) and *Rough Wallaby* (1989). His screenplay for the television miniseries on soprano Dame Nellie Melba was published as a novel in 1988.

McDonald's verse encompasses meditations on Tasmanian and Antarctic places, as well as the solitary, crazy freedom of farming or going 'over the top' in trench warfare. Items glimpsed apparently at random—as in the poems 'Components' and 'Three nineteenth century objects on a shelf'—are made strange by McDonald's attention. Synaesthetic blurring of sound and sight attracts him, as does the imagining of metaphoric other worlds, for instance in the poem 'Spider Garden'. Whether or not, as James Tulip contended in the *Penguin New Literary History of Australia* (1988), 'an undercurrent of darkish realism beneath the surface of his verse . . . has steadily drawn him across into the world of prose and history', McDonald (now

settled on a farm near Braidwood with his wife, the poet Rhyll *McMaster) seems to have stilled for good his career as a poet.   [PP

McDOWELL, Robert (1953–), was born in Los Angeles and went to local public schools. He attended the University of California, Santa Cruz, received an MFA in writing from Columbia University in 1976, and taught at Indiana State University, Evansville from 1978 to 1984. He is the most outspoken proponent of the *New Narrative movement. From 1981 through 1990 he and Mark Jarman edited *The Reaper*, which was devoted to narrative poems and became a sounding board for its editors' hyperbolic manifestos on the vitality of contemporary narrative poems in comparison to the lyric, which they once proclaimed dead. Since 1985 he has been publisher and editor of Story Line Press, a small press publishing poetry, fiction, and criticism. His first book of poems, *Quiet Money* (New York, 1987), consists of eighteen narratives focusing on the lives of ordinary men and women—businessmen, librarians, bowlers—often down on their luck, though never less than spirited. At their weakest, the poems are sentimental and melodramatic. At their strongest, they are acute renderings of character brought sharply into focus within the flux of everyday life. This is true of 'In the Photograph You See', a chilling psychological portrait of the imaginary life of a small-town tailor. The title-poem is about a bootlegger who made transatlantic flights for liquor during the depression before Lindbergh's historic trip and, in the aftermath of Lindbergh's public tragedy, learns to appreciate the compensatory pleasures of an unheroic domestic life.   [R McP

MacEWEN, Gwendolyn (1941–87), was born in Toronto and raised there and in Winnipeg. She dropped out of school at 18 to pursue a career in poetry. Following a short marriage to poet Milton *Acorn, she published the chapbooks *Selah* (1961), *The Drunken Clock* (1961), and *The Rising Fire* (1963, with Raymond *Souster's influential Contact Press), before she established her reputation with *A Breakfast for Barbarians* (Toronto, 1966).

Both *A Breakfast for Barbarians* and *The Shadow Maker* (Toronto, 1969) contain poems where the musicality of the language and vividness of image are elucidated with a surging, almost anarchic energy. An eye for the absurd in the commonplace and for emotional power in the serene are hallmarks of MacEwen's work.

Her collections *The Armies of the Moon* (Toronto, 1972), *Magic Animals* (Toronto, 1975), and *The Fire Eaters* (Ottawa, 1976), as well as the volume of travel writings about Greece, *Mermaids and Ikons* (1978), owe a debt to mythology. MacEwen's second husband, Greek singer Nikos Tsingos, introduced her to the Mediterranean mentality, and the voice she developed during this period is haunted by doubts about the border between dream and reality, a theme which underlies her novel about the Egyptian Pharoah Akhenaton, *King of Egypt, King of Dreams* (1971).

A fascination with the Arab world drew her to the subject of Lawrence of Arabia in *The T. E. Lawrence Poems* (Oakville, Ont., 1982)—her most completely integrated work. In it, the poet questions the line between psychotic delusion and rational disintegration.

MacEwen's interest in narrative was first manifested in *Terror and Erebus: A Verse Play for Radio*, written in 1965. Her treatment of the fateful Franklin Expedition of 1848 (which Northrop Frye had dubbed the 'unwritten Canadian epic') perceives the Canadian Arctic as an interior landscape rather than an exterior realm, a place inhabited by disembodied voices which exist only through the power of description, memory, and chronicle. MacEwen included the play in the 'Apocalypse' section of her final volume, *Afterworlds* (Toronto, 1987), a hauntingly poignant book; many of the poems foreshadow her death in the November of its year of publication. Throughout *Afterworlds* the poems flirt with the abstract, the inconceivable, and the ethereal, as if the voice of the poet were looking back from some point beyond life, still chronicling, still witnessing, transcribing, and describing. [BM

McFADDEN, David (1940–), lived all of his first thirty-eight years in the small-town city of Hamilton, Ontario. He has been a proof-reader, newspaper reporter, journal editor, novelist, and a prolific poet. His early *Letters from the Earth to the Earth* (Toronto, 1968) presented observations of domestic and local life, its blissful strange ordinariness, but in the 1970s his poems took on a darker tone, as in the well-known 'A Typical Canadian Family Visits Disney World'.

In 1978 McFadden's great change of life led him away from the family to British Columbia, and into a series of long poems whose subjects are darkness, chance, and the emotional and mystical elements of the everyday. The 1980s poetry is personal, but more fictive; the poet's progress is through the darker corners of life and imagination, but he still looks quirkily beyond appearances for the real forms of human life. Four novels (three in the 'Great Lakes' series) parallel this progress, which culminates in the hundred Baudelairean prose sonnets of *Gypsy Guitar* (Vancouver, 1987). In all of this work McFadden remains the comic metaphysician reporting on the experimental nature of daily life.

There are two representative selections: *My Body was Eaten by Dogs* (Toronto, 1981) and *The Art of Darkness* (Toronto, 1984). [RB

McFADDEN, Roy (1921–), was born in Belfast, read law at Queen's University in that city, and has lived there ever since with his wife and a large family, practising as a solicitor. Encouraged especially by Herbert *Read, McFadden published a promising first collection during the Second World War, but it seems to have been lost among more metropolitan voices. What may have gone against McFadden is that the vision of war he presented was largely Yeatsian. After his third book he published no major collection for twenty-four years, but the bitter circumstances of Ulster enabled a distinct narrative voice to emerge. Of the law-courts revisited McFadden says: 'Keep handy in your briefcase | A summons and a shout: | Not everyone who comes here | Is certain to get out.' By purging his voice of oratory he gained eloquence, and by remaining in Northern Ireland he has come to stand at stage centre.

There is a *Selected Roy McFadden*, ed. John Boyd (Belfast, 1943), but it is slight in relation to the total oeuvre. This includes *Swords and Ploughshares* (London, 1943); *Flowers for a Lady* (London, 1945); *The Heart's Townland* (London, 1947); *The Garryowen* (London, 1971); *Verifications* (Belfast, 1977); *A Watching Brief* (Belfast, 1979); *Letters to the Hinterland* (Dublin, 1986) and *After Seymour's Funeral* (Belfast, 1990).
[PDH

McGINLEY, Phyllis (1908–78), was born in Oregon and educated at the universities of Utah and California. She won the Pulitzer Prize for Poetry in 1960, and, with Dorothy *Parker as her only equal, she is the best woman writer of light verse that America has produced. Yet to call this poetry 'light' is not altogether accurate, if by this we mean poetry that is jokey or entirely frivolous. W. H. *Auden, introducing the prize-winning selection, claims that her poetry could not have been written by a man because it is not nostalgic, like the verse of *Betjeman. Certainly this is very much the verse of the normal wife-and-mother ('Why, if (according to A. Gesell) | The minds of children ring clear as a bell, | Does every question one asks a tot | Receive the similar answer—"What?" '). Also, in its rhyming ingenuity, it is very close to Praed or Byron ('Let sobs be broken, let tears be saline. | Charles & Company has no male line'); but, as Auden notes, it is never ostentatious in rhyme (Ogden *Nash rhymes such as 'anthropophagi/sarcophagi' don't occur). Another of McGinley's conspicuous talents is to be able to write poems about the minutiae of everyday life that are neither silly nor facetious: for example, 'My Six Toothbrushes'. When she is satirical, the satire is gentle. She can write a *Graves-like 'serious' poetry (see 'The Landscape of Love'). In her 'religious' verse, mainly about saints and theologians, she seems a little embarrassed by the sometimes conflicting demands of piety and common sense. The literary satires, such as 'Publisher's Party', seem more assured; and

some of the Second World War poems (like 'Landscape Without Figures') are both moving and difficult to reconcile with Auden's definition. She uses, exclusively, conventional forms and metres. The volume, with Auden's introduction, is *Times Three* (New York, 1960; London, 1961). [GE

McGOUGH, Roger. See Liverpool Poets.

McGRATH, Thomas (1916–90), was born the grandson of Irish Catholic homesteaders on a farm near Sheldon, North Dakota. His childhood was punctuated by often-violent labour unrest, which gave him a deep feeling for social justice. McGrath was educated in a grab-bag of places, from a one-room schoolhouse to the University of North Dakota, Louisiana State University, and New College, Oxford, where he was a Rhodes Scholar. His itinerant resumé includes work as a dockyard labour organizer in New York, two years stationed in the Aleutians during the Second World War, and stints of film-writing and college teaching that were interrupted in the 1950s when he was blacklisted as a communist.

McGrath's political views have contributed to his neglect by mainstream literary critics and publishers. His pseudo-autobiographical epic, *Letter to an Imaginary Friend* (Book I, 1970; Book II, 1985), contains vivid images from a turbulent life transmuted into verse that is alternately lyrical, fragmentary, imitative, and unruly, but often subtly controlled and poised. Written over thirty years in at least six countries, the poem builds toward a dream-vision of a better world not unlike the New Jerusalem of Blake and *Auden.

Though he occasionally succumbed to sentimentality, McGrath was a superb craftsman, comfortable with a rich variety of forms and diction. Lyrics like 'The World of the Perfect Tear' and 'The Buffalo Coat' make good use of traditional metres and rhyme. In 'The Bread of this World' one hears the full sounds of Hopkins and Dylan *Thomas. Often compared to Whitman's, McGrath's technique has, except for its occasional invective, as much in common with *Eliot's, Auden's, and *MacNeice's.

Selected Poems, 1938–1988 (Port Townsend, Wash., 1988) contains the best of McGrath's shorter work. See also *Praises and Dispraises*, by Terence Des Pres (New York, 1988) and *The Revolutionary Poet in the United States* ed. Frederick C. Stern (St Louis, Mo., 1988).   [DM

McGUCKIAN, Medbh (1950–), was born in Belfast. She studied at Queen's University, taught English at St Patrick's College, Knock, and was the first woman to be writer-in-residence at Queen's.

McGuckian has described her territory as 'the feminine subconscious or semi-consciousness'. Rivers, clouds, clothes, flowers, ferns, and shadows are her favoured archetypes, predictable in themselves but never treated predictably. There are few abstractions in her work: ideas are translated directly into imagery, giving the sense of a keen intellect at play, or opulently dreaming. Consistently inventive and witty, sometimes self-regardingly obscure, often haunting, McGuckian's work seems closer to that of John *Ashbery and the American *Language poets than to current British and Irish writing. She has published four volumes to date: *The Flower Master* (Oxford and New York, 1982); *Venus and the Rain* (Oxford and New York, 1984); *On Ballycastle Beach* (Oxford and New York, 1988); and *Marconi's Cottage* (Newcastle upon Tyne, 1992).   [CAR

McHUGH, Heather (1948–), was born in California. By the time McHugh, as a Radcliffe undergraduate, had been admitted to Robert *Lowell's graduate workshop at Harvard, her first published poem had already appeared in *The New Yorker*. Educated further at Denver University (MA 1972), she taught at SUNY Binghamton and elsewhere, most recently at the University of Washington and Warren Wilson College. She has published four poetry collections, and a French translation, *D'Apres Tout: Poems by Jean Follain* (Princeton, NJ, 1981). With her husband, Niko Boris, she has also translated the poems of Blaga Dimitrova: *Because the Sea is Black* (Middletown, Conn., 1989).

McHugh's affection for jazz and her early experiments with painting give her poems an uncommon physicality, the immediate heard quality of speech. Characteristic too are her swift, witty turns of phrase, the sense of the mind observing itself. Although rich in image, the work is often abstract rather than narrative, philosophical rather than emotional in impulse. In the later *To the Quick* and *Shades* (Middletown, 1987; 1988), McHugh's poems have grown darker, metaphysical in more complex ways, though still half-song, half-argument. Most representative is the fifth collection, *Held Sway: New and Selected Poems* (Middletown, 1993).   [MB

McKAY, Claude (1889–1948), was born in Sunny Ville, Jamaica. His father was a prosperous farmer. As a young man, he lived in Kingston, where he met the English folklorist Edward Jekyll, and it was Jekyll who encouraged him to write poems in dialect. His first two books of poems, all in dialect, *Songs of Jamaica* (Kingston, 1912) and *Constab Ballads* (London, 1912), are much concerned with the harsh lives of ordinary people, both in rural, mountainous areas, where he grew up, and in cities. He encountered the worst aspects of city life during a brief stint with the constabulary. Shortly after, McKay left Jamaica for the United States, never to return. He lived mainly in New York, but travelled widely in Europe. He was an early advocate of black liberation, both in America and in colonial Africa, and became an American citizen in 1940. In his last years he converted from communism to Roman Catholicism, and taught at a Catholic school in Chicago.

His first American volume of poems, *Harlem Shadows* (1922) inaugurated the *Harlem Renaissance. It was preceded by *Spring in New Hampshire* (London, 1920). His later poetry tended to treat politically radical themes within traditional verse-forms. Two of his most famous poems, 'If We Must Die' and 'The White House', for instance, are sonnets. The former, which was reputedly quoted by Churchill as wartime prime minister, exhorts victims of racist oppression to fight back, however hopeless the odds. The latter is a bitter indictment of presidential indifference.

Other collections include *Selected Poems* (New York, 1953) and *Selected Poetry of Claude McKay*, ed. Wayne F. Cooper (New York, 1973). *Banana Bottom* (New York, 1933) is his most successful novel. *A Long Way from Home* (New York, 1937) and *My Green Hills of Jamaica* (Washington, DC, 1975) are autobiographical works. See James R. Giles, *Claude McKay* (Boston, 1976) and Wayne F. Cooper, *Claude McKay: A Biography* (Baton Rouge, La., 1987).   [MR

MACKENZIE, Kenneth (1913–55), was born in Perth, Western Australia. He was disowned by his family after he failed to persevere in three attempts at his education: he ran away from high school, agricultural college, and a university law course.

Mackenzie went to Sydney at 21, taking his poems and arriving unannounced on Kenneth *Slessor's doorstep. Work was found for him in journalism, but he proved an unreliable employee and moved about amongst various newspapers. He married at 21 and was to have two children. At 24 he published his first novel and first volume of poetry. The novel, *The Young Desire It* (1937), appeared under the name Seaforth Mackenzie, as did all he wrote in that form, and is usually considered the best of his four works of fiction. He had already become an alcoholic and was sexually promiscuous. Drafted into the army, Mackenzie was a prison guard at Cowra in 1944 when there was a mass, intentionally suicidal breakout of Japanese prisoners of war (although he was not on duty that night). This event became the subject of his novel *Dead Men Rising* (1951). During the war he published one further book of poetry, *The Moonlit Doorway* (1944).

On his discharge from the army, Mackenzie was hospitalized for his drinking, and then separated from his wife and children. He lived in the Blue Mountains, outside Sydney, in a bark-roofed hut without electricity or water, on a block of land his wife owned. In the remaining ten years of his life he produced three novels, receiving three one-year Commonwealth Liter-

ary Fund fellowships (awarded by Slessor), and the best of his poetry, which was left unpublished until it appeared in *The Poems of Kenneth Mackenzie* (Sydney, 1972). He occasionally worked as a labourer in his last years, was hospitalized again, and was reduced at times, his wife said, to drinking methylated spirits. At the age of 42, while he was on a visit to a friend at Goulburn, south of Sydney, he was found lying drowned in a small creek.

Mackenzie's is overwhelmingly the poetry of a painful consciousness. His facile early work is full of an assertive sexuality, but for all its efforts after sensuousness has something irritable, divided, and metallic about it. He was later influenced by Edward *Thomas (too plainly so in pieces like 'By one small stream . . .'), and these poems about suffering and its occasional lapses (written either formally or in free verse) are limpid, cleanly crafted, natural, without self-pity, and full of a helpless compassion. Most notable are the poems set in hospitals, such as 'An Old Inmate'.   [RGr

MACKIE, Alasdair. See LALLANS.

MACKINNON, Lachlan (1956–), was born in Aberdeen and educated at Charterhouse and Christ Church College, Oxford. He teaches English at Winchester College and is a regular reviewer of new verse.

Mackinnon's first collection, *Monterey Cypress* (London, 1988), shows a talent for economical, evocative poems deriving from place ('Here'), identity ('Fallodon Wood'), and exile (a sequence of Parisian pieces). His interest in uncertainty provides the book's most direct and successful poem, 'In a French Court', the monologue of an abused child, although other attempts at directness can seem rhetorical and grandiose ('La Cimetière Montparnasse').

The Coast of Bohemia (London, 1991) is far more powerful, focused on the experience of breakdown and distinguished by honesty and painstaking accuracy ('Nature Poem', 'Mania').

A selection of Mackinnon's poems is contained in *New Chatto Poets* (London, 1986). His critical books are: *Eliot, Auden, Lowell: Aspects of* the *Baudelairean Inheritance* (London, 1983); *Shakespeare the Aesthete: An Exploration of Literary Theory* (London, 1988); and *The Lives of Elsa Triolet* (1992). [SO'B

MACLEAN, Alasdair (1926–), was born in Glasgow. Despite some self-regarding views on 'the pain and indignity' of writing poetry, and occasional hectoring, Alasdair Maclean's *From the Wilderness* (London, 1973) announced a late-arriving talent willing to engage with nature in the raw and the hard crofting life of Ardnamurchan in north-west Scotland from the basis of convincingly unsentimental experience. Maclean's best work is harsh and mediated through a voice which he has described as that of 'a peasant who writes poetry'. He has been ruefully conscious of the distance which has grown between him and his origins, although it could be argued that his vivid disclosures of waning Highland life make that ostensible gap unimportant.

Waking the Dead (London, 1976) closes with a sequence in memory of the poet's mother—'to draw the thin milk from two half-starved cows | she swung her sickle in a field of stones'. There is an anger and virulence in his writing about nature ('Hen Dying', for example, or 'Rams'), and in many poems a relentless, sometimes wooden iambic rhythm lends an appropriate pulse to what in the end seems the limitation of a misanthropic point of view. On the positive side, there is nothing meek, humble, or yielding in Maclean's poetry. An angry assertiveness, however, sometimes leads to a damaging contempt and a punitive relish for the hurts on which much of his vision is founded.

Night Falls on Ardnamurchan (London, 1984) is a ruminative, impressive prose account of 'the twilight of a crofting community'. [DED

MacLEAN, Sorley (1911–), was born in the island of Raasay. His people were Gaelic-speaking crofters who included notable traditional singers. At Edinburgh University he studied English literature and discovered his own voice as a poet: in English initially, but soon exclusively in Gaelic. After graduating he taught Eng-

lish at schools in the Highlands and in Edinburgh. During the war he saw active service in North Africa and was wounded at El Alamein; his major collection, *Dàin do Eimhir* (Glasgow, 1943), was prepared for publication in his absence. On returning to Scotland he married Renée Cameron and resumed his teaching career, becoming headmaster of Plockton High School in 1956. On retiring he moved to Braes in Skye, where he lives now. He was writer-in-residence at Edinburgh University, 1973–4, and has received honorary degrees from the Universities of Dundee, Edinburgh, and Grenoble and from the National University of Ireland.

MacLean's reputation was assured by 'Poems to Eimhear', with its portrayal of an individual caught in the cross-fire between personal and political imperatives. His liberation of Gaelic poetry from formal and intellectual atrophy was no less dramatic than *MacDiarmid's emancipation of Scottish literature from the 'kailyard'. The hallmarks of his poetry include warring idealism and pessimism, a dialectic of symbols drawn from the Highland landscape, and a sense of the interconnectedness of all human experience.

The bilingual collection *Reothairt is Contraigh/Spring Tide and Neap Tide* (Edinburgh, 1976) gave MacLean the opportunity to sift and group the pre-war and war poems, and to augment them with more recent compositions. The collected editions of his poetry are *Poems 1932–82* (Philadelphia, Pa., 1987: English only) and *From Wood to Ridge* (Manchester, 1989: bilingual). His life and work are discussed in *Sorley MacLean: Critical Essays*, ed. R. J. Ross and J. Hendry (Edinburgh, 1986). [WG

MacLEISH, Archibald (1892–1982), was born and brought up in Glencoe, Illinois. He graduated from Yale in 1915 and—having married and served at the front in the First World War—from Harvard Law School in 1919. After three frustrating years as a lawyer in Boston, he went to Paris to live by his poetry alone, returned to America in 1928, and spent most of the 1930s as a journalist on *Fortune* magazine. Appointed Librarian of Congress in 1939, MacLeish quickly won his way into President Roosevelt's circle of confidential advisers, becoming director of the newly created Office of Facts and Figures in 1941 (which placed him in a key position respecting wartime propaganda in America), Assistant Secretary of State in 1944, and chairman of the US delegation at the formation of UNESCO in 1945. After Roosevelt's death MacLeish's days as a government official were numbered, and in the late 1940s he turned from public to academic life, moving back to Boston to become Boylston Professor at Harvard (1949–62).

MacLeish's poetry—like his professional career—reflects the changing intellectual trends of his time. The traditional lyric forms and lilting rhythms of his first two books, *Songs for a Summer's Day (A Sonnet-Cycle)* (1915) and *Tower of Ivory* (1917), as he later commented, 'took off from Swinburne'. In Paris he discovered modernism and French Symbolism: *The Pot of Earth* (1925) and *The Hamlet of A. MacLeish* (1928), long poems on the conflict between personal desire and natural law, take many of their techniques and symbols from *The Waste Land*; and the lyrics in *Streets in the Moon* (1926) are indebted to *Pound, Laforgue, and Mallarmé. Back in America, MacLeish's new patriotic and political concerns joined an equally new declamatory style in *New Found Land: Fourteen Poems* (1930), *Frescoes for Mr. Rockefeller's City* (1933), and *Panic: A Play in Verse* (1935), and soon became vigorously partisan: *Public Speech: Poems* (1936) defines true (liberal-democratic) against specious (communist) brotherhood, while *America Was Promises* (1939) urges Americans to remain loyal to the government's New Deal doctrines. Wanting a more immediately far-reaching vehicle for his topical themes, MacLeish wrote verse plays for radio (*The Fall of the City*, 1937, and *Air Raid*, 1938), and verse illustrations to a sequence of photographs (*Land of the Free—U.S.A.*, 1938). Less choric and more personal, *Actfive and Other Poems* (1948) shows a fresh clarity and formal variety, thus launching the last phase of MacLeish's poetry. His *Collected Poems 1917–1952* (1952) won a Pulitzer Prize, a National Book Award, and a Bollingen Prize; but the later

elegies and reflections on old age in *The Wild Old Wicked Man and Other Poems* (1968) are perhaps his best (if least ambitious) poems, and the Oscar for the documentary screenplay, *The Eleanor Roosevelt Story* (1965), his most notable award. The later verse plays include *J. B.* (1958), a modern version of Job, and *Herakles* (1967), a modern version of the Greek myth. *A Time to Speak: The Selected Prose* (1941) and *A Time to Act: Selected Addresses* (1943) are good companions to his poetry of the 1930s; *Poetry and Experience* (London and Boston, 1961), however, contains more sober criticism. See also *New and Collected Poems 1917–1976* (Boston, 1976), and *MacLeish* by Signi Lenea Falk (New York, 1965).   [NE

McMASTER, Rhyll (1947–), was born in Brisbane and attended Queensland University. In her early twenties she married the poet and novelist Roger *McDonald, and much of her time in the years which followed was taken up with their three children. In the late 1970s she moved from Brisbane to Canberra, where she studied to qualify as a nurse, but before she began work in a hospital she and McDonald bought a farm near Braidwood, outside Canberra, where they have lived ever since. Farming has proved as time-consuming as child-rearing for McMaster, and for this reason her poetic output has been sparing.

Though she has only produced two slender volumes of poetry, McMaster is one of Australia's most highly regarded woman poets. *The Brineshrimp* (St Lucia, Qld., 1972) was notable for its close observation of commonplace things, and for its weight of unstated emotion. *Washing the Money* (Sydney, 1986) won a major prize, though it contained less than thirty pages of poetry. Its best poems are detailed and quirky recollections of childhood events.   [JG

McMICHAEL, James (1939–), was born in Pasadena, a poet of southern California, a region better represented in American politics —Nixon and Reagan—than in American poetry. McMichael is unusually sensitive to place: what Paterson, New Jersey, was to William Carlos *Williams, Pasadena is to him.

His father's profession—he was a real-estate developer—increased that sensitivity. McMichael has written three books of poems, as well as a study of James *Joyce, *Ulysses and Justice* (Princeton, NJ, 1991), but his claim on readers' attention rests primarily on his long poem *Four Good Things* (Boston, 1980), a sprawling autobiographical meditation on life, death, and real-estate, set in—of course—southern California. McMichael's poetic line and rhythm verge on prose; the weakly enjambed verse paragraphs allow an essayistic voice to emerge, following its own connections and associations. The poem opens with the poet's mother dying of cancer, his father pushing the development of Pasadena—two kinds of modern blight, cell division out of control. It is loose and capacious enough to hold a capsule history of Pasadena, its architectural growth amid the surrounding desert serving as a figure for the growth of the poet's mind and of the poem. McMichael's earlier books are *Against the Falling Evil* (Chicago, 1971) and *The Lover's Familiar* (Boston, 1978); a discerning essay on his work is included in Robert Hass's *Twentieth Century Pleasures* (New York, 1984). [CB

McMILLAN, Ian (1957–), is one of the new wave of young free-lance *performance poets. Born in Barnsley, Yorkshire, he learnt his stage technique as a stand-up comic in Yorkshire, before forming Versewagon with John Turner and Martyn Wiley. Later renamed the Circus of Poets, the three are a poetry performance group much in demand in schools, and at literature festivals nation-wide. McMillan has also written radio comedy and co-hosted creative-writing programmes for young people on national television.

McMillan's poems cover a wide range of contemporary subjects, but he does not write down to his audience by offering a loaded 'message'. Although primarily aiming to entertain, his poems work equally well on the printed page as in performance. He has written with verve and invention in a wide variety of verse-forms. He is never dull and can often be extremely funny, as in the satirical 'Poem Badly Translated from the Language', which sends up translatorese, 'The Soft White Pillowcase Boys', on an interview for a writer-in-residenceship, or 'Cracking Icicles in Totley Tunnel', on the 1984/5 mineworkers' strike. See: *The Changing Problem* (Manchester, 1980), *An Anthology from Versewagon* (Barnsley, 1982), *Now It Can Be Told* (Manchester, 1983), and *Selected Poems* (Manchester, 1987). [JDB

MacNEICE, Louis (1907–63), was born in Belfast and educated at Marlborough and Merton College, Oxford, where he took a first-class degree in classics and philosophy. He taught classics for a time in Birmingham and London, but for most of his working life he was a writer and producer for BBC radio, especially in the legendary Features Department.

Though MacNeice's precocious first book, *Blind Fireworks* (1929), attracted little attention, he emerged in the early 1930s as a bright, sharp, intelligent, and sophisticated poet. He was conventionally ranked with his Oxford contemporaries *Auden, *Day Lewis, and *Spender—and indeed often continues to be so ranked—but it should now be possible to see him in better perspective, relating him more interestingly to his Northern Irish background and upbringing, for example. His father was a senior clergyman in the Church of Ireland, a strict and brooding presence over the son, who often seems to have felt more at home in the less puritanical south of the island. Nevertheless, one has to bear in mind MacNeice's inherited, if deflected, notions of account-books and duty. There is also the fact of his conventional English public-school and Oxford education, in which he was both the rebel and the dandy.

Poems (1935), MacNeice's contributions to *Letters from Iceland* (prose and verse, written with Auden, 1937), and *The Earth Compels* (1938) all contain attractive and memorable poems and lines. But it was *Autumn Journal* (1939), written during the Munich crisis, that most brilliantly captures the essence of the best of MacNeice, not in miniature but at length. He had already shown a gift for sensing the temper of the time in such poems as 'An Eclogue for

Christmas' ('I meet you in an evil time') and 'Bagpipe Music' ('It's no go the merrygoround, it's no go the rickshaw'). *Autumn Journal* discursively reacts to the events of the moment, to his own public and private responses, and catches them all in a colloquial, flexible, argumentative, and yet relaxed mode which (as John Press has remarked) reminds one of Byron's *Don Juan*.

The 1940s and 1950s were prolific but difficult years for him. He wrote a great deal to order for the BBC: whatever was ruminative, occasional, and gregarious in him as a poet was perhaps given too easy a ride. Nevertheless, there are poems from these years of a dark energy (particularly those concerned with the bombing of London, such as 'Brother Fire') which are among MacNeice's best.

When he died in the autumn of 1963, MacNeice was going through a rich and extended creative phase. The evidence of this can be seen in his last two books, *Solstices* (1961) and *The Burning Perch*, which he had prepared for press and which appeared only a few days after his death. They are not in any ordinary sense the poems of a dying man, for MacNeice's death was sudden and unexpected (he died of pneumonia, brought on when making radio recordings in a damp cave); yet they are indeed much concerned with slow decline, extinction, and nullity, watched with his usual jaunty and devil-may-care insouciance.

MacNeice's *Collected Poems*, carefully edited by E. R. Dodds, appeared in London in 1966 (New York, 1967) and a *Selected Poems* (London) in 1988. There are also several verse plays (including versions of the *Agamemnon* of Aeschylus and Goethe's *Faust*, in collaboration with E. L. Stahl), and an unfinished autobiography, *The Strings are False* (London, 1965; New York, 1966), also edited by E. R. Dodds.   [AST

McNEILL, Anthony (1941–), was born in Kingston, Jamaica, and educated at Excelsior College and St George's College. He has MA degrees from both Johns Hopkins University and the University of Massachusetts (Amherst). From 1975 to 1981 he was assistant publishing director at the Institute of Jamaica.

In an interview for *Jamaica Journal* (Dec. 1970) McNeill declared: 'For poetry to have any immediate value in the West Indies, it has got to be concerned with the identity crisis which exists here.' But such a stance does not lead to parochialism in his case. 'St. Ras', for instance, scrutinizes Rastafarian behaviour in terms of a general malaise left to the reader to interpret. Indeed, his treatment of Rastafarianism, a 'local' phenomenon but of universal significance, emerges as rather more subtle, complex, and questioning than that by other poets, such as Dennis *Scott and Benjamin *Zephaniah.

His poems are available in *Hello Ungod* (Baltimore, Md., 1971), *Reel from 'The Life-Movie'* (Kingston, Jam., 1975), and *Credences at the Altar of Cloud* (Kingston, 1979).   [MR

MACPHERSON, Jay (1931–), was born in England, but she and her brother were taken to Newfoundland when she was 9, and in 1944 to Ottawa. She was educated there, at McGill University, Montreal, and at Victoria College, University of Toronto, where she was influenced by Northrop Frye, and where she now teaches. Her first collection, *Nineteen Poems* (1952), was published by Robert *Graves's Seizen Press. Her own small press, Emblem Books, published *O Earth Return* (1954), which was later to become a section of *The Boatman* (1957), the book that established her reputation. Her next collection, *Welcoming Disaster*, did not appear until 1974. These two collections were reprinted in *Poems Twice Told* (Toronto, 1981), which also contains other poems.

The Boatman is an intricately unified sequence of short poems in six sections. Though simple in diction and in metrical forms, they lightly and wittily—even colloquially—bear the weight of a whole cosmos of the poet's invention and contain biblical and classical allusions along with echoes of ballads, Elizabethan verse, carols, nursery rhymes, hymns—and of William Blake. The titles of two sections, 'O Earth Return' and 'The Plowman in Darkness', are from the 'Introduction' to Blake's *Songs of Experience*; and his idea that the human spirit must pass from innocence, through experience, to a higher innocence informs the entire collection. The boatman of the title is Noah, the 'anagogic man', who carries, 'balancing with care, | A golden bubble round and rare. | Its gently shimmering sides surround | All us and our worlds, and bound | Art and life, wit and sense, | Innocence and experience.' *Welcoming Disaster* is Macpherson's exploration—in similar light, epigrammatic, metrically strict verses—of life's 'dark places', and has as its daring and poignant central symbol Tedward, who is not only a 'guide' and 'finder of lost direction', but also a 'friendly substitute for Him'. Tedward is a teddy-bear.

[WT

McPHERSON, Sandra (1943–), was raised in San Jose, California, by foster-parents (her eventual reunion with her birth parents provides the occasion for some of her most moving poems). She went to college in California, then studied with Elizabeth *Bishop at the University of Washington, leaving after one year to have her daughter. McPherson has taught at the *Iowa and Oregon writers' workshops; she currently teaches in the creative-writing programme at the University of California, Davis.

McPherson is the younger poet who has most successfully extended the style and vision of Elizabeth Bishop into the feminist era. She shares Bishop's concern with the look of things, illuminating them through slightly odd or incongruous metaphors, often conjoining the domestic and the natural in ways that make each seem to partake of the other. Like Bishop, she speaks in a somewhat flattened, reticent tone, not given to climaxes or emotional outbursts, but pervaded by sadness and sympathy. But McPherson's subjects are often more directly human and social than Bishop's; she writes of her relationships with husband, daughter, parents, teachers, and friends with a sense of both the possibilities and limits of intimacy.

She also writes about the way gender, particularly the female, is coded and caricatured; her recent poem 'Streamers' takes a huge jellyfish as a poignant emblem for woman in her double guise of poisonous Medusa and protective mother. Her poems are oblique and often

difficult, yet are always firmly anchored in perception and experience; if we sometimes have trouble making out their biographical occasions, it is because McPherson's sensibility insists on transforming life into metaphor in such a way that neither side is subordinated. The most striking characteristic of her language is its precision, which in her case leads not to transparency but to controlled complexity. She writes equally well in free verse and fixed forms, though she tends to prefer loosely shaped stanzas of various kinds. Her most recent books are *Patron Happiness* (New York, 1983) and *Streamers* (New York, 1988).

[RG

MADDOX, Everette (1944–89), was born in Montgomery, Alabama, and lived there and later in Mobile until he entered the University of Alabama in Tuscaloosa, where he received both a BA and MA in English literature. In 1975 Maddox moved to New Orleans where he held teaching positions in creative writing and English at Xavier University and the University of New Orleans. He left teaching in 1978 to devote his energies to writing. During the next ten years Maddox wrote a considerable amount of poetry and acquired a local reputation in New Orleans as a writer and reader of his own work. His life became that of a Bohemian, and he played the role of the alcoholic poet with dedication. In the 1980s he became a fixture at *The Maple Leaf Bar* in the Carrollton section of New Orleans, and his poetry began to reach an audience of admirers throughout the southern United States.

Maddox's first full-length collection of poetry is *The Everette Maddox Song Book* (New Orleans, La., 1982), and the influences of such poets as Alan *Dugan and Frank *O'Hara are occasionally apparent in the book. But Maddox combined with these influences, and with his own comic vision, the dark surrealism found in the fiction of Donald Barthelme to produce an original voice. In his poetry Maddox is the literary equivalent of Charlie Chaplin's little tramp. His spare poems present a persona aware of and vulnerable to the inhumanities of man but still hoping for the best. His love poems in particular contain an innocent idealism rarely found in the literature of his generation. Maddox published his second book, *Bar Scotch* (Paradis, La., 1988), only months before his death from throat cancer, a complication of alcoholism and malnutrition.   [LS

MADGE, Charles (Henry) (1912–), was born in Johannesburg, South Africa, and educated at Winchester College and at Magdalene College, Cambridge, where he was a pupil of I. A. *Richards. His first book of poems, *The Disappearing Castle* (London, 1937) appeared when he was 24, by which time his work had been anthologized in the *Faber Book of Modern Verse* (1936) and the *Oxford Book of Modern Verse* (1936). Despite this acclaim, his second book of poetry, *The Father Found* (London, 1941), was followed by a gap of fifty years. In 1993 came *Of Love, Time and Places* (London), Madge's own selection from his earlier books together with more recent work. In 1936, with Tom Hopkinson, he had founded Mass Observation; and from 1950 to 1970 Madge was professor of sociology at Birmingham University.

Madge developed under the influence of slightly older poets, William *Empson and W. H. *Auden, who themselves had been influenced by modernist poetry. Madge's years at Cambridge saw the beginnings of the left-wing literary movement of the Thirties, and in 1932 he joined the Communist Party. However, his orientation to politics and society had more in common with *Surrealism, and his poetry has a visionary quality and is concerned to explore our imaginative apprehension of the world and society. This interest was also the basis of his work with Mass Observation.   [ATT

MADHUBUTI, Haki R. (1942–), was born Don L. Lee in Little Rock, Arkansas, and raised in the 'black bottom' of Detroit, Michigan. His early life was difficult: his father deserted the family when Madhubuti was still very young, and when he was 16 his mother died. After studying in Chicago and at the University of Iowa, he served in the army, 1960–3. Different jobs followed, as a cleaner, apprentice curator,

stock clerk, and post-office clerk: but after the publication of *Think Black* (1967) and *Black Pride* (1968), two collections combining autobiographical elements with a strong commitment to black activism, Madhubuti devoted himself full time to teaching, publishing, and writing. A writer-in-residence at several universities, he is also the founder and editor of *Black Books Bulletin* and Third World Press, both based in Chicago and dedicated to publishing new black writers. *Don't Cry, Scream* (1969), his third collection, continued the style of the other two: radically experimental, it used rhythmic violence and verbal play to capture the movements of black speech. However, it reflected Madhubuti's growing conviction that 'most, if not all, black poetry will be *political*' by largely discarding the personal dimension. *Directionscore: New and Selected Poems* (Detroit, 1971) is a useful selection of this earlier work.

The first collection published after Madhubuti had discarded his 'slave name', *Book of Life* (1973), retains the political commitment while moving towards the use of standard English. Political writing and activity preoccupied Madhubuti for the next ten years: but *Earthquakes and Sun Rise Missions: Poetry and Essays of Black Renewal, 1973–1983* (Chicago, 1984) continued his development of a more mainstream style. Useful information is to be found in Marlene Mosher, *New Directions from Don L. Lee* (Hicksville, NY, 1975).   [RJG

MAGEE, Wes (1939–), was born in Greenock, Renfrewshire, but grew up in Ulster and Essex. After working first as a bank clerk, then for two years in the British Army intelligence unit, he obtained a teacher's certificate at London University, and from 1967 to 1990 taught in Swindon, Welwyn Garden City, and North Humberside. He edited *Prism* magazine from 1964 to 1967, and several anthologies of poetry for children. Since 1990 he has been a full-time writer and lecturer.

Postcard from a Long Way Off (1969) and *The Radish* (1970) contributed to Magee's first full collection of poetry, *Urban Gorilla* (Leeds, 1972), which won a Leeds University New Poets award in 1973. His work reflects the violence he experienced as a child in Ulster, the violence endemic to the war-torn province but also, as the title of that collection suggests, inherent in a bleak, dark nature. Occupying a position midway between the naturalism enabled by intensely visual images, and a dramatic symbolism that owes much to his experience as a teacher, Magee's poetry depends on the juxtaposition of striking local effects and on tricksy inversions of perspective, rather than mapping out a coherent philosophical or biographical agenda. But poems in *No Man's Land* (Richmond, Surrey, 1976) and *A Dark Age* (Belfast, 1981) such as 'Visiting Belfast' and 'Cattle Trucks', nevertheless achieve an invigorating and moving composite view of history's violent freight; it is therefore somewhat to be regretted that Magee's output of accessible, witty children's poetry has recently sidelined his work for adults.   [MRW

MAHAPATRA, Jayanta (1928–), is a scientist and academic who turned to writing poetry in English in the late Sixties. Born in Cuttack, Orissa, he became known to western readers through poems in *Critical Quarterly* and **Poetry*, which awarded him the Glatstein Prize in 1975. He joined **Iowa Writers' Workshop's interna-tional writing programme (1976) and is much published in American literary journals. He is a prolific poet with twelve collections, beginning with *Close the Sky, Ten by Ten* (Calcutta, 1971) and the most recent, *Temple* (Coventry, 1989). He also translates modern Oriya poets and has edited a literary magazine, *Chandrabhaga* (Cuttack, 1979–85).

His poetry, often obscure and elliptical, draws on symbols from Orissan landscape and history, Hindu mythology and philosophy. He is preoccupied with Hindu ritual, from which he feels alienated since his grandfather converted to Christianity. In *A Rain of Rites* (Athens, Ga., 1976) there are several pieces about the great Puri temple and the poverty and squalor outside, as in his best-known poem, 'Hunger'. *Life Signs* (Delhi, 1983) includes some of his best verse, like 'The Lost Children of America', in

which vivid images of Cuttack lanes where the unkempt hippies live develop into a complex interweaving of their search and the poet's in 'haunted wood and hunted myth'. His most ambitious work, *Relationship* (Greenfield, NY, 1980) is a near-epic, some 600 lines long, in which Mahapatra delves into the self through history which he traces to mythic time when the great god Siva roamed among the wild beasts in 'the night of the wild elephants'. Guilt and ambivalent feelings towards parents are dissolved in the course of a psychic journey ending with the dance of the temple dancers.

Mahapatra's *Selected Poems* (Delhi, 1987) includes a representative sample. See also the poet's autobiographical essay, *Contemporary Authors Autobiography Series' 9* (Detroit, 1989). For critical evaluation see *Modern Indian Poetry in English*, by Bruce King (Delhi, 1987) and *Jayanta Mahapatra*, by D. Mohan (Delhi, 1987).
                                                            [RA

MAHON, Derek (1941–), was born in Belfast and educated at Trinity College, Dublin, where he took a degree in French. After leaving university, Mahon travelled in France, Canada, and the United States, teaching and doing a variety of odd-jobs, and publishing his first book, *Night Crossing* (London), in 1968, before settling in London in 1970. He was associated in the mid-1960s with the Belfast 'Group' (see HOBSBAUM, PHILIP). Apart from a return to Northern Ireland in 1977–9 as writer-in-residence at the New University of Ulster in Coleraine, he has since earned his living as a free-lance writer, reviewing widely and writing screenplays for the BBC from such sources as novels by his fellow Northern Irish writers Jennifer Johnston and Brian Moore. His Francophile enthusiasms, clearly evident in his own poetry, issued in 1984 in *High Time* (Dublin), a Molière translation for the Field Day Theatre Company, and in 1988 in his translations of the *Selected Poems* of Philippe Jaccottet (London).

Mahon is a poet of great stylistic zest whose polish ironizes a scepticism, gloom, and even apocalypticism of temperament. Admiring Louis **MacNeice's outsider attitudes, and drawn to 'Beckett's bleak *reductio*', he often evokes settings, sometimes futuristic, devoid of human beings. In 'One of these Nights' in *The Hunt by Night* (Oxford, 1982; Winston-Salem, NC, 1983) he imagines the 'radiant warplanes' of a future war as they approach London. These larger perspectives situate the plight of Northern Ireland in a context of wider contemporary breakdown and entropy. This happens strikingly in what is probably his single most admired poem, 'A Disused Shed in Co. Wicklow', in *The Snow Party* (London and New York, 1975). He discovers there an unforgettable emblem for Irish historical suffering in what begins as the almost humorous fantasy of a 'thousand mushrooms' crowding to the keyhole of a shed as the poet-photographer opens its door. A subtle and penetrating meditation on the poet's responsibility and the dangers of his appropriation of human suffering as material, the poem is eloquent testimony to an artful but scrupulously undeceived imagination. His latest collection is *Yaddo Letter* (Dublin, 1990), but in 1991 a *Selected Poems* was jointly published in Ireland, London and Oxford.

[NC

MAIDEN, Jennifer (1949–), was born in Penrith, New South Wales. After casual jobs she completed an arts course at Macquarie University, Sydney (1974). She tutors in creative writing and has received writing fellowships from the Literature Board of the Australia Council. She is married, with a daughter.

Author of two unusual novels, Maiden is best known as a poet. Critical attention has steadily increased since *Tactics* (1974) appeared in the *University of Queensland Paperback Poets series. Since then she has published eight collections: *The Problem of Evil* (1975) is the most demanding, and *For the Left Hand* (1981) the most accessible. Her *Selected Poems* (Harmmondsworth, 1989) offers a first overview. See also *The Winter Baby* (Sydney, 1991). Concentrated, idiosyncratic personal feeling and often acerbic social observation assure her of a place in any survey of Australian women writers' contribution.

[JRo

MALLALIEU, H(erbert) B(lythe) (1914–88), was born in Orange, New Jersey, but spent most of his life in England, where he was educated at Wells, Somerset. During the Second World War he served in the Royal Artillery in the Mediterranean. After the war he spent twenty years in the British Services Security Organization in Germany.

During the late 1930s Mallalieu's work appeared in Julian *Symons's *Twentieth Century Verse*, of which Mallalieu was associate editor. *Twentieth Century Verse* was sympathetic to the social, realist poetry of the left-wing literary movement of the decade, and Mallalieu's poetry of those years is marked by the rhetoric of disaster and foreboding that was characteristic of that movement. This is seen in the poems by him that appeared in John *Lehmann's first selection of *Poets of Tomorrow* in 1939, and in most of those in *Letter in Wartime* (1940). In contrast, Mallalieu's war poems are notable for the plainness and the tact with which they project the tension between the personal life and the demands of war. Several of them appear in the posthumous *On the Berlin Lakes* (Edinburgh, 1988), which includes some of the few poems that he wrote in later years.

[ATT

MALLEY, Ern. See *ANGRY PENGUINS*.

MALOUF, David (1934–), was born in Brisbane and educated at the University of Queensland. From 1959 to 1968 he lived in Europe, acquiring that unselfconscious intimacy with its history and urban sites which characterizes his poetry. Returning to Australia, he taught English at the University of Sydney until 1977. In that time three of his six volumes of verse were published. *Bicycle and Other Poems* (1970) began the *University of Queensland Press Paperback Poets series. Malouf's deep attachment to his home state (despite subsequent annual sojourns in Tuscany) is indicated in 'The Year of the Foxes', a meditative reminiscence of wartime Brisbane, and for its author 'a touchstone poem'. Here, as in much of his verse and the fictions that it presaged, Malouf showed his intense awareness of life being determined by the particulars of place, as by unsuppressible historical memories.

Neighbours in a Thicket (St Lucia, Qld., 1974), took its title from the poem 'An Ordinary Evening at Hamilton', where Malouf's remembrance of his childhood home (whose 'Familiar rooms | glow, rise through the dark—exotic islands') anticipated the memoir *12 Edmonstone Street* (London, 1985) as well as his first novel, *Johnno* (St Lucia, 1975; New York, 1978).

Malouf's fifth book of verse, *First Things Last* (St Lucia, 1980; London, 1981), was followed by his *Selected Poems* (Sydney and London) the next year. Since then the concerns of his poetry with provenance and Australianness, severance and conjunction, the primitive and the civilized have been translated into prose fiction. *An Imaginary Life* (1978) treated Ovid in exile. The Great War was the subject of *Fly Away Peter* (1981); the Second World War and its Australian aftermaths, of *The Great World* (1990). Malouf has also written the libretto for Richard Meale's opera *Voss* (based on Patrick White's novel), a volume of short stories, and a play. *David Malouf* (1990) by James Tulip contains a useful bibliography. Philip Neilsen and Ivor Indyk have written critical studies: *Imagined Lives* (1990) and *David Malouf* (1993), respectively.   [PP

MANDEL, Eli(as Wolf) (1922–), was born in Estevan, Saskatchewan, and grew up in the Jewish community of the region. During the Second World War he served with the Canadian Army Medical Corps. He received his Ph.D from the University of Toronto in 1957 with a dissertation on Christopher Smart. For many years he was professor of English literature at the University of York, Toronto.

Mandel's early poems of the late 1950s portray a speaker who wanders helplessly through a closed and violent landscape. Mythic figures such as the minotaur and Cain appear and seem to offer an explanation of the darkness and horror. In the later poems the atmosphere of terror continues, but it becomes increasingly difficult to distinguish the internal and psychic dimension from the external and public one. The poetry no longer describes an objective world to

be explained by mythic patterns, but one in which the speaker's own violent tendencies interweave with public events. The duplicity of language remains a central concern in Mandel's poetry, as is the struggle to create poems which allow us to glimpse a world of being outside language. *Dreaming Backwards* (Toronto, 1981), offers a selection of his poetry, and his essays in literary and social criticism can be found in *Another Time* (Erin, Ont., 1977) and *The Family Romance* (Winnipeg, 1986). There is an interview with Mandel and an article on his poetry, by Peter Stevens, in *Essays on Canadian Writing*, 18/19 (Summer/Fall 1980).   [RBH

MANHIRE, Bill (1946–), was born in Invercargill, New Zealand, and grew up in various small towns in the far south of the country, where his parents worked as publicans. His poems first appeared in New Zealand journals in the 1960s, while he was an undergraduate at the University of Otago. Set against the protracted, egocentric effusions of his contemporaries, his terse, cryptic imagism was immediately striking. He made his debut in British magazines in the early 1970s, when he was studying Norse sagas at University College London. He returned to New Zealand in 1973 to teach in the English Department of Victoria University of Wellington. Among his duties there, he runs a highly esteemed creative-writing course.

Much of the power in Manhire's poetry comes from the tension between the conservative and the avant-garde sides of his personality. He is continually determined to surprise, but he also wants to remain accessible. He places a high value on both imagination and common sense. Most of his poems assume a tidy stanzaic form, but his syntax is often deliberately odd, so that the reader's sense of security is undermined almost as soon as it is established. Manhire's influences are disparate enough to include both Philip *Larkin and John *Ashbery. Although he is an academic he has a dislike of jargon, which he is consequently fond of satirizing. Inimical to preciousness, he purposefully includes comic-book references, racetrack terminology, and

Manifold

other supposedly 'lowbrow' material in his poems. Yet there are also playful allusions to Spenser, Keats, Matthew Arnold, and other figures from the English literary tradition.

Manhire's first book, *Malady* (Dunedin, 1970), consisted of just four words, 'malady', 'melody', and 'my lady', arranged on the page in sundry patterns, with accompanying drawings by the New Zealand painter Ralph Hotere. Throughout his career, Manhire has never lost his fondness for word-play, experimentation, and disrupting his audience's expectations. He has a sly and unpredictable sense of humour. Nevertheless, his reputation rests on a solid, seriously intentioned body of work, notable for its oblique lyricism and sense of wonder at the strangeness of both life and language. Although he frequently embarks on surreal flights of fancy and has always shied away from the role of either autobiographer or sage, his work, viewed as a whole, can still be said to follow the trajectory of ordinary domestic life, commenting on courtship, marriage, the vicissitudes of adult love, and the anxieties of parenthood, ageing, bereavement, and death.

After the publication of his fifth book of verse, *Good Looks*, in 1982, Manhire directed his attention more towards prose fiction, producing *The Brain of Katherine Mansfield* (1988), a parody of teenagers' choose-your-own-adventure books, and *The New Land* (1990), a largely satirical collection of stories. His latest volume of poetry, *Milky Way Bar* (Wellington and Manchester, UK, 1991), also playfully manipulates narrative structures. *Zoetropes: Poems 1972–1982* (Sydney, 1984; Manchester, 1985) is the most comprehensive selection.   [IS

MANIFOLD, John (1915–85), was born in Melbourne, the eldest son of one of Australia's wealthiest pastoralists. He grew up on the family properties in the Western District of Victoria, and was educated as a boarder at Geelong Grammar School. When he was 18 his father informed him that he was not to inherit the family property; instead it was bequeathed to his younger brothers, who were not as intellectually gifted and hence less assured of earning a liv-

ing. Manifold reacted by becoming a communist. In 1934 he went to Cambridge University, where he formally joined the Communist Party; unlike his fellow students Burgess, Maclean, Philby, and Blunt, he did not conceal his membership, though like them he received a lifelong pension from the Soviet government. This assistance could not have consoled him greatly for the disappointment of being disinherited; he remained an aristocrat at heart.

Manifold never matched the fertile poetic output of another of his Cambridge colleagues, David *Campbell. His *Selected Verse* (New York, 1946; London, 1948) was published to reviews which suggested a major literary career lay before him, but thirty years later his *Collected Verse* (St Lucia, Qld., 1978) showed that he had written on average no more than three poems a year. Of these only one, 'The Tomb of Lt. John Learmonth, A.I.F.', is of the highest order. The rest of his writing consists of ballads and sonnets which commemorate such occasions as the death of Stalin or a waterside workers' strike: these are technically proficient, but seldom amount to more than light verse.   [JG

MANN, Chris(topher Zithulele) (1948–), was born in Port Elizabeth, South Africa, and educated at the University of the Witwatersrand, at Oxford as a Rhodes scholar (where he won the Newdigate Prize for Poetry), and at the School of Oriental and African Studies in London where he took a master's degree in African oral poetry. In 1982 he adopted the Zulu name Zithulele as his second name to express his solidarity with black praise-poets whose work he has translated into English. He is the director of the Valley Trust near Durban—a grass-roots organization involved in educational projects. He is married with two children.

His first volume, *First Poems* (Johannesburg, 1977), established him as a poet whose unembellished, plain-talking style was designed for oral delivery and performance. A characteristic theme—inspiration and guidance from the shades or ancestors—was further developed in his *New Shades* (Cape Town, 1982). 'Kites', the title-poem of his third volume (Cape Town,

1990), when it first appeared, had this note attached: 'These poems are written in a prosody derived from my study and practice of African oral verse.' A more recent poem of his, 'Where is the Freedom for Which We Died?' (*New Coin*, June 1991), is translated by him from his own Zulu original.

He co-edited (with Guy Butler) *A New Book of South African Verse in English* for Oxford (Cape Town, 1979). [SG

MANNING, Frederic (1882–1935), was born in Sydney, one of seven children of the sometime mayor of that city. Except for a stay of three months at Sydney Grammar School, Manning was privately educated, as he suffered severely from asthma. At the age of 21 he left Australia to live in the village of Edenham, Lincolnshire, with his former tutor, Arthur Galton, who was the local vicar. His family's wealth and their concern for his continuing ill health meant that he was never obliged to find employment, so he pursued a low-key literary career from the country vicarage, publishing three slight books and writing book reviews for the *Spectator*. In 1915, surprisingly in view of his medical history, he enlisted in the British Army as a private and was sent to the Somme; he later became an officer before being forced to resign for persistent drunkenness. Though it lasted only twenty-eight months, his time in the army was the source of all the writing for which he is remembered.

His fame now rests on the novel *The Middle Parts of Fortune* (London, 1929) which also appeared in an expurgated edition under the title *Her Privates We* (London, 1930), published pseudonymously as the work of 'Private 19022'. Except for this, one of the best novels to come out of the First World War, and a few war poems from his collection *Eidola* (London, 1917), Manning is of interest to literary historians mainly for his circle of acquaintances. He was friendly with *Pound, *Eliot (who used him as a reviewer for *Criterion* after the war), T. E. Lawrence, Richard *Aldington, and others.

[JG

MANSFIELD, Katherine (1888–1923), pseudonym of Kathleen Mansfield Beauchamp, was born in Wellington, New Zealand, the daughter of a businessman. At the age of 14 she went to school in England and spent most of her adult life there, until ill health forced her south to a series of resorts in Italy, Switzerland, and France, where she died of tuberculosis, aged 34. Mansfield's poems, which she wrote casually and in profusion from childhood onwards, are peripheral to her great achievment as a writer of short stories and are interesting mainly for biographical reasons and for the light they shed on her development as a prose writer. Under the influence of the *fin-de-siècle* poets of the Rhymer's Club and Oscar Wilde, she experimented with free verse and prose-poem 'vignettes' which explore rhythms, patterns of imagery, and themes—isolation, childhood, illness—chacteristic of her later stories. Many of her poems strive to illuminate fleeting moments of emotion in ways similar to those practised by the *Imagists, though Mansfield seems to have placed little importance on form, often using it very loosely as, in effect, an extension of note-taking. She published a number of poems during her lifetime, using a variety of pseudonyms, but did not consider herself a poet. In the year of her death, 1923, her second husband, John Middleton Murry, published a highly tampered-with selection of Mansfield's poems which established a reputation for mediocrity only rectified by Vincent O'Sullivan's 1988 edition, *Poems of Katherine Mansfield* (Auckland and Oxford). See also Antony Alpers, *The Life of Katherine Mansfield* (London and New York, 1980) and Claire Tomalin, *Katherine Mansfield: A Secret Life* (London and New York, 1987). [CPH

MAPANJE, Jack (1945–), was born in Kadango, Mangochi District, in southern Malawi. He was educated at Kadango, Chikwawa Mission, and at Zomba Catholic Secondary School. He has a BA degree and Diploma in Education from the University of Malawi, Zomba. He also holds postgraduate degrees from the University of London. In 1975 he joined the department of

Marechera

English at Chancellor College, University of Malawi, as a lecturer. He was arrested on 25 September 1987 and detained without charge until he was released in 1991. He is now living in the United Kingdom.

Mapanje is acknowledged as an authority on African oral literature and edited *Kalulu*, a Malawi-based journal of oral literature. He also co-edited with Landeg White the anthology *Oral Poetry from Africa* (London, 1983). He has published one volume of his own poetry, *Of Chameleons and Gods* (London, 1981). Mapanje's early poems are mournful in tone, lamenting the loss of the dignity of traditional Africa. The vulgarity and poverty of contemporary urban and rural communities are assiduously described. The poems which he wrote during his stay in London analysed his experience of English manners. His disappointment with English society was apparent; however, he was able to use the experience to reaffirm his own identity. The later poems are more evidently political. They are ironic and humorous in tone; the true content is veiled; the messages are transmitted through elaborate codes, sometimes derived from the oral tradition.   [FO

MARECHERA, Dambudzo (1952–87), was born in Rusape, Zimbabwe (then Rhodesia). He began his studies at the University of Rhodesia in 1972, but was expelled the following year for protesting against racial discrimination on the campus. He was awarded a scholarship to resume his studies at New College, Oxford, but was sent down two years later for his 'outrageous behaviour'. Apart from a spell as writer-in-residence at the University of Sheffield in the first half of 1979, Marechera found it impossible to settle anywhere for long. He moved from one squat to another, mostly in London, and drank heavily. In December 1977 he was arrested and charged with theft, possession of cannabis, and being an illegal immigrant, and spent three months in jail. None of this, however, stopped him writing. His first book, *The House of Hunger* (London, 1978), a collection of short stories, was joint winner of the *Guardian* fiction prize for 1979. This was followed by two further volumes

in his lifetime, *Black Sunlight* (London, 1980), a novel, and *Mindblast* (Harare, 1984), a collection of prose and poetry, and a posthumous collected poems, *Cemetery of Mind* (Harare, 1992).

Marechera returned to Zimbabwe in 1981, where he appears to have continued a 'dissipated way of life' until his death at the age of 35. A second novel, *The Black Insider* (Harare, 1990), was published posthumously, as well as another collection of assorted prose and poetry, *Dambudzo Marechera 1952–1987*, ed. Flora Veit-Wild and Ernst Schade (Harare, 1988). Marechera was unquestionably one of the most talented writers of his generation. His poems, which are largely autobiographical, explore his abiding sense of alienation within the newly liberated society, and demonstrate the eclectic range of his influences: William Blake, Rainer Maria Rilke, and Allen *Ginsberg. Unlike most of his contemporaries he had little interest in politics, which did not stop him pouring scorn on his many critics who accused him of 'irrelevance'.   [AM-P

MARKHAM, E(dward) A(rchibald) (1939–), was born in Montserrat, West Indies. He moved to Britain in 1956 and read English and philosophy at St David's University College (Lampeter). He directed the Caribbean Theatre Workshop in the West Indies (1970–1), and worked as a media co-ordinator in Papua New Guinea (1983–5). He also held writing fellowships at Hull College of Higher Education (1978–9) and the University of Ulster (1988–91), and was editor of several publications, including *Artrage* (1985–7).

Next to Derek *Walcott and Edward *Lucie-Smith, he is the most cosmopolitan of West Indian poets in style and subject-matter. He also shows great partiality for the long poem, usually autobiographical in content. Dry wit pervades much of his work, and free verse is his most frequent poetic medium. In 'Late Return', a long poem which describes a return visit to Montserrat, his wit emerges as a probing, self-critical exercise in cold detachment. 'Grandmother-poem' is more moving, drawn from childhood memories, but stern in spirit: 'I step | on the wrong end of a rake | and crack my skull: the yellow scream of grandmother burns the head.' 'Don't Talk to me about Bread' describes in great detail a woman kneading dough, but it is highly sensuous, and treats work as sublimated frustration. A delightful poem, and one of his best, it suggestively encapsulates Markham's views about the poetic process.

Recent collections include *Family Matters* (London, 1984), *Human Rites: Selected Poems 1970–1982* (London, 1984), *Living in Disguise* (London, 1986), and *Towards the End of a Century* (London, 1989). *Something Unusual* (1986) is a volume of short stories.   [MR

MARKHAM, Edwin (1852–1940), was born in Oregon, the youngest son of pioneer parents, but his father died when he was 4 and he was raised in California. Supplementing whatever education he gained from crude country schools with high-school anthologies, he reacted strongly to Ruskin, William Morris, and Karl Marx and became a schoolteacher. His poetry was conventional in means but thematically radical, broad rhetoric mated with earnest social outrage. The appearence of his powerful 'The Man with the Hoe', inspired by Millet's painting, in the San Francisco *Examiner* (15 Jan. 1899) led to national fame and publication of his first collection, *The Man with the Hoe and Other Poems* (1899). It also precipitated his move to the East Coast, to Staten Island, where he would remain until his death. Markham's 'Lincoln, Man of the People' also struck a responsive chord and contributed to the popularity of his next volume, *Lincoln, and Other Poems* (1901), but later collections—*The Shoes of Happiness* (1914), *The Gates of Paradise* (1920), and *New Poems: Eighty Songs at Eighty* (1932)—were less successful.

The 'Hoe' and 'Lincoln', poems, plus three quatrains, are in *Modern American Poetry*, ed. Louis Untermeyer (New York, 1969).   [EB

MARLATT, Daphne (Buckle) (1942–), was born in Australia, and in 1951 moved to Vancouver, Canada. In the early 1960s she became active with the poets involved in the magazine

Tish and studied with some of the major *Black Mountain poets. *Rings* (1971), with its extended poetic line to register the nuances of pregnancy and birth in the midst of a failing marriage, became part of her book of poetics and autobiography, *What Matters* (Toronto, 1980). She explores the past and present of a fishing and cannery town in *Steveston* (Vancouver, 1974/1984; anthologized in Michael Ondaatje's *The Long Poem Anthology*, Toronto, 1979), the geography and history of her city in *Vancouver Poems* (Toronto, 1972), and her mother's inheritance in *How Hug a Stone* (Winnipeg, 1983). Her stance is now strongly feminist, stimulated by collaborations with Quebec feminist writer, Nicole Brossard, and her companion, Betsy Warland, to whom *Touch to My Tongue* (Edmonton, 1984), a prose poem conflating the roles of Demeter and Persephone, is dedicated. 'Musing with Mothertongue', its accompanying essay, argues that language is 'a living body we enter at birth'. *Double Negative* (Charlottetown, PEI, 1988) is a collaboration with Warland; *Salvage* (1991) is Marlatt's feminist rewriting of her work since 1970.   [DBa

MARQUIS, Don(ald Robert Perry) (1878–1937), was born in Walnut, Illinois, and was best known as a newspaper columnist. In his early career, under the encouragement of the journalist and humorist Joel Chandler Harris, he began two columns: 'The Sun Dial' in the New York *Sun* and 'The Lantern' in the New York *Tribune*. He developed his comic and satirical perspective into a series of popular texts. *Hermione and Her Little Group of Serious Thinkers* (1916) was a satire on the social and artistic pretensions of Greenwich Village 'socialites', just as his play, *The Old Soak* (1922) offered a caustic view of American prohibition. During this period he published three books of 'serious' verse, beginning with *Dreams and Dust* (1915). However, he is best remembered for a series of books which, beginning with *archy and mehitabel* (1927), feature the rantings (in comic form) of archy the cockroach, who in a previous life was a free-verse poet. These were written at night in the deserted newspaper office. The upper case was absent because archy could not work the shift key on the typewriter. *the lives and times of archy and mehitabel*, a cat (motto: 'toujours gai'), was published in 1940 (New York and London), and included the original collections of the 'column'. Other humorous books of verse include *Sonnets to a Red-Haired Lady (by a Gentleman with a Blue Beard)* and *Famous Love Affairs* (1922) and *Love Sonnets of a Cave Man* (1928). Among Marquis's other writings are a posthumously published and unfinished autobiographical novel, *Sons of the Puritans* (1939), and *The Dark Hours*, a play based on the last period of Christ's life. See E. O. Anthony, *O Rare Don Marquis: A Biography* (1962).   [GC

MARRIOTT, Anne (1913–), was born in Victoria, British Columbia. One of the early Canadian modernists, she sought to capture in poetry the uniqueness of the Canadian experience and landscape. Along with Dorothy *Livesay, whose social concerns she shared, she co-founded in 1941 *Contemporary Verse*. She assisted with its editing until 1945, when she moved to Ottawa to work for the National Film Board; she was also assistant editor of *Canadian Poetry Magazine* (1946–8). She married Gerald McLellan in 1947, and three years later they moved to Prince George, British Columbia, where she was women's editor of the *Prince George Citizen*. The couple settled in North Vancouver in 1959. She is co-author, with Joyce Moller, of *A Swarming in My Mind* (1977), a poetry-writing workbook for elementary school students.

Her first poetry collection, *The Wind Our Enemy* (1939), is an episodic documentary of a prairie farmer's plight during the Depression; her second, *Calling Adventurers!* (1941) celebrates the romantic Canadian north. She then published little for more than a quarter-century. Her later work, primarily set on the west coast, examines the plight of the elderly and the displaced.

The fullest edition of her poetry is *The Circular Coast: Poems New and Selected* (Oakville, Ont., 1981). Her eight short stories are gathered in *A Long Way to Oregon* (Oakville, 1984).   [DS

MARSH, Sir Edward. See GEORGIAN POETRY.

MARSHALL, Tom (1938–93), was born in Niagara Falls, Ontario, and lived in the southern United States as a child. Educated at Queen's University in Kingston, Ontario, and the University of London (1966–8), he has taught in the English department at Queen's since 1964.

Marshall's major work as a poet (he has also written short stories and two novels) comprises a quartet of books—*The Silences of Fire* (London, 1969), *Magic Water* (Kingston, Ont., 1971), *The Earth-Book* (Ottawa, 1974), and *The White City* (Ottawa, 1976)—in which he creates a four-part vision of the universe based on the four elements.

Marshall sees the poet as a modern shaman, attempting to make beautiful and meaningful order in art. Although his poetry sometimes alludes to Canadian history and literature (as in 'Macdonald Park', his long poem invoking Sir John A. Macdonald, Canada's first prime minister), Marshall more frequently uses natural landscapes as ways into his reflections on more universal themes of alienation and mortality.

In his most recent book of poetry, *Playing With Fire* (Ottawa, 1984), Marshall grapples with his heightened sense of mortality and with his haunting visions of children menaced by an approaching nuclear holocaust.

Marshall has edited a collection of essays on the Canadian poet A. M. *Klein (1970) and written a book on D. H. *Lawrence's poetry, *The Psychic Mariner* (1970). His most important critical work is *Harsh and Lovely Land: The Major Canadian Poets and the Making of a Canadian Tradition* (Vancouver, 1979). *The Elements* (Ottawa, 1980) contains selections from Marshall's four previous books of poems.   [NB

MARSON, Una (1905–65), was born in Jamaica. During the early 1930s she lived in London, where she became secretary of the League of Coloured People and editor of its journal. She also became secretary to Haile Selassie, the then-exiled emperor of Ethiopia. She returned to Jamaica in 1936, where she founded the Readers and Writers Club and the Jamaica Save the

Children Fund, but was back in London in 1938 to work for the BBC World Service, finally returning to Jamaica in 1945.

Much of her poetry is characterized by experimentation with dialect, in a manner anticipating Louise *Bennett. In her 'blues' poems she experimented with jazz-derived rhythms. She could also, however, and in a strikingly witty manner, deploy traditional forms. 'To Wed or not to Wed', for instance, effectively parodies Shakespeare's most famous soliloquy from *Hamlet*, but also poses pertinent conundrums about the institution of marriage.

She published three volumes of poetry in Kingston, Jamaica: *Tropic Reveries* (1930), *Heights and Depths* (1932), and *The Moth and the Star* (1937). *Towards the Stars* (London, 1945) mostly reprints poems from the earlier volumes. [MR

Martian Poetry, took its name from Craig *Raine's poem 'A Martian Sends a Postcard Home', which shared the 1978 Prudence Farmer Award and prompted James *Fenton, dividing the prize between Raine and Christopher *Reid, to hail the new 'Martian School' (*New Statesman*, 20 Oct. 1978). Raine's poem is strikingly inventive. Misunderstanding the ignition and rear-view mirror in a car, Raine's alien declares that 'a key is turned to free the world|for movement, so quick there is a film|to watch for anything missed'. Riddling wit of this kind was partly inspired by William Golding's novel *The Inheritors* (according to Raine himself, quoted in The *Observer*, 2 Mar. 1980) and partly by similar effects in fellow-Oxonian John *Fuller's collection of poems *The Mountain in the Sea* (1975). The riddling was married in Martian poetry to the wit of 'outrageous simile', as a way of 'viewing the commonplace with wonder and innocence' (Blake *Morrison and Andrew *Motion, in their introduction to the 1982 *Penguin Book of Contemporary British Poetry*). Seven collections constitute the core of Martian poetry: Craig Raine's *The Onion, Memory* (1978), *A Martian Sends a Postcard Home* (1979), *A Free Translation* (1981), and *Rich* (1984); Christopher Reid's *Arcadia* (1979) and *Pea Soup*

(1982); and David *Sweetman's *Looking into the Deep End* (1981).

The Martian poets were widely imitated, and for a while were influential, but journalistic talk of a school was misleading. Critics complained that the reliance on visual imagery was both ostentatious and limiting, but detected affinities with the work of the Metaphysicals and of the *Imagists, and with the aesthetics of Coleridge and of the high modernists. In *Katerina Brac* (1985), a set of poems voiced for an imaginary East European poet, Christopher Reid was the first of the Martians to choose an entirely new approach. Martian elements survive in Craig Raine's stage works *The Electrification of the Soviet Union* (1986) and '*1953*' (1990), but his Martian poetry, and indeed the movement as a whole, was essentially confined to the years from the late 1970s to the mid-1980s. There is useful criticism in the special issue on British poetry since 1945 of *The Yearbook of English Studies*, 17 (1987), and in Alan Robinson, *Instabilities in Contemporary British Poetry* (London, 1988). [MHu

MARTIN, Charles (1942–), was born of German and Irish descent in the Bronx, where he attended Catholic schools, including Jesuit-run Fordham Prep and University. It was here that he acquired his training in Latin and the interest in Catullus which would ultimately lead him to write his doctoral dissertation for SUNY-Buffalo on the Latin poet's influence on *Pound, and to translating Catullus's complete works. His *The Poems of Catullus* (Omaha, Nebr., 1979; rev. ed., Baltimore and London, 1989) is notable both for its skilful rendering of Catullus's Latin hendecasyllabic line into the more natural English blank-verse line, and for its preserving his colloquial vulgarity in a contemporary American idiom.

Martin's first book, *Room for Error* (Athens, Ga., 1978), reflects the Catullan influence, particularly in 'Calvus in Ruins', a *tour de force* based upon the few extant fragments by one of Catullus's closest friends. Martin has been identified as one of the *New Formalists, and there is intelligence and wit in his treatment of a wide range of topics, from film to literature to science fiction, and of landscape, from ancient Rome to Buffalo (where he lived in the Sixties), to Brooklyn, where he has lived since 1968, teaching at Queensborough Community College and, since 1988, at Johns Hopkins University as well. His second collection, *Steal the Bacon* (Baltimore and London, 1987), confirmed his reputation for technical and thematic virtuosity and was a finalist for the Pulitzer Prize. It is highlighted by a narrative poem, 'Passages from Friday', a retelling, in eighteenth-century English, of *Robinson Crusoe* from Friday's perspective.

[RMcP

MARTIN, Philip (1931–), was born in Melbourne and educated at Xavier College and Melbourne University. His MA thesis on Shakespeare's sonnets was published by Cambridge University Press. He taught English at Melbourne University and the Australian National University before taking a lectureship at Monash University in 1964, where he remained until disabled by a severe stroke in 1988.

It was unfortunate for Martin that he did not publish his first collection of poems until 1970: *Voice Unaccompanied* appeared at the start of a decade in which fashion turned decisively against the style of poetry he represents. Elegant, civilized, and witty, more European than Australian in sensibility, his poems were hardly noticed at a time of growing nationalism and so-called modernism. *A Bone Flute* (Canberra, 1974) succeeded his first book fairly quickly, but *A Flag for the Wind* (Melbourne, 1982) took twice as long to appear, as Martin felt disheartened by a lack of response to his work. *New and Selected Poems* (Melbourne, 1988) included only fifteen new poems.

[JG

MARTIN, William (1925–), was born in Silksworth, a pit village in the Durham coalfield, and his childhood memories of its communal life form the matrix of his poetry.

A key image is the Durham Miners' Gala, when the huge silk banners of the miners' lodges are paraded through the city streets. The poems themselves are like banners, woven of many different threads—the Gnostic Gospel of

St Thomas, the legend of St Cuthbert, the industrial history of strikes and evictions, children's songs and street-games—to make emblems of community.

Locally based but wide-ranging in reference, Martin represents a development from the work of David *Jones, taking the fragments of past traditions and using them as 'rubble to build with'. He compacts his images, adding layer upon layer over long poems, and they can seem too compressed. When the language clarifies and the rhythms become songlike, he sustains a terse, haunting music. He received a Northern Arts Award in 1984, and a set of children's songs, *Battledore*, was set to music by John Woolrich in 1985.

His main collections are *Cracknrigg* (Durham, 1983) and *Hinny Beata* (Stamford, Lincs., 1987). He appears in the Morden Tower anthology *High On The Walls* (Newcastle upon Tyne, 1990).

[RGa

MASEFIELD, John (Edward) (1878–1967), was born in Ledbury, Herefordshire. His mother died when he was 6, and his solicitor father soon after, following a mental breakdown, and he was brought up by an aunt unsympathetic to his juvenile literary ambitions. A career in the merchant navy was prescribed for him, and at thirteen he joined the training ship HMS *Conway* on the Mersey. On his second voyage, however, he left his ship at New York, and worked as a bartender and in a Yonkers carpet factory before returning to London in 1897 determined to be a writer. (These adventures are recounted in the autobiographical volumes *New Chum*, 1944, and *In the Mill*, 1941.) For most of his twenties, a decade fondly remembered in the poem 'Biography' (1912), he struggled to make a living, but enjoyed the friendship of *Yeats, *Binyon, Synge, and others. He began to write poems flavoured by his youthful experiences, pledging himself in 'A Consecration' to sing of the uncelebrated, 'the ranker, the tramp of the road . . . The sailor, the stoker of steamers'. His first two volumes, *Salt-Water Ballads* (1902) and *Ballads* (1903), contained the pungent, rhythmical poems of the sea ('Sea-Fever' and

'Cargoes') which are still his best-known works.

Contemporary fame came, however, with the publication in the *English Review* in 1911 of the controversial narrative poem *The Everlasting Mercy*. This tells, in octosyllabic couplets, the story of Saul Kane, a poacher and drunkard converted by the Quaker, Miss Bourne, and juxtaposes scenes of religious fervour with pub brawls and a sort of dialogue ('You closhy put!', 'You bloody liar!') new to poetry. Further narrative poems reviving Chaucerian metres, including *Dauber* (1913), the story of the seaman-painter who proves himself and drowns, and *Reynard the Fox* (1919), an account of the Ledbury Hunt in bristling couplets, earned Masefield a high reputation on both sides of the Atlantic.

In the First World War he worked initially with the Red Cross; instead of war poems there were the prose studies *Gallipoli* (1916), *The Old Front Line* (1917), and the *Battle of the Somme* (1919). After the war he settled at Boar's Hill near Oxford, where he continued his prolific output including plays, and novels, of which *Sard Harker* (1924) and *Odtaa* (1926) are the best; but all the valuable poetry had been written by the time he was appointed Poet Laureate, succeeding *Bridges, in 1930.

Masefield's *Collected Poems*, first published in 1923, sold 200,000 copies. There is a *Selected Poems* (Manchester, 1984), a sympathetic biography by Constance Babington Smith (Oxford, 1978), and several volumes of letters.   [MI

MASON, R(onald) A(llison) K(ells) (1905–71), was born and educated in Auckland, eventually taking a classics degree. He began writing while still a schoolboy, and had written most of his major poems by the time he was 25.

Mason's work, along with Ursula *Bethell's, is widely recognized as marking the beginning of a significant New Zealand poetic tradition in the 1920s. His first properly published book, *The Beggar* (1924), was hardly noticed locally but was seen by Harold *Monro, and provided two poems for the *Chapbook Miscellany* in 1924. The earliest poems were often ornate and conven-

tionally *Georgian, though many were revised with a newly austere diction on republication. The poems have a pessimism that stresses a concern with mortality and death; their universe appears to be godless and devoid of charity, yet this harsh vision is presented in verse of considerable compassion and intensity.

At the centre of Mason's finest book, *No New Thing, Poems 1924–1929* (Auckland, 1934) is a Christ figure, the good man of the heresy of Arius, wearing the 'gallant mask' of a pretension to divinity but finally manifesting only a stoic determination to accept the fatal consequences of a humanistic commitment to goodness.

By the 1930s Mason had turned to political and trade-union activity and largely ceased writing poetry, though an interest in drama continued. A selection of his work was published as *This Dark Will Lighten* in 1941, and his *Collected Poems* (Christchurch) ed. Allen Curnow, appeared in 1962. See also, Charles Doyle, *R.A.K.Mason* (New York, 1970) and J. E. Weir, *R.A.K.Mason* (Wellington, 1977).   [WSB

MASSINGHAM, Harold (1932–), was born and grew up in Mexborough, Yorkshire, the son of a collier. After graduating in English from Manchester in 1954, he spent fifteen years as a schoolteacher, and since 1971 has taught in the extramural department of Manchester University.

In his first book, *Black Bull Guarding Apples* (1965) a determination to voice violent, animal sensations and impressions was reminiscent of that other son of Mexborough, Ted *Hughes. An early poem defines its locus, a local farm, as 'cold home for honest gutturals'. The landscape of industrial Yorkshire, and Massingham's memories of his childhood, continued to provide the source of many of his striking if also perplexing images and much of his densely, sometimes excessively textured syntax. A tendency to favour compound epithets and rugged alliteration reflects Massingham's other major influence, Anglo-Saxon poetry, and *Frost-Gods* (1971) contained an impressively energetic version of 'Creation' to add to other translations of Exeter Book riddles and poems.

Massingham then fell largely silent. But *Sonatas and Dreams* (Todmorden, Lancs., 1992) contains an admirable Pennine sequence, new work for children in the manner of his earlier 'Magician' poems, and a treatment of Van Gogh, with whom he has long been fascinated.

[MRW

MASTERS, Edgar Lee (1868–1950), was born in Garnett, Kansas, and grew up on his grandfather's farm in Illinois. Largely an autodidact, Masters spent only a single year (1889) at Knox College in Galesburg, Illinois; his mid-life tribute (in *Songs and Satires*, 1916) to William Marion Reedy 'descanting on Yeats, | With a word on Plato's symposium, | And a little glimpse of Theocritus, | Or something of Bruno's martyrdom, | Or what St Thomas Aquinas meant | By a certain line obscure to us' indicated both his willingness to be impressed by learning and a lurking sense of inferiority.

Masters began his working life as a printer, but entered his father's law office under pressure and was admitted to the Illinois Bar in 1891. He established a practice in Chicago, made a successful career, and in 1898 married Helen M. Jenkins, with whom he had three children. The same year saw publication of his first collection *A Book of Verses*, and by his mid-forties he had followed it with *The Blood of the Prophets* (1905) and the two-volume *Sons and Sonnets* (1910–12), as well as seven plays. This early work was derivative of Whitman, Swinburne, and Keats.

The book which made Masters famous was prompted partly by his mother's lively accounts of people the family had known in Petersburg and Lewistown, Illinois, and partly by J. W. Mackail's *Select Epigrams from the Greek Anthology*, given to him by Reedy (editor of *Reedy's Mirror* in St Louis). The *Spoon River Anthology* (New York and London, 1915) contained well over two hundred free-verse epitaphs. 'When the book was put together in its definitive order', Masters wrote ten years later in the *American Mercury*, 'the fools, the drunkards, and the failures came first, the people of one-birth minds got second place, and the heroes and the enlightened spirits came last, a sort of *Divine Comedy*'. Psychologically and socially acute, sympathetic in tone, the *Spoon River Anthology* marked out Masters as a leading spirit in the Chicago Renaissance, alongside Carl *Sandburg and Vachel *Lindsay. As a portrait of a community, it has often been compared with Anderson's *Winesburg, Ohio*, Wilder's *Our Town*, and Dylan *Thomas's *Under Milk Wood*. It was made into an opera (*La Collina*) by the Italian composer Mario Pergallo.

Unfortunately Masters proved to be a one-book writer, in spite of his prolific output. His next collection, *The Great Valley* (1916), included accomplished monologues which deserve to be better known ('Emily Brosseau: In Church', 'Hanging the Picture'), arresting portraits ('Theodore Dreiser', 'John Cowper *Powys'), and a poem, 'The Bay Window', which strikingly shares the tone of *Eliot's 'Portrait of a Lady'; but most of the book is little more than attitudinizing fustian. *Domesday Book* (1920) and *The Fate of the Jury* (1929) are the only other of Masters's two-dozen volumes of verse that are still read; *The New Spoon River* (1924), like the original volume, was a best-seller, but its assault on modern city life was too crude. Masters wrote several historical plays (largely in verse), seven novels (partly autobiographical), and biographies of Mark Twain, Whitman, Vachel Lindsay, and (a controversial attack) Lincoln; but he remained the Spoon River poet. Interviewed by the *New York Times* in 1942, he described himself as 'a Hellenist', claiming that the marvel of Greek civilization was that 'they thought in universals [whereas] we are provincial in our thoughts'.

In 1920 Masters gave up his Chicago law practice and moved to New York, where in 1925 he divorced his wife, marrying Ellen Coyne the following year. Towards the end of his life he was awarded a fellowship of the Academy of American Poets (1946). Masters died in 1950 and was buried in the cemetery at Petersburg amidst those he had written of in the *Spoon River Anthology*. The most useful study is John T. Flanagan's *Masters: The Spoon River Poet and His Critics* (Metuchen, NJ, 1974). [MHu

MATHEW, Ray(mond Frank) (1929–), was born in Sydney, Australia and worked as a schoolteacher, journalist, and free-lance writer. He left Australia in 1961 when his play *The Life of the Party* (1961) was produced at the Royal Court Theatre, London. He has lived for many years in New York, but his last published work to date has been his one novel, *The Joys of Possession* (London, 1967), based extensively on his personal experiences as a teacher in rural New South Wales.

Ray Mathew was the most important new poetic voice in Australia in the 1950s and the first Australian writer to reflect the stimulus of American poetic experimentalism of the period. His work, lyrical, verbally playful, and increasingly concerned with the delicate balance within interpersonal relationships, confirmed the established line of Australian lyrical poetry while at the same time infusing it with a measure of sophistication and political insight that was ahead of its time. A decade later, when the stridencies of protest-poetry in the Vietnam-War years came to dominate much Australian writing, Mathew's earlier experiments in social observation and his concern for humanistic values were largely ignored, and his work has continued to languish in comparative obscurity. Yet a rereading of his three volumes of poetry reaffirm a freshness of verbal dexterity and a sharp ear for social inflections, both rural and urban. His three collections are *With Cypress Pine* (1951), *Song and Dance* (1956), and *South of the Equator* (1961—all Sydney). [TWS

MATHEWS, Harry (1930–), has lived primarily in France since graduating from Harvard in 1952. Despite this geographical remoteness, Mathews's American audience has steadily increased in recent years, and it always made up in intensity of admiration whatever it may have lacked in size. Mathews serves an uncompromisingly experimental muse. A good portion of his work eludes classification, blurring genres and amalgamating forms. The centre-piece of *Armenian Papers* (Princeton, NJ, 1987), a retrospective selection of his poetry from 1954 to 1984, is 'Trial Impressions', a sequence of thirty versions of the text of an Elizabethan song. The song turns into a multiple-choice narrative here and an equivoque there; Mathews favours home-made forms as well as recondite ones.

Much American poetry is predicated on the repudiation of strict forms. For Mathews the problem with traditional forms is that they are not constrictive enough. In *Selected Declarations of Dependence* (Calais, Vt., 1977), Mathews devises and demonstrates a brilliantly eccentric set of formal procedures based on 'perverbs' (in which the first half of one adage is coupled with the second half of a different one) and 'paraphrases' (in which the perverbs are elaborated, transformed, made into metaphors or allegories). Mathews seems determined to create poetry out of some of the most unpromising materials that language hurls up. In 'Histoire', a madcap and hilarious sestina, the six recurring end-words are 'militarism', 'Marxism-Leninism', 'sexism', 'racism', 'fascism', and 'Maoism'.

Mathews is the only American member of the Oulipo (Ouvroir de Litterature Potentielle, or Workshop for Potential Literature), a Paris-based association of mathematicians and writers committed to the development of ingenious new forms and methods of composition. With John *Ashbery, Kenneth *Koch, and James *Schuyler, he founded the literary magazine *Locus Solus* in 1960. *The Conversions* (New York, 1962), his first novel, is a picaresque adventure based on a rich man's capricious will. He has published three novels since, most recently *Cigarettes* (New York, 1987), a fictional application of the Oulipian method of composition known as 'Mathews's algorithm'. He currently divides his time between Paris and New York. See *A Mid-Season Sky: Poems 1954–1991* (Manchester, 1992). [DL

MATHIAS, Roland (1915–), was born at Talybont-on-Usk, Breconshire, and educated at British military schools in Germany, where his father was an army chaplain, and at Jesus College, Oxford. After teaching history at schools in England, he returned to Wales to become headmaster of Pembroke Dock Grammar School in 1948, but later resumed his career as headmaster of schools at Belper in Derbyshire and in Birmingham.

In 1949 Mathias was one of the founders of *Dock Leaves* (later the *Anglo-Welsh Review*) and edited the magazine between 1961 and 1976, contributing a large number of poems, reviews, and articles, as well as substantial editorials, and in this role he was highly respected and influential.

He has published five collections of verse: *Break in Harvest* (1946), *The Roses of Tretower* (1952), *The Flooded Valley* (1960), *Absalom in the Tree* (1971), and *Snipe's Castle* (1979). Many of the poems in these volumes have to do with Wales and its history, with specific places and people, but they are also intensely personal, following no fashion and showing little significant change in theme, style, or vocabulary over the thirty years of their composition. They are sometimes difficult in their allusion and syntax, usually reflecting the poet's erudition, but they are honest and scrupulously crafted.

A selection of Mathias's writings on Anglo-Welsh literature was published under the title *A Ride through the Wood* (1985); this volume contains essays on Henry Vaughan, Vernon *Watkins, Dylan *Thomas, David *Jones, Alun *Lewis, R. S. *Thomas, and Emyr *Humphreys. The volume entitled *Anglo-Welsh Literature, an Illustrated History* (1987) is a broad survey of its subject. He is also the author of a study of the poetry of John Cowper *Powys, *The Hollowed-out Elder Stalk* (1979), and a monograph on Vernon *Watkins in the Writers of Wales series (1974), and the editor, with Raymond *Garlick, of the anthology *Anglo-Welsh Poetry 1480–1980* (1984).

Roland Mathias's Selected Poems are to be found in *Burning Brambles* (Llandysul, 1983). There is an autobiographical essay in *Artists in Wales*, ed. Meic Stephens (Llandysul, 1971), a critical essay by Jeremy Hooker in *Poetry Wales*, 7: 1, (1971), and an interview with the poet in *Poetry Wales*, 18: 4 (1983).   [MS

MATTHEWS, Harley (1889–1968), was born in Sydney and was educated at Sydney High School. He was an articled clerk in a solicitor's office until he enlisted in the Australian Infantry Forces in 1914. Matthews was among the Anzacs who landed at Gallipoli beach in a campaign against the Turks which became a legendary disaster. He survived the slaughter there to fight in France. After the war he worked for a Sydney afternoon newspaper, and in 1920 went to the United States, where he was a freelance writer for two years. In 1922 he established a vineyard at Moorebank, outside Sydney, which was to become a weekend meeting place for writers as diverse as Kenneth *Slessor and Roland *Robinson.

In 1942 Matthews was arrested and interned in an army prison camp for six months because of his association with members of the Australia First movement (an isolationist, anti-British, quasi-fascist organization), although he himself was not a member. During this time his elderly mother died and his vineyard was ruined through neglect. After the war a Royal Commission exonerated him of any connection with subversion and he was awarded £600 compensation. He lived the remainder of his life on another small farm on the outskirts of Sydney.

It was not until twenty years after the First World War that Matthews published his poems on Gallipoli. Their tone occasionally suggests Robert *Frost's narrative voice. They are written in lines of various metres and with opportunistically occurring rhymes. The long delay in these poems' appearance, their publication just before the Second World War, and their being too long for most anthologies have caused them to be overlooked. Les *Murray rediscovered 'Women Are Not Gentleman' for The *New Oxford Book of Australian Verse* (1986). At least one other long poem from *Vintage* (1938), 'Two Brothers', is equally fine, and these are among the outstanding English-language poems of the First World War. Matthews, shorter and less successful work, to be found mainly in *Patriot's Progress* (1965), has typically a note of aggrieved patriotism, along with its praise of the Australian bush. All of his books are long out of print.   [RGr

MATTHEWS, William (1942–), was born in Cincinnati, Ohio, and educated at Yale University. While he was working towards a Ph.D degree (never completed) at the University of North Carolina, Matthews founded, with Newton Smith and Russell Banks, the magazine *Lillabulero*. A prolific writer, Matthews has also served as a member of the literature panel of the National Endowment for the Arts and as president of the Poetry Society of America. Though he writes basically a free-verse line, Matthews is a master of the well-turned phrase; he is known for both the lyric and the aphoristic qualities of his poems. They are peppered with wise sayings, often cast in a metaphorical form.

The richness of Matthews's use of metaphor was already evident by the time of his third volume, *Rising and Falling* (Boston, 1979), where it can be seen in complete poems, in passages, and in single lines, as when he describes 'abandoned | mines' as 'vaccinations that didn't take'. Such resemblances lie at the heart of his best poems and account in large part for their success. Matthews's most intentionally wise book is his fifth, *A Happy Childhood* (Boston, 1984; London, 1985), which investigates the psychological basis of human life by taking its text from Freud. No simple exercise in nostalgia, the volume makes clear that we as much create our childhoods as we remember them. Matthews's next book, *Foreseeable Futures* (Boston, 1987), carried this principle even further by pointing out that a creative use of lying, or fiction, is at least as important to wisdom as an understanding of the truth.

Matthews's other books are *Ruining the New Road: Poems* (New York, 1970), *Sleek for the Long Flight* (New York, 1972), *Flood* (Boston, 1982), and *Blues if You Want* (Boston, 1989). [PS

MAURICE, Furnley. See WILMOT, FRANK.

MAXWELL, Glyn (1962–), was born of Welsh parents, but grew up in Welwyn Garden City. He took a first in English at Oxford, but abandoned research to concentrate on his writing. In 1987 he won a scholarship to Boston University, where he worked on a creative-writing programme under Derek *Walcott and George

*Starbuck. He is now a free-lance publishing editor and a regular reviewer of poetry.

Maxwell's first full collection, *Tale of The Mayor's Son* (Newcastle upon Tyne, 1990), reflected the sharp restlessness of his talent. Quirky 'tales' oscillate playfully between the realms of the library and of 'the skinhead world', in both of which the narrator emphatically and intrusively tells, and knows he tells, before he shows. Syntax is continually interrupted, broken open as readily as the ideas it governs. It is a constantly invigorating poetry, which exploits Maxwell's ear for conversational rhythms; but such immediate effects risk swamping its subjects—love in an English garden city; the ethics of advertising; small-town and national politics—with a jauntiness and an eagerness to strike a pose. *Auden has been detected as an influence, particularly in the way Maxwell establishes a conspiratorial but also meretricious relationship with his readers, and in the importance of striking rhythms in the work; a barbed Brechtian social impulse may perhaps be detectable too; but the eccentricity of Maxwell's manner is original. A second collection, *Out of the Rain* (Newcastle upon Tyne), was published in 1992. [MRW

MAZZOCCO, (William) Robert (1932–), was born in New York City, attended Columbia and Harvard, and served in the armed forces. He has lived all over the world, including Africa and the South Seas. A frequent contributor to *The New Yorker* and the *New York Review of Books*, Mazzocco has published only one volume, *Trader* (New York, 1980), a collection inspired largely by his wide travels. Many of the poems are set in the tropics and derive their unusual rhythms and phrasings from popular songs and seashanties. 'The Perfect Life', like most of his short-line, monosyllabic poems, relies on repeated phrases for its melodic effect. Dream states inspire a number of dramatic lyrics about self-immolation and the imagined death of parents, all rendered in his starkly cinematic style. Mazzocco's honest and unromantic view of the Third World draws on a wealth of observed, surreal experience, making him a 'magic realist' among poets. The title-poem, with its catalogue of dark and haunting images, establishes the inability of the traveller to penetrate the native mind. In poems about his first heterosexual experience ('Flesh') and an affair with a married sailor ('Gemini'), Mazzocco explores the mysteries of the flesh. His strange aesthetic sensibility leads him to speak in the voices of a gigolo ('Gigolo') and Vincent Van Gogh ('Dear Theo').

[TDeP

MEAD, Philip (1953–), was born in Brisbane, and attended schools in Australia, England, and the USA. He is a graduate of the Australian National University in Canberra and of La Trobe University in Victoria and is currently Lockie Fellow at Melbourne University.

Although not prolific, Mead has, in three small published collections of poetry, established himself as one of the most interesting Australian poets to emerge in the 1980s. His work displays a thorough understanding of contemporary practice and although one may detect the influence of American poets (particularly that of John *Ashbery) in his developing style, Mead has skilfully adapted the new techniques for his own purposes. His most comprehensive collection to date is This River is in the South (St Lucia, Qld., 1984). [TWS

MEHROTRA, Arvind Krishna (1947–), born in Lahore, educated at Allahabad and Bombay, is an academic in the English studies department of Allahabad University. He began writing early, and in order to promote experimental verse he started the little magazines damn you (1965–8) and ezra: an imagiste magazine (1967–71). His iconoclastic reputation was strengthened by his long poem, 'Bharatmata: a Prayer' (1966) which turns Mother India into a septic tank filled with World Bank loans. He was invited to the first international exposition of *concrete and mechanical poetry (Paris, 1967), and published his collection of concrete poems, Woodcuts on Paper (London, 1967). His association with fellow experimental poets and painters continued and two early volumes of *surrealist verse—Pomes/Poems/Poemas and Twelve Poems from the Good Surrealist—were published by avant-garde publishers in Baroda and Bombay (1971–2). The collection Nine Enclosures (Bombay, 1976) contains his best-known poem, 'The Sale', in which a single metaphor, life as a saleroom, is wittily developed.

Mehrotra, like Arun *Kolatkar and Dilip *Chitre, is an accomplished translator of verse, ranging widely from translations of second-century Prakrit love poetry to the contemporary Macedonian poet, Gjuzel. He has been influenced by the cryptic, deceptively simple aphorisms of the medieval weaver-mystic Kabir, in poems like 'After Kabir' in Distance in Statute Miles (Bombay, 1982). In 1992 he edited The Oxford India Anthology of Twelve Modern Indian Poets.

Mehrotra acknowledges the influence of André Breton's Surrealist manifestos on his own discordant images, sometimes nightmarish, often amusing and clever. His later works, even when fractured and disjointed, retain an inner rationality, as in 'Eleven Cross-sections'.

His most recent volume, Middle Earth (Delhi, 1984) is a representative selection. For criticism of his poetry, see Modern Indian Poetry in English, by Bruce King (Delhi, 1987) and Living Indian-English Poets, ed. by M. Prasad (Delhi, 1989).

[RA

MENASHE, Samuel (1925–), was born in New York City. Having enlisted in 1943, he served as an infantryman in Europe; following the Second World War he earned a doctorate at the Sorbonne. He lives in New York City.

Extremely terse poems, often no more than a few lines long, constitute the bulk of Menashe's work. Although often unpunctuated, the poems are usually syntactically complete and are more reminiscent of the Greek Anthology than of haiku. He treats the classic topics of love, loss, and time in tones that can be sombre, wry, or funny. Sometimes the poem functions like a wink, signifying a shared joke; at other times Menashe's use of imagery familiar from the Bible gives his poems a psalm-like cast.

In their cramped physical dimensions, Menashe's poems enact the limitations that form part of his subject-matter—the boundaries of the body, for example. 'The niche narrows | Hones one thin | Until his bones | Disclose him', is a characteristically laconic example. Other well-defined and vivid themes that arise in Menashe's work are tiny landscapes (most often city-scapes), momentary observations, and summaries of the evanescent: a change of weather, or waking from a dream.

Menashe's collections include *The Many Named Beloved* (London, 1961), *No Jerusalem But This* (New York, 1971), *To Open* (New York, 1974), and *Collected Poems* (Orono, Me., 1986).

[RHa

MEREDITH, William (1919–), was born in New York City, graduated from Princeton in 1940, and served as a naval aviator in the Second World War. *Love Letter from an Impossible Land*, his first poetry collection, was chosen by Archibald *MacLeish for the Yale Younger Poets Series in 1944. Five volumes followed, including *The Wreck of the Thresher and Other Poems* (New York, 1964) and *Earth Walk: New and Selected Poems* (New York, 1970). Meredith has also translated Apollinaire's *Alcools* (1964). He taught at Princeton, the University of Hawaii, Middlebury College, Bread Loaf, and for many years at Connecticut College.

Throughout his career Meredith's poetic voice has been notable for its lyrical reticence. The poems are rarely obscure but almost always noticeably, sometimes insistently, quiet, even when the subject-matter (such as Meredith's wartime experiences) might warrant drama. This characteristic tone accompanies graceful syntax and an often stately pace; the effect can be paradoxically sly or evasive, as the reader struggles to determine the poet's exact stance.

Meredith's many meditations on the New England landscape link him more strongly than most poets of his generation to Robert *Frost, but he has ties with various contemporaries as well. The war poems may recall Randall *Jarrell, the fastidious language and lurking humour James *Merrill or Richard *Wilbur, the minute yet shifting perspectives of observed nature (as in 'Whorls') Elizabeth *Bishop ('Last Things',

dedicated to Robert *Lowell, glances at both Lowell's 'Skunk Hour' and Bishop's 'The Armadillo'). Finally, though, Meredith's gift for the odd angle and the wry understatement is, however it limits his poetic range, distinctively his own.

Occasionally Meredith seems to anticipate or echo the effect of defamiliarization achieved by the *Martian poets in Britain in the 1970s. In 'Navy Field' (1944), an airman reads 'The numbered sheets that tell about weather'; in 'Hazard Faces a Sunday in the Decline' (1976), a cat is seen 'the big thrush taken from the cold | box, dressed and put in the hot'—a Thanskgiving turkey transferred from refrigerator to oven. With such eloquently clumsy periphrases Meredith evokes, in a memorably circumlocutory fashion, the things of this world. [RHa

MERRILL, James (1926–), was born in New York City, the son of the immensely wealthy financier Charles E. Merrill, the founder of Merrill Lynch, and the second of his three wives, Hellen Ingram. His parents divorced in 1939 when he was 13, a traumatic experience to which he often alludes in his poetry. Merrill attended Amherst College; he took a year off to serve in the army and graduated in 1947. Although he has since occasionally taught semesters at a variety of American universities, Merrill's freedom from financial pressures has meant that he has been able to live how and where he pleases, a privilege almost unique among modern poets. In 1954 he moved with his companion David Jackson (DJ of *The Changing Light at Sandover*) to Stonington, Connecticut. Merrill has travelled widely, and his poems are often directly concerned with the exotic discoveries and alienating displacements of his journeys abroad. For two decades starting in 1964 he spent a part of each year in Greece, where some of his best-known poems are set.

Merrill's early poems, collected in *Black Swan* (1946) and *First Poems* (1951), are stiff formal exercises in a rather remote high-symbolist rhetoric. Although they exhibit a precocious facility with a wide range of metres and rhyme-schemes, and great skill in their elaborations of stock *fin de siècle* conceits, few of these early pieces add up to more than the sum of their decorative properties. Merrill's breakthrough in the Sixties was to find a way of uniting his formal gifts with a conversational tone capable of including the more mundane aspects of life. As he realizes in 'about the Phoenix': 'But in the end one tires of the high-flown.' 'An Urban Convalescence', the opening poem of his 1962 collection *Water Street* (New York), is obviously pivotal in this transition. Merrill here rejects both the precious decadence of his earlier work and the temptation to windy denunciations of 'the sickness of our time', resolving instead to devote himself to the more practical business of day-to-day living, 'the dull need to make some kind of house | Out of the life lived, out of the love spent'.

This more personal tone allows Merrill to be autobiographical, but he is rarely *confessional. His poems are sheathed in manners in a way unusual in American poetry (Proust and *Auden are without doubt the two dominant influences on his overall poetics). Merrill has called manners 'an artifice in the very bloodstream'; his own nature poems are instinct with an unfailing courtesy, occasionally patrician, occasionally camp, and this social dimension is reflected also in the multiple frames and stylistic devices through which he habitually angles his material. His work is full of puns, extravagant word-games, mythical allusions, intricate metres, and complex rhyme-schemes. Much of it has an almost operatic lushness and self-delight.

Merrill's *chef d'oeuvre* is undoubtedly his 17,000-line epic trilogy *The Changing Light at Sandover* (New York, 1982). Its three long poems—'The Book of Ephraim' (included in *Divine Comedies*, New York, 1976; London, 1979); *Mirabell: Books of Number* (New York, 1978; London, 1979); and *Scripts for the Pageant* (New York, 1980)—are all based on Merrill's and his friend David Jackson's experiences at the ouija board. The various spirits they contact, who include the poet W. H. Auden along with other recently departed friends, gradually educate them in the ways of the scientific and the spiritual worlds, somewhat in the manner of Virgil's instructions to Dante. The poem is composed in a dazzling array of styles, ranging from blank-verse narrative to *canzone* to the upper-case shorthand of the spirits' communications through the ouija board, the different segments of which govern the poem's structure. Merrill has also written two novels, *The Seraglio* (1957) and *The (Diplos) Notebook* (1965), and a collection of his occasional prose pieces has been published under the title *Recitative* (Berkeley, Calif., 1986). See Stephen Yenser, *The Consuming Myth: The Work of James Merrill* (Cambridge, Mass., 1987)   [MF

MERTON, Thomas (1915–69), son of an English painter father and an American Quaker, was born in Southern France and brought up amongst artistic people. In the early 1930s he worked with the communists; in 1938 he joined the Roman Catholic Church, but without losing his liberal sympathies. In 1941 he entered the Cistercian Trappist Monastery at Gethsemane, in Kentucky, where he remained for six years. Eventually he was ordained priest, as Father M. Louis. *The Seven Storey Mountain* (New York, 1948), an autobiography dealing with his wild youth, conversion, and experiences as a Trappist became an international bestseller. His verse, beginning with *Thirty Poems* (New York, 1944), written 'in the first flush of his conversion', and owing more to William Blake than to Catholic devotional poets in its fervour, is perhaps best regarded as an adjunct to his main achievement as a religious thinker and mystic, or as a part of modern American Roman Catholic poetry (cf. Daniel *Berrigan) than as in the mainstream of American poetry. In the poems of the second collection, *Figures for an Apocalypse* (New York, 1947), the original fervour and passion are modified by doctrinal considerations and by a more intellectual note. Subsequent work, reflecting Merton's reading of St John of the Cross and his study of oriental religion and the Christian mysticism of the European Middle Ages, becomes more of a piece with the prose meditations of *Seeds of Contemplation* (New York, 1949), a series he continued until his premature death as a result of an accident with an electric fan. It is likely that his best poetic work has a proper place in any anthology of modern Catholic or mystical verse. See also *Cables to the Ace* (New York, 1968).   [MS-S]

MERWIN, W(illiam) S(tanley) (1927–), was born in New York City and grew up in Union City, New Jersey, and Scranton, Pennsylvania. His father was a Presbyterian minister. 'I started writing hymns for my father as soon as I could write at all', Merwin has said. He attended Princeton University, where he studied writing with John *Berryman and R. P. *Blackmur, to whom his fifth book, *The Moving Target* (1963), was dedicated. Merwin spent a postgraduate year at Princeton studying Romance languages, an interest that would lead, eventually, to his much-admired work as a translator of Latin, Spanish, and French poetry.

Having left Princeton, Merwin travelled in France, Spain, and England. He settled in Majorca in 1950 as a tutor to Robert *Graves's son. Graves, with his interest in mythology, would become a primary influence on young Merwin. Moving to London in 1951, Merwin made his living as a translator for several years. Meanwhile, back in America, his first book of poems won the Yale Series of Younger Poets Award for 1952, selected by W. H. *Auden, who remarked in his introduction on the young poet's technical virtuosity. That volume, *A Mask for Janus*, is immensely formal, neoclassical in style. For the next decade Merwin would regularly publish collections of intensely wrought, brightly imagistic poems that recalled the poetry of Wallace *Stevens as well as Robert Graves and other influences.

Merwin's early subjects were frequently tied to mythological or legendary themes, while many of the poems featured animals, which were treated as emblems in the manner of Blake. A volume called *The Drunk in the Furnace* (1960) marked a change for Merwin, in that he began to write in a much more autobiographical way. The title-poem is about Orpheus, seen as an old drunk. 'Where he gets his spirits | It's a

mystery', Merwin writes; 'But the stuff keeps him musical'. Another powerful poem of this period is 'Odysseus', which reworks the traditional theme in a way that plays off poems by Stevens and Graves on the same topic.

In the 1960s Merwin began to experiment boldly with metrical irregularity. His poems became much less tidy and controlled. He played with the forms of indirect narration typical of this period, a self-conscious experimentation explained in an essay called 'On Open Form' (1969). *The Lice* (1967) and *The Carrier of Ladders* (1970) (which won a Pulitzer Prize) remain his most characteristic and influential volumes. These poems often used legendary subjects (as in 'The Hydra' or 'The Judgment of Paris') to explore highly personal themes.

In Merwin's later volumes, such as *The Compass Flower* (1977), *Opening the Hand* (1983), and *The Rain in the Trees* (1988), one sees him transforming earlier themes in fresh ways, developing an almost Zen-like indirection. His latest poems are densely imagistic, dream-like, and full of praise for the natural world. He has lived in Hawaii in recent years, and one sees the influence of this tropical landscape everywhere in the recent poems, though the landscape remains emblematic and personal.

The best selection of Merwin's work is his *Selected Poems* (New York, 1988). See also his autobiography, *The Miner's Pale Children* (New York, 1970) and his selected essays, *Regions of Memory* (Urbana, Ill., 1983). For criticism, see W. S. Merwin, by Cheri Davis (Boston, 1981).

[JP]

MEW, Charlotte (1869–1928), was born in London into a genteel Victorian middle-class family which was neither literary nor highly educated. Her father's death when she was 29 forced Mew to take employment as a teacher, and she lived with her mother and sister all her life in varying degrees of hardship. A history of mental instability in the family dissuaded her from considering marriage. She wrote a quantity of short stories in the early years of the century and took to writing poetry when she was in her forties. Through her friendship with Alida Monro,

Mew's work was published by the *Poetry Bookshop in a slim volume, The Farmer's Bride, in 1916, and was admired by *Masefield and *Hardy, among others. In 1923 she was awarded a Civil List pension, but did not live long to enjoy it, dying by her own hand in a sanatorium five years later. Her poems are sensual, melancholy, and subjective, reflecting a lonely and eccentric life. Her use of narrative forms and the dramatic monologue is reminiscent of Browning's, which points up an interesting struggle in her poetry between form and content—the first almost wholly Victorian, the latter of the twentieth century. Her themes are death, ephemerality, love (usually lost or hopeless), God (also lost or uncompassionate), and the overriding tone is elegiac. Her work is uneven, but at its best very vivid and eloquent, rooted in the physical world and experienced through a powerful, rather morbid sensuality. The emotional intensity of many of her poems is enhanced by the use of a speaking voice and by highly personal rhythms and syntax, partly the fruit of her confessed ignorance of the rules of punctuation. A second volume, The Rambling Sailor was published posthumously in 1929 and Collected Poems in 1953. Mew's Collected Poems and Prose, ed. Val Warner, was published in 1981 (Manchester). See also Penelope Fitzgerald, Charlotte Mew and Her Friends (London, 1984).   [CPH

MEYNELL, Alice (née Thompson) (1847–1922), was born in Barnes, west London. Her father Thomas Thompson, a friend of Charles Dickens, was a cultured gentleman of independent means who insisted on a solid classical education for his two talented daughters and on frequent travel in Italy to enhance their aesthetic sensibilities.

Alice became a Roman Catholic in 1868. She married Wilfrid Meynell, also a Catholic convert, in 1877. He became a successful editor of the magazine Merry England to which the poet Francis Thompson contributed. Thompson subsequently moved in with the Meynell family and accepted their patronage. Alice also developed a friendship with George Meredith and with Coventry Patmore, but this was broken off

when Patmore insisted on its being more intimate than she desired.

Alice raised a family of seven children and yet managed to find time to be active in prominent social circles in London and in politics. She marched with the Suffragettes.

Her poems are generally low-keyed, subtle, and non-rhetorical. She employed conventional prosody and defended her use of it in her poem 'The English Metres', first published in 1921 when the *vers libre movement was at its height. The subjects she treated were usually love, religious belief, response to the beauties of nature, and war. 'Renouncement' is the most famous of her love poems.

For biographical information see Viola Meynell, Alice Meynell: A Memoir (London and New York, 1929) and June Badeni, The Slender Tree: A Life of Alice Meynell (Padstow, Cornwall, 1981). Geoffrey Cumberledge, The Poems of Alice Meynell (London and New York, 1940), is the standard collected edition of her verse.   [DS

MEZEY, Robert (1935–), was born in Philadelphia and attended Kenyon College, Ohio, for two years before entering the army in 1953—by his own account, he was discharged as a 'subversive' in 1955. He earned his BA from the University of Iowa by 1960 and spent the next year at Stanford University as a poetry fellow. He married Ollie Simpson in 1963, and they have three children. Besides teaching at the college level, he serves as poetry editor for Trans Pacific.

A gifted metaphysical poet, Mezey's strong first collection, The Lovemaker: Poems (1961), won the Lamont Poetry Award. In the volumes to follow, White Blossoms: Poems (1965) and A Book of Dying: Poems (1970), he abandoned rhyme and metre, attempting to combine his Blakean passion with Philip *Levine's freer naturalism. He also edited, with Stephen *Berg, Naked Poetry: Recent American Poetry in Open Forms (1969) and, on his own, edited and translated Poems from the Hebrew (1973).

Published in Boston by Houghton Mifflin and in London by Oxford University Press, Mezey's The Door Standing Open: New and Selected Poems 1954–1969 (1970) offers the fullest collection of his work, when supplemented by *Evening Wind* (Middletown, Conn., 1987). [EB

MICHIE, James (1927–), was born in Surrey and while an undergraduate edited *Oxford Poetry* (Oxford, 1949) with Kingsley *Amis. He became known as the able and accurate translator of Horace (1964), Catullus (1969), Martial (1973), and of *Selected Fables* by La Fontaine (1979)—the last being regarded by some as the best version so far made in this century. His translations in themselves represent a poetic achievement. His own sparse collections, *Possible Laughter* (London, 1959) and its single successor, which reprints most of it, *New and Selected Poems* (London, 1983), consist for the most part of terse and epigrammatic poems. They are very much the original occasional poems of a more-than-competent translator. A little over-influenced by *Auden and *Betjeman, they show little development, but remain the reasonable and well-crafted comments of a writer who sees his century from, so far as he can, the viewpoint of the Latin models he has rendered so well into English. [MS-S

MIDDLETON, Christopher (1926–), was born in Truro, Cornwall. He read German and French at Oxford, and subsequently taught in Zurich and London. In 1965 he emigrated and became professor of Germanic languages and literature at the University of Texas.

As a poet Middleton is compulsively experimental, which explains in part his neglect in England. The first collection he acknowledges, *Torse 3: Poems 1949–61* (1962), was awarded the first Sir Geoffrey Faber Memorial Prize, but it was with his next collection, *Nonsequences/Self-poems* (1965), that the direction he was to take became clear. An early influence was the prose of the Swiss writer Robert Walser, four of whose stories Middleton translated in the Fifties and whom he described in an early essay, included in *Bolshevism in Art and Other Expository Writings* (Manchester, 1978; Atlantic Highlands, NJ, 1980), as 'a stranger to the realm of ideas'. Throughout his work Middleton resists and subverts the demands of the 'logomorphic'

intelligence which tries to explain and interpret experience, seeking instead to disrupt poetic and linguistic modes to create unprecedented structures in which a delicate and often humorous freshness of perception is apparent.

Middleton is an outstanding translator from the German. Among his many translations are *Selected Poems* of Friedrich Hölderlin and Eduard Mörike (Chicago and London, 1972), *Kafka's Other Trial: The Letters to Felice*, by Elias Canetti (New York, 1974; Harmondsworth, 1978), *Selected Stories* of Robert Walser (New York and Manchester, 1982), and a number of Gert Hofman's novels. Translations by him can be found in *East German Poetry: an Anthology*, ed. Michael Hamburger (Manchester and New York, 1973) and *Selected Poems* of Paul Celan (Harmondsworth, 1972).

The best introduction to Middleton's work is *Selected Writings* (Manchester and London, 1989). A more recent collection is *The Balcony Tree* (Manchester, 1992). And there is a second collection of essays: *The Pursuit of the Kingfisher* (Manchester, 1983; New York, 1984). For a judicious account of his work, see *An Introduction to 50 Modern British Poets*, by Michael Schmidt (London and Sydney, 1979). [TSGH

MILES, Josephine (1911–85), was born in Chicago and educated at the University of California, Los Angeles. Severely crippled by arthritis, she taught at the University of California, Berkeley, from 1940 until her retirement in 1978. A prolific critic and scholar as well as poet, Miles's works include studies of the characteristic vocabularies of poetry in various eras. In 'Poetry and Tradition,' an essay published in *Pacific Coast Philology* (Nov. 1981), Miles stated that at the beginning of her poetic career, 'one of the assumptions I most resented was that of individual autonomy.'

Miles's early poems do not deserve Kenneth *Rexroth's famous quip ('small, very neat holes cut in the paper'), but their very modesty and attention to formal details set them apart from the broader, romantic work of Rexroth and poets such as William *Everson and Robert *Duncan with whom he was then associated.

Her later work is less formal, but extreme attention to detail remains constant. Sometimes seen as one of Rexroth's principal opponents in the mid-century poetry community in the San Francisco Bay Area, she was in fact too independent to ally herself with any poetic faction, and although her work was widely respected among her peers, she had no major disciples.

Miles's *Collected Poems* (Urbana, Ill.) was published in 1983. *To All Appearances: Poems New and Selected* (Urbana, 1974) provides a good introduction to the work. [EHF

MILLAY, Edna St Vincent (1892–1950). Though it seems surprising in the 1990s, Edna Millay, bohemian rebel and darling of Greenwich Village in the Twenties, was younger by five years than the modernist Marianne *Moore. The most gifted of three talented daughters, Edna (known as 'Sefe' or 'Vincent' to her family) was born in Rockland, Maine on 22 February 1892. Her father was a superintendent of schools, but her parents separated when their daughters were tiny, and it was principally her mother, a musician frustrated into becoming a district nurse, who brought up the family. Although encouraged to develop her gifts, the young Edna Millay had no formal teaching until, in her twenties, she was sent briefly to Barnard College and then to Vassar, from which she graduated in 1917, her reputation already established by the publication of *Renascence and Other Poems*.

Millay soon settled in Greenwich Village where she assimilated the image of the new 'free woman', undertaking to live dangerously in several roles: she acted, wrote plays in verse for the Provincetown Players, and contributed clever, satirical prose to magazines—sometimes under a pseudonym, Nancy Boyd. She also became famous for love affairs (there was an especially turbulent one with the young Edmund *Wilson), while she continued to write popular lyrics. Her second book, *A Few Figs from Thistles* (1920), included her most quoted quatrain: 'My candle burns at both ends; | It will not last the night | But ah, my foes, and oh, my friends— | It gives a lovely light.'

Edna Millay published two more collections of verse (The *Harp-Weaver and Other Poems* won the 1923 Pulitzer Prize) and produced a number of her plays before, at the end of 1923, she married Eugene Boissevain, a businessman who dedicated his life to caring for her. They travelled together and then settled for a while in New York City. After Edna had suffered several nervous breakdowns, they retreated to a farm near Austerlitz, New York State. Here, in desperately bad health, writing steadily despite a waning reputation, Millay, widowed in her later years, lived in painful seclusion until her death in 1950.

In the period between the World Wars Millay's reputation was what Sylvia *Plath's is today. But Millay, though prone to violent mood-swings and recurrent crises of health, was held prisoner, as Plath was not, by the rigidity of lyrical convention. At its most assured, Millay's ear dictated a firm, musical, economical line. Her sonnets, once compared with Shakespeare's and Donne's, to the modern ear often verge on the bathetic. Her fanciful one-act plays, though (The Princess Marries the Page, 1918, and Aria da Capo, 1919), are still performed in American schools. And Millay has a faithful following. Many women readily forgive her for sacrificing what John Crowe *Ransom stiffly identified as a woman's typical 'indifference to intellectuality' to uninhibited emotion and a gift for heart-wringing pathos.

Publications include *A Few Figs from Thistles* (1920); *Second April* (1921); *The Harp-Weaver and Other Poems* (1923); *The Buck in the Snow* (1928); *Fatal Interview* (1931); *Wine from These Grapes* (1934); *Conversation at Midnight* (1937); *Huntsman, What Quarry* (1939); *Bright these Arrows* (1940); *Murder of Lidice* (1942). Millay's *Collected Sonnets* were published in 1941 and *Collected Lyrics* in 1943. *Mine the Harvest* posthumously collected sixty-six poems in 1954. Her *Collected Poems* appeared in 1956, *Selected Poems of Edna Millay* (New York) in 1991, and *Selected Poems*, ed. Colin Falck (Manchester) in 1992. [AS

MILLER, Ruth (née Fridjhon) (1919–69), was born at Uitenhage, Cape Province. Her parents were Jewish but the ethnic influence was offset by circumstances. Deserted by her father, she and her mother lived on a farm with the family of a courtesy aunt who played a formative role in Ruth's early education. Later she attended a convent school.

The sole woman in the front rank of South Africa's English-language poets, she is the one whose work most characteristically invokes the note of tragedy. At the same time there is wit, sometimes deployed in satire. One of Miller's emotional motifs is exasperation when weakness of the flesh (such as the fatal cancer in whose grip she probably knew herself to be) or over-domestication of the spirit shrinks her capacity for joyous participation or passionate commitment. In some of her most powerful poems—'Voicebox', 'Come Not Unto Me', 'Submarine', 'Pebble', 'Rat'—the predominant theme is the confrontation of mortality.

Miller's ironical and unexpectant vision implies the possible existence of a deity whose chief attributes, however, are absence and indifference, but this does not preclude an appalled and compassionate identification with all suffering creatures (adventurous men in peril, victims of racist mean-spiritedness, a blind dog, an oil-soaked penguin). Nor does it mean that her poems cannot be celebratory—of love, courage, natural beauty. The sudden death of her 14-year-old son in 1962 brought these feelings more intensely into focus.

After her two collections *Floating Island* (Cape Town, 1965) and *Selected Poems* (London, 1969) went out of print, certain poems (notably 'The Floating Island', 'Sterkfontein', 'Penguin on the Beach', 'Fruit', 'Aliens at home', 'Plankton', 'The Stranger', 'Spider', 'Mantis') were increasingly in demand for anthologies. Both collections were incorporated, with a choice of uncollected poems and other material, in *Ruth Miller—Poems, Prose, Plays*, ed. Lionel Abrahams (Cape Town, 1990). [LA

MILLER, Vassar (1924–), was born in Houston, Texas, where she has lived all her life. Two conditions have influenced her poetry: her disease (cerebral palsy), and her religion (Christian

mysticism). Since 1956, when *Adam's Footprint* appeared, Miller has been considered an accomplished lyric poet. Her themes are intensely personal: God ('Nada'); religious faith; acceptance (her need to accept God); silence (the inexpressible); sleep (as seducer); the barren inadequacy of modern technology; the erotic; and death (as reliever of pain). She writes in both traditional and modernistic forms.

If I Had Wheels or Love: Collected Poems of Vassar Miller (Dallas, 1990) contains all the poems in her earlier eight collections, along with a sampling of her new work. The earlier collections are *Adam's Footprint* (1956); *Wage War on Silence* (1960): *My Bones Being Wiser* (1963): *Onions and Roses* (1968); *If I Could Sleep Deeply Enough* (1974); *Small Change* (1976); *Approaching Nada* (1977); and *Struggling to Swim on Concrete* (1984). *Despite This Flesh: The Disabled in Stories and Poems*, which she edited in 1984 (Austin), is an anthology of poetry and stories about the disabled. *Heart's Invention: On the Poetry of Vassar Miller*, ed. Steven Ford Brown (Houston, 1988) contains critical commentary on her work. [JT

MILLS, Neil. See SOUND POETRY.

MILNE, A(lan) A(lexander) (1882–1956), best known now for *Winnie-the-Pooh*, started life primarily as a versifier. At Cambridge he originally contributed poems to *Granta* under the initials AKM, as they were joint creations with his brother. He admired C. S. Calverley and believed in the importance of light verse: 'Light verse is not the output of poets at play but of light verse writers . . . at the hardest and most severely technical work known to authorship.' Kingsley *Amis approvingly quotes Milne on light verse in the *New Oxford Book*, but Milne's own adult verse has been little anthologized.

In the Twenties Milne began to write verse for children (which category does not include his most famous poem 'Vespers', being *about* a child, and ironic rather than sentimental). Both his children's collections, *When We Were Very Young* (1924) and *Now We Are Six* (1927), were immediate best-sellers and continue to sell.

Poems such as 'Disobedience' ('James, James, Morrison, Morrison') and 'The King's Breakfast' are as well known as any in the language.

Milne published verse in *Punch* throughout his life, most of it later collected. His adult poetry collections are *For the Luncheon Interval* (London and New York, 1925) and *Behind the Lines* (London and New York, 1940). *The Norman Church* (London, 1948) was a long poem which made little impact. His most bitter and memorable adult poem, 'OBE', is available in his biography, *A. A. Milne: His Life*, by Ann Thwaite (London and New York, 1990). [AT

MILNE, Ewart (1903–87), was born in Dublin and educated at Christ Church Cathedral Grammar School. After running away to sea and travelling to the Spanish Civil War, Milne worked variously in England and in Ireland as a farmworker and journalist.

Milne's work has been criticized for its blarney and stage Irishness, but melodious fluency is just one aspect of his style. As well as prolific, Milne was highly adaptable, ranging in subject and in tone from the bold socialism of *Forty North, Fifty West* (Dublin, 1938) to the light verse of *Once More to Tourney* (London, 1958). He seems finally to have discovered his own voice in the bitter and heartfelt poems in *Time Stopped* (London, 1967), written after the death of his wife, but he will be best remembered for the excellent declamatory anti-pub poem 'Non-Alcoholics Anonymous' in *Cantata Under Orion* (Breakish, 1976). His many other collections of verse include *Jubilo* (London, 1945), *Galion* (London, 1953), *A Garland for the Green* (London, 1962), and *Spring Offering* (Portree, 1983). [IES

MINHINNICK, Robert (1952–), was born in Neath and brought up in the village of Pen-y-fai, Mid-Glamorgan. Educated at University College, Cardiff, he has had a variety of jobs and now works for Friends of the Earth in Wales.

Minhinnick is concerned with environmental and political questions, but succeeds in avoiding rhetoric and propaganda. Many of the people in his poems live under pressure but they face a hostile world with resilience and humour. He has published five volumes of poetry: *A Thread in the Maze* (1978) and *Native Ground* (1979—both Swansea); and *Life Sentences* (1983), *The Dinosaur Park* (1985), and *The Looters* (1989—all Bridgend, Glam.). There is an interview with Robert Minhinnick in *Common Ground*, ed. Susan Butler (Bridgend, 1985). [MS

MITCHELL, Adrian (1932–), was born in London, of Scottish descent. His poems are almost all 'performance pieces', rather of the kind known by left-wing students in the Thirties as 'agitprop', verse designed to initiate, or support, political action. Free-wheeling, surrealist, rhyming or unrhyming, there is a lot of vitality in these exuberant declarations ('Snow White was in the News of the World—Virgin Lived With Seven Midgets'). However effective in performance, though, some seem simplistic and childish when written down. It is not always entirely clear whether it is socialism or anarchy that is being promoted. The tone can be hysterical; but, equally, some of the pieces are very funny, as well as subversive ('The Eggs O' God' and 'A Leaflet To Be Dropped On China'). Some even, like 'The Oxford Hysteria Of English Poetry', are funny without any political designs on the reader. A good many, with their repetitions and their banging rhythms, are like sophisticated, politically aware pop songs—'Fifteen Million Plastic Bags', warning of nuclear war, is one of the most famous of these. Other poems forsake humour completely and, however valuable in their day as propaganda, they remain prosy. The main collection is *For Beauty Douglas: Adrian Mitchell's Collected Poems 1953–79* (London and New York, 1982). His several theatre adaptations of verse plays include an English version of Peter Weiss's *Marat/Sade*. [GE

MNTHALI, Felix (1933–), was born of Malawian parents in Shurugwe, Zimbabwe. After education in Lesotho he obtained a Ph.D in English in Canada. From 1969 he taught at Chancellor College, University of Malawi. A period in detention was ended with an apology from the authorities, but from 1979 he has lived in exile, latterly as professor of English at the University of Botswana.

Mnthali's Catholic faith is a strong presence in his work: 'Corpus Christi', for instance, is a characteristically direct and sensuous hymn on his release from jail. Mnthali's free-verse rhythms are controlled towards emphatic rather than delicate effects. He deplores without affectation the negative features of Africa's recent history of colonialism and dictatorship, but is equally fervent in affirmation. His verse declaims well—'Antonina', for instance, is a compact, powerful denunciation of repression in Malawi, while 'Ads and the Man,' despite its seemingly flippant title, celebrates the country's natural grandeur on the way to a simple protestation of human love.

Mnthali's substantial collection is *When Sunset Comes to Sapitwa* (London, 1982). Adrian Roscoe discusses his work in 'Proceed with Joy: The poetry of Felix Mnthali', *The Month* (Apr. 1992). [ALRC

MOLE, John (1941–), was born in Taunton, Somerset, and teaches English, which he studied at Cambridge. He is married to the artist Mary Norman; with Peter *Scupham he runs the Mandeville Press in Hitchin. His first substantial book was *The Love Horse* (1974); since then he has published seven more, of which the most recent was *Homing* (1987), as well as four highly acclaimed collections of poems for children, to the success of which Mary Norman's delightful drawings have contributed greatly. Since *Homing* he has published poems from a series entitled *Points of Departure*, which promises to be his most impressive achievement to date.

Although Mole's concern is with the unpretentious, intelligent portrayal of everyday experience, his poems vary considerably in their degree of earnestness; what is common to all is skilled craftsmanship. He has said that regularity of form does not squeeze out feeling but squeezes it *in*—a claim justified by his successes: 'The Birthday', 'Coming Home', or the poems of *Points of Departure*. His children's poems are metrical *tours de force*; finally, the distinction between serious and juvenile is inessential, because he has the gift of writing in the child's terms at a level that also addresses adult experi-

ence. Good examples are 'Wasp Talk', which provides the title for one of Mole's best collections *In and Out of the Apple* (1984), and the haunting, Blake-like 'The Lost Boy', written for the poet's two sons.

Mole's last four collections have been published in London, and two recent children's volumes, by Peterloo Poets. Some of his *Encounter* poetry reviews were collected as *Passing Judgements: Poetry in the Eighties* (Bristol, 1989).

[BO'D

MOLL, E(rnest) G(eorge) (1900–79), was born in Murtoo, Victoria, Australia, and was educated in Australia and at Harvard University. He was professor of English at the University of Oregon, 1928–66, but retained his Australian citizenship, and published nine collections of poetry in Australia between 1927 and 1971. Of these, *Poems 1940–1955* (Sydney, 1957) represents a combination of his five previous volumes. His rural background, combined with a breadth of education, and a long period of expatriation which was no doubt intensified by occasional return visits to Australia, all brought the poet's sensibilities to bear on recapturing memorable and minute moments of Australian experience. Although Moll was not a member of the *Jindyworobak movement of the 1930s and 1940s, which sought to redefine a European Australian experience in terms of an Aboriginal understanding of the land, his work was included in some of the Jindyworobak anthologies and, in retrospect, is most securely placed in the context of a lyrical celebration of nature in its harshness and beauty. His later volume, *The Rainbow Serpent* (Sydney, 1962), included an extended sequence for several voices, 'The Lightless Ferry', based on Aboriginal death ceremonies recounted in Sir Baldwin Spencer's *Wanderings in Wild Australia*. The poem is ambitious in scope, but remains uncomfortable in its linking of Aboriginal with Greek mythologies.

[TWS

MONRO, Harold (1879–1932), was born in Brussels and read modern and medieval languages at Cambridge. He travelled and lived on the continent and studied for the Bar before taking to poetry. He co-founded the Samurai Press then, eventually, settled in London where he became founder editor of the magazines *Poetry Review* (1912), *Poetry and Drama* (1913–14), and the *Monthly Chapbook* later renamed the *Chapbook* (1919–25). In January 1913 he officially opened the *Poetry Bookshop in London, having started an imprint of the same name in 1912. Monro eventually died in a nursing home in 1932 after a long illness. His widow Alida kept the Bookshop going without him until June 1935, when it was forced to close.

Better known in his lifetime as an editor and publisher than as a poet, Monro's own poems have been highly praised by T. S. *Eliot, who wrote, in the critical note to Monro's 1933 *Collected Poems*, 'I think that his poetry, as a whole, is more nearly the real right thing than any of the poetry of a somewhat older generation than mine except Mr Yeats's'. Monro's work is serious and varied, but still rather undervalued. He wrote the unironic 'Week-end', in many ways *the* quintessential *Georgian poem, on the weekend flight of a commuter from the city to the 'comfortable joys' of his country retreat. He wrote well, too, on modern urban life in 'The Ocean in London' and 'Suburb'. In his day his best-known poem was the much anthologized 'Milk for the Cat', which manages to be simultaneously domestic and unsettling. But his real achievement is to be found in the longer poem-sequences on personal isolation such as 'Strange Meetings', 'The Silent Pool', and 'Bitter Sanctuary' (this last a bleak portrait of a terminal ward), in which his own grim and authentic voice finally breaks through, expressing what Eliot called Monro's sense of the 'ceaseless question and answer of the tortured mind'. Monro's anthology, *Twentieth Century Poetry* (1929), is a modern classic, drawing attention to the best of widely differing types of poetry by both Georgians and modernists. He wrote one critical book, *Some Contemporary Poets* (1920).

See: *Collected Poems of Harold Monro*, ed. Alida Monro with a biographical sketch by F. S. Flint and a critical note by T. S. Eliot (London, 1933) and Harold Monro *Collected Poems*, ed. Alida Monro with a preface by Ruth Tomalin (London, 1970); Joy Grant, *Harold Monro and the Poetry Bookshop* (London, 1967) and Robert H. Ross, *The Georgian Revolt: Rise and Fall of a Poetic Ideal 1910–22* (London, 1967).   [JDB

MONROE, Harriet. See *Poetry*.

MONTAGUE, John (1929–), was born into a Catholic family in New York and grew up in Co. Tyrone, and has been an important influence on the work of several younger Irish poets, including Seamus *Heaney. By them he is regarded as something of a pioneer, especially in his acute sense of the cultural and material spoliation inflicted on the Gael, and in his ambitious determination to explore its history and its effects in the present. Much of Montague's childhood, however, was spent in America, and his poetry has clearly been influenced by the *Pound tradition. He has that fear of rhetoric endemic among post-Yeatsian Irish poets: 'Enlarged profile, gun and phrase', as he nicely puts his association of gesturing politics and language. He praises Tim, the first horse he rode, for 'denying | rhetoric' and forcing him to drink from 'the trough of reality'. This aesthetic is summarized in a poem from *A Chosen Light* (London, 1967; Chicago, 1969), 'A Bright Day', where he speaks of 'The only way of saying something | Luminously as possible', which he equates with 'A slow exactness | which recreates experience | By ritualizing its details'. Montague is well able to achieve this effect, combining it with a tough urbanity of stance and diction. Formally, he has increasingly moved towards the use of fluent, run-on lines.

Perhaps his most important volume to date is *The Rough Field* (Dublin and London, 1972; Winston-Salem, NC, 1979), an ambitious attempt to link the universal and particular in a view of the current Northern Irish Troubles. Thus 'The Cave of the Night' gives a dark view of the violence on both sides, moving from legendary pre-Christian Irish child-sacrifice to the bombing of children in a community centre.

Montague has also translated much poetry

from the Irish, as can be seen from the *Faber Book of Irish Verse* (1974), which he edited. These translations are very much in the modern tradition, prizing fidelity to meaning over other values, but they are admirable in this kind.

See *New Selected Poems* (Newcastle upon Tyne, 1990), and also the John Montague Special Issue of the *Irish University Review* (Spring, 1989). [ETL

MOODY, William Vaughn (1869–1910), was born in Spencer, Indiana. He taught at Harvard (1894–1895) and the University of Chicago (1895–1902). In 1909 he married Harriet Brainard. His publications include *Poems* (Boston, 1901), and the verse dramas *The Masque of Judgment* (Boston, 1900), *The Fire-Bringer* (Boston, 1904), and *The Death of Eve* (unfinished, 1912). Two prose plays were produced in New York, *The Great Divide* in 1906 and *The Faith Healer* in 1910. He died of a brain tumour at 41.

Moody's poetry strives to affirm his idealism while addressing the corruptions of his age (e.g. 'The Brute'). His best-known poem, 'An Ode in Time of Hesitation' (1900), anticipates Robert *Lowell's 'For the Union Dead' in using Boston's monument to Colonel Robert Gould Shaw and his black Civil War regiment as a standard of heroism by which to condemn the present, but is weakened by its outdated rhetoric and thematic uncertainties. Similar flaws compromise most of his major efforts, but he shows a defter touch elsewhere, as in the humour of 'The Menagerie' or the lyric beauty of 'A Dialogue in Purgatory'. Though limited in achievement, he is an important figure in the struggle to modernize American poetry.

His work was collected in two volumes (Boston and New York, 1912). Maurice F. Brown's *Estranging Dawn* (Carbondale, Ill., 1973; London, 1973) is a solid critical biography. [MP

MOORE, Marianne (Craig) (1887–1972), was born in Kirkwood, a suburb of St Louis, Missouri. She was the second child of a father who, failing as an engineer, returned permanently to his parents after a nervous breakdown, and a mother who assumed the burden of bringing up her family. Mrs Moore housekept for her own father, a Scotch-Irish Presbyterian minister, until his death in 1894, after which she moved with her children to Carlisle, Pennsylvania. Marianne attended the Metzger School, where her mother had a teaching job, before entering Bryn Mawr College to study biology. After graduating in 1909, she qualified as a secretary and taught stenography and bookkeeping to US Indians in Carlisle. When, in 1918, her brother became a chaplain in the navy, Marianne and her mother followed him to New York, renting a basement in Greenwich Village before moving in 1929 (for the rest of their lives) to a fifth-floor apartment on Cumberland Street in Brooklyn.

The poet's literary career began, in fact, before she moved to New York, when Hilda *Doolittle (H. D.), a former Bryn Mawr classmate, then married to the English imagist Richard *Aldington, published Moore's poem 'To Military Progress' in *The Egoist* in 1915. In May of the same year, Harriet Monroe's *Poetry* (Chicago) published five poems by Marianne Moore, attracting praise from Alfred *Kreymborg and Ezra *Pound, both of whom hastened to patronize her 'flaming red hair', her innocence, and her bold, ladylike particularity. By the time H. D. and Winifred Ellerman ('Bryher') brought out Moore's *Poems* in 1921, her reputation already stood high with the avant-garde. Her second collection, *Observations* (1924) won her the *Dial* Award, and led to Moore's appointment as assistant editor of that magazine; she replaced Scofield Thayer as editor in 1926, a position she held until the *Dial*'s demise after July 1929.

During and after the Second World War Marianne Moore's reputation as *the* leading American woman poet steadily increased. In 1935 Macmillan in New York and Faber in London published her *Selected Poems*. She won the Shelley Memorial Award in 1940, the Harriet Monroe Award and Contemporary Poetry's Patron Prize in 1944, a Guggenheim Fellowship in 1945, and a joint grant from the American Academy of Arts and Letters and the National Institute of Arts and Letters in 1946. In 1947 she was elected to the National Institute for Arts and Letters. At least four honorary degrees were bestowed on her by US colleges in the 1950s, and in 1952, following the publication of her *Collected Poems*, she won, in one year, the Bollingen Award, the National Book Award, and the Pulitzer Prize. (The *Complete Poems of Marianne Moore* appeared in London in 1968, new edn. 1984.) She went on to win the NIAL Gold Medal for Poetry in 1953, and in 1955 she was elected a member of the American Academy. It seemed that Moore's eccentric, zoological, moralistic, *syllabic verses offended no one; moreover, everyone who met her delighted in her company.

To Moore's credit, she remained her unspoiled, decisive self throughout this storm of patronage and honours, producing slender new collections (*Like a Bulwark*, 1956, and *O To be a Dragon*, 1960), a version of *The Fables of La Fontaine* (1954), and a selection of essays called *Predilections* in 1955. By 1961, when Viking (New York) published *A Marianne Moore Reader*, she was already defending herself against rumbling criticism in the literary quarterlies: 'Prose: mine [she wrote] will always be "essays" and verse of mine, observations . . . Why an inordinate interest in animals and athletes? They are subjects for art and exemplars of it, are they not? minding their own business . . .', and then, quoting from Charles Ives: ' "The fabric of existence weaves itself whole. You cannot set art off in a corner and hope for it to have vitality, reality and substance." '

Although Marianne Moore was, like her puritan family, naïve, moralistic, and, as regards psychological understanding, limited as a poet, her achievement remains unique within the modernist movement. To have withstood alike sentimentality and self-indulgence, 'literariness' and philistinism, is to have survived the worst intellectual plagues of the post-Romantic period. As spokeswoman for 'literalists of the imagination' and creator of 'imaginary gardens with real toads in them', she is likely to be long celebrated as the founder of a woman's poetry that bears no stigma either of self-aggrandizement or hysteria.

[AS

MOORE, Merrill (1903–57), was born at Columbia, Tennessee, son of the state librarian. While qualifying in medicine at Vanderbilt University he became a member of the *Fugitive group of poets, specializing in the sonnet, of which he wrote about half-a-million. However, Moore's sonnets did not always contain 14 lines, and seldom rhymed in the Shakespearian or Petrarchan pattern. No one—least of all himself, perhaps—took his conversational and diagnostic poetry, or his 'Sonnetarium', a room containing 100,000 sonnets written and 'treated' by him, with the utmost seriousness; but, for a poetry that exists in such an enormous quantity (the average was thirty-five sonnets per week), his is seldom feeble or wholly without interest. Professionally, Moore was an expert on alcoholism, and perhaps did most good by treating a few worthy poets for this disease; but William Carlos *Williams thought that he had 'gone through the blinding, stupid formality' of the sonnet, and 'gone after the core' of 'the . . . form, the gist of the whole matter'. See *The Noise that Time Makes* (New York, 1929), *M: One Thousand Autobiographical Sonnets* (New York, 1938), and *Verse Diary of a Psychiatrist* (New York, 1954).

[MS-S

MOORE, Nicholas (1918–86), was born in Cambridge, England, the son of the philosopher, G. E. Moore. After leaving school he spent a year at St Andrew's University, where he met G. S. *Fraser. In 1937 he went up to Trinity College, Cambridge, where he was a contemporary of Alex *Comfort and Hamish *Henderson. From 1938 to 1940 he edited *Seven*, a magazine which published work of the writers of the *New Apocalypse movement and also that of Lawrence *Durrell, Henry Miller, and Anaïs Nin.

Between 1941 and 1945 Moore produced five books of poetry under his own name, one anonymously, and one under a pseudonym (Guy Kelly). In addition, he edited anthologies and pamphlets for the Fortune Press and Editions Poetry London, and from 1949 to 1951 he was an associate editor of *Poetry London*. *The Glass Tower* (1946) brought together his better early poetry. It was followed by *Recollections of the Gala* (1950)—perhaps his best book. After that he turned to horticulture and published little poetry until 1970, when *Resolution and Identity* appeared, followed in 1973 by *Spleen: Thirty-one Versions of Baudelaire's 'Je suis comme le roi'*, a work of Protean verve and humour. Towards the end of his life he was partially blind from diabetes; but in his last year he wrote the poems in *Lacrimae Rerum: Last Poems* (1988), some of which are among his best.

Moore wrote too much in his early years; but his best poetry is fluent, perceptive and witty, and owes more to *Auden than to the Apocalypse poets with whom he was associated. He was interested in jazz and popular song and attempted to integrate some of their effects into his poetry. He may be sampled in *Longings of the Acrobats: Selected Poems* (Manchester, 1990).

[ATT

MOORE, T(homas) Sturge (1870–1944), was born at Hastings, son of a physician. His elder brother was the philosopher G. E. Moore. Friend to *Pound, *Yeats (see *W. B. Yeats and T. Sturge Moore: Their Correspondence 1901–1937*, New York, 1953, ed. Ursula Bridge), and other literary men. Moore spent a quiet life dedicated to study of mythology, art (he wrote monographs on artists), and book design. Although of the *Georgian era, friend to Marsh and contributor to *Georgian Poetry*, his critical sensibilities were nearer to Pound's. Yet, despite the advocacy of Yvor *Winters—who believed (1933) that he had written 'more great poetry than any living writer has composed'—his work has failed to last. From the time of his first collection, *The Vinedresser* (London, 1899), Moore was conscious of the stultifying rhythms of contemporary poetry, but he lacked the energy to do anything about it. His conscientious aim for aesthetic perfection now looks like preciousness, and his unexciting and lack-lustre verse, although finely made, is weighed down by excessive use of adjectives. He continually alludes to the passions recorded in mythology, but without conviction: it is as though he was unaware of psychology. Winters mentioned

'To Slow Music' and 'The Vigil' as deeply moving, and quoted enthusiastically from the double-sonnet 'Silence'; but the inversions and archaic diction now sound even deader than they did in 1933, and Moore's poetry seems moribund. But it is true that, in Winters's words, he was never an 'actively bad poet'. See *The Poems of T. Sturge Moore* (4 vols., London, 1931–3) and his *The Unknown Known* (London, 1939); *Sturge Moore and the Life of Art* (Lawrence, Kan., 1951), by F. L. Gwynn; and *Uncollected Essays* (New York, 1973), by Yvor Winters.

[MS-S

MORAES, Dom (1938–), was born in Bombay of Goan and Indian Roman Catholic parents. His father was a famous journalist and man of letters whom he accompanied on his travels abroad. When Moraes was 7 his mother became mentally ill and had to be institutionalized. Lonely, often uprooted, brought up around books, Moraes early became interested in poetry. His youth is recalled in *My Son's Father: A Poet's Autobiography* (1968).

He went to England in 1954. While still a student at Jesus College, Oxford, he was awarded the Hawthornden Prize for *A Beginning* (1957). He was its youngest recipient. His sensitivity towards language, rhythm, and sound, use of traditional verse forms, the dreaminess and romantic diction (products of a bookish youth and reading of Spenser, Keats, and Verlaine), made him appear the successor of his friends David *Gascoyne, W. S. *Graham, and George *Barker. Famous, handsome, witty, exotic, he was for a time the darling of London's artistic circles. A love affair with a famous actress is the subject of the Cavalier lyrics in *Poems* (1960) and the verse included in *Gone Away* (1960), a maliciously witty travel-book about India. *John Nobody* (1965) alludes, in a more plain, Audenesque style, to the pains of exile, failed love, and time wasted. He became aware of political issues, especially human rights. *Beldam* (1966) introduces fantasy, surreal perspectives, unappealing personae, the grotesque, and obliqueness.

Moraes supported himself as an international journalist and editor, eventually settling uneasily in India where he married the actress Leela Naidu. The privately published *Absences* (1983) was followed by a renewal of creativity in his *Collected Poems: 1957–87* and *Serendip*. He became a more difficult poet, disillusioned, worldly wise, masking his emotions and reflections in elliptical, highly crafted dramatic monologues. There is extreme loneliness—an emotional world centred on Leela, himself, and his past—as if he were in unending exile. Multi-layered, at times hermetical, conscious of death, sometimes overwrought, the later poems are concerned with the pains, fears, and art that have gone into their making.

His poems are available in *Collected Poems: 1957–1987* (New Delhi and New York, 1987) and *Serendip* (New Delhi, 1990). See also *Three Indian Poets: Ezekiel, Ramanujan and Moraes*, by Bruce King (New Delhi, 1991).   [BK

MORGAN, Edwin (1920–), was born in Glasgow. Military service in the Royal Army Medical Corps (1940–6) interrupted Morgan's university education, which he completed 1946–7. From then until 1980 he taught in the English department of the University of Glasgow, retiring as titular professor. As professor emeritus, he retained his connection with the university of his native city.

Against the background of an academic career, and in the decade since, Morgan has produced a venturesome poetry. Often experimental, it is also defined at times by traditional forms such as the sonnet, which he uses with studied, virtuosic enthusiasm. His versification is often a form of serious play. Even an early poem in couplets, 'The Vision of Cathkin Braes' (1952), has a pronounced ludic element which he has sustained ever since with one or another kind of high-spiritedness. Comedy is a noticeable part of his poetic temperament. So, too, is a self-aware employment of literary artifice, evident in the early work but emphasized in *Glasgow Sonnets* (1972), 'New Year Sonnets', *Sonnets from Scotland* (1984), and 'Byron at Sixty-five'. It would therefore be unwise to detach the skills of his formal verse from the ingenuity and wordplay of the several experimental modes which

he also uses. 'Canedolia', 'First Men on Mercury', 'Shaker Shaken', and 'The Computer's First Dialect Poems', for example, could hardly be possible without an inventive, deliberated philology which, when identified with the self-conscious, manipulative versification of his sonnets, reveal Morgan as a poet of finely calculated risks, at least much of the time.

In the 1960s Morgan's talent began to pull together the various interests, concerns, and styles of which it is composed. As well as *concrete and science-fiction poetry, he wrote a substantial body of free-verse poems set in Glasgow. 'King Billy', 'In the Snack Bar', 'Glasgow Green', and others virtually added a new place to the map of modern poetry. Significantly, the book was called *The Second Life* (1968). It announced the arrival of a writer known until then chiefly through small-press publications, magazine appearances, and translations (especially his *Beowulf*, 1962). Many collections have followed, often in small-press editions first, as well as translations (*Rites of Passage*, 1976), sometimes into Scots (e.g. Mayakovsky, *Wi the Haill Voice*, 1972), essays and reviews (*Essays*, 1974; *Crossing the Border*, 1990), libretti, and considerable editorial work. He is among the finest verse translators of his time, and has been the most consistently interesting critic of new Scottish writing.

Poems of Thirty Years (1982) is now replaced by *Collected Poems* (Manchester, 1990). As well as critical essays about his work, there is a full bibliography in R. Crawford and H. Whyte (ed.), *About Edwin Morgan* (Edinburgh, 1990). Interviews, articles, lectures, etc. are collected in H. Whyte (ed.), *Nothing Not Giving Messages* (Edinburgh, 1990).   [DED

MORGAN, (George) Frederick (1922–), was born in New York City, the only child of well-to-do parents. Attending private schools, he had a sheltered childhood and spent much time alone reading. His father, a soap manufacturer, had enrolled him at birth in Princeton where the young Morgan began studying in 1939. At Princeton he met the newly-arrived instructor, Allen *Tate, who proved a decisive influence in shaping Morgan's literary interests. Graduating in 1943, Morgan served in the US Army's Tank Destroyer Corps. In 1947 he co-founded the *Hudson Review*, which quickly became one of the most influential American literary quarterlies. He published a few early poems, but gradually abandoned verse for editorial responsibilities. Then in 1968 the suicide of his son, John, shocked Morgan back into poetry. His first collection, *A Book of Changes* (New York, 1972), published when the author was 50, met with wide approval. But it was not until *Poems of the Two Worlds* (1977), *Death Mother* (1979), and *Northbook* (1982) that critics realized the scope and originality of his poetic talent.

While most members of his generation developed an understated *confessional style, Morgan's poetry is bold, rhetorical, and philosophical. He has also worked in a range of prosodic forms, from fixed stanzas to free verse. Unafraid of grand themes, he writes unabashedly about love, death, redemption, and despair, but while his poetry frequently contains autobiographical elements, it always strives for universal significance. His reach occasionally exceeds his grasp, but his most characteristic work—like the ambitious sequences 'Orpheus to Eurydice' and 'Northbook'—effectively combines classical clarity with direct emotionalism. With each new volume the religious character of his work has grown more apparent. Free of any denominational allegiances, his poetry—like that of Lucretius and Blake, two of his models—seeks to explore primary existential questions.

Poems: New and Selected (Urbana, Ill., and Chicago, 1987) remains the most complete collection of his work. Peter Brazeau's 'Interview with Frederick Morgan', *New England Review* (Spring 1979) is a useful source of biographical information.   [DG

MORGAN, Robert (1944–), grew up in a small town in the Blue Ridge Mountains of North Carolina. He attended the University of North Carolina at both Chapel Hill and Greensboro, where he studied with the poet Fred *Chappell. After working as a salesman, house-painter, and

farmer, he joined the faculty of Cornell University, where he teaches English and creative writing.

Both descriptively and musically, Morgan's poetry is wonderfully tactile; his writing has the consonantal roughness and density of Hopkins, a quality which makes it seem to partake of the natural textures it evokes. His poems form an extended portrait of the region in which he grew up, its ways of life, its dedication to labour and the earth. Despite this deliberate restriction of subject-matter, Morgan is able to move effortlessly when he wants to from particular events and objects to the universals they embody. The real strength and originality of his work, however, comes from his refusal to universalize too quickly or too often; from his insistence on the value of story-telling for its own sake, and on the virtues of simple, physical experience untethered to abstractions. It is perhaps not surprising, then, that he has recently turned increasingly to the short story as a medium, while continuing to produce his concrete, strongly crafted poems as well. Morgan's most recent books of poems are *At the Edge of the Orchard Country* (Middletown, Conn., 1987) and *Sigodlin* (Middletown, 1990).   [RG

MORRIS, John N(elson) (1931–), educated at the Augusta Military Academy, Hamilton College, and Columbia University. He has been the recipient of a Guggenheim Fellowship and an Award in Letters from the Academy and Institute of Arts and Letters, and at present teaches eighteenth-century literature at Washington University in St Louis. To date he has published four volumes of poetry—*Green Business* (1970), *The Life Beside This One* (1975), *The Glass Houses* 1980), and *A Schedule of Benefits* (1987—all New York).

Morris's scholarly study *Versions of the Self: Studies in English Autobiography* (New York, 1966) seems to have provided an inspiration for his poetry, which explores the same issues of consciousness, memory, and the relationship between the subjective 'I' and the outside world that are characteristic concerns of the eighteenth-century writers whom he analyses and admires. The title-poem of *The Life Beside This One* is indicative as a poem of loss and disappointment, written in a style of low-strung emotional intensity reminiscent of Philip *Larkin. Morris's subject-matter is often redolent of a cloistered life spent amongst books, but particularly in *A Schedule of Benefits* he also shows himself absorbed in the quest to make sense of his own family history and, through it, the history of America. His wilfully short lines sometimes result in a rigidity of form and tone, but his honest, straightforward poetry is always personal, if not intense.   [IES

MORRIS, Mervyn (1937–), was born in Kingston, Jamaica. He was educated at Munro College, the University College of the West Indies, and, as a Rhodes Scholar, at St Edmund Hall, Oxford. Based in the department of English at the Mona campus of the University of the West Indies, he is reader in West Indian Literature. In his day he was also a tennis player of international standing.

He is a supreme ironist, eschewing direct statement and political rhetoric in favour of poetry that yields its full meaning only after repeated reading. He also believes that poetry imposes on the poet a logic of its own, which he must follow wherever it leads. As he put it: 'In talking to people who are trying to write, I tend to stress that respect for the original impulse can be an obstacle if it prevents the "author" from seeing what the poem wants to be.' This, and other observations on the craft of poetry, are to be found in Morris's introduction to a selection of his poems in *Hinterland: Caribbean Poetry from the West Indies and Britain*, ed. E. A. Markham (Newcastle upon Tyne, 1989). 'Stripper' wittily sums up his views about poetry as a process of revelation, for both poet and reader.

Fierce irony pervades poems like 'Literary Evening, Jamaica', which attacks both militant political posturing and the poems of Philip *Larkin; 'The Early Rebels', about the corruption of political idealism; and 'The House Slave', a comment on compromise. A great admirer of Louise *Bennett, he too shows a mastery of vernacular and dialect. 'Valley Prince' is in vernacular mode, a powerful elegy on a trombone player, and is full of pent-up, explosive energy. Collections include *The Pond* (London, 1973), *On Holy Week* (Kingston, Jam., 1976), and *Shadowboxing* (London, 1979).   [MR

MORRISON, Blake (1950–), was born in Yorkshire and graduated from Nottingham University. He now works in London as a literary editor. His first book, *The Movement: English Poetry and Fiction of the 1950s* (Oxford and New York, 1980) was a detailed critical history of the trends in the new writing of that decade associated with Philip *Larkin, Kingsley *Amis, Thom *Gunn, Elizabeth *Jennings, and others. Introducing a first volume of his own poems, *Dark Glasses* (London, 1984, reissued with additional work in 1989), Morrison stated his belief that poetry 'must always be a contemplation or unravelling of mysteries'. One half of the book is a single long poem, 'The Inquisitor', which takes as its themes 'secrecy and trust' and employs cryptically handled material relating to the Falklands War, the early life of Lech Wałeşa, and the death of the Italian banker Roberto Calvi. The shorter poems are usually brief, enigmatic narratives, some suggesting personal memories ('Grange Boy', 'Metamorphoses of Childhood') or aspects of his domestic life in the present ('Pine', 'A Child in Winter'). The title-poem of his second book, *The Ballad of the Yorkshire Ripper* (London, 1987) is a monologue, in quatrains, in the accents of the notorious murderer. Like other, more oblique poems, on subjects like environmental pollution and the nuclear threat ('On Sizewell Beach', 'Havens'), it implicitly opposes a concerned humanist decency and responsibility to the forces of cruelty and waste. Morrison has also edited, with Andrew *Motion, the *Penguin Book of Contemporary British Poetry* (1982) and published a study of *Seamus Heaney* (London, 1985) and a prose work *And When Did You Last See Your Father* (London, 1993).   [AB

MOSS, Howard (1922–87), was born in New York City, the only son of a prosperous importer and manufacturer. He was a sickly infant, and for his health Moss's parents moved to nearby Rockaway Beach, Long Island, where he spent his childhood and adolescence. He entered the University of Michigan but was expelled after one year for participating in a dormitory workers' labour protest. Upon graduating from the University of Wisconsin in 1943 he worked for the War Information Office. After the war he took various editorial jobs and taught one year at Vassar College before joining *The New Yorker* as a fiction editor in 1948. Two years later he became the magazine's first full-time poetry editor, a position he held for nearly four decades until his death.

Before Moss's tenure, *The New Yorker* was not a prestigious venue for poetry and was best known for light verse. Under his discriminating leadership it became an important showcase for new poetry in America. As an editor, Moss often published sophisticated, polished, intellectually demanding poetry, but his taste was remarkably diverse. He championed many poets early in their careers and helped establish the reputations of *Roethke, *Bishop, *Sexton, *Plath, *Strand, *Dickey, *Merrill, *Kinnell, *Ashbery, *Merwin, *Justice, *Clampitt, and others.

Moss's fame as an editor often obscured his substantial achievements as a poet. Maturing early, he wrote prolifically, and his published poetry spans forty years and twelve major collections. His early work—influenced by *Auden, *Yeats, and *Stevens—was tight, formal, and lucid, but it did not share the ironic intellectuality or emotional detachment that characterized the verse of his 1950s contemporaries like *Nemerov or *Hecht. Moss's best early poems, like 'Burning Love Letters' or 'Elegy for My Father', frequently talked about love and loss in colloquial but musically precise language. Moss later experimented with free verse, often writing compressed psychological narratives, but the lyric and elegy remained his most characteristic forms. Moss's first *Selected Poems* (New York, 1972) won the National Book Award.

In addition to his poetry, Moss was a diversely talented man of letters. He wrote two plays, *The Folding Green* (for the Cambridge, Mass., Poet's Theatre in 1958) and *The Palace at 4 a.m.* (1964). He collaborated with the artist Edward Gorey on *Instant Lives* (1974), a sophisticated literary satire. He edited several anthologies, most notably *New York: Poems* (1980) which celebrated his native city. He was also an active critic, but because of his influential position at *The New Yorker*, he eventually refused to review the work of living poets (a rule he broke each time Elizabeth Bishop published a new volume). His best criticism is collected in *Minor Monuments: Selected Essays* (New York, 1986). *New Selected Poems* (New York, 1985) remains the definitive collection of his verse.   [DG

MOTION, Andrew (1952–), was born in London and educated at Radley College. He attended University College, Oxford, where he won the Newdigate Prize, and in 1975 he received a Gregory Award. His first collection, *The Pleasure Steamers* (Manchester, 1978) was greeted with critical acclaim. It is chiefly lyrical in cast, and exhibits all of his mannerisms in a forceful, concentrated form: an elusive metre, which cannot conceal the ghost of the iamb; a reticent but memorable phrasing; a plangency deriving partly from the attitude of the narrator, partly from a melancholy subject-matter. It is clear that he has learnt from two poets he much admires, Edward *Thomas and Philip *Larkin (he has written studies of both and is Larkin's authorized biographer); but he has refined the quietness of the former, and substituted sadness for the despair of the latter. He does not share the taste for rhyme of either. Nor is he as constantly observant as they, choosing his moment for precise perceptions.

Despite its similarity to a conventional collection of short lyrics, *The Pleasure Steamers* was already striking out in a direction Motion was to pursue in subsequent collections: towards narrative writing, with the use of a narrator. This is particularly clear in the sequence called 'Inland', which conveys moments in the story of a fenland village whose livelihood is threatened equally by flooding and enclosures. Motion's melancholy concentration on transience is here lent symbolic dimensions. In *Independence* (Edinburgh, 1981) Motion evokes the atmosphere of the twilight of the Raj while telling the story of a brief marriage curtailed by the death in childbirth of the narrator's young bride. *Secret Narratives* (Edinburgh, 1983), is, as the title suggests, more mysterious, in the sense that though the short poems it contains tell stories through the medium of a narrator, the general context remains unclear. *Natural Causes* (London, 1987) did not take his development much further, though there is some interesting experimentation with different linguistic registers in 'Scripture'. *Love in a Life* (London, 1991), shows a new simplicity and directness of language, along with an exactness that is sometimes startling. Although an interest in narrative fragments is still present, the reader is given more clues as to how to put these together, though never in such a way as to encourage faith in a complete, objective story.   [ETL

MOURÉ, Erin (1955–), was born and raised in Calgary, moving to Vancouver in 1974, where she worked for the Canadian National Railway and then for VIA Rail. In 1984 she moved to Montreal, where she continues to work for VIA.

Beginning with her first of six books of poems, *Empire, York Street* (Toronto, 1979), Mouré has drawn on ordinary communal and individual experience—working lives in Canada, sexuality and the politics of relationships, the allure of alcohol, the transformations within families over time—but has increasingly reflected on the powers of language to create reality. 'The Acts', the final section of *Furious* (Toronto, 1988), Mouré's fifth book, is a sequence of prose poems about the ways in which the surfaces and the depths of language create our forms of thought. Mouré proposes that language actively structures reality, rather than simply reflecting or referring to it. In her most recent writing, these thoughts on language have developed in conjunction with a more sustained focusing on the experience of women—their apprehension of language and power in relation to their own bodies and voices, and their experience of male versions and embodiments of language and power. In this area, Mouré has been influenced by her

relationship with Montreal literary critic Gail Scott.   [NB

Movement, The, was identified as a new grouping in British literature by an anonymous article, 'In the Movement', which appeared in the *Spectator* on 1 October 1954. The article (in fact written by the paper's literary editor, J. D. Scott) suggested that Movement writers admired Leavis, *Empson, Orwell, and *Graves; that they were 'bored by the despair of the Forties, not much interested in suffering, and extremely impatient of poetic sensibility'; and that they were 'sceptical, robust, ironic'. Five writers were named; the publication of *Poets of the 1950s* (1955, ed. D. J. *Enright) and the *New Lines* anthology (1956, ed. Robert *Conquest) settled the list at nine: Kingsley *Amis, Robert Conquest, Donald *Davie, Enright, Thom *Gunn, John *Holloway, Elizabeth *Jennings, Philip *Larkin, and John *Wain. The poetry of these writers, particularly in the 1950s, and the novels *Lucky Jim* (1954) and *That Uncertain Feeling* (1955) by Amis and *Hurry on Down* (1953) by Wain, together with Davie's critical study *Purity of Diction in English Verse* (1952), are now widely accepted as the core Movement texts, while a none-too-easily defined Movement tone is often detected both in post-1950s work by these writers and in the poetry of others not originally associated with the group (Alan *Brownjohn, George *MacBeth, Anthony *Thwaite). This tone is generally felt to be one of middlebrow scepticism, conformist disrespect, and ironical common sense: Larkin's poem 'Church Going' epitomizes the Movement's tone and stance. The consensus on the definition of the Movement is less secure; some have even suggested that the putative group was merely a journalistic invention.

Central and influential though the Movement writers became in post-war British literature, some critics, beginning with Charles *Tomlinson in 'The Middlebrow Muse', *Essays in Criticism*, 7 (1957), have felt parochialism, philistinism, and narrow-mindedness to be the foremost characteristics of their work. The Movement's rejection of Romantic excess links it to the post-war wave of ironical, level-headed sobriety which Chris *Wallace-Crabbe was to complain of in Australia and Robert *Lowell to react against in the USA as the 1960s began. Two useful early studies: John Press, *Rule and Energy* (London, 1963) and William Van O'Connor, *The New University Wits* (Carbondale, Ill., 1963) can still be consulted: though the best survey, placing the Movement in its societal, political, and aesthetic contexts, is Blake Morrison, *The Movement* (Oxford, 1980).   [MHu

MPINA, Edison (*c.* 1948–) is an enigmatic outsider on the edge of the remarkable generation of poets from his native Malawi which includes *Mapanje, *Chipasula, and *Chimombo. While the audiences and careers of these men have been university-based, Mpina worked until 1991 for the Commercial Bank of Malawi. His volume *Raw Pieces* (1986) has not been seen outside his home country.

He came to sudden prominence in 1981 when he beat 700 competitors to win the BBC Arts and Africa Poetry Award with 'Summer Fires of Mulanje Mountain'. Descriptive power is combined in this poem with mythic reference and cryptic political suggestiveness in a way typical of the Malawian school. 'Monkey Bay', commended by the judges of the next BBC competition (1988) is strongly reminiscent of Mapanje's work, with its casual-seeming enjambement (a technique which Mpina does not always control so well). While he has shown a capacity to handle painful subject-matter with serious wit, his output has been uneven as well as fugitive.

There are five poems by Mpina in the anthology *Summer Fires* (London, 1983), ed. Angus Calder, Jack Mapanje, and Cosmo Pieterse, and deriving from the BBC competition. Anthony Nazombe's anthology *The Haunting Wind: New Poetry from Malawi* (Blantyre, Malawi, 1990) contains four.   [ALRC

MTSHALI, Oswald (Joseph) Mbuyiseni (1940–), was born at Vryheid, in rural Natal, coming to Johannesburg only after completing his schooling. Unable to gain entry to Witwaters-

rand University, and unwilling to attend a 'tribal college', he chose to work as a messenger. His first collection of poems, *Sounds of a Cowhide Drum*, published in Johannesburg in 1971, sold 16,000 copies within a year. During and after the Soweto uprising of 1976 Mtshali aligned himself increasingly with the Black Consciousness movement, and his second collection, *Fireflames* (1980), was banned by the authorities. More recently he has worked as a journalist and is now vice-principal of a Soweto school. He writes both in Zulu and English.

Mtshali's poems give a vivid picture of urban South Africa. His spontaneous-sounding free verse evokes the frustrations of migrant workers, the humiliations of the pass laws, and the violence of Soweto shebeens. Unlike his fellow 'township poets', *Sepamla and *Serote, he has strong roots in rural tradition, contrasting its human warmth with the brittle stylishness of city life. Mtshali argues that his message is too urgent to be lost in ornate and lofty poetry, and objects that whites who claim to 'enjoy' his poems are in fact enjoying his suffering. His style is marked by simple alliterations, straightforward syntax, and a mixed, everyday vocabulary. His images are instantaneously amusing or shocking: the sun setting like a coin falling into a parking-meter slot, a convict's head shaved smooth as a potato, dogs fighting over a dead baby on a rubbish heap.

Sounds of a Cowhide Drum (London and New York, 1972) remains Mtshali's most popular collection. See also Ursula Barnett's *A Vision of Order* (London, 1983).   [JB

MUDIE, Ian (1911–76), was born in Hawthorn, South Australia, and spent most of his life in that state working as a free-lance writer, editor, and lecturer. Influenced by the *Jindyworobak movement, Mudie's early poetry contains many references to Aborigines and their beliefs, as well as a deep concern for the changes wrought on the Australian landscape and its inhabitants by European migration. Mudie was a passionate nationalist, and expressed in his poetry a vision of a potent future for Australia and its recent immigrants, but an equal distaste for the shallowness of contemporary life. His best-known poems celebrate the myth of the pioneer and the bushman, and use the vernacular freely. He wrote for a wide audience and out of a conviction that in bush life there were traditional Australian values which could be transplanted into the city. His style could be both prosaically colloquial and rhetorically ambitious. He was at his best describing landscapes and suburban living, and at his most approachable in articulating the 'bush mystique' of the mid-twentieth century. He published six books of poetry between 1940 and 1970, and a selection, containing previously uncollected poems, *Selected Poems 1934-1976* (Melbourne, 1976), appeared in the year of his death.   [JCr

MUHAMMAD, Haji Salleh (1942–) is one of Malaysia's foremost poets. In 1991 he won the highest literary honour in Malaysia, the Anugerah Sastera Negara (National Literature Award).

He began to write poetry in both English and Malay when he was undergoing teacher-training in England during the early 1960s. The poems of his apprenticeship show the fructifying influence of English poetry, and his later work evinces an intellectual quality not seen in conventional Malay poetry. He read English in the University of Singapore under D. J. *Enright, and also studied at the universities of Malaya and Michigan. His published thesis, *Tradition and Change in Contemporary Malay-Indonesian Poetry* (1977), is perhaps the best book on the subject.

Although Muhammad's last collection in English was in 1979 he continues to be an active verse translator. Some of his poems are anthologized in *Seven Poets* (Singapore, 1973) and *The Second Tongue* (Singapore, 1976). *Time and Its People* (Kuala Lumpur, 1978) is the only volume of his poetry to have been originally written in English. *The Travel Journals of Si Tenggang II* (1979) is his own translation of one of his six volumes of poetry in Malay.   [LCS

MUIR, Edwin (1887–1959), poet and translator, was born on his father's rented farm on Deer-

ness, Orkney; two years later the family moved to the neighbouring island of Wyre. His peaceful childhood gained symbolic significance through contrast with his youth in Glasgow, where the family moved in 1901, and where Muir had jobs in offices, in a beer-bottling factory, and in a factory at Fairport for reducing bones to charcoal. The sequence of personal tragedies that blighted his time in the city (both parents and two brothers dying within two years) and his horror at its slum life are recorded in *An Autobiography* (1954). In this environment Muir turned successively to evangelicalism, socialism, and the philosophy of Nietzsche, none of which could heal his injured psyche, and began to write essays and reviews for journals.

In 1919 he married Willa Anderson, setting up home in Bloomsbury and working as A. R. Orage's assistant on *The New Age*. It was at this time that he underwent psychoanalysis involving the recording of his dreams, with important consequences for his writing: he describes how his analyst warned him that his unconscious 'was far too near the surface for comfort and safety, and that I should hurry to put something soundly substantial between me and it'.

In 1921 the Muirs left for Europe. It was in Dresden that Muir began to write poetry, at the age of 35, 'too old', as he put it, 'to submit to contemporary influences'. *First Poems* was published in 1925, the year in which the Muirs began their collaborative translations from German (most notably of Kafka). After the Second World War, Muir held British Council posts in Prague and in Rome, where he became a practising Christian. He gave the 1955–6 Norton Lectures at Harvard on 'The Estate of Poetry', which allowed him to buy the Cambridgeshire cottage where he spent his last years.

Form, for Muir, was simply inherited; he set out, he observed, with 'the rhythms of English poetry on the one hand, the images in my mind on the other'. (To those English rhythms may be added the ballads he heard in his childhood— his early poems include ballads in Scots—which contributed to his instinct for narrative.) Michael Roberts excluded him from his *Faber

Book of Modern Verse on the grounds of unquestioningly traditional technique. Similarly, very little in Muir's language or imagery would seem out of place in, say, Tennyson's 'Ulysses'; he relies on a narrow stock of archetypal properties: the road, the stronghold, the labyrinth. His characters undergo psychological and political tests and traumas, often transplanted from Muir's own dreams but (despite his admiration for Wordsworth) invariably mythologized: Odysseus, Oedipus, Orpheus, Achilles, and Prometheus are among his agents. Poems are titled plainly—'The Voyage', 'The Escape', and 'The Journey Back', and are unafraid to recall literary precursors on the road: one sonnet tells how Milton 'to the dark tower came', though the horror he confronts there is distinctly Glaswegian ('the steely clamour known too well | On Saturday nights in every street in Hell'). The same sonnet uses the word 'Paradise' four times, suggesting how obsessively Muir returned to the myth of Eden and the Fall that his own early life had enacted.

Most readers of Muir's stately *Collected Poems* will feel a want of variety that a greater realism would have supplied, and regret that the heraldic atmosphere is not more often relieved by the personal tone of which Muir was a diffident master: see the elegy 'For Ann Scott-Moncrieff', the lyric sweetness of 'The Bird' and 'A Birthday', and the discursive ease of 'Reading in Wartime'. Instead, he will likeliest be remembered for the series of poems inventing atomic aftermaths: 'The Horses', 'The Shortage', and others, in which his patient pessimism is most dramatically universalized.

The best book about Muir is his *Autobiography* (1954); see also P. H. Butter, *Edwin Muir: Man and Poet* (London, 1962) and Willa Muir, *Belonging: A Memoir* (London, 1968). *The Collected Poems*, ed. W. Muir and J. C. Hall (London, 1960 and 1963, new edn. 1984), omits much early work. See also *Edwin Muir: Centenary Assessments*, ed. C. T. H. MacLachlan and D. S. Robb (1990). [MI

MULDOON, Paul (1951–), was born in Portadown, Co. Armagh, Northern Ireland, and brought up near a village called The Moy which figures prominently in a number of his poems. His mother was a schoolteacher and his father a farm labourer and market gardener. After studying at Queen's University, Belfast, where Seamus *Heaney was a tutor and where he met other poets such as Michael *Longley as part of the Belfast 'Group' (see HOBSBAUM, PHILIP), he published his first book, *New Weather* (London) in 1972, when he was only 21. He worked as a producer for the BBC in Belfast until, in the mid-1980s, he gave up his job to become a freelance writer and moved to the United States. In 1988 he edited *The Faber Book of Contemporary Irish Verse*.

'The Mixed Marriage', in his second collection, *Mules* (London and Winston-Salem, NC, 1977), concerns the opposed educational and class backgrounds of his parents: his mother's cosmopolitan literariness and his father's rural knowledge and Republican sympathies. His poetry, which frequently returns to his parents (particularly his father), itself conducts mixed marriages of various kinds. It brings his own family and rural background into a strangely dislocating relationship with an astonishing range of sophisticated literary, historical, and cultural allusion; it crosses contemporary Irish experience with Amerindian Trickster mythology; it joins early Irish legend to the thrillers of Raymond Chandler; it performs some radical formal experiments with that most traditional of poetic means, the sonnet. Wily and mischievous, these conjunctions are energetic displays of a subtle, learned, and ironic intelligence, placing the reader in a constant state of interpretative alertness and insecurity. In his influential longer poems, such as 'Immram' in *Why Brownlee Left* (London and Winston-Salem, NC, 1980) and 'The More a Man Has the More a Man Wants' in *Quoof* (London and Winston-Salem, 1983), he employs oblique, intermittent narratives of conspiracy, quest, and pursuit whose slippery air of giving nothing away, at once cajoling and unaccommodating, gracefully testifies to that most bedrock marriage of all in his work: that of a Northern Irish Catholic sensibility and the English poetic tradition. [NC

MUNGOSHI, Charles (1947–), was born in Manyene, near Chivhu, Zimbabwe, and educated at St Augustine's, Penhalonga. Well before his country gained independence in 1980 he had emerged as a prolific writer with a dawning international reputation. In 1977 his novel *Waiting for the Rain* won a PEN award, and it has been translated into several European languages. He has since published fiction and translations in Shona as well as short stories and work for children in English. Formerly an editor with the Rhodesia Literature Bureau, he has latterly exercised wide influence as director of Zimbabwe Publishing House.

The themes of his verse are those of many African poets of his generation, 'children of two worlds', distanced by education from their families, critical of urban life. He handles them, however, with a distinctive, understated elegance. He has suggested in interviews that writing verse is for him ancillary to his prose. He uses poetry to experiment in condensation of meaning. He admires the spareness of Hemingway and of such Japanese poets as Basho. A good example of his economy is 'Sitting on the Balcony', where a cryptic point about life's melancholy is made in fourteen short lines.

His one collection is *The Milkman Doesn't Only Deliver Milk* (Harare, 1981). He has sixteen poems in the definitive *Mambo Book of Zimbabwean Verse*, ed. Colin and O-Lan Style (Harare, 1986), and ten, along with an interview, in Flora Wild, *Patterns of Poetry in Zimbabwe* (Harare, 1988).   [ALRC

MURPHY, Richard (1927–), was born in the west of Ireland but spent part of his early childhood in Ceylon. He attended Magdalen College, Oxford, and the Sorbonne. Then, for some years, he ran a fishing boat in County Galway—this is the 'hooker' of 'The Last Galway Hooker'. He restored the boat himself: a revealing enterprise, suggesting as it does that concern for the objective recovery of the Irish past which is so much a feature of his verse. His cosmopolitan, colonial Anglo-Irish background fitted him to explore his Irish inheritance from a position combining intimacy with a measure of detach-

ment: an astute stance which makes itself evident both in his manner and in his subject-matter. As a lyric poet, Murphy's gift is for quiet, precise, musical phrasing but this is not his only talent. He is equally notable—indeed unusual—for his skill in narrative poems, as in 'Sailing to an Island' or 'The Woman of the House', which, though it describes itself as an elegy for his grandmother, Lucy May Ormsby, is predominantly a narrative created from memory, and one which vividly succeeds in evoking the lost world of the Ascendancy. Such poems are often written in a rhythmic, four-stress, accentual metre, with some alliteration and the use of half-rhyme: they seem, appropriately enough, indebted both to Saxon and Gaelic models. In *The Battle of Aughrim* (London and New York, 1968), Murphy examines the consequences of one of the most decisive events in Irish history. 'Aughrim's dread disaster' (1691) was the final defeat for the Catholic forces arrayed against the Williamites. It was followed by the Treaty of Limerick, and the penal period. Murphy's series was broadcast in 1968, with Ted *Hughes and Cecil *Day Lewis among the readers. It seeks to trace some of the roots of present troubles: 'Names in the rival churches are written on plaques.' But Murphy's forebears, he seems guiltily aware, are implicated in some of the wrongs committed since then.

See *New Selected Poems* (London, 1989), and Maurice Harmon, *Richard Murphy, Poet of Two Traditions* (Dublin, 1978).   [ETL

MURRAY, Les(lie) A(llan) (1938–), was born in the village of Nabiac on the remote north coast of New South Wales. An only child, he grew up on his father's dairy farm at Bunyah nearby, before attending Sydney University where he read modern languages. He worked with the translation unit at the Australian National University, 1963–7, but since 1971 he has made his living from literature. (Murray is a forceful advocate of state funding for the arts.) In 1986 he left Sydney—a city whose fashionable priorities and 'imported idiocies' he has long satirized—and returned to buy a forty-acre farm in Bunyah.

His first book *The Ilex Tree* (Canberra), co-written with his friend Geoffrey *Lehmann, came out in 1965, and he has since written prolifically, employing an unusually wide range of subject-matter and treatment. The best of his poetry is to be found in three volumes: *The Vernacular Republic: Poems 1961–1981* (Sydney, Edinburgh, and New York, 1982) and two capacious subsequent collections, *The Daylight Moon* (Sydney and Manchester, 1987; New York, 1988) and *Dog Fox Field* (Sydney, Manchester, and New York, 1990), both dedicated 'to the glory of God'.

His most ambitious single work is the novel-in-verse *The Boys Who Stole the Funeral* (Sydney), first published in 1980. Technically, its 140 deftly varied fourteen-line units, a mosaic of different kinds of writing, are a triumphant solution to the problem of how to square the demands of a prolonged narrative with the reverberating stops of lyric and meditative verse; they also keep Murray's habitual garrulousness in check. Its plot, however, a fable at the service of Murray's Roman Catholic beliefs and masculine and agrarian prejudices, is calculated to antagonize. Uncompromising views on war, abortion, and the sexes are aired between scenes of instructive violence: in one, a deplored feminist is retributively 'baptised' by scalding and disfiguring her face.

The novel reminds us of Murray's claim that white Australians should partake of the Aboriginal affinity with the environment—see also poems like 'The Buladeleah-Taree Holiday Song Cycle' from *Ethnic Radio* (Sydney, 1977). But for all its marvellous facility, it suggests a poet out of his place; and Murray's return to the country in the mid-Eighties had a measurable effect on his verse, restoring a serene non-fiction to the fore. The personality of the later poems is genial and mostly tolerant, the address muted and the technique subdued, their concerns as large and impersonal as the continent behind them. Murray has identified the distinguishing mark of Australian poetry as 'the endless detailed rehearsal . . . of Australian peculiarities that goes into it'; and neutral detail is the stuff of many spacious poems. The long piece which opens *The Daylight Moon*, for example, a voyage through flood-plains, ends on the exact and tranquil note of an 'unhurt' croc-odile's 'pineapple abdomen'. A distinguishable class of poem is content to perform quiet variations on themes of home, farm and farm machinery, family, landscape, and provincial history. Murray is also increasingly preoccupied with telling stories, which, as he explains sarcastically for urban readers, are 'a kind of spoken video'; his refinements of the fireside yarn allow him virtuoso re-creations of a range of voices, and to convey choice scraps of local non-fiction.

Murray has published two volumes of his somewhat forbidding prose; his essay on his earlier poetics, 'The Human Hair-Thread', appeared in *Meanjin* (1977). A *Collected Poems* (Sydney, Manchester, and New York, 1991) was followed in 1993 by *Translations from the National World* (Manchester, New York, and Paddington, NSW). [MI

MUSGRAVE, Susan (1951–), was born in Santa Cruz, California, of Canadian parents. She left school at 14 and has travelled widely. For long periods she has lived in the wilderness of the Queen Charlotte Islands off the coast of British Columbia, alongside the Native Indians. She regards this area as her spiritual home.

Musgrave gained recognition with her first collection, *Songs of the Sea Witch* (Vancouver, 1970), in which she projects the anarchic impulses of the authentic self seeking freedom. Written in short lines, the poems refer to blood, absence, and dismemberment. Typically, Musgrave speaks as an animistic force located between the spirit of the air and the spirit of the sea; she enacts the struggle of an unformed self to realize itself in its own unique form. Much of the imagery stems from the Pacific Northwest. Musgrave has also written a number of poems through the eyes of the Canadian native peoples to suggest that the desecration of the land and the spirit derive from the same impulse towards absolute control. When writing about the contemporary urban world, Musgrave often employs a cold, detached voice to parody what she sees as its death-in-life quality. Her selected poems, *Tarts and Muggers* (Toronto, 1982), opens with the statement: 'the embalmer's art is poetry', signalling her rejection of art that does not bring new forms into being, but rests content with embalming the dead. Her most recent volume, *Cocktails at the Mausoleum* (Toronto, 1985), proves more conversational in tone; here she reflects with wit and intelligence on the place of love and the 'shamelessness of the body' in a violent world.

Musgrave has also published two children's books, two works of fiction, and a collection of essays.

For additional information, see Dennis Brown's 'Susan Musgrave: The Self and the Other', *Canadian Literature*, 79 (Winter 1978).

[RBH

MUSKE, Carol (1945–), lives in Los Angeles, California, with her husband, actor David Dukes, and daughter. Los Angeles figures in Muske's work as a trope for the seduction of appearances; reality crosses from the Wallace *Stevens notion of the sun, 'hovering in its guise of impatient tribunal' ('The Red Trousseau') to a director's re-shooting of a tarnished sunset, so that 'the scene, infinite, rebegins' ('Unsent Letter'). Muske works in primary colours: red, blue, and yellow dominate, serving to link such disparate things as a sound-stage's fake *prie dieu*, a precinct-station map of gang activity, and a schoolgirl's model of the planets, all of which take on the red of Salem burnings, the self-immolation of a political dissident in Prague, and Eros itself, moving like a red shadow over the body in love. Muske's work derives much of its spiralling energy from Marianne *Moore. Much like Moore's paper nautilus, first protective then, freed of its fragile cargo, becoming the beautifully empty form of itself, Muske's Hollywood spirals around its version of reality, infinitely re-beginning, until it becomes wholly the form.

Carol Muske's poetry books include *Camouflage* (Pittsburgh, 1975), *Skylight* (New York, 1981), *Wyndmere* (Pittsburgh, 1985), *Applause* (Pittsburgh, 1989), and *The Red Trousseau* New York, 1993. Her novel is *Dear Digby* (New York, 1989).

[LMcM

NABOKOV, Vladimir (Vladimirovich) (1899–1977), was born in St Petersburg, the eldest son of cosmopolitan aristocrats. Mastering both French and English in childhood, Nabokov demonstrated precocious literary gifts, publishing two collections of verse while still in his teens. When his family fled revolutionary Russia in 1919, Nabokov entered Trinity College, Cambridge, where he published his first English verse. After his father, a liberal politician, was assassinated by Russian reactionaries in 1922, Nabokov moved to Berlin where he married Vera Slonim, and established himself as a leading emigré writer, usually using the pseudonym, V. Sirin. Moving to Paris in 1937 to avoid the Nazi threat, Nabokov began writing in English, and in 1940 the Nabokovs and their son Dimitri (later his father's translator), emigrated to America where he obtained university positions in literature and lepidopterology, eventually accepting a professorship at Cornell. The international success of *Lolita* following its American publication in 1958 allowed Nabokov to retire from teaching in 1959 and move to Switzerland to be near his son. Although Nabokov, an American citizen, claimed his European residency would be temporary, he died in Montreux.

Nabokov maintained that there was no generic difference between poetry and 'artistic prose', and his own verse displays the same conspicuous virtues of his fiction—playful musicality, dark wit, and narrative ingenuity. He published only a few mature poems in English, but they are uniformly strong and strikingly original. The long monologue, 'An Evening of Russian Poetry', which is spoken by an imaginary lecturer visiting a women's college, begins as gentle academic satire but builds into an exile's extravagant elegy for his lost Russia. Nabokov's finest poems, like 'The Ballad of Longwood Glen' and 'The Literary Dinner', often employ black comedy but use that savage and sophisticated humour to protect their essential innocence. Nabokov's most ambitious poem in English (or Russian) was 'Pale Fire', which formed the centre-piece of his masterful 1961 experimental novel of the same title. Purportedly written by John Shade (whom Nabokov convincingly called 'the greatest of invented poets'), this 999-line poem in heroic couplets provides the mysterious and eccentric critic, Charles Kinbote, the opportunity to project his autobiography into 200 pages of hilarious and heart-breaking footnotes. A masterful performance, *Pale Fire* became an influential model to postmodern novelists. Nabokov's poetry, however, has had little direct influence.

Nabokov also made significant contributions to verse translation and prosody. After having done many literary translations of Russian poetry, he eventually became a ferocious champion of 'honest and clumsy' literalism. His massively annotated translation of Pushkin's *Eugene Onegin* (Princeton, NJ, 1964) demonstrates scholarship and pedantry in equal measure. His book-length appendix on Pushkin's metre (later published separately as *Notes on Prosody*), which brilliantly compares English and Russian iambic tetrameter, remains a magisterial study of versification. The fullest collection of Nabokov's verse is *Poems and Problems* (New York and London, 1970). See also Andrew Field, *VN: The Life* and Art of Vladimir Nabokov (New York, 1986; London, 1987). [DG

NAIDU, Sarojini (1879–1949), Indian national leader, a pioneer of the women's movement and brilliant orator, was once highly regarded for her poetry, written in her youth. Gandhi gave her the title of 'Nightingale of India' for the musicality of her speech. Her father was a famous Bengali scientist but she was born and educated in the then-Muslim city of Hyderabad, Deccan: in her writing Hindu mythology and culture are fused with Perso-Arabic and Islamic strands. Her first collection, *The Golden Threshold* (London, 1905) had an introduction by Arthur *Symons, who noticed her Pater-like love of beauty. The book contains some of her best poems, vignettes of Indian city and village life like 'Street Cries' and 'Palanquin Bearers'. *Bird of Time* (London, 1912) proved to be very popular, with several reprints. In his introduction Edmund Gosse dwelt on her insight into the 'heart of India'; and the romantic mood of the poems of love, death, spring, Radha and Krishna, appealed to the age's fondness for Orientalism laced with philosophizing. *The Broken Wing* (London, 1917), written when Naidu had become a leading figure in India's freedom struggle and women's liberation, contains poems in which these two concerns are combined: Indian women are asked to prove their destiny as Mother India's liberators and saviours. 'The Gift of India' is Naidu's war poem, reminding the world of India's sons 'scattered like shells on Egyptian sands' and on the 'blood-brown meadows of Flanders'.

Naidu's poetry has not survived contemporary taste. She has been criticized by modern Indian-English poets for her bland romanticism and poeticized diction. Yet at her best she had a keen ear and sense of place and a delicious sense of humour. *The Sceptered Flute* (New York, 1937), which included all three collections, is sadly out of print and she can be read only in anthologies like the *Oxford Book of Mystical Verse* and the *Golden Treasury of Indo-Anglian Poetry* (Delhi, 1970). [RA

NAIR, Chandran (1945–), was born in India but his family moved to Singapore when he was still a child. He was trained as a marine biologist, but his literary interests took him into the world of publishing where he remained for many years, eventually taking up an appointment as consultant with UNESCO.

In Nair's first volume of poems, *Once the Horseman and Other Poems* (Singapore, 1972), there is a recourse to Hindu myths and legends as sources of comfort and spiritual nourishment, but in his second book, *After the Hard Hours this Rain* (Singapore, 1974), there is a shift away from Hindu themes; love is the central preoccupation. Nair is currently reworking his early stories into two novels, and these will also incorporate his latest poems. See Kirpal Singh (ed.), *Critical Engagements* (Singapore, 1986). [KS

NASH, Ogden (1902–71), was born in Rye, New York, the son of wealthy parents. After one year at Harvard, 1920–1—'it was my idea to leave, not the Dean's, and I have affidavits to prove it'—he taught, was a bond salesman, wrote streetcar ads, and (1925–31) worked in the publicity and editorial departments of first Doubleday and then Rinehart. In 1929 he joined the staff of *The New Yorker*, his preferred venue, though he also contributed to more than thirty journals. In 1931 he married and published *Hard Lines* and *Free Wheeling*. His lyrics for Broadway musicals include those for Kurt Weill's *One Touch of Venus* (1943), and for Bette Davis in *Two's Company* (music by Vernon Duke, 1962). Tall, bespectacled, elegantly suited, with fair curling hair and an intelligent, toothy smile, he was an urbane public reader of his verse and also produced Thurberish illustrations.

Though Nash belongs to entertainment, he deploys poetic resources. The inordinately lengthy, short, or alternating lines stumble along in a mix of anapaests and iambs, culminating, with expert timing, in elaborately improbable couplet-rhymes; clowning and witty by turn, his punning, ironic medleys of the sophisticated and *faux-naif* can also be epigrammatic or occasionally lyrical. Constantly revising, he crafted an instantly identifiable match for his insights—touching on sore points from family life's sex- and generation-wars, through lying, money, drink, and Englishness, to God—without which his games could and sometimes did become facetious formulas.

At his best Nash belongs with playful haters of dullness like Carroll, Lear, and W. S. Gilbert, often read when more distinguished names are mere names.

I Wouldn't Have Missed It (New York, 1975; London, 1983), selected by his two daughters, Linell Smith and Isabel Eberstadt, represents all fourteen volumes, with dates, and was republished as a paperback, *Candy Is Dandy: The Best of Ogden Nash* (London, 1985).   [HL

Native-American Poetry. Behind the established names of modern Native-American poetry lies a vast, historic legacy of oral incantation and story-telling. These legacies of word and image, each integral to the overall cultural life of all the tribal nations, together with the complexity of latter-day 'cross-blood' experience, whether reservation-based or not, has made for a dazzling eclecticism, verse at once ancestral and modern, spoken (or pictographic) in inheritance, and yet a *written* contemporary American poetry.

Much as one can point to early twentieth-century precursors like Lynn Riggs (Cherokee), Alex Posey (Creek), Pauline Johnson (Tehakionwake/Mohawk), or Frank Prewett (Iroquois), the essential poetic renaissance dates from the 1960s. In this N. Scott Momaday (Kiowa) holds a key place, both for his landmark novel, *The House Made of Dawn* (1968), and a verse-collection like *The Gourd Dancer* (1976). Poems like 'The Bear' and 'Earth and I Gave You Turquoise' reflect his deeply tribal sense of landscape and life-form. Momaday's writings have had busy company: the Alaskan-Yukon poems of *There Is No Word For Goodbye* (1981) of Mary Tall Mountain (Athabaskan); the Oklahoma-centred verse and translations of Frank Barnes (Choctaw), notably *The American Book of the Dead* (1982); chapbooks like *Then Badger Said This* (1977), by Elizabeth Cook-Lynn

(Crow Creek Sioux); the lyric, ecological compositions of *Dancing Back Strong The Nation* (1981), by Maurice Kenny (Mohawk); and the richly contemplative verse of *Songs for the Harvester of Dreams* (1981), by Duane Niatum (Klallam).

The gallery of Native-American writers, often novelist-poets, would also include Gerald Vizenor (Anishinaabe/Chippewa), for the virtuosity of collections like *Born in the Wind* (1961) and his haiku *Matushima* (1984); Paula Gunn Allen (Laguna/Sioux) for her 'womanist' *Star Child* (1980) and *A Cannon Between Her Knees* (1981); Joy Harjo (Creek), for her dramatic, highly pictorialized *What Moon Drove Me To This?* (1980) and *She Had Some Horses* (1983); Simon Ortiz (Acoma Pueblo), for his wry, 'coyote' verse in *From Sand Creek* (1982); Wendy Rose (Hopi/Me-wuk), for her unsparing *The Halfbreed Chronicles and Other Poems* (1985); James Welch (Blackfeet/Gros Ventre), for his obliquely imaged *Riding The Earth Boy 40* (1971); Ray Young Bear (Mesquakie), for his engaging *Winter of the Salamander* (1980); nila northSun (Shoshone/Chippewa), for her colloquial, often comic *Small Bones, Little Eyes* (1982); Linda Hogan (Chickasaw), for her intense, evidentiary *Seeing Through The Sun* (1985); Gail Tremblay (Onondaga/MicMac), for her ancestor-minded *Talking to the Grandfathers: Annex 21, No 3* (1987); Louise Erdrich (Turtle Mountain Chippewa), for the adept sense of community and place of her *Jacklight* (1984); and Leslie Marmon Silko (Laguna), for the intimacy and rootedness of her *Laguna Woman: Poems* (1974) and multi-form *Storyteller* (1981). An apt commentary on this diversity, and its ancestry, can be found in Simon Ortiz's 'Washyuma Motor Hotel'. He writes: 'Beneath the cement foundations | of the motel, the ancient spirits | of the people conspire sacred tricks.'

Principal anthologies and critical studies include: Alan Velie, *Four American Indian Literary Masters: N. Scott Momaday, James Welch, Leslie Marmon Silko and Gerald Vizenor* (Norman, Okla., 1981); Geary Hobson (ed.), *The Remembered Earth: An Anthology of Contemporary Native American Literature* (Albuquerque, N. Mex.,

1981); Paula Gunn Allen (ed.), *Studies in American Indian Literature* (New York, 1983); Duane Niatum (ed.), *Harper's Anthology of 20th Century Native American Poetry* (San Francisco, 1987); and Brian Swann and Arnold Krupat (eds.), *Recovering The Word: Essays on Native American Literature* (Berkeley, Calif., 1987). [ARL

NDEBELE, Njabulo Simakahle (1948–), was born in Johannesburg and spent his youth in Western Native Township, and in Charterston Location, Nigel. Having gained a first-class degree in English and philosophy he went on to take an MA at Cambridge and a Ph.D at Denver. During the 1970s he became the most articulate literary theorist of the Black Consciousness Movement, editing the student literary journal *Expression*. His poems have appeared in *Classic*, *Izwi*, and *Staffrider*. At present he lectures in African, Afro-American, and English literature at the University of Lesotho, Roma. He published a volume of short stories, *Fools*, in 1983.

Ndebele's poetry is inward-looking, evoking subjective states of being through allegory or surrealist symbolism. Unlike the 'protest poetry' of *Serote and *Sepamla, his work does not overtly proclaim an ideological or political purpose. A poem like 'Man of Smoke', for instance, seems simply a vivid evocation of a prayer-meeting from the point of view of an uncomprehending child. However, the evasive, hesitant moods of Ndebele's poetry clearly dramatize the political situation of apartheid South Africa, with its Bantustans, its censorship, and violent repression. Children dread to pass from innocence to experience; a hungry child tells her doll that her mother hates her because she herself is hated by others; the poet ironically celebrates the inert pastoral contentment of 'the old lands' away from the city. In his critical writing Ndebele insists that literature must mediate experience through the complex resonances of language. 'Protest' and political exposition alone cannot engage with the complex structures of oppression, which lie beyond the imaginative reach of mere slogans.

A selection of Ndebele's poetry can be found in *Black Poets in South Africa*, ed. Robert Royston (London, 1973). [JB

NEILL, William. See LALLANS.

NEILSON, (John) Shaw (1872–1942), was born in Penola, South Australia, of Scottish parents. When he was 9 his family moved to Minimay, Victoria, and eventually settled near Nhill, in the Horsham district. Neilson received scarcely two-and-a-half years' schooling and acquired much of his education from his parents: his father was a competent provincial poet who imbued his son with a great respect for Scottish poetry; his mother, a passionate Free Church Presbyterian, educated the boy through the Bible, focusing on the Old Testament and the letters of St Paul. In 1906 Neilson began a literary relationship with the critic A. G. Stephens, who was to become his mentor and major publisher until Stephens's death in 1933. *Heart of Spring* appeared in 1919, *Ballads and Lyrical Poems* in 1923, and *New Poems* in 1927. A *Collected Poems* was published in 1934, and was followed by *Beauty Imposes* (1938). See *Selected Poems* ed. Robert Gray (Sydney, 1992).

Neilson's work has received a range of critical response. Until quite recently he was regarded as a bush innocent with little education or knowledge of the world; a 'simple singer', or rough, uneducated navvy who wrote without thinking. Douglas *Stewart saw him as a rustic figure born with a 'gift from the sky', who only had to 'take down the words as they arrive'. Neilson indeed lived in the bush for most of his life, but his poetry bore little resemblance to his simple rustic image, and he has suffered from a critical approach that has been unable or unwilling to see past his background. Far from being a simpleton, he was a well-educated writer with a good working knowledge of English and Australian literature.

See: *Poet of the Colours* (1988), a biography by John Phillips, and Cliff Hanna (ed.), *John Shaw Neilson* (1991), which has a selection of Neilson's writings including the poet's 'Autobiography'. Hanna has also published a critical book on Neilson, *The Folly of Spring* (1990). [CHa

NEMEROV, Howard Stanley (1920–91), was born and brought up in New York City, graduated at Harvard, and served in the Canadian and American Air Forces during the Second World War. His subsequent career as poet, teacher, novelist, editor, and critic took him to many of America's most prestigious universities, and won him many of its most distinguished literary awards, culminating in the American poet laureateship (1988–90).

Nemerov's first books establish, to a large extent, the breadth of his concerns and the shapes of his expression. Relaxed and ruminative pentameters would always serve him well, whether in contemplation or celebration, satire or lament, but his relatively narrow formal horizons contrast throughout his career with the remarkable range of his interest and observation. From the outset his reach is both global and specific, ancient and contemporary, domestic and mystical. Some of the most successful early pieces (many from 1955's *The Salt Garden*) combine lyrical description of the natural with some special human detail, elevating image into parable or myth. Brief visions—of soldiers on the move, a child drowned in a pond, the flight of seagulls—crystallize and illuminate back and forth through time. *Mirrors and Windows* (1958) evinces further development of Nemerov's skills in description and dialogue, as his high-rhetorical strain makes way for the kind of low-pitched, colloquial swing one associates with the later *Frost, a poet he resembles in other ways: two measured voices ranging far and wide from a sane, stoical centre; public citizens with an abiding faith in form and reason; artists capable of great expansion and intense compression.

The Blue Swallows (1967) displays a further range, as America's accelerating, double-speaking, jargon-spouting democracy sparks against Nemerov's ever-wider and warier muse. Numerov is one of the first poets to reflect on the status and predicament of that fast-multiplying species: the poet as college professor. His next books are more epigrammatic, noting and speculating, peering at words themselves, at creativity itself with the eyes of painters, composers, novelists, or nagging at the powerful and pretentious. Nemerov becomes a wisecracker just off the public stage, blending jauntiness and wry observation into a highly accessible modern commentary, though his facility with the pentameter at times loosens its effectiveness.

In his last book, *War Stories* (1987), he rediscovers a distinct focus. The self-examination of an American in wartime, at the heart of this century, recollected with the sharpness of maturity, carries a potent charge of meaning.

Some fine, chiefly occasional poems are included in the posthumously published *Trying Conclusions: New and Selected Poems 1961–91* (Chicago, 1991). *The Collected Poems of Howard Nemerov* (Chicago, 1977) won both the National Book Award and the Pulitzer Prize of 1978. See also *The Critical Reception of Howard Nemerov: A Selection of Essays and a Bibliography*, ed. Bowie Duncan (Metuchen, NJ, 1971); *The Stillness in Moving Things: The World of Howard Nemerov*, by William Mills (Memphis, Tenn., 1975), and *Howard Nemerov*, by Ross Labrie (Boston, 1980).

[GM

New Apocalypse, The, was a movement founded by J. F. *Hendry, Henry *Treece, and Dorian Cooke at a meeting in Leeds in August, 1938. In 1939 Hendry and Treece produced *The New Apocalypse*, with contributions by Hendry, Treece, Cooke, Norman McCaig (later *MacCaig), Nicholas *Moore, Philip O'Connor, Dylan *Thomas, and Robert Melville. Dylan Thomas was a decidedly unwilling recruit; and Hendry, Treece, Cooke, and McCaig were the core group.

In his introductory essay, 'Writers and Apocalypse', Hendry wrote of the problem of writing organically and of finding a living synthesis of man and the exterior world. This, as he explained in the slightly later 'Myth and Social Integration', was to be through personal myth—the aura within which a man grows and which he makes his own.

Henry Treece had contributed an essay, 'An Apocalyptic Writer and the Surrealists'; and Apocalypse, like *Surrealism, was concerned with the relation of art to the unconscious. G. S. *Fraser called it a dialectical development of Surrealism in his essay 'Apocalypse in Poetry', which appeared in the second anthology, *The White Horseman*, in 1941. Fraser was a friend of Nicholas Moore, in whose periodical *Seven* (which ran from summer 1938 to spring 1940), several of the Apocalypse writers had first appeared, though the urbane writing of Moore and Fraser had little in common with that of Apocalypse. A third anthology, *The Crown and the Sickle*, appeared in 1943 and marked the end of the movement. Of the earlier contributors there remained only Hendry, Treece and Cooke, all of whom were away on war service; and shortly thereafter the movement faded into what Herbert *Read named the New Romanticism, of which Treece was to be a leading figure.

The poetry of the movement did not measure up to its aspirations, and Hendry's essays were the best things to come out of it. Hendry, Cooke and McCaig wrote a prophetic poetry with a surrealist tone that was uncontrolled and often violent in its imagery. Treece leaned to the banal and sentimental. McCaig, Moore, and Fraser wrote good poems in the decade, but not in the Apocalypse manner. Apocalypse and its successor, the New Romanticism, fostered much of the looseness and pretentiousness that were the vices of the worst poetry of the Forties.

Apocalypse is discussed in *The Poetry of the Thirties* (London, 1975) and *The Poetry of the Forties* (Manchester, 1985), both by A. T. Tolley, and in *Poets of the Apocalypse*, by A. E. Salmon (New York, 1983). *Aquarius*, 17/18 contains an interview with J. F. Hendry. [ATT

NEWBOLT, Sir Henry (1862–1938), was born in Bilston, Staffordshire, the son of a vicar. He was educated at Clifton, the scene of some of his most famous poems, and Corpus Christi College, Oxford, receiving his BA in 1885. In 1889 he married Margaret Edina Duckworth of Orchardleigh, Frome, the scene of his novel *The Old Country* (London, 1906; New York, 1907). He was called to the Bar, but, encouraged by the popular success of his poem 'Drake's Drum' in

1896, by the favourable response of Robert *Bridges to this poem, and by the immense popular success of *Admirals All* (London, 1897; New York, 1898), a collection of patriotic poems, he gave up the practice of law and became a man of letters.

During his busy career he edited the *Monthly Review* and published a series of novels, an autobiography, some works of criticism, books about England's military victories on land and sea (including the last two volumes of the official British naval history of the First World War), and several collections of poetry, for which he is best known today. His 'Vitaï Lampada', inspired by his experiences at Clifton, with its refrain 'Play up! play up! and play the game!' was at one time known by almost every schoolboy in England.

The best source for biographical facts is Newbolt's two-volume autobiography, *My World as in My Time* (London, 1932) and *The Later Life and Letters of Sir Henry Newbolt*, ed. Margaret Newbolt (London, 1942). A comprehensive representation of his work can be found in Patric Dickinson (ed.), *Selected Poems of Henry Newbolt* (London, 1981). [DS

New Criticism, The, is the name that has been used since 1941, when John Crowe *Ransom published a book of essays with that title, for an extraordinary body of literary criticism, written largely by poets, that began to appear in England and the United States after the First World War, reached its creative apogee in the years preceding the Second World War, and dominated Anglo-American criticism throughout the Forties and Fifties and into the Sixties. In his book Ransom discusses T. S. *Eliot, I. A. *Richards, William *Empson, Yvor *Winters, and R. P. *Blackmur, and the criticism of these writers, along with that of Allen *Tate and of Ransom himself, is still the best introduction to the New Criticism, comprising an immense Socratic dialogue on the nature of literature that is as searching, odd, and profound as the individual efforts of Sidney, Dryden, Johnson, Coleridge, Shelley, Arnold, Henry James in his prefaces, and Ezra *Pound. Eliot's *The Sacred*

Wood (London, 1920), Richards's *Practical Criticism* (London, 1929), Empson's *Seven Types of Ambiguity* (London, 1930), Winters's *Primitivism and Decadence* (New York, 1936), Blackmur's *The Double Agent* (New York, 1936), Tate's *Reactionary Essays on Poetry and Society* (New York 1936), and Ransom's *The World's Body* (New York, 1938) have at least one goal in common: they are directed, either explicitly or implicitly, towards a revaluation of past literature in the light of contemporary advanced writing, and an assessment of contemporary literary practices in the light of the advanced writing of the past. Sharing little else except a belief in the necessity of strict adherence to the text—partly a reaction to anecdotal and adventitiously dogmatic criticism, and partly a response to the monumental late-nineteenth- and early-twentieth-century editions of older English poets by scholars such as H. J. C. Grierson and E. K. Chambers—the New Critics discovered approaches to this goal as varied as their perceptions of its implications. Eliot's essays, like his poems, reveal an agonized awareness of the contradictions in Christian culture and post-medieval European history, while the criticism of Richards and his brilliant pupil Empson reflects the categorizing bias of their scientific training and the influence of Ludwig Wittgenstein's linguistic philosophy. Winters is a neoclassical traditionalist whose almost total rejection of the modernist canon is given great force by the stark clarity of his logic; Blackmur, on the other hand, is the close reader of modernist poetry *par excellence*, and his intricate exegeses of Eliot, Wallace *Stevens, Pound, and Hart *Crane, among others, have lost none of their excitement and authority. Ransom quietly pursues the philosophical ramifications of his faith in the unity of a poem's intellectual argument, emotional burden, and metrical resourcefulness, and Tate's criticism is distinguished by a keen sense of the importance of local tradition and specific incident to imaginative forms. Other writers associated with the New Criticism are Kenneth *Burke, Cleanth Brooks, Robert Penn *Warren, and Randall *Jarrell, and a truly comprehensive anthology of the movement would also include essays by Stevens, Edmund *Wilson, F. R. Leavis, Lionel Trilling, W. H. *Auden, Delmore *Schwartz, and Robert *Lowell.   [RH

New Formalism, The, is the name commonly given to the resurgence of metred and rhymed poetry among younger American poets during the 1980s. These poets came of age during the 1960s and 1970s, when the free-verse revolution instigated by *Pound, *Eliot, and William Carlos *Williams had become the accepted orthodoxy within the American university writing workshops. Sensing that free-verse conventions had become stale, resulting in solipsistic, prosaic, and unmemorable poems, the New Formalists—many of whom studied English metrics with poet and classicist Robert *Fitzgerald at Harvard, or were influenced at Stanford by the Yvor *Winters formalist aesthetic, emphasizing iambics, the plain style of Ben Jonson, and paraphrasable intellectual argument, that remained a strong presence through the Seventies—returned to traditional metres and forms and to narrative in order to give back to American poetry a clarity, a music, and an objectivity which might make it accessible to a general audience.

While there is some continuity between this generation of formalists in the United States and previous ones, there are also distinct differences between it and the academic formalism that emerged out of the *New Criticism in the 1950s. While the former eschewed emotion in favour of irony, used elevated poetic diction and inverted syntax, and frequently looked to European culture for its subject, the New Formalists, by contrast, are more direct in their depiction of emotion, more colloquial in their diction, and more at ease with American popular culture as a source for formal poems. These qualities are best exemplified in Dana *Gioia's lyrics on the landscapes of California and suburban New York; in Gjertrud *Schnackenberg's elegies to her father; in Timothy *Steele's direct yet classically restrained love lyrics.

See also the essays related to this topic in *Poetry after Modernism*, ed. Robert McDowell (Brownsville, Oreg., 1990), as well as Timothy

Steele's critique of the modernist revolt against traditional English metre, *Missing Measures* (Fayetteville and London, 1990). (See also New Narrative.) [RMcP

New Lines. The anthology, edited by Robert *Conquest and published in 1956, which brought together work by the poets collectively known as the *Movement, has become almost as celebrated for its artfully self-effacing introduction as for the poems it contains. While its editor modestly argued that the poets had in common 'little more than a negative determination to avoid bad principles', it was clear that these principles—and corresponding good ones—had been pretty thoroughly aired over the preceding years, in an article on William *Empson which John *Wain contributed to the last issue of *Penguin New Writing* (1950) and in J. D. Scott's unsigned article, 'In the Movement' (*The Spectator*, 1 Oct. 1954). By guardedly invoking *Yeats, *Graves, *Auden, and Edwin *Muir in the final section of his introduction, Conquest claimed for his poets a greater significance than his gently diplomatic tone implied.

Remarkably, Conquest's fellow-contributors without exception went on to establish distinguished literary reputations, though not exclusively as poets: Donald *Davie, D. J. *Enright, and John *Holloway have been influential academic critics; Kingsley *Amis and John Wain are principally known as novelists; while Thom *Gunn, Elizabeth *Jennings, and Philip *Larkin are among the most important English poets of the late twentieth century, whose diversity clearly rebuts the accusations of uniformity levelled at *New Lines* (see entry on The New Poetry). Among the poems in the anthology were Larkin's 'Church Going', Gunn's 'On the Move', and Davie's 'Remembering the Thirties': they may indeed have shared iambic formality and a conversational tone (qualities which, after all, would have won the approval of Wordsworth in his 1798 Preface to *Lyrical Ballads*), but their distinctive concerns—respectively, provincial religious scepticism, Californian homo-erotic hedonism, and European cultural history—are a much surer guide

to the surprising range and enduring influence of *New Lines*. [NP

NEWLOVE, John (1938–), was born in Regina and lived for a number of years in nearby farming communities in eastern Saskatchewan, where his mother taught school. He has worked in Vancouver, Toronto, and Ottawa as a warehouseman, a technical writer, and publisher's editor, and has been a writer-in-residence at several Canadian universities, but his most formative and lasting influence has been the prairies, where the rigours of climate and terrain as well as the mixture of dispossessed natives and competing ethnic minorities have created such a fascinating social and political milieu.

Newlove's earliest work focuses on derelicts, misfits, and wanderers who inhabit the margins of society; it also dramatizes the plight of the poet as outsider in a disintegrating world, finding grace in fleeting encounters and small epiphanies. The stance in these lyrics is *confessional, but the tone is more often ironic than self-indulgent; and the style, which is spare, halting, and disjunctive, is remarkable for its playfulness and its acknowledgement of the limits of language and the poetic process. There is a jazz-like, improvisational quality in Newlove's best verse that is entirely original: see, for example, 'Ride Off Any Horizon', a poem that moves from image to image by way of a repetitive structure and associational logic which allows the poet to draw into a unified whole a wide range of personal and historical materials.

Newlove's most celebrated work is 'The Pride', a longish poem that employs various levels of poetic discourse, including lyrical fragments, quasi-documentary prose pieces, and direct statement, asking the perennial Canadian question about 'the knowledge of | our origins, and where | we are in truth, | whose land this is | and is to be'. Like a cultural anthropologist, Newlove calls up the ghosts, of great moments and great Indian leaders, that must be remembered and given the permanence of art; he finds the 'roots | and rooted words', 'the pride, the grand poem | of our land, of the earth itself'. And in so doing, he accomplishes what can only be described as a poetics of recall.

Newlove's major publications are *Moving in Alone* (1965), *Black Night Window* (1968), *The Cave* (1970), *The Fat Man* (1977), and *The Night the Dog Smiled* (1986—all Toronto). [GG

New Narrative, The, is a recent movement in American poetry, often associated with the *New Formalism. In a flurry of essays New Narrative poets have defined their movement as a reaction against the solipsism of post-war American poetry. Their work, characterized by clear story-lines in both fixed and open forms, has been supported by such periodicals as the *Kenyon Review, the *Hudson Review, the *Paris Review, Verse, and The Reaper.

Christopher Clausen's *The Place of Poetry* (1981) established an historical context for the return to narrative in verse. The same year saw publication of Frederick Feirstein's *Manhattan Carnival*, a long poem in rhymed couplets. Other book-length poems include Vikram *Seth's *The Golden Gate* (1986) and Frederick *Turner's science-fiction epics, *The New World* (1985), and *Genesis* (1988). Robert *McDowell's *Quiet Money* (1987) and Mark Jarman's *The Black Riviera* (1990) contain shorter narratives. Dana *Gioia's dramatic monologues, 'The Room Upstairs', 'The Homecoming', and 'Counting the Children' are, along with Charles *Martin's 'Passages from Friday', among the best poems yet produced by writers associated with the movement.

New Narrative poets have been called reactionary for their return to traditional techniques, but they are also credited with helping to revitalize American poetry. They have written eloquently about E. A. *Robinson, *Frost, and *Jeffers as literary forebears, and have praised poets like Louis *Simpson for writing narratives of ordinary life when it was unfashionable to do so. Rita *Dove's sequence of short narrative poems, *Thomas and Beulah* (1986), may have given momentum to the movement by winning the Pulitzer Prize.

Expansive Poetry: Essays on the New Narrative and the New Formalism, ed. Frederick Feirstein

(Santa Cruz, Calif., 1989) collects critical essays by a number of these writers. [DM

New Poetry, The. This anthology, published in 1962, was intended by its editor A. *Alvarez to represent a riposte to the 'academic-administrative verse' of *New Lines. Alvarez contributed a polemical preface, subtitled 'Beyond the Gentility Principle', and began the book with poems by two exemplary Americans, John *Berryman and Robert *Lowell. As an editorial stance it was bracingly effective: readers may, therefore, have been surprised to discover that six of the nine *New Lines* poets were represented in *The New Poetry*, alongside writers with very different allegiances, such as Charles *Tomlinson, Ted *Hughes, and Geoffrey *Hill. In fact, the book is an admirably eclectic survey of British poets ranging from Norman *MacCaig (b. 1910) to John *Fuller (b. 1937). A second edition, revised and expanded though inevitably lacking some of the first's abrasive excitement, appeared in 1966. Alvarez discussed his editorial stance in a lively conversation with Donald *Davie (*The Review*, 1, 1962), reprinted in *The Modern Poet*, ed. Ian Hamilton (London, 1968). [NP

New Poets of England and America, was an influential and popular anthology published by Meridian Books in 1957, going through ten printings in the next decade. Jointly edited by American poets Donald *Hall, Robert Pack, and Louis *Simpson, it contained selections by fifty-two poets under 40 years of age, sixteen of them English and the remainder American. 'Maturity No Object', an introductory essay by Robert *Frost, bestowed an official blessing on the efforts of the younger generation. *New Poets* introduced Philip *Larkin, Kingsley *Amis, Thom *Gunn, and others to many American readers, and collected work by the post-war generation of American poets, of whom only Robert *Lowell and Richard *Wilbur were widely known at the time. In 1962 Hall and Pack produced a 'second selection' of poems by sixty-two poets, with each editor, respectively, assuming responsibility for the choices in the separate English and American sections.

Because of the age-restrictions, some poets from the first anthology were excluded, making room for Ted *Hughes, George *MacBeth, Sylvia *Plath, Anne *Sexton, and James *Dickey, to name a few. Despite the predominance of rhymed, metrical stanzas by poets with university affiliations, the two anthologies remain the most significant transatlantic gatherings of the second half of the century, and nothing of their magnitude has been attempted since.

New Poets of England and America is generally credited with having fired the first salvo in the so-called War of the Anthologies, which through the 1960s appeared to divide American poetry into two camps, 'Academics' and '*Beats', or what Robert Lowell termed schools of 'cooked' and 'uncooked' poetry. Donald Allen's 1960 anthology from Grove Press, *The New American Poetry*, was widely perceived as the Beat response to *New Poets*, presenting work by forty-four poets under 50, none of whom (including Allen *Ginsberg, John *Ashbery, Robert *Duncan, Denise *Levertov, and Gary *Snyder) had passed muster with Hall, Pack, and Simpson. Hall's own Penguin anthology of 1962, *Contemporary American Poetry*, made some concessions to changing tastes and contained poems by Robert *Creeley, Snyder, Levertov, and Ashbery. *A Controversy of Poets* (1965), ed. Paris Leary and Robert Kelly, claimed to represent all schools fairly, as did Hayden Carruth's *The Voice Which Is Great Within Us* (1970).

[RSG

New Review, The. See REVIEW, THE.

New Verse. The first issue of *New Verse* appeared in January 1933, the thirty-fourth and last in May 1939. The magazine had no wrapper, and the page-size was small, 8 by 6 inches. The first number contained no more than twenty pages, and was much exceeded only by an *Auden Double Number of forty-eight. The *New Verse Anthology* which appeared in August 1939 marked the end of the enterprise, although this was not realized at the time by its editor Geoffrey *Grigson.

Grigson said later that the magazine had come into existence because of Auden. That may have been literally true, but it was essentially a reflection of the editor's own personality and taste. Grigson was throughout his life a combative critic, and in youth a savage one. He labelled Edith *Sitwell the Old Jane, and George *Barker and Rayner Heppenstall were among those who learned that to have had poems printed in the magazine was no barrier to dismissal of their work in the harshest, most personal terms—and in Barker's case, to printing more poems in a later issue.

Although the picric nature of Grigson's criticism made *New Verse* notorious, it was the quality of his taste in choosing poems that made the magazine embody the best verse of the decade. Grigson was not immune to the fashions of the time. He printed some dud surrealist pieces, the 'Oxford Collective Poem' sponsored by Mass Observation, and the mock-metaphysical poems of Charles *Madge. Yet perhaps three-quarters of the work printed exemplified the editor's preference for poetry related to current speech, his insistence that an epic and a limerick were both poems, his alertness to what was genuine in language and emotion and not 'embedded in a stew of literature', his liking for things seen as distinct from what was only felt. Auden and *MacNeice were the magazine's poetic pillars, but behind them were many competent poets who adhered to the *New Verse* tenets.

Norman *Cameron, Kenneth *Allott, Gavin *Ewart, Bernard *Spencer, B. H. *Gutteridge, Roy *Fuller, Ruthven *Todd, and George *Woodcock are the most notable names in the list, but there was hardly a young poet of interest whose work did not appear in *New Verse*. Grigson's own taste developed during the period, so that an initial enthusiasm for Dylan *Thomas's energy was modified by increasing distrust of his windy rhetoric. There was an increasing coolness towards Stephen *Spender's poetry, and Cecil *Day Lewis, whose poems had been printed in early issues, was dismissed as 'the grease in the sink-pipe of letters who has been posing for years as spring water'. Grigson later expressed regret for the wounding language of this and other pieces, although not for the sentiment behind them, yet the intensity of feeling that marked his attacks, the determination not to be deceived by literary language and flatulence masquerading as emotion, played a large part in making *New Verse* the most notable verse magazine of its decade.

Grigson's autobiography, *The Crest on the Silver* (London, 1950) gives more information about the magazine, and so do some of the essays in *Recollections* (London, 1984), published near the end of his life. See also Ian Hamilton, *The Little Magazines: A Study of Six Editors* (London, 1976). [JGS

New Writing, was founded in 1936 by John *Lehmann, who edited it throughout its life. Lehmann had published *New Signatures* (1932) and *New Country* (1933), the defining anthologies of the left-wing literary movement of the period; and initially *New Writing*'s chief contributors came from those anthologies: W. H. *Auden, Christopher Isherwood, Stephen *Spender, William *Plomer, and Rex *Warner. *New Writing* was hospitable to the best products of the movement; though Lehmann did not make political orientation the basis of selection of what he published.

New Writing appeared every six months as a hard-cover miscellany of 150,000 words, providing space for longer short fiction that most literary periodicals could not publish. When war came, it seemed doubtful whether such an ambitious project could continue; but it did, in a reduced form, as *Folios of New Writing*, of which four issues appeared in 1940 and 1941. With the fall of France it became difficult to obtain European contributions; and in 1941, in collaboration with Czech writers in exile, Lehmann brought out *Daylight*. After one issue it was combined with *Folios* to become *New Writing and Daylight*, which endeavoured to maintain its international character until it ceased appearing in 1946. The last number was published from Lehmann's own publishing house, which produced a lavish successor in two issues of *Orpheus* in 1948 and 1949.

The most important offshoot of *New Writing* was the *Penguin New Writing*, begun in 1942 as a selection from *New Writing*, but which lived on for forty issues until 1950, becoming a fully independent quarterly in 1942. It maintained the high quality of *New Writing*, using many of the same contributors, yet over 100,000 copies each were printed in the first post-war issues.

The early volumes of *New Writing* contained work of a realist nature, some of it of the 'reporting' character favoured in the later 1930s. Poems subsequently famous by Auden and his contemporaries appeared, but the character of the periodical was given by its prose. During the war and after there was more poetry, and Lehmann found a new group of young poets whom he encouraged by steady publication: Roy *Fuller, Laurie *Lee, Terence *Tiller, Alan *Ross, Henry *Reed, and Peter *Yates. While Lehmann observed a shift from a documentary type of realism to something more introvert, he nevertheless had no time for what he saw as the glib sentimentality of many younger writers, particularly those associated with the *New Apocalypse movement. Although Lehmann's great virtue as an editor was his undoctrinaire receptiveness to new talent, *New Writing* came to define itself in terms of the type of writing he accepted: unrhetorical, humanist, perceptive, and grounded in personal experience. The limitations of *New Writing* were the limitations of the culture from which it came: despite the upheavals of the war, there was little in British experience that could lead to a wholesale questioning of human nature, as there was in Europe.

New Writing can be sampled in *The Penguin New Writing: 1940–1950*, ed. J. Lehmann and R. Fuller (London, 1985). See also *John Lehmann's 'New Writing': An Author Index 1936–1950*, by E. Whitehead (Lewiston, 1990) and *John Lehmann: A Tribute*, ed. A. T. Tolley (Ottawa, 1987). [ATT

New York School, The, is a term used since the 1960s to refer to a group of American poets who emerged in the 1950s, when the New York School of painting dominated the art world with which most of them were closely linked. Frank

*O'Hara, John *Ashbery, and Kenneth *Koch had been classmates at Harvard; in New York they met painters and wrote about them for art magazines, and O'Hara worked at the Museum of Modern Art, as did James *Schuyler. Rounding out the group were Barbara *Guest, Kenward Elmslie, and Harry *Mathews. Besides their friendship and the affinities of their verse with twentieth-century vanguard art generally, and with Abstract Expressionism in particular, these poets shared a relationship to the poetry of the immediate past that was unique at the time: thoroughly familiar with *Yeats, *Pound, *Eliot, *Stevens, Hart *Crane, and *Auden, they were influenced no less by French poetry from Baudelaire through the *Surrealists, and by translations of the Russian poets Mayakovsky and Pasternak; and their familiarity with the French and Russian modernist traditions, as well as their appreciation of maverick English and American poets such as Laura *Riding, John *Wheelwright, F. T. *Prince, David *Schubert, and Edwin *Denby, cleared the way for a common interest in what might be called the intense urbane, expressed in language that is witty, abstract, and colloquial by turns. One section of Donald Allen's anthology, *The New American Poetry 1945–1960* (New York and London, 1960; see entry on NEW POETS OF ENGLAND AND AMERICA), was devoted to Ashbery, Guest, Koch, O'Hara, and Schuyler, and the work of all seven poets was influential during the following decade, in America especially but in England as well. After reaching its zenith with the publication of O'Hara's *Collected Poems*, also edited by Allen, six years after O'Hara was fatally injured by a beach taxi in 1966, this collective influence declined somewhat, though Ashbery, O'Hara, Schuyler, and Koch were read more widely than ever during the Seventies and Eighties. Other poets associated with the New York School include Ted *Berrigan, Ron *Padgett, Joseph Ceravolo, Lee *Harwood, Tony Towle, Frank Lima, Clark Coolidge, and Trevor Winkfield. See *The Poets of the New York School*, ed. John Bernard Myers (Philadelphia, Pa., 1969), and *An Anthology of New York Poets*, ed. Ron Padgett and David Shapiro (New York, 1970). [RH

New Yorker, The. See Moss, Howard.

NICHOL, bp (Barrie Phillip) (1944–88), born into a railroad family, was brought up in various Canadian cities, most of them in the west. He trained as an elementry-school teacher, but abandoned that profession quickly to make a career as a writer and therapist.

For Nichol writing involved all the arts. He was Canada's best-known *concrete poet and *sound poet. He wrote children's books and children's television. He composed opera and pop musicals, fiction, cartoons, theory and lyric verse. He and three other Toronto poets formed The Four Horsemen, a sound-poetry performance group that gained international attention over nearly two decades.

Nichol did not recognize a line between living and art. He was an editor who encouraged and taught scores of younger writers. He turned literature into outdoor sculpture and wore clothing made of visual poems. He scored performance pieces based on French semiotic theory. He was immensely popular with other poets, and his early death occasioned ceremonies across the country.

As a poet he worked on forms derived from the examples of Gertrude *Stein and the Dadaists. A Nichol poem insists on its materiality, and the play of signifiers gives rise to much of its meaning. The most important of these poems is *The Martyrology*, which has been published in seven volumes since 1972 (Toronto). Characterized as a 'Life-poem', it is an exhaustive, cabalistic, and witty exploration of language as the writer's creed and environment.

The Martyrology is the subject of an anthology of essays, *Tracing the Paths* (Vancouver, 1988), ed. Roy Miki. Nichol's work was also the subject of another anthology, *Read the Way he Writes* (Toronto, 1986) ed. Paul Dutton and Steven Smith. A useful monograph is Stephen Scobie's *What History Teaches* (Vancouver, 1985).

[GHB

NICHOLS, Grace (1950–), was born in British Guiana, now Guyana and educated at the University of Guyana. In Guyana she worked as a teacher and journalist. She declared, in her brief autobiographical essay 'Home Truth', that it was 'only after coming to England in 1977 that poetry began to play a bigger and bigger part in my life'. Her poetry is characterized by sensitivity to the experience of women, a sensuous apprehension of mundane reality, and a piquant wit, all combining to make her a most original talent. 'Shopping', for instance, with its playful echoes of T. S. *Eliot's 'The Hollow Men', subtly hints at a domestic rift between the shopper, who is the 'voice' of the poem, and her 'old man', to make a telling point about consumer values.

Her poetry collections include I is a long memoried woman (London, 1983), which won the Commonwealth Poetry Prize, The Fat Black Woman's Poems (London, 1984), and Lazy Thoughts of a Lazy Woman (London, 1989). She has also published children's books, including the poems in Come On In To My Tropical Garden (London, 1988), and a novel, Whole of a Morning Sky (London, 1986), which is set in Guyana.

[MR

NICHOLSON, Norman (1910–87), was born at Millom, Cumberland, educated locally, and stayed all his life in the same house. In the moving poem which closes his last collection (Sea to the West, 1981) he describes how his father saw Halley's Comet in 1910 and wonders whether he himself will live to see its return in 1986. What is significant about this characteristically anecdotal poem is Nicholson's awareness that if he does see the comet he will do so from the same spot, sharing his father's 'long-ago Edwardian surprise'. Place, the local habitation of the Lake District with all its continuity and change, is of the essence in Nicholson's work, although he achieved what *Auden described as 'the poet's hope' (quoted as an epigraph to Sea to the West) to be, like some valley cheese, local but prized elsewhere.

Nicholson wrote several prose works about the Lake District—its literary figures, inhabitants and landscape—including The Lakers (1955) and his autobiography Wednesday Early Closing (1975)—but it was in his poetry, which

can be seen to become increasingly confident in the handling of blank verse and syllabic metre after beginning (Five Rivers, 1944) with a much more conventional lyricism, that he addressed most directly the forces of change he observed around him. The magnificent, gravelly 'On the Dismantling of Millom Ironworks', with its ironically lofty Wordsworthian title and its passionately meticulous itemizing of natural beauty and industrial waste, shows him at his very best, while such poems as 'Comprehending it Not' (from Sea to the West), 'The Whisperer' (from A Local Habitation, 1972), and 'Rising Five' (from The Pot Geranium, 1954) show how successful he could be in dealing, unsentimentally, with intimate personal reminiscence and building on the proverbial idiom of local dialect. His sequence of poems about Black Combe, first published as a handsome illustrated pamphlet, The Shadow of Black Combe, in 1978, is particularly distinctive in its blending of topography with anecdote. Nicholson also wrote two novels and four verse plays of somewhat lesser interest.

Although selections of Nicholson's poetry have been published by Faber—most recently Selected Poems 1940–1982 (1982)—a Collected Poems is long overdue.

[JM

NIEDECKER, Lorine (1903–70), was born and died in Fort Atkinson, Wisconsin, living much of her adult life in a small cabin on Black Hawk Island on Lake Koshkonong, Wisconsin. An active correspondent with numerous poets such as Louis *Zukofsky, Cid *Corman, and William Carlos *Williams, all of whom both influenced and praised her work, she lived an essentially isolated life, one which appealed to both her affinity for nature and her innate shyness. From her earliest work on, Zukofsky was an encouraging mentor, and his notions of objectivity and sincerity as elaborated in his essay 'An Objective' in *Poetry magazine (1931), were extremely important to her. A keen reader, her interests lay in history, the natural sciences, and pre-Socratic philosophy, subjects full of resonance for her, which informed both the content and shape of her poetry.

Niedecker is an American miniaturist; in this, her work bears some comparison with the short poems of Robert *Creeley or the terseness of J. V. *Cunningham. Her natural register is the epigrammatic mode, one which renders a life or a landscape as though it were composed of a series of small, intense moments. Her mode of construction, something she obviously took from Zukofsky, aims for fidelity to the musical phrase, the leading of sound syllables, and the sense of closure afforded by rhyme-schemes and metrical attentiveness. By such a method she invests with a satisfying density and self-containment what might ordinarily escape into ephemerality. The consequent musical completeness and condensation in the poems transforms what could easily have become effusions into something like the workings of a scientist or botanist. Whether commenting on the life of Audubon or Thomas Jefferson or on the often deeply painful events of her own life, she exhibits a rigorous detachment, all the more moving for its precision and lack of self-indulgence.

The two most useful collections of Niedecker's work are *From This Condensery: The Complete Writings of Lorine Niedecker*, ed. Robert Bertolf (Highlands, NC, 1985) and *The Granite Pail: The Selected Poems of Lorine Niedecker*, ed. Cid Corman (Berkeley, Calif., 1985). See also *Truck 16*, ed. David Wilk (1975) and Michael Heller's *Conviction's Net of Branches: Essays on the Objectivist Poets and Poetry* (1985).   [MH

NIMS, John Frederick (1913–), was born in Muskegon, Michigan, to a Catholic family, and educated at DePaul University and Notre Dame. By 1945, when he earned a Ph.D in comparative literature from the University of Chicago, he had already distinguished himself as a poet and critic: his contributions to *Five Young American Poets* (1944) display the formal acuity and urban settings characteristic of his poetry, and his 1945 review of early books by Robert *Lowell and *Merton contains prescient observations about their work. In 1947 Nims married Bonnie Larkin. They had five children, one of whom died at an early age. Nims has taught in Milan, Florence, and Madrid, as well as at several American universities; he taught at the University of Illinois at Chicago Circle from 1965 until his retirement.

In America Nims is best known for his powerful impact as editor of *Poetry* from 1978 to 1984, and as the author of an important textbook, *Western Wind* (2nd edn., 1983). In both capacities he has fostered the use of traditional forms evident in his own work. Though perhaps too cold and densely written, Nims's early poems show a talent for satire. His second full-length collection, *A Fountain in Kentucky* (1950), is more assured and emotionally profound, particularly in 'The Masque of Blackness', a sonnet-sequence touching on the death of his son George. Throughout his career Nims has been preoccupied with love and death in their most ironic correspondences, but in 'The Evergreen', from *Knowledge of the Evening* (1960), he discards ironic distance to create a moving elegy. The epigrams in *Of Flesh and Bone* (1967) are reminiscent of J. V. *Cunningham's.

Some of Nims's best work has been done as a translator and essayist. He has made important versions of the poems of St John of the Cross and Euripedes's *Andromache*. *Sappho to Valéry* (1971; rev. edn., 1990) contains not only an impressive number of translations from half-a-dozen languages, but also an introductory essay calling on translators to be poets, to make new English poems rather than versions of the originals that are merely accurate and lifeless. His lecture 'The Topless Muse' argues persuasively for reticence and restraint as ways of increasing the imaginative impact of poetry. Essays on Golding's Ovid and other subjects prove, by their lightly-worn erudition, that Nims is an important post-war American critic.

Selected Poems (Chicago, 1982) does not contain poems from *The Kiss: A Jambalaya* (New York, 1982). Sixteen of Nims's essays and introductions are collected in *A Local Habitation* (Ann Arbor, Mich., 1985). See also 'Sanctity and the Poetry of John F. Nims' by Richard Shaw, *Renascence* (Autumn 1960).   [DM

Nine, a lively monthly for the most part devoted to poetry and polemic, was founded in 1949 as a result of a meeting of nine young writers who decided that it was required to disseminate (mainly) the poetic and economic ideals of *Pound, whom they regarded as a 'hero' mistaken only in respect of Mussolini. Those present included Peter Russell (editor), Ian (then Iain) *Fletcher, G. S. *Fraser, and John *Heath-Stubbs. The first number carried a 'Message' from T. S. *Eliot, who commended the notion of a 'small number of devoted writers working together . . . seeing eye to eye about humbug'. Much attacked were socialism and Stephen *Spender. *Nine* remained Pound-orientated—the press associated with it published his wartime broadcasts from Rome as well as collections by Basil *Bunting and Tom *Scott—but was genuinely eclectic, and printed much important verse in original and in translation. Contributors included *Graves, *Bottrall, *Sisson, *Tomlinson (a fragment from an illustrated Blakean epic), Borges, Roy *Campbell, Marianne *Moore, Allen *Tate, *Eberhart, *Madge, Edwin *Morgan, and (notably) Russell and Fletcher. It ceased to appear, after nine years, in 1958. [MS-S

Nobel Prizes. Alfred Nobel (1833–96), a Swedish chemist who (with his father) developed dynamite, as well as other explosive substances, left over £2,000,000. He willed that the bulk of the interest on this sum be devoted to annual prizes for outstanding achievements in five fields: physics, chemistry, medicine and physiology, promotion of peace, and literature. He stipulated that the chosen writers should have produced work 'of an idealistic tendency', but in practice this has been interpreted very broadly by the Swedish committee which makes the awards. Between 1901 and 1992 the literature prize has been awarded eighty-three times: on three occasions to philosophers who wrote no literary works, and to Winston Churchill—ostensibly for his historical writings, but really for his skill as a war-leader against the philistine Nazis. On eighteen occasions the award has been made for an achievement exclusively poetic, although in the output of a few more winners poetry has been an important element

(e.g. *Kipling, Ivan Bunin). Of the eighteen poets chosen, four, *Yeats, *Eliot, *Brodsky (some of the time) and *Walcott, wrote in English; five in a Scandinavian language—one of these received the award posthumously. But in view of the fact that the literature award is rather more of a media than a critical event, the Swedish Academy cannot be said to have acquitted itself disastrously. The awards to Yeats and Eliot were not only expected but thoroughly deserved by any standards, even though Yeats is supposed to have greeted the news with the question, 'How much?' (today, in excess of £150,000). It has seldom been won, in the very nature of such affairs, without vigorous lobbying on the part of the supporters of those nominated, or in certain cases (Bunin, Quasimodo), without determined letter-writing campaigns on the part of the nominees themselves. On 20 November 1921, Thomas *Hardy, who had been nominated but had remained aloof, and to whom Anatole France had just been preferred, wrote to a friend: 'The prize did not come my way . . . English poetry is always at a discount on the Continent, barring Byron's, and they appreciate him rather as the wicked lord than as the poet.' This was an accurate enough summation. The committee has also—with some justification—favoured modernism and innovation in poetry; on it have been minor Swedish modernist poets whose work has been translated into various languages by subsequent prize-winners (and others less fortunate). English-language poets conspicuous for not receiving the prize include *Pound, *Frost, *Auden, and *Lowell. But Pound, like Borges, failed to get it because of his politics: it has generally been barred to proponents of right-wing or alleged right-wing views, although it has gone to very minor poets whose stand against oppression has been unequivocal (e.g. the Spaniard Aleixandre and the Czech Jaroslav Seifert). The later poetry of Lowell was accused by a critic of 'looking towards Stockholm'. This sort of condemnation in itself, whether just or unjust, together with Yeats's question quoted above, are perhaps the most accurate indicators of the prize's real status so far as serious criticism is concerned. [MS-S

NOONUCCAL, Oodgeroo (formerly Kath Walker) (1920–93), was born on North Stradbroke Island, Queensland, the home of the Noonuccal tribe. She changed her name in 1988, the bicentennial year of the European invasion of her country. Awarded the MBE in 1971 in recognition of her efforts on behalf of her people, she has since 1961 been a leader in Aboriginal activist movements. She has been much in demand as a speaker, reader, and lecturer, both in Australia and overseas.

Her book *We Are Going* (Brisbane, 1964) was the first volume of poems by an Aboriginal writer and has been one of the most successful verse publications in Australia, selling many thousands of copies. It was succeeded by *The Dawn is at Hand* (Brisbane, 1966) and a collected edition of her writings, *My People* (Brisbane, 1970). Since then she has published a charming prose book about her childhood and her Noonuccal heritage, *Stradbroke Dreaming* (Sydney, 1972), and a volume of her art-work, *Quandamooka: The Art of Kath Walker*, was edited by Ulli Beier (Bathurst, NSW, 1985).

Her poetry—direct, impassioned, and deeply committed to declaring the basic rights of her race—has its origins in the ballad tradition as much as in her search for an Aboriginal inflection through the English language. Her success in the latter aim has had a profound influence on the later striking development of Aboriginal writing in the 1980s.   [TWS

NORRIS, Leslie (1921–), was born in Merthyr Tydfil, Glamorgan. Formerly a teacher, he has earned his living since 1974 as a full-time writer and lecturer, mostly in the USA. At present he is humanities professor of creative writing at Brigham Young University, Utah.

His principal volumes of poetry are *Finding Gold* (1967), *Ransoms* (1970), *Mountains, Polecats, Pheasants* (1974), *Water Voices* (1980), and *A Sea in the Desert* (1989). He has also published two collections of short stories, *Sliding* (1978) and *The Girl from Cardigan* (1988), and with Alan Keele he is the translator of Rilke's *The Sonnets to Orpheus* (1989).

The emotional basis of Leslie Norris's writing is in his experience as a child in Merthyr, an industrial town which has continued to exercise a powerful influence on his imagination and creative skills. His poems and stories abound with the colourful characters of the place and with the rich wildlife of its rural hinterland. The energy and meticulous craftsmanship of his verse produce a wealth of images and much verbal ingenuity, and his poems usually have an impact which arises from a deep melancholy and poignancy, especially in the eclogues for childhood and youth, in which his sense of loss is most apparent.

His years in America have made his poetry more diffuse and technically more sophisticated, but his main preoccupations with place, time, and personal relationships are still firmly rooted in the Merthyr of his early years.

Two selections of Leslie Norris's verse have been published, *Walking the White Fields* (Boston and Toronto, 1980) and *Selected Poems* (Bridgend, 1986). A monograph on his work has been written by James A. Davies for the Writers of Wales series (Cardiff, 1991).   [MS

NORTJE, Arthur (1942–70), was born in Oudtshoorn (Cape Province), South Africa. His early education was in the segregated schools of Port Elizabeth. He graduated from the segregated University College of the Western Cape and taught English in South Africa until 1965 when he went to Jesus College, Oxford, to read English. He taught in Hope, British Columbia, and Toronto from 1967 until 1970 when he returned to Oxford to work for a doctoral degree. He died from an overdose of barbiturates in 1970 whilst in Oxford.

His poems first appeared in *Black Orpheus* in 1961 and he was awarded an Mbari Poetry Prize. Two collections of his poems have been published posthumously: *Lonely Against the Light* (Grahamstown, 1973) and *Dead Roots* (London, 1973). A selection of his poems was included in *Seven South African Poets* (London, 1971), ed. Cosmos Pieterse. Nortje's early poems were directly concerned with the emotional consequences of living within the inhumane structures of South Africa. The poems which he wrote whilst in England are some of the most poignant, exploring the isolation and loneliness of the exile. He was a double exile; of mixed race, he was rejected by white South Africa. This and his distance from the everyday realities of his country of birth gave emotional impetus to his best work. His later poems documented the gradual disintegration of his personality; even here his poetry was elegant, coherent, and purposeful.   [FO

NOWLAN, Alden (1933–83), was born in Stanley, a small community near Windsor, Nova Scotia. At the age of 12 he left school and worked for several years as lumber-man, mill-hand, and farmhand. At 19 he moved to Hartland, New Brunswick, and worked for the *Hartland Observer*. Later he became editor of the Saint John *Telegraph-Journal*. He published *The Rose and the Puritan*, his first volume of poems, in 1958, and *Bread, Wine and Salt* in 1967. In 1969 he was appointed writer-in-residence at the University of New Brunswick, a position he held until his death.

Many of Nowlan's poems are based on anecdotes from personal experience and are used to point up some moral. The emotions that inform his lyrics arise from his memories of growing up in a family and community that were both economically and imaginatively impoverished. His realistic imagery, conversational speech, and controlled irony allow him to avoid the sentimentality and bombast to which his subject-matter is susceptible.

Both the natural goodness of life and the evils inflicted upon us by failed institutions are central to Nowlan's poetry. He decries puritanical attitudes and moral hyprocrisy in 'All Down the Morning' and 'Beginnings'. In 'Warren Pryor', he shows how economic depression prompted well-intentioned parents to force their son into a career that crippled his spirit. He condemns anything that denies life, as, for example, in 'God Sour the Milk', or diminishes the dignity of any creature, as in 'The Bull Moose'. He is tolerant of anything that creates even the illusion of happiness and hope, as in 'Marian at the Pentecostal Meeting'.

Among his twelve volumes of poetry are: *The Rose and the Puritan* (Fredericton, 1958); *Bread, Wine and Salt* (Toronto, 1967), *Playing the Jesus Game: Selected Poems* (Fredericton, 1970); *Between Tears and Laughter* (Toronto, 1971); *I'm a Stranger Here Myself* (Toronto, 1974); *Smoked Glass* (Toronto, 1977); *I Might Not Tell Everybody This* (Toronto, 1982); *Early Poems* (Fredericton, 1983); and *An Exchange of Gifts* (Toronto, 1985), edited and introduced by Robert Gibbs.   [DRB

NTIRU, Richard (1946–), was born near Kisoro, Uganda, and educated at Ntare school, Nbarara, and Makerere University, where he acquired precocious standing as an editor, as organizer of the 1969 Arts Festival, radio playwright, short-story writer, and poet. The verse in his book *Tensions* (1971) dates from these student years. Its great promise was recognized by the inclusion of eleven items in Wole *Soyinka's *Poems of Black Africa* (London, 1975). But Ntiru fell silent after he took his first-class degree. Following a spell with the East African Publishing House in Nairobi, he remained in that city as part of the tragic Ugandan diaspora of the Amin-Obote years, working for international organizations.

In *Tensions*, admirable control of syntax and a sound ear for free-verse rhythm support an unusually wide vocabulary, displayed with evident relish. Original intelligence plays over themes of alienation and social satire characteristic of work by young African poets of the time, with some influence from the post-Poundian sequences of Christopher *Okigbo.

Ntiru is also represented in David Cook and David Rubadiri (eds.), *Poems from East Africa* (London, 1971), and is discussed by Adrian Roscoe in *Uhuru's Fire: African Literature East to South* (Cambridge, 1977).   [ALRC

NUTTALL, Jeff (1933–), born in Lancashire and educated at Hereford School of Art and Bath Academy of Art, has stated: 'I am hardly at all concerned with direct verbal/syntactical "meaning". Silly to call my verse "obscure" unless you're short-sighted.' But the epithet 'obscure' has seldom been applied to his work, although, as a critic has written, 'he is richly confused and self-contradictory in ways which are central to his time'. He edited *My Own Mag* from 1964 until 1967. His verse is discussed and enjoyed amongst small coteries and regional groups, but has not yet been widely read. He has published many small collections issued by private presses, as well as the more substantially sized *Poems 1962–1969* (London, 1970).

[MS-S

NYE, Robert (1939–), was born in London. He is best known for his novels and for his poetry reviews; but he also has a reputation as a poet. Like Robert *Graves, to whose poetry he has a debt, he has subjected his poems to a process of continuous revision, so that pieces which first appeared in *Juvenilia 1* (Northwood, 1961) or *Juvenilia 2* (Lowestoft, 1963), have resurfaced in often-drastically revised form in successive collections: *Darker Ends* (London, 1969), *Divisions on a Ground* (Manchester, 1976), and *A Collection of Poems 1955–1988* (London, 1989). The last collects all his work. Early poems were largely inchoate, and littered with phrases from his own favourite poets (*de la Mare as well as Graves); but they were always deeply felt. Many have survived into *A Collection of Poems*, purged of most of the echoes but sometimes less energetic. His direction has always been towards clarity and perfection of form. The problems for his critic are the degree of his originality and, when he seeks to be epigrammatic, the quality of his intellect. His main themes are love—which he approaches as a distinctly Celtic phenomenon—and guilt. He has written narrative poems, such as 'Crowson', in which his own voice is much more in evidence. [POM

O

OATES, Joyce Carol (1938–), was born to working-class Catholic parents in rural Williamsville, New York, near Buffalo. She attended local public schools and Syracuse University, and received an MA in English at the University of Wisconsin. During the 1960s she taught at the University of Detroit and lived through the 1967 Detroit riots, which she vividly recreates in her National Book Award-winning novel *them*. While living and teaching in Windsor, Ontario, during the Seventies she began co-editing *Ontario Review* with her husband, Raymond Smith. Since 1977 she has taught at Princeton University, where she is currently the Roger S. Berlind Distinguished Professor of Humanities.

If this prolific author is known primarily for her powerful naturalistic fiction chronicling the turbulent lives of a wide array of American characters from the Thirties through the present, she is also a distinguished poetry critic and poet whose poetry extends her fictional exploration of the harsh American landscape and of psychic extremes. She has written provocative essays on such poets as Emily Dickinson, *Lawrence, *Plath, and *Dickey. The best of her poetry is collected in *Invisible Woman: New and Selected Poems 1970–1982* (Princeton, NJ, 1982) and *The Time Traveler* (New York, 1989). If her earlier poems often seem diffuse and abstract, lacking the structure of her novels, attempting to capture the elusive lyric essence of passion rather than narrating its trajectory, those in her most recent collection are at once more structured and realistically grounded. The best of these include elegies to John Gardner, Raymond *Carver, and William Goyen; a terse meditation

on a Titian painting; thumbnail sketches of a waitress ('Waiting on Elvis, 1956') and of boxer Mike Tyson; an ingenious pantoum on excessive gambling ('An Ordinary Morning in Las Vegas'); and numerous evocations of the New Jersey landscape, rural and industrial, the most poignant being, 'Night Driving', a celebration of the trucks and smokestacks on the New Jersey turnpike, valued because they represent the proximity of home.   [RMcP

Objectivism, was a movement associated with the work of William Carlos *Williams, George *Oppen, Louis *Zukofsky, and Charles *Reznikoff. In February 1931, *Poetry (Chicago) brought out a special Objectivist issue edited by Zukofsky who specified as required reading Williams's *Spring and All*, T. S. *Eliot's *The Waste Land* and 'Marina', E. E. *Cummings's *Is 5*, Marianne *Moore's *Observations*, Wallace *Stevens's *Harmonium*, and Ezra *Pound's *XXX Cantos*. A press was established in New York financed by Oppen, and in 1932 under the name 'To Publishers' it brought out *An Objectivists' Anthology*. Edited by Zukofsky, this included work by Williams, Oppen, Reznikoff, Carl *Rakosi, and Kenneth *Rexroth. Pound and Eliot were also represented. Shortly after this, 'To Publishers' became the Ojectivist Press, under the editorship of Zukofsky and Williams.

Recalling Objectivism in his *Autobiography* (1951), Williams described it as a rejection of *Imagism: but, in fact, many of its priorities were similar. Like the Imagists, the Objectivists were concerned with precision, with dramatized experience rather than statement, and with rhythms and cadences that were the necessary products of a particular moment and voice. 'The poet' Williams argued, 'is an object'; and 'the poem being an object', he continued, 'it must be the purpose of the poet to make of his words a new form: to invent, that is, an object consonant with his day.' Of course there are differences between Objectivism and Imagism: there is a greater emphasis on the formal structure of the poem in Objectivist writing, and a more intense interest in the musical properties of poetry. But it seems fair to see Objectivism as a movement that grew dialectically out of Imagism, not in opposition to it but in fruitful tension with it. A useful introduction is the 1932 anthology. See also, Oppen, *Discrete Series* (1934), Reznikoff, *Poems 1918–36* (1976), Williams, *Collected Earlier Poems* (1951), Zukofsky, *All: The Collected Shorter Poems* (1966). [RJG

O'BRIEN, John. See HARTIGAN, P. J.

O'BRIEN, Sean (1952–), was born in London and grew up in Hull. He took degrees in English at Cambridge and Birmingham, returned to the University of Hull for three years and from 1981 to 1989 taught at a secondary school in East Sussex. He was a fellow in creative writing at Dundee University from 1989 to 1990, and now works as a free-lance writer in Newcastle upon Tyne.

O'Brien's movements about 1980s Britain have been reflected in the poetry he has written. His experience of Hull both as a place to live and as a landscape much mined by Douglas *Dunn and Philip *Larkin infected his own first collection, *The Indoor Park* (Newcastle upon Tyne, 1983). But O'Brien is both a more extravagant fabulist and a more overtly political writer than these two; while he shares with Larkin a determination to record the details of ordinary urban lives, the rhythmical and rhetorical effects his poems create are jauntier, more self-consciously rhetorical. There is also anger at the inflexibility of British social institutions. *The Frighteners* (Newcastle upon Tyne, 1987) developed this sense of anger in an inventive, historically informed group of poems, 'In a Military

Archive'; but it also included a northerner's satirical reactions to the complacency of an emphatically contemporary Thatcherite southeast. In *H.M.S. Glasshouse* (Oxford and New York, 1991) both the satire and the historical overviews continue; more revealing, however, are strange poems such as 'Hatred of Libraries', in which O'Brien comes to terms with his own involvement in the tradition he both loves and distrusts. [MRW

O'CONNOR, Frank (pseudonym of Michael O'Donovan) (1903–66), was born in Cork, and was taught in the national primary school by Daniel Corkery, later professor of English at University College, Cork—Corkery's nationalism and short-story writing were both major influences on O'Connor. In the Irish Civil War he fought on the Republican side and was imprisoned. After his release he became a librarian in 1924 and founded a theatre company in Cork. In 1928 he moved to Dublin as librarian of the Pembroke Library (until 1938) and, encouraged by *AE and *Yeats, began to write for the *Irish Statesman*. His first volume of stories, *Guests of the Nation*, was published in 1931, and the only volume of his own poems, *Three Old Brothers and Other Poems*, in 1936 (London). His poems are unsuccessful because they are metrically regular to the point of doggerel and they lack variety, being mostly a rather plaintive version of the 'randy' poetry of late Yeats.

Yeats encouraged O'Connor in the translation of Irish poetry which proved to be the major part of his poetic output. There are divided opinions about these translations: most commentators agree that the versions of the medieval monastic poems (in *The Little Monasteries*, Dublin, 1963) are apt, but there is dispute about the success of the major enterprise, *Kings, Lords and Commons* (New York, 1959), which gives translations of the poets Corkery wrote about in his pioneering study of Gaelic literature, *The Hidden Ireland* (1925). Although some commentators claim that O'Connor 'gave a voice' to poets such as Aodhagán Ó Rathaille, others feel that his English-derived quatrains are too remote from the formal intricacies of the sources.

O'Connor's enduring significance will be as one of the outstanding exponents of the short story in English and as an astute critic of fiction writing, in *The Mirror in the Roadway* (1956) and *The Lonely Voice* (1962). Apart from his translations, his principal significance in poetry is ancillary: familiarizing Yeats with the content of Irish poetry. There is a valuable (if slightly sentimental) biography by James Matthews, *Voices: A Life of Frank O'Connor* (New York, 1983), and the volumes of autobiography are *An Only Child* (New York, 1961; London, 1962) and *My Father's Son* (London, 1968; New York, 1969). For bibliography and criticism, see M. Sheehy (ed.), *Michael/Frank: Studies on Frank O'Connor* (Dublin, 1969). [BO'D

O'CONNOR, Mark (1945–), was born in Melbourne and educated at the University of Melbourne. He has worked at various jobs—editing the journal *Canberra Poetry*, 1973–5, minding houses in Europe, gardening on a Barrier Reef resort island, being for a time writer-in-residence for the New South Wales National Parks Service. Believing that in Australia there are 'thousands of different nature-feelings evoked by natural places and all requiring different words to capture them', he has assumed in his poetry the naming task of an antipodean Adam. From his first collection, *Reef Poems* (St Lucia, Qld., 1976)—which led Les A. *Murray to write of him as 'the man with a Muse a thousand miles long'—O'Connor has tried to describe with exquisite precision the flora and fauna of environments that he intimately knows. In this vein were *Poetry of the Mountains* (Leura, 1988) and *The Great Forest* (Sydney, 1989), illustrated with photographs of the Blue Mountains and of the tropical rain-forests of Australia and Papua New Guinea respectively. For all the delights of this distinctive and scrupulous poetry, its educative function—together with the author's temperament—encourages a lack of humour, while the poems do not always transcend their descriptive particulars. The human dimension is polemically absent, for O'Connor finds that in the real world 'humans are in plague proportions'. He has also written a book in favour of

phonetically accurate spelling. His *Selected Poems* was published in 1986 (Sydney). [PP

O'CONNOR, Philip (1916–), was born in Leighton Buzzard, Buckinghamshire. O'Connor describes his unconventional upbringing and early bohemian life-style in his autobiography, *Memoirs of a Public Baby* (London, 1958). As well as his collections of verse, *Selected Poems 1936–1966* (London, 1968) and *Arias of Water* (London, 1981), O'Connor's varied and eccentric corpus of work includes sociology (*Vagrancy*, Harmondsworth, 1963), personal reminiscence (*The Lower View*, London, 1960), and an autobiographical novel, *Steiner's Tour* (Paris, 1960).

O'Connor's work was first published in *New Verse* during the 1930s, and the early poems vary in style from the out-and-out surrealism of 'Blue Bugs in Liquid Silk' to the *Auden-influenced Marxist and Freudian expostulations of 'Useful Letter' and 'Poem'. His later poems are ironic and angry in tone and still deploy the associative techniques of *surrealism. Viewed as a whole his work amounts to a proclamation of uncompromising individualism.

A selection of his early work can be found in Robin Skelton (ed.), *Poetry of the Thirties* (Harmondsworth, 1964). [IES

OFEIMUN, Odia (1947–), grew up in Western Nigeria. As well as having been a journalist and an academic, Ofeimun was for several years the personal secretary of Chief Obafemi Awolowo, one time premier of the western region of Nigeria.

The scandal that led to the withdrawal of the original edition of his first collection, *The Poet Lied* (Harlow, 1981)—when J. P. *Clark decided that the title-poem pointed a finger too uncomfortably at him and threatened to sue the publishers—ensured that Odia Ofeimun's name would be well remembered. His second collection, *A Handle for the Flutist* (Ibadan, 1986) attracted wide critical applause and quickly sold out. A new edition of *The Poet Lied* (Lagos, 1990) is effectively a provisional 'collected poems', including both of his previous books, many uncollected poems, and a long interview with Ofeimun by Onwuchekwu Jemi. Ofeimun cites Quasimodo, Rilke and Martin *Carter among his formative influences, and his work acknowledges a notion of 'poetry' that transcends regional and even cultural boundaries.   [SB

O'GRADY, Desmond (1935–), was born in Limerick, and educated by the Jesuits and Cistercians; he later studied at Harvard. O'Grady spent time in Paris and Rome in the 1950s and became a friend and secretary to Ezra *Pound. He now lives mostly on the Greek island of Paros.

O'Grady's limpid lyricism in his first collection, *Chords and Orchestrations* (Limerick, 1956), soon gave way to a more blustering rhetoric under the influence of Pound—*The Dying Gaul* (London, 1968), for example, is a Poundian mélange of myth and history. The more recent collection *His Skaldcrane's Nest* (Dublin, 1979), however, contains some fine, subtle lyric verse, reminiscent of the work of O'Grady's friend Thomas *Kinsella. O'Grady's best work, which deserves much wider recognition, is his translations, ranging from versions of Armenian courtly love poems in *Off Licence* (Dublin, 1968) to his long free-verse rendering of Aneirin's heroic Middle Welsh epic *The Gododdin* (Dublin, 1977).

Other collections include *The Dark Edge of Europe* (London, 1967), *Sing Me Creation* (Dublin, 1977), *The Headgear of the Tribe* (Dublin, 1978), and *The Seven Arab Odes* (London, 1990).

[IES

O'HARA, Frank (1926–66), was born in Baltimore, Maryland, but grew up in Grafton, Massachusetts. He served in the US Navy, 1944–6, and from 1946 to 1950 he attended Harvard College, where he majored in music. After graduate school at Ann Arbor, he moved in 1951 to New York, where he was employed by the Museum of Modern Art. For the rest of his life O'Hara was deeply involved in the New York art scene, particularly with the work of abstract expressionist painters such as Willem De Kooning, Jackson Pollock, and Franz Kline. Between 1953

and 1955 he worked as editorial associate for *Art News*, for which his poet friends John *Ashbery and James *Schuyler also wrote. In 1955 he rejoined the staff of MOMA, where he was appointed assistant curator in 1960. In the early morning of 24 July 1966 he was struck and gravely injured by a beach-buggy on the beach of Fire Island, and died the following day. He is buried in Springs Cemetery on Long Island.

O'Hara's poems are a heady mixture of Whitmanian enthusiasm and explosive *surrealism. For O'Hara, as for the abstract expressionists, art is process, and many of his poems can be seen as chronicles of their own coming-into-being. His airy poetic structures are full of the random clutter of metropolitan living and casually dropped details of O'Hara's own life, his love-affairs, friendships, his responses to paintings, movies, and literature. O'Hara refused to take his poetry seriously, and often failed to keep copies of his poems, many of which were retrieved after his death only because he had included them in letters to friends. As he put it in his mock poetic manifesto, 'Personism': 'You just go on your nerve.'

O'Hara is best known for his I-do-this, I-do-that poems, such as 'A Step Away From Them', 'Why I am Not a Painter', and 'The Day Lady Died' (an elegy for Billie Holliday), but some of his later longer poems, in particular 'In Memory of My Feelings' and 'Biotherm (for Bill Berkson)' are equally effective, and have proved influential on a host of younger poets. Donald Allen edited his *Collected Poems* (New York, 1971; Manchester, 1991) and also a *Selected Poems* (New York, 1974). See also *City Poet: The Life and Times of Frank O'Hara*, by Brad Gooch (New York, 1993).   [MF

OJAIDE, Moses Tanure (1948–) was born in the Delta Province of what is now Nigeria's Midwestern State. He was educated at Federal Government College, Warri, and at the University of Ibadan, graduating in 1971. He worked for a time as a schoolteacher, and is now senior lecturer at the University of Maiduguri, where he teaches African poetry, oral and written African literature, and creative writing.

Like *Okigbo, whose poetry he admires, Ojaide fuses the gnomic, riddling quality of African oral poetry with the allusiveness and fragmentation of European modernism. His language is flavoured with West Africanisms: boldly mixed registers ('correlation', 'pep'), inventively 'incorrect' vocabulary ('fecundive', 'postcede'), and polysyllabic sonorities ('Reverberations . . . resuscitated . . . interspaces . . . evanescent'). Some of his poems are symbolic accounts of his personal love history, others focus on the beliefs and rituals of his Urhobo people. 'Where Everybody is King' is a witty satire on the unwillingness of Nigerians to accept the indignity of menial labour. 'The Fate of Vultures' expresses moral indignation at the corruption of Nigerian society, while in 'Song of My Land' the poet addresses a nation tainted by tribal antagonisms which mock his love for her.

Ojaide has published several collections, including *Children of Iroko and Other Poems* (New York, 1973). Selections of his work can be found in *The Fate of Vultures*, ed. Musaemura Zimunye, Peter Porter, and Kofi Anyidoho (Oxford, 1989).
[JB

OKAI, John Atukwei (1941–), was born in Accra and was educated in Ghana and in the Soviet Union, where he studied at the Gorky Institute in Moscow and received an MA in 1967. Since returning home Okai has taught Russian and literature at the University of Legon near Accra. He has also been involved in the organization of the Ghana Association of Writers as well as the Pan-African Writers Association.

Okai's style is that of public performance using dance, drumming, and chants. His concerns are the social and political issues of his country, his people, and of Africa in general. He has performed his poetry in North America, Europe, and in different countries of Africa. His collections include *Flowerfall* (London, 1969), *The Oath of Fontomfrom and Other Poems* (New York, 1971), and *Lorgorli Logarithms* (Accra, 1974).
[KO

OKARA, Gabriel Imomotimi Gbaingbain

(1921–), was born at Bumoundi in the Niger Delta, and educated at Government College, Umuahia, and at Yaba Higher College. After wartime service in the RAF he became a professional bookbinder, working for the Government Press in Enugu. In the late 1950s he studied journalism in the United States before becoming information officer for the Eastern Nigerian Government. His poetry first appeared in magazines, including the first issue of *Black Orpheus* (1957). *The Voice*, a poetic novella, appeared in London in 1964 (New York, 1970). During the Civil War Okara was director of cultural affairs for the Biafran Ministry of Information, and in 1969 he toured the United States with Chinua *Achebe to promote the Biafran cause. After the war he became head of the Rivers State Cultural Centre.

The two roots of Okara's poetry are the folklore and imagery of his Ijaw background, and his self-directed reading in Wordsworth, Keats, Hopkins and Dylan *Thomas. In some poems Ijaw spiritual concepts are boldly transposed direct into English ('shadow', 'inside', 'Front', 'Back'). But his lyrical free verse is by no means obscure to non-Ijaw readers; indeed, it is distinguished by its assured idiom and lucid musicality. His themes are at the same time African and universal: the conflict between tradition and modernity, homesickness, the sufferings of war. Primary images are employed with quiet conviction: the river of life flowing to the sea of death; migrating storks symbolizing the restless soul; pure stars beyond the reach of human yearning.

During the Civil War many of Okara's manuscripts were lost, and his long-awaited collection, *The Fisherman's Invocation* (London, 1978) contained only thirty-three poems. See also *West African Poetry* (Cambridge, 1986), by Robert Fraser.
[JB

OKIGBO, Christopher (1932–67), was born in Ojoto in the Igbo-speaking region of Nigeria. Intended from birth for the priesthood of the riverain goddess Idoto, he instead followed an academic career at Government College, Umuahia, and at the University of Ibadan, where he graduated in classics. Whilst teaching at Fiditi Grammar School his commitment to poetry emerged in a series of translations from the classics (notably from Virgil), followed by a spate of lyrics of increasing originality and power. For short periods he worked as a representative for the Cambridge University Press and as university librarian, but abandoned everything in 1966 to fight for the Biafran side in the Nigerian Civil War, dying in action in August of the following year. He left behind a clutch of lyrics which have gained him a reputation as the most distinguished English-language poet in Africa. Indeed, the manner of his death, the liveliness of his conversation, and the precarious devotedness of his craft have since established him as a sort of African Sir Philip Sidney, and have given rise both to a wide following and to copious imitation. His style is characterized by lyric terseness, cries from the deep wrung out of an agony both personal and archetypal. His eclecticism has attracted criticism from parochially minded critics, but on a wider view his claim to pre-eminence must be sustained.

Okigbo's major work is the interconnected sequence *Labyrinths* (1971), comprising the subsequences *Heavensgate* (1962), *Limits* (1964) and *Silences* (1965). The hortative sequence *Path of Thunder: Poems Prophesying War*, written after the first Nigerian coup of 1966, appeared for the first time in volume form in 1971. A *Collected Poems*, ed. Maja Adewale-Pearce, was published by Heinemann (London) in 1986. A detailed analysis of his poetry is to be found in Robert Fraser's *West African Poetry: A Critical History* (Cambridge, 1986). [RF

OLDS, Sharon (1942–), was raised in California, but has lived most of her adult life in New York City. She has won many awards: her first book, *Satan Says* (Pittsburgh, Pa., and London, 1980), was chosen for the San Francisco Poetry Center Award; her second, *The Dead and the Living* (New York, 1984), was a Lamont Poetry Selection; and her third, *The Gold Cell* (New York, 1987), won the National Book Critics Circle Award for Poetry. Her fourth, *The Father* (New York, 1992), was published also in London

(1993), where a selected poems, *The Sign of Saturn*, had already appeared in 1991. She writes an emotionally charged verse, centring her negative feelings on abusive members of her childhood family and on cruel figures drawn from political history. Against these Olds sets the power of love, directed primarily towards her adult family (particularly her two children), but also towards the physical world: 'I am | paying attention to small beauties, | whatever I have— as if it were our duty to | find things to love, to bind ourselves to this world.'

Though her poems seem literally expressed when first encountered—because of their clarity and directness—in fact they are carefully designed and cunningly figurative. One poem speaks of a broken elbow as a 'fine joint that | used to be thin and elegant as | something made with Tinkertoy, then it | swelled to a hard black anvil, | softened to a bruised yellow fruit'. Though Olds is sometimes seen by critics as a shriller Sylvia *Plath who deals with less important subjects, she really does not take herself so seriously. Her poems have the saving grace of humour: 'When I take my girl to the swimming party | I set her down among the boys. They tower and | bristle, she stands there smooth and sleek, | her math scores unfolding in the air around her.' [PS

OLIVER, Mary (1935–), was born in Ohio and attended Ohio State University and Vassar College; she has taught at Case Western Reserve. Her first four collections—*No Voyage and Other Poems* (1965), *The River Styx and Other Poems* (1972), *The Night Traveler* (1978), and *Sleeping in the Forest* (1979)—revealed a poet in full command of considerable technical resources who delighted in odd line-breaks and varying rhyme placements. Her work has been compared to that of Theodore *Roethke, James *Wright, and Emily Dickinson, although it is the former's intense identification with nature's remorseless processes that most strikingly characterizes her lyric approach. Unlike Roethke, however, she exhibits a didactic tendency which sometimes attenuates her keen, empathetic observations.

Oliver's fifth collection, *American Primitive*

(Boston, 1983), earned her a Pulitzer Prize, and since then she has published *Dream Work* (Boston, 1986), and *New and Selected Poems* (Boston, 1992), which won a National Book Award.   [EB

OLSON, Charles (1910–70), was born and raised in Worcester, Massachusetts, and educated at Wesleyan University and Harvard, where he studied American civilization. During the Second World War he worked for the Democratic Party and for the Office of War Information as assistant chief of the Foreign Language Division. His first two books, *Call Me Ishmael* (1947), a study of Melville's *Moby-Dick*, and *The Mayan Letters* (1953), written to Robert *Creeley from Mexico where he was studying Mayan hieroglyphics, cover a range of subjects—mythology, anthropology, language, and cultural history—and use the fervent informal style that were to distinguish all his discursive prose. Olson's influential manifesto, *Projective Verse*, was published in pamphlet form in 1950 and then quoted generously in William Carlos *Williams's *Autobiography* (1951). In the *'projective', or 'open', verse it recommends, which aims to transfer energy from the world to the reader without artificial interference, syntax is shaped by sound, not sense; sense is conveyed by direct movement from one perception to another, not rational argument; and the reader's rendition directed by freely varied spacing between words and lines on the page. Olson himself had started writing poetry in the late 1940s, and 'The Kingfishers', the longest poem in his first collection, *In Cold Hell, In Thicket* (1953), remains his most striking demonstration of projective verse. *The Distances* (1960), his second collection, is less formally innovative but more ambitious in treating personal dreams and universal myths. In 1951 Olson succeeded the artist Josef Albers as rector of *Black Mountain College, North Carolina, and remained there until it closed in 1956. He taught again—at the State University of New York, Buffalo (1963–5)—but, settling in Gloucester, Massachusetts, devoted most of his time and energy in subsequent years to *The Maximus Poems*, his most substantial work.

Begun in 1950 as a sequence of verse letters to his friend Vincent Ferrini, and modelled formally on *Pound's *Cantos*, *The Maximus Poems* is, in Olson's words, 'a poem of a person and a place'. In the first volume, *The Maximus Poems* (1960), Maximus (named after an itinerant Phoenician mystic of the fourth century, but referring also to Olson, who was six feet eight inches tall), dismayed by the culture of contemporary Gloucester, examines its origins in the European settlement of America. In the second volume, *The Maximus Poems, IV, V, VI* (1968), his interest widens to embrace ancient myths and religious texts, and narrows to scrutinize certain documentary details of Gloucester's past. The unfinished final volume, *The Maximus Poems, Volume Three* (1975), imagines a new Gloucester in which material and commercial values have been abandoned and spiritual and communal values restored. The complete work, *The Maximus Poems* (Berkeley, Calif. and London, 1983), and the rest of Olson's verse, *The Collected Poems of Charles Olson* (Berkeley, 1987), have both been edited by George F. Butterick. *Human Universe and Other Essays*, ed. Donald Allen (Berkeley, 1965), is the most generous selection of his prose. See also *Charles Olson and Robert Creeley: The Complete Correspondence*, ed. George F. Butterick and Richard Blevins, 9 vols. (Berkeley, 1980–90), and *The Poetry of Charles Olson: A Primer*, by Thomas F. Merrill (Delaware, 1982).   [NE

OLSON, Elder (1909–92), was a member of the Neo-Aristotelians, so named by Kenneth *Burke, a group of critics based at the University of Chicago, where Olson taught from 1942 to 1977. He was by no means exclusively an Aristotelian, however, and a great range of theoretical positions are adopted in his well-regarded critical works, which include *Tragedy and the Theory of Poetry* (Detroit, 1961), *The Theory of Comedy* (Bloomington, Ind., 1968), and *On Value Judgment in the Arts, and Other Essays* (Chicago, 1976).

As a poet, Olson was by no means a programmatic Aristotelian either. He is perhaps best known as a dramatic lyricist, but his work resists easy categorization and ranges from meditative poems to comic verse. An exceedingly demanding precisionist and craftsman, he worked slowly, and in a prefatory note to *Last Poems* (Chicago, 1984), wrote that the book was so named 'not because I think I shall write no more, but because—considering my rate of production—I think it unlikely that I shall make another collection'.

Olson was also a playwright and a pianist, who once considered a professional career as a musician.

His *Collected Poems* (Chicago, 1963) was followed by *Olson's Penny Arcade* (Chicago, 1975) and *Last Poems*. See Thomas E. Lucas, *Elder Olson* (New York, 1972), and James L. Battersby, *Elder Olson: An Annotated Bibliography* (New York and London, 1983). [EHF

ONDAATJE, Michael (1943–), was born in Ceylon, where he lived for eleven years. He was educated at Dulwich College in England, before emigrating to Canada, where he studied at Bishop's University, University of Toronto, and Queen's University, completing an MA thesis on Edwin *Muir. Ondaatje has lived in Toronto for more than twenty years and has taught intermittently at Glendon College at York University. He has been involved in the staging of some of his work and has long been intersted in film-making, producing a film about bp *Nichol called *Sons of Captain Poetry* and a documentary about Theatre Passe Muraille's 'The Farm Show', called *The Clinton Special*. Ondaatje's writings are numerous and have been enthusiastically received. The poems include *The Dainty Monsters* (Toronto, 1967), *The Collected Works of Billy the Kid* (Toronto, 1970; New York, 1974; London, 1981) *There's A Trick With A Knife I'm Learning to Do* (Toronto and New York, 1979), and *Secular Love* (Toronto and New York, 1986). His prose works include *Coming Through Slaughter* (1976), *Running in the Family* (1982), *In the Skin of a Lion* (1987), and *The English Patient* (1992) which was joint-winner of the 1992 Booker Prize in England.

There is a startling intimacy, or physicality, in Ondaatje's work, that derives from an imagina-

tion closely attuned to the body and its processes. The personae in his poems notice the movement of bones in a wrist, the archaeology of scars, and the politics of personal space. His method is that of the cinematic close-up or the image that conjures the inscape of a human or animal figure.

If Ondaatje is a subtle student of human behaviour, he is also a dramatist of disaster, charting transformations in the personal fortunes of his characters as they spiral towards madness. His short narratives, including 'Peter', 'Elisabeth', and *The Man With Seven Toes*, move with the slow-motion quality one associates with the dream state, where violence is all the more powerful because it is indirect or understated. And the figures of Buddy Bolden in *Coming Through Slaughter* and Pat Garrett in *The Collected Works of Billy the Kid*, who is described as a sane assassin, embody the full measure of the irrational energy that underscores Ondaatje's situations and characters. [GG

O'NEILL, Michael (1953–), was born in Aldershot and grew up in Liverpool. He completed a D.Phil. at Exeter College, Oxford, and has lectured in English at the University of Durham since 1979. In 1982 he co-founded *Poetry Durham*, under an editorial banner of deliberate eclecticism; he still edits the magazine. He has published a literary life of Shelley and a study of his language, and is the co-author, with Gareth *Reeves, of *Auden, MacNeice, Spender* (1992).

O'Neill received an Eric Gregory Award for his poetry in 1983, and selections of his work appeared in *The Gregory Poems 1983–84* (1985) and *New Poetry 8* (1982). His first full-length collection was *The Stripped Bed* (London, 1991). O'Neill's poems draw variously on his Liverpool childhood, particularly his sense of Irishness as caught in the evidence of his name and his family's accents; on the tense interaction between a life spent reading and the married life he leads beyond books; and, most movingly, on the experience of adopting a child. [MRW

Open Form. See PROJECTIVE VERSE

OPPEN, George (1908–84), was born in Alsace-Lorraine and grew up in San Francisco. Oppen had a small income from a trust fund on which he and his wife Mary could live. In the Fifties the Oppens lived in Mexico, where George ran a small carpenter's shop. His first book, *Discrete Series*, appeared in 1934.

Though associated with William Carlos *Williams and the *'Objectivists', Carl *Rakosi, Charles *Reznikoff, and Louis *Zukofsky, Oppen felt a greater kinship with the anonymous poet of 'O Western Wind' and Blake than with poets who kept their eye on the object. He was interested in images which retain a trace of the sacred. His poems have an intensity of vision that he took from the *Imagists—seeing, as Blake prescribed, '*through*' the eye.

Oppen wrote no poetry for twenty-eight years after *Discrete Series*, and while he always tended to explain the hiatus in terms of other commitments and concerns, he acceded to Hugh Kenner when Kenner interrupted his narrative of lost time in an interview to say, 'in other words, it took you twenty-eight years to write the next poem'. After that his work rapidly gathered velocity and momentum: he wrote like a man reborn. *The Materials* appeared in 1962 and *This In Which* in 1965, but only with *Of Being Numerous* (1968) does Oppen begin doing his best work.

Oppen is a modernist with a populist streak, and a conscience. There is a sense in his work that every increment of the poem has meaning, that the placement of each word, each line-break, is of primary importance. There is no appealing flow in Oppen, no narrative. Everything about him bespeaks a certain spareness, an obsession with the 'unearthly bonds | Of the singular | Which is the bright light of shipwreck' ('Of Being Numerous'). A poem, for Oppen, is a realm of pure attention. His goal is always 'to somehow see the one thing'.

In the 1970s Oppen returned to San Francisco and just as he had captured New York and 'a language, therefore, of New York' in *Of Being Numerous*, in *Seascape: Needle's Eye* he grasps San Francisco and the feel of the late Sixties from an interested, engaged, yet sceptical perspective.

He did not want 'things themselves' but 'to construct a method of thought from the imagist technique of poetry—from the imagist intensity of vision'. Oppen's work is notable for what it leaves out: it abounds in gaps, white space.

Oppen's main collections are: *Discrete Series* (1932–4), *The Materials* (1962), *This In Which* (1965), *Of Being Numerous* (1968), *Seascape: Needle's Eye* (1972), *Myth of the Blaze* (1972–5), *Primitive* (1978). *The Collected Poems of George Oppen 1929–1975* appeared in New York and London in 1975. See also: *Meaning a Life*, by Mary Oppen, *Ironwood* 26 (Oppen issue), and *George Oppen: Man and Poet*, ed. Burton Halen (Maine, 1981). [MRu

OPPENHEIMER, Joel (1930–88), was one of the principal members of the 'second generation' of *Black Mountain poets. A student at Black Mountain College for three years, where his mentors included Charles *Olson and Paul *Goodman, he became professionally a printer and later a teacher. He was also the first director of the *St Mark's Church Poetry Project in New York (1966–8), a columnist for the *Village Voice*, a playwright, a fiction writer, and the author of popular books on baseball and Marilyn Monroe. He is best known for his deeply personal poetry, in which the 'I' (or 'i' as he prints it) is central. Oppenheimer's poetics are grounded in Jungian psychology, however, and the personal in his poems can often be read as a manifestation of the archetypal. Like Robert *Creeley's work, Oppenheimer's tends to be written in short, abrupt lines, but it is generally less conflicted and jagged in its rhythms.

Poetry, the Ecology of the Soul (Buffalo, NY, 1983), ed. David Landrey and Dennis Maloney, includes several talks and a selection of the poetry. David Thibodaux's *Joel Oppenheimer: An Introduction* (Columbia, SC, 1986) is a useful critical study. See also George F. Butterick, *Joel Oppenheimer: A Checklist of His Writings* (Storrs, Conn., 1975). [EHF

Origin (1951–86), a quarterly magazine principally of poetry but also of fiction and criticism, was founded and edited by Cid *Corman and published in five series, first from Massachusetts, then from California, and later from Japan. Aiming in the first series (1951–7) to print 'new/unknown writers who have shown maturity/insight into their medium' and 'to demonstrate the directions . . . of contemporary creativity', Corman extended editorial policy in subsequent series (1961–4; 1966–71; 1977–80; 1983–6) to include any work he felt deserved a wider audience, whenever it had been written. Series One and Two devoted a great deal of space to the poets associated with *Black Mountain College and influenced by William Carlos *Williams and Era *Pound: Charles *Olson dominated two of the first eight issues; Paul *Blackburn and Denise *Levertov were among the early guest editors; and work by Robert *Creeley, Robert *Duncan, and Larry *Eigner also featured prominently. Thereafter the magazine became more diverse, though it continued to favour poems in free and experimental forms. Perhaps its strongest feature, however, was the translations—from a wide range of languages—which helped establish or extend the American reputations of a number of European and Far-Eastern poets, most of them modern (Antonin Artaud, Gottfried Benn, René Char, Paul Celan), but a few (like Basho) whose work is centuries old. *The Gist of Origin, 1951–1971,* edited and introduced by Cid Corman (New York, 1973), is an anthology of poems, short stories, and essays from the magazine's first three series. [NE

ORMOND, John (1923–90), was born at Dunvant in Swansea and educated at the University College in that town. He joined the staff of *Picture Post* in 1945.

His early verse (written under the name Ormond Thomas) appeared in the volume *Indications* with that of James *Kirkup and John Bayliss in 1943, but on the advice of Vernon *Watkins he wrote little more until the mid-1960s, when he began contributing to the magazine *Poetry Wales.* By that time he had had a distinguished career with BBC Wales as a maker of documentary films about Welsh painters and writers, including Ceri Richards, Dylan *Thomas, Alun *Lewis, and R. S. *Thomas.

The volume *Requiem and Celebration* (1969) collects work written over a period of twenty-five years; it is uneven in quality but provided evidence of his struggle to find his own voice. It was followed by *Definition of a Waterfall* (1973) which consolidated his reputation as one of the best Welsh poets of his generation.

There is a brilliance and eloquence about John Osmond's poems that are recognizably Welsh. Many are rooted in Swansea: local and elegiac they may sometimes be, and wryly affectionate for the people who made him—family, neighbours, and village characters—but they also tackle more complex themes such as personal identity, communal loyalty, the natural world, and love between men and women, confronting the numinous with an attractive wit and fortitude. His best poems are unsentimental but emotionally effective, and they are usually meticulously crafted.

John Ormond's best work appeared in his *Selected Poems* (Bridgend, 1987); another selection is to be found in *Penguin Modern Poets,* 27 (1978). There is an autobiographical essay by the poet in *Artists in Wales,* ed. Meic Stephens (Llandysul, 1973); see also *In Place of Empty Heaven,* a study of Wallace *Stevens (the W. D. Thomas Memorial Lecture at University College, Swansea, 1982). [MS

ORMSBY, Frank (1947–), was born in Enniskillen, Co. Fermanagh, and has stayed in Northern Ireland. Educated at Queen's University, Belfast, he began editing *Honest Ulsterman* magazine as a student, and remained its editor until 1989. Since 1971 he has taught English at the Royal Belfast Academical Institution, and has consistently championed the work of other Ulster poets. He edited *Poets from the North of Ireland* (1979), anthologies of Ulster autobiography (1987) and twentieth-century Irish love poems (1987), an anthology of Northern Irish prose and poetry, *Rage for Order* (1992), and the *Collected Poems* of John *Hewitt (1992). Ormsby won an Eric Gregory Award for his own poetry in 1974.

His first full collection, *A Store of Candles* (London, 1977), concentrates with a defiant exactness of phrase and observation on the life existing behind and around the headlines that make the province's public history. His poems resemble 'The Practical Farms' with which the book starts: making use of detail, asserting a faith in form which survives violent, off-stage eruptions almost intact. Unobtrusive half-rhymes suggest equivalences that work against or above political allegiances, and allow for surprisingly tender explorations of a family's movements through the troubles. The impressive sequence which provides the title of Ormsby's next collection, *A Northern Spring* (London, 1986), complicates these despatches from 'My Careful Life' by adopting personae and different voices to relive his family's experiences of the two world wars as retailed in their journals. [MRW

ORR, Gregory (1947–), was born in Albany, New York, the son of a physician. He attended Hamilton College from 1964 to 1966 but completed his BA at Antioch College in 1969 and his MFA at Columbia University in 1972. He teaches at the University of Virginia in Charlottesville.

Burning the Nests Empty (1973), his widely praised first collection, was followed by *Gathering the Bones Together* (1975) and *The Red House* (1980). In 1985 he published *Stanley Kunitz: An Introduction to the Poetry* in the Columbia University series on twentieth-century American poetry, and a fourth book of his own poems, *We Must Make a Kingdom*, the next year. His spare poetry often seems an odd mixture of Charles *Simic, James *Tate, and David *Ignatow in its use of small personal anecdotes to link together a chain of surreal associations and juxtapositions, often grotesque or morbid in content. Orr's *New and Selected Poems* (Middletown, Conn., 1987) offers the fullest sampling of his achievement to date. [EB

O'SULLIVAN, Vincent (1937–), was born in Auckland, New Zealand. He graduated from Auckland University (1959) and Oxford (1962), where he was a Commonwealth Scholar at Lincoln College. After lecturing at the universities of Victoria, Wellington (1963–6) and Waikato (1968–78), he became literary editor of the *New Zealand Listener* (1978–80). This was followed by free-lance writing and (from 1981) literary and research fellowships in New Zealand and Australia. He was appointed to a chair in the English department at the University of Victoria, Wellington, in 1987.

O'Sullivan's works include plays, a novel, a critical monograph, four volumes of short stories, the five-volume *Letters of Katherine Mansfield* (co-editor), and anthologies, including the most reliable guide to New Zealand verse, *An Anthology of Twentieth Century New Zealand Poetry* (Auckland, third edn., 1987).

O'Sullivan's first two volumes of poetry, *Our Burning Time* (Wellington, 1965) and *Revenants* (Wellington, 1969), make revealing reading. Though introspective and convoluted, they contain lines of force that anticipate the satirical poems to come, and they provided early literary exercises in the tense and sinewy compressions that characterize his later work.

Bearings (Wellington, 1973) was followed by *From the Indian Funeral* (Dunedin, 1976). Here the poems deal with personal observation, experience and feeling, and the themes that illuminate his mature poetry can be detected.

The later volumes are: *Butcher and Co.* (Auckland, 1977); *Brother Jonathan, Brother Kafka* (Auckland, 1980); *The Butcher Papers* (Auckland, 1982); *The Rose Ballroom and Other Poems* (Dunedin, 1982); *The Pilate Tapes* (Auckland, 1986); and *Selected Poems* (Auckland, 1992).

[KI

OSUNDARE, Niyi (1947–), lectures at the University of Ibadan and is a leading figure among a new generation of English-language poets in Nigeria. He might be described as a committed poet, as a self-consciously political writer, for his work deals with profoundly serious and topical themes. But this could be misleading. His collection *The Eye of the Earth* (Ibadan, 1986) is as much a celebration of the natural world and the peasant traditions of his Ikere people as it is a political critique. Osundare seems always conscious of the priorities of his craft; his poetry is by turns lyrical and declamatory, carefully structured and full of vivid, original imagery. His other collections include *Village Voices* (Ibadan, 1986), *Moonsongs* (Ibadan, 1988), and *Waiting Laughters* (Lagos, 1989).   [SB

OWEN, Jan (1940–), was born in Adelaide, South Australia, of Australian and Hungarian ancestry. She is married with three children. Her first book, *Boy With A Telescope* appeared in 1986, and her second, *Fingerprints on Light* (Sydney, 1990) confirmed the range of her subject-matter, which includes character-studies, historical vignettes, and an extended impressionistic series of monologues based on the 1780s French expedition to explore the Pacific, commanded by La Perouse.

Owen's verse holds an easy equilibrium between a contemporary use of traditional forms and the breath-related experiments of *projective-verse composition initiated by Charles *Olson. Her awareness of a distinctively Australian pace holds a poise between laconics and enthusiasm.   [JRo

OWEN, Wilfred (Edward Salter) (1893–1917), was born in Oswestry. His parents were then living in a comfortable house owned by his grandfather, Edward Shaw. At his death two years later this former mayor of the city was found to be almost bankrupt, and Tom Owen was obliged to move with his wife and son to lodgings in the back-streets of Birkenhead. They carried with them vivid memories of their vanished prosperity, and Susan Owen resolved that her adored son Wilfred should in time restore the family to its rightful gentility. She was a devout woman, and under her influence Wilfred grew into a serious and slightly priggish boy. At school in Birkenhead and later in Shrewsbury—where Tom Owen was appointed assistant superintendent of the Joint Railways in 1906—he worked hard and successfully, especially at literature and botany.

Leaving school in 1911, Owen took up a post as lay assistant to the vicar of Dunsden in Oxfordshire. Removed from his mother's influence, he became less enamoured of evangelical religion and more critical of the role of

the Church—as represented by the vicar—in society. His letters and poems of this period show an increasing awareness of the sufferings of the poor and the first stirrings of the compassion that was to characterize his later poems about the Western Front. He attended botany classes at Reading University and was encouraged by the professor of English to read and write more poetry. In February 1913, on the verge of a nervous breakdown, he left Dunsden and, when he had recovered, crossed to France where he taught at the Berlitz School of Languages in Bordeaux.

He was in the Pyrenees, acting as tutor in a cultivated French household, when war was declared. A visit to a hospital for the wounded soon opened his eyes to the true nature of war, but it was not until September 1915 that he finally decided to return to England and enlist. Commissioned into the Manchester Regiment, Owen crossed the Channel on 30 December 1916 and, in the first days of 1917, joined the 2nd Manchesters on the Somme near Beaumont Hamel. In March he fell into a cellar and suffered concussion, and some weeks later, after fierce fighting near St Quentin, was invalided home with shell-shock. At Craiglockhart War Hospital, on the outskirts of Edinburgh, he met Siegfried *Sassoon. Discharged in October, he was posted successively to Scarborough and Ripon, where many of his finest poems were written. At the end of August, he was certified 'fit to proceed overseas' and, a month later, was again in action. He was awarded the Military Cross for his part in a successful attack on the Beaurevoir-Fonsomme Line and, before sunrise on the morning of 4 November, led his platoon to the west bank of the Sambre and Oise Canal. They came under fire from German machine-guns behind the parapet of the east bank, and at the height of the ensuing battle Owen was hit and killed.

He had begun writing poems when he was 10 or 11 and soon fell under the influence of Keats, who was to remain the principal influence on his work, at least until at Dunsden he discovered the more political Shelley and, later, the Romantics' successors, the English and French poets of the Nineties. In a poem of 1912 Owen sees himself as 'a meteor, fast, eccentric, lone', moving through darkness; a prophecy to be fulfilled when—in the words of his sonnet '1914'—'War broke: and now the Winter of the world | With perishing great darkness closed in.' Having survived his first exposure to that murderous darkness, he met Sassoon, whose 'war poems' had just been collected in *The Old Huntsman and Other Poems* (1917). This introduced him to a colloquial language (to which Sassoon had himself been introduced by *Hardy) suitable for rendering the experience of battle. Under Sassoon's influence, and with his sympathetic encouragement, Owen purged his style of archaism and poetic diction to find a voice of his own. At Craiglockhart, probably in August 1917, he read the anonymous 'Prefatory Note' to an anthology, *Poems of Today* (1916), that spoke of one contributor who had 'gone singing to lay down his life for his country's cause', and ended with the statement that the poets' themes 'mingle and interpenetrate throughout, to the music of Pan's flute, and of Love's viol, and the bugle-call of Endeavour and the passing bell of Death'. It is not difficult to imagine Owen responding to this euphemistic rubbish with his 'Anthem for Doomed Youth', beginning: 'What passing bells for these who die as cattle?' There is no time to give them the trappings of a Christian funeral that Owen remembers from his Dunsden days; instead, they receive a brutal parody of such a service ('demented choirs of wailing shells'), and bitterly but obliquely he assigns responsibility for their deaths. The manuscript of this poem shows Owen and Sassoon working on it together, but although one can detect Sassoon's influence in the target of its protest—the *old* men of the Army, Church, and Government who send *young* men to their deaths—its metaphorical and musical texture is more complex than anything Sassoon had so far achieved: for example, the word-play in Owen's line, 'The pallor of girls' brows shall be their pall'. This device was to find its fullest expression in the system of pararhyming that would prove his major contribution to the technique of English poetry. The second pararhyme of a pair would usually be lower in pitch than the first

('escaped/scooped', 'grained/groaned'), which gives the musical movement of a poem like 'Strange Meeting' a dying fall that underscores the tragic unfulfillment that is its theme.

'Anthem for Doomed Youth' is only one of a number of Owen's poems triggered by an indignant response to a prior text. 'Dulce et Decorum Est' is another, prompted by Horace's Latin sentence and the jingoistic verse of Jessie Pope, to whom Owen's manuscripts reveal the poem was originally dedicated. Sassoon showed his young friend how to articulate and direct his indignation, and the intensity of Owen's compassion for suffering boys probably owes something to the homosexual orientation that he must latterly have recognized but may have resisted. It is clear that a principal cause of his distress at Craiglockhart was to prove a principal factor in the liberation and organization of his poems: the recurrent dreams that are a symptom of shell-shock. The realities of battle, banished from his waking mind, now erupt into his dreams and into his poems: dreams and poems alike are often haunted by tormented eyes (as in 'Dulce et Decorum Est')—those, perhaps, of the sentry he saw blinded in January 1917, the subject of his late poem 'The Sentry'. The dream-like intensity of this, and the dreamscapes of 'Strange Meeting' and 'The Show', contribute to the mythic power of Owen's best work and set him in a tradition that extends back to Dante, Virgil, Homer, and beyond. His vision of a subterranean Hell, its mouth agape, can be traced through these and other poems of his brief maturity and adolescence to the Calvinist Hell of which he heard at his mother's knee. Owen's descents into the Underworld have a curious common denominator: in each case the earth is described in terms of the human body (mouth, throat, womb), and usually with a marked sense of physical revulsion. This is the more strange and tragic since his early poems abound in lyrical descriptions of beautiful bodies and celebrations of the natural world.

Owen may have repudiated the Church of England in which his mother hoped he would make his career, but he never wavered in his belief in the person and teachings of Christ.

This left him on the battlefield, as he said, 'a Conscientious Objector with a very seared conscience'. In his celebrated draft Preface for the book of poems he was never to see in print, he wrote: 'All a poet can do today is warn. That is why the true Poets must be truthful. It sounds easy, but it is not easy to tell the truth in a poem, especially a truth from which the memory recoils.' He tells the truth when he says in 'The Sentry': 'I try not to remember these things now.' But, when he tries to forget them, 'Eyeballs, huge-bulged like squids' | Watch my dreams still'. In those dreams the horror is reborn, the reality of battle reshaped to the dimensions of the poem; poems to which we, his readers, owe—more than to any others— our vision of the reality of the Western Front, of Hell on earth.

The most recent and comprehensive edition of Owen's poetry is *The Complete Poems and Fragments*, ed. Jon Stallworthy (Oxford 1983; New York, 1984). He also edited the paperback *Poems of Wilfred Owen* (London, 1985), and wrote the standard biography, *Wilfred Owen* (London,

Oxford, and New York, 1974). See also *Owen the Poet*, by Dominic Hibberd (London, 1986).

[JHS

OYEBODE, Femi (1954–), grew up in Lagos and studied medicine in Ibadan before going to England to study psychiatry. He has lived and practised as a psychiatrist in Birmingham since 1980. His first collection of poems, *Naked to Your Softness and Other Dreams* (Birmingham, 1988), was much admired by reviewers in both Britain and Nigeria. His second, *Wednesday is a Colour* (Birmingham, 1990), is similar in style: constructed of five sequences that seem—but are not directly—linked, charting a personal effort to understand the experience of exile. Oyebode's manner is a distinctive combination of the imagistic lyric and the densely referential prosaic. There is a narrative unfolding in the sequences but it is hardly linear or transparent. There is a surreal edge to Oyebode's work, but its 'difficulty' evolves as much from his absorption in Yoruba mythology and the ideas of contemporary psychology. [SB

P

PADGETT, Ron (1942–), was born in Tulsa, Oklahoma, and attended Columbia University. He is married and lives in New York City, where he is a member of the Teachers and Writers Collaborative, a project that introduces schoolchildren to poetry. Although he resists the label, he is generally viewed as a second-generation member of the *New York School, following in the footsteps of Frank *O'Hara, John *Ashbery, and Kenneth *Koch. In Padgett's case the seminal influence is probably that of Koch, with whom he studied at Columbia. Padgett's poems lack both the thematic complexity and depth of Ashbery and the documentary texture of O'Hara; their appeal lies chiefly in their bright, zany sense of humour and their cartoon imagery. Like Koch, Padgett cultivates a childlike sensibility. Convention, artifice, and cliché provide the primary stuff of his imagination, together with a fluid, discontinuous sense of form inherited from French *Surrealism.

A number of books have been produced in collaboration with other writers, like Ted *Berrigan, and with artists like Jim Dine and Joe Brainard. In addition to his poetry, Padgett has translated the French poets Apollinaire, Larbaud, and Cendrars. His books of poems include *Tulsa Kid* (New York, 1979), and *Triangles in the Afternoon* (New York, 1980).   [RG

PAGE, Geoff(rey Donald) (1940–), was born in Grafton, New South Wales, and educated in Canberra, where he teaches English and history.

His interest in history is evident throughout his verse, and in the anthology he edited, *Shadows from the Wire: Poems and Photographs of Aus-*tralians in the Great War* (1983), and is voiced too in the novels *Benton's Conviction* (1985) and *Winter Vision* (1989), and in the short prose pieces of *Invisible Histories* (1990). Influenced by Les A. *Murray, Page's linguistic range is, however, narrower than Murray's, his subject-matter and its handling more conservative, even nostalgic. Music, especially jazz, is another continuing interest, informing a range of formal experiments. These are most notable in *Footwork* (Sydney, 1988), which is Page at his most metrically and linguistically innovative. More typically, in volumes such as *Smalltown Memorials* (St Lucia, Qld. 1975), *Cassandra Paddocks* (Sydney, 1980), and *Collected Lives* (Sydney, 1986), his poetry is spare, almost reticent, though flashes of vivid imagery often fix a poem's image of the historic past with a modern tone or gesture. *Selected Poems* (Sydney, 1991) gives Page's own choice of the best from his previous eight volumes—a distillation of the careful voice of a craftsman poet. It was followed by *Gravel Corners* (Sydney, 1992).   [JD

PAGE, P(atricia) K(athleen) (1916–), was born in Swanage, England, but raised on the Canadian prairies by parents who migrated to Canada in 1919. After attending St Hilda's School in Calgary, she was employed initially as a shop assistant and radio actress in Saint John, New Brunswick, and worked later as a researcher and scriptwriter in Montreal at the National Film Board. From 1942 to 1945 she was associated with F. R. *Scott, A. M. *Klein, and Patrick *Anderson on the editorial board of *Preview*, an avant-garde literary magazine, and she published *As Ten as Twenty*, her first collection of poems, in 1946. In 1950 she married W. A. Irwin, who was then commissioner of the National Film Board and later Canada's ambassador to Australia, Brazil, and Mexico. It was while living abroad that she took up drawing and painting. In 1954 she published *The Metal and the Flower*, and followed this with *Cry Ararat* (1967), illustrated with her drawings, *Poems: Selected and New* (1974), and *Evening Dance of the Grey Flies* (1981—all Toronto), which contains one of her stories, 'Unless the Eye Catch Fire'. Page was made a member of the Order of Canada in 1977 and lives in Victoria.

Page's earlier work is written, mostly, in a modernist, 'metaphysical' mode, and is characterized by density of metaphor, extraordinary juxtapositions, and attitudes that range from the whimsical to the ironic. Some of her later work is in a plainer style and expresses her symbolic search for a sense of unity of being. Several of her verses, like her drawings, are rich in images of plant life. Among her best-known poems is the frequently anthologized 'The Stenographers'.

Most of Page's poetry, together with a few of her drawings and two brief essays on poetics, has been published in *The Glass Air: Poems Selected and New* (Toronto and New York, 1991). Her publications also include *Brazilian Journal* (1987), a diary written while abroad.   [JSt

PALMER, Michael (1943–), was born in New York City and educated at Harvard. Since 1969 he has lived in San Francisco with his wife, the architect Cathy Simon, and daughter. Palmer teaches intermittently but, unlike most poets of his generation, has not pursued a teaching career. He translates from the French, has collaborated on books with the painters Irving Petlin and Sandro Chia, and on dance with the Margaret Jenkins Dance Company.

Beginning with *Blake's Newton* (Los Angeles) in 1974, six full-length books of poetry have appeared—each a more radical exploration of his poetics than the last. Often grouped with the *Language poets and considered one of their precursors, Palmer's poems are an original synthesis of Louis *Zukofsky, *Surrealism, reading in philosophy and linguistic theory, *Beckett,

Jack *Spicer, and Paul Celan. For all his daunting range of reference, Palmer's work has a sense of humour based on dead-pan assertion and a use of misheard and mis-spoken speech. He builds his books around serial poems. *Notes for Echo Lake* (1981) and *SUN* (1988—both Berkeley, Calif.) are his most accomplished. Constantly subverting their own lyric impulse, intelligent and somewhat dry, yet supple in their inclusiveness, Palmer's poems speak in many voices at once.

A useful introduction to his method and interests is Palmer's anthology *Code of Signals: Recent Writings in Poetics* (Berkeley, 1983).
                                                    [WC

PANKEY, Eric, (1959–), was born in Kansas City and educated at the University of Missouri and the University of Iowa. He was a member of the *Iowa Writer's Workshop and is presently director of the Writing Programme at the Washington University in St Louis. His first volume, *For the New Year* (New York, 1984), won the Walt Whitman Award of the Academy of American Poets.

Pankey's three volumes, from the first, *For the New Year*, through *Heartwood* (New York, 1988), and on to *Apocrypha* (New York, 1991) have shown a development from an innocent, intelligent lyric poetry influenced by Robert *Frost towards a more complex poetry of argument dealing with difficult philosophical subject-matter. What has remained constant is Pankey's sharp observational skills, careful structural formality, and religious sensibility. The shift may be seen by comparing the too-easily won satisfactions of the early poem 'Elegy' with the later poem 'Prayer', which not only admits the possibilities of pain and suffering but actually performs a struggle with them. In *Apocrypha*, which is split into six sections with names like 'Depositions', 'Arguments', and 'Reconstructions', Pankey's whimsy has matured into a poetry of methodical wisdom that is reminiscent of *Eliot. Like Eliot's later work, however, the privilege of this increase in dialectical intensity has been the sacrifice of tonal variety and ambiguity.   [IES

Paris Review, The. Begun in Paris in 1953 by Harold Humes and Peter Matthiessen, the magazine quickly shifted to include New York as its other publishing base. Its contents are coterminous with the cosmopolitan catholicism of its origins, yet it has avoided shapeless eclecticism by its astute choice of editors, some of whom, like the American poet Tom *Clark, have brought a more specific, even subversive, tone to their choice of contents. George Plimpton and Donald *Hall became editors in the second issue, thereby ensuring that the magazine's policy would stay both open and stimulating, a fact which may be quickly gauged by a brief list of the writers who have appeared in its pages—Philip *Larkin, Wole *Soyinka, Charles *Olson, Samuel *Beckett, Jack Kerouac, V. S. Naipaul, William Burroughs, Simone Weil. While the periodical is not noted for its critical commentary, it has given rise to a famous series of interviews; T. S. *Eliot, Ezra *Pound, Boris Pasternak, and Robert *Frost were relatively early subjects, but the list has grown to include Harold Brodkey, Thomas McGuane, and Doris Lessing. The sixth volume of collected interviews, known as *Writers At Work*, was published in 1984, although it has to be said that the bewildering diversity of current practice poses a real threat to the periodical's distinctiveness. Despite its relatively restricted format, it has fostered the work of graphic artists and has included work by such luminaries as Picasso, De Kooning, and Chagall.   [CM

PARKER, Dorothy (1893–1978), was born in New York, was famous in her day (the Twenties and Thirties) as the foremost American wit and as a writer of short prose pieces for *The New Yorker*. Her light verse is excellent ('Byron and Shelley and Keats | Were a trio of lyrical treats', etc.), but the more 'serious' poems, mainly love poems, can be mawkish ('Oh, gallant was the first love, and glittering and fine'), full of much unresolved romanticism. Constantly 'betrayed' by unsatisfactory and unreliable lovers, Parker fought back in sharp epigrammatic verse, critical of men—particularly of the highbrows and Bohemians who were her usual companions:

'Oh, hard is the struggle, and sparse is | The gain of the one at the top, | For art is a form of catharsis, | And love is a permanent flop.' She published several books of verse, but the easiest way to find the poems now is to consult *The Penguin Dorothy Parker* (1981), which has the best prose pieces too.   [GE

PARSONS, Clere (Trevor James Herbert) (1908–31), was born in India, where his father worked in the Indian Civil Service. He was educated at St Paul's School and Christ Church, Oxford. He suffered from a severe form of diabetes, which brought about his early death.

While at Oxford he was active in undergraduate poetry circles, founding a poetry society with the help of *MacNeice, *Spender, Bernard *Spencer, and others, editing issues of *Oxford Poetry* and *The Oxford Outlook*, and contributing poems, essays, and reviews to them; he was also involved in the publication of a short-lived avant-garde magazine, *Sir Galahad*. Faber published a slim volume containing eighteen of his poems in 1932.

Although, according to MacNeice in *The Strings are False* (London, 1965), Parsons had 'an invalid's fanaticism' in politics, his poetry is radically unlike that of most of his generation's at Oxford, since it is unconcerned with the great events of the day and draws on French and American models: Mallarmé is invoked in the fine poem 'Introduction', and the example of E. E. *Cummings was at one time important. There is apparent in Parsons's best poems an extreme and wholly individual sensitivity to what Parsons called the 'melody of words', a sensitivity which makes his poems, once read, hard to forget. Had he lived, our view of the poetry of this century might have been different.

There is an excellent selection of the poems, *The Air Between: Poems of Clere Parsons*, ed. T. W. Sutherland (Newcastle upon Tyne, 1989). A single uncharacteristic poem is included in the Penguin *Poetry of the Thirties* (1964). For brief and sympathetic accounts of the poetry, see C. H. Sisson's *English Poetry 1900–1950: An Assessment* (London, 1971) and the same author's *The*

Avoidance of Literature (Manchester, 1978), as well as *Recollections*, by Geoffrey Grigson (London, 1984). [TJGH

PARTHASARATHY, Rajagopal (1934–), was born in Tirupparaiturai, Tamil Nadu, and educated in Bombay. Between 1959 and 1971 he taught English in various colleges in Bombay and Madras, joining Oxford University Press, Madras as regional editor. For the past decade he has lived in the United States, where he teaches at Skidmore College.

Though Parthasarathy's earliest published poems date from 1956, it was another twenty years before he brought out *Rough Passage* (Delhi, 1977; rev. edn. 1980), his first and so far only book. Its individual poems are of varying length but written in the same three-line stanza, and the whole is divided in three parts, 'Exile', 'Trial', and 'Homecoming'. In a preface, Parthasarathy says *Rough Passage* should be read as one poem. It begins in a basement flat in London where, in his thirtieth year, after a taste of exile, he learns 'roots are deep', and ends fifteen years later, when he tries to initiate a dialogue between himself and his 'Tamil past'. Disappointingly, the Tamil past turns out to be 'an unrecognizable carcass', and the poet reconciles himself to going 'through life/with the small change of uncertainties'. Indian readers of Parthasarathy's generation, especially those who spent their youth 'whoring/after English gods', are particularly responsive to the poem, while the younger generation are less sympathetic.

Parthasarathy is also the editor of *Ten Twentieth-Century Indian Poets* (Delhi, 1976), a widely used anthology of Indian verse in English. For a discussion of his work, see *Modern Indian Poetry in English* by Bruce King (Delhi, 1987). [AKM

Partisan Review (1934–), an American literary and political journal, was founded twice: first as 'a bi-monthly of revolutionary literature' published by the John Reed Writers' Club, an intellectual wing of the American Communist Party; then in 1937 (by original—and longest-standing—editors William Phillips and Philip

Rahv, along with F. W. Dupee, Dwight Macdonald, Mary MacCarthy, and George L. K. Morris) as an independent magazine, still politically radical but hospitable to a wider variety of views. Throughout its history, first in New York City (1934–63), then in New Jersey (1963–78) and Boston (1978–), the magazine has reflected—and influenced—the development of American political and literary thought, remaining partisan only in name, but quick none the less to question the culture and politics of mainstream America.

Poetry and reviews of poetry have always been a strong, if never a dominant, feature of *Partisan Review*. The most substantial single poems to which it has given first American publication are two of T. S. *Eliot's Four Quartets (1940–1) and John *Berryman's 'Homage to Mistress Bradstreet' (1953). As associate editor (1946–55), Delmore *Schwartz printed poems by many prominent American and British poets, including W. H. *Auden, Elizabeth *Bishop, and Wallace *Stevens, and essays on poetry by R. P. *Blackmur and Randall *Jarrell among others. Since then a series of guest editors has been largely responsible for the inclusion of traditional and experimental verse alike. There are several selections of work from the magazine, and *The Little Magazine in America*, ed. Elliot Anderson (New York, 1978) contains a history of its editorial policies by William Phillips. [NE

PASTAN, Linda (1932–), was raised in New York City but has lived for most of her life in Potomoc, Maryland, a suburb of Washington, DC. The problems her work deals with are familiar ones—loneliness and death—and in her early books Pastan's control of her images was now and then uncertain, as in this lament at her inability to prevent her father's death: 'my father [is] running out upstairs, and me without a nickel | for the meter.' Later she became more successful at harmonizing her metaphors. Though known as a 'domestic' poet who is fond of recording everyday happenings, she is at her best when writing elegiacally. *PM/AM: New and Selected Poems* (New York, 1982) reprints what

Pastan wishes to save from her first four volumes; it was followed by *A Fraction of Darkness* (New York, 1985) and *The Imperfect Paradise* (New York, 1988). [PS

PATCHEN, Kenneth (1911–72), was born in Niles, Ohio. After a short education at Alexander Meikeljohn's Experimental University of Wisconsin, where he distinguished himself as an athlete, Patchen did a variety of menial jobs, until Random House published his first collection of poems, *Before the Brave* (New York, 1936), after which he was taken up as a leftist and rebel. He thereafter wrote poetry prolifically, but never managed to gain any real control over his work, which was 'furious', sometimes powerful, and increasingly prophetic in tone, in the manner of the poet who most influenced him, William Blake. Critics deplored his 'carelessness', which was always evident, and also the contempt with which he seemed to regard his own lyrical gifts. But Henry Miller and others (including, latterly, Jonathan *Williams) admired and excused him, and funds were raised for him by people as eminent as T. S. *Eliot and W. H. *Auden, who regarded him as worth supporting. He was for a long period incapacitated by a spinal illness, although the extent of this has recently been questioned. A few critics saw him as one of 'America's great poet-prophets', but a more moderate view applauded flashes of real power and cherished, rather, the prose memoir, *Memoirs of a Shy Pornographer* (New York, 1945; London, 1948). He was taken up and published in England by *Poetry Quarterly. See: *Selected Poems* (New York, 1946 rev. edn., 1958, 1964), *Selected Poems* (London, 1968); *Collected Poems* (New York, 1969). [MS-S

PATEL, Essop (1943–), was born in Germiston but grew up in Ladysmith, Natal, and spent seven years in London from 1962, working and studying law. He gained his LLB at the University of the Witwatersrand and practises as an advocate in Johannesburg. He has edited the work of the *Drum* writers Nat Nakasa and Can Themba and, with Tim Couzens, an anthology of black South African poetry, *The Return of the Amasi Bird* (1982). His poems were published in literary magazines such as *Staffrider* and *The Classic* before the appearance of his first volume, *They Came at Dawn* (1980).

His poems exhibit characteristics of what has become known as 'Soweto poetry': an aesthetics of resistance, shot through with a strongly imaged black consciousness. But they gain a poignancy from their tenderness towards all victims of dispossession: Patel calls them love poems because, in their contempt for the oppressor, they affirm love for the oppressed. The poems in his most recent volume, *The Bullet and the Bronze Lady* (Braamfontein, 1987), experiment with formal techniques, word-play, and satire. Some are the poems of a Muslim revolutionary, revealing his solidarity with all who fight against oppressive regimes. [CWo

PATEL, Gieve (1940–), was born in Bombay, and educated there at St Xavier's College and Grant Medical College. After working for two years (1969–71) as a medical officer in rural Gujarat, he returned to Bombay where he now has his own clinic. Beginning in 1966, the year in which his first book, *Poems*, appeared, he has held several exhibitions of his paintings, and in 1971 his first play, *Princes*, was produced. He has since written two others.

Patel's preoccupation is with the human body, which he views with objectivity, bemusement, and, at times, exasperation. 'I am continuum with the century's skin', he writes, and his poems explore both the body's and the world's vulnerability and resilience. Like *Daruwalla and *Jussawalla, Gieve Patel is a Parsi. This fact, together with the wryness and detachment of much of his work, is reflected in the title of one of his best-known poems, 'The Ambiguous Fate of Gieve Patel, He Being Neither Muslim Nor Hindu in India'.

Patel's second collection of poems, *How Do You Withstand, Body* (Bombay, 1976), was followed by *Mirrored, Mirroring* (Madras, 1991). For a discussion of his work, see *Modern Indian Poetry in English* by Bruce King (Delhi, 1987). [AKM

PATERSON, A(ndrew B(arton) 'Banjo' (1864–1941), was born near Orange, New South Wales. Due to financial and rural misfortune, his family moved to Illalong Station, close to Yass, when Paterson was 6. He was educated at the Sydney Grammar School, and later became a solicitor.

In 1889 Paterson began to publish, under the pseudonym 'The Banjo', with the *Bulletin*. 'Clancy of the Overflow' and 'The Man from Snowy River' were immediatley popular, and in the following years Paterson conducted a poetic 'debate' with Henry *Lawson, championing his heroic and romantic vision of the bush against Lawson's battling vision of flies and dust and floods. These poems were collected in *The Man from Snowy River and Other Verses* (1895), which has remained one of the biggest-selling books of verse in Australia. This was followed by *Rio Grande's Last Race and Other Verses* (1902) and *Salt Bush Bill J. P. and Other Verses* (1917). All three volumes are contained in the *Collected Verse of A. B. Paterson* (Sydney, 1923), which is regularly reprinted. See also *Selected Poems* (Sydney, 1992). Paterson edited the first collection of Australian bush ballads (1905), and wrote three books of fiction: *An Outback Marriage* (1906), *Three Elephant Power and Other Stories* (1917), and *The Shearer's Colt* (1934). He covered the Boer War as a correspondent, served in the Remount Service during the First World War, and edited various Sydney journals.

Paterson's popularity rests on his ability to create characters which capture cultural stereotypes. His best ballads are told with sturdy galloping rhythms and cavalier rhymes, generating the humour of the tall bush story, or the pathos or glory of the sporting hero. He is credited with the composition of Australia's unofficial national anthem, 'Waltzing Matilda'.

Clement Semmler's *The Banjo of the Bush: The Work, Life and Times of A. B. Paterson* (Melbourne, 1966) gives a good account of the cultural importance of Paterson's poetry. [AU

PATTEN, Brian (1946–), one of the *Liverpool Poets, was born and brought up in Liverpool. His fey, sincere, breathless, and schoolboyish lyrics once sold in large numbers to a public which enjoyed poetry readings, of which he has given many. He was occasionally influenced by traditional poetry, in such lines as 'Our love like a whale from his deepest ocean rises'. He is satirical of what he takes to be a 'cultured élite', and salutes the masses as the 'rightful owners of the song'. See *Walking Out: The Early Poems of Brian Patten* (Leicester, 1970), *Storm Damage* (London, 1988), and *Grinning Jacks: Selected Poems* (London, 1990). [MS-S

PAULIN, Tom (1949–), was born in Leeds but brought up after 1953 in Belfast. Educated at the universities of Hull and Oxford, he has been a lecturer in English literature at the University of Nottingham since 1972. An acerbic commentator on both literature and politics, he has collected his critical work in *Ireland and the English Crisis* (1984) and *Minotaur* (1992) and edited the *Faber Book of Political Verse* (1986). Since his first volume, *A State of Justice* (London, 1977), his poetry has been continuous with this prose effort, engaging the political and cultural realities of Northern Ireland in a variety of forms and from a flexible position in which the secular, non-sectarian republicanism of the eighteenth century is a point of frequent recourse. The commentary has also been pursued in a number of plays, including a version of Sophocles' *Antigone* (London, 1985). The play was first performed by the Field Day Theatre Company, of which Paulin is a director together with Seamus *Heaney, Brian Friel, and others.

Paulin's is not, however, a politicized poetry in any simple or single sense. Particularly since *Liberty Tree* (London, 1983), when his style altered radically from an earlier tight-lipped, rather dour formalism towards a greater suppleness and musicality, he appears to have been emulating the James *Joyce whom he admiringly describes as a 'politicized aesthete'. He takes a playful, lingering delight in the world's surfaces and textures, implying a politics through the sensuous apprehension and fragmentary evocation of ordinary moments and episodes, as in the sequence 'The Book of Juniper', where a utopian desire for a 'sweet | equal republic' is conjured out of a series of vivid evocations (religious, historical, and even culinary) of the juniper plant. Where *Liberty Tree* is by turns luxuriant and ascetic, *Fivemiletown* (London, 1987) is more desolately the latter, paring Paulin's natural eloquence back to the bone. In thin, disconsolate poems combining a wide range of dictions (including Belfast dialect), Paulin writes abrupt narratives of joyless sexuality and political oppression, creating insinuating vignettes of the Northern Protestant condition.   [NC

p'BITEK, Okot (1931–82), was one of the most significant voices in African literature in English. As a poet he drew his inspiration, and adapted his techniques, from the Acoli oral tradition that was his particular cultural heritage. Born in Gulu in Northern Uganda, he became a scholar of distinction, finally taking a B.Litt at Oxford. He returned to Uganda as director of the National Cultural Centre, but after independence his outspoken criticism of politicians in *Song of Lawino* (1966) led to his dismissal. He took up a post at the University of Nairobi and was only able to return to Uganda, as professor of creative writing at Makerere University, in 1982. He died just a few months later.

Lawino, in *Song of Lawino*, is a 'traditional' Acoli woman who laments her displacement in the affections of her husband, Ocol, by an educated, westernized Christian girl who 'aspires' | to look like a white woman'. But Lawino is expressing more than jealousy; she is, as it were, defending indigenous African ways of thought and behaviour against the insidious corruption of those values by the alien forces of colonialism and Christianity. Ocol, who once admired her for the very qualities he now despises, has changed only since he was exposed to those 'civilizing' forces. *Song of Ocol* (1970) allows Ocol to reply to the criticisms Lawino has made, though in the process he concedes and confirms many of her points. The issues these poems raise were, and indeed still are, of great importance in Uganda and across the whole of Africa, but it is the music and humour of the poetry which speaks to all readers. *Song of Lawino and Song of Ocol* were published as one volume in the Heinemann African Writers Series (London, 1984).

Two other long poems by p'Bitek, in a similar style, 'Song of a Prisoner' and 'Song of Malaya', were published in one volume as *Two Songs* by the East African Publishing House in Nairobi in 1971. He also published a collection of translations from Acoli oral poetry, *Horn of My Love* (London, 1974), and a collection of folk-tales, *Hare and Hornbill* (London, 1978).   [SB

PEACOCK, Molly (1947–) was born in Buffalo, New York and graduated from the State University of New York at Binghamton in 1969. From 1970 to 1976 she held administrative posts at the college, then earned her MA at Johns Hopkins University in 1977 as an honorary fellow. After moving to Manhattan, she became a learning specialist at Friends Seminary and was elected president of the Poetry Society of America in 1988.

Peacock's first two poetry collections, *And Live Apart* (Columbia, Mo., 1980) and *Raw Heaven* (New York, 1984), displayed a virtuoso gift for using formalist means in a fluid fashion to scan the psychological dilemmas of contemporary life, often lightened by humour or ironic distance. Her most recent volume, *Take Heart* (New York, 1989), is more intimate and intense than its predecessors, more willing to confront confessional themes, such as the lingering impact of an abusive father.   [EB

PEAKE, Mervyn (Lawrence) (1911–68), was born at Kuling in China, the son of a medical missionary. He came to England aged 11, was educated at Eltham College, and trained as an artist. He was invalided out of the army in 1943 after a nervous breakdown, but later (as a war artist) visited Belsen. He was by then at work on a novel, *Titus Groan* (1946), the first of the Gothic trilogy for which he is best known, though he also earned renown as an illustrator (of his own work and others'). He suffered latterly from what was diagnosed as 'premature senility'.

Peake's first published work was poetry

(*Sights and Sounds*, 1941) and he produced three further volumes of verse: *The Glassblowers* (1950); *The Rhyme of the Flying Bomb* (1962), a ballad of the blitz; and *A Reverie of Bone* (1967); but his oeuvre is not substantial. The products of mental distress, most of the poems exist to give vent to violence of expression ('Thunder the Christ of it . . .') or monstrousness of image. Not many refer to the external world, as 'London, 1941' does; and the standard length is eight or ten jagged lines. The creative energy of Peake the novelist is glimpsed in 'Reverie of Bone', whose length (thirty-eight six-line stanzas), as well as its subject, may reflect his experience of mass graves; the poem is covered with striking phrases ('arctic filigree of feet', 'the dumb bullion of the shrouding clay') but itself lacks a skeleton.

A thin *Selected Poems* was first published in 1970 (London). See also the memoir, *A World Away* (1970) by his widow, Maeve Gilmore. [MI

PECK, John (Frederick) (1941–), was born in Pittsburgh, Pennsylvania. He studied at Allegheny College and, under Yvor *Winters, at Stanford University, where he wrote a doctoral thesis on *Pound. He has lectured in English at several universities and, since 1984, has been studying analytical psychology at the Jung Institut, Zürich. He has published four books of verse: *Shagbark* (New York, 1972), *The Broken Blockhouse Wall* (Boston, 1978; Manchester, 1979), *Poems and Translations of Hï-Lö* (Manchester, 1991), and *Argura* (Manchester, 1993).

Peck's poetry draws consciously on two seemingly incompatible models: Pound and Winters. A subtle practitioner of standard metres, he now writes mainly in free or *syllabic verse with a musical sensitivity to relative degrees of stress that only a student of Pound could hope to achieve. From Pound, too, he has learnt to value the integrity of the line and the firmly defined sensuous particular, but he rejects the associated fragmentation of syntax, assuming with Winters that poetry belongs to a necessary human order defended against the vegetable flux of nature. The consequent

preoccupation with the space between consciousness and 'the stout weave | Of what is' accounts for the fascination of his work, but also for some regrettable obscurity. [CW

PEERADINA, Saleem (1944–), was born in Bombay, and educated at St Xavier's College, Bombay, and Wake Forest University in the United States. During the Seventies and Eighties he taught English in various colleges in Bombay, and he has also worked as reviews editor of *Express Magazine,* and as advertising copywriter. He now lives in the United States, where he teaches.

Peeradina's first book, *First Offence* (Bombay, 1980), opens with poems that look at Bombay's suburbs and shanty towns, its Hindu, Muslim, and Christian places of worship, and its streets and crowds. Peeradina is not particularly observant, however, and offers only a generalized picture, sometimes satirical, of life in the metropolis. *First Offence* ends with 'Wife's Touch', a poem whose title prefigures the theme of his next collection, *Group Portrait* (Madras, 1992). In it Peeradina celebrates domestic bliss, and if his concerns have narrowed, the writing is far more assured. Whether describing a family scene or expressing parental anxiety, Peeradina goes about his business in a brisk, straightforward manner.

Apart from publishing two collections of verse, Peeradina has edited *Contemporary Indian Poetry in English: An Assessment and Selection* (Bombay, 1972). This early anthology is important both for its critical assessments, made by diverse hands, and its discriminating selection of poets. For a discussion of his work, see *Modern Indian Poetry in English* by Bruce King (Delhi, 1987). [AKM

PERELMAN, Bob. See LANGUAGE POETRY.

Performance Poetry, a genre which grew from a number of sources, including music-hall and burlesque, jazz poetry, and the *Beat movement.

In true Performance Poetry, poems are learned (or, very rarely, improvised) rather than read from a book. Because of this, some fine performers of their written work, such as the *Liverpool Poets, are not strictly performance poets. Most performance poetry is transient, existing at the time of performance and then in memories of that performance. Attempts to capture the performance, whether on record or in book-form, seldom do justice to the work.

There are three distinct waves of twentieth-century performance poetry. The first came from America, via jazz, and can be said to begin with the poetry of Vachel *Lindsay (1879–1931) and Langston *Hughes (1902–67). A major factor in the relative health of performance poetry is the availability of cheap venues to perform in, and the anti-establishment Beat poets of the 1950s created and popularized the idea of the coffee-house and folk-club reading. Beat poets who read and performed their work included Allen *Ginsberg, Gregory *Corso, and (though he was primarily a novelist) Jack Kerouac. At the same time, Lawrence *Ferlinghetti was leading a *San Francisco movement similar to, and often confused with, the Beats, centred on his City Lights bookshop, another reading and performing venue. In Britain the Beat spirit was picked up by, amongst others, Michael Horovitz (b. 1935), poet, performer, and publisher, whose Live New Departures poetry circus included, from 1959 onwards, poets such as Jeff *Nuttall and Pete Brown (also a pop-lyric writer for such bands as Cream and his own Piblokto: the relationship between performance poetry and pop lyrics is a complex one, and at times the two seem to be part of one discipline). Horovitz remains an important figure on the performance-poetry circuit, with his Poetry Olympics gigs which bring together poets, musicians, and story-tellers. His two anthologies Children of Albion (London, 1969) and Grandchildren of Albion (Stroud, Glos., 1992) are important snapshots of their time.

With the arrival of Punk Rock in Great Britain in 1976 came the second wave of performance poetry, or 'Ranting', again tied to the availability of venues. Punk bands performed in tiny clubs and often used a poet as MC or support act. The pioneer and leader of this group was John

Cooper Clarke (b. 1950) whose rapid-fire monologues gave him a brief celebrity outside the poetry world. He was older than many of the other Ranters, and has carried on doing the same kind of work while others who were prominent at that time have developed or faded away. Prominent ranters included Joolz, Seething Wells, Attilla the Stockbroker, along with many others with names like Ginger John the Doomsday Commando and Mark MiWurdz.

Many of these performers, including Henry Normal, Nick Toczek, and Kevin Fegan, were subsumed into the third wave of performance poetry in Great Britain, which was led by the newly created alternative-cabaret scene, a London-based movement of the mid-Eighties. It was common for these clubs to put two comedians, a musician, and a performance poet on the same bill. Poets who worked on this circuit included many of the aforementioned, but also Liz *Lochhead and John Hegley. The centre of the cabaret-poetry scene is the Apples and Snakes venue, which has published (London) two important anthologies, both called Apples and Snakes (1985 and 1992).

In parallel with, and sometimes overlapping these waves of performance poetry there is a highly developed black performance-poetry scene. In America, Gil Scott-Heron and his band The Last Poets are notable, as is the rise from the street of rap and hip-hop, which are purely performance forms. Notable rappers include Ice T, and, from the more 'pop' end of the culture, Hammer. In Great Britain in the mid-Seventies Linton Kwesi *Johnson was the catalyst for a scene that included such notable performance poets as John *Agard, Benjamin *Zephaniah, Grace *Nichols, Lemn Sissay, and Valerie Bloom. These black rappers and performance poets continue to influence the literary as well as the performance-poetry scene.

A final strand of performance poetry which sometimes, though not often, overlaps with the others, is that which stems from the Dadaist movement of the Twenties and includes *sound poetry. Notable performers in this area include Bob Cobbing, Bill Griffiths, Peter Finch, and Ivor Thomas.

As well as the anthologies mentioned, see *News for Babylon*, ed. James Berry (London 1984). Individual collections include Valerie Bloom, *Touch Mi, Tell Mi* (London 1983); John Cooper Clarke, *Ten Years in an Open-Necked Shirt* (London 1982); Peter Finch, *Selected Poems* (Bridgend, 1987); John Hegley, *Can I come down now, Dad?* (London, 1991); Joolz, *Emotional Terrorism* (Newcastle upon Tyne, 1990). Recordings include: Gil Scott-Heron, *Small Talk at 125th and Lennox* (1978); *Poetry Olympics* (1982); Linton Kwesi Johnson, *LKJ Live in Concert* (1985); John Cooper Clarke, *Zip Style Method* (1982).

[IMcM

Personal Landscape. See DESERT POETS.

PETERS, Lenrie (1932–) grew up in the Gambia and Sierra Leone, studied medicine at Trinity College, Cambridge, and worked as a doctor in the English Midlands for several years. He has been settled back in the Gambia for the last twenty years, where he practises as a surgeon in Banjul. He is also the current chairman of the West Africa Examinations Council.

Peters published one novel, *The Second Round* (London, 1965), but is best known as a poet; the appearance of his *Selected Poems* (London, 1981) was a major event in African poetry. In some ways Peters is an untypical African poet; his verse is measured and articulated in the traditions of European poetry, and he is a man of the world who draws on the mythologies of the whole planet as his legitimate cultural heritage. But the heart of Peters's poetry is his commitment to Africa, and in particular to the people of the Gambia. *Selected Poems* collects work written over twenty years, including selections from *Poems* (Ibadan, 1964), *Satellites* (London, 1967), and *Katchikali* (London, 1971), as well as a selection of previously uncollected poems. The title-poem of *Katchikali* is in many ways characteristic of his work as a whole: a lament for the desecration of an ancient Gambian holy place by developers and tourists, it offers a vigorous critique of a society that can sell out its shrines to 'hide-hunters'. What happened to the crocodile pool at Katchikali seems to the poet a metaphor for what is happening to spiritual values across the continent. Such a sensitivity to the conflict between an apparent short-term good and the values that would promote real, long-term development underpins much of Peters's poetry.

[SB

PETERSEN, Donald (1928–), was born in Minneapolis, Minnesota, and educated at the Sorbonne and at Carleton College. Subsequently he did graduate work at Indiana University and the University of Iowa. Petersen began his teaching career at Iowa, but in 1956 he moved to the State University of New York College at Oneonta, where he has taught ever since.

Petersen's reputation as a poet rests almost entirely upon one book, *The Spectral Boy* (Middletown, Conn., 1964). A strict and traditionally formal poet, Petersen has over the years published poems and criticism occasionally in some of the literary periodicals in the United States, particularly the *New Criterion*—generally at the request of editors, for Petersen does not take the initiative to submit his work. He has circulated a manuscript, 'Later Poems' (Oneonta, *c*.1988), among his friends. In a brief forenote for the collection he wrote that, for reasons such as 'scope', the 'often intractable' materials, and the 'variable, refractory tone', he has had to keep the poems private, but in fact it is not apparent that Petersen's problems are much different from those of any other poet. The later poems are as well-written and as worthy of publication as any of those to be found in his first book.

[LT

PHILLIPS, Robert (1938–), was born and grew up in rural Laurel, Delaware, and attended the local public schools. He received both BA and MA degrees in English from Syracuse University, where he edited *Syracuse 10*, the literary magazine where he published his own early work as well as that of classmates Joyce Carol *Oates and Dick *Allen. In 1965 he left Syracuse and academia to pursue an advertising career in Manhattan, and moved shortly thereafter to Westchester County.

The poems in his first book, *Inner Weather* (Francestown, NH, 1966), are juvenilia but they confirm his strong grounding in traditional poetic metre, as well as establishing his affinity for the elegy and the pastoral and his interest in music and art as poetic subjects. His poetic development was significantly advanced both by his collection of stories set in Delaware, *The Land of Lost Content* (New York, 1970), and by his critical book, *The Confessional Poets* (Carbondale, Ill., 1973). His examination of *Roethke, Robert *Lowell, *Plath, *Sexton, and others enabled him to view his own life as a legitimate poetic subject, though his autobiographical poems eschew the sensational subjects of the most extreme *confessional poets. Instead, the persona that emerges in his work is that of a congenial, sensitive individual who has survived a somewhat less-than-idyllic Southern boyhood to achieve a precarious middle-aged stability in suburbia. This persona evolved in three volumes of poetry published in the Seventies and reached its fruition in his definitive volume, *Personal Accounts: New and Selected Poems 1966–1986* (Princeton, NJ, 1986). His sequence 'Middle Age Nocturnes' contains many affecting poems on how natural and domestic details reflect the condition of a marriage, as in 'Middle Age: A Nocturne' and 'Autumn Crocuses'. Another sequence, 'Ninety Miles from Nowhere', by contrast, portrays the poet's Southern childhood; in 'Once' he celebrates the single occasion his father took the family to the nearby beach, while in 'Running on Empty' he equates driving on an empty gas tank with creating poetry despite his father's withheld love. As literary executor, he has edited numerous posthumous volumes of Delmore *Schwartz's work.

[RMcP

PICKARD, Tom (1946–), was born in Newcastle upon Tyne. He was co-founder, with Basil *Bunting, of the poetry centre, the Morden Book Tower, and managed it (1963–73). Pickard was one of the more interesting of those British poets to base their procedures on the *Black Mountain school: he attracted the attention of Bunting because, instead of merely imitating them, he tried to remain true to his locale (which was that of the elder poet). Bunting

wrote a preface to his first (and by most judged as his best to date) collection, *High on the Walls* (London, 1967), and praised the 'music' of its *Williams-like short lines, which were touchingly evocative of the Northumberland landscape, and of adolescent love. Bunting hoped he would develop to learn 'to sing with a longer breath'; but Pickard's talent developed in other directions, notably that of documentary film, several of which he scripted or directed for television. The best of his later work is to be found in the poems contained in radio and television documentaries such as *The Jarrow March* (1976). His work has been analysed in depth by Eric Mottram in *Poetry Information* 18 (London, 1978). His other verse collections are: *The Order of Chance* (London, 1971) and *Custom and Exile* (London, 1985).

[MS-S

PIERCY, Marge (1936–), was born in Detroit, Michigan, attended the University of Michigan on a scholarship, and now lives with her husband, writer Ira Wood, on Cape Cod. Well known as both novelist and poet, Piercy has published eleven novels and more than twelve volumes of poetry. Among her best novels are the utopian feminist *Woman on the Edge of Time* (1976) and the autobiographical *Braided Lives* (1982). Her most recent work of fiction is *He, She, and It: A Novel* (1991).

Her poetry, from *Breaking Camp* (1968) to *Mars and Her Children* (1992), reflects the influence of Whitman and *Ginsberg, as well as her own Jewish-Welsh working-class background. Long seen as a political poet, the ardent Marxist, feminist, and environmentalist argues for race- and class-equality, decries traditional male-female roles and relationships, and explores tensions between nature and technology. Sometimes criticized as a propagandist, Piercy nevertheless achieves a successful balance of ideology and aesthetics, particularly in *My Mother's Body* (1985) and *Available Light* (1988).

Circles on the Water: Selected Poems of Marge Piercy (New York, 1982) provides a representative sampling of her work, and *Ways of Knowing: Essays on Marge Piercy* (Mobile, Ala., 1991), ed.

Sue Walker and Eugenie Hamner, contains useful critical commentary. [EDF

PINKERTON, Helen (1927–), was born in Butte, Montana. She received her BA and MA from Stanford University and her Ph.D in 1966 from Harvard. At Stanford she became a member of the Yvor *Winters circle and published seven poems in Winters's anthology *Poets of the Pacific: Second Series* (Stanford, Calif., 1949). She continues to live in California, engaged in teaching, writing poetry, studying and translating her favourite Greek poet, Pindar, and in researching her favourite American writer, Herman Melville.

Her carefully crafted poetry is profoundly philosophical and religious. Her subject-matter is the metaphysical problems of the nature of reality, evil, divinity, and self, together with the possibility of Christian or theistic belief in the twentieth century. Her style is austere and conventional. Among her notable poems are 'Indecision', 'Good Friday', 'The Gift', and two 'Holy Sonnets', all of a religious nature. Recently she has turned to the arts for her inspiration, as in *The Harvesters and Other Poems on Works of Art* (Florence, Ky., 1984).

Her poems have been collected in *Poems 1946–1976* (Huntsville, Tex., 1984). Her basic metaphysical views are discussed in her article (published, like her other prose, under her married name Helen Trimpi) 'Contexts for "Being", and "Self" in Valéry and Edgar Bowers', *The Southern Review*, 13 (1977). Among her prose works are *Melville's Confidence Men and American Politics* (Hamden, Conn., 1987). [DS

PINSKY, Robert (1940–), was born in New Jersey and educated at Rutgers University and afterwards at Stanford under Yvor *Winters. He has taught at various American universities, including Wellesley College and the University of California at Berkeley. Complimented by Robert *Lowell for belonging 'to that rarest category of talents, a poet-critic', Pinsky published an outstanding critical book, *The Situation of Poetry* (Princeton, NJ), in 1976, and he has also been poetry editor of *New Republic*. His first volume was *Sadness and Happiness* (Princeton,

1975), followed by *An Explanation of America* (Princeton and Manchester, 1979) and *History of My Heart* (New York, 1984). He has also, with Robert *Hass, translated some of the poems of the Polish poet Czeslaw Milosz.

Pinsky's work aims very deliberately at a return, after the various forms of modernism and confessionalism, to a new discursiveness in American poetry, a rationality and temperateness in which the objects and feelings of the ordinary suburban world may be given their due. Decisively rejecting the Poundian advice to 'go in fear of abstractions', Pinsky positively welcomes them, in poems which approach the reader in the tone of civilized, slightly earnest conversation. In the long poem *An Explanation of America*, for instance, the Vietnam War is absorbed into the ratiocinative texture: 'I think it made our country older, forever. | I don't mean better or not better, but merely | As though a person should come to a certain place | And have his hair turn gray, that very night.' Such discursiveness may, of course, turn lax or prolix, reminding the reader of nothing so much as a slow, funereal, late-Wordsworthian chunter; but Pinsky has absorbed the lessons of the moderns too, and this long passage on Vietnam concludes with a memorably well-focused figure which proposes that the war will be taken into the American 'family' like 'A new syllable buried in their name'. If it was ever his poet-critic's intention, Pinsky has probably failed in any attempt to establish a 'New Discursive' school of American poets; but his own work, measured and scrupulous, makes a proper case for itself. [NC

PINTER, Harold (1930–), was born in London. It is usual to consider that the playwright Pinter's command of rhythm and nuance makes his drama poetic, although his poems, which were not collected until the 1970s, have tended to be overshadowed by his other writings. The poems contain shifts of register familiar from the plays (as in 'Message': 'I was well acquainted with the pong myself, | I told him, and I counselled calm. | Don't let the fuckers get you down.'), as well as the characteristic air of menace. While the earliest poems ('New Year in the Midlands', 'I Shall Tear Off My Terrible Cap') are clearly touched by Dylan *Thomas, the most striking influence is the William *Empson of 'Missing Dates', 'Success', and 'Let it Go': 'It is the test they set that will not go, | The failing of the doing so, | Ungainly legacy that they bestow.' ('The Doing So'). More recently Pinter has written stripped-down dramatic lyrics ('Before They Fall'), and 'Partners', an outburst of political fury paralleled in his recent writing for the stage.

Poems and Prose 1949–77 was published in London in 1978. *Collected Poems and Prose* (London, 1986) updates the earlier collection.   [SO'B

PITTER, Ruth (1897–1992), was born in Ilford, Essex, a suburb of London. Her parents, artisans and East End school-teachers, reared their daughters to love the countryside and to that end rented a cottage in the Essex forest where Ruth spent the happiest hours of her childhood. During the First World War she worked as a clerk in the War Office. After the war she earned her living in London as a painter and decorator of tea-trays and pots. She set up a gift shop with her companion Kate O'Hara which was twice bombed in the Second World War. She then engaged in war work again. By 1952 she had established her reputation as a poet, and she and Kate were able to buy a house in the country where Ruth could indulge her passion for gardening.

She started writing verse at the age of 5 and achieved her first publication in 1912, in *The New Age* edited by A. R. Orage, who became a dominant influence on her. Her earliest book of poems was *First Poems* (London, 1920) but it was not until *A Mad Lady's Garland* (London, 1934; New York, 1935) that she received substantial attention from reviewers, partly because her friend Hilaire *Belloc wrote the preface.

Pitter's poetry, usually but not always written in conventional prosody, is classical and traditionalist. Her subject-matter reflects her wide-ranging response to a variety of experiences, ranging from the pleasures of gardening, in *The Rude Potato* (London, 1941), to transcen-

dental religious experience, as in 'Six Dreams and a Vision' in *The Ermine: Poems, 1942–1952* (London, 1953) written after her conversion in the 1940s to Anglicanism under the influence of C. S. *Lewis.

Her *Collected Poems* (London, 1968; New York, 1969), with a preface by herself, contains her best work. Helpful biographical information and critical evaluation will be found in Arthur Russell (ed.), *Ruth Pitter: Homage to a Poet* (London, 1969).   [DS

PITT-KETHLEY, Fiona (1954–), was born in Middlesex. She trained as a painter at Chelsea College of Art, and now lives in St Leonard's, Sussex, writing full-time. She has produced three collections of poetry (all published London): *Sky Ray Lolly* (1986), *Private Parts* (1987), and *The Perfect Man* (1989), as well as a travelogue, *Journeys to the Underworld* (1989).

Fiona Pitt-Kethley's work is unflinchingly anti-romantic. She has been criticized for rhythmic flatness, and her largely iambic lines can seem monotonous over a whole collection. Yet her forthright, down-to-earth tone and lack of squeamishness combine with her rhythmically rather dignified manner to lend a nice sense of bathos to her treatment of erotic and, more especially, pornographic mythology. Once banned by the Poetry Society for her use of four-letter words, Pitt-Kethley is in fact a moral and even a didactic writer, a crusader against sexual hypocrisy. There is some risk, however, of both her work and reputation being hijacked by a version of the porno-myth she at first set out to undermine.

[CAR

PLATH, Sylvia (1932–63) was born in Boston, Massachusetts, on 27 October (she shared a birthday with Dylan *Thomas), and spent her childhood in Winthrop. When she was 8 her German father, a professor at Boston University, died of diabetes. Two years later her mother moved the family inland to Wellesley, where she struggled to give Sylvia and her younger brother every advantage of a superior education. Self-consciousness and anxiety about status and money during adolescence contributed to the profound insecurity Plath concealed all her life beneath a façade of brassy energy and brilliant achievement.

Plath discovered that writing was her vocation very early. By the time she was at Smith College in the early 1950s she had published precocious poems in newspapers and written over fifty short stories, some of which won prizes from ladies' magazines. At Smith she went on winning prizes, but after a third year of feverish overwork, she broke down and attempted suicide. Six months in a private hospital set her on her feet again, but in reality she never recovered.

After she had graduated, *summa cum laude*, from Smith in 1955, she went to Cambridge University on a Fulbright scholarship, and there she met the poet Ted *Hughes. They were married in London in June 1956. The marriage was for six years a strong union of supremely dedicated writers. Sylvia's wholehearted enthusiasm for Hughes's work, which she sent off to the competition that won him fame, was balanced by his steadfast belief in her exceptional gift. They lived in Massachusetts (Cambridge, Northampton—where Sylvia taught for a year at Smith—and Boston), then in London and Devon. A daughter, Frieda, was born in April 1960, and a son, Nicholas, in January 1962.

Sylvia Plath's early poems—already drenched in typical imagery of glass, moon, blood, hospitals, foetuses, and skulls—were mainly 'exercises' or pastiches of work by poets she admired: Dylan Thomas, W. B. *Yeats, Marianne *Moore. Late in 1959, when she and her husband were at Yaddo, the writers' colony in New York State, she produced the seven-part 'Poem for a Birthday', which owes its form to Theodore *Roethke's 'Lost Son' sequence, though its theme is her own traumatic breakdown and suicide attempt at 21. After 1960 her poems increasingly explored the surreal landscape of her imprisoned psyche under the looming shadow of a dead father and a mother on whom she was resentfully dependent.

A fanatical preoccupation with death and rebirth informs her sad, cynical novel, *The Bell Jar*, as it does her first book of poems, *The Colossus*, published in London by Heinemann in October 1960, and by Knopf in New York, in 1962. Plath's mature poetry, too exalted to be merely *'confessional', frequently treats of this resurrection theme, together with a related one which attempts to redeem meaningless life through art. Lines like 'I am lost, I am lost, in the robes of all this light' ('Witch Burning'), and 'On Fridays the little children come | To trade their hooks for hands' ('The Stones') foreshadow the powerful, wholly convincing voice of poems like 'The Hanging Man', published posthumously in *Ariel*: 'By the roots of my hair some god got hold of me. | I sizzled in his blue volts like a desert prophet.'

Ted Hughes has described how Sylvia Plath underwent a searing, 'curiously independent process of gestation' during the spring of 1962, when, two months after giving birth to a son, she produced a powerful radio drama, 'Three Women'. The first deathly Ariel Poems appeared soon afterwards with 'The Moon and Yew Tree', 'Little Fugue', 'Elm', 'Event', 'Berck-Plage', and others. During the summer of 1962 her marriage to Hughes began to buckle; she was devastated when she learned that he had been unfaithful to her. Although she and Hughes travelled to Ireland together in September, the marriage was by then in ruins, and in October she asked her husband to leave for good.

It was after Hughes's departure that Plath produced, in less than two months, the forty poems of rage, despair, love, and vengeance that have chiefly been responsible for her immense posthumous fame. Throughout October and November of 1962 she rose every day at dawn to take down, as from dictation, line after miraculous line of poems like 'The Bee Meeting', 'Stings', 'Daddy', 'Lady Lazarus', 'Ariel', and 'Death & Company', as well as those heartbreaking poems to her baby son: 'Nick and the Candlestick' and 'The Night Dances'.

In December 1962 she moved with her children from Devon to London. What she recognized as the 'genius' of her poetry temporarily restored her self-confidence, but in January

1963, after the publication of *The Bell Jar*, and during the coldest winter of the century, she descended into a deep, clinical depression, and in the early morning of 11 February, she gassed herself.

In the quarter-century following her suicide Sylvia Plath has become a heroine and martyr of the feminist movement. In fact, she was a martyr mainly to the recurrent psychodrama that staged itself within the bell jar of her tragically wounded personality. Twelve final poems, written shortly before her death, define a nihilistic metaphysic from which death provided the only dignified escape.

Sylvia Plath's *Collected Poems* were published in London and New York in 1981. There are biographies by Lindsay Wagner-Martin (1987) and Anne Stevenson (1989). [AS

PLOMER, William (Charles Franklyn) (1903–73), who was born in Pietersberg, South Africa, founded the satirical magazine *Voorslag* (Whiplash) in 1926 with Roy *Campbell, the venture being joined later by Laurens van der Post. In 1926 Leonard Woolf published at the Hogarth Press *Turbott Wolfe*, a novel about South Africa. After spending two years teaching in Japan Plomer published two further novels, *Paper Houses* (1929) and *Sado* (1931). In 1929 he emigrated to England, where he was welcomed by Bloomsbury and by Bohemian literary London. His first collection of verse, *The Fivefold Screen* (1932), contained poems whose visual clarity, musical resonance, and atmospheric intensity he never recaptured, perhaps because after 1932 his memories of his native land lost their freshness and poignancy. In 1937 Plomer became chief reader to Jonathan Cape, a task he performed with skill and assiduity. He at once recognized the unique quality of the diary kept from 1870 to 1879 by Francis Kilvert, curate of a parish on the Welsh borders, and edited a three-volume selection between 1938 and 1944.

Plomer wrote a number of satirical poems and ballads in the late 1930s and early 1940s. Some portray the sleazier aspects of sexual transactions in London. We meet Mews-Flat Mona; French Lisette and Dublin Dan fleecing a client in a Maida Vale flat; and D'Arcy Honeybunn, 'A rose-red sissy half as old as time'. The wartime ballads recount incidents as grotesque as the cruel surrealistic comedy of Dali and Buñuel. In 'The Flying Bum', a bomb plants on the dining-room table of a vegetarian guesthouse 'A lightly roasted rump of horse'. Such poems and those that dwell lovingly on a severed human thigh, or on the strangling of a girl with a stocking, may reflect Plomer's forays into the dangerous underworld of homosexual promiscuity that marked his conduct from the late 1920s until the mid-1940s.

After the war Plomer brought out some highly successful works of prose fiction and embarked on a career as one of Benjamin Britten's librettists, happily subduing his own artistic inclinations to the composer's imperative demands. His post-war verse became more benign and wider in its human sympathies. 'Mrs Middleditch' concerns an elderly woman who is suddenly overcome, while shopping in a supermarket, by a vision of the poor and hungry of the world. It is a far cry from Mews-Flat Mona and French Lisette. 'A Young Jackdaw' sounds a note of lyricism, less sharp-edged and ironical than in his early poems, but with a new tenderness. During the last years of his life Plomer made a tentative return to the Anglicanism of his devout mother. In 'The Bungalows', surveying the drab uniformity of suburban houses, he envisages the birth of a Saviour as once in Bethlehem: 'It may be born, it may be born.'

See *Collected Poems* (London, 1973) and Peter F. Alexander's *William Plomer* (Oxford, 1989).

[JPr

PLUMLY, Stanley (1939–), was born in Barnesville, Ohio, and grew up in the lumber and farming regions of Virginia and Ohio. His father was a lumberjack and welder. He was educated at Wilmington College, a Quaker school in Ohio, and Ohio University. In 1985 he married the poet Deborah Digges. He is a professor of English at the University of Maryland. His first collection, *In the Outer Dark* (Baton Rouge, La., 1970), won the Delmore Schwartz Memorial

Award; his third, *Out-of-the-Body-Travel* (New York, 1978), was nominated for the National Book Critics Circle Award.

For his Keatsian eye to nature, Plumly has been called the most English of American poets, and his quiet poems are unmistakable. His more autobiographical work, often depicting a working-class rural childhood, suggests that he may have inherited the mantle of James *Wright, his fellow Ohioan. One is more astonished, however, by the garden found there than by the resolute bleakness of the life. Plumly writes compact, descriptive lyrics and more prosaic narrative poems. Both types are rooted in nature and both assert themselves melodically. In his earlier books Plumly used his mother and father as dual-axes for his poetry, but with time the machinery has enlarged, rotating history, family, and nature.

In addition to the two volumes named earlier, Plumly has published three collections of poetry: *Giraffe* (Baton Rouge, 1973), *Summer Celestial* (New York, 1983), and *Boy on the Step* (New York, 1989). He has also written *The Abrupt Edge* (New York, 1993), a book of personal and critical essays.   [HC

PLUTZIK, Hyam (1911–62), was born in Brooklyn, the son of Jewish immigrants from Russia. He grew up in the countryside near Southbury, Connecticut, and did not speak English until he was 7. He studied English at Trinity College in Hartford and, after two years of graduate study at Yale at the beginning of the Depression, worked as a reporter for several newspapers (including Walt Whitman's *Brooklyn Eagle*). In 1936–7 Plutzik spent a crucial year of Thoreauvian solitude near Quaker Farms, Connecticut, meditating on his purposes as a writer, and then returned to Yale, earning an MA in English in 1940. In 1942 he enlisted in the US Army; he was commissioned in 1943, and married Tanya Roth of Brooklyn, before being posted to duty as an ordnance officer with the 44th Heavy Bomb Group of the Eighth Air Force, in Norfolk. Discharged at the end of 1945, Plutzik joined the English faculty of the University of Rochester (New York), becoming Deane Professor of Poetry and Rhetoric in 1961. He died of cancer in 1962, leaving his wife and two sons and two daughters.

Plutzik's first collection, *Aspects of Proteus* (New York, 1949) marked him as a seasoned poet already, lyrically inclined but sturdily independent of the pieties of post-war formalism. He found his main themes early—the tragic meanings of the war, the interplay of science and the imagination, the ways ordinary private lives attain to myth, the enigmatic witnessing of nature to human life and death—and in his second book, *Apples from Shinar* (Middletown, Conn., 1959), these themes took on a new depth and resonance, infused with Jewish mysticism and a distinctive phenomenological awareness, as in 'Jim Desterland', 'For My Daughter', and 'The Bass'. His third book, *Horatio* (New York, 1961) is something of a surprise: a long and absorbing narrative account of what happens to Hamlet's friend after he promises to represent Hamlet faithfully to the world.

The last lines of one of Plutzik's last, unpublished poems read: 'Out of my life I fashioned a fistfull of words. | When I opened my hand, they flew away.' The durability of his achievement is manifested by generous selections of his work in recent British and American anthologies and by the recent publication of a sumptuous *Collected Poems*, including previously uncollected and unpublished work, with commentary by Anthony Hecht and Ted Hughes (Brockport, NY, 1987).   [JRa

PN Review. See POETRY NATION.

Poetry: A Magazine of Verse (1912–), published monthly from Chicago, was founded by Harriet Monroe to create an American audience for contemporary poetry at a time when even literary magazines were printing poems, if at all, merely to fill gaps. As editor till 1936, Monroe played a central part in reviving poetic activity in America and in promoting experimental and avant-garde poetry. Never limited to a single conception of poetry, however, she published— and advanced the careers of—Midwesterners like Carl *Sandburg, Edgar Lee *Masters, and Vachel *Lindsay, of modernists like William

Carlos *Williams, Marianne *Moore, Wallace *Stevens, and T. S. *Eliot, and of more traditional regional poets like Edwin Arlington *Robinson and Robert *Frost. In its first few years, when Ezra *Pound was sending work by H. D. (Hilda *Doolittle), Richard *Aldington, and others from England, the magazine provoked controversies about free verse and poetic experimentalism, but it soon became, and has remained under such editors as Karl *Shapiro (1950–65), Henry Rago (1955–69), and Daryl *Hine (1969–77), the most established and prestigious American magazine devoted exclusively to poetry. Although it has always sought especially to discover and foster new American talent, it has also helped disseminate the modern verse of other cultures, periodically filling issues with translations. No other magazine has so comprehensively reflected the development of verse and ideas about verse in America in this century. *Harriet Monroe and the Poetry Renaissance*, by Ellen Williams (Urbana, Ill., 1977) gives a detailed account of the magazine's first ten years; and *Poetry (1912–1977)* is an anthology of poems from the magazine edited by Daryl Hine (Boston, 1978). See also Ian Hamilton, *The Little Magazines: A Study of Six Editors* (London, 1976).   [NE

Poetry Australia. For many years one of the most important poetry magazines in Australia, this began as a quarterly in 1964 but later changed to six issues a year. It was founded by Dr Grace Perry as a breakaway movement from the Poetry Society journal *Poetry Magazine* (later *New Poetry*), and immediately established itself as a wide-ranging journal of eclectic interest. It featured many special overseas issues (New Zealand, Canadian, Italian, American, Dutch, Japanese, Swedish, etc.), as well as special issues on young poets, poetry of the various Australian states and commemorative issues on particular poets. It introduced the innovative gesture of devoting whole issues as, in effect, books of poems by new writers (e.g. John *Tranter and Jennifer *Maiden). Editorial assistance from such poets as Bruce *Beaver and later Les *Murray helped attract major works. In the years

before the formation of the Literature Board (1973), it played a leading part in organizing poetry readings, workshops, seminars, and visits by overseas poets. In the 1970s its substantial position was consolidated, but by the later 1980s, although it continued to produce a number of important theme issues and individual collections, Grace Perry's failing health and a loss of innovative vitality relegated it to a minor position. Other, newer magazines, had taken over. No survey of Australian poetry, however, should underestimate the contribution of *Poetry Australia* over its first twenty years.   [TWS

Poetry Book Society, The (PBS), is a London-based book-club, in receipt of an annual Arts Council subsidy, devoted to contemporary poetry and with a current membership of 1,800. It was founded in December 1953. The original board of management included Basil Blackwell, Joseph Compton, T. S. *Eliot, and Erica Marx, with Eric W. White, literature director of the Arts Council, as founder secretary. The basic format of membership has never changed: members receive, post-free, four books of new poetry each year, selected for the board of management by two independent selectors. In addition to the quarterly book (the 'choice') the PBS has always recommended a number of other new books which may be purchased by members. With the quarterly choice comes a printed bulletin containing poems from the recommendations and a short prose statement from the author of the choice. Each winter since 1956 the PBS has published an annual anthology of new poems—recently published by Hutchinson—compiled by an editor who is a retiring selector.

Under the chairmanship of Philip *Larkin in the early 1980s the PBS became a simultaneous book-club, offering books to members at discounted prices. The PBS estimates it can distribute over 8,000 books to members annually. Over the years the choice has often been the first book by poets such as Douglas *Dunn, Ted *Hughes, or Tom *Paulin, who were later to achieve fame. Its ability to help shape the taste, and extend the readership, of the British poetry-reading public is not to be underestimated.

In the early 1960s the PBS organized a series of poetry festivals which evolved into the hugely successful Poetry International, directed variously by Ted Hughes, Patrick Garland, and Charles Osborne. Poetry International featured leading poets of the world reading from their work, including W. H. *Auden, Pablo Neruda, Vasko Popa, and John *Berryman, and often filled the Queen Elizabeth Hall on the South Bank Centre for several nights each summer until 1975.

See: *Poetry Book Society: The First Twenty-Five Years*, ed. Eric W. White (London, 1979), and *Thirty Years of the Poetry Book Society*, ed. Jonathan Barker, preface by Blake Morrison (London, 1988) [JDB]

Poetry Bookshop, The, was founded in January 1913 by the poet and critic Harold *Monro at 35 Devonshire Street, Theobalds Road, London, near the British Museum. The Poetry Bookshop was a specialist retail outlet and a centre for poets and readers of contemporary poetry. Monro edited magazines such as *Poetry Review* and *Poetry and Drama* from the shop. He arranged regular readings by poets—including W. B. *Yeats, Walter *de la Mare, W. H. *Davies, T. S. *Eliot, Ezra *Pound, Robert *Graves, and dozens more—from their own work. The poets W. W. *Gibson, Robert *Frost, T. E. *Hulme, and Wilfred *Owen at various times stayed in the shop's attic rooms. F. S. *Flint rightly called Monro a 'romantic idealist'. He was certainly hospitable and generous in his encouragement of unpublished poets such as the young Wilfred Owen. In 1926 the shop moved to 38 Great Russell Street. Following Monro's death in 1932, his widow Alida Monro struggled to continue, but the shop had been in financial difficulties for some time and she was forced to close in June 1935.

Monro also founded an influential publishing imprint named The Poetry Bookshop, which published books and pamphlets by many contemporary poets such as Frances *Cornford, Eleanor Farjeon, James Elroy *Flecker, and Edward *Shanks. The imprint published each of the five best-selling *Georgian Poetry* anthologies

edited by Edward Marsh, and published between the years 1912 and 1922. The anthologies launched the *Georgian poets (who included W. H. Davies and Walter de la Mare in their number), and were read by a very wide non-specialist audience. Monro also published the first anthology of *Imagist poetry, *Des Imagistes*, in 1914. Monro's taste as editor and publisher was wide yet conservative and, at times, flawed: astonishingly, he rejected T. S. Eliot's 'The Love Song of J. Alfred Prufrock' and the poems of Edward *Thomas when offered to him for publication (he was later to acknowledge the importance of both poets.) Yet, these major failures apart, he published poems by many writers, such as Ford Madox *Ford (Hueffer), F. S. Flint, Robert Graves, and Charlotte *Mew, whose work was later to achieve prominence.

Two books on the subject are Joy Grant, *Harold Monro and the Poetry Bookshop* (London, 1967), and Robert H. Ross, *The Georgian Revolt: Rise and Fall of a Poetic Ideal 1910–22* (London, 1967). [JDB]

Poetry London, was the leading poetry magazine of the 1940s and caught much of the character of the decade. It was started in 1939 by Anthony Dickins and the Ceylonese James Tambimuttu, who became one of the most colourful and influential literary figures of the period. The founders raised money by subscription for six issues, but this ran out after two. A gift enabled the magazine to appear bimonthly for four more issues, starting November 1940. Issues 7 and 8 did not appear until 1942; issue 9 came out in 1943; and issue 10, in the form of a large book, in 1944. By that time Tambimuttu was engrossed in a new publishing venture, Editions Poetry London, under the imprint of Nicholson and Watson; they also supported *Poetry London*, which did not, however, appear again until the autumn of 1947. By then Nicholson and Watson had begun to find the venture too expensive; but Tambimuttu found a new backer in Richard March. March and the poet Nicholas *Moore appeared as associate editors for issues 14 and 15; after which, in the autumn of 1949, March took control of *Poetry London* and edited it with Moore until its twenty-third and final issue in the winter of 1951.

Tambimuttu had returned to Ceylon in 1949. In 1956 he started *Poetry London–New York*; but again money ran out after a couple of years. His final try was *Poetry London / Apple Magazine*, with a first issue in 1979 and a second in 1982. He died in 1983.

The early issues of *Poetry London* opened with 'Letters', almost all by Tambimuttu, in which he argued for a poetry that was spontaneous, incantatory, and responsive to the unconscious. He criticized *New Verse*, a main organ of the social-realist poetry of the 1930s, as advocating a poetry in which objects replaced emotions. *Poetry London* became a voice of the New Romanticism of the 1940s (see NEW APOCA-LYPSE); yet the amount of rubbish published by Tambimuttu was small. Among the poets whose early work appeared in *Poetry London* were W. S. *Graham, David *Wright, Kathleen *Raine, Lawrence *Durrell, and Michael *Hamburger. Tambimuttu published the first books of Bernard *Spencer, Raine, and Wright, as well as David *Gascoyne's *Poems 1937–43* and Durrell's *Cefalu*. He was among the first to recognize the talent of Keith *Douglas.

Tribute is made to his achievements in *Tambimuttu: Bridge Between Two Worlds*, ed. J. Williams (London, 1989). [ATT

Poetry Nation, was founded in 1973 by Michael *Schmidt, with C. B. Cox, professor of English at Manchester University, initially as co-editor. Schmidt intended the title 'to suggest a republic of letters, but it was immediately perceived as nationalistic and right-wing' (Mark Fisher, *Letters to an Editor*, Manchester, 1989). The first issue in fact included an essay by Terry Eagleton and an interview with Edgell *Rickword; Michael Schmidt, strongly influenced by the example of Octavio Paz's magazine *Plural*, pursued a policy of oppositional openness, and was concerned to attack the intellectual orthodoxies of the day rather than to take political positions. The magazine included poetry, fiction, essays, memoirs, reviews, and reports from abroad. In

1976 the hardback *Poetry Nation* was superseded by the A4-format *PN Review* (the form in which the magazine still continues), and C. H. *Sisson and Donald *Davie joined Schmidt as editors (remaining until Issue 37 in 1984). Davie's 'Reflections on PNR' (*Yearbook of English Studies*, 16, 1986) looked back on the magazine's history to the point of his own departure, interpreting its influence as a corrective against the 'long-standing Leftist monopoly in the intellectual market-place'—a view which arguably misrepresented the plurality Schmidt upheld throughout. Three issues of *PN Review* were particularly widely noticed: Issue 13, which accused the Church of England of neglecting the Authorized Version of the Bible and the Book of Common Prayer; Issue 36, an anthology of contemporary British and Irish poetry conceived as a response to the *Penguin Book of Contemporary British Poetry*; and Issue 49, a debate on post-structuralist criticism. [MHu

Poetry Quarterly, founded in 1940 at just the time when the public demand for verse had increased, was dedicated to the publication of work by contemporary poets, and to reviews of and essays on individual poets. It was published by Grey Walls Press, a small literary firm financed by a business man and Conservative MP. *Poetry Quarterly* ceased in 1953 when this proprietor was convicted of fraud, although not in connection with his literary enterprises. The editor throughout was Charles Wrey Gardiner. The sales were comparatively high during the war, but later fell off. Its chief rival was *Poetry London*, but this appeared much less regularly. The editorial policy was never coherent, and is best summed up by an editorial pronouncement: 'the publication of a poem is an accident and its audience an irrelevance.' Inasmuch as *Poetry Quarterly*, the standing of which was never high, had a direction, this was (nominally) anti-*Georgian, vaguely neo-romantic—and 'neo-Apocalyptic' (see NEW APOCALYPSE); but it performed a function in providing encouragement to new young poets. Contributors included James *Kirkup, G. S. *Fraser, John *Heath-Stubbs, and Nicholas *Moore. [MS-S

Poetry Review, was the magazine of the Poetry Society, founded in 1909, and initially edited by Harold *Monro, who soon departed to found the *Poetry Bookshop, edit *Poetry and Drama* and publish the anthologies of *Georgian Poetry*. For most of its life *Poetry Review* has been conservative, generous, and intellectually modest, often aptly reflecting the Poetry Society's tranquil amateurism: the editorial stance was self-effacing, the critical values shaped more by enthusiasm than by discernment. Such tranquillity was much disrupted in 1970, however, when the retiring editor, Derek Parker, was briefly succeeded by Eric Mottram, an advocate of *concrete poetry and the avant-garde. Subsequently the magazine has once again become more conventionally welcoming, though far less comatose than its earlier self: each issue is now built around a particular topic, which may be geographical (Europe, Ireland, America) or more broadly thematic ('Poetry among the Arts', 'Poetry and Science', 'Work', 'The Green Issue'). The present editor is Peter Forbes.

[NP

Poets Laureate. Although their predecessors include Dryden, Wordsworth, and Tennyson, the Poets Laureate of the twentieth century have not been especially distinguished. The universally derided Alfred *Austin, who held the office from 1896 until 1913, was succeeded by Robert *Bridges (to 1930), John *Masefield (to 1967), C. *Day Lewis (to 1972), Sir John *Betjeman (to 1984), and Ted *Hughes. The list all-too-neatly illustrates the difficulty of finding candidates who combine originality with orthodoxy, outstanding literary talent with impeccable respectability. The paradoxical nature of the office is perhaps most clearly embodied in Day Lewis, an interesting minor poet and an admirable translator of Virgil; yet as publishing-house director and pseudonymous author of detective stories, he was undeniably the safe bet of the *Auden generation. The most appropriate recent incumbent was Betjeman, a deftly witty occasional poet as well as an unusually popular one, though hardly a characteristic literary figure of his time; his natural successor would have been Philip *Larkin, who is said to have declined the post. Instead, Ted Hughes was a surprising choice, a writer decisively outside the prevailing tradition of formal urbanity, though no more inspired than most of his predecessors by the quaint task of turning royal occasions into poems.

[NP

PORTER, Hal (1911–84), was born in Melbourne. By his own account, he wrote much but published little until he was over 40, believing that his writing was too far removed from the social realism that dominated literary fashion. When his poems and short stories eventually began to appear in the mid-1950s his reputation as Australia's most conscious stylist was quickly established. His first book, apart from the privately printed *Short Stories* (1942), was a collection of verse, *The Hexagon* (Sydney, 1956). In the following year he was invited to edit the prestigous anthology, *Australian Poetry 1957*.

Porter's verse forms a comparatively small part of his published work. By the time his second collection, *Elijah's Ravens* (Sydney), appeared in 1968 he had published two volumes of short stories, two volumes of autobiography, one of theatrical biography, two plays, and had edited the short-story anthology, *Coast to Coast 1961–1962*. Very early in his publishing career Porter's reputation as a poet began to be overshadowed by his successes in the short story, where his verbal exuberance was matched by witty, often satirical, observations of contemporary Australian life. Between *Elijah's Ravens* and his third and final book of verse, *In an Australian Country Graveyard* (Sydney, 1974), which he illustrated himself, Porter published another novel, two more plays and two further short-story collections. Porter's first volume of autobiography, *The Watcher on the Cast-Iron Balcony* (London, 1963), has become an Australian classic. It is on this work and a number of short stories that his reputation presently rests. His verse, both lyrical and descriptive, is distinguished by a formal conservativism and a surprising mixture of conventional subject-matter and verbal pyrotechnics. At its best, it shimmers with intense imagery and sensuous word patterns; at its less successful, it is clotted by verbal density and self-conscious extravagance.

[MLo

PORTER, Peter (1929–), was born in Brisbane. He came to England in 1951 and, apart from short periods as writer-in-residence at English, Scottish, and Australian universities, has lived in London ever since. In the 1950s he was associated with the *Group, and felt a particular affinity for the work of Martin *Bell (whose *Complete Poems*, edited by Porter, appeared in 1988). For some years in the 1960s Porter worked in an advertising agency—fellow employees included Peter *Redgrove and Gavin *Ewart—but since 1968 he has earned his living as a free-lance writer and broadcaster, and was for many years regular poetry critic for the *Observer*. He has two daughters by his marriage to Jannice Henry, who died in 1974.

Porter is a prolific poet, and an uneven one. He regards fecundity as a virtue (as did *Auden, who has been an important influence), and one suspects that obscure or awkward passages, the occasional impression of impatience or carelessness, particularly in his handling of rhyming, stanzaic forms, are prices he has been willing to pay for a substantial and varied oeuvre. Critics were quick to cast him—on the strength of a few muscular, overwrought poems in his first book which parade their author's queasy fascination with the London 'scene', consumer goods, and casual sex—as a privileged outsider, the satirist of a new Elizabethan age. In fact some of the poems are strikingly Elizabethan in a different sense—steeped in corruption, plucking anatomies of decay from the fashionable decadence; while others energetically recall an Australian background shadowed by illness, loneliness, and childhood fears (Porter's mother died when he was 9). A fruitful sense of unbelonging, and scathing irony at the expense of what 'belonging' might mean, inform Porter's satirical verse, which at its best (as in the pointed 'recreations' of Martial) is witty and scabrous, full of what one commentator has called 'the provincial's sour relish for attacking the vices and absurdities of the world he has entered'.

With hindsight, though, the targets (fatuous officialdom, artistic pretension, sexual greed) seem softer than they might once have seemed, the attack too neatly tailored to the demands of the poetry reading. The real fulfilment of Porter's early promise is in his mature persona: that of an elegiac moralist, stoical, compassionate, sardonic, preoccupied with mortality and 'the sadness of the creatures', and most memorable when confessing more than hopeless lust or moral torpor—notably in the tender, self-accusing poems that followed his wife's suicide.

Porter has said that his poetry deals with 'the art and life of the past, the everyday life of the present'. This is true as far as it goes, but it drastically understates the intellectual richness and the—sometimes impenetrable—allusiveness of his manner. In Australia 'alienated', as his compatriot Clive *James wrote, by his 'European sensibility', suspicious of his homeland's 'dreadful health' (though prepared in more recent poems to celebrate its natural glories), Porter has set about imaginatively possessing Europe with determination and an impressive range of cultural and historical reference. Baroque music, opera, Renaissance painting, and the Italian landscape are regularly invoked as consolations for the vanity and imperfection of the world, while 'God' and 'the gods' also recur frequently as the origins both of injustice and mysterious benediction. In all this the poet's voice is pained, urbane, sententiously aphoristic or stately and oracular, ready to generalize, and to reach for lapidary or discursive extravagance.

The volumes published since *Collected Poems* have shown the increasing influence of Wallace *Stevens and John *Ashbery—a marked interest in dreams, in the opulence and irrational punning vitalism of words, and in varieties of ironic parable—though not to the point where Porter would be prepared to relinquish his customary, controlled eloquence (a matter of phrasing more than formal or musical properties) for, say, Ashbery's colloquialism and 'directionless drift'. Warily noting the decline of civilization in an age of nuclear threat and literary theory, Porter as warily (and controversially) recognizes the limitations of his own art, continuing to find a role for the poet as self-deprecating scourge.

Porter was awarded the Duff Cooper Memorial Prize for his *Collected Poems* (Oxford, 1983), which contains virtually all the poems published in nine volumes up to and including *English Subtitles* (1981). He has also published *Fast Forward* (Oxford, 1984), *The Automatic Oracle* (Oxford, 1987), *Mars* (illustrations by Arthur Boyd; London, 1988), *A Porter Selected* (1989), *Possible Worlds* (1989), *Millennial Fables* (1994), and *The Chair of Babel* (1992—all Oxford). See also Bruce Bennett, *Spirit in Exile* (1991) and Peter Steele, *Peter Porter* (1992—both Melbourne). [AJ]

POUND, Ezra Loomis (1885–1972), was born in Hailey, Idaho, but grew up and was educated mainly in Pennsylvania.

In 1908, when a projected academic career was cut short, he set sail for Europe, spending several months in Venice and finally settling in London, where he was befriended by his hero, W. B. *Yeats. Between 1908 and 1911 he published six collections of verse, most of it dominated by a passion for Provençal and early Italian poetry. This is filtered through the medievalizing manner of Browning and the Pre-Raphaelites. Under the influence of Ford Madox *Ford and T. E. *Hulme he modernized his style, and in 1912 launched the *Imagist movement, advocating concreteness, economy, and free verse. The oriental delicacy of his brief Imagist lyrics (e.g. 'In a Station of the Metro') soon gave way to the more dynamically avant-garde manner of Vorticism. Association with Vorticist visual artists (e.g. Henri Gaudier-Brzeska and Wyndham *Lewis) helped him to see how poems could be made up, like post-Cubist sculptures, of juxtaposed masses and planes. These lessons were reinforced by his work on Ernest Fenollosa's literal versions of classical Chinese poems, which he turned into the beautiful free-verse lyrics of *Cathay* (1915). Fenollosa had argued that Chinese written characters were ideograms—compressed and abstracted visual metaphors. In this interplay of concrete signs Pound saw the model for a new

kind of poetry, dynamic and economical, which juxtaposed not only images but diverse 'facts'—allusions, quotations, fragments of narrative. Such a method, soon to be tried out in his major work *The Cantos* (on which he tentatively embarked in 1915), would permit the use of quotations from other languages and even gobbets of prose.

The range and brilliance of Pound's contacts in all the arts convinced him that London was to be the centre of a new Renaissance. He cast himself in the role of impresario, editor, and advocate, contributing to Yeats's mature style, discovering and promoting *Joyce and *Eliot, advising an American businessman on the modern works of art to buy in London. But his hopes foundered in the waste of the First World War, and the consequent disappointment was to colour the rest of his life's work. In the short term it provoked his first major poems, 'Homage to Sextus Propertius' (1919) and *Hugh Selwyn Mauberley* (1921). These two ironic sequences represent a contrast. The free-verse 'Homage', an ironic persona poem based on the lyrics of the first-century Roman poet, is a defence of the private and erotic in poetry against the imperialistic jingoism promoted by war. *Mauberley*, in tautly rhymed satirical stanzas, depicts the war as the *Götterdammerung* of an emasculated and philistine culture, condemned by the limitation of its own horizons. The poem is also evidence of Pound's close working relationship with Eliot, whose taste it reflects (cf. the 'Sweeney' poems of the same period). The relationship was to culminate in the crucial part played by Pound in cutting *The Waste Land* (1922).

Mauberley has been described as Pound's farewell to London. In 1920 he left, spending four years in Paris then moving on to Italy, where he settled in Rapallo in 1924. He was now concentrating on *The Cantos*, his 'poem including history', and the first section was published in 1925.

As *The Cantos* shows, he was now preoccupied with economics. The war, as he saw it, had been caused by the rivalries of international capitalists. He thought he had found a solution to the evils of unchecked capitalism, one especially favourable to the arts, in the Social Credit theory of Major C. H. Douglas, who argued that a system of state credit could increase purchasing power in the population at large, thus promoting creativity and removing power from bankers and financiers. Attracted to Mussolini by his energy and his promises of monetary reform, Pound naïvely assumed that the Italian leader could be persuaded to put Douglas's theory into practice. At first, the main target of Pound's attacks is 'usury', which he depicts (e.g. in Canto 45) as an unnatural force that pollutes the creative instinct in humanity. By about 1930 the usurers he condemns are usually Jews, and his language is vitiated by virulent anti-Semitism.

A Draft of XXX Cantos (1930) presents the poet as wandering Odysseus, travelling among the dead. Through juxtaposition, he uncovers repeated patterns in history and experiences moments when the world of time is transfigured by the eternal world of the gods. The mainly Mediterranean emphasis of the first thirty Cantos then gives way (in Cantos 31–70, published 1934–40) to the economic policies of early US presidents and the governance of ancient China. Despite an increase in prosy didacticism and much consequent turgidity, these sections contain some of Pound's finest poetry (e.g. Cantos 36, 45, 47, and 49).

In the later 1930s Pound devoted much of his energy to defending fascism and trying to avert war. When war broke out, he embarked on a series of fanatical addresses to American troops, which were broadcast on Rome Radio. As a result, he was arrested by partisans in 1945 and handed over to the US forces, who held him for six months at a Disciplinary Training Centre near Pisa, pending trial on a treason charge. It seems likely that the inhuman conditions he endured there for the first three weeks accelerated the breakdown in rationality already to be glimpsed in his writings. Repatriated to the United States to stand trial, he was found unfit to plead on grounds of insanity and incarcerated in St Elizabeths Hospital, Washington DC, from 1946 to 1958.

His imprisonment brought about an artistic recovery. *The Pisan Cantos* (1948), drafted in the DTC, are the most directly personal poems he wrote. In adversity, and conscious of the tragedy of Europe, he contemplates his own past in that context, especially the watershed years of the modern movement. Suffering and retrospection induce a new humility, exemplified in his care for the life around him—the insects, the animals, the camp guards. In St Elizabeths he completed two rather more cryptic sections of the poem—*Section: Rock-Drill* (1955) and *Thrones* (1959)—as well as a programme of translations from the Confucian classics.

On his release he returned to Italy, dying in Venice in 1972. Despite moments of defiance, his last years were overshadowed by self-doubt and consciousness of his 'errors and wrecks'. In rare public utterances he condemned *The Cantos* as a failure, a view he seems not consistently to have held; but the poem was never completed. In 1969 he concluded its publication with *Drafts and Fragments of Cantos CX–CXVII*: thirty-two pages of verse, mostly serene but poignant in its fragmentation.

Pound was the central figure in the modern movement, personally responsible for the renewal of English poetry in the 1910s. Yet he remains a controversial figure. His brutal politics have been damaging to his lofty view of the artist and civilization; he is also condemned as an élitist, an obscurantist, and a charlatan—a man deficient in self-knowledge, with no real understanding of the modern world despite his avant-gardiste posturing. None of these charges quite shakes the substance of his achievement, which is fundamentally a matter of technical accomplishment to a point where refinement of skill becomes a moral quality. Such is the sensitivity of his verse movement that it seems to release independent life and otherness in his subjects, as if it had discovered them by chance. This is so whether he seeks to evoke the movement of olive leaves in the wind or the character of a Renaissance *condottiere*. The same quality lies behind his genius for translation, an art he has been said to have invented for our time: uncannily, he creates a language for each author which registers the remoteness of the author from our world while at the same time making his work available to us. If Pound is obscure, it is largely because of his wide frame of reference; he was also an educator, who used poetry to introduce his readers to works and ideas he had discovered for himself. It is hardly his fault that his syllabus has never been adopted.

Pound's poetry is collected in two volumes: *Collected Shorter Poems* (London, 1984)—the American edition is entitled *Personae: Collected Poems* (New York, 1971)—and *The Cantos of Ezra Pound* (New York, 1972; London, 1981). *The Translations of Ezra Pound*, ed. Hugh Kenner (New York and London, 1953), is a large selection with major omissions. The *Literary Essays of Ezra Pound*, ed. T. S. Eliot (London and New York, 1954), suggests the scope of his criticism, while *Selected Prose, 1909–1965*, ed. William Cookson (London and New York, 1973), includes much of his polemical writing as well. The fullest biography is Humphrey Carpenter, *A Serious Character* (London, 1988), though it has been severely criticized. See also two critical introductions: Hugh Kenner, *The Poetry of Ezra Pound* (London and Norfolk, Conn., 1951) and Donald Davie, *Ezra Pound: Poet as Sculptor*, now reprinted in *Studies in Ezra Pound* (Manchester, 1991). [CW

POWELL, Craig (1940–), was born in Wollongong, New South Wales, graduated in medicine from Sydney University in 1965, and went on to qualify as a psychiatrist. In 1972 he left Australia and spent ten years in Manitoba and Ontario, Canada. He returned to Sydney in 1982, where he practises psychiatry.

Powell won the Australian *Poetry Magazine* Award in 1964 and two years later published *A Different Kind of Breathing*, the first of seven collections of poetry. These include *I Learn by Going* (1968), *A Country without Exiles* (1972), *Rehearsal for Dancers* (1978), and *A Face in Your Hands* (1984). In 1983 he was awarded the Mattara Poetry Prize.

Powell's poetry, influenced by the ideas of the Chicago analyst Heinz Kohut, expresses a tragic view of existence. Many of his poems develop around people he has come to know in his profession as a psychiatrist. The central section of *A Country without Exiles* consists of compassionate portraits of the inmates of a mental hospital. Powell has also written a number of poems to fellow poets, including Francis *Webb, reflecting on the emotional and spiritual sources of poetry. His accounts of personal experience and that of the characters he recreates balance the imperfections of human nature against an affirmation of shared humanity.

See *Selected Poems 1963–1977* (London, Ont., 1978), and *The Ocean Remembers It Is Visible: Poems 1966–1989* (Princeton, NJ, 1989), and for criticism, 'One Person Speaking Truthfully', *Poetry Australia*, 92 (1984); 'The Language of the Poem', *The Phoenix Review*, 3 (1988); and an interview, 'Tenderness Towards Existence', *Poetry Australia*, 107/108 (1986). [PK

POWYS, John Cowper (1872–1963), is the subject of a long-standing dispute: is he an unduly neglected master, or an extravagantly verbose and largely empty writer—or a mixture of both? This dispute centres, however, on the status of his novels, which are regarded as either major or monstrosities. He began as a poet (*Odes and Other Poems*, London, 1896), but there is little that is suggestive of, or gives much clue to, the nature of his later achievements in either this volume or its successors: *Samphire* (New York, 1922) and *Lucifer* (published in 1956 but written in 1906). There is not much sign of the eccentricity, wildness, and other-worldliness of the prose in Powys's late Victorian volumes of verse, although Kenneth Hopkins in *John Cowper Powys: A Selection from his Poems* (London, 1964) makes a modest claim for them.

[MS-S

PRATT, E(dwin) J(ohn) (1882–1964), was born in Western Bay, Newfoundland. He was an ordained Methodist minister and long-serving member of the English department at Victoria College in the University of Toronto, from which he retired in 1953. Educated in schools in Newfoundland, Pratt attended the University of

Toronto from which he received a BA and MA, and a Ph.D. He also held a degree in divinity.

A self-described 'writer of tragic situations relating to the sea', Pratt established a reputation as a poet of strong conventional rhythms which lent themselves readily to the telling of his 'story-poems'. A convivial yarn-spinner and friendly presence on the poetry scene in Canada in the first half of the twentieth century, Pratt exerted considerable influence on fellow writers, publishers, and magazine editors of this period. He was founding editor (1936–43) of the *Canadian Poetry Magazine*, and a prominent member of the Canadian Authors' Association, and he was awarded many medals, distinctions, and honorary degrees for his services to Canadian writing in his role as chronicler of the heroics and the history of the raw Canadian experience.

Newfoundland Verse (1923), Pratt's first collection, gives evidence of the essentially traditional approach of this poet to his art. It was followed by *The Witches Brew* (1925) which, in style and content, announces Pratt's whimsical interest in primordial creatures and conflict on an epic scale. The behaviour of man in heroic and self-sacrificing conflict with forces of nature, ideology, or history greater than himself became the substance of much of his work from the 1930s onwards. *The Roosevelt and the Antinoe* (1930) deals with rescue at sea; *The Fable of the Goats and Other Poems* (1932) frames that bellicose decade; while *The Titanic* (1935) is a study in the hubristic arrogance of technological man. In 1940 Pratt published *Brébeuf and his Brethren*, a narrative concerned with the clash of Christianity and Amerindian culture. During the war and immediately thereafter Pratt produced four collections of verse—*Dunkirk* (1941), *Still Life and Other Verse* (1943), *They Are Returning* (1945), *Behind the Log* (1947)—which were overtly patriotic and celebratory of the allied war effort, as well as his first *Collected Poems* which appeared in 1944. In 1952 Pratt published *Towards the Last Spike*, aptly described in the subtitle as a verse panorama of the struggle to build the first Canadian transcontinental railway. 1958 saw the publication of *The Collected Poems of E. J. Pratt*

(Toronto), with an introduction by Northrop Frye who had been one of Pratt's students.

In spite of his reliance on traditional verse-patterns and rhythms, his tendency to see life in terms of a slightly dated equation of struggle and redemption, and his predisposition to robust story-telling in his poems, Pratt remains a compelling and influential figure in twentieth-century Canadian poetry.   [MG

PREWETT, Frank (James 'Toronto') (1893–1962), was born in Kenilworth, near Mount Forest, Ontario, on his maternal grandfather's pioneer farm. He was raised in Toronto and educated at the University of Toronto, and later at Christ Church, Oxford. During the First World War he was transferred from the Canadian Expeditionary Force to the Royal Artillery, wounded and shell-shocked in April 1918, and sent to Lennels near Coldstream, Scotland, where he was placed under the care of the psychologist/anthropologist W. H. R. Rivers. There Prewett met Siegfried *Sassoon who introduced him to the literary figures and circles associated with both war-writing and the later *Georgian poetry, including Robert *Graves, Edmund *Blunden, Wilfred *Owen, and Lady Ottoline Morrell and the Garsington circle.

Prewett stands apart from other 'Georgian' poets in two respects: that he was the only Canadian to participate in the stylistic movement (Edward Marsh included eight of Prewett's poems in *Georgian Poetry 1920–1922*); and that his images are shaped not by the gentility of English nature but by the exacting harshness of the Canadian environment and the war.

Prewett's first volume, *Poems* (1920), handset by Virginia Woolf and published by the Hogarth Press, contains many of the poet's finest trench verses, such as 'Voices of Women', 'The Somme Valley, 1917', and 'Burial Stones', interspersed with more truly 'Georgian' poems of bucolic landscapes observed during his recuperation. A second volume, *The Rural Scene* (1924), continued many of the themes of love, death, and nature that Prewett had explored in his previous collection.

Prewett died in poverty and obscurity in 1962 and was buried in Inverness. See *Collected Poems of Frank Prewett* (London, 1964); *The Selected Poems of Frank Prewett*, ed. Bruce Meyer and Barry Callaghan (1987); Bruce Meyer, *Profiles in Canadian Literature: Frank Prewett* (1991); Andrew Coppolino, 'A Canadian in the Garsington Circle: Frank Prewett's Literary Friendships,' *Studies in Canadian Literature*, 12: 2 (1987).

[BM

PRINCE, F(rank) T(empleton) (1912–), was born in South Africa. He was educated there and at Oxford and Princeton universities. During the Second World War he served in Army Intelligence. From 1957 to 1974 he was professor of English at Southampton University. In 1973 he gave the Clark Lectures at Cambridge. His critical works include *The Italian Element in Milton's Verse* (1954) and *William Shakespeare: The Poems* (1963).

Prince's best-known single poem is probably the personal and deeply Christian 'Soldiers Bathing', which was first collected in the volume of that title in 1954. By the year of publication (1963) of his *The Doors of Stone*, the good Prince poem is readily definable. It is well made; it tends to be long; the poet projects his imagination into the realities of named people (e.g. Edmund Burke, the Zulu king Chaka, Michelangelo); the clarity and subtlety of perception challenges the reader's attentiveness and willingness to think, albeit within a familiar context of mainstream ideas and attitudes.

Beginning in 1970, Prince has given us a succession of long poems, each amounting to several hundred lines. Much of this later work confirms the trends already indicated. Some of the pieces are informed with a remarkable idealism, a concern with the possibility and fact of self-transcendence, which is traditional in that its roots are in Plato, Shelley, Judaism, and Christianity, but original in its personal presence, its particular statements and fervour. The derivation and overt subject-matter of such writings might be pre-judged as bookish (c.f. the titles *Drypoints of the Hasidim* and *Afterword on Rupert Brooke*), but in fact the poetry impinges

urgently on ethical, moral, and religious aspects of daily reality. Yet it is not didactic: it is concerned with spiritual work in progress, not with the exposition of finalized wisdom.

Prince is an outstanding craftsman, as can be seen from even cursory attention to his prosody. This includes free verse of exemplary precision in the placing and relative emphasis of stressed syllables, lively but 'natural' iambics, and *syllabics (based on *Bridges) whose arithmetical count does not prejudice the verve of English speech.

The *Collected Poems* (London and New York) of 1979 was revised and brought up to date in 1992.

[WGS

Projective Verse is a formal designation most famously developed by Charles *Olson in his 1950 essay of that name. Though the essay had considerable impact at the time, setting forth the poetics of what came to be known as the *Black Mountain school while elaborating principles that had already been announced and put into practice by older poets like *Pound and William Carlos *Williams, the term has not generally been adopted for descriptive purposes; critics and poets tend to prefer simpler labels like 'open form' to designate the kind of poetry Olson champions in his essay.

What the term 'projective' conveys that 'open' does not is the heavy emphasis that Olson and his Black Mountain associates laid on the kinetics of poetic form. For Olson the poem is a 'high energy-construct' that embodies or enacts 'the *process* of the thing'. Olson's own verse offers an especially clear illustration of how all the elements of the poem—typography, rhythm, syntax, the page as 'field of action'—can be mobilized to create a strong sense of movement or forward thrust. For Olson two factors are crucial in allowing the poet to translate the moment-by-moment process of composition into language. One is the poet's own breathing, which Olson insists must generate the poem's shape and rhythms; the other is the typewriter (Olson assumes that modern poets compose on it), which allows for a precise mechanical registering of 'the intervals of its composition'. This peculiar combination of the organic and the technological lies at the heart of Olson's poetics, and may suggest some of the contradictions lurking within it. But the real problem with Olson's conception of projective verse is its abstract formalism; to make a poem that embodies the process of its composition may be worthwhile, but it does not guarantee that the poem will have a specific value of its own. None the less, Olson's essay considerably enlarged poets' thinking about the possibilities of form, and so deserves credit for some of the more exciting developments of the 1950s and 1960s. The essay may be read in *The Poetics of the New American Poetry* (New York, 1973).   [RG

PROKOSCH, Frederic (1906–89), was born in Madison, Wisconsin, and educated at Haverford College, King's College, Cambridge, and Yale. His father was a professor at Yale and wished him to take up an academic career; but, following the success of his novel, *The Asiatics*, in 1930, Prokosch travelled widely and devoted himself entirely to writing. His first book of poems, *The Assassins* (1936), was followed by *The Carnival* (1938), *Death at Sea* (1940), and *Chosen Poems* (London, 1944; New York, 1948), which was to be his last collection; though a few poems have since been published privately. He is best known for his numerous novels. His translations include *Some Poems of Friedrich Hölderlin* (1943) and the *Medea* of Euripides (1947). His memoirs, *Voices*, appeared in 1983.

Prokosch's poetry is accomplished and initially impressive. Its diction is fresh and contemporary, and there is an underlying unease reminiscent of *Auden; but one senses a discontinuity between the often brilliant images and the containing vision of the poems, which sometimes seems contrived and commonplace. He is sampled best in *Chosen Poems*. *Frederic Prokosch*, by Radcliffe Squires (New York, 1964) is a valuable study.   [ATT

PRYNNE, J(eremy) H(alvard) (1936–), was born in England and is a university lecturer in English at Cambridge. His name has become synonymous, for some, with all that is most rebarbative in the work of the contemporary English avant-garde. Yet of all the writers who might fit that description he has attracted the most widespread notice and approval. His originality and ambition are evident, and the fact that these are conveyed in pungent phrasing and a free verse of evident craft has commanded a fascination and a willingness to work at his meaning. He is the subject of respectful discussion in Donald *Davie's *Thomas Hardy and British Poetry* (1973), and his collected works, *Poems* (Edinburgh and London, 1983), were well received.

Prynne's handling of free verse is similar to that of Charles *Olson, about whom he has written. Like Olson he sets out to trace the movement of the mind before it becomes subject to the tidying-up of secondary formulations: 'The first essential is to take knowledge | back to the springs'—which simultaneously refers to the subjective source and to the historical past. Also like Olson, he is unafraid of the discursive. In this mode he delights to explore the mutual dependence of the economic, the social, and the subjective, as in 'Sketch for a Financial Theory of the Self' (*Kitchen Poems*, 1968). He conveys a sense of the mind working at an intellectual problem on the spot, complete with various highly adventurous quirks of thought and expression which would be out of place in a straightforwardly discursive poem. He can be accessible in this manner, as in certain poems in *The White Stones* (1969), such as 'Acquisition of Love' or 'Questions for the Time Being', but the archaeology of thought can lead to poems where the associations are so incongruous and unfathomable as to seem arbitrary. Such works are probably best seen as variations on the modern tradition of collage, and as opportunities for the reader to exercise a playfully inventive role. In this respect Prynne looks less like the vitalist Olson, and more akin to the early *Ashbery.   [ETL

PUDNEY, John (Sleigh) (1909–77), was born in Langley, Buckinghamshire, and educated at Gresham's School, Holt. During the Second World War he served with the Royal Air Force.

433

He worked for the BBC, and for the *News Chronicle* and other newspapers, and was a director of the publishers Putnam.

The war was his most prolific period as a poet; and his 'For Johnny' was one of the best-known war poems. His *Selected Poems* (1947) was one of the first books in the wide-circulation Guild Books. In the fifteen years following the war he wrote eight novels, two volumes of short stories, and many books on aviation history and other subjects. He returned to poetry with *Spill Out* (1967) and *Spandrels* (1969).

His wartime poems often captured the emotional feel of being involved in the war; but little of the particularity of wartime experience comes through the conventional rhetorical gestures he seems drawn to in his serious poetry. He is best in his lighter, less adventurous pieces, where directness and natural diction are his strengths. He may be sampled in *Selected Poems* (London, 1973).   [ATT

Pulitzer Prizes, were established in 1917 under the terms of the will of the American newspaper proprietor Joseph Pulitzer. The original awards, which were confined to American citizens, were given annually for journalism and literature; the prizes for poetry were inaugurated in 1922, although special poetry prizes had been awarded in 1918 and 1919. Winners include Edna St Vincent *Millay, Robert *Frost (three times), Amy *Lowell, Conrad *Aiken, Robert *Lowell, W. H. *Auden, Marianne *Moore, Wallace *Stevens, Elizabeth *Bishop, Richard *Wilbur, W. C. *Williams, John *Berryman, Anne *Sexton, John *Ashbery, and Sylvia *Plath. Other names have proved less enduring: Margaret Widdemer, Leonora Speyer, George Dillon (who collaborated with Edna Millay in translating Baudelaire), Audrey Wurdemann, and Robert Coffin.   [POM

PURCELL, Sally (Anne Jane) (1944–), read Medieval French at Lady Margaret Hall, Oxford, and has since published a translation of Dante's *De vulgari eloquentia* (*Literature in the Vernacular*, Manchester, 1981) and an edition of *The Poems of Charles of Orleans* (Manchester, 1973). Her versions of Provençal troubadour poems appeared in 1969, and her own poetry has depended closely on the classical and medieval legends she grew up studying. Precise, stylized evocations of Queen Proserpina or Merlin have dominated her work from *The Devil's Dancing Hour* (London, 1968) and *The Holly Queen* (London, 1972) to *By the Clear Fountain* (Bath, 1980), *Guenever and the Looking Glass* (Warwick, 1984), and *Lake and Labyrinth* (Durham, 1985); while her poems have always exploited the superstition inherent in their subjects, they have also increasingly emphasized intricate, occasionally precious patterns of reflection operating between the landscapes of her poems and the characters who inhabit them. Her lyrics have been criticized as a little too ethereal, and for their avoidance of the earthier physical realities of the situations they conjure; if one of her *Four Poems* (Leamington, 1985) is to be believed, however, Purcell prefers to see 'God's pattern | linking all the gardens'.

                     [MRW

PURDY, Al(fred) (Wellington) (1918–), was born at Wooler, Ontario, a hamlet near Lake Ontario. His father, a farmer of United Empire Loyalist stock, died when Purdy was 2; the boy was then raised by his religious mother in the nearby city of Trenton. After leaving school, Purdy worked at a variety of jobs in Trenton, Belleville, Vancouver, and Montreal. He also served in the Royal Canadian Air Force from 1940 to 1944. In recent years, he has lived at Roblin Lake, near Trenton. Although he brought out his first book of poems in 1944, his reputation as a poet was not securely established until the publication of *The Cariboo Horses* (Toronto, 1965). He has been the recipient of several Canada Council grants and has been appointed a writer-in-residence at a number of Canadian universities.

While Purdy's poetic world includes places as remote as the Cariboo country of central British Columbia, villages in the Canadian Arctic, and the 'long road' to Newfoundland, the rural landscape around Trenton figures most significantly in his verse. Much of the charm of his poetry lies in the variety and extravagance of its descriptive detail, its somewhat folksy similes, and its sudden turns of thought. He typically subordinates his poetic lines to the casual, emergent syntax of colloquial speech. In many of his poems, a past and a present state of affairs are contrasted nostalgically.

Most of Purdy's poetry can be found in *The Collected Poems of Al Purdy* (Toronto, 1986) and *The Woman on the Shore* (Toronto, 1990). His many publications include his edition of a collection of statements by Canadians on their attitudes towards the United States, *The New Romans* (New York and Edmonton, 1968); a collection of semi-autobiographical essays, *No Other Country* (Toronto, 1977); and an historical novel, *A Splinter in the Heart* (Toronto, 1990). For critical comments and biographical information, see Laurie Ricou, 'Al Purdy', *Profiles in Canadian Literature*, 2, ed. Jeffrey M. Heath (Toronto, 1980). [JSt

PUTNAM, H. Phelps (1894–1948), was born and raised near Boston, Massachusetts. After graduating from Yale he worked as a miner in Colorado, as a bureaucrat in Washington, and as an advertising copy-writer in Boston, and travelled in Europe during the heady years following the First World War, before publishing *Trinc* (New York, 1927), a collection notable for several haunting short stories in verse, one of which, 'Ballad of a Strange Thing', a retelling of the fable of Pan and Syrinx set in the Massachusetts countryside, is perhaps his single most accomplished poem. When *Trinc* came out he was planning an epic of modern life to be modelled on Dante, and his next book, *The Five Seasons* (New York, 1931), introduces the protagonist, a wanderer named Bill Williams, and his Virgilian *alter ego*, Hasbrouck. But the poem never went any further, in part because Putnam seems to have been overwhelmed by his own ambition, and in part because of his worsening health. Asthmatic from an early age, he spent much of the Twenties and Thirties in the south-western United States, but the asthma eventually weakened his heart and he died of a stroke after seventeen years of writing little and publishing less.

See *The Collected Poems of H. Phelps Putnam*, ed. Charles L. Walker (New York, 1971).

[RH

Q

QUENNELL, Sir Peter (Courtney) (1905–93), was born in London. He is best known as a critic, but for a brief period in his earliest career was held to be a poet of high promise. 'The Sunflower' appeared in many anthologies. Accomplished poems appeared in Marsh's *Georgian poetry anthology while he was still at school, and he published *Masques and Anti-Masques* (Waltham St Lawrence, 1922) at the age of 17. This was followed by *Poems* (London, 1926), the New York edition (1930) of which added Quennell's Ariel poem, 'Inscription on a Fountainhead'. It is clear that the author of these rather stately and elaborate verses was sensitive to modernism, although it was more the limited modernism of *Graves and *Riding than that of *Pound or *Eliot; but he was not committed to it, nor, perhaps, to anything more than the development of a sophisticated style.

[MS-S

R

RAFAT, Taufiq (1927–), was born in Sialkot and educated in Lahore. His first collection, *Arrival of the Monsoon* (Lahore), appeared only in 1985. He has also translated two Punjabi folk poets, Bulleh Shah (1680–1758) and Qadir Yar (1802–50).

Rafat is not prolific—*Arrival of the Monsoon* has 116 poems written over thirty years (1947–78)—but he has an easy, entertaining way of describing local customs, rituals, and seasonal festivities. Dull or exotic (according to the reader's point of view), the work invites anthropological interest: see 'Eve of Eid-ul-Azha', 'The Kite-flyers', 'Sacrifice', and 'Arrival of the Monsoon'. In these the craftsmanship is deft and the line is generally uncluttered and colloquial. Rafat writes mainly in the narrative-descriptive mode, but sometimes lapses into abstract moralizing. The social facts in 'Sialkot Bombed', 'Kitchens', 'Circumcision', and 'Divorce' are familiar, and the anti-Western sneers are comfortably populist: 'Their divorce is final | but they still meet by appointment | and are helpful and friendly to each other. | They call it civilized behaviour.'   [SbinH

RAGO, Henry. See POETRY.

RAINE, Craig (1944–), was born at Shildon, Co. Durham. His father, Norman Edward Raine, appears in the prose centre-piece of the 1984 collection *Rich* as a one-time boxer who once beat Olympic featherweight champion Otto Kästner, and latterly as a jack-of-all-trades, raconteur, spiritualist and faith-healer. His mother, Olive Marie Raine, is portrayed as an intense, Lawrentian woman; poems in *A Mart-*ian Sends a Postcard Home describe her dressmaking or at Roman Catholic mass.

Raine attended Barnard Castle School and Exeter College, Oxford. Subsequently he obtained a B.Phil. at Oxford (1968) and read for a D.Phil. on Coleridge (abandoned in 1973). From 1971 to 1981 Raine combined periods of teaching at Oxford colleges with work on the *New Review, Quarto,* and the *New Statesman.* Critical work dating from that time is collected with essays of the 1980s in *Haydn and the Valve Trumpet* (1990). From 1981 to 1991 Raine was poetry editor at Faber & Faber and is now a fellow of New College, Oxford. In 1972 he married Ann Pasternak Slater.

Raine's first two collections of poems, *The Onion, Memory* (Oxford, 1978) and *A Martian Sends a Postcard Home* (Oxford, 1979), accompanied competition successes and attracted a great deal of attention. His hallmark in both books was vitality in metaphor and simile. Some critics complained of an over-reliance on ostentatious effects; others defended the plurality and vigour of Raine's imagination. James *Fenton and others saw Raine as the founder of the *Martian school, which took a fresh, transforming look at the everyday. *A Free Translation* (Edinburgh 1981) and *Rich* (London, 1984) were as strikingly inventive (and tender, even sentimental) as the debut volumes. They also demonstrated once again Raine's affinity with the modernist writers he has repeatedly written on (*Eliot, *Joyce, *Stevens). Since *Rich* Raine has written two adaptations for the stage: *The Electrification of the Soviet Union* (London, 1986), an opera libretto after a novella by Pasternak, and '*1953*' (London, 1990), a version of Racine's *Andromaque.*

437

Useful studies of Raine's work include Michael Hulse, 'Alms for every beggared sense: Craig Raine's aesthetic in context', *Critical Quarterly*, 23: 4 (1981); Charles Forceville, 'Craig Raine's Poetry of Perception: Imagery in *A Martian Sends a Postcard Home*', *Dutch Quarterly Review*, 15: 1 (1985); the feature (various authors) in *Ploughshares*, 17: 3 (1987); and Alan Robinson, *Instabilities in Contemporary British Poetry* (Basingstoke and London, 1988). [MHu

RAINE, Kathleen (1908–), was born in London but spent much of her childhood in Northumberland. She took her MA in Natural Sciences at Girton College, at a time when the Thirties generation of Cambridge poets, including *Empson, *Bottrall, and Charles *Madge (who became her husband), was beginning to make its mark. Cambridge, however, was not a formative influence on her work, and she felt she had to break free of its analytic and scientific ethos before finding her own poetic voice. During a long and prolific career she has produced ten volumes of poetry, the first two, *Stone and Flower* (1943) and *Living in Time* (1945) appearing under Tambimuttu's *Poetry London* imprint. Her poetry criticism includes volumes on Coleridge, Hopkins, and *Yeats, and she is particularly noted for her Blake scholarship. She has so far produced three volumes of autobiography and, since 1981, has been a co-editor of the little magazine, *Temenos*.

Influenced by Swedenborg and the Neo-Platonists, Kathleen Raine is interested in archetypal forms of being. Her work is in many ways the polar opposite of *Imagism and the notion of 'no ideas but in things'. Though the natural world is important to her, 'things' for Raine are only the beginning. The appeal to the big, abstract ideas of time, eternity, and so on, and the constantly elevated tone produce a somewhat amorphous effect, more sacred text than life-study.

The *Selected Poems* of 1988 (Ipswich; Rochester, Vt., 1989) covers her career fairly generously, if less fully than the *Collected Poems* of 1981 (London) which includes, together with work from the two volumes mentioned above,

poems from all her collections up to *The Cathedral in the Heart* (1979). Her most recent single volume of verse is *The Presence* (Ipswich and Rochester, Vt., 1987). [CAR

RAKOSI, Carl (name legally changed to Callman Rawley) (1903–), the son of Hungarian nationals, was born in Berlin and went to the United States in 1910. His family settled in Wisconsin, where he was raised. He majored in social work at the University of Wisconsin at Madison, which led to a lifelong career in the social-welfare field.

While still a student Rakosi had begun writing poetry, and by the late 1920s *Pound was taking his poems for the *Exile* and the *Literary Review*. *Zukofsky, recognizing Rakosi's clear, distinctive voice, championed his work and included him in the important *'Objectivist' issue of *Poetry* magazine and the subsequent *An 'Objectivists' Anthology*. After having published actively throughout the late Thirties Rakosi, like many politically left-wing American writers of the period, became disillusioned with writing and gave up poetry. In 1965, at the urgings of the young British poet Andrew Crozier, Rakosi took up poetry again, producing the vast bulk of his work, including much aphoristic prose and autobiography, by which he is known.

Rakosi's poetry, marked by clarity and a quiet, yet compelling intensity, is a form of American plainsong. His work, broad in scope, ranges from poems of deep, meditational seriousness, like 'Association with a View from the House' or 'Yaddo', to the probing, often hilarious social commentary of his 'Americana' series, a sustained poetic rendering of American mores, politics, and polyvocalisms.

The fullest editions of Rakosi's work are *The Collected Poems of Carl Rakosi* (1986) and *The Collected Prose of Carl Rakosi* (1983—both Orono, Me.). See also *Conviction's Net of Branches: Essays on the Objectivist Poets and Poetry* (Carbondale, Ill., 1985), by Michael Heller.

[MH

RAMANUJAN, A(ttipat) K(rishnaswami) (1929–93), born and educated in Mysore, was a fellow of Deccan College, 1958–9, and Fulbright Scholar at Indiana University, 1960–2. He has been at the University of Chicago since 1962, where he is now William E. Colvin Professor in the departments of South Asian Languages and Civilizations, and Linguistics. Besides being a distinguished translator of poetry and prose in Tamil and Kannada—notable, especially, are his translations from classical Tamil verse, *Speaking of Siva* (London, 1972) and *Poems of Love and War* (New York, 1985)—he is one of the most consistently rewarding of the Indian poets writing in English. Though his output is relatively small, he seems to have created, in his three books of poems, *The Striders* (London and New York, 1966), *Relations* (London, 1971), and *Second Sight* (New Delhi and New York, 1986), a recognizably 'Ramanujanesque' world from the dailiness of South Indian small-town life, populated with relations and Hindu gods.

There is a sense of rootedness in Ramanujan's poetry, which often exists in tension with the curious and anxious sense of cultural displacement an educated post-colonial Indian sometimes feels. His involvement with Indian culture is, in all senses of the word, intimate: both deeply knowledgeable and loving; it is an involvement he allows to filter into, and enrich, his English verse. By his own definition, there are two genres in South Indian Kannada folklore: *akam* consists of narratives or songs performed by women inside the house, usually describing familial relationships; *puram* genres are performed in public by men, and describe battles, and historical and communal events. If we extend this distinction to his poetry, we find that Ramanujan is an *akam* poet, and that his best poems—such as 'Small-scale Reflections on a Great House', 'Still Another for Mother', 'History'—deal with domestic interiors and the fabric of family life; it is also perhaps no accident that many of the protagonists of his poems are women—mothers, grandmothers, cousins, and aunts. The tone of his poetry is tolerantly humorous, ostensibly unambitious, but fastidiously accurate in evoking surface-texture and detail; a seemingly innocent detail in an anecdote—a grain of rice on a kitchen floor, the noise of his father slapping soap on his back during a bath—might set off intangible echoes and resonances. [AC

RAMKE, Bin (1947–), was born in Port Neches, Texas. Educated at Ohio University, Ramke has taught at Columbus College in Georgia and the University of Denver in Colorado.

Ramke is a regionalist: his scenarios—domestic, romantic, and sexual—are generally set in the southern and south-western United States. Concentrating on this segment of American society, Ramke's responses are intelligent and humane. He relies upon imagery to carry meaning; he rarely editorializes. When he does allow himself the luxury of comment, he usually means it as just that—comment, not pronouncement.

Ramke's books include *The Erotic Light of Gardens* (Boston and London, 1989), *The Language Student* (Baton Rouge, La., and London, 1986), *White Monkeys* (Baton Rouge and London, 1981), and *The Difference Between Night and Day* (New Haven, Conn., and London, 1978). [RS

RANASINGHE, Anne(liese Katz) (1925–), born of a German-speaking Jewish family in Essen, left Germany for England in January 1939. Her parents and most of her family circle died in Nazi concentration camps. Her education, begun in Cologne, was completed at Parkstone Girls' Grammar School in Britain.

Ranasinghe trained as a nurse in London, studied journalism, and speaks five languages. Settling in Colombo following her marriage in 1949 to a Sri Lankan physician, she began writing poetry in 1968 and published her first poems in 1971. Her experience of the Nazi holocaust helped her to write of Sri Lanka's 1971 insurrection in powerful poems that have imparted a new strength to Sri Lankan poetry, especially that written by women.

Writing articles about Hitler's Germay for a Sri Lankan newspaper, Ranasinghe began a journey back into her past which culminated in a return to Essen in 1983 that has profoundly influenced her subsequent writing. She has won several awards and prizes, including the Sri Lanka Arts Council Prize for Poetry (1985). Her publications, all printed in Colombo, include *Poems* (1971), *With Words We Write Our Lives Past Present Future* (1972), *Plead Mercy* (1976), *Love, Sex and Parenthood* (1977), *Of Charred-Wood Midnight-Fear* (1983), *Against Eternity and Darkness* (1985), and *Not Even Shadows* (1989). Her work has been translated into four languages, and is included in Y. Gooneratne (ed.), *Poems From India, Sri Lanka, Malaysia and Singapore* (Hong Kong, 1979). See also Le Roy Robinson, 'An Interview with Anne Ranasinghe', *Annual Review of Economics*, 6 (Nagasaki, Mar. 1990).

[YG

RANKIN, Jennifer (1941–79), born Jennifer Mary Haynes in Sydney, grew up there and at a small property near Mittagong. She graduated from Sydney University, where she had been a fringe-member of the Downtown Push, a loose group of artists, bohemians, and libertarians which included Clive *James and Germaine Greer.

With her first husband, John Roberts, she lived in Adelaide and later Canberra. She then lived briefly with the novelist Frank Moorhouse before marrying David Rankin, an artist, in 1969. Her earliest poems, fostered by friendships with Robert *Adamson, John *Tranter, and others of the *'Generation of '68', date from this period, although her first collection, *Ritual Shift*, did not appear until 1976.

Although her later poetry shows traces of Ted *Hughes, Margaret *Atwood, and Galway *Kinnell, she had already a distinctive style. *Earth Hold* was published in London in 1978. At the time of her death from cancer a third collection, *The Mud Hut*, had just appeared in *Exile* in Canada.

Her short career and the dispersed nature of her publication has retarded the growth of Rankin's reputation. Her *Collected Poems* (St Lucia, Qld., 1990), however, was hailed as revealing one of the most significant Australian poets of the 1970s.

[DBr

RANSOM, John Crowe (1888–1974). Associated with the American South, Ransom was an early member of the group of writers known as *Fugitives, many of whom met at Vanderbilt University in the period after the First World War (in which he served as a lieutenant). Born in Pulaski, Tennessee, Ransom received his AB from Vanderbilt in 1909; he was afterwards a Rhodes Scholar at Christ Church, Oxford, from which he took another degree in 1913. In his poem, 'Philomela' he describes how unimpressed he was with the famous song of the nightingale while walking with some Oxford students in Bagley Wood.

Ransom's reaction against the nightingale is typical of his anti-Romantic, neoclassical stance as a poet—a stance he shared with T. S. *Eliot and other modernists. Unlike Eliot, however, Ransom was deeply committed to his native region, and he returned to his home state of Tennessee to teach at Vanderbilt, where he remained until 1937 and where he met Robert Penn *Warren, Allen *Tate, Donald *Davidson, and Randall *Jarrell, all of whom considered him a friend and mentor.

The Fugitives had much in common with T. S. Eliot, though Ransom personally disliked his poetry. Eliot declared himself a classicist, a Catholic, and a royalist, and there are echoes of this in Ransom's self-description: 'In manners, aristocratic; in religion, ritualistic; in art, traditional.' In his first critical work, *God Without Thunder* (1930), Ransom urged the return to religious values, suggesting that a belief in the supernatural was necessary if one wished to 'represent the fullness of the natural'. In returning to religion, Ransom stressed the importance of orthodoxy, advocating 'a virile and concrete God', also described as 'the Demigod who came to do honour to the God'. The son of a minister, Ransom seemed very like a typical Southern fundamentalist in this early prose work; he modified this view somewhat in *The World's Body* (1938), where he was less prescriptive and, in the tradition of Matthew Arnold, saw poetry as taking on many of the tasks formerly performed by religion. In another important book of prose essays, *The New Criticism* (1941), Ransom argued for an 'ontological critic' who could show the ways in which the logical structure of poetry embodied the world by summoning creation in all its variegated detail and natural, organic form.

This organic theory of poetry was illustrated perfectly by the poems. As Robert Penn Warren once noted, Ransom is a critic whose theories of poetry and poems uniquely mirror each other. There is, in fact, a decidedly academic, if not archaic, quality apparent in Ransom's poetry. Critics have, variously, described his poems as 'metaphysical' and 'formalist', both terms which fit rather well, although there is an unruly energy in Ransom's finest poems, such as 'Janet Waking', 'The Equilibrists', or 'Bells for John Whiteside's Daughter'.

Ransom was not a prolific poet. He published three relatively slim books of verse between 1919 and 1927; after that he turned his attention largely to criticism and to editing the *Kenyon Review*, which he founded at Kenyon College, Ohio, where he taught from 1937 until his retirement in 1959. Nevertheless, Ransom's poetry has consistently attracted interest for its poise, its idiosyncratic language, its cultivated obliquity, and its wry humour.

The inevitability and pity of human failure and the evanescence of life are primary subjects for Ransom, and the elegy is his most natural form, as in 'Here Lies a Lady', which begins: 'Here lies a lady of beauty and high degree, | Of chills and fever she died, of fever and chills, | The delight of her husband, an aunt, an infant of three | And medicos marveling sweetly on her ills.' In 'Blue Girls' Ransom describes the pampered young students of a seminary for girls, advising them: 'Practise your beauty, blue girls, before it fail.' The poem ends with a typical Ransom twist: 'For I could tell you a story which is true; | I know a woman with a terrible tongue, | Blue eyes fallen from blue, | All her perfections tarnished—yet it is not long | Since she was lovelier than any of you.'

Summing up the work of Ransom, Robert Penn Warren said that his old teacher's prose and poetry together amounted to 'a celebration of life, as manifested in the virtues of charity and endurance, tenderness and gaiety'. These deeply human values shine through Ransom's small but luminous body of writing. For selections, see Ransom's *Selected Poems* (New York, 1963) and *Selected Essays* (Baton Rouge, La., 1984). A *Selected Poems* was published in Manchester in 1991. There is a good biography of Ransom, *Gentleman in a Dustcoat*, by Thomas Daniel Young (Baton Rouge, 1976). For criticism, see Miller Williams, *The Poetry of John Crowe Ransom* (New Brunswick, NJ, 1972) and Thornton H. Parsons, *John Crowe Ransom* (Boston, 1969). [JP

RATTENBURY, Arnold (1921–), was born in China, where his father served as a Wesleyan minister. He was educated at Kingswood School, and while there became friendly with such kindred spirits as E. P. Thompson and Geoffrey Matthews. He then proceeded to Cambridge University. However, the outbreak of the Second World War put an end to his formal education. War service came to a premature end in 1943, and in the following years Rattenbury was first an editor at *Our Time* and *Theatre Today* and then an exhibition designer, which he remains.

Rattenbury's first volume of poems, *Second Causes* (London, 1969), is notable for its close weave of social satire and political vision. Like many of his generation Rattenbury had early become a Marxist but he has never reneged on his ideals or thought it appropriate to apologize for them. His poems are often prompted by an angry contempt for social arrangements that commit the majority of people to thwarted lives; but his wit and relish for the things that make up the observable world keep his work well clear of didacticism. This is apparent in his second collection *Man Thinking* (Nottingham, 1972), with its epigraph taken from a letter of Gorky's to Chekhov: 'I'm a very rough, clumsy man and my soul is incurably sick. Incidentally, this is how the soul of a thinking man should be.' A similar vein of hard-edged wit can be discerned in his most recent volume, *Dull-Weather Dance* (Calstock, Cornwall, 1981). [JL

RAWORTH, Tom (Thomas Moore) (1938–), is a prolific experimental poet, the author of more than twenty-five books brought out by various small presses. He himself published a number of the better-known contemporary avant-garde poets at the Goliard Press, which he helped to found. He has given many readings in Europe and America, a fact which squares with the non-literary and informal approach of his work and with his interest in jazz. He is well regarded by poets in the modernist tradition. He appeared in Michael Horovitz's *Children of Albion* anthology (1969) and in *Penguin Modern Poets*, 19 (1971) where his work stood alongside selections from Lee *Harwood and John *Ashbery. The company he kept there is instructive about his own work which, like theirs, often attempts to transcribe the immediate present. But various tricks can be played with this idea. One may treat the moment as subjective, or try to be objective, concentrating on sense-perception, or pay attention to the creation of the text. Raworth uses all these approaches, sometimes within the space of one poem. This can be illustrated from 'Stag Skull Mounted', a series of poems each of which is given a date and time of day. In '9.30 p.m. May 13th 1970' Raworth, letting his thoughts flow, announces: 'i am a ping pong ball from face to face | idea to idea and what i do | is a disservice.' But in '8:00 p.m. May 5th 1970' we are treated to a more objective view: 'each evening a girl with a twisted spine | passes my window as the weather warms | her dresses thin and shorten.' But at any moment we may be reminded that the poet is making artefacts out of his stray perceptions: the brief entry for '11:08 a.m. May 7th 1970' ends 'found poem'. This last emphasis, on poem as object, has produced some adventurous work in his 'Logbook' series. The conceit of this is that we are given the few remaining pages of the logbook of what appears, at first, to be a voyage. But our construction of a chronology is deliberately hindered, so that we cannot identify the text with the reflection of reality.

The odd juxtapositions in some Raworth poems have led critics to use the word 'surrealism'. But while this is an undoubted influence, it is idle to pin labels to his work. Raworth improvises. This informal approach is mirrored in his language. For whatever licence he permits himself in subject-matter, his diction and rhetoric are the opposite of bardic. He has no special poetic register. This may help to account for his popularity, which was confirmed and extended by the publication of *Tottering State: New and Selected Poems 1963–1984* (Barrington, Mass., 1984; revised, with the dates emended to 1963–1987, London, 1988). [ETL

RAY, David (1932–) was born in Oklahoma. He is professor of English at the University of Missouri. His poetry, usually in unrhymed but regular lines, is for the most part personal, dealing with his family and his domestic experiences, although he has written some political poems—for example, protests at American involvement in Vietnam, and at treatment of minority groups. His most poignant work is to be found in *Sam's Book* (Middletown, Conn., 1987), dealing in a direct manner with the death of his young son. His output as a whole, while liberal in spirit and deeply felt, lacks the stamp of individuality or any rhythm to characterize it as his own. However, its content, personal and detailed, is remarkably free from stridency or pretentiousness. He has been influenced by his experiences in India as an Indo-US Fellow (1981–2) in the poems of *Elysium in the Halls of Hell* (Jaipur, 1986); and he has edited, with Amritjit Singh, *India: An Anthology of Contemporary Writing* (Athens, Ohio, 1983). He is a generous and useful critic of the work of other poets. See also *The Maharaji's New Wall* (Middletown, 1987). [MS-S

RAYMOND, Vicki (1949–), was born in Victoria, but grew up in South Australia and Tasmania, where her first collection was published, although she had already become an expatriate, employed at the Australian High Commission in London. *Holiday Girls and other poems* (Sandy Bay, Tasmania, 1985) won the Commonwealth Poetry Prize for best first volume, and the consequent reading tour introduced her to British audiences. *Small Arm Practice* (Richmond, NSW,

1989) includes selections from *Holiday Girls* with a large amount of new work. *Selected Poems* was published in Manchester in 1993. Some poems have been set to music by English composer Patrick Morris.

Raymond is most clearly a satirist, whose sharp observation penetrates the evasions and deflates the pretensions present in everyday life, popular psychology, and high culture. 'Don't talk about your childhood', she commands, 'say what you are now'; and her versions of Horace have a corresponding lively anachronistic irreverence.

However, while her characteristic combination of idiomatic language and tight form particularly suits satire, it is well-adapted to such quirkiness as cornering 'the market in poems about snails' and capable of comically evoking the distinctly sinister ('Love Poem'), or sympathetically perceiving that behind the mundane surfaces of holiday camps, laundromats, and offices 'something will always be strange'.

[JS

READ, Sir Herbert (Edward) (1893–1968), was born in rural Yorkshire and educated (after years of struggle) at Leeds University. He fought in the First World War—winning the DSO and MC—and attracted some attention as a minor war poet. He became very influential as a champion of modernism in art and poetry, and as a pioneer of Jungian depth-psychology in criticism. A lifelong anarchist, he was knighted in 1953. Of all his imaginative work, the allegorical novel *The Green Child* (London, 1935) attracted the most praise; but he seldom achieved a comparable synthesis of thought and feeling in his poetry. This, although respected and published by his friend T. S. *Eliot at Faber, has fallen into near oblivion. Read was a determined modernist; but the modernist procedures did not come as easily or as naturally to him in poetry as in criticism. As a result of meeting *Pound and others while a serving soldier, he began to write in the manner of the *Imagists (*Songs of Chaos*, London, 1915). But Robert *Bridges always seemed as strong an influence as any other poet—and this he acknowledged. His war

poetry was admirably laconic and lacking in heroics, but somewhat flat. However, *The End of a War* (London, 1933), a long poem, remains his most notable achievement. See *Collected Poems* (London, 1966), and *Herbert Read* (London, 1961), by Francis Berry. [MS-S

READING, Peter (1946–), was born in Liverpool. He has worked as a teacher, lecturer in art history, and as a weighbridge operator. His strongly anti-romantic, disenchanted, and usually satirical verse began to attract attention—and some reprobation—with *The Municipality's Elderly* (London, 1974). Reading's often mechanically ironic verse, which deliberately assaults 'good taste' for its hypocrisy, depends on his reader's understanding that he is not a 'gutter-press racist'. He is not; but after fifteen years the manner of his verse—owing much to E. E. *Cummings, to the deadpan pseudo-syllabic verse (which employed syllable-count without regard to duration) common in the years just before he began to publish, and to newsprint conventions—has worn somewhat thin. *C* (London, 1984), 100 prose poems of 100 words each, displays him at his least effective: the pieces are supposed to be composed by a man dying of cancer, and are no more horrible or interesting than the clinical notes would be: it works to no point. Such writing, not in verse, seems to operate as an oblique defence of the writer's own sensibility, which the reader now inevitably begins to suspect may be commonplace or sentimental. On the other hand, Reading, in his relentless pursuit of shocking subject-matter, is often clever or funny in his presentation of it, putting parodic emphases where news items do not, and vice versa. But with these more-or-less amusing experiments he continues to muffle his own voice, as though any natural lyricism or alternative kind of narrative eludes him. See *Stet* (London, 1986) and *Shitheads: New Poems* (London, 1989). [MS-S

REANEY, James (1926–), was born on a farm near Stratford, Ontario, and was educated at the University of Toronto—his thesis title was 'The Influence of Spenser on Yeats'. Like Jay

Redgrove

*Macpherson, Reaney is one of the Canadian 'mythopoeic' poets influenced by Northrop Frye (who supervised his thesis). Since 1960 he has taught in the English department of the University of Western Ontario, London. The poems he published as a student and the forty-two lyrics in *The Red Heart* (1949) announced a striking and original new voice in Canadian poetry: childlike, playful, witty, steeped in knowledge, given to wayward fantasy, technically assured, and coloured by a childhood in southern Ontario. This region is also the background of *A Suit of Nettles* (1958; 1975), a series of twelve eclogues modelled on Spenser's *Shepheardes Calender*, though the intention is satirical: the dialogues are between learned geese, and the twelve-month cycle ends in ritual slaughter. Exuberantly, and sometimes comically, in a virtuoso display of verse forms the poet treats a variety of subjects that include sterility and fertility, education, religion, and Canadian history. By contrast, *Twelve Letters to a Small Town* (1962) is quiet and charming—recollections of a childhood in Stratford, Ontario, in the form of lyrics, dialogues, and prose poems, written as a libretto that was set to the music of Canadian composer John Beckwith and broadcast in July 1961. This same voice is also heard in the quatrains that make up most of *The Dance of Death in London, Ontario* (1963), illustrated by the late Jack Chambers. Since the 1960s Reaney has concentrated on playwriting. His poetry was first collected in *Poems: James Reaney*, ed. with an introduction, by Germaine Warkentin (Toronto, 1972), who also edited his *Selected Shorter Poems* (1975) and *Selected Longer Poems* (1976)—both Erin, Ont.   [WT

REDGROVE, Peter (1932–), describes himself as 'poet and analytical psychologist'. His poetry is central to a crusading and controversial body of work that also includes novels, short stories, radio and television plays, and volumes of psychology and sociology.

Born into an English middle-class family and educated at a public school, Redgrove's first breach of convention was painful and involuntary. Conscripted into the army at 18, he suffered a mental breakdown and was given insulin-shock treatment, an experience that underlies the first of his narrative poems, 'Lazarus and the Sea'. At Cambridge, where he read natural sciences, he was a contemporary of Ted *Hughes, with whom he has strong affinities. In London, where he worked as a scientific journalist and copy-writer, he was a member of the *Group and was particularly influenced by Martin *Bell, who encouraged him to give his poems narrative and dramatic form.

Redgrove's work made an immediate impact. He became visiting poet at Buffalo University, Gregory Fellow in Poetry at Leeds University, O'Connor Professor of Literature at Colgate University, and resident author at Falmouth School of Art, an association that lasted from 1966 to 1983. But the early books, culminating in *The Force* (London, 1966), have an unfocused energy.

Redgrove might be termed a scientific visionary. The more idiosyncratic he has allowed himself to become, the clearer the work has become. In *Dr Faust's Sea-Spiral Spirit* (London and Boston, 1972), confirmed by his studies with the Jungian analyst, John Layard, and by a close working partnership with his second wife, Penelope *Shuttle, he began to fashion the concentrated, expository style he has refined through subsequent books. He deploys a range of techniques that may appear surreal, but all proceed from a consistent vision of the universe as a living entity, in which the human species plays only a small part. Typical is his acceleration and deceleration of time, so that trees 'Lope away over the red-hot fence | Or stand for a three-hundred-year moment'.

Never arbitrary, his inventive visual images are really links in a chain of argument. He draws on scientific data, dream images, the arcana of myth and magic, whatever will serve as a metaphor for the 'intense wholenesses' he wishes to convey. In the course of this impassioned pleading, he has developed an extraordinary range of tones, humorous, erotic, and ecstatic—often within the same poem. He is a prolific poet and, once the procedures become familiar, the poems can seem formulaic. At their best, though, they have an undeniable transforming power.

The Moon Disposes (London, 1987) contains Redgrove's selected poems, 1954–87. Given the narrative element, his poems can gain from being heard as well as read, and *The Apple-Broadcast* (London and Boston, 1981) was published with an accompanying cassette. Eight essays on his work appear in a special issue of *Poetry Review*, 71: 2/3 (London, Autumn 1981), and there is an extended interview with Philip Fried in *The Manhattan Review*, 3: 1 (New York, Summer 1983). [RGa

REED, Henry (1914–86), was born in Birmingham and educated at King Edward VI School and Birmingham University, where he studied language and literature and wrote an MA thesis on *Hardy. He worked as a teacher and freelance journalist, 1937–41. After a short period in the army he was transferred to the Foreign Office to work in Naval Intelligence, 1942–5. Thereafter Reed made his career in radio as a journalist, broadcaster, and playwright. The BBC's Third Programme was inaugurated in October 1946, and he became a member of the legendary group of writers—including Louis *MacNeice, Dylan *Thomas, Terence *Tiller, P. H. Newby, Patric *Dickinson, W. R. *Rodgers, and Rayner Heppenstall—who were attached to the network during its golden period. Later he was a visiting professor and associate professor of English at the University of Washington, Seattle.

Reed published only one book of poems, *A Map of Verona* (London, 1946), which in turn is famous chiefly for one poem, 'Lessons of the War'. It is probably the most celebrated English poem, and certainly the most popular, to emerge from the Second World War. Part I in particular, 'Naming of Parts', has entered the collective folk-memory. Reed told the poet Vernon *Scannell that the poem began as a comic monologue recited for the amusement of his fellow recruits. Its good-natured humour, broad sexual innuendo, and lyrical evocations of nature make it instantly memorable. By juxtaposing dry and faintly absurd technical language

about the cleaning of guns with the immemorial goings-on of flowers and bees in spring Reed dramatizes both the ridiculousness and boredom of war—time out of time, as it were—and its relationship to the awkward, unbalanced lives of the individuals haplessly caught up in it.

The other two sections, 'Judging Distances' and 'Unarmed Combat', employ the same strategy of juxtaposing military jargon with the ordinary-language meaning of such terms as 'proper issue' and 'dead ground'. Part of the poem's success is bound up in its formal rhythmic brilliance, which cleverly mixes prosaic and lyric modes of speech and versification.

The volume's other success is the famous parody of *Eliot, 'Chard Whitlow' ('As we get older we do not get any younger'), which Eliot himself commended for its accuracy. Elsewhere in the book Eliot proves rather more of a hindrance than a help, for example in the title-poem, whose wistful sensitivities ('underground whispers of music', 'shifting crowds in the causeways . . . discerned through the dusk') recall the perplexities of Prufrock and *The Waste Land*. *Lessons of the War* (New York, 1970) reprints Reed's most famous poem and adds two new sections to it, 'Movement of Bodies' and 'Returning of Issue'.

Reed worked for many years on a biography of Hardy, which he never finished. Much of this research went into his first 'Hilda Tablet' radio play, *A Very Great Man Indeed* (see *Hilda Tablet and Others: Four Pieces for Radio*, London, 1971). Others of his many radio plays include an adaptation of *Moby-Dick* (London, 1947), several versions of plays by the Italian playwright Ugo Betti, and *The Streets of Pompeii and Other Plays for Radio* (London, 1971), some of which are based on incidents in the life of Leopardi. The plays belong partly to BBC radio's period of achievement and experimentation, under the producer Douglas Cleverdon, and partly to the general attempt to revive *verse drama of the 1940s and 1950s, led by Eliot and Christopher Fry. Outside literature Reed's main interest was in music, especially opera. A *Collected Poems*, ed. Jon Stallworthy, was published in 1991 by Oxford University Press. [WS

REED, Jeremy (1951–), was born in Jersey. Deprecated by many for his Firbank-like, *poète maudit* persona, Reed is much admired by a minority, including David *Gascoyne and Kathleen *Raine (who see or have seen him as lone inheritor, respectively, of the English *surrealist and the Neo-Platonic traditions). He has continued to be able to write in the formal manner which characterized his first substantial collection, *By the Fisheries* (London, 1984). Here such poems as 'John Clare's Journal' show him to be a potentially rich and capable, if somewhat over-sonorous and derivative nature-poet, writing under the influences of 'mad' poets such as Smart, as well as Eugenio Montale, whom he has translated in *The Coastguard's House* (Newcastle, 1990). His glances towards more fashionable themes such as AIDS, cross-dressing, and pop- and drug-culture in general have been less successful, and judged by most critics not of his coterie as ill-advised, banal, and a distraction from his real capabilities as a poet writing—if only intermittently—in the British surrealist tradition of *Scarfe, Roger Roughton (see entry on *Contemporary Poetry and Prose*), and, above all, his mentor Gascoyne. The direction he chooses to take remains to be seen; of his technical capacities there is little doubt. His book about poetry, *Madness: The Price of Poetry* (London, 1990), was generally seen as disappointingly trite. See *Selected Poems* (London, 1987), *Nineties* (London, 1990), and *Red-Haired Android* (London, 1992). [MS-S

REESE, Lizette (Woodworth) (1856–1935), grew up in a rural Maryland village and became a teacher of English at Western High School in Baltimore, where she would remain until her retirement in 1921. Although an admirer of the seventeenth century and of the entire English pastoral tradition, her first two collections, *A Branch of May* (1887) and *A Handful of Lavender* (1891), were surprisingly modern in their supple directness and lack of excessive sentiment. A later volume, *A Wayside Lute* (1909), contains her best-known poem, the sonnet 'Tears', and in many ways—high polish, sharp observations, concise clarity of images—her verses invite comparison with the more original work of Emily Dickinson and seem to anticipate the terse lyricism of *Millay, *Wylie, and the later *Teasdale, despite lingering traces of a Victorian sensibility. *Pastures* (1933) was her tenth and final collection.

A generous selection of her poems is scattered throughout *The Home Book of Modern Verse*, ed. Burton Egbert Stevenson (New York, 1963), but the smaller group in *Modern American Poetry*, ed. Louis Untermeyer (New York, 1969), which includes 'Tears' and the equally effective 'A Puritan Lady', is better chosen. [EB

REEVES, Gareth (1947–), read English at Oxford and was a postgraduate at Stanford University, California, where he held a Wallace Stegner Writing Fellowship from 1973 to 1974. He lectures in English at the University of Durham, and is a co-founder and editor of *Poetry Durham*. Reeves has fashioned a style that is idiomatic, often ironic, and yet capable of a terse lyricism. *Real Stories* (Manchester, 1984), his only book-length collection to date, is divided into three sections. Several elegies appear in the first. Given the fineness of these elegies and of others—especially about Reeves's father, the poet James *Reeves—published subsequently in periodicals, it is unsurprising that in *T. S. Eliot: A Virgilian Poet* (Basingstoke and London, 1989) Gareth Reeves writes well about the 'Hades of memory'. The first section of *Real Stories* also touches wryly on the poet's 'English' schooling: the plaited comedy of 'Can We Interest You in God?' is an example. The second section includes poems set in America; they show a vigorous relish for the 'alien' and the 'random'. The final section's mainly domestic pieces number some of the best poems in a precisely observed and emotionally mature collection. See also *Listening In* (Manchester, 1993). [MO'N

REEVES, James (1909–78), was born in Middlesex and educated at Stowe and Jesus College, Cambridge. Thereafter, he held various schoolteaching and lecturing jobs until 1952, when he turned to full-time writing and editing. He was responsible for over forty titles, several as general editor of the Heinemann 'Poetry Bookshelf' series, whose selections of English poets were widely used in schools. His varied output included four books of verse for children and collections of folk-song texts.

He was not, however, a prolific or assertive poet. His first volume, *The Natural Need*, was published in 1936 by Robert *Graves and Laura *Riding's Seizin Press; in the same year, Graves tells us, *Yeats excluded him from the *Oxford Book of Modern Verse* as 'too reasonable, too truthful', since the Muses prefer 'gay, warty lads'. (From this early connection Reeves has frequently been conscripted into a Graves 'school'.) Reeves's five subsequent volumes are full of well-proportioned poems, many in tuneful quatrains, but there is a general lack of passion or even character, despite the privacy of the subject-matter. In the introduction to his first *Collected Poems* (London, 1960) he explains why none of the momentous events of his times had got into his writing: 'To me poetry is rooted in the particular and the immediate.' The smooth, inhibited lyricism is, however, varied by the angry local satire of such poems as 'Greenhallows', 'Planning Permission', and 'Converting the Vicarage'.

Reeves's *Collected Poems 1929–1974* (London) supplanted the earlier volume, and presents a debate on his own limitations. Some poems stand up for timidity: one of them prefers his 'backwater' to a mainstream fouled with ambition, another condemns the noisy egos of the Dylan *Thomas era, 'where every other poet is a megaphone'. But the verdict of 'Voices Loud and Low' is ambiguous, and later poems like 'The Solvers' and 'A Stoical Robin' ridicule their author's procedure. His alert self-doubt is encapsulated in the foreword to *Subsong* (London, 1969); 'Subsong' is explained as the quietest form of birdsong, performed for the sole benefit of the performer; but at times it can sound as if the bird 'is prevented from singing normally by being strangled'. [MI

REID, Alastair (1926–), was born in Whithorn, Scotland. His mother was a physician, his father a minister in the Church of Scotland. Reid's

studies at the University of St Andrews were interrupted by the Second World War, in which he served in the Pacific with the Royal Navy. Returning to St Andrews after the war, he graduated with a degree in classics. He soon migrated to America, where he took a position in classics at Sarah Lawrence College.

It was during this period that he began writing poems, many of which were published in *The New Yorker*, a magazine with which Reid has had a continuing association for over three decades as a staff writer. Reid's first book of poems, *To Lighten My House* (1953), was influenced by Dylan *Thomas and Gerard Manley Hopkins, though his particular voice—intensely musical, alliterative—was present even in his apprentice work.

In the mid-Fifties Reid began to spend part of each year in Majorca, where he befriended Robert *Graves, with whom he translated Suetonius. Graves has been an abiding influence on Reid's poetry. Reid's work as a translator, especially of Spanish poetry, began in the late Fifties, though it was during the Sixties and Seventies that he did his much-admired translations from Pablo Neruda, Jorge Luis Borges, and other Latin American writers. *Oddments, Inklings, Omens, Moments* appeared in 1959.

Reid is primarily a poet of awe, gazing at the world with a childlike vision, registering its bright surfaces in melodic language and arresting phrases. There is wistfulness in his work, too: a sense that in this post-Edenic world one can hope for little except the chance occurences of love or good weather. The landscapes of his verse—North American, Mediterranean, Scottish—are deeply inward places, often sunswept, occasionally drenched by rain.

Reid, married twice, has one son, Jasper. For many years he and his son wandered from country to country, with Reid's only permanent address being *The New Yorker*. In recent years, he has divided his time evenly between New York and a rustic, self-built house in the Dominican Republic. *Weatherings* (New York, 1978) contains most of Reid's published verse. See also *Passwords* (Boston, 1964), a collection of poems and essays, and *Whereabouts* (San Francisco,

1987), a book of essays. Reid has also written several books for children. [JP

REID, Christopher (1949–), was born in Hong Kong but educated in England. At Exeter College, Oxford, he was taught for a term by Craig *Raine, a poet with whom he is often associated. Yet, for all their shared interest in metaphor, butchers, children, and couplets, they are quite different poets. Raine's poetic presence is exuberant, edgy, vigorous; Reid's is droll, self-contained, cool. Raine's love poems are erotic, Reid's affectionate. Raine admires Picasso's bold distortions; Reid invokes the intimate interiors of Vermeer and Vuillard. Raine's finest poems are capable of a surprisingly raw directness; Reid's best work is elegantly oblique.

In Reid's attractive first collection, *Arcadia* (Oxford, 1979), a close, if partial, reading of Wallace *Stevens shows in the finicky diction and the ring of certain titles: 'A Holiday from Strict Reality', 'Big Ideas with Loose Connections', 'The Meaning of Morning'. The dandy in Stevens offers a model for the way Reid advertises the artifice of his language, usually to witty effect. In 'From an Idea by Toulouse-Lautrec', associations mingle as Reid depicts preparations for a meal: if the eucharist is brought to mind, so too is St Laurence's martyrdom. The more formally compacted poems in *Pea Soup* (Oxford, 1982) sustain the ingenuity and graceful good humour of *Arcadia*, but they reveal, too, greater tonal range; their span includes reflections on fictiveness, poker-faced confrontations between chaos and a wish for order, and affectingly wry love poems (such as the Nabokovian 'At the Wrong Door'). The writing's comic poise never lapses, yet an awareness of poetry as a ritual that keeps suffering at arm's length is rarely absent.

Reid's interest in personae and parody shapes his third and finest collection, *Katerina Brac* (London, 1985), where he assumes the role of an invented female poet, and mimics the intonations of Eastern European poetry in translation, employing a suppler, lower-key style than in previous volumes. Skirting bathos and banality, the book contrives quirky, half-serious variations on serious themes, especially the relation between history and poetry, experience and representation. *Auden's 'poetry makes nothing happen' appears to lie behind the volume's deadpan uses of 'happen'. Christopher Reid is interviewed by John Haffenden in *Poetry Review*, 72: 3 (Sept. 1982). His poetry is discussed in Alan Robinson, *Instabilities in Contemporary British Poetry* (Basingstoke and London, 1988). [MO'N

Review, The. Despite the parish-magazine-like appearance of its early issues in 1962, *The Review*, edited by Ian *Hamilton, rapidly established itself as the most influential and stylish of postwar British poetry magazines. The poems of its regular contributors—among them Douglas *Dunn, Colin *Falck, John *Fuller, David *Harsent, Hamilton himself, and Hugo *Williams—tended to be sparse, intense, and intelligent; but the magazine will be more widely recalled as a forum for rigorous and sometimes ferocious critical writing. Over ten years, in thirty numbers, *The Review* covered most important English and American poets of the time, giving particularly sympathetic, sustained attention to Robert *Lowell, who was in some respects its literary mentor; the final double number included a substantial and entertaining symposium on 'The State of Poetry' in 1972. Less serious but equally entertaining were the regular satirical columns of 'Edward Pygge'. A selection of essays from the first fifteen issues, compiled by its editor, was published as *The Modern Poet* (London, 1968). The magazine was succeeded in 1974 by *The New Review*, an ambitious literary monthly. [NP

REXROTH, Kenneth (1905–82), was born in South Bend, Indiana, but lived in San Francisco from 1927, and was thereafter associated with all its literary manifestations, eventually as a kind of elder statesman. He encouraged successive 'movements', especially the *Beat poets, but tended to lose patience with each one and abandon it as a misguided job. He always hoped for a total change in humanity. He was on the board of *Black Mountain Review* (see BLACK

MOUNTAIN POETS), but resigned early on (1954) because he felt a critic had been 'unfair' to *Roethke. He did not approve of adverse criticism of anyone except officials and politicians. His voice, exemplified at its least enduring in such lines as 'Never | Give up this savage religion | For the blood-drenched civilized | Abstraction of the rascals | Who live by killing you and me', was frequently raucous and careless. His best poems, all in the tradition of the *Imagists and *Objectivists, were written despite his politics, although very occasionally the rhetoric of the political verse takes on an impassioned and bitter tone which has verbal, if not intellectual, power. Thus, when in 'Thou Shalt Not Kill: A Lament for Dylan Thomas', Rexroth laments that the poet was murdered by politicians, lawyers, publishers, and 'bosses', rather than by unwise ingestive habits, he does it with such sincerity that he temporarily persuades the reader. But the best work is about nature, and much of it is in the manner of his translations from the Chinese and Japanese. This kind of poem is, surprisingly, precise, carefully worked out, and above all, quiet. See *The Complete Collected Shorter Poems* (New York, 1967); *The Collected Longer Poems* (New York, 1968); and *New Poems* (New York, 1974).

[MS-S

REYNOLDS, Oliver (1957–), was born in Cardiff into a Quaker family. After leaving school he spent a year as a porter at Whitchurch Mental Hospital before going on to study drama at the University of Hull, 1977–80. Since then he has worked intermittently in the theatre, and has been Judith E. Wilson Junior Fellow in creative writing at Cambridge University and a writer-in-residence at the universities of Glasgow and Strathclyde. Reynolds is a prolific and restless poet who, with three books published, still seems far from settling into a single voice or style. *Skevington's Daughter* (London, 1985), *The Player Queen's Wife* (London, 1987), and *The Oslo Tram* (London, 1991) variously contain love lyrics, sequences on photography and Wales, contemporary urban vignettes, and brief monologues spoken by other artists, actors, or musi-

cians; but his strongest work is in a vein of oblique or fragmentary historical narrative, in which (often horrific) details of violent death or suffering are treated with extreme detachment, and the poem derives power from the indirection it employs in circling towards a centre of bizarrerie or cruelty. Some of Reynolds's most memorable poems to date deal with madness and the institutionalized lives of mental patients; his approach is that of the compassionate observer. Reviewers have pointed, not always approvingly, to Reynolds's 'cleverness' and facility; he is a witty poet, with a predilection for mock-learned word-play, for punning both linguistically (where playfulness is used to make political points, in particular about the Welsh language) and visually. He has produced elegant versions of poems by Baudelaire and Rilke, and these, like some of his more consciously light-verse pieces, gain from the use of regular (if flexible) rhyme and metre. Elsewhere, the flatness of Reynolds's verse can be deadening, the tone less wittily insouciant than irritatingly coy; variety sometimes looks like uncertainty, and the language does not always show an unfaltering sureness of touch.   [AJ

REZNIKOFF, Charles (1894–1976), was born in Brooklyn, New York, and educated at New York University's School of Law. Except for an abortive year at journalism school in Missouri when he was 16 and a year working in Hollywood in the 1930s—the source of some of his most mordant and witty poetry—Reznikoff was a lifelong resident of New York City. He briefly practised law, then worked at a number of writing and editing jobs, including one for an encyclopedia of law for lawyers. A tireless walker, covering five or six miles of the city every day until the end of his life, he found his natural subject-matter in the life of the streets, the ethnic neighbourhoods, and the urban poor. Influenced by the example of *Pound and other early modernists, he had begun writing poetry when he was a teenager. In the Twenties his work came to the attention of Louis *Zukofsky, who saw in it *the* prime example of *'objectivist' poetics. Reznikoff's work was neglected by editors and critics alike until the mid-Fifties, when his association with Zukofsky and other poets such as *Oppen and *Rakosi brought him to the attention of a younger generation. Over the last twenty-five years all of his previous work, much of it self-published, has been reprinted, and his reputation as one of the foremost poets of his generation is now well established.

Reznikoff's poetry, precise, authoritative, and subtle, has its roots in the modern free-verse revolution of the early part of the century, in particular the *Imagist programme of Pound and *Hulme. Equally, Reznikoff's preference for a poetry of statement rather than metaphor, for observation and image over interiority, is deeply related both to his legal training, with its emphasis on unambiguous clarity, and to his sense of the Jewish poet as an objective moral witness, one whose relation to language is traditionally held as sacred.

Reznikoff's work ranges widely from short, darkly sarcastic, epigrammatic jottings to long autobiographical and historical poems and verse dramas which make use of biblical parallelism and a tonal 'recitative' close to colloquial prose rhythms. Shunning rhetorical flourish, the poems achieve, through reticence and understatement, an almost documentary or photographic effect, which contributes to their felt solidity and sense of 'truthfulness.' These effects are particularly pronounced in Reznikoff's masterpiece, 'Autobiography of a Writer', and in the historical volumes Holocaust and Testimony, works which rely mainly on the use of edited court-room material. Throughout all of his work one is aware of Reznikoff's probing historical vision as it renders the effect of history's impersonal forces on the individual. Such a vision powerfully animates the city poetry with its vignettes of immigrant life, of petty hopes and failure, which seem finally illuminated not only by the poet's attentive eye but also by the light of time itself.

The most complete edition of Reznikoff's work is Poems 1918–1975: The Complete Poems of Charles Reznikoff, ed. Seamus Cooney (Santa Rosa, Calif., 1989). See also Holocaust (Los Ange-les, 1975), Testimony (New York, 1965), and The Manner Music, a novel, with introduction by Robert Creeley (Santa Barbara, Calif., 1976); and for criticism, Charles Reznikoff, by Milton Hindus (Santa Barbara, 1977), Charles Reznikoff: Man and Poet (Orono, Me., 1984), ed. Milton Hindus, and Conviction's Net of Branches: Essays on the Objectivist Poets and Poetry, by Michael Heller (Carbondale, Ill., 1985). [MH

Rhyme. Contrary to common opinion, the twentieth century is not so much the era of free verse as the century of rhyme—into which more experiment has gone than during any previous period. The first useful innovation was Wilfred *Owen's development of pararhyme, in which he matched initial and final consonants of rhymes around vowels dissimilar in each rhyme-partner ('hall / Hell'). His 'Strange Meeting' and 'Exposure' are rhymed consistently in this way. *Yeats independently simplified this technique in two ways, reducing the sound-match to the final consonants only ('spot / cut'), in each partner, and using it unsystematically as an extension of other rhyming licences such as eye-rhyme. 'In Memory of Major Robert Gregory' offers many examples. Geoffrey *Hill, in poems like 'The Mystery of the Charity of Charles Péguy' is a major follower. It is often known as half-rhyme. Both techniques were anticipated in the eccentric rhyming habits of Emily Dickinson. Traditional pure rhyme has been developed by the innovations of *Mac-Neice and *Auden. One development of theirs might be called syllable rhyme, since it depends on rhyming the stressed syllables of polysyllabic words and ignoring the dissonant terminations ('speaking / Greek'; 'mastered / last'). Auden's 'Music is International' is a fine example. Keith *Douglas uses it as a licence.

Another innovation on dissyllabic rhyme, favoured by MacNeice, is to rhyme on the unstressed syllable, as in 'Prognosis'. This type of rhyme mixed with traditional and pararhyme has been used by *syllabics writers like Marianne *Moore and Thom *Gunn to try to give lines of syllabics more definition; Moore's 'Critics and Connoisseurs' and Gunn's 'The Feel of Hands' give instances (eg. 'desperate/that'). The problem often is to rhyme on and off the stress ('lonely/sea'). The finest example of this is probably Auden's villanelle 'Miranda' in *The Sea and the Mirror*. 'Dirty Story' by Kingsley *Amis provides another example.

Along with *Eliot, in the minor poems and elsewhere, and *Pound, in 'The Classic Anthology defined by Confucius', MacNeice also experimented with eccentric shifts of medial rhyme, for example in 'The sunlight on the garden'—as did Dylan *Thomas in 'The Conversation of Prayer'. Many modern poets have been fascinated with the idea of running rhyme from stanza to stanza. Interesting samples are 'The Pedigree' by *Hardy; 'I Remember, I Remember' and 'The Building' by *Larkin; and 'Statement by a Responsible Spinster' by Iain Crichton *Smith who employs pararhyme as part of the scheme. John *Fuller uses a running off-stress rhyme ('furrow/harrow') in 'Song for a Condemned Queen'.

In the United States, Archibald *MacLeish used a simpler idea of assonance syllable rhyme on the stress of polysyllables ('victory/conspicuous') to ease the running-rhyme problem of *terza rima* in 'Conquistador'. (This was parodied down to the rhyme in Edmund *Wilson's 'The Omelette of A. M. MacLeish'.) Eliot simplified the *terza rima* problem further by merely alternating stressed and light endings. MacNeice offers many other examples of assonance rhyme, such as 'Donegal Triptych I'. His 'Bagpipe Music' offers an example of double assonance rhymes. Dylan Thomas developed simple assonance ('boughs/towns') as a rhyme system in such poems as 'Fern Hill'. He also developed what might be called consonant chime, where lines continuously end with the same consonant. In 'I, in my Intricate Image' most of the lines conclude with l sounds of various types. Later poets have enhanced assonance rhyme by matching initial consonants, as in 'feast/feed'. Obviously, these new systems can be used in combination to produce a very complex and subtle music. Auden has an early example in 'Five Songs II', where he makes opposite partners of pararhymes assonate

('began/flush/flash/gun'). His late work has more varied use of such features, as may be seen from 'Dame Kind'. Wilfred Owen, a tireless experimenter, may have been approaching this subtle use of varied rhyme-links in the last stanza of 'Insensibility', where several rhyme-groups share sounds and echo sounds within the lines. These experiments mean that rhyme is not the problem it was in English, but a much more expressive tool.

Few successors have chosen to use these techniques as systematically as the originators, taking them opportunistically as extra aids to traditional rhyme-schemes—though consistent examples of some may be found in Geoffrey *Hill, Peter *Dale, and others. Austin *Clarke, clearly influenced by the wider variety of rhyme in Gaelic, has used most of these techniques in an intuitive way, and the tradition may have influenced the technique of Irish poets like Seamus *Heaney in poems with pararhymes and final consonance, on and off the stress, mixed with pure rhyme, as in his 'Alphabets'.

[PD

RICH, Adrienne (1929–), was born in Baltimore, Maryland. The elder of two sisters, Rich grew up in an upper-middle-class environment and was educated at Radcliffe College, from which she graduated in 1951. She won the Yale Series of Younger Poets Award that same year. Her book, *A Change of World*, was selected by W. H. *Auden, who wrote in his preface: 'The poems a reader will encounter in this book are neatly and modestly dressed, speak quietly but do not mumble, respect their elders but are not cowed by them, and do not tell fibs.'

Rich married in her early twenties and bore three children before her thirtieth birthday; she also published *The Diamond Cutters* (1955), a graceful, neatly crafted book much in the vein of her first volume. It was not until the mid-Sixties, when she and her husband began to work actively to end the war in Vietnam, that her poetry acquired the tense, angry voice that has been characteristic of her mature work. *Necessities of Life* (1966) was a breakthrough work for Rich, followed quickly by *Leaflets* (1969), *The*

Will to Change (1971), and Diving into the Wreck (1973). The poems of this middle period are those of a poet who has happily shed the conventions of formal poetry. Images gather like bright shards: phrases from letters, public speech, intimate moments from the poet's past and present. Among the significant poems of this period are 'Face to Face', 'Orion', 'Leaflets', 'I Dream I'm the Death of Orpheus', and 'Waking in the Dark', all written with a fierce new urgency.

Rich's later work has come directly out of her experience as an early leader in the feminist movement. Her essays were seminal in the redefinition of patriarchy and motherhood, pointing a way towards a non-sexist future. In poetry and prose, Rich's work of the Seventies and Eighties examines the connections between the literary imagination and history, between ethics and action; she writes in a deeply autobiographical vein about the experience of being white, Jewish, and lesbian in America. The struggle of the individual for freedom is seen, by Rich, as coincident with wider struggles for freedom. Her major collection of recent years is The Dream of a Common Language (New York, 1978), a book in which she explores the 'technology of silence' as well as 'these words, these whispers, conversations | from which time after time the truth breaks moist and green'. In a more recent collection, Time's Power (New York, 1989), she wrestles with time itself, with the contradictions of memory, with the meaning of human responsibility in the face of change and death. Her work is, always, grounded in a non-sexist, non-racist political perspective.

The Fact of a Doorframe (New York, 1985) is a recent selection of her poems. A selection of her prose is Blood, Bread, and Poetry (New York, 1986). For criticism, see Barbara C. Gelpi and Albert Gelpi, Adrienne Rich's Poetry (New York, 1975) and Terrence Des Pres, Praises and Dispraises (New York, 1988). [JP

RICHARDS, I(vor) A(rmstrong) (1893–1979), was educated at Clifton and Magdalene College, Cambridge, where he became a fellow. Famous as the author of Principles of Literary Criticism

(1925) and Practical Criticism (1929), and as the inventor, with C. K. Ogden, of Basic English, Richards was one of this century's best literary critics. His poems, because of this, are often considered side-efforts. Yet, although they do not have the imagination and beauty to be found in the verse of his brilliant pupil William *Empson, they still have many virtues. This is a dense lyrical 'metaphysical' verse, tightly constructed and rhymed, punning ('fain' and 'feign'), with occasional old-fashioned inversion of word-order ('What a word means who'ld say | Will new words choose and use') and quibbling play with words. Complicated argument is attempted, and in every way these poems are thoughtful. Although nothing romantic or exotic is aimed at, some of the philosophy can remind us of Fitzgerald's Omar Khayyam: 'Am I not the original Ball | Tossed into Court to call | The players to their Game. | Those tireless Players who | Do what they have to do | That's never twice the same?' It's nice to see 'TV'd' rhymed with 'need'; but sometimes, in the forest of rhymes, the thread can be lost.

Richards's collections are Goodbye Earth and Other Poems (New York, 1958; London, 1959), The Screens and Other Poems (New York, 1960; London, 1961), and Internal Colloquies: Poems and Plays (London, 1972). I. A. Richards: New and Selected Poems came out in 1978 (Manchester). [GE

RICKWORD, Edgell (1898–1982), was born in Colchester, Essex, into an educated, middle-class family. He joined the Artists' Rifles in 1916, as soon as he was of an age to enlist, lost an eye in the war, and was invalided out of service. He was awarded the MC. After the war Rickword went up to Oxford to read French, but did not complete the degree. He became a reviewer for the Times Literary Supplement and the New Statesman (writing one of the few perceptive early reviews of The Waste Land in 1923) and published a study of the poet Rimbaud in 1924. He edited the short-lived but influential *Calendar of Modern Letters (1925–7) and two volumes of Scrutinies (1928, 1931), and published three volumes of poetry, Behind the Eyes (1921), Invocations to Angels (1928), and Twittingpan (1931) before he all but gave up the writing of verse. After that time his increasing involvement in Marxist politics turned his energies to political activism. In the Thirties and Forties he was an important member of the British Marxist intelligensia, founded and edited Left Review (1934–8) and Our Time (1944–7), and was instrumental in the formation of the Left Book Club. As a poet, writing in the Twenties, he reacted strongly against the insipidity he perceived in the work of his contemporaries and strove to develop an aesthetic of 'negative emotions', deriving his use of form and symbol from the poets he specially admired, the French Symbolists and English metaphysical poets. In these tastes, and in his outstanding ability as an essayist and editor, he has more in common with *Eliot than any other of his contemporaries. Rickword's poetry is trenchant, skilful, and capable of encompassing a wide range of styles, from powerful satire to unusual and lyrical love poems. In metre and diction, as well as politically, he prefigures the *Auden generation of poets, but unlike them wrote in an atmosphere of self-determined isolation. Even in the period of his greatest political involvement, Rickword was a lone figure, pursuing his own way.

See Behind the Eyes: Selected Poems and Translations (Manchester, 1976) and Collected Poems (Manchester, 1991); also two prose collections: Essays and Opinions 1921–1931 and Literature in Society 1931–1978, both ed. A. Young (Manchester, 1974 and 1978).   [CPH

RIDDELL, Elizabeth (1910–), was born in New Zealand but moved to Australia immediately she left school to work as a journalist, invited by a Sydney editor on the strength of some schoolgirl verses she had published. She became one of Australia's most respected newspaper-women, and continues to work as a book reviewer for a television programme.

Riddell has published four collections of poetry, the latest, From the Midnight Courtyard, in 1989, and a Selected Poems (1992—both Sydney). She has remarked that her work is strongly influenced, in both style and content, by her career as a journalist, and she does have an admirable readability, a sureness at finding the emotive centre in a seemingly ordinary subject, lightness of touch, and concision. There is also a very unjournalistic aestheticism about her poetry, in tension with its spareness, which seems influenced by Kenneth *Slessor. Her early work is rhymed, her later is less formal; it is lightly but skilfully affecting in either mode.

[RGr

RIDGE, Lola (1871–1941), was born in Dublin but raised in Australia and New Zealand without a father. She married a mine manager in 1895 but left him and arrived in New York in 1908, where she supported herself by factory work, modelling, and writing advertising copy. Politically and aesthetically she identified with the city's radical faction, an admirer of Emma Goldman and contributor to Alfred *Kreymborg's Others magazine. Her first collection, The Ghetto and Other Poems (New York, 1919), offered a free-verse portrait of poor Jewish immigrants that both romanticized them and portrayed them with naturalistic fidelity in the mode of Carl *Sandburg. Sun-Up and Other Poems (New York, 1920) also revealed the influence of Amy *Lowell, its title-poem a psychologically acute and unsentimental treatment of her Australian childhood. She married David Lawson, an engineer twelve years younger than herself, in 1919. Politics dominate Red Flag (New York, 1927), a celebration of the Russian Revolution and fellow artists, and Firehead (New York, 1929), which uses the crucifixion of Christ to protest against the execution of Sacco and Vanzetti, but her last collection, Dance of Fire (New York, 1935), plays with an obscure fire symbolism in a very mannered fashion.   [EB

RIDING Laura (1901–91), was born Laura Reichenthal in New York. The daughter of an Austrian émigré and his second wife, a New Yorker, she was educated at high school in Brooklyn. While at Cornell University she began to write poetry and married a teaching assistant in history, Louis Gottschalk, though the marriage was dissolved in 1925 shortly after she had abandoned her studies and moved with him to the University of Louisville.

At this time she became involved with the *Fugitive Group and with John Crowe *Ransom and Allen *Tate in particular, both of whom were struck by the intensity and commitment with which she had dedicated herself to poetic truth. 'Her intelligence is pervasive,' Tate wrote in 1924. 'It is in every inflexion of her voice, every gesture . . . But always you get the conviction that the Devil and all Pandemonium couldn't dissuade her of her tendency'. This ambivalence has tended to characterize all subsequent critical and personal response, and is inseparable from the often rancorous and partisan assessments of her turbulent and productive literary association with Robert *Graves.

Following the publication of her first collection of poetry, *The Close Chaplet* (1926), in the same year that she took the name Riding, a correspondence with Graves who particularly admired her poem 'The Quids' led to her coming to England and to the beginning of a productive partnership. This produced such seminal works as their joint *A Survey of Modernist Poetry* (1926) and, after their move to Majorca, the founding of the Seizin Press 'to print necessary books by various particular people' and the occasional miscellany *Epilogue*, the aim of which was to 'clarify a standard of reality'. During this time both Graves and Riding supported themselves very largely through 'pot-boiling' writing projects for which he showed more aptitude and enthusiasm than she did.

Riding's complex devotion to 'truth' and linguistic purity resulted in her abandonment of poetry in 1938. She returned to the USA, married Schuyler Jackson, of *Time*, who had written admiringly of her work, and with him devoted herself to a long work on language-study, *Rational Meaning: A New Foundation for the Definition of Words*. This was unfinished at the time of his death in 1968 but has been completed subsequently.

Despite her rejection of poetry for a polemical voice which, for all its undeniable brilliance, is determinedly unattractive and combative, *The Poems of Laura Riding* (Manchester and New York, 1980) is a remarkable book. Often, as a poet, dismissed as austere, Riding delights in the play of abstraction, and the more she races over the switchback of her paradoxes the more engrossing her poetry becomes. From the nursery-rhyme rhythms of 'Forgotten Girlhood' to much longer and involved meditations such as 'Laura and Francisca' what Graves, in a poem, referred to as her 'bladed mind' is always evident. In danger of being relegated by reputation to the ranks of the unreadable, Riding's poetry deserves to be come to afresh, freed from its author's denigration and the strictures of the lengthy apologia which she insists on printing as preface and appendices.

Laura Riding's *Progress of Stories* is available in a companion edition (Manchester and New York, 1982), and a study of her life-work, *Riding's Pursuit of Truth*, by T. P. Wexler, was published (Athens, Ohio) in 1977.   [JM

RIDLER, Anne (1912–), was born in Rugby and educated at King's College, London. Married with four children, she worked on the editorial staff of Faber & Faber for a number of years. Her first book, *Poems*, was published in 1939, and she has produced ten further collections and pamphlets. She has also published a number of translations of opera libretti, including Monteverdi's *Orfeo*, and her verse-plays (*Cain, The Shadow Factory*, etc.) have been performed in London and Oxford.

Her poetic development owes much to Wyatt and *Auden, as well as *Eliot, 'who first made me despair of becoming a poet'. Her dramatic work shows more of *Eliot's influence, perhaps, than her poetry, in which even her freer verse has a formal, cadenced air; and an Elizabethan quality of musical grace pervades her most metrical stanzas. She is a Christian poet and there is a vein of erotic mysticism in her work. However, it is via the calm, dry observation of everyday matters that she moves towards her moments of vision and 'the Third Eye, which sees where sense is dark'. Despite the Latinate elegance, the consoling cadences, and the occasional archaism or inversion, the tone is modern in its 'less-deceived' and searching honesty.

Anne Ridler's *Collected Poems* (Manchester) is forthcoming in 1994. Her most significant earlier volumes, besides *Poems*, are *The Nine Bright Shiners* (1943), *The Golden Bird and other poems* (1951), *A Matter of Life and Death* (1959), *Some Time After and other poems* (1972), and *New and Selected Poems* (1988—all London).

[CAR

RILEY, John (1937–78), was born in Leeds. He read English at Cambridge, becoming part of the group known as the *Cambridge School of poets, and forming a close association with Tim Longville, with whom he translated Hölderlin, wrote several books, and founded Grosseteste Press and *Grosseteste Review*. After nine years teaching in secondary schools, he returned to Leeds to write full-time and was killed there by muggers in 1978.

Although Riley shared some characteristics with the Cambridge poets—the influence of *Pound and Charles *Olson, a structuralist concentration on language—he was distinguished by his response to the Russian tradition, particularly to Mandelstam, whose 'Octets' and 'Stalin Ode' sequence he translated. Riley was received into the Russian Orthodox Church in 1977. His long poem 'Czargrad' is an impressive fusion of these influences, Byzantium being glimpsed, not in changeless metal, but in the movement of consciousness.

The Collected Works (Leeds, 1980) contains poetry, prose, and translations. He is represented in the Cambridge poets' anthology, *A Various Art* (Manchester, 1987). Critical essays appear in a memorial volume, *For John Riley* (Leeds, 1979), and in *Poetry Review*, 71: 1 (London, June 1981). There is a useful discussion of 'Czargrad' by Douglas Oliver in *PN Review*, 20 (Manchester, 1981). [RGa

ROBERTS, Michael (William Edward) (1902–48), was born in Bournemouth and brought up on a farm in the New Forest. He read chemistry at King's College, London, mathematics at Cambridge, and held a succession of senior teaching posts in Newcastle and

London. During the war he worked for the BBC's European Service and later became principal of a teacher-training college. He died of leukaemia in 1948. Roberts was a left-wing humanist, scientist, poet, mountaineer, and perhaps the best interpreter of contemporary poetry of his generation, a successor to T. E. *Hulme, of whom he wrote a critical study in 1938. He edited *New Signatures* and *New Country* in the early 1930s, ushering in the *Auden generation of poets, and wrote an influential *Critique of Poetry* in 1934. His two philosophical books, *The Modern Mind* (1937) and *The Recovery of the West* (1941), reveal his deep concern about the fate of the earth, but his most enduring work was as editor of the *Faber Book of Modern Verse* (1936). His poems, published in *These Our Matins* (1930), *Poems* (1936), and *Orion Marches* (1939), are generally meditative and undramatic, reflecting his love and understanding of the natural world. His control of form is perhaps too great to allow much scope to his poetry, but what he does, he does with insight, intelligence, and a great deal of poetic skill. His work is directly spoken and full of a sort of spiritual integrity, often self-effacing and always well made. Roberts's *Selected Poems and Prose*, ed. F. Grubb, was published in Manchester in 1980. [CPH

ROBINSON, Edwin Arlington (1869–1935), was born in Head Tide, Maine, and raised nearby in Gardiner which, as 'Tilbury Town', became the setting for many of his poems. He enrolled at Harvard in 1891 but had to leave after only two years when the family's finances collapsed shortly after his father's death. On his return to Gardiner he decided to become a professional poet and for the next decade endured poverty—and sometimes almost dereliction— to fulfil this ambition. His first collection, *The Torrent and the Night Before* (1896), privately printed, and an expanded version, *The Children of the Night* (1897), were barely noticed when they appeared, though they contain several lyrics, such as 'Luke Havergal' and 'Richard Cory', which later became his most popular. Robinson settled in New York City in 1899 and held various jobs—including subway-construction inspector—until 1904, when President Roosevelt, who admired his work, arranged a virtual sinecure for him in the New York Customs House. From 1910 Robinson devoted himself entirely to writing, spending summers at the MacDowell colony in New Hampshire and winters in New York. With *The Town Down the River* (1910) and *The Man Against the Sky* (1916) he emerged from obscurity to become, in the 1920s, the most highly regarded and widely read poet of his generation: the *Collected Poems* (1921, Pulitzer Prize) finally relieved him of dependence on friends and patrons; and *Tristram* (1927, Pulitzer Prize)—the third, after *Merlin* (1917) and *Lancelot* (1920), of his Arthurian trilogy—was a bestseller.

Robinson's is a poetry of ideas and characters presented in traditional forms. Once his reputation was secure, he turned more frequently from short lyric forms to long blank-verse narratives (completing thirteen book-length poems—from *Merlin* to *King Jasper* (1935)—in the second half of his career), which enabled him to indulge expansively in characterization and social and metaphysical discussion. The title-poem of *The Man Against the Sky*, which came, he said, 'as near as anything to representing my poetic vision', considers a variety of philosophical attitudes, eventually stripping them away to reveal the certain need beneath all philosophies for endurance in the face of adversity. This Hardyesque stoicism, fortified by an Emersonian celebration of the individual, is repeatedly expressed by the many learned and eccentric old failures depicted in his work, 'Miniver Cheevy' and *The Man Who Died Twice* (1924) among them. Indirectness is the most persistent device in Robinson's poetry and accounts both for its best and its worst effects. The cool, cryptic reporting of tragic events has earned shorter poems like 'The Mill' a permanent place in anthologies. The more diffuse verse novels (*Roman Bartholow*, 1923, and *Cavender's House*, 1925), however, which fail to root their Jamesian subtleties in a sufficiently clear context, are now largely neglected. The *Collected Poems of Edwin Arlington Robinson* (New

York, 1937) is still the standard edition of his work; *Edwin Arlington Robinson*, by Emery Neff (London and New York, 1948), is the most thorough biography: and *Edwin Arlington Robinson: A Critical Study*, by Ellsworth Barnard (New York, 1952; repr. 1969) is the best critical introduction. [NE

ROBINSON, Roland (1912–92), born in Ireland of English parents, went to Australia when he was 9, began working as a houseboy on a sheep station when he was 14, and was later a boundary rider, horse-trainer, jockey, fencer, dam builder, factory worker, railway fettler, cleaner, art-school model, member of a ballet company, gardener, assistant to a collector of crocodiles and snakes for a menagerie, and the greenkeeper of a golf course in Sydney. Until very recently he was the only white poet to collect the anecdotes and oral traditions of the Aborigines, both the tribal people of the Northern Territory and the detribalized blacks of the south coast of New South Wales, and he set these down alongside his own work in verse and prose.

Robinson wrote eight small volumes of poetry, five prose works on Aboriginal myths and legends, and three volumes of autobiography. These last reveal an extremely emotional, driven nature. They record how he regularly fled to the bush to escape routine or the complications and demands of his relationships with women. In his old age he lived on the coast near Newcastle, New South Wales, leonine and impassioned as ever, with the last of his companions. He received the Patrick White Award.

The poetry of Edward *Thomas was Robinson's ideal, for its purity. His own work is more vehement and vivid, though less original and subtle, than his master's. Its real achievement is the assimilation of its unique setting—Robinson's best poetry burns and gleams with the colours of the outback, and suggests all the sweep of the coastal bush and heathland within its simple lyric forms. His work is narrow in its range and repetitive, and it lacks any intellectual scheme, but its intensity does much to justify these limits. There is a very slim, judicious *Selected Poems* (Sydney, 1989).   [RGr

RODEFER, Stephen. See LANGUAGE POETRY.

RODGERS W(illiam) R(obert) (1909–69) was generally and affectionately known as Bertie Rodgers. Educated in his native Belfast, he graduated from Queen's University in 1931 and was ordained to the Presbyterian ministry in 1935. He was installed as minister to the rural parish of Loughgall, Co. Armagh, and for his non-sectarianism became known locally as 'the Catholic Presbyterian'.

He began writing poetry in 1939. *Awake!* appeared in 1941, and this first collection borrowed a pre-war idiom of wit and dread, reworking it lyrically and inventively to probe and value everyday living. In 1946 his wife moved to Edinburgh to train as a psychoanalyst and he relinquished the ministry, taking an appointment as producer at the BBC in London offered him by Louis *MacNeice. Following the death of G. B. Shaw, Rodgers was elected to his place in the Irish Academy of Letters in 1951. He remarried in 1953.

Europa and the Bull (1952) was his second collection. and it harnessed Christian and classical mythologies alike to a frank and joyful assertion of sexual exuberance—'Lent' and 'The Net' are outstanding and widely anthologized. At the BBC Rodgers wrote a radio play evoking Belfast—'The Return Room' (1955, unpublished)—but little poetry. For his broadcast series of *Irish Literary Portraits* (published London, 1972)—among which are intimate and mischievous accounts of *Yeats and *Joyce from their friends and contemporaries—Rodgers became known as oral historian of the Irish literary movement.

In 1966 he moved to California and held fellowships in creative writing. He died in Los Angeles in 1969, and is buried in Loughgall churchyard. *Collected Poems*, ed. Dan Davin (London, 1971), includes the pithy 'Home Thoughts From Abroad' and a terse elegy on MacNeice. Darcy O'Brien's biographical study (Lewisberg, 1970) draws with sensitivity on unpublished

dream-notebooks and other uncollected writings.   [PL

RODMAN, Selden (1909–), was born in New York. He founded and edited several magazines, such as *Common Sense* (1932–43), and worked on others, including *New World Writing*. He is best known for his biography of the American painter Ben Shahn, and for his books about Haiti and its art—he was co-director of the Centre d'Art at Port-au-Prince. *Lawrence: The Last Crusade* (New York, 1937) is a narrative poem on T. E. Lawrence. *The Airmen* (New York, 1941), another long poem, celebrates man-in-flight, from Icarus to modern pilots. *The Revolutionists* (New York, 1942) is a verse play, commissioned by the Haitian government and produced (1941) at Port-au-Prince at its expense, about the slave revolt of 1791. *The Amazing Year: A Diary in Verse* (New York, 1947) another narrative poem, in which Rodman juxtaposes personal and international events in the post-war year 1945–6. The poems are in a loose style, lying somewhere between those of Richard *Eberhart (with whom he compiled the anthology *War and the Poet*, New York, 1945) and Peter Viereck, but without any marked individual features.

[MS-S

RODRIGUEZ, Judith (1936–), although born in Perth, Western Australia, grew up in Queensland, where she first published under her maiden name, Green, in a joint volume, *Four Poets* (Melbourne, 1962). She has travelled widely, especially in the Americas, her first marriage being to a Colombian academic. She is now married to Thomas *Shapcott, teaches creative writing in Melbourne, is editor for the Penguin Australian Poetry Series, and has recently edited the *Collected Poems* of Jennifer *Rankin (St Lucia, Qld., 1990).

New and Selected Poems (St Lucia, 1988) draws on six earlier collections, including the PEN Award winner, *Mudcrab at Gambaro's* (St Lucia, 1980). Like previous volumes, it is illustrated by her accomplished linocuts, which reflect, in their boldness and flowing lines, poems that are substantial and sensual. She is particularly successful in the celebratory mode, combining generosity of spirit with sharp observation and a robust wit and intelligence applied alike to domestic existence, literary occasions, and international politics and places.   [JS

ROETHKE, Theodore (1908–63), was born in Saginaw, Michigan. He was the son of Otto Roethke, of Prussian extraction, who owned a large greenhouse that figured as a central image in many of Roethke's finest poems. Roethke graduated from the University of Michigan and later took courses at Harvard. He taught English literature and creative writing at Lafayette College, at Penn State University, and at Bennington College before moving permanently to the University of Washington in Seattle in 1948, where he was poet-in-residence.

Roethke's first book, *Open House* (1942), was composed of short, tightly rhyming poems, much influenced by Stanley *Kunitz, Louise *Bogan, and W. H. *Auden, with all of whom he had close personal ties. Roethke's breakthrough as a poetic stylist occurred with *The Lost Son* in 1948, a book which re-created the poet's lost youth among the flowers of the greenhouse. A major lyric sequence in the book contained brief, vividly concrete poems in which flowers—carnations, roses, chrysanthemums—took on an almost spiritual life. 'Cuttings', 'Flower Dump', 'Child on Top of a Greenhouse', 'Big Wind', and 'My Papa's Waltz'—all from this volume—are among the permanent achievements of modern American poetry, as is the title-sequence, 'The Lost Son', an autobiographical poem that is highly innovative in technique.

During the early Fifties Roethke experimented with oblique autobiographical poems that made use of nursery rhymes and Freudian psychology. These were gathered in *The Waking* (1953). In the mid-Fifties he returned to formal poetry, often echoing *Yeats, whom he deeply admired: 'I take this cadence from a man named Yeats', he wrote in 'Four for Sir John Davies'—'I take it, and I give it back again.' One also sees the influence of Dylan *Thomas, Hopkins, and the Elizabethan lyricists in the exuberant love poems of this period, many of which were written for his young wife, Beatrice Heath O'Connell, who had been a student at Bennington when he taught there. Among these is 'Words for the Wind', the title-poem of Roethke's first *Selected Poems* (1958). There is a great deal of metaphysical wit in these poems, too, as in 'I Knew A Woman', where he writes: 'She was the sickle; I, poor I, the rake, | Coming behind her for her pretty sake | (But what prodigious mowing we did make).' Another important poem of the Fifties was 'The Waking', a haunting villanelle.

A consistent strain of Emersonian romanticism runs through Roethke's work from the beginning, with its emphasis on the emblematic aspects of the natural world. Roethke was a latter-day Transcendentalist, finding spiritual correspondences in physical things. In his deeply inward symbolism, 'wind' is synonymous with 'spirit'. The poet, in works such as 'In a Dark Time', broods on the natural world, pursuing an intensely subjective *via negativa*: 'In a dark time, the eye begins to see.' Arriving at the end of this negative path, the poet emerges into an almost ecstatic, mystical vision, in which 'The mind enters itself, and God the mind, | And one is One, free in the tearing wind.'

Like so many poets of his generation— *Plath, *Berryman, *Lowell—Roethke suffered bouts of mental illness. He was briefly institutionalized several times. 'This shaking keeps me steady', he wrote in 'The Waking', and he did indeed view his periodic breakdowns as spiritual crises. He liked, in fact, to identify himself with such 'mad' poets of the past as William Blake and Christopher Smart.

The primary influence on Roethke's final work was clearly Walt Whitman, whose spirit presides over *The Far Field*, published posthumously in 1964. Roethke broke free of the formal constraints of the Fifties and began writing long free-verse poem-sequences in sprawling lines reminiscent of *Leaves of Grass*. This last volume contains many of Roethke's most memorable poems, including 'The Far Field', 'Meditation at Oyster River', 'Journey to the Interior', and 'The Rose'. These exquisite nature poems are deeply spiritual, depicting fiercely private journeys from blindness to vision in sensuous, musical, highly concrete language. One of the most effective techniques of these poems is the use of Whitmanian catalogues, which included detailed lists of natural flora and fauna.

Roethke died of a heart attack while swimming at the age of 55. His influence has been profound on many poets, including Sylvia Plath, James *Dickey, James *Wright, Ted *Hughes, and Seamus *Heaney. See his *Collected Poems* (New York, 1966; London, 1968 and 1985). See also, *On the Poet and His Craft: Selected Prose of Theodore Roethke*, ed. Ralph J. Mills, Jr. (Seattle, 1965) and *Selected Letters of Theodore Roethke* (Seattle, 1968; London, 1970). For biography, see Allan Seager, *The Glass House* (New York, 1968). For criticism, see *Theodore Roethke: Essays on the Poetry*, ed. Arnold Stein (Seattle, 1965) and Jay Parini, *Theodore Roethke: An American Romantic* (Amherst, Mass., 1979).   [JP

ROGERS, Pattiann (1940–), was born in Joplin, Missouri. She married John Rogers, a geophysicist, in 1960 while she was an undergraduate at the University of Missouri, from where she graduated in 1961. She moved with her family to Texas where she received an MA in creative writing from the University of Houston in 1981. Soon after this Rogers published her first book of poems, *Expectations of Light* (1981). She currently lives with her husband in Castle Rock, Colorado.

Rogers's poetry is based firmly in the subjects and images found in the natural sciences. She uses the things of this natural world as conceits to explain and understand the human condition. It has become a signature technique of her poetry to select a particular metaphor and then extend and examine it throughout the poem from every possible angle and point of view. This methodology is used in the title-poem of Rogers's second book, *The Tattooed Lady in the Garden* (1986), in which the poet is symbolized as a woman in a lush garden who is covered with tattoos of the images of nature that surround her. By the poem's conclusion it is impossible to tell where the lady ends and the garden begins. Rogers has also used this technique successfully

in her writing of love poems. Her most recent collection is *Splitting and Binding* (Middletown, Conn., 1989).   [LS

ROLLS, Eric (Charles) (1923–), was born in Grenfell, New South Wales, and was for many years a farmer. He is best known for two prose works, *They All Ran Wild* (Sydney, 1969) about the destructiveness of introduced flora and fauna in Australia, and *A Million Wild Acres* (Sydney, 1981), a natural and social history of the Pilliga scrub in New South Wales, which received major awards. Rolls, however, first gained wide literary acclaim for a poem written when he was 15: 'Death Song of the Mad Bush Shepherd', which was eventually included in his first verse collection, *Sheaf Tosser* (Sydney, 1967).

Rolls's poetry has maintained a vigorous link with the tradition of Border ballads in its wry lyricism and sometimes macabre playfulness. His first collection is dominated by pastoral subject-matter and earthy humour. *The Green Mosaic* (Melbourne, 1977) uses his New Guinea experiences during the Second World War to explore similarly sensuous and observant lyrical accounts of human, animal, and vegetable quiddities. His collection of children's rhymes, *Miss Strawberry Verses* (Melbourne, 1978) is not for the faint hearted; it is a pity none of these amiable ferocities is included in his *Selected Poems* (Sydney, 1990), which does, however, restore to circulation the work of a verbally resourceful and playful poet whose essential concerns are summed up in the title of another of his bestselling prose works, *Celebration of the Senses* (Sydney, 1984).   [TWS

ROMER, Stephen (1957–), was born in Hertfordshire and educated at Cambridge. *Idols* (Oxford, 1986), his first collection of poems, is marked by an assured stylishness: influences (notably Corbière and Geoffrey *Hill) have been creatively absorbed. The poems in the first half are written in off-rhyming couplets, a form put to elegant yet expressively jittery use. Here Romer's main concerns are love, poetry, and their attendant complications: narcissism, 'the mind', art's dubious triumphs over experience. The pervasive mood is one of dandified, if heartfelt, irony. Romer's lines move with a finicky grace, yet they remain open to what 'Higher Things' calls 'the sublime'. He trains a quasi-philosophical eye on his emotions and explores fictive parallels with a mixture of wit and anguish. Composed in a variety of forms (including blank verse and off-rhyming tercets), the poems in the second half have a less guarded feel, and yet the better pieces (such as 'How Things Continue') retain stylistic control while striking affirmative, even visionary, notes. *Plato's Ladder* (Oxford, 1992) continues in a similar vein, but also includes a sequence about post-Communist Poland, where Romer taught for a year. [MO'N

ROOK, (William) Alan (1909–90), was born in Ruddington, Nottinghamshire, and educated at Uppingham and Oxford. He served in the Royal Artillery in the Second World War; and, as deputy assistant adjutant general, reached the rank of major. *Soldiers, This Solitude* (London, 1942), which contained the poem 'Dunkirk', received considerable acclaim. He became a co-editor of the magazine *Kingdom Come* after it was taken over in 1941 by Henry *Treece and Stefan Schimanski. After the war he went into the family wine business.

Rook published two further volumes of poetry, *These are my Comrades* (London, 1943) and *We who are Fortunate* (London, 1945). The title of the last book echoes important preoccupations of his poetry: the relationship between death in war and death as an aspect of life; and the relationship of those who survive to those who are killed. His treatment of these themes tends, however, to be poetically conventional and little reflective of the realities of war. In 1948 he published *Not As A Refuge*, a prose meditation on the role of the poet. After that he published no poetry. [ATT

ROOT, William Pitt (1941–), was born in Austin, Minnesota, and attended the universities of Washington at Seattle and North Carolina.

Among figures he most admires, Root has included W. C. *Williams, *Frost, Whitman, Lorca, and Blake, confessing a special regard for Theodore *Roethke's 'Greenhouse' and 'North American' series. His first two collections, *The Storm and Other Poems* (1969) and *Striking the Dark Air for Music* (1973), both of which revolve obsessively around the early death of his father, reflect a steady shift from Williams to Blake and Roethke, from direct statements and concrete scenes to a more introspective quest for allegory and mystical resolutions in nature. His willingness to take risks, to expose the close relationship between narrator and poem-making self, does not always save his work from a tunnel lexicon and focus.

Root has yet to publish a selected or collected volume; his most recent books are *Reasons for Going It on Foot* (New York, 1981) and *Faultdancing* (Pittsburgh, Pa., 1986). [EB

ROSE, Peter (1955–), was born into a famous footballing family and grew up in Wangaratta, Victoria. He works as commissioning editor for an international publishing house in Melbourne and has published two books of poetry. *The House of Vitriol* (1990) established his style distinctly; it was soon followed by *The Catullan Rag* (1993—both Sydney), the shapes and quirks of which are clearly the products of the same sensibility.

Rose's is a post-realist poetry which enjoys the modernist habit of incorporating a diversity of cultural materials and proper names. It offers collages without easy signposts, events without manifest conclusions: one of his trade-marks is the strategically weak ending.

The poems in Rose's second collection tend to be larger and more assured than those in *The House of Vitriol*, pointing beyond the operatic or historical materials which bedeck them to the occasions of flat-life in the days and nights of inner suburbia. The persona tends to be mercurial, evasive, and ruefully hedonistic. There is also a suite of fourteen poems spoken by a modern Catullus. Swagged with adjectives, Rose's busy poems refuse the well-made turn and counter-turn. Although obscure at times, they are crammed with the stuff of colourful dailiness.   [CW-C

ROSENBERG, Isaac (1890–1918), was born in Bristol, the son of poor Jewish immigrants from Eastern Europe. The family moved to the East End of London when Rosenberg was 7. He showed early talent as a graphic artist, and on leaving school at the age of 15 was apprenticed to a firm of engravers. Private and institutional charity from Jewish sources subsequently enabled him to attend the Slade School of Art. During his time there he exhibited a few pictures in various galleries, without much success, and printed and published, with no success whatever, his first small collection of poems, *Night and Day* (1912). The outbreak of the First World War found him in Cape Town, where he had gone in hope of being cured of a serious pulmonary illness. He returned to England early in 1915, enlisted towards the end of that year (he was posted initially to a special unit for under-sized recruits, the 'Bantam' battalion of the Suffolk Regiment), and was sent to France six months later. He was killed in action on 1 April 1918.

Throughout his life Rosenberg was undecided as to whether he should devote himself chiefly to his painting or his poetry. Once he had joined the army, the matter was effectively settled for him: it became impossible for him to continue painting, but even in the front line, or just behind it, he could and did go on writing. Today he is best known as a 'war poet'; his name and reputation are indissolubly linked with those of *Sassoon and *Owen; he is seen as one who tried to write realistically, as they did, about life (and death) in the trenches. In fact his mode of writing is as different from theirs as they are from each other. What Sassoon and Owen do have in common is that they are poets of disillusionment; their subject is not just the horrors of trench warfare, but the falsity of the patriotic emotions and the ideas of military glory which, they felt, had made such horrors possible.

Rosenberg, by contrast, appears never to have had any interest in these ideas and emo-

tions, or any illusions about them. As a civilian he had scarcely known anything but penury, isolation, and illness; even the extreme rigours of army and trench life seem, therefore, to have been for him merely a continuation of peace by other means (to adapt von Clausewitz's famous maxim). As a result he was able to write about his experiences in France with a stoic sensitivity, a mixture of sardonic poise and passionate fellow-feeling, that is distinctively his own. Indeed, something strangely resembling a note of relish is to be found in the handful of poems which keep his name alive today: 'Break of Day in the Trenches', 'Returning, We Hear the Larks', 'Dead Man's Dump', 'The Burning of the Temple', and perhaps a few others. These poems are as bleak and sombre as any to have emerged from the trenches; but the muscularity of their diction and the energy of their vision reveal how much appetite and ambition there was in his nature. At the same time, and no less importantly, they reveal also how great was his capacity for self-detachment.

The most recent, and fullest, edition of Rosenberg's poetry and letters is to be found in *The Collected Works of Isaac Rosenberg*, ed. Ian Parsons (London, 1979). See also *Journey to the Trenches: The Life of Isaac Rosenberg*, by Joseph Cohen (London, 1975) and *Isaac Rosenberg: the Half Used Life*, by Jean Liddiard (London, 1975).

[DJ

ROSENBLATT, Joe (Joseph) (1933–), was born in Toronto, where he grew up in the Kensington Market district and attended Central Technical School. He moved to British Columbia in 1967 and now lives on Vancouver Island. Since 1969 he has edited the literary magazine *Jewish Dialog*.

Launching his career in 1963 with *The Voyage of the Mood*, Rosenblatt has fashioned a distinctive body of work that draws on *sound poetry and experiments in typography related to the work of bp *Nichol and bill *bissett. But Rosenblatt's vision is unique in Canadian poetry in its evocations of a unified, eroticized cosmos in which animal life unabashedly celebrates its being. Rosenblatt is also an accomplished artist;

his quirky humour is complemented by the delicate line drawings with which he illustrates his work.

The opening section of one of his best known books, *Bumblebee Dithyramb* (Erin, Ont., 1972), re-creates in passionate detail the rituals of a broad range of animal and natural life, including bees, spiders, toads, mantises, fish, cockroaches, a mushroom, a venus flytrap, and various flowers. Drawing resourcefully on typographical experiment and repetition, Rosenblatt's poems about bumblebees are powerful enactments of the bees' sound and sense.

Topsoil (Erin, 1976) includes work from several of Rosenblatt's earlier books.   [NB

ROSENTHAL, M(acha) L(ouis) (1917–), was born in Washington, DC. He is one of the few contemporary poets to have been deeply influenced by the eclectic Chicago Critics (R. S. Crane and others) who flourished alongside, and reacted to, the *New Criticism. The key to his methods, which are traditional and lyrical, may be found in *The Modern Poetic Sequence: The Genius of Modern Poetry* (New York and Oxford, 1983), a critical book he wrote with Sally M. Gall. An interesting and skilful poet who has learned from *Pound and W. C. *Williams as well as from more traditional poets like *Yeats, he has worked out what amounts to a theory of modern lyrical poetry which must, he feels, exist most effectively in sequences rather than in single poems. Such a theory bears more than a passing resemblance to that of Robert *Graves, who believed that the essential poetry in epics was carried at points of high stress in the narrative; but he has not mentioned Graves in this connection. He admires such poems as *The Waste Land* and 'Song of Myself', and his own lyrics are intended to be read as making up a single long poem. Sometimes these poems read oddly, because 'sense' (events, structure) is made subordinate to 'affect'; but they are usually interesting, and frequently make intelligent use of irony. See *Blue Boy on Skates* (New York and London, 1964); *Poems 1964–1980* (New York, 1981); *All For Love* (New York, 1987).
                                                        [MS-S

ROSS, Alan (1922–), was born in Calcutta and educated at Haileybury and at St John's College, Oxford. He served in the Royal Navy from 1942 to 1947, his final post being interpreter to the British Naval C-in-C, Germany. After working for the British Council from 1947 to 1950 he was on the staff of the *Observer* from 1950 to 1971, reporting international cricket tours of South Africa, Australia, and the West Indies.

Many of the poems in *The Derelict Day* (London, 1947) and *Something of the Sea: Poems 1942–1952* (London, 1954; Boston, 1955), reflect Ross's experience of war. The subtitle of the first volume, *Poems from Germany*, points to its theme—the drab, dispirited, and sleazy world of post-war Germany, defeated and occupied. Various poems in the second collection convey with remarkable power every aspect of life on a warship in the Arctic. 'J. W. 51B A Convoy', while shirking nothing of the pain and horror of a naval battle, celebrates the heroism and the exhilaration that combat at sea may generate. It is unsurpassed by any narrative poem of the Second World War.

In 1961 Ross took over from John *Lehmann the *London Magazine* and, while maintaining its literary standards, gave more space than before to the other arts. In 1986 he edited a selection of the verse and prose from the years of his editorship.

Ross followed his early volumes with *To Whom it may Concern* (1958), *North from Sicily* (1965), and the substantial *Poems 1942–67* (1968—all London). Later collections include *Tropical Ice* (1972), *The Taj Express: Poems 1967–73* (1973), *Open Sea* (1975), and *Death Valley* (1980—all London), a grim evocation of an oppressive landscape. Much of his work displays the immediacy of impressionistic journalism, and of snapshots on a Mediterranean cruise; his best poems attain a fine solidity and depth, especially when they are concerned with people, places, and erotic encounters. His achievements as poet, writer on cricket and travel, editor, and anthologist were recognized by the award of the CBE in 1972.

See his two volumes of autobiography, *Blindfold Games* (London, 1986) and *The Coastwise Lights* (London, 1988).   [JPr

ROSS, W(illiam) W(rightson) E(ustace) (1894–1966), Canadian poet and geophysicist, was born in Peterborough, Ontario, and was educated at the University of Toronto. Deliberately aloof from the mainstream of Canadian literary life, Ross developed a self-contained and highly private version of a modernist sensibility. His tightly wound, Giacommeti-like *imagist verse began to appear in *Poetry (Chicago) in 1923 and in the *Dial. Not a prolific writer, Ross published privately his first collection, *Laconics*, in 1930. This was followed by *Sonnets* (1932), a collection less concentrated in its imagism. For most of his life Ross was content to immerse himself in his work as a scientist at the Dominion Magnetic Observatory, and he distanced himself successfully from his fellow poets until Raymond *Souster published a modestly mimeographed booklet, *Experiment 1923–1929* (1956). The appearance of this crudely produced pamphlet helped to draw attention to the unique quality of Ross's style. He was recognized as a pioneer who had jettisoned the conventional baggage of European literary modernism, and had constructed a poetry of the sparest contemporary forms into which he had worked the sharp images and the frequently lonely echoes of his native land. In 1968, in a collaborative effort, Raymond Souster and J. R. Colombo edited a representative collection of Ross's poetry entitled *Shapes and Sounds: The Poems of W. W. E. Ross* (Toronto), for which Barry Callaghan wrote a 'Memoir'. [MG

ROTHENBERG, Jerome (1931–), was born in New York City, and educated at City College of New York and the University of Michigan. From 1959 to 1970 he taught in New York, where he was associated with the poet Robert *Kelly; since 1976 he has taught chiefly at the University of California, San Diego.

Rothenberg follows in the footsteps of such figures as *Pound, *Olson, and *Bly as a teacher, anthologizer, and consolidator of an alternative poetic tradition with its own eccentric genealogy, and his work in these roles has tended to overshadow his own poetry. The literary canon that Rothenberg has been developing over the past three decades is a diverse blend of so-called 'primitive' or oral poetries from many cultures, especially the Native American tribes; the twentieth-century literary avant-garde, especially Dadaism and its tributaries; and the entire Jewish tradition from ancient times to the present, Rothenberg's own primary inheritance. In each of these areas he has produced large anthologies that are particularly noteworthy for their innovative presentations of unfamiliar materials. Most recently Rothenberg has been exploring the larger implications of what he terms 'ethnopoetics', investigating ways in which contemporary poetry can draw on the resources of oral and tribal cultures.

Rothenberg's own poetry freely makes use of all these traditions in varying combinations and proportions. His *New Selected Poems 1970–1985* (New York, 1986) gathers work from his moving volume *Poland/1931* (New York, 1974), devoted to the experience and culture of European Jews; from *A Seneca Journal* (New York, 1978), written while Rothenberg was an honorary member of an Indian tribe in upstate New York; and from *That Dada Strain* (New York, 1983), a volume that pays homage to the literary experiments of an earlier generation. Yet while each of these books emphasizes a single tradition, each contains elements of the others as well, producing a heady and unpredictable mix of stylistic and thematic ingredients. One of Rothenberg's most interesting formal inventions, derived from his ethnopoetic research, is the 'event' poem, which takes the form of a set of instructions for performing some ritual procedure; he includes a number of these in *Poland/1931*, characteristically adapting a tribal form to Jewish concerns and sensibility. His most recent book, devoted in large part to the Jewish holocaust, is *Khurbn and Other Poems* (New York, 1989). [RG

ROUGHTON, Roger. See *Contemporary Poetry and Prose*.

ROWBOTHAM, David (Harold) (1924–), was born in Toowoomba, Queensland, and served in the RAAF in the Pacific in the Second World War. His first poems appeared in Australian journals in the immediate post-war years and drew attention to a regional poet of lyric talent. Although he published two prose collections (*Town and City: Tales and Sketches*, 1956, and *The Man in the Jungle*, a novel, 1964), it is as a poet that Rowbotham has established himself. His sixth collection, *The Pen of Feathers* (1971), was second prize-winner in the Cook Bicentenary literary competition, and in 1991 he was awarded an Order of Australia. He has also been made an emeritus fellow of the Australia Council in the form of a life pension.

Rowbotham's literary career has been centred in Queensland, where for many years he was literary editor, arts editor, and theatre critic for the *Courier Mail* newspaper. He retired in 1987. Although there is a strong vein of regional colour and tone in his poetry, an overview reveals that Rowbotham has developed a continuing interest in the fields of science, technology, and other aspects of late twentieth-century civilization. His *Selected Poems* (St Lucia, Qld., 1975) will be revised and updated in an edition due from Penguin Australia. Although his writing reveals the metrically conservative influence of his literary precursors in Australia, notably Douglas *Stewart and R. D. *Fitzgerald, Rowbotham has become something of a loner, with a doggedly individual if non-flamboyant tone: his characteristic later poetry teases out meanings and resonances from some initial image or 'pretext'. Although sometimes witty and even biting, the poetry maintains an essential seriousness of purpose which refuses to compromise with postmodernist 'play'. It is this very unfashionableness which may in the long term reveal Rowbotham's best poems as enduring and original.

A critical book on his work by John Stungnell, *Focus on David Rowbotham* (Brisbane) was published in 1969, and *Modern Australian Poetry, 1920–1970*, by Herbert C. Jaffa (Detroit, 1979) includes an essay on Rowbotham. [TWS

ROWLAND, J(ohn) R(ussell) (1925–), was born at Armidale, New South Wales, and after joining the Australian Department of Foreign Affairs in 1944, served in London, Washington, Saigon, Malaysia, Paris, Moscow, and other East European countries. He was ambassador in Moscow (1965–8) and Paris (1979–82).

Not surprisingly, Rowland's wide experience during his diplomatic career contributed to the subject-matter of his poetry, much of which is concerned with reflections and observations of the public world that was his daily life for so many years. His poems of family life and personal concerns complement those of the controlled observer, and such poems as 'Canberra in April' and 'At Noosa' have been frequently anthologized.

In the best sense, his are 'occasional' poems which reflect an urbane and sensitive response to a wider range of contacts and experiences than are experienced by many, reflecting a conservative but caring sensibility. His best-known collections are *The Feast of Ancestors* (1965), *The Clock Inside* (1979), and *Sixty* (1989—all Sydney). [TWS

RUARK, Gibbons (1941–), was born in Raleigh, North Carolina, the son of a Methodist minister. Ruark was educated at the University of North Carolina and the University of Massachusetts, and since 1968 has taught at the University of Delaware. His first collection, *A Program for Survival* (Charlottesville, Va.), was a National Arts Council selection in 1971. Subsequent books include *Reeds* (Lubbock, Tx., 1978), *Keeping Company* (Baltimore, Md., 1983), and *Rescue the Perishing* (Baton Rouge, La., 1991). Fred *Chappell has praised Ruark's elegies and love lyrics, noting his 'insistence on the virtues of quietness and simplicity . . . in noisy and chaotic times'. While the poet has usually favoured subjects drawn from locale and autobiography, he has also written powerful poems of social protest, like 'Nightmare Inspection Tour for American Generals'. The surrealistic title-piece of his first collection describes a close encounter between a UFO and a ring of copulating men and women: 'Let us admire ourselves in the mirroring surface | While the machine is gentled and admires us all'. Travel in Italy, England, and Ireland has provided Ruark with material for poems like 'Basil', 'Miles from New-grange at the Winter Solstice', and 'North Towards Armagh', which alludes to an IRA terror bombing, the details of which the poet is told are 'no use in my peaceable poems'. Unlike most of his contemporaries, Ruark has successfully experimented with a number of traditional verse-forms, among them the sonnet, *terza rima*, and Sapphics.   [RSG

RUBADIRI, David (1930–), was born in Malawi (formerly Nyasaland), but educated at King's College, Budo, and Makerere University, both in Uganda. After a period of detention by the British for his opposition to Central African Federation, he spent two years (1960–2) at King's College, Cambridge. Publishing widely, he could already be clearly seen as a pioneer of verse in English by black Africans and was represented as such in the early anthologies of Moore and Beier (Harmondsworth, 1963) and Reed and Wake (London, 1964).

He had other striking gifts, pedagogic and political. In 1964, after Malawi became independent, he was the country's first ambassador to the United States and United Nations. However, his leader, Banda, turned against the young men who had brought him to power and Rubadiri soon began a life as university teacher in exile—back at Makerere, then in Nairobi, with spells in the US and Nigeria. His warm encouragement of student drama and of younger writers made him a well-loved figure. Eventually, in the Eighties, he found a niche as professor of education at the University of Botswana.

Rubadiri has published little new creative work since the 1960s. His novel, *No Bride Price* (Nairobi, 1967), continues to attract critical attention, and his verse is found in many anthologies, including *Poems from East Africa* (London, 1971), which he co-edited with David Cook, and his own selection for secondary schools, *Growing Up With Poetry* (London, 1989). Such poems as 'African Thunderstorm' achieved, and maintain, wide currency because they show with taste and clarity how English free verse can be applied to African material. Typically, as in this case, Rubadiri confronts a strong subject with symbolic overtones in a pos-

ture ultimately derived from the Romantics, though in 'Stanley Meets Mutesa' the echoes are from *Eliot's 'Journey of the Magi'.   [ALRC

RUKEYSER, Muriel (1913–80), was born and raised in New York City. She was educated at Vassar College (where her fellow students included Elizabeth *Bishop and Mary McCarthy) and Columbia University, and taught at Sarah Lawrence College. Her nonliterary involvements were unusually eclectic, encompassing aviation, science, photography, and above all political activism. In addition to poetry and translations, Rukeyser wrote biographies and children's books.

Rukeyser's work provides a crucial bridge between the politically engaged poetry of the 1930s and the 1960s in America. Like many intellectuals during the Depression, she was strongly involved in left-wing political causes, including the socialist and labour movements and the resistance to fascism in Spain. Her poetry during this period reflects the influence of 'engaged' poets like Horace *Gregory and, especially, W. H. *Auden, whose intricate formal techniques and eccentric diction offered Rukeyser a way to avoid the heavy-handedness of much social protest poetry. Her first book, *Theory of Flight* (New Haven, Conn., 1935), derived in part from her experience as a novice pilot, received the Yale Younger Poets Award. Subsequent books show a gradual loosening of technique; Whitman begins to replace Auden as a formal model, until by the Sixties she is writing a sweeping, eclectic free verse that inspired younger women like Adrienne *Rich and Anne *Sexton, both of whom acknowledge their debt to Rukeyser. Rukeyser's voice in her late poetry also becomes less mediated, more open and direct in its assumption of responsibility to lessen the world's suffering; in a famous line that has been taken up as a rallying cry for feminist poets, she announced: 'No more masks!' If few of Rukeyser's poems have become anthology pieces, she nevertheless is a key figure in the transformation of women's poetry over the last sixty years. Her work is available in *The Collected Poems of Muriel Rukeyser* (New York, 1978).   [RG

RUMENS, Carol (-Ann) (1944–), was born in London and attended Bedford College, University of London. After working in publicity and advertising she became a free-lance writer and poetry editor of *Quarto* and the *Literary Review* (London). She was creative-writing fellow at Kent University, Canterbury, 1983–5, and Northern Arts Literary Fellow (Newcastle), 1988–90. In 1991 she took up an appointment at Queen's University, Belfast.

From the outset (*Strange Girl in Bright Colours*, London, 1973) Rumens has insisted on the fusion of the personal and the political. Her feminist-socialist perspective has combined with formal versatility to produce work of considerable variety and scope. *Unplayed Music* (London, 1981) and *Star Whisper* (London, 1983) contain vivid, melancholy, lyrical, and dramatic poems of love and domestic life, with a firm sense of social and political context, while hinting at the theme of exile and atrocity which emerge fully in *Direct Dialling* (London, 1985). Here Rumens addresses large historical themes ('Revolutionary Women', 'A Jewish Cemetery', 'Outside Osweicim'), and strikes the international note which now characterizes her work. That she has for the most part avoided the pitfalls of this approach—moralizing, abstraction—is due partly to a developing dramatic imagination and also to the sensual particularity which has often distinguished her poems. A visit to Russia produced *The Greening of Snow Beach* (Newcastle upon Tyne, 1988), containing some of her most impressive work ('A Moscow Wife, Waiting', 'The Fire Fighter's Widow on her First Memorial Day Outing'). *From Berlin to Heaven* (London, 1989) charts further travels, while also marking an intriguing and estranged return to English themes.

Selected Poems (London, 1987) draws on Rumens's first four collections. She has published a novel, *Plato Park* (London, 1987), and has edited *Making for the Open: The Chatto Book of Post-Feminist Poetry* (new edn., London, 1988) and *New Women Poets* (Newcastle upon Tyne, 1990). She is, with Richard McKane, a principal translator of *The Poetry of Perestroika*, ed. Peter Mortimer and S. J. Litherland (Newcastle upon

Tyne, 1991). Her play *Almost Siberia* was staged at Newcastle Gulbenkian Theatre and Soho Polytechnic in 1989–90.

[SO'B

RUSSELL, George William. See AE.

RUSSELL, Peter. See *NINE*.

RUTSALA, Vern (1934–), was born in McCall, Idaho, and educated at Reed College in Portland, Oregon, where he took his BA in 1956. Subsequently he served as an enlisted man in the US Army for two years, then attended the *Iowa Writers' Workshop, where he earned an MFA in 1960. Rutsala has spent his entire academic career at Lewis and Clark College in Portland, except for visiting appointments at the University of Minnesota and Minneapolis and Bowling Green State University in Ohio.

With his first book. *The Window* (Middletown, Conn., 1964), Rutsala had already developed the style that has continued to run through all his work, even the book of prose (but not prosaic) poems titled *Paragraphs* (Middletown, 1978). Characteristic elements include: statements laid out in prose lines; images that might best be described as 'a surrealism of the everyday'; an existential stolidity in the face of the incursions of time and the world upon our minds and bodies; a sense of the idiocy of it all, of self-satire.

Small Songs (Iowa City, 1969), a sequence of epigrams, *The Harmful State* (Lincoln, Nebr., 1971), and *The New Life* (Portland, Oreg., 1978) were all chapbooks. Rutsala continued, in *Laments* (New York, 1975), *The Journey Begins* (Athens, Ga., 1976), and *Walking Home from the Icehouse* (Pittsburgh, Pa., 1981) to force the reader to see himself clearly, but the poet's sadistic good humour took the edge off the pain. In 1985 Rutsala published two collections, a book, *Backtracking* (Santa Cruz, Calif.), and a chapbook, *The Mystery of Lost Shoes* (Amherst, Mass.).

[LT

RYAN, Gig (Elizabeth) (1956–) was born in Melbourne, Australia. Since 1978 she has lived mainly in Sydney, where she was instrumenal in forming a band, *Disband*, whose album *Six Goodbyes* was released in 1988.

Her first book of poems, *The Division of Anger* (Sydney, 1981), established her as an abrasive and vivid new writer. Her subsequent verse collections, *Manners of an Astronaut* (Sydney, 1984) and *Excavation* (Sydney, 1990) have been equally commanding, and disturbing. The poet and critic Martin *Johnston early on described her writing as 'hallucinatory', but it is also concerned with an increasingly sophisticated manipulation of heard speech, especially the staccato and disjointed speech of inner cities and the environment of rock bands and the drug culture. The politics of sex, power, and the victim mentality remain her chief concerns, though her most recent work gives hints of an abiding lyrical impulse beneath the habitual stance of aggressive, hurt bravado.

[TWS

RYAN, Michael (1945–), was born in St Louis, Missouri. He studied at Notre Dame University and Claremont Graduate School, and gained an MFA and Ph.D from the University of Iowa. Ryan's first volume, *Threats Instead of Trees* (New Haven, Conn., 1974), won the Yale Series of Younger Poets Award. He has since published two volumes of poetry, *In Winter* (New York, 1981, selected by Louise Glück for the National Poetry Series) and *God Hunger* (New York, 1989). He has received numerous prizes for poetry, including fellowships from the National Endowment for the Arts and the Guggenheim Foundation. Ryan has also supported himself by teaching at such institutions as the University of Iowa (where he was an editor of *The Iowa Review*), Southern Methodist University, Goddard College (where he directed the writing programme in 1978–9), and currently at Warren Wilson College. A practitioner of the meditation-in-verse and the self-presentational lyric, Ryan attempts to infuse the commonplace with mystery and drama through conversational free verse and, on occasion, traditional forms. Too often, however, he does not transcend the mundane, settling instead for a less-than-edifying poetry of remarks.

[RMcD

S

SACKS, Peter (1950–), was born in Port Elizabeth, South Africa and grew up in Durban. He now teaches English and writing at Johns Hopkins University.

Sacks writes a strong, clear-sighted poetry that is deeply rooted in place. But if the poems begin in particular locales, the poet's meditative intelligence soon brings the moral topography into view. In his first collection, *In These Mountains* (New York and London, 1986), Sacks manifested his characteristic concerns—with romantic love, memory, political accountability, and the spiritual impulse—but managed to sustain a subdued lyricism throughout. The title-poem, an imaginative re-creation of the lives of the Bushmen of the Kalahari, summons up the void left behind after their all-but total eradication, but does so in an elegiac manner. The poet hears: 'no bird cry,│no river sound, no spirits travelling quickly│with their quivers under the cold drift of stars,│their bone-chip rattles and their voices│streaming in the darkness and the wind.'

Promised Lands (New York and London, 1990), Sacks's second collection, reveals a perceptibly more stringent vision. While the majority of the poems are bound to locale—notably the sequence 'States' which surveys the American terrain—Sacks is more inclined than before to historical, mythic, and religious speculation. The result is that the sensuous particulars encountered in the first book recede to make place for more emblematic treatment of subject. Place is not so much seen for itself as seen *through*. A starkly beautiful natural world is also a place for moral and spiritual self-reckoning. In his powerful long poem 'Alaska', Sacks concludes: 'Between destruction and redemption│we who know nothing of purity except the word,│move through the waters,│move into the fire no breath can name,│the fire that will not say *it is enough*│until we breathe again.'

Sacks is also the author of *The English Elegy: Studies in the Genre from Spenser to Yeats* (1985).

[SPB

SACKVILLE-WEST, V. (Victoria Mary) (1892–1962), was born into a wealthy and aristocratic family and brought up at Knole, the ancestral home of the Sackville family. She became a prolific novelist and biographer, but never shook off the air of a dilettante and is best remembered for her literary friendships (notably with Virginia Woolf), her well-documented marriage to writer and diplomat Harold Nicolson, and her expertise as a creative gardener. The garden she made with Nicolson at their home, Sissinghurst Castle, became the subject for many gardening books in the later years of her life. Her reputation as a poet rests on *The Land*, a popular success ever since its publication in 1926, which relates at length (2,500 lines) and in the first-person the cycle of a farming year in Kent. The poem was deliberately anti-modernist and provincial, using regular iambic lines and archaic diction, but was not deliberately modelled on Virgil's *Georgics*, of which the author was ignorant. A better poem, started soon after publication of *The Land* but not finished until 1946, is *The Garden*, also a long poem, but by no means so artificial. It was in effect a treatise on gardening, and also a meditation, written in time of war and expressive of an inner landscape as well as a realized, physical one. Sackville-West published several volumes of verse privately, and *King's Daughter* (1929) with the Hogarth Press. *Collected Poems* (vol. 1) appeared in 1933 and *Selected Poems* in 1941 (both London). There was no second volume of *Collected Poems*. See also Victoria Glendinning, *Vita, The Life of Vita Sackville-West* (London, 1983). [CPH

SADOFF, Ira (1945–) was born in Brooklyn, New York. His father abandoned the family when Sadoff was 13. Sadoff attended Cornell University and did graduate work at the University of Oregon. He served as the founding editor of the literary magazine, the *Seneca Review*, and poetry editor of the *Antioch Review* during the 1970s. He is currently professor of English at Colby College in Maine.

Although his first book of poems, *Settling Down* (1975), was positively received, Sadoff's initial style now seems dated. Influenced by the *Deep Image style popularized in the early Seventies by poets such as Robert *Bly and James *Wright, Sadoff's early work emphasized a mix of the transcendental and absurdist functions of *surrealism. By the time of his second book, *Palm Reading in Winter* (1978), however, Sadoff's work had changed, and his mature work is characterized by its discursive intelligence, as well as its responsiveness to the demands of personal history and memory.

Family life, the frailty and complexity of family roles and relationships, are among Sadoff's most prominent subjects and themes. Many poems, including 'Meditation' and 'The Vacation in Miami: July, 1954', explore confusion, guilt, and anger from the point of view of a boy abandoned by his father. Other poems focus on the troubled relationship between the boy and his mother after the father's departure. Sadoff's poems drift between dream-like uncertainties and moments of absolute, often terrifying clarity as his adolescent speakers come into self-consciousness. Sadoff also examines family life from an adult's perspective in poems which explore the speaker's marriage.

Another of Sadoff's principal subjects is American politics and culture. Sadoff believes in the political witness of poetry, and he rages against class structure (often in ironic or humorous tones), and especially against the socially privileged. His later work, including poems such as 'Nazis' and 'Mahler', explores his own complex feelings about being a Jew in a Christian culture.

Recent collections include *A Northern Calendar* (Boston, 1982) and *Emotional Traffic* (Boston, 1989). [TSw

SAIL, Lawrence (1942–), was born in London. He read French and German at St John's College, Oxford, and taught in Kenya for five years before moving to Exeter, where he taught until 1991. He edited the magazine *South West Review* for nearly five years, and compiled the anthology *First and Always: Poems for Great Ormond Street Children's Hospital* (London, 1988). He is currently chairman of the Arvon Foundation and was programme director of the Cheltenham Festival of Literature in 1991.

Sail is a taut and sinewy poet, drawn to the epiphanies of nature, particularly the sea, and the sacraments of personal life. There is a development from the poems in *Opposite Views* (London, 1974), which attempt, often successfully, to catch the voice of the times—titles such as 'Consumer Poems', 'Curriculum Vitae', 'Report from the Planet Proteus' give the flavour—to the more intense, sometimes religious, poems of *Devotions* (London, 1987). His second book was *The Kingdom of Atlas* (London, 1980); his most recent is *Out of Land: New and Selected Poems* (Newcastle upon Tyne, 1992).

Sail's poems are usually short to medium-length. His descriptions are pithy, crisp, sometimes witty in the *Martian manner. In his mature work even the secular occasions are sacramental: 'Snooker Players' celebrates the Newtonian simplicity and perfection of the game, counterpointing the murkiness of the fallen world beyond the illuminated table; 'Allotments' are seen as the 'last real estate of common prayer'. [PF

ST JOHN, David (1949–), was born in California. He has taught in the writing seminars of

Johns Hopkins University and now teaches at the University of Southern California. In St John's lyrics there is a fusion of *confessional, meditative, epistolary, and narrative elements. In 'Dolls' and 'You', from *Hush* (Boston, 1976), the over-valued desire for individuality is posed against the desire for romantic communion; as the two desires violate one another, each lover has the choice of betraying either one's self or one's mate. This conflict is further explored in St John's later, more ambitious books.

Lyrical and extravagantly emblematic, 'Of the Remembered', a long poem from *The Shore* (Boston, 1980), is a postmodern reply to *Eliot's Four Quartets*; it is an effort to find a redemption through memory and language. A prismatic sequence of related dramatic monologues and cinematic vignettes, *No Heaven* (Boston, 1985) is a powerful presentation of a more fragmented and troubled spirituality, confronting the seductive delusions of godless desire, and finding that antique faiths may be absurd, or impossible to embrace. 'The Man with the Yellow Gloves' is a parable of how the self may become disfigured by appropriating obsolete ancestral spirits.

[DWF

Saint Mark's Poetry Project, The, or, more properly, the Poetry Project at Saint Mark's Church-in-the-Bowery, located on the north-east corner of Second Avenue and East 10th Street in New York City, has played a vital part in the development and dissemination of new American poetry since 1966, when it was started with the help of the Episcopalian church's rector, Father J. C. Michael Allen, and with money from a federal grant for the social rehabilitation of New York's lower East Side. The Project's first director, poet Joel *Oppenheimer, initiated a roster of activities which remains basically unchanged: open readings on Monday nights, invitational readings on Wednesday nights, weekly workshops conducted by neighbourhood poets, and the irregular publication of a poetry magazine, *The World*. During the tenure of the Project's second director, poet Anne Waldman, the church became the unofficial campus of the *New York School of poetry, though both

the Project and its publications have always been hospitable to a wide range of poets, and the church has been the site of memorable readings not only by poets associated with the New York School, but also by Robert *Lowell, Allen *Ginsberg, Adrienne *Rich, John Cage, Amiri *Baraka, John *Wieners, and many others. Father Allen was succeeded as rector by the equally co-operative Father David Garcia, and since Waldman the Project's poet-directors have included Ron *Padgett, Bernadette Mayer, Eileen Myles, and Ed Friedman.

[RH

SALKEY, Andrew (1928–), was born in Colón, Panama, of Jamaican parents. He was educated at St George's College and Munro College in Jamaica, and at the University of London. He is now associate professor of writing at Hampshire College, Amherst, Massachusetts.

Though better known for his novels, Salkey has published much poetry and continues to do so. Political commitment, very much from a leftist perspective, dominates his poems, but they rise above purely ideological rhetoric. They accentuate personal allegiances, avoid tendentiousness, and are generally tough-minded. Consequently many are occasional in nature, addressed or dedicated to friends. His 'postcard' poems, particularly, make the primacy of the personal clearly evident, 'sent', as their titles indicate, from such developing countries as Mexico, Brazil, and Uganda, and each is precisely dated. Other poems express considerable unease at his comfortable 'exile'. 'I Never Left', for instance, ends with 'I left the island | I never left'.

His books of poems include *Jamaica* (London, 1973), a long, historical work in verse, *In the Hills Where Her Dreams Live* (Havana, 1979), and *Away* (London, 1980). Two of his best novels are *A Quality of Violence* (London, 1959) and *The Late Emancipation of Jerry Stover* (London, 1968).

[MR

SALOM, Philip (1950–), was born near Perth and grew up on a dairy farm at Brunswick Junction in the south-west of Western Australia. After graduating from an agricultural college he worked in New Zealand, before returning to Western Australia to study, and later teach, creative writing.

Salom has won Commonwealth poetry awards for his first book, *The Silent Piano* (Fremantle, 1980) and his third, *Sky Poems* (Fremantle, 1987). The environment of the dairy farm and its 'natural' activities links Salom's first book with those of other Australian rural poets such as Les A. *Murray and David *Campbell. But Salom's imagination is not restricted to observed detail and ranges very widely: the title-poem of his first volume tells how a prisoner 'escapes' his confinement by making a silent piano from old bits of wood.

Salom's second volume, *The Projectionist* (Fremantle, 1983) develops the character of a country-town projectionist, using the device for a variety of cinematic effects. In the *livre composé*, *Sky Poems*, the poetic self is very mobile, displaying an audacious range of imagery and speculation, questioning settled notions of subject and object. In *The Barbecue of the Primitives* (St Lucia, Qld., 1989) a wide-ranging, original intelligence at times recalls Peter *Porter's poetry. *Feeding the Ghost* (Ringwood, Victoria) came out in 1993. [BB

SALTER, Mary Jo (1954–), born in Grand Rapids, Michigan, grew up in Baltimore, Maryland. She was educated at Harvard, and in 1982 married Brad *Leithauser, the poet and novelist, with whom she has two children. Salter has lived for several years in Kyoto; then in Rome, London, Reykjavik, and now Paris. In the United States she shares a post with her husband at Mount Holyoke College.

Like her teacher Elizabeth *Bishop, Salter values craftsmanship. Her poems colour a world of 'Order gloved as Beauty', while constantly subverting elements we count on most as safe and innocent: home, family, and even art. To think of Salter as a placid or comfortable poet is to misunderstand her. Though her range may exclude anger, there is frustration and joy, gratitude and grief. Her poems range from domestic to large, sometimes tragic subjects with uncommon fluency.

Salter has published two collections of poetry, *Henry Purcell in Japan* (New York, 1985) and *Unfinished Painting* (New York, 1989), which was the 1988 Lamont Poetry Selection of the Academy of American Poets. She has also written a children's book, *The Moon Comes Home* (New York, 1989). [HC

SANCHEZ, Sonia (1934–), was born in Birmingham, Alabama, and educated at Hunter College, New York. Graduate work in poetry with Louise *Bogan at New York University was followed by growing involvement in the civil-rights movement. Her first collection, *Homecoming* (1969), was notable for its political militancy, its commitment to the black community and scorn for 'white America', and for its daring use of African-American rhythms and language. Combining political activism with an energetic career as writer and teacher, Sanchez has taught at many universities, including Rutgers, Pennsylvania, and Temple. Her interest in developing an understanding of their African inheritance among young black people is reflected in her several books for children, among them *It's A New Day* (1971) and *A Sound Investment* (1986); while she has also produced significant autobiographical work, most notably the prose-poem collection *homegirls & handgrenades* (1984).

In her poetry of the last three decades Sanchez has restructured conventional grammatical forms in order to dramatize black speech rhythms: *We a BaddDDD People* (1970) best illustrates her experiments with sound, idiom, and grammar. *Love Poems* (1973) records some of the more intimate details of the poet's life as woman, lover, and mother. In 1972 Sanchez joined the Nation of Islam and, although she resigned three years later, her 1973 volume, *A Blues Book for Blue Black Magical Women* openly supports that movement while offering a statement on the historical condition of black women. *I've Been A Woman: New and Selected Poems* (Sausalito, Calif., 1981) is a useful selection of her work. Information on her life and writing may be found in *Black Women Writers (1950–1980): A Critical Evaluation*, ed. Mari Evans (Garden City, NJ, 1984). [RJG

SANDBURG, Carl (1878–1967), was born in Galesburg, Illinois, and lived mostly in Chicago. He is now best remembered for his monumental biography of Abraham Lincoln, but there was a period in the early 1920s when his reputation as a poet was extensive in America and growing in England. The young Rebecca West was one of his early admirers and introduced a selection of his work for Jonathan Cape. Nevertheless, with a brief revival during the period of the *Beat generation (with whom he had little in common), Sandburg has largely dropped from sight.

This is a pity. Sandburg's poetry retains two claims on our attention. As Daniel *Hoffman pointed out, Sandburg was the first important American writer to grow up in a household where English was the second language—the first was Swedish—and this gives his approach to rhythm and diction something more than idiosyncrasy. William Carlos *Williams broke the grip of the iambic line with more subtlety, but Sandburg smashed it open with greater naturalness. Poems like 'Skyscraper' and 'Cool Tombs' offer the paragraph as a verse unit in a way that no one had quite done before, not even Whitman.

The rhythms of Sandburg, refined by his wide experience as a reader of his own verse in public, have still to be fully assimilated, though they echo in poets like C. K. *Williams and Philip *Levine. But the subject-matter of his large opus is perhaps more important. In the age of Dreiser and Sinclair Lewis, Sandburg was the only poet who offered a full portrait of the industrial scene, managing some sort of challenge in verse to the sweep and range of the Zolaesque novel. What Sandburg often catches is the tacky bravura and breezy sentimentality of his midwest subjects, a sense of pulsating energy still unsure of itself and sometimes lapsing into the maudlin, the vicious, or the grotesque. Poems like 'Mag', 'Grass', and 'Fog' illustrate the sketchbook vitality of this kind of work.

The Complete Poems of Carl Sandburg (New York, 1950) won him a Pulitzer Prize. There is, alas, no selection in print in England; but see

Carl Sandburg: His Life and Works, by North Callahan (University Park, Pa., and London, 1987). Those visiting Chicago should seek out the Carl Sandburg Village, a memorial sequence of skyscrapers on the site of the St Valentine's Day Massacre.   [GMacB

San Francisco Group, The, grew out of a poetry reading held in 1955 at the Six Gallery, a small cooperative arts centre located in the Marina District of San Francisco and run by painters associated with the San Francisco Art Institute. The reading, recorded by Jack Kerouac in his novel *The Dharma Bums* (1958), brought together Allen *Ginsberg, Gary *Snyder, Michael *McClure, Philip *Whalen, and Philip *Lamantia, each of whom was introduced by Kenneth *Rexroth, a San Francisco poet from an earlier generation. Further readings at different venues, including the City Lights bookshop run by Lawrence *Ferlinghetti, helped to promote what came to be known as the San Francisco Renaissance. Among other poets associated at one time or another with this movement were Robert *Duncan, William *Everson, Jack *Spicer, Robin Blaser, and Lew Welch. Although it was predominantly a white, male group, a few black writers, like Bob Kaufman, and some women writers, such as Helen Adam, Madeline Gleason, Joanne Kyger, and Diane *di Prima, were actively involved.

The movement was more notable for its spirit of camaraderie than its unanimity of purpose: it in fact incorporated a variety of styles, among them prophetic rapture, *imagist precision, *surrealism, satire, and personal *confession. Also, several writers associated with the group were equally, if not more, involved with the activities of the *Black Mountain movement and the *Beat generation. If there was a common objective uniting the San Francisco writers, however, it was summed up by Ferlinghetti, who declared in 1955 that the kind of poetry that was 'making most noise' in his city was 'what should be called street poetry'. 'It amounts', he said, 'to getting poetry back into the street where it once was, out of the classroom . . .

and—in fact—off the printed page.' Believing that 'the printed word has made poetry so silent', the San Francisco poets aimed at a language and line shaped by the *voice*, an oral poetry frequently accompanied by jazz. Ironically, since the ending of the movement, usually associated with the death of Jack Spicer in 1965, anyone interested in its work has to rely on the printed page, although some poets have made recordings of their poems. A useful selection is to be found in *The New American Poetry*, ed. Donald M. Allen (New York, 1960). See also, Michael Davidson, *The San Francisco Poets: Poetics and Community at Mid-Century* (Cambridge, Mass., 1989). [RJG

SANT, Andrew (1950–), was born in London and educated in both England and Australia. Although he has frequently returned to England for extended visits, Sant has spent most of his adult life in Hobart, Tasmania, where until 1990 he co-edited the literary magazine *Island*. He has worked in a number of occupations, including the management of a hostel for juvenile delinquents, labouring for the Forestry Commission, and teaching. In 1989 he was made a member of the literature board of the Australia Council.

Sant's poetry is notable for its quizzical and analytic teasing out of resonances from initial (and graphic) evocations of such universal endeavours as bee-keeping, apple-growing, kelp-harvesting, and wine-making. His earlier work was to a certain extent indebted to such English models as *Hughes and *Larkin, but the stimulus of the Tasmanian environment led him to hone his spare and contemplative style to a new precision, though underlying his close attention to detail is a sophisticated poet's 'raid on reality' in order to bring back multiple possibilities and a continuing search for clarification.

His major collections are *The Caught Sky* (Sydney, 1982), *The Flower Fable* (Sydney, 1985), and *Brushing the Dark* (Melbourne, 1989). [TWS

SANTAYANA, George (1863–1952), was born in Spain but brought to Boston in 1872 to live with his American mother. He graduated from

Harvard in 1886 and three years later was teaching in its philosophy department. His first book was a poetry collection, *Sonnets and Other Verses* (1894), followed by *The Sense of Beauty* (1896), which inspired countless Harvard aesthetes to burn with Pater's 'gem-like flame.' Poetry remained the focus with the publication of *Lucifer: A Theological Tragedy* (1899, revd. edn., 1924) and *A Hermit of Carmel* (1901), but the five volumes of *The Life of Reason* (1905–6) established his reputation as a philosopher, essentially a naturalist, though convinced that a 'supernatural' element existed somewhere. His mother's legacy freed him to move abroad in 1912, settling permanently in Rome by 1924.

Santayana's prose, including *Three Philosophical Poets* (1910), had more of an impact on American poetry than his verse. As *Poems* (1923) conceded, his prosody was 'worn and traditional', and his best work is an elegiac series of scrupulous Platonic sonnets, although his only novel, *The Last Puritan* (1935), was a surprise best-seller. William G. Holzberger has edited *The Complete Poems of George Santayana* (Lewisburg, Pa., and London, 1979). See also *The Letters of George Santayana*, ed. Daniel Cory (New York, 1955) and *George Santayana: A Biography* (New York, 1987), by John McCormick. [EB

SAROYAN, Aram. See CONCRETE POETRY.

SARTON, (Eleanor) May (1912–95), was born in Belgium and taken to America in 1916; after a partly Belgian education she was naturalized as an American in 1924. She won a readership less for her technical skill than for her (as she puts it) 'unbuttoned ego'. Apart from many love poems, she wrote observantly (and most successfully) on nature, on paintings and artists, and writers (her novel about F. O. Matthiessen, *Faithful Are the Wounds*, is regarded as one of her most notable achievements). Her greatest debt is to *Millay, in whose tradition she wrote; but she lacked Millay's bite and ability to end a poem. Her verse none the less gives pleasure at a certain level, has been awarded many prizes, and sounds an authentic emotional note of a perhaps more feminist than literary sort. See *Collected Poems 1930–1973* (New York, 1973); S. S. Hilsinger and L. Brynes (eds.), *Selected Poems* (New York, 1978); and A. Sibley, *May Sarton*, (New York, 1972). [MS-S

SASSOON, Siegfried (Loraine) (1886–1967), the son of a rich Jewish father and an Anglican mother, was educated at Marlborough and at Clare College, Cambridge, where he failed to take a degree. In the years before 1914 he enjoyed hunting, golf, and cricket, read widely, and issued privately a number of small verse collections, of which the most accomplished was *The Daffodil Murderer* (1913), published under the pseudonym of Saul Kain. Begun as a parody of *Masefield's *The Everlasting Mercy*, it developed into a serious poem in which Sassoon remarked, 'I was at last writing physically'.

Sassoon, who had joined up on the first day of the war, won the MC during the Somme offensive of July 1916. But by then he had begun to write what he called real trench poems; and in July 1917, having thrown his MC into the Mersey, he protested publicly against the continuation of the war. He was persuaded by Robert *Graves to enter the Military Hospital at Craiglockhart, where he became friends with his fellow-patient Wilfrid *Owen. He was discharged, returned to active service, received a head wound, but survived the war.

Sassoon's war poems were published in *The Old Huntsman* (1917) and *Counter-Attack* (1918). Some describe with horrifying detail the nature of trench-warfare: the filth, the stench of decomposing corpses, the rats, the moral degradation. Others satirize the brass-hats and their apparent indifference to the futility of their military operations. The most ferocious lash civilians in Britain who delude themselves with jokes and slogans about the war.

In 1919 Sassoon became literary editor of the socialist *Daily Herald*, and in 1923 his *Satirical Poems* attacked conservative politicians and plutocracy. But 'At the Grave of Henry Vaughan', written in 1924, points in a new direction: 'And this lowly grave tells Heaven's tranquillity | And

here stand I, a suppliant at the door.' For years afterwards Sassoon's poetry mirrors his spiritual desolation and his search for the peace that he found at last in the Roman Catholic faith to which he was converted in 1957, and which inspired a number of unpublished devotional poems.

In 1928 Sassoon published *Memoirs of a Fox-Hunting Man*, the first of six prose autobiographies of which the last, *Siegfried's Journey* (1945), carried the story to 1920. His study of Meredith was published in 1948.

Sassoon valued his later poems more highly than his war poems, which were, he said, 'improvised by an impulsive, intolerant, immature young creature under the extreme stress of experience'. Nevertheless, they are the poems by which he is most likely to be remembered and honoured.

Rupert Hart-Davis has edited three volumes of Sassoon's diaries covering the years 1915 to 1925, *Letters to Max Beerbohm* (1986), and *War Poems* (1983—all London), which includes seven poems from periodicals and thirteen from MSS. See also *Collected Poems 1908–56* (London, 1961, 1984); Michael Thorpe, *Siegfried Sassoon: A Critical Study* (Leiden and Oxford; 1961); and Dame Felicity Corrigan, *Siegfried Sassoon: A Poet's Pilgrimage* (London, 1973). [JPr

SCAMMELL, William (1939–), was born in Hythe, Hampshire, but is most commonly associated with Cumbria, where he now lives. He had little early formal education and soon dropped out of school, working at a number of odd jobs, including a spell as a photographer on Cunard liners. He took a degree in English literature from Bristol University as a mature student in 1967, then worked in adult education in Gloucester and Cumbria until early retirement in 1991.

Given the Cumbrian association, it is no surprise that Scammell's six books of poems, including *Yes & No* (1979), *A Second Life* (1982), *Jouissance* (1985), *Eldorado* (1987), and *Bleeding Heart Yard* (1992), all published by Peterloo Poets (Calstock, Cornwall), show the influence not only of Wordsworth but also of Norman

*Nicholson; an admirer and friend of the latter, Scammell edited a Festschrift in his honour, (*Between Comets: for Norman Nicholson at 70*, Durham, 1984). The Wordsworthian legacy is particularly displayed in Scammell's emotive descriptions of landscape, showing not only its affective power on the human subject but also the ravages of industrialization. Though his usual mode is robust, that of the earthy provincial outsider, Scammell can nevertheless be whimsically metropolitan, as in *The Game: Tennis Poems* (Calstock, 1992), a set of verse parodies describing famous tennis players.

In addition to poems, he has published a critical book (*Keith Douglas: A Study*, London, 1988) and has edited two anthologies, *The New Lake Poets* (Newcastle upon Tyne, 1991) and *The Poetry Book Society Anthology* 3 (London, 1992). He is currently editing a selection of Ted *Hughes's critical prose and an anthology of nature poems. Scammell is also well known as a reviewer. His most recent book of poems is *Five Easy Pieces* (London, 1993).   [GF

SCANNELL, Vernon (1922–), was born in Lincolnshire, studied at Leeds University, served in the 51st division of the Gordon Highlanders, and has been—among various short-term occupations—a professional boxer and a prep-school teacher; in his autobiography *The Tiger and the Rose* (1971) he provided a fascinating account of the colourful early life which shaped his subsequent career.

A free-lance writer and broadcaster who has published a further autobiography about his wartime experience, several novels with a boxing background, anthologies, and a variety of highly professional occasional criticism as well as many volumes of poetry, Scannell has always valued 'a concern with style, an unfussy elegance, wit and intelligence . . . a real involvement with living experience'. A quick glance at the titles of some of his collections—*A Sense of Danger* (1962), *Walking Wounded* (1965), *The Loving Game* (1975), and *Funeral Games* (1987)—immediately suggests what, in fact, has distinguished his best work; a fascination with risk-taking, and a resilient, compassionate con-

cern for ordinary human life, in which tenderness is qualified by a kind of brusque disenchantment.

Whether his settings are the battlefield (about which he writes in his prose account *Argument of Kings*, 1987), or the home-front of domesticity, Scannell's sympathies are for the casualties, the 'walking wounded'. While often expressing both the exhilaration and abandon of combat, knowing at first hand how 'a fighter can't pack pity with his gear', he is equally skilful in suggesting the depths of guilt and remorse, perhaps most dramatically in what is probably his most anthologized poem 'A Case of Murder'. Scannell's work, however raw its subject-matter, is always carefully written, and it is a clear indication of his concerns that one of his books for younger readers is entitled *Mastering the Craft* (1970).

Vernon Scannell was granted a Civil List Pension in 1981 for services to literature. See *New and Selected Poems 1950–1980* (London, 1980).

[JM

SCARFE, Francis (Harold) (1911–86), was born on Tyneside and educated at King's College, Durham, Fitzwilliam House, Cambridge, and the Sorbonne. Before the Second World War he was a university lecturer. He entered the army in 1941, and by 1945 was lieutenant-colonel in the Education Corps. He taught French at Glasgow University until 1959, when he became director of the British Institute in Paris, a post he held until 1978. In that year he was made Chevalier de la Légion d'Honneur.

In the 1930s he showed an interest in *Surrealism and contributed to Roger Roughton's *Contemporary Poetry and Prose*. Later in the decade his work appeared in Julian *Symons's *Twentieth Century Verse*; and, like several other poets associated with that periodical, he had his first books, *Inscapes* (1940) and *Forty Poems and Ballads* (1941), published by the Fortune Press. His third volume, *Underworlds* (London), appeared in 1950, and was to be his last until *Grounds for Conceit* (Walton-on-Thames, Survey, 1984), all the poems in which were written in the year 1982–3.

His best poems are notable for their simple and direct handling of personal themes. His pioneering study, *Auden and After* (1942), had a wide circulation in its day. [ATT

SCHMIDT, Michael (1947–), was born in Mexico. He studied at Harvard and at Wadham College, Oxford, where he edited the magazine *Carcanet* and went on to found Carcanet Press. This began with small pamphlets but rapidly progressed to the production of full-size books when it moved, with Schmidt, to Manchester. It has become one of the most important poetry presses in Britain. Schmidt also founded and edits the magazine *Poetry Nation*.

Schmidt's first phase as a poet is strongly marked by his American connection: by the influence of Elizabeth *Bishop, W. C. *Williams, and of Melville's prose. There are no grand gestures, and the occasion of the poem may seem unremarkable, but the phrasing is often memorable: a tough, quiet music pervades his free-verse lines. Lineation is often significant, though sometimes awkwardly handled. A good book from which to gauge Schmidt's first style is *Bedlam and the Oak Wood* (Oxford, 1970). In the Eighties he has moved towards lines that are rhythmically looser and emotionally more straightforward and personal, as in *The Love of Strangers* (London, 1989), though he retains a careful, dry approach to diction. [ETL

SCHNACKENBERG, Gjertrud (1953–), was born of second-generation Norwegian Lutheran parents in Tacoma, Washington, where she attended local public schools. She began writing poetry as a student at Mount Holyoke College, from which she graduated in 1975, and received an honorary doctorate in 1985. As an undergraduate she earned a reputation as a poetic prodigy, twice winning the Glascock Award for Poetry, as well as the admiration of Harvard classicist and poet Robert *Fitzgerald.

Her two books of poetry, *Portraits and Elegies* (Boston, 1982; revd. edn., New York, 1986; London, 1986) and *The Lamplit Answer* (New York,

1985; London, 1986), marked by her fluency with metre and rhyme, have established her as one of the strongest of the *New Formalists and confirmed her early promise. Much of her poetry is related to the death of her father, a history professor, in 1973. This includes a graceful sequence of elegies in the first book, 'Laughing with One Eye', about her shared past with him and her subsequent feeling of loss, and, from the second, 'Supernatural Love', a *tour de force* in rhymed tercets which recalls a childhood scene in her father's study where an inquiry into the roots of the word 'carnation' becomes at once a meditation on Christ's crucifixion and on her own poetic origins. 'Darwin in 1881', published in both books, is an ambitious narrative poem on Charles Darwin's melancholy final year, while 'Heavenly Feast', from the second, is a contemporary prayer, a powerful rendering of Simone Weil's self-starvation. The second volume contains less successful narrative poems based on Sleeping Beauty and the life of Chopin which seem overly academic. Stronger is a sequence addressed to an absent lover which, if too self-conscious, also uses rhyme and wit playfully to balance the at-times desperate mood of the persona. [RMcP

SCHUBERT, David (1913–46), was born in New York City of Russian parents. His father, severe, restless, with artistic inclinations, left the family in Schubert's childhood, and not long after he found his mother hanged. Living with relatives, Schubert displayed a brilliance at school that brought him early to Amherst College. Robert *Frost, befriending him, did his best to keep Schubert there; but his absorption in writing left no time for studies. Encountering him in New York, Frost offered financial help. A little later he married Judith Ehre, a support in every way. After several near-misses with publishers, New Directions printed him in its *Five Young American Poets* (1941). His difficulties mounting, he fled his home, required hospitalization, and died in 1946.

At the end he tried to destroy all his work. Mrs Schubert salvaged what she could, and in 1961 Macmillan published his *Initial A*. Finally, in 1983, the *Quarterly Review of Literature* brought out *David Schubert: Works and Days*, a volume including all his poems, a biography Renée Karol Weiss composed of letters, interviews, and memoirs, and articles by James *Wright, John *Ashbery, David *Ignatow, and others. William Carlos *Williams had already declared Schubert 'a nova in the sky', and on reading the volume Ashbery judged Schubert one of America's great poets. His work was hailed at home and abroad.

Immediately perceptible is the poetry's bulk of colour, action, mercuriality. Not that it is blind to human havoc. On the contrary, Schubert worked constantly within that havoc. But even desperation takes on a sombre gaiety, a more-than-melancholy amusement of the kind that Charlie Chaplin embodied. In Schubert's own words: 'What I see as poetry is a sample of the human scene, its incurably acute melancholia redeemed only by affection.'

[TW

SCHULMAN, Grace (1935–), was born Grace Waldman in New York City, the only child of a Polish-Jewish immigrant father and a seventh-generation American mother. In 1959 she married Jerome L. Schulman, a research virologist. Since 1972 she has been poetry editor of the *Nation* and professor of English at Baruch College, New York City. From 1974 to 1984 she was director of the Poetry Center at the 92nd Street YM-YWHA.

Although at the age of 14 Schulman was introduced to Marianne *Moore, who would become a friend and artistic mentor until her death, Schulman's poems were not influenced by this association. They are not hewn or fabulist, but choose instead a vatic, ungainly style that is clear and intelligent. The poems range from unabashed love lyrics to prayer-like blessings.

Schulman has published two volumes of poetry, *Burn Down the Icons* (Princeton, NJ, 1986) and *Hemispheres* (New York, 1984), and a critical appreciation of Marianne Moore (1986). She has also published translations from Hebrew and Spanish.

[HC

SCHUYLER, James (1923–91), was born in Chicago but grew up in Washington, DC, and in western New York State. He lived in Italy for several years in the Fifties, staying for a while with W. H. *Auden at his summer retreat at Ischia. A fine elegy for the older poet is included in Schuyler's 1980 collection, *The Morning of the Poem* (New York and London). Like fellow New York poet and friend Frank *O'Hara, Schuyler has worked on the staff of both the Museum of Modern Art and of the magazine *Art News*. In 1959 he commented: 'New York poets, except I suppose the colour blind, are affected most by the floods of paint in whose crashing surf we all scramble.'

While some of Schuyler's early poems experiment with surreal imagery and avant-garde narrative techniques, his later work is conversational and direct. In long poems such as 'The Morning of the Poem' and 'Hymn to Life' (1974) Schuyler meditates fluently on the random happenings of successive days, eschewing grand climaxes and keeping close to the arbitrary flow of his mental processes. Many of his poems are urbane and witty responses to the changing seasons. Schuyler evokes the natural world with a cool, elegant precision that suggests the influence of Elizabeth *Bishop, though his free verse is looser and more ramblingly open to the contingent than Bishop's ever is. Schuyler's love poems are also characterized by a colloquial intimacy and straightforwardness, but these often rear dangerously close to the mawkish. His best-known poem is his restrained and moving elegy for Frank O'Hara called 'Buried at Springs', included in his collection *Freely Espousing* (New York, 1969). His *Selected Poems* was published in New York (1988) and Manchester (1990).

Schuyler has also written three novels: *Alfred and Guinevere* (New York, 1958), *A Nest of Ninnies* (with John *Ashbery) (New York, 1969; Manchester, 1987), and *What's for Dinner* (Santa Barbara, Calif., 1978). All three are amusing comedies of manners, and reflect his immersion in the works of Ronald Firbank, Ivy Compton-Burnett, and E. F. Benson.

[MF

SCHWARTZ, Delmore (1913–66), was born in Brooklyn, New York, where he spent his childhood. Schwartz's highly autobiographical stories often depict the milieu of the middle-class Jewish families who had recently emigrated to America (Schwartz's family had Romanian roots), and of the generation of young intellectuals born of those families; he came to be regarded as their most incisive chronicler. Schwartz's own family suffered the difficulties of his parents' failing marriage; when Delmore was 9 his father left the family for good. The repercussions can be felt most memorably in Schwartz's famous story, 'In Dreams Begin Responsibilities'.

After attending the University of Wisconsin, Schwartz graduated in 1935 from New York University; he then attended Harvard Graduate School in philosophy. At 24 he published *In Dreams Begin Responsibilities* (1938), a volume of poems and stories, which brought high praise from *Eliot, *Pound, W. C. *Williams, Wallace *Stevens, John Crowe *Ransom, and Allen *Tate, who called it 'the first real innovation we've had since Eliot and Pound'. In the words of Schwartz's biographer James Atlas, it was 'heralded as the flowering of a new generation'. Two of Schwartz's best-known poems, 'In the Naked Bed, in Plato's Cave' and 'The Heavy Bear Who Goes With Me', appeared in this volume.

Schwartz became a prominent figure of New York intellectual life. Handsome, a witty and brilliant talker, Schwartz developed a reputation as a compelling presence in his person as well as his poetry. His cultural commentaries and literary essays received widespread praise and continue to be regarded as important documents of the period ('The Isolation of Modern Poetry' and 'The Vocation of the Poet in the Modern World' are considered seminal essays). In his stories, Schwartz's wry portraits of New York intellectuals of the Thirties and Forties are without equal.

Schwartz taught somewhat dissatisfiedly at several universities: Harvard, Kenyon College, Princeton (with friends John *Berryman, Randall *Jarrell, and Saul Bellow), and Syracuse.

Literary friendships were essential to Schwartz; also of note include those with R. P. *Blackmur, Robert *Lowell, James Agee, William Barrett, and Dwight Macdonald. Of Schwartz, Lowell said, 'I've never met anyone who has somehow as much seeped into me'. Berryman considered him the century's 'most underrated poet'. Bellow used Schwartz as the model for the brilliant and tortured poet Von Humboldt Fleisher in his novel *Humboldt's Gift*.

Schwartz published *Summer Knowledge* (1959), a selection of poems, to high acclaim. It received the prestigious Bollingen Prize in a year that also saw the publication of Robert Lowell's *Life Studies*. Schwartz's poems resonate with philosophical inquiry; they often consider the conflicts of the self (and its imperatives) with the external world—including those social, cultural, and political demands illuminated by an individual conscience. Late in his life Schwartz looked to nature for the healing premisses that might assuage the agony of those philosophical conflicts detailed in his work. Irving Howe called Schwartz 'the poet of the historical moment quite as Auden was in England'.

Schwartz was married twice: to Gertrude Buckman in 1938, and to Elizabeth Pollet in 1949. He spent the last dozen years of his life struggling against mental illness. His paranoid denunciations of even his closest friends left Schwartz alone at the end. He died of a heart attack in July 1966 in a Times Square hotel.

Major works include: *In Dreams Begin Responsibilities* (New York, 1938, 1978), *Selected Poems: Summer Knowledge* (New York, 1959), and *Selected Essays* (Chicago and London, 1970). See also *Delmore Schwartz: The Life of an American Poet*, by James Atlas (New York, 1977; London, 1979). [DStJ]

SCHWARTZ, Lloyd (1941–), was born in Brooklyn, New York. He graduated from Queens College (City University New York) in 1962, and received his MA (1963) and Ph.D (1976) from Harvard University, where he studied informally with Robert *Lowell 'on and off for fourteen years'. Schwartz wrote his doctoral thesis on Elizabeth *Bishop and co-edited

Elizabeth Bishop and Her Art (Ann Arbor, Mich., 1983). A well-known writer on classical music, he has served as classical music editor of the *Boston Phoenix* (since 1977) and as classical music critic for the *Fresh Air* programme on National Public Radio (since 1987). A professor of English at the University of Massachusetts, Boston, he lives in Somerville, Massachusetts.

Schwartz's first book of poems, *These People* (Middletown, Conn., 1981), consisted of a provocative sequence of dramatic monologues. For his vivid portrait-poems—'Mug Shots', 'Mental Cases', and the sly 'Self Portrait'—Schwartz probed his disturbing, sometimes shocking subjects with novelistic rigour and compact technique. His shrewd timing and darting prosody counterbalanced his characters' dead-end obsessions and broken speech.

In his most recent book, *Goodnight Gracie* (Chicago, 1992), Schwartz expanded his reconnaissance of identity and otherness to include prickly poems on domestic life, documentary-style re-creations of American crossroads, and ambitious meditations on art and artists. For these brash, unpredictable, often moving inventions he used a language that veered from overheard comic conversation to plangent elegy.

[RP

SCOTT, Alexander (1920–89), was born and brought up in Aberdeen, and attended that city's university, his studies interrupted from 1941 to 1945 by war service with the Gordon Highlanders. He was awarded the MC. Subsequently Scott taught at Edinburgh for a year, but spent most of his life at the University of Glasgow, where for many years he headed the department of Scottish literature.

'Coronach', Scott's elegy for the dead of his battalion, is probably his finest poem. His best work is in Scots—he originated the term 'aggrandized Scots' as an alternative to Synthetic Scots or *Lallans or Plastic Scots or Doric, all attempts to describe a literary Scots language in poetry which draws its diction from more than one part of the Scots-speaking districts of the country.

Scott's long poem 'Heart of Stone' (originally

written for television) celebrates his native place with indigenous relish. Several others direct themselves to Isadora Duncan, Jayne Mansfield, Marilyn Monroe, and, in 'Ballade of Beauties', to 'Miss Warsaw Ghetto Nineteen-Forty-Two' (as the poem's refrain goes), with a disconcerting fascination for dead glamour. Elsewhere in Scott's work there is a decidedly satirical strain, at its best in his series of short squibs 'Scotched', but at times his writing in that vein could be sour and malicious. His best work tends to prove that the Scots language works best when tied to rhyme, metre, and stanza.

Scott also wrote plays, and it seems likely that an admirable ambition in poetic drama was suffocated by the inability of Scottish audiences to take his approaches seriously. The Scots language is especially suited to drama; and this ostensible 'failure' (his last play was produced in 1958) could explain his general cynicism in later years.

Scott contributed to Scottish literature through his biography of William Soutar, *Still Life* (London, 1958), and his edition of Soutar's *Diaries of a Dying Man* (Edinburgh, 1955). His more-readily available books are *Cantrips* (Preston, Lancs., 1971) and *Selected Poems 1943–1974* (Preston, 1975). With Norman MacCaig, he edited *Contemporary Scottish Verse* (London, 1970), and, with Michael Grieve, *The Hugh MacDiarmid Anthology* (London, 1972). [DED

SCOTT, David (1947–) was born in Cambridge, studied theology at Durham, and, after an urban curacy and a spell as school chaplain, became vicar of the Cumbrian parishes of Torpenhow and Allhallows in 1980. Scott's gentle, contemplative intelligence can be found at work in his quiet but firm poems which invest the parochial and the domestic with a sense of mystery, so that seemingly routine activities take his reader by surprise with the accuracy of their detail. In his best work a small-scale but vivid itemizing is charged with unsentimental affection and often wryly humorous relish. A number of the poems, such as 'Quodlibet' and 'Hopkins Enters the Roman Catholic Church', celebrate the life of dedicated scholarship and discreet conduct, and if there is sometimes a slight air of sententious piety about them it is usually given an edge by his characteristic wit. Like Andrew *Young, another parson-poet whom in some ways he resembles, he has a keen eye for the natural world and for figures in a landscape. As if to declare his witness to the tradition to which he belongs, he has also attempted free-verse translations of George Herbert's Latin Poems.

David Scott has collaborated with Jeremy James Taylor on several plays for the National Youth Music Theatre, and has written a book of poems for young children, How Does It Feel? (London, 1989). His two main collections are A Quiet Gathering (Newcastle upon Tyne, 1984), which won the Geoffrey Faber Memorial Prize, and Playing for England (Newcastle upon Tyne, 1989). [JM

SCOTT, Dennis (1939–91), was born in Kingston, and educated at Jamaica College, and the University of the West Indies at Mona. He is principal of the Jamaica School of Drama, and has been associate professor of directing at Yale University, and editor of Caribbean Quarterly.

Dennis Scott's poetry is notable for its dramatic personae, and its densely archetypal symbolism. His occasional use of dialect goes beyond the vernacular to delve into the psyche. 'Uncle Time', for instance, seems traditional in its linking of time with foreshadowed death, but it becomes very West Indian in the way he approaches the subject. Not only is the poem in dialect, but Scott also relates the personification of Time to the folkloric figure of Anancy, the cunning spider-man. Other poems about time, 'Time Piece' and 'Time-slip', are in standard English, but equally powerful in suggesting corrosion of life and expectations.

Scott's later poems, particularly in Dreadwalk (London, 1982), appear to construct an aesthetic based on Rastafarian beliefs. Poems like 'Dreadwalk' and 'Apocalypse Dub', though very different from those of a true Rastafarian and 'dub poet', like Benjamin *Zephaniah, are immersed in fluid, surrealistic imagery, and suggest increasingly complex personae. His search for

archetypal imagery, from whatever source, produced a verse adaptation of Sir Gawain and the Green Knight (New Orleans, 1978).

See also Uncle Time (Pittsburgh, Pa., 1973). Scott's play, An Echo in the Bone, was published in Plays for Today, ed. Errol Hill (London, 1985).

[MR

SCOTT, F(rancis) R(eginald) (1899–1981), was born in Quebec City and educated at Bishop's College School and University in Lennoxville, Quebec, and at Oxford University, where he was a Rhodes Scholar. Returning to Canada, Scott schoolmastered briefly before entering the law faculty at McGill University, where he obtained his BCL in 1926, was called to the bar in 1927, and became a member of faculty in 1928, ending his career as dean of law, 1961–4.

As a result of his exposure to Fabianism at Oxford, and following upon the Great Depression, Scott became active in left-wing politics and was a founding member of the League for Social Reconstruction (1932), which led to the formation of a socialist political party, the Co-operative Commonwealth Federation, now the New Democratic Party of Canada. He served the United Nations in Burma in 1952, and was a member of the Royal Commission on Bilingualism and Biculturalism from 1963 to 1971.

The poet in Scott was manifested in 1921 when he began to publish light verse of a decidedly *Georgian flavour. At McGill he fell in with A. J. M. *Smith and other budding modernists who were instrumental in publishing a university-based, avant-garde literary paper called The McGill Fortnightly Review (1925–7). This initial experience led to a series of involvements with reviews, little magazines, and publishing ventures, most of which had a significant impact on the development of modernism in Canadian poetry. In 1936 he edited New Provinces: Poems of Several Authors, the first modernist anthology of Canadian verse. Scott was late in publishing his own first book. Overture appeared in 1945, but from then on he had a steady, if measured, output with Events and Signals (1954), a collection of satirical poems called The Eye of the Needle (1957), and Signature (1964). His poetry embraces a wide variety of subjects and forms—nature poems, poems of social, political, and humanitarian dedication, metaphysical and love poems, 'found poems', and translations of French-Canadian verse; but he is best known as a social critic whose cutting satires about hypocrisy, stupidity, and injustice express a deep indignation.

Scott's *Selected Poems* appeared in 1966, to be followed by *The Dance is One* (1973), and *The Collected Poems* (1981—all Toronto). An anglophone native of Quebec, Scott was passionately committed to the building of bridges between Canada's two premier European founding cultures. This dedication is evidenced in his translations of the poetry of such leading French-Canadian poets as Saint-Denys Garneau and Anne Hébert. See Sandra Djwa, *The Politics of the Imagination: A Life of F. R. Scott* (Toronto, 1987). [MG

SCOTT, John A(lan) (1948–), was born in Littlehampton, Sussex, and emigrated to Melbourne, Australia, in 1959. With *Wearne and Laurie *Duggan he participated in the Monash University poetry readings in the late Sixties. He has taught media and creative-writing courses in Canberra, Melbourne, and Wollongong.

His early verse swung between *confessionalism and an impersonality made more difficult by his fascination for codes and the visual arts. Claustrophobic *symboliste* atmospheres pointed to an absorption with French models, but it was the compression of narrative implications (from crime or dystopian fiction) into terse sequences which opened out his work. Both tendencies dovetailed in *St Clair* (1986), the three verse-novellas of which show sexual obsession and political repression alternately restricting and being dissolved by free poetic discourse. Scott explores transactions between discourses in *Translation* (1990). His 'Orpheus' sequence imitates the viscous punning of the Elizabethans as well as the play of Ovid's Latin, while 'The Apology', sharing a cast with Scott's melancholy, mad, campus novel *Blair* (1988), worries over a writer's traducings of his experience.

Scott's three most important volumes are *Singles* (St Lucia, Qld., 1989), *St Clair* (Sydney, 1990), and *Translation* (Sydney, 1990). [CP

SCOTT, Margaret (1934–), was born in Bristol, read English at Cambridge, and emigrated to Australia in 1959. From 1966 until her retirement in 1990 she taught at the University of Tasmania and published principally in the field of Renaissance drama. Her first volumes of verse, *Tricks of Memory* (1980) and *Visited* (1983), show a robust attentiveness to familiar landscapes allied with a rueful sense of the figure that she cuts within them. Editor, with Vivian *Smith, of an anthology of Tasmanian poetry, *Effects of Light* (1985), and an associate editor of the *Oxford Literary Guide to Australia* (1987), Scott's most accomplished and varied verse collection to date is *The Black Swans* (Sydney, 1988). Notably extending her previous range, the book begins with a detailed, wryly celebratory sequence on 'Housework' and includes poems that evoke the Tasman Peninsula where she now lives, before modulating into the desolately loving 'Elegies' for her late husband, Michael Scott. More recently she has completed an historical novel, *The Baby-Farmer* (1990), dealing with the Victorian trade in the adoption and murder of unwanted children. [PP

SCOTT, Tom (1918–95), was brought up in Glasgow and St Andrews. His education was postponed by family hardships and the Second World War. Later, as a mature student, he took degrees from the University of Edinburgh, including a doctorate.

By the 1960s Scott was writing successfully in Scots. The title-poem of *The Ship and Ither Poems* (London, 1963) is long and ambitious, showing a tasteful distribution of Scots lexis and an accessible management of learning. Its ultimate effect is one of erudition and feeling released by a voice as cultured as it is colloquial. Other poems in the volume exemplify equal artistry, especially 'The Mankind Toun' and 'Fergus'.

Much of his subsequent work is on a large scale. *At the Shrine o The Unkent Sodger* (Preston, Lancs., 1968) stumbles over its own directness, with the result that its indignation appears worthy but inert. *Brand the Builder* (Epping, 1975) has its moments, but its sustained blank verse is permitted to carry a colloquial dismissiveness and, at times, comes close to the Scottish personality at its sourest and worst. *The Tree* (Dunfermline, 1977), a blank-verse poem in English of some 230 pages, subsides frequently into learned chatter and the unremittingly prosaic. Occasionally its pages are redeemed by passages of interesting lore. *The Dirty Business: A Poem About War* (Barr, Ayrshire, 1987) is, again, worthy and shrill.

As a critic and literary historian Scott published *Dunbar: A Critical Exposition of the Poems* (Edinburgh, 1966), while a comprehensive literary history of Scotland was announced but has never appeared. He co-edited the *Oxford Book of Scottish Verse* (1966), and edited the *Penguin Book of Scottish Verse* (Harmondsworth, 1970). His work is discussed in a special issue of *Agenda* (1993). [DED

SCOTT, Winfield Townley (1910–68), was born in Newport, Rhode Island. He spent an idyllic childhood in Newport and wrote about it in a memoir, 'The Owl in the Hall', in *Alpha Omega* (Garden City, NY, 1971). He wrote prize-winning poems in high school and edited the literary magazine. He graduated from Brown University, where he went with the literary crowd and fell under the influence of professor S. Foster Damon. A visit with Edwin Arlington *Robinson, then the most prominent American poet, was influential; but much as he admired his work, Scott spent most of his life trying to avoid writing like Robinson. From 1929 to 1951 he worked for the Providence (Rhode Island) *Journal*, writing book reviews and becoming editor of its weekly book page, considered the finest in New England and the best in the United States outside of New York. Handsome, ambitious, yet for a long time repressed and lacking in self-confidence, he was a gracious, socially adept, and well-liked member of the New England literary community.

His most successful poems chronicle momentary, surprising personal victories in a normally bleak world, whose meanings are informed chiefly by the agonies of self-doubt, the play of the imagination, and heterosexual love and longing. A plain and direct diction makes his poems accessible, while a consistent colour symbolism involving green, gold, and red expresses romantic passion and projects it on to the natural and human world. Most of his best work can be found in his *Collected Poems 1937–1962* (New York, 1962). Scott Donaldson's *Poet in America: Winfield Townley Scott* (Austin, Tex., 1972) is an excellent biography. [JTT

SCOTT-HERON, Gil. See Performance Poetry.

Scottish Renaissance. First used either by the French man-of-letters Denis Saurat in the 1920s, or by Lewis *Spence in 1926, the idea of a modern 'Scottish Renaissance' was very quickly colonized by Hugh *MacDiarmid and promoted by him. Indeed, the phrase has come to be closely associated with MacDiarmid, and is used to describe the impetus and influence of his poetry and criticism.

No coherent movement actually existed. Instead, MacDiarmid, together with other poets, novelists, dramatists, artists, and musicians, subscribed to an amorphous but challenging set of principles and desires, which, it was hoped, would rescue the Scottish arts and culture in general from provincial stagnation and the status of second-hand Englishness.

In one way, the phrase simply recognizes a new confidence in Scottish writing in the 1920s—that of MacDiarmid, Lewis Grassic Gibbon, *Soutar, Linklater, and others. However, by having identified the energy and achievement that were undoubtedly there, the idea of a 'renaissance' became a useful catalyst. It helped to encourage an enhanced or clearer national identity among writers and artists. [DED

SCOVELL, E(dith) J(oy) (1907–), was born in Sheffield and educated at Casterton School, Westmorland, and Somerville College, Oxford. Regarded by Geoffrey *Grigson as 'the purest of women poets of our time', she published her first volume, *Shadows of Chrysanthemums*, in

1944. The poems in this and two subsequent volumes, *Midsummer Meadows* (1946) and *The River Steamer* (1956), are the work of a strong lyrical intelligence, achieving a delicate air of mystery which arises from close observation of the physical world. Whether meditating on the 'innocent wild head' of a baby, 'the look of utterance on the silent flower', or, minutely, the progress across a sandy yard of leaf-cutting ants 'under their little sails of green', Scovell combines a naturalist's precision (she is married to the distinguished ecologist Charles Elton) with what she has called her betrothal at birth to a sense of otherness which she takes for granted.

Perhaps too quiet for the noisy poetic climate of the late 1940s and too numinous for the period which reacted against the *New Apocalypse, Scovell's work did not receive the attention it deserved. Between 1956 and the early 1980s she published few poems and no book. In 1982, however, *The Space Between* collected the work of this interim period, including some of the translations from the Italian of Giovanni Pascoli on which she had begun to work, and confirmed the consistency and continuity of her vision. Although she has been described as a religious poet, she would prefer to avoid such labelling—indeed, her poem 'Agnostic' is the closest she has come to a declaration—and it would be more accurate to regard her as a poet constantly astonished by the world. By no means confined to her home ground of Oxford, she has travelled widely, working with her husband in tropical America, and a number of her poems give as rapt an attention to exotic landscapes as they do to her garden or to the quiet stretches of the river Isis.

E. J. Scovell's *Collected Poems* (Manchester, 1988) contains her complete set of Pascoli translations and a generous selection of later work. There is also a *Selected Poems* (Manchester, 1991). [JM

SCUPHAM, (John) Peter (1933–), was born in Liverpool and brought up in Cambridge. His father was controller of BBC Educational Broadcasting. He graduated from Emmanuel College, Cambridge, where he read English, in

1957, and married in the same year. He lives in Norfolk where he runs writers' weekends while remaining co-proprietor (with John *Mole) of one of Britain's best small presses, the Mandeville Press.

He published his first pamphlet, *The Small Containers* (Stockport, 1972), relatively late, when he was 39, but has produced eight full-length collections at regular intervals since. His early poems established a continuing tendency towards private rumination: decorous and fragile—like the title of one of them, 'Painted Shells'—they are products of an essentially fugitive (the word is a favourite of Scupham's) temperament. Toys and games are a recurring subject-matter. A fastidious craftsman, he is comfortable with demanding forms: the title-piece of *The Hinterland* (London, 1977) is a Hungarian sonnet-sequence (compare John *Fuller's 'The Labour of Hercules', 1972). His later work is less ornate in manner, and its treatment of autobiographical materials has a firmer cultural and historical grounding. *The Air Show* (Oxford, 1988), a reconstruction of his boyhood experience of the Second World War, is his most successful single work to date. His *Selected Poems* was published (Oxford) in 1990. [MI

Secession (1922–4). Edited by Gorham B. Munson, Kenneth *Burke, and Matthew Josephson, *Secession* appeared first from Vienna and Berlin, then died in New York when the first two of its editors became (temporarily) interested in the teachings of Gurdjieff as interpreted by A. R. Orage in America. It was most notable for its publication of the early poems of Hart *Crane. It also printed many *Imagist poems, Marianne *Moore's appreciation of H. D. (Hilda *Doolittle), and Malcolm *Cowley's of the French writer Raymond Roussel's *Locus Solus*. See *The Little Magazine* (New York, 1947), by F. Hoffman, C. Allen, and C. Ulrich. [MS-S

SEEGER, Alan (1888–1916), was born in New York City into relatively affluent circumstances. His family moved to Mexico in 1900, and at the age of 12 he was sent to the Hackley School in Tarrytown, New York, entering Harvard in

1906. College classmates included T. S. *Eliot and Walter Lippmann, but Seeger was defiantly isolated, although he did edit the *Harvard Monthly* in his senior year. After graduation he spent two years in lower Manhattan as a Bohemian rebel, then left for Paris to work and write in the Latin Quarter. When the First World War began he enlisted in the Foreign Legion, true to his often proclaimed contempt for danger and bourgeois security, and was killed at the Battle of the Somme on 4 July 1916.

Despite his swaggering nonconformity Seeger remained tied to traditional forms, as seen in 'I Have a Rendezvous with Death'. If he is remembered at all, it is for this moving evocation of a romantic stance already obsolete by the war's end; some critics have praised 'Broceliande' and a few of his Mexican poems as well. His *Collected Poems* (New York) was published in 1916, followed a year later by his *Letters and Diary* (New York).   [EB

SEIDEL, Frederick (1936–), was born in St Louis, attended Harvard, and lives in New York City. He has taught English at Rutgers University and served as Paris editor of the *Paris Review*. His second book of poems, *Sunrise* (New York, 1980), was the Lamont Poetry Selection for 1979, and also won the National Book Critics Circle Award for 1980. Seidel's first book, *Final Solutions* (New York, 1963), was an unusually powerful debut, remarkable for its combination of an impeccable formal aesthetic with a dark and gritty vision. Seidel's self-revelations and his obsessional personae make the *confessionalism of Robert *Lowell, his most obvious influence, seem tame by comparison. Seidel's early poems revel in their lack of conviction, marking both the modern loss of faith and the poet's abandoned Jewishness. His frankly erotic poems discuss voyeurism and masturbation, and identify the body parts as well as their functions. With *Sunrise*, Seidel's poetry becomes more of a chronicle of the times, a gossipy insider's view of art and politics during the Sixties that finds the poet at an exclusive fund-raiser for Robert Kennedy ('1968'), pub-crawling with Francis Bacon ('Fucking'), attending the Finnish

Grand Prix at Imatra ('Men and Woman'), and visiting the set of Antonioni's *Zabriskie Point* ('Death Valley'), a movie that shares the same apocalyptic sensibility as *Sunrise*. Having celebrated the New Frontier and witnessed its sad aftermath, Seidel explores a private emotional realm in *These Days* (New York, 1989), though his bitter view of American politics is still present in poems such as 'Our Gods' and 'Empire'. Many of the poems also return to a more controlled style after the open forms of *Sunrise*, and his main subject is the painful memory of a difficult adolescence. Kinky sex still preoccupies Seidel, and he further develops, in some obscure poems, a more symbolic poetic language.

Poems: 1959–1979 (New York, 1989) reprints most of *Final Solutions* and all of *Sunrise. Men and Woman* (London, 1984), an English edition of Seidel's selected poetry, also draws from both volumes and adds some of the poems that appear in *These Days*. His latest collection is *My Tokyo* (New York, 1993).   [TDeP

Seizin Press. See GRAVES, ROBERT, and RIDING, LAURA.

SENIOR, Olive (1943–), was born in Jamaica, and educated there and in Canada. She is managing editor of Jamaica Publications Ltd., and editor of *Jamaica Journal*. She has also been involved in the Women in the Caribbean Research Project for the University of the West Indies in Barbados.

According to E. A. *Markham, 'Senior must be—apart from *Walcott—our most elegant and graceful poet'. Although she has said in an interview that 'Jamaica is still a society of great spirituality, of great psychic energy', many of her poems are highly sceptical in tone, most notably 'Epitaph'. It commemorates the death of a young child, but ends with the following lines: 'old superstitions | are such lies'. Her poems vividly convey, as do her short stories, village life in Jamaica, but always in an unsentimental and tough-minded fashion.

Olive Senior's poems have been published in *Talking of Trees* (Kingston, Jam., 1985). Her collections of short stories include *Summer Light-*

ning (London, 1986) and *Arrival of the Snake Woman* (London, 1989). [MR

SEPAMLA, Sipho (Sydney) (1932–), belongs to the group of 'township poets', including *Mtshali and *Serote, who emerged in South Africa during the 1970s. He was born in Krugersdorp on the Witwatersrand, and trained to be a teacher. In the late 1960s he was stimulated to write by the new-found confidence of younger blacks in their opposition to apartheid. During the mid-1970s he relaunched the journal *The Classic* as *The New Classic*, and was active in organizing poetry readings, conferences, and art exhibitions. He also edited the theatre magazine *S'ketsh*. Both journals were subject to constant censorship, and he also suffered the banning of a novel and a volume of poetry. In 1980 he was given a passport to visit Germany and England, and in 1981–2 he was a fellow at Iowa University.

Having lived almost all his life in Johannesburg, Sepamla asserts an urbanized identity, satirizing the apartheid 'Bantu culture' of mudhuts and primitive agriculture. He writes only in English: sometimes in urban dialect, sometimes (as in the much-anthologized 'To Whom It May Concern') in a parody of the inhuman officialese of apartheid. Underlying all his poems, even the elegies for children murdered by the police, is a confidence that time is running out for white domination. Sepamla dismisses 'fine points' of literary discrimination, and his verse lacks punctuation, relying for effect on rhythmic parallelism and repetitions. His verse can seem short-winded and idiomatically insecure, but sometimes it achieves a rhetorical power reminiscent of oral praise-song.

The Soweto I Love (London, 1977) is Sepamla's most easily obtainable collection. See also *The Poetry of Commitment in South Africa* (London, 1984), by Jacques Alvarez-Peyreyre. [JB

SEROTE, Mongane (Wally) (1944–), belongs to the group of 'township poets', including *Sepamla and *Mtshali, who came to prominence in South Africa during the 1970s. He was born in Sophiatown, Johannesburg, and attended school in Alexandra Township and in Leribe, Lesotho. He became active in the Black Consciousness Movement, and in 1969–70 was imprisoned for nine months in solitary confinement, only to be released without charge. His second volume of verse, *Tsetlo* (1974) was banned on publication. A Fulbright scholarship took Serote to the United States, and in 1979 he completed a fine arts degree at Columbia University, after which he went to work with the Nedu Arts Ensemble in Gaberone, Botswana.

Serote's intense, expressionist poetry gives lyrical voice to the suffering of blacks under apartheid. In passionate addresses to Alexandra or Johannesburg, he dramatizes the grim violence of township life and celebrates black endurance. Serote mastered English only after leaving school, and the linguistic tensions and dislocations of his writing echo the frustrations of his political theme. He breaks lines in midphrase or even mid-word, and in one poem subverts 'Whitey's' language to an incoherent babble. Out of Serote's sharp subjectivity, however, grows the collective confidence of black revolt. He celebrates the spiritual strength of blacks who cannot bring themselves to return hatred for hatred, though his patient musings over injustice frequently modulate into the menacing tone of one driven beyond endurance. In the later 1970s Serote turned to longer poems of explicit political commitment, and his latest volume, *A Tough Tale* (London, 1987), addresses itself primarily to his companions in the struggle.

A selection from Serote's work can be found in *Poets to the People*, ed. Barry Feinberg (London, 1980). See also *Black Writers from South Africa*, by Jane Watts (London, 1989). [JB

SETH, Vikram (1952–), was born in Calcutta and educated at Oxford, Stanford, and Nanjing universities, training as an economist. His years in India, England, California, and China have given his work a distinctly cosmopolitan flavour; in addition to poetry he has written a book about his travels in China and Tibet. He resides in California and New Delhi.

Seth has published several volumes of elegant, finely crafted formal poetry, the most recent of which is *All You Who Sleep Tonight* (New York and London, 1990); but he is best known as the author of *The Golden Gate* (New York, 1986), a novel in verse modelled on Pushkin's *Eugene Onegin*, tracing the fortunes of a group of young professional Californians as they come to terms with various problems ranging from nascent homosexuality to the nuclear threat. Urbane, inventive, and rigorous in its adherence to Pushkin's sonnet-like tetrameter stanza, the book enjoyed surprising success when it appeared, perhaps because it was deliberately marketed as a novel rather than a poem. Its appearance placed Seth squarely at the crossroads of two allied movements in recent American poetry loosely referred to as the *New Formalism and the *New Narrative. Whether the feat is one that bears repetition is another matter. Seth's best lyric pieces appear in *The Humble Administrator's Garden* (Manchester and Delhi, 1985) and in *The Oxford India Anthology of Twelve Modern Indian Poets*, ed. A. K. Mehrotra (Delhi, 1992). He has also written a novel, *A Suitable Boy* (London, 1993).   [RG

SEXTON, Anne (née Harvey) (1928–74), was born in Newton, Massachusetts, and went from boarding school to a Boston finishing school in 1947. The next year she eloped with Alfred Muller Sexton II, who later entered his father-in-law's firm. The birth in 1951 of her first daughter helped trigger a series of mental breakdowns, suicide attempts, and consequent hospitalizations that would pattern the rest of her life.

Sexton began writing poetry in 1957, at first as therapy. She then honed her skills in several workshops, including one with Robert *Lowell, where she met Sylvia *Plath. She was also friends with Maxine *Kumin and W. D. *Snodgrass, whom she viewed as a mentor. His candid approach to intense personal material clearly influenced her first collection, *To Bedlam and Part Way Back* (1960), though her intimate female perspective and use of simple rhyme and metre effects to simulate a regressive state were original, as was the extremes to which she

pushed her *'confessional' stance. This held true through *All My Pretty Ones* (1962) and *Live or Die* (1967), which won the Pulitzer Prize. In *Live or Die* there is a poem addressed to the dead Sylvia Plath, in which Plath is reproached for having gone alone 'into the death I wanted so badly and so long'. It was only in *Transformations* (1971), ribald, often wryly Freudian or feminist versions of Grimm fairy tales, that Sexton was able to transcend narrow technical and narrative boundaries. At the time of her suicide in October 1974 she was Professor of Creative Writing at Boston University. A posthumous volume, *45 Mercy Street*, appeared in 1976. This book Sexton had said in 1974, 'is too personal to publish for some time'.

All her verse is in *The Complete Poems* (Boston, 1981). See also *Anne Sexton: A Self-Portrait in Letters*, ed. Linda Gray Sexton and Lois Ames (Boston, 1977), *Anne Sexton* (Boston, 1989), by H. Caroline Bernard-King, and *Anne Sexton: A Biography*, by Diane Wood Middlebrook (Boston, 1991). The Middlebrook biography caused much controversy when it appeared: the biographer made use of 'session tapes' recorded during Sexton's interviews with her psychiatrist.   [EB

SEYMOUR, A(rthur) J(ames) (1914–90), was born in British Guiana (now Guyana), and educated at Queen's College. His career as a senior civil servant included a stint as information officer at the central secretariat of the Caribbean Organization in Puerto Rico (1962–4). He was also founder and editor (1945–61) of *Kyk-over-al*, a highly influential literary periodical, which he resumed editing a few years before his death. His poetry-pamphlet series, 'Miniature Poets', featured early work by such writers as the poet Martin *Carter and the novelist Wilson Harris.

Seymour's poems, particularly the early ones, have been criticized as being too tame and overly conventional. The poetry he wrote from *The Guiana Book* (Georgetown, 1948) onwards, however, often displays a vivid, complex, and quirky historical imagination. 'For Christopher Columbus', for instance, focuses on the great voyager's perplexities. He ambiguously emerges as a kind of poet: 'as architect of a new age | the solid world would build upon his poem.'

His larger collections include *Selected Poems* (Georgetown, 1965) and *Images of Majority* (Georgetown, 1978). [MR

SEYMOUR-SMITH, Martin (1928–), was born in London. At Oxford he was poetry editor of *Isis*, and after National Service in the Near East tutored Robert *Graves's son in Mallorca before becoming a schoolteacher in 1954. His study of Graves was published in 1956; since 1960 Seymour-Smith has been an eclectic freelance writer, whose work—from a *Guide to Modern World Literature* (London, 1973, etc.) and *How to Succeed in Poetry Without Really Reading or Writing* (1986), to biographies of Graves (1982), *Kipling (1989), and *Hardy (1994)—has variously popularized, debunked, and respected its literary subjects.

Seymour-Smith's poetry is less voluminous than his other writing, but it is equally difficult to define. *Tea With Miss Stockport* (London and New York, 1963) contained several narratives, including the title-poem, which blended farce with the suggestion that an appetite for violence is common to us all. Among several deftly described characters, the poem's persona is, typically, 'complicated and cleverer'; it falls to him to negotiate the disturbing and amusing consequences of the sexual encounter that ensues. That negotiation curiously involves much fastidious reticence, a quixotic refusal to be explicit, and a similar mixture of social satire and hints of darker, more private sexual anxiety characterizes his other collection, *Reminiscences of Norma* (London, 1971). Again, the title-sequence boasts of being an imaginative exercise in rearrangement of fact and fantasy in which the poet hopes not to participate; it remains taxing, precise, and occasionally frustrating work. [MRW

SHANKS, Edward (Richard Buxton) (1892–1953), was born in London and educated at Trinity College, Cambridge, where he edited *The Granta*, 1912–13. Invalided out of the army

in 1915, he returned to literary journalism. He subsequently wrote for the *London Mercury*, under J. C. *Squire, and the *London Standard*, as well as producing books on Shaw, *Graves, and *Kipling, and several generally light-hearted novels.

Shanks's early escape from the First World War and a precocious technical facility helped his early poetry embrace an obviously *Georgian attitude to nature; the unaffected airiness of his verse was initially much admired, and his volume *The Queen of China and Other Poems* (1919) won the first Hawthornden Prize for Imaginative Literature. He never pretended to great originality, but made a virtue of allusions to a literary tradition which included Shelley and Spenser. But by 1933, and the publication of his *Poems 1912–1932* (London), his whimsical narratives and lyrics had begun to look dated, and though in the 1940s he tried to turn his Georgian manner to a bleak modern world, in his poems 'written under the various influences of war', and collected in *Poems 1939–1952* (London, 1953), these never looked like more than period pieces. Their value, as Shanks himself began to accept, is largely autobiographical: they function as a fragmentary diary of a poet who uneasily spanned two separate periods and modes of writing, those of Rupert *Brooke and of modernism.

Shanks's work is briefly discussed in Robert H. Ross's book *The Georgian Revolt* (Carbondale, Ill., 1965). [MRW

SHAPCOTT, Jo (1953–), was born in London, educated at Trinity College, Dublin, and St Hilda's College, Oxford, and later won a Harkness Fellowship to Harvard. She has worked as Education Officer at the South Bank Centre, and for the Arts Council Literature Department. Her first collection, *Electroplating the Baby* (Newcastle upon Tyne, 1988) won the Commonwealth Prize, and her second, *Phrase Book* (Oxford, 1992) was a Poetry Book Society Choice. She was twice a winner of the National Poetry Competition.

Using a precise, colloquial diction, Shapcott draws her subjects and imagery from unusual sources, including popular culture and the sciences. She excels in narrative forms, often written from a displaced, oblique but controlled point of view and employing a surreal wit with which to explore the balances of sexual, political, or human versus animal power.   [CAR

SHAPCOTT, Thomas W(illiam) (1935–), was born in Ipswich, Queensland, and maintained an accountancy business there until he chose literature full time in 1978. In that year his *Selected Poems* drew on nine collections. He had influenced perceptions of contemporary poetry through three anthologies: *New Impulses in Australian Poetry* (St Lucia, Qld., 1968, with Rodney *Hall), *Australian Poetry Now* (Melbourne, 1970), and *Contemporary Australian and American Poetry* (St Lucia, 1976). He had served (1973–6) on the National Literature Board of which he was to be director, 1983–90.

Also in the future were three further verse collections, a substantially extended *Selected Poems* (St Lucia, 1988), and six novels. Of these, *The Search for Galina* (London, 1989; Sydney 1990) involved devising poems for the Russian woman poet of its title, while *White Stag of Exile* (London and Ringwood, Vic., 1984) is structurally dominated by its long concluding poem, 'Canticle'.

Shapcott's early poetic explorations of environment are conventional in evoking the substance of a natural world, but as his literary allegiances realigned towards America a different voice could be heard, self-conscious about form and perception, fracturing syntax and narrative sequence. There remains, however, an alert responsiveness to particularities and to dramatic presences; in short, to the world of substance. See also: *Biting the Bullet: A Literary Memoir* (Brookvale, 1990).   [JS

SHAPIRO, Alan (1952–), was born in Boston, Massachusetts, and educated at Brandeis University. He has since taught at Stanford University, California, and at the University of North Carolina.

The early poems of *The Courtesy* (Chicago and London, 1983) explore the need to be a part of the general human experience. In the best of these poems, of which 'Simon, the Barber' is representative, the speaker yearns for acceptance by old friends and family members.

In his more recent poems Shapiro speaks no longer as an outsider but as a willing participant in his extended family of men and women. His love poems celebrate the mundane moments of life. A pregnant wife regards herself in the mirror; a man joins a woman for a swim: casual moments, imbued with stature in Shapiro's poems.

Shapiro's other books include *Covenant* (Chicago and London, 1991) and *Happy Hour* (Chicago and London, 1986).   [RS

SHAPIRO, Harvey (1924–), born in Chicago and educated at Yale and Columbia universities, has served as an editor with a number of prestigious publications, including *Commentary*, *The New Yorker*, and the *New York Times Magazine*. Between 1975 and 1983 he was the editor of *The New York Times Book Review*. Shapiro's success as an editor has sometimes obscured his achievement as a poet.

Shapiro's poetry, which owes much stylistically to the work of William Carlos *Williams and Charles *Reznikoff, generally deals with urban experiences, the poet's family, and his identity as a Jew. He is very much a modernist poet of alienation, one at times with nowhere to turn but an inhospitable city: 'The self, humiliated', he says in 'Cityscape', 'has no recourse but to the world'. Perhaps his finest poem is 'National Cold Storage Company', the name of a Brooklyn storage building which becomes for the poet an emblem of the American past, and in which there may be '[a] monstrous birth'.

For an introduction to Shapiro's work, see *National Cold Storage Company: New and Selected Poems* (Middletown, Conn., 1988).   [EHF

SHAPIRO, Karl (1913–), was born in Baltimore, Maryland, the grandson of Russian-Jewish immigrants. He was educated at the University of Virginia and Johns Hopkins University, although he never took a degree. Beginning to write while still at high school, his first substantial group of poems appeared in *Five Young American Poets* (1941). His first major collection, *Person, Place, and Thing* (1942), consists of poems that are usually metrically regular with fixed, though untraditional stanza forms and written in a tough, flat idiom. Attentive to the person, place, or incident they describe, they can occasionally move towards satire. Serving in the US Army from 1941 to 1945, Shapiro wrote of his wartime experiences in *V-Letter and Other Poems*, which won him a Pulitzer Prize. Working as poetry consultant to the Library of Congress from 1946 to 1947, and editing both *Poetry magazine (1950–6) and *The Prairie Schooner (1956–66), Shapiro has also taught at several universities, including Johns Hopkins, Nebraska, and California, and served as a visiting professor in Australia, India, and Japan. An influential figure in contemporary American poetry, he has written many critical works: among them, *In Defence of Ignorance* (1960), an attack on the influence of T. S. *Eliot and Ezra *Pound, and *The Poetry Wreck: Selected Essays 1950–1970* (1975).

Later collections of Shapiro's poetry show several changes of direction. *Trial of a Poet* (1947) and *Poems of a Jew* (1958), for instance, are frequently ironic in attitude and written in taut, disciplined forms. *The Bourgeois Poet* (1964) shows Shapiro moving towards a longer, flowing line somewhere between free verse and prose poetry. Intensely personal and virulently anti-authoritarian, the poems of this period offer random celebrations of gaiety and spontaneity. Subsequent collections, however, such as *White-Haired Lover* (1968) and *Adult Bookstore* (1976), mark a return to more traditional forms and a retreat into more conservative values. In 1990 Shapiro completed the second volume of his autobiography, *Reports of my Death*. See *Collected Poems 1940–1978* (New York, 1978).

[RJG

SHETTY, Manohar (1953–), was born in Bombay and educated at St Peter's High School, Panchgani, and the University of Bombay. Except for a short period when he worked in a restaurant owned by his family, Shetty has been a journalist since 1974, and at present lives in Panjim, Goa, where he is editor of *Goa Today*.

Shetty's themes—loneliness, boredom,

ennui—are born of the 'daily groove' of living, and make him very much a poet of the city. The poems operate not in wide open spaces but inside enclosed and enclosing ones, observing in great detail the life lived behind shut doors, in the company of domestic creatures (lizards, spiders, cockroaches) and shadowgraphs ('Two flat palms part | and a bored crocodile yawns'). Once in a while, though, he takes in the outside world, looking at it with the same precision, as if through a magnifying glass.

Shetty's collections of poems, *A Guarded Space* (1981) and *Borrowed Time* (1988—both Bombay), appeared from small presses, and were little noticed except by other poets, among them *Moraes, *Mahapatra, and *Jussawalla (who, in fact, published *Borrowed Time*). For a discussion of his work, see *Modern Indian Poetry in English*, by Bruce King (Delhi, 1987). [AKM

SHOVE, Fredegond (1889–1949), was the daughter of F. W. Maitland, jurist and biographer of Leslie Stephen. She married Gerald Shove, an economics professor at King's College, Cambridge. Not long after she had published her first collection, *Dreams and Journeys* (Oxford, 1918), and Marsh had included her in *Georgian Poetry* (in preference to Charlotte *Mew), the Woolfs issued *Daybreak* (Richmond, Surrey, 1922) from their prestigious Hogarth Press. As a result, her verse was discussed for a short period. However, she published no more except a critical study, *Christina Rossetti* (Cambridge, 1931). Shove was pleasantly sensitive to nature—and had a technique superior to that of run-of-the-mill *Georgians, often writing in complex stanza forms ('Love As He Is In the World'). She as often expressed a strong sense of personal sin ('Liturgy' begins, 'O deliver me, deliver me from myself') but never sufficiently defined this, or the rather fervent Christianity of which she apparently felt unworthy. There was justice in the verdict that she resembled a house 'in which all the fittings for electric light are in position but which is not yet connected to the mains'. She took trouble with her poems, and discerning readers followed her in the hope that a connection would be made, but it was not.

Poems (Cambridge, 1956), a selection by her sister Ermengard, selects some previously unpublished poems, and has a short memoir.   [MS-S

SHUTTLE, Penelope (1947–), was born in Staines, Middlesex, and educated at Staines Grammar School and Matthew Arnold County Secondary School. Her output covers radio drama, fiction, and non-fiction, and includes several books written in collaboration with her husband, the poet Peter *Redgrove, though all her work springs from an essentially poetic imagination. Unusually for a woman poet, she began publishing while still in her twenties, and won early recognition in the form of the Greenwood Prize (1972) and an Eric Gregory Award (1974). Of her numerous poetry collections, the most recent full-length volumes are *The Orchard Upstairs* (1980), *The Lion from Rio* (1986), *Adventures with my Horse* (1986), and *Taxing the Rain* (1992—all Oxford).

Though Sylvia *Plath is clearly an influence, Shuttle's work conveys a less pressured sensibility and diction. Female experiences and processes are often mythologized in a style that may be inventive and surreal or discursively relaxed. She is more interested in using language expressionistically than as a precise instrument of observation, and her best effects are often cumulative. Dreams and archetypes are a prevailing influence.   [CAR

SILKIN, Jon (1930–), was born in London, the son of a solicitor, and educated at Dulwich College. He worked as a labourer before becoming a magazine editor—he founded the quarterly *Stand*—and teacher. His early poems, in *The Peaceable Kingdom* (London, 1954; New York, 1969) and especially in *The Re-ordering of the Stones* (London, 1961) are reminiscent of *Auden in their clipped and unabashed use of abstract terms and ellipsis: 'To hold | In sex and affection, | The adored human creature | Making of both a unit | In love, and procreate.' But unlike Auden's, Silkin's style serves a stringent, thoughtful, and indignant compassion for the suffering and exploited. Sometimes the suffering may be close to the poet, as in the often-anthologized 'Death of a Son'. But in general Silkin's stance implies a wider political attitude. Sometimes his terse style results in a dense and tortuous obscurity, and sometimes the assault on liberal complacency is crude and self-righteous. The recurrent imagery of small animals and birds (vulnerable) and stones (invulnerable) can seem perfunctory and mechanical.

The poems in *Nature with Man* (London, 1965) represent a change and an advance. There is a closer attention to physical appearance, married to Silkin's gifts with language. The 'Flower Poems' are especially impressive. Daisies 'Look unoriginal | Being numerous. They ask for attention | With that gradated yellow swelling | Of oily stamens. Petals focus them: | The eyelashes grow wide.' The attention to these flowers is made to seem analogous to a considerate attention to humanity. Silkin has learnt something from William Carlos *Williams here, but his language, with its quirky phrasing and inventive diction, is more self-conscious. In *Amana Grass* (London and Middletown, Conn., 1971) are a number of poems of place, some about Israel: Silkin now explores the links between the political and the personal (his Jewishness) in a more profound manner. The style is sometimes reminiscent of Neruda in its capacious lines and exalted meditativeness. Perhaps his most impressive volume so far is *The Little Time-Keeper* (Manchester, 1976; New York, 1977), which fuses public and private, sensuous and abstract, in a rich, authoritative, compact style. See also *The Lens-Breakers* (London, 1992).   [ETL

SILLIMAN, Ron. See LANGUAGE POETRY.

SIMIC, Charles (1938–), was born in Yugoslavia and emigrated with his family to the United States at the age of 11. Perhaps it is because his formative years were spent in a country occupied by the Nazis that Simic's most persistent thematic concern should be with the effect of cruel political structures upon ordinary human life. It is this context that explains the series of almost miniaturist poems, on such subjects as 'Fork', 'Spoon', 'Knife', 'Ax', and 'Stone', that Simic included in his first book, *Dismantling the Silence* (1971). Rather than constituting the poet's major achievement, as some critics insist, these poems should be seen as defining momentary stays against confusion. The world of Simic's poems is frightening, mysterious, hostile, dangerous; by focusing on such unimportant, everyday objects, he is able to create, however briefly, some degree of order, comprehension, and control. Elsewhere in his early books Simic presents himself only as a clown, joking the night away; it is this sort of poem that he chose, wisely, not to reprint in his *Selected Poems: 1963–1983* (New York, 1985, revd. edn., 1990; London, 1986), which collects from his first six volumes. In his most typical poems, Simic tells stories that are amusing and sinister at the same time: in 'Rough Outline', the 'famous torturer' meets a bride in a wedding-dress, who begs him to spare her beloved. I can't do that, he replies, for he must be tortured tonight, but 'You can come along and help him lament his fate'. The bride declines this invitation, and as the poem ends, 'a dog-like creature' howls 'Down by the slaughterhouse' and 'the snow start[s] to fall again'. As befits the professor of literary theory and creative writing at the University of New Hampshire, the texture of Simic's poems is conceptual and sophisticated; he regularly alludes to a wide range of western thought and literature.

Since *Selected Poems*, Simic has published three volumes: *Unending Blues* (1986), *The World Doesn't End* (1989), and *The Book of Gods and Devils* (1990—all San Diego, Calif.). His prose is collected in *The Uncertain Certainty* (Ann Arbor, Mich., 1988).   [PS

SIMMONS, James (1933–), was born in Derry into a family of singers. He started singing in his father's bar in Portrush, and is popular in Ireland as a singer and songwriter as well as poet, although he does not make a clear division between these activities: several poems in his *Poems 1956–1986* (Newcastle upon Tyne, 1986) are also songs. He seeks his models in the lyrics of popular music and jazz, and is sometimes overtly hostile to what he sees as the preten-

sions of high art, especially that of the modern period, as in *No Land is Waste, Dr. Eliot* (Richmond, Surrey, 1972): 'What roots? What stony rubbish? What rats? Where? | Visions of horror conjured out of air, | the spiritual D.T.s. The pompous swine . . . | that man's not hollow, he's a mate of mine.' Not surprisingly, he wishes his poems to have an appeal outside literary circles. As he says in the first issue of *The Honest Ulsterman*, the literary journal he founded in 1968: 'I hope this magazine gets into the hands of school children and the so-called man in the street, people who think a dull life is inevitable, normal.' Simmons's poems have a wry, bittersweet, ironic flavour. His directness can make his treatment of the Troubles acutely painful, as in 'Claudy', which describes the effects of a car-bomb.   [ETL

SIMPSON, Louis (1923–), the son of a lawyer of Scottish descent and a Russian mother, was born in Jamaica and emigrated to the United States at the age of 17. He interrupted his studies at Columbia University to serve in the US Army in Europe during the Second World War. Returning to Columbia after the war, Simpson earned a Ph.D, then taught in California for some years before moving to Long Island, where he has lived and taught since 1967.

Simpson is among that group of American poets who made a radical change in style in mid-career. The poems in his early books are tightly written in traditional forms, with careful use of metre and rhyme. Some of these poems—for example 'As Birds Are Fitted to the Boughs'—have been seen by critics as comparable to the great Elizabethan lyrics. The real world also enters Simpson's early work in poems dealing with his war experiences, notably 'Carentan O Carentan' and 'The Runner'. In the early Sixties, however, Simpson began to feel that his forms were distancing his work from real life, and he started to write free-verse poems in which both structure and meaning are created by patterns of imagery. He also at this time became critical of American society, particularly for its warmongering in Vietnam and its lack of cultural seriousness. *At the End of the Open Road* (1963), for which Simpson was awarded the Pulitzer Prize, portrays the United States as a superficial country stalled at a moral dead-end. With *Adventures of the Letter I* (1971), Simpson began writing poems about Russia and his Russian ancestors and about the most ordinary forms of American life, finding his materials for these on the streets or in the shopping-malls and living-rooms of the American suburbs. In 'Quiet Desperation' a nondescript middle-aged man watches a little television, chops a little wood, walks his dog, and broods about his own mortality. In 'The Beaded Pear' a mother goes shopping with her family, converses with them over dinner ('Why don't you get transferred, Dad?'), and later constructs her pear out of styrofoam and sequins.

Collected Poems (New York, 1988) includes all the poems that Simpson wants preserved from his earlier books. His *Selected Prose* (New York, 1989) is supplemented by *Three on the Tower: The Lives and Works of Ezra Pound, T. S. Eliot, and William Carlos Williams* (New York, 1975) and *A Revolution in Taste: Studies of Dylan Thomas, Allen Ginsberg, Sylvia Plath, and Robert Lowell* (New York, 1978; London, 1979). He has written one novel, *Riverside Drive* (1962), an autobiography, *North of Jamaica* (1972), and (much later) an autobiographical essay, *Contemporary Authors: Autobiography Series*, vol. 4. See also Hank Lazer (ed.), *On Louis Simpson: Depths Beyond Happiness* (1988), and *Louis Simpson* (1972), by Ronald Moran. [PS

SIMPSON, R(onald) A(lbert) (1929–), was born in Melbourne, studied with the Christian Brothers, then at Melbourne Teachers' College and the Royal Melbourne Institute of Technology. He was an art teacher in various secondary schools until 1968, when he began lecturing in drawing at the Caulfield Institute of Technology, from which he retired in 1987. He travels frequently to the United States and is poetry editor for the *Melbourne Age*. He still combines drawing with the writing of lyric poetry, though he is far better known as a poet.

At once personal, terse, and dispassionate, Simpson has assimilated a variety of influences (*Graves, *Ransom, Camus, *Gunn, and William Carlos *Williams) in the process of arriving at his clear, understated poetry of loss and resignation. The early poetry collected in *The Walk along the Beach* (1960) and *This Real Pompeii* (1964) faces annihilation with a *Movement-like concern for lyric shapeliness and measured anticlimax, while the critical sestina. 'All Friends Together' is uncharacteristically hilarious. Simpson's later poetry modulates into free verse, a shorter line, and flattened endings. Affinities might be discerned between this verse and his cubist drawings. It often glumly shows its autobiographical hand.

From his early 'Landscape' to his recent 'The Performer, the Feather and the Dogs', there is a familiar low-toned Simpson world of large fears and small expectations. His work can be found in *Selected Poems* (St Lucia, Qld., 1981) and *Words for a Journey* (Melbourne, 1986). See the critical judgements of Harry Heseltine, 'Poetry, Nature, Counterstatement', *Overland*, 105 (1986). [CW-C

SINGER, (James) Burns (1928–64), was born in New York of mixed Polish, Jewish, and Celtic blood. Singer remained an American citizen all his life, though his family left the US for Scotland when he was 4. He began an English degree course at Glasgow University but left to teach mathematics in London, roamed Europe for two years, and returned to Glasgow to read zoology. He made a successful career as a marine biologist while maintaining a separate life as a poet and literary essayist, married psychologist and painter Marie Battle in 1956, and died of a heart-attack in Plymouth, aged 36. As a student he had met and fallen under the influence of W. S. *Graham, and was also an admirer of George *Barker, but his poetry was not significantly like anyone else's, writing as he did in an intellectual register very different from, and almost alien to, the familiar English literary one. His language and rhythms are simple, his arguments complex, rigorously complete, and worked out with acute observation of mental and physical processes. His imagery and themes draw heavily on the scientific world he moved in. His idiosyncratic brand of lyricism is all the more powerful for appearing in an essentially rationalist context. Singer's was the sort of philosophical writing guaranteed not to win a large audience—Hugh *MacDiarmid found him obscure, and Singer's one collection published during his lifetime, *Still and All* (1957), received little attention—yet Singer held strong views on the need for poetry to be open to any sort of reader. His prose writings, which remain uncollected, are illuminating on this and many other points. His *Selected Poems*, ed. Anne Cluysenaar, appeared in 1977 (Manchester). See also *Collected Poems* (London, 1970), ed. W. A. S. Keir, which contains a memoir by Hugh MacDiarmid and further biographical information.

[CPH

SIRIWARDENA, Reggie (1929–), was educated at Royal College, Colombo, and at the University of Ceylon.

Editor of the first Sri Lankan anthology to include the work of Sri Lankan writers (1982), Siriwardena has written during the last decade a small body of finely crafted and deeply moving original poems which appear regularly in *The Thatched Patio*, in-house journal of the International Centre for Ethnic Studies in Colombo. He has published *Waiting for the Soldier* (Colombo, 1989), the ten poems in which are reprinted, together with new poems and two essays on verse-form, in *To The Muse of Insomnia* (Colombo, 1990). Other publications include several books for children, and a play, *Prometheus: An Argumentative Comedy for Two Characters* (Colombo, 1989).

Siriwardena's translations (all published in Colombo) include *Many Voices* (1974), English verse translations of fifty Spanish, Italian, French, and Russian poems; a broadsheet of translations from Anna Akhmatova's poetry (1979); *Two Plays of Aleksandr Pushkin* (1979); and *Marina Tsvetaeva* (1985), a small volume of translations with a biographical and critical commentary.

[YG

SISSAY, Lemn. See PERFORMANCE POETRY.

SISSMAN, L(ouis) E(dward) (1928–76), was a precocious only child brought up in Detroit, who at 13 became national champion in a radio spelling bee, and three years later went to Harvard, already six-foot four and overweight. He was rusticated, readmitted, elected class poet, and graduated *cum laude*. At Harvard, the editor of his collected poems tells us, 'his poetic technique set and was varnished', but it remained unused for more than a decade, during which he became a successful advertising man.

In 1965 Sissman learned that he was suffering from the then-incurable Hodgkin's disease. The knowledge moved him to the writing and publication of poems, written during and between periods of hospitalization and treatment that included chemotherapy. *Dying: An Introduction* (Boston, 1968) was followed by two other volumes and a collection of essays. His posthumous collected poems, *Hello, Darkness*, appeared in 1978 (Boston). He was twice married.

The expectation such a life might give of gloomy self-regarding poetry would be wrong. Most of Sissman's poems are written in iambic pentameter, and deal cheerfully or ironically with the universe of things known and seen. He felt more kinship with British than with contemporary American poets, mocked and imitated *Empson, dedicated a poem to Kingsley *Amis and Robert *Conquest, and wrote a tribute to Orwell. His originality rests in working against the poetic grain of almost all the American writing round him, as well as in what John Updike called his 'antic exactitude'. He needed space to achieve his full effects, so that the finest poems are the longer ones, like 'Going Home, 1945' (evidently written much later), 'The Marschallin, Joy Street', 'A Day in the City (Boston-New York)', and the partly autobiographical 'A War Requiem'. He also needed, as it seems at times, reassurance about the existence of the world in which he lived, so that there is much naming of shops, restaurants, and houses. No doubt the need for reassurance was also connected with the death-sentence under which he lived, which is looked at glancingly but courageously in some of the last poems, like 'Cancer: A Dream'.

Sissman's limitation rests in that set, varnished technique. There is little change or variation in his poems, which are chatty, comic, at times rhetorically powerful, but rarely delicate or tender. Yet his achievement was remarkable, nothing less than a hymn to American urban man.   [JGS

SISSON, C(harles) H(ubert) (1914–), was born in Bristol. He was a higher official in the Ministry of Labour, and as a poet became known late, with *Collected Poems 1943–1983* (Manchester, 1984). Sisson has adhered to the position made famous by *Eliot: Anglican, monarchist, Tory; but his Anglicanism, still central to his poetry even though he now refuses to attend church on account of the changes in the Prayer Book, is less high-church, and his austere poems in no way resemble Eliot's. The cast of mind of *Hardy is quite as strong an influence; so is French poetry from Malherbe onwards. Sisson believes that the 'truth lies at the bottom of a well of rhythm', and seeks to reproduce the rhythms of speech. 'In London' is a characteristic early poem: an ironic note of pastoral is introduced into a squalid urban scene incorporating a shabby erotic encounter; punctuation is light, and treats line-endings as commas or semicolons. A power of feeling of Hardyean intensity is fully acknowledged in Sisson, but expression of it is, more often than not, deliberately denied. The meaninglessness of existence is also acknowledged, countered only tentatively: 'If we have reasons, they lie deep.' Extreme bitterness about contemporary life is most evident in 'The Spectre', a satirical account of a successful modern intellectual going through familiar stages of pseudo-development: Poundian disenchantment sharpened by an uncompromising Augustinian Christianity, from which every consolatory supernatural element has been stripped. This relentless theological position is most fully worked out in 'The Usk'. Sisson has his advocates, but his poetry has not yet entered the mainstream, owing to its persistently exasperated tone and its apparently anti-liberal stance. But it is powerfully representative of what is left of the Christian tradition in

English poetry. Since his *Collected Poems* he has published one collection, *God Bless Karl Marx* (Manchester, 1988). He has also translated Horace, Lucretius, Virgil, Dante, and La Fontaine, among others. His prose works include *The Avoidance of Literature: Collected Essays* (1978) and *Anglican Essays* (1983—both Manchester). In 1993 he was made a Companion of Honour.   [POM

SITWELL, Dame Edith (Louisa) (1887–1964), was the eldest child of Sir George and Lady Sitwell of Renishaw Hall, near Scarborough. Lonely and unconventional-looking, she was always to feel that, unlike her younger brothers, Osbert and Sacheverell (to whom she was none the less devoted) she had been deprived of her due share of maternal affection. She was educated at Renishaw, from which she was finally rescued by her governess, Helen Rootham. In 1914 they moved to London, and were companions for many years. It was Helen Rootham who introduced Sitwell to the French Symbolists, of whom Rimbaud made the strongest impression on the young writer. She published her first book, *The Mother*, at her own expense a year later, and the following year began to edit, with Nancy Cunard, the magazine *Wheels*. This ran for six issues and roused controversy by championing literary modernism against the *Georgians.

Famously accused by F. R. Leavis of belonging, with her brothers, 'to the history of publicity rather than that of poetry', Sitwell undoubtedly had an enormously theatrical sense of herself. The famous iconic image of her photos and portraits seems reflected in her poems, with their bright, stately, brocade-like figures. The constant procession of emblems throughout her work—lions, peacocks, roses, gold, blood, bone—often seems a rather easy shorthand for unearned symbolic resonance, though in small doses her pictures are quaintly appealing, like Pre-Raphaelites in primary colours.

Façade, a sequence of poems set to music by William Walton, drew jeers at its first performance in 1922, but later became her most popular work. Arguably it is her best, the derogation of sense to sound for once fully justified. In her own way she responded seriously and passionately to public events, and her two wartime collections, *Street Songs* (1942) and *Green Song* (1943), caught the heroic mood of the time, and may have helped instigate the later, neo-romantic school of poets, dubbed the *New Apocalypse.

Whatever her credibility as a poet, Sitwell is undoubtedly an important figure in the literary history of England in the present century. She was a crusading force against the native tendencies to philistinism and conservatism. Though her most sustained loyalty was to the emigré Russian artist Pavel Tchelitchew, she selflessly championed many young and deserving writers. Under constant pressure to earn her living, she almost certainly published too much, not only poetry but critical pot-boilers and historical works. Her prose is patchy but can be vivid and immediate and, especially in her letters, harshly witty.

The fullest representation of her poetry is in the *Collected Poems* (London, 1957; new edn., and paperback, 1993). For a detailed and sympathetic account of her life and work, see *Edith Sitwell: A Unicorn among the Lions*, by Victoria Glendinning (London, 1981).   [CAR

SITWELL, Sir (Francis) Osbert (Sacheverell) (1892–1969). Osbert Sitwell's verse was the least considerable part of an oeuvre that has mostly dated, except for the novel *Before the Bombardment* and his long and informative autobiography—he having been, mainly, the witty controversialist and polemicist of a famous and eccentric family. The best of his verse, written early in his career, is strongly pacifistic, and satirical of what he called the 'muddle made by profiteers, scamps, fools and the selfishly sentimental' after the First World War, in which he fought, and which confirmed him in a lifelong hatred of war. It is usually conventional in form, but occasionally experimental or anti-*Georgian (he co-edited the modernist journal *Wheels*), though showing little originality of diction, and he all but abandoned the form in later

life. He wrote a skilful libretto for William Walton's oratorio *Belshazzar's Feast* (1931). See *Collected Poems and Satires* (London, 1931).   [MS-S

SITWELL, Sir Sacheverell (1897–1989), was unexpectedly included in Michael *Roberts's *Faber Book of Modern Verse* (1936)—a book of almost classic status in the history of English modernism—and thus gained some wide attention for a few years. But his inclusion as a genuinely modernist poet proved to be one of Roberts's few errors: interest in his rather eccentric but frequently diffuse and inconsequential poetry diminished. Sitwell, as an early critic suggested, believed that as much poetry could be 'extracted from a banana as a battlefield'; but he lacked his sister Edith's liveliness and deftness of technique, and it is hard to believe that he was very carefully studied by his readers. He had, however, an unlikely advocate in G. S. *Fraser, who believed that Sitwell would have his due when it was recognized that his poetic work, especially his scarcely heeded post-war poems, incorporated a 'criticism of language' rather than of 'life'. Between 1918 and 1972 he published nineteen collections of verse and a further forty-three were privately printed between 1972 and 1978. The tally of other publications—most of them art criticism and travel but including two plays—amounts to about sixty. But see *Collected Poems* (1936), *An Indian Summer: 100 Recent Poems* (1982), D. Parker, (ed.), *Sacheverell Sitwell: A Symposium* (1975), and *Sacheverell Sitwell: Splendours and Miseries*, by Sarah Bradford (1993—all London).   [MS-S

Sixties, The, a magazine founded in 1958 by Robert *Bly and William Duffy; after 1962 it was edited by Bly alone. For the first two years (three issues) of its existence, the magazine was known as *The Fifties*. Seven additional issues (numbered four through ten) were produced under the title by which the magazine is best known, *The Sixties*, and one was later produced under the title *The Seventies* (Number 1). The magazine is inextricably linked with Bly's name and was the chief vehicle for the expression of his ideas about poetry during the time of its existence.

The issues are therefore polemical in their orientation and intended to prove that American poetry has gone dead by becoming too logical in its content, too iambic in its rhythms, and too removed from the real (mostly political) concerns of everyday life. One of Bly's remedies was to prescribe what has been called the *'deep image'—of which he found exemplars in non-American poets; thus each issue of the magazine contains translations of such writers as Neruda, Jiménez, Trakl, Vallejo, Machado, and Hernandez. Bly presented his ideas in essays (at least one per issue) written by himself. Perhaps most important among these are those on such younger American poets as Louis *Simpson, Donald *Hall, W. S. *Merwin, John *Logan, Gary *Snyder, James *Dickey, and James *Wright, that Bly printed under the pseudonym 'Crunk'. The issues also contain surprisingly small selections of poems by American writers. Perhaps the most interesting parts of *The Sixties* are those devoted to parody and invective.   [PS

SKELTON, Robin (1925–), was born in Yorkshire. Educated at Christ's College, Cambridge, and the University of Leeds, Skelton lectured for a time in English literature at the University of Manchester. In 1963 he emigrated to Canada where he taught in the department of English at the University of Victoria, before becoming the university's first chairman of the department of creative writing. In addition to his own creative writing, he has published widely on the Irish literary renaissance. He has influenced many Canadian writers as a teacher and through his work with the *Malahat Review*, which he cofounded in 1967 and edited until 1983. He has also written on sorcery and witchcraft.

Skelton has written in many different poetic styles and voices, and has exercised in many forms. Most notably, perhaps, he has been influenced by the *Surrealists (he has commented that he sees himself as a 'messenger'), and like them he would claim to be in search of the secret world beneath the 'lying intimacies' of everyday life.

Much of Skelton's poetry to 1977 can be found in the two companion volumes *Collected Shorter Poems 1947–1977* (1981) and *Collected Longer Poems 1947–1977* (1985—both Victoria, BC). Skelton's own books about poetry include *The Practice of Poetry* (1971), *The Poet's Calling* (1975), and *Poetic Truth* (1978—all London and New York).

His most recent books are: *Limits* (1981), *Distances* (1985), and *Openings* (1988).   [RH

SKOVRON, Alex (1948–), was born in Poland. In 1956 his family moved to Israel, and then in 1958 to Sydney. Since taking degrees in political science at the universities of New South Wales and Sydney, Skovron has worked as an editor for several publishing firms.

In 1976 he married Ruth Paluch, and in 1979 moved to Melbourne. Skovron had begun seriously to write poetry in 1968, but published nothing until 1982. After that he rapidly won recognition and began for the first time to meet other poets and move in literary circles. Nor does he seem before this to have taken an especial interest in any poet more recent than *Eliot.

Where one might expect naïvety, isolation produced in Skovron a brooding complexity of form and imaginative organization. In his first book, the award-winning *The Rearrangement* (Melbourne, 1988), the most striking poems are long and extraordinarily intricate. The title-poem is formally a remarkable *tour-de-force*, done with such cunning that the patterning almost escapes notice; suitably, perhaps, it is a study of obsession. Other poems are more accessible, but most demand an alert reader. *The Rearrangement* was followed by *Sleeve Notes* (Sydney, 1992).   [EJ

SKRZYNECKI, Peter (1945–), was born in Germany of Polish/Ukrainian parents. He emigrated to Australia in 1949 and grew up in Sydney, where he gained degrees from Sydney University and the University of New England. He is a teacher. His poems have been translated and published in Polish and in 1990 he received from the Polish government the medal of *L'ordre du Mérite culturel* for his contribution to Polish culture in Australia.

Skrzynecki was one of the first writers in Australia of his generation to articulate the contours of the post-war migrations in the 1950s, and his anthology *Joseph's Coat* (Sydney, 1985) was one of the major collections to cover the increasingly multicultural nature of the evolving Australian society.

Although he has published a notable collection of short stories, *The Wild Dogs* (St Lucia, Qld., 1987) and one novel, *The Beloved Mountain*. (Sydney, 1988), it is as a poet that Skrzynecki has made his mark. He has published six collections, the most notable being *Immigrant Chronicle* (St Lucia, Qld., 1975), *The Polish Immigrant* (Brisbane, 1983), and *Night Swim: Poems 1978–1988* (Sydney, 1989). He has won a number of literary awards.

Skrzynecki's poetry is imbued with a sense of introspection and a European sensibility. Although he frequently writes about direct experience and the natural environment of Australia, his best work has a driven, worrying quality that reflects both an autobiographical obsession and a deep-seated alienation.   [TWS

SLATER, Montagu (1902–56), was born in Cumberland into a strict Wesleyan family. After winning a scholarship to Oxford and graduating in 1924, Slater began work in Liverpool as a reporter. By 1930 he had joined the Communist Party, to which he remained loyal for the rest of his life. Marxist ideas profoundly influenced all that he wrote. He published his first novel in 1931, his second three years later, and others followed at regular intervals thereafter. However, it seems that by the early 1930s he had discovered that his deepest allegiances were to drama, including verse drama. During the decade he wrote many plays, including his great *Stay Down Miner* (1936), published as *A New Way to Win* (London, 1937), and several pageant plays. There followed much work as a writer of film-scripts and, most famously, collaborations with Benjamin Britten, including the opera *Peter Grimes*.

Peter Grimes and Other Poems (London, 1946) is Slater's only published collection of poetry. Yet he wrote and—less often—published poetry throughout his life. Much of this work is either satiric doggerel or dramatic ballad, in both of which forms he scores a number of important

successes. A generous selection of these and other poems, together with an informed and appreciative memoir, has been made by his friend Arnold *Rattenbury, and is to be found in *The 1930s: A Challenge to Orthodoxy*, ed. John Lucas (Brighton, Sussex, 1978). There is also a memoir by J. R. St John in *The New Reasoner*, 1:4 (1958).   [JL

SLEIGH, Tom (1953–), was born in Mount Pleasant, Texas. He attended the California Institute of Arts and Johns Hopkins University, and has made his home in Cambridge, Massachusetts, since the early 1980s. Sleigh teaches in the English department at Dartmouth College.

Sleigh's poetry, while anchored at every point to concrete particulars, can also be read as an exploration of Simone Weil's polar terms— 'gravity' and 'grace'. Gravity recognizes suffering and the often-harsh exactions of circumstance, and Sleigh probes these in a number of unflinching poems about the lives of family members and his own encounter with illness. Grace, in Sleigh's vision, may not be God-given, but it brings the redemptive recognition of beauty and, at rare moments, a near-mystical surety of connection to a deeper ground of being.

'Ending', Sleigh's most ambitious work to date, brings the terms of the opposition into high relief. The poem, chronicling his struggle with illness, is harrowing in its particulars, and shows to full advantage the poet's supple and rhythmic idiom. Sleigh's two collections are *After One* (Boston, 1983) and *Waking* (Chicago, 1990).   [SB

SLESSOR, Kenneth (1901–71), is widely held to be Australia's first modern poet as well as one of its finest. His writing career was comparatively short. He published his first volume in 1924 and the last of his hundred-odd poems appeared in the mid-1940s. Yet, with the possible exception of his contemporary R. D. *Fitzgerald, it was Slessor who did more than anyone to propel Australian poetry into the twentieth century and help it shake off the 'colonial' tag. Commentators on his first mature poems were quick to find in them evidence of the influence of T. S. *Eliot. Slessor himself always claimed Tennyson as an early master. It has been suggested that his poems mingle Eliot's edgy toughness with Tennyson's tender fantasy and feeling. However, any attentive reader of such characterstic poems as 'Heine in Paris', 'Captain Dobbin', and above all 'Five Bells', will recognize the originality of Slessor's ample rhetoric and of his technical assurance. This is not to say he is free of influences. But while these exist they are well absorbed into work which represents a blend of the ironic, poised tone of such French poets as Corbière and Laforgue together with the sumptuous cadences of *Yeats and, just possibly, the Wallace *Stevens of *Harmonium*.

Slessor's poetry is entirely professional. Its polish is the result of hard work. It is also dense with the actualities of Australian life, and in this Slessor seems to be the source for much of Les *Murray's poetry. The second edition of his *Poems* was published in 1957 (London and Sydney) and *Selected Poems* in 1975 (Sydney).   [JL

SMITH, A(rthur) J(ames) M(arshall) (1902–80), was born in Montreal and was educated at McGill University and the University of Edinburgh. Smith developed a taste for the new poetry as a young browser in Harold *Monro's bookshop in London where he lived from 1918 to 1920. At McGill University he teamed up with F. R. *Scott, recently returned from Oxford, to launch a literary supplement to the student newspaper. This was followed by a more mature effort in the form of the *McGill Fortnightly Review* (1925–27). The effect of Smith's enterprise both as a practising poet and a budding critic was to draw like-minded and aspiring young writers into a circle which became known as the 'McGill Movement'. They read *Eliot, *Yeats, the Symbolists, and followed the literary currents of international modernism in the avant-garde periodicals of the times. Smith himself published in the *Measure* and the *Dial* in the middle Twenties, and would go on to win the Harriet Monroe Memorial Prize from *Poetry (Chicago) in 1943. All of this helped to solidify his strong antiparochialism, and to turn Smith into a sophisticated and witty internationalist in his literary outlook. After his return from Edinburgh, Smith drifted to the United States where he eventually settled into a long and distinguished career at Michigan State University as professor of English and poet-in-residence. In 1936 he collaborated with F. R. *Scott in assembling *New Provinces: Poems of Several Authors*, a milestone anthology of modernist Canadian verse. A meticulous craftsman, Smith took a long time to produce his first book, *News of the Phoenix and Other Poems* (1943). This was followed eleven years later by *A Sort of Ecstasy: Poems New and Selected* (1954) which offered twenty new poems. This pattern of worrying, polishing, and reworking material became a hallmark of Smith's method, and has meant that the sum total of his life's published work stands at some 200 poems. In spite of this, Smith has managed to produce poems in a great variety of modes. A versatile and playful stylist, his poetry ranges from the stark image and the simple lyric to the allusive conceits of a literary imagination schooled in Donne and the metaphysical poets. Smith's *Collected Poems* came out in 1962, and was followed by *Poems New and Collected* (1967) and *The Classic Shade: Selected Poems* (1978—all Toronto).

In addition to his poetry, Smith carved out a prominent role for himself as an anthologist and influential critic. He edited *The Book of Canadian Poetry* (Toronto and Chicago, 1943, 1948, 1957) and the *Oxford Book of Canadian Verse in English and French* (Toronto and New York, 1960). His critical writings can be found in *Towards a View of Canadian Letters: Selected Critical Essays 1928–1971* (Vancouver, 1973). See also Michael E. Darling, *A. J. M. Smith: An Annotated Bibliography* (Montreal, 1981).   [MG

SMITH, Dave (David Jeddie) (1942–), was born in Portsmouth, Virginia. He attended local schools and graduated from the University of Virginia. He served in the US Air Force and, later, studied in the graduate schools of Southern Illinois University and Ohio University. Married to Dee Smith, with three children, he is professor of English at Virginia Commonwealth University.

The author of over a dozen books of poetry, Smith has been widely praised for his lyricism and narrative powers, both of which are brought forcefully to bear in poems which are often set in the rural south. His talent for the gradual release of narrative details gives his longer poems, such as 'Night Fishing for Blues' or 'In the House of the Judge', a sustained drive. As in 'Goshawk, Antelope', Smith regularly invokes a 'country of blue sedge' populated by wild animals and birds that, in this poet's hands, become powerful natural symbols. His poetic stage is crammed with workers: fishermen, oystermen, clam-diggers; the natural landscape of the poems is frequently a backdrop to country revels at sundown, to old railroad roundhouses, racial fights, and dusty roads—a landscape reminiscent of Robert Penn *Warren, whose poetry has had a profound influence on Smith.

As in 'The Roundhouse Voices', Smith is primarily a poet of memory, summoning his own childhood and family in haunting ways. He can vividly recall a childhood swimming-hole in 'Hole, Where Once in Passion We Swam', an old family heirloom in 'The Spinning Wheel in the Attic', a lost cousin in 'De Soto', or the discovery of an old chest filled with pornographic photos in 'The Pornography Box', one of many poems that invoke the poet's father. Helen Vendler has called Smith 'a distinguished allegorist of human experience', describing his poems as 'solemn, harsh, driven, obdurate, hungry for some guarantees—which he wants as much to create as to experience—of promises kept, love exchanged, hope confirmed'. Smith has said that 'Poetry is the knight doing psychic combat for us', and his poems frequently aspire to an almost heroic stance, with the acts of memory and vision viewed as something akin to restitution and recovery.

Smith's selected poems is *The Roundhouse Voices* (New York, 1985). A more recent collection is *Cuba Night* (New York, 1990). A new *Selected Poems* came from Newcastle upon Tyne in 1992. He has also written a novel, *Onliness* (Baton Rouge, La., 1981), a book of stories, and a collection of critical essays, *Local Assays* (Urbana, Ill., 1985). [JP

SMITH, Iain Crichton (1928–). Born in Glasgow, Smith was taken as an infant to the island of Lewis where he remained until entering the University of Aberdeen in 1945. After National Service he taught in various schools in the west of Scotland. He has been a free-lance writer since 1977.

Smith has been prolific in both English and Gaelic (of which he is a native speaker). As well as poetry he has published novels, collections of stories, plays, essays, and reviews. His major themes are the contest of the individual with repressive religious, social, and political forces which result in the displacement of the poet; the offensiveness of a superficial, consumerist society; and the vulnerability of the Gaelic language and its culture in the face of corrosive modern pressures. The first and third of these themes originate in his upbringing on Lewis where the power of the Presbyterian United Free Church (the 'Wee Frees') is evoked as personally and culturally negative. Smith's term for this 'patriarchal' sway is Law, which he counters with Grace, the values of which he takes from poetry, art, classical mythology, and the 'endlessly various, real, human | world which is no new era, shining dawn', as he writes in 'Lenin', where he tackles a political version of strait-jacketing denial.

Much of Smith's poetry in English is stanzaic, iambic, and uses rhyme. The much-anthologized 'Old Woman', and 'At the Sale', are good examples. Other work, perhaps his best—'The Clearances', 'Poem in March', 'Chinese Poem', and a good deal in his recent collections—is usually freer. Ostensibly casual forms permit the release of often eccentric imagery. He refers widely to literature, art, history, and philosophy, but also introduces vivid observations of contemporary life ('By the Sea'). Many influences are detectable—*Auden, *Lowell, *Larkin, and *Stevens among them—but there are others which appear momentarily and suggest that Smith is a restless and perhaps uncertain writer for whom the issues raised by a bilingual poetic endeavour have not always been fruitful. However, they also help to identify Smith as an eclectic poet who has been willing to take stylistic and emotional risks. His sense of humour is evident in 'Chinese Poem' and especially in his satirical poems in Gaelic (which he translates himself), such as 'The TV' and 'Gaelic Stories'.

Smith has published fifteen major separate collections in English and/or Gaelic. *Selected Poems* (London and Chester Springs, Penn., 1970), *Selected Poems 1955–80*, ed. R. Fulton, (Edinburgh, 1981), and *Selected Poems* (Manchester, 1985) offer a cross-section of his generous productivity. More recent collections (all Manchester) are *The Exiles* (1984), *A Life* (1986), and *The Village* (1989). There is now also a *Collected Poems* (Manchester, 1992). *Towards the Human: Selected Essays*, appeared in 1986 (Edinburgh). There is a full bibliography by G. F. Wilson (1990), and see *Iain Crichton Smith: New Critical Essays*, ed. C. Nicholson (Edinburgh, 1991) and Carol Gow, *Mirror and Marble* (Edinburgh, 1992). [DED

SMITH, Ken(neth John) (1938–), was born in Yorkshire, the son of an itinerant farm-labourer. He read English at Leeds during the University's literary flowering in the early Sixties, when Wilson Knight and Geoffrey *Hill were on the teaching staff and Jon *Silkin and Peter *Redgrove were Gregory fellows in poetry. *The Pity* (London, 1967) shows the social commitment associated with *Stand*, of which he was co-editor from 1963 until he moved to America in 1969.

That move precipitated a change, not simply in his style, but in his conception of poetry. Influenced by the work of James *Wright and Robert *Bly, and even more by the primitive poetry collected in *Technicians of the Sacred* (New York, 1968), he became impatient with an art of framed observations. *Work, distances/poems* (Chicago, 1972) marks the beginning of what is really one lifelong poem, an intermittent narrative that fluctuates from lyrics and epigrams to extended sequences. He develops myths and discovers personae, telling stories in order to understand his own story, finding 'a language to speak to myself'.

Such a project was not widely understood in

England. He returned in 1973 but did not re-establish his reputation until *The Poet Reclining* (Newcastle upon Tyne) appeared in 1982, bringing together ten years' work that had been published only in fugitive pamphlets. The poems have immediate virtues—rhythmic vitality, clarity of image—but their importance lies in their cumulative power, in the way they seem to grow from a sustained and necessary activity.

When Smith becomes journalistic, jotting down graffiti, eavesdropping on buses, trying to catch the mood of the times, his forms become casual and repetitive. But in *Wormwood* (Newcastle upon Tyne, 1987), based on his experiences as writer-in-residence at Wormwood Scrubs Prison, he modulates his voice skilfully. *A Book of Chinese Whispers* (Newcastle upon Tyne, 1987) is a collection of Smith's prose pieces. [RGa

SMITH, Michael (1954–83), was born in Kingston, Jamaica. Working-class in origin (his father was a mason, and his mother a factory worker) he enrolled at the Jamaica School of Drama, and by the time he graduated in 1980, he was one of the most popular 'dub' performance poets in Jamaica. In 1982 he toured Britain and Europe with great success. His life, however, was tragically cut short when four hired thugs stoned him to death during the Jamaican general-election campaign of 1983. When challenged, he had reputedly said: 'I-man free to walk anywhere in this land.'

Michael Smith's most famous poem, 'Me Cyaan Believe It', is a sardonic protest against any limits which hedge the lives of ordinary people, and his Rastafarian contempt for the merely political bares its teeth in the following lines from 'I an I Alone': 'Hey, lady, yuh believe in Socialism?' | 'No, sah, me believe in social livin.'

It a Come (London, 1986), his only book of poetry, received a Poetry Book Society Recommendation. The Island LP record, *Me Cyaan Believe It* (1982) records his style of public performance, and was produced by fellow 'dub' poet Linton Kwesi *Johnson. [MR

SMITH, Stevie (Florence Margaret) (1902–71), was born in Hull, but from the age of 3 lived in a north London suburb, Palmers Green. Until 1953 she worked as a secretary, mainly in a publishing company. Most of her adult life she lived with an aunt. She never married.

She first came to prominence as the author of a novel, *Novel on Yellow Paper* (London, 1936), a book which shares some qualities with her poetry: quirky, sardonic, disconcerting in its varying tones of voice. Her first book of poems, *A Good Time Was Had By All* (1937), established from the beginning several of her characteristics: quick changes of tone, abrupt veerings between comic and tragic, absurd and solemn, and a range of lyrical, satirical, discursive, and flippant modes.

'I can't make up my mind', she wrote, 'if God is good, impotent or unkind.' She scratched obsessively at the Christian Church and the Christian faith, as if they were sores which would not quite heal. Her lectures to university societies ('The Necessity of Not Believing' at Cambridge, 'Some Impediments to Christian Commitment' at Oxford) are variations on the themes of many poems: 'There is a god in whom I do not believe | Yet to this god my love stretches | This god whom I do not believe in is | My whole life, my life and I am his.'

Throughout the entire period of her writing life, and since her death (when, incidentally, she was at the height of her fame and popularity), Stevie Smith's 'seriousness' and 'importance' have been frequently questioned. Was she naïve, or *faux-naïf*? Childlike or childish? Ingenuous or disingenuous? To some, she was William Blake rewritten by Ogden *Nash. The drawings that accompanied many of her poems, and the curious combination of ceremony and levity she brought to the reading aloud of her work, have been called in question. In the best full-length book so far written about her (*Stevie Smith: A Critical Biography*, London, 1988; New York, 1989), Frances Spalding convincingly argues for her importance without abandoning her acclaimed role as an idiosyncratic and often very funny entertainer.

In her lifetime, she produced seven books of poems, including a *Selected Poems* (London and New York, 1964). If any distinction can be made between poems written at different periods, it is that the theme of death increasingly preoccupied her in her later work, often seen in a whimsical and even sprightly way, as if death were almost someone to be comfortably welcomed, like a neighbour. She drew on many invented voices, controlling a range of personae unequalled since *Eliot, and possibly Browning, but always recognizably issuing from the same tormented, lyrical, hymn-haunted, Poe-addicted, teasing, inconsequential, truth-telling mouth.

After her death, her *Collected Poems* was edited by her literary executor, James MacGibbon (London, 1975; New York, 1976). There is a miscellaneous collection of her prose pieces and several otherwise unpublished or uncollected poems, *Me Again* (London, 1981; New York, 1982). [AST

SMITH, Sydney Goodsir (1915–75). For a poet who wrote in vigorous Scots (or *Lallans), it is remarkable that Smith was born in New Zealand, settled in Edinburgh only in his late teens, and was educated in English public schools and at Oxford (having failed first-year medicine at Edinburgh). His work draws from the spirit of the Scottish poetry of the fifteenth and sixteenth centuries more than the epoch of Fergusson and Burns. Not having lived a childhood in Scotland, he was perhaps sufficiently free of the latter-day class associations of the Scots language to appropriate it for his poetry with what can seem a mixture of instinctive, sentient scholarship on the one hand, and recklessness on the other. While Hugh *MacDiarmid was his master, and MacDiarmid's poetry of the 1920s his enabling exemplum, Smith shares with other outstanding writers in Scots (Robert *Garioch, William *Soutar) a distinctive idiom that differs from MacDiarmid's.

In very general terms, Smith's work is of two kinds. 'The Grace of God and the Meth-Drinker', 'Gowdspink in Reekie' (i.e. Oliver Goldsmith in Edinburgh), 'Kynd Kittick's Land', or 'Slugabed' (Part V of 'Under the Eildon Tree'), present a rumbustious humour with directness, bravura, and speed. He distrusted passages of figurative imagery (the mainstay of much English and other poetry), and, indeed, anything other than incidental metaphor can be seen as unusual in poetry in Scots until this century. The wilder side of Smith's poetic temper found expression in prose too, in *Carotid Cornucopius* (1947, repr. 1964), which owes something to Rabelais, Urquhart, Jarry, and *Joyce, but more to an individual release of inspired linguistic lunacy.

Smith's other main line of work is lyrical, passionate, and controlled. Lyrics like 'Aa my Life' and 'Time be Brief' exclude that fanciful, supercharged prolixity to which Scots diction can be prone, achieving instead the chaste quality of timeless song. Despite passages where his language can feel more artificial than it need be, Smith's work as a whole reaches for a classic Scottish imbalance of daftness and common sense, broad comedy and seriousness.

Smith also wrote *The Wallace* (1960), a verse drama on the Scottish hero, a good deal of criticism, and undertook editing—for example, (with J. Barke) Burns's *The Merry Muses of Caledonia* (1959) and *A Choice of Burns's Poems and Songs* (1966). Almost all his collections were published in Edinburgh, with the exception of *Collected Poems* (London, 1975). *For Sydney Goodsir Smith* (1975) contains essays on his poetry, poems, a checklist and memoirs of a writer still remembered by his nickname, 'The Auk'. He was also an artist and cartoonist.   [DED

SMITH, Vivian (1933–), was born in Hobart, and in the 1960s was associated with *Harwood and *McAuley as establishing a Tasmanian regional school of meditative landscape lyrics. While objects of the natural world are evoked (and celebrated) in the present as they 'dance a meaning for the mind', his human figures are often treated elegiacally. Summoned up 'At an Exhibition of Historical Paintings, Hobart', they demonstrate the 'pathos of the past, the human creature'; their presence haunts such places as a 'Deserted Bandstand, Kingston Beach' or

declares itself in the things they have left behind ('Old Men are Facts', 'In the Colonial Museum').

He also writes of Paris, Tuscany, and Sydney, to which he moved as reader in English at Sydney University, changing fields from French literature, although this interest is pursued in the closing section of *Selected Poems* (Sydney, 1985) where the 'Translations and Variations' series is drawn from a number of modern European poets, notably Paul Celan.

His combination of intelligence and feeling and the subtle musicality of his traditional verse-forms have commanded critical respect. Apart from editing of several anthologies, his substantial contribution to Australian literary criticism includes authorship of the poetry section of the *Oxford History of Australian Literature* (Melbourne, 1981).   [JS

SMITH, William Jay (1918–), was born in Winnfield, Louisiana. Soon after his birth, Smith's father, an unsuccessful farmer, re-enlisted to become a clarinettist in the US Army band. In 1921 the family moved to Jefferson Barracks near St Louis, where Smith spent his entire youth—memorably recounted in his elegant memoir, *Army Brat* (New York, 1980). He took a BA and MA in French from Washington University. During the Second World War he served in the US Navy as liaison officer on board a French frigate in both the Atlantic and Pacific theatres of operation. After the war he taught briefly before winning a Rhodes scholarship in 1947 to study at Wadham College, Oxford. That year he also married the poet Barbara *Howes. This marriage ended in divorce in 1964. Two years later he married Sonja Haussman of Paris. Smith's career has been remarkably diverse. He taught at several colleges and universities as well as serving two years in the Vermont House of Representatives. In 1968–70 he worked as poetry consultant to the Library of Congress. A pre-eminent translator of modern poetry, he has also lectured abroad, especially in Eastern Europe. He currently divides his time between New York, Paris, and Cummington (Massachusetts).

Smith has been a prolific writer, publishing

over forty books of poetry, translation, children's verse, literary criticism, and memoirs in addition to editing several influential anthologies. His best poems are unlike anything else in contemporary American literature. His early lyric poetry is as close as any verse by the French Symbolists to the unattainable ideal of *poésie pure*. Although often based on realistic situations, Smith's compressed, formal lyrics develop language musically in a way which summons an intricate, dreamlike set of images and associations. The poems sometimes use simple syntax and diction—as in 'American Primitive' or 'The Closing of the Rodeo'—to create dark and ambiguous effects. Smith likewise uses tight formal patterns—as in 'Galileo Galilei' or 'Miserere'—to present nightmarish scenes which defy rational explanation. Without abandoning formal verse, Smith also explored a unique brand of free verse in later volumes like *The Tin Can* (New York, 1966). Written in long, powerfully rhythmic lines reminiscent of St John Perse's *versets*, these poems avoid the pseudo-Biblical sound of the Whitmanian tradition but none the less grant Smith the expansive freedom of unmetred verse. Although Smith is often grouped with the formalist poets of his generation (*Wilbur, *Nemerov, *Hollander, etc.), his work remains original and distinctly personal, ultimately bearing as much relation to French as to American literature.

Collected Poems: 1939–1989 (New York, 1990), remains the most comprehensive edition of Smith's poetry. *Laughing Time: Collected Nonsense* (New York, 1990) is the best gathering of his polished light verse. A substantial selection of his literary criticism can be found in *The Streaks of the Tulips* (New York, 1972). For a sampling of his voluminous translations, see *Collected Translations* (St Paul, Minn., 1985).   [DG

SMITHER, Elizabeth (1941–), was born in New Plymouth, New Zealand, and has lived there most of her life. She works part-time as a librarian.

Smither has published prolifically since 1975, producing eight substantial collections of poetry and several lighter booklets, as well as two novels and a book of short stories. Her poetry, conservative in form, is distinguished by, for the most part, epigrammatic brevity, a dry wit, and a pleasure in syntactic complexity to the point of ambiguity. In a period when many New Zealand poets adopted American models of poetry, fraught with local reference, she has preferred a more British idiom of restrained, cosmopolitan intellectualism, with an occasional personal poem: there is a perpetual re-negotiation of the boundaries between the poet's life, art, and mythology. Typical are her book-titles, such as *You're Very Seductive William Carlos Williams* (1978), *Casanova's Ankle* (1981), *The Legend of Marcello Mastroianni's Wife* (1981), and *Professor Musgrove's Canary* (1986).

Smither continues to publish frequently in British poetry magazines. Her most recent collection, *A Pattern of Marching*, (Auckland, 1989), won the 1990 New Zealand Book Award for poetry.   [KJ

SMITHYMAN, Kendrick (1922–), was born in Te Kopuru, Northland, New Zealand. He moved to Auckland as a child and has lived there ever since. In 1946 he married the poet Mary Stanley and has remarried since her death in 1980. In 1963 he joined the teaching staff of Auckland University, retiring in 1987. His first significant collection, *The Blind Mountain*, was published by the Caxton Press in 1950. Like James K. *Baxter and Louis *Johnson, Smithyman is a major middle-generation New Zealand poet who turned away from the overt 'nationalism' of a previous generation (*Curnow, *Brasch, *Fairburn) in order to create a densely detailed syntax which explores relationships between language and locality. If Johnson's post-war contribution to New Zealand poetry was to widen subject-matter, and Baxter's to humanize the life of the spirit, then Smithyman's equally significant gift was in his persistent struggle to get away from 'the English line'. Turning to the early American modernists for inspiration (particularly *Ransom, Marianne *Moore, and Robert Penn *Warren), he was probably the first New Zealand poet to cultivate a highly developed personal language on purely modernist terms. His early collections are sometimes dominated by 'poetic' considerations but, following an extended visit to England and Canada in 1969, his poetry relaxed, and in *The Seal in the Dolphin Pool* (1974), *Dwarf with a Billiard Cue* (1978), *Stories About Wooden Keyboards* (1985), and his *Selected Poems* (1989—all Auckland), a tendency to garrulousness is more than compensated for by the increasing wit, irony, and sheer weight of knowledge that his poems have learned to carry. He published a collection of essays on New Zealand poetry, *A Way of Saying*, in 1965, and in 1987 he edited a selection of stories by the New Zealand domiciled English writer Greville Texidor. Essays on Smithyman's poetry can be found in *Landfall*, 168, and in the excellent introduction to his *Selected Poems*, by Peter Simpson.   [PB

SNODGRASS, W(illiam) D(e Witt) (1926–), was born in Wilkinsburg, Pennsylvania. He attended Geneva College before he enlisted in the US Navy, where he served in the Pacific. On his return from military service he became a student at the University of *Iowa Writers' Workshop, spending seven years there. He has subsequently taught at various universities, including Cornell, Wayne State, Syracuse, and (currently) the University of Delaware.

Snodgrass's first collection, *Heart's Needle*, came out in 1959 and brought him widespread notice and a Pulitzer Prize. It was evidence of a copious and restless talent. It included some very funny, self-deprecating light verse ('April Inventory'), alongside exercises, only just this side of laborious, in Donneish metaphysical conceits ('Riddle', 'These Trees Stand'), poems on heroic classical themes ('Orpheus'), poems about music that are themselves unusually musical in tone and form, and a sequence of poems about his recent divorce and his separation from his baby daughter.

In any other year *Heart's Needle* would have been noteworthy for its wide-ranging, sometimes hit-and-miss experimentalism and for its orthodox technical facility: Snodgrass rhymed and scanned—and appeared to rhyme and scan about everything in sight. But 1959–60 was a year that saw the publication of Robert *Lowell's *Life Studies*, Anne *Sexton's *To Bedlam and Part Way Back*, and Sylvia *Plath's *The Colossus*, and on the strength of his poems about his divorce, Snodgrass was press-ganged as a *'Confessional Poet'.

Much later, reviewers were prone to describe Snodgrass as an imitator of Lowell—which was utterly untrue of his plangent and oblique private poems, although some of his historical-metaphysical verse does recall the Lowell of the 1940s. Lowell himself once nicely distanced Snodgrass, with due respect, calling him 'the American Philip Larkin'.

The poem 'Heart's Needle' is long, intricate, tender, and formal in its verse manners; a world away from the stripped-to-the-bone technique of *Life Studies*. It is—in an almost Victorian way—unafraid of sentiment, a solemn threnody lightened by continuous, skilful changes of landscape and metrical pattern. It speaks of deep distress, but does so in a tone of triumphant virtuosity.

In subsequent collections Snodgrass continued to widen his already impressively wide range, zigzagging between 'public' and 'private' themes with an ambitious series of poems about paintings, exuberant poems for children, and pained, exact, sometimes lacerating poems about his family. 'A Flat One' (collected in *After Experience*, 1967) represents Snodgrass at his finest: it combines a jolting emotional frankness with confident technical mastery. Addressed by a hospital nurse to an old man, a veteran of the First World War, who has just died in the nurse's care, the poem has the pungent detail, the recessed narrative, and the unabashed feeling of a nineteenth-century genre painting.

Snodgrass's major project since 1977 has been an epic verse cycle, designed for dramatic delivery, titled *The Fuehrer Bunker*, which is still apparently incomplete. It consists of a series of monologues by Hitler, Eva Braun, Himmler, Goebbels, Goering, and other leading Nazi figures in the spring of 1945 during the Allied capture of Berlin. From the first appearance of these poems critical opinion has been violently divided over their merits. Reviewing the 1977 collection, Hugh Kenner wrote (in the *New York Times Book Review*) that it was a mystery why 'Snodgrass should be wasting his gifts on attempts to outdo "the banality of evil"' — a sentiment that was echoed by the many reviewers who referred to Snodgrass's 'wasting' of his talent on this theme. However, Harold Bloom (in the *New Republic*) admired the sequence: 'Granted the immense difficulties he has taken on, Snodgrass demonstrates something of the power of a contemporary equivalent of Jacobean drama at its darkest.' In general, Snodgrass's reputation has been in eclipse since the *Fuehrer Bunker*, although he has continued to publish poems unrelated to his Nazi epic (including a quantity of high-spirited light verse).

Selected Poems 1957–1987 (New York, 1987) gathers material from *Heart's Needle* (New York, 1959; Hessle, Yorks., 1960); *After Experience* (New York, 1967; Oxford, 1968); *Remains* (Mount Horeb, Wis., 1970; revd. edn., Brockport, NY, 1985); *The Fuehrer Bunker* (Brockport, 1977); *If Birds Build With Your Hair* (New York, 1979); *The Boy Made of Meat* (Concord, NH, 1982); *A Locked House* (Concord, 1986); and *The Death of Cock Robin* (Newark, Del., 1989). Further collections include *W.D's Midnight Carnival*, with paintings by DeLoss W. McGraw (Encinitas, Calif., 1988). *In Radical Pursuit* (New York, 1975) is a collection of lectures and essays. [JR

SNYDER, Gary (1930–), was born in San Francisco, and brought up in Oregon and Washington State. He received his BA in anthropology at Reed College, Portland, in 1951. His subsequent career has been a remarkable combination of the academic and the contemplative, spiritual study and physical labour. Between working as a logger, a trail-crew member, and a seaman on a Pacific tanker, he studied Oriental languages at Berkeley (1953–6), was associated with *Beat writers such as *Ginsberg and Kerouac, lived in Japan (1956–64), later studied Buddhism there, and won numerous literary prizes, including a Guggenheim fellowship (1968) and the Pulitzer Prize (1975). He now teaches literature and 'wilderness thought' at the University of California at Davis.

The shapes and strengths of Gary Snyder's craft were established at the outset of his career. His first book, *Riprap* (Kyoto, 1959), demonstrates the clarity of his seeing, his desire to crystallize moments, his striking ability to convey the physical nature of an instant: 'I cannot remember things I once read | A few friends, but they are in cities. | Drinking cold snow-water from a tin cup | Looking down for miles | Through high still air' ('Mid-August at Sourdough Mountain Lookout'). Simplicity, distance, accuracy of atmosphere: these are hallmarks of the work throughout. The laid-back, jotted-down tone masks an acute sensitivity to rhythm and, in particular, assonance. Though his formal spectrum is narrow, from terse, rhythmic observation with a resonant conclusion ('I feel ancient, as though I had | Lived many lives', 'An Autumn Morning in Shokoku-ji') to lengthy, free-associative odysseys through the American 'back country', his territory is vast, and his resources of phrase and juxtaposition seemingly endless. Such a ranging strategy does not always pan gold from the water, but when it does Snyder comes face to face with a wide, gladdening openness, or touches wellsprings of healing profundity.

Snyder's poetry blends America's native past with the grandeur and detail of nature, and the mental disciplines of Zen Buddhism: his long apprenticeship in the latter has harvested a tough simplicity and freshness of expression (at its best in *Cold Mountain Poems*, San Francisco, 1965), a trust in the way words lead him, the faith of a traveller through an interior, whether continental or psychological. He writes in the first person, as individual in the wilderness, but the beauty and glory of the wilderness allows that individual the status of common man. He tells no tales: what he says is what he heard or saw; imagination is not for invention, but for finding the forms of expression that most perfectly mirror the world outside. For Snyder, symbol and metaphor cause a distancing from the thing itself: as *Pound suggested, the thing itself is at least enough.

Love and respect for the primitive tribe, honour accorded the Earth, the escape from city and industry into both the past and the possible, contemplation, the communal, peace, and the ascetic: what came to fruition and influence in the Beat waves of the Fifties and Sixties has stood the test of the cynical decades that followed. Though Snyder's later work has not surpassed his early, his philosophy seems, in the fashionably 'green' 1990s, as deep-rooted and prophetic as his best work has remained fresh and unique: 'There is not much wilderness left to destroy, and the nature in the mind is being logged and burned off. Industrial-urban society is not "evil" but there is no progress either . . . A gas turbine or an electric motor is a finely-crafted flint knife in the hand. It is useful and full of wonder, but it is not our whole life . . . I try to hold both history and the wilderness in mind, that my poems may approach the true measure of things and stand against the unbalance and ignorance of our times' (quoted in David Kherdian, *Six San Francisco Poets*, Fresno, Calif., 1969).

Among his other collections are *Turtle Island* (New York, 1974), *Axe Handles* (Berkeley, Calif., 1983), and *Left Out in the Rain: New Poems 1947–1985* (Berkeley, 1986).　　　　[GM

SORLEY, Charles Hamilton (1895–1915), was born in Aberdeen, of Lowland Scottish descent on both sides. In 1908 he gained an open scholarship to Marlborough College where, in his father's words, 'he abounded in the mysteries of its etiquette and slang' and distinguished himself as a member of the school literary society to which, among other contributions, he presented 'John Masefield and the Twentieth Century Renaissance'. The whole of this paper can be found in the posthumous edition of Sorley's letters, edited by his father and published by the Cambridge University Press in 1919. Appreciative, incisive, convinced that 'one of the worst traits of modern literature, as of modern conversation, is its inability to call a spade a spade', it is an invigorating performance. Sorley's literary promise was clearly outstanding, and although his output as a poet was small it is an indication of the impact his work made on the keenest poetic intelligences among his contemporaries that, on learning of his death at Loos in 1915, Robert *Graves should have written in one of his own letters home 'what waste!'

At the outbreak of war—before, as he hoped, taking up an Oxford scholarship—Sorley was studying and travelling in Germany, and the poems he later wrote while an officer on active service are characterized by a refusal to endorse the jingoism prevalent in the early stages of the war. Openly critical of what he considered Rupert *Brooke's adoption of 'the sentimental attitude', and attacking Thomas *Hardy's 'Victory crowns the just' as the worst line he ever wrote, Sorley's position was passionately clear-sighted. His sonnet 'To Germany' describes the opposing sides as 'gropers both through fields confined' who 'stumble' and 'do not understand'.

Perhaps inevitably Sorley's juvenilia outweigh his achieved successes, and not surprisingly in a writer neither ambitious for publication nor benefiting (as did *Owen, Graves, and *Sassoon) from mutual criticism amongst peers, he is often self-consciously romantic and stilted in his diction, but at least one poem—'All the hills and vales along'—is a small masterpiece and his achievement remains considerable. His poems are available in *Collected Poems*, ed. Jean Moorcroft Wilson (London, 1985), who has also written *Charles Hamilton Sorley: A Biography* (London, 1985); and Hilda Spear has edited *Poems and Selected Letters* (Dundee, 1978).　　　　[JM

SOTO, Gary (1952–), a leading presence in Chicano poetry, grew up in a *campesino* family in California, the memory of whose landscape and field-hands underwrites nearly all his verse from *The Elements of San Joaquin* (Pittsburgh, Pa., 1977) to *Who Will Know Us?* (San Francisco, 1991) and *Learning Religion* (San Francisco, 1991). His appeal lies in the sparenesses of his language and imagery, and a respect—usually within a frame of Californian locale and history—for the insistent particularity of experience. An early poem like 'October' makes the point. A field-worker sees animals readying themselves for the change of seasons: sparrows from 'a bare sycamore', 'an owl shuffled into a nest | Of old leaves and cotton', and a coyote 'squatted behind granite, | His ears tilting | Towards a rustle, eyes dark | with the winter to come'. This same quiet, vivid alertness, and Soto's command of measure, runs variously through a magic-realist composition like 'The Space', in *The Tale of Sunlight* (Pittsburgh, 1978), a compassionate worker poem like 'Mission Tire Factory, 1969', in *Where Sparrows Work Hard* (Pittsburgh, 1981), or the title-poem of *Black Hair* (Pittsburgh, 1985), which calls up Soto's own Chicano, yet wholly self-particular, childhood in describing its narrator as 'Mexican, | a stick | Of brown light'. See also *Father is a Pillow Tied to a Broom* (Pittsburgh, 1980) and *Lesser Evils: Ten Quartets* (Houston, Tex., 1988).

[ARL

Sound Poetry in the twentieth century began with the Dadaists and artists/writers like Man Ray and Kurt Schwitters. The leading sound poet currently working in the UK is Bob Cobbing, an iconoclastic figure whose 'writing' encompasses visual and sound poetry in an exhilarating mixture. Quoting lines like 'YARR YAUP YARK YOWL YAK' does no justice to the power of sound poetry when performed. It is, in fact, the ultimate *performance poetry and should be treated as such. Other recent sound poets include dsh (Dom Sylvester Houedard), Neil Mills, Peter Finch, and Edwin *Morgan; bp *Nichol, bill *bissett, and Steve McCaffrey from Canada; and Jackson Mac Low from the USA. Apart from live performance, the place to search out these poets is in small but influential magazines such as *Kroklok* and *Second Aeon* from the 1970s, and *Stereo Headphones* magazine.

Bob Cobbing: books, pamphlets, and records available from Writers Forum Press, London; Peter Finch: *Selected Poems*; Poetry Wales Press (1987); dsh: books available from Writers Forum Press, London; Edwin Morgan: books available from Carcanet Press, Manchester.

[IMcM

SOUSTER, Raymond Holmes (1921–), was born in Toronto where he was educated at the University of Toronto schools and Humberside Collegiate Institute, and where, except for wartime service in the RCAF, he has lived and worked in banking all his life. Souster's literary activities began in the 1940s when he became involved in editing two avant-garde periodicals, *Direction* (1943–6) and *Enterprise* (1948), which led to involvement with a group of Montreal poets who were first associated with First Statement Press in that city. Souster went on to edit two other important literary periodicals, *Contact* (1952–4) and *Combustion* (1957–60), thus establishing himself firmly at the heart of mid-century poetry in Canada. Introduced in the anthology *Unit of Five* (1944), Souster had his first independent collection, *When We Are Young*, in 1946, followed by *Go to Sleep World* (1947). Of the Canadian poets of his generation Souster was the one most overtly interested in, and influenced by, American contemporaries. He was first attracted to Henry Miller, and later entered into lasting friendships and correspondence with Robert *Creeley and Cid *Corman. Souster's *Selected Poems* were published in 1956 and brought him his first serious critical attention. In the decade of the 1960s Souster entered upon a prolific and distinguished period in his creative life. His collected poems, *The Colour of the Times* (Toronto) appeared in 1964. He was one of the founders of The League of Canadian Poets, serving as its president, 1968–9.

Very much a cautious modernist, Souster has been involved in the quiet promotion of young talent, both through the agency of a poets' co-operative publishing venture called Contact Press, which he co-founded with Louis *Dudek and Irving *Layton in 1952, and by editing *Poets '56* (Toronto) and *New Wave Canada: The New Explosion in Canadian Poetry* (Toronto, 1966). In the late 1960s he embarked on the revision of his early poetry with a view to its reissue. *Selected Poems* (Ottawa, 1972) was the result of that process, and served to lead up to a four-volume *Collected Poems* (Ottawa), which began to appear in 1980 and confirmed a strong colloquial tone in a poetry of urban images informed by the modest emotions of a middle-class nostalgia.

Souster has also written fiction, publishing *The Winter of Time* (1949) and *On Target* (1972) under the pseudonym of R. and J. Holmes, and has co-authored *From Hell to Breakfast* (1980) with Douglas Alcorn. He has made much use of his experiences in the RCAF in his fiction. Souster has collaborated, as well, in the compiling of several school anthologies.   [MG

SOUTAR, William (1898–1943), went to school in his native Perth. After First World War service in the Royal Navy, from which he was invalided out with the disease that led to his relatively early death, he attended the University of Edinburgh. His first poems in Scots coincided with the momentum generated by Hugh *Mac-Diarmid, but a devotion to the fifteenth- and sixteenth-century Makars and balladry was closer to Soutar's inspiration than the modernism expounded by MacDiarmid.

Spondylitis led to seven years as a semi-invalid from 1923, after which Soutar was bedridden until his death. He published ten collections in his lifetime and there was a posthumous volume in 1944. Only two of these are in Scots, but there were many uncollected poems and it is for his Scots poetry that he is chiefly remembered. Some of his lyrics are pure and haunting ('The Tryst', 'Sang'), as are several of his ballads. A vigorous, grotesque poem like 'The Hungry Mauchs' (maggots) shows him at his best and working close to the taproot of the Scottish imagination—fantastic, earthy, folkish, and direct.

In English, his anti-war satires ('The Guns') and poems attacking unemployment, privilege, rank, and other ills of the times rise occasionally to forcefulness. His epigrams, of which he wrote many, suffer from a lack of the necessary malice.

It was Soutar's conviction that a long-lasting and authentic revival of poetry in Scots (or Doric as he called it) depended on impressing the young with the worth of the native language. 'If the Doric is to come back alive, it will come first on a cock-horse.' His Scots verse for children ('bairn rhymes') is among his best work and still enjoys a degree of currency.

Collected Poems (London, 1948) was edited by Hugh MacDiarmid. There is a biography by Alexander Scott, *Still Life* (1958), who also edited a selection from Soutar's diaries, *Diaries of a Dying Man* (1954; repr., 1991). *Poems of William Soutar: A New Selection*, ed. W. R. Aitken (Edinburgh, 1988) is the most readily available edition.   [DED

Southern Review, The. Original Series (1935–42), edited by Cleanth Brooks and Robert Penn *Warren. New Series (1965–), edited by Donald E. Stanford and Lewis P. Simpson, published at Louisiana State University. Stanford retired in 1983 and was replaced by James Olney. Simpson retired in 1987 and was replaced by Fred Hobson until 1989, and then by Dave *Smith. Stanford and Simpson remain on the staff as advisory editors.

The original *Review* established a national and international reputation as one of America'a outstanding literary quarterlies. It was the first journal to bring Eudora Welty and Katherine Anne Porter to national attention. It published Allen *Tate, Yvor *Winters, R. P. *Blackmur, Caroline Gordon, Peter Taylor, and other now well-known writers early in their careers. Among the older distinguished contributors were T. S. *Eliot, John Crowe *Ransom, F. R. Leavis, Thomas *Hardy, and Ford Madox *Ford.

The editors of the new *Southern Review* followed the policy of the original journal in emphasizing the culture of the South but at the same time publishing contributions of high quality from anywhere in America and Europe. Also, there was a definite attempt to bring together the work of authors of established reputation with that of talented younger writers in the same issue; such writers as N. Scott Momaday, Joyce Carol *Oates, and Anne Tyler, all of whom appeared in the *Review* early in their careers. There were special issues devoted to the works of Wallace *Stevens, Eric Voegelin, Robert *Frost, Caroline Gordon, Yvor Winters, W. B. *Yeats, and Writing in the South. Because one of the editors (Stanford) was associated with the *'Stanford School' of poets, the new *Southern Review* was one of the few periodicals in America to welcome poetry written in conventional prosody. [DES

SOYINKA, Wole (Oluwole Akinwande) (1934–), was born in Ijebu Isara, Nigeria. He grew up in Abeokuta, where his father was a schoolteacher. He was educated at Abeokuta Grammar School and Government College, Ibadan. He studied at University College, Ibadan (1952–4) and then at Leeds University (1954–7), where he graduated with an honours degree in English. He has been at various times on the academic staff of the universities of Lagos, Ibadan, and at Ife, where he was professor of comparative literature and dramatic arts. Between 1973 and 1974 he was overseas fellow, Churchill College, Cambridge, and visiting professor, department of English, University of Sheffield. He was awarded the Nobel Prize for Literature in 1986.

Soyinka's influence and impact in Africa is evident in drama, poetry, fiction, and autobiography. In addition to his poetical works, he has published two novels, two volumes of autobiographical writing, critical essays, and several plays. He has also edited an impressive anthology, *Poems of Black Africa* (London, 1975). As a consequence of his political activities during the Nigerian Civil War he was detained in August 1967 until October 1969 by the Federal Military Government of Nigeria.

The early poems which were included in his first volume, *Idanre and Other Poems* (London, 1967), were often self-consciously impenetrable. The images were startling but remote. *A Shuttle in the Crypt* (London, 1972) emerged from Soyinka's prison experience. It is a companion volume to *The Man Died* (London, 1972) in which he gave an account of his prison experience in prose. The poems served several different functions; some were 'animystic spells' designed to modulate his thinking processes, whereas others were descriptive of his environment and his internal awareness of his predicament. *Ogun Abibiman* (London, 1976), a narrative poem, was written to celebrate Mozambique's declaration of war against the white regime in erstwhile Rhodesia. It was regarded by observers as Soyinka's first explicit avowal of a wider political vision. This and his latest volume, *Mandela's Earth and Other Poems* (London, 1989), mark a structural departure for Soyinka; the old opacity is less evident and there is a more natural correspondence of language and meaning.

The Writing of Wole Soyinka (London, 1973), by Eldred D. Jones, and *Critical Perspectives on Wole Soyinka* (London, 1980), ed. James Gibbs, give a critical background to Soyinka's writings. [FO

SPARK, Muriel (Sarah) (née Camberg) (1918–), was born in Edinburgh to a Jewish father and English mother. She was educated at James Gillespie's School for Girls in Edinburgh, which she left at the age of 18 to live in Rhodesia where, in 1937, she was married (she is divorced, with one son); returning to England in 1944, she worked for the Intelligence Service in a department producing anti-Nazi propaganda. Between the end of the war and her early successes as a novelist she worked at a variety of jobs connected with publishing; she became secretary of the *Poetry Society in 1947, and in 1948–9 was editor of *Poetry Review*. In the early 1950s she wrote or edited, in collaboration with Derek Stanford, a critical biography of Emily Brontë, a selection of Brontë's poems, and selections from the letters of Mary Shelley, the Brontës, and John Henry Newman. She also published biographical studies of Mary Shelley and John *Masefield, and a volume of poems. In 1954 Spark became a Roman Catholic. Her first novel, *The Comforters*, appeared in 1957, and has been followed by eighteen further novels to date, for which Spark has been awarded numerous prizes and honours; she has also published short stories and radio plays. From 1962 to 1966 she lived in New York, but for the last twenty-five years has made her home in Italy.

Though there is nothing in it to match the quality and originality of her achievement in fiction (which sets a high standard), the little poetry Spark has written—and continues to write—is important to her, and is not negligible. Those characters in her fiction to whom Spark extends a (rare) indulgence tend to write metrical verse, quote the English classics, translate from the Latin. In her own verse there is a fair sprinkling of neat, consciously archaic forms (ballads, roundels, villanelles, jaunty quatrains and couplets), and, correspondingly, of epigrammatic neatness of statement, as well as riddling narrative (parables and cautionary tales), plangent lyricism, heavy-handed satire, and Stevie *Smith-like whimsy. She has said that important early influences were the Old Testament and the border ballads; the visionary extravagance and strong emotions of such sources take on a whiff of Nineties-ish decadence in 'The Ballad of the Fanfarlo', an ambitious 'recreation' from Baudelaire on themes of atonement, death, damnation, and salvation, and in those poems which explore the workings of religious mystery in a 'Kensington of dreadful night'.

See *Going Up to Sotheby's and Other Poems* (London, 1982), which supersedes *Collected Poems I* (London, 1967; New York, 1968). [AJ]

SPARSHOTT, Francis (1926–), was born in Chatham, England. He served with the Intelligence Corps, attended Oxford University, and went to the University of Toronto in 1950. He is now that university's professor in philosophy. Sparshott is an accomplished satirist, elegant or rough as the occasion demands. At ease with a large number of forms, he is especially striking in his command of rhyming effects. His poetic voice and range of subject-matter are reminiscent of some of the classical lyric poets. His eight collections of poetry are: *A Divided Voice* (Toronto, 1965): *A Cardboard Garage* (Toronto, 1969); *The Rainy Hills: Voices After a Japanese Fashion* (Toronto, 1979); *The Naming of the Beasts* (Windsor, Ont., 1979); *The Cave of Trophonius and Other Poems* (Coldstream, Ont., 1983); *The Hanging Gardens of Etobicoke* (Toronto, 1983); *Storms and Screens* (Toronto, 1986); and *Sculling to Byzantium* (Toronto, 1989). [EC]

SPEAR, Charles (1910–85), was born in Owaka, South Otago, New Zealand, and educated at Canterbury and Otago universities. He worked as a journalist and teacher, and then as a lecturer in Middle English at the University of Canterbury until his retirement in 1976. He spent the last decade of his life in London. His reputation as a poet rests on a single slim volume, *Twopence Coloured* (Christchurch, 1951), from which substantial selections have been made by every significant anthologist of New Zealand verse. Spear's 'muse' is, as he himself claimed in 'Remark', 'Studiously minor, yet attuned to doom'. It is as though an 1890s aesthete had been infected by a post-war malaise. Spear is a miniaturist, compressing into his neatly rhymed stanzas a phantasmagoria of the fictional and the historical. Spear also wrote, with L. A. Baigent, the novel *Rearguard Actions* (London, 1936). [MacDJ]

Spectra Hoax. See BYNNER, WITTER, and FICKE, ARTHUR DAVISON.

SPENCE, Lewis (1874–1955). Although he wrote little, Spence's position in modern Scottish poetry rests on his introduction of a richer Scots idiom than the rural dialect of his contemporaries prior to Hugh *MacDiarmid's more sweeping innovations. His best-known poem is 'The Prows O'Reekie', an impassioned, proud, excitable, and memorable piece about Edinburgh, and 'Great Tay of the Waves', 'The Siller Bullet', and 'Kinrick' are not without their exhilarations. 'The Stown Bairn' and 'The Ferlie' draw from his interest in fairy lore, mythology, and the occult, in which subjects Spence was a scholar, publishing many books, some of them possibly crazed—*Will Europe Follow Atlantis?*, for example.

Spence shared with MacDiarmid the distinction of being a founder of the National Party of Scotland; indeed, he was the first to stand for a parliamentary seat in the party's cause.

His poems in English are more backward-tending in style than his work in Scots, although there, too, his modernity is probably marginal, if sometimes original and gripping. *Collected Poems* appeared in 1953 (Edinburgh). [DED]

SPENCER, Bernard (1909–63), was born in Madras, son of a high-court judge, and was educated at Marlborough College and Corpus Christi College, Oxford, where he took a degree in Greats. From 1932 to 1940 he was, in turn, a preparatory schoolmaster, an advertising copywriter, and a script-writer in a film company. After that, and until his apparently accidental but certainly mysterious death (he was found dead by a railway track in Vienna), he worked for the British Council in Greece, Egypt, Italy, Spain, Greece again, Turkey, and Austria.

Spencer began, and to some extent continued, in the shadow of those Oxford contemporaries who quickly achieved a reputation: *Auden, *MacNeice (who was his senior at Marlborough), and *Spender. He was co-editor of *Oxford Poetry 1930* and *1931*. The first poem by which he can clearly be distinguished is 'Allotments: April', which Geoffrey *Grigson published in *New Verse* in 1936: it has a pertinacious sensuousness which was his own, to be seen later in more exotic settings in his Mediterranean poems of the 1940s and 1950s.

A central characteristic of Spencer's poems is a sense of loneliness, of being someone apart. Living most of his working life in non-English-speaking communities, professionally having to do the work of a bonhomous British Council officer, Spencer seems almost to have cultivated a kind of gregarious isolation. He became, quite consciously, 'a stranger here', a man fixing and defining modes of unease.

But equally there are those moments which signal 'things amazingly connected'. Spencer, early and late, was good in an unexpected way at memorializing moments of precarious happiness, with 'an importance of beauty' (from a poem written in celebration of his first wife in 1937) or, in one of his last poems in 1963, a moment of hilarity on 'that fine particular day' ('Traffic in April').

Spencer's rhythms were very personal, sometimes uncertain, tantalizing, full of indirections; but increasingly they carried his own individual voice, his own quizzical view of things. Sometimes he wrote with a strong sense of the living past: in an interview he commented that: 'The fact of being in some sort of continuity with earlier civilisations does have an exciting effect on me.' He collaborated with Nanos Valaoritis and Lawrence *Durrell in producing versions of the modern Greek poet George Seferis, *The King of Asine*, which reflect such archaeological excitement.

In his lifetime Spencer published *Aegean Islands and Other Poems* (1946), *The Twist in the Plotting* (1960), and *With Luck Lasting* (1963). After his death, Alan Ross edited a *Collected Poems* (London, 1965), to be followed by a definitive *Collected Poems* (Oxford, 1981), ed. Roger Bowen. [AST

SPENCER, Theodore (1902–49), was born in Pennsylvania. He became a much-valued teacher at Harvard, and in 1946 was appointed Boylston Professor of Rhetoric and Oratory. Spencer was a noted scholar of Shakespeare, Elizabethan drama, and metaphysical poetry; his own carefully wrought verse—in the same tradition as that of Allen *Tate and John Peale *Bishop, but less contemporary in its outlook—reflects this, as well as the pervasive influence of *Yeats and *Eliot. His slender and elegant output offers an example of the very best that a literary critic who is deeply educated in his craft, but who lacks native inspiration or the capacity to discover a language of his own, can do. Spencer understood and wrote well about the essentially dramatic nature of lyric poetry, but the situations implied by his own lyrics precisely lack drama—being, rather, exquisitely judged inventions, as if the poet were divorced from his own (not feeble) emotions, which, however, were fulfilled in his teaching. The long philosophical poems in *An Act of Life* (New York, 1944) are finely worked out and finely crafted, but owe too much to Yeats, whose voice (but not passion) they echo. His best poems are brief nature lyrics, particularly ones about birds, of which he had, said his friend F. O. Matthiessen, 'an eager knowledge'. See *The Paradox in the Circle* (New York, 1941); *Poems 1940–1947* (New York, 1948); *An Acre in the Seed* (New York, 1949). [MS-S

SPENDER, Sir Stephen (Harold) (1909–95), was born in London, and educated at University

College School, Hampstead, and Oxford (University College), where he was a contemporary and friend of *Auden, Isherwood and *MacNeice. Thus began a famous association with other writers who developed social and political themes from a left-wing standpoint; though his political affiliation (with the Communist Party) was brief. He visited Spain during the Civil War (1936–9), assisting the Republican cause with propaganda activity. During the Second World War he served in the National Fire Service in London, and was for two years co-editor, with Cyril Connolly, of the literary monthly *Horizon*. His contribution to the volume of essays *The God that Failed* (1951), and his reversal of the critical position he adopted in *The Destructive Element* (1935) with the publication of *The Creative Element* (1953), establish his rejection of Communism in favour of a liberal individualism. In the latter year he became inaugural co-editor of *Encounter*, an anti-Communist political and literary monthly supported initially by the US Central Intelligence Agency. By this time his main period of creativity as a poet had virtually ended, though his work as a critic, and as a translator of Spanish and German (and later, Greek) poetry and drama continued and expanded.

Spender's early verse (in books such as *Poems*, 1933, and *The Still Centre*, 1939) catches movingly the alarm and confusion in the atmosphere of 1930s Europe, and affirms, in poems like 'The Funeral' and 'An Elementary School Classroom in a Slum', the political values he then held (a very personal, humanistic socialism). It also deliberately substitutes for the traditional English poet's devotion to nature a celebration of technological achievement ('The Express' and 'The Pylons'). At this time he displays at his best an eloquent Romantic pity for the poor and the oppressed, and a gift for rendering scenes of wartime suffering and destruction (in Spain, and in London during the air-raids) with photographic accuracy, even if the images sometimes remain somewhat unfocused. These prominent features of his poetry diverted attention at first from the presence of a deeply self-questioning personality, unsure how to match poetry to either external events or his own feelings. How he should, or could, commit himself emotionally is a recurrent theme; reassessment and revision of the poems is a constant habit. He is only too aware of a heritage of daunting greatness (in Beethoven, say, or Hölderlin) which transcends his untidy and violent modern experience.

There is more emotional directness in the poems of love and tribute to be found in *Ruins and Visions* (1942) and *Poems of Dedication* (1947); notably in 'Elegy for Margaret', a dead sister-in-law. As before, he attempts rhetorical effects, but it is rarely his best vein, the poems becoming turgid and overreaching; though the rhetoric of 'Returning to Vienna, 1947' produces one of his finest sustained passages. A calmer, even informal, style employed in later poems of a retrospective kind, in *The Generous Days* (1971) and the second *Collected Poems* of 1985, shows a more relaxed side to his talent; the tributes to Auden and MacNeice are entertaining as well as moving. Spender's ultimate reputation may depend on how future readers will assess the appropriateness of his nakedly Romantic approach to the stresses of twentieth-century life. The most original poems deserve to remain famous. But the characteristic quality of undisguised vulnerability, tenderness, and even gaucheness in the endeavour to be truthful, may have the more enduring appeal.

His *Collected Poems 1928–53* (London and New York, 1955) presents a highly selective and substantially revised body of work from the individual books published up to that point; his development as a poet may be traced in much closer detail in those. This volume in turn was revised and re-ordered, with further poems added, for its reissue as *Collected Poems 1928–1985* (London and New York, 1985). *World Within World* (London and New York, 1951) is a work of candid autobiography. A volume of memoirs, *The Thirties and After* (London and New York) appeared in 1978, and his *Journals 1939–83* ed. John Goldsmith (London and Franklin Center, Pa.), were published in 1985.

[AB

SPICER, Jack (1925–65), was born in Hollywood and attended the University of California, Berkeley, where he met Robert *Duncan and Robin Blaser, and was deeply impressed by the poetry of *Yeats, though Duncan and Charles *Olson would have the most impact on his own verses. He became a professional linguist with a strong interest in semiotics, philosophy, and cosmology. A leading member of the so-called *San Francisco Group, his poetry favoured open, serial forms, especially after 1961. Spicer's second collection, *Billy the Kid* (1959), is his most impressive performance, using the outlaw as an admittedly romanticized culture hero who engages in archetypal mythic rituals and pursues a, not always convincing, Neo-Platonic line of thought. Later volumes, *The Holy Grail* (1964), *Language* (1965), and *Book of Magazine Verse* (1966), are often linguistically rich but thin on lyric orchestration and emotional intensity.

Robin Blaser edited *The Collected Books of Jack Spicer* (Santa Barbara, Calif., 1980).   [EB

SPIRES, Elizabeth (1952–), was born in Lancaster, Ohio. She was raised in nearby Circleville and attended Vassar College and Johns Hopkins University. She married the Southern novelist Madison Bell in 1985; she lives in Baltimore, Maryland, and teaches at Goucher College (since 1982) and Johns Hopkins (since 1989).

The poems of Elizabeth Spires are notable for both their secular and spiritual subjects. Like Elizabeth *Bishop (whom Spires interviewed in the *Paris Review* series), Spires is a poet attentive to the physical world; yet while relishing description, she approaches pain and ecstasy more immediately than Bishop. Though for many years a lapsed Catholic, Spires is essentially a religious poet, meditating on human suffering and annunciations of good and evil. Other poems suggest a kind of allegorical autobiography through archetypal Jungian terms instead of conventional *'confessional' details.

Spires has published three volumes of poetry, *Globe* (Middletown, Conn., 1981), *Swan's Island* (New York, 1985), and *Annonciade* (New York, 1989). A fourth volume, tentatively titled *Worldling*, is forthcoming.   [HC

SQUIRE, Sir John (Collings) (1884–1958), was born in Plymouth and educated at Blundell's School, Tiverton, and St John's College, Cambridge. From 1913 he was literary editor of the *New Statesman*, for which he wrote under the pseudonym 'Solomon Eagle'; in 1919 he founded the monthly *London Mercury*, which he edited until 1934, and used to combat the 'anarchical cleverness' of modernism. As chief literary critic of the *Observer* he had further opportunity to promote those writers who shared his Edwardian tastes and values, derisively dubbed 'the Squirearchy' by the *Sitwells. He was knighted in 1933.

Squire was a talented parodist, and his *Collected Parodies* (1921) may oddly capture more of his own character than his poems do. His assimilative sensibility gives a derivative taste to much of his serious verse, which began with *Three Hills* (1913); and Squire's low regard for originality in general can be gauged from his Second World War poem, 'Arnhem by Zutphen': 'We are waging the old warfare where Sir Philip Sidney died.' To an age which increasingly prized difficulty and precision, Squire offered poems which were not only easy to read but seemingly easy to write. Some pieces carry the impression of haste, as if, surmised John *Betjeman, 'they have been finished off after some interruption in a busy editor's life had diminished the force of the original inspiration'.

Two of Squire's efforts are more sustained than the rest: 'The Stockyard', a sickened response to a visit to the slaughterhouses of Chicago; and, in a different mood, 'The Rugger Match', a comprehensive account of a Twenties Varsity game. There are a handful of other notable poems. In the brightly coloured sonnet 'Discovery', an Indian trembles as Columbus's 'doom-burdened caravels' nudge his shore. His best work gives simple expression to his keen sense of mortality: 'Winter Nightfall', a surprisingly tough elegy for a retired colonel; another elegy, 'To a Roman' (Catullus); and 'Meditation in Lamplight', in which a contemporary reviewer saw a characteristic mixture of 'tragedy and chat'.

The posthumous *Collected Poems* (London, 1959) was edited by Betjeman. Squire also wrote short stories and an autobiography, *The Honeysuckle and the Bee* (1937). [MI

SQUIRES, (James) Radcliffe (1917–), was born the son of a barber in Salt Lake City, Utah. He received his BA in 1940 from the University of Utah. In the same year Squires published *Cornar*, his first book of poetry. After wartime service as a naval officer, he earned an AM from the University of Chicago. He married Eileen Mulholland, who had been one of his junior high-school teachers, in 1945. Two years of teaching at Dartmouth were followed by a fellowship at Harvard University, where he received a Ph.D in 1952. That year Squires moved to the University of Michigan at Ann Arbor, remaining on its faculty until his retirement in 1981. In 1959 a Fulbright scholarship took him to Salonica, Greece; two years spent there and in Athens deeply influenced his work.

A fruitful preoccupation with history and place distinguishes Squires's eight books of poetry. The mannered formality of his early verse has given way to poems that are powerfully evocative of travel as travail, a struggle for knowledge and insight in a world often mysteriously cruel. Though he is compared to *Frost and *Jeffers, both for his narratives and his tragic view of life, his recent poems are, in their allusive meldings of past and present, reminiscent of Cavafy. Squires has written about America, Greece, and Spain, and many of his best poems are unassumingly personal, such as the powerful sequence from *Journeys* (1983) in which, after the death of his wife in 1976, he faces the shattering prospect of a life without love.

Squires's five books of criticism include studies of Jeffers, Frost, and the American novelist Frederic *Prokosch. His excellent literary biography of Allen *Tate is marred only by having been written while its subject was still alive, which precludes a fuller view of Tate's life.

Poetry readers will have to seek out Squires's individual collections: *Fingers of Hermes* (Ann Arbor, Mich., 1965); *The Light Under the Islands* (Ann Arbor, 1967); *Waiting in the Bone* (Omaha,

Nebr., 1973); and *Gardens of the World* (Baton Rouge, La., 1981). See also 'In the Garden of Talos', by Brewster Ghiselin, *Sewanee Review* (Fall, 1975), and 'Temenos and Transcendence', also by Ghiselin, *Western Humanities Review* (Fall, 1984). [DM

STAFFORD, William (1914–93), was raised in various small towns in rural Kansas, then earned bachelor's and master's degrees at the University of Kansas. During the Second World War he was a conscientious objector, an experience later described in his prose memoir, *Down in My Heart* (1947). After the war Stafford earned a Ph.D at the newly formed *Iowa Writers' Workshop. In 1948 he moved to the West Coast, and from 1956 to 1979 was professor of English at Lewis and Clark College in Portland, Oregon. His poetry is generally seen as emerging intimately from the landscape of the Pacific Northwest, though he has written at least as many poems with homey, Midwestern settings. Stafford started writing poems as a child and began accumulating mature work and publishing it in magazines in approximately 1948. His first book, *West of Your City*, did not come out until 1960, however—simply because no publisher asked until then, according to the poet. Stafford had a good many poems stockpiled, as it were, and his procedure for most of his books has been to select a group of poems written over a long period of time, rather than just gather his most recent work together. Critics have often commented on the consistency in his work in terms of theme, style, and content, meaning to imply a lack of development. During this phase as an astute critic, however, James *Dickey commented that Stafford never wrote a bad poem, that lyric poetry seemed to spring almost spontaneously from his pen. Stafford's first five books were collected into *Stories That Could Be True* (New York, 1977), which also contains several new poems.

Stafford is among the most visible of poets and appears with great regularity in classrooms and at readings, symposia, and writers' conferences. He is fond of counselling young writers not to be critics of their own work; the key to writing good poetry is not to censor what wants to come out. Stafford has described his own writing process: he gets up early in the morning, before anyone else is awake, reclines on his couch with a pad of paper and a pen, and lets the words flow. He does not revise heavily, preferring only to correct obvious mistakes and harmonize his rhythms.

Thematically, Stafford celebrates familiar human virtues and has great respect for quiet, contemplation, and hidden significances. Thus, in his most characteristic poems he seeks a place in the wilderness, an almost sacred location untouched by man, where an answer to the ultimate mysteries of the universe might be approached. Stafford is not foolish enough to try to express what this answer or insight might be; the process of the search, along with its implications, is enough for him.

In addition to *Stories that Could Be True*, readers should consult the later volumes, *A Glass Face in the Rain* (New York, 1982) and *Smoke's Way* (Port Townsend, Wash., 1983). Stafford's critical prose is collected in *Writing the Australian Crawl* (Ann Arbor, Mich., 1978). See also Jonathan Holden, *The Mark to Turn: A Reading of William Stafford's Poetry* (1976); Peter Stitt, *The World's Hieroglyphic Beauty: Five American Poets* (1986); and George S. Lensing and Ronald Moran, *Four Poets and the Emotive Imagination: Robert Bly, James Wright, Louis Simpson, and William Stafford* (1976).   [PS

STAINER, Pauline (1941–), read English at St Anne's College, Oxford, and gained an M.Phil from Southampton University. She has worked in a mental hospital, pub, and library. Married, with four children, she lives in Essex. She has won a variety of prizes in poetry competitions and festivals and, in 1987, was awarded a Hawthornden Fellowship. Her two collections have been Poetry Book Society Recommendations.

Stainer's poems juxtapose elemental ice, glass, and stones with fibre-tip pens, hang-gliders, and the red-light district of Bangkok. Artists, musicians, archetypal figures, angels, and virgins are blended into Christianity, chemistry,

optics, and medicine. Reminiscent of pre-Raphaelite paintings, her poems are coloured predominantly by blacks, whites, and reds, usually blood red, as they move smoothly from the sacramental and mystical to the sexually implied and explicit.

Her first collection, *Honeycomb* was published in 1989 and her second, *Sighting The Slave Ship*, in 1992 (both Newscastle upon Tyne).   [PMcC

STALLWORTHY, Jon (Howie) (1935–), was born in London. He worked for many years as poetry editor of Oxford University Press before taking up a teaching post at Cornell which he held for a decade. He is now Professor of English Literature at Wolfson College, Oxford. Well known for his meticulous edition of the poems of Wilfred *Owen, whose biography he wrote, and for his work with *Yeats's manuscripts, Stallworthy is a graceful, fastidious, and emotive poet who has been content, for the most part, to work in conventional forms. His poems are much concerned with 'family, England and "good form" ', although the last-named quality is often dealt with in an ironic and impatient manner. His sequence *A Familiar Tree* (London, Oxford and New York, 1978), about the history of his own family, provides a British and well-bred counterpart to similar poems by Americans such as *Lowell, but is in no way less sophisticated.

See also *The Apple Barrel: Selected Poems 1956–1963* (London, 1974); *The Anzac Sonata: New and Selected Poems* (London, 1986; New York, 1987); *The Guest from the Future* (Oxford, 1989).   [MS-S

Stand, a British magazine, at first devoted to poetry and criticism of poetry, and latterly also to short fiction, was founded by Jon *Silkin, with others. in 1952: it has had the longest run of any of the British little magazines', with the exceptions of the *Poetry Review*, *Outposts*, and Miron Grindea's more irregular *Adam* (which, however, has seldom printed original verse). Since 1964 *Stand* has been closely associated with Northern House Publishers, Newcastle upon Tyne, also co-founded by Silkin. Tony *Harrison

515

and Ken *Smith joined Silkin as co-editors for the year 1968/9. *Stand* has always carried the imprint of the busily 'engaged' personality, and the concerns, of its London-born founder. It has thus expressed Silkin's own 'stand' as one who mixes 'rationalist agnosticism and dilute Orthodox Judaism', together with, from the time he settled in Newcastle, what has been called 'the voice of the Northumbrian'. However, *Stand* has been notably eclectic in giving space to critics of its left-wing or 'committed' stance. The exact nature of the commitment, which has been described as one of 'responsibilities, community and moral probings', may conveniently be studied in *Poetry of the Committed Individual: A 'Stand' Anthology* (London, 1973). The technical standard of the verse, and of the criticism, in *Stand* has seldom drooped, and it is probably now the outstanding representative of politically oriented theories of verse in the English-speaking world. It notably eschews humour or levity, and has published many contemporary European poets in translation. [MS-S

STANFORD, Ann (1916–87), was born in LaHabra in southern California, a beautiful farming area with orange, lemon, and walnut groves and a view of the distant coastal range of mountains, a landscape frequently described in her poetry. At Stanford University, from which she was graduated in 1938, she became a member of the Yvor *Winters circle, and was the youngest poet to contribute to his anthology *Twelve Poets of the Pacific* (Norfolk, Conn., 1937). In 1942 she married the architect Ronald White, who built her a study near their home in the Santa Monica mountains where she worked daily, writing in longhand her highly personal, luminescent, lyrical poetry, as well as two volumes of dramatic poetry, a translation of the *Bhagavad Gita* (New York, 1970), and a critical biography of Anne Bradstreet (New York, 1974). She also found time to obtain a doctor's degree at UCLA, to raise a family, and to teach English literature at California State University at Northridge. She died in Los Angeles.

Of her eight volumes of poetry, the best-known are *The Weathercock* (New York, 1966),

The Descent (New York, 1970), and *In Mediterranean Air* (New York, 1977), all published by Viking. There is an interview with her by Karla M. Hammond in the *Southern Review*, 18 (Apr. 1982). [DES

STANFORD, Frank (1948–78), was born in Mississippi and raised by adoptive parents in Memphis and north central Arkansas. After his stepfather died in 1963, Stanford was sent to a Benedictine monastery and academy in Subiaco, Arkansas, where he spent his last three years of high school. He entered the University of Arkansas in 1967, and in 1969 enrolled in the graduate poetry workshop there. From this time until his death ten years later Stanford dedicated his life to the writing of poetry. He left the University of Arkansas in 1971 without a degree, and for most of the next seven years earned his living as a land-surveyor in north-west Arkansas. At the time of his death at the age of 29 Stanford had published seven volumes of poetry. Most significant among these are his first book, *The Singing Knives* (1972), and a five-hundred page epic poem entitled *The Battlefield Where the Moon Says I Love You* (1977). Two posthumous volumes, *You* (1979) and *Crib Death* (1979), were also published.

Stanford embodied in his work those themes and attributes that are usually associated with the literature of the southern United States. Preoccupations with the elegiac, the past as personal history, narrative, the natural world, and a sense of Gothic romanticism, permeate his poetry much as they do the works of *Faulkner, Carson McCullers, and James *Dickey. Stanford's early work centred on narrative creations of a mythic lost world of childhood in rural Arkansas. The prolific outpouring of these poems about his childhood was an attempt to deny time and mutability, and to create a past on the poet's own terms. Stanford's last poems, however, are direct confrontations with death. This theme becomes so obsessive in the late work that Death occasionally appears as a character in his narratives and lyrics of this period. Stanford died in Fayetteville, Arkansas, from self-inflicted gunshot wounds. The fullest collection of his work is *The Light the Dead See: The Selected Poems of Frank Stanford* (Fayetteville, Ark., 1991). [LS

Stanford School, The, is the name sometimes given to the writers associated with Yvor *Winters during his career (1927–66) at Stanford University, California. Between May 1929 and February 1930, Winters, his wife Janet *Lewis, and the poet Howard *Baker published four issues of a magazine, the *Gyroscope*, which included work by themselves, Caroline Gordon, and Katherine Anne Porter. In the course of the 1930s, Winters's dissatisfaction with the forms and ideas of modernism hardened into the systematic reaction expressed in his criticism, notably in the short books later collected as *In Defense of Reason* (Chicago, 1947; London, 1960) and in the manifesto-foreword to *Before Disaster* (Tryon, NC, 1934), a pamphlet of his poems. His ideas were also forcefully expressed in his verse-writing classes, which led in time to two anthologies: *Twelve Poets of the Pacific* (Norfolk, Conn., 1937) and *Poets of the Pacific: Second Series* (Stanford, Calif., 1949). Among the poets included were, in the former, J. V. *Cunningham, and in the latter, Edgar *Bowers. Among other poets who attended the writing classes were Thom *Gunn, Donald *Hall, Philip *Levine, and Robert *Pinsky. [CW

STARBUCK, George (Edwin) (1931–), was born in Columbus, Ohio, and graduated from the California Institute of Technology in Pasadena, majoring in mathematics. A distinguished university career was interrupted only by two years in the army and three in publishing.

An early poem, 'Named Individual' (from *Bone Thoughts*, 1960) shows Starbuck in characteristic pose, as citizen menaced or circled by shapeless inhuman forces, whether Government, the Bomb, or the Universe itself. He is equipped, however, with a veritable arsenal of strategies against the darkness, and the very qualities that make his work seem at first wilfully odd—ceaseless formal exploration, Byronic ingenuity in rhyme, and playful linguistic whimsy—proclaim his strength and sanity,

while at the same time dramatizing the idiocy of what he opposes.

Throughout the Sixties and Seventies America's wars, leaders, laws, and broadcasters are caught in the roving spotlights of his craft, either in short, comic diplodactyls and clerihews, or in long, zigzagging rambles, culminating in *Talkin' B. A. Blues* (1980), a Dylanesque satire on higher education. But the poet's own practice does not escape: in 'Tuolomne' (from *Desperate Measures*, 1978) he apologizes to heaven for his tangential habits ('I scribble sidenotes to the fall of nations'), displaying, alongside his self-awareness, signposts to a couple of roads he might have taken: descriptive lyric, and ruminations on 'serious' matters in 'serious' metres. That he has continued instead to experiment at the edges of formal possibility, while delighting in America's Absurd, demonstrates his intelligence about what truly constitutes poetic 'seriousness': knowledge of the powers and limits of words themselves, and awareness that to don a joker's mask is merely one of the oldest and swiftest ways into the palace. The best of his unique work is collected in *The Argot Merchant Disaster* (Boston and London, 1982). [GM

STEAD, C(hristian) K(arlson) (1932–), was born in Auckland, New Zealand. In his essays on New Zealand literature, *In the Glass Case* (Auckland, 1981), Stead writes of his excitement at moving from the suburbs to the University of Auckland in 1951. His association with that university as student, lecturer, and professor of English was to last until he retired in 1986 in order to write full time. At the university he quickly became part of a talented older generation of Auckland-based writers and academics, including Allen *Curnow, Robert Chapman, Frank Sargeson, Rex *Fairburn, Maurice Duggan, Keith Sinclair, and Kendrick *Smithyman. This early discovery of New Zealand voices that were 'distinct and in which each believed he had a subject-matter ready to hand', gave him an immediate sense of belonging and a considerable critical zeal. He is probably New Zealand's most influential literary critic and an early advocate of modernism in that country. His book *The New Poetic: Yeats to Eliot* (London,

1964; New York, 1966) was an international success, and in 1986 he published a further critical study of *Pound and the modernist movement. His poem 'Pictures in an Undersea Gallery' (1958) was voted the most popular poem ever printed in the quarterly *Landfall. Strongly influenced by Pound, Stead's poetry is notable for its linguistic elegance and exotic appeal. It has a literary sophistication often somewhat at odds with the day-to-day realities of the New Zealand scene, but in *Walking Westward* (Auckland, 1979) and, particularly, *Between* (Auckland, 1988), there has been a growing interest in the invention of personae and dramatized voices that has given his poetry a sharper contemporary edge. This may have something to do with his parallel development as a novelist. His early novel, *Smith's Dream*, was followed by *All Visitors Ashore* (1984), *The Death of the Body* (1986), and *The End of the Century at the End of the World* (1992). He has been awarded the CBE for his services to New Zealand literature.   [PB

STEELE, Peter (1939–), was born in Perth, Western Australia, and educated at the University of Melbourne, graduating BA in 1966, MA in 1968, and Ph.D in 1976. He has taught at the University of Melbourne since 1966 and is now reader in English. From 1973 to 1977 Steele was rector of Campion College, Melbourne, and from 1985 to 1991 was provincial superior of the Society of Jesus in Australia.

Steele's first important work was his magisterial *Jonathan Swift: Preacher and Jester* (Oxford, 1978), in which he emerges not only as an acute critic of Swift but also as a remarkable prose stylist in his own right. His next critical work was *Expatriates: Reflections on Modern Poetry* (Melbourne, 1985), in which it becomes clear that Steele is better approached as an essayist than as a literary critic in any narrow sense. In prose that dazzles as it informs, Steele's essays often trace eccentric orbits around their topics, combining close analysis with aphoristic energy. An abiding interest in the self and its disguises is embodied in *The Autobiographical Passion* (Melbourne, 1989). A host of uncollected and fugitive papers explore a rich variety of religious and literary themes.

Steele's prose and verse are of a piece in terms of their absorption with play, imagination, and the quest for meaning. Yet the poems adopt and work with a plainer style than the essays. The title of his first collection, *Word from Lilliput* (Melbourne, 1973), reminds us that Swift remains a guiding spirit; while a fellow-feeling with the *Auden of 'In Praise of Limestone' is apparent in *Marching on Paradise* (Melbourne, 1984). Perfectly at home in a variety of formal modes, Steele writes as wittily and sharply about modern manners as he does about age-old moral and spiritual perplexities.   [KH

STEELE, Timothy (1948–), was born in Burlington, Vermont, where he attended the local public schools. He was educated at Stanford and received his Ph.D from Brandeis, where he was strongly influenced by his teacher J. V. *Cunningham. He returned to Stanford as a Wallace Stegner fellow, and has lived in California through the Seventies and Eighties, teaching at Stanford and UCLA. He currently lives in Los Angeles and teaches at that campus of California State University.

Among the most notable of the *New Formalists, he is also the poet who most successfully embodies the tenets associated with Cunningham and *Winters (whose legacy at Stanford was still strong long after his death in 1968), which include strict adherence to traditional, usually iambic, metre and to the plain style of Ben Jonson, with an emphasis upon paraphrasable intellectual argument and on reason controlling emotion. In his two books of poetry, *Uncertainties and Rest* (Baton Rouge, La., 1979) and *Sapphics Against Anger* (New York, 1986), he writes with quiet authority, passion, and wit about the landscapes of Vermont ('Incident on a Picnic', 'Learning to Skate', 'The Sheets') and California ('California Street, 1975–76', 'Near Olympic', 'Will Rogers Beach'), as well as about such abstractions as culture, faith, and friendship. Both books contain a sequence of epigrams in the tradition of Cunningham and *Auden, as well as classically restrained yet delicately sensual love lyrics, including 'Last Night as You Slept', 'An

Aubade', and 'Love Poem'. His belief that poetic form should reflect the reasoned balance of strong passions is concisely stated in 'Sapphics Against Anger'. His critique of modernism, *Missing Measures: Modern Poetry and the Revolt Against Meter* (Fayetteville, Ark., and London, 1990), is a carefully argued and lucidly written work of scholarship as well as being the strongest defence yet of the New Formalists' return to metred verse. [RMcP]

STEIN, Gertrude (1874–1946), was born in Pennsylvania and educated at Radcliffe College and Johns Hopkins. In 1902 she settled in Paris, where she established a literary and artistic salon for the avant-garde. Stein used poetry as she habitually used prose: for experimental purposes. There is little difference between the two forms as they appear in her work. But she held, or purported to hold, different theories about her poetry and her prose. In the latter she liked to avoid nouns, preferring verbs; in poetry, though (she wrote), 'you can love a name and if you love a name then saying that name any number of times only makes you love it more'—'poetry is really the name of anything'. This, characteristically, is a theory of her own poetry rather than anyone else's; it is bound up with her often very abstract exploration of the deadening consequences of denotation. Poetry for her could deal with everything that did not involve 'movement in space' (implying verbs). She was an influence in literature, but mainly on the novel; only a few poets (e.g. Robert *Duncan) were directly affected by her specifically poetic procedures. Poets, she thought, were 'drunk with nouns'. She wrote: 'When I said.|A rose is a rose is a rose is a rose.|And then later made that into a ring I made poetry and what did I do I caressed completely caressed and addressed a noun.' Her theory is most conveniently found in the lecture 'Poetry and Grammar', in *Look at me and here I am* (London, 1967), ed. Patricia Meyerowitz. *Tender Buttons* (New York, 1914) consists of prose poems. See also *Stanzas in Meditation and Other Poems 1929–33* (New York, 1956).

[MS-S

STEPHENS, James (1880–1950), was born in Dublin. Recognized as important in the Irish Revival, he is now a neglected figure. *Joyce at one point thought him the only man capable of completing the composition of *Finnegans Wake*. Stephens was a poet of great prosodic ability, whose work, firmly rooted in Irish lore, changed little from *Insurrection* (Dublin, 1909), his first collection, to *Kings and Moons* (London, 1938), his last. He possessed simplicity, but his frequently nonchalant manner concealed a profound melancholy. His robust enjoyment of life was always jostled by a metaphysical and religious unease. This blend of feelings comes across as brilliantly anecdotal in his best poems, such as 'What Thomas an Buille Said in a Pub'. He kept his verse, if not consistently light in tone, then at least only briefly tragic, as in the famous 'The Snare'. His work cries out for judicious selection, only partly fulfilled in *Collected Poems* (London, 1954) or in *James Stephens: A Selection* (London, 1962), ed. Lloyd Frankenberg. It is in his novel *The Crock of Gold* (London, 1912) that his comic genius is most substantial. See *Stephens* (London, 1965), by Hilary Pyle, and *The Writings of James Stephens* (London, 1979), by Patricia McFate. [MS-S

STERN, Gerald (1925–), was born in Pittsburgh, and studied at the University of Pittsburgh and Columbia. After serving in the Air Corps he taught at many colleges and universities, for the longest period at Somerset County College in New Jersey. Since 1982 he has taught at the University of *Iowa Writers' Workshop.

To say that Stern's distinctive and endearing voice combines the bluster of Allen *Ginsberg with the tenderness of James *Wright may seem unhistorical, given that Stern is in fact a year or two older than those poets. Yet while Wright and Ginsberg published their first books in the mid-Fifties, Stern did not make his debut until 1971, when *The Pineys* appeared. Even then he received little attention until the publication of *Lucky Life* in 1977. Thereafter he has come to be recognized as a major poet of celebration, indeed one of the few writing today who has been able to sustain the Whitmanian note convincingly. Together with the characteristic sense of plenitude reflected in his fondness for parataxis, catalogue, and anaphora, Stern's poetry displays an avowedly Jewish attitude towards suffering (see his poem 'Behaving Like a Jew', in which he refuses to be consoled for the death of an opossum on the highway); the amalgamation of these two strains, the Whitmanian and the Judaic, produces a bitter-sweet music unlike any other in contemporary poetry. Stern's focus on his solitary experience, his comically narcissistic portrayals of his own epiphanies and ecstasies, make him in many ways an old-fashioned poet, limited in the range of contemporary reality he can encompass. Yet by the same token he demonstrates the continued viability of a poetic mode that may well nourish the psyches of its readers more than other, less solipsistic modes can. His work may be sampled in *Leaving Another Kingdom: Selected Poems* (New York, 1990); his most recent book is *Bread Without Sugar* (New York, 1992).   [RG

STEVENS, Wallace (1879–1955), was born in Reading, Pennsylvania, and grew up in a comfortable, upper-middle-class family. He attended Harvard from 1897 to 1900, where he studied French and German and became friendly with George *Santayana, the philosopher, to whom he would later address one of his finest poems, 'To an Old Philosopher in Rome'. At Harvard, Stevens was editor of the college literary magazine, *The Advocate*.

After leaving Harvard, Stevens planned to become a journalist; he worked briefly with the *New York Herald Tribune*, but he did not like the daily routines of journalism. Following advice from his father, he left his job at the paper to enter New York Law School in 1901. In 1904 he was admitted to the New York bar. For several years he practised law with mediocre success, moving from firm to firm while, at the same time, reading and writing poetry. In 1908 he began working for the legal department of an insurance company, a shift of emphasis that led to his ultimate appointment with the Hartford Accident and Indemnity Company, of which he became vice-president in 1934. 'It gives a man

character to have this daily contact with a job', he would later say, dividing his life sharply between his literary and business lives.

Stevens married Elsie Moll in 1908, a woman whom he had met five years earlier in Reading. They had one child, a daughter, Holly, and lived a secluded, upper-middle-class life in Hartford, Connecticut. Stevens did not travel, though he relished postcards from friends abroad, and he delighted in fine wines, French cheeses, paintings, and flowers. He acquired an impressive collection of classical recordings and spent a good deal of time gardening. He continued to work at the insurance company until his death, often composing poems on his way to the office and revising them while there.

Though Stevens began publishing in magazines such as *Poetry as early as 1914, he did not actually publish a book until 1923, when he was 44 years old. That book, *Harmonium*, is a landmark volume in modern American poetry. It contains many of Stevens's best-known poems, such as 'Earthy Anecdote', 'The Snow Man', 'Ploughing on Sunday', 'Sunday Morning', 'Tea at the Palace of Hoon', 'Peter Quince at the Clavier', and 'Thirteen Ways of Looking at a Blackbird'. These poems exhibit a dandified, almost baroque quality of language typical of Stevens's early work, which is much in contrast to the later, barer style. *Harmonium* suggests that Stevens had been closely reading the English Romantics—especially Keats—as well as the French Symbolists. The poems of this period are marked by high spirits, a fascination with sensual experience, and a fine sense of parody and pastiche. The influence of *Imagism can be seen throughout, with sharply defined images everywhere. The linguistic medium itself is brought to the fore, with a huge emphasis on the musicality of the line. In contrast to the brightness so pervasive in this volume, there is a sombre tone that occasionally enters the work, as in 'The Snow Man', wherein the poet, like the snowman of the poem, 'beholds | Nothing that is not there and the nothing that is'.

'The poet's subject is his sense of the world', Stevens once wrote. His principal, almost obsessive, subject was in fact the interplay between reality and the imagination. Like the great Romantics he admired, he believed in the ultimate value of imagination, in the ability of the imagination to transform reality. In this, Stevens echoes Coleridge and Nietzsche, Bergson and Santayana, all of whom he read avidly. One long poem of his middle period, 'The Man with a Blue Guitar' (1936), is a brilliant sequence of couplets that explores the meaning and complex figural workings of imaginative vision, represented here by the colour blue. Green, here as elsewhere, represents 'reality' in Stevens's developing symbology, which is remarkably consistent throughout his work. This polarity is similarly represented by north and south, wind and stone, and other oppositional terms.

There is a consistent anti-clerical, atheistical strain in Stevens, who is none the less a deeply 'religious' writer in a sense. 'Poetry', he writes in 'Blue Guitar', '. . . must take the place | Of empty heaven and its hymns.' But the music of imagination, in Stevens, is not supernatural. Later in life, in an essay called 'Imagination as Value', he remarks that 'the great poems of heaven and earth have been written and the great poem of the earth remains to be written'. Thus, Stevens set out to write what, in a poem called 'Of Modern Poetry', stands as something of a credo: 'The poem of the mind in the act of finding | What will suffice.' The poet's job in an age of disbelief is, he suggests elsewhere, to supply the 'satisfactions of belief, in his measure and in his style'. This quasi-religious quest became, increasingly, his central preoccupation as he explored the dialectic of reality and the imagination throughout the Thirties, Forties, and early Fifties.

Transport to Summer appeared in 1947, and it contained the major poem of Stevens's later period, 'Notes Toward a Supreme Fiction', a poem which examines the notion of 'fiction' and its relation to 'fact'. Stevens declares: 'The poem refreshes life so that we share, | For a moment, the first idea.' That is, poetry takes us back to an 'immaculate beginning'. It quickens our sense of the world we inhabit. Stevens celebrates the 'war between the mind | And sky, between thought and day and night'. He finds endless new ways to provide 'the bread of faithful speech'. In a remarkable book of essays, *The Necessary Angel* (1951), Stevens explained his concept of the poet's role: 'What makes the poet the potent figure that he is, or was, or ought to be, is that he creates the world to which we turn incessantly and without knowing it and that he gives to life the supreme fictions without which we are unable to conceive of it.'

Stevens's last book (apart from his *Collected Poems* of 1954, which included the famous sequence 'The Rock'), was *The Auroras of Autumn* (1954), a book markedly different in texture from *Harmonium*, though one sees the same fundamental preoccupations. Stevens in his later work wrote poetry very much in opposition to Ezra *Pound's version of Imagism. Increasingly, blank verse became his medium, with its regularity of rhythm, though he also cultivated highly idiosyncratic forms of abstraction and narrative indirection that have strongly influenced many contemporary poets.

Typical of the later Stevens is the fine meditative sequence, 'An Ordinary Evening in New Haven', where he argues that 'The poem is the cry of its occasion, | Part of the res itself and not about it'. With characteristic obliquity and wit, the poet searches out 'the inner men | Behind the outer shields', contemplating the objective world from a supremely subjective viewpoint.

One observes throughout Stevens's career a deepening sense of duality; indeed, the life of the successful insurance company executive and the life of the great modernist poet never coincided, except in the most superficial ways. The outer shields that Stevens wore correspond in some ways to the famous masks of W. B. *Yeats; they were projections meant to aid the poet in his antithetical quest. This quest, for Stevens, is a holy one, and the poet is regarded as a vatic philosopher in the ancient Roman sense: a high priest of the imagination. 'If one no longer believes in God (as truth)', Stevens says in a letter, 'it is not possible merely to disbelieve; it becomes necessary to believe in something else.' That 'something else' is, of course, poetry itself, seen as a self-defining quest for meaning, an attempt to conjure a world of bright, hard things that, in the Emersonian sense, become inner objects. The final unity towards which all poetry leans is a blending of subject and object, of self and other.

In 'To an Old Philosopher in Rome', a very late poem, Stevens invokes his old Harvard teacher and friend, George Santayana, celebrating 'a kind of total grandeur at the end'. In this total grandeur the physical objects of the world are all 'enlarged'. Yet they remain themselves, too: 'No more than a bed, a chair and moving nuns.' Santayana is seen to pause upon the threshold of death with a sudden waft of understanding: 'He stops upon this threshold, | As if the design of all his words takes form | and frame from thinking and is realized.' This realization is a form of embodiment that Stevens sought perpetually through his life as a poet. It is what he called in 'Not Ideas About the Thing But the Thing Itself' a 'new knowledge of reality'. This is the knowledge, the transmogrification, that Stevens looked for and, often enough in the poetry itself, found.

The Collected Poems of Wallace Stevens (New York, 1954; London, 1955 and 1984) remains the definitive volume. In addition, there is *Opus Posthumous* (New York, 1957, expanded edn., 1989; London, 1959 and 1990), a collection of posthumous poems, plays, and prose, originally edited by Samuel French Morse. *The Letters of Wallace Stevens* (New York, 1966; London, 1967) was edited by his daughter, Holly Stevens. See also Stevens's *The Necessary Angel* (New York, 1951; London, 1960). Among innumerable critical works of note are Frank Kermode, *Wallace Stevens* (Edinburgh, 1969, rev. edn., London, 1989); Helen Vendler, *Wallace Stevens: Words Chosen out of Desire* (Knoxville, Tenn., 1984); Harold Bloom, *Wallace Stevens: The Poems of our Climate* (Ithaca, NY, 1977); Milton Bates, *Wallace Stevens: A Mythology of the Self* (Berkeley, Calif., 1985). For biographical studies, see Peter Brazeau, *Parts of a World: Wallace Stevens Remembered* (New York, 1983); Holly Stevens, *Souvenirs and Prophecies: The Young Wallace Stevens* (journals) (New York, 1977); and J. Richardson, *Wallace Stevens: The Early Years, 1879–1923* (New York, 1986), the first of two volumes.   [JP

STEVENSON, Anne (1933–), was born of American parents in Cambridge, England. Educated in the USA at the University of Michigan, she began to write poetry in response to her researches into the breakdown of puritanism as a moral force. This concern is reflected in her 1974 volume, *Correspondences* (Middletown, Conn. and London), a warm and vividly colloquial sequence of verse-letters, fictional but inspired by her family archive. In 1954 she settled in England, where she was a founder of the Poetry Bookshop in Hay-on-Wye. She has held literary fellowships in Scotland and the North-East, and currently lives in Grantchester and Wales.

Her next volume, *Travelling Behind Glass; Selected Poems 1963–1973* (London, 1974), contains poems that voice feminist concerns in a strikingly composed, never self-indulgent manner. She has written emotionally about landscape and the natural world, but seems at her best as a chronicler of human behaviour and concerns. Technically her reach is wide and consistently accomplished. Her *Selected Poems* (Oxford and New York, 1987) contains work from all her earlier volumes, including *Enough of Green* (1977), *Minute by Glass Minute* (1982), and *The Fiction-Makers* (1985). Since then she has published *The Other House* (1990) and *Four and a Half Dancing Men* (1993—both Oxford and New York). Her controversial biography of Sylvia *Plath appeared in 1989.   [CAR

STEWART, Douglas (1913–85), was born at Eltham, Taranaki Province, New Zealand, and moved to Sydney in 1938 to work on the *Bulletin*, becoming literary editor of the Red Page in 1940. In 1961, when the *Bulletin* changed ownership, he became literary editor with the publishers Angus & Robertson until he retired in 1971.

Editor, dramatist, poet, and anthologist, Stewart was one of the most influential literary figures in the Australia of his time. He first made his reputation with the verse plays *Ned Kelly* (1943), *The Fire on the Snow* and *The Golden Lover* (both 1944), and *Shipwreck* (1947), explorations of the meaning of heroism and the struggle of passionate feeling against convention. Stewart also wrote short stories, belles-lettres, and reminiscence, and edited fifteen volumes of poetry and prose, most notably the collections *Australian Bush Ballads* (1955), *Old Bush Songs and Rhymes of Colonial Times* (1957), and *The Pacific Book of Bush Ballads* (1967), all in collaboration with Nancy *Keesing. His reputation as a poet rests on thirteen volumes of poetry. After his move to Sydney his early New Zealand landscape poetry was followed by a series of attempts to come to terms with Australian nature, history, and landscape, and to write poems that combined popular and traditional Australian elements. He was much influenced by the Australian landscape and nature poetry of the 1940s, which he fostered in the *Bulletin*, and in *Sun Orchids and Other Poems* (1952) and *The Birdsville Track and Other Poems* (1955) found his own voice in a poetry of sparse, meticulous, and often humorous observation. The search for the meaning of heroism continued in *Rutherford and Other Poems* (1962), where his earlier concern with historical exploration led to poems about scientific discovery. Stewart became more and more aware of the fragility of civilized values in a world of increasing violence and fanaticism, and some of his finest poems like 'B Flat', 'Silkworms', the elegy for Kenneth *Slessor, and 'Terra Australis' celebrate the virtues of wise passivity, and the acceptance of the inevitable restrictions of life. See *Collected Poems 1936–67* (Sydney, 1967); *Selected Poems* (Sydney, 1992).

[VS

STEWART, Harold (1916–95), was born in Sydney, Australia, where, after study at Sydney University, he was a member of the Australian army's directorate of research and civil affairs from 1942 to 1946, during which time he became a close friend of the poet James *McAuley. In 1944 Stewart and McAuley devised the infamous 'Ern Malley' hoax, as an attack on the experimental modernism being lauded in the magazine *Angry Penguins* by its editor, the poet Max *Harris. The fictitious 'Ern Malley', though created by a collage technique that sought to dislocate logic and common sense, has survived the context of his creation,

because of an essential playfulness and gently erotic tone that overrides the more obvious disjunctions of the pieces (which, after all, were designed to hoodwink a canny, if enthusiastic, editor).

The shadow of this hoax lies over all of Stewart's later poems, which in his two first individual collections, *Phoenix Wings: Poems 1940–46* (1948) and *Orpheus and Other Poems* (1956), retain a rigid formalism of language and metre. A deep interest in Oriental culture informs these poems, and in 1965 Stewart took up residence in Kyoto, Japan, where he studied at the Shinshu Buddhist University.

Harold Stewart established an international reputation with his two volumes of translations from Japanese haiku, *A Net of Fireflies* (1960) and *A Chime of Windbells* (1969—both Tokyo and Rutland, Vt.). Since then he has published a long poem in twelve parts, *By the Old Walls of Kyoto* (New York, 1979), which, in a formal style clearly related to his early Australian poems, expresses his deep-felt understanding of his adopted culture and its philosophies.   [TWS

STICKNEY, (Joseph) Trumbull (1874–1904), was born in Geneva of an established New England family. His early years were spent travelling in Italy, England, France, Switzerland, and the USA. He was educated in classics at home by his father, then in England, and finally (1891–5) at Harvard, where he made friends with William Vaughn *Moody and contributed poems and reviews to the *Harvard Monthly*. He returned to Europe to study classics at the Sorbonne where, in 1903, he became the first American ever to be awarded the *Doctorat ès Lettres*. His interests included Greek and Sanskrit, and he experimented with writing verse dramas. A small book of poems, *Dramatic Verses*, was published in Boston in 1902. He returned to teach Greek at Harvard in 1903, where he died of a brain tumour in October 1904, aged 30.

Stickney was steeped in Greek thought and literature, yet his poems exhibit a curiously tortured modern sensibility. Intellectually gifted, he was an outsider prone to hopeless and idealized love-affairs, who dedicated his short life to poetry. His work has often been underestimated by critics and has usually been ignored by anthologists. In spite of this, his best poems are rhythmically memorable and have an impressive stylistic cohesion. His emotional range is narrow and intense, and often expresses a sense of overwhelming loss and melancholy, perhaps reminiscent of other 1890s poets such as Ernest Dowson. At times his diction is too archaic for modern taste, but his best poems, such as the sonnet 'Be still. The Hanging Gardens were a dream', 'An Athenian Garden', 'In Summer', and 'Mnemosyne' are none the less subtly original in their delicacy of cadence and intensity of mood.

See *Dramatic Verses* (Boston, 1902); *The Poems of Trumbull Stickney*, ed. George Cabot Lodge, John Ellerton Lodge, and William Vaughn Moody (Boston, 1905); *Homage to Trumbull Stickney*, ed. James Reeves and Seán Haldane, (London, 1968); and *The Poems of Trumbull Stickney*, ed. Amberys R. Whittle (1972). [JDB

STONE, Ruth (1915–), was born in Roanoke, Virginia, and attended the University of Illinois. The mother of three daughters, Stone has taught creative writing at many institutions, including Indiana and Brandeis universities. She currently teaches at State University New York at Binghamton.

One of the more neglected poets of her generation, Stone has published five books, most recently *Second-Hand Coat: Poems New and Selected* (Boston, 1987) and *Who is the Widow's Muse?* (Cambridge, Mass., 1991). What many readers first notice in her poetry is its humour, which ranges from delicate whimsy to verbal slapstick ('Then I picked at the tiling | And the house fell down'). It quickly becomes apparent, however, that Stone's comic energies are placed in the service of a humane and tender vision that gives a special place to the experience of ordinary women. While many of her poems are autobiographical lyrics, other lives, however dimly known, exert a powerful claim on her imagination: in one poem she summons up an android composed of the particles left by all the past occupants of a particular hotel room;

another poem depicts the speaker passing a crowd on a train platform, ending with the line: 'I feel their entire histories ravish me.' Elsewhere Stone explores individual histories, giving them the circumstantial weight of fiction while still maintaining the light-footed poise of her language, with its quick puns, quirks of diction, and startling metaphors. Her poetry balances the immediate life of the self with the inferential life that surrounds it, with results that are both funny and affecting. [RG

STOW, Randolph (1935–), was born into a long-established pastoralist family in Geraldton, Western Australia, and had published a volume of poetry and two novels by the time he graduated from university in Perth. He worked first as a storeman at an isolated mission station in the Kimberley Ranges, then as a cadet patrol officer in New Guinea. While on duty in the Trobriand Islands he contracted a severe form of malaria and was invalided home with a suicidal depression. For three years he was in London, being treated at a hospital for tropical diseases, then lived in Malta and the United States, writing fiction. Having settled in East Anglia, from where his forebears had emigrated, Stow left off the writing of his seventh (and best) novel, *Visitants*, for ten years, partly because of an addiction to the drug Mandrax which had been prescribed for him after a car accident. When eventually finished, this book, which draws on his painful experiences in the Trobriands, helped him to win the Patrick White Award. In his lost years Stow lived in complete obscurity in a farm cottage, on a trickle of royalties and working at a village pub for the price of his drinks. He now has a small terrace house in Old Harwich, where he lives alone, frugally and self-effacingly. Once among the most recognizably Australian poets and novelists, he intends to remain in England because of the greater social and linguistic complexity in that country, which he feels his work needs.

Stow's poetry is impressive but there is little of it. *Act One* (1957) contained his accomplished juvenilia; *Outrider* (1962), his main book of verse, was illustrated with paintings especially done for it by Sidney Nolan; *A Counterfeit Silence* (1969) is a slim selected volume; and there are nine new poems in the anthology *Randolph Stow* (St Lucia, Qld., 1990).

The main theme of both Stow's poetry and prose is isolation, a sense of 'otherness', within nature and society. His poetry is introspective and quiet, but there is a *frisson* of neuroticism about it. His imagery is subjective, and his lines are usually loose and lapsing, arranged in couplets or short stanzas. The manner is feverish, piercing, and yet frail. There is patrician reserve and anguish together.

Stow has been influenced, he says, by Rimbaud, Whitman, and St John Perse, but perhaps just as important to him has been the Australian poet Francis *Webb. The best of his fiction, including *Tourmaline* (1963), is as effective as his verse.   [RGr

STRAND, Mark (1934–), was born in Canada on Prince Edward Island. He studied at Antioch College, where he took a BA. He also received a BFA from Yale, where he studied painting. At the University of Iowa, he worked closely with poet Donald *Justice, completing an MA in 1962. He spent a year in Italy on a Fulbright scholarship, and later taught at Iowa for three years. In 1965 he spent a year as Fulbright Lecturer at the University of Brazil, where he was deeply influenced by contemporary Latin American poets (especially the Brazilian poet Carlos Drummond de Andrade). Strand has moved around a good deal, teaching at many American universities, including Columbia, Princeton, Harvard, and the University of Utah, where he is now professor of English.

Strand's poetry is known for a clarity reminiscent of the paintings of Edward Hopper, and for a deeply inward sense of language. Many of the poems aspire to the condition of dreams, shot through with images possessing a strangely haunting vividness, as in 'The Ghost Ship', which summons a mysterious ship that floats 'Through the crowded streets . . . | Its vague | tonnage like wind'. He frequently invokes everyday images, as in 'The Mailman', where a wraith-like mailman visits the narrator at midnight to deliver 'terrible personal news'. In 'The Last Bus' the poet imagines Rio de Janeiro, calling the sea 'a dream' in which the city 'dies and is reborn'. The poem is surreal in a manner that combines the dreamlike quality of Pablo Neruda with aspects of nightmare that recall such European expressionists as Georg Trakl.

Strand's first book, *Sleeping with One Eye Open* (was published in 1964). His second, *Reasons for Moving* (1968), attracted widespread attention from critics; it includes 'Eating Poetry' which begins: 'Ink runs from the corners of my mouth. | There is no happiness like mine. | I have been eating poetry.' This antic surrealism also animates poems like 'Moontan', 'The Man in the Tree', and 'The Marriage'. *Darker* (1970) was an obliquely autobiographical volume, containing such poems as 'My Life' and 'My Death'. These poems are full of a quiet, ironically pictured anguish as the poet teeters on the brink of self-consciousness in pursuit of his *via negativa*. In 1973 Strand published *The Story of Our Lives*, more explicitly autobiographical than anything he had written before. It includes a striking elegy for the poet's father.

The Late Hour (1978) is among the strongest of Strand's several books, containing poems for the poet's son and daughter, and a number of poems (such as 'The Late Hour', 'Snowfall', and 'The Garden') that possess a deeply elegiac quality. In this book, Strand began writing with a freshness and simplicity that recall the poetry of ancient China.

As the Mexican poet Octavio Paz has written: 'Mark Strand has chosen the negative path, with loss as the first step towards fullness: it is also the opening to a transparent verbal perfection.' Strand's *Selected Poems* (New York, 1980) adds to previously published work a number of beautifully realized autobiographical poems, including 'Shooting Whales' and 'Nights in Hackett's Cove'. Strand has also published a book of short stories, several translations from European and Latin American poets, and an anthology of contemporary poetry. For criticism, see Richard Howard, *Alone with America* (New York, 1969).

[JP

STRAUSS, Jennifer (née Wallace) (1933–), was born at Heywood, Victoria, Australia, and graduated from Melbourne University. Married in Scotland to fellow-expatriate Werner Strauss, she has studied and taught in England, Germany, the USA, and Canada. Since 1964 she has lectured, specializing in medieval English literature, at Monash University in Melbourne. She has published three collections: *Children and other Strangers* (1975); *Winter Driving* (1981); and *Labour Ward* (1988—all Melbourne), and edited the *Oxford Book of Australian Love Poems* (1993). Strauss provides sharply focused insights into injustice, especially the oppression of women, from literature ('Wife to Horatio') and legend ('Bluebeard Re-Scripted'), as well as history ('The Anabaptist Cages, Munster', 'Ignaz Semmelweis Enters the Vienna Insane Asylum, 1865'). Her latest book includes responses to military oppression in Argentina. [JRo

STRYK, Lucien (1924–), was born in Poland and now teaches at the Northern Illinois University at DeKalb. A deliberately 'minor' poet, wishing in his own words 'to avoid the hateful evidence of our will to impress', Stryk has been decisively influenced by Zen poetry, some of which he has translated (e.g. *Triumph of the Sparrow: Zen Poems of Shinkichi Takahashi*, Urbana, Ill., 1986). His first substantial book, published by the Fantasy Press in Oxford, *The Trespasser* (1956), was *Pound-influenced and artificial, but full of ably and conscientiously made poems of a generally *imagist variety. Fear of 'impressing' may well have robbed his later work of impact, for its subject-matter is frequently far from that of Zen Buddhism, covering both his war and domestic experience. He has even been described as a 'tourist poet', because of his vivid snapshots of people (usually deprived) and places all over the world. Like many American poets, Stryk is suspicious of rhetoric and linguistic excitement; but he seldom declines into the prosaic. His highest achievement lies in his successful adaptation of Japanese procedures into English. See *Collected Poems 1953–1983* (Athens, Ohio, 1984) and *Of Pen and Ink and Paper Scraps* (Athens, 1989). [MS-S

STUART, Dabney (1937–), was born in Richmond, Virginia. He was educated at Davidson College and Harvard University and teaches at Washington and Lee University in Lexington, Virginia, where since 1988 he has edited the literary quarterly *Shenandoah.* Stuart's first book, *The Diving Bell* (New York, 1966), was widely praised by reviewers for its formal polish and its inventiveness with autobiographical subject-matter, particularly in poems about the poet's extended Southern family. His early work is indebted to the *confessional poets, especially Robert *Lowell and *Snodgrass, but his eight published collections display a wide variety of other formal modes, from *surrealism in *The Other Hand* (Baton Rouge, La., 1974), to the songs and ballads of *Yeats and *Muir in *Round and Round: A Triptych* (Baton Rouge, 1977). Stuart writes personal poetry of unusual honesty, and many of his love poems are marked by their directness and absence of false sentiment. His most recent collections—*Common Ground* (1982), *Don't Look Back* (1987), and *Narcissus Dreaming* (1990—all Baton Rouge) reveal the poet's familiarity with contemporary psychoanalytical literature, particularly in poems which rework and further develop family material. These books also contain poems of lyric meditation, occasional pieces of social and literary satire, and serious examples of acrostic verse. Stuart has also written a critical study of Vladimir Nabokov and a book of children's verse, *Friends of Yours, Friends of Mine.* [RSG

SUKNASKI, Andrew (1942–) was born in Wood Mountain, Saskatchewan, to immigrant parents. Exposed only to Polish-laced Ukrainian in his early childhood, his first contact with English was not until he turned 6. Suknaski ran away from home at 16 and spent seventeen years travelling the world, working at various jobs. He attended Simon Fraser University and the University of British Columbia, as well as the Kootenay School of Fine Arts and the Montreal Museum School of Art and Design. He has published four substantial collections: *Leaving* (1974); his most celebrated book, *Wood Mountain Poems* (1976); *the ghosts call you poor* (1978), and *In the Name of Narid* (1981), as well as numerous chapbooks and collections of *concrete poetry.

Suknaski's poems are simultaneously a personal search for identity and self, and an attempt to define Canada's multicultural dimension. When asked which ethnic group he identifies with, Suknaski allies himself with the eclectic nationalities of Wood Mountain, ranging from Romanian and Metis to Irish and Dutch. Dialect, heavily-accented pidgin English, and beer-parlour slang are all rendered on the page in their phonetic simplicity. Influenced by the immigrant's heritage, the dialect is neither English nor the language which infiltrates it; the poems depend on the vividness of the anecdote for their analogies.

The National Film Board of Canada produced an informative film, *Wood Mountain Poems* (1982), on Suknaski, his heritage, and his poems, directed by Harvey Spak. His poetry collections are all published by small, independent presses, with the exception of *Wood Mountain Poems* and *the ghosts call you poor*, published in Toronto by Macmillan of Canada.   [MQA

Surrealism had its origins in France. It was concerned with the resolution of the two seemingly contradictory states of dream and reality in an absolute 'Surreality', by means of which freedom from the shackles of reality would be attained. The Surrealists advocated an art that was free of control by reason; and Freud's theories concerning the unconscious had great importance for them. The movement originated in the group that directed the review *Littérature* from 1919 to 1924—Louis Aragon, André Breton, and Phillipe Soupault—and in 1924 Breton produced *La Manifeste du Surréalisme* (the First Surrealist Manifesto).

Surrealism came to public attention in England with the International Surrealist Exhibition at the New Burlington Galleries in June 1936, which was accompanied by the publication of *Surrealism*, edited by Herbert *Read. An earlier account had been *A Short Survey of Surrealism* (1935) by the 19-year-old David *Gascoyne, one of the young poets who were to be seen in

David Archer's bookshop in Parton Street, at once a home for Surrealism and for left-wing ideas. It was among certain writers born between 1911 and 1915 that Surrealism had its impact on English poetry: David Gascoyne; Charles *Madge; Kenneth *Allott; Lawrence *Durrell; Francis *Scarfe; Philip *O'Connor; and Dylan *Thomas (in his stories); though the older Hugh Sykes-Davies and Humphrey Jennings also espoused it.

The most notable British organ of Surrealist literature was *Contemporary Poetry and Prose*, which ran from May 1936 to autumn 1937 and was edited from Parton Street by Roger Roughton, then 19. Other periodicals hospitable to surrealism were: *Janus*, edited by Reginald Hutchins and John Royston Morley for two issues in 1936; *Delta*, published from Paris by Alfred Perlès, Henry Miller, and Lawrence Durrell; and Nicholas *Moore's *Seven*, which ran from summer 1938 to spring 1940.

From these years the most notable works influenced by Surrealism were David Gascoyne's poems, *Man's Life Is This Meat* (1934), and Lawrence Durrell's fiction, *The Black Book* (1938). The impact of Surrealism on literature in England was much less than it was on the visual arts. However, cultural manifestations as various as the *New Apocalypse movement and Mass-Observation owed a great deal imaginatively to Surrealism. Many of the younger writers associated with the movement stopped writing at an early age, perhaps because the coming of the Second World War destroyed the adventurous climate in which Surrealism thrived. *The Poetry of the Thirties*, by A. T. Tolley (London and New York, 1975) discusses Surrealism and British poetry.   [ATT

SWART (Edward) Vincent (1911–62), was born in the Orange Free State into a bilingual home. A benefactor paid for his education at the University of the Witwatersrand. He was an outstanding student and thereafter worked briefly as a lecturer in English, publishing poetry in local and overseas journals. After a short period studying at Cambridge he returned to South

Africa at the outbreak of the Second World War. His charismatic personality and bohemian life-style attracted a wide circle of acolytes. During the Forties and Fifties he became increasingly involved in anti-government activity, being detained in 1960, and thereafter banned. Influenced by modernism and *surrealism, his bold use of imagery and his experimentation with new literary directions challenged the traditional nature of contemporary South African poetry. But his personality was always unstable and his health declined rapidly. His poetry analyses the private world of his own damaged psyche, exploring personal relationships and the nature and function of the poet. Although he continued to write, no further poetry was published during his lifetime. *Collected Poems* (Johannesburg, 1981) contains all his finished work.   [MLe

SWEENEY, Matthew (1952–), was born in Co. Donegal, Ireland. He moved to England in 1973 and studied German and English at the Polytechnic of North London and the University of Freiburg, 1975–9. Since then he has lived in Bloomsbury and made a profession of creative writing, doing many readings and school visits, and holding (at different times) three separate posts as an Arts Council-sponsored writer-in-residence.

Sweeney's first volume, *A Dream of Maps* (Dublin), was published in 1981 with his name inauspiciously misspelt on the title-page. In subsequent books—*A Round House* (Dublin, 1983), *The Lame Waltzer* (Dublin, 1985), and *Blue Shoes* (London, 1989), he has developed an economical, naïve style of narration for his lugubrious fables, in which domestic rituals are intruded on, and sometimes overtaken, by the surreal. Contemporary landscapes, whose features include the golf courses, lighthouses, and cold seas of Donegal, are peopled by eccentrics and solitaries, when not with mysterious pronouns. His chief concern is mortality; there are deaths (especially by drowning) and resurrections, but it is in the mixed realm of the moribund—as when he charts the functionless survival of his character the Lame Waltzer—that his imagina-

tion has probed most distinctively. See also *Cacti* (London, 1992).

Sweeney has also published poems (*The Flying Spring Onion*) and a novel (*The Snow Vulture*) for children (both 1992).   [MI

SWEETMAN, David (1943–), was born in Northumberland, and educated at the universities of Durham and East Africa. He has worked as a publisher's editor in Paris and a producer for the BBC; he is now a free-lance writer, and lives in London and France. He has published several children's books and a biography of Vincent van Gogh. His only full-length collection of poems to date, *Looking Into the Deep End* (London, 1981), appeared at the height of the fashion for *'Martian' poetry, and is clearly indebted to Craig *Raine's confident use of vivid similes, visual conceits, and riddling metaphors. If in Sweetman's work the style seems less self-congratulatory than in Raine's, that may be because Sweetman also lacks some of the latter's aptness and vigour. He occasionally moves outside Raine's very English, domestic or pastoral scenarios, but his references to Hiroshima, Dresden, Vietnam, and civil war in Africa risk sounding like short-cuts to the more inclusive historical awareness his poems reach for. His most affecting poems deal with his own family history. Elsewhere, what is original about Sweetman's sensibility—a guilty exoticism, a note of troubled erotic release—is all but muffled by the arty sophistication that compares miners to 'Coptic saints' and refers in a knowing way to Huysmans, Telemann, Gibbon, Degas, etc.; uncertainty of tone and signs of strain in the use of similes, lend less a fruitful tension than an air of the precious and *voulu*.   [AJ

SWENSON, May (1919–89), was born in Logan, Utah and educated at Utah State University. She moved to New York during the 1930s and worked for the Writer's Project (a part of the Works Progress Administration). During those years Swenson practised and refined her craft; many of the poems that first made her reputation were published in *The New Yorker*, beginning in the 1940s.

Swenson was a poet of strong formal instinct who was drawn to the particulars of her natural and domestic surroundings. In her early publications—as in the book *Another Animal* (New York, 1954)—formal considerations guided most of her choices of subject and presentation. Nevertheless, from the start Swenson showed herself capable of keenly registering the sensuous, and was willing to let sounds and rhythms inscribe a confined world.

Swenson's poems published in the 1960s suggest a struggle in her art. She essayed a number of ambitious visual effects; many of her 'iconographs' incorporated a vertical split in the text. Later, she brought more of her own experience forward as subject-matter. Her poems took on a new kineticism; they seemed less concerned with stilling an object or animal in the amber of pure perception. The surface is altogether friendlier and more inviting.

In 1980 Swenson succeeded Elizabeth *Bishop as chancellor of the Academy of American Poets; in 1981 she was awarded the Bollingen Prize for Poetry; and in 1987, just two years before her death, she received a fellowship from the MacArthur Foundation. Swenson's books include: *A Cage of Spines* (1958), *To Mix With Time: New and Selected Poems* (1963), *Half Sun Half Sleep* (1967—all New York); *New and Selected Things Taking Place* (Boston, 1978); and her last volume, *In Other Words* (New York, 1987).   [SPB

SWINGLER, Randall (1909–67), was educated at Winchester and Oxford. In 1934 he joined the Communist Party and in 1937 became editor of *Left Review*. During the Second World War he served in North Africa and Italy and was awarded the MM. After the war he lived by lecturing and editing. He left the Communist Party in 1952.

His first books, *Poems* (1932) and *Reconstruction* (1933), were followed by *Difficult Morning* (1933), which had an impressive fluency. However, its tone of loosely focused aspiration and its conventional imagery belied an appearance of modernity largely confined to a rejection of puritanical restrictions. This liberal, middle-class ambience seemed more congenial to

Swingler than the call for change of the party with which he aligned himself; and in his best poem, 'Sussex in Winter', he responds movingly to the conflict.

The Years of Struggle (1946) was presented as an account of the inner development of one involved in the struggle to prevent war and then build a new society. His last collection, *The God in the Cave* (London, 1950), consists of two short sequences that deal with the struggle to accept the forces of life and change—a theme common to all Swingler's poetry. A great deal of his poetry remains uncollected, including words for the music of Alan Rawsthorne, Benjamin Britten, and others.

Swingler wrote two novels, *No Escape* (1937) and *To Town* (1939). A memoir and a selection of his poetry can be found in *The 1930s: A Challenge to Orthodoxy*, ed. J. Lucas (Hassocks, Sussex,1978).
                                    [ATT

SYKES, Roberta (Bobbi) (1943–), was born in Townsville, Queensland, the eldest of three daughters. An Aborigine, she spent much of her early life combating racist taunts. Forced to leave school at 14 because of her colour, she experienced a succession of 'life-or-perish' situations as a dishwasher, floor-scrubber, factory-worker, and trainee nurse. She left Townsville for Sydney in the early 1970s, ultimately working with a range of urban Aboriginal organizations. Sykes became a recognizable public figure when arrested in mid-1972 as the secretary of the Aboriginal (tent) Embassy, erected on the lawns of Parliament House, Canberra, as a symbol of indigenous pride and defiance.

Encouraged by the black American scientist, Professor Chester Pierce, she obtained an Ed.M (Harvard, 1981) and an Ed.D (1984), and later turned her doctoral thesis into the Sydney University Press publication *Incentive, Achievement and Community* (1986)—an analysis of black viewpoints on Aboriginal education. *Black Majority*, an analysis of the first twenty-one years (1967–88) of black Australian citizenship, was published in 1989 to much critical acclaim. She is currently a lecturer in the department of English, Macquarie University.

Syllabics

Sykes's only volume of poems, *Love Poems and Other Revolutionary Actions* (St Lucia, Qld., 1979; republished, 1988) is divided into three sections—'The Revolution', 'For Love', and 'Of People'. *Love Poems* catalogues the poet's confusions, joy, sense of communal pain, and political intentions in verse stylistically reminiscent of much African-American poetry of the Sixties and Seventies. Powerful poems such as 'Counselling', 'Ambrose', and 'Black Women' depict the stark realities of being black in Australia in the second half of the century. Sykes is not a revolutionary; she writes in order to publicize revolutionary ideas about race, women's issues, and the political system.

The best source on Sykes is Sykes herself—in works such as *Black Power in Australia* (1975), the biography *Mumshirl* (1981), *Incentive, Achievement and Community* (1986), *Black Majority* (1989), and *Connections—Essays on Black Literatures* (1988), ed. Emmanuel S. Nelson.   [DH

Syllabics have been written by poets in need of an alternative to stress and quantitative metre and to free verse. Two main twentieth-century traditions can be identified. One derives from Robert *Bridges, who began in 1913 to experiment with what he termed 'neo-Milton syllabics', on the grounds that '[the] accentual (dot and go one) bumping' of traditional isochronous metre 'is apt to make ordinary words ridiculous'. Syllabic prosody observed a syllable-count but dispensed with a stress pattern, and was thus better able to accommodate natural spoken rhythms, in the view of Bridges. 'Poor Poll' (published in 1921) was the first of these poems; Bridges developed his twelve-syllable 'loose Alexandrines' for use throughout *The Testament of Beauty* (1929). Book-length studies of Bridges by Elizabeth Cox Wright (1951) and Donald E. Stanford (1978) argue that, in the British poet's use, the syllabic line replaces the traditional foot as the unit of rhythm. Writers in the Bridges tradition of consistent line-length have included Thom *Gunn (see the seven-syllable line of 'Considering the Snail' and other poems in *My Sad Captains*, 1961) and John *Hollander, whose *Powers of Thirteen* (1983)

offers 169 (13 x 13) thirteen-line poems written in thirteen-syllable lines. Critics complain of the monotony of this kind of syllabic prosody.

The other main tradition offers greater variety through its use of changing line-length, complex stanzas, and occasional rhyme. Marianne *Moore's 'The Steeplejack' uses six-line stanzas, the lines 11/10/14/8/8/3 syllables in length, the second and fifth lines of every stanza rhyming; in 'The Fish' her pattern is 1/3/9/6/8, rhyming *aabbc*. Dylan *Thomas used syllabics for certain poems ('Poem in October', 9/12/9/3/5/12/12/5/3/9, unrhymed; 'Fern Hill', 14/14/9/6/9/15/14/7/9, rhymes and consonances placed variably). Poets as different as Sylvia *Plath and Allen *Curnow have also written syllabics of this kind. Other poets in this tradition include Kendrick *Smithyman ('Waikato Railstop', 10/13/12/12/6/4 with variations, unrhymed; 'Colville', 7/9/10/7/10/9 with variations, *abcbcd*); Michael *Hulse ('Getting a Tan', 2/4/12/6/6/6, *abccab*; 'Raffles Hotel', 12/12/8/10, unrhymed); and Roger Finch, an American resident in Tokyo, who used the Japanese *tanka* as a precedent for lines using only odd numbers of syllables ('The Bat Tree', 9/13/11/11/ 9/11, fourth and sixth lines rhyming), but subsequently relaxed his rule ('What is Written on the Ceiling', 5/9/12/11/7/9/11, third and seventh lines rhyming; 'What is Written on the Floor', 5/7/11/11/3/10, fourth and sixth lines rhyming).   [MHu

SYMONS, Arthur (William) (1865–1945), was the son of a Cornish Methodist minister. His childhood was spent in Guernsey, Alnwick, and St Ives according to his father's various appointments. He did not learn to read until he was 9, but by his late teens was writing dozens of poems. His first book, a study of Browning, appeared when he was 21, and *Days and Nights*, a collection of poems dedicated to Walter Pater, in 1889. His attitudes and activities are at the heart of the Nineties movement, and the magazine he edited, the *Savoy*, is far more typical of Nineties writing than the *Yellow Book*. In 1901 he married the daughter of a Newcastle ship-owner, and seven years later suffered a nervous breakdown in Italy. He was diagnosed as suffering from GPI (General Paralysis of the Insane), and put into a mental home, from which he emerged in 1910. He lived for another thirty-five years in Kent, writing many books in order to keep his wife and himself financially afloat. A Collected Works began to appear (London, 1924), but only nine volumes of the projected sixteen were published. A biography by Roger Lhombreaud appeared in 1963 (London), another by Karl Beckson in 1987 (Oxford).

The best of Symons's poetry belongs to the Nineties, and indeed is super-typically of the period. His considerable influence on later poets, *Eliot, *Pound, and Conrad *Aiken among them, was exerted partly through his own poetry but more directly by The Symbolist Movement in Literature (1899), which served for many as an introduction to Rimbaud, Verlaine, and the Symbolists. In a note written near the end of his life he said: 'I have believed more than I have doubted: I conceived more things than I have executed. I have never reasoned deeply on deep questions. I have generally hated logic.' Yet the attraction of Symons's criticism, and even his poetry, is its clarity, generosity, logic, and good sense. Almost everything he wrote is sensible, and the anguish expressed particularly in the sonnets of Amoris Victima gives them a power mostly lacking in his work. Except in the destructive breakdown in which he suffered delusions, he was never granted the mystical experience he believed to transcend logic.

[JGS

SYMONS, Julian (Gustave) (1912–94), was born in London. He left school aged 14 and worked as an advertising copy-writer. During the Second World War he served in the Royal Armoured Corps and was invalided out in 1944. Since 1947 he has been a free-lance writer. He is best known for his crime novels, though he has written many volumes of non-fiction, and is one of the few notable literary critics of his generation.

Symons founded *Twentieth Century Verse in 1937 and edited it until it closed in 1939. Its main contributors wrote a poetry in the realist,

humanist line of *Auden and his associates; and Symons, in Confusions About 'X' (London, 1939) and The Second Man (London, 1944), was influenced by Auden. The first of these, with its sense of a conflict within the self of several personae, shows the contemporary impact of psychology; but Symons is better in more direct poems of person or place. His second book is marred by a hardening of attitudes. After the war the impulse to write languished under a sense that the world would not change. Symons returned to poetry later in life with two short but attractive books, The Object of an Affair and Other Poems (1974) and Seven Poems for Sarah (1979—both Edinburgh). Notes from Another Country (London, 1972) are his memoirs.

[ATT

SZIRTES, George (1948–), was born in Hungary and came to England with his parents, following the uprising in Budapest in 1956. His education and formative experiences have all been in England, but he has never lost sight of his Central European origins. In the Eighties he returned to Hungary on extended visits, and the major poem-sequences of his last two books have had Hungarian subjects and settings. His discovery of his Jewish background, as much as the thawing of relations between the Communist world and the West, have led him to revalue the experience of his family, and to pioneer a coming-together of English and European identity which should prove influential both in Britain and abroad.

One further important agent in Szirtes's poetry is his training in art, particularly as an etcher, painter, and graphic artist. It was while he was studying for his diploma that he met Martin *Bell, then teaching liberal studies at Leeds Art School. Bell, with his affection for French poetry and Italian opera, saw in Szirtes an ideal amalgam of English individualism and European culture. Szirtes has fulfilled Bell's confidence. His first collection, The Slant Door, (London, 1979), though sometimes stiff in its devotion to formality, has much of the surrealist charm and eccentricity of his own painting and etching. From this book onwards Szirtes has grown in confidence, raiding the great store of European myth, fairy-tale, legend, and history, to produce a poetry where proverbial charm joins hands with Audenesque wisdom. Szirtes has never abandoned his English models: behind his pictures of Central European persecution (see especially his sequence 'Courtyards') there lies the moral clarity of Marvell or Herbert. Since *The Slant Door* he has published five books—*November and May* (1981), *Short Wave* (1983), *The Photographer in Winter* (1986—all London); and *Metro* (1988) and *Bridge Passages* (1991—both Oxford).

[PNFP

SZUMIGALSKI, Anne (1922–), was born in London. Raised in a family that loved language, she began composing poems as a young girl, feeling that this would be her lifelong vocation. She was educated privately in languages and literature.

Szumigalski emigrated to Canada in 1951, moving to Saskatoon, Saskatchewan, in 1956, where she has established herself as a force in Canadian poetry written on the prairies. She was a founding member of the Saskatchewan Writers' Guild, a founding editor of the literary magazine *Grain*, and a co-founder of the Saskatchewan Writers' Colony, and has worked as a teacher, editor, writer-in-residence, and translator. In addition to poetry she has also written prize-winning short fiction, and several works in collaboration with Saskatoon writer Terrence Heath—most recently, *Journey/Journée* (1988).

Szumigalski's first book, *Woman Reading in Bath* (1974), while powerfully evoking the cycles of natural, mortal, and passionate life, frequently intermingles the surreal or the holy in the domestic and mundane scenes she re-creates. Her ten other books include: *Doctrine of Signatures* (1983) and *Instar: Poems and Stories* (1985). Her most recent work, *Rapture of the Deep* (Regina, 1991), shows her abiding skill with narrative forms.

The fullest selection of Szumigalski's work is *Dogstones: Selected and New Poems* (Saskatoon, 1986). The journal *Arc* (Ottawa) devoted a special issue to Szumigalski in Fall, 1989. See also Szumigalski's autobiographical work, *The Word, The Voice, The Text: The Life of a Writer* (Saskatoon, 1990).

[NB

T

TAGGARD, Genevieve (1894–1948), was born in Waitsburg, Washington, to teacher parents who took her to Hawaii to live when she was 2. Due to her father's lung problems the family shifted back and forth several times before 1914, when Taggard entered Berkeley, where she was encouraged in her writing by Witter *Bynner. In 1920 she moved to Manhattan, worked for an avant-garde publisher, and helped found *Measure: A Magazine of Verse* a year later, the same year she married novelist Robert Wolf.

The marriage was marred by several clashes before its dissolution in 1934. Taggard's poetry, first gathered in *For Eager Lovers* (1922), *Hawaiian Hilltop* (1923), and *Travelling Standing Still* (1928), was highly polished, occasionally touching, backed by sure erudition, as was her study, *The Life and Mind of Emily Dickinson* (1930). She also taught at Mount Holyoke and Sarah Lawrence. Her taste for the metaphysical vied with an equally intense commitment to leftist politics, evident in the protest poetry of *Calling Western Union* (1936), and her editing both *May Days: An Anthology of Verse from Masses-Liberator* (1925) and *Circumference, Varieties of Metaphysical Verse, 1456–1928* (1929). She married an American representative of *Tass* in 1935. Her last volumes, *Long View* (1942) and *Slow Music* (1946) returned to a metaphysical mode.

Her daughter, Marcia D. Liles, has edited *To the Natural World* (Boise, Idaho, 1980), a generous selection of her work with bibliographical notes. [EB

TAMBIMUTTU See POETRY LONDON.

TATE, Allen (1899–1979), was born in Winchester, Kentucky. At Vanderbilt University he joined John Crowe *Ransom's literary discussion group (his friend Robert Penn *Warren was also a member), and co-founded and edited its journal, *The *Fugitive*, thus beginning a lasting alliance with the *Agrarian group of Southern writers. In 1924 he married the novelist Caroline Gordon, and over the next ten years, living variously in West Virginia, New York, Paris, and Tennessee, published biographies of Stonewall Jackson (1928) and Jefferson Davis (1929), and made his name as a poet with *Mr. Pope and Other Poems* (1928), *Three Poems* (1930), and *Poems, 1928–31* (1932). During the 1930s he took up his first teaching post, in Tennessee (1934–6), and published his first book of criticism, *Reactionary Essays on Poetry and Ideas* (1936); like much of his poetry, his only novel, *The Fathers* (1938), set in antebellum Virginia, is an attempt to understand his regional and cultural origins. Tate was poet-in-residence at Princeton in the early 1940s. Then, as editor of the *Sewanee Review* (1944–6), he encouraged and influenced writing on Old Southern and New Critical issues alike. His version of *New Criticism, most forcefully defended and practised in *Reason in Madness* (1941) and *On the Limits of Poetry* (1948), holds that poetry is not a vehicle for imprecise feeling but an autonomous structure, an objective frame for a tension between themes. His commentaries, however, are usually as alert to a poem's intellectual, cultural, and biographical context as to its formal qualities. From 1951 Tate was professor of English at the University of Minnesota, making frequent trips elsewhere to lecture, and continuing to publish volumes of well crafted poems: *Poems* (New York, 1960), *The Swimmers* (London, 1970;

533

New York, 1971). His first marriage, always troubled (he and Gordon had divorced and remarried in 1946), was finally annulled in 1959; and Tate was married again twice.

Tate's poetry is marked by classical erudition, strong and carefully worked metrical effects, and an elevated tone—a baroque manner which has been traced to the rhetoric of the preachers and politicians of the Old South. Present in all his work are the preoccupations he identified in his most celebrated poem, 'Ode to the Confederate Dead': the tension between ' "active faith" which has decayed, and the "fragmentary cosmos" which surrounds us'; and 'heroism in the grand style, elevating even death from mere physical dissolution into a formal ritual'. Tate's conversion to Catholicism in 1950, then, was not surprising, and is reflected in his later work: throughout *The Forlorn Demon* (critical essays, 1953) he draws on Catholic doctrine to organize his perceptions; and 'The Swimmers' and 'The Buried Lake', late poems in Dante's *terza rima*, find in Christian rather than classical tradition a religio-moral context for assessing Southern experience. Tate was in a sense a poet's poet: his advice was crucial in guiding poets—as diverse as Hart *Crane and Robert *Lowell—whose work is more likely to endure than his.

See *Collected Poems, 1919–1976* (Baton Rouge, La., 1977) and *Collected Essays* (Denver, Col., 1959). [NE

TATE, James (1943–), was born in Kansas City, Missouri, attended the University of Missouri and Kansas State College, and took an MFA at the *Iowa Writers' Workshop in 1967, the same year in which he won the Yale Younger Poets competition for his book *The Lost Pilot*. He has taught at the University of California, Berkeley, and Columbia University; he now teaches at the University of Massachusetts.

Tate is the funniest and most prolific of the group of young American surrealists who emerged in the late Sixties, a group which included *Simic, *Strand, Bill *Knott, and Charles *Wright. While much of this poetry aims for a bare, primitive quality that involves a restricted palette of images, Tate from the start has opted for a more wide-ranging, quirky, idiosyncratic brand of imagery less concerned with purity of effect than with surprise and bewilderment. His lines are often clotted with colourful nouns that release energy through their clashing associations, as in the title of his early poem 'The Wheelchair Butterfly'. Tate also makes brilliant use of folksy Midwestern idioms, which bring a casual, demotic air to his derangements of reality. His most memorable poems are those which temper his surrealist manner with a recognizable sense of subject or occasion; he writes wonderfully of the suburbs, of formal events like weddings and funerals, and of other areas of life in which his verbal anarchy can wreak havoc on the routine complacency it encounters. Tate is more than a poetic Marx brother, however; his sense of fun is inextricably bound up with darker emotions like fear, anxiety, and repulsion. These flit about the edges of his landscapes, deepening their shadows and revealing a kind of desperation as the primary motive for his manic play, as hinted by the title of his early book *The Oblivion Ha-Ha*. Tate has published nine volumes of poetry, the most recent of which are *Constant Defender* (Middletown, Conn., 1983) and *Reckoner* (Middletown, 1986). [RG

TAYLOR, Andrew (1940–), was born in the fishing port of Warrnambool, Victoria. He studied at Scotch College, at the University of Melbourne, and in Italy. For much of his adult life he has taught at the University of Adelaide. In recent years, his second wife being German, he has spent a good deal of time in Germany and this has had its effect on his poetry, which has moved away from much of its early zest and jauntiness into a plangency which has slippery, dark affinities with European modernism. He was at his liveliest in an early sequence, 'The Cat's Chin and Ears: A Bestiary' but the dominant tone of his writing was signalled by the titles of his first two books, *The Cool Change* (1970) and *Ice Fishing* (1972); it is a poetry of cool spaces, of silence, of dividing waters, and of absences. He has also practised that disconcerting form, the prose poem.

Taylor's poetry may be read in *Selected Poems* (St Lucia, Qld., 1982, revd., 1988). He published little poetry in the 1980s but would seem to have devoted his energies to the theory-driven study, *Reading Australian Poetry* (St Lucia, 1987), a book which throws much light on his own poetic concerns. [CW-C

TAYLOR, Eleanor Ross (1920–), was born in South Carolina and educated at the Women's College of the University of North Carolina at Greensboro. Since 1943 she has been married to the fiction writer Peter Taylor. Her first book, *Wilderness of Ladies*, appeared in 1960 with a fulsome introduction by Randall *Jarrell—so fulsome, indeed, that some commentators wondered if it might not somewhat impede Taylor's development. In 1972, though, she published *Welcome Eumenides* (New York)—a book notable for the fieriness and economy of its lyrics and for two resourceful narratives: 'A Few Days in the South', which has been described by Richard *Howard as 'the best poem since Whitman about the War Between the States', and the title-poem, a dramatic work done in the voice of Florence Nightingale. Taylor's *New and Selected Poems* appeared in 1986. [POM

TAYLOR, Henry (1942–), was born to Quaker parents and grew up in Lincoln, Virginia in the farm country west of Washington, DC, attending local public schools through the ninth grade. His father was a dairy farmer and he himself a trainer of jumping horses which he began to ride at horse-shows at an early age. He spent his last three years of high school at the Quaker George School in Pennsylvania before going on to the University of Virginia where he began writing poetry, eventually under the tutelage of George *Garrett. He graduated from the writing programme at Hollins College in 1967. Though he spent three years teaching at the University of Utah, he never overcame the feeling of being a displaced Southerner—a situation wittily captured in 'Buildings and Grounds'— and returned to Virginia in 1971 when he began teaching at American University in DC, in 1977

building a house on his family farm in Lincoln. It is not surprising then that the majority of the poems in his three collections, *The Horse Show at Midnight* (Baton Rouge, La., 1966), *An Afternoon of Pocket Billiards* (Salt Lake City, Utah., 1975), and *The Flying Circus* (Baton Rouge, 1985)— which won the Pulitzer Prize—grow out of his experience in this pastoral setting. He captures the visual texture and the rhythm of the changing seasons as well as the subtle tensions and continuities of relationships within families and between generations, the latter most poignantly in 'At the Swings', centred on his interactions with his sons as his wife's mother is dying of cancer. His poetry is notable for its wit, as in his parodies of *Bly, James *Dickey, and others in his first volume, and his epigraph 'Divorce'; for the chilling detail with which he captures the violence inherent in farm life, as in 'Barbed Wire', on the death of a frightened horse; and for finding metaphors from farming and horse-training which embody the elements of craft and grace that characterize the writing of poems, as in 'The Flying Change'. [RMcP

TEASDALE, Sara (1884–1933), was born in St Louis, Missouri. The child of elderly, over-protective parents, the delicate Teasdale was raised in an atmosphere of Victorian constraint. She moved to New York, and in 1914 married businessman Ernst Felsinger whom she divorced in 1929. Her poetic output declined during the 1920s and she became increasingly depressed and reclusive until, in 1933, she committed suicide.

Influenced by the work of Sappho, Christina Rossetti, Dickinson, and later *Yeats, but curiously unaffected by contemporary movements, Teasdale developed as a skilled lyricist. Her fragile, musical verse, usually in rhymed quatrains, originally dealt with idealized love and beauty, but later focused on death. *Love Songs* (1917) brought her international recognition and a Columbia (now Pulitzer) Poetry Prize. Poems in *Flame and Shadow* (1920), *Dark of the Moon* (1926), and the posthumously published *Strange Victory* (1933) illustrate Teasdale's artistic maturity and growing fascination with death.

The Collected Poems of Sara Teasdale (New York, 1937) is widely available; *Mirror of the Heart: Poems of Sara Teasdale* (New York, 1984) includes nearly seventy previously uncollected or unpublished poems. See also Margaret Haley Carpenter's *Sara Teasdale: A Biography* (New York, 1960), William Drake's *Sara Teasdale: Woman and Poet* (San Francisco, 1979), and Carol B. Schoen's critical study, *Sara Teasdale* (Boston, 1986). [EDF

TESSIMOND, A(rthur) S(eymour) J(ohn) (1902–62), was born in Birkenhead, an only child. Educated at Charterhouse, he refused to re-attend at the age of 16, running away to London—to return home in a fortnight. A year later he went to Liverpool University, after which he moved to London, working in bookshops then settling down as an advertising copywriter. During the Second World War, deciding he would be a useless soldier, dangerous to the cause, he went into hiding, only to find later that he was unfit to fight. Inheriting £4,000 from his father in 1945, he spent half on various psychoanalysts, the rest on his night-life. In later years he underwent shock treatment, which may have contributed to the brain haemorrhage from which he died.

The early influence of *Imagism, and, for all his depressive tendencies, an exhilaration with form, give his work a honed and memorable succinctness and clarity—which produces some delightful humour, as in 'Pets'. Night-lifer, loner, *flâneur*, Tessimond is an excellent recorder of the general, of the stereotypes of the city. His 'Man in the Bowler Hat', 'The British' and 'Cats: II' are justly in many anthologies, especially for schools. He also has a genre of conversation-poems, such as the fine 'Middle-aged Conversation', that capture succinctly his sense of the melancholy of existence.

Three volumes were published during his life (all London): *The Walls of Glass* (1934): *Voices in a Giant City* (1947), and *Selection* (1958). Three posthumous collections, ed. Hubert Nicholson, have appeared from Reading: *Not Love Perhaps* . . . (1978), *Morning Meeting* (1980), and finally *The Collected Poems*, with translations from

Jacques Prévert (1985), containing previously uncollected poems. [PD

THESEN, Sharon (1946–), was born in Saskatchewan and went to school in Prince George, British Columbia, a northern pulp-mill town curiously full of poets. She studied poetry with Robin Blaser at Simon Fraser University, and spent some years teaching at a community college in North Vancouver.

She published four books in the 1980s, and was hailed as a bright lyric poet. Her voice is sweet and ironic at the same time: a poem is likely to allude to classical literature or recent philosophy, but also to offer the energy of colloquial quips. A singular book is the sequence called *Confabulations: Poems for Malcolm Lowry* (Lantzville, BC, 1984). Thesen lets the poem range from *Lowry's Vancouver home, forward to England, back to Mexico, the pronouns sliding through all persons as she exhibits the struggle between the talent to compose and the urge towards drunkenness. It is an ambitious poem, and like those of Lowry, sometimes more intelligent than beautiful.

More successful are Thesen's poems about being a woman in the late twentieth century. They are filled with rueful delight and wisdom's pain; not overtly feminist, their images present a woman's life in writing, including its political necessities. A volume of selected poems, *The Pangs of Sunday* (Toronto) was published in 1990. [GHB

This Quarter (1925–32). Founded by Ernest Walsh and edited by him and others, *This Quarter* was published from various European cities, and was irregular in its appearances. Walsh had a habit of disappearing with such properties as James *Joyce's 'Shem' chapter from *Work in Progress* (which he duly published), and then reappearing only after alarmingly long intervals. The magazine was largely published in honour of Ezra *Pound, who printed various fragments in it. The work of Natalie Barney and Gertrude *Stein also appeared in its pages. Despite its championship of Pound it was less concerned with poetry than the other magazines in its expatriate group. See *The Little Magazine* (New York, 1947), by F. Hoffman, C. Allen, and C. Ulrich. [MS-S

THOMAS, D(onald) M(ichael) (1935–), was born in Redruth, Cornwall, and educated at New College, Oxford. He was senior lecturer in English at Hereford College, 1964–78.

D. M. Thomas's obsessions are plain: love, death, and place. From his earliest work sexual fantasy is to the fore, sometimes in a violent context. Greater tenderness is apparent in poems of familial love—'The Journey' (*Love and Other Deaths*, London, 1975) addresses the poet's mother: 'we are water and moor | And far journeyers together. Whatever else we are'—and in dealing with his Cornish inheritance in 'For Doll Pentreath', an elegy for the last native Cornish speaker. There is a strong narrative element in his work, incorporating dream and myth (as in 'Diary of a Myth Boy' and 'The Dream Game' from *The Honeymoon Voyage*, London, 1978). In recent years much of Thomas's energy has been applied to fiction (though he disputes the separation of forms) and translation.

The Bronze Horseman and other Poems by Pushkin appeared in 1981 (London and New York), *Selected Poems* in 1983 (London and New York), *The Puberty Tree: New and Selected Poems* in 1992 (Newcastle upon Tyne), and an autobiography, *Memories and Hallucinations* in 1988 (London and New York). Thomas's novels include *The White Hotel* (1981) and *Ararat* (1983). [SO'B

THOMAS, Dylan (1914–53), was born in Swansea. He worked for a short time as a junior reporter on the *South Wales Evening Post*, then moved to London to embark on a literary career. His first book of poems, *Eighteen Poems*, was published in 1934. Thomas's poetry, although it has attracted admiration and adulation—increased in some of his hearers to a state of worship by the booming bardic readings he gave in public—has also seemed to some formless, incoherent, and over-wordy. When the poems are analysed, however, it is clear that the charge of formlessness must be dropped. He worked out his stanzas very carefully, with exact syllable-counts for the lines so that they correspond in each stanza. Likewise, the rhymes are scrupulously observed—though they are very unusual rhymes. Some rely on assonance ('Heaven/pheasants'), some are 'vowel-rhymes' ('kind/night'), and some are assonantal vowel-rhymes ('planets/valley'), while in the same poem comparatively conventional rhymes can occur ('fires/friars'). Since the rhymes are usually separated from one another by intervening lines, they are seldom obvious. His habit of declaiming the poems non-stop, running on from line to line and stanza to stanza, increased the impression of formlessness.

Of course the poems are rhetorical, and can sometimes sound like a preacher in full flow—it has been suggested that Thomas's remembrances of chapel sermons played their part—but they also have originality and beauty, which his marvellous readings displayed to advantage. The main impetus came from Thomas's romanticized, idealized childhood; 'Fern Hill', one of his greatest poems, is entirely about this, a rustic idyll that has nothing to do with the respectabilities of lower-middle-class Swansea (his father was a schoolmaster) but everything to do with summer holidays in the country. 'The ball I threw while playing in the park | Has not yet reached the ground', as he wrote in 'Should lanterns shine'. In other words, his childhood was present to him at all times, a 'land of lost content'.

Thomas could also write much tighter, more conventional, verse. 'In my craft or sullen art' is a good example of this, and so is the famous villanelle on the death of his father, 'Do not go gentle into that good night'. These poems are exceptional, as they contain none of the theatricality and posturing that one finds in the more flamboyant pieces. The effort that went into the longer poems is legendary—there are supposed to be more than 300 drafts of 'Fern Hill'—and this is even more remarkable when one considers his life-style, which was that of an alcoholic, a talkative and witty one, but irreclaimable.

Thomas did not produce a huge body of

work; there are only ninety-nine poems in his *Collected Poems*, two of them added posthumously by the editors. There is also the radio play *Under Milk Wood* (New York and London, 1954). He died, though, just before he was 40, and a lot of his time was taken up by his work for the BBC (free-lance and as a member of the staff), by writing short stories and other prose pieces, and by the never-ending drunkenness.

Thomas's poems are full, not so much of 'the most heterogeneous ideas yoked by violence together' (Dr Johnson's description of metaphysical verse), but of heterogeneous *images*, from books as well as from life. He also used clichés ('animals thick as thieves') and unexpected metonymy ('tangled with chirrup and fruit'). Some epithets seem to be there for surprise value only—'the religious wind'. There is lurking Blake—'worms' are everywhere—and the repetitive key-words can be wearisome— 'green', 'bones', 'marrow', 'thighs', etc. Although Thomas makes great use of the countryside and its creatures he was, as he confessed, unmoved by such things. In the poems, however, they work well (like the heron on Sir John's Hill). In the first two books there are good lines ('I see the boys of summer in their ruin'—paunchy, middle-aged men lying on the beach, as he later explained) and some good poems; mostly the more straightforward ones ('The force that through the green fuse', 'The hand that signed the paper'), but also some that are more Dionysiac ('If I were tickled by the rub of love', 'Especially when the October wind', and 'Light breaks where no sun shines'). But he could also, at all stages of his career, write extremely bad individual lines ('His mother's womb had a tongue that lapped up blood').

The later poems include some that are undistinguished—and one long failure, 'The ballad of the long-legged bait'—but they also include some that could be called great, by most standards: 'Fern Hill', 'Over Sir John's Hill', 'In my craft or sullen art', 'Do not go gentle into that good night', 'Poem in October', 'In the White Giant's Thigh', and 'Elegy'. Just a few are untypical but rewarding: 'Now', 'Paper and stick'. In general, the later verse is less compact and dra-

matic, easier to get on with, and a good deal more moving in human terms. See *The Poems of Dylan Thomas*, ed. Daniel Jones (London and New York, 1971); also Paul Ferris's biography (London, 1977) and Constantine FitzGibbon's edition of the Letters (London, 1966).   [GE

THOMAS, Edward (1878–1917). Edward Thomas wrote all his poems in the last two-and-a-half years of his life. In the previous sixteen years he had published thirty volumes of topography, biography, criticism, and belles-lettres, compiled sixteen editions and anthologies, and produced over a million-and-a-half words of reviews. The poetry came in a burst of creative activity; the prose was soul-destroying. It kept him, he said, 'so confoundedly busy I feel as if the back of my head would come out'.

Relatively little of the prose has stood the test of time. Although some titles (the best of them is *The South Country*) were carried back into print on the wave of interest in turn-of-the-century rural writers which broke across popular taste in the 1970s, the majority are too deeply bogged down in antiquated locutions and attitudes to attract more than specialist interest. What they represent is generally cherished and admired: stable country values in the moment before they were destroyed by the First World War; but in substance and detail their pastoralism seems not so much remote as fusty.

Thomas's poems, on the other hand, embody similar virtues but manage to wrestle them free from late Victorian encumbrances—and in the years since Philip *Larkin and other writers associated with the *Movement began to espouse a specifically English poetic line, their stock has risen steadily. For all their occasional lapses (they were written hurriedly) and traces of an earlier idiom (inverted syntax, sweetly sentimental ruralism), they are now clearly and rightly established as part of the tradition of English pastoral lyricism which runs forward from Wordsworth through *Hardy and *Housman to Larkin himself.

The strength of Thomas's poems lies in their ability to enact with great subtlety and discretion the emergence of a recognizably modern sensibility. More profoundly than his contemporary *Georgians (whom he resembles in many superficial respects), more often and more steadily than Ivor *Gurney, his poems function as a hinge between old and new worlds. Their account of country things (in 'Lob', for instance) itemizes particular idioms as well as particular ways of life, but their reflections on time and its passing describe how these things are destroyed; their intelligent shyness charts the growth of a familiar self-consciousness; and their skilful testing of time-honoured forms—notably their use of long, pensive sentences to conduct the rhythm of a thinking voice through the whole length of a poem—challenges received technical conventions and looks forward to the more radical experiments of the modernists.

The material for Thomas's lyrics and little dramas of displacement came directly from his own experience. Born in Lambeth, south London, he was the eldest son of 'mainly Welsh' parents whose principle adult sense of their homeland was nostalgia. As a town-boy Thomas was nostalgic for the nearer country of southern England too, and by the time he came to the end of his career at Saint Paul's school in Hammersmith he had begun writing essays and articles celebrating his rural walks and expeditions. His first collection of these pieces, *The Woodland Life*, appeared when he was 19.

Before taking his degree at Oxford (in 1900) he had married Helen, the daughter of his early mentor James Ashcroft Noble, had a son, and resolved to live by his pen. The decision brought him freedom of a desperately restricted kind, and he spent most of the next fourteen years on a treadmill of hack-work, increasingly prone to depression, occasionally contemplating suicide, and painfully aware that he had 'lost his way'. Various Georgian friends (W. H. *Davies, Walter *de la Mare) suggested that he try writing poems, but Thomas was too far gone in self-doubt to make the attempt. When he did, it was only by force of accident, as well as intervention. Robert *Frost, whose *North of Boston* Thomas had reviewed enthusiastically, urged him to try his hand at precisely the same time as

war broke out, and this advice from a poet he respected more than most others living, combined with the sense of danger which suddenly clouded everything he valued, finally persuaded him.

Thomas wrote his first poem in December 1914 and his last—his one hundred and forty-third—shortly before he was killed at Arras on 9 April 1917, when he was 39. In a sense they are all war poems, and not only because they were all written after the outbreak of war. Sometimes openly—in the Frost-like dramatic dialogue 'As the Team's Head-brass'—they chronicle the impact of the fighting in France on the Home Front; sometimes obliquely—in 'The Green Roads'—they sketch the unique tenuousness of life in wartime; sometimes with delicate lyric yearning—in 'Lights Out'—they record the hope and fear of an individual soldier expecting to die. Whatever their form, their tone is strikingly consistent. When Thomas began writing poems his voice was already fully mature, and although for many years after his death he was regarded as a 'poet's poet', the careful scrutiny of his gaze, the tact of his rhythms, and the deftness with which he assimilates large social and political issues into a delicate lyric framework, have meant that he has gradually become one of the most generally admired, as well as one of the most influential poets of the century.

See *The Collected Poems of Edward Thomas*, ed. and introduced by R. George Thomas (Oxford, 1978). There is a biography by R. George Thomas (Oxford, 1985) and interesting memoirs by Helen Thomas (*As It Was*, London, 1926; *World Without End*, London, 1935) and Eleanor Farjeon (*Edward Thomas: The Last Four Years*, Oxford, 1958). The Helen Thomas memoirs can be had in a combined edition, *Under Storm's Wing* (Manchester, 1988).   [AM

THOMAS, Ivor. See PERFORMANCE POETRY.

THOMAS, R(onald) S(tuart) (1913–), was born in Cardiff and brought up and educated in Holyhead. His parents were not Welsh-speaking, though it is probable that his father had some Welsh as a child but lost it after being sent to sea as an apprentice at 16. However, through chance encounters while a classics student at the University College of North Wales, Bangor, Thomas learnt that his father's mother was Welsh-speaking, and this discovery encouraged what had already become his own intention to learn the language. The intention became a commitment which developed while he trained in theology at St Michael's College, Llandaff.

Thomas's relationship to the language and the Welsh literary tradition is central to an understanding of his growth as a poet. Although it was important for him to speak Welsh in order to communicate, as an Anglican priest, with his first parishioners—in Denbighshire and Flintshire between 1936 and 1942—the ability to do so enabled him to fulfil what he had come to regard as 'the necessary qualifications of a truly Anglo-Welsh writer, namely that he should steep himself in all things Welsh to justify the hyphen'. That hyphen—a contentious mark of unease, ambivalence, and intense, agitated enquiry—has in many ways proved to be the mainspring of Thomas's poetic career, in that for him it can never entirely disappear. Although much of his prose, including the untranslated autobiography *Neb* (no-one / anyone) and his lecture on the spiritual Good Place 'Abercuawg', has been written in Welsh, he has only been able to write poetry in his mother tongue, since it requires a naturalness and instinctiveness he realizes he cannot achieve in a second language. This dilemma has had a profound effect on his work as a whole.

Thomas's first collection from an English publisher, *Song at the Year's Turning*, was published in 1955, the year after his move to the parish of Eglwysfach. It contained poems selected from his first two volumes privately printed in Wales—*The Stones of the Field* (1946) and *An Acre of Land* (1952)—as well as *The Minister* (1953), a long radio poem for several voices. With this work Thomas achieved a reputation for addressing the harsh realities of the depopulated hill country in a verse which is uncompromisingly austere and rooted in an unforgiving landscape. The scenic emptiness and arid conditions are matched by an appalled sense of men-

tal vacancy and emotional impoverishment in the inhabitants. 'A Peasant', the first poem to introduce the archetypal peasant farmer Iago Prytherch, sets the tone of what is to come although its stately, almost Yeatsian, rhetoric and sonorous closing couplet are soon to be replaced in Thomas's stronger poems by harsher cadences, more arbitrary line-breaks, and a conspicuous absence of consoling rhymes. In these 'bleak litanies' (to borrow a title from one of the most recent poems) lives and landscapes become a focus of Thomas's entirely unsentimental compassion for the individual and his often bitter scorn and resentment of the dehumanizing social conditions which have cut a community off from the tradition which would have given its life meaning. The abiding issue remains implicit in the priest's understanding of the bald question asked in 'Here'—'Does no God hear when I pray?'—while the last line of 'Kneeling' offers the provisional, loaded answer which recurs in all Thomas's poetry, with varying degrees of patience, up to the present: 'The meaning is in the waiting.'

In the period between 1955 and 1968 Thomas continued to work at these themes, though with increasing evidence of metaphysical speculation and inner debate developing alongside the more earth-bound poems of character and place. The main volumes of this period are *Poetry for Supper* (1958), *Tares* (1961), *The Bread of Truth* (1963) *Pieta* (1966), and *Not that he Brought Flowers* (1968).

In 1967 Thomas moved to the parish of Aberdaron on the Lleyn Peninsula, and in the work which followed there has been a distinct change of style. This is evident at first in the watershed volume *H'm* (1972) with its resonant abstraction, occasionally apocalyptic imagery not a little reminiscent of Ted *Hughes's *Crow*, and its experimentation with indented lines under the conscious influence of William Carlos *Williams. In *Laboratories of the Spirit* (1975) and *Frequencies* (1978), with a vocabulary often drawn from mechanics, physics, and biology, he continues to contend with 'the disposer of the issues | of life', exploring interior worlds of private doubt in the search for consolation. As in the earlier work, he remains waiting 'somewhere between faith and doubt | for the echoes of arrival', while often, even in the same poem, pursuing a protean *deus absconditus*. There has been much debate about this development. Some see him as having abandoned the rocky acres for a nebulous cosmos, and a firm footing in metaphor for an inconclusive and often prosaic space-walking. Others regard his recent work as his finest, as an enlargement of his concerns and a refinement of his technique. What is certainly interesting is that, as the poetry has moved away from its precise Welsh location, and with his retirement from the Church in 1978, Thomas has become increasingly active as a public figure in nationalist politics. It is as if direct political involvement has eased the tension between his imagination and his conscience, and resulted in the achievement of a greater poise, a more resonant austerity.

Thomas's most recent collections are *Experimenting with an Amen* (1986), *The Echoes Return Slow* (1988), *Counterpoint* (Newcastle upon Tyne, 1990), and *Mass for Hard Times* (Newcastle upon Tyne, 1992). His *Selected Poems: 1946–1968* (Newcastle upon Tyne, 1986), *Later Poems 1972–1982* (London, 1983), and *Selected Prose* (Bridgend, 1986) are currently available, along with *Complete Poems* (London) which was published to coincide with his eightieth birthday in 1993. An extensive and revealing interview, conducted by Ned Thomas, appeared in the Welsh Internationalist magazine *Planet*, 80 (Aberystwyth, 1990). R. S. Thomas received the Queen's Gold Medal for Poetry in 1964.   [JM

THOMPSON, John (Michael) (1938–76), was born in Manchester, England. His father died during the Second World War. His mother remarried and moved to Australia. Thompson was educated at Manchester Grammar School and the University of Sheffield. After completing compulsory military service in 1960, he became a graduate student at Michigan State University. He obtained a Ph.D in comparative literature in 1966, with a thesis on the recent poetry of René Char. Among those on his guidance committee was A. J. M. *Smith.

Between 1966 and 1976 Thompson taught English and American literature and creative-writing classes at Mount Allison University, Sackville, New Brunswick. During the three years following publication of *At the Edge of the Chopping There Are No Secrets* (Toronto, 1973), Thompson's marriage ended in separation, he experienced depression and mental instability, began drinking heavily, and suffered the loss through fire of his old farmhouse on the Tantramar Marshes. Early in 1976 he died in a coma judged to have been accidentally induced by medication and alcohol. *Stilt Jack* (Toronto), a collection of thirty-eight *ghazals* which Thompson completed just before his death, was published in 1978.

Thompson is considered one of the most important Canadian poets of the 1970s. *Atwood, Phyllis *Webb, D. G. *Jones, and Douglas *Lochhead have all written poems alluding to him, as have numbers of other Canadian poets. Thompson's first book, written in free verse, with frequent stepped lines, is stylistically related to the poems of Denise *Levertov. Like Char, Thompson's intent was to make language synonymous with the natural existence of such things as stones, birds, and fish, transforming all into a state of archetypal perfection. *Stilt Jack* persists in this ambition, but also phrases those recoils, lapses, and imperfections inevitably attendant upon it. The apparent obscurity of *Stilt Jack* and its radical parataxis are the result of the collection's extraordinary allusiveness. *Yeats, Char, *Roethke, Wallace *Stevens, and Emily Dickinson are among the poets engaged. *Hamlet* and *King Lear* are the sources of several defining lines. One of the poet's personae is Orestes. *Stilt Jack* may be read as the record of a Jungian quest for individuation and as an attempt to recover and personally integrate one interpretation of western poetic tradition.

See also *Sea Run: Notes on John Thompson's Stilt Jack* (Antigonish, Nova Scotia, 1986), by Peter Sanger.   [PMS

THOMSON, Derick (1921–) also known as Ruaraidh MacThómais, belongs to the island of Lewis. His father was a headmaster and a published Gaelic poet. After completing his schooling at the Nicolson Institute, Stornoway, he attended Aberdeen and Cambridge universities. Deciding to pursue an academic career in Celtic he held, successively, an assistantship at Edinburgh, a lectureship at Glasgow, a readership at Aberdeen, and finally the chair of Celtic at Glasgow (1964–91). He has been an active Gaelic publisher, writer, scholar, critic, and publicist. He was co-founder and subsequently editor of *Gairm*, the Gaelic literary quarterly (1950–)

Thomson was one of the first to exploit the freedom of form and subject won for Gaelic poetry by Sorley *MacLean. His own most important innovation has been at the metrical-formal level, where he has explored and developed the possibilities of free verse in the Gaelic context. At the thematic level his verse shows a satisfying consistency and sense of purpose. He delights in irony, and his poetry is acute, honed, and sometimes barbed. His most deeply pondered themes are alienation and fragmentation, as found embedded in the personal experience of émigré Gaels, and in the breakup of traditional Gaelic community life. In his more recent collections Scottish nationalism has also been a strategic concern.

Thomson's collections of poetry, from *An Dealbh Briste* ('The Broken Image': Edinburgh, 1951) to the most recent, contain English versions of some poems. In *Creachadh na Clàrsaich/Plundering the Harp* (Edinburgh, 1982), which is in effect his collected poems for the years from 1940 to 1980, English translations have been supplied throughout. D. MacAulay's bilingual anthology *Nua-bhàrdachd Ghàidhlig/Modern Scottish Gaelic Poems* (Edinburgh, 1976) contains a selection and critical introduction.

[WG

THORPE, Adam (1956–), was born in Paris, and brought up in Beirut, Calcutta, Cameroon, and the south of England. After graduating from Magdalen College, Oxford, in 1979, he founded Equinox Travelling Theatre, touring villages with actors, puppets, and mime. In 1984 he won the Time Out Mime Street Entertainer of the

Year Award, and he taught in London from 1983 until moving to France to complete his first novel, *Ulverton* (London 1992).

Thorpe's first full-length verse collection, *Mornings in the Baltic* (London, 1988), reflects a wide range of subjects presented through a series of first-person voices, both autobiographical and historical. His best poems bring together very different types of experience with something of a Flaubertian attention to detail and sensitivity to illusion. His second volume, *Meeting Montaigne* (London, 1990), is shorter, more sombre and restrained, gesturing towards Dante's *Inferno* as a model for London life, while, at the same time, looking to the family and the artistic traditions of France as sources of consolation.

For discussions of his work see Peter Robinson's review in *Poetry Durham*, 22 (Durham, 1989) and an interview with Mark Wormald in *Oxford Poetry*, 5: 2 (Oxford, 1990).   [CLB

THUMBOO, Edwin Nadason (1933–), was born in Singapore and read English at the then University of Malaya. In 1967 he joined the University of Singapore, now the National University of Singapore, where he is still head of the department of English language and literature. He took his Ph.D there, and rose to become a full professor in 1979, serving also as dean of the faculty of arts and social sciences until late 1991.

His three volumes of poetry have established him as the Republic's unofficial poet laureate. Since the early 1970s Thumboo has had more influence over the course of Singapore writing than any other individual. *Rib Of Earth* (1956), *Gods Can Die* (1977), and *Ulysses By The Merlion* (1979—all Singapore) are marked by courageous social and political statement. Thumboo's verse has a strong sense of the nascent history of an emerging nation struggling to find new roots out of the soil of colonialism and a diverse multiracial immigrant culture. *Gods* and *Ulysses* won the National Book Development Council of Singapore Award for poetry in 1978 and 1980.   [KBS

THWAITE, Anthony (Simon) (1930–), was born in Chester, the son of a bank employee, and spent his childhood in Yorkshire. After four wartime years in the USA he finished at Kingswood School and did his national service, going up to Christ Church, Oxford, in 1952. From the time of his first lectureship at Tokyo University (1955–7), Thwaite combined periods of academic life with literary and media work. He was a producer with the BBC from 1957 to 1962, literary editor of the *Listener* (1962–5) and of the *New Statesman* (1968–72), and co-editor of *Encounter* from 1973 till 1985; in the intervals he was assistant professor of English at the University of Libya (1965–7) and visiting professor at the University of Kuwait (1974), and in 1985 returned to Tokyo University for a year as Japan Foundation Fellow. He has been a director of André Deutsch Ltd since 1986.

His first two collections of poetry, *Home Truths* (1957) and *The Owl in the Tree* (1963), shared the Empsonian tone, common sense, and emotional empiricism of the *Movement writers, particularly *Larkin ('Death of a Rat', 'Mr Cooper', 'Manhood End'). Thwaite's archaeological and cultural interests were broad, though, and in *The Stones of Emptiness* (1967), *Inscriptions* (1973), and *New Confessions* (1974) he developed a resourceful historical imagination ('The Letters of Synesius', 'Monologue in the Valley of the Kings').

The mastery of the dramatic monologue which Thwaite demonstrated in these volumes was suspended in the more anecdotal *A Portion for Foxes* (1977) but persuasively displayed once again in *Victorian Voices* (1980). In the 1980s two collected editions followed—*Poems 1953–1983* (London, 1984) and *Poems 1953–1988* (London, 1989)—with *Letter from Tokyo* (London, 1987) renewing Thwaite's engaging tussle with Japan.

The qualities of civil accessibility, curiosity, and even-handedness which distinguish Thwaite's poetry have also been characteristic of his work as critic, reviewer, and editor, as travel-writer, as broadcaster, and (in 1986) as chairman of the Booker Prize panel of judges. He edited Philip Larkin's *Collected Poems* in 1988 and his *Selected Letters* in 1992. His wife Ann is a well-known biographer and children's writer.

[MHu

TIETJENS, Eunice (1884–1944), was born in Chicago, her mother a European-trained artist, and moved easily among the theatre and bohemian crowd associated with the Chicago Renaissance, friend of the Floyd Dells and Sara *Teasdale. She travelled and lived for a while in the Orient, which resulted in *Profiles of China: Sketches in Free Verse of People and Things Seen in the Interior* (1917), subsequently complemented by *Profiles from Home* (1925) and several prose works, including *Japan, Korea, and Formosa* (1924) and *China* (1930). In 1913 Tietjens became Harriet Monroe's assistant at *Poetry magazine, but her two collections of verse on personal themes, *Body and Raiment* (1919) and *Leaves in Windy Weather* (1929), demonstrate scant originality. In the 1930s she moved permanently to Miami with her second husband, where she was active in various women's clubs, lecturing and teaching, although her literary energies were devoted to prose, producing five children's books and an autobiography, *World at My Shoulder* (1938).

No biography of Tietjens exists, and her poetry has virtually disappeared, although nine of her poems are in *The Home Book of Modern Verse*, ed. Burton Egbert Stevenson (New York, 1963).

[EB

TILLER, Terence (Rogers) (1916–87), was born in Cornwall and educated at Latymer Upper School, Hammersmith, and Jesus College, Cambridge. From 1939 to 1946 he taught at Fuad I University in Cairo, where he was associated with *Personal Landscape* (See DESERT POETS) and with Bernard *Spencer, Lawrence *Durrell, and other writers exiled in Egypt by the Second World War. After the war he worked as a producer with the BBC.

Poems (1941) was followed by *The Inward Animal* (1943) and *Unarm Eros* (1947—all London), his most satisfying book. Since 1947 Tiller has produced only three volumes of poetry, *Reading a Medal* (1957), *Notes for a Myth* (1968), and *The Singing Mesh* (1979—all London), the last of which he said contained his final poems.

His poetry is introspective and concerned with the remoteness of the self within the individual and the relationship of the self to that which is other. Traditional in form and imagery, it is enigmatic and allusive, owing much to the metaphysical poets and to William *Empson; but, particularly in the later books, the linguistic complexity seems to stand between the reader and any emotional impact the poetry might have. Tiller is best in his Egyptian poems, where there is a fruitful interplay between the figurative and the actual. [ATT

TILLINGHAST, Richard (1940–), was born in Memphis, Tennessee, and educated at the University of the South (Sewanee) and at Harvard, where he studied with Robert *Lowell. The author of three books of poems, Tillinghast has taught at Harvard and Berkeley and currently directs the writing programme at the University of Michigan at Ann Arbor.

The early poems in Tillinghast's first volume, *Sleep Watch* (Middletown, Conn., 1969) reflect both the poet's Southern roots and the influence of such poets as Allen *Tate, but the most characteristic work in this book is more casual: evocative phrases float in a loose syntax. Tillinghast's later volumes, *The Knife and Other Poems* (1980) and *Our Flag Was Still There* (1984—both Middletown), venture beyond the contingencies of self and towards history, but a wistful, elegiac, and tentative tone remains. Poems bear witness to both the Vietnam War and the Civil War, through the vicarious filter of the poet's life. 'Sewanee in Ruins', perhaps this poet's most ambitious sequence, traces the fortunes of the Sewanee campus from 1860 to the present (1983). [RHa

TIPPING, Richard Kelly (1949–), while still an undergraduate in his native Adelaide, edited the little magazine *Mok*, which was influential on the so-called *Generation of '68. Apart from travel, he has lived mostly in Sydney or Adelaide, and now teaches media studies at the University of Newcastle, New South Wales. The range of his work keeps faith with the countercultural programme of the Sixties: a productive sculptor and photographer, video- and filmmaker, he also plays a selection of little-practised instruments. *Signs of Australia* (1982) illustrates his devotion to visual puns and found poems.

The enduring verse from Tipping's first two volumes is minimalist, concatenating gently reworked clichés with haiku-like *aperçus*. The overtly political poems (some composed in adolescence) now seem derivative, the attempts to sing himself and his times, portentous. *Nearer by Far* (1986) gainsays his early acclaim as an Australian 'revolutionary' poet. It includes engaging poems on the bizarreries of the moment, but discursive and satirical themes make for bathos. Tipping's work always seems more found than made.

Three volumes, *Soft Riots* (1972), *Domestic Hardcore* (1975), and *Nearer by Far* (1986), have all been published by University of Queensland Press, St Lucia. [CP

TODD, Ruthven (1914–78), was born in Edinburgh and educated at Fettes School and Edinburgh College of Art. Before the Second World War he worked at various trades, including that of farm labourer, and spent time in the Orkneys. His work appeared in Julian *Symons's magazine, *Twentieth Century Verse*, and in the first selection of John *Lehmann's *Poets of Tomorrow* (1939). *Until Now* (London, 1942) brought together most of the poems he had written up to that time. *The Acreage of the Heart* (Glasgow, 1943) and *Planet in My Hand* (London, 1946) contained rather few new poems; but, after he had emigrated to America in 1947 he wrote more steadily until 1956, the year of the last poem in his final, retrospective volume, *Garland for a Winter Solstice* (London and Boston, 1962). His career as an art critic had already been established with his collection of essays *Tracks in the Snow* (London and New York, 1946). He later went to live in Spain.

Todd's best poems were written before 1939 and are personal rather than political. They measure up to his own contention that they try merely to be poems and to be simple. His political poems are marred by an ill-adapted Audenesque rhetoric; and there is little sense of emotional involvement in the poems he wrote in America. [ATT

TOLSON, Melvin B. (1898?–1966), was born in Moberley, Missouri. He attended Fisk University, took a BA with honours from Lincoln University in Pennsylvania in 1923, and an MA from Columbia University in New York City in 1940. He began his working life as a manual labourer, but became an academic when he taught at Wiley College in Marshall, Texas, from 1924 to 1947. He continued his career at Langston University, in Langston, Oklahoma, from 1947 to 1965, where he was mayor of the city from 1952 to 1958. His last post was at Tuskegee Institute during the final two years of his life.

Tolson's first book was *Rendezvous with America* (1944) which contained protean and technically various poems, including some written in traditional forms and others in experimental prose patterns. It was ignored by the critics. *Libretto for the Republic of Liberia* (New York and London, 1953) got considerably more notice and resulted in Tolson's being appointed poet laureate of the Republic of Liberia. *Harlem Gallery: Book One, The Curator* (1965) had been planned as an epic in five parts, but the poet's premature death intervened. This book was a fusion of Tolson's earlier formal style with a more idiomatic expression derived from the world of jazz.

A Gallery of Harlem (New York and London, 1979) was made up of earlier and, some maintain, livelier versions of the poems in *Harlem Gallery*. In the late 1930s and early 1940s Tolson wrote a column for the Washington *Tribune*; these pieces were gathered posthumously as *Caviar and Cabbages* in 1984. A critical work by Mariann Russell, *Melvin B. Tolson's Harlem Gallery*, appeared in 1980, and in 1984 Robert M. Farnsworth published *Melvin B. Tolson: Plain Talk and Poetic Prophecy*. Over the years Tolson's has been a steady and steadying influence in Afro-American literature. [LT

TOMLINSON, Charles (1927–), was born in Stoke-on-Trent and went to Queens' College, Cambridge, where he studied with Donald *Davie. His reputation was first established in the USA, where his collection *Seeing Is Believing* appeared in 1958, two years before the British

edition. Since then Tomlinson has published numerous individual books, and his *Collected Poems* (Oxford, 1985). He has taught at the University of Bristol since 1957, where he was made professor of English Literature in 1982.

Tomlinson's work has been somewhat against the tide of contemporary British poetry. His 1961 essay 'Poetry Today' took issue with the 1950s poetry of the *Movement, and argued instead for poets such as Basil *Bunting and Hugh *MacDiarmid. His own early verse was influenced by the prosody of poets such as the Italian Giuseppe Ungaretti and the Americans Wallace *Stevens and William Carlos *Williams. However, his debt to modern American, Italian, or French poetry has been rather overestimated. His essential sense of the 'otherness' of things in the visible world is nearest in spirit to the native English meditative tradition of Wordsworth and Coleridge. He has written: 'In both graphic and poetic art, I like something lucid surrounded by something mysterious'. His poetry accommodates both the exotic and the local and this has led him to be described variously as both Augustan and modernist, the latter through his co-authorship of the multilingual *Renga: A Chain of Poems* (Harmondsworth, 1979) with Octavio Paz, Jacques Roubaud, Edoardo Sanguineti.

Tomlinson's *Collected Poems* provides evidence of his range: from poems linking chance encounters between things seen in his local Gloucestershire landscape, to descriptive pieces about travels in the United States, France, Mexico, and Italy. Tomlinson also writes on music, historical situations, and, in *The Way In* (1974), on his youth in the Potteries. His poems since his *Collected Poems*, gathered in *The Return* (1987), *Annunciations* (1989), and *The Door in the Wall* (1992—all Oxford) show a deepening religious sense.

Tomlinson is also an artist and has written poems on painters, including Cézanne and Constable. His own graphic works are executed in surrealist decalcomania, consisting of black gouache pressed between two sheets. An Arts Council touring exhibition of his work was launched at the Hayward Gallery in 1978, later published as *Eden*.

Tomlinson has also written critical prose and edited the *Oxford Book of Verse in English Transla-tion* (1980). He has translated poets, including Tyutchev, Machado, Vallejo, Paz, and Ungaretti, collected in *Translations* (Oxford, 1983). [JDB

TONKS, Rosemary (1932–), was born in Lon-don and educated at Wentworth School, from which she was expelled at the age of 16. In the same year she published her first book, a chil-dren's adventure-story. She married at 19 and worked for a time as poetry reviewer for the BBC European Service. She has written three novels, the most recent being *The Halt During the Chase* (1972), and two collections of poems, *Notes on Cafés and Bedrooms* (London, 1963) and *Iliad of Broken Sentences* (London, 1967).

Reflecting her early travels in Europe and the Middle East, her usual poetic territory is the seedy underworld of the modern city, with its shifting, nomadic population of survivors. The angle of vision is that of the *flâneur*, Baudlairean but more good-humoured than splenetic. If there is a youthful naïveté about her celebra-tions of the louche and derelict, she can also be attractively self-mocking. Her imagery, often near-surreal, is accessible and vivid. Since con-verting to evangelical Christianity in the early Seventies, she has ceased to publish. [CAR

TOOMER, Jean (Eugene) (1894–1986), was born in Washington, DC, and raised there by his divorced mother in the home of his maternal grandfather, P. B. S. Pinchback, who was the pri-mary influence on the poet's early life. Although the Pinchbacks were light enough in skin colour to pass as Caucasians, and lived in what was essentially a white middle-class neighbourhood, the grandfather insisted that Eugene attend a school for blacks outside the neighbourhood. In 1907 his mother remarried and moved, first to Brooklyn and then to New Rochelle, a suburb of New York City. Here, in the public library, Toomer expanded his early interest in litera-ture. When his mother died in 1909 he moved back to Washington, and from 1914 to 1919 shunted back and forth between there and New

York, attending various colleges but never earn-ing a degree. In the latter year he decided to cast his lot as a professional writer.

His first book was a collection of poems and stories, *Cane* (1923), and his reputation rests almost exclusively on this one volume, although in 1921 and 1922 he wrote two plays, *Balo* and *Natalie Mann*, a drama satirizing mid-dle-class Washington blacks. He had little luck publishing other works during his lifetime, but in 1988, two years after his death, Darwin T. Turner edited *The Wayward Seeking*, a collection of writings by Toomer, and in the same year *The Collected Poems of Jean Toomer* appeared, ed. Robert B. Jones and Margery Toomer Latimer (Chapel Hill, NC, and London).

Toomer was not a part of the *Harlem Renaissance, and despite the Afro-American themes of *Cane*, his relationships with both whites and blacks remained ambivalent. See *The Lives of Jean Toomer: A Hunger for Wholeness* (1987), by Cynthia Earl Kerman and Richard Eldridge. The only substantial study to appear in Toomer's lifetime was Brian Joseph Benson's and Mabel Mayle Dillard's *Jean Toomer* (1980). [LT

TORRENCE, Ridgely (1875–1950), born in Florida, spent two years at Miami University before going on to Princeton for his degree. He moved to New York City, where he married Olive Howard Dunbar, also a writer, was befriended by Edwin Arlington *Robinson, and worked for six years at the New York Public Library. After a stint as an editor at *Cosmopolitan*, he served as the *New Republic*'s poetry editor from 1920 to 1933. His own small body of verse was marked by a wide diversity of content and styles, extending from 'The Bird and the Tree', a ballad about a lynching, to the city-scape explored in 'Three O'Clock', often exhibiting a Pre-Raphaelite dreaminess that flowed easily into cosmic allegory.

Fascinated by both the theatre and black life, Torrence wrote for the Negro Theatre in the 1910s, producing verse plays in 1914 and 1917, and in 1939 began the National Survey of the Negro Theatre for the Rockefeller Foundation.

A year later he edited *Selected Letters of Edwin Arlington Robinson*; his *Poems* (New York) appeared in 1941. [EB

TOWLE, Tony. See NEW YORK SCHOOL.

Traditional forms have, despite modernist upheavals, throughout the century been at least as popular as *vers libre*. In fact, accentual-syllabic metres (metres with regular numbers of syllables and of stressed syllables in each line) have dominated English verse only slightly less in this century than in the last four.

Blank verse, however, the unrhyming iambic pentameters in which over half of all English verse is composed, has become increasingly difficult for modern poets to use successfully. It evolved in the nineteenth century—and especially in the work of Wordsworth and Browning—into the most pliable, unobtrusive, and conversational poetic form. This century, its supremacy in lyric, narrative, and dramatic verse has been challenged by looser, accentual metres and quatrains, tercets, and distichs of various kinds. Where it has survived it contributes to a formal (*Frost, *Eliot) and sometimes even a 'grand' (*Stevens, Hart *Crane) manner. The heroic couplet, pervasive in 1700 but already in decline by 1800, has proved even harder to sustain as a medium for serious subjects (*Pound wrote of the weariness of waiting for the other shoe to drop), although its comic potential has frequently been demonstrated, and *Merrill's long poem *The Changing Light at Sandover* (1982) suggests that in the right hands it is still capable of a wide range of tones.

The early Italian forms have thrived in modern English verse, partly perhaps because of their ability to absorb so much experimentation without being disfigured beyond recognition. Almost all poets have written sonnets, if not sequences of sonnets. (Composing over ten thousand in his life, Merrill *Moore was probably the most prolific sonneteer of all time). The form has broadened to accommodate every kind of subject (from personal love to genocide), technique (from complete regularity to complete freedom), and genre (from extended narra-

tive to brief meditation). *Terza rima*, invented by Dante and introduced into English by Chaucer, has also been used across the whole thematic spectrum, though some poets, such as Allen *Tate and *Hardy, have sought to exploit its traditional Christian associations. The longer stanza of early Italian epics, *ottava rima*, is an equally versatile if more demanding form. Its triple rhymes have yielded rich comic effects in long poems by *Auden and *Koch, and a grave, lyrical resonance in shorter poems by *Yeats.

At the end of the nineteenth century, Swinburne, *Austin, Dobson and other British poets revived the Old French forms which involve repeated refrains. The ballade and the triolet have continued more recently to occasion ingenious exercises in light verse. The villanelle and the sestina, however, have been transformed and account for some of the most powerful lyrics in modern poetry. Dylan *Thomas's 'Do not go gentle into that good night' and *Empson's 'Missing Dates' are memorable examples of the former, *Ashbery's 'The Painter' and Elizabeth *Bishop's 'A Miracle for Breakfast' of the latter.

Despite the continued dominance of accentual-syllabic metres, some pure accentual and pure *syllabic metres have been adopted, and some restored, in modern poetic practice. The systematic alliterative metre of Old English verse, for example, fell from favour at the end of the Middle Ages and was not resuscitated until this century. Auden's *The Age of Anxiety* (1947) is only the most extended and accomplished of recent experiments in the many varieties of this form. Hopkins's 'sprung rhythm' is also an almost entirely accentual metre; its capacity to hold stressed syllables both closer together and further apart than iambic metres helps to vary the pace of his poems and thus to produce their great emotional intensity. One pure syllabic form now thoroughly assimilated into English poetic tradition is the Japanese haiku. Impressed by its succinct presentation of images unqualified by subjective or discursive comment, the *Imagist poets started imitating it around 1910. Syllabic verse has also been effectively employed at greater length, particularly in Marianne *Moore's ornate stanzas.

Many nineteenth-century poets, including Tennyson, Clough, and *Bridges, attempted English versions of quantitative classical metres. The impossibility of scanning English in this way doomed such experiments, and modern translations of classical texts tend instead to use accentual equivalents of their metres, traditional English metres, or free verse. Richmond *Lattimore's alcaics and *Day Lewis's hexameters are notable adaptations, respectively, of Alcaeus's and Virgil's forms. One of the few recent poets to adapt classical metres in his own compositions was Auden, whose work, it should be added, displays exceptional facility in the whole range of forms this entry has covered.

The most engaging introduction to prosody is *Rhyme's Reason: A Guide to English Verse*, by John Hollander (New Haven, Conn., and London, 1981; enlarged edn., 1989). For a comprehensive bibliography of writings on prosody, see *English Versification, 1570–1980: A Reference Guide with a Global Index*, by T. V. F. Brogan (Baltimore, Md., 1981). See also entries on New Formalism, New Narrative, and Rhyme.   [NE

transition. Subtitled 'An International Quarterly for Creative Experiment', *transition* was founded in Paris in 1927 by Eugene and Maria Jolas. Strongly influenced by the *Surrealists, Eugene Jolas sought a 'revolution of the word', where sensitivity to the realm of dream and hallucination would lead to the creation of what he termed 'paramyths'. He quickly fastened on James *Joyce's *Finnegans Wake* as the ideal exemplum of his aesthetic determinations; known initially as 'Work in Progress', excerpts from Joyce's novel appeared in almost every issue of the magazine, together with supporting critical articles, many of which formed the basis for *Our Exagmination Round his Factification for Incamination of Work in Progress* (1929). Joyce was not entirely happy with aspects of Jolas's thought; he disliked psychoanalysis and would hardly have supported Jolas's inclusion of Carl Jung, particularly considering Jung's article on *Ulysses*. Jolas none the less stayed close to Joyce and was the first person to guess the title of Joyce's novel. In addition to Joyce, *transition*

published the first translations of Franz Kafka, as well as work by Gertrude *Stein, W. C. *Williams, H. D. (Hilda *Doolittle), Hart *Crane, Laura *Riding, Paul Eluard, Samuel *Beckett, and many others. Picasso and Mirò designed covers for *transition*, their work reflecting the accurate and persuasive treatment of art which also graced its contents. The last issue appeared in 1938, bringing to a close one of the most important and influential magazines of its time.   [CM

Translation of foreign poetry into English has been dominated in the twentieth century by the precepts and practice of Ezra *Pound. Not since Shelley and Browning has a poet of comparable stature loaned so much energy to the task of importing other literatures into the English language, and Shelley's adaptations of the Homeric hymns and Browning's version of the *Agamemnon* did not have so livening an effect on subsequent translators as did Pound's supernal renditions of the eighth-century Chinese poet Li Po, done largely from the notes of the sinologist Ernest Fenollosa, and of Sextus Propertius, in which Pound transposes the Latin elegist's biting love poems from Caesar's Rome to Edwardian London. In these poems, in the many other translations—from Greek, Old English, Italian, Provençal, and French—that stand out among the shorter poems collected in *Personae*, and in the glittering fragments laid into *The Cantos* from the very beginning, Pound created a modern standard for the translation of verse that has yet to be rivalled, much less bettered.

Even so, there have been many fine translations since Pound pointed the way, both of poems that might not have been translated so extensively or so well without his example, and of poems that fell outside either the wide range of his interests or the long span of time during which he was actively translating. In the first group is an entire family of translations of Homer that includes a remarkable prose version of the *Odyssey* by T. E. Lawrence and an equally vivid prose-and-verse adaptation of the *Iliad*, entitled *The Anger of Achilles*, by Lawrence's friend Robert *Graves; translations by Richmond *Lattimore of both poems into loose equivalents of the original hexameters, and by Robert *Fitzgerald into suave iambic pentameter; and Christopher *Logue's harshly cinematic 'performance version' of the *Iliad*, several books of which have been published in the two volumes *War Music* and *Kings*. Fitzgerald and Lattimore have each translated plays by the Greek dramatic poets as well, and Lattimore has also translated Pindar, Sappho, and many of the poets in the *Greek Anthology*, while Fitzgerald has given English-language readers what is probably the best verse translation of the *Aeneid* since Dryden's. Other distinguished translations from the Latin are Basil *Bunting's handful of excellent versions of Horace, Louis *Zukofsky's bizarre but compelling phonetic translation of Catullus, and Robert *Lowell's tight-lipped imitations of poems by Horace and Juvenal.

Among the century's many translations of Dante, especially noteworthy are Laurence *Binyon's tapestry-like rendition of *The Divine Comedy*, Lowell's stinging translation of the Brunetto Latini canto from the *Inferno*, and James *Schuyler's exquisite version of the sestina from the *Rime* that begins 'Al poco giorno . . .'. Although the intensely musical verse of the Provençal troubadors has been left alone for the most part since Pound made his sparkling rescensions of Arnaut Daniel and Bertrans de Born, Paul *Blackburn's gritty translations of Peire Vidal and other Provençal poets provide a salutary exception to this general neglect, and of the later French poets Villon has been translated with great care and skill by Anthony Bonner and by Galway *Kinnell. Neither Corneille nor Racine really exists in English yet, and the same is virtually true of Nerval, Baudelaire, Rimbaud, Corbière, and Mallarmé, although the poetry of at least one nineteenth-century French symbolist, Jules Laforgue, has been rendered at length and handsomely by William Jay *Smith. The ancient Chinese poets, on the other hand, have been extremely fortunate: in addition to Pound's versions of Li Po, there are Arthur *Waley's magnificent blank-verse translations of hundreds of poems by scores of poets, and

William Hung's curiously neglected but definitive translations of Tu Fu, as well as F. T. *Prince's brilliant recasting, in *The Yüan Chên Variations*, of some of Waley's translations of Po Chü-i.

Distinctive translations from the second large group—of poems for one reason or another remote from the force-field of Pound's commanding interests—include Frank O'Connor's spirited adaptations of Irish Gaelic poetry; two entirely different translations of Pushkin's *Eugene Onegin*, one into unadorned free verse by Vladimir *Nabokov and the other into rhyme-and-metre-faithful stanzas by Charles Johnston; the eloquent translation by George Reavey of a sizeable selection of poems by Mayakovsky, and the translation by B. G. Guerney of the great book of poems that ends Pasternak's novel *Doctor Zhivago*; Michael *Hamburger's sensitive adaptations, both into prose and into poetry, of Friedrich Hölderlin's maze-like odes; the still unsurpassed version by Stephen *Spender and J. B. Leishman of Rilke's *Duino Elegies*, and the accomplished versions by Babette *Deutsch, by Randall *Jarrell, and by Robert Lowell of some of Rilke's shorter poems; the hyperkinetic translations by Robert *Bly, by James *Wright, by H. R. Hays, by John Knoepfle, and by Hardie St Martin of twentieth-century Spanish and Spanish-American poets such as Lorca, Antonio Machado, Juan Ramón Jiménez, Pablo Neruda, César Vallejo, and Miguel Hernández; and the successive attempts, by John Mavrogordato, by Rae Dalven, and by Edmund Keeley and Philip Sherrard, to fix in English the spectral poems of the Alexandrian Greek, C. P. Cavafy. Other verse translations of note are Elizabeth *Bishop's beautifully paced versions of the Brazilians Carlos Drummond de Andrade and João Cabral de Melo Neto; James *Merrill's soaring recreation of Valéry's 'Palm'; John *Ashbery's rare and elegant translations of Baudelaire, Max Jacob, and Arthur Cravan; and Ted *Berrigan's lively interpretations of Catullus, Rimbaud, Rilke, Ungaretti, and Henri Michaux. Of special interest, too, are the translations by Samuel *Beckett, by Cseszlaw Milosz, and by Joseph *Brodsky of poems they wrote originally in French, in Polish, and in Russian respectively.

For Pound's theories of translation, see especially the notes to his redaction of Fenollosa's essay, 'The Chinese Written Character as a Medium for Poetry', and the analyses in *ABC of Reading* of his own touchstones for translation: Gavin Douglas's powerful Chaucerian version of the *Aeneid*, and Arthur Golding's sumptuous, late-sixteenth-century rendition of Ovid's *Metamorphoses*.   [RH

TRANTER, John (1943–), was born at Cooma in the south-east of New South Wales. He read English at Sydney University but did not pursue an academic career. He has worked in printing and publishing and as a radio producer. In the Sixties he travelled to the East and to Europe, though he was never tempted to become an expatriate. He began to publish early. His first four books, *Parallax*, *Red Movie*, *The Blast Area*, and *The Alphabet Murders* were in print by 1976, and show a poet attempting to find an equivalent in verse to the urban discontents of the age. The young Rimbaud has always been Tranter's ideal, and there is a calculated *deréglement du sens* about his early work. A key book in his development is his sequence of 100 sonnets, *Crying in Early Infancy* (Brisbane, 1977). Here a near-*confessional abruptness meets the ludic language-centred poetry of the *New York School. It is characteristic of both Tranter and his age that often the hero of his poetry is the poem itself. Tranter sealed his importance in contemporary Australian letters with his influential anthology *The New Australian Poetry* (Brisbane, 1979). *Under Berlin* (St Lucia, Qld., 1988), his richest collection yet, reveals the unexpected influence of *Auden in its fondness for surveying multiple historical vistas, and its witty psychological dramatizing. Since then he has published *The Floor of Heaven* (Sydney, 1992).

Tranter's example has been decisive among Australian poets of his generation, those who began writing in the Sixties and during the Vietnam War. Tranter's revolution may be expressed simply as an orientation of Australian sympathies away from the 'bush' tradition of Australian verse, which was still being promulgated in journals such as the *Bulletin* and *Meanjin* when he was growing up, but also away from Britain and any decorous or academic style. The models to hand were American—more West Coast aestheticism (Robert *Duncan) than *Beat or *Black Mountain. Young Australian poets looked to Tranter as their stylistic mentor, not so much for his polemical force as for his practical example. He has never been a strenuous theorist of poetry, but always a brilliant strategist. Whether poets in Sydney and Melbourne tuned in to New York or followed notions from Parisian theorists mattered less to him than that they should devote themselves to creating a new Australian poetry which could take its place unapologetically on the world stage.   [PNFP

TREECE, Henry (1912–66), was born in the West Midlands of (he claimed) 'Welsh extraction originally'. He took a degree at Birmingham University, and until the war was a schoolmaster. He served in the RAF, and then wrote radio scripts for adults (including the trilogy *The Dark Island*, *The End of a World*, and *The Tragedy of Tristram*) and children. Finally he settled to the writing of historical novels, which were highly successful. As a poet, he found his first mentor in Michael *Roberts. With J. F. *Hendry, and encouraged by Herbert *Read, he founded the *New Apocalypse movement. He was a close friend of Stefan Schimanksi (killed in an air crash on his way to Korea in 1950), and with him edited the magazine *Kingdom Come* and the bi-yearly *Transformation*. Treece's verse arose from his and the New Apocalyptic belief in the priestly role of the poet; had T. S. *Eliot not published (at Faber) *Invitation and Warning* (London, 1942), and had there not been a wide market for poetry of all kinds during the wartime years, it is unlikely that it would have found many readers. But Treece's poems, although self-consciously 'Celtic', 'Bardic', and unoriginal, were technically not inefficient. See *Towards a Personal Armegeddon* (New York, 1940), *Collected Poems* (New York, 1946), and *How I See Apocalypse* (London, 1946).   [MS-S

TREVELYAN, R(obert) C(alverly) (1872–1951), was born in Weybridge, the son of Sir George Otto Trevelyan, and brought up in London and in Wallington Hall, Northumberland. He attended Trinity College, Cambridge, 1891–5, where he was an Apostle. He travelled frequently in Europe, especially Italy, where he paid annual visits to Bernard Berenson at I Tatti. After his marriage to Elizabeth des Amorie van der Hoeven, he settled in The Shiffolds near Dorking where he and his Dutch wife (a violinist) entertained a constant flow of musicians, painters, and poets.

His prolific original verse, from his first book, *Mallow and Asphodel* (1898), to his last, *From the Shiffolds* (1947), was written usually in conventional metres, although he occasionally experimented within the bounds of a formulable prosody. His prose tract *Thamyris* (1925) is an attack on the *vers libre* movement. He frequently made use of Greek and Latin mythologies, yet just as frequently indulged in descriptions of the beauties of rural England. He was steeped in Greek and Latin literature and he was an indefatigable translator. Especially noteworthy is the *De Rerum Natura* of Lucretius translated into English verse. Of his many verse plays, *The Bride of Dionysus* (1912), made into an opera by Sir Donald Tovey and produced in Edinburgh in 1929 and 1932, and *The New Parsifal* (1914) are the most readable today. Trevelyan's collected works are in two volumes (London, 1939). [DES

TRIMPI, Helen. See PINKERTON, HELEN.

TRIMPI, Wesley (1928–), was born in New York City. He received his AB from Standford University in 1950, his Ph.D from Harvard in 1957. He is a professor of English at Stanford. As an undergraduate student at Stanford he came under the influence of Yvor *Winters, who published fourteen poems by Trimpi in *Poets of the Pacific: Second Series* (Stanford, Calif., 1949). His *Ben Jonson's Poems: A Study of the Plain Style* (Stanford, 1962), which is dedicated to 'J. V. *Cunningham: a master of the plain style', is indicative of some of the major influences at

work on his own verse, a poetry of plain statement, substantial rational content, non-rhetorical, usually rich in classical allusion, and of low intensity of feeling.

'The Growth of Perseus', which summarizes the Perseus myth, 'Oedipus to the Oracle', which summarizes the Oedipus tale, 'Venus', and 'To Persephone' are among his most successful poems which make use of classical literature. 'The Betrothal' and 'Song' are moving personal poems, and 'Epitaph for an English Department' illustrates his satirical bent. There is excellent descriptive writing in 'Adirondacks: Late Summer 1948', 'Lake Tahoe: Early Summer 1949', and 'Los Gatos Hills'.

His two volumes of verse are *The Glass of Perseus* (Denver, Col., 1953) and *The Desert House* (Florence, Ky., 1982). In his *Muses of One Mind: The Literary Analysis of Experience and Its Continuity* (Princeton, NJ, 1983) Trimpi is primarily concerned with classical literature, but the literary theories he defends are relevant to his own work as a poet. [DES

TRIPP, John (1927–86), was brought up in Whitchurch, a suburb of Cardiff, and worked as a journalist in London until 1969, when he returned to Wales and lived thereafter as a freelance writer, often precariously. His early poems, contributed to *Poetry Wales* and subsequently published in the booklet *Diesel to Yesterday* (1966), were mostly concerned with aspects of Welsh history, often from a nationalist point of view. An English-speaking Welshman with left-wing and pacifist convictions, he felt compelled to write about what he saw as the shoddy materialism afflicting the Welsh people and the decay of the community's traditional values, as in the volumes *The Loss of Ancestry* (1969), *The Province of Belief* (1971), and *The Inheritance File* (1973).

His view grew more bitter after the failure of the devolution referendum in 1979, but he then turned to more contemporary subjects such as the social dereliction of south Wales. The sequence of poems entitled 'Life under Thatcher' is perhaps the most typical of his later mode, turning a laconic eye not only on social deprivation but on himself as poet-observer. But he was also capable of humour, compassion, and anger, as in the volume *Passing Through* (1984). These qualities were widely appreciated at the many public readings which the poet gave during his last years. He was also passionately engaged in Welsh literary affairs, first as a member of the editorial board of *Planet* between 1973 and 1979 and later with the Welsh Academy and the Welsh Union of Writers.

A selection of John Tripp's work (with that of John *Ormond and Emyr *Humphreys) appeared in the *Penguin Modern Poets* series (1978). A posthumous volume of his *Selected Poems* (Bridgend, 1989) was edited by John Ormond. A monograph on the poet's life and work was contributed to the Writers of Wales series (Cardiff, 1989), by Nigel Jenkins.   [MS

TSALOUMAS, Dimitris (1921–), was born on the Greek island of Leros. Among poets not native speakers (such as *Skrzynecki and *Kefala), he is distinctive in having arrived in Australia in 1952 with an established poetic reputation in his original language, and he continues to publish in Athens.

His first two Australian-published collections were in Greek, translated by Philip Grundy. *The Observatory* (St Lucia, Qld., 1983) won a National Book Council Award and the 100 pithily concentrated short poems of *The Book of Epigrams* (St Lucia, 1985) received an enthusiastic critical reception. Editing the anthology *Contemporary Australian Poetry* (St Lucia, 1986), he prepared the translations for the dual-language Greek edition (Thessalonika, 1985).

Falcon Drinking (St Lucia, 1988) is his first collection 'conceived and written in English'. The qualities of his Greek poetry—intense and densely metaphoric lyricism and sardonic observation of the self and its surrounding world—persist, and the Australian poems, even when not specifically linked to Greece, as in 'Note with Interlude from the Banks of the Brisbane in September', are perhaps most interesting when they suggest palimpsests, cultural inscriptions written over a shadow text of memory and attitudes.   [JS

TURNBULL, Gael (Lundin) (1928–), was born in Edinburgh and worked as a medical practitioner in England before emigrating to Canada in the 1950s. He became a Canadian citizen before returning permanently to Great Britain, where—in his magazine *Migrant*—he was active as the publisher of many lesser known, often avant-garde, poets. Although Turnbull was associated with *Origin, his work does not in fact much resemble that of the *Black Mountain poets, except that it is resolutely low-key and suspicious of rhetoric. *Twenty Words, Twenty Days* (Birmingham, 1966) is characteristic in being interesting, honest, but slightly pallid: he takes a word randomly from the dictionary for each of twenty days, and builds an autobiographical poem around it. This reads inconsequentially to some, but as a set of remarkably truthful impressions to others. He is, at the least, persistent and original; the most evident influences on his work are the poetry of Robert *Duncan and the *Imagists, but these are not obtrusive. See *A Gathering of Poems 1950–1980* (London, 1983).   [MS-S

TURNER, Brian (1944–), born in Dunedin, has been a publisher's editor, free-lance writer, playwright, and university writer-in-residence. Having come from a background of sport (he represented New Zealand at hockey, and his father and two brothers have competed internationally in their sports), he came rather late to poetry. However, with his first book, *Ladders of Rain* (Dunedin, 1978) he established a personal style which was identifiably local. The subjects are rooted in his own territory of Dunedin and the South Island of New Zealand. Turner rejects travel as dislocating and refuses the influences of imported trends in poetry. Unlike many New Zealand poets of the Seventies and Eighties he does not look to American poetry, preferring a more conservative British model while citing the particular influence of W. S. *Merwin and Ian *Hamilton. Of his five volumes, *All that Blue Can Be* (Dunedin, 1989) is the most consistent and least mannered.   [RB

TURNER, Frederick (1943–), was born in Northamptonshire, grew up in England and Africa, and was educated at Oxford. His first book, *Between Two Lives* (1972), consists of lyrics in various stages of metamorphosis as they try to become narrative poems. *The New World* (Princeton, NJ, 1985) recounts the adventures of a rather chivalric science-fiction hero around whom a fascinating cosmos of good and evil, wisdom and folly, springs up.

The sources of Turner's story-telling lie on the one hand in the great epics (Greek, Christian, Indian, Welsh, Nordic), and on the other in the detail of modern scientific theory and the magical, dangerous technology to which it has given rise. His characters are warriors who fight with intelligent swords guided by solar-powered microprocessors; in Turner's exuberant, Lamarckian materialism, the right configuration of chemicals is as good as a soul. His people create themselves bodily as well as culturally, choosing beauty generation after generation in the midst of tragic conflict. Their adventures lead them always further into trouble, which however teaches them 'that we cannot fall back on the comfort of despair | but are bound to build the world in the human image, | and cleanse ourselves only with fluids of past pollutions'. The new world is thus never a return to innocence, but a surprising new twist, lovely and threatening, in the traffic of angels up and down nucleic acid's symbolic ladder.   [EG

TURNER, W(alter) J(ames) (1884–1946), was born and educated in Melbourne, Australia. In 1907 he went to London to become a writer. His first success came with satirical sketches which Orage published in *The New Age*. He earned his living from music criticism (principally for the *New Statesman*) and literary editing.

Sir Edward Marsh first brought Turner's poetry to prominence when he included it in his *Georgian poetry anthology for 1916–17. Influenced by *de la Mare, Turner was committed to rhythm, music, sensibility, and imagination, but his early work also shows the inspiration of the Australian landscape and his interest in anthropological study and what it revealed about the relationship between art and religious yearning. In 1922 Turner refused to be included in the fifth Georgian anthology, which did not, he later argued, include 'the most complex art of the age'. Turner's enthusiasms for Symbolist poetry, Plato, Kierkegaard, and 'philosophical-religious explanations of human life' distinguish his poems. *Yeats included a generous selection of Turner's poems in the *Oxford Book of Modern Verse* (1936). He confessed himself 'lost in admiration and astonishment' at Turner's 'majestic song', but also praised his modernity, 'strange philosophical poems', and intellectual subtlety.

The only available edition of Turner's poetry is *W. J. Turner: Selected Poetry*, ed. Wayne McKenna (Kensington, NSW, 1990), but see *Selected Poems* (London, 1939) and *Fossils of a Future Time?* (1946). See also McKenna's *W. J. Turner: Poet and Music Critic* (Gerrards Cross, Bucks., and Kensington, 1990).   [WMcK

TUWHARE, Hone (1922–), was born in Kaikohe, New Zealand. His mother died when he was young, and he was brought up by his father, who worked on market gardens. Tuwhare remembers lying awake at night, hearing his father chant in Maori or tell ghost stories. His father also introduced him to the King James Bible, a lasting influence on his work.

In 1939 Tuwhare joined the Railway Workshops at Otahuhu and served his apprenticeship as a boilermaker tradesman. He became a Marxist, read a range of left-wing writers, and met the poet R. A. K. *Mason. After the Soviet invasion of Hungary in 1956 he left the Communist Party and at about the same time began writing poetry seriously. *No Ordinary Sun* (1964) was welcomed as the first book of verse in English by a Maori poet and became one of New Zealand's best-selling poetry collections.

Tuwhare's poetry can be anecdotal, political, and sometimes—as in 'Rain'—effortlessly lyrical. His earliest poems adopted a high, rhetorical, formal manner; later work is more conversational, open to the vernacular. Often a

Tuwhare poem is a piece of direct address—to a friend, to the spirits of the dead, to a Maori meeting house. Tuwhare writes usually in a flexible English (in the space of a few lines he can sound as if he is both in church and at the pub), but the oral and oratorical elements in his work, along with a gound-note of lament and an informing animism, have their roots in Maori spirituality.

A collected poems, *Mihi*, is published by Penguin (Auckland, 1987); an extended interview with Hone Tuwhare appears in *Landfall*, 167 (1988). [WM

Twentieth Century Verse. The first issue of this magazine appeared in January 1937, the eighteenth and last in July 1939. A pamphlet offshoot of the magazine, *Some Poems In Wartime*, was published early in 1940. The magazine was edited throughout by Julian *Symons, and shortly after the war began he and Geoffrey *Grigson, editor of *New Verse, discussed the possibility of amalgamation. This idea came to nothing and both magazines closed down, their place taken by Tambimuttu's 'vast junk shop or oriental bazaar', *Poetry London.

'Our chief object is to print the work of young poets who from one reason or another, the cut of their jacket or the colour of their tie, do not get much of a hearing elsewhere', said the editorial in the first issue, and *Auden, *MacNeice, *Spender, and *Day Lewis never appeared in the magazine. Symons looked instead for poets outside the Oxbridge circles, and after the uneasy first three or four issues found them in Roy *Fuller, Ruthven *Todd, George *Woodcock and H. B. *Mallalieu, as well as the editor himself. Dylan *Thomas, Gavin *Ewart, and Kenneth *Allott were also frequent contributors.

The magazine suffered from the fact that Symons's view of poetry was very similar to Grigson's. Both were wary of grand rhetorical poetic gestures and stances, both preferred poets who thought they were dealing with 'an explicable, if not with a calculated and an orderly, universe'. Since *New Verse* had the benefit of better poets and stricter editing, it was

much the better magazine. It would be wrong, however, to regard *Twentieth Century Verse* as a mere echo of the other paper. Symons swam against the tide of fashion in his support of Wyndham *Lewis (who was given a celebratory double number to coincide with a new exhibition), and in printing American poets then very little known in England. An American double number included work by Allen *Tate, Conrad *Aiken, Wallace *Stevens, Theodore *Spencer, John Peale *Bishop, Delmore *Schwartz, Yvor *Winters, John *Berryman, and Theodore *Roethke. The later issues show perhaps more clearly than *New Verse* the qualities and limitations not of the best, but the most typical Thirties poetry. [JGS

TWICHELL, Chase (1950–), received a BA from Trinity College and an MFA from the University of Iowa. For years she lived in Florence, Massachusetts, and worked there for a small press as an editor and typesetter while also doing free-lance editorial work. Her first book of poems, *Northern Spy* (Pittsburgh, Pa., 1981), was one of the first collections by poets of her generation to integrate poetry's traditional field of experience and the language and subjects of contemporary science. Her second book, *The Odds* (Pittsburgh, 1986), expands this effort and adds to the poet's spare, crisp execution of line and rhythm an anecdotal narrative impulse. Notable in this collection are two long poems, 'My Ruby of Lasting Sadness', which looks back with bitter-sweet precision on a youthful romance, and 'A Suckling Pig', an ambitious rendering of psychological torment and physical excesses among an artistic, Yuppie set of New England friends. *Perdido* appeared in London in 1992.

Twichell taught at the University of Alabama and received fellowships in poetry from the Artists' Foundation (Boston), the Guggenheim Foundation, and the National Endowment for the Arts. She lives in Princeton, New Jersey with her husband, the American fiction writer Russell Banks.

[RMcD

U

University of Queensland Press. Under Frank Thompson, UQP in the late 1960s began a major series of Australian poetry titles, beginning with Roger *McDonald's *Citizens of the Mist* (1968) and the anthology *New Impulses in Australian Poetry*, ed. R. Hall and T. Shapcott (1968). UQP appointed Roger McDonald as poetry editor. As the result of a suggestion by David *Malouf in 1970, Paperback Poets began. This was to feature virtually all the outstanding writers who emerged over the next decade: Malouf, Michael *Dransfield, Judith *Rodriguez, Rhyll *McMaster, Andrew *Taylor, Geoff *Page, Robert *Gray, Alan *Wearne, Jennifer *Maiden, and others. The series also published already established writers (Bruce *Beaver, Rodney *Hall, Thomas *Shapcott, R. A. *Simpson). *The First Paperback Poets Anthology*, ed. R. McDonald, was published in 1974 and the second (ed. T. Shapcott) in 1982. Thirty-seven poets appeared in this series alone. Subsequently UQP continued with poetry, though in a more formal format. Many titles published in the 1980s were awarded major literary prizes. After the success of the Paperback Poets series UQP embarked on fiction publication by new writers, beginning with Rodney Hall, Peter Carey, and David Malouf, and this has become a major feature of contemporary Australian literature. Poetry, however, provided the impetus for UQP to become one of Australia's major publishers.

[TWS

UNTERMEYER, Louis (1885–1978), was born in New York. As a famous and at one time influential anthologist Untermeyer attracted praise from Allen *Tate (his anthologies of American poetry were the 'best available') and rude dispraise from E. E. *Cummings ('Mr u will not be missed | who as an anthologist | sold the many on the few | not excluding mr u'). Tate was right about the quality of the anthologies: as works for the general reader they are admirably eclectic, and they give useful representative selections from interesting poets otherwise difficult of access. Untermeyer's knowledge of modern poetry was extensive. The best of his own poetry consists of enjoyably sharp parodies (*Collected Parodies*, New York, 1926), in which poets such as *Yeats, Poe, Vachel *Lindsay, and *Masefield tell Mother Goose tales: their excesses as well as virtues are amusingly brought out. The rest of his poetic output, which is competent, is most of all influenced by Heine, of whose poems he made many translations. It is pallid, since he seemed to need the parody form to bring out his undoubted wit. But Edwin *Muir praised his 'opulence'. *From Another World* (New York, 1939), is valuable for its anecdotes of the large number of poets he knew. See *Selected Poems and Parodies* (New York, 1935) and *Long Feud: Selected Poems* (New York, 1962).

[MS-S

URDANG, Constance (1922–), was born in New York City. She graduated from Smith College and the University of Iowa. Married to the poet Donald *Finkel, she now divides her time between St Louis, Missouri (her home for many years) and San Miguel de Allende, Mexico.

All three geographical locations figure in her first works of fiction, *Natural History* (1969), *Lucha* (1986), and *American Earthquakes* (1988) and her recent novellas, *The Woman who Read Novels* and

Peacetime (1990). Her five volumes of poetry, from *Charades and Celebrations* (New York, 1965) to *Alternative Lives* (Pittsburgh, 1990), use a similar geography to explore the multiple roles of women and changing sense of self.

Urdang's poetry, while intensely private and introspective, transcends the merely personal. Her ironic humour and clarity of detail, particularly in *The Picnic in the Cemetery* (New York, 1975) and *The Lone Woman and Others* (Pittsburgh, 1980), allow her to explore self-alienation with an objective compassion.　　　[EDF

V

VALENTINE, Jean (1934–), was born in Chicago, and educated at Radcliffe College. In 1965 she won the Yale Younger Poets Award for her book *Dream Barker*. She has taught at several colleges and universities, and is currently on the faculty of Sarah Lawrence College.

Jean Valentine writes a deeply personal poetry that seems to withhold its secrets from us, yet in doing so opens itself to a different kind of attention. Her poems make frequent references to family, lovers, and events that remain obscure, unnarrated; but these bits of experience furnish germs for Valentine's extraordinary, incantatory spells of language. Syntax in her work often seems to dissolve into a series of nouns or namings, as though summoning the presences she desires. Like other poets who came of age in the Fifties, Valentine moved from a carefully worked, somewhat brittle style to a freer, less rational mode, in her case perhaps influenced by Mandelstam, whom she has translated. Her poems can be virtually opaque in the way they pass from image to image; at their best, however, a lucid dream logic makes itself felt in the absence of story or argument. Her work can be sampled in *Home Deep Blue: New and Selected Poems* (Cambridge, Mass., 1988). [RG

VAN DOREN, Mark (1894–1972), was born in Hope, Illinois, grew up there and in Urbana, Illinois, and was educated at the University of Illinois and Columbia University. He taught at Columbia, 1920–59, where he was considered an outstanding educator.

Van Doren, who owned a farm and farmhouse in Connecticut, is best known for his poetry about the people of New England who are depicted with sympathy and understanding, usually in a rural setting which is described with sharp-eyed, loving detail. He was well aware, however, that New England culture was in a state of decline, and hence much of his poetry was elegiac in tone. He wrote in conventional prosody in carefully crafted lines and stanzas and in a style that has been described as autumnal and dry. In his foreword to *Good Morning: Last Poems by Mark Van Doren* (New York, 1973), Richard *Howard placed him in the tradition of E. A. *Robinson and *Frost.

Van Doren published more than a thousand poems. Among those praised by critics are 'Most Difficult', 'Private Worship', 'Return to Ritual', 'This Amber Sunstream', and 'Young Woman at a Window'. A long verse narrative of note is *The Mayfield Deer* (New York, 1941), derived from an historical account of a nineteenth-century Illinois hunter and his tame deer. *Collected and New Poems 1924–1963* (New York, 1963) is a substantial compilation of his shorter poems. *The Autobiography of Mark Van Doren* (New York, 1958) supplies details of his life up to 1957. [DES

VAN DUYN, Mona (1921–), was born in Waterloo, Iowa, and earned a BA from the University of Northern Iowa in 1942, followed by an MA from the University of Iowa in 1943, the same year she married Jarvis Thurston. Since 1944 she has taught at various universities and (beginning in 1947) edited *Perspective: A Quarterly of Literature* with her husband.

From the start of her writing career Van Duyn has enjoyed unusual critical acceptance.

The traditional nature of her lyric gift, which often involves complex rhyme-schemes, in tandem with her sensitivity to the web-fine nuances of ordinary experiences have made her popular with prize-awarding juries. On the basis of only two undramatic but impressive collections, *Valentines to the Wide World: Poems* (1959) and *A Time of Bees* (1964), she won the Bollingen Prize in 1970, and her third volume, *To See, To Take: Poems* (1970), received a National Book Award a year later.

Van Duyn's most recent collections, *Letters from a Father, and Other Poems* (New York, 1982) and *Near Changes* (New York, 1990), are also well crafted, though the latter is more occasional than impelling. Her *Merciful Disguises: Poems Published and Unpublished* (New York, 1973) offers a representative sampling of early work.   [EB

VAN WYK, Christopher (1957–), was born in Johannesburg, where he has worked as a clerk, an educational writer for the independent South African Council for Higher Education, and also as the editor of *Staffrider* magazine, a literary journal which was particularly influential in South Africa in the 1980s.

Van Wyk showed early promise, his first collection having been published when he was barely out of his teens. Entitled *It Is Time To Go Home* (1979), it at once placed him among the several protest poets who emerged in South Africa in the 1970s. Written largely in the years immediately after the Soweto Revolt of 1976, it dealt with the poet's initiation into the oppressive South African reality of that time. Many of the best poems in the volume establish a link between the poet's coming of age and his growing awareness of the fraudulence of apartheid. Other poems included are an impressive demonstration of Van Wyk's satirical gifts. Although many South African poets have drawn attention to the evils of racism, few before Van Wyk have focused with a more bitter wit on the grotesque distortions of language for which apartheid has been responsible. This is the subject of his 'In Detention', still his best-known and most widely anthologized poem.

Although he has not published another collection since *It Is Time To Go Home*, his more recent work shows that he has grown wary of the more obvious themes of black South African protest poetry. Increasingly, his poems have revolved around family memories, using these as a means of exploring a past both personal and collective. There are examples of this recent work in the anthology *Soundings* (Cape Town, 1989), while some of his earlier work is included in the South African reader, *A Land Apart* (London, 1986).   [SW

Vers libre, a term used to describe verse without traditional metrical arrangement. Though authorities have cited many precedents for *vers libre*, it was not until the 1880s that young French and Belgian Symbolist poets, such as Gustave Kahn, Jules Laforgue, Édouard Dujardin, Jean Moréas, Albert Mockel, and Francis Vielé-Griffin launched a concerted movement devoted to verse without metre. In his *Premiers poètes du vers libre* (Paris, 1922), Dujardin gives 1886–8 as the years of the seminal publications. The phrase itself appears to have been popularized by Vielé-Griffin, who opens his prefatory manifesto to *Joies* (Paris, 1889) with the sentence: 'Le vers est libre.' The new medium spread quickly, and its significance was immediately noted. In 1891 Mallarmé remarked, in an interview with Jules Huret, that 'every poet is going off by himself with his own flute, and playing the songs he pleases. For the first time since the beginning of poetry, poets have stopped singing bass.'

Vers libre soon passed to other countries, though in many cases parallel movements had already been developing. In English, such works as Blake's 'Prophetic Books', Tupper's *Proverbial Philosophy*, Whitman's *Leaves of Grass*, and Henley's Edinburgh Infirmary poems now seem to anticipate *vers libre*. *Hulme, *Ford, and *Pound were among the earliest to champion *vers libre* in English; if the Symbolists were the principal pioneers of the medium in French verse, the *Imagists could claim an analogous role in English.

Overall, the *vers libre* movement is part of that general revolution in the arts which began in the last two decades of the nineteenth century and culminated in the early decades of the twentieth. So far as *vers libre* expresses a desire to free poetry from regulation, it may be seen as an outgrowth of Romantic aesthetics, with its emphasis on the autonomy of the individual poet and poem. So far as *vers libre* represents an interest in 'experiment', it expresses a desire to emulate modern science and to claim for poetry the kinds of 'breakthroughs' and progressive advances of apparatus of which science is capable. So far as *vers libre* reflects the belief that metrical composition is overly marmoreal, and that poetry should imitate the methods and sophistications of modern prose fiction, it reflects the feeling that we live in an age of prose and that verse is, in Edmund *Wilson's phrase, 'a dying technique'.

Critics of *vers libre* have noted that, whereas it was originally intended to lead to a renewal of conventional poetry or to the discovery of new metric, wide adoption of the medium was followed instead by increasingly varied and idiosyncratic procedures of versification. As Valéry commented in 1921 in his 'Concerning *Adonis*': 'Our epoch has seen the birth of almost as many prosodies as it has counted poets.' Others have expressed the related concern that once its revolutionary energy was spent, *vers libre* lapsed into the vices it had been designed to remedy. As early as his 'Retrospect' of 1918, Pound lamented that '*vers libre* has become as prolix and as verbose as any of the flaccid varieties that preceded it'. Defenders of *vers libre* have countered by arguing that it is the most prevalent means of poetic expression in the twentieth century and should be considered a legitimate form in its own right.

Vers libre should not be confused with *vers libres*. The latter term refers to a kind of classical French verse exemplified by La Fontaine's *Fables*; 'free verses' of this sort are 'free' only in that they admit a mixture of different conventional metres and different kinds and sequences of rhymes. Nor should *vers libre* be confused with *vers libérés*, which indicate verses which, though 'liberated' from certain conventions of classical

French verse, such as the proscription against lines longer than alexandrines, still maintain syllabic correspondences. The English term 'free verse' is a translation from the French; though current today, it is noteworthy that the early English-language experimentalists— Hulme, Ford, Pound, and the young *Eliot—use the French term.

Dujardin's study remains the most important historical document of the *vers-libre* movement in France; Henri Morier's *Le Rythme du vers libre symboliste et ses relations avec le sens* (3 vols., Geneva, 1943–4; repr. Geneva, 1977) is a standard prosodic investigation. Eliot's 'Reflections on *Vers Libre*' (orig. pub. 1917 in the *New Statesman*, repr. in *To Criticize the Critic*, New York, 1965) and Ford's *Thus to Revisit* (New York, 1921) are especially pertinent to the *vers libre* movement in England. Recent studies include Timothy Steele, *Missing Measures: Modern Poetry and the Revolt Against Meter* (Fayetteville, Ark., 1990) and Clive Scott, *Vers Libre: The Emergence of Free Verse in France 1886–1914* (Oxford, 1990).

[TS

Verse Drama. The dramatic conventions inherited by the twentieth century from the nineteenth—the charged naturalism of Chekhov and Ibsen and its impoverished British relation, the 'well-made play'—could scarcely have been less encouraging for the production of verse drama. W. B. *Yeats's work for the theatre during the 1890s had included *The Countess Cathleen* (1892, subsequently revised), but *Cathleen ni Houlihan* (1902), like a number of his subsequent plays, was in prose: in any case, his mythological-political subjects and distinctive rhetorical manner were unlikely to provide a useful model for subsequent writers apart from essentially anachronistic figures such as Gordon *Bottomley. Furthermore, the subsequent development of cinema, television, and video served to reinforce a general assumption that dramatic language should make some attempt at verisimilitude: the mainstream English dramatists of the post-war years—Osborne, *Pinter, Wesker—are, despite their differences, essentially engaged in presenting a language which purports to be that of 'real life', in which characters are unlikely to speak poetry.

It follows, therefore, that the twentieth-century writer of verse drama will be working, consciously or unconsciously, against the main cultural currents of his time: thus it seems wholly appropriate that the century's best-known English verse play, T. S. *Eliot's Murder in the Cathedral* (1935), should be set in 1170. Occupying a mid-point between Eliot's liturgical pageant *The Rock* (1934) and his later plays set in unconvincing domestic interiors, *Murder in the Cathedral* is a work as suited to the church as to the theatre, and it remains an anachronistic triumph. Eliot's remaining plays are *The Family Reunion* (1939), *The Cocktail Party* (1950), *The Confidential Clerk* (1954), and *The Elder Statesman* (1959): the last three were first performed at the Edinburgh Festival, directed by E. Martin Browne, in the years immediately preceding book publication.

The work of Christopher Fry, the other principal verse dramatist of the time, has proved similarly to consist of one clear winner against the odds and a number of also-rans. In *The Lady's Not for Burning* (1948), dramatic energy and coherence alleviate the problems which would otherwise arise from Fry's inordinately stilted diction; the remaining three plays in his seasonal cycle (*Venus Observed*, 1950; *The Dark is Light Enough*, 1954; and *A Yard of Sun*, 1970) are less successful, though *A Sleep of Prisoners* (1951) has its admirers. A slightly younger writer, Henry *Reed, brought something of Fry's timelessness to verse plays for radio, including a two-hour version of *Moby Dick* (1947) and the Italia Prize-winning *The Streets of Pompeii* (1951).

Essentially, though, both Eliot and Fry were attempting to merge conventions borrowed from naturalistic drama with incompatible literary techniques. But while twentieth-century verse drama thus seems to have been doomed to failure, the rather different concept of verse *in* drama offered livelier possibilities. Drawing upon Brecht's well-documented ideas of 'Epic Theatre', which substituted the disruptive challenges of alienation for the smooth certainties of illusion, such drama broke through the sym-

bolic barrier of the proscenium arch and allowed prose, verse, and song to mingle in creative juxtaposition. Once the limitations of naturalism had been swept aside, a Shakespearian freedom could be re-established, in which apparently incompatible elements became a source of rich diversity. With apt, if accidental, timing, in the same year that Eliot turned church into theatre *Auden and Isherwood turned theatre into cabaret.

The combination of Brechtian techniques with English public-school humour in Auden and Isherwood's *The Dog Beneath the Skin* (1935) is as improbable as it is invigorating. Two further collaborations—*The Ascent of F6* (1936) and *On the Frontier* (1939)—swiftly followed, and mention should also be made here of Auden's other main variations on the theme of verse drama: the 'charade', *Paid on Both Sides* (1928); the 'Christmas Oratorio', *For the Time Being* (1941–2); the 'Commentary on Shakespeare's *The Tempest*', *The Sea and the Mirror* (1942–4); and the 'baroque eclogue', *The Age of Anxiety* (1944–6).

More recently, the most notable English beneficiary of Brecht's influence has been John Arden, who has made extensive use of verse and of folk-song, notably in *Serjeant Musgrave's Dance* (1959), but also in *Left-Handed Liberty* (1965), a chronicle play about King John and Magna Carta, as Shakespearian as it is Brechtian. The inescapable presence of Shakespeare's verse also informs, in a rather different way, Tom Stoppard's *Rosencrantz and Guildenstern are Dead* (1966); fascinated by the linguistic patterning, adept at puns and word-play, Stoppard is a writer who brings many of the poet's skills to his prose.

The insecure, and indeed peripheral status of twentieth-century verse drama has produced relatively little critical writing; however, *The Third Voice*, by Denis Donoghue (Princeton, NJ, and Oxford, 1959) is, unusually, a full-length study of the subject.　　　　　　　　[NP

VETTESE, Raymond. See LALLANS.

VIERECK, Peter (Robert Edwin) (1916–), was born in New York. He taught history at Mount

Holyoke College, Massachusetts. His first collection, *Terror and Decorum: Poems 1940–1948* (New York, 1948) won the Pulitzer Prize. This and its successors contained tricksy poems, many of them parodic, which risked everything on a rather trite, or folksy, humour: undoubtedly serious themes were juxtaposed with deliberately absurd expositions of them, so that the impression conveyed was either of banality or cleverness. Thus, a comment on Keats's odes, 'To A Sinister Potato', began: 'O vast earth-apple, waiting to be fried.' This kind of nervous zest has prevented Viereck, despite a certain proportion of lyrical successes in his earlier work, from being accepted into the mainstream. *Archer in the Marrow: The Applewood Cycles 1967–1987* (New York, 1987), a long poem with a huge *apparatus criticus*, has its moments, but is similarly flawed by a not-quite-coherent zaniness, as if the poet had given up on his audience. See *New and Selected Poems 1932–1967* (Indianapolis, Ind., 1967) and M. Henault, *Peter Viereck* (New York, 1969).   [MS-S

VLIET, R(ussell) G(ordon) (1929–84), was born in Chicago to a naval medical officer and his wife. The family spent two years in American Samoa before moving to Texas, where Vliet attended high school and college. Although he lived principally in New England after his marriage in 1951, it was Texas and the American Southwest which had the most visible effect on his writing. Vliet died of cancer in 1984.

From the beginning of his literary career in the 1950s, Vliet thought of himself primarily as a poet and playwright, although by the mid-1970s he also began to achieve success as a 'poetic prose' novelist with *Rockspring* (New York, 1974) and *Solitudes* (New York, 1977, rev. as *Soledad* in 1986). His first collection of poetry, *Events and Celebrations* (New York, 1966), contains the highly praised ballad 'Clem Maverick', which was later published separately as *Clem Maverick: The Life and Death of a Country Music Singer* (Bryan, Tex., 1983).

Vliet's second book, *The Man with the Black Mouth* (Santa Cruz, Calif., 1970), was virtually ignored by critics, but many of the same poems

are included in *Water and Stone* (New York, 1980), which also contains the autobiographical poem 'Passage' and the Noh drama which gives the book its title. Although Vliet said that poetry should be 'unkempt . . . bulbous-eyed from old astonishments', his own most notable effects are low-key, and rather mutedly specific. Certainly his observations are more impressive than his exclamations.   [CMW

VOIGT, Ellen Bryant (1943–), was born in Danville, Virginia, in the Piedmont South and raised on a farm owned by her father. The rural world of her childhood—and of her adult years in Vermont—is one of the major forces in her poetry. Ten years after earning an MFA at the *Iowa Writers' Workshop she published her first collection of poems, *Claiming Kin* (Middletown, Conn., 1976). The book's title attests to the importance of family memories and family relationships throughout Voigt's poetry. Though candid and intensely personal at times, her poems also embrace a human community beyond the self. Her attention to nature aligns her with the pastoral tradition, but Voigt rejects any consoling equation between the human and natural worlds, as 'Liebesgedicht' and the ironically titled 'Pastoral' of her second collection, *The Forces of Plenty* (New York, 1983), indicate. For Voigt nature is both beautiful and terrifying, nurturing and flatly indifferent.

All of Voigt's poetry, including *The Lotus Flowers* (New York, 1987), is marked by her sense of human vulnerability. The forces of plenty contend against the forces of loss. Yet, especially in her last two volumes, she has become a poet of survival as well as of evanescence. Moving with ease from narrative to descriptive to meditative poems, alert to the music of her language and to the moral implications of the experiences and emotions she records, Voigt creates elegant and accessible poems of quiet authority, particularly in 'The Spire', 'Year's End', 'At the Movie: Virginia, 1956', and 'The Farmer'.   [JLa

Vorticism. See *Blast*.

WADDINGTON, Miriam (1917–), was born Miriam Dworkin, the daughter of Jewish-Russian immigrants, in Winnipeg, Manitoba. In 1931 her family moved to Ottawa. Waddington received her BA from the University of Toronto in 1939, the year she married journalist Patrick Waddington; they had two sons. During the Second World War she published poems, stories, and reviews while studying social work at the universities of Toronto and Pennsylvania. She moved to Montreal in 1945, taught at McGill's School of Social Work, and was later a case-worker for various social organizations. In 1960 she separated from her husband and returned to Toronto, where she continued her social work and, in 1964, joined the English department of York University, where she is professor emeritus and senior scholar.

Spare and deceptively simple, and often lyrical, joyous, and humorous, the poems in Waddington's thirteen volumes—from her first collection, *Green World* (1945), to *The Last Landscape* (1992)—explore her prairie childhood, her social concerns, landscape, people, Jewish folklore, love and loss, memory and isolation, ageing and death.

Waddington has paid homage to A. M. *Klein in her 1970 monograph on him and in her edition of *The Collected Poems of A. M. Klein* (1974). Her own *Collected Poems* (Toronto, 1986) is complemented by selections from her short fiction in *Summer at Lonely Beach and Other Stories* (Oakville, Ont., 1982), and from her memoirs and essays in *Apartment Seven* (Toronto, 1989).   [DS

WAGONER, David (1926–), was born in Massillon, Ohio. At Pennsylvania State University he studied under Theodore *Roethke and received his BA in 1947. Two years later he took an MA from Indiana University and subsequently taught at DePauw University for a year, 1949–50, and at Pennsylvania State for four years, 1950–4. In the latter year he went to the University of Washington in Seattle, which he has ever since maintained as his home-base and where, for many years, he edited *Poetry Northwest*, a highly regarded quarterly.

A 1950s competence was the main feature of Wagoner's first book, *Dry Sun, Dry Wind* (Bloomington, Ind., 1953). *A Place to Stand* (Bloomington, 1958), went in two directions simultaneously: there was greater formality of structure, but a loosening of language giving, in certain poems, an almost jazz-like effect. The most engaging aspect of the poems in *The Nesting Ground* (Bloomington, 1963) was their colloquial music. That remained true of *Staying Alive* (Bloomington, 1966), and particularly of the title-poem, simultaneously a handbook about surviving in the woods and a parable about how to stay human in the process. *New and Selected Poems* (Bloomington, 1969) sampled the best of these volumes.

The outdoors of the Pacific Northwest figures prominently in Wagoner's work, as in *Riverbed* (Bloomington, 1972), but manifesting itself at times in poems having to do with Native Americans and their lore, such as 'Seven Songs for an Old Voice' which concludes *Sleeping in the Woods* (Bloomington and London, 1974). In *Who Shall Be the Sun* (Bloomington and London, 1978) Wagoner personified natural forces and gave them Indian names in his retelling of the myths of the tribes. The poems of *First Light*

(Boston and Toronto, 1983) were crisp, the imagery evocative, the sensibility contemplative; they exhibited a keen sense of narrative, an insight into character, an eye for composition, and a feeling for atmosphere, light, and colour. Wagoner's most representative collections are the *Collected Poems 1956–1976* (Bloomington and London, 1976) and *Through the Forest: New and Selected Poems* (Boston and Toronto, 1987).

[LT

WAH, Fred (1939–), was born in Swift Current, Saskatchewan, and grew up in the West Kootenay mountains of south-eastern British Columbia. He entered the University of British Columbia as a music student, but became interested in poetry there, where he was one of the founders of the poetry newsletter *Tish*. He pursued his education at the universities of New Mexico and Buffalo, studying with Robert *Creeley and Charles *Olson. He returned to the Kootenays to teach writing at colleges for two decades. In 1990 he took a post at the University of Calgary.

Wah has always been active as an editor, founding and co-editing numerous magazines and books. He is on the editorial board of *Open Letter*, a journal of postmodern theory and criticism. He is also a fervent talent-scout, and has helped launch the careers of many younger poets, often during writer-in-residencies at western universities and retreats.

His early experience in music (including his jazz trumpet playing) shows in his poetry, where sound and improvisation are more important than syntax. In recent years he has explored his own childhood and the early life of his half-Chinese father, who was born in Canada and raised in China. He has also, since a trip to China and Japan, been finding verse-forms which will accommodate Asian and Native North American practices.

Wah has been writing sequential criticopoetic prose for the past decade. The first collection of these pieces, *Music at the Heart of Thinking 1–69*, was published in 1987. See *Waiting for Saskatchewan* (Winnipeg, 1985).

[GHB

WAIN, John (Barrington) (1925–), was born in Stoke-on-Trent, Staffordshire, and educated at the High School, Newcastle-under-Lyme. A damaged eye kept him out of military service, and he became a wartime undergraduate at St John's College, Oxford, where he was taught by C. S. *Lewis (see his early volume of autobiography, *Sprightly Running*, London, 1962; New York, 1963). In 1947 he was appointed lecturer in English at Reading University; but after the success of his first novel, *Hurry on Down* (1953), a picaresque account of a lower-middle-class life after college, he gave up teaching to live as a full-time writer. As well as eleven novels, he has published volumes of literary criticism and a biographical study of Samuel Johnson, but he has continued to regard his poems as 'the best things I have done'. He was Professor of Poetry at Oxford, 1973–8.

His career as a poet has had two clear phases. The poems he wrote in the 1950s, some of which Robert *Conquest published in *New Lines*, are archetypal *Movement pieces: they aim at discipline, a chilly sort of wit, measured understatement; favoured forms include villanelle and terza rima; the prevailing influence is *Empson. The last of Wain's poems in this style are gathered in *Weep Before God* (London and New York, 1961); among them is 'Au Jardin Des Plantes', whose gorilla suffers the 'prodigal idleness' of unemployment, a subject to which Wain's occasional habit of superfluous restatement is well suited. This and several other pieces put the world scathingly to rights.

A radical break is marked by the publication in 1965 of *Wildtrack* (London and New York), a long philosophical poem whose opening barrage—'BAM BAM WHEE CRUMP'—blows away all traces of Empsonian restraint. Wain has taken up Anthony Hartley's challenge to the maturing Movement poet to 'let it rip' and 'risk making a fool of himself'. Subsequent volumes confirm his belated commitment to modernist principles; the best of them is *Feng* (London and New York, 1975), a sequence of poems dealing with the Hamlet story.

Poems 1949–1979 (London, 1981) is highly selective, tending to suppress the compact earlier work. It shows Wain's preference for 'short-long' poems of between seventy-five and 150 lines, the length (he says) 'in which Pound was a master in his early days'.   [MI

WAINWRIGHT, Jeffrey, (1944–), was born in Stoke-on-Trent, Staffordshire, read English at Leeds University, and is senior lecturer in English at Manchester Polytechnic.

Wainwright has been bracketed with Douglas *Dunn and Tony *Harrison as a working-class poet, but in output and method his work is markedly different from theirs. The brief *Selected Poems* (Manchester, 1985) reveals a political poet who aims at an intensity usually thought of as religious. His best-known poem, 'Thomas Muntzer', is a series of dramatic lyrics in which the sixteenth-century Protestant reformer meditates on his visions and eventual defeat; elsewhere, in dealing with his central themes of power and love, Wainwright offers a sense of the commonwealth of human life as— in the absence of another adequate term— sacred ('Transitive').

Whilst Wainwright's poems continually imply the scope of imperial history, they derive their force from regard for people— the drowned girl and the dead of Waterloo in '1815', a drowned sailor in 'The War with Japan'. The poems are characterized by extreme economy and clarity, and Wainwright moves deftly between terseness and full-throated feeling. Because he dramatizes (rather than merely asserting) the field of force binding private and public concerns, the love poems and the more evidently historical-political poems show themselves as part of a single endeavour.

Wainwright's adaptation of Charles Péguy's *The Mystery of the Charity of Joan of Arc* (Manchester, 1986) was first performed in Stratford-upon-Avon in 1984.   [SO'B

WAKOSKI, Diane (1937–), was born in Whittier, California, and in 1960 earned a BA from the University of California at Berkeley. She taught English in a Manhattan junior high from 1963 to 1966, and was granted a Guggenheim fellowship in 1972. Twice married and divorced,

she has supported herself for many years by giving workshops and readings around the country.

Wakoski is often associated with the *'deep image' poets, such as Robert *Bly and James *Wright, although her concern for plumbing archetypal depths has always exhibited strong surreal and *confessional drives as well, leading to comparisons with Sylvia *Plath. Her first collection was *Coins and Coffins* (1962), but *The George Washington Poems* (1967), which cleverly uses the first president as an avatar for various male roles, *Inside the Blood Factory* (1968), *The Magellanic Clouds* (1970), and *The Motorcycle Betrayal Poems* (1971) are disturbing books that confirmed her reputation.

Wakoski's *The Collected Greed* (Los Angeles, 1984) completes a sequence begun in the 1960s, and her critical prose can be found in *Towards a New Poetry* (Ann Arbor, Mich., 1979). See also *Emerald Ice: Selected Poems 1962–1987* (Los Angeles, 1988).   [EB

WALCOTT, Derek (1930–), was born and raised in the West Indies and has been publishing poetry and plays for some four decades. He apprenticed himself early on to the English tradition and has never strayed far from the declamatory lyrical line. His mentors include the Elizabethans and Jacobeans, Wordsworth, Tennyson, *Yeats, *Hardy, and Robert *Lowell (who himself sought to incorporate that tradition into his work). Reverberating against this diction one hears the local influences, the dialect phrases and constructions of the Caribbean. The whole heritage is there, but it is quickened and jazzed.

Educated in the West Indies, Walcott spent some years teaching there. He gradually discarded his early ambition to be a painter, devoting himself instead to poetry and drama. From the time of his first departure for the United States in the 1950s, he has shuttled back and forth between Boston, New York, and St Lucia. The work manifests the contrasts, collisions, and convergences of urban American and West Indian cultures.

In the crisis-ridden decades of the 1950s and

1960s, when poets took up various cudgels—for free verse, *projective verse, *Beat prosody, *confessionalism, and so on—Walcott's work was little heeded. He was always to one side of the current excitement. In the last ten years, though, he has moved forward to claim his rightful place.

Walcott's breakthrough volume, so far as his own development was concerned, was probably *Another Life* (New York and London, 1973), a book-length lyrical saga in which the poet, modulating between first and third persons, dramatized the artistic struggles that finally led him to leave the Caribbean. The staging of episodes reveals something of the playwright's instinct, while the lines themselves manifest an unquenchable lyricism.

Walcott's next collections, *Seagrapes* (New York and London, 1976), *The Star Apple Kingdom* (New York and London, 1979), and *The Fortunate Traveller* (New York, 1981; London, 1982) show the poet taking firm control of his idiom—fusing the diction of his masters with his own particularly sensory drives. *Midsummer* (New York and London, 1983), a fifty-four-poem sequence, delights throughout in the freedom that arrives when form and craft become second-nature: 'My palms have been sliced by the twine | Of the craft I have pulled at for more than forty years. | My Ionia is the smell of burnt grass, the scorched handle | of a cistern in August squeaking to rusty islands; | the lines I love have all their knots left in.'—from *XXV* (London, 1990).

In 1990, he published (New York and London) the ambitiously epical *Omeros*, in which he not only reinterpreted but fundamentally reimagined our core Western legend. The work, widely praised—indeed, deemed by many to be Walcott's crowning achievement—can be read as the poet's bid to gather the many strands of Caribbean culture into an emblematic statement that can be read alongside, as well as against, the canonical Homeric text. Walcott's *Collected Poems* (New York) was published in 1987 (London, 1990). He teaches at Boston University and travels frequently to give readings or in connection with performances of his many plays. He spends part of every year on St Lucia. In 1992 he was awarded the Nobel Prize for Literature. [SPB

WALEY, Arthur (David) (1889–1966), was born at Tunbridge Wells and, after being educated at Rugby and King's College, Cambridge, he settled in Bloomsbury for most of his life. From 1913 to 1929 he was an assistant to Laurence *Binyon in the Department of Prints and Drawings at the British Museum, where he had the opportunity to immerse himself in Oriental history and culture while teaching himself Japanese and Chinese and composing the translations of Chinese and Japanese poetry and prose which made him famous. In his verse translations he succeeded in creating poems which were faithful to the text yet possessed the vitality and freshness of original compositions. He frequently employed a stress accent reminiscent of the experimental verse of *Bridges and Hopkins. His extensive prose works include a critical biography of Po Chü-i, his favourite Chinese poet.

His most important volumes of verse translations are *A Hundred and Seventy Chinese Poems* (London, 1918, revd. and repr., 1987; New York, 1919, 1929); *Japanese Poetry: The Uta* (Oxford, 1919, 1929), and *The No Plays of Japan* (London, 1921, 1965; New York, 1957; Rutland, Vt., 1976). *The Secret History of the Mongols and Other Pieces* (London and New York, 1964) contains examples of his original verse. Biographical information will be found in Ivan Morris (ed.), *Madly Singing in the Mountains* (Berkeley, Calif., 1981) and Alison Waley, *A Half of Two Lives* (London, 1982). The standard bibliography is Francis A. Johns, *A Bibliography of Arthur Waley* (London and New York, 1988). [DES

WALKER, Kath. See NOONUCCAL, OODGEROO.

WALKER, Ted (Edward Joseph) (1934–), was born in Sussex and educated at St John's College, Cambridge. He is now professor of creative writing at New England College, Arundel, Sussex. His prize-winning collections, *Fox on a Barn Door* (London, 1965) and *Solitaries*

(London, 1967), consisted for the most part of nature poems reflecting the landscape of West Sussex. The chief, and slightly obtrusive, influence upon these was Ted *Hughes; but Walker's technique was more conventional. Personal themes were expressed through observations of landscape in a manner reminiscent of *Hardy, but often remained somewhat underresolved. *Gloves for the Hangman* (London, 1973), which marked an advance, cast off the earlier influences and attempted a more direct approach with some success; but the book met with less attention. He has made some good translations from European poets. See *Hands at a Live Fire: Selected Poems* (London, 1987), and a prose work, *The Last of England* (London, 1992).

[MS-S

WALLACE, Bronwen (1945–89), was born and lived most of her life in Kingston, Ontario, where she worked in a centre for battered women and children and taught part-time at Queen's University. In addition to free-lance writing and editing, she collaborated with Chris Whynot on two films: *All You Have To Do* (1982) and *That's Why I'm Talking* (1987).

Wallace claimed to be concerned with the 'hidden lives' of people and the 'unexpected rituals' by which these hidden lives may be revealed. Thus her fascination with narrative and 'how we tell the story of our lives', which consists of 'detours and double-backs, leaps' of ordinary story-telling. The digression, or lateral shift, which she uses so cleverly, has the effect of increasing the reader's attention and bringing new and unexpected ideas into play. While her poetry, recorded conversations, and interviews reveal the influence of poets such as Al *Purdy and Galway *Kinnell, Wallace's social and domestic parables owe their largest debt to what she calls 'kitchen-table conversation', and the nitty-gritty of confession, self-deception, and denial that can be involved in our attempts to communicate.

Her publications include *Signs of the Former Tenant* (Ottawa, 1983), *Common Magic* (Ottawa, 1985), and *The Stubborn Particulars of Grace* (Toronto, 1987). Her first collection of short stories, *People You'd Trust Your Life To*, was published posthumously in 1990. [GG

WALLACE-CRABBE, Chris(topher) (1934–), was born in Melbourne and is currently professor of English and director of the Australian Centre at Melbourne University. Periods in America include a Harkness fellowship (1965–7) and a visiting professorship of Australian Studies at Harvard (1987–8).

His early advocacy of American poets (Robert *Lowell, Wallace *Stevens) demonstrated the sharp eye for shifts in poetic preoccupations which has been a feature of critical work such as his influential essay 'The Habit of Irony: Australian Poets of the Fifties,' in *Meanjin*, 20 (1961); *Melbourne or the Bush* (Sydney, 1974), which examines different cultural values; *Toil and Spin* (Melbourne, 1980), which considers different modes of poetic creativity; and *Falling into Language* (Melbourne, 1990), which deals with postmodernist issues like 'The Textual Self', or 'Struggling with an Imperial Language'.

In poetry which is equally at home in Melbourne's suburbs (the setting of his 1981 novel *Splinters*) and the great international cities, an interest in complexities and ambiguities of tone, in slippages of language, has been consistent throughout a prolific and protean performance. This began in coolly stoic and intelligent formalism; its most recent manifestations sometimes confuse a prevailing Australian taste for straightforward melancholy by mixing both sombreness and a jauntily epigrammatic despair with wittily sensuous celebrations of worldly pleasures and glimpses of Gothic nightmares. For discussion of his work, see *Stop Laughing! This is Serious: Three Studies in Wit and Seriousness in Contemporary Australian Poetry*, by Jennifer Strauss (Townsville, Qld., 1990).

Selected Poems (Sydney, 1973) drew on five collections; three more preceded *The Amorous Cannibal* (1985), *I'm Deadly Serious* (1988), *For Crying Out Loud* (1990), *Rungs of Time* (1993), and *Selected Poems 1956–94* (1995), all in the Oxford Poets series (Oxford and Melbourne). [JS

WANGUSA, Timothy (1942–), was born in Bugisu, Uganda. A student at Makerere University, he returned after postgraduate work at Leeds to teach there, becoming full professor in 1981. He was one of the few leading academics, and the only widely published creative writer, to live in Uganda throughout the dictatorship of Amin and Obote's horrific second term. In 1985–6 he was briefly minister of education in the cabinet of a transitional government: in 1989 he was elected MP for Bubulo County, Mbale.

His novel, *Upon This Mountain* (London, 1989), deals with the conflicts experienced by a village boy educated under colonialism. His verse is charged with a strong sense of African mythologies and speech forms. It confronts a wide range of themes, from the mysteries of Christian faith to topicalities. An ambitious, uneven sequence, 'Anthem for Africa', sets the evils of Amin's Uganda in the context of the entire continent's history. Traces of Shakespeare, Milton, and *Eliot flavour a diction which is at times Parnassian but which at its best is straightforwardly eloquent.

His book *Salutations* was published in Nairobi (1977). *Anthem for Africa* is forthcoming.

[ALRC

WANTLING, William (1933–80), was born in Peoria, Illinois, and after leaving high school at 16 enlisted in the US Marine Corps. Volunteering for combat duty he fought in the Korean War until discharged in 1955. Having experienced morphine in Korea (following an injury), he quickly became addicted to hard drugs on his return to the USA. A failed marriage, and continued use of narcotics, eventually led to his imprisonment in 1958. After release on parole in 1960 Wantling was soon back in San Quentin prison.

Psychic and addiction problems, plus a long list of briefly held jobs, gave Wantling the drifter's aura of an 'on the road' poet typical of the Fifties. His poetic output was small but what was published indicated a vibrant, fresh talent allied to great sensitivity. His highly colloquial poems, often unstructured, dealt with experiences (prison life; addiction; violence) well outside the usual subject-matter for poetry.

The Awakening (Paradise, Calif., 1967) con-

tains poetry of pain and despair in brutal urban situations. The love poems are especially poignant and resonant. A British edition of *The Awakening* (London) appeared in 1968, and Wantling was included in *Penguin Modern Poets 12* (Harmondsworth) in the same year. *10,000 r.p.m. and diggin' it, yeah* (1970) and *San Quentin Blues* (1973—both Cardiff) offered further outlets for his distinctive work, but like his earlier collections both booklets are now out of print.

[WM

WARNER, Rex (Ernest) (1905–86), was educated at St George's School, Harpenden, and Wadham College, Oxford, where he was a contemporary of Cecil *Day Lewis and W. H. *Auden. With them he was part of the left-wing literary movement of the 1930s and appeared in the anthology *New Country* in 1933. His *Poems* was published in London in 1937 (New York, 1938), and in revised form as *Poems and Contradictions* in 1945. He made a reputation as a classicist and translator, producing versions of *The Medea of Euripides* (London, 1944; New York, 1949), Aeschylus's *Prometheus Bound* (London, 1947; New York, 1949), and other classical Greek dramas in verse. He also translated the poetry of George Seferis.

Warner's most famous works were his novels. He was one of the first British writers to use creatively the example of Kafka. His poetry is less notable. Like Day Lewis, whose poetry Warner's often resembles, he was influenced by Hopkins, though the influence was often ill-absorbed. In the 1930s he wrote political poems that were sometimes bald versifications of political positions. He saw himself as one who delighted in nature, but was moved by the torture of man by man. His poems of nature are much his best, particularly those about birds, of which he was a sensitive observer.   [ATT

WARNER, Sylvia Townsend (1893–1978), was born and brought up at Harrow School, where her father was a history master. She trained as a composer and musicologist before turning to writing in the mid-1920s. In 1930 she left a busy London literary life and moved to Dorset with the woman poet Valentine Ackland in what turned out to be a lifelong commitment. Warner was a successful novelist in the Twenties, with her early books (especially *Lolly Willowes*, 1926) in the fantastic mode popularized by her friends David Garnett and T. F. Powys, and later she became well known for her short stories, many of which appeared in *The New Yorker*. Warner joined the Communist Party in 1935 and was a prominent political activist, travelling to Spain twice during the Civil War. Her poetry, which was the least public face of a varied writing career, is characterized by sharp wit, rich vocabulary, and a deliberately ambiguous tone. Using mostly traditional forms, domestic themes, and blessed with a gift for lyricism, her work can at first seem an odd off-shoot of the *Georgian school, but the subversive vision and mischievous humour of even her earliest volumes, *The Espalier* (1925) and *Time Importuned* (1928), are determinedly counter-Georgian. A disparate body of work published, often obscurely, over a period of fifty years is distinguished by linguistic and syntactical verve. A significant quantity of her poetry was not published until after her death (*Collected Poems*, Manchester, 1982); see also *Selected Poems* (Manchester, 1985). Warner wrote seven novels, ten volumes of stories, a biography of T. H. White, and translations from the French. Her *Letters* were published in 1982 (London). See also Claire Harman, *Sylvia Townsend Warner: A Biography* (London, 1989).   [CPH

WARREN, Robert Penn (1905–88), was born in Guthrie, Kentucky, and came in at the tail-end of the Southern renaissance, whose main luminaries included William *Faulkner, Cleanth Brooks, and John Crowe *Ransom. Warren shared something of the gifts of all three. He collaborated with Cleanth Brooks on the seminal studies *Understanding Poetry* and *Understanding Fiction*, and his own *Selected Essays* reveal insights into a variety of topics in verse and prose. His fiction ran to a long list of novels and two books of short stories; his most famous novel, *All The King's Men* (New York, 1946; London, 1948), a study of small-town and state poli-

tics based on the career of the Louisiana governor Huey Long, was made into a successful film in the 1940s.

But the central thrust of Warren's literary career lay in the field of poetry, though it was not until late in his career—after the age of 50 in effect—that his best work and his major acclaim were to come. The bridge work between his early and later verse career is the narrative poem—or verse novel—*Brother To Dragons*, which draws on an actual set of events, the murderous Oedipal fixation of Lilburn Lewis, a nephew of Thomas Jefferson. The brooding violence and Southern guilt of this poem surface increasingly in Warren's later verse, though here they may owe something to the extended narratives of Robinson *Jeffers. Indeed, the controlled ruggedness of Jeffers's free verse may be an important contributor to the formation of Warren's distinctive later style. The shift in this between autobiographical anecdote and meditation and a repeated interest in exploring objective narratives with a moral to them may be seen as the special polarity of Warren's career, something which marks a comparison with the verse of Thomas *Hardy, another poet whose rough-hewn individual style was only perfected in older age.

Poems like 'Star-Fall' and 'The Mission' illustrate how Warren increasingly worked. An everyday incident is clearly described, the human elements are outlined against the vast unyielding continuity of the universe, and a gloomy or inspiring moral is drawn. This is a crude analysis, and fails to unveil the grandeur and huge emotion Warren can deploy through these bare frameworks; but the frameworks themselves, prosaic and humble, enable the vast sensations to stoop to an earthy dimension, and the poems avoid—almost always—the airy emptiness which ventures of this kind so often drift into. There is much of the honesty of *Frost in Warren, but none of his cracker-barrel flippancy. On the other hand, there is rarely Frost's sense of balance, at line level, between a rigid metre and a varying rhythm, and when Warren attempts rhyming and metrical poems he is not often at his best.

Selected Poems 1923–1975 (New York and London) appeared in 1976, and *New and Selected Poems 1923–1985* (New York) in 1985. [GMacB

WARREN, Rosanna (1953–), the daughter of Robert Penn *Warren and Eleanor Clark, was born in Fairfield, Connecticut, and educated at Yale and at Johns Hopkins universities. She teaches at Boston University and is on the staff of *Partisan Review*.

She developed an early interest in Latin and French poetry and an apprehension of or sense of poetic form when required to memorize French poems in her *lycée*. Her father encouraged her to read the poetry of Donne, Blake, *Hardy, and *Ransom. Of these, Hardy has remained an abiding influence together with Baudelaire, whom she read earlier, in addition to her more recent study of Greek lyric poetry, especially Sappho.

In her undergraduate years at Yale she was introduced to the poetry and painting of Max Jacob, whose work she especially admires. Some of her best poems are inspired by or are about painting and about the relationship of art to nature, but her subjects also include domestic life, love, war, and death. One of her most moving poems is on the Civil War Battle of Antietam Creek. All of her poetry is written in carefully crafted free verse combining strong cadences with freshly perceived particulars, and creating a density of style reminiscent of Greek sculpture, as in 'Painting a Madonna' and 'A Cypress'.

Warren's first book, *Snow Day* (Winston-Salem, NC, 1981) has been incorporated into *Each Leaf Shines Separate* (New York, 1984). She is the editor of *The Art of Translation: Voices from the Field* (Boston, 1989), a collection of lectures given at Boston University. [DES

WATKINS, Vernon (Phillips) (1906–67), was born in Maesteg in Wales and educated at Repton and at Magdalene College, Cambridge, where he was a contemporary of William *Empson and Kathleen *Raine. Out of sympathy with the prevailing positivism at Cambridge, he left without taking a degree. In 1927 he had a breakdown, following a vision that he

had conquered time. After he recovered he went to work at Lloyds Bank in Swansea, where he remained for the rest of his life, refusing promotion to devote himself to poetry. He died of a heart attack while playing tennis in Seattle, where he had gone as a visiting professor.

Watkins wrote steadily throughout his career, and by the time he met Dylan *Thomas in 1934 he had written a thousand poems and published none. Encouraged by Thomas, he allowed his poems to appear in *Wales* and *Life and Letters Today*; but his first book, *The Ballad of the Mari Lwyd*, did not appear until 1941 when he was 35.

Watkins was a great admirer of *Yeats, a visit to whom in 1938 was the occasion of a long poem, 'Yeats in Dublin'. However, Watkins's serene simplicity had little in common with Yeats's rhetorical grandeur. Another important formative influence was his friendship with Dylan Thomas; and their correspondence, published as *Dylan Thomas: Letters to Vernon Watkins* (1957) and later as *Letters to Vernon Watkins* (1988) and *Letters to Dylan Thomas* (1988), constitutes an important poetic document.

Watkins said that he could never write a poem dominated by time: constancy within change he recognized as the theme that engaged his imagination. His poetry draws on and attempts to create myth, because he saw myth as a redemptive process constantly re-enacted. For all his insistence on simplicity of impulse, Watkins was a learned poet: he translated Heine's *The North Sea* (1957), and his *Selected Verse Translations* appeared in 1977.

His *Collected Poems* were published in 1986 (London). He may be sampled in *Unity of the Stream: Selected Poems* (Wantage, Berks., 1983). See also *Vernon Watkins*, by R. Mathias (Cardiff, 1974) and *Portrait of a Friend* by Gwen Watkins (Llandysul, 1983; also as *Dylan Thomas: Portrait of a Friendship*, Seattle, 1985). [ATT

WAYMAN, Tom (Thomas Ethan) (1945–), was born in Hawkesbury, Ontario. He took his BA at the University of British Columbia and his MFA at the University of California, Irvine. In the late 1960s he became involved with the radical left on a number of American campuses. On his return to Vancouver he experienced difficulty in finding a teaching job and worked for a time as a building labourer.

Wayman's first book, *Waiting for Wayman* (Toronto, 1973), records his discovery that all human relations, even the most intimate, are distorted by the economic forces of capitalism. Influenced by Pablo Neruda, he places everyday North American events within an international context. His later collections continue this vein but emphasize the lives of average workers, explaining how the economic system impoverishes their lives. In *Inside Job: Essays on the New Work Writing* (Madeira Park, BC, 1983), he argues that poetry needs to express the actual moment in which we live, and that since work takes up a large part of our lives, poetry must similarly be about work. His most recent collection of poetry, *In A Small House on the Outskirts of Heaven* (Madeira Park, 1989), also contains a prose Afterword entitled 'Work, Money, Authenticity'. In his accounts of the workplace and the treatment of workers, Wayman writes in the narrative mode and in free verse. He employs a hard-hitting vernacular, is often anecdotal, and expresses anger at particular people and institutions; his poetry also contains much wit and quiet irony about his own place as a poet and worker in society.

Stephen Scobie has an interview with Wayman, 'Everyone is an Expert on the Present', in *NeWest Review*, 4: 9 (Jan. 1979).   [RBH

WEARNE, Alan (1948–), grew up in the eastern Melbourne suburb of Blackburn. He joined with John *Scott and Laurie *Duggan in the Monash University poetry readings, and in the 1979 Victorian elections stood as the Labour candidate for Nunawading.

The knotty diction and scrimmaging syntax of his verse compose a shorthand which chews over and spits out social codes (like that of the Anglican Church of Australia). Dramatic monologues save this language from pure idiosyncrasy: Wearne's narrators, wresting their stories from speech conventions, give an index to their personalities. In *Out Here* (Newcastle upon Tyne, 1987), nine monologuists attempt to extract the meaning from one enigmatic act, a teenager's self-mutilation in the school toilets.

In *The Nightmarkets* (Ringwood, Victoria, 1986) Wearne adopted a final strategy of Browning's—length. The 11,000 lines (many cast as sonnets) and ten monologues revolve around two actions: a journalist's investigation of the links politics has with prostitution and his erotic obsession with a 'hostess'; and a feminist's affair with a charismatic political leader. A survey of sexual and political mores, chronicling the extinction of the radical idealism which fired the Vietnam and Whitlam years, *The Nightmarkets*'s tone is not sufficiently detached from the ennui which afflicts its speakers. In 'Nothing But Thunder' (in *Scripsi*, 1989), Wearne is better able to place the reflections of a drug-runner, whose flagging hedonism leaves him craving for converts.   [CP

WEBB, Francis (1925–73), was born in Adelaide and raised in Sydney by his paternal grandparents after his mother died when he was 2. He was educated by the Christian Brothers, then joined the Royal Australian Air Force in the Second World War, and trained in Canada as a gunner. He was never involved in combat. Demobilized, he enrolled at the University of Sydney, but within a year went back to Canada and then moved to England. There he had the first of his mental breakdowns, and was diagnosed a schizophrenic at 24. He came back to Australia for three years, returned to England, suffered another attack, and was hospitalized for six years. Returning for the last time to Australia, he spent virtually the rest of his life in mental institutions. He was usually in open wards, without privacy, where even the radio on which he listened to classical music was stolen from him. It was only at the end of his life that he was transferred, by a doctor involved in literature, to a hospital for mental retards, so that he could have a small room to himself. Released for a time in the Sixties, Webb would go daily to Sydney's Bondi Beach to swim, but was tormented by the sight of the young people there. He went to confession twice a day and to mass every day and several times on Sundays. He returned to hospital at his own request, obsessed by fears of communism and by the need for piety, and died in an institution, aged 48. In his last years a number of writers would visit him. One of these was Sir Herbert *Read, who ranked Webb with *Eliot, Rilke, and Pasternak as the century's major poets.

Webb is considered in Australia (where he has had virtually his only audience) as either the country's finest poet (David *Campbell claimed that he 'went higher' than anyone else who has written there) or as a turgid rhetorician. His early poems are heavily metred and rhymed, influenced by the early Robert *Lowell; the best of his later work is usually his quietest, like his own justifiable favourites, 'A Death at Winson Green' and 'Five Days Old'.

Webb relies heavily on personification, which often becomes grotesque. He worked in large formal stanzas, and the feeling in reading him of a sombre, dark architecture reminds one of his devotion to the music of Bruckner and Mahler. The writhing sense of sin and the stretching after grace in his work issues, at its best, in an experience of compassion. 'Harry', in the sequence 'Ward Two', is one of the finest instances of this. The poem 'Morgan's Country', about a bushranger, is unmatched as a brief evocation of madness. The ambiguity in Webb's work repays struggle, because there is never bad faith but always a completely serious theme beneath it. Despite his failings—the lumbering of many of his poems, their often musty, airless quality—it is a supportable claim that Webb has produced some of the most moving poetry of the century. There were five books, between 1948 and 1964. The first biography— *God's Fool*, by Michael Griffiths—and a new selection—*Cap and Bells: The Poetry of Francis Webb*, ed. Michael Griffiths and James A. McGlade—appeared in 1991 (both Sydney).

[RGr

WEBB, Harri (1920–), was born in Swansea into a family whose roots were in Gower, and educated at Magdalen College, Oxford, where he read Romance languages. After serving in the

Second World War as an interpreter with the British Naval Mission to the French Provisional Government, he worked with Keidrych Rhys at the Druid Press in Carmarthen, and eventually as a librarian, first at Dowlais in Merthyr Tydfil and later at Mountain Ash in Glamorgan. He entered politics in the ranks of the Welsh Republican Movement, but from 1959 was active on behalf of Plaid Cymru (the Welsh nationalist party), editing the party's newspaper. In 1965, while living in Merthyr Tydfil, he was associated with Meic Stephens in the launching of the magazine *Poetry Wales*, and they collaborated in the writing of political ballads.

His early poems appeared in the magazine *Wales* during the 1940s and (with those of Meic Stephens and Peter Griffith) in the volume *Triad* (1963), but he found his mature voice as a contributor to the early numbers of *Poetry Wales*. Most of the poems in his first collection, *The Green Desert* (Llandysul, 1969), are about the history and social condition of the Welsh people. They are witty, erudite, and iconoclastic, and although sometimes propagandist, they are never crude or hectoring. His reputation as a poet of the Welsh nationalist cause was consolidated by his second volume, *A Crown for Branwen* (Llandysul, 1974), which included one of his few poems in Welsh, 'Colli Iaith' (Losing a Language), which has achieved the status of a folk-song.

During the 1970s Harri Webb began writing scripts for television, and his work was frequently to be heard on the BBC programme *Poems and Pints*. Thereafter his verse aimed at a wider audience: he still wrote about Welsh historical characters but more often in a light-hearted or satirical way. See the volumes *Rampage and Revel* (Llandysul, 1977) and *Poems and Points* (1983).

An autobiographical essay by Harri Webb will be found in *Planet*, 30 (Jan. 1971) and in *Artists in Wales*, ed. Meic Stephens (Llandysul, 1977). For a critical discussion of his work, see the article by Belinda Humphrey in the *Anglo-Welsh Review*, 21 (1972).

[MS

WEBB, Phyllis (1927–), was born in Victoria, British Columbia. She has lived and worked all over Canada, and has in recent years settled on Saltspring Island off Canada's west coast. She has been a politician, secretary, radio producer, and university lecturer. Notorious for her long silences, she has nevertheless produced a considerable body of lyrical poems and is an influence on writers of two generations.

Her third book, *Naked Poems* (Vancouver, 1965), has become a key text in contemporary Canadian literature. It is a suite of intimate stanzas often cited as the source for what many critics call the characteristic Canadian invention—the lyric become a long poem.

Her subject is often suicide or other deaths. The territory is variously the personal psyche, world politics, or other literatures. The poetry itself is the means by which one may avoid despair and seek beauty, a tactic for survival. Webb's persona often seems highly strung, given to a music whose source is next to pain. It often celebrates heroes who have been to the edge of death—Jacobo Timmerman, the Old Testament's Daniel, Dostoyevsky. In recent years it has named other women poets and their need to be heard.

Webb's work before 1980 can be found in *The Vision Tree: Selected Poems* (Vancouver, 1982). Her writings about poetry appear in *Talking* (Montreal, 1982). [GHB

WEDDE, Ian (1946–), was born in Blenheim, New Zealand. After early years spent largely overseas, Wedde returned to New Zealand for university study, gaining an MA from Auckland in 1968. He began publishing poetry in 1966. After travelling through Asia, Europe, and North Africa, Wedde worked in Jordan and Syria, and then in England, where he was poetry critic for the *London Magazine*. A poem sequence, *Homage to Matisse* (1971), was published in London. The years of travel inform Wedde's New Zealand-published first collection, *Made Over* (1974). The book made clear his interest in the poetics of William Carlos *Williams.

Returning to New Zealand, Wedde settled in Otago, 1972–5. The birth of his first son in 1972 inspired *Earthly: Sonnets for Carlos* (1975), a highly reticulated sequence of sixty free-form sonnets embodying Wedde's ambition to connect domestic and political landscapes. Outside the sonnets, Wedde explored other 'worlds within worlds' and diverse notions of responsibility ('the ability to respond'). The long poem *Pathway to the Sea* (1975) denounced the proposed siting of an aluminium smelter near a local bird sanctuary. A second collection, *Spells For Coming Out* (1977), also belongs to the Otago period.

In 1975 Wedde moved to Wellington, where his literary activities ranged from script-writing for experimental theatre to co-editing the tabloid *Spleen*. A first novel, *Dick Seddon's Great Dive*, was published in 1976, and Wedde began the research on Pacific whaling that became crucial to his poetry and fiction from 1976 on.

Longer forms and a darker vision characterize the poems of *Castaly* (Auckland, 1980; Oxford, 1981) and *Tales of Gotham City* (Auckland, 1984). *Georgicon* (Wellington, 1984) proposes new uses for the elements of irony and affectionate parody which are strongly developed in Wedde's writing. Other projects of the 1980s included publication of *The Shirt Factory and Other Stories* (1981) and co-editing the *Penguin Book of Contemporary New Zealand Verse* (1985, revd. edn., 1989). In 1986 Wedde published an epic novel, *Symmes Hole* (Auckland and London), and in 1987 assembled a selected poems, *Driving into the Storm* (Auckland). A comic novel, *Survival Arts*, followed in 1988. His most recent collection of poems is *Tendering* (Auckland, 1988). [ML

WEISS, Theodore (1916–), was born in Reading, Pennsylvania, and educated at Muhlenberg College and Columbia University. He married Renée Karol in 1941; in 1943 the Weisses founded an influential literary magazine, the *Quarterly Review*. The recipient of many honours, including a Guggenheim fellowship, Weiss is the subject of a documentary film, *A Year in the Life of a Poem* (1988). He taught at Yale, Bard, Washington University, the Massachusetts Institute of Technology, and, for over twenty years, at Princeton. Weiss lives in

Princeton and continues to edit the *Quarterly Review* together with his wife.

Weiss is a prolific essayist and critic as well as poet. His criticism includes a selection of the notebooks of Gerard Manley Hopkins (New York, 1945) and *The Breath of Clowns and Kings: Shakespeare's Early Comedies and Histories* (New York and London, 1971). He is the author of twelve volumes of poetry, most recently *From Princeton One Autumn Afternoon: Collected Poems* (New York, 1989).

Weiss's poetry, while not at all inaccessible, is perhaps best summed up as quirky in style. A tone of jocular alertness informs poems which take bird-like hops down or across the page: short lines often seem to articulate brief arcs of somewhat fragmented thoughts. Weiss's poetry evokes the visible world of nature and cities, domestic interiors and artefacts, but it is also constantly pulled toward the kind of abstract questions posed in the title-poem of *From Princeton One Autumn Afternoon*, an epistolary meditation on language, fame, and mortality. Weiss's work manages to combine a serene sense of the absurd with an anxious awareness of the clutter and detritus of a crowded century, a chaotic culture.   [RHa

WELLESLEY, Dorothy (Violet), Duchess of Wellington (1889–1956), was born in Berkshire. Her father died young; her mother married the Earl of Scarborough in 1899, thus introducing Dorothy to a world in which her own subsequent marriage to Gerald, seventh Duke of Wellington, in 1914, firmly established her.

Wellesley liked to experiment with an erudition never quite suited to her romantic impulsiveness; her first book, *Poems* (1920), betrayed this mixture of languor and aspiration. Not until 1934, and her *Poems of Ten Years*, did she benefit from any critical reassessment: she was praised for the detail with which she observed natural objects, and for the vigorous, if melodramatic, intensity of her laments over the suppression of the natural world by the commercial. But it was only when W. B. *Yeats read her poem 'Horses', which he included in his *Oxford Book of Modern Verse* (1936), that Wellesley found an influential

champion. He wrote his *Letters on Poetry* (1940) to her, and enthusiastically introduced a new selection of her work in 1936. 'Matrix', which Yeats proclaimed one of the most moving philosophical poems of the age, is a strange, visionary assertion of the womb as the origin of the masculine soul; 'Fire' exhibits Wellesley's 'frenzied grandeur', as Yeats termed it, as well as her recurrent preoccupation with the elements, and the sequence 'Deserted House' is a luminous, if grotesque, revisitation of childhood.

Wellesley collected her poems in *Early Light* (London, 1956). See also her autobiography, *Far Have I Travelled* (London, 1952).   [MRW

Wellington Group, The. The term refers to a loose association of New Zealand poets in Wellington, in the years between 1950 and 1965. New Zealand poetry after the Second World War tended to polarize around debate on the precepts that Allen *Curnow had outlined in his *A Book of New Zealand Verse 1923–1945*. What Curnow sensed as a 'common problem of the imagination' seemed to some of the younger poets to have become a prescription for thematic concerns, and Curnow's editorial practice became the subject of ongoing controversy.

The Wellington group saw themselves as establishing poetic practices that differed from those of Curnow as anthologist and, to a lesser degree, of Charles *Brasch as *Landfall*'s editor. Controversy flared over the withholding of permission for some work that Curnow wished to include in the *Penguin Book of New Zealand Verse* in 1960, and over the editorial introduction and practice when that anthology appeared. Yet seen retrospectively, the idea of a 'Wellington group' is more a term of geographical convenience than of poetic identity.

Certainly James K. *Baxter and Louis *Johnson, both Wellington residents during the period, seemed to draw a number of poets around them: Alastair *Campbell, for example, and the immigrants Peter *Bland and Charles *Boyle. Yet Baxter was a poet less at odds with Curnow than the rhetoric of his criticisms might have suggested. Only Louis Johnson, the editor of *Poetry Yearbook*, which published ten issues between 1951 and 1964, might be argued to have been at the centre of a school. The identification of a Wellington presence occurs in a paper Baxter gave to the 1951 Writers' Conference, and it underpins the ongoing critical rhetoric of the next decade. The issues in contention became those of the 'universal', as opposed to regional, concerns of local poetry, the primacy of 'content' as opposed to notions of academic formalism, and an increasing focus upon the suburban, the domestic, and the personal in much of the new work.

It is arguable that the sense of community asserted by the Wellington group was based less on poetic practice than on literary politics, in which a century of antipathy between the cities of Auckland and Wellington simply found a new focus. The notion of a 'group' and the polemics associated with it seem to have disappeared by about 1966.

For further information, see Kendrick Smithyman, 'Wellington and the Fifties,' in *Essays on New Zealand Literature*, ed. Wystan Curnow (Auckland, 1973); Patrick Evans, *Penguin History of New Zealand Literature*, chapter 8 (Auckland, 1990); Peter Simpson, 'The Trick of Standing Upright', *World Literature Written in English*, 26: 2 (1986). [WSB

WELLS, Robert (1947–), was born in Oxford. He read classics and English at King's College, Cambridge, has lived in Iran, and farmed in England and Italy.

His farming experience is closely associated with a prevalent theme in his poetry—love of the earth and the spiritual benefit of labouring in the fields, of establishing a union and communion with the earth, as expressed in his poems 'The Winter's Task' and 'Further on Down' in his first volume of verse, *The Winter's Task* (Manchester, 1977). It naturally followed that the poem chosen for his first major translation would be Virgil's *Georgics* (Manchester, 1982), a poem that he says demonstrates the value of cultivating the land with one's own hands. In his next translation, *The Idylls of Theocritus* (Manchester, 1988), he explains in his introduction his

endeavour to reveal the poems as they truly are, unobscured by the pastoral tradition they stimulated. Both translations, written in unrhymed lines of five accents, succeed in conveying the sense and tone of the original text without being exactly literal.

The best of Wells's verse is available in his *Selected Poems* (Manchester, 1986). [DES

WEVILL, David (Anthony) (1935–), a Canadian citizen, was born in Japan, educated in Canada and Cambridge, England, and now teaches at the University of Texas. His early poems, particularly those collected in *A Christ of the Ice-Floes* (London, 1966), gained attention in England owing to his association with the *Group and with Peter *Redgrove. The chief influences on his work have remained the psychological theories of Jung, and such Spanish-language poets as Paz, Neruda and Lorca. A much-praised early poem, 'Birth of a Shark', is typical in its sincere vagueness and its thrusting about in the seas of *'deep imagery'. The Jungian 'search', an admittedly circular one, is Wevill's main theme, and so his is a poetry that needs to be read in its entirety to be fully appreciated. Moreover, in later work, such as that collected in *Figure of Eight* (Toronto, 1984; Plymouth, Devon, 1988), a somewhat more epigrammatic quality became apparent, even though the mage-like narrator continued to be present. Wevill translated, with Edwin *Morgan, *Selected Poems* by the Hungarians Sandor Weöres and Ferenc Juhász. See also *Other Names for the Heart; New and Selected Poems* (Toronto, 1985). [MS-S

WHALEN, Philip (1923–), was born in Portland, Oregon, and educated there at Reed College, where he roomed with the poets Lew Welch and Gary *Snyder. He served in the US Air Force during the Second World War. His growing involvement with Zen Buddhism culminated in 1973 with his ordination as a priest. He now lives on a Buddhist commune in San Francisco.

Whalen is an eccentric but respected figure in recent American poetry, with strong links to the *Beat movement and the *San Francisco group.

His spiritual authority as a Buddhist priest consorts oddly with his garrulous, quirky manner; many of his poems are long, free-associative meditations that snake their way among references to food, politics, classical music, science, Greek literature, and similarly eclectic topics. Whalen is fond of various visual tricks involving typography and spacing, and he occasionally even incorporates little drawings and diagrams in his poems. At times his more recent poems move towards the contemplative quietness associated with Zen, but for the most part he attempts to wed his spiritual concerns with a restless, self-consciously rhetorical sensibility that is more American than Japanese. While his poetry is always entertaining, it offers few striking felicities of word or image; this may be why Whalen has not produced many individually memorable poems. His published volumes resemble notebooks, filled with miscellaneous jottings and doodlings, with here and there a fresh observation or an interesting phrase. His work can be sampled in *Decompressions: Selected Poems* (Bolinas, Calif., 1977).   [RG

WHEELOCK, John Hall (1886–1978), might well be described as the last nineteenth-century American poet. Throughout his long career he clung stubbornly and, some might say, heroically to a diction and manner that had long been repudiated by most of his contemporaries. The sentimental lyric, the philosophical poem, the ballad: all these forms were taken up by Wheelock with no trace of irony, no attempt at 'modernization'. Beside him *Frost looks like a radical experimenter (which of course he was). Wheelock's chief influences in the American tradition were the genteel 'Fireside' poets— Longfellow, Whittier, and so on—rather than the more iconoclastic Transcendentalists like Emerson, Whitman, and Dickinson, who fostered, the major strain of modern American poetry. Perhaps the chief interest of Wheelock's work for us today lies in the way that, despite his early predilections for nineteenth-century modes, we can see him gradually assimilating the tamer devices of modern verse, until by the end of his life he is writing with a directness and descriptive freedom that make for some moving lyrics on age, death, and nature.

Wheelock was born in Far Rockaway, New York; he grew up on Long Island, in an area which provides the setting for many of his poems. He attended Harvard, where he became close to the critic Van Wyck Brooks, a lifelong friend. After a sojourn in Europe he went to work for Scribner's, where he stayed for most of his life, acting at one point as assistant and successor to the famous editor Maxwell Perkins. He also began an intense friendship with the poet Sara *Teasdale, which ended with her death in 1933. He married late in life, at the age of 54. In 1954 he initiated and edited the Scribner's series Poets of Today, which did much to promote the work of young, unknown poets. His own work can be read in *This Blessed Earth: New and Selected Poems, 1927–1977* (New York, 1978).   [RG

WHEELWRIGHT, John (1897–1940), was born in Milton, Massachusetts, the descendant of two state governors and a Puritan divine expelled from Boston in 1637 for his nonconformist views, and religion and politics played as prominent a part in Wheelwright's life and poetry as they had played in his family's past. After graduating from Harvard he toured expatriate Europe, then returned to Boston and settled into a superficially eccentric life made possible by inheritances. Publication of his verse in the 1920s was confined for the most part to circulation among friends, perhaps because of an intuition that his Anglo-Catholic poems, despite their heresies, were unlikely to find a wider audience among the extravagances of the Jazz Age; but shortly after the stockmarket crash in October 1929 he joined the Socialist Labor Party, and he published his first book, *Rock and Shell* (Boston, 1933), at a time when similarities between the sacrament of Communion and the ritual of the breadline, and between the persecution of a new faith and government-sanctioned strike-breaking, would be apparent even to readers who weren't steeped in Marxist doctrine and the history of primitive Christianity. It was, however, his less tendentious poems, crisply phrased and scrupulously fanciful, that made the deepest impression on his contemporaries and on later advocates such as John *Ashbery and Frank *O'Hara. Two more collections followed, and a fourth manuscript was ready for print when he was killed by a drunken driver while crossing a street. Thirty years passed before the publication of his *Collected Poems*, ed. Alvin H. Rosenfeld (New York, 1972). [RH

WHIGHAM, Peter (1925–87), was born in England, lived for some years in Italy and in 1966 took up a teaching post in Santa Barbara. A classicist and translator, he found inspiration for his own poetry in his impressively eclectic reading. The title of the first, slight, collection he published with Denis Goacher, *Clear Lake Comes from Enjoyment* (1959), suggests an ideal of limpidity resulting from immersion in a pure source, and the epigrammatic style he continued to favour proved both imitation and homage to the manner of unimpeachable models. His translations of *The Poems of Catullus* appeared in 1966, and he later edited and contributed to *Epigrams of Martial Englished by Divers Hands* (1987). He also translated two books by the traveller and anthropologist Boris de Rachewiltz, *Black Eros* (1964) and *Introduction to African Travel* (1966). The poems collected in Whigham's next two volumes, *The Ingathering of Love* (1967) and *The Blue Winged Bee* (1969), somewhat uneasily blended Catullan questioning and self-deprecation with a tribute to the less stylized poetry of the Dalai Lama, whose work 'suggested' several of the poems. Whigham was keen to roughen the metrical pattern of his poetry, and repeatedly attempted to inject into it a colloquial register—*Astropovo* (1970) contains a number of experiments in musical and metrical form. But he remained a student of the classics. Poems about natural subjects repeatedly hinge on allusions to his masters; what he called the 'Honey of memory' is the dominant influence and note in *Things Common, Properly: Selected Poems 1942–1982* (London, 1984).

Whigham's poems are represented in John Matthias (ed.), *23 Modern British Poets* (Chicago, 1971). [MRW

WHISTLER, (Alan Charles) Laurence (1912–), distinguished glass-engraver and memoirist, younger brother of the designer Rex Whistler, is a graceful minor poet whose work, at first merely conventional and occasional (*The Emperor Heart*, London, 1936), gained depth after the death of his much-loved first wife, the actress Jill Furse, in 1944. Whistler wrote a book about her, *Jill Furse: Her Nature and Her Poems 1915–1944* (London, 1945), and remained preoccupied by her loss for a long period, culminating in *To Celebrate Her Living* (London, 1967). Technically, his poems have something of the meticulous nature of his famous engravings on goblets and on church windows all over England. The best of them, particularly those in *A View from this Window* (London, 1956), which are elegies, possess a power reminiscent of Crashaw and other late metaphysical poets. Whistler is for some a paradigm of what a 'minor poet' ought to be: not flashy, modest, and with his own small but distinct voice. See *The World's Room: Collected Poems* (London, 1949) and *Enter* (London, 1987) [MS-S

WHITE, Kenneth (1936–), was born in Glasgow and educated at the universities of Glasgow, Munich, and Paris. He was a lecturer in French at Glasgow in the mid-1960s, but since 1967 has lived in France. From 1983 he has been professor of twentieth-century poetics at the Sorbonne.

Two early collections appeared in France, *White Coal* (1963) and *En Toute Candeur* (1964). Two others then appeared in London, *The Cold Wind of Dawn* (1966) and *The Most Difficult Area* (1968). Almost ten years were to pass before White's poetry began to appear again, this time in France in bilingual editions. One consequence of this was that his work was relatively little known among English-language readers until 1989 and the appearance simultaneously of *The Bird Path: Collected Longer Poems* and the prose work *Travels in the Drifting Dawn* (both reissued by Penguin Books, 1990). *Handbook for the Diamond Country: Collected Shorter Poems 1960–1990* (1990) and *The Blue Road* (1990—both Edinburgh) have been published since. As his publishing history suggests, White was well known in his adopted country, France—enough for him to be hailed as 'the foremost English-language poet'—and hardly known at all in his native Scotland until 1989, where, however, his work has now received considerable critical attention and attracted a number of followers.

White's poetry is founded on a need to replace what Thoreau called a 'desponding creed' with attempts and beliefs that might contribute to 'chances of wholeness' otherwise confounded by technological and materialist society. In questing after 'something else', White's poetry proposes a shift from history to geography. He has written about what he calls 'geopoetics', assuming the stance of an 'intellectual nomad' (the idea is originally Norman Douglas's) and a 'laughing anarchist'. The objective is to win through to 'the space won at the end of the personal journey'.

*MacDiarmid, *Pound, *Snyder, *Olson, Chinese and Japanese poetry, are among White's sources and influences, although the biggest impact on his work could have been the places where he has travelled. A satisfyingly outdoors poetry (often with much naming of places) is made to co-exist with more bookish, philosophical impulses. Its best effect is one of wind-swept contemplation in remote places. A genuinely meditative, sometimes mystical, beauty, can be the result.

White has also written critical works not yet published in the UK, including La Figure du Dehors (Paris, 1982) and Une Apocalypse Tranquille: Crise et Creation dans la Culture Occidentale (Paris, 1985). [DED

WHITTEMORE, (Edward) Reed (II) (1919–), was born in New Haven, Connecticut. He taught English at the University of Maryland, and is now emeritus professor there. He co-edited (1939–53) the magazine *Furioso, was literary editor of the New Republic, 1969–73, and poet laureate for Maryland, 1985–8. His poetry follows in the tradition created by William Carlos *Williams, of whom he has written a useful critical biography, with more than a glance at

the quasi-surreal side of Wallace *Stevens in the long poem 'The Self-Made Man', in the book of that title (New York, 1959). Much of his poetry is light, satiric, and somewhat inconsequential in a now-accepted American manner. But he was much praised for his vigorously defiant poem 'Lines Composed on Reading an Announcement by Civil Defense Authorities Recommending That I Build A Bomb Shelter in My Backyard'. His later work is generally more sombre in theme. It sometimes deals, ironically but never bitterly, with American 'culture', and it expresses an agreeable liberal humanism, but usually lacks bite or much individuality. See Poems New and Selected (Minneapolis, Minn., 1967) and The Past, the Future, the Present: Poems Selected and New (Fayetteville, Ark., 1990).

[MS-S

WICKHAM, Anna (1884–1947), was born in 1884 in Wimbledon, where her father kept a music shop. She was taken to Queensland, Australia, as a small child, and returned to England at the age of 20 to train as a singer. An unhappy marriage frustrated this ambition, and she increasingly turned to poetry. Her first poems were printed by Harold and Alida *Monro of the *Poetry Bookshop, and she went on to produce many collections, including Songs of Oland (1911), The Contemplative Quarry (1915), The Man with the Hammer (1916), and The Little Old House (1921). Anna Wickham hanged herself in London in 1947.

She wrote in both free and rhymed forms, and though her distinctive, forthright voice is always audible, what she called her 'free rhythms' can sound rather inert and unsure. Her short, formal pieces are often more successful, with a crispness that enhances the social observation of, for example, men 'of the Croydon class' and women 'passionate about pins and pence and soap'. A substantial collection of her poetry and essays, The Writings of Anna Wickham: Free Woman and Poet, was published by Virago (London) in 1984. [CAR

WIENERS, John (1934–), was born in Milton, Massachusetts, the son of working-class parents of Irish descent. After graduating from Boston College he studied at *Black Mountain College with Charles *Olson, Robert *Duncan, and Robert *Creeley, and at the age of 24 published *The Hotel Wentley Poems* (San Francisco, 1958), in which he writes about his experiences with drugs, his homosexual love-affairs, and his bouts of mental illness in powerful unmetred verse influenced by Forties jazz and Abstract Expressionist painting. In subsequent collections he widened his thematic scope to include explorations of feminine psychology and imaginings of moneyed leisure, and the end of this intensely lyrical period was marked by the publication of his first *Selected Poems* (New York, 1972). His next book, *Behind the State Capitol or Cincinnati Pike* (Boston, 1975), is one of the strangest in the history of American poetry. Poems of civic protest alternate with harrowing fantasies about movie stars, socialites, and kingpins of organized crime, and the media-obsessed subject-matter is reflected in radically distorted syntax and bizarre physical properties: letters are capitalized wilfully, often in the middle of a word; words are hyphenated mid-syllable, sometimes at the end of a line; and lines and sentences begin and end without warning. After this bath in the static of consciousness, Wieners fell silent until the appearance of *Selected Poems 1958–1984*, ed. Raymond Foye (Santa Rosa, Calif., 1985), which closes with a group of new and more accessible poems. See also *Cultural Affairs in Boston: Poetry and Prose 1956–1985*, ed. Raymond Foye (Santa Rosa, 1988). [RH

WIKKRAMASINHA, Lakdasa (1941–78), was educated at St Thomas's College, Mount Lavinia, Sri Lanka, and studied law before becoming an English teacher. His interest in Sinhala literature led him to experiment with methods of fusing the Western and Oriental traditions creatively in his own writing.

A bilingual poet, whose career ended prematurely with his death by drowning, Wikkramasinha's first book of verse, *Lustre. Poems* (Kandy, 1965), was written entirely in English in the contrary spirit of one who, finding himself constrained by his education to write in the language of 'the most despicable people on earth', had set himself to write as anarchically as possible. This mood did not last. His work appeared in *Madrona, Eastern Horizon, New Ceylon Writing, Outposts, University of Chicago Review*, and other local and international journals, and was published privately by him in *Janakiharana and Other Poems* (1967), *Fifteen Poems* (1970—both Kandy), and *Nossa Senhora dos Chingalas* (1973), *O Regal Blood* (1975), and *The Grasshopper Gleaming* (1976—all Colombo). In honour of a Sri Lankan artist of a previous generation, Wikkramasinha edited and privately published *Twelve Poems to Justin Daraniyagala 1903–67* (Kandy, 1971).

See also Y. Gooneratne (ed.), *Poems From India, Sri Lanka, Malaysia and Singapore* (Hong Kong, 1979), and *New Ceylon Writing* 4 (Sydney, 1979), which include Wikkramasinha's work; the latter also contains biographical information and critical assessments of his poetry by several hands. [YG

WILBUR, Richard (1921–), was born in New York and educated at Amherst College and Harvard University. He began writing poetry while serving in the United States Army during the Second World War and later explained this as his way of attempting to restore order to a world gone mad. His first book, *The Beautiful Changes and Other Poems* (1947), was published shortly after the war and only one year after Robert *Lowell's *Lord Weary's Castle* (1946). There were many more similarities than differences in the work of the two young writers, but when Lowell turned to a *'confessional' subject-matter with his *Life Studies* in 1959—leading the turn towards the personal that has dominated American poetry ever since—Wilbur did not follow. He thus stands apart from his literary age in at least three ways: he exhibits a classic, objective sensibility in a romantic, subjective time; he is a formalist in the midst of a relentless informality; and he is a relative optimist among absolute pessimists.

Wilbur has never stopped writing in the carefully metred and rhymed forms with which he began; he is the only contemporary poet to whom the term 'elegant' has regularly, and appropriately, been applied. But though Wilbur's consistency of form has allowed him to develop his skills and earn praise, it has also opened him to the charge that his work lacks development. His second book, *Ceremony and Other Poems* (1950), was followed by *Things of This World* (1956), generally thought by critics to be his best volume. *Advice to a Prophet and Other Poems* (1961), Wilbur's fourth volume, is his least attractive because in it he essentially abandons the positive quest for spirituality that underlies his best poems. Here he adopts a negative stance and satirically condemns modern mankind for its materialism and lack of depth. However, for his next volume, *Walking to Sleep: New Poems and Translations* (1969), Wilbur was awarded the Bollingen Prize for poetry, indicating that his reputation had not fallen excessively far. Interestingly, Wilbur had already been awarded the Bollingen Prize for translation in 1963, in honour of his rendering of Molière's *Tartuffe* (his version of *The Misanthrope* was performed in 1955). He has also written two books for children, and his literary essays are collected in *Responses: Prose Pieces, 1953–1976* (New York, 1976). His last separate volume of poetry, *The Mind-Reader* (1976), contains a few unrhymed poems, but nothing that could truly be called informal (regular metres are retained). In 1987 Wilbur was named the second poet laureate of the United States, succeeding Robert Penn *Warren.

As he indicated in his lecture 'The Bottles Become New Too', Wilbur has a deep regard for the physical world: 'poets can't afford to forget that there is a reality of things which survives all orders great and small . . . No poetry can have any strength unless it continually bashes itself against the reality of things.' This sense of regard is balanced, both in his view of the world and in his work, by an equally strong sense that an unseen power of spirituality underlies that physical realm. As Wilbur said during an interview with Peter Stitt: 'To put it simply, I feel that the universe is full of glorious energy, that the energy tends to take pattern and shape, and that the ultimate character of things is comely and

good.' It would seem to be the ultimate goal of Wilbur's poetry to praise both of these aspects of reality and to show their inherent union.

It is through the power of the imagination to create metaphor that Wilbur attempts to unite these two realms, as he himself has indicated: 'the imagination . . . when in best health neither slights the world of fact nor stops with it, but seeks the invisible through the visible.' Metaphor allows Wilbur to point out a close physical resemblance (between wings and leaves, for example), to transform one thing into another (ferns into ocean waves), or to suggest the presence of the unseen within the seen (Arcadia within an ordinary grove of trees). It is thus through metaphor that Wilbur's poetry accomplishes technically what he has conceived as true of the world in a philosophical sense. Motion seems always an aspect of his most effective metaphors, reflecting Wilbur's high regard for the concept of *grace*, which combines beautiful movement with a sense of benediction. His conception of God would seem similarly dual, something that exists both within the poet—as creative intelligence, an aspect of the imagination—and outside him. These two facets work in consort in a Wilbur poem: for the spirituality that exists within the universe to be both recognized and expressed, what is required is a perceiving creative intelligence within the observer that can somehow faintly match that of God.

Wilbur's work is gathered in *New and Collected Poems* (San Diego, Calif., 1988; London, 1989). See also Donald Hill, *Richard Wilbur* (New York, 1967); Wendy Salinger (ed.), *Richard Wilbur's Creation* (Ann Arbor, Mich., 1983); and Peter Stitt, *The World's Hieroglyphic Beauty: Five American Poets* (1986). [PS

WILCOX, Ella Wheeler (1850–1919), was born in Wisconsin, her father a dance-teacher, her precocity encouraged—at the age of 8 she was earning a substantial writing income. Poetry remained her favourite mode, starting with her first collection, *Drops of Water* (1872), which preached temperance, although she also wrote a number of prose volumes, including *The Story of a Literary Career* (1905) and *The Worlds and I*

(1918). She snared a national audience when her innocuous *Poems of Passion* (1876) was rejected by the first publisher approached on grounds of 'immorality'. In 1884 she married Robert Wilcox, and they moved to Connecticut. The forty-odd volumes of verse perpetrated by Wilcox, which evolved from prosy didacticism and pseudo-eroticism to Theosophist mysticism, have deservedly disappeared, her sole claim to poetic fame two lines paraphrased from Shakespeare in 'Solitude': 'Laugh, and the world laughs with you; | weep, and you weep alone.'

[EB

WILKINSON, Anne (1910–61), was born Anne Gibbons in Toronto. Through her mother she was related to the prominent Osler family and enjoyed a privileged upbringing; she was educated by private tutors and at progressive schools in England, France, and the United States. In 1932 she married Frederick Robert Wilkinson, a Toronto surgeon, and they had five children, two of whom died in infancy; their marriage ended in divorce in 1953. After a long battle with cancer, Wilkinson died in Toronto.

Encouraged by E. J. *Pratt and Alan Crawley, editor of *Contemporary Verse*, Wilkinson published two poetry collections, *Counterpoint to Sleep* (1951) and *The Hangman Ties the Holly* (1955), that revealed an extraordinary imagination and poetic gift—combining light and lively diction, and elegance and wit—in poems that explored her sensuous identification with nature and love, and life itself, including its pain and the omnipresence of death. A founding editor and patron of *The Tamarack Review*, Wilkinson also wrote *Lions in the Way* (1956), a history of the Osler family, and *Swann and Daphne* (1960), a fantasy for children.

Wilkinson's poetry, and an autobiographical fragment, 'Four Corners of My World', are available in *The Poetry of Anne Wilkinson and a Prose Memoir* (Toronto, 1968, with an introduction by A. J. M. Smith; Toronto, 1990, with an introduction by Joan Coldwell). See also *The Tightrope Walker: Autobiographical Writings of Anne Wilkinson* (Toronto, 1992), ed. Joan Coldwell. [DS

WILLIAMS, Charles (1886–1945), was born in London and for most of his life worked for the Oxford University Press. Williams's personal influence exceeded his general literary reputation, even though his novels, effective supernatural thrillers, were popular. T. S. *Eliot believed him to be a 'man who was always able to live in the material and spiritual world at once', and W. H. *Auden, when he first met him in 1936, said that in his presence he felt 'for the first time in my life in the presence of personal sanctity . . . I felt transformed into a person who was incapable of doing anything base or unloving'. Williams had also a profound influence upon the life and work of C. S. *Lewis, who admired his poetry. This poetry has received little attention outside a circle which included Eliot, Lewis (of whose group, the Inklings, Williams was a member) and, more recently, John *Heath-Stubbs. After beginning with somewhat pallid and more or less *Georgian lyrics in such volumes as *The Silver Stair* (London, 1912) and *Windows of Night* (London, 1924), he published a long series of poems on Arthurian themes, *Taliessin Through Logres* (London, 1938). It is this volume, and its successor *The Region of the Summer Stars* (London, 1944), that attracted the attention of his fellow Anglicans. Lewis's *Arthurian Torso* (London, 1948) contains a posthumous fragment by Williams called 'The Figure of Arthur' and a full commentary. This body of work has struck more than one reader uninitiated into higher Anglicanism as resembling the agnostic *Bridges of *The Testament of Beauty* crossed with the Eliot of *Murder in the Cathedral*: well and carefully wrought, meticulous, somewhat self-consciously 'beautiful'.

See John Heath-Stubbs's introduction to *Collected Plays* (London, 1963), and his *Charles Williams* (London, 1955); *Further Papers on Dante* (London, 1957), by Dorothy L. Sayers; and the article 'The Mathematics of the Soul' (*Poetry London*, 11, 1947), by M. Diggle. [MS-S

WILLIAMS, C(harles) K(enneth) (1936–), was born in Newark, New Jersey, and now lives in Paris, but spends part of each year teaching at George Mason University, Virginia. In 1975 he married Catherine Mauger; they have a son, and Williams also has a daughter by a previous marriage. He has been contributing editor to *American Poetry Review* (Philadelphia) since 1972. An exalted—though often comic or rueful—sense of the ties of marriage, family, and friendship, and an acute sympathy for 'flesh and blood'—in both senses—exposed to cruelty or indignity, colour Williams's uncompromising and distinctive poems. He is, as one reviewer has pointed out, 'almost synonymous' with the very long, unrhymed line that seems to owe something to Whitman and the Psalms; and he shows a novelist's or short-story writer's absorption in the matter of neglected, humble, or humiliated lives and places. His run-down urban settings are inhabited by the vulnerable and the walking wounded: hobos, misfits, war-veterans, invalids, lovers, and especially children and the old; a tendency to voyeurism inherent in Williams's meditative luxuriance is mostly transcended, and harsh or squalid subjects are invested with raw urgency, sombre tenderness, even reverence.

Williams has been publishing for almost thirty years, but his first books seem as misjudged in their bid for originality as his later ones seem confident and unerring. His work of the 1960s and early 1970s is crippled by its wilful commitment to extremes—an extreme horror and outrage, an equally extreme, anguished compassion, expressed in a poetic idiom that is, for the most part, unpunctuated, unfocused, and full of inarticulate ferocity. With his third book appeared the longer, more relaxed line, the spacious, clause-rich syntax (all patient modification and qualification), and the engagement with a populous, impressively detailed reality. This is the vein which—with occasional lapses into bathos or a garrulous self-fascination—Williams has worked to greatest effect ever since.

Poems 1963–1983 (Newcastle upon Tyne, 1988) contains a generous selection from Williams's first two books, and his subsequent three volumes in their entirety; *Flesh and Blood* (New York and Newcastle upon Tyne, 1988), won the National Book Critics' Circle Award; it

was followed by *A Dream of Mind* (New York and Newcastle upon Tyne, 1992). He has also published translations of Sophocles's *Women of Trachis* (with Gregory Dickerson) and *The Bacchae* of Euripides.   [AJ

WILLIAMS, Hugo (1942–), was born at Windsor. His father, the actor Hugh Williams, is portrayed in *Writing Home* (1985) as 'handsome', 'masterful', a man who was once 'on Famous Film Star | Cigarette Cards' but later had little work and less money. Stylish in his thirties before the war, a soldier in Tunisia during it, Hugh Williams was glamorously unknowable for his young son, and 'Death of an Actor', for all its affection, remembers the remoteness of a 'stiff theatrical man'. The poet's mother, Margaret Vyner Williams, is rarely mentioned in the poems.

Hugo Williams was educated at Eton College (1955–60) and then spent two years as editorial assistant on the *London Magazine* before leaving to spend twenty months travelling around the world. Those travels were recorded in *All the Time in the World* (1966), which appeared the year after Williams's first book of poems, *Symptoms of Loss*. In 1965 Williams married, and soon went back to work on the *London Magazine*, where he remained until 1970, the year in which his second collection of poems, *Sugar Daddy*, was published.

These early years, which brought him an Eric Gregory Award (1966) and Cholmondeley Award (1971), also saw the beginnings of Williams's association with Ian *Hamilton's *Review*. The brevity and restraint of poems in *Sugar Daddy* and *Some Sweet Day* (1975) linked Williams to other *Review* poets, including Hamilton himself, David *Harsent, and Colin *Falck; but poems in *Love-Life* (1979) showed him opening out towards a more relaxed, anecdotal and (auto)biographical style. With further awards and a reading tour of the USA (recorded in his frank *No Particular Place to Go*, 1981), Williams finally emerged from the 'record-breaking dole-run' which he described as the 'real background story' of his 1970s. *Writing Home* and *Self-Portrait with a Slide* (1990), together with the 1989 *Selected Poems* (all Oxford), established Williams as a poet of candour, irony, and brio. [MHu]

WILLIAMS, John Hartley (1944–), was born in Cheshire, grew up in North London, and was educated at William Ellis School and the universities of Nottingham and London. He has lived and worked in France, Francophone Africa, and Yugoslavia, and, since 1976, in Berlin where he teaches English at the Free University. His first collection, *Hidden Identities* (London, 1982), showed the influence of American modernism—particularly *Cummings—but was also notable for its interest in narrative and its presentation of English poetry as part of a wider European experience. *Bright River Yonder* (Newcastle upon Tyne, 1987) expanded the fictionalizing aspect into a sequence of poems set in a Wild West frontier town which assembled a story from a variety of differing voices and perspectives. *Cornerless People* (Newcastle upon Tyne, 1990) collected restless poems of journeying and cultural dislocation set against the background of capitalist Europe. [DK]

WILLIAMS, Jonathan (Chamberlain) (1929–), was born at Asheville, North Carolina. Out of the *Black Mountain school (he was at Black Mountain itself from 1951 until 1956), although he had started at Princeton, Williams is more relaxed and humorous than most of the poets thus associated. He lists ninety-nine (almost all very small) publications of his poetry up to 1990. Titles of these collections (often single poems) are evocative of the kind of poet he is: *Green Corn thru a Cow or Where Were You When the Culture Explosion Hit the Fan?* (1965); *50! Epiphytes, -taphs, -tomes, -grams, -thets! 50!* (1967), *Uncle Gus Flaubert Rates the Jargon Society in 101 Laconic Présalé, Sage Sentences* (1987). It is not hard to be pleased or amused by this, but it is hard to take it seriously, or Williams as a serious poet. But he has never claimed to be one. 'This' as he says, 'is your friendly local, Ecological Logodaedalist talking'; and he has aptly been described as a 'folk remedy'. He has a liking for Stevie *Smith, Lorine *Niedecker, Basil *Bunting, and for composers such as Satie and Mahler, and celebrates them jokily. He is an institution rather than a poet in the usually understood sense. But he has done serious work as a publisher dedicated to what he believes enduring: he published Charles *Olson, wrote on Bunting, and published the many letters *Patchen wrote to him. See *An Ear in Bartram's Tree: Selected Poems 1957–67* (Chapel Hill, NC, 1969); *Elite/Elate Poem: Poems 1971–1975* (Highlands, NC, 1979); *Get Hot or Get Out: A Selection of Poems 1957–1981* (Metuchen, NJ, 1982). [MS-S]

WILLIAMS, Miller (1930–), was born in Hoxie, Arkansas. After holding a number of academic appointments and other positions, he has taught since 1970 at the University of Arkansas, where he is university professor of English and foreign languages. He is also the director of the University of Arkansas Press, which he has developed into a leading literary publisher. His books include critical studies of *Ransom and *Ciardi; translations of Nicanor Parra, Pablo Neruda, and G. G. Belli; and several anthologies.

A prolific poet as well, Williams has published since 1964 seven full collections, and two volumes of new and selected poems. His work is uneven; many poems are more clever in inspiration than they are satisfying in execution. But he has always been capable of powerful and concentrated work ('Late Show'), and has written a number of impressive poems—including 'Original Sin', 'And When in Scenes of Glory . . .', 'In Your Own Words . . .', 'Getting Experience', and 'Wiedersehen'—about his Southern boyhood and adolescence. His poetry has grown in depth and sureness from book to book; his latest full collection, *Imperfect Love* (Baton Rouge, La., and London, 1986), is his best. 'In Extremis in Hardy, Arkansas' is an especially effective blend of his strengths: wit, colloquialism, technical fluency, and a wry tenderness concerning the complexities of the human heart.

Living on the Surface: New and Selected Poems (Baton Rouge and London, 1989) is a severe and judicious selection from all his published work. Michael Burns has edited *A Habitation and a*

Name: Essays on the Poetry of Miller Williams (Missouri, 1991). [MP

WILLIAMS, Tennessee (1911–83), was christened Thomas Lanier Williams, a name which he said 'sounds like it might belong to the sort of writer who turned out sonnet sequences to Spring'. Perhaps for this reason he changed it to Tennessee Williams—his forebears had fought Indians in the State of Tennessee, although he himself was born in Mississippi. The fact is, Williams did win a prize as a young man for a poem about Spring. His first appearance between book covers was in *Five Young American Poets* (1944). After establishing himself as a playwright with *The Glass Menagerie* (1944–5), he continued to write poems. Two collections followed: *In the Winter of Cities* (1954) and *Androgyne, Mon Amour* (1977).

While Williams's best poetry is found in his plays, in dialogue such as Quixote's outcry in *Camino Real*: 'The violets in the mountains have broken the rocks!'—Williams's fame as a playwright has overshadowed his accomplishment as a lyric poet. If there is an influence, it is the poetry of D. H. *Lawrence. The poems are sometimes self-conscious and marred by old-fashioned inversions. But there is a range—from songs, ballads, and blues to soliloquies, love poems, and elegies. The primary subject is the outcast in society, and the prevailing emotion is tenderness, as in 'Little Horse' and 'Recuerdo'. There are also poems of great humour, including 'Kitchen Door Blues' and 'Life Story'.

At present there is no collected edition. The best poems are available in the revised, expanded version of *In the Winter of Cities* (New York, 1964). See also *The Kindness of Strangers: The Life of Tennessee Williams*, by Donald Spoto (Boston, 1985).

[RSP

WILLIAMS, William Carlos (1883–1963), was a medical student at the University of Pennsylvania, where he began his lifelong friendship with *Pound (a 'special student' there) and H.D. (Hilda *Doolittle), the daughter of an astronomer whose observatory was associated with the university. Williams had a serious medical career. He studied advanced pediatrics in Germany after his internship, set up private practice in Rutherford, New Jersey (his native town), and eventually became head pediatrician of the General Hospital in the nearby city of Paterson.

Meanwhile, he played an active role in the avant-garde poetic movements centred in New York City and was also constantly in touch with Pound's literary activities and associates in Europe. His major difference with Pound (apart from Williams's acutely responsive and realistic presentations of women and his revulsion against fascism; see especially *Paterson* III–V) lay in his desire to create a specifically American poetics based on the rhythms and colorations of American speech, thought, and experience. His little prose work *In the American Grain* (1925) is a highly original and intense effort to present—in a sense, to create—the key events and figures of what Horace *Gregory, in his introduction to the 1939 reprint, called America's 'mythical history'. Without being so intended, it is something of a companion volume to D. H. *Lawrence's *Studies in Classic American Literature* (1923). The two books complement one another, and in fact Lawrence reviewed Williams's book with respectful interest. The reciprocal preoccupations of these two dynamic intelligences is one demonstration among many that Williams, like Whitman, was not a provincial despite his passionate search for a truly American poetry. His art and his larger interests were ultimately cosmopolitan.

His *Autobiography* (New York, 1951) is partly devoted to the medical side of his life and its crucial relation to his poetry—which, like his fiction, draws heavily on his experience as a doctor. His working-class patients, especially the women whose babies he delivered and whose hardy courage he vastly admired, absorbed his sympathetic if sometimes irritated attention much as Chekhov's peasant patients did his. They were of a different order of ethnic and class background, often, from the essentially middle-class world of Rutherford where he had spent his childhood and where he settled after his marriage to Florence Herman, the 'Floss' of his poems, who also appears in his plays and is the central figure of his novel *White Mule* (1937)—the first in a trilogy based on the lives of her Swedish mother and German father as immigrants in America.

Williams has gradually emerged as one of the great forces in twentieth-century American verse. His experiments, though striking, may have lacked the brilliance of Pound's and *Eliot's at their best, and they may lack the elegance of Wallace *Stevens in *Harmonium* or *The Auroras of Autumn*. But Williams's work is more expressive of American sensibility, and more saturated with American speech and its rhythms, than any poet's since Whitman. For these reasons he has entered the bloodstream of later American poetry: Allen *Ginsberg, Robert *Lowell, Paul *Blackburn, and many others show strong traces of his influence. (And indeed his poetry has also cast a net of 'Americanization' overseas, in the form of some poets' stylistic reorientation. We find writers like Charles *Tomlinson and John *Montague, for example, reflecting this influence while adapting it to their own countries' colloquial turns and poetic traditions.)

Robert *Frost, of course, rivals Williams in his use of the native idiom—his poems are true to the speech and the trapped psyches of the New England country-people he knew; the dark elegiac and tragic strains running through so much of what he wrote carry it far beyond mere pastoral charm. Williams, however, expresses the whole nation's character, and especially its urban volatility: its multiracial and immigrant streams of speech and behaviour, its violence and exuberance, its ignorance of its own general and regional history. His important sequence *Paterson*, published serially between 1946 and 1961 in five 'Books' and part of a sixth, is an exploration of all these matters. It is presented as a search for the elements of a 'common language': a shared cultural and historical awareness to counteract the fragmentation of American society. Williams saw this fragmentation as a pressure for 'divorce' (i.e., inability to

connect or communicate), not only between the sexes but among the people at large.

Williams's *Selected Essays* (New York, 1954) are most useful as clues to his artistic and intellectual affinities. *Joyce, Pound, Gertrude *Stein, Marianne *Moore, and Kenneth *Burke loom large in this respect, together with Alfred Stieglitz and certain painters: Brueghel, Matisse, Tchelitchew, Sheeler. Williams had far more of a painter's eye than do most poets; see, for instance, his *Pictures from Brueghel* (1962). His famous, somewhat baffling, yet nevertheless valuable concept of the 'variable foot' (each 'foot'—or line-fragment—a held moment or unit of measure within an unfolding apperception) gives the typographical movement of his later poems something of the character of animated abstract painting. It is clear that he felt a compelling convergence of visual and aural patterns as he wrote.

At the same time, his poems project a sensuous and associative immediacy of extraordinary vivacity. Their aura of spontaneous improvisation has misled many younger poets into overlooking his artistry. ('Rigor of beauty is the quest,' he wrote at the start of the 'Preface' to *Paterson*.) Perhaps it was his apparently relaxed colloquialism—often coupled, however, with startling shifts of focus and with eloquent passages of beautifully controlled rhythm and phrasing—that delayed recognition of his achievement even in the United States.

Since his first published book, *The Tempers* (1913), Williams's poems have appeared in numerous individual volumes and collected editions. Except for *Paterson* (New York, 1963; London, 1964; Manchester, 1992), they have now been gathered together in chronological order, and with scrupulous scholarly care, in the two-volume *The Collected Poems of William Carlos Williams* (New York, 1986 and 1988; Manchester, 1987 and 1989), ed. A. Walton Litz and Christopher MacGowan. M. L. Rosenthal brought out *The William Carlos Williams Reader* (New York, 1966; London, 1967), and Charles Tomlinson edited a *Selected Poems* (New York, 1985; Harmondsworth, 1990). See also the biography by Paul Mariani, *William Carlos Williams:*

A New World Naked (New York and London, 1981) and Emily Mitchell Wallace, *A Bibliography of William Carlos Williams* (Middletown, Conn., 1968). [MLR

WILMER, Clive (1945–), was born in Harrogate, Yorkshire, grew up in London, and was educated at King's College, Cambridge. He has lived in Florence and Padua and has taught at the University of California at Santa Barbara. He lives in Cambridge, where he was a founder-editor of the periodical *Numbers* and is a presenter of the BBC programme 'Poet of the Month'.

His poetry at times has affinities with the **Stanford School' founded by Yvor *Winters in its employment of the plain style and substantial rational subject-matter, and it frequently reflects his long-standing admiration for George Herbert. A careful craftsman, he aims at what he calls 'exactness of form', with each poem having its own distinctive structure. He frequently expresses a religious feeling derived from his Anglican upbringing and social and aesthetic thought as represented by the works of John Ruskin and William Morris, both of whom he has edited.

Wilmer's poems are in *The Dwelling Place* (Manchester, 1977); *Devotions* (Manchester, 1982); *A Catalogue of Flowers* (Florence, Ky., 1986); and *Of Earthly Paradise* (Manchester, 1992). He has edited John Ruskin's *Unto this Last and Other Writings* (London, 1985). Among his critical essays is 'An Art of Recovery: Some Literary Sources for Geoffrey Hill's *Tenebrae*', *The Southern Review*, 17 (Jan. 1981). [DES

WILMOT, Frank (1881–1942), was born in Melbourne, subject of his most significant work, *Melbourne Odes* (Melbourne, 1934), published under the pseudonym 'Furnley Maurice'. In representations of depression life such as 'Upon a Row of Old Boots and Shoes in a Pawnbroker's Window', these expressed the radicalism which had led him to attack Australian involvement in the First World War: 'To God from the Weary [later 'Warring'] Nations', published 1916, became the centre-piece of the anti-war *Eyes of Vigilance* (Melbourne, 1920).

However, *Melbourne Odes* also celebrated the city as a place of social dreams and vivid activity, challenging the dominance of nature poetry such as Wilmot himself had written in *The Gully and Other Poems* (Melbourne, 1925). And in their formal experimentation, they put into practice his conviction that Australian writers should look to American modernism for methods to develop the 'National Poetry' he advocated in the essay collected in *Romance* (Melbourne, 1922)

Wilmot, who managed Melbourne University Press, remained active in literary life but published little after *Melbourne Odes*. E. Morris Miller's account in *Australian Literature 1795–1938* (Melbourne, 1940; facsimile Sydney, 1973) compares interestingly with David Headon's 'Frank Wilmot: The First Australian Modernist', *Meanjin*, 41: 4 (1982). [JS

WILSON, Edmund (1895–1972), was born in Red Bank, New Jersey, the only child of well-to-do parents who gave their son an unwavering belief in the importance of good writing. After graduating from Princeton University and serving with the American Expeditionary Force in France, Wilson settled in Jazz Age New York and worked as an editor for *Vanity Fair* and the *New Republic*. Though he published a book of poems and a novel in 1929, neither had the impact of *Axel's Castle*, his 1931 study of post-Symbolist writers such as Valéry, *Stein, *Joyce, and *Eliot. Many other influential works of criticism followed—most notably, perhaps, *Patriotic Gore* (New York and London, 1962), a survey of the literature of the American Civil War. Of the poems collected in *Night Thoughts* (New York, 1961), the two most powerful are 'A Young Girl Indicted for Murder' and 'On Editing Scott Fitzgerald's Papers', the latter an elegy in heroic couplets written while he put together *The Crack-Up*, a selection of notebook entries, character sketches, and magazine articles by his old Princeton friend. Wilson died in Talcottville, New York, where he and his fourth wife had lived for more than twenty years in a home inherited from his mother's family. The best guide to his poems is the autobiography drawn from his diaries (all published New York): *A Prelude* (1967), *The Twenties* (1975), *The Thirties* (1980), *The Forties* (1983), *The Fifties* (1987), and *Upstate* (1972). Leon Edel edited the intermediate volumes in the series.   [RH

WINGFIELD, Sheila (1906–92), was born in Hampshire and attended Roedean School. In her childhood she was obliged to hide her literary interests from her parents, and later came a ban 'on meeting literary personalities' from her husband. History and mythology in particular became compelling objects of study for her in her isolation, interests reflected in her richly allusive writing. Her first collection, *Poems* (1938) was praised by *Yeats. She went on to produce a further six volumes, including the symphonic meditation, 2,000 lines long, on war and love, *Beat Drum, Beat Heart* (1946). She also wrote two volumes of memoirs, *Real People* (1952) and *Sun Too Fast* (1974).

Her sonorous, dignified tone and her intellectual range are suggestive of Geoffrey *Hill, but without a trace of pomp. Her most philosophical flights are always tempered by precise observation. The fullest selection of work by this underrated poet may be found in her *Collected Poems* (London, 1983).   [CAR

WINKFIELD, Trevor. See NEW YORK SCHOOL.

WINTERS, Yvor (1900–68), was born in Chicago. His father, who had a nervous and physical breakdown before Winters was 4, took the family to Los Angeles and Seattle and, in 1914, back to Chicago in search of secure and lucrative employment. Winters spent one year at the University of Chicago, three years in bed in Santa Fe, New Mexico, with tuberculosis, and two more as a schoolteacher in the coal camps of Madrid and Cerillo, south of Santa Fe. He took an MA in Romance languages from the University of Colorado in 1925, and taught French and Spanish at the University of Idaho (1925–7). In 1926 he married Janet *Lewis, and the following year was enrolled as a graduate student at Stanford University, where he stayed for the rest of his working life, becoming professor of English in 1949.

Winters's poetry falls clearly into two phases. His first three volumes (thought by many to be his best), *The Immobile Wind* (1921), *The Magpie's Shadow* (1922), and *The Bare Hills* (1927), all collected in *The Early Poems: 1920–28* (1966), were written under the technical influence of *Pound, William Carlos *Williams, Marianne *Moore, H.D. (Hilda *Doolittle), and other modernists. Their imagistic free verse is emotionally charged, vividly evocative of the New Mexican landscape, and—as Winters himself later observed—redolent of his youthful solipsistic and deterministic philosophy. In the late 1920s and early 1930s Winters tired of modernist innovations and found inspiration in the conventional prosody of Dryden, Pope, *Hardy, E. A. *Robinson, and others. *The Proof* (1930) begins with *imagist poems but ends with traditional metres; and all eight poems in *The Journey* (1931) use heroic couplets. As Western editor of *Hound & Horn* during its last two years (1932–4), and in his first three critical books, collected as *In Defense of Reason* (1947), Winters gave trenchant and dogmatic expression to his revised opinions; he believed that poetry should be a clear statement using traditional metres (since they alone could exploit the full emotional potential of language) to convey feeling informed by understanding. Not only, he felt, were *Bridges and T. Sturge *Moore better poets than *Eliot and Pound; free verse and imagism were themselves temporary aberrations from the Anglo-American poetic tradition. These views involved Winters in some bitter critical disputes. Meanwhile, he continued publishing his neoclassical poems, in *Before Disaster* (1934), *Poems* (1940), which he printed on his own press, *The Giant Weapon* (1943), and *Three Poems* (1950); 'Sir Gawaine and the Greene Knight' and 'A Summer Commentary', in particular, succeed in combining effective use of imagery with ordered and precise statement. In *The Function of Criticism* (1957) and *Forms of Discovery* (1967), Winters sustained and developed his anti-modernist polemic, championing the 'post-symbolist' style of poetry which made 'no sacrifice of rational intelligence'. His poetic output diminished towards the end of his life, but his *Collected Poems* (1952; revd. and enlarged, Athens, Ohio, 1960; Manchester, UK, 1978; repr., Athens, 1980) won a Bollingen Prize in 1960. See also *In Defense of Reason* (1947; repr., Athens, 1986) and *An Introduction to the Poetry of Yvor Winters*, by Elizabeth Isaacs (Athens, 1981).

[NE

WOJAHN, David (1953–), was born in St Paul, Minnesota, and lived in the Twin Cities until earning a BA in English from the University of Minnesota in 1977. He next completed an MFA at the University of Arizona and has since taught at five universities, currently at Indiana. In 1981, Richard *Hugo selected *Icehouse Lights* (New Haven, Conn., 1982) for the Yale Younger Poet Award.

Both *Icehouse Lights* and Wojahn's second book, *Glassworks* (Pittsburgh, Pa., 1987), repeatedly pursue the theme of memory as a source of endurance rather than loss. In brief narratives such as 'The Astral Body' and 'Porch Lights' Wojahn creates purely personal juxtapositions of past and present. But in some longer poems like 'Cold Glow: Icehouses' and 'Steam' he blends personal memory and present context with historical analogues, such as the origins of a resort town's defunct mineral baths. Besides first-person narratives, Wojahn sometimes writes dramatic monologues; 'Song of Burning' adopts the voice of rock-singer Jim Morrison. Along the same lines, *Mystery Train* (Pittsburgh, 1990) contains a series of imaginative character-sketches about rock musicians from Elvis Presley to Bob Marley. [MCB

WOLFE, Humbert (1885–1940), was born in Italy. During the 1930s he was an under-secretary at the then Ministry of Labour. Wolfe was a quintessentially middle-brow poet, with some small lyric talent ('The dust on Agamemnon's shield' is a typical line), but no genius. He graduated from acid romantic to rude epigrammatist. His poems are almost always brief and to the point, and are in their way well made. His sharpest work is concerned with the prejudice he encountered as a 'clever Jew'; he wrote an effective pamphlet attacking G. K. *Chesterton

for his anti-Semitism. It is ironic that his best essay, an official-inspired one about how to use the stirrup-pump (with which the population was supplied in 1939 to deal with incendiary bombs), was hardly put to the test. See *London Sonnets* (London, 1919) and *Kensington Gardens in Wartime* (London, 1940). [MS-S

WONG, Phui Nam (1935–), was born in Kuala Lumpur. English was the main medium of his education, but as a schoolboy he also attended Chinese school in the afternoon for some years and later studied Chinese classical poetry under a tutor. Between 1955 and 1959 he studied in the University of Malaya (then in Singapore), majoring in economics but also studying philosophy and English. He has worked mainly in development and merchant-banking and finance, and is now an investment consultant.

Wong started writing verse as an undergraduate. His mature poems are among the best Malaysian poems in English, unsurpassed in their eloquence and linguistic richness. Most of them are contemplative or introspective and draw their images from the Malaysian landscape. In his introduction to the collection *How the Hills are Distant* (Kuala Lumpur, 1968), Wong expresses the need to naturalize English, his adopted language, for his poetic purposes, just as a Malaysian of immigrant ancestry like himself would have to be naturalized to the culture of the country his forefathers have adopted.

The other collection of his poems is *Remembering Grandma and Other Rumours* (Singapore, 1989). [FA

WOODCOCK, George (1912–), was born in Winnipeg, Manitoba. His parents returned to England when he was five months old, and he was educated there. During the 1930s Woodcock worked as a railway clerk and began contributing poems to Julian *Symons's *Twentieth Century Verse*. His first collection, *Six Poems*, was published in 1938. He founded the magazine *Now* in 1940, and under the influence of Herbert *Read became an anarchist. In 1949 he married the artist Ingeborg Linzer and they emigrated to Canada. A man of letters, Woodcock has written on many subjects, including anarchism, and has written biographies of Godwin, Gandhi, and Orwell. He has also published extensively on the social history of Canada. As well, in 1959 he became the first editor of *Canadian Literature*, and for the next eighteen years worked closely with Canada's writers and critics.

In his *Collected Poems* (Victoria, BC, 1983), Woodcock notes that he virtually stopped writing poetry when he left England in 1949 and began again only in the late 1960s. His early poetry owes much to the *Imagists: brief, suggestive renderings of landscape which intimate a coming storm. He was influenced also by *Eliot and *Auden: many of his poems re-create an abstract landscape, a world of innocence which might extend to humanity, except that mankind's rapacity and greed intrude. His poems often employ mythic figures, in particular an Odysseus figure who returns from his wanderings and finds himself unable to prevent civilization from destroying itself. Woodcock's later poetry, in which he draws on Canada's west-coast imagery, tends to be more affirmative. The emphasis falls on metamorphosis, the power to change 'the eternal dark to light'.

Woodcock's two volumes of autobiography, *Letter to the Past* (Don Mills, Ont., 1982) and *Beyond the Blue Mountains* (Markham, Ont., 1987), contain valuable insights into his development as a poet. *A Political Art: Essays and Images in Honour of George Woodcock* (Vancouver, 1978) also contains interesting material.   [RH

WRIGHT, C(arolyn) D. (1949–), was born in Mountain Home, Arkansas, in the Ozark Mountains. She was educated at Memphis State University and the University of Arkansas, and in 1983 she married the poet Forrest Gander. Wright has lived in Providence, Rhode Island, since 1983 and is an associate professor of English at Brown University.

The first real influence on Wright was Frank *Stanford, a land surveyor and poet, who lived in a neighbouring town. From him she learned a sense of narrative in a rural Southern idiom. Wright's poems are colloquial in diction, and their subjects 'half pulled out of earth and rivers'.

Wright has written of herself: 'I am, irrevocably, a purebred hill person.' And of her work: 'My poems are about desire, conflict, the dearth of justice for all. About persons of small means.'

Wright has published six collections of poetry, most recently *Translations of the Gospel Back into Tongues* (Albany, NY, 1982), *Further Adventures with You* (Pittsburgh, Pa., 1986), and *String Light* (Athens, Ga., and London, 1991).
                                                    [HC

WRIGHT, Charles (1935–), was born in Pickwick Dam, Tennessee. Educated at Davidson College and the University of Iowa, he began writing poems while stationed in Verona, Italy, with the Army Intelligence Unit between 1957 and 1961. He has since taught at the University of Padua as a Fulbright lecturer and studied in Rome. During his early years in Italy he came under the poetic spell of Ezra *Pound, whom he addresses as 'Cold-blooded father of light' in one of his finest early poems, 'Homage to Ezra Pound', in *Hard Freight* (1973). Wright has also been deeply influenced by Dante and such modern Italian poets as Eugenio Montale and Cesare Pavese, both of whom he has translated. Wright's translation of Montale's *The Storm and Other Things* won a PEN translation award in 1979.

Before taking his current post as professor of English at the University of Virginia, Wright taught for many years at the University of California at Irvine. The various landscapes of Wright's life—the South, California, Italy—have inevitably found their way into his poems, but his landscapes are deeply interior, often surreal. His poems, from *The Grave of the Right Hand* (1970) to *Zone Journals* (1988), are austere and difficult of access. As Helen Vendler has said 'they defy exposition. They cluster, aggregate, radiate; they add layers, like pearls.'

Wright is fundamentally a religious poet, his poems subverting the traditional imagery of eastern (*China Trace*, 1977) and western (*The Southern Cross*, 1981) spiritual traditions in unusual ways. His densely imagistic poems, with their inescapable rhythms and insistent musicality, explore possibilities for a spiritual life in a world overwhelmed by concrete objects. He often, as in *Bloodlines* (1975), works in obliquely autobiographical poem-sequences. More recently, as in *Zone Journals*, he has adapted the journal form to his own uses, creating complex meditations on the mysteries of memory and creation. See Wright's selected volume of early poems, *Country Music* (Middletown, Conn., 1982). For an interview with Wright, see the *Paris Review*, 113 (Winter 1989).

[JP

WRIGHT, David (1920–94), was born in Johannesburg. He became deaf in childhood and, at the age of 14 was brought to England to attend the Northampton School for the Deaf. He graduated from Oriel College, Oxford, in 1942. His first collection, *Poems*, was published by *Poetry London* in 1949 (though it had been in the publisher's hands since 1943); his second collection, *Moral Stories* (1954), showed a strong reaction against his earlier manner. From 1959 to 1962 he edited, with the painter Patrick Swift, the quarterly review X (see *An Anthology from X*, ed. Wright, Oxford, 1988). Also with Patrick Swift, he wrote three books about Portugal. There is an autobiographical work, *Deafness: A Personal Account* (1969), and one critical work about a fellow South African, Roy *Campbell (1961). As an anthologist, Wright edited a number of excellent volumes, among them *Longer Contemporary Poems* (1966), the *Penguin Book of English Romantic Verse* (1968), and the *Penguin Book of Everyday Verse* (1976). He lived in the Lake District.

His poetry is remarkable for its quiet intelligence and humour, and the integrity of its style. The tone is conversational, though not in the sense of reproducing a factitious chattiness; rather, it creates the lively curve of an eminently humane mind's thinking and speaking. The perceptions are romantic, elegiac, exact. The subjects are various: there are recollections of childhood and of friends; poems about places and things observed, as well as on his deafness; some attractive poems about animals and birds; and noble elegies to Patrick *Kavanagh, Patrick Swift, Jean Murray Wright, and Philippa Reid.

After *To the Gods the Shades: New and Collected Poems* (Manchester, 1976) appeared, Wright published two collections: *Metrical Observations* (1980) and *Elegies* (1990). There is also a *Selected Poems* (Manchester, 1988). A warmly appreciative essay on Wright's work can be found in *In Two Minds: Guesses at Other Writers*, by C. H. Sisson (Manchester, 1990).   [TJGH

WRIGHT, James (1927–80), was born into the family of an Ohio steelworker and educated in that state. After military service Wright went to Kenyon College where he studied under *Ransom, later completing his university training in Seattle with Theodore *Roethke. He taught for many years in the University of Minnesota and was attached to other academic institutions, latterly to Hunter College, New York.

There is a paradox at the heart of Wright's poetry: this most finely tuned of stylists, this clear delineator of language's own needs, is able to appeal directly to the feelings of his readers as few other American poets of his generation can. It is customary to speak of Wright's shifts of allegiance from formal versification to open-ended composition as a conversion to populism, but a Wright poem from any period will have a high emotional tension fitted to striking directness of utterance. When he came into prominence in the late Fifties and early Sixties, Wright seemed a cuckoo in each partisan's nest—a formalist (by Roethke out of *Yeats) in the age of the *Beats, a 'Minnesotan-Peruvian' (see DEEP IMAGE) among the *Confessionals, and a master translator eschewing the academy in favour of Whitmanesque vernacular.

Such stylistic ambiguity sprang from Wright's impassioned identification with poor and unrepresented minorities in the United States, fused with an equally characteristic American fondness for the pressures of high art. Martin's Ferry, the mining town in Ohio where Wright grew up, recurs in his poetry like a tocsin of doom. It is both the source of many of his most terrible stories of poverty and wretchedness and the focus of his pantheism. Early in his career, he stated: 'I try to say how I love my country and how I despise the way it is treated. I try to speak of the beauty and again of the ugliness in the lives of the poor and neglected.'

Perhaps the most significant of early influences on Wright's work were two great European expressionist masters, Trakl and Rilke: indeed, if any one stylistic term might be applied to every stage of his development it would be expressionism. Wright's most celebrated conversion, immediately visible in the progression from *Saint Judas* (1959) to *The Branch Will Not Break* (1963), was seen at the time as deriving from the influence of his friend Robert *Bly, who championed the objective lyricism of Spanish-American poetry against the prevailing 'Confessional' mode of *Lowell and his followers. Finely stitched impacted stanzas, usually rhymed, were replaced by lyrical statements of an *Imagist sort. The language of these poems is direct and addresses personal and emotional concerns in a manner almost *en plein air*.

Wright's affection for and critical esteem of Vallejo and other South American poets, however, does not fully account for his stylistic shift; nor can his practice be held to resemble Bly's. Wright's originality has always shone more brightly when he appears to be imitating some prevailing mode. The poems from *The Branch Will Not Break* and *Shall We Gather at the River* (1968) show Wright experimenting with an open language appropriate to the increasing desperation of life in the USA. While Vallejo's poetry challenges political injustice in authoritarian regimes, Trakl's is wrought from the internal drama of the Central European mind, and Wright's, in turn, follows Trakl's tendency. From the beginning Wright was concerned with extremes of mental suffering, with poverty of hope as well as material poverty, and with murderers, hobos, and dispossessed American Indians. 'At the Executed Murderer's Grave' is one of the most powerful of his earlier poems.

The Branch Will Not Break reprinted one of his most notorious works, a poem which exemplified his changed style and which was so conspicuously misunderstood it became a rallying point for those suspicious of Wright—'Lying in a Hammock at William Duffy's Farm in Pine Island, Minnesota'. Long and facetiously elaborate titles, occasionally exceeding the body of the poem in length, are a feature of his work in the Sixties, and in this case a short passage of natural observation culminates in the line: 'I have wasted my life.' Years afterwards, Wright explained reasonably that this was a statement of mood, not an Augustinian confession. At the time it seemed a veritable polemic in favour of poetic detachment.

Wright travelled widely and often, and some of the most moving among his later poems are set in Italy. Whether he is rescuing a bee from a suicidal orgy in a ripe pear, 'among the gasworks at the edge of Mantua', watching the fast-flowing Adige river at Verona, or pausing at Leonardo's and Michelangelo's town of Aghiara, Wright finds occasion for many exquisite sorties into Latin elegy, and ties them to a specifically American *lacrimae rerum* from his Ohio childhood. The Italian poems are central to his book *To a Blossoming Pear Tree* (New York, 1977; London, 1979). Before this Wright had published a *Collected Poems* (Middletown, Conn., 1971). He died in 1980. *Above The River: The Complete Poems* (New York and Newcastle upon Tyne, 1992) contains also some prose pieces and translations. [PNFP

WRIGHT, Judith (1915–), was born and brought up in the New England area of New South Wales. For many years she made her home at Mount Tambourine, Queensland, but more recently has returned to New South Wales and now lives in Braidwood. With the publication of her first volume *The Moving Image* (1946) Wright established herself as a poet of the first rank, and subsequent volumes have brought her a well-deserved international reputation. She has published work other than poetry, including criticism, short stories, and studies of conservation and of Australian history. Nevertheless, it is the poetry which counts for most.

Her range is wide. She is technically adroit over a variety of forms, and in all her volumes the poems, meditative, lyrical, and combative by turns, move easily from the personal to the social, and from the world of nature to the world of politics. Through them all, however, runs a tough connecting thread, a conviction that the created world and its inhabitants have been touched by a grace they repeatedly deny. Over the years her poems have become darker. Yet the conviction survives. In her early poetry she tended to concentrate on the intensely personal, as in the beautiful 'The Company of Lovers', 'Woman to Man', and 'Our Love is so Natural'; and even the much-anthologized 'Bullocky', a deftly constructed fable at whose heart is the archetypal figure of the ploughman, can be read as a poem which gathers together the possibilities of several kinds of fruition, including the personal. Going with these poems are others about Australia's native flora and fauna, and some of these were gathered together in the delightful volume *Birds*, first published in 1962 and then reprinted in 1967, this time with some unfussy illustrations by the Australian artist Annette Macarthy Onslow.

With the publication of *The Other Half* (1966) it is possible to detect a change, not so much of direction as of tone. There had been poems of social awareness in previous volumes, but when Wright turns to such matters in the new collection the poems have about them a distinctively sharpened note of displeasure at the despoiling of 'green earth'. The volume's final poem, called 'Turning Fifty', ends with her raising her cup to the 'new sun', but there is nothing bland or absolving about the gesture. The poem is taut with anger. It may be that this is at least one reason why she says in a late poem, 'Skins', that she no longer wishes to read the poems she wrote in her thirties. 'They dropped off several incarnations back.' That poem comes from *Phantom Dwelling* (London, 1986). Her earlier work may be most conveniently consulted in the *Collected Poems* (London and Sydney, 1970). See also *A Human Pattern: Selected Poems* (Sydney, 1991; Manchester, 1992). [JL]

WRIGHT, Kit (1944–), was born in Kent, and educated at Oxford. He has lectured in Canada, was fellow-commoner in creative art at Cambridge, 1977–9; from 1970–75 he was education secretary at the Poetry Society. He now lives in London, where he works as a free-lance writer, broadcaster, and editor, and is a well-known figure on the poetry-workshop scene. Both the Home Counties background and unfashionable urban life elicit Wright's lyricism, and his poetry is profoundly English in its combining of jaunty rhythms, comic rhymes, a detached or impersonal air, with subject-matter that is frequently bleak, blackly funny, and grimly personal. Bereavement, breakdown, failure (particularly in love), the 'tears and terror' or the quiet desperation beneath the surfaces of ordinary English life, a recurring note of grief or sympathy for victims and underdogs—and a persistent strain of remorse and self-reproach, often connected with drinking: these are fairly constant in Wright's work, but so are the metrical ingenuity, the levity, and verbal panache.

Poems 1974–1983 (London, 1988) contains all the poems from Wright's first two full collections and his contributions to *Treble Poets I*; subsequently he has published *Short Afternoons* (London, 1989). He is also the author of several books for children. [AJ]

WYLIE, Elinor (Morton Hoyt) (1885–1928), was born in New Jersey and grew up in Philadelphia and Washington, DC. Married at 20 to socialite Philip Hichborn, she eloped five years later with Horace Wylie, with whom she lived, partly in England, from 1911 to 1915. Divorced from Wylie in 1923, she married William Rose *Benét, a man of letters and brother of the poet Stephen Vincent *Benét. She lived in Greenwich Village from 1922 until her death from a stroke in 1928.

Elinor Wylie's first book of poems was privately printed in London in 1912 and was followed in 1921 by *Nets to Catch the Wind*; three more collections, and four novels, followed in quick succession.

During and immediately after Wylie's lifetime her striking beauty combined with a social persona both aristocratic and artistic to cast an adulatory spell. Edmund *Wilson, no gusher as a rule, called Wylie in an essay after her death 'master of a divine language' and 'a free spirit as few Bohemians are'. This aura has dissipated, and Wylie is now regarded as a minor poet. Her novels, precious period pieces, are now hardly read; but some poems, particularly from the earlier collections, retain both force and charm. With firmly chiselled lines and colourful images, lyrics like 'August', 'Wild Peaches', or 'Bronze Trumpets and Sea-Water' stand out from the *Imagist practices of the period. More closely resembling the traditionally shaped lyric intensities of Edna St Vincent *Millay, Wylie's best poems have a distinctively worldly voice, as they ruefully limn the tensions between experi-ence and idealism. Wylie's burnished diction and supple rhymes influenced the poetry of the young James *Merrill.

Wylie's work is to be found in *Collected Poems of Elinor Wylie* (1932), *Collected Prose of Elinor Wylie* (1933), and *Last Poems* (1943—all New York). See also *Elinor Wylie*, a largely hostile study of the work by Thomas A. Gray (New York, 1969); *Elinor Wylie: A Life Apart* by Stanley Olson (New York, 1979); and *The Life and Art of Elinor Wylie* by Judith Farr (Baton Rouge, La., 1983).

[RHa

Y

YAP, Arthur (1943–), was born in Singapore, and educated locally, at Leeds University, and at the National University of Singapore, where he is a senior lecturer.

His poems are original, but can also be demanding: elliptical, dense, dry, sometimes droll. At their best, they shuttle between playfulness and sobriety and are alert to the rhythms and contours of the natural and the peopled landscape, seasoning insight with compassion.

Yap's stories can be sampled from *Singapore Short Stories: Volume 1,* ed. Robert Yeo (Singapore, 1978). His paintings have been exhibited locally, in Adelaide, and in Bangkok. His poetry collections (all published Singapore) are: *Only Lines* (1971); *Commonplace* (1977); *Down the Line* (1980); and *Man snake apple and other poems* (1986). For criticism of Yap's work see D. J. Enright, *TLS* (24 Nov. 1978); Anthony Burgess, *Straits Times* (9 Aug. 1983); *Singapore Studies,* ed. Basant K. Kapur (Singapore, 1986); *Critical Engagements,* ed. Kirpal Singh (Singapore, 1986). [RPa

YATES, Peter (1914–), was born of British parents in India and educated at Sevenoaks School and London University. Before the Second World War he lived a wandering life in America, Sumatra, and Europe. After a brief period in the army, he was invalided out. His first book of poems, *The Expanding Mirror,* appeared to some acclaim in 1942. It was followed by *The Motionless Dancer* in 1943 and *Light and Dark* in 1951. He wrote two verse dramas, *The Assassin* (1945) about John Wilkes Booth, the actor who shot Lincoln; and *The Burning Mask* (1948), about the actor Edmund Kean. *The Assassin* was produced at the Lyric theatre, Hammersmith—one of the few verse dramas of the period to achieve theatrical success. During the 1950s he was involved in a motorcycle accident that left him incapacitated for many years. Nothing more by him appeared until a selection of old and new poems, *Petal and Thorn,* was published in 1983.

Unusually for the image-dominated period in which he wrote, Yates frequently structured his poems in terms of the interplay of abstractions that reflect his often tortured vision of a shattered world made unclean by the loss of unreflective innocence. He is best sampled in *Petal and Thorn* (London, 1983). There is a brief memoir in *John Lehmann: A Tribute,* ed. A. T. Tolley (Ottawa, 1987). [ATT

YEATS, W(illiam) B(utler) (1865–1939), was born in Dublin, son of the painter John Butler Yeats and Susan Pollexfen. His family moved to London when he was 2, and back to Dublin when he was 16. His childhood holidays were spent in Co. Sligo, which came to share with Lady Gregory's Coole Park the central place in his poetry's imaginative geography. After it was decided that he would not go to Trinity College, Dublin (where his father's friend Edward Dowden was professor of English), he studied at the Dublin Metropolitan School of Art from 1884 to 1886. His first published poems appeared in the *Dublin University Review* in 1885; his first volume of poems, *The Wanderings of Oisin and Other Poems* (1889), already suggests the three major preoccupations of his writings: Ireland, spiritualism, and love—unsurprising concerns in the context of both English and Irish poetry of his time. The preponderance of one or other of these depended on who Yeats was currently influenced by (though Conor Cruise O'Brien argues in his essay 'Passion and Cunning' that the poet's declared passions were always controlled by his determination to be a significant poet). He was a founder-member of the Irish National Literary Society in 1892.

The first major influence was Yeats's father, whom he both revered and reacted against. But as early as the mid-1880s he was reading Sinnett's *Esoteric Buddhism*; in 1890 he joined the Hermetic Order of the Golden Dawn, and in 1892 he wrote to John O'Leary that his interest in the occult was, after his poetry, the most important pursuit of his life. His interest in Irish affairs was fanned by meeting O'Leary, the exiled Fenian leader who returned to Dublin from Paris in 1885; Yeats first encountered him in the exclusive, Trinity-based Contemporary Club to which he was introduced by his father. O'Leary was in turn responsible for Yeats's first meeting with Maud Gonne in London in January 1889: an event which he described in the Dantesque phrase 'the troubling of my life'. As a passionate Irish nationalist of great beauty, she represented the poet's ideal, and his largely (though not entirely) unrequited love for her obsessed him for the next quarter-century. The volumes of poems up to *The Green Helmet* (1910) are dominated by Yeats's love for her and the despair caused by her marriage to John MacBride in 1903, culminating in the love-lament 'No Second Troy'.

In this period Yeats was by no means a prolific poet. His friend (and later enemy) George Moore testifies that his poetic career was thought to have largely ended in the early years of the new century, something which is partly corroborated by the appearance of an eight-volume *Collected Works* in 1908. In that period Yeats was most active in the successful attempt to set up an Irish National Theatre, started in 1899 in collaboration with Augusta, Lady Gregory, and Edward Martyn. He found in writing for the theatre a literary way of combining through mythology his interests in Irish nationalism and the mysterious, and it also afforded acting parts for Maud Gonne. In 1902 Maud played the title-role in the nationalistic play *Cathleen Ni Houlihan* (of which Yeats wondered in his late poem 'The Man And The Echo', 'Did that play of mine send out | Certain men the English shot?'—Stephen Gwynn said it did have an emotionally rousing impact). But strangely, despite his energetic involvement with the theatre throughout his life, Yeats's plays lack a natural sense of the theatrical; though they have moments and subjects of high drama, they are often defeated by their brevity and by verging on the ludicrous. He was, though, a very effective promoter of other playwrights, most importantly Synge, whom he encouraged to return to Ireland from Paris in the 1890s. Whether or not Yeats has the principal responsibility for Synge's inspiring sojourns in the Aran Islands from 1899 to 1902, there is no doubting his defence of Synge's *The Playboy of the Western World* (1907) against what he saw as the small-minded prudery and nationalism of the protesting audience in his Abbey Theatre in Dublin. The occasion was the first of many when Yeats accused the new Irish (and indeed English) middle classes of debased materialism—though it must be said that it was a charge which had general fashionable currency in literary circles long before, and after, Yeats.

From *Responsibilities* (1914) onwards, Yeats's poetry develops great dramatic power and scope. As public events in Ireland became more crucial, his poetry becomes correspondingly more public, beginning with the disillusioned but rhetorical 'September 1913': 'Romantic Ireland's dead and gone, | It's with O'Leary in the grave.' These poems of Yeats's 'middle period' combine to great effect a declamatory voice with a diction which is more spare than in his earlier, 'Celtic twilight' verse. 'Easter 1916' notes the new 'terrible beauty' that the rebellion represents, and Yeats traces with horror the growing violence of the period, through 'Nineteen Hundred And Nineteen' on to 'Meditations in Time of Civil War' (both published in *The Tower*, 1928). Outside his poetry, he was practically active in the public sphere, and he was nominated to the Senate, the Upper House of the new Free State, in 1922. He made some historically significant speeches there, many arguing the Anglo-Irish Protestant interest which he felt was insufficiently represented in the new state: something which led to increasing political disillusion and disengagement on his part. But by the 1920s, under the pressure of political events around him, Yeats had become an important public poet.

There were major developments in Yeats's private and intellectual life in the middle period too. In 1917, after Maud Gonne's daughter Iseult had also refused him, he married Georgie Hyde Lees whom he met in 1911. The marriage was very happy and they had two children. A week after the wedding, George (Yeats's name for her) started to produce automatic writing which greatly excited her husband. Her communications were the basis of Yeats's pseudo-philosophical, mystical book *A Vision* (1925); more importantly, they provided material for several powerful visionary poems, such as 'The Second Coming' (published 1921) and 'Leda and the Swan' (in *The Tower*). A further literary stimulus was Yeats's introduction by Ezra *Pound to the Japanese Noh plays. This led to the production in 1916 of *At the Hawk's Well*, the first of Yeats's *Four Plays for Dancers*, plays which used masks, which Yeats saw as shifting the emphasis from the actor to the language. Like the thought of *A Vision*, the notion of the mask extended into Yeats's poetry to salutary effect.

Perhaps the most important aspect of Yeats's poetry in this period was the development of his theory of symbolism as mediating between life and art, a dichotomy which was to be the principal concern of his poetry for the rest of his life. To represent this concern, he refined the symbols which he had used throughout his writing (the swan and the rose, for example), in a process which is brilliantly traced in Frank Kermode's *Romantic Image* (1957). To those he added some new symbols, derived from his own life, particularly the tower which was Thoor Ballylee, near Gort, Co. Galway, not far from Coole Park. Yeats bought it in 1917 and, though he lived in it only very briefly, it afforded an important artistic domicile for him. Many critics (C. K. *Stead, for example) have felt that his greatest achievement was this development of a

symbolic language to express an equilibrium between the conflicting demands on the poet of the outside world and his art: what he called in a late poem, 'The Choice', the intellect's dilemma of choosing between 'Perfection of the life, or of the work'. This theme is central to the two volumes which are often thought to be Yeats's best, *The Tower* (1928) and *The Winding Stair* (1933). The maintenance of this equilibrium is the subject of the complementary Byzantium poems; 'Sailing to Byzantium' (1927) declares the physical world to be 'no country for old men', and takes the poet to the holy, artistic city of Byzantium (as extolled by the Nineties aesthetes) where, 'out of bodily form', the soul can sing. In 'Byzantium' (1930), the objective has ostensibly been reached, as 'the unpurged images of day recede'. But the tension is sustained by the use of sexual language (the images in Byzantium *beget*, for instance) to keep the demands of the physical world in contention.

Yeats remained unreconciled to growing old (at least in his poetry; Louis *MacNeice reported that in reality Yeats viewed approaching death with surprising equanimity), and one of the principal subjects of his *Last Poems* is the raging against old age which is the central issue in the poem 'The Tower' (1926). But it is by no means the only topic in Yeats's later work; there is a development in the language of his masterly reverie poems, in 'Among School Children' (1926), 'In Memory of Eva Gore-Booth and Con Markiewicz' (1927), 'Coole Park, 1929' and 'Coole Park and Ballylee, 1931', for example. His health—physical, and to some extent mental—came under increasing strain as he attempted to 'hammer his thoughts into unity' and to make his complete poems represent that unity. His prose writing, which was voluminous throughout his life, becomes increasingly central to his work in later years. Yeats was not a good critic of other people's writing, but he was a compelling commentator on his own and a vitally important analyst of the poet in action. His self-commentary and his manuscripts have been used very effectively by Curtis Bradford and Jon *Stallworthy to trace the evolution of his poetry.

In his last years he shared with *Eliot the undisputed central place in English poetry (*Hardy was drafted in later to provide a more English and less complex alternative); he was awarded the Nobel Prize for Literature in 1923. In 1936 he edited the Oxford Book of Modern Verse 1892–1935 (eccentrically—he represented *Auden minimally and his own friends generously), and he spent part of his later years in France, where he died in January 1939, prompting a great elegy by Auden. His body was returned to Ireland in 1948 and buried, as he had wished, in Drumcliffe churchyard, Co. Sligo (where his paternal grandfather had been rector), under the epitaph from the end of his 'Under Ben Bulben': 'Cast a cold eye | On life, on death. | Horseman, pass by!'

Yeats's Last Poems (1939) present serious problems of editing and interpretation. The standard one-volume edition (the 1952 extended 2nd edition of the 1933 Collected) ended in a fine climax with 'Under Ben Bulben'. But all the major editions (which are seriously divided on other issues) agree that Yeats's intention—left unfulfilled at his death—was that that volume should be left divided as first published, with New Poems (1938) ending with 'Are You Content?' and the separate volume called Last Poems beginning with 'Under Ben Bulben'. As a result, these Last Poems, beginning with this epitaph poem, become a voice from the grave: something which suits the theme of many of them ('Cuchulainn Comforted', for instance). Whatever form of Last Poems is preferred, there is no doubt that they are a remarkable and powerful swan-song, some written within a week of the poet's death and all in the face of illness. Perhaps the poems which make the best epitaph for his work (as distinct from his life) are two describing the enduring discontent with his achievement that gives his poetry such unflagging energy, 'What Then?' (from New Poems) and 'The Circus Animals' Desertion' (from Last Poems).

The critical evaluation of Yeats will always be problematical because of controversy over his political views (Irish nationalist or right-wing eugenicist in the 1930s) or the seriousness with which he took the occult (which Yvor *Winters said reduced his poetry to nonsense). But there is no disputing his influence. As Eliot prophesied, he created a poetic language for the twentieth century, as is evident throughout the writing of poets such as *Larkin and *Heaney.

No fully definitive version of Yeats's poems is possible, for reasons which are evident in the Variorum Edition, ed. P. Allt and R. K. Alspach (1957). The fiftieth anniversary of Yeats's death in 1989 saw several new editions of the poems, but there are two major contenders, representing two separate traditions: W. B. Yeats: The Poems Revised, ed. R. J. Finneran (New York, 1989) which ultimately derives (with important changes) from the one-volume Collected Poems; and Yeats's Poems, ed. A. N. Jeffares (London, 1989) which derives from the limited editions The Poems of W.B. Yeats (London, 1949), overseen by the poet's widow George, the publisher Harold Macmillan, and the publisher's reader Thomas Mark. The Jeffares edition has an appendix by Warwick Gould, the editor of the Yeats Review, arguing the case for regarding this as nearly the definitive edition. The most obvious difference between the editions is that the longer pieces, headed 'Narrative and Dramatic' in the Collected Poems are kept as a separate category at the end by Finneran but incorporated chronologically into the whole corpus by Jeffares, following the 1949 edition. Gould's forthcoming Yeats's Permanent Self: Canon, Arrangement and Order in the Collected Works is intended to resolve the whole matter.

Perhaps inevitably in the case of a poet as public as Yeats, the most prominent work on him has tended to be scholarly-historical rather than critical, as is evident from the volumes of the valuable Yeats Review. Of this work the most important is John Kelly's monumental edition of the Letters, the first volume of which appeared in 1986. Pending the appearance of the 'official' biography by R. F. Foster, J. B. Hone's 1942 W. B. Yeats: 1865–1939 (revd. edn., 1952) and A. N. Jeffares's W. B. Yeats: A New Biography (London, 1988) are the best lives of Yeats. Finneran's edition of the poems was the first volume of a new standard edition of the complete works; in the meantime most of his writings exist in a series of lightly edited Macmillan volumes: *A Vision* (2nd edn., 1937); *Collected Plays* (2nd edn., 1952); *Autobiographies* (1955); *Mythologies* (1959); *Essays and Introductions* (1961); *Explorations* (1962). More fully edited are a series of volumes of various prose writings: *The Senate Speeches of W. B. Yeats*, ed. D. R. Pearce (1960); *Uncollected Prose by W. B. Yeats*, vol. 1, ed. J. P. Frayne (1970) and vol. 2, ed. J. P. Frayne and C. Johnson (1975); *Memoirs*, ed. D. Donoghue (1972). Of criticism on the poetry, the pioneering works by Richard Ellmann, *Yeats: The Man and the Masks* (London, 1949) and *The Identity of Yeats* (London, 1954) have not been superseded; also useful are H. Bloom, *Yeats* (Oxford, 1970) and D. Donoghue, *Yeats* (London, 1971). The most useful guide to the poems is certainly Jeffares's *A Commentary on the Collected Poems of W. B. Yeats* (London, 2nd edn., 1984). But there is a huge volume of writing on Yeats; for further guidance, see the extensive bibliographies in the volumes of the *Yeats Review*, or the brief bibliography in Jeffares's edition of the poems.   [BO'D

YOUNG, Andrew (John) (1885–1971), was born at Elgin, Morayshire, where his father was station-master. The family later moved to Edinburgh and he attended the Royal High School there and Edinburgh University. Taking an arts degree in 1907, he seemed set on a career in the law, but after a brief period spent studying art and ecclesiastical architecture in Paris he entered New College, Edinburgh, to prepare himself for the Presbyterian ministry. During the First World War he served at an army rest-camp near Boulogne. In 1920 he was appointed minister of the Presbyterian church at Hove, Sussex, but in 1939 he joined the Anglican communion and was made vicar of Stonegate, Sussex, later becoming a canon of Chichester Cathedral.

His first collection of poems, *Songs of the Night*, was published in 1910, while he was still a student at New College. Despite a steady output in the years that followed, it was not until his eighth book, significantly entitled *Winter Harvest* (1933), that he felt satisfied he had found his true voice. This was also the first volume in which he showed his practice of reworking old material in his new manner, the ultimate fruits of which were displayed in his radically selective *Collected Poems* of 1950.

Young's earliest poems betray something of the influence of Swinburne and his Decadent disciples, and he later passed through a phase that might be classified as *Georgian. His mature style, however, is quite distinctive, and while the occasional line may be coloured by the influence of one of the poets he continued to admire—*Hardy perhaps above all—the discovery of a personal voice, sturdily independent of fashion and at the exclusive service of a highly idiosyncratic vision, is at the very heart of his achievement.

What connects Young with the Georgians is his abiding interest in landscape, flora, and fauna as poetic subjects; what differentiates him from them is the use he made of those subjects. His extensive knowledge of wild flowers and intimacy with the places where they grew give his descriptive writing a rare authority. Employing traditional lyric forms, terse in utterance and argument, pointed with simile and paradox in a manner that recalls the work of Herbert, Marvell, and other metaphysical poets, constantly upsetting preconceptions and seeking to accommodate the profoundest mysteries within the smallest span of words, his finest poems are to be read as meditations on death and the impermanence of worldly attachments. A pawky humour and relish of the tricks played by the perceiving mind are also characteristic of his stance. Young continued his investigation of favourite themes in two long, blank-verse poems, 'Into Hades' and 'A Traveller in Time', which purport to recount other-worldly journeys made by the poet himself and which were published in 1958 under the joint title, *Out of the World and Back*.

Because Young revised or rejected so much of his early work, the establishment of a canonic text has been no simple matter. After the poet's own 1950 edition, a *Collected Poems* edited by Leonard Clark was published in 1960, and this was followed in 1974 by a *Complete Poems*, also edited by Clark. The most satisfactory text, however, is provided by *The Poetical Works of Andrew Young* (London, 1985), ed. Edward Lowbury and Alison Young. This includes early poems thought to have been worth rescuing, as well as a number of verse plays. Young's essays on wild flowers, topography, architecture, and kindred matters give a strong impression of his wit and breadth of learning, and are to be found in such volumes as *A Prospect of Flowers* (1945), *A Prospect of Britain* (1956), and *The New Poly-Olbion* (1967). [CJR]

YOUNG, Douglas (1913–73), was born in Tayport, Fife, and spent some of his younger years near Calcutta where his father worked in the jute trade. He took degrees in classics from the universities of St Andrews and Oxford, and taught Latin and Greek at the universities of Aberdeen, University College Dundee, St Andrews, McMaster (Ontario), and North Carolina, where he died.

A lifelong Scottish nationalist, Young's academic career was interrupted during the Second World War by controversy and imprisonment arising from his conscientious objection to the right of the British parliament to conscript Scots into the armed forces. His first poems appeared around this time as *Auntran Blads* (1943), followed by *A Braird o Thristles* (1947), and a brief *Selected Poems* (1950).

At its best Young's use of Scots is stark, lyrical and philologically astute as well as affecting—see 'Thonder They Ligg', 'For a Wife in Jizzen', and 'The Shepherd's Dochter'. He translated Aristophanes's *The Frogs* into Scots as *The Puddocks* (1957) and *The Birds* as *The Burdies* (1959). In 1968 he translated (into English verse) Euripides's *Hippolytus* (as *Venus with a Vengeance*, Hamilton, Ont., 1974) and *The Oresteia* of Aeschylus (Norman, Okla., 1974). Other books include *Chasing an Ancient Greek* (London, 1950), *St. Andrews* (London, 1969), and *Scotland* (London, 1971). He also edited Theognis for the Bibliotecha Teubneriana. His anthology *Scottish Verse: 1851–1951* (London, 1952) is still a valuable survey of its period. *A Clear Voice: Douglas Young, Poet and Polymath*, ed. C. Young and D. Murison (Edinburgh, 1976) contains a memoir and selections from Young's work in verse and prose.

[DED

Z

ZAMORA, Bernice (1938–), born and raised in Colorado, has won an extensive reputation largely on the basis of a single volume, *Restless Serpents* (1976), a collection both of her own poems and those of José Antonio Burciaga. Her poetry has been notable, in both Spanish and English, for its subtlety of idiom, her command, often colloquial, of a distinctively crafted *chicana* speaking voice. Even so, Robinson *Jeffers and Theodore *Roethke have been prime influences. Her versatility shows through on a number of related fronts: as a poet of feminine sexuality and consciousness ('Gata Poem', 'Notes From a Chicana "Coed"' or 'When We Are Able'), of childhood ('Angelita's Utility'), of eroticism ('Pueblo 1950', 'Bearded Lady', and 'And All Flows Past'), of chicano linguistic and cultural tradition ('Let the Giants Cackle'), of landscape and place (the Jeffers-like 'California'), and of creativity itself (the impressively wrought title-poem 'Restless Serpents', alongside 'Without Bark' or 'Metaphor and Reality'). Long a critic of 'Anglo' oppression and insensitivity to cultural difference, she none the less avoids all polemical calls to arms or self-pity. She especially parodies stereotypes, both cultural and sexual.

See *Restless Serpents* (Menlo Park, Calif., 1976); also *Flor y Canto IV and V: An Anthology of Chicano Literature*, ed. Bernice Zamora and José Armas (Albuquerque, NM, 1980); and *Contemporary Chicana Poetry: A Critical Approach to an Emerging Literature*, by Marta Ester Sánchez (Berkeley, Calif., 1985).   [ARL

ZATURENSKA, Marya (Alexandrovna) (1902–82), was born in Kiev, Russia. Her mother's family was Polish, and worked for generations for the Radziwill family. Her father served in the Russian Army during the Russo-Japanese War and the Boxer Rebellion. As a little girl Zaturenska loved Polish and Russian folk-songs, and before she could read or write, created lyrics for the tunes. In 1909, when she was 8, the family moved to America, residing on Henry Street in New York City near the Settlement House. She was educated in public schools, but had to drop out. She attended high school at night, worked in a factory by day—and wrote poetry. Her first published poems appeared in national magazines, including *Poetry, when she was still in her teens, and she won the John Reed Memorial Award in 1922, when she was 20. She graduated from the University of Wisconsin Library School in 1925. That same year she married the poet and critic Horace *Gregory, of a patrician Milwaukee family. They later collaborated on anthologies and *A History of American Poetry, 1900–40* (New York, 1946).

Threshold and Hearth, her first collection, appeared in 1934. It received the Shelley Memorial Award. But it was her second book, *Cold Morning Sky*, which put her on the literary map. Published in 1937—a year which saw new collections by *Bogan, H.D. (Hilda *Doolittle), *Jeffers, *Millay, *Pound, *Stevens, and *Tate, among others—it was awarded the Pulitzer Prize. It was reprinted twice the following year.

Her greatest influence was the English Decadent school, particularly Christina Rossetti, of whom she wrote a biography. Zaturenska's meditative and mystical lyrics are admired for their delicacy, mastery of metre and rhyme, and her ability to make something fresh out of lyric conventions. As late as 1974, when she published her eighth and last collection, *The Hidden Waterfall*, she had not altered her style or subjects to make them more fashionable. With the rise of the *New Formalism in America in the late 1980s her poems may continue to be admired. Mention should also be made of her fine translations from the Italian, including works by Monti, Stampa, and Tasso.

The largest edition is *Collected Poems of Marya Zaturenska* (New York, 1965). See also 'The Real Thing: An Interview with Marya Zaturenska', by Robert Phillips, *Modern Poetry Studies*, 9: 1 (Spring 1978). [RSP

ZEPHANIAH, Benjamin (1958–), was born in Birmingham, but brought up in Jamaica. He spent his early teens at various approved schools in England, and also had a spell in prison. In his late teens he made his way as an impersonator of famous stars, eventually branching out as a very popular *performance poet.

He seems to be a cruder kind of 'dub' poet than Linton Kwesi *Johnson or John *Agard, but the very rawness of his verse is true to the emotions and attitudes of dispossessed people submerged even within the Afro-Caribbean community in Britain. His poetry also displays the prophetic vein of a Rastafarian, and ranges from pure rhetoric to visionary rapture. At its best, it is full of ambivalent tension between these two poles. He can also be refreshingly down-to-earth. In 'Just Like David' he makes it clear that the function of the poet is to smite oppressive Goliaths everywhere.

The Dread Affair (London, 1985) contains his collected poems. See also *City Psalms* (Newcastle upon Tyne, 1992). Published plays include *Hurricane Dub* in *BBC Radio Drama: Young Playwrights Festival*, ed. Jeremy Mortimer (London, 1988) and *Job Rocking*, in *Black Plays: Two*, ed. Yvonne Brewster (London, 1989). [MR

ZIEROTH, Dale (1946–), was born in Neepawa, Manitoba, the son of a farming couple. Before settling in North Vancouver, where he

teaches creative writing at Douglas College, he worked as a park ranger in the Banff-Kootenay region, a problematic 'wilderness' experience which forms the basis for his second collection of poems, *Mid-River* (Toronto, 1981). Zieroth has taught at the Banff Centre for the Fine Arts, holds an MA from Simon Fraser University, British Columbia, and since 1985 has edited the literary magazine *event*.

Zieroth's first book, *Clearings: Poems from a Journey* (Toronto) appeared in 1973. His latest collection, *When the Stones Fly Up* (Toronto, 1985) moves in and out of past and present, memory and dream, with impressive fluidity, exploring the configurations of urban living and domestic interrelations, and also the haunting lacunae inherited from his German family's experience of immigration. Zieroth's latest book of poems is *The Weight of my Raggedy Skin* (Nelson, BC, 1991). [JKK

ZIMUNYA, Musaemura (1949–), was born in Mutare, Zimbabwe (then Rhodesia), and studied at the University of Kent. He is currently a lecturer in English at the University of Zimbabwe.

Much of Zimunya's poetry is concerned with the war of liberation and its aftermath. It is a poetry of disillusion. The poet sees little sign that the move from Rhodesia to Zimbabwe has effected any profound transformation in the society: 'Bulawayo was a place of killing again | to remind us that our peace was a hasty marriage . . .'. He has published a book of criticism, *Those Years of Drought and Hunger: The Birth of African Fiction in English* (Gweru, 1982) and has co-edited a number of anthologies.

He has published four collections: *Zimbabwe Ruins* (Harare, 1979); *Thought Tracks* (Harlow, 1982); *Kingfisher, Jikinya, and Other Poems* (Harare, 1982); and *Country Dawns and City Lights* (Harare, 1985). [AM-P

ZUKOFSKY, Louis (1904–78), was born in New York City, the son of Yiddish-speaking immigrant parents. Educated at Columbia University, he lived and worked mainly in New York. By his early twenties he was already an accomplished poet and critic, earning the respect and admiration of *Pound, William Carlos *Williams, and *Eliot. Williams, especially, came to rely on Zukofsky as an important adviser and editor for his own poetry, and as something of a guide amidst the highly politicized literary community before the Second World War. Pound constantly promoted Zukofsky as both editor and critic, seeing in him an exceptional advocate of the new poetry. Not yet 30, Zukofsky, through Pound's efforts, was asked to edit and to write a manifesto for the now-famous 1931 *'Objectivist' issue of *Poetry magazine, in effect creating a poetic movement whose influence is more widely felt today than ever. Zukofsky's own career in the late Thirties and Forties seemed to be in eclipse while critical interest focused on poets influenced by the *New Criticism. In the early Fifties, however, Zukofsky's work was rediscovered by such poets as *Duncan, *Creeley, and *Corman. Today, Zukofsky's reputation as a poet and theorist is at its highest, especially among younger poets who see him as one of the founding figures of modernist poetry.

Two traits, a sensitivity to the sound-forms of the language and a high degree of intellection, mark all of Zukofsky's poetry and other writings. If he is one of the most musical poets of the modern era, he is also one of the most intellectually difficult. Varied in tone and subject-matter, as in the comic ode beginning 'To my wash-stand', or in the long travel-poem, 'Barely and Widely', his works can be gems of sonic counterpoint and verbal compression. Typically, as in the complex sestina 'Mantis' with its moving coda, ' "Mantis", An Interpretation', he skilfully weaves social commentary and philosophy into an ongoing ars poetica, and in A, a poem of twenty-four movements composed throughout his life, he creates an epic collage of autobiography, history, and reflection, replete with theatre pieces, music, word-play, and punning. An act of intense attentiveness to the associative power of word and thought, 'A' is, like Pound's Cantos, profoundly serious, prolix, and irreducible to easy exegesis.

Of equal note among Zukofsky's works is his massive study, Bottom: On Shakespeare, which invokes much of Western literature and philosophy as it elaborates a highly original reading of the key tropes of the Shakespearian canon. Zukofsky's essays, including studies of Henry Adams, Pound, *Stevens, and Williams, and appreciations of such diverse figures as William Blake and Charlie Chaplin, are important documents in our understanding of modernist art and literature.

The most complete editions of Zukofsky's work are 'A' (Berkeley, Calif., 1978); All: The Collected Short Poems (New York, 1971—earlier editions of All were published also in London in 1966 and 1967); Bottom: On Shakespeare (Berkeley, 1986); and Prepositions: The Collected Critical Essays of Louis Zukofsky: Expanded Edition (Berkeley, 1981). See also Louis Zukofsky: Man and Poet, ed. Carroll F. Terrell (Orono, Me., 1979), Hugh Kenner's A Home Made World (New York, 1975) and The Pound Era (Berkeley, 1971), and Michael Heller's Conviction's Net of Branches: Essays On The Objectivist Poets and Poetry (Carbondale, Ill., 1985). [MH

ZURNDORFER, Lotte (1929–), was born in Dusseldorf. Her father, Adolf, managing director of a publisher's, Ed. Lintz, and theatre critic for the Frankfurter Zeitung and Theaterwelt, married his niece, Else. After their home was smashed by Kristallnacht Brownshirts, Lotte and her elder sister Hannele caught the last children's train, 3 May 1939. The parents' attempts to follow were deliberately frustrated, and both died at Łódź concentration camp. After harrowing resettlement and evacuation, the girls were given motherly care by a Dr Salmon's wife, Mary. Lotte graduated from St Hugh's, Oxford, in 1951, was a publications officer in Manchester, taught at the Sorbonne, and settled as an English literature lecturer at Helsinki University. Married to Henry Troupp, professor of neurosurgery there, she has two daughters.

In her finely tuned poems, their careful perceptions archly fixed in 'combed' and 'shaggy' words, the pain and exile are never directly touched on; yet the generalized and lightly brushed-in allusions to death and agony are meant: art is serene, 'and all Art false': to Rodin's 'Douleur' she comments: 'how you cannot scream.'

After her *The Fantasy Poets: Number Nine* (Oxford, 1952), Cecil *Day Lewis published her *Poems* (London, 1960). See also the autobiography *The Ninth of November*, by Hannele Zürndorfer (London, 1983).   [HL

ZWICKY, Fay (1933–), was born in Melbourne, to an old-established Jewish family (Rosefield) and has been successively a concert pianist, an academic, and a full-time writer of poetry, short stories (*Hostages*, Fremantle, 1983), and literary criticism. *The Lyre in the Pawnshop: Essays on Literature and Survival 1974–1984* (Nedlands, WA, 1986) illuminates Zwicky's poetics by its defence of humanist values and seriousness of mind and by its commitment to the power of language to integrate both social fabric and individual consciousness.

Zwicky's poetic truth-telling can be fierce, celebratory, witty, compassionate—sometimes all combined. Neither in style nor content does she slot easily into any poetic group, including the 'feminist', although much of her work can be seen as challenging the definition of Australian identity as strong, silent, and masculine. While her argument with her personal and cultural heritage, with the love that she can deny neither to her Jewish father nor to traditional European culture, may be most vividly present in the title poem of *Kaddish and Other Poems* (St Lucia, Qld., 1982), similar preoccupations occur in *Isaac Babel's Fiddle* (Adelaide, 1975) and *Ask Me* (St Lucia, 1989). They are also dramatized in her revisions of traditional representations of figures such as Mrs Noah, Penelope, or Devi. *Poems, 1970–1992* (St Lucia) came out in 1993.

[JS

OXFORD

MORE OXFORD PAPERBACKS

This book is just one of nearly 1000 Oxford Paperbacks currently in print. If you would like details of other Oxford Paperbacks, including titles in the World's Classics, Oxford Reference, Oxford Books, OPUS, Past Masters, Oxford Authors, and Oxford Shakespeare series, please write to:

UK and Europe: Oxford Paperbacks Publicity Manager, Arts and Reference Publicity Department, Oxford University Press, Walton Street, Oxford OX2 6DP.

Customers in UK and Europe will find Oxford Paperbacks available in all good bookshops. But in case of difficulty please send orders to the Cash-with-Order Department, Oxford University Press Distribution Services, Saxon Way West, Corby, Northants NN18 9ES. Tel: 01536 741519; Fax: 01536 746337. Please send a cheque for the total cost of the books, plus £1.75 postage and packing for orders under £20; £2.75 for orders over £20. Customers outside the UK should add 10% of the cost of the books for postage and packing.

USA: Oxford Paperbacks Marketing Manager, Oxford University Press, Inc., 200 Madison Avenue, New York, N.Y. 10016.

Canada: Trade Department, Oxford University Press, 70 Wynford Drive, Don Mills, Ontario M3C 1J9.

Australia: Trade Marketing Manager, Oxford University Press, G.P.O. Box 2784Y, Melbourne 3001, Victoria.

South Africa: Oxford University Press, P.O. Box 1141, Cape Town 8000.

OXFORD PAPERBACK REFERENCE

From *Art and Artists* to *Zoology*, the Oxford Paperback Reference series offers the very best subject reference books at the most affordable prices.

Authoritative, accessible, and up to date, the series features dictionaries in key student areas, as well as a range of fascinating books for a general readership. Included are such well-established titles as Fowler's *Modern English Usage*, Margaret Drabble's *Concise Companion to English Literature*, and the bestselling science and medical dictionaries.

The series has now been relaunched in handsome new covers. Highlights include new editions of some of the most popular titles, as well as brand new paperback reference books on *Politics*, *Philosophy*, and *Twentieth-Century Poetry*.

With new titles being constantly added, and existing titles regularly updated, Oxford Paperback Reference is unrivalled in its breadth of coverage and expansive publishing programme. New dictionaries of *Film*, *Economics*, *Linguistics*, *Architecture*, *Archaeology*, *Astronomy*, and *The Bible* are just a few of those coming in the future.

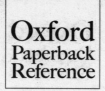

Oxford Paperback Reference

THE CONCISE OXFORD COMPANION TO ENGLISH LITERATURE

Edited by Margaret Drabble and Jenny Stringer

Derived from the acclaimed *Oxford Companion to English Literature*, the concise maintains the wide coverage of its parent volume. It is an indispensable, compact guide to all aspects of English literature. For this revised edition, existing entries have been fully updated and revised with 60 new entries added on contemporary writers.

* Over 5,000 entries on the lives and works of authors, poets and playwrights

* The most comprehensive and authoritative paperback guide to English literature

* New entries include Peter Ackroyd, Martin Amis, Toni Morrison, and Jeanette Winterson

* New appendices list major literary prize-winners

From the reviews of its parent volume:

'It earns its place at the head of the best sellers: every home should have one'
Sunday Times

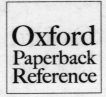

Oxford
Paperback
Reference

THE CONCISE OXFORD DICTIONARY OF OPERA

New Edition

Edited by Ewan West and John Warrack

Derived from the full *Oxford Dictionary of Opera*, this is the most authoritative and up-to-date dictionary of opera available in paperback. Fully revised for this new edition, it is designed to be accessible to all those who enjoy opera, whether at the opera-house or at home.

* **Over 3,500 entries on operas, composers, and performers**

* **Plot summaries and separate entries for well-known roles, arias, and choruses**

* **Leading conductors, producers and designers**

From the reviews of its parent volume:

'the most authoritative single-volume work of its kind'
Independent on Sunday

'an invaluable reference work'
Gramophone